Pro Football Prospectus

2005

Aaron Schatz

with

Ben Alamar • Jim Armstrong • Al Bogdan

Will Carroll • Tim Gerheim • Russell Levine

Dan Lewis • Ned Macey • Jason McKinley

Michael David Smith • Mike Tanier • Ryan Wilson

WORKMAN PUBLISHING • NEW YORK

Library of Congress Cataloging-in-Publication Data is available.

ISBN-13: 978-0-7611-4019-1
ISBN-10: 0-7611-4019-0

Workman books are available at special discounts when purchased in bulk for premiums and sales promotions as well as for fund-raising or educational use. Special editions or book excerpts can also be created to specification. For details, contact the Special Sales Director at the address below.

Design by Barbara Balch
Cover design by Paul Gamarello

Workman Publishing Company, Inc.
708 Broadway
New York, NY 10003-9555
www.workman.com

Printed in the U.S.A.
First printing July 2005

10 9 8 7 6 5 4 3 2 1

Contents

Skill Players

Further Research

Introduction

Aaron Schatz

Coming off a 6–10 season, not many people expected much from the Pittsburgh Steelers last year. So it was a bit surprising when, led by an untested rookie, the Steelers went 15–1 and easily won the AFC North. Nobody from ESPN.com, *Sports Illustrated,* or the *Sporting News* saw it coming. Internet sportswriter King Kaufman of Salon.com, who tracks the predictions of NFL experts from leading magazines and websites, found only a single website that correctly predicted Pittsburgh's finish: an upstart statistical analysis site just entering its second year, FootballOutsiders.com.

In fact, FootballOutsiders.com made more accurate predictions about the 2004 NFL season than any writer for a major sports website or magazine. The site correctly predicted 10 of 12 playoff teams. It predicted that the New York Jets, 6–10 the previous season, would be the breakout team of the year. Its stats-based forecast system projected the New England Patriots as the best team in football. And it projected one other strange result, something nobody could have possibly imagined—that the 4–12 San Diego Chargers would turn things around and feature one of the top offenses in football.

How did a group of football *outsiders* manage to get so inside the NFL? As the founder of FootballOutsiders.com and the head writer of the staff that made all those wise predictions about 2004, I can tell you that it all started with this question: "Do teams have to establish the run?"

It was December 2002 and my hometown team, the New England Patriots, was finishing up a disappointing season in which it would miss the playoffs despite winning the previous Super Bowl. To a number of local sportswriters, it was quite obvious why the Patriots didn't win—they had failed to establish the run early in games.[1]

Interestingly, at the same time, some of these writers were proclaiming the Oakland Raiders to be a major Super Bowl contender, with a significant chance of winning the AFC and going on to beat either Tampa Bay or Philadelphia in Super Bowl XXXVII. But the Oakland Raiders had an offense built almost entirely around the pass, and a running back, Charlie Garner, who ranked in the NFL's top ten in receptions.

Bill James, the godfather of advanced baseball analysis ("sabermetrics," as it is often called), started by adding up numbers from box scores to answer fundamental questions about the game. Things have come a long way since 1978, when James self-published his first *Baseball Abstract,* and every NFL game now has play-by-play available on the Internet. "OK," I thought to myself, "let's go through every game, and figure out how many times each team ran during the first half, and see if teams that run more in the first half have a tendency to win games."

I started counting manually, and about four games in I realized this was silly. Why not just paste the text of each game's play-by-play into a spreadsheet and use another column to add up the rushing attempts? And once I thought of this, I realized, there was no need to count only rushing attempts. You could count passes and compare receivers, or quarterbacks.

The end result was a database of every single play in the 2002 NFL season. It turned out that there is virtually no correlation between teams that ran the ball more often in the first quarter and the teams that won the most games—the winning teams are the ones that ran the most in the fourth quarter. Teams run when they win, not win when they run.

But now that I had this huge spreadsheet, there was nothing stopping me from answering other questions. Who was worth more, a running back with 500 yards and ten TDs, or one with 1,000 yards but only five TDs? How much did strength of schedule affect the performance of different players? Which was more likely to convert on third and one, a pass or a run?

Hundreds of books and websites were and are devoted to statistical analysis of, and critical thinking about, why baseball teams win or lose. Why was nobody doing the same thing for professional football, the most popular sport in the country?

Advanced NFL analysis did exist, if you looked hard enough. Bud Goode first began creating advanced football statistics 30 years ago, and he was the first person to popularize the idea that net yards per pass is the statistic that most accurately indicates the quality of an NFL team. But

---

1. The original article inspired by this question is online at http://www.footballoutsiders.com/ramblings.php?p=3.

he rarely wrote in the public sphere, instead working primarily as a consultant for coaches around the league.

Two writers from the world of baseball analysis, Pete Palmer and John Thorn, collaborated with Bob Carroll, the president of the Professional Football Researchers Association, to put out a book called *The Hidden Game of Football* in 1988. *Hidden Game* came out before the era of the Internet, however, which today makes it much easier than in the past to share and discusss research and then apply it to whatever happens the following season. *Hidden Game* was briefly updated ten years later, but remained stuck in the 1987 and 1997 seasons.

The Internet created an explosion of statistical analysis telling NFL fans how to build a winning fantasy football team or how to make more money gambling on point spreads. But there still wasn't a central home for NFL research that broke through the bias inherent in conventional statistics and applied critical thinking to professional football. There was no place to find analysis that reached down to the play-by-play level. No place that evolved new statistics necessary to a true understanding of the game, then explained them in language that normal people could understand. In other words, there wasn't really a football equivalent to *Baseball Prospectus.*

So I decided to create one.

I launched FootballOutsiders.com in August 2003 with just two regular columns, my weekly statistical analysis and a fantasy-oriented fan commentary called Scramble for the Ball. Then word of what we were doing began to spread around the Internet, which generated some attention from newspapers and other websites that recognized our informed perspective on the NFL. We hosted Gregg Easterbrook's Tuesday Morning Quarterback column on our site for a month after ESPN.com let him go (over a controversy related to a column he wrote in his other life, as a political and cultural writer for *The New Republic* and its website). Football fans asking the same questions, fans hungry for a regular forum for intelligent discussion of the NFL, started popping up on our discussion boards. The writing staff slowly grew from just me and my college buddies to a network of fans across the country and even the globe: a Lions fan in Chicago, a Bucs fan in Jersey, a Colts fan in Australia.

Last year the writers of *Baseball Prospectus* approached me to ask if we would be interested in producing a football annual that shared their name. This book is the result—a mind-altering experience for the football fan that drills down deeper into the game than any book that's come before and then takes that knowledge and applies it to the 2005 season to tell you what to expect from your favorite teams and players.

We'll show you how to look at what football statistics mean *in context*—the context of down and distance, where three yards can be success or failure depending on the situation, and the context of schedule, where a good player can look average because he has faced a string of difficult defenses. You'll learn why third down performance is a strong indicator of a team's future prospects, why it is better to run than to pass on third and short, and why you never draft a kicker in the second round.

What's remarkable is how many teams already think this way. In baseball, the gospel of statistical research was spread from amateur writers to the major national columnists and only then into front offices. In football, most teams already do statistical analysis in order to plan for future opponents as well as manage their budgets under the salary cap.

The Boston Red Sox are often celebrated as the first "Moneyball" team to win a championship, but the New England Patriots have won three of the last four Super Bowls using very similar methods. Both teams have been built using a combination of scouting and statistical analysis to gather as much information as possible and efficiently use every space on the roster while staying within budget. Both teams pick up players deemed expendable by other organizations and utilize them in ways that maximize their skills. The result is a roster with depth at nearly every position, which can be used to emphasize offense or defense depending on what is needed in a particular game situation.

But while teams have become more advanced in their approach to the game, most journalists have not. Television commentators spout off about what went wrong when the team that went 10–6 despite getting outscored by opponents turns around and goes 6–10 the next year. Sportswriters mistake cause and effect by writing about how teams win only if they have a running back who gains 100 yards. Official statistics judge wide receivers on total receptions without considering which receivers *miss* the most passes. Fantasy football magazines expect most players to simply repeat the previous year's numbers.

And even though NFL teams have gone much farther down the path of objective analysis than their baseball counterparts, coaches still make decisions based on hunches that turn out to be statistically irrational, and general managers still make roster decisions that run counter to everything that we've learned in studying professional football. The Lions can't stop passing on third and short, and the Jets drafted a kicker in the second round despite all evidence that this is a waste of a pick. The insiders could learn something from an outside perspective, and we're here to provide it.

Football vs. Baseball

Unfortunately, there are many obstacles to doing objective analysis of the NFL, and we would be remiss if we didn't acknowledge these issues.

As far as baseball analysis has come in 30 years, one subject has still defied efforts at comprehensive analysis:

defense. It is the one area of baseball with multiple-player interaction rather than a one-on-one battle between pitcher and hitter, and it is the one area where the conventional box score does not explain exactly what happened on the play. (How hard was the ball hit? Exactly where in right field did it land?) Sabermetric writers like our partners at *Baseball Prospectus,* as well as the more analytic front offices, are still searching for a method that clearly and accurately judges defensive performance.

With the possible exceptions of field goal percentage and kickoff distance, every action on a football field is the equivalent of defense in baseball in terms of complexity of measurement.

Every action on a football field is the result of a multiple-player interaction, and most of those players do not have their performance listed in a box score, let alone assessed. When Peyton Manning throws a 20-yard touchdown pass to Reggie Wayne, we don't know whether the coverage was man or zone, which defensive player was closest to Wayne, or whether Wayne was open because coverage was focused on Marvin Harrison. We don't know which defensive players were rushing Manning and which offensive players were blocking them. We don't know whether Wayne caught the ball in the end zone, or caught the ball on the 15-yard line and then gained 15 yards after the catch.

To some people, the fact that not everything on a football field is accurately measured means that any attempt to do advanced analysis of professional football is useless. Others point to the 16-game NFL season and argue that so small a sample size undermines any statistical analysis.

Our motto is that the best is the enemy of the better. The fact that we cannot develop perfect analysis is not a reason to give up on better analysis.

It is important to understand that we are in the very early stages of our work, and we are really just starting to scrape the surface of what is possible. In the life cycle of analysis, we are much closer to where Bill James was in his first few *Baseball Abstracts* than we are to where our partners at *Baseball Prospectus* are in 2005. But those early Abstracts contained the foundation for everything that came afterward, and so do the studies in this book. We have plans to analyze more data, improve our methods, and track events not even included in standard play-by-play in order to better our knowledge of professional football.

If you have any questions or comments about this book, feel free to email us at book@footballoutsiders.com.

The Setup

The first section of the book is a long explanation of all the new statistics that we use to analyze the NFL: what they mean and how they are derived. It's long, so feel free to read some of it, flip around the rest of the book, and then come back.

Each NFL team gets a chapter featuring an essay on what happened during the 2004 season as well as what we can expect in 2005. Many of the team chapters also feature a second essay concerning primary research on a topic related to that team. Then come statistics for every team, including weekly performance in 2004, the statistical record for the past five years, and individual statistics for both offensive and defensive players. The chapters end with commentary on each of the major units of the team: offensive line, defensive front seven, defensive secondary, special teams, and coaching staff, along with appropriate statistics for each unit over the past three seasons.

You'll notice the words "skill players" missing from that paragraph. That's because skill players have their own section in the back of the book. Unlike our partners at *Baseball Prospectus,* we haven't developed intricate ratings for each individual player yet, just for skill players, so they're grouped by position with commentary as well as 2005 projections that will also help you plan for your fantasy football draft.

Finally, there are a series of longer research essays on various topics, including injuries, drive momentum, fantasy football preparation, and what every NFL fan should know about the 2005 college football season.

Acknowledgments

There are a lot of people who have helped Football Outsiders go from a bunch of goofy equations on my computer to the book you hold in your hands right now. In fact, the list of people to thank is so long that you may confuse this book with a rap album (*DVOA Gets Crunk, Vol. 1*). However, there are a few people who need to be thanked above all others.

First, Gregg Easterbrook, whose temporary setback became the launching pad for our long-term success. Thank you for all your support over the past two years and for letting us publish your column ever so briefly.

Second, Benjy Rose and Bob Sawyer, two Football Outsiders whose work you won't see in this book. They are the architects responsible for the great design on our website and for keeping things running all season long. Benjy in particular had to deal with upping our server subscription every time I wrote another controversial column for ESPN.com. Thanks also to the FO staff, past and present, who aren't found in this book, including cartoonist Jason Beattie, programmer Pat Laverty, and writers Vivek Ramgopal and Ian Dembsky.

Third, the folks at Prospectus Entertainment Ventures Inc., who gave us their support and their name in the interest of spreading the statistical analysis revolution past the world of baseball. In particular, Chris Kahrl for finding us first, Nate Silver and Jonah Keri for all their work making this book happen, and Will Carroll for being our Bo Jackson.

Some of the ideas in this book, or portions of the essays, originally appeared as part of my work at ESPN.com or in the *New York Sun,* and I thank Michael Woodsworth and Matt Oshinsky at the *New York Sun,* as well as David Schoenfield and Michael Knisley at ESPN.com, for the opportunities they've given me and the permission to include that work here.

Thanks to our editor, Richard Rosen, to layout guy Don Rodgers, and to Katherine Camargo, who is really good at scheduling things. Thanks to our inspirations: Bill James, Bud Goode, Allen Barra, Doug Drinen, and the authors of *The Hidden Game of Football,* Pete Palmer, John Thorn, and Bob Carroll. Thanks to Jim Schwartz, Matt Burke, Mike Eayrs, Paraag Marathe, Kevin Lewis and the Pro Trade gang, Roland Beech and TwoMinuteWarning.com, Dean Oliver and Kevin Pelton from the world of hoops, David Leonhardt and Bob Goetz at *The New York Times,* Richard Just at *TNR,* Jenny Schuessler at *The Boston Globe,* Luc Rheaume from Sports Forecaster (who loans us Mike Tanier), Chris Creed (who originally gave Russell Levine the forum that we later picked up), William Krasker, Carl Prine, Eddie Epstein, Bruce Allen, King Kaufman, Jeff Merron, John Faure, Royce Webb, Bob Cook, Peter King, Tom Curran, Jascha Hoffman, Josh Levin, Jon Chait and Paul Campos, Michael "not David" Smith, Chris Hoeltge, Jordy Singer, Steve Deutsch, Dale and Neumy, Brad Davies and Dan Morello, Chris "The Fullback" Mooney, Sean Benak, Fritz Holznagel, Frank Mulcahy, all the brothers and alumni of Zeta Delta Xi at Brown University, and Ron Mexico for filling our summer with laughter. I'm sure we forgot someone.

Thanks to all of the readers of Football Outsiders, everyone who participates in our online discussions, everyone who writes a guest column, and those readers who helped us put together data for this book, primarily Bill Moore but also Melissa Cain, Brian Hook, and Ryan Maxwell. Thanks to Eliot Horowitz and Dennis Doughty, who wrote the data parser, as well as John Argentiero and Evan Davidson, who wrote the stat compiler.

Finally, and most important, thanks to our wives and families for dealing with this odd hobby that has become, for me at least, an even stranger profession. This book is dedicated to my wife, Kathryn, who was basically a single parent for three weeks this spring, and my daughter, Mirinae, who wanted to know why daddy always kept her from hitting the "delete" key.

And thank you for buying this book and taking the chance on something unlike any football book you've ever read before. We hope you enjoy it.

Aaron Schatz
Framingham, MA
June 2005

Statistical Toolbox:

Or Everything You Ever Wanted to Know About Pro Football but the Stats Hadn't Been Invented Yet

Aaron Schatz

While baseball and even basketball have been subjected to a multitude of fancy statistical measures over the last two decades—Wherefore art thou, TENDEX?—football numbers have remained remarkably simplistic. Until now. There are a lot of new numbers in this book and new statistics for measuring NFL performance. We feel they are far better than what came before, and we've done our best to present them in a way that makes them easy to understand.

In our quest to improve NFL analysis, we are limited by what is available in the play-by-play. We don't have length of incomplete passes, for example, or numbers for missed tackles or missed blocks. We don't know all the players who are on the field at any one time, so we can't judge the impact that a top receiver has on the performance of the other receiver on the other side of the field who gets less defensive attention. But we can learn a lot more from the publicly available information than the standard numbers would indicate.

What follows is an explanation of the original statistics you'll find in this book: how we calculate them, what the numbers mean, and what they tell us about why teams win or lose football games.

Defense-Adjusted Value Over Average (DVOA)

One running back runs for three yards. Another running back runs for three yards. Which is the better run?

This sounds like a stupid question, but it isn't. In fact, this question is at the heart of nearly all the analysis in this book.

What is the down and distance? Is it third and 2, or second and 15? Where on the field is the ball? Does the player get only three yards because he hits the goal line and scores? Is this player's team up by two touchdowns in the fourth quarter, so that he is running out the clock, or down by two touchdowns so that the defense is playing purely against the pass? Is our running back playing against Baltimore, or Kansas City?

All of these are crucial questions in judging a particular play's success, and yet conventional NFL statistics account for plays based solely on their yardage. The NFL determines the best players by adding up all their yards, no matter in what situations they came or how many plays it took to get them. Now why would they do that? Football has one objective—to get to the end zone—and two ways to achieve that, by gaining yards and getting first downs. These two goals need to be balanced to determine a player's value or a team's performance. All the yards in the world aren't useful if they all come in eight-yard chunks on third-and-tens.

The popularity of fantasy football only exaggerates the problem. Fans have gotten used to judging players based on how much they help fantasy teams win and lose, not how much they help real teams win and lose. But fantasy scoring skews things by counting the yard between the one and the goal line as 61 times more important than all the other yards on the field. Let's say Keyshawn Johnson catches a pass on third and 15 and goes 50 yards but gets tackled two yards from the goal line, and then Julius Jones takes the ball on first and goal from the two-yard line and plunges in for the score. Or, let's say that the Giants take a touchback on the opening kickoff, and the Dallas defense stuffs Tiki Barber twice, and, on third and 10, Eli Manning throws the ball into the arms of Roy Williams, who gets taken down by Jeremy Shockey at the two-yard line. Then on the ensuing first and goal, Jones scores a touchdown.

Has Jones done something special? Not really. When an offense gets the ball on first and goal at the two-yard line, they are going to score a touchdown five out of six times. In the first situation, Jones is getting the credit that primarily belongs to the passing game. In the second situation, Jones is getting the credit that primarily belongs to the defense.

Can we do a better job of distributing credit for scoring points and winning games? That's the goal of DVOA, or Defense-adjusted Value Over Average. DVOA breaks down every single play of the NFL season to see how much success an offense or defense achieved in each specific situation compared to the league average. It uses a value based both on total yards and yards towards a first down, based on work done by Pete Palmer, Bob Carroll, and John Thorn in their seminal book, *The Hidden Game of Football*. On first down, a play is considered a success if it gains 45% of needed yards; on second down, a play needs to gain 60% of needed yards; on third or fourth down, only gaining a new first down is considered success.

We then expand upon that basic idea with a more complicated system of "success points." A successful play is worth one point, an unsuccessful play zero points. Extra points are awarded for big plays, gradually increasing to three points for 10 yards, four points for 20 yards, and five points for 40 yards or more. There are fractional points in between. (For example, eight yards on third and ten is worth 0.54 "success points.") Losing three or more yards is valued at −1 point, an interception is −8 points, and a fumble is worth anywhere from −2.15 to −6.54 points depending on how often a fumble in that situation is lost to the defense—no matter who actually recovers the fumble. Red zone plays are worth more, as are plays between the offense's own 20- and 40-yard lines, and there is a bonus given for a touchdown.

(The system is a bit more complex than the one in *Hidden Game,* thanks to a number of developments, including the larger penalty for turnovers, the fractional points, and a slightly higher baseline for success on first down. The reason why all fumbles are counted, no matter whether they are recovered by the offense or defense, is explained in the New Orleans chapter. The reason why plays in the red zone as well as between the offense's own 20- and 40-yard lines are worth more is explained later in the book in an essay titled "The Most Important Real Estate in Football.")

Every single play run in the NFL gets a "success value" based on this system, and then that number gets compared to the average success values of plays in similar situations for all players, adjusted for a number of variables. These include down and distance, field location, time remaining in game, and current scoring lead or deficit. Teams are always compared to one standard, as the team made its own choice whether to pass or rush. However, when it comes to individual players, rushing plays are compared to other rushing plays, passing plays to other passing plays; tight ends get compared to tight ends, wideouts to wideouts.

Going back to our example of the three-yard rush, if Player A gains three yards under a set of circumstances where the average NFL running back gains only one yard, it can be argued that Player A has a certain amount of value above others at his position. Likewise, if Player B gains three yards on a play where, under similar circumstances, an average NFL back would be expected to gain

four yards, it can be argued that Player B has negative value relative to others at his position. Once we have all our adjustments, we can find the difference between a particular player's success and the expected success of an average running back in the same situation (or between a particular defense and the average defense in the same situation, etc.). Add up every play by a certain team or player, divide by the total baseline for success in all those situations, and you get VOA, or Value Over Average.

Of course, the biggest variable in football is the fact that each team plays a different schedule. By adjusting each play based on the defense's average success in stopping that type of play over the course of a season, we get DVOA, or Defense-adjusted Value Over Average. Rushing and passing plays are adjusted based on down and location on the field; receiving plays are also adjusted based on how the defense performs against passes to running backs, tight ends, and wide receivers. Defenses are adjusted based on the average success of the *offenses* they are facing.

(Confusion alert: Originally, we called the adjusted VOA for defense something else, but finally we decided that it was better to call opponent-adjusted VOA the same thing in every instance, and most people thought "DVOA" just sounded better than "OVOA" or "AVOA" even though, yes, when we're talking about defenses the "D" can't stand for "defense." Think of it as standing for "dependent on opponent" or something.)

The biggest advantage of DVOA is the ability to break teams and players down to find strengths and weaknesses in a variety of situations. In the aggregate, DVOA may not be quite as accurate as some of the other, similar "power ratings" formulas based on comparing drives rather than individual plays, but, unlike those other ratings, DVOA can be separated not only by player but also by down, or by week, or by distance needed for first down. This can give us a better idea of not just which team is better but why, and what a team has to do in order to improve itself in the future. You will find DVOA used in this book in a lot of different ways—because it takes every single play into account, it can be used to measure a player or a team's performance in any situation. All Minnesota third downs can be compared to how an average team does on third down. Kurt Warner and Eli Manning can each be compared to how an average quarterback performs in the red zone, or with a lead, or in the second half of the game.

Since it compares each play only to plays with similar circumstances, it gives a more accurate picture of how much better a team really is compared to the league as a whole. The list of top DVOA offenses on third down, for example, is more accurate than the conventional NFL conversion statistic because it takes into account that converting third and long is more difficult than converting third and short and that a turnover is worse than an incomplete pass because it doesn't provide the opportunity to move the other team back with a punt on fourth down.

One of the hardest parts of understanding a new statistic is grasping the idea of what numbers represent good performance or bad performance. We try to make that easy with DVOA, because it gets compared to average. Therefore, 0% always represents the league average. A positive DVOA indicates that the offense is more likely to score, and a negative DVOA indicates that the defense is more likely to stop them. This is why the best offenses have positive DVOA ratings (Indianapolis: +38.9%) and the best defenses have negative DVOA ratings (Pittsburgh: −15.0%).

Ratings for teams and starting players generally follow that scale, with the best being around 30% and the worst being around −30% (opposite for defense). However, because the baseline represents multiple years, and 2004 was the strongest year for NFL offense in at least two decades, the overall NFL average DVOA in 2004 was actually 1.5%, not 0%. The best offenses are higher than in years past, and the best defenses are less negative.

Team DVOA totals combine offense and defense, and the team total is given by offense minus defense to take into account that better defenses are more negative. (Special teams performance is also added, as described later in this essay.)

Does it work? Using correlation coefficients, we can show that only points are better than DVOA at indicating how many games a team has won (table 1) and DVOA does a better job of predicting wins in the coming season than either wins or points scored in the previous season (table 2).

TABLE 1. CORRELATION OF VARIOUS STATS TO WINS, 2000–2004

Stat	Offense	Defense	Total
Points Scored/Allowed	.69	−.67	.91
DVOA	.63	−.49	.84
Yards Gained/Allowed	.51	−.44	.67
Yards Gained/Allowed per Play	.50	−.36	.70

TABLE 2. CORRELATION OF VARIOUS STATS TO WINS FOLLOWING YEAR, 2000–2003

Stat	Correlation
DVOA	.30
Wins	.24
Point Differential	.24
Yardage Differential	.18

(Correlation coefficient is a statistical tool that measures how two variables are related by using a number between 1 and −1. The closer to −1 or 1, the stronger the relationship; the closer to 0, the weaker the relationship.)

Defense-Adjusted Points Above Replacement (DPAR)

After working with DVOA for a few months, we had to deal with a strange phenomenon: Well-regarded players, particularly those known for their durability—including Deuce McAllister, LaDainian Tomlinson, and Jeremy Shockey—had DVOA ratings that came out around average. The reason is that DVOA doesn't take into account the value of having a player involved in a greater number of plays, even if his performance is league-average. A player who is involved in more plays can draw the defense's attention away from other parts of the offense. If that player is a running back, he can take time off the clock with repeated runs.

Let's say you have a running back who carries the ball 300 times in a season. What would happen if you were to remove this player from his team's offense? What would happen to those 300 plays? Well, the player would not be replaced by thin air. This is why you have to compare performance to some kind of baseline; two yards is not two yards better than the alternative. On the other hand, while comparing players to the league average works on a per play basis, it doesn't work on a total basis because a player removed from an offense is not generally replaced by a similar player. Nearly every player is a starter for a reason: He is better than the alternative. Those 300 plays will generally be given to a significantly worse player, someone who is the backup because he doesn't have as much experience and/or talent.

To take this into account, we borrowed the concept of replacement level from our partners at *Baseball Prospectus.* Using a scale similar to the scale *BP* uses to determine baseball's replacement level, we've determined that a replacement level player has a DVOA of roughly −13.3%. Instead of determining value by comparing each play's "success value" to the average, as in DVOA, each play is instead compared to a number roughly 13.3% below the average success value of similar plays. That gives us value over a replacement level player, a better representation of a player's total contribution to his team on all his plays.

Actually, while in general replacement level is −13.3%, technically it is different for each position depending on whether we are measuring passing, rushing, or receiving. And, of course, the real replacement player is different for each team in the NFL. Pittsburgh's backup quarterback (Roethlisberger) was better than its starting quarterback (Maddox) from the beginning of the year. Two guys who started the season as backup running backs in Denver (Bell and Droughns) were better than the guy who began the year as a starter (Griffin). Both of Priest Holmes's backups performed well. On the other hand, of course, the drop from the starter to the backup is sometimes greater than the average drop to replacement level. Imagine if Peyton Manning broke his leg, for example. Since you need to generalize for the league as a whole, and since no starter is responsible for the performance of his backup, we use the same general replacement level across the league.

Of course, giving a number of "success value points over replacement level" would be fairly useless to the average fan and even the nonaverage fan. If we wrote that Ben Roethlisberger was worth 158 success value points over replacement in 2004, you would have no idea what the heck we were talking about. So we translate those success value points into a number that represents actual points. After working through statistics from the past five seasons, our best approximation is that a team made up entirely of replacement level players would be outscored 407 to 260, finishing with a 4–12 record. Conveniently, this is close to the average record of the last four expansion teams. But part of the reason this team gives up so many more points than it scores is that it has replacement level special teams. Those replacement level special teams are worth −27 points, making the actual baseline for determining offensive value 274 points (the baseline for defensive value is 394 points).

With a bit of math, it works out that each "success value point" over replacement level is worth about .48 actual points above this offensive baseline. We also adjust this number for the strength of the opponents each player has faced. Now I can tell you that Ben Roethlisberger was worth 76 points more than a replacement level quarterback in 2004, or 76.0 DPAR (which stands for Defense-adjusted Points Above Replacement). The year before, Pittsburgh starting quarterback Tommy Maddox was worth 37.0 DPAR.

Problems with DVOA and DPAR

Football is a game in which nearly every action requires the work of 2 or more teammates—in fact, usually 11 teammates all working in unison. Unfortunately, when it comes to individual player ratings, DVOA and DPAR are still far away from the point where we can figure the value of a player separate from the performance of his 10 teammates that are also involved in each play. That means that when we say, "Priest Holmes has a DVOA of 17.6%," what we are really saying is "Priest Holmes, playing in the Kansas City offensive system with the Kansas City offensive line blocking for him and Trent Green selling the fake when necessary, has a DVOA of 17.6%."

DVOA is limited by what's included in the official NFL play-by-play, so we can't say which teams have the best offensive DVOA when play-faking, or the best defensive DVOA against three-receiver sets, or the best DVOA facing a blitz.

Because we need to have the entire play-by-play of a season in order to compute DVOA and DPAR, these metrics are not yet ready to compare players of today to players of history. As of this writing, we have processed seven seasons, 1998–2004.

Special Teams

The problem with a system based on measuring both yardage and yardage towards a first down, of course, is what to do with plays that don't have the possibility of a first down. Special teams are an important part of football and we needed a way to add that performance to the team DVOA ranking. Our special teams metric includes five separate measurements: field goals (and extra points), net punting, punt returns, net kickoffs, and kick returns.

The foundation of most of these special teams ratings is the concept that each yard line has a different value based on how the likelihood of scoring changes with better field position. In Hidden Game, the authors suggested that the value of field position for the offense existed on a straight line with your own goal line being worth −2 points, the 50-yard line 2 points, and the opposing goal line 6 points. (−2 points isn't just the value of a safety; it also reflects the fact that when you are backed up in your own zone, you are likely going to see your drive stall, and you'll need to punt and give the ball to the other team in good field position. Thus, the defense is more likely to score next.)

Our studies have updated this concept to reflect the actual likelihood that the offense or defense will have the next score based on field position over the past three seasons. The line that represents the value of field position is not straight but curved, with the value of each yard increasing as teams approach either goal line (figure 1).

FIGURE 1. VALUE OF FIELD POSITION 2001–2004

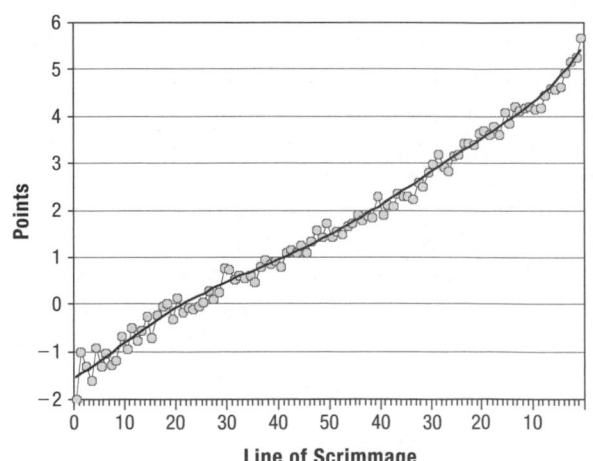

Line of Scrimmage

The special teams ratings compare each kick or punt to the league average based on the point value of field position at the yard line where each kick begins and ends, and where each return begins and ends. We've determined a league average for how far a kick goes based on the yard line from where the kick occurs (almost always the 30-yard line for kickoffs, variable for punts) and a league average for how far a return goes based on the yard line where the ball is caught (for kickoffs) or where the ball is caught as well as where it was kicked (for punts).

On kickoffs, the kicking team is rated based on net points compared to average, taking into account both the kick and the return if there is one. For the return team, the rating is based only on how many points the return is worth compared to average, based on the location of the catch. Return teams are not judged on the distance of kicks, nor are they judged on kicks that cannot be returned, such as touchbacks and kicks out of bounds.

Punt ratings work very similarly to kickoff ratings. The difference is the assumption that, unlike with kickoffs, the punt return team has some effect on the length of the punt itself. Sometimes they block it, but more often they force the punter into an imperfect kick because he needs to get the ball off before a block can occur. Kickoff ratings count the net value of the kickoff for the kicking team, but only the return for the returning team. Punt ratings, however, count the net point value of the punt for both the punting team and the return team.

Field goal kicking is measured differently. Measuring kickers by field goal percentage is a bit absurd, as it assumes that all field goals are of equal difficulty. In our metric, each field goal is compared to the average number of points scored on all field goal attempts from that distance. The value of a field goal increases as distance from the goal line increases.

Kickoffs, punts, and field goals are then adjusted based on weather and altitude. It will surprise no one to learn that it is easier to kick the ball in Denver or a dome than it is to kick the ball in Buffalo in December. These adjustments are explained further in the Denver chapter later in the book.

Once we've totaled how many points above or below average can be attributed to special teams, another formula then transforms these numbers from points to DVOA so the ratings can be added to offense and defense to get total team DVOA.

There are two aspects of special teams that don't show up in our numbers because a team has little or no influence on them—and yet, these plays do have an impact on wins and losses. The first is the length of kickoff by the opposing team, because no matter how strong your return

man you can't make the other guy kick it shorter. The second is field goals against your team. There is very little indication that this number has any correlation to a team with strong special teams, and even blocked field goals are—Carolina in the first couple weeks of 2003 notwithstanding—pretty much random. These two items represent "hidden indicators" of team performance that do not show up in our ratings. Special teams ratings also do not include two-point conversions or onside kick attempts, which are so infrequent as to be statistically insignificant in judging future performance.

Kickers have a player comment section with individual numbers for the last three years; other individual special teams ratings appear in an appendix at the end of the book.

Pythagorean Projection

The Pythagorean projection is an approximation of each team's wins based solely on points scored and allowed. The basic concept was made famous by baseball analyst Bill James, who discovered that the record of a baseball team could be very closely approximated by taking the square of team runs scored and dividing it by the square of team runs scored plus the square of team runs allowed. Statistician Daryl Morey later extended this theorem to professional football, although the exponent is 2.37 rather than 2. The Pythagorean projection has done a remarkable job of predicting Super Bowl champions. Out of 17 Super Bowls played since the 1987 strike season, 11 were won by the team that led the NFL in Pythagorean Wins, while only 7 were won by the team with the most actual victories. That includes Super Bowl XXXIX, as the 14–2 Patriots led the league with 12.4 Pythagorean Wins while the 15–1 Steelers had only 11.5 Pythagorean Wins (as did the 13–3 Eagles and 12–4 Colts). Other Super Bowl champions that led the league in Pythagorean Wins but not actual wins include the 2000 Ravens, 1999 Rams, and 1997 Broncos. Teams that win a game or more over what the Pythagorean projection estimates tend to regress the following year; teams that lose a game or more under what the Pythagorean projection estimates tend to win more the following year, particularly if they were 8-8 or better despite underachieving.

Adjusted Line Yards[1]

One of the most difficult goals of statistical analysis in football is somehow isolating how much responsibility for a play lies with each of the 22 men on the field. Nowhere is this as obvious as the running game, where one player runs while up to nine other players—including wideouts, tight ends, and a fullback—block in different directions.

---

1. Note to veteran FootballOutsiders.com readers: This method is significantly updated from the method used previously.

None of the statistics we use for measuring rushing—yards, touchdowns, yards per carry—differentiate between the contribution of the running back and the contribution of the offensive line. Neither do our advanced metrics DVOA and DPAR.

We have enough data amassed that we can try to separate the effect that the running back has on a particular play from the effect of the offensive line (and other offensive blockers) and the effect of the defense. A team might have two running backs in its stable: RB A, who averages 3.0 yards per carry, and RB B, who averages 3.5 yards per carry. Who is the better back? Imagine that RB A doesn't just average 3.0 yards per carry, but gets exactly 3 yards on every single carry, while RB B has a highly variable yardage output: sometimes 5 yards, sometimes −2 yards, sometimes 20 yards. The difference in variability between the runners can be exploited to not only determine the difference between the runners, but the effect the offensive line has on every running play.

We know that at some point in every long running play, the running back has gotten past all of his offensive line blocks. From here on, the rest of the play is dependent on the runner's own speed and elusiveness, combined with the speed and tackling ability of the defensive players. If Tiki Barber breaks through the line for 50 yards, avoiding tacklers all the way to the goal line, his offensive line has done a great job—but they aren't responsible for most of that run. How much are they responsible for?

For each running back carry, we calculated the probability that the back involved would run for the specific yardage on that play, based on that back's average yardage per carry and the variability of their yardage on every play. We also calculated the probability that the offense would get the yardage based on the team's rushing average and variability *without* the back involved in the play, and the probability that the defense would give up the specific amount of yardage based on its average rushing yards allowed per carry and variability. For example, based on his rushing average and variability, the probability in 2004 that Tiki Barber would have a positive carry was 80% while the probability that Giants would have a positive carry without Barber running was only 73%.

Yardage ends up falling into roughly the following combinations: losses, 0–4 yard gains, 5–10 yard gains, and gains of 11-plus yards. In general, the offensive line is 20% more responsible for lost yardage than it is for yardage gained up to 4 yards, but 50% less responsible for yardage gained from 5–10 yards, and not responsible for yardage past that. Thus, the creation of Adjusted Line Yards.

Adjusted Line Yards takes every carry by a running back and applies those percentages. (We don't include carries by receivers, which are usually based on deception rather than straight blocking, or carries by quarterbacks, which are busted passing plays except in Atlanta.) Those numbers are then adjusted based on down, distance, and situation as well as opponent (similar to DVOA) and then normalized so that the league average for Adjusted Line Yards per carry is the same as the league average for RB yards per carry (in 2004, 4.19).

Runs are listed by the NFL in seven different directions: left/right end, left/right tackle, left/right guard, and middle. Further research showed no statistically significant difference between how well a team performed on runs listed middle, left guard, and right guard, so we list runs separated into five different directions. Note that there may not be a statistically significant difference between right tackle and middle/guard either, but until we can research further (and for the sake of symmetry) we do still split out runs behind the right tackle separately.

Success Rate

Success rate is a statistic for running backs that measures how consistently they achieve the yardage necessary for a play to be successful. Some running backs will mix a few long runs with a lot of failed runs of one or two yards. Other running backs will consistently gain five yards on first down, or as many yards as necessary on third down.

Work on DVOA has shown us that five yards on first and ten is a good indicator that the team will eventually convert for another set of downs, but teams aren't used to requiring five yards from their running backs on every carry. Most teams consider a four-yard carry on first and ten a success—which it is, somewhat. It isn't as good as a five-yard run, but it is close, and it gets a partial credit in the DVOA system to recognize this. Since Success Rate compares rush attempts to other rush attempts, without consideration of passing, the standard for success on first down is slightly lower than for DVOA.

In addition, the metric changes slightly in the fourth quarter when running backs are used to run out the clock. A team with the lead is satisfied with a shorter run as long as it stays in bounds; for a team down by a couple of touchdowns in the fourth quarter, four yards on first down isn't going to be a big help.

The formula for Success Rate is as follows:

- A successful play must gain 40% of needed yards on first down, 60% of needed yards on second down, and 100% of needed yards on third down.

- If the offense is behind by more than a touchdown in the fourth quarter, the benchmarks switch to 50%/65%/100%.

- If the offense is ahead by any amount in the fourth quarter, the benchmarks switch to 30%/50%/100%.

The league-average Success Rate in 2004 was 46.4%. **Success Rate is not adjusted based on defenses faced.**

Quarterbacks and wide receivers who occasionally are used on rushing plays do not get Success Rates.

Similarity Scores

Similarity scores were first introduced by Bill James to compare baseball players to other baseball players from the past. It was only natural that the idea would spread to other sports as statistical analysis spread to other sports. NBA analyst John Hollinger has created his own version to compare basketball players, and we have created our own version to compare football players.

Similarity scores have a lot of possible uses, and we aren't the only football analysts who use them. Doug Drinen of the website footballguys.com has his own system that is specific to comparing fantasy football performances. The major goal of our similarity scores, however, is to compare career progressions and try to determine when players have a higher chance of a breakout, a decline, or—due to age or usage—an injury. Therefore we compare not only numbers like attempts, yards, and touchdowns, but also age and experience. We often are looking not for players who had similar seasons, but for players who had similar two- or three-year spans in their careers.

Similarity scores have some important weaknesses. The method compares standard statistics like yards and attempts, which are of course subject to all kinds of biases from strength of schedule to quality of receiver corps. The database for player comparison begins in 1978, the year the 16-game season began and passing rules were liberalized (a reasonable starting point to measure the "modern" NFL). We also project statistics for 1982 and 1987 as if the strikes did not happen, although we cannot correct for players who crossed the 1987 picket line to play more than 12 games.

Our similarity scores system is still in its infant stages, and we use it on a limited basis in the book. You'll see it mentioned in a few places (particularly in the player comments) but there isn't one particular article that specifically revolves around similarity scores. If you are interested in the computations behind our similarity scores system, we have listed the standards for each position online at http://www.footballoutsiders.com/stats/similarity.php.

2005 Win Projection System

Each team receives a 2005 Projection at the beginning of its chapter. Many preseason books and magazines will give an exact prediction of a team's win-loss record, but that's a bit of a fool's exercise because:

a. With only 16 games in a season, a team's performance may vary wildly from its actual talent level due to a couple of random bounces of the ball or badly timed injuries, and

b. The economic structure of the NFL causes teams to suddenly jump or drop in overall ability more often than in other sports.

Instead, we are providing a look at the probability of each team to have a given type of season based on what we know about them at press time. The projections begin with three equations that forecast 2005 DVOA for offense, defense, and special teams based on a number of different factors including two years of DVOA in various situations, improvement in the second half of 2004, recent draft history, and both quarterback and coaching experience. This is an updated version of a formula that we used on our website to predict the 2004 standings, the one that unexpectedly, but correctly, foresaw that San Diego would have one of the league's best offenses.

These three equations produce precise numbers representing the most likely outcome, but also produce a range of possibilities because of unforeseen changes, not to mention the usual variation in performance. The Colts, for example, are projected to have the best offense in the AFC this year, yet due to injury, free agency, the draft, schedule strength, Belichick's mind games with Manning, and other factors, there is a chance that the Colts offense will regress. The variation in the equations can be used to define the probability of each possible DVOA for each team. Each team then has a set of possible DVOA levels for each category and each possible DVOA has a related probability of occurring. The set of possible DVOA ratings for all 16 opponents also creates a set of possible schedule strength ratings.

Then we created a simulation that calculates total wins for the season by randomly picking ratings for offensive, defensive, special teams, and schedule strength out of each team's set of DVOA possibilities according to the probability of each outcome. We ran this simulation for each team 1,700 times and compared the results to the historical probability that an NFL team would win a certain number of games over a 16-game season. (None of the calculated probabilities, for the entire league, was more than 1.7% different from the historical probability of each win total for the entire league.)

The resulting possible win totals are then separated into five categories:

- Leinart Land (0–4 wins)
- Bad Team (5–6 wins)
- Mediocre (7–8 wins)
- Playoff Contender (9–10 wins)
- Super Bowl Contender (11+ wins)

Yes, we know that an 8–8 team was a playoff contender in last year's NFC, but that's not something that happens very often. You'll notice the best AFC teams have much lower chances of winning 11 or more games; this is because the AFC is very evenly balanced, with many teams that have a decent chance to be good, while the NFC is distinctively split between haves and have-nots.

The percentage given for each category is dependent not only on how good we project the team to be in 2005, but the level of variation possible in that projection and the expected performance of the teams on the schedule. For example, while both Jacksonville and Oakland have a median of 7.0 expected wins, you'll notice that Oakland's probability of entering the playoff race is higher, but so is their probability of entering the Matt Leinart Sweepstakes. There is more variation when we look at Oakland's possible performance than when we look at Jacksonville's.

KUBIAK Projection System

Most "skill position" players whom we expect to play a role this season receive a 2005 projection of their standard NFL statistics using the KUBIAK projection system. KUBIAK takes into account a number of different factors including expected role, performance over the past two seasons, age, height, weight, historical comparables, and projected team performance on offense and defense. KUBIAK got its name because if Baseball Prospectus was going to name their projection system after a little-known utility infielder, we wanted to name ours after the man who held John Elway's clipboard for so long that they made him offensive coordinator.

Drive Stats

In a statistical appendix at the back of the book you'll find drive stats for the last three years, compiled by Jim Armstrong. These are also occasionally mentioned throughout the book. Drive stats are computed from NFL drive charts and are not adjusted for strength of schedule or situation. Take-a-knee drives at the end of a half are discarded.

These stats are generally self-explanatory, giving each team's total number of drives as well as average yards per drive, points per drive, touchdowns per drive, punts per drive, and turnovers per drive, interceptions per drive, and fumbles lost per drive. LOS/Drive represents average starting field position (line of scrimmage) per drive from the offensive point of view. Drive stats are given for offense and defense, with NET representing simply offense minus defense.

How to Read the Prospectus Box

Here is a rundown of all the tables and stats that appear in the 32 team chapters. Each team chapter begins with a box in the upper-right-hand corner that gives a summary of our statistics for that team, as follows:

2004 Record gives the team's actual win-loss record.

DVOA Estimated Wins projects how many games the team would be expected to win based on 2004 perfor-

mance in specific situations, normalized to average luck and an average schedule. The formula emphasizes consistency and overall DVOA as well as DVOA in the most important specific situations: red zone defense, first quarter offense, and performance in the second half when the score is close. Rank is given in parentheses.

Pythagorean Wins gives the approximate number of wins expected last year based on the team's raw totals of points scored and allowed, along with NFL rank.

DVOA gives the team's total DVOA rating, with rank. We also give each team's **weighted DVOA,** based on a formula that gives more emphasis to performance in games later in the season. This gives a more accurate picture of where each team stood at the end of the regular season, a useful indicator for which teams may improve or decline in 2005 (particularly on defense).

Adjusted Offense will look new even to readers of Football Outsiders, but it isn't really a new stat, just a different way to look at DVOA. Plays are analyzed using the same measures of success and the same league-wide baselines from the DVOA system, then translated into points using the same ratio as Points Above Replacement for individual players, with 0% DVOA corresponding to the 2004 league average of 23.5 points per game. The resulting number gives the number of points per game that a team would score if you separated out the offense from all outside factors. It assumes the team has an average defense and average special teams, running an average number of 61.5 plays per game against an average schedule of opponents. For example, the New England offense would score 28.4 points per game if all other factors were neutral. The league's top offense, Indianapolis, would score 31.7 points per game. The league's worst offense, Chicago, would score 11.1 points per game. In reality, the Bears scored 14.4 points per game because their pathetic offense had the benefit of better field position thanks to an above-average defense and special teams.

Adjusted points per game can only be used to rate the entire offense, not to split out the offense into different situations, so we're still using standard DVOA as well. You'll find DVOA listed next to adjusted offense along with rank out of all 32 NFL teams. **Adjusted Defense** provides the same two measures for the defense. Remember that a negative DVOA (or under 23.5 adjusted points per game) means better defense.

Adjusted Special Teams gives the value of special teams in points per game, above or below league average, plus the value translated into DVOA and rank out of 32 teams.

Variance measures a team's consistency over the 2004 season. Teams are ranked from least consistent (number 1, greatest variance, Buffalo) to most consistent (number 32, least variance, New Orleans).

2005 Projection gives the team's chances of finishing in five different win categories based on the 2005 Win Projection system described earlier in this chapter.

Projected Average Opponent gives the team's strength of schedule for 2005 based not on last year's record but on median projected DVOA for each opponent. A positive schedule is harder, a negative schedule easier. Teams are ranked from the hardest projected schedule (number 1, San Diego) to the easiest (number 32, Chicago). This strength of schedule projection does not take into account which games are home and which are away, or the timing of the bye week.

After the prospectus box, each team then gets an essay discussing its 2004 season and prospects for 2005, followed in some chapters by a research essay (or two) on a particular issue related to that team. Then come statistical tables and comments related to that team and its specific units.

Table 3 gives a quick look at the team's week-to-week performance in 2004. This includes the playoffs for those teams that made the postseason, with the four weeks of playoffs numbered 18 (wild card) through 21 (Super Bowl). All other tables in the team chapters represent regular season performance only, unless otherwise noted.

Looking at the first week for the New England Patriots in table 3, the first five columns are fairly obvious: The Patriots beat Indianapolis in Week 1, and the score was 27–24. YDF and YDA are total net yards on offense and total net yards against the defense. These numbers do not include penalty yardage or kick and punt return yardage. TO represents the turnover margin. Unlike other parts of the book where we consider all fumbles as equal, this represents only actual turnovers: fumbles lost and interceptions. +2 here means that the Colts turned the ball over two more times than the Patriots did.

Finally, you'll see DVOA ratings for this game: total DVOA first, then offense, defense, and special teams. Note that these are DVOA ratings, adjusted for opponent. Therefore, if you were to compare the same week for two teams that played each other, the team with the higher rating did not necessarily play better and "deserve" to win that game. A good example of this is New England's 24–10 win over Miami in Week 5. Although New England outplayed Miami in that game, the Patriots are listed with a total DVOA of −14.6% and the Dolphins with a total DVOA of 15.8%. When you consider that Miami was one of the league's worst teams, the Patriots actually played below-average football that day despite winning the game. The Dolphins actually played above-average football when we consider the level of competition represented by New England.

Included in table 3 is a graph representing each team's weekly performance throughout the season, based on total DVOA. Opponent and week are listed on the x-axis; the breaks in the line represent the bye week (or, for the Patriots and three other teams, bye weeks). The curved line that

TABLE 3. WEEKLY PERFORMANCE

Wk	vs.	W-L	PF	PA	YDF	YDA	TO	DVOA Total	Off	Def	ST
1	IND	W	27	24	404	446	+2	61.8%	44.8%	-21.8%	-5.8%
2	@ARI	W	23	12	376	167	0	83.8%	30.8%	-43.8%	10.8%
3	BYE										
4	@BUF	W	31	17	399	357	+1	60.8%	84.8%	-3.8%	-27.8%
5	MIA	W	24	10	207	296	+1	-15.8%	-17.8%	-3.8%	-1.8%
6	SEA	W	30	20	363	443	0	42.8%	20.8%	-11.8%	11.8%
7	NYJ	W	13	7	347	270	0	65.8%	40.8%	-24.8%	2.8%
8	@PIT	L	20	34	244	420	-4	-35.8%	-9.8%	31.8%	5.8%
9	@STL	W	40	22	377	336	+1	48.8%	32.8%	7.8%	23.8%
10	BUF	W	29	6	429	123	+4	146.8%	43.8%	-111.8%	-8.8%
11	@KC	W	27	19	411	417	0	56.8%	37.8%	-14.8%	4.8%
12	BAL	W	24	3	310	130	+2	75.8%	26.8%	-48.8%	1.8%
13	@CLE	W	42	15	410	293	+1	31.8%	1.8%	-14%	16.8%
14	CIN	W	35	28	354	482	+3	19.8%	65.8%	46.8%	0.0%
15	@MIA	L	28	29	323	222	-3	-8.87%	-18.8%	40.8%	-30.8%
16	@NYJ	W	23	7	374	278	+3	76.8%	41.8%	-33.8%	2.8%
17	SF	W	21	7	405	318	-1	3.8%	13.8%	8.8%	-1.8%
18	BYE										
19	IND	W	20	3	325	276	+3	90.8%	30.8%	-56.8%	4.8%
20	@PIT	W	41	27	322	388	+4	88.8%	50.8%	-35.8%	4.8%
21	PHI	W	24	21	331	369	+3	-100.0%	-100.0%	-100.0%	-50.8%

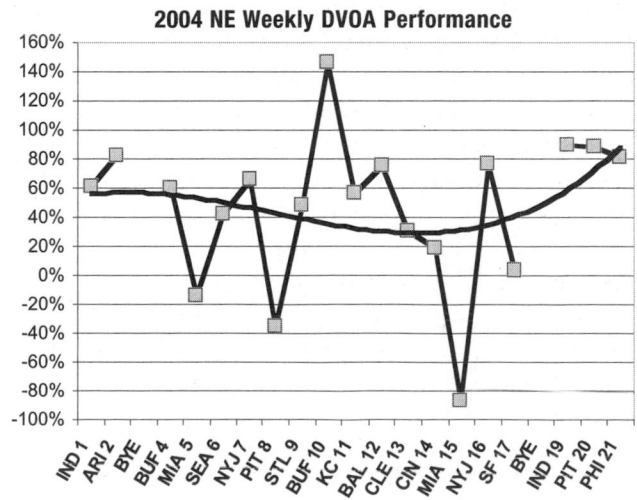

2004 NE Weekly DVOA Performance

runs through the graph represents the trend of the team's performance as the season progressed. (For you math types, this curve is the closest-fit third-order polynomial equation. For you nonmath types, that means it bends twice.)

Trends and Splits

This section gives DVOA split into different portions of a team's performance, for both offense and defense. Each split is listed with the team's rank among the 32 NFL teams. These numbers represent regular season performance only.

Total DVOA gives total offensive and defensive DVOA in all situations. **Unadjusted VOA** represents the breakdown of play-by-play considering situation but not opponent. A team whose offensive DVOA is higher than its offensive VOA played a harder-than-average schedule of opposing defenses; a team with a lower defensive DVOA than defensive VOA played a harder-than-average schedule of opposing offenses.

Weighted Trend lowers the importance of earlier games to give a better idea of how the team was playing at the end of the regular season. The final six weeks of the season are full strength; each week then gets less weight until the first three weeks of the season, which are not included.

Variance is the same as noted above, with a higher percentage representing less consistency. This is true for both offense and defense: Atlanta, for example, had the league's least consistent offense with 20.5% variance, but the most consistent defense with only 3.0% variance.

Passing and **Rushing** are fairly self-explanatory. Note that rushing includes all rushes, not just those by running backs, and this includes quarterback scrambles that may have began as pass plays. Unfortunately, we cannot yet separate intended and nonintended quarterback runs in the play-by-play.

The next three lines split out DVOA on **First Down**, **Second Down**, and **Third Down.** Third Down here includes fourth downs where a team runs a regular offensive play instead of punting or attempting a field goal. Next comes DVOA in the **Red Zone**, which is any offensive play starting from the defense's 20-yard line through the goal line. The final split is **Late and Close,** which includes any play in the second half or overtime when the teams are within eight points of each other in either direction—the offense leading by up to eight points, or losing by up to eight points. (Eight points of course is the biggest deficit that can be made up with a single score, a touchdown and two-point conversion.)

Five-Year Performance

This table gives each team's performance over the past five seasons. It includes win-loss record, Pythagorean Wins, Estimated Wins, and total DVOA, along with DVOA for offense, defense, and special teams. The four DVOA ratings are listed with the team's rank among that season's 32 NFL teams (for 2000 and 2001, 31 teams).

The league-average baseline for DVOA is calculated from multiple seasons, so league-average DVOA will be higher or lower than 0% for each particular season. Over the past five years, 2002 and 2004 have higher offensive levels, and 2000, 2001, and 2003 have higher defensive levels. To give an example of how this affected a specific team, New England's offensive DVOA rating dropped from 2002 to 2003 but the 2003 Patriots have a higher rank among the 32 teams because the context of the league was slightly different.

Individual Offensive Statistics[2]

Each team chapter contains a table giving passing and receiving numbers for any player who either threw at least five passes or was thrown at least five passes, along with rushing numbers for any players who carried the ball at least three times. These numbers also appear in the player comments at the end of the book (except for wide receiver rushing attempts) but by putting them together in the team chapters we hope we make it easier to compare the performances of different players on the same team.

All players are listed with DPAR, PAR, and DVOA. The purpose of listing both DPAR and PAR is to compare how different players on the same team were affected by the schedule. For example, Eli Manning had a higher DPAR than PAR, because he played a particularly difficult schedule. His teammate, Kurt Warner, had a lower DPAR than PAR, because he played an easier schedule before losing the quarterback job to Manning.

Passing statistics (table 4) then list total pass plays **(Plys),** net yardage **(NtYds),** and net yards per pass **(Avg).** These numbers include not just passes (and the positive yardage from them) but aborted snaps and sacks (and the

TABLE 4. SAMPLE PASSING TABLE

Passing (min. 5 plays)

Player	DPAR	PAR	DVOA	Plys	NtYds	Avg	Cmpl	TD	Int
Tom Brady	113.4	95.6	41.8%	499	3520	7.1	60.8%	28	13

---

2. An important note: Individual numbers in the team tables will differ from individual numbers in the player comments. The team tables feature our numbers, which are edited to remove plays such as kneeldowns, Hail Marys, and clock-stopping spikes, and include aborted snaps as passes rather than rush attempts. The tables in the player comment chapters at the end of the book are official NFL totals.

TABLE 5. SAMPLE RUSHING TABLE

Rushing (min. 3 plays)

Player	DPAR	PAR	DVOA	Plys	Yds	Avg	TD	Fum	Suc
Corey Dillon	50.4	49.5	19.8%	345	1636	4.7	12	4	54%
Kevin Faulk	-11.5	-11.2	40.8%	54	255	4.7	2	0	50%

TABLE 6. SAMPLE RECEIVING TABLE

Receiving (min. 3 plays)

Player	DPAR	PAR	DVOA	Plys	Ctch	Yds	Y/C	TD	CPct
WR									
David Givens	21.4	19.8	16.8%	106	56	872	15.6	3	53%
David Patten	18.6	17.2	15.8%	95	44	800	18.2	7	46%
Deion Branch	-16.7	-17.2	36.8%	51	35	454	13.0	4	69%

negative yardage from them). The final three numbers are completion percentage **(Cmpl),** which does not include aborted snaps or sacks, plus passing touchdowns and interceptions.

Rushing statistics in table 5 start with DPAR, PAR, and DVOA, than list rushing plays and yards along with average yards per carry and rushing touchdowns. The final two columns are fumbles—both those lost to the defense and those recovered by the offense—and Success Rate, explained earlier in this chapter.

Receiving statistics in table 6 start with DPAR, PAR, and DVOA and then list the number of passes thrown to the receiver (Plys), the number of passes caught (Ctch), the total receiving yards, yards per catch (Y/C), total receiving touchdowns, and catch percentage (CPct), which is the percentage of passes intended for the receiver that were caught.

Individual Defensive Statistics

Defensive players make plays. Plays aren't just tackles—interceptions and pass deflections change the course of the game, and so does the act of forcing a fumble or beating the offensive players to the ball. And while some plays stop a team on third down and force a punt, others merely stop a receiver after he's caught a 30-yard pass. The numbers in this book are the first step toward giving some kind of context to the official record of defensive performance (table 7).

Defensive players are listed in the team chapters if they made at least 20 plays during the 2004 season. Players are separated into defensive line, linebackers, and defensive backs and listed with the following numbers:

Age: The player's age, listed simply as the difference between birth year and 2005.

Plays: The total plays, including tackles, pass deflections, interceptions, fumbles forced, and fumble recoveries.

TABLE 7. SAMPLE DEFENSIVE PLAYERS TABLE

Defensive Players (min. 20 plays)

Player	Age	Plys	Stop	Dfts	AvYds	StpRt	Sack	Int	FR
Linebackers									
Tedy Bruschi	32	126	68	22	3.8	54%	3.5	3	0
Ted Johnson	33	79	44	8	3.5	56%	1.0	0	0
Mike Vrabel	30	72	39	17	3.5	54%	5.5	0	0
Willie McGinest	34	58	41	20	1.7	71%	9.5	1	1
Roman Phifer	37	44	18	9	5.7	41%	1.5	1	1
Roosevelt Colvin	28	31	17	8	3.6	55%	5.0	0	0

Stops: The total number of plays that prevent a "success" by the offense (45% of needed yards on first down, 60% on second down, 100% on third or fourth down).

Defeats (Dfts): The total number of plays that stop the offense from gaining first down yardage on third or fourth down, stop the offense behind the line of scrimmage, or result in a fumble or interception.

Average Yards (AvYds): The average number of yards gained by the offense when this player is credited with making the play.

Stop Rate (StpRt): The percentage of Plays that are Stops.

The final three columns represent official NFL totals of sacks, interceptions, and fumble recoveries.

We would like to thank Roland Beech and the staff of TwoMinuteWarning.com for allowing us to publish their individual defensive player statistics in our book this year. We have plans to build upon this work in the future, but for now, the defensive player statistics are not adjusted for situation or opponent like our offensive metrics. The numbers unfortunately do not reflect the opportunities a player has to make plays, but they do show us which players were most active on the field. A large number of plays could mean a strong defensive performance, or it could mean a cornerback that opposing quarterbacks tried to pick on. In general, the defensive player numbers should be taken as information that tells us what happened on the field in 2004, not as a strict, unassailable judgment of which players are better than others.

How to Read the Offensive Line Tables

The offensive line tables (see table 8) list the last three years of Adjusted Line Yards and other statistics for each team.

The first column gives standard yards per carry by each team's running backs **(Yds).** The next two columns give Adjusted Line Yards **(AdjLineYd)** followed by rank among the 32 teams.

Then come three other rushing statistics. **Power** gives the percentage of runs in "power situations" that achieved a first down or touchdown. Those situations include any

TABLE 8. SAMPLE OFFENSIVE LINE TABLE

Offensive Line

Year	Yds	AdjLineYd	Rank	Power	Rank	10+ Yds	Rank	Stuff	Rank	Sack	AdjSack%	Rank
2002	4.00	4.00	14	76%	7	12%	28	22%	6	31	5.0%	8
2003	3.62	4.01	23	60%	23	10%	31	23%	10	32	5.4%	12
2004	4.42	4.56	5	76%	7	16%	21	22%	11	26	4.8%	5

Year	LEnd	Rank	LTckl	Rank	MdGrd	Rank	RTckl	Rank	REnd	Rank
2002	4.00	18	4.00	18	4.40	7	3.20	27	3.06	27
2003	3.76	22	3.76	28	4.18	16	4.64	8	3.06	26
2004	4.98	5	4.76	8	4.24	16	5.19	2	4.56	5

third or fourth down with one or two yards to go, and any runs in goal-to-go situations from the two-yard line or closer. Unlike the other rushing numbers on the Offensive Line table, Power does include quarterbacks.

10+ Yards gives the percentage of a team's rushing yards that came more than ten yards past the line of scrimmage. A team with a high ranking in Adjusted Line Yards but a low ranking in 10+ Yards is heavily dependent on its offensive line to make the running game work. A team with a low ranking in Adjusted Line Yards but a high ranking in 10+ Yards is heavily dependent on its running back breaking long runs to make the running game work.

Stuff gives the percentage of runs that are stuffed based on the following parameters:

On first down, zero or negative gain

On other downs, less than one-fourth the yards needed for another first down.

Note that this is a slightly different definition than the one used by STATS, Inc., for its "stuffs" statistic. Since being stuffed is bad, teams are ranked from stuffed least often (number 1) to most often (number 32).

The final number on the first part of the table is Adjusted Sack Rate **(AdjSack%),** which is a better measurement than total sacks, and rank among the 32 teams. Some teams allow a lot of sacks because they throw a lot of passes; Adjusted Sack Rate accounts for this by dividing sacks by total pass plays. It is also adjusted for situation (sacks are much more common on third down, particularly third and long) and opponent. Remember that quarterbacks share responsibility for sacks, and two different quarterbacks behind the same line can have very different Adjusted Sack Rates. Particularly if one is named "Rob Johnson."

The second part of the offensive line table gives Adjusted Line Yards in each of the five directions, with rank among the 32 teams. Note that the league average is higher on the left than the right. Specifically in 2004, the league average was 4.23 on runs left end, 4.38 on runs left tackle, 4.20 on runs middle and guard, 4.18 on runs right tackle, and 3.90 on runs right end.

How to Read the Defensive Front Seven Tables

The defensive front seven section contains a table that looks exactly like the table in the offensive line section. The difference is that the numbers here are for all opposing running backs against this team's defensive front. Teams are now ranked in the opposite order, as well, so the number one defensive front seven is the one that allows the fewest Adjusted Line Yards, the lowest percentage in Power situations, and has the highest Adjusted Sack Rate. Directions for Adjusted Line Yards are given from the offense's perspective, so runs left end and left tackle are aimed at the right defensive end and (assuming the tight end is on the other side) weakside linebacker.

How to Read the Defensive Secondary Tables

The defensive secondary table (table 9) gives DVOA figured against different types of receivers. Each offense's wide receivers have one receiver designated as number one, and another as number two. (Occasionally this is difficult, due to injury or a particularly screwed-up offense like Cleveland's, but usually it isn't rocket science.) The other receivers form a third category, with tight ends and running backs as fourth and fifth categories. The defense is

TABLE 9. SAMPLE DEFENSIVE SECONDARY TABLE

Year	DVOA vs. #1 WR	Rank	DVOA vs. #2 WR	Rank	DVOA vs. Other WR	Rank	DVOA vs. TE	Rank	DVOA vs. RB	Rank
2002	-8.8%	25	-16.6%	12	4.7%	21	4.6%	26	-36.5%	3
2003	-62.9%	1	-39.1%	3	-36.4%	5	-30.7%	2	12.2%	26
2004	-49.7%	1	41.5%	30	11.4%	22	-31.0%	5	16.2%	28

then judged on the performance of each receiver based on the standard DVOA method, with each rating adjusted based on strength of schedule. (Opponents with Terrell Owens and Torry Holt as top receivers, for example, are tougher than opponents with David Terrell and Amani Toomer as top receivers.)

The defensive secondary table is actually more of a general pass defense table, as the ratings against tight ends and running backs are in large part due to the performance of linebackers. Ranks go from the top defense (number 1) to the worst defense (number 32).

How to Read the Special Teams Tables

The special teams tables (table 10) list the last three years of kick, punt, and return numbers for each team.

The first two columns list total special teams DVOA and rank among the 32 teams. The next two columns list the value in actual points of field goals (and extra points) when compared to how a league-average kicker would do from the same distances, adjusted for weather and altitude, and rank among the 32 teams. The two columns after that list the estimated value of field position over or under the league average based on net punting, translated into actual points, and rank among the 32 teams. The final sets of columns list the estimated value of field position and rank for punt returns, net kickoffs, and kick returns.

Administrative Minutiae

Receiving statistics include all passes intended for the receiver in question, including those that are incomplete or intercepted. The word "passes" refers to both complete and incomplete pass attempts. When rating receivers, interceptions are treated as incomplete passes with no penalty.

For the computation of DVOA and DPAR, passing statistics include sacks as well as fumbles on aborted snaps. We do not include kneeldown plays or spikes for the purpose of stopping the clock. Some interceptions that we have determined to be Hail Mary plays at the end of the first half or game are counted as regular incomplete passes, not turnovers.

Unless we say otherwise, when we refer to third down performance in this book we are referring to a combination of third down and the handful of rushing and passing plays that take place on fourth down (primarily fourth-and-one). One major exception to this is the article on the effect of sacks that appears in the Chicago chapter.

Thank you to Dr. Benjamin Alamar for help with the calculation of both the improved Adjusted Line Yards formula and the 2005 Win Projection system, as well as the explanations for each.

TABLE 10. SAMPLE SPECIAL TEAMS TABLE

Year	DVOA	Rank	FG/XP	Rank	Net Punt	Rank	Punt Ret	Rank	Net Kick	Rank	Kick Ret	Rank
2002	15.2%	5	13.9	1	-10.0	19	1.2	14	-12.5	13	-13.9	24
2003	-15.2%	13	-11.6	30	2.6	17	-4.2	20	5.3	7	14.6	3
2004	0.2%	16	15.2	1	-0.5	23	-16.2	29	-4.8	24	7.2	8

The Best Quarterback Season Ever

Aaron Schatz

Did Peyton Manning have the greatest quarterback season of all time?

Looking at raw numbers, the answer seems to be yes. Manning broke Dan Marino's NFL passing touchdown record, and he did it without playing more than a couple snaps in his team's final game. He averaged more than nine yards per pass attempt and threw just ten interceptions. He smashed the NFL passer rating record of 112.8 with a passer rating of 121.1.

On the other hand, Manning set that record during one of the most all-around offense-oriented seasons in NFL history. Thanks in part to stricter enforcement of illegal contact by defensive backs, the league-wide completion percentage was the highest in NFL history, 59.8%. The average team threw 23 passing touchdowns, the highest number in NFL history. (Take out the 51 thrown by Manning and Jim Sorgi, and the average becomes 22 passing touchdowns, which is still higher than any season except 1995 and 1983.) The average team threw 16.4 interceptions, lower than any season other than 1997. Quarterbacks averaged seven yards per pass attempt for the first time since 1990.

Was Manning really having the best season ever, or was he just helped by the rules?

With four weeks left in the season, that's the question that ESPN.com asked me to answer. At that time, Manning's numbers projected over the full 16-game season to 4,833 yards and a ridiculous 59 touchdowns with just 12 interceptions. Was this really the best quarterback season in history after the offensive environment of 2004 was taken into account?

The best way to determine this would be to go through the play-by-play from every NFL season, breaking down each play to create DVOA and DPAR, with different baselines for quarterback performance based on the offensive environment of each era. This would allow a correction for quarterbacks who received great field position from their defenses, quarterbacks who benefited from strong running games, and quarterbacks who played particularly easy schedules.

Unfortunately, play-by-play from every NFL season is a little tough to find. At the time, only six seasons of play-

TABLE 1. AVERAGE TEAM PASSING, 1998 VS. 2004

Year	Comp	Att	Yds	TD	INT
1989	286	512	3659	20.8	20.0
2004	306	511	3605	22.9	16.4
Ratio	107%	100%	99%	110%	82%

by-play had been broken down for DVOA ratings (it's now seven). Accurate play-by-play for Jack Kemp and Len Dawson in the mid-1960s AFL probably doesn't even exist.

Since I couldn't break down actual play-by-play, the next best thing was to translate the standard statistics for every quarterback season into the offensive environment of 2004. For example, table 1 shows a comparison of the average team's passing numbers in 1989 and the average team's passing numbers in 2004:

Since quarterbacks in general threw 7% more completions in 2004, every quarterback from 1989 got 7% more completions. They also got 10% more touchdowns, 1% fewer yards, and 18% fewer interceptions. I did this for each season since the 1950 NFL-AAFC merger. Quarterbacks from 1977 and earlier were projected to 16 games instead of 14 or 12. And Manning and the other quarterbacks of 2004 were projected over a 16-game season instead of the 12 games they had played at the time.

Through statistical regression, I created a formula that turned passes, yards, touchdowns, and interceptions into a rough estimate of the Football Outsiders PAR (Points Above Replacement) metric, which was also being run every Monday as part of ESPN's Snap Judgment column. The resulting list of the best quarterback seasons of all time looked like this:

1. Peyton Manning, 2004 Colts
2. Otto Graham, 1953 Browns
3. Dan Marino, 1984 Dolphins
4. Bert Jones, 1976 Colts
5. Warren Moon, 1990 Oilers
6. Donovan McNabb, 2004 Eagles
7. Ken Anderson, 1975 Bengals

8. Kurt Warner, 1999 Rams
9. Rich Gannon, 2002 Raiders
10. Kurt Warner, 2001 Rams

The analysis showed that 2004, even after correcting for the overall rise in offense, was a historic year for great quarterbacks. Since Daunte Culpepper was the next player on the list, 2004 had put three quarterbacks in the top 11.

But the method had some flaws. It wasn't a list of the best quarterback seasons, but rather a list of the best passing seasons. It didn't include rushing numbers, and it didn't include sacks. It didn't correct for strength of schedule. And, of course, it didn't take into account what happened over the last four weeks of 2004. Peyton Manning didn't finish the year with 59 touchdowns—he threw only 5 in his last three games and then sat out the last game of the year. Donovan McNabb had mediocre games against Dallas and Washington and then sat out the last *two* games of the year. And Daunte Culpepper, with Randy Moss back in the lineup, finished the year with four of his best games.

So with the entire season in the books, I went back and revisited my list of the top quarterback seasons in modern NFL history.

This time, I included rushing statistics, translating numbers into the context of 2004 based on how many runs, yards, and rushing touchdowns the average team had from its quarterbacks each season. I included sacks, except for years where those numbers are not available. (That meant two different formulas to determine PAR, with a second, slightly less accurate formula for the 1960 AFL, 1963 AFL, and 1960–1962 NFL.)

I translated numbers not into Points Above Replacement, but into Points Above Average, to increase the value of quarterbacks who were truly great, and decrease the value of those who were very good and happened to throw the ball a ton.

The next step was adding strength of schedule. Since we estimate the influence of the offense and the defense to be roughly 50–50, each quarterback was adjusted based on half the difference between the average pass defense he faced and the average pass defense in the league that season. As you might expect, nearly every quarterback at the top of the list faced a below-average schedule of pass defenses—in large part because those pass defenses had to face a quarterback having one of the best seasons of all time.

Finally, with apologies to Otto Graham, I redefined modern NFL history to start with the beginning of the AFL in 1960 rather than the NFL-AAFC merger in 1950. It just doesn't make sense to try translating Graham into a modern context, because he was driving a Porsche while other quarterbacks had barely invented the wheel. Cleveland was the first team whose offensive linemen formed a pass-

ing pocket instead of trying to block a pass play like a running play. Coach Paul Brown also originated timing routes, sideline passes, and the draw play. At the same time, Brown believed in running the ball in the end zone, so Graham had 8 rushing touchdowns and only 11 passing touchdowns despite throwing for 250 more yards than any other quarterback. Translated to a 2004 context, Graham's 1953 season looks like this: 302-for-369, an 81.8% completion percentage, with 4,232 yards but only 16 touchdowns and six interceptions.

I left out quarterbacks from the strike-shortened 9-game 1982 season, although quarterbacks from the strike-shortened 1987 season were prorated from 12 games to 16. It's also important to note that I counted only regular season performance, and I counted only the quarterback's personal performance—there was no adjustment based on how many games the team won, so that quarterbacks would not be penalized for sharing a locker room with subpar defenses.

The top seasons are listed both with the actual numbers and with the numbers projected to today's offensive environment: a league-average 2004 schedule. We'll look at the top ten as well as some other interesting seasons lower down on the list. The top 100 seasons appear in tables 2 and 3.

Based on the results, it turns out that a Colts quarterback did have the best season in modern NFL history. It just turns out we had the wrong Colts quarterback.

1. Bert Jones			1976 Baltimore Colts			
	Cmpl	Att	Pct	Yds	TD	INT
Actual:	207	343	60.3%	3104	24	9
Projected:	328	479	68.5%	4521	33	9

When people talk about the great quarterbacks from the 1970s, you hear about Terry Bradshaw, Fran Tarkenton, Roger Staubach—never Bert Jones. But for a short, three-year stretch, from 1975 to 1977, Bert Jones was the best quarterback in the league. People knew who he was then—he was the second-overall pick in the 1973 draft, and he won the 1976 MVP award. Jones's 1976 season is the best, not because it stands out in one area, but because it ranks so high in every area. Quarterbacks who threw for more yards per attempt threw more interceptions. Quarterbacks who threw for more touchdowns had a lower completion percentage. Quarterbacks who threw for more yards couldn't tuck it and run (Jones was second among quarterbacks that year with 214 yards on the ground).

As a high draft pick, Jones started nothing like Kurt Warner, but his career pattern was very similar. After three amazing years, Jones lost most of 1978 and 1979 to injury and eventually was traded to the Rams where he rotted on the bench behind Vince Ferragamo. But according to our

TABLE 2. TOP 100 QUARTERBACK SEASONS: ACTUAL NUMBERS

Rank	Name	Year	Team	G	Cmpl	Att	Pct	Yds	Y/At	TD	Int	RuYD	RuTD	Sack
1	Bert Jones	1976	BAL	14	207	343	60.3%	3104	9.0	24	9	214	2	29
2	Peyton Manning	2004	IND	16	336	497	67.6%	4557	9.2	49	10	38	0	13
3	Dan Marino	1984	MIA	16	362	564	64.2%	5084	9.0	48	17	−7	0	13
4	Daunte Culpepper	2004	MIN	16	379	548	69.2%	4717	8.6	39	11	406	2	46
5	Steve Young	1992	SF	16	268	402	66.7%	3465	8.6	25	7	537	4	29
6	Ken Anderson	1975	CIN	13	228	377	60.5%	3169	8.4	21	11	188	2	32
7	Ken Stabler	1976	OAK	12	194	291	66.7%	2737	9.4	27	17	−2	1	19
8	Ken Anderson	1974	CIN	13	213	328	64.9%	2667	8.1	18	10	314	2	36
9	Steve Young	1994	SF	16	324	461	70.3%	3969	8.6	35	10	293	7	31
10	Warren Moon	1990	HOU	15	362	584	62.0%	4689	8.0	33	13	215	2	36
11	Roman Gabriel	1973	PHI	14	270	460	58.7%	3219	7.0	23	12	10	1	31
12	Kurt Warner	1999	STL	16	325	499	65.1%	4353	8.7	41	13	92	1	29
13	Peyton Manning	2003	IND	16	379	566	67.0%	4267	7.5	29	10	29	0	18
14	Fran Tarkenton	1976	MIN	13	255	412	61.9%	2961	7.2	17	8	45	1	25
15	Steve Young	1998	SF	15	322	517	62.3%	4170	8.1	36	12	454	6	48
16	Steve Young	1993	SF	16	314	462	68.0%	4023	8.7	29	16	407	2	31
17	Neil Lomax	1984	STL	16	345	560	61.6%	4614	8.2	28	16	184	3	49
18	Kurt Warner	2001	STL	16	375	546	68.7%	4830	8.8	36	22	60	0	38
19	Rich Gannon	2002	OAK	16	417	616	67.7%	4676	7.6	26	10	156	3	36
20	Len Dawson	1962	KC	14	189	310	61.0%	2759	8.9	29	17	252	3	—
21	Dan Fouts	1981	SD	16	360	609	56.9%	4802	7.9	33	17	56	0	19
22	George Blanda	1961	HOU	14	187	362	51.7%	3330	9.2	36	22	12	0	—
23	John Brodie	1970	SF	14	223	378	59.0%	2941	7.8	24	10	29	2	8
24	Roger Staubach	1977	DAL	14	210	361	58.2%	2620	7.3	18	9	171	3	30
25	Johnny Unitas	1963	BAL	14	237	410	57.8%	3481	8.5	20	12	224	0	42
26	Sonny Jurgensen	1961	PHI	14	235	416	56.5%	3723	8.9	32	24	27	2	—
27	Roger Staubach	1971	DAL	13	126	211	59.7%	1882	8.9	15	4	343	2	23
28	Joe Montana	1989	SF	13	271	386	70.2%	3521	9.1	26	8	227	3	33
29	Donovan McNabb	2004	PHI	15	300	469	64.0%	3875	8.3	31	8	220	3	32
30	Sonny Jurgensen	1967	WAS	14	288	508	56.7%	3747	7.4	31	16	46	1	19
31	Johnny Unitas	1967	BAL	14	255	436	58.5%	3428	7.9	20	16	89	0	25
32	Joe Namath	1967	NYJ	14	258	491	52.5%	4007	8.2	26	28	14	0	26
33	Jeff Garcia	2000	SF	16	355	561	63.3%	4278	7.6	31	10	415	4	24
34	Roger Staubach	1979	DAL	16	267	461	62.5%	3586	7.8	27	11	172	0	36
35	Archie Manning	1978	NO	16	291	471	54.5%	3416	7.3	17	16	202	1	37
36	Johnny Unitas	1964	BAL	14	158	305	51.8%	2824	9.3	19	6	162	2	37
37	Ken Anderson	1981	CIN	16	300	479	56.7%	3754	7.8	29	10	320	1	25
38	Randall Cunningham	1998	MIN	16	259	425	60.9%	3704	8.7	34	10	132	1	20
39	Daunte Culpepper	2000	MIN	16	297	474	62.7%	3937	8.3	33	16	470	7	34
40	Roger Staubach	1973	DAL	14	179	286	62.6%	2428	8.5	23	15	250	3	43
41	Peyton Manning	2000	IND	16	357	571	62.5%	4413	7.7	33	15	116	1	20
42	Milt Plum	1960	CLE	12	151	250	60.4%	2297	9.2	21	5	−24	2	—
43	John Elway	1993	DEN	16	348	551	63.2%	4030	7.3	25	10	153	0	39
44	Dan Fouts	1980	SD	16	348	589	62.2%	4715	8.0	30	24	15	2	32
45	Daryle Lamonica	1968	OAK	13	206	416	49.5%	3245	7.8	25	15	98	1	27
46	Bart Starr	1966	GB	14	156	251	62.2%	2257	9.0	14	3	104	2	26
47	Fran Tarkenton	1973	MIN	14	169	274	61.7%	2113	7.7	15	7	202	1	31
48	Bernie Kosar	1987	CLE	12	241	389	62.0%	3033	7.8	22	9	22	1	22
49	Ken O'Brien	1985	NYJ	16	297	488	60.9%	3888	8.0	25	8	58	0	62
50	Brett Favre	1995	GB	16	359	570	63.0%	4413	7.7	38	13	181	3	33

(continued on page 18)

TABLE 3. TOP 100 QUARTERBACK SEASONS: PROJECTED TO 2004 OFFENSIVE ENVIRONMENT

Rank	Name	Year	Team	Cmpl	Att	Pct	Yds	Y/At	TD	Int	RuYD	RuTD	Sack	PAA*	Def†
1	Bert Jones	1976	BAL	328	479	68.5%	4521	9.4	33	9	222	1	30	163.8	−9.6
2	Peyton Manning	2004	IND	333	497	67.0%	4478	9.0	47	10	38	0	13	155.6	−7.7
3	Dan Marino	1984	MIA	382	564	67.7%	4965	8.8	46	14	0	0	10	154.9	−8.8
4	Daunte Culpepper	2004	MIN	378	548	69.0%	4697	8.6	37	11	406	2	46	154.1	−4.1
5	Steve Young	1992	SF	297	429	69.3%	3792	8.8	30	6	483	4	27	148.1	−1.3
6	Ken Anderson	1975	CIN	349	507	68.7%	4475	8.8	29	9	217	2	35	147.9	−1.7
7	Ken Stabler	1976	OAK	318	414	76.6%	4170	10.1	40	15	0	1	20	146.1	3.1
8	Ken Anderson	1974	CIN	338	458	73.7%	4016	8.8	27	8	345	1	43	144.3	−1.9
9	Steve Young	1994	SF	315	438	71.9%	3882	8.9	36	10	345	6	35	143.1	−6.4
10	Warren Moon	1990	HOU	410	618	66.3%	5020	8.1	36	13	158	2	35	140.4	−0.6
11	Roman Gabriel	1973	PHI	462	691	66.8%	5107	7.4	35	11	11	1	35	132.1	−7.7
12	Kurt Warner	1999	STL	318	472	67.3%	4180	8.9	40	12	74	1	27	132.0	−13.4
13	Peyton Manning	2003	IND	382	561	68.0%	4483	8.0	34	10	29	0	20	131.2	0.0
14	Fran Tarkenton	1976	MIN	413	580	71.1%	4456	7.7	26	8	47	1	26	131.2	1.5
15	Steve Young	1998	SF	335	512	65.4%	4206	8.2	36	11	384	4	45	129.5	−4.2
16	Steve Young	1993	SF	320	459	69.8%	4164	9.1	35	17	413	2	31	129.2	−6.9
17	Neil Lomax	1984	STL	368	560	65.8%	4613	8.2	29	13	194	2	39	128.0	3.8
18	Kurt Warner	2001	STL	368	535	68.7%	4799	9.0	38	20	44	0	37	127.7	−8.2
19	Rich Gannon	2002	OAK	394	583	67.5%	4598	7.9	27	10	114	2	37	127.5	−4.0
20	Len Dawson	1962	KC	280	367	76.5%	3366	9.2	29	8	223	2	—	126.9	2.0
21	Dan Fouts	1981	SD	398	615	64.7%	4864	7.9	35	13	66	0	19	126.3	−1.6
22	George Blanda	1961	HOU	268	408	65.7%	3910	9.6	33	11	10	0	—	126.2	−0.5
23	John Brodie	1970	SF	348	509	68.5%	4066	8.0	32	9	35	3	9	125.8	11.3
24	Roger Staubach	1977	DAL	357	528	67.7%	4143	7.8	29	8	220	2	33	125.5	−2.0
25	Johnny Unitas	1963	BAL	366	542	67.6%	4385	8.1	22	9	234	0	44	125.5	6.0
26	Sonny Jurgensen	1961	PHI	365	563	64.9%	4758	8.5	35	16	23	1	—	124.7	2.4
27	Roger Staubach	1971	DAL	213	301	70.6%	2854	9.5	23	3	430	1	29	124.4	2.8
28	Joe Montana	1989	SF	286	385	74.2%	3371	8.7	28	6	186	2	31	124.2	−7.6
29	Donovan McNabb	2004	PHI	301	469	64.2%	3902	8.3	31	8	220	3	32	123.6	1.3
30	Sonny Jurgensen	1967	WAS	419	623	67.2%	4692	7.5	33	11	59	1	21	122.9	−13.1
31	Johnny Unitas	1967	BAL	375	535	70.1%	4393	8.2	23	12	115	0	27	122.8	−4.1
32	Joe Namath	1967	NYJ	381	583	65.4%	4942	8.5	27	17	18	0	27	121.8	−3.3
33	Jeff Garcia	2000	SF	350	545	64.3%	4242	7.8	32	9	261	3	23	121.7	−9.1
34	Roger Staubach	1979	DAL	327	508	64.2%	4086	8.0	31	8	190	0	36	120.5	2.4
35	Archie Manning	1978	NO	400	570	70.2%	4408	7.7	25	12	247	1	38	120.4	6.3
36	Johnny Unitas	1964	BAL	242	402	60.2%	3650	9.1	22	5	149	1	32	119.8	−1.4
37	Ken Anderson	1981	CIN	329	484	68.1%	3748	7.8	30	8	378	1	26	119.8	−5.3
38	Randall Cunningham	1998	MIN	270	421	64.2%	3752	8.9	35	11	112	1	19	117.9	−5.5
39	Daunte Culpepper	2000	MIN	298	460	64.7%	4038	8.8	37	15	296	4	32	117.8	4.8
40	Roger Staubach	1973	DAL	304	430	70.7%	3799	8.8	35	14	265	2	49	117.2	−10.9
41	Peyton Manning	2000	IND	357	554	64.4%	4494	8.1	37	14	73	1	19	117.0	1.7
42	Milt Plum	1960	CLE	259	365	70.9%	3196	8.8	25	4	0	1	—	116.5	−6.9
43	John Elway	1993	DEN	357	547	65.3%	4227	7.7	32	9	155	0	39	116.2	3.4
44	Dan Fouts	1980	SD	388	615	63.1%	4994	8.1	32	16	15	1	32	116.2	6.4
45	Daryle Lamonica	1968	OAK	362	577	62.7%	4488	7.8	32	11	130	1	30	115.9	−2.5
46	Bart Starr	1966	GB	228	315	72.2%	2902	9.2	18	2	113	1	25	115.6	1.5
47	Fran Tarkenton	1973	MIN	293	412	71.2%	3448	8.4	23	6	214	1	35	115.3	1.9
48	Bernie Kosar	1987	CLE	349	516	67.6%	4082	7.9	28	9	27	1	26	114.5	0.4
49	Ken O'Brien	1985	NYJ	320	484	66.2%	3844	7.9	27	6	64	0	50	114.0	−1.7
50	Brett Favre	1995	GB	335	523	64.0%	4126	7.9	39	12	211	2	34	113.9	−6.2

(continued on page 19)

* PAA: Projected Points Above Average.
† Def: Effect of schedule on projection; the lower this number, the easier the schedule.

TABLE 2. TOP 100 QUARTERBACK SEASONS: ACTUAL NUMBERS *(continued from page 16)*

Rank	Name	Year	Team	G	Cmpl	Att	Pct	Yds	Y/At	TD	Int	RuYD	RuTD	Sack
51	Roger Staubach	1978	DAL	15	231	413	55.9%	3190	7.7	25	16	182	1	32
52	Ken Stabler	1974	OAK	14	178	310	57.4%	2469	8.0	26	12	−2	1	18
53	Jim Hart	1976	STL	14	218	388	56.2%	2946	7.6	18	13	7	0	17
54	Boomer Esiason	1988	CIN	16	223	388	57.5%	3572	9.2	28	14	248	1	30
55	Fran Tarkenton	1967	NYG	14	204	377	54.1%	3088	8.2	29	19	306	2	29
56	Y. A. Tittle	1963	NYG	13	221	367	60.2%	3145	8.6	36	14	99	2	24
57	Greg Landry	1971	DET	14	136	261	52.1%	2237	8.6	16	13	530	3	29
58	Trent Green	2003	KC	16	330	523	63.1%	4039	7.7	24	12	83	2	20
59	Joe Montana	1983	SF	16	332	515	64.5%	3910	7.6	26	12	284	2	33
60	Daryle Lamonica	1969	OAK	14	221	426	51.9%	3302	7.8	34	25	36	1	11
61	Bert Jones	1977	BAL	14	224	393	57.0%	2686	6.8	17	11	146	2	26
62	Mark Rypien	1991	WAS	16	249	421	59.1%	3564	8.5	28	11	6	1	7
63	Joe Montana	1984	SF	16	279	432	64.6%	3630	8.4	28	10	118	2	22
64	Len Dawson	1966	KC	14	159	284	56.0%	2527	8.9	26	10	167	0	—
65	Fran Tarkenton	1974	MIN	13	199	351	56.7%	2598	7.4	17	12	120	2	17
66	Brian Sipe	1980	CLE	16	337	554	60.8%	4132	7.5	30	14	55	1	23
67	Peyton Manning	1999	IND	16	331	533	62.1%	4135	7.8	26	15	73	2	14
68	Fran Tarkenton	1975	MIN	14	273	425	64.2%	2994	7.0	25	13	108	2	27
69	Joe Montana	1987	SF	13	266	398	66.8%	3054	7.7	31	13	141	1	22
70	Earl Morrall	1968	BAL	14	182	317	57.4%	2909	9.2	26	17	18	1	24
71	Joe Namath	1968	NYJ	14	187	380	49.2%	3147	8.3	15	17	11	2	15
72	Trent Green	2004	KC	16	369	556	66.4%	4591	8.3	27	17	85	0	32
73	John Hadl	1967	SD	14	217	427	50.8%	3365	7.9	24	22	107	3	9
74	John Brodie	1965	SF	13	242	391	61.9%	3112	8.0	30	16	60	1	14
75	Joe Theismann	1983	WAS	16	276	459	60.1%	3714	8.1	29	11	234	1	34
76	Steve McNair	2003	TEN	14	250	400	62.5%	3215	8.0	24	7	138	4	19
77	Steve Beuerlein	1999	CAR	16	343	571	60.1%	4436	7.8	36	15	124	2	50
78	Len Dawson	1968	KC	14	131	224	58.5%	2109	9.4	17	9	40	0	19
79	Dan Marino	1986	MIA	16	378	623	60.7%	4746	7.6	44	23	−3	0	17
80	Daryle Lamonica	1967	OAK	14	220	425	51.8%	3228	7.6	30	20	110	4	37
81	Steve Young	1997	SF	15	241	356	67.7%	3029	8.5	19	6	199	3	35
82	Steve Deberg	1990	KC	16	258	444	58.1%	3444	7.8	23	4	−5	0	22
83	Daunte Culpepper	2003	MIN	14	295	454	65.0%	3479	7.7	25	11	422	4	37
84	Brett Favre	1996	GB	16	325	543	59.9%	3899	7.2	39	13	136	2	40
85	Lynn Dickey	1983	GB	16	289	484	59.7%	4458	9.2	32	29	12	3	40
86	Boomer Esiason	1986	CIN	16	273	469	58.2%	3959	8.4	24	17	146	1	26
87	Troy Aikman	1993	DAL	14	271	392	69.1%	3100	7.9	15	6	125	0	26
88	Rich Gannon	2001	OAK	16	361	549	65.8%	3828	7.0	27	9	231	2	27
89	Vinny Testaverde	1998	NYJ	15	259	421	61.5%	3256	7.7	29	7	104	1	19
90	Fran Tarkenton	1970	NYG	14	219	389	56.3%	2777	7.1	19	12	236	2	36
91	Dan Marino	1987	MIA	12	263	444	59.2%	3245	7.3	26	13	−5	1	7
92	Scott Mitchell	1995	DET	16	346	583	59.3%	4338	7.4	32	12	104	4	31
93	Vinny Testaverde	1996	BAL	16	325	549	59.2%	4177	7.6	33	19	188	2	34
94	Roman Gabriel	1967	RAM	14	196	371	52.8%	2779	7.5	25	13	198	6	—
95	Dan Fouts	1979	SD	16	332	530	62.6%	4082	7.7	24	24	49	2	28
96	Jim Everett	1989	RAM	16	304	518	58.7%	4310	8.3	29	17	31	1	29
97	Len Dawson	1971	KC	14	167	301	55.5%	2504	8.3	15	13	24	0	30
98	Terry Bradshaw	1977	PIT	14	162	314	51.6%	2523	8.0	17	19	171	3	26
99	Jeff George	1997	OAK	16	290	521	55.7%	3917	7.5	29	9	44	0	58
100	Marc Bulger	2004	STL	14	321	485	66.2%	3964	8.2	21	14	89	3	41

TABLE 3. TOP 100 QUARTERBACK SEASONS: PROJECTED TO 2004 OFFENSIVE ENVIRONMENT (continued
from page 17)

Rank	Name	Year	Team	Cmpl	Att	Pct	Yds	Y/At	TD	Int	RuYD	RuTD	Sack	PAA*	Def†
51	Roger Staubach	1978	DAL	316	500	63.2%	4065	8.1	34	11	223	1	33	113.7	2.5
52	Ken Stabler	1974	OAK	278	429	64.9%	3644	8.5	40	10	0	1	21	112.5	−5.1
53	Jim Hart	1976	STL	349	541	64.5%	4390	8.1	28	13	7	0	17	112.3	0.1
54	Boomer Esiason	1988	CIN	247	393	62.9%	3639	9.3	31	12	222	1	30	112.0	−5.3
55	Fran Tarkenton	1967	NYG	298	463	64.4%	3903	8.4	33	14	396	1	32	111.9	−6.9
56	Y. A. Tittle	1963	NYG	338	490	69.0%	3840	7.8	37	11	104	1	25	111.8	−9.5
57	Greg Landry	1971	DET	227	369	61.5%	3340	9.1	26	10	657	2	37	111.6	4.5
58	Trent Green	2003	KC	332	519	64.1%	4246	8.2	26	12	83	1	22	110.7	−2.8
59	Joe Montana	1983	SF	357	525	68.0%	3946	7.5	28	9	298	2	28	110.4	2.3
60	Daryle Lamonica	1969	OAK	364	585	62.2%	4625	7.9	47	17	43	1	12	110.4	0.1
61	Bert Jones	1977	BAL	380	575	66.1%	4218	7.3	26	9	187	1	28	110.0	−5.0
62	Mark Rypien	1991	WAS	266	432	61.6%	3736	8.6	35	10	7	1	7	109.8	−1.2
63	Joe Montana	1984	SF	294	432	68.1%	3545	8.2	29	9	124	1	18	109.1	−5.6
64	Len Dawson	1966	KC	236	326	72.4%	2997	9.2	25	7	181	0	—	109.0	−1.8
65	Fran Tarkenton	1974	MIN	317	490	64.7%	3945	8.0	27	10	132	1	20	109.0	0.6
66	Brian Sipe	1980	CLE	374	579	64.6%	4331	7.5	31	10	56	1	23	109.0	−2.2
67	Peyton Manning	1999	IND	331	504	65.6%	4154	8.2	29	13	59	1	13	108.7	7.5
68	Fran Tarkenton	1975	MIN	408	566	72.1%	4083	7.2	32	11	123	2	29	108.5	−15.4
69	Joe Montana	1987	SF	355	487	72.9%	3790	7.8	36	13	159	1	24	108.5	−0.2
70	Earl Morrall	1968	BAL	274	414	66.1%	3806	9.2	27	14	24	1	26	107.0	−5.9
71	Joe Namath	1968	NYJ	326	522	62.6%	4344	8.3	19	13	14	1	17	107.0	0.3
72	Trent Green	2004	KC	367	556	66.0%	4544	8.2	28	16	85	0	32	106.9	−1.4
73	John Hadl	1967	SD	322	507	63.6%	4188	8.3	26	13	138	2	9	106.9	1.0
74	John Brodie	1965	SF	379	523	72.6%	3982	7.6	32	13	71	1	14	106.6	4.9
75	Joe Theismann	1983	WAS	295	468	63.0%	3692	7.9	29	8	246	1	29	106.5	−2.8
76	Steve McNair	2003	TEN	251	397	63.2%	3350	8.4	28	7	139	3	21	106.4	−2.8
77	Steve Beuerlein	1999	CAR	336	540	62.2%	4275	7.9	36	13	100	1	46	106.3	−8.1
78	Len Dawson	1968	KC	230	308	74.8%	2944	9.6	22	7	52	0	21	106.3	1.7
79	Dan Marino	1986	MIA	402	616	65.2%	4693	7.6	46	18	0	0	15	105.8	−5.7
80	Daryle Lamonica	1967	OAK	327	504	64.8%	4022	8.0	32	13	142	3	39	105.3	−1.6
81	Steve Young	1997	SF	247	347	71.2%	3043	8.8	21	6	179	2	31	105.2	−5.6
82	Steve Deberg	1990	KC	290	470	61.6%	3626	7.7	25	4	0	0	22	105.0	−4.2
83	Daunte Culpepper	2003	MIN	296	450	65.8%	3631	8.1	26	11	424	3	41	104.6	−4.3
84	Brett Favre	1996	GB	326	522	62.5%	3996	7.7	43	12	144	2	41	104.1	3.6
85	Lynn Dickey	1983	GB	311	493	63.0%	4494	9.1	34	21	13	2	34	104.0	4.6
86	Boomer Esiason	1986	CIN	293	464	63.2%	3994	8.6	26	14	149	1	23	103.0	2.6
87	Troy Aikman	1993	DAL	276	389	71.0%	3211	8.2	18	6	127	0	26	102.9	−2.6
88	Rich Gannon	2001	OAK	358	538	66.7%	3899	7.3	29	9	169	1	26	101.5	−2.2
89	Vinny Testaverde	1998	NYJ	270	417	64.8%	3300	7.9	29	6	88	1	18	101.2	−1.1
90	Fran Tarkenton	1970	NYG	347	524	66.4%	3960	7.6	26	11	286	3	40	100.9	−3.2
91	Dan Marino	1987	MIA	381	589	64.7%	4373	7.4	34	14	0	1	8	100.7	1.8
92	Scott Mitchell	1995	DET	325	535	60.8%	4119	7.7	31	11	121	3	32	100.3	−2.7
93	Vinny Testaverde	1996	BAL	324	527	61.5%	4246	8.1	35	16	199	2	34	100.0	3.3
94	Roman Gabriel	1967	RAM	287	455	63.1%	3535	7.8	29	9	256	4	0	99.8	−4.6
95	Dan Fouts	1979	SD	403	585	68.9%	4581	7.8	28	19	54	1	28	99.7	−3.4
96	Jim Everett	1989	RAM	323	517	62.4%	4182	8.1	32	14	25	1	27	99.5	−4.8
97	Len Dawson	1971	KC	274	425	64.5%	3636	8.6	24	10	30	0	38	99.5	−4.6
98	Terry Bradshaw	1977	PIT	275	459	60.0%	3986	8.7	27	15	220	2	28	99.4	−0.4
99	Jeff George	1997	OAK	299	508	58.9%	3985	7.8	31	9	40	0	52	99.2	−3.3
100	Marc Bulger	2004	STL	322	485	66.5%	4001	8.2	22	14	89	3	41	99.2	4.0

* PAA: Projected Points Above Average.
† Def: Effect of schedule on projection; the lower this number, the easier the schedule.

formula, Bert Jones—not Johnny Unitas, not Peyton Manning—had the greatest season not just by a Colts quarterback, but any modern quarterback.

2. Peyton Manning   2004 Indianapolis Colts

	Cmpl	Att	Pct	Yds	TD	INT
Actual:	336	497	67.6%	4557	49	10
Projected:	333	497	67.0%	4478	47	10

After adjusting every quarterback season both for the offensive environment of the time and strength of schedule, Manning still has the most passing touchdowns of any season in history. But he loses the top spot on this list for two reasons. First, unlike Jones, he did not have positive value rushing to add to his value as a passer. Second, he sat out the final game of the season. Project the final game based on the idea that Manning would have matched his average performance of the season, and Manning's 2004 would pass Jones's 1976 to rank as the greatest quarterback season in modern history. But project the final game based on how Manning played in the three previous games, since he was slowing down at the end of the year, and Jones would still rank number one. Since Jim Sorgi took the field after two passes, we'll never know if Manning could have passed Jones to hold the title of best season ever.

3. Dan Marino   1984 Miami Dolphins

	Cmpl	Att	Pct	Yds	TD	INT
Actual:	362	564	64.2%	5084	48	17
Projected:	382	564	67.7%	4965	46	14

Many people assumed that Manning surpassed Marino's record under easier conditions. But 1984 was a very strong year for offense around the NFL, so Marino set the record in an offensive environment pretty similar to today's. The main differences were lower completion percentages for quarterbacks around the league in 1984, and a lot more interceptions thrown.

4. Daunte Culpepper   2004 Minnesota Vikings

	Cmpl	Att	Pct	Yds	TD	INT
Actual:	379	548	69.2%	4717	39	11
Projected:	378	548	69.0%	4697	37	11

Daunte Culpepper's 2004 season comes out higher than it probably should because I could not consider fumbles in the equation we used to estimate value. But that doesn't take away from the fact that Culpepper's season was nearly as historic as Manning's season. Much of the difference between the two quarterbacks is made up by Culpepper's value on the ground. He also faced a slightly harder schedule than Manning, because of games against strong NFC defenses like those of Washington and Philadelphia.

5. Steve Young   1992 San Francisco 49ers

	Cmpl	Att	Pct	Yds	TD	INT
Actual:	268	402	66.7%	3465	25	7
Projected:	297	429	69.3%	3792	30	6

After the original ESPN.com list, I got the most e-mail complaining about the absence of two quarterbacks: Steve Young and Brett Favre. The changes made for this new list don't do much to help Favre, who has generally had a completion percentage close to the league average. But Steve Young now has four seasons in the top 20 because we're recognizing the value of his rushing yardage to go with his passing performance. In 2002, to go with the great numbers above, Young had 537 rushing yards and four rushing touchdowns. The only quarterbacks with more valuable rushing seasons than Steve Young's 1992 are Randall Cunningham, Greg Landry, Michael Vick, and Bobby Douglass.

6. Ken Anderson   1975 Cincinnati Bengals

	Cmpl	Att	Pct	Yds	TD	INT
Actual:	228	377	60.5%	3169	21	11
Projected:	349	507	68.7%	4475	29	9

Ken Anderson's great seasons in the mid-1970s marked the first significant success for the Bill Walsh offense that now pervades the NFL (and is known as the "West Coast Offense" despite the fact that it has nothing to do with the original "West Coast Offense" of Sid Gillman and the San Diego Chargers). To understand how a quarterback with only 228 completions and 3,169 yards can somehow project to 349 completions and 4,475 yards under current conditions, you have to remember how much different the NFL was before the liberalization of passing rules in 1978. In 1975, the average quarterback completed barely half his passes. Teams averaged 4.5 fewer passes a game than today and ran the ball eight more times a game. There were two fewer games per season. Fran Tarkenton won the MVP this season, but Anderson threw for 175 more yards on 48 fewer attempts. The Bengals had to play in Oakland in the first round of the playoffs, and Anderson led a two-touchdown comeback in the fourth quarter, but the Bengals couldn't recover a last-minute onside kick and lost 31–28.

7. Ken Stabler   1976 Oakland Raiders

	Cmpl	Att	Pct	Yds	TD	INT
Actual:	194	291	66.7%	2737	27	17
Projected:	318	414	76.6%	4170	40	15

Stabler had a season nearly as great as Jones, but very different. He had a higher completion percentage, but threw more interceptions. Stabler had more yards per attempt, Jones more yards per completion. Jones ran for 214 yards, while The Snake slithered for a whopping −2 yards. Of course, while Jones may have had the better season when it comes to personal achievement, Stabler had the better season period, because he got a ring at the end. This is also the list's best performance by a quarterback who faced a harder-than-average schedule of defenses.

8. Ken Anderson   1974 Cincinnati Bengals

	Cmpl	Att	Pct	Yds	TD	INT
Actual:	213	328	64.9%	2667	18	10
Projected:	338	458	73.7%	4016	27	8

Yes, he's here twice, and the Bengals were only 7–7 this year, as opposed to their 11–3 record in 1975. But Anderson's completion percentage was even higher in 1974, and he had 314 rushing yards on just 43 carries. Many people criticize Anderson because those Bengal teams couldn't make the Super Bowl, but in an era still heavily oriented toward the running game, the Bengals had the worst run defense in the league. Anderson also had these great years despite missing a game in each season, and these projected stats are for just 15 games to reflect that. If we projected him to 16 games, he would be even higher.

9. Steve Young   1994 San Francisco 49ers

	Cmpl	Att	Pct	Yds	TD	INT
Actual:	324	461	70.3%	3969	35	10
Projected:	315	438	71.9%	3882	36	10

This was the top-rated season of all time according to the official NFL passer rating until Peyton Manning blew the record away last year. The main difference between this season and Young's 2002 season is an easier schedule. (Atlanta and New Orleans, both NFC West teams in those geographically challenged days, each allowed 4,000 yards passing in 1994.)

10. Warren Moon   1990 Houston Oilers

	Cmpl	Att	Pct	Yds	TD	INT
Actual:	362	584	62.0%	4689	33	13
Projected:	410	618	66.3%	5020	36	13

Ah, the run and shoot. Some might object to the presence of Moon on this list, since he was playing in an offense that allowed him to throw, throw, and throw some more. It is hard to take a football strategy seriously when it is invented by a guy named "Mouse." But Moon's performance was based on more than just some gimmick offense. No team ran less often than the Oilers, so opposing defenses could play with extra defensive backs the whole game. Moon led the league in completion percentage anyway. Despite the run and shoot, he led the league in pass attempts by only 30, but he had an astonishing 700 more yards than

the quarterback in second place, Jim Everett. The scary part is that if a team put together the run and shoot in 2004, they might be throwing *more*. The average NFL team in 2004 passed 5% more often than in 1990, with a higher completion percentage and more yardage. Imagine the run and shoot with stricter pass interference calls making things easier on the receivers.

11. Roman Gabriel   1973 Philadelphia Eagles

	Cmpl	Att	Pct	Yds	TD	INT
Actual:	270	460	58.7%	3219	23	12
Projected:	462	691	66.8%	5107	35	11

This was the season I had the most problem with. When you take every quarterback season since 1960 and translate them to the offensive environment of 2004, Gabriel's 1973 season blows the others away in terms of pass attempts. The only year that comes close is Drew Bledsoe's 1994, a year when Bledsoe actually *did* attempt 691 passes, which is the NFL record by a whopping 36 attempts. Gabriel threw all these passes because the Eagles were a 5–8–1 team with the worst defense in the league. But Gabriel didn't have a good season because of a ridiculous number of attempts. He had a great season that just happened to include a ridiculous number of attempts. He had the league's fourth-best completion percentage and third-best ratio of touchdowns to interceptions. He led the league in pass completions by 77, even though he led the league in pass attempts by only 84. If you normalize yardage totals to the league average, no quarterback has ever thrown for more yards. He just kept throwing and connecting and the defense just kept giving it back. I can only imagine how good his DVOA would be considering the horrifying field position he was usually starting from.

12. Kurt Warner   1999 St. Louis Rams

	Cmpl	Att	Pct	Yds	TD	INT
Actual:	325	499	65.1%	4353	41	13
Projected:	318	472	67.3%	4180	40	12

In 1999, Kurt Warner set a record for most fantasy football leagues won by the guy with waiver priority in the first week. Both this season and his 2001 are in the top 20, but what's scary is that according to DVOA the best year for the Rams offense was 2000. That was the year that Warner missed five games due to injury and Trent Green took over without missing a beat, but the Rams were betrayed by a defense that completely imploded.

Most Seasons in the Top 100

Frank Tarkenton: 6 (1967, 1970, 1973–1976)

Steve Young: 5 (1992–1994, 1997, 1998; in addition, his 1991 season, when he played only 11 games, is #101)

Roger Staubach: 5 (1971, 1973, 1977–1979)

Peyton Manning: 4 (1999, 2000, 2003, 2004)

Joe Montana: 4 (1983, 1984, 1987, 1989)

Len Dawson: 4 (1962, 1966, 1968, 1971)

Both Ken Anderson and Dan Fouts would have four seasons in the top 100 if we counted the 1982 strike season.

Franchises with Most Quarterbacks in the Top 100

San Francisco 49ers: 12 (Steve Young 5, Joe Montana 4, John Brodie 2, Jeff Garcia 1)

Baltimore/Indianapolis Colts: 10 (Peyton Manning 4, Johnny Unitas 3, Bert Jones 2, Earl Morrall 1)

Minnesota Vikings: 8 (Frank Tarkenton 4, Daunte Culpepper 3, Randall Cunningham 1)

Los Angeles/Oakland Raiders: 8 (Daryle Lamonica 3, Rich Gannon 2, Ken Stabler 2, Jeff George 1)

Franchises with No Quarterbacks in the Top 100

(Besides the Texans and Browns v2.0)

Atlanta: Steve Bartkowski 1983 is highest at #134

Buffalo: Jim Kelly 1991 is highest at #121

Chicago: Rudy Bukich 1965 is highest at #152

Jacksonville: Mark Brunell 1996 is highest at #119

New England: Babe Parilli 1962 is highest at #166

Seattle: Jim Zorn 1978 is highest at #137

Tampa Bay: Doug Williams 1981 is highest at #260

Best Rookie Quarterback

Greg Cook, 1969 Cincinnati Bengals, is ranked #170. Ben Roethlisberger's 2004 season (#296) is the only other rookie season in the top 300.

Seasons Producing Most Quarterbacks in the Top 100

1967: 7 (Sonny Jurgensen, Johnny Unitas, Joe Namath, Fran Tarkenton, John Hadl, Daryle Lamonica, Roman Gabriel)

2004: 5 (Peyton Manning, Daunte Culpepper, Donovan McNabb, Trent Green, Marc Bulger)

1968: 4 (Daryle Lamonica, Earl Morrall, Joe Namath, Len Dawson)

1976: 4 (Bert Jones, Ken Stabler, Fran Tarkenton, Jim Hart)

2003: 4 (Peyton Manning, Trent Green, Steve McNair, Daunte Culpepper)

The list of the five quarterbacks from 2004 who made the top 100 does show one of the problems with this method. No matter how accurate an equation that esti-

mates one of our advanced metrics, we aren't going to get complete accuracy without having detailed play-by-play that lets us take into account field position and defense and other such things. So Tom Brady, who finished third among 2004 quarterbacks in DPAR and second in DVOA, finishes in seventh place for the year using this method, behind the five quarterbacks listed above as well as Drew Brees.

What About Standard Deviations?

From looking at the list of top seasons, it is clear there are three particularly strong periods for quarterbacks: the late 1960s, the mid-1970s, and right now. Can we really call Bert Jones's 1976 season the greatest of all time if Ken Stabler's 1976 season was almost as good? Or is the greatest season of all time one where a quarterback completely dominated the competition by having a strong season while every other quarterback in the league was close to average?

If we believe the latter, the correct way to rank quarterbacks would not be by estimated Points Above Average, but by estimated standard deviations away from the league average. Standard deviation is a mathematical concept that measures the variation among numbers in a certain set. A season with low standard deviation is one where the best and worst quarterbacks are relatively close to each other, such as 1994. A season with high standard deviation is one where the best quarterbacks are really great, and the worst quarterbacks are really terrible, such as 2004 or 1976 (the latter being an expansion year). The best quarterback of all time would be one who had a magnificent season in a year with a low standard deviation.

That was the method used to rank teams in Eddie Epstein's book *Dominance: The Best Seasons of Pro Football's Greatest Teams*. But I chose not to use it to rank quarterbacks, because quarterbacks don't face each other. If a team has a great season, it has to beat other teams. But a quarterback doesn't have to beat other quarterbacks—he has to beat defenses. So it is unfair to penalize one quarterback because another quarterback elsewhere in the league—say, I don't know, his brother—is struggling.

Nonetheless, for those who are curious, here are the top ten quarterback seasons from 1972–2004 based on standard deviations of Points Above Average away from the mean:

Steve Young, 1994

Warren Moon, 1990

Roger Staubach, 1979

Kurt Warner, 2001

Steve Young, 1992

Archie Manning, 1978

Roger Staubach, 1977

Rich Gannon, 2002

Dan Marino, 1984

Roger Staubach, 1978

You'll notice that neither Bert Jones nor Peyton Manning makes this list. On the other hand, Steve Young's 1994 performance benefits, in part, from the fact that there really were no bad quarterbacks that year and the league average he deviated from was extremely high. Rick Mirer, who had the lowest yards per attempt, threw 11 touchdowns and only 7 interceptions. Heath Shuler, who may have been the league's worst passer, had 10 touchdowns and just 12 interceptions.

Baltimore Ravens

People started calling Brian Billick an offensive mastermind sometime during the 1998 season. (They started calling him Neo midway through last season when he could be seen sporting sunglasses and all-black leather outfits on the sidelines—even when it was cloudy—but that's a story for another time.) At the time, he was the offensive coordinator for the Minnesota Vikings, who had just completed one of the most prolific displays of offensive firepower in NFL history. They finished the season 15–1, led the league in touchdowns (41), and ranked second in total passing yards (4,492) and yards per attempt (8.4). All this happened even with 35-year-old Randall Cunningham, who had been out of football two years earlier, as starting quarterback. Almost as an afterthought, halfback Robert Smith managed to run for almost 1,200 yards.

Fast-forward to 2005. Billick is now entering his seventh season as the head coach in Baltimore, and the Ravens have never ranked higher than 16th in total offensive DVOA. They didn't even manage a ranking that high until last year; in the four previous years, the Ravens ranked 30th, 24th, 25th, and 20th, respectively—and this *includes* their dominant running game. If we consider only their DVOA rating for passing offense, they never climbed above 20th.

So what happened? For the past few seasons, Baltimore has been only a player or two away from being a legitimate Super Bowl team. The dominating nature of its defense is legendary. The two missing pieces of the puzzle happen to be on the other side of the ball—quarterback and wide receiver.

Baltimore has a reputation for using the draft only to stock the defense, but that's not really accurate. The Ravens have done a good job of drafting a mix of players on both sides of the ball. The problem is not that the quarterback and wide receiver positions were never addressed during the draft, but rather that the otherwise well-managed Ravens seem to have a blind spot when it comes to evaluating talent at those positions. Throw in a little bad luck in free agency and you're staring at a team that played like they discovered the forward pass sometime during training camp.

In 2000, Baltimore drafted QB Chris Redman, who was to learn the job while holding a clipboard for Trent Dilfer and later Elvis Grbac. After a disagreeable experience with

RAVENS PROSPECTUS

2004 Record: 9–7

DVOA Estimated Wins: 10.1 (9th)

Pythagorean Wins: 9.6 (9th)

DVOA: 18.9% total (9th), 15.1% weighted (10th)

Adjusted Offense: 21.0 points/game (−2.5% DVOA, 16th)

Adjusted Defense: 17.0 points/game (−16.6% DVOA, 2nd)

Adjusted Special Teams: +1.6 points/game (4.7% DVOA, 5th)

Variance: 22.0% (10th)

2004: Lewis and Lewis had off years and the Ravens still almost made the playoffs.

2005: Derrick Mason and Samari Rolle make the Ravens a legitimate Super Bowl contender—now it's up to Kyle Boller.

2005 Projection

Leinart Land (0–4): 8%

Bad Team (5–6): 13%

Mediocre (7–8): 21%

Playoff Contender (9–10): 25%

Super Bowl Contender (11+): 34%

Projected Average Opponent: −2.5% DVOA (25th in NFL)

Grbac in 2001 (and this experience was mutual—instead of renegotiating his contract going into the next season, Grbac opted to retire), the Ravens finally gave Redman his shot in 2002. But after six mildly promising games, he suffered a season-ending injury. Redman played two games as a backup in 2003, missed all of 2004 after yet more surgery, and can currently be found in Foxboro waiting for Tom Brady and Rohan Davey to be run over by trucks.

Since its quarterback of the future got injured after six games, Baltimore decided to go out and get another quarterback of the future. The Ravens dealt New England their 2004 first-round pick and 2003 second-round pick (which became Vince Wilfork and Eugene Wilson) to move up and take Kyle Boller with the 19th-overall selection. The Ravens actually wanted Byron Leftwich, but he was gone by the seventh pick.

Baltimore's track record with wide receivers has been even worse. In that same 2000 draft when they took

25

Redman, the Ravens used their two first-round picks on running back Jamal Lewis and wide receiver Travis Taylor. The Ravens thought they had two franchise players for the foreseeable future. Well, they were half right. Lewis single-handedly rushed the Ravens to victory on a regular basis over the next few seasons, while Taylor never clicked in Baltimore. In his five years, he never had more than 869 receiving yards and never caught more than 61 passes in a season. Last year he didn't catch a single touchdown pass. The Ravens made no attempt to re-sign him when he entered free agency this off-season, and he signed with the Vikings.

In 2002, the Ravens used three of their ten draft picks on wide receivers: Ron Johnson in the fourth round and LaMont Brightful and Javon Hunter in the sixth round. These three receivers combined for 16 career receptions over two seasons. Contrast that with New England's seventh-round pick in the same draft, David Givens, who has amassed 99 receptions and ten touchdowns in that same span. The next year, despite pledging to build their offense around another promising first-round passer, the Ravens did nothing to upgrade the wide receiver position. Shocker of shockers, a Baltimore team with a rookie under center and no clear receiving threat turned out to be one of the worst passing teams in the NFL in 2003.

And just when you thought things couldn't get any worse, they did. Early in the 2004 off-season, Baltimore made a trade with San Francisco for the rights to Terrell Owens. Unfortunately for the Ravens, Owens had other ideas. Specifically, he wanted to play in Philadelphia for a team with a proven quarterback. By the time the smoke had cleared, Owens was an Eagle, the free agency cupboard was bare except for the most elder of elder statesmen, and Baltimore got stuck with the consolation prize: a fifth-round pick in the upcoming draft to let Philadelphia trade with the 49ers instead.

The Ravens eventually traded their fourth-round pick to Jacksonville for Kevin Johnson, then took three more receivers in last year's draft. Johnson led the team in receptions with a whopping 35. Of the three drafted receivers, only sixth-rounder Clarence Moore was actually useful; second-round pick Devard Darling was lost for the year after three weeks, and seventh-rounder Derek Abney never played.

So while Baltimore successfully used the draft to build one of the most dominating defenses ever and maintain that defense year after year, the team has been unable to build even an average offense through the draft. Instead, Baltimore has constantly been forced to venture into free agency to find some much-needed upgrades. It's sometimes the case that teams overpay in free agency when they would be better served building their teams through the draft, but given Baltimore's spotty track record culti-

vating homegrown talent on offense, the Ravens wisely used free agency to address some glaring weaknesses on that side of the ball.

Which brings us to the 2005 off-season. Not known for being particularly active in free agency, especially when compared to their NFC neighbors to the south, the Washington Redskins—perennial *off-season* Super Bowl champs—the Ravens took a decidedly hands-on approach this time around. After a disappointing 2004, the Ravens wasted little time in upgrading their roster, and in just over a week, several key acquisitions immediately put them back in the "potential Super Bowl contenders" conversation.

A salary cap purge shook up the Tennessee Titans, and the Ravens were the beneficiaries, grabbing two ex-Titan Pro Bowlers: WR Derrick Mason should finally give Billick (and Boller) the outside weapon he's been looking for since coming to Baltimore; CB Samari Rolle is one of the best cover guys in the league and he'll step in for the departed Gary Baxter. Not quite as glamorous, but just as important, is the signing of former Steelers offensive lineman Keydrick Vincent. The Baltimore offensive line has always been successful making room for the running game, but it struggled in pass blocking last season. Vincent was an integral part of a Pittsburgh team that led the AFC in rushing while protecting rookie QB Ben Roethlisberger. He'll be an immediate upgrade at guard over Bennie Anderson.

And things only got better during the NFL draft. The Ravens got arguably the most polished wideout in the class when they selected Mark Clayton with the 22nd-overall pick. He's been compared to Marvin Harrison with Hines Ward's toughness, and he'll immediately upgrade last season's mediocre receiving corps. Baltimore also landed defensive end Dan Cody, offensive tackle Adam Terry, and center Jason Brown with consecutive picks. All three players could contribute this season and at the very least will add some much-needed depth along the defensive and offensive lines.

Of course, there are still some big question marks heading into training camp. First, will Boller improve after two mediocre seasons? In his rookie campaign he sported a –26.7 DPAR (46th among all quarterbacks) that can be chalked up to youthful exuberance and inexperience. Last season he showed signs of maturing as the season progressed—his 23.1 DPAR was 20th-best in the NFL. In 2005, he'll have no excuses because tight end Todd Heap should be fully recovered from an injury and Mason should team up with Clayton, Darling, or Moore on the outside to give him plenty of targets.

If Boller progresses on schedule, the only wild card will be the effect a four-month prison term had on RB Jamal Lewis. If he doesn't return to the form that made him one of the most dangerous backs in the NFL, Baltimore could face a new kind of problem. In seasons past, the Ravens would often have to combat opposing defenses putting eight and nine guys in the box both to stop Lewis and to dare Boller to beat them with his arm. If Lewis struggles next season, expect the Ravens to turn to backup running back Chester Taylor and also rely more on guys like Heap and Mason to take some of the pressure off the running game. Still, the success of this team will ultimately come down to how well Boller plays within the parameters of the offense.

The Ravens believe they will field the most balanced team since Billick took over in 1999. If that turns out to be true, they could be the team to break the New England dynasty. If that turns out to be false, they could be looking up at Cincinnati and Pittsburgh in the division standings.

Ryan Wilson

Research: Are the Ravens Telegraphing Their Plays?

In perhaps the only memorable episode of *Coach,* the Minnesota State Screamin' Eagles made it to some NCAA bowl game. Truth be told, it was not so memorable that we can tell you which bowl game it was, but hey, nobody's perfect. In any event, defensive coordinator Luther Van Damm falls ill before game time—something stress related—and is hospitalized. Because of the nature of his malady, Van Damm is barred from tuning into the game, but, this being a sitcom, he violates the doctor's orders. Hilarity is supposed to ensue, but what actually happens is an impossible triumph. Van Damm notices that an opposing offensive lineman has two different stances, one for a run and another for passing downs. Through much difficulty, Luther gets this message to Coach Hayden Fox, and, on the last play of a close game, Fox makes a key substitution leading to a game-ending interception. All because of how some nondescript lineman shifted his weight.

This is called "telegraphing." Such a flaw, once detected, can be fatal. Even if the information is limited to a signal that team is just "thinking pass," defenses can adapt: They can bring in personnel—adding a nickelback, for instance—or they can be sure that a linebacker picks up the tight end. Similarly, they can bring the safeties up into the box when the offense signals rush. The point is, you do not need to know *exactly* what your opponent is going to do; any informational advantage is a big one.

Fortunately for the telegraphing team, the clues are hard to detect. When telegraphing is discovered, teams keep quiet about it, since once it gets around it's useless. Therefore, we do not hear much about telegraphing. Which is why we were surprised when, in the course of one dis-

cussion thread on Football Outsiders.com this summer, two different comments suggested the same thing: The Ravens were telegraphing their pass plays.

The comments were replying to a post discussing the blocking skills of NCAA running backs; those who were better blockers, the linked-to article suggested, were more likely to get playing time in the NFL. After all, most highly drafted running backs can hit the hole or push a pile, can run downfield, and can get outside the tackles. (The others are Ron Dayne.) But not all have sound blocking skills, and lacking this fundamental trait makes such a player a liability on passing downs. And one of these blocking-deficient backs, claimed the discussers, was a well-known rusher named Jamal Lewis.

The theory is a simple one. Lewis, despite being a strong rusher, is such a poor blocker that Brian Billick pulls him on passing downs in favor of Chester Taylor. To make matters worse, this appears to be common knowledge—both posts stated that other teams are keen to the maneuver. Could this be right?

If this telegraphing theory were correct, we would expect that the Ravens would pass more often when Taylor was in the game than Lewis, and rush more often in the opposite situation. Sadly, NFL play-by-play data severely hamstrings our ability to measure this, because there is no listing of which players are on the field except for the ones who touch the ball or make the tackle. Without going through unavailable video, we cannot tell which running back was on the field when Kyle Boller was told to throw the ball. All we can do is try discern some signal from the statistical noise of standard numbers.

Let's start by looking at how Lewis and Taylor were used when they were the center of the offense (table 1). Clearly, when Lewis was the focus, the team was almost certainly running. Taylor also ran plenty of times, but was thrown a pass three times as often as Lewis.

But does that really tell us anything? After all, if the Ravens were going to run, they would clearly prefer to do so with Lewis. We are missing the downs in which the Ravens passed but the running back—whomever he was—was there primarily to block. And that is what we are truly after.

Luckily for us, though not for him, Jamal Lewis had some trouble with the law last year, and then he had some trouble with his ankle. Between the two, he missed four games during the season (Weeks 7–8 and 12–13) and was

TABLE 1. RUNS AND PASSES FOR BALTIMORE RB

Player	Runs	Passes	Pct. Runs
Lewis	235	12	95.1%
Taylor	160	36	81.6%

TABLE 2. KYLE BOLLER, BASED ON BACKFIELD, PRORATED TO 16 GAMES

Backfield	Comp %	Yd/ Pass	Yd/ Comp	TD:Int Ratio	P:R Ratio	TD%	Int%
Lewis and Taylor	55.0%	5.7	10.3	0.75	0.86	2.2%	3.0%
Just Taylor	56.6%	5.3	9.4	2.33	1.10	3.6%	1.6%

extremely limited in two more (Weeks 11 and 14). During those weeks, Taylor was the primary running back, and without Lewis in the lineup, it was impossible for the Ravens to telegraph plays by removing Lewis for Taylor.

Now, if the Ravens are telegraphing, the defense should be benefiting from it. (If they aren't, then we don't even care that the Ravens *are* tipping their plays.) And while we cannot isolate the rushing stats—we cannot tell if the difference is because of the drop of quality from Lewis to Taylor—we *can* isolate the passing stats.

Let's start by taking a look at Kyle Boller's stats from the games with Lewis as the primary back versus those with Taylor as the primary back. This includes P:R Ratio, simply passes divided by rushes. After compiling the numbers and prorating them over a 16-game season, we get some interesting results (table 2).

The stat to focus on is Boller's touchdown-to-interception ratio. Boller threw only six touchdowns in ten games with Lewis as the primary running back, but seven touchdowns in six games with Taylor as the primary back. Some might suggest that the benefit came from a less conservative passing game, but the evidence suggests otherwise. Boller's interceptions dropped, from eight during Lewis's ten games to just three during Taylor's six games. His completion percentage and yards per attempt (or completion, take your pick) reflected either no strategic change whatsoever—the numbers are relatively close—or, if anything, a *more* conservative passing game with Taylor in the backfield.

The data suggests that it is certainly possible that the Ravens were tipping off the defense during games both Lewis and Taylor were active. But to feel stronger about it, we would like to be able to control for the quality of the defense itself. With DPAR, we can do that. Table 3 shows

Boller's average and median DPAR values based on the weeks with and without Lewis.

The difference is phenomenal. Defenses handled Boller far more effectively when Jamal Lewis was a viable part of the offense. What is causing this? One possibility is that Todd Heap, Boller's best target (before the off-season signing of Derrick Mason), missed ten weeks of the season. Unfortunately, there were only two weeks during the 2004 season in which Taylor was the main running back and Heap was healthy. Similarly, there were a mere four weeks with both Heap and Lewis in the game *and* four with neither of them in the game. The statistical significance of such data is minor at best.

What we can do is measure Kyle Boller's DPAR with Heap in the game and without (table 4). What that provides us with is the effect of Heap, all else equal. As expected, we see a positive correlation between Heap's presence and Boller's results. What is surprising is how muted the difference is compared to the Lewis vs. Taylor difference. This suggests two things: First, while Heap does help the passing game, he does not affect it enough to explain the difference seen by using Chester Taylor as the primary back; and second, when Taylor is the primary back, the advantage felt is far bigger than one would originally think.

Is it due to telegraphing? Maybe not. That is certainly the sexy explanation, but there is a more likely one: Lewis is such a bad blocker (or Taylor a good one) that Boller suffers significantly. If that is the reason, there is an important question: How significantly does Boller fall?

Let's revisit the prorated DPAR numbers seen in table 3, but, to err on the side of caution, let's slash the Taylor-created DPAR by 50%. That gives Boller a DPAR of 18.6 (rounded down) for those weeks.

Now, let's add Boller's DPAR in Lewis weeks to Lewis's rushing DPAR. We will do the same for Taylor weeks and Taylor's rushing numbers (see table 5). We prorated Lewis's DPAR for a full season; that is, to 390 carries—2 more than his 2003 total. We capped Taylor at 260 carries (two-thirds as many as Lewis), figuring that the Ravens would run less often if he were the feature back, and also to take into consideration the fact that his 160 carries last year was a career high, and we do not know if he can be a near-400-carry workhorse. Remember, we are trying to bias the data so that any error in it favors Lewis.

TABLE 3. DPAR FOR KYLE BOLLER, BASED ON BACKFIELD

Backfield	Avg. DPAR	Median DPAR	Prorated to 16 Games
Lewis and Taylor	0.9	2.2	14.4
Just Taylor	2.3	4.3	37.3

TABLE 4. PASSING DPAR OF KYLE BOLLER WITH AND WITHOUT TODD HEAP

	Avg. DPAR	Median DPAR	Prorated to 16 Games
Todd Heap healthy	1.8	3.9	28.5
Todd Heap injured	1.2	2.2	19.7

TABLE 5. ESTIMATE OF RUNNING BACKS' AGGREGATE DPAR EFFECT

Player	Boller's DPAR	RB's DPAR	Total
Lewis	14.4	27.1	41.5
Taylor	18.6	23.4	42.0

Regardless of the cause, it seems that even a ridiculously conservative estimate has the Ravens slightly better off with Taylor in the game. If the cause is telegraphing, this can be solved by allowing Lewis to remain in the game on passing downs. If the cause is poor blocking by Lewis, perhaps Brian Billick's off-season regimen should include running back blocking drills. In either case, the Ravens should further investigate the cause and rectify the error.

Dan Lewis

Ravens 2004 Stats by Week

Wk	vs.	W-L	PF	PA	YDF	YDA	TO	DVOA Total	Off	Def	ST
1	@CLE	L	3	20	254	250	-3	-78.8%	-46.3%	18.4%	-14.1%
2	PIT	W	30	13	259	310	+3	92.5%	38.6%	-43.0%	10.8%
3	@CIN	W	23	9	380	398	+2	62.5%	20.0%	-25.2%	17.3%
4	KC	L	24	27	207	398	0	0.4%	-17.6%	13.4%	31.4%
5	@WAS	W	17	10	202	107	-1	51.4%	-21.2%	-40.1%	24.5%
6	BYE										
7	BUF	W	20	6	160	270	+4	68.0%	3.3%	-65.6%	-0.9%
8	@PHI	L	10	15	327	298	-1	5.7%	-0.3%	-3.3%	2.7%
9	CLE	W	27	13	240	217	+1	16.9%	-6.2%	-29.2%	-6.2%
10	@NYJ	W	20	17	262	305	0	27.5%	3.0%	-22.1%	2.3%
11	DAL	W	30	10	287	222	+1	34.1%	-3.4%	-38.7%	-1.1%
12	@NE	L	3	24	130	310	-2	-29.6%	-44.7%	-7.6%	7.5%
13	CIN	L	26	27	356	453	0	-32.5%	26.6%	54.1%	-4.9%
14	NYG	W	37	14	353	196	+5	103.6%	4.4%	-83.0%	16.2%
15	@IND	L	10	20	354	316	-2	-1.3%	-17.8%	-16.6%	-0.2%
16	@PIT	L	7	20	248	404	+1	-12.8%	17.1%	28.5%	-1.3%
17	MIA	W	30	23	332	345	+3	10.7%	10.9%	-8.2%	-8.5%

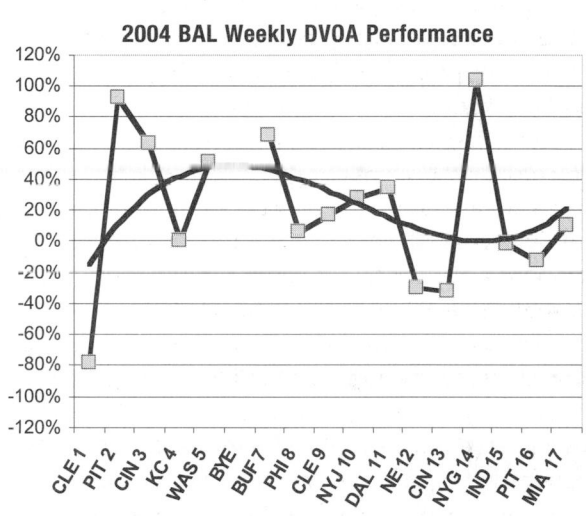

2004 BAL Weekly DVOA Performance

Trends and Splits

	Offense	Rank	Defense	Rank
Total DVOA	-2.5%	16	-16.6%	2
Unadjusted VOA	-8.5%	26	-17.4%	3
Weighted Trend	-0.8%	16	-14.7%	5
Variance	5.5%	28	12.5%	5
Passing	-6.1%	20	-20.8%	2
Rushing	0.9%	15	-12.3%	3
First Down	0.7%	18	-30.1%	2
Second Down	-0.3%	20	2.4%	14
Third Down	-12.8%	20	-17.6%	10
Red Zone	33.8%	1	-47.4%	2
Late and Close	19.9%	4	3.5%	22

Five-Year Performance

	2004	2003	2002	2001	2000
W-L	9-7	10-6	7-9	10-6	12-4
Pythagorean Wins	9.6	11	6.9	9.3	13.5
Estimated Wins	10.1	10.1	8.7	8.9	11.8
Total DVOA	18.9%	18.4%	-1.2%	4.7%	32.6%
Rank	9	6	17	12	2
Offense	-2.5%	-20.6%	-4.3%	-12.7%	-6.5%
Rank	16	30	24	25	20
Defense	-16.6%	-32.0%	-5.4%	-18.1%	-31.5%
Rank	2	1	8	5	1
Special Teams	4.7%	7.0%	-2.3%	-0.7%	7.6%
Rank	5	1	22	18	2

Passing (min. 5 plays)

Player	DPAR	PAR	DVOA	Plys	NtYds	Avg	Cmpl	TD	Int
Kyle Boller	23.1	3.1	-2.0%	492	2328	4.7	55.6%	13	10

Rushing (min. 3 plays)

Player	DPAR	PAR	DVOA	Plys	Yds	Avg	TD	Fum	Suc
Jamal Lewis	16.2	14.5	2.4%	235	1011	4.3	7	2	46%
Chester Taylor	14.0	12.5	7.8%	160	714	4.5	2	1	41%
Kyle Boller	1.5	0.5	-12.0%	37	206	5.6	1	2	—
Jamel White	-0.5	0.0	-23.9%	14	62	4.4	0	0	36%
Musa Smith	0.9	0.5	0.6%	12	48	4.0	0	0	33%
Alan Ricard	1.2	1.1	7.5%	10	36	3.6	0	0	70%
B. J. Sams	1.8	1.6	75.1%	4	19	4.8	1	0	75%

Receiving (min. 5 plays)

Player	DPAR	PAR	DVOA	Plys	Ctch	Yds	Y/C	TD	CPct
WR									
Travis Taylor	-7.8	-9.2	-29.1%	80	34	421	12.4	0	43%
Kevin Johnson	0.2	-0.8	-14.0%	58	35	345	9.9	1	57%
Clarence Moore	-2.2	-4.1	-20.0%	56	24	282	11.8	4	41%
Randy Hymes	2.5	1.8	-6.0%	44	26	255	9.8	2	55%
TE									
Todd Heap	8.6	7.5	19.9%	44	27	303	11.2	3	61%
Daniel Wilcox	4.6	1.9	10.7%	35	25	226	9.0	1	71%
Terry Jones	-0.5	-1.5	-15.4%	24	17	114	6.7	1	71%
Darnell Dinkins	2.1	1.8	9.5%	15	9	94	10.4	1	60%
RB									
Chester Taylor	0.2	1.3	-9.6%	36	30	175	5.8	0	78%
Alan Ricard	-2.9	-2.9	-47.5%	14	11	39	3.5	0	79%
Jamal Lewis	3.5	3.6	47.1%	12	10	116	11.6	0	83%

Defensive Players (min. 20 plays)

Player	Age	Plys	Stop	Dfts	AvYds	StpRt	Sack	Int	FR
Defensive Line									
Marques Douglas	28	74	46	21	2.7	62%	5.5	0	0
Kelly Gregg	29	64	42	11	2.5	66%	1.5	0	1
Tony Weaver	25	43	34	16	1.6	79%	4.0	1	1
Maake Kemoeatu	26	27	11	2	3.1	41%	0.0	0	0
Linebackers									
Ray Lewis	30	155	92	26	4.5	59%	1.0	0	2
Ed Hartwell	27	97	43	12	4.5	44%	0.0	0	1
Adalius Thomas	28	69	49	23	2.5	71%	8.0	1	0
Terrell Suggs	23	61	49	25	0.0	80%	10.5	0	2

Player	Age	Plys	Stop	Dfts	AvYds	StpRt	Sack	Int	FR
Secondary									
Gary Baxter	27	104	39	20	6.8	38%	2.0	1	0
Ed Reed	27	97	43	27	8.8	44%	2.0	9	2
Will Demps	26	90	34	11	10.3	38%	2.5	1	2
Chris McAlister	28	56	22	9	8.1	39%	0.0	1	2
Chad Williams	26	37	23	16	4.0	62%	2.0	3	0

Offensive Line

Year	Yards	AdjLineYd	Rank	Power	Rank	10+ Yds	Rank	Stuff	Rank	Sack	AdjSack%	Rank
2002	4.25	4.25	13	75%	8	18%	12	22%	10	42	7.3%	24
2003	5.11	4.39	6	59%	24	27%	2	23%	8	41	8.6%	31
2004	4.31	4.31	11	59%	19	18%	8	22%	10	35	6.8%	18

Year	LEnd	Rank	LTckl	Rank	MdGrd	Rank	RTckl	Rank	REnd	Rank
2002	5.60	2	3.36	30	4.24	17	4.04	18	4.29	12
2003	3.90	19	4.53	13	4.67	4	4.34	14	3.18	21
2004	4.13	20	4.76	7	4.59	5	3.76	24	3.23	25

LT Jonathan Ogden is still one of the best linemen in the game, but a preseason leg injury slowed him for most of 2004. This had a ripple effect on the offensive line, which is clear when you look at Baltimore's Adjusted Sack Rate before the bye week (10.1%) and after the bye week (5.7%). RT Orlando Brown's chronic knee condition didn't help matters, but without a viable replacement, he'll return this season. RG Bennie Anderson was largely ineffective and he won't be back. Baltimore signed Keydrick Vincent from Pittsburgh to take his place. And given his proficiency at both run and pass blocking, coupled with his modest three-year $4.6 million contract, he might be the best free agent pickup of the off-season. Free agent C Casey Rabach signed with the Redskins, but 2000–2003 starter Mike Flynn has fully recovered from an injury that caused him to miss most of last season and will return to the starting lineup. This line is also very disciplined, second in the league with just 14 false starts and fourth with just 12 offensive holding calls.

Defensive Front Seven

Year	Yards	AdjLineYd	Rank	Power	Rank	10+ Yds	Rank	Stuff	Rank	Sack	AdjSack%	Rank
2002	3.97	4.28	21	71%	23	13%	7	21%	26	34	5.4%	25
2003	3.40	3.53	1	53%	3	10%	7	29%	8	48	7.9%	1
2004	3.65	3.99	8	65%	20	9%	4	26%	11	39	6.7%	15

Year	LEnd	Rank	LTckl	Rank	MdGrd	Rank	RTckl	Rank	REnd	Rank
2002	5.20	32	4.56	24	4.14	15	3.92	11	3.95	16
2003	2.24	1	3.59	6	3.57	3	4.30	19	3.05	6
2004	3.61	6	4.26	13	4.08	12	4.15	13	3.55	11

Rex Ryan replaces Mike Nolan as the new defensive coordinator and the Ravens will return to the 4-3 defense. DE Anthony Weaver is a better fit in the 3-4 and DE Marques Douglas followed Nolan to San Francisco as an unrestricted free agent, which may precipitate OLB Terrell Suggs taking over the position he played in college. (He's pretty much already there anyway—Suggs was the only linebacker in the league to make his average play zero yards past the line of scrimmage.) The Ravens landed Oklahoma DE Dan Cody, widely considered to be a first-round talent, when he surprisingly fell all the way to the 53rd selection. He's a natural pass rusher who could team nicely with Suggs to wreak havoc on opposing quarterbacks. DT Kelly Gregg and 2004 second-round pick DT Dwan Edwards should help take up space and allow Ray Lewis to make more plays near the line of scrimmage. The other linebackers teaming up with Lewis are Adalius Thomas and T. J. Slaughter, who replaces departed Edgerton Hartwell. Peter Boulware did not play all season due to knee injuries and while he might be able to help some team part-time, it won't be the Ravens, who cut him for salary cap relief roughly five minutes before this chapter was finished.

Defensive Secondary

Year	DVOA vs. #1 WR	Rank	DVOA vs. #2 WR	Rank	DVOA vs. Other WR	Rank	DVOA vs. TE	Rank	DVOA vs. RB	Rank
2002	3.9%	20	16.7%	19	2.2%	15	-17.1%	6	-45.6%	1
2003	-28.7%	3	-10.7%	14	-78.4%	1	-10.6%	11	-24.1%	4
2004	-13.0%	5	2.0%	11	-16.0%	10	5.1%	17	-42.8%	3

Amazingly, the Ravens secondary actually got better this off-season. They already had the best defensive player in the league in S Ed Reed, but the addition of CB Samari Rolle almost seems unfair. Opposite Rolle will be Pro Bowler Chris McAllister. And whenever you have Deion Sanders—arguably the best cornerback in the history of the game—playing nickelback, it's probably a good sign. Lost in the mix is the *other* safety, Will Demps. He's certainly not as flashy as his secondary mates, but he's strong against the run and is above average defending the pass.

Special Teams

Year	DVOA	Rank	FG/XP	Rank	Net Punt	Rank	Punt Ret	Rank	Net Kick	Rank	Kick Ret	Rank
2002	-2.3%	22	3.9	7	-14.5	29	15.4	3	-7.9	26	-9.5	29
2003	7.0%	1	11.0	3	17.0	1	0.8	12	7.3	4	2.9	9
2004	4.7%	5	11.9	4	11.3	8	7.1	4	-2.8	17	-1.2	17

B. J. Sams was an undrafted free agent who added an element to the return game not seen since Jermaine Lewis was returning kicks. He occasionally battled turnovers last season, but given that he was a rookie, he should only get better with experience. Punter Dave Zastudil has a strong leg and plays an underrated yet important part in setting up Baltimore's defense through the field position battle. And the Ravens are one of the teams that understand that kickoffs and field goals are equally important parts of the kicking game. Matt Stover is one of the best field goal kickers in the league and the Ravens have certainly needed him due to their inability to consistently score touchdowns. But historically he hasn't been so great on kickoffs, so in 2003 Baltimore signed Wade Richey as a kickoff specialist. The mediocre net kickoff rating for 2004 is the fault of the kickoff coverage, not Richey, who has averaged exactly a touchback per game over the past four seasons.

Coaching Staff

Brian Billick is known as a players' coach, but the Ravens' offensive woes have quelled the genius talk. Firing offensive coordinator Matt Cavanaugh and replacing him with Jim Fassel is the first step in revitalizing an offense that was stuck in neutral. Defensive coordinator Rex Ryan comes from the first family of defensive coordinators (his father is Buddy Ryan, originator of the 46 defense, and his brother, Rob, is the coordinator in Oakland) and should have no trouble picking up where predecessors Mike Nolan and Marvin Lewis left off. Rick Neuheisel also joins the staff as the quarterbacks coach as he looks to put his recent troubles at the University of Washington behind him.

Buffalo Bills

There are three elements that make up a football team: offense, defense, and special teams. Despite ranking at the top of the NFL in two of these three elements, the 2004 Buffalo Bills did not make the playoffs. They came close. When the Bills stood at 1–5 after six weeks, they never could have imagined they would be in control of their own playoff destiny in Week 17. But they won their next two games, paused to have the stuffing pounded out of them by the Patriots, and then reeled off another six wins by an average score of 38–15.

Amazingly, Buffalo held the advantage on all tiebreakers going into the season's final week; all the Bills had to do to make the playoffs was beat a visiting Pittsburgh team that was resting nearly all of its starters since it had already clinched the AFC's top seed. The defense allowed a 58-yard run by Willie Parker but otherwise did its job, keeping the Steelers to 3.7 yards per play while forcing three turnovers. But Buffalo's weak link, the offense, as usual could not hold up its end of the bargain, converting just two third downs and turning the ball over three times itself, including a Drew Bledsoe fumble to start the fourth quarter that was returned for a touchdown, effectively ending Buffalo's season.

The team's 9–7 record was a surprise, but the ultimate failure of the offense should not have been. The Bills' defense inflated the scoring numbers, so despite scoring at least 33 points in each of those six straight wins, Buffalo's offense never really played well, with the exception of an unexpected Week 13 shootout with Miami. Defense and special teams drove Buffalo's winning streak.

After seven weeks of the season, the 1–5 Bills ranked 19th-overall in our DVOA ratings (see table 1). They had a good run defense and special teams, an average pass defense, and an atrocious offense. Over the final ten weeks of the season, Buffalo's defense was the best in the league against the pass and number two against the run. The special teams made huge plays in nearly every game.

The result for the offense was absurdly good field position. During the 1–5 start, Buffalo's average offensive drive began on its own 28.4-yard line. During the final 8–2 run, the average offensive drive started on Buffalo's 39.2-yard line. The offense doesn't have to improve much to score a lot more if it gets to start 11 yards closer to the goalposts each time.

An even closer look at the turnaround of the defense shows that the improvement came almost entirely on third down (see table 2). For the first seven weeks of the season, Buffalo was having success keeping teams to short gains on first and second down, but teams converted third or fourth downs at a rate well above the league average of 38.6% success, and gained plenty of yards in the process. However, in the final ten weeks, Buffalo's defensive DVOA on third down improved to match its performance on first and second down. (This is not an uncommon phenomenon, as you'll learn from an essay in the San Diego chapter.) Opponents converted on third down less often, and one third down per game they turned the ball over, which robbed them of an opportunity to push the Buffalo offense back with a punt on fourth down.

The Buffalo defense was so strong that DVOA rates the Bills as the best team in football over the second half of the season—better than the Patriots, better than the Colts, and

TABLE 1. 2004 BUFFALO DVOA WEEKS 1–7 VS. WEEKS 8–17

	W–L	Pass Def	Rank	Run Def	Rank	Offense	Rank	Sp Teams	Rank	Total	Rank
Weeks 1–7	1–5	0.3%	15	−11.9%	7	−13.0%	25	2.7%	11	−7.0%	19
Weeks 8–17	8–2	−52.2%	1	−17.4%	2	−0.5%	18	13.1%	1	47.6%	1

TABLE 2. 2004 BUFFALO DEFENSE BY DOWN, WEEKS 1–7 VS. WEEKS 8–17

	Weeks 1–7	Weeks 8–17
First Down DVOA	−7.7%	−43.4%
Second Down DVOA	−36.7%	−24.0%
Third/Fourth Down DVOA	53.0%	−36.4%
Conversion Rate	43%	36%
Yards/Play	6.0	4.3
Turnovers	0	10

TABLE 3. YEAR-TO-YEAR CORRELATION OF PERFORMANCE, OFFENSE VS. DEFENSE

Statistic	Offense	Defense
Points	.492	.207
Yards	.553	.335
Yards/Play	.568	.350
Points/Drive	.517	.236
Yards/Drive	.516	.318
DVOA	.553	.398
VOA*	.534	.339
Turnovers/Drive	.270	.062
Interceptions/Drive	.280	.133
Fumbles Lost/Drive	.186	.051

* DVOA, but not adjusted for opponent

better than the Steelers. This news is sure to warm the hearts of Buffalo fans and have them exploring hotel reservations for Super Bowl XL. There's just one problem: It's doubtful that Buffalo's defense will be this good again in 2005.

The reason is simple: Offense is far more consistent from year to year than defense. It's true in every study of the NFL, no matter what statistic is used to measure performance. To demonstrate, let's look at the variability of offensive and defensive performance from one year to the next by using year-to-year correlations. Correlation coefficients are a common statistical method giving a number between −1 and 1 that measures how closely two variables are related. A positive correlation means that a team that is good in an area tends to be good in that area the next year, and the closer the number to 1, the more consistency there is from year to year. A negative correlation, closer to −1, means that when a team is good in an area one year, it tends to be worse in that area the next year. A correlation of 0 means two numbers are unconnected.

We computed the year-to-year correlation of several metrics, including points, points/drive, yards/drive, and DVOA for both offense and defense over the five seasons from 2000 through 2004 (table 3).

There are a number of possible reasons for this defensive instability, but the biggest reason is the importance of turnovers. A defense that is able to "force" turnovers radically affects the outcome of games. However, as the last three entries on table 3 show, turnover totals have very little year-to-year predictability, especially in the case of fumbles. A defense may or may not be better than the next at "causing" fumbles, but the recovery of loose fumbles is completely random. (This is discussed further in the New Orleans chapter.)

A second likely reason for defensive unpredictability is injuries. Carl Prine, an investigative journalist with the *Pittsburgh Tribune-Review,* recently took a break from covering important stories such as the Gulf War and heroin trade to conduct some groundbreaking research on NFL injuries. He studied the official injury reports from each season between 2000 and 2003 and authored a lengthy series of articles printed in January 2005.[1] Among his findings was that injuries are more prevalent among defensive players than offensive players. That means a greater chance that the defense will lose that one key player whose absence will damage the team's overall performance, with a domino effect that puts replacement-level benchwarmers into important positions and forces other players to use skills they don't really have. Prine also found that injuries in the defensive front seven have a far greater effect on a team's performance than injuries in the secondary.

Prine's studies have major implications for the Bills, whose defense went through an astonishingly injury-free 2004 campaign. Of the 11 defensive starters, only two were

---

1. These articles can be found online at this address: http://www.pittsburghlive.com/x/tribune-review/specialreports/specialnfl/.

forced to miss games due to injuries: safeties Lawyer Milloy, who lost five games to a broken arm, and Troy Vincent, who lost nine games to a knee injury. It would defy probability for Buffalo to go through another season without losing at least one member of the front seven to a major injury. The Bills have already lost an important player, defensive tackle Pat Williams, to free agency.

So if Buffalo can't count on having the best defense in the league again, that puts even more pressure on the offense to improve to a point where this team can make the playoffs. And the Buffalo offense is a big fat question mark thanks to a quarterback whose career consists of just five NFL passes.

Last year, the Bills traded up to take J. P. Losman in the first round, only to see him lose most of his rookie season to a broken leg. They decided to hand him the ball for 2005 anyway. Scouting reports on Losman always emphasize his athletic ability and strong arm, but Losman's negatives all portend a long, slow learning process: "Rushes through his progressions"; "Forces balls into traffic"; "Scrambles too often instead of letting the play develop." At Tulane, Losman ran a wide-open offense with lots of shotgun, and he's going to have to adapt to an offense that requires him to limit mistakes and hand the ball to Willis McGahee a lot. Otherwise he'll have the same problem that Bledsoe has, never taking an 8-yard dump-off on first down when he could throw a 40-yard incomplete pass instead.

Other AFC teams that missed last year's playoffs have spent the off-season retooling and filling holes on their rosters. The Ravens added two big-time wide receivers, a veteran and a rookie. The Bengals used draft picks to try to fix their run defense. Oakland brought in Randy Moss. Kansas City tried to sign every defensive player on the market. But Buffalo is counting on addition by subtraction. Its free agent signings consisted of an insurance policy for Losman (Kelly Holcomb) and an offensive lineman who might not even start (Bennie Anderson). The Bills traded their first-round pick last year to get Losman, and they already know third-round tight end Kevin Everett is out for the year after tearing his ACL at minicamp. What they have is second-round wide receiver Roscoe Parrish and a big, heaping bowl of Not Drew Bledsoe.

Buffalo has to get past one of the league's hardest schedules and a division rival that has won two straight Super Bowls. But our projection system indicates that Buffalo's defense was so good by the end of last year that a couple steps backward will still leave the unit among the NFL's top defenses. Combined with an average offense, that would make Buffalo a Super Bowl contender. Drew Bledsoe couldn't be the average quarterback that this team needed. Can J. P. Losman?

Aaron Schatz
Jim Armstrong

Bills 2004 Stats by Week

Wk	vs.	W-L	PF	PA	YDF	YDA	TO	DVOA			
								Total	Off	Def	ST
1	JAC	L	10	13	242	225	0	9.1%	-25.0%	-38.6%	-4.5%
2	@OAK	L	10	13	243	273	-1	-68.4%	-43.2%	23.4%	-1.8%
3	BYE										
4	NE	L	17	31	357	399	-1	-0.7%	2.6%	32.3%	29.1%
5	@NYJ	L	14	16	252	383	+1	19.2%	14.1%	-5.5%	-0.4%
6	MIA	W	20	13	341	212	+1	53.3%	33.0%	-21.8%	-1.5%
7	@BAL	L	6	20	270	160	-4	-48.8%	-58.5%	-14.4%	-4.7%
8	ARI	W	38	14	209	213	0	21.6%	-4.9%	13.8%	40.4%
9	NYJ	W	22	17	341	282	+2	39.1%	21.5%	-19.9%	-2.3%
10	@NE	L	6	29	123	429	-4	-86.8%	-108.6%	-6.8%	15.0%
11	STL	W	37	17	294	270	+3	99.0%	-3.8%	-51.8%	50.9%
12	@SEA	W	38	9	434	230	-2	61.5%	18.2%	-37.2%	6.1%
13	@MIA	W	42	32	362	403	+6	44.5%	31.2%	-5.3%	8.0%
14	CLE	W	37	7	321	17	+2	99.1%	-16.7%	-131.2%	-15.4%
15	@CIN	W	33	17	212	275	+3	29.5%	-37.9%	-38.4%	29.0%
16	@SF	W	41	7	441	189	+3	115.1%	38.6%	-56.3%	20.3%
17	PIT	L	24	29	267	262	0	52.4%	10.0%	-62.9%	-20.6%

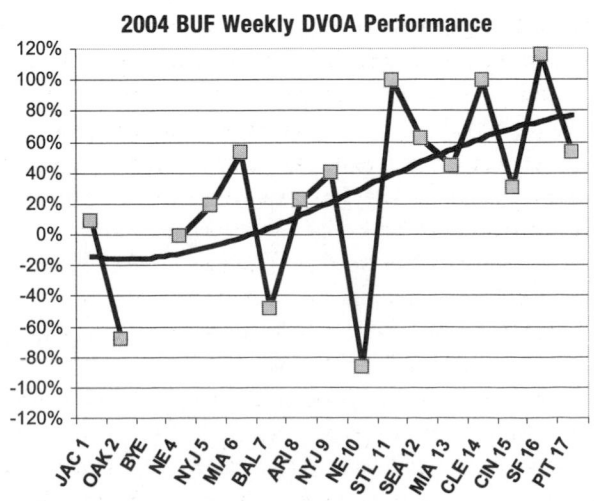

2004 BUF Weekly DVOA Performance

Trends and Splits

	Offense	Rank	Defense	Rank
Total DVOA	-5.1%	21	-24.5%	1
Unadjusted VOA	-7.7%	24	-29.7%	1
Weighted Trend	-1.6%	17	-34.2%	1
Variance	15.4%	3	15.5%	31
Passing	-8.8%	23	-32.5%	1
Rushing	-1.7%	19	-16.1%	2
First Down	-6.3%	24	-30.9%	1
Second Down	-6.5%	23	-28.3%	1
Third Down	0.7%	15	-4.7%	15
Red Zone	-7.8%	19	-21.1%	6
Late and Close	11.1%	10	-37.5%	1

Five-Year Performance

	2004	2003	2002	2001	2000
W-L	9-7	6-10	8-8	3-13	8-8
Pythagorean Wins	11	6.7	7.6	4	7
Estimated Wins	11.6	6.4	6.6	3.7	7.7
Total DVOA	28.6%	-9.2%	-13.4%	-32.2%	0.1%
Rank	5	22	24	30	17
Offense	-5.1%	-20.5%	-1.0%	-13.3%	3.4%
Rank	21	29	21	26	13
Defense	-24.5%	-12.1%	8.6%	11.4%	-11.0%
Rank	1	7	24	27	10
Special Teams	9.2%	-0.7%	-3.8%	-7.5%	-14.4%
Rank	1	20	26	29	31

Passing (min. 5 plays)

Player	DPAR	PAR	DVOA	Plys	NtYds	Avg	Cmpl	TD	Int
Drew Bledsoe	22.5	13.7	-2.0%	481	2662	5.5	56.9%	20	15
J. P. Losman	-4.9	-5.2	-167.4%	6	30	5.0	60.0%	0	1

Rushing (min. 3 plays)

Player	DPAR	PAR	DVOA	Plys	Yds	Avg	TD	Fum	Suc
Willis McGahee	19.6	18.3	1.2%	284	1131	4.0	13	3	46%
Travis Henry	1.4	0.2	-10.6%	94	326	3.5	0	0	43%
Shaud Williams	3.2	4.4	5.1%	42	167	4.0	2	0	48%
Joe Burns	-1.0	-1.1	-25.6%	20	73	3.7	0	0	25%
Drew Bledsoe	-1.4	-1.4	-41.5%	11	53	4.8	0	1	—
Lee Evans	3.7	4.0	86.5%	5	85	17.0	0	0	—
Eric Moulds	-0.3	-0.3	-38.0%	5	19	3.8	0	0	—

Receiving (min. 5 plays)

Player	DPAR	PAR	DVOA	Plys	Ctch	Yds	Y/C	TD	CPct
WR									
Eric Moulds	11.1	10.5	-4.0%	152	88	1048	11.9	5	58%
Lee Evans	26.7	26.9	39.4%	75	48	843	17.6	9	64%
Josh Reed	-5.1	-5.7	-36.8%	36	16	153	9.6	0	44%
Sam Aiken	1.6	0.8	-1.1%	18	11	148	13.5	0	61%
Bobby Shaw	-1.6	-1.3	-37.8%	12	5	59	11.8	0	42%
Jonathan Smith	-1.4	-1.3	-48.8%	6	3	21	7.0	0	50%
TE									
Mark Campbell	4.1	3.0	9.3%	30	17	203	11.9	5	57%
Tim Euhus	3.8	2.9	28.1%	15	11	98	8.9	2	73%
Ryan Neufeld	-1.3	-1.9	-25.8%	14	6	61	10.2	0	43%
RB									
Willis McGahee	-0.5	-2.1	-12.2%	36	22	167	7.6	0	61%
Daimon Shelton	0.7	-0.8	-3.3%	24	17	114	6.7	0	71%
Travis Henry	-0.2	-0.3	-13.8%	14	10	45	4.5	0	71%

Defensive Players (min. 20 plays)

Player	Age	Plys	Stop	Dfts	AvYds	StpRt	Sack	Int	FR
Defensive Line									
Aaron Schobel	28	80	61	31	1.6	76%	8.0	0	3
Pat Williams	33	55	47	16	0.4	85%	2.5	1	1
Sam Adams	32	43	33	18	-0.1	77%	5.0	1	0
Chris Kelsay	26	41	32	16	-0.1	78%	4.5	1	2
Ryan Denney	28	33	20	5	2.7	61%	3.0	0	0
Ron Edwards	26	22	16	11	2.1	73%	4.0	0	0
Linebackers									
London Fletcher	30	152	78	27	4.6	51%	3.5	0	1
Takeo Spikes	29	117	78	38	3.1	67%	3.0	5	1
Jeff Posey	30	67	34	12	3.3	51%	1.0	1	1

Player	Age	Plys	Stop	Dfts	AvYds	StpRt	Sack	Int	FR
Secondary									
Terrence McGee	25	103	36	15	9.1	35%	2.0	3	1
Nate Clements	26	94	41	24	7.3	44%	0.5	6	2
Lawyer Milloy	32	66	26	8	6.5	39%	4.0	2	0
Kevin Thomas	27	42	18	5	6.0	43%	1.0	0	0
Izell Reese	31	37	9	3	11.5	24%	0.0	1	0
Troy Vincent	34	30	12	3	6.1	40%	1.0	1	1
Pierson Prioleau	28	24	15	6	4.9	63%	0.0	0	1
Rashad Baker	23	21	7	5	10.1	33%	0.0	1	0

Offensive Line

Year	Yards	AdjLineYd	Rank	Power	Rank	10+ Yds	Rank	Stuff	Rank	Sack	AdjSack%	Rank
2002	4.35	4.36	9	70%	12	13%	26	23%	14	54	8.4%	28
2003	3.95	4.07	21	67%	15	12%	26	24%	20	51	8.8%	32
2004	3.86	3.94	25	57%	22	17%	19	27%	25	39	7.8%	22

Year	LEnd	Rank	LTckl	Rank	MdGrd	Rank	RTckl	Rank	REnd	Rank
2002	3.84	21	4.49	7	4.36	9	4.38	13	4.71	6
2003	3.91	18	3.97	22	4.08	20	4.67	6	3.13	23
2004	5.10	4	4.68	11	3.85	27	2.94	32	3.62	20

The best player on the Bills' line last year, by far, was left tackle Jonas Jennings. The 49ers offered Jennings a big contract, so he represents a very large hole that they need to fill. Mike Gandy, signed as a free agent from Chicago, is supposed to take his place. Not only is Gandy a huge drop-off in talent, he also has had shoulder injuries, which can be problematic for an offensive lineman whose job is to constantly use his arms to hold people off. Trey Teague could move back to tackle, the position he played in Denver before coming to Buffalo three years ago, but then who plays center? Over at right tackle, Mike Williams has been a rare disappointment at the position where first-round picks represent the lowest risk. The Bills took Williams with the fourth-overall selection in 2002, but he was good at the University of Texas because he weighed 360 pounds and no one could get around him. In the NFL it doesn't work that way. NFL linemen, no matter their size, need skill, and Williams is lacking it. Some combination of Chris Villarrial, Ross Tucker, and Bennie Anderson will man the guard positions. This offensive line has been a disappointment, and we don't have a lot of reason to be optimistic that it will get better.

Defensive Front Seven

Year	Yards	AdjLineYd	Rank	Power	Rank	10+ Yds	Rank	Stuff	Rank	Sack	AdjSack%	Rank
2002	4.63	4.47	29	70%	19	21%	27	20%	28	31	6.1%	17
2003	3.64	4.04	16	62%	7	10%	6	24%	16	36	6.9%	7
2004	3.68	3.73	3	42%	1	15%	12	29%	5	45	8.4%	3

Year	LEnd	Rank	LTckl	Rank	MdGrd	Rank	RTckl	Rank	REnd	Rank
2002	3.94	15	4.22	18	4.38	23	4.59	23	6.39	32
2003	2.31	2	4.52	19	3.99	11	4.47	23	3.62	13
2004	3.30	4	4.83	27	3.53	3	4.11	12	3.55	12

A single adjustment in the defensive lineup can have a huge impact on a team—not because of the new player's ability, per se, but because the change allows the rest of the defense to switch into roles where they have a better chance to succeed. Nobody would call left defensive end Chris Kelsay a star, but his move into the starting lineup at midseason roughly coincided with the defensive surge that drove Buffalo's second-half improvement. With Kelsay and Aaron Schobel rushing the passer, Sam Adams, and Pat Williams could do what they do best: stand in the middle being fat and impassable. Williams is gone to Minnesota and backup Ron Edwards will try to replace him. The other issue is that Adams is 32; like many tackles his size, Adams looks good in the first quarter, but his mobility declines rapidly until, late in the game, he looks like he can hardly move. It's nice to be big enough that no one can push you around, but sometimes football players need the ability to run, too. Adams-type players—Grady Jackson, Gilbert Brown, Ted Washington—have a tendency to lose a great deal of their effectiveness very quickly.

Behind this line may be the best collection of starting linebackers in the NFL. Takeo Spikes had a phenomenal year and led the league in Defeats. That means that 38 times last year, Spikes made a play that stopped the offense short of the line of scrimmage or, on third down, short of the yards necessary to continue the drive. London Fletcher is the kind of middle linebacker who's always around the ball—the only linebacker in a 4-3 scheme who made more plays was Keith Bullock of Tennessee. And Jeff Posey is a very underrated outside linebacker who can occasionally put his hand down and play a little defensive end as well. All three are strong in pass coverage, a major reason why the Bills were the best in the league at preventing passes to both running backs and tight ends.

Defensive Secondary

Year	DVOA vs. #1 WR	Rank	DVOA vs. #2 WR	Rank	DVOA vs. Other WR	Rank	DVOA vs. TE	Rank	DVOA vs. RB	Rank
2002	-1.9%	13	39.0%	30	18.6%	28	-1.9%	14	-7.7%	9
2003	6.9%	19	-14.8%	12	17.6%	27	7.5%	20	-52.1%	1
2004	-4.3%	11	-0.6%	10	17.5%	24	-45.7%	1	-66.5%	1

No one saw it coming, but the Bills' secondary metamorphosed from lousy in 2002 to solid in 2003 to one of the league's best in 2004. They found just the right blend of experienced safeties in Lawyer Milloy and Troy Vincent, with youthful cornerbacks in Terrence McGee and Nate Clements. We much prefer experience in our safeties, who rely on reading quarterbacks, and youth in our cornerbacks, who rely on keeping pace with speedy receivers, rather than experienced corners and youthful safeties. The problem with this strategy is that cornerbacks usually struggle for a year or two until they learn to play in the NFL. That's what happened with 2001 first-rounder Clements, and as he has matured, so has this unit. Everyone's aware that Clements is fast, but he doesn't get enough credit for his hitting ability—when a cornerback forces five fumbles, you know he's popping some people, and it's those hits that make Clements the complete package. Aside from drafting corner depth with Wake Forest's Eric King in the fifth round, the Bills didn't make any changes in their secondary in the off-season, and who can blame them?

Special Teams

Year	DVOA	Rank	FG/XP	Rank	Net Punt	Rank	Punt Ret	Rank	Net Kick	Rank	Kick Ret	Rank
2002	-3.8%	26	2.0	13	1.2	16	-2.9	22	-14.9	31	-6.4	28
2003	-0.7%	20	-5.7	25	5.2	12	-8.1	27	2.4	14	2.3	11
2004	9.2%	1	-2.0	22	11.9	7	9.7	3	9.9	7	21.7	2

The Bills had the best special teams in the league, which is good news but not as good as you might think. Like defensive performance, special teams performance is less consistent from year to year than offense. The year-to-year correlation for special teams DVOA is a little higher than the year-to-year correlation for defensive DVOA, although it is actually lower if you don't adjust for weather and altitude. Making it even less likely that Buffalo will approach last year's greatness in 2005 is the fact that Buffalo's high rating is based more on a few game-changing plays rather than consistent week-to-week performance. The Bills had a positive special teams rating in only half their games. That being said, game-changing plays do in fact change games and so this unit should be lauded. Bills special teams coach Bobby April, who was fired by Mike Martz in St. Louis, put together a great unit for an organization that had struggled with special teams in the past. April was delighted when punt returns powered the Bills to a victory over the Rams last season, with Nate Clements returning a punt 86 yards for a score and Jonathan Smith returning another punt 53 yards. And while Terrence McGee played a little corner and a little special teams in 2003, he didn't show any signs that he'd become the terrific return man he was in 2004. Brian Moorman is one of the league's top punters, but kicker Rian Lindell is below average at both parts of his job and got off easy because the kickoff coverage was the league's third best when it came to preventing returns.

Coaching Staff

In his first year as a head coach, Mike Mularkey implemented the kind of run-heavy offense he likes. But despite the emphasis on the run, the most important member of the staff is quarterbacks coach Sam Wyche. Wyche has a great reputation for developing young passers and J. P. Losman may be the biggest project of his career. If Losman turns out well, Wyche deserves more credit than any other coach. Defensive coordinator Jerry Gray, a former defensive back for Buddy Ryan's Houston Oilers defense and a holdover from the Gregg Williams era, did excellent work with his unit.

Cincinnati Bengals

The Cincinnati Bengals have finished the last two seasons with identical 8–8 records, but they are a combined 10–6 during the second half of those seasons. Considering the Bengals averaged four wins over the four seasons before they hired Marvin Lewis, he should be given a star on the Hollywood Walk of Fame.

Cincinnati's slow start the last two seasons isn't that surprising. In 2003, the Bengals were coming off a 2–14 record and Marvin Lewis was just learning how to be an NFL head coach. In the early days he spent much of his time convincing ownership to loosen the purse strings, ridding the clubhouse of deadwood, and persuading skeptical fans to support a historically hapless home team. Plus, to quote Steve Spurrier, Lewis still had to "coach 'em up." Despite the long odds, the Bengals managed to win eight games for the first time since 1996. In 2004, there were more big changes. Lewis turned the offense over to QB Carson Palmer, the first-overall selection in the 2003 draft, who had spent his rookie season as Jon Kitna's apprentice. Palmer suffered through growing pains during the first half of the season, resulting in some ill-timed interceptions and the occasional Chad Johnson temper tantrum. It didn't help that Cincinnati's first six opponents included three playoff teams as well as the defensively strong Ravens and Dolphins. Eventually, Palmer became more comfortable, the schedule got easier, and as a result the Bengals won five of their last eight games.

It was a breakout year for several other Bengals. Chad Johnson was already considered one of the best receivers in the league, but there were questions about T. J. Houshmandzadeh's durability behind Johnson and Peter Warrick. Houshmandzadeh, who didn't catch a pass in 2003 because of a nagging hamstring injury, answered his critics with 73 catches for almost 1,000 yards and moved ahead of the injured Warrick as the number two receiver on the depth chart. That production also made him some money—deciding they could not let that 2004 production go elsewhere, the Bengals re-signed him to a four-year, $13 million deal before he could hit free agency.

Backup running back Rudi Johnson moved up to starter, replacing Corey Dillon, the all-time leading rusher in Bengals history. No problem there: Johnson rushed for more than 1,400 yards last season and put to rest any concerns about the running game. Like Houshmandzadeh, Johnson signed a new contract with Cincinnati before he became eligible for free agency in February.

The disgruntled Dillon had been traded to the Patriots in return for a second-round pick days before the 2004 draft. It turned out to be one of the most mutually beneficial trades in recent NFL history. The Pats got a bruising runner who helped them to a third Super Bowl title. The Bengals ditched a malcontent and used the pick on safety Madieu Williams, who immediately paid dividends in the secondary and looks like a future star.

In fact, the entire secondary took a major step forward in 2004. Deltha O'Neal, motivated to prove he was underappreciated in Denver, was one of the league's top cornerbacks during the 12 weeks he was healthy, and his partner Tory James had a career-high eight interceptions. Keiwan

BENGALS PROSPECTUS

2004 Record: 8–8

DVOA Estimated Wins: 8.8 (12th)

Pythagorean Wins: 8.1 (15th)

DVOA: 9.8% total (11th), 20.2% weighted (7th)

Adjusted Offense: 23.5 points/game (7.6% DVOA, 11th)

Adjusted Defense: 21.8 points/game (1.1% DVOA, 17th)

Adjusted Special Teams: +1.1 points/game (3.2% DVOA, 10th)

Variance: 19.4% (14th)

2004: Carson Palmer came along quicker than expected and the Bengals finished 8–8.

2005: Rumors that the Bengals are installing orange turf with black stripes are untrue, but the uniforms stay.

2005 Projection

D'Brickashaw D'erby (0–4): 13%

Bad Team (5–6): 18%

Mediocre (7–8): 25%

Playoff Contender (9–10): 23%

Super Bowl Contender (11+): 21%

Projected Average Opponent: −1.2% DVOA (20th in NFL)

Ratliff, another second-round pick, had a solid rookie campaign at nickelback. Only Washington had a better overall defensive DVOA against opposing wide receivers.

Unfortunately, the Bengals' front seven still couldn't stop the run. Cincinnati's ranking in run defense DVOA improved from last in the league in 2003 to 22nd in 2004. But the reasons had nothing to do with the front seven. Better tackling in the secondary led to fewer long runs, while the decline of the NFC meant the Bengals improved in the rankings without improving their performance. Of the ten teams below them in run defense, only three were from the AFC: Kansas City, Tennessee, and Cleveland.

The Cincinnati defense also struggled to pressure the quarterback on a consistent basis, finishing 22nd in Adjusted Sack Rate with 33 sacks. This was an improvement from 2003, when the Bengals ranked 28th with 30 sacks, but it wasn't enough to save defensive coordinator Leslie Frazier's job. Lewis promoted Chuck Bresnahan to defensive coordinator, the same job he held for three straight divisional championship teams in Oakland from 2000 through 2002. Bresnahan's run defense struggled in 2001, but ranked in the top ten for DVOA run defense in both 2000 and 2002. First-round draft pick David Pollack will make the move from defensive end to outside linebacker and could make an immediate impact. Pollack and former Dolphin defensive end Bryan Robinson—not a great pass rusher, but very physical at the point of attack—should bolster Cincinnati's run defense.

Since the NFL went to an eight-division format in 2002, fans have casually dismissed the AFC North as a pool of mediocrity, like the NBA Atlantic Division or ABC's sitcom lineup. That's all about to change and the Bengals have a lot to do with the shift in perception.

In two years, Lewis has done a superb job of using the draft to restock his team for the immediate future while also grooming players to be successful after some apprenticeship. Some players, like Williams, Ratliff, and defensive tackle Langston Moore, made an immediate impact. Others, like Palmer and wide receiver Kelley Washington, took a season or two to develop but should be important contributors this year. (Last year's first-round pick, running back Chris Perry, remains a question mark.)

The last draft brought another wave of young talent into Cincinnati, and at a certain point all of this talent has to gel. Heading into 2005, this team is very well positioned for a playoff run. This is probably the same regurgitated song-and-dance you read somewhere last season, but this time it's legit. The Bengals have a well-respected head coach, a maturing quarterback, genuine offensive weapons in Rudi Johnson, Chad Johnson, and T. J. Houshmandzadeh, and a defense on the brink of a breakthrough. In the ultra-competitive AFC, a winning season does not come easily. But not every team that was sitting at home last January is going to be stuck sitting at home this coming January. It won't be easy to unseat any of last season's AFC playoff teams, but somebody new will end up in the postseason. For the first time in a very long while, it isn't crazy to think it could be the Bengals.

Ryan Wilson

Research: Carson Palmer vs. Byron Leftwich: The Effect of Schedule on Statistics

Almost every year, an NFL team compiles a gaudy record thanks to a friendly schedule. Historically, people still question the undefeated 1972 Dolphins due to their weak opposition. More recently, the 1999 Rams charged to a 13–3 record despite never beating a team with a winning record. Even last year, the Falcons won only 1 of their 11 games against a team with a winning record. For some reason, however, the effect of schedule on individual player's statistics has not entered our common discourse. Each week, fantasy players across the nation scout for a running back playing against Minnesota and fear a quarterback facing Baltimore. Nobody ever seems to realize, however, that each player's schedule does not even out over the course of a season. The opponents a player plays during the year can have a profound impact on his year-end statistics.

Consider the first two quarterbacks taken in the 2003 draft, Carson Palmer and Byron Leftwich. While Leftwich played most of his rookie season with the Jaguars, Palmer did not take a single snap for the Bengals. In their second season, the two put up very similar conventional statistics (table 1), although Leftwich seems to have a small advantage with fewer interceptions. But, as is often the case, conventional statistics are misleading. Palmer and Leftwich faced very different levels of competition, and that's

TABLE 1. BYRON LEFTWICH AND CARSON PALMER, 2004

Player	Att	Comp	Pct	Yds	Y/P	TD	INT	DVOA	DPAR
Leftwich	441	267	60.5%	2941	6.67	15	10	2.3%	30.2
Palmer	432	263	60.9%	2897	6.71	18	18	7.2%	39.0

why our statistics show Palmer superior in both DVOA and DPAR.

What sort of crazy math are we doing? DVOA and DPAR do account for context, like field position, down, and distance. These numbers also include sacks and ignore intentional spikes and Hail Mary interceptions. But those differences cannot account for the size of this discrepancy. The bulk of the disparity is attributable to the relative strength of each player's opponents.

As we explained in the "Statistical Toolbox" in the front of the book, the D in DPAR and DVOA is the adjustment based on the defense. We also have statistics called PAR and VOA that analyze performance based on down and distance in the same fashion, but without adjusting for opponent. With these numbers, Leftwich leaps back in front, posting a PAR of 43.6 and VOA of 9.2% compared to 15.8 PAR and −5.0% VOA for Palmer.

Consider the schedules of the Bengals and Jaguars last year. The Bengals played in the AFC North, where each team faced the AFC East and NFC East. The Jaguars played in the AFC South, where each team played the AFC West and NFC North. That means that while Palmer played Baltimore and Pittsburgh twice, as well as New England, Washington, and Buffalo, Leftwich got the Colts and Titans twice, plus the Chiefs, Raiders, Vikings, and Packers. (Each quarterback missed time due to injuries, so Palmer did not actually face the Eagles, Bills, or Giants, and Leftwich missed games against the Titans and Lions.)

Overall, Palmer ended up playing 8 of his 13 games against teams ranked in the top 11 of DVOA in pass defense (table 2). He faced only two of the ten worst pass defenses. Leftwich did play against three of the top four pass defenses, but the next best pass defense he faced was San Diego, which ranked 14th. He played games against four of the seven worst pass defenses, including three of the bottom four. Palmer's average opponent ranked 12th in DVOA pass defense with a DVOA of −5.5%. Leftwich's average opponent ranked 17th in DVOA pass defense with a DVOA of 2.9%.

Compare each player's conventional stats to those posted by quarterbacks against the teams on each player's respective schedule. We took each quarterback one at a time and subtracted his statistics from the overall passing statistics allowed by his opponents. (Divisional opponents counted twice.) Then, we figured out what each team allowed per pass attempt on a percentage basis. For instance, the Steelers allowed to all quarterbacks besides Palmer a 56% completion rate, with 5.8 yards per attempt. They allowed a TD on 2.6% of pass attempts and intercepted nearly 4%. We then multiplied these per attempt ratios by the number of attempts Palmer had against Pittsburgh. The result gives the approximate numbers that an average NFL quarterback would have posted against Pitts-

TABLE 2. DVOA RANK OF OPPONENT PASS DEFENSES, 2004

Carson Palmer		Byron Leftwich	
Team	Rank	Team	Rank
BAL	2	BUF	1
BAL	2	PIT	3
PIT	3	DEN	4
PIT	3	SD	12
DEN	4	CHI	13
WAS	7	HOU	14
MIA	9	HOU	14
NE	11	IND	18
TEN	20	IND	18
CLE	21	TEN	20
CLE	21	KC	26
NYJ	24	MIN	29
DAL	27	GB	30
—	—	OAK	31

burgh, given the same number of pass attempts as Palmer. Add this together for each team, and the result tells us how an average quarterback would have fared against the schedule faced by Palmer or Leftwich.

Note that everything is balanced by pass attempts, so Leftwich does not lose ground because he attempted only 20 passes against Green Bay, and Palmer gains no ground for having attempted an average of 44 passes per game in his two contests against Baltimore. They are compared to what an average quarterback would have done in 20 passes against Green Bay or 44 per game against Baltimore.

In this context, Palmer is certainly the superior quarterback. He averaged 6% more completions, nearly 8% more yards per attempt, and 14% more touchdowns than the average quarterback playing his schedule. He did, however, throw 19% more interceptions. Leftwich, on the other hand, was extremely average. His completion rate was 1% off the other quarterbacks, and his YPA was 2% off. He did throw 33% fewer interceptions, but he also threw 31% fewer touchdowns.

We can also use this method to estimate how each quarterback would have done facing his counterpart's schedule (see table 3). Our calculations assume that Leftwich would have attempted the same number of passes in each game against Palmer's opponents that Palmer did and vice versa.

If the schedules had been reversed, nobody would even consider comparing the two. In this hypothetical, Palmer still throws more interceptions, but he also throws more than twice as many touchdowns and averages 1.3 more yards per pass attempt. Of course, these numbers

TABLE 3. PALMER AND LEFTWICH WITH REVERSED SCHEDULES

Player	Att	Comp	Pct	Yds	Y/P	TD	INT
Leftwich with CIN schedule	432	247	57.1%	2628	6.08	11	10
Palmer with JAC schedule	441	284	64.4%	3242	7.35	25	18

have a pro-Palmer bias similar to the pro-Leftwich bias in the actual 2004 stats. Had Leftwich actually played the opponents that Palmer faced, and Palmer the opponents that Leftwich faced, this article would appear in the Jacksonville chapter arguing that Leftwich was not the bust that he appeared to be.

So to get the best idea of how the two players compare, we have to estimate their numbers against a league-average schedule. We took the overall numbers posted by every NFL quarterback and calculated the league-average completion percentage as if Leftwich or Palmer did not play in 2004. We did the same for yards per attempt, touchdown rate, and interception rate. We then combined this with our earlier numbers that showed how each player compared to an average quarterback on a per play basis to approximate each player's stat line against average competition (table 4).

These numbers show that the two players were very close in value, but while Leftwich holds the slim advantage in actual statistics, Palmer holds the slim advantage here. Palmer is clearly much more of a high risk, high reward quarterback, who throws for more yards per attempt, more touchdowns, and more interceptions. While this could be a true difference in the quarterbacks, it could also be related to the strength of the Cincinnati and Jacksonville defenses. Palmer needs to put more points on the board to win, so he is more aggressive. Leftwich's main goal is to protect the football and take advantage of those opportunities that present themselves.

Both Palmer and Leftwich are just entering their third seasons and have yet to turn 25. Each has proven that he can start in the NFL, and each has emerged as an above-average quarterback according to DVOA. Looking forward, it is impossible to predict how they will develop. A little troubling is that Palmer's closest comparable in similarity scores is Tim Couch in 2002. However, similarity scores do not include any adjustment for level of competition, so the similarity with Couch is based on Palmer's pedestrian counting stats. Palmer's third-closest comparable is Tom Brady in 2001, which is a pretty good demonstration of how uncertain the future is for a promising quarterback who has not yet reached superstar status. Oh, and second, between Couch and Brady on Palmer's list of comparable quarterbacks? Why, that would be Byron Leftwich in 2004. (Palmer also shows up high on Leftwich's list of comparables, behind Brian Griese in 1999 and Brady.)

For now, all we can conclusively say is that Palmer had a better 2004 season than Leftwich, a fact greatly obscured by the difficulty of his schedule. In the NFL, where each team plays only 13 of the other 31 teams, ignoring the impact of schedule when evaluating individual performances would seem foolhardy at best. By making an adjustment for schedule, we can see that Palmer, despite his mediocre conventional numbers, was the most developed second-year quarterback in the league last season.

Ned Macey

TABLE 4. PALMER AND LEFTWICH VS. LEAGUE-AVERAGE SCHEDULE

Player	Att	Comp	Pct	Yds	Y/P	TD	INT
Leftwich w/average schedule	441	263	59.6%	2844	6.45	14	10
Palmer w/average schedule	432	274	63.4%	3070	7.11	22	16

Bengals 2004 Stats by Week

Wk	vs.	W-L	PF	PA	YDF	YDA	TO	Total	Off	Def	ST
								DVOA			
1	@NYJ	L	24	31	351	438	-1	1.9%	31.2%	43.5%	14.2%
2	MIA	W	16	13	210	226	+2	-13.7%	-25.1%	-6.1%	5.2%
3	BAL	L	9	23	398	380	-2	-45.9%	-10.9%	24.4%	-10.7%
4	@PIT	L	17	28	293	333	-1	4.4%	3.2%	-3.8%	-2.6%
5	BYE										
6	@CLE	L	17	34	189	449	+3	-55.8%	-33.8%	18.8%	-3.2%
7	DEN	W	23	10	321	318	+2	72.4%	16.4%	-37.7%	18.3%
8	@TEN	L	20	27	274	358	-1	-43.1%	-24.1%	21.9%	2.9%
9	DAL	W	26	23	328	311	+5	63.7%	15.2%	-40.5%	8.1%
10	@WAS	W	17	10	316	268	0	8.1%	-3.5%	-19.6%	-8.1%
11	PIT	L	14	19	209	235	0	9.4%	16.3%	-4.5%	-11.4%
12	CLE	W	58	48	504	462	-1	-12.1%	27.3%	52.7%	13.3%
13	@BAL	W	27	26	453	356	0	50.7%	66.7%	32.1%	16.1%
14	@NE	L	28	35	482	354	-3	12.9%	57.2%	46.2%	2.0%
15	BUF	L	17	33	275	212	-3	-1.2%	-14.3%	-33.9%	-20.8%
16	NYG	W	23	22	233	326	-1	-23.2%	-24.4%	10.4%	11.6%
17	@PHI	W	38	10	308	342	+5	109.4%	24.3%	-68.4%	16.8%

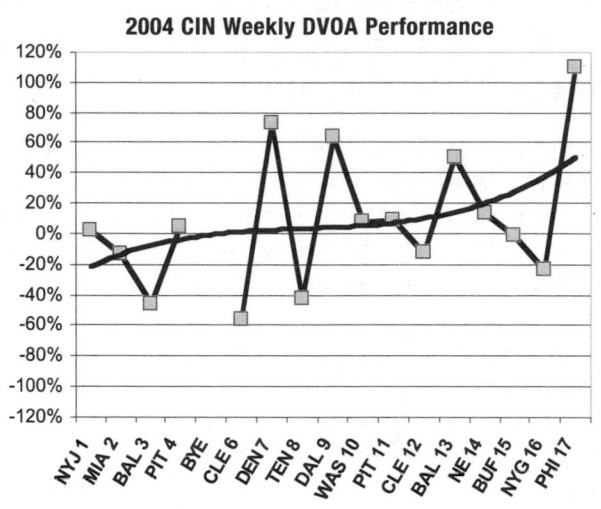

2004 CIN Weekly DVOA Performance

Trends and Splits

	Offense	Rank	Defense	Rank
Total DVOA	7.6%	11	1.1%	17
Unadjusted VOA	-3.8%	21	-1.4%	15
Weighted Trend	13.6%	9	-3.2%	15
Variance	8.8%	16	12.4%	7
Passing	9.5%	11	-2.1%	15
Rushing	5.6%	10	4.4%	22
First Down	1.7%	15	10.1%	23
Second Down	8.3%	13	-3.9%	10
Third Down	18.4%	8	-8.8%	14
Red Zone	21.5%	5	10.0%	24
Late and Close	-5.8%	15	9.8%	27

Five-Year Performance

	2004	2003	2002	2001	2000
W-L	8-8	8-8	2-14	6-10	4-12
Pythagorean Wins	8.1	7.0	3.8	5.2	2.8
Estimated Wins	8.8	7.0	3.4	5.6	3.7
Total DVOA	9.8%	-9.3%	-33.9%	-22.8%	-40.4%
Rank	11	23	29	27	29
Offense	7.6%	6.6%	-1.7%	-15.6%	-18.9%
Rank	11	10	22	28	26
Defense	1.1%	15.2%	20.7%	-2.0%	13.6%
Rank	17	32	30	21	27
Special Teams	3.2%	-0.8%	-11.5%	-9.2%	-7.9%
Rank	10	21	32	31	30

Passing (min. 5 plays)

Player	DPAR	PAR	DVOA	Plys	NtYds	Avg	Cmpl	TD	Int
Carson Palmer	39.0	15.7	7.2%	452	2716	6.0	60.9%	18	18
Jon Kitna	8.7	0.8	5.9%	111	580	5.2	58.7%	5	4

Rushing (min. 3 plays)

Player	DPAR	PAR	DVOA	Plys	Yds	Avg	TD	Fum	Suc
Rudi Johnson	30.6	21.8	5.1%	362	1462	4.0	12	4	46%
Kenny Watson	1.2	0.3	-2.0%	25	158	6.3	0	2	48%
Carson Palmer	3.5	3.3	51.2%	9	59	6.6	1	0	—
Jon Kitna	1.1	0.8	10.0%	7	44	6.3	0	0	—
T. J. Houshmandzadeh	2.8	2.8	51.4%	6	51	8.5	0	0	—
Chad Johnson	1.9	1.9	46.9%	4	39	9.8	0	0	—
Cliff Russell	0.3	0.2	-11.7%	3	15	5.0	0	0	—
Jeremi Johnson	-3.9	-3.8	-241.0%	3	5	1.7	0	1	0%

Receiving (min. 5 plays)

Player	DPAR	PAR	DVOA	Plys	Ctch	Yds	Y/C	TD	CPct
WR									
Chad Johnson	24.0	20.8	6.7%	169	95	1274	13.4	9	56%
T. J. Houshmandzadeh	31.0	27.5	28.8%	109	73	978	13.4	4	67%
Kelley Washington	9.5	9.5	14.8%	50	31	377	12.2	3	64%
Peter Warrick	3.0	3.6	12.0%	17	11	127	11.5	0	65%
Kevin Walter	1.1	0.7	4.6%	9	8	67	8.4	0	89%
TE									
Matt Schobel	3.9	0.8	11.2%	33	21	201	9.6	4	64%
Tony Stewart	-6.4	-8.1	-50.3%	25	10	48	4.8	1	40%
Reggie Kelly	-3.1	-3.6	-34.1%	21	15	85	5.7	0	71%
RB									
Kenny Watson	2.7	0.0	9.1%	35	25	171	6.8	1	71%
Rudi Johnson	-5.3	-6.4	-48.6%	28	15	84	5.6	0	54%
Jeremi Johnson	-2.5	-3.4	-31.9%	18	16	53	3.3	1	89%

Defensive Players (min. 20 plays)

Player	Age	Plys	Stop	Dfts	AvYds	StpRt	Sack	Int	FR
Defensive Line									
Justin Smith	26	73	45	18	1.3	62%	8.0	0	2
John Thornton	29	59	40	14	2.4	68%	3.0	0	0
Duane Clemons	31	51	39	19	0.6	76%	6.5	0	0
Langston Moore	24	30	20	6	1.9	67%	1.0	0	0
Carl Powell	31	20	14	8	1.1	70%	2.0	1	0
Linebackers									
Brian Simmons	30	109	45	18	5.8	41%	1.0	2	1
Landon Johnson	24	90	37	14	4.5	41%	2.0	0	1
Kevin Hardy	32	70	38	12	3.9	54%	4.0	0	0
Caleb Miller	25	28	12	4	5.5	43%	0.0	0	1
Nate Webster	28	24	12	5	4.0	50%	1.0	0	1

Player	Age	Plys	Stop	Dfts	AvYds	StpRt	Sack	Int	FR
Secondary									
Madieu Williams	24	103	39	25	7.0	38%	2.0	3	2
Tory James	32	79	26	16	8.4	33%	0.0	8	1
Kim Herring	30	68	22	10	9.1	32%	0.0	1	0
Kevin Kaesviharn	29	66	23	9	10.0	35%	0.0	0	1
Deltha O'Neal	28	54	24	16	6.9	44%	1.0	4	0
Keiwan Ratliff	24	41	18	10	8.1	44%	0.0	0	3
Rogers Beckett	28	20	4	2	8.6	20%	0.0	0	0

Offensive Line

Year	Yards	AdjLineYd	Rank	Power	Rank	10+ Yds	Rank	Stuff	Rank	Sack	AdjSack%	Rank
2002	4.19	4.33	10	88%	1	14%	25	22%	9	35	5.2%	9
2003	4.07	4.08	20	58%	28	18%	10	24%	15	38	6.6%	18
2004	4.15	4.15	18	58%	20	18%	13	26%	21	31	4.9%	6

Year	LEnd	Rank	LTckl	Rank	MdGrd	Rank	RTckl	Rank	REnd	Rank
2002	3.24	28	4.46	8	4.73	3	4.51	11	3.44	22
2003	3.72	24	4.10	19	4.15	17	4.19	19	4.08	14
2004	4.52	11	4.43	16	4.16	18	3.87	20	3.92	15

One of the Bengals' biggest needs along the offensive line heading into 2005 is grooming a replacement for center Rich Braham. He's battled injuries the last few years and he'll be 35 in November. Cincinnati drafted center Eric Ghiaciuc in the fourth round, but he probably won't be ready to assume the starting role for at least a season. (This gives the public address announcer at Paul Brown Stadium ample time to figure out how to pronounce his name.) The Bengals also signed center Ben Wilkerson out of Louisiana State. Highly rated heading into the 2004 season, he suffered a knee injury and went undrafted. If he can return to his college form, he could be a steal. Other than at center, this unit is solid, particularly in pass blocking. Left tackle Levi Jones is gradually fulfilling his first-round potential, veteran Willie Anderson is still making Pro Bowls, and guards Eric Steinbach and Bobbie Williams are both reliable.

Defensive Front Seven

Year	Yards	AdjLineYd	Rank	Power	Rank	10+ Yds	Rank	Stuff	Rank	Sack	AdjSack%	Rank
2002	3.86	4.25	19	49%	3	12%	5	23%	22	25	4.6%	31
2003	4.90	4.49	27	66%	18	23%	29	23%	22	30	4.7%	28
2004	4.68	4.53	29	71%	26	18%	21	23%	18	37	6.3%	22

Year	LEnd	Rank	LTckl	Rank	MdGrd	Rank	RTckl	Rank	REnd	Rank
2002	4.25	22	4.12	16	4.50	27	4.61	24	3.45	9
2003	4.64	26	3.47	4	4.80	31	4.63	27	3.79	17
2004	4.39	18	5.34	32	4.68	29	3.41	1	4.46	24

Cincinnati's defensive problems are all up front and that's why the Bengals took defensive end David Pollack in the draft's first round. Pollack will move to outside linebacker, where he'll team up with his college teammate and new inside linebacker Odell Thurman. With tackle John Thornton and end Justin Smith, these players should not only improve a pass rush that registered 37 sacks last season, but also bolster one of the worst run defenses in the AFC. In 2004, the Bengals drafted linebackers Caleb Miller and Landon Johnson, and both players saw a lot of playing time as rookies. Former Tampa Bay Buccaneer Nate Webster started last season at middle linebacker but played in only three games due to injury. There's some concern that he may not be back in Cincinnati this season, which is why the Bengals drafted Thurman. If you like statistical flukes, check out that rating for the Cincinnati defense against runs behind the offense's right tackle.

Defensive Secondary

Year	DVOA vs. #1 WR	Rank	DVOA vs. #2 WR	Rank	DVOA vs. Other WR	Rank	DVOA vs. TE	Rank	DVOA vs. RB	Rank
2002	22.0%	28	40.6%	31	14.5%	24	37.5%	31	8.6%	19
2003	33.5%	30	-22.6%	9	-9.0%	17	-21.2%	5	40.3%	32
2004	-24.0%	4	-13.8%	6	-6.9%	16	32.3%	28	1.9%	26

In 2004 Cincinnati drafted CB Keiwan Ratliff and S Madieu Williams in the second round, and they were keys to the much-improved pass defense. With Deltha O'Neal joining Tory James at cornerback, the Cincinnati secondary showed drastic improvement from the year before. In DVOA pass defense, they improved from 28th in the league in 2003 to 15th last season, and things will improve even more if they can find somebody to effectively cover tight ends. Going into the draft the Bengals were looking for a run-stuffing safety but didn't land one, which puts even more pressure on the front seven.

Special Teams

Year	DVOA	Rank	FG/XP	Rank	Net Punt	Rank	Punt Ret	Rank	Net Kick	Rank	Kick Ret	Rank
2002	-11.5%	32	2.2	10	-35.7	32	-23.7	32	-13.8	29	7.0	8
2003	-0.8%	21	10.2	5	-5.1	26	-3.2	18	3.5	11	-9.5	29
2004	3.2%	10	12.1	3	6.1	14	-11.2	27	12.3	3	-1.2	18

Cincinnati lost its veteran punter, Kyle Richardson, to AFC North rival Cleveland, and the job is now Kyle Larson's to lose. Kicker Shayne Graham made several game-winning kicks last season and he's quietly becoming one of the most consistent young kickers in the AFC. Cliff Russell and Kenny Watson do a reasonable job on kick returns, and while rookie corner Ratliff and starting receiver Houshmandzadeh handled punt returns last season, someone else may take on this task in 2005.

Coaching Staff

Going into his third season, head coach Marvin Lewis has kept his coaching staff pretty much unchanged except for hiring Chuck Bresnahan to replace ousted defensive coordinator Leslie Frazer. Frazer struggled to shore up the Bengals run defense; now that's on Bresnahan's plate. Offensive coordinator Bob Bratkowski is underrated—with all the problems of the Cincinnati defense, very few people have really noticed how good the offense has been over the past two seasons. Secondary coach Kevin Coyle deserves plaudits for the improvement of the defensive backs last season, but the real name to watch (and try to learn how to spell) is his assistant, Sigismondo Cioffi. Cioffi coaches safeties but also handles defensive preparation and film study. He turns 32 early in the season, but this is already his ninth year on the Bengals' coaching staff. In fact, he started as a game preparation intern under Bruce Coslet in 1993, when Coslet was with the Jets and Cioffi was just 20 years old.

Cleveland Browns

It can't be easy to root for the Cleveland Browns. For four years, Cleveland fans have watched a team coached by their former head coach, assisted by their former defensive coordinator, win three Super Bowls. In the meantime, their organization gradually gave over most of its power to a big-name college coach, Butch Davis, who never adapted to the NFL and ended up looking more Michael "Dauber" Dybinski than Hayden Fox.

Finally, Cleveland fans can stop swearing every time they see the words "New England" in the newspaper. When Butch Davis arrived from the University of Miami, the Browns fired Romeo Crennel as defensive coordinator. Now he comes back as head coach to clean up the Davis disaster.

The troubles in Cleveland begin with personnel decisions. In his four years with the Browns, Davis drafted Gerard Warren, William Green, Quincy Morgan, Jeff Faine, and Kellen Winslow in the first or second round. To call Warren an underachiever wouldn't be fair to underachievers. Green hasn't come close to playing like a 16th overall pick and has had more run-ins with the law than Tommy Lee. Morgan, drafted ahead of Chad Johnson, Steve Smith, and Justin McCareins, never materialized into a number one receiver, and was traded midseason to the Cowboys. Winslow is about to lose a second year to injury, this time one not even related to football. The only player who looks like he has a promising future in Cleveland is Faine.

A year ago, Browns fans were dancing in the streets when it was announced that free agent quarterback Jeff Garcia would be the man to get this team back to the playoffs. Little did Garcia know that he and Davis would get along about as well as Shannon Doherty and Paris Hilton at a Rick Solomon birthday party.

But Garcia had the worst year of his career after signing a three-year, $25 million deal before the season. Between the off-field issues—including Terrell Owens questioning his sexuality, a much-publicized bar fight that included his current and ex-girlfriend, and a DUI arrest—and the myriad on-field problems that led to him second-guessing Butch Davis's game-planning acumen, it's amazing Garcia was actually able to make it to Week 11.

Garcia struggled, in part, because Davis never completely drew an offensive blueprint. The Browns had no proven running back and a roster stocked with number two receivers without a player who could step forward to

BROWNS PROSPECTUS

2004 Record: 4–12

DVOA Estimated Wins: 5.6 (27th)

Pythagorean Wins: 4.9 (30th)

DVOA: −19.4% total (28th), −22.3% weighted (27th)

Adjusted Offense: 18.4 points/game (−11.9% DVOA, 27th)

Adjusted Defense: 24.1 points/game (9.7% DVOA, 24th)

Adjusted Special Teams: +0.8 points/game (2.3% DVOA, 12th)

Variance: 21.6% (11th)

2004: It was bad, and then worse, and then even worse.

2005: This season won't be quite as painful as 2004; it'll just seem like it.

2005 Projection

Leinart Land (0–4): 31%

Bad Team (5–6): 25%

Mediocre (7–8): 22%

Playoff Contender (9–10): 13%

Super Bowl Contender (11+): 9%

Projected Average Opponent: −1.8% DVOA (23rd in NFL)

be number one. To add injury to insult, they lost their first-round draft pick (Winslow) for the season after Week 3.

The Browns also never addressed their offensive line problems. In 2003, the Browns finished 18th in Adjusted Line Yards and 21st in Adjusted Sack Rate. During the 2004 off-season, they lost two linemen, signed one free agent, and didn't draft an offensive lineman until the sixth round. The resulting line dropped to 30th in Adjusted Line Yards and 27th in Adjusted Sack Rate. At times, Garcia looked more like Dr. Richard Kimball on the run from the law than an NFL quarterback trying to go through his progressions. Later, Luke McCown took over at quarterback and proved that he was, in fact, a McCown. The Browns struck rock bottom during Week 14 with five turnovers, eight sacks, and a whopping 17 yards of total offense against Buffalo.

On defense, the Browns were consistent against both the run and the pass—consistently bad, ranking 21st and 30th in DVOA respectively. The defense was showing signs of improvement around midseason, but completely melted down in a 58–48 shootout loss to the Bengals that was followed by Davis's hasty resignation. If not for a Week 17 win against the Texans, the Browns would have finished the season with a nine-game losing streak.

It took about four minutes for Crennel to accept the Cleveland Browns job after the New England Patriots won their third Super Bowl. It will take a little longer than that to turn the Browns around. But Crennel and new general manager Phil Savage (previously director of player personnel for Baltimore) quickly made improvements to the Cleveland roster.

Jeff Garcia didn't figure in Crennel's long-term vision, so he was released. So were veteran safety Robert Griffith and the disappointing defensive lineman Courtney Brown. The rest of the defensive line was shipped off to Denver in various deals that netted the Browns a fourth-round draft pick and running back Reuben Droughns. Cleveland then signed one of the best young cornerbacks in the league, two offensive linemen, and a proven punter and traded for a veteran quarterback. And all of this happened a month before the draft.

For the first time in a long time, this team has a plan, and it starts with a more consistent running game. Early in the off-season, the Browns signed Ravens running back Chester Taylor to an offer sheet only to have Baltimore match it less than a week later. Casting about for another option at running back, Cleveland sent defensive linemen Ebenezer Ekuban and Michael Myers to Denver for Droughns. Even without the legendary Denver offensive line, Droughns is a bruising runner who should help take some of the pressure off the passing game. He will likely end up the winner in a training camp battle with incumbent running back Lee Suggs, who showed some promise last season but has battled injuries during his career. The odd man out is Cleveland's first pick in the 2002 draft, William Green; the Browns are tired of his inconsistent play and off-field troubles, and it would be a bit surprising if he hasn't been released by the time this book hits the shelves.

The passing game was supposed to be built around two strengths: this year's first-round pick, wide receiver Braylon Edwards—considered by many to be the most talented player in the draft—and last year's first-round pick, tight end Winslow. But Winslow's motorcycle accident will keep him on the shelf for another season (and possibly longer). That puts more pressure on both Edwards and the running game. With Winslow off pondering the idea that "wheelies" are not as cool as he expected, the tight end duties will again fall to Steve Heiden and Aaron Shea, but they will primarily be used as blockers and third or fourth receiving options.

All the changes on the offensive side of the ball pale in comparison to the upheaval on the defensive side, which will convert to a 3-4 formation similar to the one Crennel ran in New England. Since linebackers are critical to the success of this defense, Cleveland has a problem. The current Cleveland linebackers are prone to injury, a bit undersized, and have trouble shedding blocks. The Browns took five defensive players in the draft, but only one linebacker, and that was in the sixth round.

The 3-4 defense is just one of the many facets of the Patriots style that Crennel will now apply to his new team. Don't forget, the Patriots were 9–7, 8–8, and 5–11 in the three years prior to their first Super Bowl championship, and what they accomplished had more to do with execution than athleticism. Crennel will try to bring the same philosophy to the Browns, but the problems of this team are more acute than the ones Belichick inherited in Foxboro five years ago.

It's obvious this team has a lot of work to do before making a playoff run. But with a new GM, a new coach, and a new philosophy, the turnaround time should be considerably shorter. If third-round pick Charlie Frye progresses into a starting quarterback, if Kellen Winslow can actually get on the field, and if the players buy into what Crennel is trying to do, it is reasonable to believe that the Browns will be contending for the playoffs in three years. A lot of the near-term success of this franchise will be determined by how quickly the current players learn the nuances of the 3-4 defense, and also by how much of a contribution the newly acquired free agents and draft picks make. In the long term, it's up to Crennel to develop players who exemplify the "whole is greater than the sum of the parts" meme perfected in New England.

Ryan Wilson

Research: Yards vs. Reality

The Browns had the fifth-ranked pass defense in the NFL last year.

Seriously.

The NFL ranks defenses by yards allowed, not by any sophisticated measure of quality. With passing yards allowed as the criteria, the Browns (3,091 gross yards allowed, 2,901 net yards) ranked just between the Steelers and Broncos.

Alert readers can smell the rat: Passing yards allowed is an awful measure of defensive quality, especially for bad teams. Teams like the Browns are blown out several times in a season; in these situations, opponents sit on the ball during the second half, and they don't throw for very many yards.

But the Browns pass defense had solid peripheral statistics, too. The Browns allowed just 17 passing touchdowns last season, tied for fourth in the NFL. They allowed just 6.9 yards per attempt, which ranked ninth. Yards per attempt are a legitimate indicator of quality. Maybe the Browns pass defense *was* good.

Or, maybe not. Cleveland's passing defense DVOA of 5.9% ranked 21st in the league. Once again, DVOA illustrates facts that observant fans know (there was nothing good about the Browns defense last year) but ordinary statistics fail to show.

DVOA adjusts for the quality of the opponent. The Browns played two games against the pass-challenged Ravens, and they also faced the Redskins, Bills, and Dolphins. They faced the Jets during their anemic Quincy Carter period. They lost two games to the Steelers, a team that can throw the ball but often chooses not to. The Browns had an above-average VOA of −1.4% before fine-tuning for schedule, but the adjustments reflect that it is easy to prevent the pass when you face opponents who aren't very good at it, or don't like to do it when they can hand the ball to Jerome Bettis 30 times instead.

Even before adjusting for opponents, DVOA reveals that the Browns' low total of touchdown passes allowed is misleading. The Browns gave up 22 rushing touchdowns, the highest total in the NFL (tied with the 49ers). While the Browns run defense was also terrible, it wasn't to blame for every one of those touchdowns. Many of them were quick plunges that occurred after breakdowns in the pass defense:

- Week 2 vs. Dallas: Eddie George scores a 3-yard touchdown, two plays after a 37-yard catch by Antonio Bryant.
- Week 4 vs. Washington: Clinton Portis scores a 1-yard touchdown, two plays after a 30-yard catch by Laveranues Coles.
- Week 5 vs. Pittsburgh: Ben Roethlisberger's 6-yard sneak for a touchdown comes on the heels of a 48-yard hookup with Plaxico Burress.

- Week 13 vs. New England: Two short Corey Dillon touchdowns are set up by (1) a 25-yard catch by Christian Fauria that puts the ball on the Browns' 11-yard line and (2) a 39-yard pass interference penalty against David Patten by Lewis Sanders.

The raw figures suggest that the Browns pass defense effectively kept opponents out of the end zone. In fact, the Browns secondary was scorched for several long touchdowns: They allowed seven touchdown passes of 30 or more yards. The Browns didn't give up many 10- to 15-yard touchdowns, mainly because opponents were confident that they could run the ball in the red zone.

The feeble Cleveland offense also had an impact on the low total of yards allowed, even though they weren't actually on the field covering opposing receivers. Because the Browns often went three-and-out and had numerous turnovers, the average drive against the Cleveland defense started on the opposing 32.5-yard line. Only St. Louis and San Francisco gave the ball back to the other team with shorter field position, and shorter field position means giving up fewer yards because it takes fewer yards to score.

In sum, the poor play of the Browns pass defense is largely hidden on the stat sheet. DVOA can't cut through every distortion; the Chargers attempted just six passes in a 21–0 rout of the Browns, so it's hard to account for how badly the Cleveland pass defense might have performed if it had to. But DVOA strongly indicates that the Browns pass defense wasn't an asset, but simply the team's least glaring weakness. It's an accurate statement, much more useful than the official stats that show the 2004 Browns finishing high in any meaningful category.

Mike Tanier

Browns 2004 Stats by Week

Wk	vs.	W-L	PF	PA	YDF	YDA	TO	Total	Off	Def	ST
								\<DVOA\>			
1	BAL	W	20	3	250	254	+3	57.8%	5.9%	-34.5%	17.3%
2	@DAL	L	12	19	202	441	+1	-94.3%	-86.3%	14.4%	6.4%
3	@NYG	L	10	27	285	390	-3	-74.3%	-9.8%	62.8%	-1.6%
4	WAS	W	17	13	280	265	+1	13.0%	18.3%	12.2%	6.9%
5	@PIT	L	23	34	296	401	0	5.6%	32.1%	24.3%	-2.2%
6	CIN	W	34	17	449	189	-3	28.2%	-1.7%	-26.3%	3.6%
7	PHI	L	31	34	394	488	-2	0.0%	38.2%	27.7%	-10.5%
8	BYE										
9	@BAL	L	13	27	217	240	-1	-20.4%	-36.3%	8.3%	24.1%
10	PIT	L	10	24	228	300	-3	-47.2%	-45.3%	2.2%	0.4%
11	NYJ	L	7	10	216	235	0	15.1%	9.1%	-22.8%	-16.7%
12	@CIN	L	48	58	462	504	+1	-6.9%	35.3%	37.0%	-5.2%
13	NE	L	15	42	293	410	-1	-30.6%	-22.4%	-6.8%	-15.0%
14	@BUF	L	7	37	17	321	-2	-119.2%	-123.2%	1.9%	6.0%
15	SD	L	0	21	231	257	0	-29.6%	-31.0%	11.3%	12.7%
16	@MIA	L	7	10	285	280	-2	-61.5%	-19.5%	31.2%	-10.8%
17	@HOU	W	22	14	364	238	-1	15.1%	1.1%	6.6%	20.6%

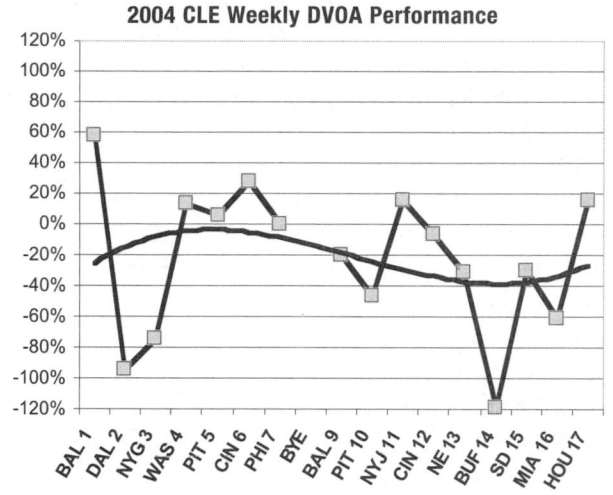

2004 CLE Weekly DVOA Performance

Trends and Splits

	Offense	Rank	Defense	Rank
Total DVOA	-11.9%	27	9.7%	24
Unadjusted VOA	-23.6%	29	6.8%	22
Weighted Trend	-15.5%	28	7.8%	22
Variance	19.1%	2	6.2%	25
Passing	-13.0%	24	5.9%	21
Rushing	-10.9%	26	12.9%	30
First Down	-3.1%	22	15.6%	28
Second Down	-21.8%	29	7.3%	21
Third Down	-13.1%	21	1.6%	22
Red Zone	-1.5%	17	35.4%	30
Late and Close	-8.2%	20	-3.5%	16

Five-Year Performance

	2004	2003	2002	2001	2000
W-L	4-12	5-11	9-7	7-9	3-13
Pythagorean Wins	4.9	5.8	8.7	6.9	1.5
Estimated Wins	5.6	6.8	8.4	7.5	3.5
Total DVOA	-19.4%	-7.9%	-2.9%	-3.9%	-45.5%
Rank	28	21	22	19	30
Offense	-11.9%	-12.7%	-6.4%	-22.9%	-31.9%
Rank	27	27	26	30	30
Defense	9.7%	-4.0%	-1.2%	-22.1%	11.8%
Rank	24	12	14	2	25
Special Teams	2.3%	0.9%	2.3%	-3.1%	-1.7%
Rank	12	15	10	26	20

Passing (min. 5 plays)

Player	DPAR	PAR	DVOA	Plys	NtYds	Avg	Cmpl	TD	Int
Jeff Garcia	11.2	-4.3	-2.8%	277	1627	5.9	57.1%	10	8
Luke McCown	-20.0	-26.9	-58.0%	112	474	4.2	49.0%	4	7
Kelly Holcomb	13.7	11.4	21.4%	92	706	7.7	67.8%	7	5

Rushing (min. 3 plays)

Player	DPAR	PAR	DVOA	Plys	Yds	Avg	TD	Fum	Suc
Lee Suggs	-0.5	-6.5	-14.9%	199	755	3.8	2	6	45%
William Green	-1.8	-3.8	-17.4%	163	594	3.6	2	3	36%
Jeff Garcia	7.5	7.0	22.1%	28	175	6.3	2	0	—
James Jackson	2.2	2.1	29.2%	12	81	6.8	0	0	50%
A. Echemandu	-2.9	-3.3	-83.8%	8	25	3.1	0	1	38%
Dennis Northcutt	-1.0	-1.3	-47.9%	8	19	2.4	0	0	—
Terrelle Smith	1.2	1.0	31.8%	4	9	2.3	0	0	100%
Luke McCown	1.1	0.9	47.6%	3	26	8.7	0	0	—

Receiving (min. 5 plays)

Player	DPAR	PAR	DVOA	Plys	Ctch	Yds	Y/C	TD	CPct
WR									
Dennis Northcutt	5.7	4.6	-5.4%	94	55	806	14.7	2	59%
Antonio Bryant	9.9	8.8	7.1%	72	42	546	13.0	4	58%
Andre' Davis	10.2	8.6	34.1%	33	16	416	26.0	2	48%
Quincy Morgan	0.5	0.0	-11.1%	21	9	144	16.0	3	43%
Frisman Jackson	6.4	5.6	37.7%	19	13	168	12.9	0	68%
Andre King	-0.4	-0.3	-24.6%	8	5	49	9.8	0	63%
TE									
Aaron Shea	2.1	0.3	-4.4%	48	26	252	9.7	4	54%
Steve Heiden	6.7	5.5	12.6%	42	28	287	10.3	5	67%
Kellen Winslow	-1.0	-0.6	-28.4%	11	5	50	10.0	0	45%
RB									
Lee Suggs	-0.7	-1.4	-13.5%	35	20	178	8.9	1	57%
William Green	-1.0	-1.8	-19.7%	22	14	84	6.0	0	64%
Terrelle Smith	-1.7	-2.0	-33.7%	12	7	39	5.6	0	58%
James Jackson	-1.5	-1.1	-67.4%	8	6	22	3.7	0	75%

Defensive Players (min. 20 plays)

Player	Age	Plys	Stop	Dfts	AvYds	StpRt	Sack	Int	FR
Defensive Line									
Kenard Lang	30	67	46	24	1.6	69%	7.0	0	0
Alvin McKinley	27	53	33	14	2.8	62%	3.0	0	2
Orpheus Roye	32	44	34	7	3.0	77%	1.0	0	0
Ebenezer Ekuban	29	43	30	19	1.5	70%	8.0	0	2
Michael Myers	29	35	20	7	2.4	57%	1.0	0	1
Linebackers									
Andra Davis	27	77	41	15	3.8	53%	0.5	3	1
Warrick Holdman	30	76	41	8	4.6	54%	0.5	0	0
Chaun Thompson	25	62	26	7	4.9	42%	2.5	0	1
Kevin Bentley	26	52	24	17	5.3	46%	0.0	0	0
Barry Gardner	29	29	16	5	5.9	55%	0.0	1	1
Tyrone Rogers	31	23	10	4	3.5	43%	1.5	0	0

Player	Age	Plys	Stop	Dfts	AvYds	StpRt	Sack	Int	FR
Secondary									
Robert Griffith	35	121	45	22	7.6	37%	1.0	1	0
Anthony Henry	29	90	29	16	7.6	32%	0.0	4	0
Daylon McCutcheon	29	58	23	8	8.4	40%	0.0	2	0
Earl Little	32	54	12	7	8.6	22%	0.0	1	1
Chris Crocker	25	50	18	8	6.8	36%	2.0	1	0
Lewis Sanders	27	31	13	6	6.6	42%	0.0	2	0

Offensive Line

Year	Yards	AdjLineYd	Rank	Power	Rank	10+ Yds	Rank	Stuff	Rank	Sack	AdjSack%	Rank
2002	3.91	3.89	26	61%	25	17%	15	25%	22	35	5.9%	12
2003	4.07	4.11	19	45%	32	15%	17	26%	24	40	7.0%	21
2004	3.75	3.66	30	64%	14	17%	17	30%	31	42	8.2%	27

Year	LEnd	Rank	LTckl	Rank	MdGrd	Rank	RTckl	Rank	REnd	Rank
2002	4.05	16	3.91	23	3.69	29	3.71	27	4.53	9
2003	3.45	27	4.66	9	4.06	21	4.36	11	4.16	12
2004	4.33	16	3.30	30	3.72	28	3.74	25	3.06	26

Injuries and poor play have plagued the offensive line for the past few seasons. The Browns upgraded the guard position when they signed former Patriot Joe Andruzzi, and Cosey Coleman will battle Kevin Garmon for the other guard spot. Both tackles, Ryan Tucker and Ross Verba, are grizzled veterans, but they must avoid injuries just to give the Browns a chance to compete offensively. Cleveland's first-round pick in 2003, Jeff Faine, is coming off a mediocre season, but he's still the best option they have at center.

Defensive Front Seven

Year	Yards	AdjLineYd	Rank	Power	Rank	10+ Yds	Rank	Stuff	Rank	Sack	AdjSack%	Rank
2002	4.41	4.09	15	48%	2	22%	31	26%	10	31	5.1%	27
2003	4.76	4.26	21	63%	11	25%	30	23%	21	33	6.1%	18
2004	4.34	4.62	31	67%	22	12%	7	21%	27	32	6.2%	23

Year	LEnd	Rank	LTckl	Rank	MdGrd	Rank	RTckl	Rank	REnd	Rank
2002	4.10	19	2.95	1	4.59	29	4.00	15	3.06	8
2003	4.69	27	4.28	17	4.41	24	3.81	10	3.49	11
2004	4.19	14	4.32	14	4.85	31	4.15	15	4.59	27

There's more stability in Iraq than there is along Cleveland's defensive line. Without Courtney Brown and Gerard Warren, it will be up to Orpheus Roye and Kenard Lang to adjust to both new coaches and a new defensive scheme. The Browns also took some steps in the right direction when they signed DT Jason Fisk from the Chargers and LB Matt Stewart from the Falcons, two players who have experience in the 3-4 with their previous clubs. Fisk started only one game last season in San Diego, and he might be more effective at the DE position in the 3-4 because he's a bit too small to play nose tackle. Nonetheless, he'll add depth to a largely new defensive line that replaces the one that, for the most part, relocated to Denver this off-season. Stewart, who started 45 games for Atlanta over the last three seasons, is versatile enough to play either the inside or outside linebacker position. He's a solid open-field tackler and led Atlanta linebackers in Stop Rate last year. Neither is known as an impact player, but Crennel proved with the Patriots that putting people in position to make plays is much more critical than having a bunch of first-round picks on the field. How else do you explain Mike Vrabel?

Defensive Secondary

Year	DVOA vs. #1 WR	Rank	DVOA vs. #2 WR	Rank	DVOA vs. Other WR	Rank	DVOA vs. TE	Rank	DVOA vs. RB	Rank
2002	-14.6%	7	6.1%	15	-3.2%	13	-29.9%	5	-2.8%	13
2003	-11.1%	10	21.6%	26	-48.7%	2	-22.0%	4	7.9%	23
2004	6.0%	18	15.5%	23	30.7%	30	-9.0%	11	-24.8%	6

There's a lot of turnover in this unit, with two of Cleveland's three leading tacklers gone to other teams as free agents. Anthony Henry, now in Dallas, will be replaced by Gary Baxter. Baxter immediately brings big-play ability and physicality, not to mention that Baltimore Ravens swagger, to a decidedly mediocre unit. The other corner, Daylon McCutcheon, is a solid but unspectacular player. Last year's opening week safeties, Robert Griffith and Earl Little, are also gone. Chris Crocker replaced Little halfway through last season, but he isn't as good against the run as the Browns would like, especially in the run-heavy AFC North. That explains why the Browns used their second-round pick on Oklahoma's Brodney Pool, perhaps the most athletic safety in this year's draft class. It was the second straight season that the Browns took a safety in round two, and second-year prospect Sean Jones will be back from an injury that cost him all of his rookie season. Pool's college teammate Antonio Perkins, a cornerback chosen in the fourth round, will provide depth.

Special Teams

Year	DVOA	Rank	FG/XP	Rank	Net Punt	Rank	Punt Ret	Rank	Net Kick	Rank	Kick Ret	Rank
2002	2.3%	10	-2.4	20	5.1	12	6.3	9	2.0	14	1.9	13
2003	0.9%	15	1.9	16	5.9	11	-7.6	26	4.3	8	0.4	15
2004	2.3%	12	3.3	14	17.0	4	-2.0	11	-0.9	13	4.0	20

Cleveland's special teams numbers require a bit more breakdown to be fully understood. For example, if the Browns finished fourth in the league in net punting value, why did they replace punter Derrick Frost with veteran Kyle Richardson, formerly of the division rival Bengals? The answer is that Cleveland's 17.0 points of field position on punts can be broken down into −1.9 points from below-average punt distance and 18.9 points of value from limiting opposing punt returns. The Browns weren't exactly downing it before the other team could get to the ball; only 5 of Frost's 85 punts came down within the ten-yard line, and not a single one came down behind the five. Another misleading number is the negative value for kick returns. For the first half of the year, Cleveland tried everyone short of Orpheus Roye as a kick returner and got a whole bunch of below-average returns. Rookie receiver Richard Alston took over the kick return duties for good in Week 9 and over the course of the season his 46 returns combined for 4.7 points worth of field position over league average. The mediocre numbers for kicker Phil Dawson are not misleading, but he had an off year and should bounce back in 2005.

Coaching Staff

Romeo Crennel is the new sheriff in town, and his main deputies will be former Dallas offensive coordinator Maurice Carthon and former Texans defensive line coach Todd Grantham. Carthon began his coaching career in 1994, working as Bill Parcells's offensive assistant in New England. He then followed Parcells to New York where he was the running backs coach. Before reuniting with the Big Tuna in 2003 as Dallas's offensive coordinator, Carthon held the same position in Detroit in 2002. At every stop, he's been very effective at getting the most out of his running backs, and that is something Crennel hopes he can accomplish in Cleveland. Coming from the Texans, Grantham is very familiar with the 3-4 defense that Crennel wants to install. There are also a few familiar names among the position coaches. Terry Robiskie, interim coach after the Browns fired Butch Davis last year, stuck around to be wide receivers coach. Former New England great Ben Coates will oversee the tight ends. And the offensive quality control coach is some fellow named Carl Crennel II, who may have gotten his job through a random résumé submission.

Denver Broncos

Why are the Broncos stuck in this strange holding pattern of above-average-ness?

In a parity-crazed league where teams seem to randomly rise and fall each season, the Denver Broncos have been remarkably consistent for the past five years. The Broncos have not had a losing record since 1999, but they have also not won their division or a playoff game since John Elway's retirement after the 1998 season.

The last two seasons in particular are uncanny duplicates. For two straight years the Broncos have gone 10–6, won a wild card, and been blown out at Indianapolis in the first round of the playoffs. Two years ago Denver outscored regular-season opponents 381–301; last year, it was 381–304.

Although the gradations of improvement were minimal, the 2004 Broncos were probably the best team that Denver has put on the field since Elway's departure. Yet the team was not a serious Super Bowl contender, and there isn't much reason to expect a major step forward (or, for that matter, backward) in 2005.

Most football observers marvel at Mike Shanahan's ability to stick an unknown player into his backfield to produce a new 1,000-yard rusher seemingly at will. But the emergence of a mystery running back isn't the only plot thread that repeats in Denver year after year. For three straight years, the Broncos have ranked better in both yards gained and allowed than in both points gained and allowed. For three straight years, this can be explained primarily by Denver's negative turnover margin, particularly when it comes to interceptions.

Two years ago, the Broncos rid themselves of quarterback Brian Griese, who despite strong numbers had been inconsistent and unable to lead Denver past the first round of the playoffs. His replacement, Jake Plummer, has strong numbers, but is inconsistent and has been unable to lead Denver past the first round of the playoffs.

Another example of *Groundhog Day* in Denver: Year after year, the Broncos have good placekicking and terrible punting that, because of the effects of altitude, looks like great placekicking and reasonable punting.

Denver fans can be forgiven if they think their team has been running in circles for the last five years. At least Denver's circles intersect with the playoffs most of the time, which is better than the circles that New Orleans has been running in.

BRONCOS PROSPECTUS

2004 Record: 10–6

DVOA Estimated Wins: 10.2 (8th)

Pythagorean Wins: 10.1 (8th)

DVOA: 19.6% total (7th), 19.4% weighted (8th)

Adjusted Offense: 23.7 points/game (8.2% DVOA, 10th)

Adjusted Defense: 17.7 points/game (−14.2% DVOA, 5th)

Adjusted Special Teams: −1.0 points/game (−2.8% DVOA, 23rd)

Variance: 26.1% (7th)

2004: I swear I've seen this movie before.

2005: If San Diego regresses, the Broncos probably win the division, which should postpone their exit from the playoffs by a whopping seven days.

2005 Projection

Leinart Land (0–4): 9%

Bad Team (5–6): 15%

Mediocre (7–8): 23%

Playoff Contender (9–10): 24%

Super Bowl Contender (11+): 28%

Projected Average Opponent: 4.7% DVOA (7th in NFL)

The one area of development in Denver in 2004 was pass defense—the Broncos were fourth in pass defense DVOA after ranking just below the top ten for five straight seasons. Improved pass defense was the goal behind the team's biggest move of the 2004 off-season: the trade of running back Clinton Portis to Washington for cornerback Champ Bailey. That's why Broncos fans were so stunned during the playoffs when Peyton Manning picked apart the Denver secondary yet again.

They should not have been. Bailey can only do so much; while he covered Marvin Harrison closely, the Colts repeatedly picked on undrafted rookie cornerback Roc Alexander, who was stuck covering Reggie Wayne. In fact, Denver had trouble all season against teams with multiple talented wideouts whose quarterbacks would throw again and again to anyone Bailey wasn't covering. While Bailey covered Tony Gonzalez, Eddie Kennison twice torched the Broncos for 100 yards. While Bailey kept Muhsin Muhammad to 9 yards, Keary Colbert and Ricky Proehl combined for 150. Atlanta wideouts, possibly the league's worst, had more yards against Denver (170) than against any other team because Bailey was busy covering Alge Crumpler.

Denver's defensive DVOA on passes to wide receivers was 2.5% in 2003, 21st in the league. It was 12.2% in 2004, 23rd in the league, which means that Bailey by himself didn't help the secondary's overall performance against opposition wideouts. But Denver's DVOA on passes to tight ends went from 23rd in the NFL to 2nd. That's partly the effect of Bailey on teams with top tight ends like San Diego or Kansas City, and partly the effect of rookie strong-side linebacker D. J. Williams on teams with average tight ends. When the Broncos had to depend on the rest of the secondary, things didn't turn out so well.

Did the Broncos fill their remaining defensive holes for 2005? Well, they didn't have a Clinton Portis-sized trading chip again, and they didn't have much salary cap room to sign a big-name free agent. In fact, free agency opened new holes in their secondary, with strong safety Kenoy Kennedy going to Detroit and starting cornerback Kelly Herndon to Seattle. The pass rush was hit as well as defensive end Reggie Hayward, the team's sack leader, signed with Jacksonville.

Denver's response to these losses has to stand as one of the odder personnel decisions of recent NFL history. Stuck with a shallow secondary that lost two starters on top, Denver decided not to sign defensive backs but instead imported most of the 2004 Cleveland Browns defensive line. That includes ex-Dallas defensive end Ebenezer Ekuban, who had a good year after signing with Cleveland, but it also includes defensive linemen Gerard Warren and Courtney Brown, who rank, literally, among the biggest draft disappointments in NFL history.

The Broncos have taken the defensive line that ranked 6th in Adjusted Line Yards and 9th in Adjusted Sack Rate and replaced most of its starters with the defensive line that ranked 31st in Adjusted Line Yards and 23rd in Adjusted Sack Rate. Hello? Perhaps the Broncos will be able to finally coach a great performance out of Warren and Brown, but it is hard to see how that will happen when Denver's new defensive line coach, Andre Patterson, was Cleveland's defensive line coach of the last two seasons.

Meanwhile, having ignored the secondary in free agency, the Broncos used their first three picks of the draft on cornerbacks. This could pay dividends down the road, but in the short term, the learning curve for NFL defensive backs is steep. Just ask the Green Bay Packers.

Things aren't perfect on the offensive side of the ball, either. Like many older wide receivers, Rod Smith had a strong year because, at 35, he was helped considerably by the new rules on illegal contact, but at 36 he'll probably return to a steady annual decline next year. Ashley Lelie is a strong number two receiver but doesn't look like he'll ever be a true number one target. And while Tatum Bell will probably be ready to take over as the starting running back, meaning yet another new 1,000-yard rusher in Denver, Plummer will likely continue his still maddening ways, mixing amazing plays involving a lot of scrambling and firing a bullet to an open receiver with foolhardy interceptions that fill the television repair shops of Colorado with shoe-smashed picture tubes.

And so the Broncos are stuck in a strange holding pattern they can escape only with small improvement in a lot of different places. Some of that improvement may come from young players, but repeated first-round playoff exits have resulted in poor draft position, and even for a team with a record of finding late-round gems like Denver, picking outside the top 20 means it's harder to find impact players. For every late-first-round find like Williams, there's a late-first-rounder who doesn't quite live up to expectations, like 2001's top pick, corner Willie Middlebrooks.

Without a way to add major impact players, Denver has two options. One is to shake things up by hoping to turn another team's lemons into lemonade. The other way is to try new schemes and new motivational techniques. If the first option doesn't work in 2005, Denver may need to explore the second option in 2006. If Denver has another early playoff exit, it will be time to consider changing the head coach.

Fans always call for a coaching change when they are frustrated with the direction of their team, and Shanahan has been blamed for some shortcomings that aren't directly his fault, from the failures of specific players to plain old bad luck. But coaches do settle into patterns. As trends in the league change from year to year, innovative strategies become outmoded. Tools that motivated players when they were young cease to motivate those players when they are older.

You can't fault a coach for almost being really successful; Shanahan has had only one losing season since arriving in Denver in 1995. But the Broncos continue to run similar teams onto the field because every year their team reflects the personality of their coach. Shanahan is a gambler, and by that we don't mean that he takes risks. Andy Reid and Bill Belichick take risks, but only after weighing potential gain against the possibility of loss. A gambler takes a shot without fully weighing the risks. Too often in the past few years, Shanahan and the Broncos have made critical mistakes at critical times because they chose a bad time to take a gamble. Jake Plummer has this problem; so do defensive players like Trevor Pryce and the (now-departed) Kenoy Kennedy. If the Broncos want a team that does something different, they need a coach with a different personality.

It also needs to be acknowledged that the "plug in running back, get 1,000 yards" mentality has started to become a problem, almost as if Shanahan is determined to prove that he can turn anyone into a valuable running back. Instead of finding someone cheap and letting him grow into the position, Shanahan is busy cluttering the roster with mediocre players like Quentin Griffin, blowing cap space on proven failures like Ron Dayne, and spending a third-round pick on Maurice Clarett so that he can be fourth on the depth chart.

There are plenty of examples, in all sports, of coaches who have early success but then settle into stagnation. When the players tune out someone known as a players' coach, you bring in a taskmaster; when they tune out the taskmaster, you bring in the players' coach. The same jolt can occur when you replace an offensive-minded coach with a defensive-minded one, and vice versa.

The organizational adjustment related to a coaching change can itself be an important coaching tool. Tony Dungy, for example, built the defense in Tampa Bay, but couldn't seem to win in the playoffs. Jon Gruden came in, gave a bit of a shock to the system, and the Buccaneers won the Super Bowl. Dungy, meanwhile, went on to Indianapolis, where he was as different from his predecessor Jim Mora as Gruden was from him, and he has turned the Colts into perennial contenders.

There is always a possibility that Denver can all at once improve in all the different places where they need just a little improvement. After all, that's what happened last year in Pittsburgh, home of the league's longest-tenured head coach. Denver also figured out a way to possibly snag a franchise-level player without losing ballgames, dealing this year's first round pick to the Redskins for a package that included Washington's top pick in 2006. Given the way things have been going in Washington, the Broncos may want to start printing up those "Leinart 11" jerseys immediately.

But if this team ends another wild card year with an early playoff exit, it is time to take the risk that a new coach with new ways can spark the Broncos to a 12–4 season. It is the best thing for the Broncos and the best thing for Shanahan. Since Shanahan is an offensive guru, the best switch might be to find a defensive innovator hungry for his first head coaching position, such as Minnesota's Ted Cottrell, Buffalo's Jerry Gray, or New England's Eric Mangini.

Under new leadership, the Broncos might succeed immediately or, more likely, improve after two or three losing years and some rebuilding with high draft picks (starting with the one they will get from Washington). The alternative is what you'll probably see in 2005: another year of 9–10 wins and a first- or second-round playoff exit. Lather, rinse, repeat.

Aaron Schatz

Research: The Effect of Weather and Altitude on Special Teams

According to the NFL, the top ten kickers in 2004 based on kickoff distance, with a minimum of 40 kickoffs are shown in table 1.

Let's see, that would be four kickers that play their home games indoors, two from Florida, and one each from Arizona, California, and Colorado. Only one kicker in the top ten plays outdoors in a northern city roughly near sea level. And if this list had a minimum of 30 kickoffs, it would include three more dome kickers: Mitch Berger of New Orleans and both Aaron Elling and Jose Cortez of Minnesota.

In 2003, this same list had five dome kickers, plus Mare and Knorr, and three kickers from cold weather cities: Akers, Wade Richey of Baltimore, and Jeff Reed of Pittsburgh. Do the best kickers in the NFL really all play indoors or at altitude?

No, of course not. Everybody knows that it is easier to kick indoors, and everyone knows that the ball travels farther in the thin air of Denver. But nobody ever bothers to quantify this and apply it to rating kickers and punters. Because they missed this step in player evaluation, the Broncos have suffered through the worst punting in the NFL year after year, from both Tom Rouen and Micah Knorr, until they waived Knorr and tried Jason Baker in the middle of last season.

When we first developed special teams ratings at FootballOutsiders.com in the middle of the 2003 season, we compared everything to an average baseline from the 2002 season. And we noticed that early in the year, nearly every team came out as above average on special teams. Then, as the season went on, the average team gradually became average, but Denver and the dome teams still dominated.

TABLE 1. TOP 10 KICKERS IN 2004, (MINIMUM 40 KICKOFFS)

Rank	Kicker	Team
1	Neil Rackers	ARI
2	Josh Scobee	JAC
3	David Akers	PHI
4	Olindo Mare	MIA
5	Micah Knorr	DEN
6	Jason Hanson	DET
7	Sebastian Janikowski	OAK
8	Jay Feely	ATL
9	Kris Brown	HOU
10	Jeff Wilkins	STL

What we were seeing was the effect of weather and altitude on the kicking game.

In order to correct for this issue, we separated every stadium in the NFL into four categories. Domed stadiums, including the retractable roof in Houston, are one category. The second category includes outdoor fields from Nashville south, plus the Bay Area, which we call "warm" stadiums. (No, 40 degrees in December isn't warm, but it isn't Buffalo either.) The rest of the stadiums are grouped together as "cold" stadiums, with one mile-high exception: Denver.

This obviously is not the most precise method for quantifying the effects of weather on the kicking game. It would be more exact to measure the wind speed, temperature, and specific precipitation for each game during the past few seasons. But until we've collected that data, this method provides a reasonable estimate of weather effects.

With only 24 regular season games in Denver during that period, sample size for our fourth category is small. Unfortunately, going back before 2002 would create problems because of a change in the enforcement of the "K-ball" rule. The league began using special new balls specifically for kicks and punts in 1999, part of an attempt to keep home teams from doctoring the balls to give an advantage to their kickers, but the enforcement of the rule was haphazard for the first three seasons. As a result, kicking distances generally dropped in 2002.

(Eventually, we hope to also measure the effect of altitude and weather on passing and rushing, but we have not done such a study as of yet.)

Figure 1 shows the average distance of NFL kickoffs over the past three years, by week and separated into our four categories. (For purposes of clarity, lines represent general trend rather than zigzagging actual numbers.) At the beginning of the season, the average kickoff distance indoors and outdoors is roughly the same. But as the season progresses, kickoff distance indoors stays flat, while outdoor kickoffs gradually become shorter. The effect is stronger in cold weather cities than in warm weather cities.

But Denver is its own animal. At the start of the season, the average kickoff in Denver goes roughly four yards farther than the average kickoff in the other 31 stadiums around the NFL. As the weather gets colder, Denver kickoffs gradually decline the same way they do in other cities, but Denver kickers still have a tremendous advantage over those in other northern cities.

The effects are the same whether the kickers involved are wearing Bronco uniforms or not. Punter Micah Knorr took over Bronco kickoffs in the middle of 2002; he was released in the middle of 2004. In the two years between, his average kickoff at home went 66.2 yards, and his average kickoff when Denver played outdoors on the road went just 62.0 yards. (The difference is even larger for Jason Elam, who kicked off for the first half of 2002, and Jason Baker, who kicked off for the second half of 2004.) Opposing kickers over the past three seasons have averaged 66.2 yards per kickoff in Denver, and 60.7 yards per kickoff when facing Denver at home (not counting domes).

Punts show the same trend as kickoffs (figure 2). While kickoffs are nearly always taking place at the 30-yard line, punts take place all over the field, which could result in biased numbers out of Denver because the Broncos have been a strong offense for three years. Therefore, instead of

FIGURE 1. AVERAGE KICKOFF DISTANCE TREND BY WEEK, 2002–2004

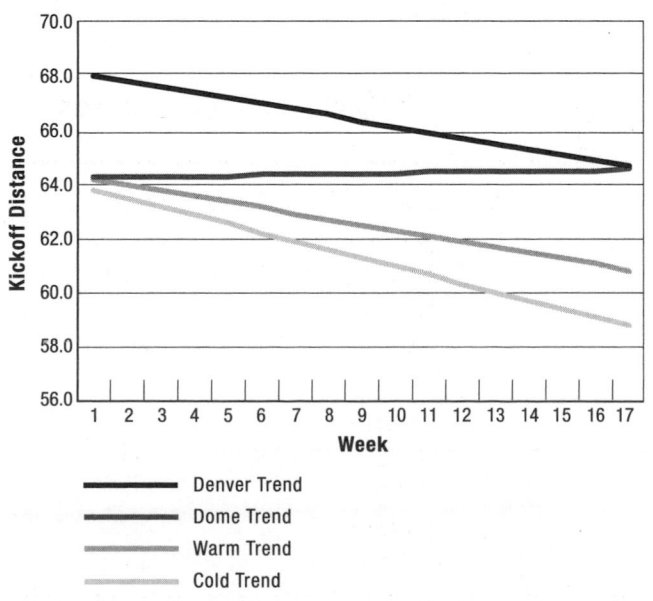

FIGURE 2. AVERAGE PUNT VALUE TREND BY WEEK, 2002–2004

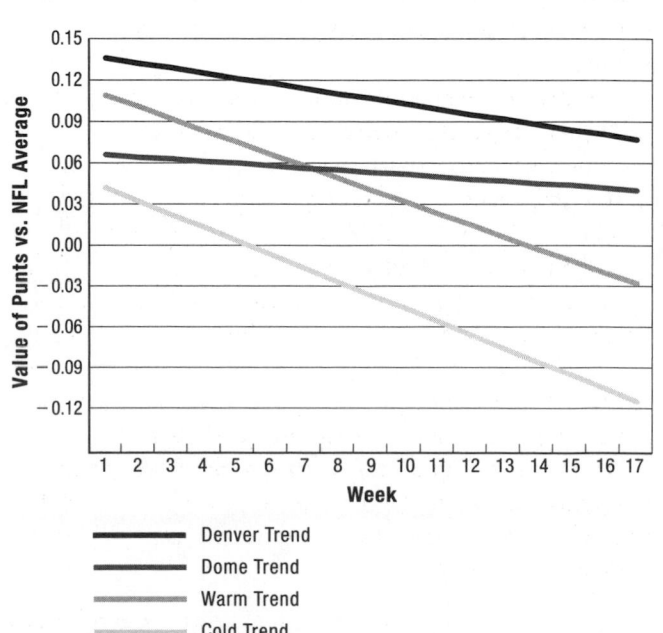

using gross punt distance, we're using here our computation of the value of field position that is gained by each punt based on the average punt from that line of scrimmage. (Explained in the statistical introduction to the book.)

The effects of altitude have hidden just how bad the Denver punters—primarily Micah Knorr—have been. The average NFL punt over the last three seasons has traveled 41.3 yards. The average Bronco punt has traveled 41.0 yards. It really doesn't seem like much of a problem.

Except that half those punts have come in the thin air of altitude. In Denver, the average Bronco punt travels 42.8 yards—and the average punt by Denver's opponents goes two yards farther. When the Broncos are on the road, their average punt goes just 39.4 yards—and the average punt by Denver's opponents goes 2.3 yards farther.

The final element of special teams is the one people pay the most attention to: field goal kicking. Unfortunately, the effects of weather on field goal kicking don't easily translate to a chart showing value by the week. Weather and altitude do not affect field goals of all distances in the same way. Longer field goals get harder in the season's final months in all outdoor stadiums, but short field goals become more difficult in cold weather only. Domed stadi-ums have a larger impact on medium-range field goals than the altitude of Denver, but Denver has a stronger impact on both short-range (under 25 yards) and long-range (47 yards and longer) field goals.

But the effect of the Denver altitude is pretty obvious when looking at Jason Elam's numbers at home and on the road. In Week 12, of course, Elam famously had a 43-yard game-winning field goal attempt in the final minute blocked by the Oakland Raiders. But his other 15 field goal attempts at home last year went through the uprights, and over the past three years, he is 41-for-47 including 6-for-6 on field goals of 50 yards or more. On the road, however, he is 41-for-54 over the past three years, and has hit just 3 of 7 attempts from 50 yards or more.

Next year, Denver will probably have a new punter and a new kickoff specialist, either ex-Panther Todd Sauer-brun or seventh-round rookie Paul Ernster. Whoever gets the job, it will be almost impossible for them to put up superficial numbers below the league average. Remember that in Denver, when it comes to kicking, you aren't aver-age unless you look good, and you aren't good unless you look like the best in the league.

Aaron Schatz

Broncos 2004 Stats by Week

Wk	vs.	W-L	PF	PA	YDF	YDA	TO	DVOA Total	Off	Def	ST
1	KC	W	34	24	413	318	-2	14.1%	-18.8%	-15.1%	17.8%
2	@JAC	L	6	7	356	176	-1	14.5%	4.6%	-22.7%	-12.9%
3	SD	W	23	13	328	214	0	71.6%	24.5%	-45.6%	1.5%
4	@TB	W	16	13	249	269	+1	6.1%	6.1%	8.8%	8.8%
5	CAR	W	20	17	434	227	-2	16.8%	26.9%	4.6%	-5.5%
6	@OAK	W	31	3	444	145	+1	88.3%	24.7%	-57.5%	6.1%
7	@CIN	L	10	23	318	321	-2	-45.5%	-22.0%	7.2%	-16.3%
8	ATL	L	28	41	567	467	-2	-34.5%	14.8%	46.1%	-3.2%
9	HOU	W	31	13	364	331	0	11.4%	33.2%	15.2%	-6.6%
10	BYE										
11	@NO	W	34	13	389	411	+4	63.3%	39.7%	-7.0%	16.6%
12	OAK	L	24	25	367	395	0	-45.5%	-37.1%	-6.0%	-14.4%
13	@SD	L	17	20	337	208	-2	5.7%	-47.5%	-66.5%	-13.2%
14	MIA	W	20	17	415	214	-2	-9.2%	-6.0%	-2.7%	-6.0%
15	@KC	L	17	45	402	410	-3	-40.1%	-10.7%	17.9%	-11.4%
16	@TEN	W	37	16	496	153	0	97.4%	45.1%	-62.3%	-10.0%
17	IND	W	33	14	453	200	+1	118.3%	38.9%	-74.9%	4.5%
18	@IND	L	24	49	338	629	0	-21.7%	14.1%	38.5%	2.6%

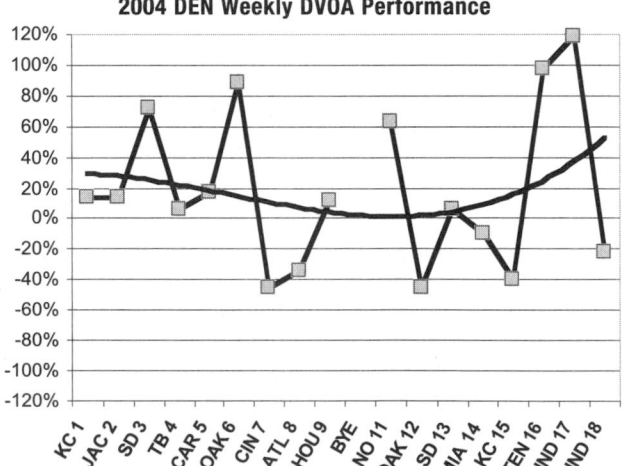

2004 DEN Weekly DVOA Performance

Trends and Splits

	Offense	Rank	Defense	Rank
Total DVOA	8.2%	10	-14.2%	5
Unadjusted VOA	13.4%	9	-6.8%	7
Weighted Trend	8.3%	11	-15.4%	4
Variance	8.1%	18	12.5%	6
Passing	17.1%	10	-18.9%	4
Rushing	0.3%	16	-8.8%	7
First Down	6.9%	10	-8.1%	7
Second Down	14.7%	10	-10.6%	5
Third Down	0.3%	14	-32.0%	2
Red Zone	-10.2%	21	-12.5%	11
Late and Close	-7.5%	18	-10.9%	12

Five-Year Performance

	2004	2003	2002	2001	2000
W-L	10-6	10-6	9-7	8-8	11-5
Pythagorean Wins	10.1	10.2	9.2	8.0	10.5
Estimated Wins	10.2	9.4	9.5	8.2	10.8
Total DVOA	19.6%	11.3%	11.7%	2.6%	20.0%
Rank	7	12	12	14	7
Offense	8.2%	2.8%	12.2%	-7.6%	14.6%
Rank	10	12	6	18	6
Defense	-14.2%	-10.1%	-0.9%	-8.5%	-7.6%
Rank	5	8	15	13	13
Special Teams	-2.8%	-1.6%	-1.3%	1.7%	-2.2%
Rank	23	24	19	9	22

Passing (min. 5 plays)

Player	DPAR	PAR	DVOA	Plys	NtYds	Avg	Cmpl	TD	Int
Jake Plummer	56.4	72.5	11.5%	537	3983	7.4	58.2%	27	21

Rushing (min. 3 plays)

Player	DPAR	PAR	DVOA	Plys	Yds	Avg	TD	Fum	Suc
Reuben Droughns	17.0	21.2	-0.3%	275	1240	4.5	6	5	51%
Quentin Griffin	-6.9	-6.0	-33.0%	85	311	3.7	2	2	33%
Tatum Bell	15.5	17.5	33.9%	75	396	5.3	3	0	57%
Jake Plummer	-2.6	-1.7	-27.4%	44	223	5.1	1	2	—
Garrison Hearst	2.9	3.8	16.9%	20	81	4.1	1	0	45%
Rod Smith	0.7	0.8	-13.1%	5	33	6.6	0	0	—
Darius Watts	1.5	1.6	24.5%	5	33	6.6	0	0	—
Cecil Sapp	2.3	2.3	117.8%	4	32	8.0	0	0	100%
Ashley Lelie	-0.2	-0.2	-35.3%	3	5	1.7	0	0	—

Receiving (min. 5 plays)

Player	DPAR	PAR	DVOA	Plys	Ctch	Yds	Y/C	TD	CPct
WR									
Rod Smith	20.9	23.8	7.5%	136	79	1144	14.5	7	58%
Ashley Lelie	25.4	26.5	22.7%	101	54	1084	20.1	7	53%
Darius Watts	3.4	4.3	-5.3%	53	31	386	12.4	1	50%
Nate Jackson	1.1	1.0	1.5%	11	8	73	9.1	0	73%
Triandos Luke	-0.7	-0.2	-29.5%	8	6	52	8.7	0	75%
TE									
Jeb Putzier	16.8	19.6	35.9%	54	36	572	15.9	2	67%
Dwayne Carswell	-1.3	0.0	-19.3%	36	22	198	9.0	1	61%
Patrick Hape	-1.3	-0.7	-25.1%	17	8	35	4.4	4	47%
RB									
Reuben Droughns	4.9	5.2	10.6%	44	32	241	7.5	2	73%
Quentin Griffin	-1.9	-2.6	-32.8%	14	10	68	6.8	1	71%
Kyle Johnson	5.6	5.1	62.1%	13	9	126	14.0	2	69%
Tatum Bell	-2.5	-2.7	-82.7%	7	5	80	16.0	0	71%

Defensive Players (min. 20 plays)

Player	Age	Plys	Stop	Dfts	AvYds	StpRt	Sack	Int	FR
Defensive Line									
Reggie Hayward	26	46	35	26	0.1	76%	10.5	1	1
Marco Coleman	36	28	18	4	2.5	64%	2.5	0	1
Monsanto Pope	27	26	21	5	1.6	81%	1.0	0	0
Mario Fatafehi	26	25	21	10	-0.6	84%	2.5	0	1
Linebackers									
D. J. Williams	23	111	72	19	3.3	65%	2.0	1	0
Al Wilson	28	109	65	28	4.3	60%	2.5	2	0
Donnie Spragan	29	71	37	14	4.1	52%	1.0	0	1

Player	Age	Plys	Stop	Dfts	AvYds	StpRt	Sack	Int	FR
Secondary									
Kelly Herndon	29	94	57	27	4.7	61%	1.0	2	1
Champ Bailey	27	94	45	24	8.5	48%	0.0	3	0
Kenoy Kennedy	28	90	27	12	8.9	30%	2.0	1	1
John Lynch	34	73	28	16	6.4	38%	2.0	1	0
Willie Middlebrooks	26	27	16	8	7.4	59%	1.0	0	1
Lenny Walls	26	25	12	8	8.0	48%	0.0	0	0

Offensive Line

Year	Yards	AdjLineYd	Rank	Power	Rank	10+ Yds	Rank	Stuff	Rank	Sack	AdjSack%	Rank
2002	5.16	5.05	1	65%	19	18%	10	15%	1	45	7.9%	26
2003	4.76	4.35	10	65%	17	25%	5	21%	4	25	5.4%	11
2004	4.49	4.44	8	56%	27	17%	15	21%	5	17	3.8%	3

Year	LEnd	Rank	LTckl	Rank	MdGrd	Rank	RTckl	Rank	REnd	Rank
2002	5.86	1	5.32	1	4.83	1	4.88	4	5.33	2
2003	4.37	12	4.01	21	4.32	13	4.32	15	5.29	1
2004	5.44	1	3.89	26	4.53	10	4.25	14	4.37	9

When Mike Shanahan took over the Broncos in 1995, the most important addition to his staff was offensive line coach Alex Gibbs. Ever since, fans have had a vague understanding that there was something controversial about the blocking methods taught by Gibbs and later by his protégé Rick Dennison. That vague understanding became crystal clear on a Monday night last year, when Broncos lineman George Foster delivered a block directly into the side of Bengals defensive lineman Tony Williams's lower leg. That play (commonly called a cut block) was the last of Williams's season, and many people called it a cheap shot, but the NFL ruled the play legal and didn't discipline Foster. Oddly, up until that moment, Foster was the least likely of the Broncos' offensive linemen to deliver cut blocks. As by far the biggest member of the Broncos' line, he tended to use the old lineman's standby of overpowering his opponents, rather than trying to take them down by hitting them low.

Shanahan doesn't deny that Foster and, even more, his other offensive linemen—Matt Lepsis, Tom Nalen, Dan Neil, and Ben Hamilton—rely on cut blocks. But Shanahan says his team doesn't do it any more than several other teams. To prove his case, Shanahan invited the media into a film session and showed what he called cut blocks delivered by offensive linemen on other teams. But none of the plays Shanahan showed featured a lineman blindsiding an opponent away from the play, as Foster did to Williams. Moreover, Denver's success isn't just about dancing on the line between legal and illegal blocks. It is also about dancing on the line between legal and illegal holding. Denver was called for 26 offensive holding penalties, the most in the NFL, but for every time they were called for holding, there were countless other times when they used the same techniques with impunity.

Defensive Front Seven

Year	Yards	AdjLineYd	Rank	Power	Rank	10+ Yds	Rank	Stuff	Rank	Sack	AdjSack%	Rank
2002	3.97	3.95	10	74%	26	19%	21	25%	15	41	7.8%	9
2003	4.37	4.01	14	60%	5	22%	26	25%	14	35	6.8%	12
2004	3.83	3.90	6	68%	24	12%	8	27%	7	38	7.6%	9

Year	LEnd	Rank	LTckl	Rank	MdGrd	Rank	RTckl	Rank	REnd	Rank
2002	3.81	11	3.69	6	4.30	22	3.11	2	3.72	12
2003	4.02	13	4.67	22	4.12	16	3.45	5	3.34	8
2004	3.91	10	3.96	6	4.18	15	3.66	5	2.79	5

We almost ran Cleveland's numbers here instead of Denver's. Of all the strange moves this off-season, none is stranger than the wholesale importation of the Cleveland defensive line (31st in Adjusted Line Yards, 23rd in Adjusted Sack Rate) to replace the Denver defensive line (6th in Adjusted Line Yards, 9th in Adjusted Sack Rate). As we point out in the main chapter, it isn't like new Denver defensive line coach Andre Patterson is a far better coach than former Cleveland defensive line coach Andre Patterson. Denver, planning a switch to the 3-4 defense, thinks that Courtney Brown has the skills to be a two-gap, run stopping end, but Cleveland—also planning a switch to the 3-4 defense, with Super Bowl-winning coordinator Romeo Crennel now running the show—doesn't really agree. You also have to wonder about switching to the 3-4 when the Broncos have just added four defensive linemen to a roster that still has three of last year's four starters (end Marco Coleman, tackles Mario Fatafehi and Monsanto Pope) and wasn't able to trade 1998–2003 starter Trevor Pryce. The one lineman not here anymore is the best one, Reggie Hayward, who takes his 10.5 sacks to Jacksonville.

At least they didn't mess around with the linebackers. As you'll see in the numbers below, Denver's pass defense was driven not by the cornerbacks but by suffocating pass coverage from the linebackers that made the Broncos the second-best defense in the league on passes to tight ends and running backs. D. J. Williams would have easily stood out as the best rookie linebacker in any season that didn't feature a guy named "Vilma," and while we throw around the word "underrated" a little too often, Al Wilson certainly does qualify. How many times did you see a feature on this two-time

Pro Bowler during any national pregame show? How many times has Al Wilson been "miked up" by ESPN? How many times has Al Wilson showed up in an NFL Network commercial? The answer is zero, zero, and zero.

Defensive Secondary

Year	DVOA vs. #1 WR	Rank	DVOA vs. #2 WR	Rank	DVOA vs. Other WR	Rank	DVOA vs. TE	Rank	DVOA vs. RB	Rank
2002	4.8%	22	34.7%	28	-30.1%	6	16.4%	24	0.4%	14
2003	23.7%	25	-9.1%	15	-13.4%	14	10.0%	23	-16.0%	6
2004	7.4%	19	14.4%	22	16.4%	23	-43.6%	2	-48.8%	2

Our rating of Denver as the season's fourth-best passing defense conflicts with public perception. Some of that comes from our opponent adjustments, since the AFC West is a division of strong offenses. But the issue in Denver is not whether the Broncos can stop the pass, but which pass. The strength of Denver's pass defense came from the linebackers and, to a lesser extent, the safeties, John Lynch and the now-departed Kenoy Kennedy. Champ Bailey made a difference, but mostly just in direction; wherever Bailey was, the quarterback would usually just throw somewhere else. Bailey is partially responsible for Denver having the second-best defense against tight ends, because he would usually cover the players of Gonzalez/Gates caliber, but that just freed up the wide receivers. Eddie Kennison, for example, had two 101-yard days against the Broncos while Gonzalez had 17 and 44 yards. While Bailey was keeping Muhsin Muhammad to a season-low 9 yards, Keary Colbert was ringing up 115 yards. And of course, there was the playoff game, where Bailey covered Marvin Harrison while Reggie Wayne abused rookie corner Roc Alexander for 221 yards and two touchdowns.

The depth problems got worse in the off-season when Herndon and Kennedy both signed elsewhere, so the Broncos devoted their first *three* picks to cornerbacks. Darrent Williams of Oklahoma State is fast but undersized. Karl Paymah of Washington State is strong in press coverage but has trouble with zone. Domonique Foxworth of Maryland has natural talent but his technique needs work. At least one of these players should eventually overcome his weaknesses. In the meantime, while the rookies learn, Lenny Walls will be healthy again and start opposite Bailey, while backups Nick Ferguson and Chris Young will compete to replace Kennedy at safety.

Special Teams

Year	DVOA	Rank	FG/XP	Rank	Net Punt	Rank	Punt Ret	Rank	Net Kick	Rank	Kick Ret	Rank
2002	-1.4%	19	-5.9	24	-14.3	28	1.9	14	4.8	9	5.7	10
2003	-1.6%	24	6.1	12	-19.5	32	6.8	7	3.9	9	-6.3	25
2004	-2.8%	23	6.3	10	-5.2	30	-10.0	25	-5.4	26	-1.1	16

As we note in the main part of this chapter, Denver has not had good special teams for years, in part because they accept poor performance that looks average, thanks to altitude-enhanced numbers. Last year, the Broncos seemed to finally understand they had a problem, and so with four weeks left in the season they waived punter/kickoff specialist Micah Knorr and hired punter/kickoff specialist Jason Baker. The problem is that while Knorr was above average on kickoffs but horrible on punts, Baker was above average on punts but horrible on kickoffs. The Broncos traded for disgruntled Carolina punter Todd Sauerbrun, who will be a huge improvement on the field and a huge distraction off the field, but they also spent a seventh-round pick on kicker/punter Paul Ernster from Northern Arizona, who led NCAA Division I-AA with a 47.8-yard punting average in 2004. His kickoffs were said to lack hang time, but in Denver nothing lacks hang time, so he may end up as a kickoff specialist while Jason Elam continues to be a consistent field goal kicker. All the mediocre return men of last year should be forgotten with the arrival of second-round cornerback Darrent Williams, who had three punt returns for touchdowns over the past two college seasons. Triandos Luke is next in line if Williams can't handle both kick and punt returns.

Coaching Staff

Shanahan has kept intact much of the same offensive staff that he had when he first became the head coach. Offensive line coach Rick Dennison, offensive coordinator Gary Kubiak, tight ends coach Brian Pariani, and running backs coach Bobby Turner all joined the staff when Shanahan did, in 1995. Turner spent time on the staff at Ohio State before he joined Denver and has kept in close contact with the Buckeyes. He's known Maurice Clarett for years and lobbied for the Broncos to draft him. Larry Coyer enters his sixth season coaching in Denver and his third as defensive coordinator. Not only has he improved the defense since his arrival, he also coaches this team's best unit, the linebackers.

Houston Texans

Some NFL teams are like oatmeal—each spoonful is essentially the same. Sure, you may get more raisins in one spoonful and extra brown sugar in the next, but it's only a matter of degrees. The 2004 Indianapolis Colts resembled oatmeal: The offense was always good, some days more than others, and the defense, though occasionally opportunistic, was always shaky.

The 2004 Houston Texans were like gumbo. The taste and texture differed wildly from spoonful to spoonful—sometimes fans would get a shrimp or oyster, sometimes just a spoonful of overcooked okra. Sometimes the Texans delivered a satisfying defensive performance, sometimes a spicy offensive explosion—but, after a while, all the flavors merged into mush.

Although the Texans ranked 15th in DVOA and rated as the 7th most-consistent team from week to week, they rarely played like an average team. They typically paired a good defensive game with a poor offensive game, or a lame first half with a spirited second-half comeback, resulting in an average day overall. You expect a mediocre team to have its ups and downs—that's what makes it mediocre. What's interesting about the Texans is that when one part was up, another part was down, and the aggregate looks average even if nobody played average football.

Going into 2004, the biggest issue for the Texans was when and if they would win back-to-back games; QB David Carr even vowed during the off-season not to cut his hair until the team won two straight. They were supposed to turn the corner in 2004, establishing themselves as a legitimate team with the potential week in and week out to beat any opponent.

To the delight of everyone in Houston, not least the Carr family barber, the Texans achieved their preseason goal with victories against Kansas City and Oakland in Weeks 3 and 4. Cheers and shears followed. They enjoyed two in a row so much that after losing a close game to the Vikings, the Texans beat Tennessee and Jacksonville to rise to 4–3 at midseason. And that's as good as it got; Houston went 3–6 the rest of the way to finish 7–9.

The Texans sparkled intermittently throughout the 2004 season. WR Andre Johnson caught two highlight-reel touchdown passes against the Vikings. David Carr notched the second and third 300-yard passing days of his career, combining for five touchdowns against only one interception in those two games. In two games against Jacksonville,

TEXANS PROSPECTUS

2004 Record: 7–9

DVOA Estimated Wins: 8.0 (17th)

Pythagorean Wins: 7.1 (19th)

DVOA: −1.2% total (15th), −1.6% weighted (17th)

Adjusted Offense: 21.5 points/game (0.2% DVOA, 14th)

Adjusted Defense: 20.9 points/game (−2.4% DVOA, 14th)

Adjusted Special Teams: −1.3 points/game (−3.7% DVOA, 27th)

Variance: 13.6% (26th)

2004: Another year of biding time on the path from expansion to the playoffs.

2005: Look, Dad, I'm a real boy!

2005 Projection

Leinart Land (0–4): 9%

Bad Team (5–6): 15%

Mediocre (7–8): 22%

Playoff Contender (9–10): 24%

Super Bowl Contender (11+): 30%

Projected Average Opponent: −0.2% DVOA (16th in NFL)

the defense allowed only six points while forcing four turnovers. Rookie CB Dunta Robinson had a two-interception game against the Raiders and a two-sack game against the Colts. But RB Domanick Davis lost four fumbles in the first two games of the season, David Carr had an under-40 passer rating in the Jets game, and against Indianapolis, the defense allowed Peyton Manning to throw five touchdown passes almost in spite of himself—it wasn't Manning who stopped the Texans from tackling Dallas Clark while he ran 50 yards for a late touchdown—and the offense gave up two more Colts touchdowns. The team watched a winnable game with Detroit get away on a 99-yard Eddie Drummond kick-return touchdown.

The Texans could be great finishers at times. They scored 21 points in the fourth quarter in Week 5 against Minnesota, but still lost in overtime thanks to a horrid first 18 minutes. In Week 14 the Texans failed to show up for the Colts' 14-point first quarter, but won the last three, 14–9. At other times, they were great starters. They gave up 23 second half points in Week 13 to the Jets after leading 7–6 at the half. Against the Packers in Week 11, the Texans led 13–3 after three quarters, but gave up 13 fourth quarter points and lost by a field goal on the last play of the game.

The Texans are no longer an expansion team. Their fans now expect the team to be a legitimate contender for the AFC playoffs in 2005, and general manager Charley Casserly and head coach Dom Capers understand their team's adolescence and behaved accordingly.

The 2002, 2003, and even 2004 Texans lived in a world unencumbered by salary cap issues. Players could survive even if their play didn't match their price tag. Free agents were easily affordable.

Things changed in the spring of 2005. The team decided the defense was getting old and slow and released 29-year-old inside linebacker Jay Foreman, then shopped around 30-year-old inside linebacker Jamie Sharper before releasing him, too. Then they released 32-year-old CB Aaron Glenn after trading second- and third-round draft picks to the Raiders for cornerback Philip Buchanon.

Those three players, along with outside linebacker Kailoo Wong, nose tackle Seth Payne, safety-nee-cornerback Marcus Coleman, and defensive end Gary Walker (aged 29, 30, 31, and 32, respectively) formed the veteran core of both the defense and the entire team. Despite being cut, these are still good players, as evidenced by Glenn and Sharper getting snapped up soon after hitting the free market (by the Cowboys and Seahawks, respectively). But the Texans—acting just like a mature NFL team—felt that these players, with their cap numbers growing and their productivity shrinking, had outlived their usefulness in Houston.

The Texans have traded the veteran leadership of Glenn and Sharper for the speed and athleticism of Buchanon and ex-Dolphin linebacker Morlon Greenwood. But this defense's weakest link hasn't been the pass coverage. It's been the pass rush, 30th in Adjusted Sack Rate in 2003 and dead last in 2004. Wong led the team with 5.5 sacks because rookie Jason Babin, drafted to be the sack artist of the future, failed to play up to expectations. (Babin was already behind the eight ball—by which I don't mean Gary Walker's big bald head—because he was making the difficult transition from a defensive end in Division I-AA to an outside linebacker at the NFL level.) Capers and the coaching staff have a lot of faith in his ability to develop, which they've shown by doing nothing to bolster the position this off-season.

Prior to the 2004 season, the Texans featured an aging defense with a new cornerback (rookie Dunta Robinson), a new linebacker (Babin), and a new lineman (Robaire Smith, late of the Titans). The biggest concern was the pass rush, which had been terrible in 2003.

Flash-forward to 2005: The Texans sport a young defense with a new cornerback (Buchanon), two new linebackers (Greenwood and a player to be named later), and a new lineman (rookie first-rounder Travis Johnson from Florida State). Still, the biggest concern is for the pass rush. The more things change, the more they stay the same.

The story is remarkably similar on the other side of the ball. In their first season, the Texans had a promising young quarterback and a porous offensive line. In 2003, they had promising young players at all the skill positions, but the line remained porous. To try to solve this problem, the Texans signed Todd Wade from the Dolphins to play right tackle and promoted second-year man Seth Wand to starting left tackle. Then they slid Chester Pitts into the guard position he was originally drafted to play.

The result was better run blocking, but the pass blocking didn't improve. Wade played well enough (against defensive ends not named Robert Mathis), but Wand is not yet a good NFL left tackle; though he has all the physical tools, he is still developing his skills after playing at Division III Northwest Missouri State. As with Babin, the coaches expect Wand to learn on the job—they didn't sign or draft anyone to compete for his starting spot.

The Texans expect their young players to improve with experience, and usually, that's what young players do. Last season's offense was young and promising; this year's offense should be just a little older but a lot better. Last year's defense was a little old, with the exception of a couple of rookie first-rounders in major roles. This year's defense will be younger, but Robinson and Babin are more experienced—and likely better.

The Texans didn't boast any standout unit last year, and it doesn't look like they will in 2005, either. So it's hard to imagine the Texans winning the AFC South without a major collapse from Indianapolis. But all it takes is a little improvement on both sides of the ball to make the Texans an above-average team. Thanks to a schedule that includes the feeble NFC West and rebuilding teams like Tennessee and Cleveland, a little improvement may be just enough to give the Texans their first trip to the postseason.

Tim Gerheim

Texans 2004 Stats by Week

Wk	vs.	W-L	PF	PA	YDF	YDA	TO	DVOA Total	Off	Def	ST
1	SD	L	20	27	336	324	-4	4.4%	-4.3%	1.3%	10.0%
2	@DET	L	16	28	386	266	-2	-50.5%	-10.8%	19.9%	-19.9%
3	@KC	W	24	21	286	364	0	-31.7%	-33.5%	-0.7%	1.0%
4	OAK	W	30	17	386	375	+4	26.9%	13.0%	-14.8%	-0.9%
5	MIN	L	28	34	410	510	0	22.9%	32.1%	20.1%	10.9%
6	@TEN	W	20	10	345	305	+2	42.8%	-6.0%	-45.0%	3.8%
7	BYE										
8	JAC	W	20	6	369	287	0	32.1%	21.8%	-11.6%	-1.3%
9	@DEN	L	13	31	331	364	0	5.1%	28.3%	30.0%	6.8%
10	@IND	L	14	49	302	398	-2	-36.3%	-49.7%	-24.1%	-10.7%
11	GB	L	13	16	251	473	+2	-31.3%	-23.0%	12.9%	4.7%
12	TEN	W	31	21	328	355	+2	9.8%	29.8%	21.9%	1.9%
13	@NYJ	L	7	29	230	360	-1	-60.4%	-26.8%	21.0%	-12.7%
14	IND	L	14	23	273	382	-2	27.4%	11.9%	-10.5%	5.0%
15	@CHI	W	24	5	314	203	+4	32.9%	15.3%	-40.2%	-22.6%
16	@JAC	W	21	0	333	126	+1	67.4%	5.6%	-80.2%	-18.4%
17	CLE	L	14	22	238	364	+1	-41.6%	5.5%	30.3%	-16.8%

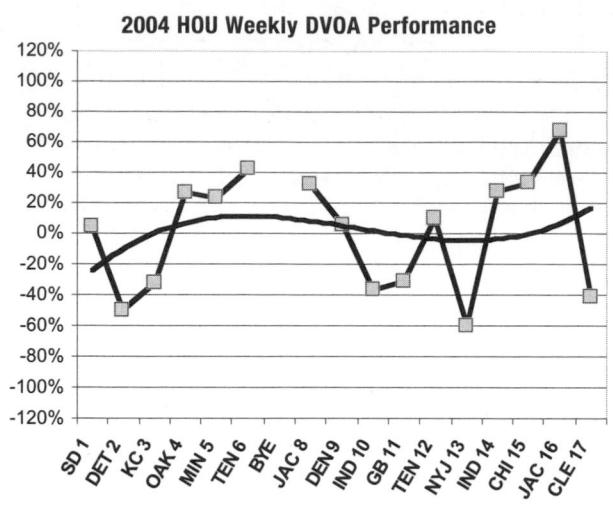

2004 HOU Weekly DVOA Performance

Trends and Splits

	Offense	Rank	Defense	Rank
Total DVOA	0.2%	14	-2.4%	14
Unadjusted VOA	4.5%	13	6.8%	21
Weighted Trend	-0.3%	15	-4.1%	12
Variance	5.9%	27	9.7%	17
Passing	1.4%	16	-2.2%	14
Rushing	-1.0%	17	-2.5%	14
First Down	-0.2%	19	-3.1%	14
Second Down	-3.7%	22	-8.1%	7
Third Down	7.0%	12	9.8%	24
Red Zone	13.8%	9	-8.2%	13
Late and Close	-9.4%	22	-16.9%	7

Five-Year Performance

	2004	2003	2002	2001	2000
W-L	7-9	5-11	4-12	—	—
Pythagorean Wins	7.1	4.5	3.7	—	—
Estimated Wins	8.0	5.9	2.1	—	—
Total DVOA	-1.2%	-19.6%	-42.1%	—	—
Rank	15	29	32	—	—
Offense	0.2%	-11.0%	-38.0%	—	—
Rank	14	24	32	—	—
Defense	-2.4%	12.7%	8.5%	—	—
Rank	14	29	23	—	—
Special Teams	-3.7%	4.0%	4.5%	—	—
Rank	27	4	7	—	—

Passing (min. 5 plays)

Player	DPAR	PAR	DVOA	Plys	NtYds	Avg	Cmpl	TD	Int
David Carr	27.5	46.3	-0.6%	519	3259	6.3	61.2%	16	14

Rushing (min. 3 plays)

Player	DPAR	PAR	DVOA	Plys	Yds	Avg	TD	Fum	Suc
Domanick Davis	14.5	19.8	-2.9%	301	1185	3.9	13	2	43%
Jonathan Wells	0.9	3.6	-11.6%	82	299	3.6	3	1	48%
David Carr	5.9	6.2	-0.4%	55	315	5.7	0	0	—
Tony Hollings	1.7	1.5	21.3%	11	47	4.3	0	0	64%
Andre Johnson	0.0	0.0	-30.5%	4	12	3.0	0	0	—
Jabar Gaffney	-0.5	-0.4	-44.4%	4	30	7.5	0	1	—

Receiving (min. 5 plays)

Player	DPAR	PAR	DVOA	Plys	Ctch	Yds	Y/C	TD	CPct
WR									
Andre Johnson	18.4	22.8	4.5%	137	79	1151	14.6	6	58%
Jabar Gaffney	16.7	18.7	20.9%	68	41	632	15.4	2	60%
Corey Bradford	3.1	4.3	-7.4%	54	27	399	14.8	3	50%
Derick Armstrong	14.5	16.6	42.9%	39	29	415	14.3	1	74%
TE									
Billy Miller	-1.7	-1.8	-20.9%	34	17	178	10.5	1	50%
Mark Bruener	-1.8	-1.5	-38.2%	10	4	52	13.0	0	40%
RB									
Domanick Davis	12.3	15.0	19.1%	85	68	596	8.8	1	81%
Jonathan Wells	1.6	2.3	9.2%	16	11	79	7.2	2	69%
Tony Hollings	0.2	-0.3	-1.8%	7	5	46	9.2	0	71%
Moran Norris	-1.0	-1.2	-43.9%	5	4	13	3.3	0	80%

Defensive Players (min. 20 plays)

Player	Age	Plys	Stop	Dfts	AvYds	StpRt	Sack	Int	FR
Defensive Line									
Robaire Smith	28	59	44	17	2.5	75%	2.0	0	0
Seth Payne	30	50	33	7	1.8	66%	2.0	0	0
Gary Walker	32	30	23	7	1.5	77%	0.5	0	0
Jerry DeLoach	28	28	22	6	2.4	79%	0.0	0	0
Linebackers									
Jamie Sharper	31	147	75	28	4.9	51%	2.0		1
Kailee Wong	29	84	49	19	3.2	58%	5.5	3	1
Jay Foreman	29	81	35	8	5.1	43%	0.0	0	1
Jason Babin	25	69	44	22	2.5	64%	4.0	0	2
DaShon Polk	28	30	15	5	5.0	50%	1.0	0	1

Player	Age	Plys	Stop	Dfts	AvYds	StpRt	Sack	Int	FR
Secondary									
Dunta Robinson	23	106	45	25	6.7	42%	3.0	6	0
Aaron Glenn	33	79	27	13	8.3	34%	0.0	5	1
Marcus Coleman	31	64	16	5	10.4	25%	0.0	2	0
Demarcus Faggins	26	49	19	11	9.3	39%	0.0	3	0
Glenn Earl	24	44	12	3	9.2	27%	0.0	0	0
Jason Simmons	29	40	15	8	8.7	38%	0.0	1	0
Marlon McCree	28	26	10	4	10.1	38%	0.0	1	0

Offensive Line

Year	Yards	AdjLineYd	Rank	Power	Rank	10+ Yds	Rank	Stuff	Rank	Sack	AdjSack%	Rank
2002	2.96	3.10	32	56%	29	9%	30	36%	32	76	14.0%	32
2003	3.73	3.68	29	66%	16	16%	15	30%	30	35	7.3%	25
2004	3.86	4.14	19	67%	11	13%	31	25%	20	50	10.5%	30

Year	LEnd	Rank	LTckl	Rank	MdGrd	Rank	RTckl	Rank	REnd	Rank
2002	3.31	26	2.68	32	3.30	31	2.20	32	2.95	29
2003	3.89	20	3.70	29	3.60	31	4.04	20	3.80	18
2004	4.85	7	3.85	27	4.35	12	3.96	19	2.83	30

Let's just say the O-line's not a strength. The first year of the Seth Wand experiment at left tackle didn't work out, based on the increased sack numbers in 2004 over 2003 (although still mercifully lower than David Carr's record-setting 76 in 2002). When they were unable to pry Pro Bowler Orlando Pace away from the Rams, the Texans signed former New Orleans right tackle Victor Riley to provide competition for Wand, but passed on all of the available tackles in the draft. (They didn't choose an offensive lineman until they picked center Drew Hodgdon in the fifth round.) Left guard Chester Pitts is a penalty machine—he led the league with 21 flags in 2003 and in 2004 tied for second with 14 penalties. (To put this in perspective, the next-highest Houston offensive lineman was Wand with 4 penalties.) The rest of the line—Todd Wade, Zach Wiegert, and Steve McKinney—is capable and durable, but unspectacular. Nobody is going to mistake these guys for the Chiefs or Broncos; however, if Wand does improve, this unit should allow the offense to be productive. If Wand doesn't get better, the rest of the line isn't good enough to pick up the slack, and it will be another long, painful year for Carr and company.

Defensive Front Seven

Year	Yards	AdjLineYd	Rank	Power	Rank	10+ Yds	Rank	Stuff	Rank	Sack	AdjSack%	Rank
2002	4.22	4.24	18	71%	24	17%	16	24%	16	34	6.4%	13
2003	4.62	4.61	31	64%	13	18%	18	18%	31	20	4.6%	30
2004	4.50	4.37	24	47%	2	17%	18	22%	21	24	4.6%	32

Year	LEnd	Rank	LTckl	Rank	MdGrd	Rank	RTckl	Rank	REnd	Rank
2002	4.44	23	3.13	4	4.26	18	3.94	12	4.67	27
2003	4.53	22	5.23	29	4.68	30	4.56	25	4.31	25
2004	3.77	7	5.06	29	4.42	24	4.15	14	4.60	28

The Texans hung a sign in the window of Reliant Stadium saying "Linebackers wanted. Inquire within." Dissatisfied with Jay Foreman's play and Jamie Sharper's cap number, the Texans released the two inside linebackers who had started the vast majority of their games. They'll be replaced by Morlon Greenwood, newly arrived from Miami, and Kailee Wong, who moves back to the inside where he played in Minnesota during the first four years of his career. On the outside, Jason Babin needs to polish his skills and demonstrate that the Texans didn't err in trading up to pick him in the first round of last year's draft. The Texans love Antwan Peek's athleticism and are promoting him from third-down pass rushing specialist to starter. They only hope he keeps his head in the game and one eye on his playbook. Depth is provided by two free agent signings, Frank Chamberlin from Cincinnati and Zeke Moreno from San Diego, plus holdover DaShon Polk.

(continued next page)

Defensive Front Seven *(continued)*

The defensive line relies on the trio of Robaire Smith, Gary Walker, and Seth Payne, backed up by a gaggle of uninspiring but experienced players. Smith is in his prime and adding him as a free agent from the division rival Titans paid big dividends. The big difference in Houston's run defense came from catching guys going around left end, and that's a direct result of Smith tying up blockers so Wong can make tackles. (Smith also helps stop screen passes before they develop, as you can see below from the improvement in pass defense against running backs.) Walker and Payne are talented but aging, so the Texans began the rejuvenation of the defensive line by drafting defensive tackle Travis Johnson from Florida State. He figures to play end in the Texans' 3-4 alignment and his arrival is a strong sign that Walker will be released come 2006.

Defensive Secondary

Year	DVOA vs. #1 WR	Rank	DVOA vs. #2 WR	Rank	DVOA vs. Other WR	Rank	DVOA vs. TE	Rank	DVOA vs. RB	Rank
2002	34.3%	31	-3.1%	14	-33.7%	4	-11.5%	11	16.0%	25
2003	23.7%	24	-21.7%	11	-25.6%	8	21.0%	26	34.1%	31
2004	-3.3%	15	20.0%	27	-20.0%	6	-0.2%	14	-35.4%	4

The Texans best defensive player in 2004 was cornerback Dunta Robinson, first runner-up to Jets' linebacker Jonathan Vilma for defensive rookie of the year. Robinson's partner, Aaron Glenn, played well but began to show his age, and the Texans released him after trading for Philip Buchanon of the Raiders. Buchanon should upgrade the speed of the defense. Demarcus Faggins has one of the NFL's best names and is also an excellent nickel corner. Marcus Coleman is no Ed Reed at free safety, but he performed admirably in his first year after switching from cornerback. By the middle of the year rookie Glenn Earl had won the starting strong safety job over veterans Eric Brown and Jason Simmons. Simmons and free safety Jammal Lord, the converted Nebraska quarterback who spent most of 2004 on the practice squad, figure to hold the top backup spots at safety.

Special Teams

Year	DVOA	Rank	FG/XP	Rank	Net Punt	Rank	Punt Ret	Rank	Net Kick	Rank	Kick Ret	Rank
2002	4.5%	7	2.1	12	16.0	2	17.2	2	1.7	15	-12.0	31
2003	4.0%	4	5.3	13	9.4	4	-0.1	14	6.9	6	0.9	14
2004	-3.7%	27	-4.2	29	-3.9	26	-5.5	17	-2.6	16	-4.4	24

Houston's special teams had a severe off year in 2004 after being a top ten unit in 2002 and 2003, but this can primarily be blamed on injuries. Kicker Kris Brown and punter Chad Stanley both played through injuries for weeks and required surgery early in the off-season. They should be completely recovered by Week 1, so the kicking game should be in good hands—er, feet. Speaking of good feet, the return game figures to be the area in which speedy rookie receiver Jerome Mathis contributes the most in 2005. He averaged 35.5 yards per kick return last year at Hampton and has shown great promise in very limited action as a punt returner (two returns for 47 yards in his college career). Philip Buchanon may also be called on to return punts, but he was actually less effective last year in Oakland than J. J. Moses was in Houston. Buchanon has been a superlative return man in the past, though, so if he regains his old form he'll give the Texans terrific flexibility on special teams. Moses was cut in May.

Coaching Staff

The honeymoon in Houston is over, a fact that is more meaningful to the coaches than anyone. If the Texans don't live up to playoff expectations in 2005, Dom Capers and his staff will face some tough questions. Capers is a fairly popular coach, because while he is conservative and defensive minded, he likes to take calculated risks—à la the David Carr touchdown dive on the last play of the game against Jacksonville in 2003. Fittingly, the staff has taken some real risks in the off-season: Capers, along with GM Charley Casserly, elected to stick with left tackle Seth Wand, and they released three of the most senior players on defense—Jamie Sharper, Jay Foreman, and Aaron Glenn. Offensive coordinator Chris Palmer has been criticized for the conservativeness of the offense, particularly the underutilization of Andre Johnson—a consequence of the offensive line's struggles. Defensive coordinator Vic Fangio has run a remarkably solid expansion-team unit, but in 2005 he will be judged on how well the new-look defense gels.

Indianapolis Colts

For the Indianapolis Colts, the 2004 postseason was déjà vu all over again—ending the season again on a snowy day in Foxboro with an anemic offensive performance. In both 2003 and 2004, the Colts went 12–4 and won the AFC South. Three of the four regular season losses were the same: New England, Jacksonville, and Denver. Both years, the Colts were the third seed in the AFC playoffs. Both years, they blew out Denver at home on wild card weekend. Last year, they had to face New England in the second round, ending their season one week earlier than 2003, but in an all too familiar way.

The 2004 campaign mirrored the 2003 campaign in so many ways that it might appear as though the Colts are simply treading water. That's not an analysis we shy away from—you'll find that prognosis elsewhere in this book for teams like New Orleans and Denver. But while this may be the popular perception of the Colts, we do not agree. Below the superficial similarities, last year's Colts took another step forward.

Nobody paid much attention to the similarities between the two seasons until the repeat egg-laying in New England, because all attention was on Peyton Manning's chase of Dan Marino's single-season touchdown record. Manning finally passed Marino in Week 16, not on a meaningless toss but on a game-tying touchdown in the final minute of regulation that led to a huge Colts victory over AFC West champion San Diego. Manning's pursuit grabbed most of the headlines, but the Colts offense as a whole was a dominant force. They easily posted the highest offensive DVOA of this decade at 38.9%, topping the 31.4% of the 2000 Rams. Edgerrin James had his best season since his 2001 knee injury, ranking second in the NFL in yards from scrimmage. The receiving corps became the first in league history to have three receivers each with over 1,000 yards receiving and ten touchdowns.

The yardage numbers are impressive in themselves, but the Colts offense also scores well in our more advanced metrics. According to DPAR, James was the third-most valuable back in football if you include rushing and receiving. Brandon Stokley and Reggie Wayne ranked first and second in DVOA among receivers, and Wayne ranked first in DPAR. This offensive unit's regular season ranks up there with the greatest of all-time. A league-wide rise in scoring just slightly tempers the impact of these numbers, but the offense was truly amazing.

INDIANAPOLIS PROSPECTUS

2004 Record: 12–4

DVOA Estimated Wins: 12.3 (3rd)

Pythagorean Wins: 11.5 (2nd)

DVOA: 34.7% total (3rd), 43.1% weighted (1st)

Adjusted Offense: 31.7 points/game (38.9% DVOA, 1st)

Adjusted Defense: 22.1 points/game (2.3% DVOA, 18th)

Adjusted Special Teams: −0.6 points/game (−1.8% DVOA, 22nd)

Variance: 14.4% (25th)

2004: Peyton Manning chases Dan Marino to 49.

2005: Peyton Manning chases Trent Dilfer to 1.

2005 Projection

Leinart Land (0–4): 6%

Bad Team (5–6): 11%

Mediocre (7–8): 19%

Playoff Contender (9–10): 26%

Super Bowl Contender (11+): 38%

Projected Average Opponent: −0.9% DVOA (18th in NFL)

Of course, this offensive output means little when the team scores only three points in a playoff game. The Colts have made the playoffs five times in six years, and all five times they have come up short of the Super Bowl. Only once in that period have they even made it as far as the conference championship. However, a closer look at DVOA since Tony Dungy took over in 2002 shows steady improvement, not stagnation (see table 1).

The Colts have actually taken quantum leaps forward in each season under Dungy. They have improved by over 12% in each year, a remarkable level of consistent improvement. Dungy took over a team that was, in all honesty, not very good. Indianapolis progressed to playing at a championship level in 2004—and the quality of competition in 2004 was extremely high.

The Colts' 2004 DVOA of 34.7% would have ranked second among all AFC teams between 2000 and 2003, behind only the 2000 Titans (see table 2). But in the ultra-competitive environment of 2004, the Colts had only the

TABLE 1. INDIANAPOLIS BY DVOA, 2001–2004

Year	DVOA	Rank
2001	−14.3%	24
2002	−2.1%	20
2003	18.9%	4
2004	34.7%	3

TABLE 2. TOP TEAMS BY TOTAL DVOA, 2000–2004

Year	Team	DVOA
2002	TB	40.9%
2001	STL	39.6%
2000	TEN	36.1%
2004	NE	35.6%
2004	PIT	35.4%
2004	IND	34.7%
2000	BAL	32.6%
2001	PHI	32.4%
2002	OAK	29.8%
2003	KC	29.6%

third-highest DVOA in the AFC, behind Pittsburgh and New England. Three times the Dungy-led Colts have lost in the playoffs, and all three losses came on the road, in cold weather, against a team with a higher DVOA.

In 2005, there is no reason to believe that the offense will not be among the two or three best in the league yet again, and the only two major players from the unit who are not returning are TE Marcus Pollard and G Rick DeMulling. Pollard, the longest-tenured Colt last season, became expendable because of the emergence of TE Dallas Clark and WR Brandon Stokley. With Stokley enjoying so much success in three-receiver sets, the Colts have moved away from using two tight ends in their base offense. As for DeMulling, he missed five games during the 2004 season, yet the offense did not miss a beat.

The other key to the offense's continued success is its relative age. The only major contributor over the age of 30 is Marvin Harrison. Harrison, who will be 33 this season, is clearly on the downward slope of his career, but that slope can still be impressive when you're one of the best receivers of all time: 86 receptions for 1,113 yards and 15 touchdowns in 2004. Furthermore, the emergence of Wayne as one of the top receivers in football will curtail, if not eliminate, the amount of double coverage Harrison faces. The Colts may undergo a change similar to that in St. Louis, where Torry Holt has replaced Isaac Bruce as the primary receiver. Nothing could help slow Harrison's sta-

tistical decline as much as a few Bruce-like seasons feasting on number two cornerbacks.

The problem with the Colts, of course, is a defense that does not exactly conjure up images of the 1985 Bears, or even the 2004 Bears for that matter. By conventional measures, the 2004 team appears to have taken a step back, ranking 29th in yards allowed after ranking 11th in 2003. Fortunately, we have DVOA to sort through the noise, and it shows the Colts defense remaining roughly the same, going from 2.2% DVOA to 2.3% DVOA. Because of the 2004 rise in offense, that actually represents improvement, from 20th in the NFL to 18th. The improvement becomes clearer if you consider that the Colts ranked 16th in defense with a 0.0% DVOA before the meaningless Week 17 game against Denver. A weighted defensive DVOA of −3.7% (which does include the Denver game) demonstrates that the defense improved not only year to year, but also from September to December.

In 2005, the Colts are likely to put out their best defense of the Tony Dungy era. They have said goodbye to two starters in free agency—S Idrees Bashir and MLB Rob Morris—but those players had limited talent. Bashir is going to be replaced by intriguing youngster Bob Sanders, who despite his small size (5′ 8″) is a hard hitter with a nose for the football.

Morris has always been a liability, particularly because middle linebacker in Dungy's Cover 2 defense has extensive pass coverage responsibilities. He's also a terrible open-field tackler—Fred Taylor faked him out so badly during Jacksonville's fourth quarter comeback in Week 7 that his shoes ended up somewhere in Kentucky. Morris's inability to control the middle of the field was a major reason for the Colts' abysmal pass defense DVOA of 42.4% on first downs and why they were one of the worst teams defending passes to tight ends and running backs. Combine all situations other than first down passes, and the Colts' defensive DVOA was −10.4%, which would have ranked sixth in the league, just ahead of the Patriots.

Morris will be replaced by the much more agile Gary Brackett, but this will come at the expense of run defense because Morris, despite his faults, was adequate at stuffing the run. In the draft, the Colts focused on pass defense, drafting cornerbacks Marlin Jackson and Kelvin Hayden in the first two rounds and adding safety Matt Giordano in the fourth. The only addition to the Colts' run defense was Vincent Burns, a solid third-round defensive tackle, but a player not likely to contribute much immediately. Right before we went to press, the Colts re-signed the still available Morris as a backup. He could prove quite valuable in short-yardage defense, a situation he thrived in a year ago.

The Indianapolis defense is still very young; if Jackson beats out Nick Harper as the starting cornerback, their oldest starter will be Josh Williams at age 29. The team's best defensive player, Dwight Freeney, is only 25. Sometimes too much youth is cause for concern, but young does not always mean inexperienced, and this youthful defense includes at least eight returning starters. A defense growing into its prime, combined with the stability Dungy and defensive coordinator Ron Meeks provide, should give the Colts their first above-average defense since Peyton Manning arrived in 1998.

The Colts have reached a position somewhat akin to the 2004 Eagles. Each year they are among the best teams in their conference, but at a certain point, they need to break through and reach the Super Bowl. This team is young, but its future is very cloudy after the 2005 season. If they do not agree to contract extensions, both Reggie Wayne and Edgerrin James will be free agents. In 2006, Peyton Manning will receive the first of several large bonuses that will require plenty of cap manipulation. The Colts have an enormous amount of money invested long term in Manning, Harrison, and tackle Ryan Diem. This year the Colts will look similar to the last few seasons, but a year from now the core of this team may be very different.

Peyton Manning is not the first star quarterback with a specific bête noire. In 1996, Brett Favre was the best quarterback in football and the reigning NFL MVP. Yet for three straight years, the Packers had faced the Dallas Cowboys in both the regular season and the playoffs, and the Packers had lost all six games. They played again during the 1996 regular season and the Cowboys won yet again. But in the playoffs, the Panthers beat the Cowboys, the Packers beat the Panthers, and Brett Favre became a Super Bowl champion instead of that guy who couldn't win when it mattered.

The Colts have been building a team for the past three seasons, going from 6–10 and out of the playoffs to 12–4 and among the best teams in football. With the offense intact, points will be scored in bunches. A young, athletic defense should build upon recent improvements. If Brett Favre could conquer a demon named Barry Switzer, there's no reason why Peyton Manning can't conquer his demon named Bill Belichick.

Ned Macey

Colts 2004 Stats by Week

Wk	vs.	W-L	PF	PA	YDF	YDA	TO	DVOA Total	Off	Def	ST
1	@NE	L	24	27	446	402	-2	-2.0%	21.0%	27.8%	4.9%
2	@TEN	W	31	17	373	389	+1	33.1%	49.6%	19.6%	3.1%
3	GB	W	45	31	453	459	+2	30.2%	52.8%	12.7%	-9.9%
4	@JAC	W	24	17	337	408	0	27.1%	45.3%	18.7%	0.5%
5	OAK	W	35	14	338	269	+2	35.8%	4.6%	-35.6%	-4.4%
6	BYE										
7	JAC	L	24	27	446	414	0	30.3%	61.2%	24.6%	-6.3%
8	@KC	L	35	45	505	590	+1	-11.4%	33.7%	36.4%	-8.8%
9	MIN	W	31	28	408	292	+1	34.8%	63.7%	5.2%	-23.7%
10	HOU	W	49	14	398	302	+2	66.3%	15.6%	-52.0%	-1.3%
11	@CHI	W	41	10	486	224	+4	121.4%	77.5%	-41.7%	2.1%
12	@DET	W	41	9	356	386	+5	72.6%	69.3%	8.1%	11.4%
13	TEN	W	51	24	567	340	-1	71.1%	52.2%	-24.3%	-5.5%
14	@HOU	W	23	14	382	273	+2	17.5%	26.9%	11.5%	2.1%
15	BAL	W	20	10	316	354	+2	37.3%	40.2%	-8.7%	-11.6%
16	SD	W	34	31	464	374	0	32.3%	19.9%	1.6%	14.1%
17	@DEN	L	14	33	200	453	-1	-47.3%	-16.9%	34.9%	4.5%
18	DEN	W	49	24	529	338	0	72.6%	84.5%	8.3%	-3.6%
19	@NE	L	3	20	276	325	-4	-4.4%	8.6%	12.2%	-0.8%

2004 IND Weekly DVOA Performance

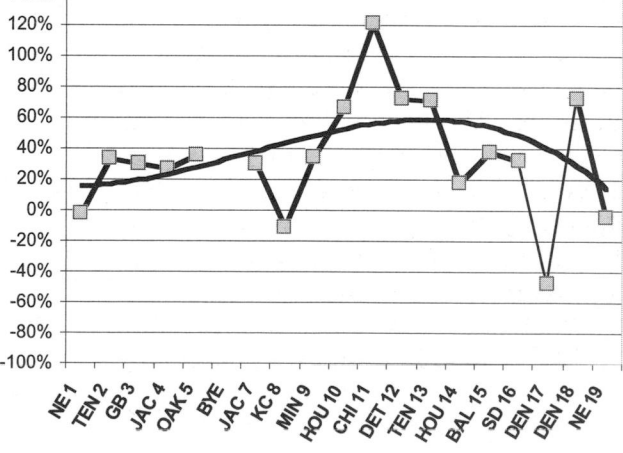

Trends and Splits

	Offense	Rank	Defense	Rank
Total DVOA	38.9%	1	2.3%	18
Unadjusted VOA	45.7%	1	7.9%	23
Weighted Trend	40.8%	1	-3.7%	14
Variance	6.5%	24	7.6%	21
Passing	63.1%	1	1.4%	18
Rushing	9.4%	8	3.5%	21
First Down	35.7%	1	23.5%	31
Second Down	47.3%	1	5.5%	18
Third Down	30.0%	7	-44.4%	1
Red Zone	13.5%	10	-20.1%	8
Late and Close	38.8%	2	15.7%	30

Five-Year Performance

	2004	2003	2002	2001	2000
W-L	12-4	12-4	10-6	6-10	10-6
Pythagorean Wins	11.5	10.6	9.0	6.5	10.5
Estimated Wins	12.3	10.2	8.1	6.6	10.0
Total DVOA	34.7%	18.9%	-2.1%	-14.3%	16.8%
Rank	3	4	20	25	9
Offense	38.9%	20.0%	7.1%	6.8%	27.5%
Rank	1	2	13	5	2
Defense	2.3%	2.2%	7.4%	16.1%	9.0%
Rank	18	20	22	30	24
Special Teams	-1.8%	1.1%	-1.8%	-4.9%	-1.6%
Rank	22	14	20	27	19

Passing (min. 5 plays)

Player	DPAR	PAR	DVOA	Plys	NtYds	Avg	Cmpl	TD	Int
Peyton Manning	170.1	189.2	62.8%	509	4451	8.7	67.6%	49	10
Jim Sorgi	2.6	1.3	4.8%	31	162	5.2	58.6%	2	0

Rushing (min. 3 plays)

Player	DPAR	PAR	DVOA	Plys	Yds	Avg	TD	Fum	Suc
Edgerrin James	34.8	41.0	9.9%	334	1551	4.6	9	5	57%
Dominic Rhodes	4.6	4.3	8.1%	53	254	4.8	1	1	45%
Peyton Manning	0.8	0.9	-3.1%	8	53	6.6	0	0	—
James Mungro	0.4	0.3	12.7%	5	19	3.8	0	0	60%

Receiving (min. 5 plays)

Player	DPAR	PAR	DVOA	Plys	Ctch	Yds	Y/C	TD	CPct
WR									
Marvin Harrison	28.6	31.4	14.6%	139	86	1113	12.9	15	62%
Reggie Wayne	44.0	46.5	40.8%	115	77	1210	15.7	12	67%
Brandon Stokley	38.4	40.8	41.7%	102	68	1081	15.9	10	67%
TE									
Marcus Pollard	10.6	11.8	27.1%	41	29	309	10.7	6	71%
Dallas Clark	7.6	7.4	17.2%	39	25	423	16.9	5	64%
Ben Hartsock	-1.3	-2.4	-33.4%	8	4	33	8.3	0	50%
RB									
Edgerrin James	14.7	15.4	40.2%	60	51	483	9.5	0	85%
James Mungro	3.4	3.2	50.3%	8	7	36	5.1	3	88%

Defensive Players (min. 20 plays)

Player	Age	Plys	Stop	Dfts	AvYds	StpRt	Sack	Int	FR
Defensive Line									
Raheem Brock	27	51	38	23	1.1	75%	6.5	0	2
Montae Reagor	28	44	34	18	1.9	77%	5.0	0	1
Josh Williams	29	40	27	9	2.4	68%	0.0	0	2
Dwight Freeney	25	34	27	19	-1.4	79%	16.0	0	0
Larry Tripplett	26	27	17	3	3.7	63%	0.0	0	0
Robert Mathis	24	26	22	18	-2.3	85%	10.5	0	3
Linebackers									
Cato June	26	112	55	27	5.7	49%	0.0	2	2
David Thornton	27	85	38	13	5.5	45%	0.0	1	0
Rob Morris	30	78	47	15	3.5	60%	3.0	1	0
Jim Nelson	30	56	27	9	6.6	48%	0.0	1	2
Gary Brackett	25	23	8	3	6.3	35%	0.0	2	0

Player	Age	Plys	Stop	Dfts	AvYds	StpRt	Sack	Int	FR
Secondary									
Nick Harper	31	88	26	10	8.6	30%	0.0	3	1
Jason David	23	65	28	15	8.0	43%	0.0	4	0
Idrees Bashir	27	59	8	5	12.7	14%	0.0	0	1
Mike Doss	24	47	14	9	8.1	30%	1.0	2	0
Von Hutchins	24	42	12	6	8.0	29%	0.0	1	0
Anthony Floyd	24	36	6	0	11.0	17%	0.0	0	0
Bob Sanders	24	31	9	4	8.8	29%	0.0	0	2
Cory Bird	27	29	6	2	9.1	21%	0.0	0	0
Joesph Jefferson	25	26	10	7	8.8	38%	0.0	1	0
Donald Strickland	25	21	4	0	9.2	19%	0.0	0	0

Offensive Line

Year	Yards	AdjLineYd	Rank	Power	Rank	10+ Yds	Rank	Stuff	Rank	Sack	AdjSack%	Rank
2002	3.50	3.87	28	62%	22	11%	29	27%	26	23	3.8%	2
2003	3.90	4.39	7	52%	30	10%	30	23%	12	20	3.6%	2
2004	4.65	4.83	1	46%	32	15%	26	19%	4	14	1.8%	2

Year	LEnd	Rank	LTckl	Rank	MdGrd	Rank	RTckl	Rank	REnd	Rank
2002	3.27	27	4.07	18	4.30	14	3.86	24	3.04	27
2003	4.80	7	4.91	6	4.12	18	4.29	16	4.50	6
2004	5.42	3	5.05	4	4.87	1	4.20	15	4.39	7

Howard Mudd's offensive line is one of the most underappreciated in football. Mudd, who was a Pro Bowl lineman with the 49ers in the 1960s, believes in trapping and pulling and has put together a line that succeeds more with mobility than with power. Despite ranking first in Adjusted Line Yards and second in Adjusted Sack Rate, they have only one Pro Bowl player on the roster, left tackle Tarik Glenn. These numbers are partially attributable to the unique talents of Edgerrin James and Peyton Manning, but the line's role is too frequently overlooked. The base play of the Colts offense is the stretch play, which they run in either direction. The Colts frequently show this look and go play action for big plays. Peyton Manning's mastery of play action is often acknowledged, but none of it would work without the line selling each play as if they were run blocking. The Colts' offense requires agile linemen who are able to sprint out to the corner and get in front of James on running downs. The one place this line struggles is when the Colts need just a yard or two, which may explain why Manning is constantly throwing the ball instead of handing it to James at the goal line.

Both tackles, Glenn and Ryan Diem, are big players at over 320 pounds, yet agile enough to move outside on running plays. The Colts were much more effective running behind left tackle than right, in general because this is the usual direction for the stretch play. Glenn is the top player on this line, but he appears to be getting a bit confused by Peyton Manning's constant presnap signaling—he led the league with both nine false starts and 16 penalties total. Diem is only 25 years old and was signed to a sizable long-term extension in the off-season. The other key member of the unit is center Jeff Saturday, who has enormous responsibility in the Colts' check-with-me offense. The guards last season were Rick DeMulling and Tupe Peko. DeMulling moved to Detroit as a free agent, and Peko was released. This year the Colts will use Ryan Lilja and Jake Scott, effective in six and nine starts last season, respectively, while filling in for the injured DeMulling and Peko. Second-day draft picks Dylan Gandy and Robert Hunt should provide depth.

Defensive Front Seven

Year	Yards	AdjLineYd	Rank	Power	Rank	10+ Yds	Rank	Stuff	Rank	Sack	AdjSack%	Rank
2002	4.30	4.40	27	79%	30	14%	8	24%	19	36	6.0%	19
2003	4.61	4.45	24	64%	14	19%	21	23%	23	31	6.8%	11
2004	4.82	4.56	30	52%	6	19%	22	23%	20	45	8.1%	4

Year	LEnd	Rank	LTckl	Rank	MdGrd	Rank	RTckl	Rank	REnd	Rank
2002	4.16	21	4.99	29	4.45	26	3.96	14	3.83	14
2003	4.25	15	4.62	20	4.35	22	4.71	28	4.73	3
2004	4.52	21	4.50	19	4.63	28	4.75	31	3.83	16

The Colts' front seven is among the lightest in football. The two tackles, Monte Reagor and Josh Williams, both are listed at 285 pounds. Star defensive end Dwight Freeney is only 268 pounds. Even the linebackers are small, with converted college safety Cato June playing outside linebacker at 225 pounds. Dungy's defense is based on speed, and the Colts are certainly quick. The plan is for the offense to get a lead and then let the defense attack the quarterback with Freeney and pass rush specialist Robert Mathis. But small size means that when the offense struggles, the front seven can be worn down. This is what happened in the playoffs, as the Colts held the Patriots to just six points in the first half but were exhausted by two long, clock-killing drives in which Corey Dillon ran over the smaller Colt defenders.

Freeney deserves the credit he gets for being a good pass rusher, but he deserves more blame than he gets for being lousy against the run. He frequently takes an angle toward the quarterback that completely takes him out of the play on handoffs. The individual defensive stats show that Freeney had remarkably few plays for a starting lineman in a 4-3 defense. And because Freeney and Mathis are so focused on rushing the passer, they are the only two players in the league who made their average tackle more than a yard *behind* the line of scrimmage.

(continued next page)

Defensive Front Seven *(continued)*

The Colts also lack playmaking linebackers. In recent years they have watched Mike Peterson and Marcus Washington leave, and this year they send middle linebacker Rob Morris to the bench. Morris was drafted before Dungy arrived and never quite fit into his defense. The in-house replacement for Morris is Gary Brackett, who is quick but—you guessed it—a little undersized. As we note in the main part of this chapter, Brackett will improve the pass defense but struggle against the run. Fortunately for the Colts, middle linebacker is not the playmaking position in Dungy's Cover 2 defense. Instead, plays are funneled to the weakside linebacker, a position occupied by June last season. June did lead the team in tackles, but he made almost no big plays. The Colts also have second-year players Gilbert Gardener, Keyon Whiteside, and Kendyll Pope to provide solid depth at the position.

Defensive Secondary

Year	DVOA vs. #1 WR	Rank	DVOA vs. #2 WR	Rank	DVOA vs. Other WR	Rank	DVOA vs. TE	Rank	DVOA vs. RB	Rank
2002	5.8%	23	-3.3%	13	4.5%	18	10.5%	22	2.7%	15
2003	25.3%	27	-21.8%	10	-11.0%	16	-13.9%	9	-16.2%	5
2004	-8.0%	8	3.1%	14	5.6%	20	12.8%	19	16.7%	29

Considering the pressure applied by Freeney and Mathis, ranking 18th in pass defense DVOA is an indictment of the secondary. Injuries, combined with a lack of depth, meant the Colts frequently shuttled different players in and out of their nickel package, which in turn meant struggles against multiple-receiver sets. Week 1 starting cornerback Donald Strickland missed the last 12 games of the season, starting safeties Idrees Bashir and Mike Doss each missed several games, and promising rookie safety Bob Sanders missed 10 games. These injuries forced the Colts to use fourth-round rookie Jason David at starting cornerback opposite Nick Harper, with sixth-round rookie Von Hutchins in the nickel.

Hoping health cures all ills, the Colts are bringing back all of their contributors from last season save Bashir, who is easily replaced by Sanders. They also bucked their recent draft history by taking cornerbacks with their first two picks. Marlin Jackson will presumably compete for a starting job along with Harper, David, and maybe Strickland. Second-round pick Kelvin Hayden, who played wide receiver and running back for most of his college career before switching to cornerback as a senior, is considered a bit of a project and will likely not be much of a factor this season. With the drafting of Jackson, Strickland could move back to safety, where he played as a rookie. The cornerbacks are not an exceptional group, but they will find protection in Dungy's Cover 2 and serve their role if they prevent the big play. For the Colts to really improve on the defensive side of the ball, they need a cornerback to emerge as a dominant player. Jackson showed flashes of this potential in college, but for this season the most likely candidate is David, who picked off 4 passes and broke up 11 more as a rookie. You can make plays when the quarterbacks are always passing in your direction, but these are still encouraging numbers for a rookie. This young unit has shown flashes of promise, and its development is the key for the Colts in 2005.

Special Teams

Year	DVOA	Rank	FG/XP	Rank	Net Punt	Rank	Punt Ret	Rank	Net Kick	Rank	Kick Ret	Rank
2002	-1.8%	20	-3.9	21	5.9	11	-8.3	29	-0.3	17	-3.2	21
2003	1.1%	14	18.1	1	3.6	15	-13.9	30	-7.2	29	5.6	8
2004	-1.8%	22	-3.6	26	5.6	15	-4.5	15	-13.3	29	5.8	11

The Colts special teams are a steaming pile of mediocrity somewhat masked by Mike Vanderjagt's perfect field goal record of 2003. But Vanderjagt is actually a problem because of his inability to get consistent distance or hang time on kickoffs. To remedy this, the Colts tried several different kickoff specialists and even tried letting the punter kick off. Nobody was successful. This table shows the five different kickers who attempted kickoffs last year, along with their value based on both the net kickoff and the kickoff distance alone:

Kicker	Weeks	Kickoffs	Net Kick	Kick Only
Jeff Baker	10–13	33	-0.8	-1.0
Mike Vanderjagt	1–4, 7–8	32	-6.5	-4.9
Martin Gramatica	14–17	21	-2.8	-2.0
Hunter Smith	4, 9	8	-2.5	-1.1
Matt Bryant	5	6	-0.7	-0.8

Aware of this problem, the Colts spent a sixth-round pick on Michigan State's Dave Rayner, the second-best kicker in the draft. Rayner has a strong leg and will likely handle kickoffs this season before taking over as the full-time kicker when Vanderjagt's contract expires at the end of the season. In fact, with a salary cap figure over $2 million, Vanderjagt might find himself out of Indianapolis much sooner if Rayner has a strong enough preseason.

Punter Hunter Smith (Phunter?) had a fine season with 21 kicks inside the 20 and only three touchbacks. Kickoff returns were handled by backup running back Dominic Rhodes, who averaged nearly 25 yards a return. But Brad Pyatt, Jason David, and Troy Walters all struggled on punt returns. Walters will be back, but the Colts really need to upgrade this unit.

Coaching Staff

Tony Dungy is universally respected by his peers and players, and the Colts have played well for him. One of his most important decisions has been to let offensive coordinator Tom Moore have free reign. The Colts' triplets have been around since 1999, but only in the last two years, with the development of Wayne and the switch to the no huddle, has the offense become a dominant unit. Moore and Peyton Manning work well together, and Moore is comfortable enough to let Manning call his own plays. The offense was basically unstoppable until it came to a screeching halt against the Patriots. Moore has been criticized for the game plan in that contest because the Colts did not throw the ball down the field. Wide receivers coach Clyde Christensen, who worked with Dungy throughout his Tampa Bay tenure, has done strong work in an offense that requires receivers to adjust their routes on the fly.

Defensively, the Colts are run by Ron Meeks, a former secondary coach for Dungy in Tampa. Meeks runs Dungy's "Tampa 2" scheme, designed to create turnovers and limit big plays by the opposing offense. The unit is vastly improved over the defense Meeks inherited, but there's plenty of opportunity for further growth, particularly with the defensive focus of this year's Indy draft. If the Colts are not able to move comfortably into the top half of NFL defenses, then either their defensive scheme or their offense-heavy philosophy needs to change.

For all of Dungy's success, both in Indianapolis and in Tampa Bay, he has acquired a stigma of not being able to win the big game. He is 5–7 in the playoffs, a fairly pedestrian record. Of course, all seven losses have been road games, five of which were during the divisional round, a round where the home team almost always wins. The fact that Jon Gruden won the Super Bowl in Tampa Bay the year after Dungy was fired will be held against him until he wins his own. He has had no better opportunity than he will this year to prove he can do just that.

Jacksonville Jaguars

In 2004, the Jacksonville Jaguars won a number of early games with late comebacks. It looked like they had found the same magic recipe that their expansion brethren, the Carolina Panthers, had used to make it to the previous Super Bowl. So it is no surprise that we felt that the 2004 Jaguars, like the 2003 Panthers, weren't quite as good as their record. And lo and behold, we were right.

At the peak of their season, when they were 5–2, Jacksonville's opponents had outscored the Jaguars 126–122. Our DVOA ratings at that point had them as the 16th-best team in the league. They continued to win close games for the rest of the season—of Jacksonville's nine wins in 2004, the only one that came by more than a touchdown was a 22–3 shellacking of the Chicago Bears. Clutch performance, however, is a cruel mistress. The same Jacksonville team that depended on fourth quarter comebacks early in the season fell to fourth quarter comebacks by both Tennessee and Pittsburgh late in the season.

For the season, Jacksonville scored only 261 points, while giving up 280 points. According to the Pythagorean projection based on points scored and allowed, the Jaguars played closer to a 7–9 team than a playoff contender. Most teams that outperform their point differential in the actual standings regress the next season. Nine teams won at least a game more than their Pythagorean projection in 2003, but only Philadelphia and Arizona had improved records in 2004. The additions of Terrell Owens and Denny Green likely played a role in this.

The Jaguars are not making any similar big-name additions. Instead, they are banking on the continuing improvement of quarterback Byron Leftwich to help increase offensive efficiency while the talented defense strives to become a dominant unit. In his second season, Leftwich developed into a solid, if unspectacular, quarterback. After struggling as a rookie, when he was rushed into the starting lineup in Week 4, Leftwich improved his numbers across the board in his second season. His completion percentage rose from 57% to 60%, he threw six fewer interceptions, and his DVOA rose from −6.7% to 2.3%. He ranked 17th in the league in DPAR, ahead of more established quarterbacks such as Aaron Brooks and David Carr. It was an encouraging season for the future of the franchise.

But other than Leftwich, the Jaguars had only one legitimate offensive threat, veteran wide receiver Jimmy Smith. Smith, at age 36, is clearly on the downside of his

JAGUARS PROSPECTUS

2004 Record: 9–7

DVOA Estimated Wins: 8.4 (14th)

Pythagorean Wins: 7.3 (18th)

DVOA: −0.1% total (14th), −1.7% weighted (18th)

Adjusted Offense: 19.5 points/game (−7.5% DVOA, 25th)

Adjusted Defense: 19.2 points/game (−8.5% DVOA, 8th)

Adjusted Special Teams: −0.4 points/game (−1.0% DVOA, 20th)

Variance: 8.4% (31st)

2004: They were great in the first half, but it was something of a mirage.

2005: Chances for improvement rest on Leftwich's enormous shoulders.

2005 Projection

Leinart Land (0–4): 22%

Bad Team (5–6): 25%

Mediocre (7–8): 24%

Playoff Contender (9–10): 16%

Super Bowl Contender (11+): 13%

Projected Average Opponent: 1.2% DVOA (14th in NFL)

career, but he's still putting up strong seasons and commanding respect from opposing secondaries. He ranked only 30th in the NFL in DPAR, but his value to the Jaguars is more apparent when you compare him to the other receivers on his own team. Smith was the only wide receiver or tight end on the Jaguars with a positive DVOA rating. Rookie Reggie Williams, who started alongside Smith, ranked 79th in DPAR (out of 84 receivers who were thrown 50 or more passes). Slot receiver Troy Edwards was 75th. Fourth receiver Ernest Wilford was slightly above replacement level thanks to his penchant for catching touchdowns. Jacksonville's tight ends were the worst in the league; Todd Yoder had the highest DVOA at −27.1%.

On the ground, longtime running back Fred Taylor has finally stayed healthy for several seasons. But while his average of 4.7 yards per carry looks very good, in reality, his effectiveness is declining. As the situation becomes more important, Taylor struggles. He converted only 6 of

18 third or fourth down runs, and he had a −44.1% DVOA in the red zone. He ran the ball nine times within the opponent's five-yard line and managed to gain positive yardage only twice. Because of these propensities, Taylor ranked 31st in the league in DPAR among running backs after ranking 3rd, 7th, and 12th in his previous three healthy seasons.

Of course, the offense isn't supposed to be the unit winning games for Jacksonville. Head coach Jack Del Rio, a former assistant in Baltimore and Carolina, is clearly modeling the Jaguars after the teams of his past, trying to pair a dominant defense with an efficient, ball control offense.

Del Rio's transformation of the Jaguars was a bold move, considering that the team he took over after the 2002 season was instead weighted toward offense. According to DVOA, it ranked 8th in the league in offense but only 26th in defense. Over the past two seasons, the team has inverted completely to the point where, in 2004, the Jaguars ranked 25th in the league in offense and 8th in defense. That's not quite dominant yet, but Del Rio has done his job well.

Like a winning baseball team's, the Jaguars' defense is strongest up the middle. Talented young tackles John Henderson and Marcus Stroud held firm against the run and also contributed an impressive 11 sacks from the tackle position. Middle linebacker Mike Peterson and safety Donovan Darius are also important contributors to a unit that was equally strong against the run (8th in DVOA) and the pass (11th in DVOA). Much of this quality was obscured by a schedule littered with powerful offenses, from the division rivals in Indianapolis to the AFC West to NFC North opponents Green Bay and Minnesota. Jacksonville's pass defense VOA, the rating that does not account for quality of opponent, was only 3.0%, 21st in the league.

Going 9–7—despite being outscored—is not the best omen for 2005, but the Jaguars went into the off-season with several glaring holes that, if properly filled, could greatly improve the team. The holes were at wide receiver and defensive end. As mentioned, Williams and Edwards were among the worst receivers in football. At defensive end, the Jaguars got only eight sacks from Bobby McCray and Greg Favors combined. Just as bad, according to our Adjusted Line Yards, the Jaguars ranked in the top ten defending runs up the middle, but in the bottom ten on runs behind the offense's two tackles.

The Jaguars struck out on every attempt to acquire a legitimate secondary receiver through free agency and resorted to re-signing the underwhelming Edwards and using their first-round pick on former Arkansas quarterback Matt Jones, a projected wide receiver in the NFL. Jones is a physical specimen, and recently converted college quarterbacks Antwaan Randle El, Ronald Curry, and Drew Bennett have all made a successful switch to receiver at the pro level. Unfortunately for the Jaguars, none of those players made a big impact as rookies, with only Randle El playing regularly as a slot receiver. Jones is a better athlete than all of them, but expecting more than a token contribution this year would be unrealistic.

The receiving corps may not be upgraded for 2005, but the Jaguars did manage to land the top free agent defensive end available. Reggie Hayward had a career year for Denver last year, posting 11 sacks. He likely benefited from the internal pressure of Trevor Pryce, but playing with Henderson and Stroud in the middle should allow Hayward plenty of one-on-one opportunities on the outside. The addition of Hayward could give the Jaguars a dominant pass defense, as even with the anemic output from their defensive ends, the Jaguars actually ranked 12th in our Adjusted Sack Rate metric.

Offensively, the key will be if Leftwich can take that proverbial next step. In order to make Del Rio's vision work, Leftwich must develop into the type of quarterback Tom Brady is: efficient, poised, and extremely clutch. Leftwich is an ideal candidate to run this sort of team for two reasons. First, despite his youth, he makes few mistakes with the ball. He turned the ball over only 12 times last season, third fewest among all quarterbacks who attempted at least 400 passes. Second, he has a knack for making big plays late in the game. In half of the eight games he won as the starter, he led a game-winning drive in the fourth quarter. Heck, he even led a game-winning drive in the fourth quarter of a game he didn't actually win—he drove the Jaguars down the field for a field goal that gave them a 16–14 lead against Pittsburgh with two minutes left, only to watch Ben Roethlisberger lead a similar drive that gave Pittsburgh a 17–16 victory.

With Leftwich entering his third season, it is time for Del Rio to open up the offense. While division rival Tennessee hired celebrated USC offensive coordinator Norm Chow to take over their offense, Jacksonville contented itself with not-so-heralded USC quarterback coach Carl Smith. Del Rio's realization that the offense needed to improve is admirable, but his choice of Smith to replace Bill Musgrave is questionable. Smith was the offensive coordinator for the New Orleans Saints between 1986 and 1996. During that time, he never had a team ranked in the top ten in yards.

While Smith's track record is average at best, what may be most troubling is his adherence to a run-first philosophy. As mentioned, Fred Taylor is clearly on the decline, and putting an increased burden on him seems like an unwise use of resources. The opportunity for improvement is in the passing game, with the untapped potential of Leftwich. Jones, though unpolished, should at least provide a deep threat that will open up other receivers underneath. One would imagine that Reggie Williams could not be worse; only ten other rookie receivers since 1978 had 15 catches and less than ten yards per reception. A look at rookies most similar to Williams includes some promising names such as Carl Pickens, Eric Moulds, Qadry Ismail, and Terance Mathis. Then again, it also includes Freddie Mitchell. OK, Jaguars fans, everyone step down from the ledge.

Jacksonville's most persistent offensive problem last season came on first downs, when they had an offensive DVOA of −18.9% compared with −6.9% on second down and 12.8% on third down. The Jaguars had 415 first downs last season, and more than half were followed by second and seven-or-more yards. Their first down efficiency ranked 29th in the NFL, ahead of only the offensively inept Redskins, Dolphins, and Bears. All those first downs with little gain led to plenty of third downs where Leftwich was asked to do the impossible. Sometimes, Leftwich actually responded, but his occasional magic on difficult third downs was often canceled by Taylor's failure on the easy ones. As a result, despite one of the better third down DVOA ratings in the league, the Jaguars ranked 21st in the league in third down conversion percentage.

Del Rio's rhetoric following the change in coordinators leaves it unclear as to whether he understands the weaknesses of the Jaguars' offense. Del Rio has rightly commented that the West Coast attack favored by Musgrave may not have played to the strengths of the strong-armed Leftwich and downfield threat Williams. Smith says he favors a more vertical passing attack, but he is by nature conservative and prefers a run-heavy offense. The Jaguars need to be more creative in their offensive sets and more efficient on first down. Incomplete passes mixed with two-yard runs just aren't going to cut it.

The Jaguars appear to be an up-and-coming team, anchored by a strong defense and a promising young quarterback. But Leftwich is surrounded by an unfortunate mix of fading stars and unproven young skill players. Del Rio's desire to mold a conservative offense doesn't take advantage of what skills Jimmy Smith and Fred Taylor have left. Hayward may improve the defense a bit more, but the real room for growth on the Jaguars is on the offensive side of the ball, and nothing that has happened since the end of the 2004 season indicates that they will come out significantly improved in 2005.

Ned Macey

Jaguars 2004 Stats by Week

Wk	vs.	W-L	PF	PA	YDF	YDA	TO	DVOA			
								Total	Off	Def	ST
1	@BUF	W	13	10	225	242	0	8.8%	-11.2%	-18.0%	2.0%
2	DEN	W	7	6	176	356	+1	10.5%	-10.2%	-7.1%	13.5%
3	@TEN	W	15	12	253	249	+1	7.1%	-14.9%	-22.3%	-0.3%
4	IND	L	17	24	408	337	0	4.4%	8.2%	3.7%	-0.1%
5	@SD	L	21	34	429	386	-3	-26.9%	8.0%	25.4%	-9.5%
6	KC	W	22	16	378	350	+1	40.8%	15.2%	-21.7%	3.9%
7	@IND	W	27	24	414	446	0	10.6%	13.6%	11.3%	8.2%
8	@HOU	L	6	20	287	369	0	-39.3%	-23.2%	17.2%	1.2%
9	BYE										
10	DET	W	23	17	415	190	+1	1.6%	13.5%	-35.2%	-47.1%
11	TEN	L	15	18	274	295	0	-8.1%	-31.5%	-14.9%	8.5%
12	@MIN	L	16	27	379	330	0	-16.7%	-27.2%	-5.8%	4.7%
13	PIT	L	16	17	359	316	0	-29.4%	28.4%	54.2%	-3.6%
14	CHI	W	22	3	332	210	+1	2.2%	5.9%	6.8%	3.1%
15	@GB	W	28	25	312	444	+3	25.6%	1.1%	-38.8%	-14.3%
16	HOU	L	0	21	126	333	-1	-85.6%	-90.3%	-0.5%	4.2%
17	@OAK	W	13	6	242	281	+2	17.8%	-54.1%	-63.0%	8.9%

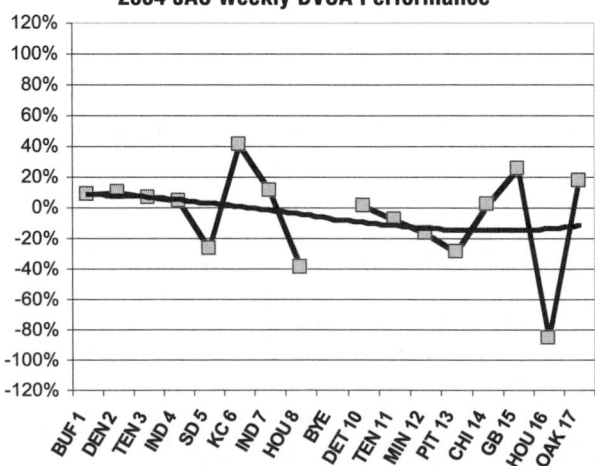

2004 JAC Weekly DVOA Performance

Trends and Splits

	Offense	Rank	Defense	Rank
Total DVOA	-7.5%	25	-8.5%	8
Unadjusted VOA	-3.0%	17	0.2%	18
Weighted Trend	-10.9%	25	-11.8%	7
Variance	9.1%	15	7.8%	20
Passing	-6.7%	21	-10.8%	8
Rushing	-8.4%	24	-5.8%	11
First Down	-18.9%	29	-12.1%	6
Second Down	-6.9%	24	2.5%	15
Third Down	12.8%	11	-19.1%	9
Red Zone	-20.5%	27	-48.0%	1
Late and Close	-8.4%	21	-21.6%	4

Five-Year Performance

	2004	2003	2002	2001	2000
W-L	9-7	5-11	6-10	6-10	7-9
Pythagorean Wins	7.3	6.3	8.4	8.3	9.1
Estimated Wins	8.4	7.6	8.1	7.3	7.9
Total DVOA	-0.1%	-5.0%	1.8%	-1.3%	6.5%
Rank	14	19	16	15	15
Offense	-7.5%	-2.4%	11.9%	2.4%	12.0%
Rank	25	15	8	7	7
Defense	-8.5%	-4.0%	10.3%	4.2%	7.0%
Rank	8	13	26	23	23
Special Teams	-1.0%	-6.6%	0.2%	0.6%	1.6%
Rank	20	32	14	12	14

Passing (min. 5 plays)

Player	DPAR	PAR	DVOA	Plys	NtYds	Avg	Cmpl	TD	Int
Byron Leftwich	30.2	43.6	2.3%	466	2831	6.1	60.5%	15	10
David Garrard	1.2	1.0	-9.5%	78	339	4.3	52.8%	2	1

Rushing (min. 3 plays)

Player	DPAR	PAR	DVOA	Plys	Yds	Avg	TD	Fum	Suc
Fred Taylor	10.1	13.7	-3.5%	260	1224	4.7	2	3	45%
Greg Jones	-3.2	-2.2	-24.2%	62	162	2.6	3	1	48%
LaBrandon Toefield	0.4	1.6	-11.5%	51	169	3.3	0	0	49%
Bryon Leftwich	0.1	0.5	-17.7%	30	156	5.2	2	0	—
C. Fuamatu-Ma'afala	3.2	2.9	16.2%	20	69	3.5	1	0	65%
David Garrard	2.8	3.3	20.1%	11	77	7.0	1	0	—

Receiving (min. 5 plays)

Player	DPAR	PAR	DVOA	Plys	Ctch	Yds	Y/C	TD	CPct
WR									
Jimmy Smith	19.7	20.8	6.6%	137	74	1179	15.9	6	54%
Troy Edwards	-2.6	-0.8	-20.9%	80	50	533	10.7	1	63%
Reggie Williams	-7.7	-7.0	-36.3%	54	27	268	9.9	1	50%
Ernest Wilford	2.5	4.1	-5.4%	35	19	271	14.3	2	54%
Cortez Hankton	3.3	3.7	42.0%	9	9	81	9.0	2	100%
TE									
Kyle Brady	-3.4	-2.1	-36.9%	23	14	103	7.4	1	61%
Todd Yoder	-1.9	-1.2	-27.1%	22	14	157	11.2	0	64%
Brian Jones	-2.7	-2.3	-35.5%	19	6	87	14.5	1	32%
George Wrighster									
RB									
Fred Taylor	3.8	5.2	3.2%	58	36	345	9.6	1	62%
LaBrandon Toefield	2.0	2.8	1.3%	34	28	151	5.4	1	82%
Greg Jones	-3.4	-3.7	-72.1%	10	3	13	4.3	0	30%
Marc Edwards	-0.5	-0.7	-20.8%	8	7	41	5.9	0	88%
C. Fuamatu-Ma'afala	-0.6	-0.6	-29.7%	6	4	19	4.8	0	67%

Defensive Players (min. 20 plays)

Player	Age	Plys	Stop	Dfts	AvYds	StpRt	Sack	Int	FR
Defensive Line									
John Henderson	26	81	58	19	2.2	72%	5.5	0	1
Marcus Stroud	27	57	39	12	1.7	68%	4.5	0	1
Greg Favors	31	36	24	8	3.6	67%	5.5	0	0
Bobby McCray	24	22	14	9	1.5	64%	3.5	0	0
Rob Meier	28	21	18	7	1.3	86%	0.5	0	0
Linebackers									
Mike Peterson	29	126	62	21	4.1	49%	5.0	0	1
Akin Ayodele	26	100	46	10	5.0	46%	2.0	0	1
Daryl Smith	23	54	33	11	3.6	61%	2.0	1	1

Player	Age	Plys	Stop	Dfts	AvYds	StpRt	Sack	Int	FR
Secondary									
Donovin Darius	30	100	32	19	8.6	32%	0.0	5	4
Dewayne Washington	33	87	23	8	9.6	26%	0.0	2	0
Rashean Mathis	25	79	33	18	6.5	42%	0.0	5	0
Deon Grant	26	79	18	13	11.9	23%	1.0	2	1
Deke Cooper	28	26	10	9	9.5	38%	1.0	1	0
Juran Bolden	31	22	7	4	8.6	32%	0.0	0	0

Offensive Line

Year	Yards	AdjLineYd	Rank	Power	Rank	10+ Yds	Rank	Stuff	Rank	Sack	AdjSack%	Rank
2002	4.54	4.38	7	70%	13	20%	8	25%	19	42	8.6%	30
2003	4.39	4.37	8	69%	11	17%	12	21%	5	27	4.7%	6
2004	4.13	4.10	20	51%	29	18%	9	27%	23	32	6.1%	12

Year	LEnd	Rank	LTckl	Rank	MdGrd	Rank	RTckl	Rank	REnd	Rank
2002	4.64	8	4.07	19	4.57	4	4.51	12	3.50	21
2003	3.38	30	4.11	18	4.46	6	4.34	13	4.97	2
2004	2.77	29	4.33	20	4.24	17	3.81	22	4.50	6

The Jaguars' offensive line had four players start all 16 games last season, but the one injury they did suffer was major. Left tackle Mike Pearson was lost for the season in Week 4. The other four starters, all returned from the 2003 season, were right tackle Maurice Williams, guards Chris Naeole and Vince Manuwai, and center Brad Meester. Pearson was replaced by Ephraim Salaam, who did a credible job filling in but was not as powerful a blocker as Pearson, so the effectiveness of the line declined.

This season, the Jaguars return the entire unit intact, including Salaam and second-round pick Khalif Barnes. Everyone but Meester is 26 or younger. New offensive coordinator Carl Smith wants to emphasize the run this season, so this young and talented offensive line needs to turn its potential into results. Bigger holes to run through will do a lot to slow Fred Taylor's inevitable decline.

Defensive Front Seven

Year	Yards	AdjLineYd	Rank	Power	Rank	10+ Yds	Rank	Stuff	Rank	Sack	AdjSack%	Rank
2002	3.92	4.46	28	64%	11	8%	2	23%	20	36	6.3%	16
2003	3.11	3.58	2	66%	19	7%	2	29%	6	23	4.6%	29
2004	4.10	4.15	14	63%	19	15%	14	25%	12	36	7.2%	12

Year	LEnd	Rank	LTckl	Rank	MdGrd	Rank	RTckl	Rank	REnd	Rank
2002	5.10	30	4.37	21	4.44	24	4.16	17	4.50	23
2003	4.07	14	3.62	8	3.42	2	3.77	9	4.17	22
2004	4.64	23	4.56	23	3.99	9	4.42	24	3.94	19

Pro Bowl tackles Marcus Stroud and John Henderson are the center of everything Jacksonville does defensively. Despite being big men, they are not cut in the mold of space-eating tackles like Gilbert Brown and Ted Washington. They are able to make the plays themselves, as seen by their combined 129 tackles and ten sacks. Their play created open space in the defense for middle linebacker Mike Peterson, and he had the best season of his career with 126 tackles and five sacks of his own.

The rest of the front seven left something to be desired. The Jaguars cut Hugh Douglass in training camp and went with a rotation of defensive ends that neither stopped the run nor got to the quarterback. There aren't a lot of teams where the defensive tackles make twice as many plays as the ends. To alleviate this problem, they have imported Reggie Hayward from the Broncos and Marcellus Wiley from the Cowboys. Hayward had 11 sacks and 26 Defeats, more than all the Jacksonville ends combined. As right defensive end, he helped the Broncos rank in the top ten against runs left end and left tackle. The Jaguars, using converted linebacker Greg Favors at defensive end, ranked 23rd in the league against similar runs. At linebacker, the Jaguars got solid play from Akin Ayodele, but little from rookie Daryl Smith. Hayward's arrival means Favors can shift back to linebacker and compete with Smith for the starting position.

Defensive Secondary

Year	DVOA vs. #1 WR	Rank	DVOA vs. #2 WR	Rank	DVOA vs. Other WR	Rank	DVOA vs. TE	Rank	DVOA vs. RB	Rank
2002	-2.1%	12	19.9%	22	-45.0%	2	37.9%	32	5.3%	17
2003	9.1%	20	6.8%	21	-4.4%	20	-4.3%	13	-13.2%	8
2004	-4.0%	12	7.7%	19	-31.6%	2	-5.8%	13	-1.4%	22

The Jaguars were one of the few teams in football who had all four starters in their secondary play all 16 games. Safety Donovan Darius had arguably the best season of his seven-year career, setting career highs in tackles and interceptions. Darius, always known for his hard-hitting style and ability to stuff the run, developed over the past year into one of the league's strongest safeties in pass coverage as well as contract whining. The other safety, ex-Panther Deon Grant, is solid in pass coverage and a nice complement to Darius.

The top cornerback is Rashean Mathis, a physical corner who broke in as a safety. An emerging star, he was unfazed by the new emphasis on illegal contact and collected five interceptions. The other starter, veteran DeWayne Washington, serviceable though nothing special, was released. The Jaguars will turn to nickelback Kiwaukee "The Ming of Beers" Thomas to step in as the starter. Thomas has performed well in a reserve role for the last several seasons, but he will likely be tested early and often by opposing teams' quarterbacks. His promotion to starter leaves the Jags thin at corner with undersized (5'8") third-round draft pick Scott Starks serving as the nickelback. At Wisconsin, Starks was great in man coverage and always aware of where the play was, but his stone hands made him king of the interception-turned-pass deflection.

Special Teams

Year	DVOA	Rank	FG/XP	Rank	Net Punt	Rank	Punt Ret	Rank	Net Kick	Rank	Kick Ret	Rank
2002	0.2%	15	-11.1	30	12.4	6	8.1	8	-5.5	22	-2.8	19
2003	-6.6%	32	-19.5	32	-4.3	24	0.7	13	-7.1	28	-6.4	26
2004	-1.0%	20	-2.5	23	-3.2	25	-3.2	12	8.0	8	-4.8	25

Jacksonville's slightly below average special teams were still a major improvement from the black hole of 2003. Much of that improvement came from the powerful leg of kicker Josh Scobee, a fifth-round pick who took over for the disastrous Seth Marler. The change accounted for an improvement of 32 points, roughly equivalent to trading Eddie George for Priest Holmes.

Punter Chris Hanson will always have a special place in our hearts as the inspiration for the "Keep Choppin' Wood" award, given weekly on our website to the player who does the most to help his team lose. (This was the Jacksonville motivational slogan two years ago, which Hanson took literally by swinging an ax in the locker room—accidentally cutting into his foot and ending his 2003 season early.) Hanson was never considered for the award himself, since his punts were worth 6.7 points worth of field position, but he might want to nominate the porous coverage team, which turned those punts into a net negative. As for returns, the Jaguars brought Jermaine Lewis in to run back kicks before the 2003 season, but he has played only 11 games in two seasons. With Lewis missing most of the season, David Allen filled in returning punts and Troy Edwards returned kickoffs. Both replacements did better than Lewis had done in the first half of the year.

Coaching Staff

Jack Del Rio was hired as the Jaguars head coach after only one season at the coordinator level. It was a bold move considering more experienced coordinators such as Charlie Weis, Romeo Crennel, and Ted Cottrell were available. Two years of experience have helped Del Rio learn from his mistakes—he no longer keeps sharp-bladed lumberjack equipment in the locker room, for example—and he has successfully molded the Jacksonville franchise in his image. This off-season he shook things up by changing most of his offensive staff, including hiring a new offensive coordinator, Carl Smith. Smith has not been a coordinator since his days with Jim Mora almost ten years ago, but he sees eye to eye with Del Rio on a run-heavy offense that, when it does pass, takes advantage of Leftwich's arm with long throws down the field. On the defensive side, coordinator Mike "not David" Smith returns for his third season. He suffers from the same fate as many coordinators who work under a head coach who built his reputation on the same side of the ball as the coordinator. The Jaguars' defensive improvement is usually credited to Del Rio, and the excellent job being done by Smith is ignored. His ability to build schemes that pressure the quarterback despite terrible performances from his defensive ends is just one example of his considerable skill.

Kansas City Chiefs

Great news, Chiefs fans: The defense has been repaired. The woeful unit that finished 31st in the league in weighted DVOA in the last two seasons, the one that gave up 85 plays of 20 or more yards and 11 scoring drives of 80-plus yards, has been patched, buttressed, spackled, and repainted. There will be as many as five new starters, including top-dollar free agents and first-round draft picks, so the defense won't be nearly as inept as the 2003 and 2004 editions.

Now the bad news: The offense is about to fall apart. The Chiefs have the oldest starting offense in the NFL. Top wide receiver Eddie Kennison is 32. Trent Green is 35, just nine months younger than Brett Favre. Priest Holmes is 31 and failed to finish two of the last three seasons because of injuries. The offensive linemen spent the off-season perusing their pension plans. There are very few young players ready to step up. It will be almost impossible for the offense to repeat the success of 2003 and 2004, and they're more likely to slip a lot than a little.

Since Joe Montana's retirement, the Chiefs have been a one-dimensional team, winning exclusively with either their offense or defense. In the Marty Schottenheimer era, the defense was loaded with Pro Bowlers like Derrick Thomas, Neil Smith, and Dale Carter, while the offense consisted of Marcus Allen and his Amazing Friends (Steve Bono! Kimble Anders! Chris Penn!). When Schottenheimer gave way to Gunther Cunningham and then Dick Vermeil, the offense surged to life, but the defense crumbled. In 1995, the Chiefs finished 1st in the league in fewest points allowed, 12th in points scored, went 13–3— and lost their first playoff game. In 2003, they finished 1st in the league in points scored, 19th in points allowed, went 13–3—and lost their first playoff game. In between, there was one other 13–3, early-playoff-exit season, mixed in with an endless string of 7–9 and 9–7 finishes.

This year, GM and Semi-Benevolent Despot Carl Peterson recognized the telltale signs of collapse. Vermeil announced that he would retire (again) at the end of the year. It was no secret that the core of the offense was getting old. So Peterson spent the off-season gearing up for one last Super Bowl surge. He abandoned the defensive philosophy of the last two seasons—"just make it good enough"—and girded the lineup with serious acquisitions like cornerback Patrick Surtain, linebacker Kendrell Bell, safety Sammy Knight, and rookie linebacker Derrick Johnson.

CHIEFS PROSPECTUS

2004 Record: 7–9

DVOA Estimated Wins: 9.5 (10th)

Pythagorean Wins: 9.0 (11th)

DVOA: 12.1% total (10th), 4.2% weighted (14th)

Adjusted Offense: 29.1 points/game (29.0% DVOA, 2nd)

Adjusted Defense: 25.8 points/game (16.2% DVOA, 28th)

Adjusted Special Teams: −0.3 points/game (−0.8% DVOA, 19th)

Variance: 15.7% (22nd)

2004: For weeks we thought they would be the sleeper second half team, until we discovered they died in their sleep.

2005: The Vermeil era ends not with a bang, but with a whimper.

2005 Projection

Leinart Land (0–4): 11%

Bad Team (5–6): 16%

Mediocre (7–8): 24%

Playoff Contender (9–10): 23%

Super Bowl Contender (11+): 26%

Projected Average Opponent: 5.1% DVOA (4th in NFL)

The Chiefs have tried this before—two seasons ago, when they signed Vonnie Holliday and Shawn Barber while drafting defensive tackles Ryan Sims and Eddie Freeman. But the logic behind those signings was different. Holliday and Barber were younger free agents, acquired to plug major holes and provide a modest upgrade. Surtain and Knight are old mercenaries; Bell and DE Carlos Hall are boom-or-bust types, expected to provide an immediate spark. Bell and Hall (and certainly Johnson) may still be around in 2007, but the two defensive backs are in the fold for one last roundup before Vermeil sings "Happy Trails."

The defensive changes will allow Cunningham—the former head coach who last year returned as defensive coordinator—to implement properly his defensive system in 2005. After the Chiefs defense imploded late in the 2003 season (yielding 45 points to the Vikings in Week 16 before surrendering 38 to the Colts in the playoffs), Cunningham replaced Greg Robinson, a coach who favored a two-gap approach on the line and a read-and-react style in

TABLE 1. CHIEFS RAW DEFENSIVE STATS, 2003–2004

Year	Rush Yds	Pass Yds	Yd/Rush	Yd/Pass	Int	Sacks
2003	2344	3363	5.2	6.4	25	36
2004	1834	4203	4.6	8.5	13	41

the secondary. Cunningham prefers man coverage, frequent blitzes, and a one-gap philosophy on the line. (One-gap assignments allow defensive lineman to be more aggressive at the snap; two-gap assignments are more conservative.) Cunningham's schemes promised more big plays, but as the 2004 season played out, the difference in coaching styles was barely noticeable on the stat sheet (table 1).

Under Cunningham the Chiefs were marginally better against the run and had a few more sacks. However, the pass defense got worse, and the team's defensive strength in 2003—the ability to force turnovers—evaporated. The Chiefs went from a bad defense that could hide some of its deficiencies by intercepting passes to a bad defense that could not.

Cunningham's philosophy was the same as when he ran the great Kansas City defenses of the mid-1990s: He eschewed zone coverage so he could bring a heavy pass rush, daring you to beat his corners man-to-man. In the NFL of 1995 with Dale Carter and James Hasty at cornerback, this worked. In the NFL of 2005, when the average receiver is taller and faster and you have Dexter McCleon and Eric Warfield at cornerback, you're screwed. In today's NFL, offensive coordinators believe their best receivers can beat your best corners, and even if the defensive back is with the receiver when the ball leaves the quarterback's hand, the quarterback believes the receiver will have separation by the time the ball gets there.

The constant blitzing did have some impact—Kansas City's defensive line had 59 tackles for a loss (sixth in the league) as blockers peeled off to battle linebackers—but it came at a horrible cost. Opposing wide receivers averaged 17.4 yards per catch against the Chiefs, almost two yards more than the second-worst team in the NFL. Our breakdown of pass defense by receiver type shows that the Kansas City cornerbacks simply could not cover the other team's best receivers. The Chiefs had a 32.7% defensive DVOA against opposing number one wideouts, 27th in the NFL. They had a −19.1% DVOA against opposing number two wideouts, 2nd in the NFL. They kept Jerome Pathon to 33 yards while Joe Horn was getting 167. They kept Eddie Berlin to 4 yards while Drew Bennett was getting 233.

Adding to the problem was the play of the linebackers and safeties. Last year the Chiefs were 26th in the league against opposing third or fourth receivers and 31st defending passes to running backs. For two straight years now, the Chiefs have been one of the worst teams in the league against opposing tight ends, which is inexcusable. Don't these guys practice against Tony Gonzalez? Forget Antonio Gates; the Chiefs gave up 47 receiving yards to Ken Dilger and 50 receiving yards to Shad Meier.

Cunningham's scheme won't change much this year, but it won't have to—the newcomers can make the system work. Surtain can handle most top wide receivers one-on-one; McCleon or Warfield will be able to handle second wideouts. Bell comes from a 3-4 system where he usually was allowed to attack the line of scrimmage at the snap. Cunningham will allow him to run blitz and fill gaps; he'll be much more effective in that role than Kawika Mitchell and the others who tried to play the middle last year. When Bell shoots the gap, other players will have to seal cutback lanes. Knight is an effective in-the-box safety, and while Johnson is similar to Barber in many ways (a speedster who will run around some blocks), his field smarts help him range over a wider area while his ability to strip the ball gives the Chiefs a better shot at that game-changing turnover. Hall will play on third downs, teaming with Jared Allen, last year's rookie surprise, to provide an effective pair of rush ends.

Put it all together and the Chiefs defense won't be awful anymore—it will probably be a bit better than mediocre. The offense just has to keep it together for one more year. Unfortunately, there's plenty of evidence that the offense may burn up in reentry.

Take a moment to thumb through the projections in the player comments—we'll wait. Holmes is due for a decline. Gonzalez is due for a decline. Eddie Kennison is due for a decline. Johnnie Morton is now gone. Exacerbating the situation is that three offensive linemen are aged 32 or older. There might be less cause for alarm if a few hot young stars were ready to grab the reins of the offense, but the most exciting young player on the team is a guy Peterson would have traded for a cleat cleaner this time last year, backup running back Larry Johnson.

Three years of intense work on the defense has taken a predictable toll on the offense. No major free agent dollars have been spent on the offense since the team acquired Morton and Willie Roaf in 2002. The draft strategy over the past three seasons has been to spend one first-day pick on an offensive player—Johnson, Kris Wilson, Craphonso Thorpe—then go back to defense, defense, and more defense. The offense behind the frontline talent is now gutted. Johnson could replace Holmes with only a slight drop-off, but if Wilson or Jason Dunn had to replace Gonzo, or if Thorpe or Sammie Parker had to step in for Kennison, or if anyone had to replace the durable Green or Roaf, it would get ugly real fast at Arrowhead.

The question for Chiefs fans, then, is one of timing. Have Surtain and company arrived in time? Can the offense sustain 30-point-per-game production for another year while the revamped defense cuts opponents under 20 points per game? Can the new defense succeed in a division where there are no weakling offenses, against a schedule that also features the Eagles and Patriots?

Maybe. The statistics suggest that the Chiefs shaved about ten points off their defensive stats at just about the same time the offense shed ten points of its own. That would leave the Chiefs between seven and nine wins again, with a roster full of even more 30-somethings, with the same dearth of young talent on offense, and with a new coach facing the task of sorting things out. That new coach could be offensive coordinator Al Saunders, but if the offense does flop, Peterson will look outside the organization. Peterson, with a new contract extension, is the one man whose job is safe. He'll be the one operating the bulldozer when this latest renovation plan fails.

Mike Tanier

Research: Tony Gonzalez, Past and Future

In 2004, Tony Gonzalez led the Kansas City Chiefs in receiving yards for the third time in four years and the fourth time in six years.

It's not unusual for a tight end to lead his team in receiving yards for a season or two, but it's rare for a tight end to do so for an extended period of time. Most of the great receiving tight ends of recent history—Winslow, Novacek, Brett Jones—shared the spotlight with a great wide receiver or two. Even tight ends who are the focal point of the passing game often finish second or third on the team in receiving yards. Jimmie Giles was a four-time Pro Bowler for the Buccaneers, but he led the team in receiving only once; Kevin House, a deep-threat receiver, usually gained more yards.

Table 2 shows the only tight ends to lead their teams in receiving yards three or four out of four years in the Super Bowl era. Apologies to Mike Ditka, who did it in the early 1960s when many teams still had just "ends."

What do these teams have in common? Surprisingly, their offenses were pretty good. Newsome's Browns didn't have great yardage totals but finished 3rd, 16th, and 10th in points scored in three of his seasons. Christensen's Raiders never finished below 15th in the league in points or 16th in yards. Odoms's Broncos were in the top ten in points all three years. Smith's Cardinals were fourth in points in the 16-team NFL in 1968. Only Tucker, playing for some miserable Giants teams, was a "default" guy who

TABLE 2. TEs WHO LED THEIR TEAM IN RECEIVING YARDS THREE OR MORE TIMES

Team	Player	Years
Chiefs	Tony Gonzalez	1999, 2001, 2003–2004
Browns	Ozzie Newsome	1981–1985
Broncos	Riley Odoms	1973–1975
Raiders	Todd Christensen	1983–1986
Cardinals	Jackie Smith	1966–1968
Giants	Bob Tucker	1971–1974, 1976

led the team in receiving because the team was consistently so terrible that there was no one else to throw to.

Newsome, Christensen, Smith, and Odoms were all great players, but they didn't last long. Newsome's last productive season was 1985, when he was 29 years old. Christensen made the Pro Bowl at age 31, but retired a year later. Odoms didn't catch over 40 passes in a season after he turned 30. Smith made his last Pro Bowl in 1970 at age 30, and although he hung around for eight years after that, only once did he gain over 425 yards receiving—a mark he had surpassed in every one of his first eight seasons. Tight end is a grueling position, and many of the best receivers at the position, from Mark Bavaro to Ben Coates, are too beaten up by age 30 to sustain their production.

Gonzo will turn 30 next February, and the Chiefs hope he can join the players on table 3 as one of the most productive older tight ends in history. But three of those players reached the age of 29 without much wear and tear. Shuler didn't top 30 catches in a season until 1984, when he was 28. Christensen was strictly a special-teamer his first two seasons and didn't play a full season as the starter until 1983, when he was already 27. Walls was a scrub in San Francisco for five years and had a total of 11 recep-

TABLE 3. BEST TE SEASONS, AGE 29 AND OLDER

Player	Team	Year	Rec	Yds	TD	Age
Todd Christensen	RAI	1986	95	1153	8	30
Shannon Sharpe	DEN	1997	72	1107	3	29
Todd Christensen	RAI	1985	82	987	6	29
Mickey Shuler	NYJ	1985	76	879	7	29
Wesley Walls	CAR	1999	63	822	12	33
Shannon Sharpe	BAL	2001	73	811	2	33
Shannon Sharpe	BAL	2000	67	810	5	32
Mickey Shuler	NYJ	1988	70	805	5	32

tions until he finally became a starter at the age of 28. Gonzalez, on the other hand, has been a regular from the time he joined the league in 1997 at the tender age of 21.

Gonzalez will have one or two more seasons in the 65-catch, 800-yard range. Then, one of two things will happen—he'll hang around for several years like Sharpe, Newsome, and Smith, or he will age quickly and suddenly walk away from the game. For Gonzalez, who once spent an off-season trying out for the NBA, a long, lingering second career as a 30-catch brawler seems unlikely.

If the Chiefs resemble any of the teams in table 2, offensively, it's the Christensen-era Raiders. That team had a star running back in Marcus Allen who was also a major part of the passing game, as is Priest Holmes. Those Raiders teams had receivers like Dokie Williams, Jessie Hester, and Malcolm Barnwell (as well as the aging Cliff Branch)—guys who went deep but didn't rack up a lot of yards on possession receptions. Eddie Kennison and company play similar roles. The Raiders won a Super Bowl with Christensen leading the team in receptions and yards, but that was when both Christensen and Allen were young. By 1986, both players were past their peak and the Christensen-Allen formula was yielding 8–8 records. The similarities between those teams and the 2003–2005 Chiefs are apparent.

Once Christensen left the Raiders, the offensive suffered an identity crisis. Al Davis kept shouting "Throw it deep!" but it was useless with no great tight end to work the middle. The Raiders kept finishing in the middle of the pack offensively despite big-name running backs like Allen, Bo Jackson, and Roger Craig. The Broncos of Odoms's era suffered a similar fate. Odoms tailed off, Red Miller tried to build around aging wide receivers Haven Moses and Ricky Upchurch (the Eddie Kennison and Dante Hall of the 1970s), and the offense sunk to below the league average. Only Newsome's Browns got better as Newsome declined, thanks to the rise of Bernie Kosar at quarterback.

So while it's possible to win a Super Bowl with an offense centered around the tight end, it's also very rare, and it had better happen while that tight end is at the peak of his powers. The best bet for the Chiefs would be to start making adjustments now by developing better receivers and designing plays that will allow Gonzo to remain as fresh as possible for as long as possible. Unfortunately, the team had to devote 90 percent of its resources over the last three years to fixing the defense. The Chiefs are now primed to watch their Pro Bowl tight end run a fade route, taking the team's fortunes with him.

Mike Tanier

Chiefs 2004 Stats by Week

Wk	vs.	W-L	PF	PA	YDF	YDA	TO	Total	Off	Def	ST
1	@DEN	L	24	34	318	413	+2	25.1%	24.2%	-7.4%	-6.5%
2	CAR	L	17	28	281	358	0	6.0%	-2.8%	-12.0%	-3.2%
3	HOU	L	21	24	364	296	0	45.1%	22.7%	-16.0%	6.4%
4	@BAL	W	27	24	398	207	0	21.1%	56.1%	12.5%	-22.4%
5	BYE										
6	@JAC	L	16	22	350	378	-1	-49.9%	11.4%	43.8%	-17.5%
7	ATL	W	56	10	540	222	+1	104.5%	66.6%	-57.0%	-19.2%
8	IND	W	45	35	590	505	-1	58.1%	59.3%	-0.3%	-1.6%
9	@TB	L	31	34	459	418	-3	-27.3%	36.5%	67.9%	4.2%
10	@NO	L	20	27	497	374	-3	0.8%	12.8%	16.3%	4.3%
11	NE	L	19	27	417	411	0	-5.5%	30.4%	38.0%	2.1%
12	SD	L	31	34	310	498	-2	11.0%	25.9%	36.7%	21.8%
13	@OAK	W	34	27	500	364	-1	-23.8%	35.3%	59.5%	0.3%
14	@TEN	W	49	38	383	542	+2	-5.6%	13.3%	35.7%	16.8%
15	DEN	W	45	17	410	402	+2	71.5%	55.2%	-3.0%	13.3%
16	OAK	W	31	30	433	300	-1	-19.7%	5.6%	21.1%	-4.2%
17	@SD	L	17	24	443	363	-2	-19.1%	-3.6%	8.3%	-7.2%

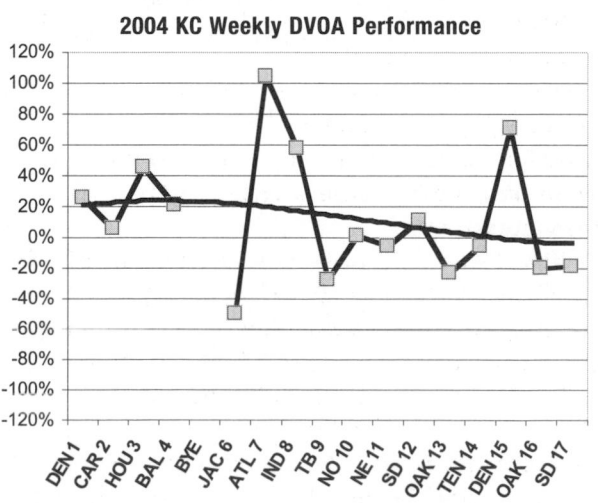

2004 KC Weekly DVOA Performance

Trends and Splits

	Offense	Rank	Defense	Rank
Total DVOA	29.0%	2	16.2%	28
Unadjusted VOA	31.1%	3	26.4%	32
Weighted Trend	27.8%	2	25.8%	31
Variance	4.9%	31	10.0%	15
Passing	36.7%	4	20.6%	26
Rushing	21.1%	1	10.5%	27
First Down	25.4%	3	3.3%	15
Second Down	21.0%	5	27.8%	30
Third Down	56.9%	2	29.5%	28
Red Zone	9.1%	12	7.2%	22
Late and Close	14.2%	9	24.2%	32

Five-Year Performance

	2004	2003	2002	2001	2000
W-L	7-9	13-3	8-8	6-10	7-9
Pythagorean Wins	9.0	11.4	9.5	7.3	8.0
Estimated Wins	9.5	11.0	9.5	7.2	8.2
Total DVOA	12.1%	29.6%	17.4%	-1.7%	-0.1%
Rank	10	1	6	17	18
Offense	29.0%	28.4%	29.6%	4.4%	8.1%
Rank	2	1	1	6	9
Defense	16.2%	4.5%	13.3%	6.0%	4.1%
Rank	28	21	28	24	19
Special Teams	-0.8%	5.7%	1.2%	-0.1%	-4.1%
Rank	19	2	12	16	27

Passing (min. 5 plays)

Player	DPAR	PAR	DVOA	Plys	NtYds	Avg	Cmpl	TD	Int
Trent Green	102.9	114.3	27.7%	587	4360	7.4	66.4%	27	16
Todd Collins	0.8	0.6	25.8%	5	42	8.4	20.0%	0	0

Rushing (min. 3 plays)

Player	DPAR	PAR	DVOA	Plys	Yds	Avg	TD	Fum	Suc
Priest Holmes	26.9	26.0	16.3%	196	892	4.6	14	4	53%
Larry Johnson	24.0	21.8	28.0%	120	581	4.8	9	0	53%
Derrick Blaylock	22.1	22.0	25.9%	118	539	4.6	8	0	57%
Trent Green	4.4	4.2	37.3%	14	94	6.7	0	0	—
Tony Richardson	2.4	2.2	33.8%	12	56	4.7	0	0	58%
Dante Hall	1.5	1.6	0.2%	8	56	7.0	0	0	—
Johnnie Morton	-1.0	-0.9	-51.8%	7	43	6.1	0	1	—
Omar Easy	-1.1	-1.2	-99.8%	4	1	0.3	0	0	25%

Receiving (min. 5 plays)

Player	DPAR	PAR	DVOA	Plys	Ctch	Yds	Y/C	TD	CPct
WR									
Eddie Kennison	24.7	27.1	19.2%	106	62	1086	17.5	8	58%
Johnnie Morton	19.3	21.0	24.4%	74	55	731	13.3	3	68%
Dante Hall	1.1	2.1	-11.2%	36	25	206	8.2	0	64%
Chris Horn	2.8	3.0	9.1%	17	15	118	7.9	1	59%
Samie Parker	4.5	5.0	36.8%	13	9	137	15.2	1	69%
TE									
Tony Gonzalez	43.1	43.6	35.9%	141	102	1216	11.9	7	70%
Jason Dunn	1.3	1.5	-3.1%	21	17	97	5.7	3	67%
RB									
Derrick Blaylock	4.6	4.8	17.6%	36	25	244	9.8	1	69%
Larry Johnson	13.0	13.1	76.9%	28	22	278	12.6	2	79%
Priest Holmes	3.6	4.0	18.5%	25	19	190	10.0	1	76%
Tony Richardson	-1.5	-1.0	-23.4%	23	19	108	5.7	0	74%

Defensive Players (min. 20 plays)

Player	Age	Plys	Stop	Dfts	AvYds	StpRt	Sack	Int	FR
Defensive Line									
John Browning	32	40	30	10	2.4	75%	4.5	0	0
Eric Hicks	29	34	25	11	1.5	74%	5.0	0	0
Jared Allen	23	30	24	12	-0.4	80%	9.0	0	0
Lionel Dalton	30	22	18	11	-0.2	82%	4.0	0	1
Linebackers									
Scott Fujita	26	93	50	20	6.5	54%	4.5	0	0
Kawika Mitchell	26	75	46	19	4.3	61%	1.0	0	2
Monty Beisel	27	53	28	9	4.5	53%	2.5	1	1
Shawn Barber	30	37	22	11	5.5	59%	1.0	1	0
Quinton Caver	27	30	12	3	6.9	40%	0.0	0	0

Player	Age	Plys	Stop	Dfts	AvYds	StpRt	Sack	Int	FR
Secondary									
Greg Wesley	27	75	23	14	11.1	31%	0.0	4	0
Eric Warfield	29	73	26	17	12.4	36%	0.0	4	0
Dexter McCleon	32	50	17	9	9.2	34%	0.0	2	1
William Bartee	28	48	15	7	9.9	31%	1.5	0	0
Jerome Woods	32	45	10	6	12.6	22%	1.0	0	0
Shaunard Harts	27	44	7	3	12.5	16%	0.0	0	0
Willie Pile	25	30	7	2	9.5	23%	0.0	0	0

Offensive Line

Year	Yards	AdjLineYd	Rank	Power	Rank	10+ Yds	Rank	Stuff	Rank	Sack	AdjSack%	Rank
2002	4.72	4.54	3	76%	5	16%	17	22%	12	26	5.5%	11
2003	4.34	4.49	3	67%	14	14%	22	23%	13	20	4.1%	4
2004	4.60	4.70	3	70%	8	16%	23	18%	2	32	6.6%	17

Year	LEnd	Rank	LTckl	Rank	MdGrd	Rank	RTckl	Rank	REnd	Rank
2002	5.15	4	5.18	2	4.79	2	4.01	20	3.31	25
2003	5.01	3	5.02	4	4.36	10	4.67	7	4.11	13
2004	4.81	8	4.35	18	4.76	3	3.97	17	4.91	3

Like the rest of us, guards usually have to take I-77 to get to Canton, but Will Shields has a legitimate claim for enshrinement. He has eight Pro Bowl appearances and has blocked for superstars like Joe Montana, Marcus Allen, and Priest Holmes. He's also one of the few offensive linemen who ever earned major endorsement deals (remember the Subway ads?), so he has name recognition. If the Chiefs can reach the Super Bowl while Shields is still starting, that could propel him into the Hall. But Shields considered retirement in the off-season, which reveals the downside of starting a potential Hall of Famer—chances are, the guy's pretty old. Shields turns 34 at the start of the season, left tackle Willie Roaf is 35, and center Chris Weigmann turns 32 in July. Last year, Derrick Blaylock and Larry Johnson showed that it is easy to have success behind this line. But this line is just a couple of high ankle sprains or Achilles tendon tears away from a complete collapse.

Defensive Front Seven

Year	Yards	AdjLineYd	Rank	Power	Rank	10+ Yds	Rank	Stuff	Rank	Sack	AdjSack%	Rank
2002	4.72	4.34	23	74%	25	21%	29	19%	30	33	5.7%	22
2003	5.15	4.43	23	67%	23	27%	32	22%	25	35	5.6%	23
2004	4.63	3.97	7	67%	23	25%	29	29%	4	42	7.8%	7

Year	LEnd	Rank	LTckl	Rank	MdGrd	Rank	RTckl	Rank	REnd	Rank
2002	4.54	26	4.63	26	4.08	10	4.79	30	4.52	25
2003	4.86	31	5.31	31	4.39	23	4.77	29	2.92	5
2004	4.51	20	4.41	18	3.83	6	4.28	20	2.86	6

The shocking truth about the Kansas City run defense is that part of it was actually very good in 2004. That part would be the defensive line, which was near the top of the league at stuffing runners at the line of scrimmage. Once a running back got to the second level, however, he could basically run until he hit Mexico. Against Carolina, the crowd resorted to holding up signs that said "Stop, DeShaun Foster, Stop." Foster was just one of the Low Success Rate All-Stars that had big games against the Chiefs because every run went for either 2 or 20. All four backs who rung up 100-yard days against the Chiefs had a Success Rate of 43% or less: Foster, Quentin Griffin, Michael Pittman, and Deuce McAllister.

The right side of the defense (defending left-side runs) was a huge problem. Right end Vonnie Holliday got hurt and was replaced by Jared Allen, a long snapper turned pass rusher who isn't the most instinctive run defender. A revolving door of linebackers started on the right side: Shawn Barber, Quentin Caver, and Monty Beisel. Beisel is now in New England, and Patriots fans are still trying to figure out why. Caver was re-signed but will be beaten by rookie Derrick Johnson for the starting job.

Kendrell Bell was known as a blitzer in Pittsburgh, but he has the athletic ability to be a fine all-around middle linebacker. He has the size and strength to fill the hole, something most of last year's starters lacked. He'll replace Kawika Mitchell, who often looked lost in coverage and got blocked too easily in run defense.

Defensive Secondary

Year	DVOA vs. #1 WR	Rank	DVOA vs. #2 WR	Rank	DVOA vs. Other WR	Rank	DVOA vs. TE	Rank	DVOA vs. RB	Rank
2002	7.6%	24	6.9%	16	17.4%	27	33.9%	30	21.7%	29
2003	46.6%	32	-47.2%	1	-31.9%	7	36.8%	30	4.5%	18
2004	32.7%	27	-19.1%	2	21.2%	26	36.9%	29	17.7%	31

After years of watching Dexter McCleon, Eric Warfield, and William Bartee run with their receivers, fail to track the ball in the air, and get out-jumped for 40-yard receptions, Chiefs fans will be thrilled to see Patrick Surtain covering opponents' top receivers. Similarly, safety Sammy Knight's smarts and hard hitting will provide relief from four years of Greg Wesley and Jerome Woods, who specialized in missing open field tackles and tracking down running backs after 12-yard gains. Surtain and Knight will be 29 and 30 when the season starts, so they are "win now" additions, not long-term solutions. Knight has already become somewhat limited in coverage, so opponents will go out of their way to match him up man-on-man with slot receivers or Antonio Gates-type tight ends. Wesley and Woods, meanwhile, both grumbled about having to compete for a starting job, and both have suggested that they won't accept a bench role. That, boys and girls, is why there is something called a "waiver wire."

Special Teams

Year	DVOA	Rank	FG/XP	Rank	Net Punt	Rank	Punt Ret	Rank	Net Kick	Rank	Kick Ret	Rank
2002	1.2%	12	6.3	6	-9.1	25	5.7	10	-6.2	25	10.1	5
2003	5.7%	2	5.1	14	2.9	16	12.0	4	-3.5	22	15.1	2
2004	-0.8%	19	-3.6	27	-13.4	32	-5.8	19	-4.2	23	22.7	1

Dante Hall had "only" two kick return touchdowns last year, leading some analysts to wonder why the Chiefs' special teams had slipped. The phrase is "regression to the mean," but that fact didn't stop color commentators from saying that Hall was tired from playing too much on offense or whatever. Hall actually had very few punt return opportunities—opponents only punted against the Chiefs 60 times, the fourth-lowest total in the NFL. When they did punt, they were often close to midfield, leading to touchbacks and hard-to-return kicks near the end zone. Thanks to the defense, Hall got plenty of kickoff return practice, but if the Chiefs want to use their punt returner as a weapon, they'll have to get opponents to punt more often.

    The Chiefs chose punter Dustin Colquitt in the third round, which is almost as absurd as taking a kicker in the second round. But unlike the Jets, who wasted a pick so they could fill a hole that didn't actually exist, the Chiefs at least were trying to fix an area where they were at the bottom of the league. Opponents averaged 34.1 yards per drive against the Chiefs last year (31st in the NFL), so moving them back three or four more yards will prevent a few scores. Lawrence Tynes missed two extra points last year, which sums his problems up rather nicely.

Coaching Staff

Dick Vermeil has stated that he will retire for a third time after this season—if Vermeil was a rock band, he would be the Rolling Stones, who have a farewell tour every eight years. Offensive coordinator Al Saunders appears to be Vermeil's heir apparent. Saunders was 17–22 as the Chargers coach in the mid-1980s, the era when the Marx Brothers (Mark Hermann, Mark Malone, Mark Vlasic) were trying to replace Dan Fouts at quarterback. But that's ancient history. Saunders is the architect of a unique offense that allows Trent Green to serve as a point guard, distributing the ball to playmakers like Priest Holmes and letting them create in the open field. Saunders was also wide receivers coach for the Greatest Show on Turf (the 1999 Rams), so he knows offense. Unless the Chiefs really tank, look for this insular organization to promote from within.

    Vermeil's staff is a virtual Who's Who of assistant coaches. Defensive line coach Bob Karmelowicz has a rep as one of the best position coaches in the game, yet Coach Karm hasn't developed many top prospects in the past few years. DE Jared Allen may become a gem if he can improve as a run defender, and Ryan Sims still has potential if he can stay healthy and focused for 60 snaps per game, but several players like Eddie Freeman turned out to be busts on Karmelowicz's watch. The defensive line is the one unit of the defense that got minimal attention in the off-season, with Carlos Hall as the only significant addition. Coach Karm will have to make the most of his unproven line of Hall, Sims, Allen, Lional Dalton, and Junior Siavii.

Miami Dolphins

Miami Dolphins fans are not used to losing. Winning for most of the season only to fall apart in December or the playoffs? Absolutely—that they are used to. But outright failure? This was new. The 2004 Miami Dolphins lost more games than any team in the history of the franchise. The team had not lost more than ten games in a season since the AFL and NFL merged in 1970. In fact, until last year's debacle, the Dolphins had only *two* losing seasons since 1970: 6–10 in 1988 and 6–8 in 1976.

From the very start of the 2004 off-season, nothing seemed to go right for the Dolphins. Living legend Dan Marino was hired as general manager and quit three weeks later. Offensive coordinator Norv Turner was hired away by Oakland to be head coach. His replacement, Joel Collier, quit due to "exhaustion" within three months.

The coaching issues paled, however, compared to the sudden retirement of star running back Ricky Williams on the eve of training camp. Williams proceeded to change his mind about retiring, un-retiring and re-retiring roughly 146 times over the course of the next six months, all the while being publicly psychoanalyzed by everyone from Dr. Phil to Mike Ditka. The Dolphins vowed to run a similar ground-oriented offense without Williams and spent the season flailing about in search of a running back who could stay healthy for five or six minutes.

They traded a third-round draft pick to St. Louis for Lamar Gordon, only to see him go down for the season with a separated shoulder in his third game. Both backups, Travis Minor and Sammy Morris, went down with sprained ankles in the first game of the season and missed several weeks. The Dolphins continued to run an offense built on a straight-ahead ground attack even when that ground attack consisted of practice squad player Leonard Henry and third-string Chicago washout Brock Forsey.

The correct response to the Williams retirement would have been to shift the team's style to reflect the its remaining offensive strength. Although its quarterbacks were never impressive, Miami had two good receivers in Chris Chambers and Marty Booker and a strong tight end in Randy McMichael. But Dave Wannstedt changed nothing. The Dolphins continued the battering ram approach— 74% of their runs had a listed direction of middle or guard, the most in the league by far. Only one other team, Oakland, was above 60%.

DOLPHINS PROSPECTUS

2004 Record: 4–12

DVOA Estimated Wins: 6.3 (25th)

Pythagorean Wins: 5.7 (27th)

DVOA: −15.5% total (25th), −7.3% weighted (22nd)

Adjusted Offense: 13.9 points/game (−28.5% DVOA, 31st)

Adjusted Defense: 19.7 points/game (−7.5% DVOA, 9th)

Adjusted Special Teams: +1.9 points/game (5.4% DVOA, 4th)

Variance: 18.8% (15th)

2004: Dude, I am like, so wasted right now.

2005: If you liked the 2000 Patriots, you'll love the 2005 Dolphins.

2005 Projection

Leinart Land (0–4): 31%

Bad Team (5–6): 26%

Mediocre (7–8): 22%

Playoff Contender (9–10): 12%

Super Bowl Contender (11+): 9%

Projected Average Opponent: 5.6% DVOA (2nd in NFL)

Even so, the biggest problem wasn't the parade of replacement-level runners but the men blocking for them— or, rather, not blocking for them. The Dolphins blew through three quarterbacks and a half-dozen different running backs and every single one of them had problems because the line was horrible. The Miami line was last in Adjusted Line Yards, last in allowing runners to be stuffed at the line of scrimmage, and 26th in Adjusted Sack Rate. Nobody on the right side of the line had started a single game the year before, while third-year center Seth McKinney had started a grand total of three. Over on the left, tackle Wade Smith was so bad in his second year that he was yanked from the starting lineup after only two games.

The inept offense meant that the skilled Miami defense spent a lot of time on the field, and it clearly showed. Table 1 shows how the Dolphins controlled opponents in the first quarter, but gradually gave up more yards per play as the game progressed and the defense became exhausted.

TABLE 1. MIAMI DEFENSE BY QUARTER, 2004

Qtr	NFL Avg. Yd/Play	MIA Yd/Play	MIA DVOA
Q1	5.39	4.56	−15.6%
Q2	5.45	4.92	−4.1%
Q3	5.24	5.33	−3.3%
Q4	5.20	5.02	−4.2%

TABLE 2. MIAMI DEFENSE BY WEEK, 2004

Weeks	MIA DVOA	Yd/Play	Turnovers per Game*
1–5	−30.1%	4.12	1.8
6–9	30.4%	6.01	0.5
11–17	−12.6%	4.89	3.4

* Includes fumbles both lost and kept

The Dolphins went into their bye week 1–8 and Wannstedt finally saw the writing on the wall and quit. He was replaced by defensive coordinator Jim Bates, who somehow convinced the team to play hard over the final seven weeks. The defense, which had given up after the first five losses, returned to its early-season form. The difference between Miami in Weeks 6–9 and Miami the rest of the season is fairly substantial, as table 2 shows.

Bates didn't just change the defensive attitude of this team, he also changed the offensive philosophy. Bates had the offense throw more passes, and when he did run, he ran his backs to the outside more often (table 3). With Bates as head coach and every unit on the team playing better, the Dolphins went 3–4, including a shocking upset of the Super Bowl champion Patriots on *Monday Night Football*.

After the season, the Dolphins had two alternatives. They could have kept Bates as the head coach, used draft picks and free agent dollars on offensive linemen so as to

TABLE 3. MIAMI PLAY CALLING UNDER DAVE WANNSTEDT AND JIM BATES, 2004

First Half Plays*	Pass	Rush
Wannstedt	55%	45%
Bates	63%	37%

Runs by Direction	Middle	Guard	End/Tackle
Wannstedt	47%	27%	26%
Bates	40%	28%	32%

* Includes first half only to filter out influence of the score late in the game

improve the offense to league average, and tried to ride their great defense back to respectability. Or, they could have made a big splash with a big-name head coach who would be given substantial power and a directive to rebuild the franchise from the ground up.

Miami chose the latter, hiring Nick Saban and giving him full reign over the entire operation. Saban had been a rumored candidate for numerous NFL and college jobs over the past couple of seasons, and the Dolphins were finally able to entice him away from Louisiana State.

Saban's record as a head coach is impressive: 9–2 with Toledo, 34–24–1 with Michigan State, 48–15 (and a national championship) with LSU. But his record as a defensive coordinator might be even more impressive. Table 4 looks at the Cleveland Browns during the four seasons that Saban was defensive coordinator (1991–1994), as well as the season before he arrived and the season after he left. The Browns' defense improved enormously when Saban arrived. Now, we'll be the first to acknowledge that had a lot to do with the fact that Bill Belichick had arrived as the head coach. But while Belichick was still the head coach in 1995, Saban was gone and the defense declined significantly.

Perhaps the greatest myth surrounding Saban is that he believes a 3-4 defense is the way to win. In reality, Saban thinks the way to win is whatever defense fits your talent and the circumstances of the game. The Dolphins will almost certainly employ both a 3-4 and a 4-3, depending on the circumstances and the personnel. Saban's defensive coordinator, Richard Johnson, actually has more experience with a 4-3 than a 3-4.

Saban could have asked Jim Bates to remain as defensive coordinator. Although having the head coach go back to a coordinator role might have been a little odd for the players, Bates and Saban are friends and both were on Belichick's staff in Cleveland. (That was quite a staff, by the way. It also included three guys who are now having a lot of success in college: Fresno State head coach Pat Hill, Iowa head coach Kirk Ferentz, and Virginia head coach Al Groh. The two guys doing quality control and film breakdowns, Chuck Bresnahan and Jim Schwartz, are now the defensive coordinators in Cincinnati and Tennessee, respectively. Eric Mangini, now defensive coordinator in New England, showed up in Belichick's final year.)

But letting Bates go was the first signal that this was now Saban's team and it would be rebuilt in his image. This message was reinforced by Miami's free agent signings. Saban turned over numerous defensive positions despite inheriting an already strong defense. The Dolphins will have three new starters in the secondary next year, and the team signed two big-name defensive ends, Kevin Carter and Vonnie Holliday, even though both of last year's starting defensive ends are still on the roster. Meanwhile,

TABLE 4. CLEVELAND BROWNS DEFENSE, 1990–1995

Year	Pts	Rush Yds	Pass Yds	INT	Fumbles (Recovered)	Sacks	Yd/Pass	Yd/Rush
1990	462	2105	3296	13	32 (11)	32	6.5	4.1
1991	298	1875	3445	15	33 (18)	35	5.8	4.2
1992	275	1605	3467	13	33 (20)	48	5.9	3.7
1993	307	1654	3466	13	28 (9)	48	6.4	3.7
1994	204	1669	3425	18	26 (13)	38	5.8	3.6
1995	356	1826	4013	17	20 (7)	29	6.4	3.8

on offense, Saban signed only three free agents—one was a much-needed tackle, Stockar McDougle, but the other two were a fullback and a backup quarterback.

On draft day, Saban's strategy was no different. He chose running back Ronnie Brown with the second-overall selection, but then spent Miami's next three picks on defensive players: defensive end Matt Roth of Iowa, linebacker Channing Crowder of Florida, and cornerback Travis Daniels from—surprise, surprise—Louisiana State. The Dolphins chose only one offensive player other than Brown, tackle Anthony Alabi, and that wasn't until the end of the fifth round.

The lack of attention to the offense leads us to believe that Saban is designing his defense first and will take care of offense later. Miami fans should get used to a lot of three-and-outs while they wait for later to show up.

In fact, "later" will be the buzzword for the entire season around Miami. This year is all about change, as Saban gradually puts his stamp on the entire organization. The worry about Saban is that he's in the "Belichick in Cleveland" portion of his career. Some of his early moves in Miami—trouble hiring a defensive coordinator, taking a super hard line with the media—set off alarm bells that evoke Belichick in Cleveland, circa 1994. But while Belichick had been around the NFL for a long time when he got the Cleveland job, he had never been a head coach and has admitted he struggled with some of the added responsibilities. Saban is used to all that responsibility; he just hasn't been in the league for a decade. If he can spend 2005 reacclimating himself to the professional game and next off-season upgrading the offense, this team will make a lot of noise in 2006.

Aaron Schatz
Michael David Smith

Dolphins 2004 Stats by Week

Wk	vs.	W-L	PF	PA	YDF	YDA	TO	Total	Off	Def	ST
1	TEN	L	7	17	262	243	-2	-62.4%	-78.2%	-22.5%	-6.7%
2	@CIN	L	13	16	226	210	-2	-2.8%	-41.9%	-35.3%	3.7%
3	PIT	L	3	13	169	314	-3	-46.1%	-59.1%	-22.2%	-9.2%
4	NYJ	L	9	17	293	235	-3	-20.1%	-51.3%	-24.9%	6.3%
5	@NE	L	10	24	296	207	-1	15.8%	-24.8%	-43.5%	-2.9%
6	@BUF	L	13	20	212	341	-1	-60.7%	-30.4%	32.3%	2.0%
7	STL	W	31	14	323	372	+1	18.1%	23.1%	25.6%	20.7%
8	@NYJ	L	14	41	259	472	-3	-104.8%	-49.9%	53.6%	-1.4%
9	ARI	L	23	24	403	270	-1	-3.0%	0.7%	7.7%	3.9%
10	BYE										
11	@SEA	L	17	24	288	293	-1	12.1%	-41.8%	-43.8%	10.2%
12	@SF	W	24	17	200	224	+1	-33.6%	-55.4%	-16.6%	5.2%
13	BUF	L	32	42	403	362	-6	-42.7%	-6.3%	31.4%	-5.1%
14	@DEN	L	17	20	214	415	+2	3.8%	-27.7%	-23.9%	7.6%
15	NE	W	29	28	222	323	+3	89.7%	14.7%	-42.2%	32.8%
16	CLE	W	10	7	280	285	+2	12.6%	-4.8%	-7.9%	9.5%
17	@BAL	L	23	30	345	332	-3	-29.2%	-29.6%	9.4%	9.8%

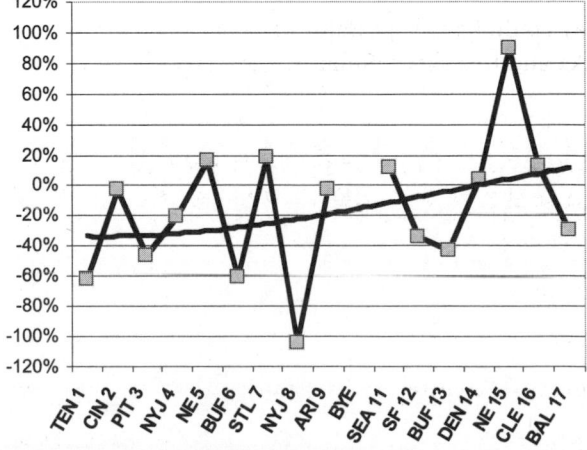

2004 MIA Weekly DVOA Performance

Trends and Splits

	Offense	Rank	Defense	Rank
Total DVOA	-28.5%	31	-7.5%	9
Unadjusted VOA	-33.4%	31	-5.8%	9
Weighted Trend	-18.9%	29	-3.7%	13
Variance	7.9%	20	9.4%	18
Passing	-35.7%	31	-9.4%	9
Rushing	-17.9%	30	-6.0%	10
First Down	-31.6%	32	-6.1%	10
Second Down	-23.4%	30	-6.8%	9
Third Down	-27.4%	25	-12.6%	11
Red Zone	-49.1%	31	-18.3%	9
Late and Close	-44.7%	31	-15.7%	9

Five-Year Performance

	2004	2003	2002	2001	2000
W-L	4-12	10-6	9-7	11-5	11-5
Pythagorean Wins	5.7	9.6	10.1	9.6	11.2
Estimated Wins	6.3	9.5	10.1	8.4	11.0
Total DVOA	-15.5%	11.7%	24.1%	8.7%	24.7%
Rank	25	11	4	11	3
Offense	-28.5%	-9.9%	3.2%	-11.9%	-5.1%
Rank	31	21	18	23	19
Defense	-7.5%	-18.4%	-18.1%	-15.9%	-21.1%
Rank	9	4	2	6	4
Special Teams	5.4%	3.2%	2.9%	4.6%	8.6%
Rank	4	7	9	5	1

Passing (min. 5 plays)

Player	DPAR	PAR	DVOA	Plys	NtYds	Avg	Cmpl	TD	Int
A. J. Feeley	-11.6	-33.0	-20.5%	381	1765	4.6	53.7%	11	15
Jay Fiedler	-22.9	-27.2	-39.0%	215	1021	4.7	53.2%	7	8
Sage Rosenfels	-9.8	-13.3	-67.8%	42	240	5.7	41.0%	1	3

Rushing (min. 3 plays)

Player	DPAR	PAR	DVOA	Plys	Yds	Avg	TD	Fum	Suc
Sammy Morris	12.4	11.3	6.2%	132	524	4.0	6	1	45%
Travis Minor	4.2	3.3	-5.1%	110	395	3.6	3	0	37%
Leonard Henry	-3.7	-5.9	-34.2%	45	132	2.9	0	1	29%
Lamar Gordon	-9.1	-7.8	-81.6%	35	64	1.8	0	1	29%
Brock Forsey	-3.8	-4.8	-55.9%	19	54	2.8	0	1	37%
Chris Chambers	0.6	0.7	-15.3%	9	66	7.3	0	1	—
Jay Fiedler	-1.5	-2.2	-40.7%	9	62	6.9	0	1	—
A. J. Feeley	-0.6	-0.5	-33.3%	7	17	2.4	1	0	—
Vick King	0.0	-0.1	-14.1%	4	9	2.3	0	0	25%

Receiving (min. 5 plays)

Player	DPAR	PAR	DVOA	Plys	Ctch	Yds	Y/C	TD	CPct
WR									
Chris Chambers	5.0	2.8	-9.2%	138	69	878	12.7	7	50%
Marty Booker	-3.2	-3.9	-19.6%	105	50	638	12.8	1	48%
Derrius Thompson	8.5	8.2	14.3%	47	23	359	15.6	4	49%
Bryan Gilmore	0.2	-0.3	-13.6%	34	15	212	14.1	1	44%
TE									
Randy McMichael	11.1	4.5	3.9%	118	73	791	10.8	4	62%
Donald Lee	-2.2	-3.7	-28.1%	20	13	119	9.2	1	65%
RB									
Sammy Morris	-0.3	-1.7	-11.0%	28	22	124	5.6	0	79%
Travis Minor	-2.5	-6.0	-26.5%	27	13	75	5.8	0	48%
Lamar Gordon	-2.4	-2.2	-37.2%	19	13	74	5.7	0	68%
Rob Konrad	-0.2	-1.6	-10.4%	18	8	69	8.6	1	44%
Jamar Martin	-3.9	-5.2	-90.1%	8	4	16	4.0	0	50%
Leonard Henry	-1.2	-1.3	-60.4%	6	3	12	4.0	0	50%

Defensive Players (min. 20 plays)

Player	Age	Plys	Stop	Dfts	AvYds	StpRt	Sack	Int	FR
Defensive Line									
Jason Taylor	31	79	57	30	1.5	72%	9.5	1	3
Jeff Zgonina	35	66	48	14	1.9	73%	5.0	0	0
David Bowens	28	46	36	19	1.1	78%	7.0	0	0
Bryan Robinson	31	45	32	6	2.1	71%	0.0	0	0
Jay Williams	34	40	34	13	2.4	85%	2.0	1	0
Dario Romero	27	22	14	8	1.0	64%	3.5	0	0
Linebackers									
Zach Thomas	32	148	74	20	4.1	50%	2.0	0	0
Morlon Greenwood	27	104	54	12	4.9	52%	0.0	0	0
Junior Seau	36	58	33	9	3.9	57%	1.0	0	1
Derrick Pope	23	39	25	6	3.3	64%	2.0	0	1
Eddie Moore	25	28	21	5	3.4	75%	0.0	0	2

Player	Age	Plys	Stop	Dfts	AvYds	StpRt	Sack	Int	FR
Secondary									
Sammy Knight	30	101	39	16	6.9	39%	0.0	4	1
Patrick Surtain	29	70	35	17	6.3	50%	1.0	4	2
Sam Madison	31	59	19	9	10.1	32%	0.0	0	0
Antuan Edwards	28	42	14	9	12.5	33%	1.0	0	0
Will Poole	24	37	15	8	7.7	41%	1.0	0	0
Arturo Freeman	29	33	10	6	10.4	30%	0.0	4	0
Reggie Howard	28	30	9	8	12.2	30%	0.0	0	1

Offensive Line

Year	Yards	AdjLineYd	Rank	Power	Rank	10+ Yds	Rank	Stuff	Rank	Sack	AdjSack%	Rank
2002	4.76	4.38	6	69%	14	21%	6	21%	4	28	6.2%	16
2003	3.61	3.76	28	71%	8	13%	25	26%	23	32	6.5%	17
2004	3.48	3.48	32	73%	4	17%	18	30%	32	52	8.2%	26

Year	LEnd	Rank	LTckl	Rank	MdGrd	Rank	RTckl	Rank	REnd	Rank
2002	5.60	3	4.44	9	4.06	24	4.36	16	5.17	3
2003	2.73	32	3.25	32	3.87	24	3.69	25	4.73	4
2004	2.48	32	3.25	31	3.52	32	3.45	30	4.06	13

Although Ricky Williams was a popular scapegoat for Miami's offensive ineptitude, the real problem with this team was an offensive line so bad that Jim Brown would struggle to run behind it. There were times during the season where you half expected them to invite opposing pass rushers in for tea and crumpets. Nick Saban doesn't seem to agree with our diagnosis of the problem, however, as he took just one offensive lineman in the draft, fifth-rounder Anthony Alabi out of Texas Christian. Could this line possibly undergo a sudden renaissance without a major influx of new talent? Last year's first-round pick, guard Vernon Carey, is likely to improve in his second season. Free agent signing Stockar McDougle will be an upgrade over previous right tackle John St. Clair, who followed his four seasons of never blocking anyone in St. Louis by never blocking anyone last season in Miami. Otherwise there's no reason to believe this line won't keep Ronnie Brown from enjoying an up close and personal introduction to the wide world of NFL linebackers.

If you ever want to upset a Dolphins fan, raise the fact that they dealt a 2004 second-round pick to New England for the 2003 third-round selection, which Miami used on left tackle Wade Smith, who was abysmal in his rookie season and lost his starting job after two games in his second year. In the meantime, New England sent Miami's former pick to Cincinnati for Corey Dillon, which means that Miami effectively dealt the ability to get a 1,500-yard rusher for a subpar offensive lineman who couldn't effectively block a tic-tac-toe game even if he was in charge of all nine squares.

Defensive Front Seven

Year	Yards	AdjLineYd	Rank	Power	Rank	10+ Yds	Rank	Stuff	Rank	Sack	AdjSack%	Rank
2002	3.72	3.99	12	71%	22	10%	3	24%	18	47	8.7%	2
2003	3.31	3.66	29	47%	1	9%	4	29%	7	45	7.7%	2
2004	4.37	4.25	17	50%	4	20%	23	23%	17	36	7.2%	13

Year	LEnd	Rank	LTckl	Rank	MdGrd	Rank	RTckl	Rank	REnd	Rank
2002	3.67	7	4.02	13	4.22	17	4.72	28	2.39	3
2003	4.31	16	2.94	1	3.88	7	4.05	15	1.32	1
2004	4.75	26	3.99	8	4.43	25	3.94	10	3.75	15

This is where Nick Saban is beginning the reconstruction of the Dolphins, and while there was already plenty of talent to work with, he went and brought in loads more. It is unclear who will start where and whether the Dolphins will be playing more 3-4 or 4-3. Given the number of defensive linemen, we're guessing 4-3. The line starts with Jason Taylor, a rare breed of Pro Bowl defensive end who plays a balanced game, equally effective against the pass and the run. Saban, who loves sizable defensive ends, signed two big-name, big-weight free agents: Kevin Carter (formerly of Tennessee) and Vonnie Holliday (formerly of Green Bay and two horrible years in Kansas City that he wants to forget). Both are listed at 290 pounds, compared to just 255 for Taylor. Don't be surprised to see either at defensive tackle some of the time. The Dolphins also added 340-pound veteran nose tackle Keith Traylor, who stuffed runners in the middle of New England's defense last year. But wait, there's more—2004 starter Jeff Zgonina is still here too, as is second-round pick Matt Roth, considered one of the top pass rushers in the draft. Backup defensive tackle Dario Romero fights through double teams like crazy, but with all the players added in front of him you have to wonder how often he'll get onto the field. He doesn't have big stats because he's more about taking on blockers so that others can get the glory. If you are looking for a below-the-radar defensive free agent to make a big splash in a year or two, he's a good bet.

Middle linebacker Zach Thomas, despite missing three games, led the team in tackles last year by a sizable margin, but the lineup on either side of him is a bit up in the air. Junior Seau is close to the end, and Morlon Greenwood signed with Houston. They could be replaced by some combination of Eddie Moore (who led the team's linebackers in Stop

(continued next page)

Defensive Front Seven *(continued)*

Rate, albeit in limited playing time), ex-Bronco Donnie Spragan, rookie Channing Crowder, and last year's seventh-round steal out of Alabama, Derrick Pope. Pope is basically Zach Thomas Jr.: a sure tackler with speed who lasted into the second day of the draft because of concerns about his size. Pope started the games that Thomas missed due to injury, and he didn't miss a beat.

Defensive Secondary

Year	DVOA vs. #1 WR	Rank	DVOA vs. #2 WR	Rank	DVOA vs. Other WR	Rank	DVOA vs. TE	Rank	DVOA vs. RB	Rank
2002	-8.3%	9	-34.3%	5	-93.1%	1	-0.1%	15	5.7%	18
2003	-21.8%	5	-25.9%	7	-19.6%	10	-17.3%	7	2.8%	17
2004	-9.1%	7	38.4%	29	-19.0%	8	-11.2%	9	-13.2%	14

The days of Sam Madison and Patrick Surtain as the best pair of corners in the league are over, but while Surtain is now in Kansas City, Madison is still here and played well last year at age 30. Surtain's replacement was set to be Will Poole, who showed flashes of talent in his first year out of USC, until Poole tore the anterior cruciate ligament in his left knee during May minicamp. With Poole out for the year, the job is expected to go to either free agent pickup Mario Edwards, who was in Tampa Bay last season, or backup Reggie Howard, who was a starter with the 2003 NFC champion Panthers. But do not be surprised if fourth-round selection Travis Daniels is starting by midseason. Last year, the Patriots were unafraid to start rookie Randall Gay at cornerback because the system he learned from Nick Saban at Louisiana State was similar to the one used by the Patriots and Bill Belichick. Daniels isn't just used to the system used by Miami's new head coach—the coach is the same guy. As for the safety position, Miami will start two free agents, free safety Tebucky Jones from New Orleans and strong safety Travares Tillman from Carolina. Jones is a hard hitter who has flourished since his original team, the Patriots, gave up on trying to make him a cornerback. Tillman has talent but has been limited by injuries to only 13 games in the last three years.

Special Teams

Year	DVOA	Rank	FG/XP	Rank	Net Punt	Rank	Punt Ret	Rank	Net Kick	Rank	Kick Ret	Rank
2002	2.9%	9	-2.1	18	13.3	4	-7.9	28	3.6	11	9.0	7
2003	3.2%	7	0.7	19	9.5	3	-6.2	24	15.7	3	-1.8	19
2004	5.4%	4	4.0	12	12.7	6	-3.9	13	7.5	10	9.7	6

Miami is one of three teams, along with Detroit and Philadelphia, that have bucked the general rule that special teams do not remain consistently strong from year to year. Wes Welker started the year in San Diego and ended it as the most versatile special teams player in the league. Welker was an undrafted free agent out of Texas Tech who signed with the Chargers and played one game before he was waived and claimed by the Dolphins. In Miami, he returned kickoffs and punts, made tackles in coverage, played a little bit of receiver, and even filled in as a kicker when Olindo Mare was hurt—making his only field goal attempt and only extra point attempt and kicking off three times. Mare should be healthy this year and no kicker booms it past the end zone more often. Matt Turk is a reliable punter, and Brendon Ayanbadejo has become one of the best coverage men in the league. Like his brother, Cardinals fullback Obafemi Ayanbadejo, he entered the league as an undrafted free agent but showed that he was a hard worker and good athlete.

Coaching Staff

One of the most intriguing moves by Nick Saban was bringing along Scott O'Brien as director of football operations. O'Brien coached the special teams in Carolina for the past six seasons. He also worked with Saban under Bill Belichick in Cleveland, and Saban hopes he and O'Brien can form the same type of relationship that Belichick and Scott Pioli have (without O'Brien marrying Bill Parcells's daughter). Scott Linehan was a good choice as offensive coordinator for the Dolphins. The Vikings didn't want Linehan to leave, but Red McCombs didn't want to pay him what he's worth. Linehan favors a system similar to the one that Joe Gibbs developed during his first term in Washington: heavy use of a blocking H-back, running back by committee, and lots of motion and changing formations. Since Miami took Ronnie Brown with the second-overall selection in the draft, we thought the "running back by committee" part of Linehan's strategy was going to be chucked, but a possible Ricky Williams comeback could change things.

New England Patriots

To summarize for those of you who may have been introduced to professional football in, say, the last 15 minutes, the New England Patriots have won three of the past four Super Bowl championships. Only one other franchise, Dallas in the early 1990s, has ever won three Super Bowls in the same period of time. Fifteen years ago, the Patriots were the Montreal Expos of the NFL: horribly mismanaged, lagging in popularity compared to a crosstown team in a different sport that had far more tradition, and rumored weekly to be moving to any city with a population of at least six people. Today, New England is widely acclaimed as the best-run franchise in professional sports.

Before Super Bowl XXXIX had even been played, sportswriters and fans had already begun debating New England's status as an NFL dynasty. On one hand, the scoring-differential gap between the Patriots and their competition has been much smaller when compared to dynasties of the NFL's past—all three of their Super Bowl wins have come by just three points. On the other hand, the Patriots have won three championships in an era where free agency and the salary cap are supposed to prevent teams from building the kind of core group of players that could go on an extended run of this magnitude.

The irony of the Patriots' dominating run is that it hasn't disproved this assumption at all. There are huge differences between the roster of the team that beat Philadelphia in Super Bowl XXXIX and the roster of the team that upset St. Louis in Super Bowl XXXVI. The 2001–2004 Patriots need to be understood not as an extended dynasty but as a team that on the way to building a Super Bowl champion somehow stumbled its way into being a Super Bowl champion.

The Patriots were in terrible salary cap shape when head coach and general manager Bill Belichick took over, $6.5 million over the salary cap after 2000, thanks to the previous regime's habit of doling out large contracts to declining veterans. Spotty drafting had left the team bereft of talented younger players. Building 19 opened three new warehouses filled with nothing but unsold Andy Katzenmoyer jerseys on markdown.

The strategy that became known as the "Patriots way" was actually a stopgap measure. The Patriots signed 20 low-cost free agents before the 2001 season with the idea that these players would allow the Patriots to put a com-

petitive team on the field while gradually installing Belichick's system, jettisoning players who weren't with the program, and building with younger talent.

But instead of just keeping the team above water, most of these free agents played at a level higher than they had ever played before, and the Patriots rode a remarkable run of serendipity to an upset Super Bowl title. In the end, the biggest break was not any single play, but an injury that allowed Belichick to replace the declining Drew Bledsoe with a talented second-year player whose skills exactly fit Belichick's quarterback ideal, a player who had somehow been overlooked by 31 other teams in the previous year's draft: Tom Brady.

When the team went 9–7 in the year after the Super Bowl title, everyone assumed that the 2001 team was a one-year wonder. But according to our DVOA ratings, the Patriots have improved in each year of Belichick's five-year tenure. New England ranked 22nd of 31 teams in 2000, Belichick's first season. The Patriots' upset win in

PATRIOTS PROSPECTUS

2004 Record: 14–2

DVOA Estimated Wins: 13.2 (1st)

Pythagorean Wins: 12.4 (1st)

DVOA: 35.6% total (1st), 33.0% weighted (4th)

Adjusted Offense: 28.4 points/game (26.3% DVOA, 4th)

Adjusted Defense: 19.1 points/game (−9.1% DVOA, 6th)

Adjusted Special Teams: +0.1 points/game (0.2% DVOA, 16th)

Variance: 28.4% (3rd)

2004: Yop, they're a dynasty.

2005: The odds against them winning a third straight title are long, but no longer than the odds faced by any of the other 31 teams.

2005 Projection

Leinart Land (0–4): 6%

Bad Team (5–6): 11%

Mediocre (7–8): 21%

Playoff Contender (9–10): 25%

Super Bowl Contender (11+): 36%

Projected Average Opponent: 5.0% DVOA (5th in NFL)

the 2001 Super Bowl belied their low regular-season ranking of 16th, partly the reflection of adjustments for an easy schedule. In 2002, the Patriots ranked 11th; the continued development of young stars was concealed by a far more difficult schedule and a 9–7 season that ended without a playoff berth because of a tiebreaker.

The 2003 team—which won its final 12 regular-season games—ranked second in DVOA; Kansas City, despite fading late in the season, ranked number one thanks to its dominating first half. With the 2004 team, the Patriots finally ranked number one. (The actual DVOA ratings are found in the Five-Year Performance table at the end of this chapter.)

These ratings tell the story of a team gradually improving itself from also-ran to two-time Super Bowl champion, but which, thanks to a remarkable three-game streak of playoff football, just happened to win an extremely unlikely championship in the second year of its rebuilding project.

Because of the makeup of the 2001 championship team, most NFL fans have an image of the 2003–2004 Patriots as a team built on older veterans. But a remarkable four-year streak of drafting has allowed New England to constantly cycle out its declining veterans in favor of young talent. Only five of those veteran free agents from 2001 still remained on the team in 2004, and only one, linebacker Mike Vrabel, was a starter. The off-season release of LB Roman Phifer and free agent departures of WR David Patten and DB Je'Rod Cherry means that only Vrabel and Pro Bowl special teams specialist Larry Izzo are left from the 2001 signing bounty.

(The makeup of the 2001 championship team, unfortunately, also contributes to the massive chip on the shoulder of most Patriots supporters. It seems ridiculous after two 14–2 seasons, but some sportswriters still write that the Patriots are a lucky team of overachievers. This, in turn, is why New England fans have become so attached to their insufferable "nobody respects us" complex, an affectation that made sense in 2001 when the Patriots really did get no respect, but now serves only to make many Patriots fans just seem like spoiled brats.)

The neighboring Red Sox were celebrated as the first "moneyball" team to win a world championship, but in fact no team in professional sports understands the concept of economic efficiency as well as the Patriots. New England makes every roster decision based on a simple cost-benefit analysis: Is a player's future value to the team higher than the cap space he will take up? If the answer is no, the team does not hesitate to release a player, no matter his skill, work ethic, or popularity among the fans. This unemotional approach to roster construction has not only made New England the best team in the NFL, it has also served to keep the Patriots from falling prey to the most common undoing of dynasties: aging.

When safety Lawyer Milloy became overpriced, he was replaced with a second-round rookie, Eugene Wilson. New England did not need to match Detroit's exorbitant free agent offer for offensive lineman Damien Woody, because fifth-round rookie Dan Koppen had already forced Woody to move over from center to guard. Ty Law was a perennial Pro Bowler and possibly the best player on the team, but the Patriots unceremoniously dumped him this off-season because no cornerback, especially one coming off a broken foot, is worth $12 million in cap space.

None of these moves, however, affected fans like the February release of wide receiver Troy Brown. A diminutive wideout taken in the no-longer extant eighth round of the 1993 draft, Brown had been a scrappy fan favorite since the Tuna roamed the Foxboro sideline. His willingness to switch from offense to defense in the middle of the 2004 season symbolized New England's "anything for the team" persona. The Patriots had Brown practice with the secondary before the season began as a precaution, in case they ever faced a scenario where injuries left the team without enough defensive backs to put on the field. They faced it by midseason, when Patriots were down their top three defensive backs. For the rest of the year and through a successful run to the Super Bowl championship, Brown served as the nickelback even though he had never played defense in his life. Though he sacrificed his role as New England's third receiver, he still played offense for a few plays each game and also returned punts.

But for all his hard work and past value to the Patriots, Brown was an aging third receiver set to make $5 million in 2005. Loyalty is not a luxury that a team can afford in a league with a zero-sum salary cap. Brown's release doesn't mean that the team did not appreciate his contributions in 2004, it simply meant that they could not let that appreciation cost them a chance at winning again in 2005. (In May, Brown re-signed with New England at a lower salary.)

The constant roster turnover means that the Patriots, despite their multiple championships, are actually one of the youngest teams in the league. With the exception of Corey Dillon, every single starter on offense is 28 years old or younger, and that includes the franchise quarterback. The starting defensive line averages 25 years of age and consists of three first-round picks: Vince Wilfork (2004), Ty Warren (2003), and Richard Seymour (2001). The secondary mixes veterans in their early thirties with younger players like Wilson and Asante Samuel. The only positions where the Patriots primarily use older players are running back and linebacker.

How does a team with three recent Lombardi Trophies manage to acquire so many useful young players? The team depth that has allowed the Patriots to weather constant injuries over the past two seasons is due in large part to success with late-round draft picks and rookie free agents.

Rather than simply assign a value to a player and then draft or sign him based on that value, the Patriots seek players that will fit their specific style. Undrafted free agent cornerback Randall Gay is a perfect example. Belichick and Vice President of Player Personnel Scott Pioli knew that Gay would fit the team because he had played in a similar defensive system under former Belichick assistant (and now Miami head coach) Nick Saban at Louisiana State. Gay played at a high enough level to render worries about the Patriots "patchwork secondary" meaningless during the playoffs and to allow the Patriots to relieve themselves of Law's exorbitant salary in the upcoming season. The Patriots continued this strategy in the most recent draft. First-round offensive lineman Logan Mankins and fourth-round defensive back James Sanders both come from Fresno State, whose head coach Pat Hill was the offensive line coach on Belichick's Cleveland staff.

Belichick and Pioli have built a team that is young, talented, and deep. The 2003–2004 Patriots, not the 2001 Patriots, represent the goal that Belichick had when he came to New England five years ago. The 2005 Patriots will be the first to have to overcome turnover on the sidelines as well as the roster, with offensive coordinator Charlie Weis gone to Notre Dame and defensive coordinator Romeo Crennel now head coach in Cleveland. But with so many young and talented players playing pivotal roles, there's no reason to doubt that the 2005 Patriots will make a run at a third straight Super Bowl championship.

Aaron Schatz

Research: Wherefore Art Thou Romeo?

While Bill Belichick has deservedly gotten the bulk of the credit for the Patriots' amazing run, former coordinators Charlie Weis and Romeo Crennel also received their fair share of plaudits. Weis's offense morphed from a conservative game plan, designed to protect a rookie quarterback, to an aggressive short-passing game, to the powerful and diverse run/pass attack the Pats featured last season. Crennel has been a major part of frustrating the best offenses in football, from the innovative 2-5 employed against the Eagles in the Super Bowl to the uncompromising game plans that confuse Peyton Manning over and over.

After many years of excellent work, both these men finally received well-deserved promotions after the 2004 season. Weis was tapped to be head football coach at his alma mater, Notre Dame, and Crennel will take over the Cleveland Browns. Many observers have reacted to these departures by suggesting that, while the Patriots have survived the loss of numerous players, replacing these important coordinators will not be so easy.

But a close examination of recent teams facing a similar situation shows that the impact of a coordinator may not be as great as many people think. Teams do generally regress after losing their coordinators. However, elite units such as those coached by Weis and Crennel generally see a greater falloff when they *retain* their coordinators than when their coordinators move on to become head coaches.

We went back and looked at every coordinator who received an NFL head coaching job over the past 15 seasons. All told, 47 coordinators were named head coaches. Of these, 12 were promoted to head coach of the team that already employed them. These 12 saw very minimal decline in the performance of their units, an understandable phenomenon given that their imprint remained on the team. In some cases, such as Mike Martz in St. Louis, they retained their coordinator duties even as head coach.

That leaves us with 35 coordinators who left one team when they were hired to be head coach for a different NFL team. This sample size is admittedly small, but it should provide some indication of the impact of unwillingly losing a top coordinator. Unfortunately, to get even a sample of this size, we had to stretch back before the DVOA era. This means that, after spending the rest of the book telling you how yards and points are not the best measure of a team, we have no choice in this study but to use yards and points.

For each of the 35 examples, we looked at how the offense/defense did, both in the coordinator's final season with the team and again the following year with the coordinator now employed elsewhere. We were looking for the immediate impact to see how important the loss of both coordinators would be for the Patriots this season. We looked at how the unit did both in overall points and yards as well as its relative league rank, to account for some variation in year-to-year trends. What we found was that units that lost their coordinator did regress, but not by as much as one might predict.

On average, these 35 units dropped 2.9 places in the NFL rankings for points and 3.3 places in the rankings for yards. The average unit was 22.5 points and 189.2 yards worse with the new coordinator. The difference of 22.5 points is roughly equivalent to a half a win. The 2004 Patriots, for example, scored 437 points and allowed 260 points, totals that would project to 12.4 wins. Had they given up 22 more points, they would have been projected to win 11.8 games. Since the Patriots lost two coordinators, 22 fewer points scored and 22 more points allowed equals 11.4 wins, a full win difference if they suffer the average fate of other teams that lost their coordinators.

These averages may be slightly misleading because most units that lost their coordinator were among the best in the NFL. For instance, the San Francisco 49ers lost Mike Shanahan to the Broncos in 1994 after ranking first in both points scored and yards gained the previous season.

Without Shanahan, the 49ers still ranked first in the league in both categories, and while they gained fewer overall yards in 1994, they scored 32 more points.

With that in mind, it may be more instructive to look at the median change in performance. The median performance was a decrease in rank of three spots in points and four spots in yards. However, in actual points, the median drop was only seven points, while the drop in yards was a more substantial 247. Altogether, 21 out of 35 teams declined in points and 25 out of 35 declined in yards. Twenty-seven of the 35 dropped in at least one category (and for all those English majors out there, that means 19 declined in both). The fact that 21 out of 35 declined in points but the median drop is only seven points clearly shows that a good number of teams stayed roughly around the same level.

Of course, not all coordinators are created equal. Last season the Patriots ranked in the top five in points scored and allowed. Breaking out only those coordinators who were in the top five in points, our sample is whittled down to 16. This of course means that more than half the coordinators who have gotten jobs do not have a unit ranked among the top five in points. Since John Fox, Jon Gruden, Marvin Lewis, and Tony Dungy number among those who got jobs after coaching units in the bottom half of points, we won't quibble with the GMs' decisions in this case.

In this more rarefied air, 11 out of 16 teams did better in points before losing their coordinator. The teams under a new coordinator were on average over 44 points worse. Of course, that includes several major declines, including the Titans giving up 197 more points in an injury-riddled season after Gregg Williams left, and the Vikings scoring 157 fewer points after they set the all-time scoring record under Brian Billick in 1998. The greatest improvements under the new coordinators were the 1993 49ers, who scored 38 more points when Mike Shanahan replaced Mike Holmgren, and the 1994 Cowboys, who scored 38 more points after Norv Turner headed to the Redskins and was replaced by Ernie Zampese.

The story for yards is even scarier, as these top five teams did on average 318 yards worse the year after losing their coordinator. Only 3 out of 16 teams improved in yards, led by the 341-yard improvement of the 1993 49ers. The biggest losers were the aforementioned Titans, in their disappointing 2001 campaign, and the 1993 Cowboys, who gave up 720 more yards after losing Dave Wannstedt to the Bears. No wonder Jimmy Johnson was so high on Wannstedt.

The consistent decline of units after they lost their coordinator is fairly clear, but the final question remaining is how much of this decline is attributable to simple regression to the mean. Coordinators are often promoted to head coach after exceptional seasons, and following excellent seasons, even teams that retain their coordinators often face a decline. To measure this impact, we looked at every team that ranked in the top five for points scored or allowed between 1989 and 2003. If we subtract the 16 teams who had a coordinator get promoted, we have a sample of 135 teams (one season there was a tie for fifth place, so the original sample was 151). Among these 135 teams, the average unit scored/gave up 55 more points than the year before.

Looking back at the top five units with new coordinators the following year, the average change in points scored/given up was just under 45 points. Not only is the normal regression to the mean more substantial, but only 7 out of 16 teams saw point changes as substantial as 55 after losing their coordinators. Further, only 28 out of 135 (21%) teams whose coordinators did not get promoted saw improvements in points, while of the original 16, 5 (31%) saw improvements after losing the coordinator. Teams who did not change coordinators were therefore likely to decline by more points and less likely to improve than those teams whose coordinators were hired to be head coaches.

When we are talking about relatively small sample sizes, it is difficult to form any strong conclusions. But the numbers here seem fairly clear: Teams that lose their coordinators decline by no more than any other top-level team. Having watched Weis and Crennel work for the last several seasons, this is a hard conclusion to come to terms with. But it might be easier to understand when you consider that the new defensive coordinator, Eric Mangini, has worked with Belichick since 1995 and Crennel since 2001, while the new offensive coordinator is basically Belichick himself. There are plenty of reasons to believe that New England will decline next year—roster changes, a difficult schedule, good old regression to the mean—but it doesn't seem like the departure of the coordinators is one of them.

Ned Macey

Patriots 2004 Stats by Week

Wk	vs.	W-L	PF	PA	YDF	YDA	TO	Total	Off	Def	ST
								\multicolumn{4}{c}{DVOA}			
1	IND	W	27	24	402	446	+2	60.9%	44.5%	-21.0%	-4.5%
2	@ARI	W	23	12	376	167	0	82.6%	30.0%	-42.7%	9.9%
3	BYE										
4	@BUF	W	31	17	399	357	+1	60.1%	84.4%	-2.8%	-27.1%
5	MIA	W	24	10	207	296	+1	-14.6%	-17.1%	-3.1%	-0.6%
6	SEA	W	30	20	363	443	0	41.9%	20.2%	-11.2%	10.5%
7	NYJ	W	13	7	347	270	0	65.4%	40.2%	-23.5%	1.7%
8	@PIT	L	20	34	244	420	-4	-35.1%	-9.4%	30.6%	4.8%
9	@STL	W	40	22	377	336	+1	47.9%	32.5%	7.2%	22.7%
10	BUF	W	29	6	429	123	+4	145.6%	42.8%	-110.9%	-8.1%
11	@KC	W	27	19	411	417	0	55.9%	37.4%	-14.4%	4.2%
12	BAL	W	24	3	310	130	+2	75.4%	26.4%	-47.7%	1.3%
13	@CLE	W	42	15	410	293	+1	31.0%	0.7%	-14.2%	16.1%
14	CIN	W	35	28	354	482	+3	18.7%	64.9%	46.4%	0.3%
15	@MIA	L	28	29	323	222	-3	-87.2%	-18.0%	39.6%	-29.6%
16	@NYJ	W	23	7	374	278	+3	76.0%	40.8%	-32.9%	2.3%
17	SF	W	21	7	405	318	-1	3.4%	12.5%	7.7%	-1.4%
18	BYE										
19	IND	W	20	3	325	276	+4	89.8%	29.9%	-56.3%	3.7%
20	@PIT	W	41	27	322	388	+4	87.8%	49.5%	-34.8%	3.5%
21	PHI	W	24	21	331	369	+3	80.6%	38.2%	-34.2%	8.2%

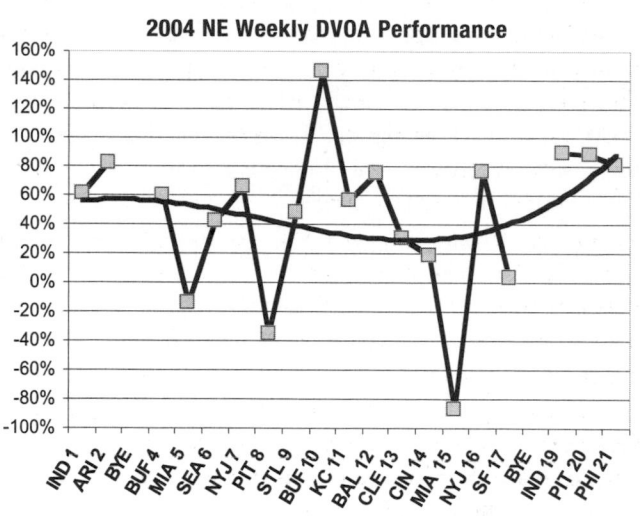

2004 NE Weekly DVOA Performance

Trends and Splits

	Offense	Rank	Defense	Rank
Total DVOA	26.3%	4	-9.1%	6
Unadjusted VOA	18.6%	6	-14.0%	5
Weighted Trend	24.4%	4	-7.4%	10
Variance	8.0%	19	14.3%	3
Passing	42.1%	2	-6.5%	11
Rushing	12.2%	5	-12.3%	4
First Down	17.4%	4	-13.6%	5
Second Down	32.3%	3	4.2%	17
Third Down	36.1%	5	-21.2%	7
Red Zone	16.7%	7	-39.7%	2
Late and Close	45.5%	1	-33.9%	2

Five-Year Performance

	2004	2003	2002	2001	2000
W-L	14-2	14-2	9-7	11-5	5-11
Pythagorean Wins	12.4	11.4	8.9	10.8	6.1
Estimated Wins	13.2	11.7	9.1	7.4	6.9
Total DVOA	35.6%	22.4%	12.5%	-1.4%	-9.7%
Rank	1	2	11	16	22
Offense	26.3%	-0.8%	4.0%	-8.7%	-7.5%
Rank	4	13	17	21	21
Defense	-9.1%	-22.0%	-3.4%	-3.4%	5.7%
Rank	6	3	10	19	22
Special Teams	0.2%	1.2%	5.2%	3.9%	3.5%
Rank	16	13	5	6	12

Passing (min. 5 plays)

Player	DPAR	PAR	DVOA	Plys	NtYds	Avg	Cmpl	TD	Int
Tom Brady	113.4	95.6	41.6%	499	3520	7.1	60.8%	28	13
Rohan Davey	2.3	2.3	49.0%	10	54	5.4	40.0%	0	0

Rushing (min. 3 plays)

Player	DPAR	PAR	DVOA	Plys	Yds	Avg	TD	Fum	Suc
Corey Dillon	50.3	49.5	19.7%	345	1636	4.7	12	4	54%
Kevin Faulk	11.4	11.2	39.8%	54	255	4.7	2	0	50%
Patrick Pass	1.2	0.6	-6.7%	39	141	3.6	0	0	46%
Cedric Cobbs	-5.4	-4.7	-76.0%	22	50	2.3	0	1	32%
Tom Brady	1.1	1.1	-8.1%	16	52	3.3	0	1	—
Rabih Abdullah	-0.3	-0.9	-19.6%	13	13	1.0	1	0	23%

Receiving (min. 5 plays)

Player	DPAR	PAR	DVOA	Plys	Ctch	Yds	Y/C	TD	CPct
WR									
David Givens	21.4	19.8	16.6%	106	56	872	15.6	3	53%
David Patten	18.6	17.2	15.5%	95	44	800	18.2	7	46%
Deion Branch	16.7	17.2	36.2%	51	35	454	13.0	4	69%
Troy Brown	3.6	3.0	5.2%	29	17	184	10.8	1	59%
Bethel Johnson	1.3	2.3	-6.5%	21	10	174	17.4	1	48%
TE									
Daniel Graham	13.6	12.2	32.5%	48	30	364	12.1	7	63%
Christian Fauria	8.0	8.1	42.3%	20	16	195	12.2	2	80%
Jed Weaver	2.5	3.1	16.8%	12	8	93	11.6	0	67%
RB									
Patrick Pass	2.9	1.3	11.2%	32	28	215	7.7	0	88%
Kevin Faulk	8.2	7.2	46.8%	30	26	248	9.5	1	87%
Corey Dillon	1.0	-1.0	0.8%	21	15	103	6.9	1	71%

Defensive Players (min. 20 plays)

Player	Age	Plys	Stop	Dfts	AvYds	StpRt	Sack	Int	FR
Defensive Line									
Ty Warren	24	50	37	12	1.5	74%	3.5	0	0
Vince Wilfork	24	48	31	7	2.3	65%	2.0	0	2
Richard Seymour	26	41	24	9	1.4	59%	5.0	0	1
Jarvis Green	26	25	17	8	0.5	68%	4.0	0	3
Keith Traylor	36	28	21	4	1.7	75%	0.0	0	0
Linebackers									
Tedy Bruschi	32	126	68	22	3.8	54%	3.5	3	0
Ted Johnson	33	79	44	8	3.5	56%	1.0	0	0
Mike Vrabel	30	72	39	17	3.5	54%	5.5	0	0
Willie McGinest	34	58	41	20	1.7	71%	9.5	1	1
Roman Phifer	37	44	18	9	5.7	41%	1.5	1	1
Roosevelt Colvin	28	31	17	8	3.6	55%	5.0	0	0

Player	Age	Plys	Stop	Dfts	AvYds	StpRt	Sack	Int	FR
Secondary									
Rodney Harrison	35	135	51	21	7.0	38%	3.0	2	0
Eugene Wilson	25	74	15	12	12.2	20%	0.0	4	2
Asante Samuel	24	51	22	13	10.1	43%	0.0	1	0
Randall Gay	23	45	17	12	7.7	38%	0.0	2	2
Ty Law	31	34	15	6	7.8	44%	0.0	1	0
Troy Brown	34	23	8	7	8.9	35%	0.0	3	2

Offensive Line

Year	Yards	AdjLineYd	Rank	Power	Rank	10+ Yds	Rank	Stuff	Rank	Sack	AdjSack%	Rank
2002	4.01	4.33	11	76%	7	12%	28	22%	6	31	5.0%	8
2003	3.62	4.01	23	60%	23	10%	31	23%	10	32	5.4%	12
2004	4.42	4.56	5	69%	9	16%	21	22%	11	26	4.8%	5

Year	LEnd	Rank	LTckl	Rank	MdGrd	Rank	RTckl	Rank	REnd	Rank
2002	3.95	19	5.00	4	4.52	6	4.53	10	2.51	32
2003	3.76	22	3.76	28	4.18	16	4.64	8	3.06	26
2004	4.98	5	4.76	8	4.24	16	5.19	2	4.56	5

New England has put together an underrated offensive line that rarely makes mistakes—they were called for only 13 false start penalties, the lowest total in the league. The line combines one well-paid star, left tackle Matt Light, and a group of somewhat interchangeable low-round picks and free agents. (Center Dan Koppen, a 2003 fifth-round pick, has started since the second game of his rookie year and plays at a near-Pro Bowl level; he's the exception to the "interchangeable" part of that description.) Of course, New England's game planning is known for constantly shifting strategies to ensure that opponents never see what they expected. Why should their approach to roster construction be any different? And so, after winning two straight Super Bowls with undrafted players starting at both guard positions, the Patriots used two of their first three draft picks this year on players who are projected as guards: first-rounder Logan Mankins of Fresno State and third-rounder Nick Kaczur of Toledo. Mankins should slip right into the lineup at left guard, with Joe Andruzzi leaving for Cleveland. After a year or so of apprenticeship, Kaczur is likely destined to eventually replace either right tackle Brandon Gorin or right guard Stephen Neal, the weaker members of the line when it comes to pass protection. The

Patriots frequently had to hold tight end Daniel Graham back to help out, which is why he averaged 4.3 passes in the first six games of the season but only 2.2 passes per game after Tom Ashworth's injury moved Gorin into the starting lineup in Week 8.

Defensive Front Seven

Year	Yards	AdjLineYd	Rank	Power	Rank	10+ Yds	Rank	Stuff	Rank	Sack	AdjSack%	Rank
2002	4.51	4.38	26	71%	21	19%	18	20%	27	35	6.3%	14
2003	3.49	3.99	13	62%	8	6%	1	25%	15	40	5.8%	22
2004	3.80	4.36	23	57%	10	7%	1	20%	31	46	7.6%	10

Year	LEnd	Rank	LTckl	Rank	MdGrd	Rank	RTckl	Rank	REnd	Rank
2002	5.08	29	4.46	22	4.20	16	4.12	16	4.84	29
2003	3.34	4	5.13	28	4.04	13	4.06	16	2.72	4
2004	5.91	31	4.14	10	4.40	23	4.04	11	2.50	2

Forget Ty Law's talk and Tom Brady's fame. The Patriots' athletic, intelligent, and multifaceted front seven is the heart of the New England dynasty. They can easily switch between the 3-4 and 4-3 formations, usually with linebacker Willie McGinest as a down lineman. They also excel with weird Belichickian creations like the no-down-linemen defense used against Miami and Buffalo last year and the 2-5 introduced to pressure Donovan McNabb in the Super Bowl. New England's Adjusted Line Yards number suffers because, even more than with other 3-4 teams, the linemen tie up the blockers rather than penetrate, while the linebackers make the plays. Because those linebackers are so good at pursuit and tackling, the Patriots have allowed the fewest long runs in the league for two straight years, but they rarely stuff opposing runners at the line. (Though, as you may notice from that power run success percentage, they are pretty good at it when they need to be.)

While the defensive line—discussed in the main essay of this chapter—is still the youngest and deepest unit on the team, the aging linebacker corps has some question marks. None is bigger than the health of Tedy Bruschi, who is unlikely to play this year after suffering a mild stroke a week after the Pro Bowl. The Patriots signed two free agents who will likely share time as his replacement: Chad Brown, a three-time Pro Bowler known for his strong tackling and pass rush skills who was released in a salary cap move by Seattle after an injury-plagued 2004, and Monty Beisel, who is fine in pass coverage but was a major reason why last year's Kansas City defense could not wrap up any runner who made it past four yards. The other starting inside linebacker, 33-year-old Ted Johnson, has watched his skills rapidly crumble over the past two seasons, and the backup is Dan Klecko, a converted lineman who missed most of 2004 with an injury. Lots of teams are moving toward the 3-4 thanks to New England's success, but don't be surprised to see the Patriots often using only three linebackers because of these depth problems.

Defensive Secondary

Year	DVOA vs. #1 WR	Rank	DVOA vs. #2 WR	Rank	DVOA vs. Other WR	Rank	DVOA vs. TE	Rank	DVOA vs. RB	Rank
2002	-18.7%	4	-15.1%	12	5.4%	21	2.7%	16	-36.7%	3
2003	-62.9%	1	-39.1%	3	-36.4%	5	-30.7%	2	12.2%	26
2004	-49.7%	1	41.5%	30	11.4%	22	-31.0%	5	16.2%	28

Even though at times they were reduced to pulling people out of the stands to play cornerback, DVOA says that the Patriots actually had the best defense in the league against number one receivers both before and after Ty Law's injury. They intercepted a league-high 11 passes intended for opposing number one receivers. They also had one of the worst defenses in the league against number two receivers, even before getting hit by injuries, and allowed big games to guys like Antonio Bryant, Johnnie Morton, and Marty Booker. That's a pretty good sign of depth issues, which is why the Patriots traded for ex-Cardinal and Raven Duane Starks, signed free agent Chad Scott from the Steelers, and drafted Ellis Hobbs from Iowa State. Asante Samuel will likely start at one corner spot with either Starks or Randall Gay at the other. The main man in the secondary will still be Rodney Harrison, *for whom we have the utmost respect.* As you can see from the numbers, Harrison eats tight ends for breakfast, but his aggression has its downside—Harrison had 11 penalties called against him, more than twice any other Patriots defender. We're not sure what's up with New England's weakness on passes to running backs, but it goes away on third down when it would really be a problem.

Special Teams

Year	DVOA	Rank	FG/XP	Rank	Net Punt	Rank	Punt Ret	Rank	Net Kick	Rank	Kick Ret	Rank
2002	5.2%	5	13.9	1	-3.0	19	1.2	15	2.5	13	13.9	4
2003	1.2%	13	-11.6	30	2.6	17	-4.2	20	5.3	7	14.6	3
2004	0.2%	16	15.2	1	-0.5	23	-16.2	29	-4.8	24	7.2	8

Kicker Adam Vinatieri is considered by many to be the greatest clutch field goal kicker of all time. Larry Izzo has been elected the "special teams" Pro Bowler in three of the past five years. New England is known for having starters play on special teams. Put those three facts together and you are probably surprised to see that New England's special teams are actually mediocre. Vinatieri is the best field goal kicker in the league when he's not suffering from a back injury, but his kickoffs are average, and while punter Josh Miller was a step up from Ken Walter, that's not much of a compliment. Kick-off and punt coverage went from good in 2003 to poor in 2004. Bethel Johnson has been one of the best kickoff return-ers in the league for two years now, and the team's weakness on punt returns should be solved with the addition of Tim Dwight from San Diego.

Coaching Staff

Bill Belichick had a great run of keeping a successful coaching staff intact. Only one coach on the 2004 team, lineback-ers coach Dean Pees, wasn't with the team for its Super Bowl wins in 2001 and 2003. As noted earlier in this chapter, 2005 will end that run with both coordinators leaving the team for head coaching positions elsewhere. Promoted from secondary coach to defensive coordinator is Eric Mangini, who put together the patchwork secondary that held through the 2004 Super Bowl run. Like Belichick, he's a graduate of Wesleyan University, known more for musicians than foot-ball coaches, and a bit of an intellectual. The experiment will be at offensive coordinator, because the Patriots will not have one, instead splitting those duties between Belichick, receivers coach Brian Daboll, and offensive line coach Dante Scarnecchia.

New York Jets

The New York Jets were the NFL's most misunderstood team in 2004. The conventional wisdom is that the Jets combined one of the league's top defenses and a near-unstoppable running game to overcome a mediocre, conservative passing attack and mistake-prone special teams. The reality is that the Jets' offense was just as efficient through the air as it was on the ground, and the special teams were above average in every area except punt returns. It was gaping holes in the defensive secondary that nearly cost this team its playoff spot.

This analysis of the Jets generated a slew of caustic comments, both on our website and on various Jets message boards around the Internet. To put it bluntly, most Jets fans think we are idiots. The idea that a team that finishes 4th in points allowed, but 17th in points scored, actually is much better on offense than defense seems, at first glance, to be completely absurd. However, a closer look at the data shows how New York's raw scoring and yardage totals are severely affected by three factors: schedule, style, and special teams.

Schedule

The Jets' offense consistently faced above-average defenses. They play in a division where all three rivals have strong defenses, and half of their games in 2004 came against teams that finished in the top ten for defensive DVOA. The defense, on the other hand, faced an easy schedule of weak offenses from the AFC North and NFC West, not to mention two games each against Buffalo and Miami—both among the worst offensive teams in the NFL.

Adjusted only for situation, and not opponent, our ratings move the New York defense up from 19th to 12th, (we call these ratings VOA, instead of DVOA), a position more in line with the public perception of the Jets, though it may still seem low to some.

Conversely, removing the schedule adjustment drops the offensive rating, though not quite as much as it improves the defensive rating—offense goes from 23.4% to 20.4%. More important to the evaluation of the offense is not the quality of the schedule but its timing—the timing of quarterback Chad Pennington's shoulder injury. With the season half over, the Jets were 6–2 with an offensive DVOA of 36.6%, third behind Indianapolis and Kansas City. The offense was averaging 7.3 net yards per pass. Pennington then missed the next three games (with tears

in his rotator cuff and labrum), and played the final five games even though the injury was not fully healed. In those eight games with Quincy Carter or a gimpy Pennington under center, the Jets went 4–4 with an offensive DVOA of 11.1% and only 5.7 net yards per pass.

When Jets fans gripe about their passing game, they are actually complaining about issues from the second half of the season: Pennington seemingly robbed of his ability to throw long, LaMont Jordan's inability to throw the ball out of bounds on a failed halfback option, or the very fact that Quincy Carter even exists. Quincy Carter won't be here in 2005, and Pennington, the Jets and all their fans fervently hope, will be and stay healthy.

Style

Of course, Quincy Carter was not number one on the list of men Jets fans wanted run out of town after last season. That distinction belonged to former offensive coordinator

Paul Hackett, who drove New Yorkers (particularly the sportswriters) insane with his conservative play calling. It is crucial to recognize, however, that the conservative nature of Hackett's game plan didn't affect just the Jets offense; it affected the Jets defense as well.

Hackett's style is manifested not only in a reluctance to throw the ball downfield and a high ratio of run plays to pass plays—the Jets were one of only four NFL teams to run more often than they passed in 2004—it is also apparent in the astonishingly slow pace of the New York offense.

Those readers who may be familiar with our statistical analysis counterparts from the world of basketball, such as John Hollinger and Roland Beech, are aware of the major impact a team's pace has on NBA statistics. In 2004–2005, the expansion Charlotte Bobcats scored more points per game than the defending champion Detroit Pistons did. Did this mean they had a better offense? No, of course not. The Pistons scored fewer points because they played a slow-down style that constantly milked the 24-second clock and emphasized their defense. The Bobcats scored more points only because they took more shots.

The same principle applies in the NFL. Simply put, the Jets gain fewer yards and score fewer points because they run fewer plays than other NFL teams, yet use gobs of time doing it. This makes their defense look better, because their opponents are running fewer plays and thus gaining fewer yards and scoring fewer points. The Jets faced only 966 plays on defense, fewer than all but five NFL teams.

A good way to gauge a team's pace is by examining how many game-clock seconds the offense uses per play. In the second half of this chapter, a further exploration of the idea of game pace, we analyze numbers in situations likely to be dictated by a team's specific strategy rather than the score of the game.

In 2000, the last season before Hackett took over as offensive coordinator, the Jets averaged 28.0 seconds per play in defined game pace situations, making them the third-fastest offense in the league. In each of Hackett's four seasons, the Jets ranked among the five *slowest* offenses in the league, culminating in the 2004 season when the Jets ranked fifth-slowest with 31.45 seconds per play.

A conservative style of play also minimizes turnovers and penalties. The Jets turned the ball over less often than any other offense in 2004, with 11 interceptions and 5 lost fumbles. Simply judging the offense by yards per play ignores the importance of keeping the ball out of the hands of the other team.

Has there been any offensive coordinator in the NFL as conservative as Hackett over the last few years? Well, yes, actually, there has been. The Tennessee Titans ranked among the six slowest offenses in the NFL every year from 2000 through 2004. The architect of that offense was—

drum roll, please—new Jets offensive coordinator Mike Heimerdinger, the very man Jets fans are expecting to transform their offense with a wide-open, fast-paced passing game.

Special Teams

As we noted earlier, the Jets were above average in nearly every area of special teams. (In the case of Doug Brien, of course, the playoffs were a different story.) The Jets punting game truly stood out, where they gained 16.9 points worth of Adjusted Field Position. Meanwhile, the one area where the Jets were below average was punt returns, where they lost 6.8 points worth of adjusted field position.

The confluence of these two stats shows that the Jets tended to play with a longer field than most other teams, both on offense and on defense. The defense, in particular, rarely faced defending a short field because Toby Gowin was booming his punts and the offense almost never turned the ball over.

The average NFL drive in 2004 began on the 30.9-yard line. New York's average drive started on its own 30, the 22nd-best starting position among offenses. The average drive for Jets' opponents started on the 29.5-yard line, the 7th-best starting position among defenses. Those fractions of a yard may not seem like much, but over the course of a season they build up. This is why the Jets ranked 4th in points allowed, yet 7th in yards allowed; and 17th in points scored, but 12th in yards gained. They could gain more yards and still not reach the end zone, give up more yards and still not allow the other team into the end zone.

Even those who are not convinced that the Jets had a better offense than defense in 2004 have to admit that there's a good chance that will be the case in 2005. The reason is less about schedule strength and statistical bias and more about the roster changes that occurred during the off-season.

In Chad Pennington, the Jets have a gifted young quarterback—assuming his recovery from labrum surgery goes well. Jay Fiedler, protected by an actual offensive line—instead of Miami's Five Guys Named Moe—provides a wily veteran backup whose similar style should allow him to easily step in for Pennington if necessary. The difference between Laveranues Coles and Santana Moss is overstated, but the trade certainly increases Pennington's comfort level and his desire to throw to his number one receiver. On the ground, a drop-off from Curtis Martin in 2005 is inevitable—no running back above the age of 30 had ever led the league in rushing yards before—but Derrick Blaylock provides the best possible solution to the problem of replacing LaMont Jordan. He brings a strong résumé, an acceptance of the backup role, and a much lower price tag.

While the front office has made plenty of moves on offense, however, it has not done on the same on defense. The Jets went into the off-season needing an upgrade at cornerback and strong safety, and they now have questions at defensive tackle as well.

This off-season, the Jets had two major free agents on the defensive line. One would be given the franchise tag to keep him in New York, and the other would go where the grass, and money, was greener. By franchising defensive end John Abraham and allowing defensive tackle Jason Ferguson to test the market and sign with Dallas, the Jets made a conscious choice of pass rush over run defense. It was the wrong decision.

The Jets took a step forward on defense last year because of their ability to stop the run, not the pass. They were 5th in the NFL in yards allowed per carry, but 18th in net yards allowed per pass attempt. These numbers don't take into account a schedule filled with teams that had better running games than passing games, including Buffalo, Seattle, Baltimore, and Pittsburgh. That's why DVOA ranks the Jets' pass defense a lowly 24th. In the AFC, only Kansas City and Oakland ranked below them.

Abraham is a gifted pass rusher, but he is overvalued because his sacks are easier to count than the number of times Ferguson requires a double team from the opposing offensive line. Abraham is maddeningly inconsistent; Ferguson is always reliable. Abraham missed 13 games over the past two seasons; Ferguson missed none.

When it comes to the mismanagement of football resources, however, the mistake of keeping Abraham over Ferguson is trivial compared to what the Jets did in this year's draft. After dealing their first-round pick to Oakland for veteran tight end Doug Jolley and a second-round pick 24 slots lower, the Jets then used that pick not on a player to fill one of their defensive holes, not on a much-needed replacement for departed right tackle Kareem McKenzie, but on a kicker.

After last year's playoff choke, there was no way that the team could bring Doug Brien back to face the angry fans at the Meadowlands. But blowing a second-round draft pick on kicker Mike Nugent of Ohio State was a monumental overreaction.

There is no doubt that Nugent was the best kicking prospect to come out of college in a number of years. But the key word there is "prospect." Kickers are drafted so rarely that you would assume no team would draft one unless they were certain they were getting a sure thing. Yet the number of drafted kickers who develop into productive, enduring NFL players is astonishingly low.

Not counting Nugent, since 1993 13 different kickers have been chosen in the first five rounds of the NFL draft (table 1). Only five of those kickers spent all of last season

TABLE 1. KICKERS DRAFTED IN ROUNDS 1–5, 1993–2005

Year	Round	Name	Team	College	Games
1993	3	Jason Elam	DEN	Hawaii	172
1993	5	Scott Sisson	NE	Georgia Tech	29
1994	3	Doug Brien	SF	California	151
1995	3	Steve McLaughlin	STL	Arizona	8
1997	3	Brett Conway	GB	Penn State	51
1999	3	Martin Gramatica	TB	Kansas St.	93
2000	1	Sebastian Janikowski	OAK	Florida St.	77
2001	4	Bill Gramatica	ARI	South Florida	34
2001	5	John Markham	NYG	Vanderbilt	0
2002	4	Jeff Chandler	SF	Florida	13
2002	4	Travis Dorsch	CIN	Purdue	1
2004	3	Nate Kaeding	SD	Iowa	16
2004	5	Josh Scobee	JAC	Louisiana Tech	16
2005	2	Mike Nugent	NYJ	Ohio State	—

on an NFL roster. One of them was—yes—Doug Brien, who in 1994 was a promising young prospect deemed worthy of a third-round pick by the San Francisco 49ers. Another was 2004 third-round pick Nate Kaeding of San Diego. Without a missed field goal in the wild card game by last year's hot kicking prospect, of course, there would have been no opportunity for Brien to miss two field goals against Pittsburgh, and the Jets would not have spent a second-round pick on this year's hot kicking prospect.

Kickers are notoriously inconsistent from year to year, and even kickers good enough to be drafted high end up no differently. Martin Gramatica was as highly lauded as Nugent when Tampa Bay used a third-round pick on him in 1999; last year he was booed out of town after he missed two field goals in a close loss to St. Louis and three in a close loss to Carolina. Arizona chose his brother Bill in the fourth round of 2001; the younger Gramatica was out of the league within three years.

Green Bay wasted a third-round pick on Brett Conway in 1997; he didn't even make the roster. He later kicked for six teams over a five-year period. The Rams used a third-rounder on Steve McLaughlin in 1995; he played only one season, missing half his field goals. Cincinnati spent a fourth-rounder on Travis Dorsch; he lasted all of one game. John Markham, taken by the Giants the year before, didn't even get that far.

Of course, any player chosen in the second round of the draft could turn out to be a bust, be it a kicker or any other position. However, stats bear out that the higher in the draft a position player is taken, the more likely he is to succeed in the NFL. That's not true for the specialists like kickers and punters.

Last year's two Pro Bowl kickers, Adam Vinatieri and David Akers, were both undrafted free agents. So were the two Pro Bowl kickers from the year before, Mike Vanderjagt and Jeff Wilkins. Contrast that to the other positions where the Jets had holes going into the draft: offensive tackle, defensive tackle, cornerback, and safety. A great majority of Pro Bowlers at these positions were first-round picks, and the rest were primarily second- and third-rounders.

The Jets did choose cornerback Justin Miller with their own pick in the second round and defensive tackle Sione Pouha in the third. They used their fourth- and fifth-round picks on safeties to add depth to the secondary. But they took no offensive linemen. Two tackles, Marcus Johnson of Mississippi and Khalif Barnes of Washington, went off the draft board in the next five picks after the Jets took Nugent. Instead of one of those players, the Jets, as of press time, have Adrian Jones, the final player taken in the fourth round of the 2004 draft, on top of the depth chart at right tackle.

Johnson and Barnes could turn out to be flops. But since most second-round offensive linemen become productive starters and most fourth-round linemen do not, the difference in value between those players and Jones is far greater than the difference in value between Nugent and a league-average free agent kicker. This would be true even if Nugent were guaranteed to immediately become the best kicker in the NFL, and of course there is no such guarantee. The choice to take Nugent rather than a position player looks even worse based on a recent study by two business professors showing that, because of the exorbitant salaries paid to first-round selections, the picks that offer the best chance to maximize return on investment come in the second round. (This study is discussed further in the New York Giants chapter.)

A common refrain is that the Nugent pick made sense because the Jets were just a kicker away from a trip to New England for the AFC championship game. But that assumes that the 2004 Jets and the 2005 Jets are the same except for Nugent, and they aren't. The team has holes on the offensive and defensive lines that will make a repeat of last year's 10–6 record extremely difficult. They are depending on rookies to upgrade the secondary, and first-year cornerbacks have a steep learning curve. The team's biggest additions are either backups (Blaylock and potentially Fiedler) or replacements for similar players (Coles, Jolley). It's nice that Nugent might be more likely than Brien to connect on a last-minute field goal to win the game. But as bad as it might be to miss that field goal, it is even worse to lose by two touchdowns because of inexperienced players throughout the rest of your roster.

Aaron Schatz

Research: The Effect of Pace in Football

The Jets, under the reign of head coach Herman Edwards and offensive coordinator Paul Hackett, have been one of the slowest-paced teams in the NFL. As mentioned above, Tennessee has also been a slow-paced team in recent years. Conversely, teams perennially ranking among the fastest paced seem to come from the Mike Holmgren family tree of head coaches. Bill Walsh taught Holmgren how to script the first 15 plays of a game, and apparently that script also dictates an aggressively paced offense. The Seahawks, Eagles, and Packers all have been fast-paced teams under Holmgren, Andy Reid, and Mike Sherman, respectively. This makes the Eagles' fourth quarter Super Bowl slowdown seem even more bizarre. (By the way, new Tennessee offensive coordinator Norm Chow worked with both Holmgren and Reid at BYU in the 1980s, so things may be changing for the Titans.)

Is it unusual for a team to maintain a consistent game pace, year after year? Yes—it turns out that most teams do not show much consistency at either end of the rankings. For example, the Denver Broncos' offense has been slow, fast, and everywhere in between despite many years of coaching stability under head coach Mike Shanahan and offensive coordinator Gary Kubiak.

Game pace in football has not been studied as extensively as pace in basketball. One reason is that it is tricky to define pace in football because sometimes the clock is running between plays and other times it is stopped. There are actually several ways an offense can control the pace of a game, including deciding how much of the play clock to run down before the next snap, play calling (obviously, passing plays are more likely to result in clock stoppages), and the execution of the play (running out of bounds or committing penalties).

Pace can also be greatly influenced by game situations. A team with a lead late in the game is likely to slow down and grind out the clock as much as possible. And a team down by a couple of touchdowns in the fourth quarter is probably running a fast-paced, no-huddle offense in an attempt to catch up before time runs out.

When the concept of pace was introduced on Football Outsiders during the past season[1], our intent was to de-

---

1. You'll find the articles here: http://www.footballoutsiders.com/ramblings.php?p=1867 and http://www.footballoutsiders.com/ramblings.php?p=1880.

scribe pace as dictated by each team's game plan or style of play, not pace that was situation induced. In that study, we limited our discussion of pace to only the first half of games. We calculate a team's pace from NFL drive charts, which list time of possession and number of plays, resulting in a pace definition of time (in seconds) per play. A high value indicates slow pace, whereas a low value indicates fast pace. Note that this is based on game-clock time, not real time. An alternate definition might consider real time, or perhaps be based on how much time is left on the play clock when the ball is snapped. In reality, there is probably not much difference, for two reasons. With today's NFL rules, the game clock is running more often than not between plays, especially during the situations we're interested in. Secondly, an offensive philosophy that dictates different speeds depending on whether the game clock is running just isn't realistic.

In order to accurately describe a team's pace as determined by its style or philosophy, the current score and time remaining must also be considered. In our revised definition of game pace, only drives where the score was within six points are considered. Further, drives starting in the last five minutes of the first half are thrown out since these drives are very likely to be hurry-up drives in an attempt to score before halftime. Finally, we also discard all fourth quarter drives, since the pace of late-game drives are usually situation induced, regardless of the score. Applying this refined definition of game pace to the 2004 season, we ranked the 32 teams according to their game pace. Table 2 shows the results, ranked from slowest to fastest.

The results show that over the course of a season there isn't any apparent connection between a team's pace and its ability to score points or win games. Teams can win with either a slow- or fast-paced style, and as mentioned earlier, only a few teams tend to consistently employ just one approach.

Perhaps more interesting are the game-day strategy implications of pace. Commentators often talk about a team's ability to "control the clock" as being a key to victory. Others advocate a "ball control" offense against a stronger team in order to keep the opposing team's offense off the field. Of course, barring turnovers on punts and kickoffs, football rules require teams to alternate possessions, so generally a team can't give itself more chances to score than its opponent gets. But by slowing the pace, a team can reduce the total number of possessions by *both* teams. As the theory goes, creating a shorter game gives the weaker team a better chance of staying with the stronger team, which would certainly win in a game with an infinite number of possessions. The complementary theory is that stronger teams should run a hurry-up offense in order to lengthen the game and create more opportunities to impose their might.

Several years ago statistics Professor Harold Sackrowitz and his son Daniel, writing in the statistical journal *Chance,* examined the strategic aspects of football pace in a theoretical manner. They concluded that because the probability of winning is so sensitive to changes in scoring efficiency, it is misguided to employ a ball control offense. They argue that a team attempting to deviate from its optimal pace will likely reduce its ability to score so much that the strategy will not be worthwhile.

In order to examine the effects of such strategies, we undertook an empirical study of pace using all 1,752 regular season games from 1998 to 2004. In order to evaluate the relative strength of teams (which theoretically would dictate their pace strategy), we obtained point spreads for all the games and grouped them into three bins—(1) evenly matched teams with betting lines of 3 points or less, (2) moderately mismatched teams with lines between 3.5 to 6.5 points, and (3) heavily mismatched teams with lines of 7 points or greater. Each team's game pace was determined

TABLE 2. 2004 SITUATION NEUTRAL GAME PACE

Rank	Team	Seconds/Play	Rank	Team	Seconds/Play	Rank	Team	Seconds/Play	Rank	Team	Seconds/Play
1	NYG	32.412	9	STL	30.878	17	CLE	29.979	25	NO	29.112
2	JAC	32.049	10	ATL	30.771	18	MIN	29.705	26	BUF	29.086
3	HOU	31.514	11	PIT	30.658	19	DEN	29.641	27	NE	29.079
4	ARI	31.461	12	DAL	30.629	20	DET	29.561	28	CIN	28.872
5	NYJ	31.451	13	BAL	30.563	21	KC	29.548	29	PHI	28.685
6	TEN	31.448	14	CHI	30.511	22	SF	29.497	30	OAK	27.627
7	WAS	31.057	15	CAR	30.508	23	GB	29.324	31	MIA	27.550
8	TB	31.033	16	SD	30.281	24	IND	29.195	32	SEA	27.519

by applying our revised game pace definition (as described above). In order to measure only that pace deliberately established by a team (prior to being affected by a lopsided score), any game that didn't have a minimum of four qualifying drives by each team during the game was discarded from the data set, leaving us with 1,704 team-game pace data points (852 games) over the seven-year span. Each team's game pace was labeled as being fast, medium, or slow, such that each pace bucket contained exactly one third of the values. Finally, the winning percentage of each combination of groupings was determined. Figure 1 shows the results, using the convention of negative point spreads to represent the stronger teams and positive point spreads to represent the weaker teams.

We see that in games between heavily mismatched teams, a medium pace works best, both for the stronger *and* the weaker team. There appears to be no evidence that weaker teams have improved their chances of winning by

FIGURE 1. GAME PACE EFFECTS 1998–2004

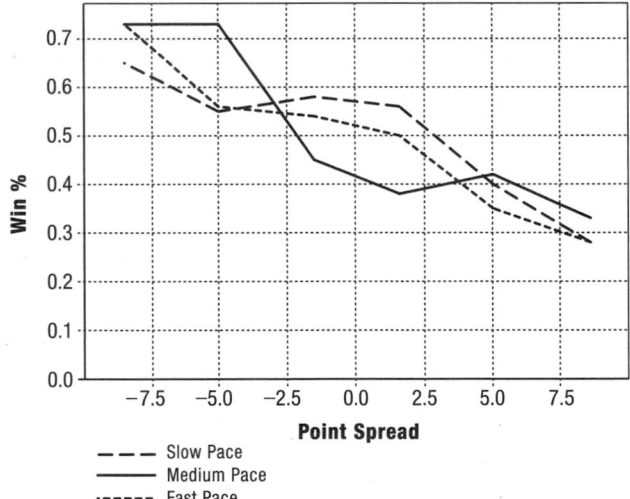

running a slowdown-ball-control offense. Stronger teams haven't helped themselves by running a hurry-up offense, although among the heavily favored group, it hasn't hurt. A more curious result is that in games between evenly matched teams, a medium pace seems to be the least effective. Perhaps there is a positive psychological effect of running an extreme pace when the teams are equally matched.

Of course, these are just general conclusions. Teams can win with either fast- or slow-paced offenses. Generally, it would seem a team's pace doesn't have a major impact on its chances of winning. From 1998 through 2004, slow-paced teams have won 49.7% of their games, fast-paced teams have won 49.8%, and the teams in between have won 50.4%.

Perhaps the best approach a team can take is to stay with whatever pace seems to work best in order to maintain optimal offensive efficiency. To test this theory, we measured the variance of each team's games in the seven-year period and divided the results into two groups, those with high variance and those with low variance. We then determined how many wins each group averaged. The results suggest that teams can expect an average of one additional win per season just by maintaining a relatively consistent pace from game to game. The high-pace-variance teams averaged 7.51 wins per season, while the low-pace-variance teams averaged 8.48 wins per season.

It may actually be counterproductive for an offense to adjust its pace philosophy based on a game mismatch because it leads to reduced efficiency. Although there is some evidence that a slow or fast pace can help in an evenly matched game, in general, a medium pace works best. Teams are better off staying with their optimal pace at least until game situations dictate otherwise.

Jim Armstrong

Jets 2004 Stats by Week

Wk	vs.	W-L	PF	PA	YDF	YDA	TO	DVOA Total	Off	Def	ST
1	CIN	W	31	24	438	351	+1	18.5%	61.8%	30.9%	-12.5%
2	@SD	W	34	28	380	327	+4	62.0%	32.5%	-35.1%	-5.6%
3	BYE										
4	@MIA	W	17	9	399	357	+1	20.9%	1.5%	-14.1%	5.2%
5	BUF	W	16	14	235	293	+3	25.7%	45.0%	19.8%	0.5%
6	SF	W	22	14	383	252	-1	10.7%	35.4%	32.5%	7.8%
7	@NE	L	7	13	270	347	0	-11.0%	3.0%	13.6%	-0.4%
8	MIA	W	41	14	472	259	+3	97.6%	76.0%	-12.0%	9.7%
9	@BUF	L	17	22	282	341	-2	2.5%	23.4%	20.8%	-0.1%
10	BAL	L	17	20	305	262	0	0.8%	5.5%	8.9%	4.2%
11	@CLE	W	10	7	235	216	0	-44.7%	-17.8%	25.9%	-1.0%
12	@ARI	W	13	3	325	245	+4	34.3%	6.1%	-22.0%	6.2%
13	HOU	W	29	7	360	230	+1	89.9%	35.6%	-36.3%	18.0%
14	@PIT	L	6	17	296	262	-1	16.7%	-13.7%	-25.6%	4.8%
15	SEA	W	37	14	482	275	+3	83.8%	85.7%	-2.1%	-4.1%
16	NE	L	7	23	278	374	-3	-15.6%	-1.0%	11.1%	-3.5%
17	@STL	L	29	32	342	479	+3	-13.3%	-12.4%	21.6%	20.8%
18	@SD	W	20	17	396	408	+1	52.2%	42.4%	-9.0%	0.7%
19	@PIT	L	17	20	275	364	0	29.1%	10.4%	-11.7%	7.0%

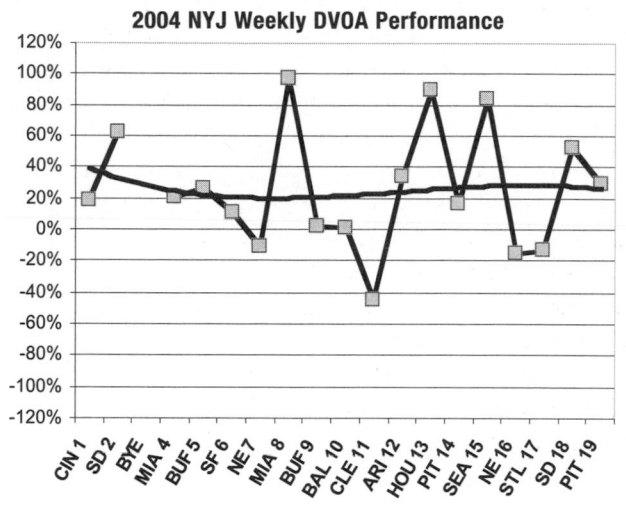

Trends and Splits

	Offense	Rank	Defense	Rank
Total DVOA	23.4%	5	2.8%	19
Unadjusted VOA	20.4%	5	-3.4%	12
Weighted Trend	16.9%	6	2.8%	19
Variance	10.3%	13	5.5%	29
Passing	30.9%	6	15.1%	24
Rushing	17.3%	2	-10.4%	5
First Down	33.4%	2	13.2%	26
Second Down	15.3%	8	-8.0%	8
Third Down	16.4%	9	-1.1%	20
Red Zone	32.9%	2	2.9%	21
Late and Close	17.3%	6	-7.2%	14

Five-Year Performance

	2004	2003	2002	2001	2000
W-L	10-6	6-10	9-7	10-6	9-7
Pythagorean Wins	10.2	7.5	8.6	8.4	8.0
Estimated Wins	11.1	7.9	9.8	10.4	9.9
Total DVOA	23.8%	-4.0%	15.2%	14.0%	13.3%
Rank	6	18	8	7	11
Offense	23.4%	8.0%	18.7%	-1.1%	-4.4%
Rank	5	9	4	11	17
Defense	2.8%	13.9%	11.0%	-13.2%	-21.6%
Rank	19	30	27	8	3
Special Teams	3.1%	2.0%	7.5%	1.8%	-3.9%
Rank	11	10	2	8	25

Passing (min. 5 plays)

Player	DPAR	PAR	DVOA	Plys	NtYds	Avg	Cmpl	TD	Int
Chad Pennington	77.2	60.5	31.6%	390	2576	6.6	65.4%	16	9
Quincy Carter	8.8	4.9	15.9%	70	429	6.1	60.3%	3	1
Brooks Bollinger	0.7	0.3	4.2%	10	52	5.2	55.6%	0	0

Rushing (min. 3 plays)

Player	DPAR	PAR	DVOA	Plys	Yds	Avg	TD	Fum	Suc
Curtis Martin	54.4	51.1	19.7%	370	1685	4.6	12	2	53%
LaMont Jordan	19.2	20.6	36.0%	93	479	5.2	2	0	55%
Chad Pennington	5.3	4.3	15.5%	24	135	5.6	1	1	—
Quincy Carter	-2.5	-2.8	-72.5%	8	26	3.3	0	1	—
B. J. Askew	-0.3	-0.2	-23.2%	6	23	3.8	0	0	33%
Santana Moss	-1.8	-1.9	-65.3%	6	23	3.8	0	1	—

Receiving (min. 5 plays)

Player	DPAR	PAR	DVOA	Plys	Ctch	Yds	Y/C	TD	CPct
WR									
Justin McCareins	20.8	20.0	19.8%	90	56	772	13.8	4	62%
Santana Moss	24.6	22.9	32.6%	78	45	838	18.6	5	58%
Wayne Chrebet	6.2	6.6	2.6%	54	31	397	12.8	1	57%
Jonathan Carter	6.1	5.8	42.0%	16	10	173	17.3	1	63%
Jerricho Cotchery	-0.1	-0.3	-16.1%	11	6	60	10.0	0	55%
TE									
Chris Baker	5.3	3.5	14.1%	29	18	182	10.1	4	62%
Anthony Becht	-2.4	-3.7	-25.4%	28	13	100	7.7	1	46%
RB									
Jerald Sowell	7.1	3.2	13.0%	59	45	342	7.6	1	76%
Curtis Martin	4.7	1.9	10.7%	50	41	248	6.0	2	84%
LaMont Jordan	4.4	4.1	42.7%	16	15	112	7.5	0	94%

Defensive Players (min. 20 plays)

Player	Age	Plys	Stop	Dfts	AvYds	StpRt	Sack	Int	FR
Defensive Line									
Jason Ferguson	31	60	40	11	1.9	67%	3.5	0	0
Shaun Ellis	28	58	46	25	1.0	79%	11.0	0	1
Dewayne Robertson	24	52	35	15	1.7	67%	3.0	0	0
John Abraham	27	50	38	22	0.0	76%	9.5	0	1
Bryan Thomas	26	44	33	14	2.4	75%	1.5	0	0
Linebackers									
Jonathan Vilma	23	113	64	23	3.7	57%	2.0	3	1
Eric Barton	28	113	59	22	4.3	52%	2.5	1	4
Victor Hobson	25	48	25	6	4.6	52%	0.0	1	0
Sam Cowart	30	26	16	4	3.1	62%	0.0	0	0

Player	Age	Plys	Stop	Dfts	AvYds	StpRt	Sack	Int	FR
Secondary									
Eric Coleman	23	102	33	19	10.0	32%	2.0	4	1
David Barrett	28	94	36	18	7.9	38%	0.0	2	0
Reggie Tongue	32	78	20	10	10.6	26%	0.0	1	1
Donnie Abraham	32	70	30	17	6.4	43%	0.0	2	2
Jon McGraw	26	34	17	10	7.5	50%	0.0	2	0
Terrell Buckley	34	23	13	6	4.4	57%	0.0	3	0

Offensive Line

Year	Yards	AdjLineYd	Rank	Power	Rank	10+ Yds	Rank	Stuff	Rank	Sack	AdjSack%	Rank
2002	4.09	4.08	17	52%	30	16%	20	26%	25	33	6.4%	18
2003	4.06	4.23	14	65%	18	13%	24	24%	17	30	5.5%	13
2004	4.70	4.82	2	84%	1	14%	30	18%	3	31	6.3%	14

Year	LEnd	Rank	LTckl	Rank	MdGrd	Rank	RTckl	Rank	REnd	Rank
2002	3.94	20	3.69	28	4.16	20	4.66	6	3.64	19
2003	4.59	9	4.57	10	3.83	25	4.69	4	4.68	5
2004	4.93	6	4.71	10	4.61	4	5.17	3	5.29	1

Center Kevin Mawae is probably the best in the league at getting out in front of his running back. Quickness is an under-appreciated attribute for a center, and Mawae is incredibly quick. The dramatic improvement that transformed this from an average line to one of the league's best came on either side of him. In 2003, Mawae was flanked by Dave Szott, a fading veteran in his 14th season, and Brent Smith, who had not played a single down in 2001 or 2002. Szott retired and was replaced at left guard by Pete Kendall, who had a very good year after Arizona coach Dennis Green made the surprising decision to cut him. Smith was replaced in the starting lineup by Brandon Moore, who is the answer to the question, "Has NFL Europe ever developed a significant player at a position other than quarterback or special teams?" The Jets have been one of the league's top teams running to the right for two years, which means the loss of right tackle Kareem McKenzie to the Giants is a big one. Every time Jason Taylor or Willie McGinest blows by Adrian Jones or Marko Cavka to drop Pennington and knock the Jets into deep field goal range, at least Jets fans can feel assured that Mike Nugent will absolutely, positively never miss from 55-plus yards. I mean, the guy was a *second-round draft pick,* for crying out loud.

Defensive Front Seven

Year	Yards	AdjLineYd	Rank	Power	Rank	10+ Yds	Rank	Stuff	Rank	Sack	AdjSack%	Rank
2002	4.67	4.72	32	77%	28	14%	9	15%	32	30	5.6%	24
2003	4.30	4.86	32	63%	9	10%	5	16%	32	35	6.7%	13
2004	3.68	3.87	5	61%	15	15%	11	28%	6	36	6.7%	17

Year	LEnd	Rank	LTckl	Rank	MdGrd	Rank	RTckl	Rank	REnd	Rank
2002	4.70	28	4.63	25	4.60	30	4.69	26	5.55	31
2003	4.82	30	5.27	30	4.56	29	5.17	31	5.71	32
2004	2.71	1	4.68	26	4.00	10	3.45	2	4.26	22

This group was the biggest reason the Jets made the playoffs last season, but the departure of Jason Ferguson might be one of those losses that creates a domino effect. With Ferguson gone, other players will have to be responsible for larger areas of the field or duties that don't quite fit their skill sets. The retirement of Josh Evans, expected to be one of the players to help replace Ferguson, further complicates things. The Jets have signed Lance Legree from the cross-town (yet same stadium) Giants, but he's never started on a regular basis and has a hard time shedding blockers. The other possibility is third-round pick Sione Pouha, a 329-pound run stuffer out of the University of Utah. Pouha struggles against complicated blocking schemes and wears down late in games, which is why many scouts considered him a development project. But there are no Mormon development projects. Because Pouha spent three years as a missionary, he is a 26-year-old rookie. While we do not fault Pouha for putting his religious beliefs ahead of his career, the Jets must understand that by the time he "develops" the proper technique to play defensive tackle in the NFL, he'll already be into his physical decline.

While defensive tackle is a mess, though, the rest of this group is top notch. During the playoffs Dewayne Robertson showed that quick first step that made the Jets trade up to get him. The Steelers could not pull effectively because Robertson got into the backfield as soon as the guard moved. The most surprising thing about the Jets' front seven is the faith first-year defensive coordinator Donnie Henderson put in rookie middle linebacker Jonathan Vilma, who called all the defensive alignments on his way to being named defensive rookie of the year. Our numbers seem to indicate that the weak link in the linebacking corps is Victor Hobson, who made far fewer plays than either Vilma or Eric Barton and made those plays farther from the line of scrimmage.

Defensive Secondary

Year	DVOA vs. #1 WR	Rank	DVOA vs. #2 WR	Rank	DVOA vs. Other WR	Rank	DVOA vs. TE	Rank	DVOA vs. RB	Rank
2002	-38.6%	2	17.3%	20	4.4%	17	8.3%	20	11.4%	23
2003	24.7%	26	30.3%	31	3.6%	23	-13.0%	10	10.4%	24
2004	33.0%	28	20.9%	28	-13.9%	11	-19.0%	8	-11.2%	15

First the good news: Erik Coleman had a very strong rookie season, possibly the best of any second-day draftee from 2004, and he's a big part of why the Jets were stronger against tight ends and slot receivers than against standard wideouts. The bad news is that this secondary needed an upgrade in the off-season, and didn't quite get it. Cornerback Donnie Abraham, who will turn 32 this season, is nowhere near the cornerback he was as an important member of the Bucs' defense in the 1990s. The corners were a huge liability last year. The other corner, David Barrett, is really a nickelback forced into the starting lineup, and he doesn't shut down receivers the way the Jets need him to. He may be replaced by Justin Miller of Clemson, who surprised many (and delighted the Jets) by dropping into the middle of the second round when most people projected him to go in the first. Cornerbacks take time to adapt to the NFL, though, so the Jets will probably have to stick with Barrett for the time being. Fourth-rounder Kerry Rhodes out of Louisville and fifth-rounder Andre Maddox out of North Carolina State will compete to replace strong safety Reggie Tongue, waived in early June.

Special Teams

Year	DVOA	Rank	FG/XP	Rank	Net Punt	Rank	Punt Ret	Rank	Net Kick	Rank	Kick Ret	Rank
2002	7.5%	2	-2.2	19	7.3	8	14.9	4	2.7	12	19.2	1
2003	2.0%	10	8.9	10	-8.1	28	3.1	24	14.3	4	-0.1	17
2004	3.1%	11	3.7	13	16.9	5	-6.8	21	1.8	11	1.8	14

Things are going to be just a little weird around the Jets' special teams in 2005. Start with the Mike Nugent controversy, discussed earlier in this chapter—there aren't a lot of teams where the kicker gets more press coverage than the quarterback. The departed Toby Gowin had a strong year as both kickoff specialist and punter. Nugent will try to fill one role but the other is up in the air. At press time, it looked like New York's punter this season will either be 31-year-old Australian Rules Football veteran Ben Graham (who is trying to follow in the footsteps of fellow Aussie punter Darren Bennett), or ex-Denver punter Micah Knorr. Jets fans should root for Graham because he would make a more fun interview and because Knorr was our worst-rated punter last year—he cost the Broncos 10.5 points worth of field position with his punts after adjusting for altitude. Near the end of the season the Jets moved rookie receiver Jerricho Cotchery into the kick return role, and he was dynamite, so they would be well advised to try him in both return slots. Finally, the Jets are one of the few teams with a long snapper controversy. Although James Dearth (who was the first free agent signing of the Terry Bradway era) has been a solid player, the Jets drafted Colorado State tight end Joel Dreessen in the sixth round. They might use Dreesen as their long snapper because he may be able to contribute more on the offense.

Coaching Staff

As noted in the first part of this chapter, Paul Hackett, after being continuously ripped in New York for his play calling, quit as offensive coordinator and will be replaced by ex-Tennessee coordinator Mike Heimerdinger. Defensive coordinator Donnie Henderson was part of Marvin Lewis's staff in Baltimore when the Ravens built the league's best defense, and he hopes to repeat that success with the Jets. It will help, of course, if Jonathan Vilma can play like Ray Lewis.

The most interesting name on the coaching staff, however, is Dick Curl. Curl was the ex-Dick Vermeil assistant brought in last year by Herman Edwards specifically to handle clock management. On one hand, we heartily endorse the allocation of resources to improving clock management. On the other hand, it didn't really seem like clock management actually improved. Curl's story got even stranger this past off-season when he somehow became the beneficiary of the memorable sideline confrontation between Edwards and running backs coach Bishop Harris during the playoff game in San Diego. Harris went off to San Francisco after the season, and Curl is now clock management assistant/running backs coach.

Oakland Raiders

Norv Turner has now coached 124 NFL games. He has made the playoffs only once. That's an amazing feat: There aren't many coaches who last long enough to post a 54–70 record. In fact, as table 1 shows, there are only ten coaches in NFL history who have logged 100 games but reached the playoffs no more than once.

Turner's record looks worse when you realize that he was the offensive coordinator for the Chargers in 2001 and the Dolphins in 2002 and 2003. That's three more years of high-level coaching with no playoff appearances, despite the fact that those Dolphins teams had good talent and winning records.

Starr survived because he was a local legend; Van Brocklin and Capers spent years building expansion teams. The Skins kept Turner on for six years in DC primarily because of his Super Bowl pedigree: two championships in Dallas as offensive coordinator under Jimmy Johnson.

The Chargers then hired him, presumably, on the success of his offenses in Washington. The Dolphins hired him because good friend Dave Wannstedt was the coach. And Al Davis hired him because everybody else had.

NFL reporters tout Turner as an offensive mastermind, with *Pro Football Weekly* calling him "one of the best offensive coordinators and QB coaches in the game" when the Chargers hired him in 2001. But if Turner is an offensive mastermind, he's really going out of his way to hide it.

The Cowboys' offense actually had its two highest-scoring seasons after Turner left for Washington. The Redskins offense was parked in neutral for most of Turner's tenure, with a single breakout season. In San Diego and Miami, the story was the same (see table 2). Since leaving Dallas, Turner's offenses, except in 1999, have barely risen above mediocrity. The point is hammered home further by looking at DVOA ratings for Turner's teams in the seven seasons for which we have play-by-play data.

In fairness to Turner, the Chargers offense ranked 31st in DVOA when he took over and dropped to 20th after he left. The Redskins slipped to 22nd after he left. The Dolphins ranked 23rd before he arrived and slipped somewhere below Eastern Nazerene College after his departure. Turner really hasn't had top offensive talent to work with on his last three teams. But after acquiring Randy Moss and LaMont Jordan in the off-season, Turner is out of excuses. Jordan led the NFL in DVOA, outpacing teammate Curtis Martin. DVOA figures for running backs tend to favor play-

RAIDERS PROSPECTUS

2004 Record: 5–11

DVOA Estimated Wins: 5.9 (26th)

Pythagorean Wins: 5.1 (28th)

DVOA: −19.1% total (26th), −21.0% weighted (26th)

Adjusted Offense: 20.6 points/game (−3.2% DVOA, 17th)

Adjusted Defense: 25.3 points/game (14.3% DVOA, 27th)

Adjusted Special Teams: −0.5 points/game (−1.6% DVOA, 21st)

Variance: 16.0% (20th)

2004: Well, um, they had a nice Sunday night game against Tampa.

2005: 54–40 and Fight: Once a historical slogan, now a typical loss for the 2005 Raiders.

2005 Projection

Leinart Land (0–4): 24%

Bad Team (5–6): 23%

Mediocre (7–8): 24%

Playoff Contender (9–10): 17%

Super Bowl Contender (11+): 12%

Projected Average Opponent: 5.2% DVOA (3rd in NFL)

ers with limited carries, but his DPAR rating (13th) is also excellent. Moss, battling injuries, snatched 13 TD passes in 13 games last season and ranked 15th among wide receivers in DPAR despite missing time. In 2003, playing without injury, he was second in the league in DPAR.

Moss and Jordan will be backed by an impressive supporting cast. Jerry Porter was hurt and had an off year, but still caught eight TD passes; his low DPAR ranking (56th) says more about the team's tendency to force him the ball than about his skills. Ronald Curry caught 71% of the passes thrown to him and finished tenth among wide receivers in DVOA; if he returns from an Achilles tendon injury, he'll be the best slot receiver outside of Indianapolis. Kerry Collins, terrible early on, threw 16 TD passes and eight interceptions in seven games after the Raiders' bye week. The offensive line, bolstered by rising stars like Robert Gallery, finished eighth in Adjusted Sack Rate.

This is the best collection of talent Turner has had to work with since he had Brad Johnson, Stephen Davis,

TABLE 1. COACHES WITH 100+ GAMES BUT NO MORE THAN ONE PLAYOFF APPEARANCE

Coach	Wins	Losses	Ties	Playoff Rcrd
Norv Turner	54	70	—	1–1
Marion Campbell	34	80	1	0–0
Dom Capers	46	66	—	1–1
Bruce Coslett	47	77	—	0–1
Dan Henning	30	73	1	0–0
Mike Holovak	52	47	9	1–1
Joe Kuharich	58	81	3	0–0
Ray Perkins	42	75	—	1–1
Bart Starr	52	73	3	1–1
Norm Van Brocklin	66	100	7	0–0

TABLE 2. OFFENSIVE RANK OF TURNER-COACHED TEAMS

Year	Team	Points	Yards	DVOA
1994	Was	13	19	N/A
1995	Was	18	16	N/A
1996	Was	8	16	N/A
1997	Was	15	19	N/A
1998	Was	17	12	12
1999	Was	2	2	3
2000	Was	24	11	11
2001	SD	14	15	16
2002	Mia	12	15	18
2003	Mia	17	24	21
2004	Oak	18	20	17

The Raiders defense finished a respectable 15th in Adjusted Line Yards, but it was 30th in Adjusted Sack Rate and 29th in percentage of runs stuffed. Ryan will have another year to develop his system and a new set of younger defensive linemen: ex-Eagle free agent Derrick Burgess and rookies Ryan Riddle (who had 14.5 sacks last year at Cal) and Antaaj Hawthorne. There's an influx of youth in the secondary as well, with rookie Fabian Washington likely starting at cornerback and fellow rookie Stanford Routt as nickelback.

But the front seven must pressure the quarterback for the secondary to contain the powerful offenses of the AFC West. And while the Raiders' division schedule figures to be difficult, the rest of the schedule is downright brutal. The Raiders face both defending conference champions on the road. Opponents like the Jets, Bills, and Cowboys won't be pushovers. According to average projected DVOA of opponent, only San Diego and Miami face harder schedules in 2005.

The difficult schedule is bad news for Turner, a coach whose teams have a history of flat performances in critical situations. Fans in Washington remember a Redskins team that stormed out to a 7–1 record in 1996, only to lose six of their last eight games. They also remember a 2000 Redskins team that started out 6–2 but missed the playoffs, losing to Cowboys and Cardinals teams that would finish 5–11 and 3–13 and ending the year with a .500 record. Raiders fans saw a little of that in 2004: The Raiders blew a chance to go 3–1 when they lost to the Texans in Week 4, kicking off a five-game losing streak. Turner's teams seem to have a knack for losing streaks and banana peel games; stacking the deck against them with a rough slate of games is almost cruel.

This team could easily go into the tank at the first sign of trouble. Turner may be too laid back to challenge the me-first attitudes of Moss, Sapp, and Charles Woodson, and Collins isn't a strong clubhouse leader. One bad early-season loss could sink the ship.

Al Davis is not a patient man, the Raiders are not in rebuilding mode, and there will be nowhere to hide if Turner does not lead Oakland to the playoffs in 2005. Moss, Porter, Collins, and Jordan are players tailor-made for Turner's offensive scheme. Woodson, Burgess, and Danny Clark can be the building blocks of a quality defense. If they played in the depleted NFC, this team might be dangerous. But in the AFC, they'll win eight or nine games and add to Turner's resume of playoff near misses.

A 9–7 record won't save Turner's job, but it could earn him his next one, as a coach or coordinator. Then another team can dream of an offense like the 1993 Cowboys, only to get one that looks more like the 1996 Redskins.

Mike Tanier

Michael Westbrook, Albert Connell, and Larry Centers in Washington in 1999. That was Turner's playoff team, the one that finished second in the NFL in points scored. They excelled on offense but were inconsistent on defense, leading to the firing of coordinator Mike Nolan. Now Nolan is in San Francisco, where he will take on Turner in an epic Bay Area battle of "who can win eight games."

The 1999 Redskins, like the current Raiders, were a year removed from a spending spree on the defensive line. The Redskins were ultimately disappointed by the play of Dana Stubblefield and Dan Wilkinson, two big names who never played up to their billing. Their counterparts on the 2004 Raiders were Warren Sapp, Ted Washington, and John Parrella. Washington was satisfactory late in the year, but Sapp and Parrella gave the team little return on a hefty investment. This veteran decline was a major reason why Rob Ryan's defense was one of the weakest in the NFL.

Raiders 2004 Stats by Week

Wk	vs.	W-L	PF	PA	YDF	YDA	TO	Total	Off	Def	ST
1	@PIT	L	21	24	353	234	-3	-23.0%	-11.7%	-4.3%	-15.7%
2	BUF	W	13	10	273	243	+1	60.7%	49.0%	-9.0%	2.7%
3	TB	W	30	20	399	389	-1	32.9%	48.3%	16.8%	1.3%
4	@HOU	L	17	30	375	386	-4	-53.6%	-24.4%	28.6%	-0.6%
5	@IND	L	14	35	269	338	-2	-40.9%	-47.9%	-9.5%	-2.6%
6	DEN	L	3	31	145	444	-1	-93.2%	-55.2%	33.3%	-4.7%
7	NO	L	26	31	432	322	-2	-35.4%	6.6%	27.2%	-14.9%
8	@SD	L	14	42	281	448	-2	-67.2%	-23.8%	53.5%	10.2%
9	@CAR	W	27	24	297	304	-1	25.3%	29.9%	14.4%	9.9%
10	BYE										
11	SD	L	17	23	273	402	0	3.8%	21.2%	12.8%	-4.6%
12	@DEN	W	25	24	395	367	0	20.5%	-3.6%	-29.3%	-5.2%
13	KC	L	27	34	364	500	+1	6.6%	29.9%	29.3%	5.9%
14	@ATL	L	10	35	296	354	-3	-46.1%	-0.3%	36.9%	-8.8%
15	TEN	W	40	35	415	527	+1	-10.7%	28.6%	37.3%	-2.0%
16	@KC	L	30	31	300	433	+1	-4.2%	-12.3%	4.0%	12.2%
17	JAC	L	6	13	281	242	-2	-47.4%	-69.4%	-30.3%	-8.3%

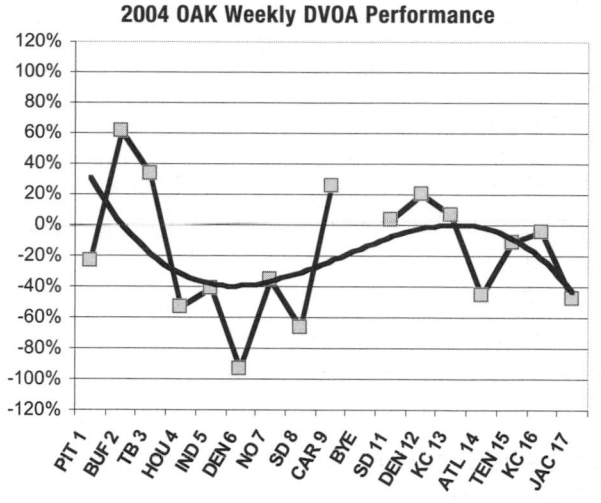

2004 OAK Weekly DVOA Performance

Trends and Splits

	Offense	Rank	Defense	Rank
Total DVOA	-3.2%	17	14.3%	27
Unadjusted VOA	-5.5%	22	21.4%	29
Weighted Trend	-4.7%	20	15.6%	28
Variance	12.9%	6	6.0%	26
Passing	-4.2%	19	34.3%	31
Rushing	-1.6%	18	-3.6%	13
First Down	12.6%	6	7.7%	22
Second Down	-15.7%	27	13.3%	26
Third Down	-16.6%	23	29.6%	29
Red Zone	-15.6%	24	22.8%	28
Late and Close	-22.4%	25	4.9%	24

Five-Year Performance

	2004	2003	2002	2001	2000
W-L	5-11	4-12	11-5	10-6	12-4
Pythagorean Wins	5.1	4.9	11.5	9.9	12.1
Estimated Wins	5.9	5.8	11.3	10.2	11.2
Total DVOA	-19.1%	-15.9%	29.8%	16.4%	24.5%
Rank	26	27	2	6	5
Offense	-3.2%	-10.9%	22.7%	15.4%	14.8%
Rank	17	23	2	3	5
Defense	14.3%	8.7%	-8.9%	-3.4%	-4.8%
Rank	27	25	5	18	15
Special Teams	-1.6%	3.7%	-1.9%	-2.4%	4.9%
Rank	21	5	21	22	7

Passing (min. 5 plays)

Player	DPAR	PAR	DVOA	Plys	NtYds	Avg	Cmpl	TD	Int
Kerry Collins	4.8	19.4	-11.1%	540	3322	6.2	56.3%	21	20
Rich Gannon	15.7	5.7	39.8%	72	502	7.0	60.3%	3	2

Rushing (min. 3 plays)

Player	DPAR	PAR	DVOA	Plys	Yds	Avg	TD	Fum	Suc
Amos Zereoue	0.2	1.2	-14.3%	112	430	3.8	3	1	42%
Tyrone Wheatley	12.1	8.0	14.0%	85	327	3.8	4	0	51%
Zack Crockett	7.4	8.7	17.6%	49	232	4.7	2	0	61%
Justin Fargas	3.1	3.7	6.0%	35	126	3.6	1	0	54%
J. R. Redmond	-0.1	-0.5	-15.1%	21	119	5.7	0	2	43%
Kerry Collins	1.1	1.4	11.8%	8	41	5.1	0	0	—

Receiving (min. 5 plays)

Player	DPAR	PAR	DVOA	Plys	Ctch	Yds	Y/C	TD	CPct
WR									
Jerry Porter	5.3	6.9	-9.5%	136	64	998	15.6	9	47%
Doug Gabriel	1.5	2.8	-12.6%	79	33	551	16.7	2	42%
Ronald Curry	20.8	22.6	29.7%	70	50	679	13.6	6	71%
Alvis Whitted	2.4	2.6	-0.7%	25	9	227	25.2	2	36%
Jerry Rice	-0.8	-1.3	-23.1%	15	5	67	13.4	0	33%
John Stone	2.1	2.3	50.5%	5	3	80	26.7	0	60%
TE									
Doug Jolley	2.4	2.7	-4.8%	48	27	313	11.6	2	56%
Courtney Anderson	3.5	3.1	11.6%	21	13	175	13.5	1	62%
Teyo Johnson	5.7	6.1	51.7%	13	9	131	14.6	2	69%
RB									
J. R. Redmond	-3.5	-4.0	-24.8%	50	32	233	7.3	0	64%
Amos Zereoue	6.8	6.2	18.2%	47	39	284	7.3	0	83%
Zack Crockett	1.0	0.8	-0.6%	20	16	87	5.4	0	80%
Tyrone Wheatley	1.6	0.6	13.0%	15	15	78	5.2	0	100%
Justin Fargas	-1.2	-1.5	-26.2%	14	11	68	6.2	0	79%

Defensive Players (min. 20 plays)

Player	Age	Plys	Stop	Dfts	AvYds	StpRt	Sack	Int	FR
Defensive Line									
Bobby Hamilton	34	60	41	9	1.7	68%	1.0	0	0
Tyler Brayton	26	50	29	11	3.7	58%	2.5	1	0
Warren Sapp	33	44	32	11	2.0	73%	2.5	0	2
Ted Washington	37	42	26	5	2.3	62%	3.0	0	0
Sam Williams	25	29	16	5	4.4	55%	0.0	0	0
John Parrella	36	23	17	2	2.7	74%	0.0	0	0
Tommy Kelly	25	22	18	10	0.7	82%	4.0	0	1
Terdell Sands	26	21	12	3	4.3	57%	0.0	0	0
Linebackers									
Danny Clark	28	135	68	23	4.5	50%	2.0	0	0
Napoleon Harris	26	62	28	5	4.5	45%	0.0	0	0
Travian Smith	30	44	19	9	4.6	43%	0.0	0	1
Tim Johnson	27	26	19	13	3.9	73%	0.5	1	0
DeLawrence Grant	26	21	9	4	3.1	43%	2.0	0	0

Player	Age	Plys	Stop	Dfts	AvYds	StpRt	Sack	Int	FR
Secondary									
Ray Buchanan	34	93	23	8	9.7	25%	0.0	1	0
Charles Woodson	29	90	30	12	7.3	33%	2.5	1	1
Marques Anderson	26	77	33	13	5.4	43%	0.0	1	2
Patrick Buchanon	25	68	23	9	8.4	34%	0.0	3	2
Denard Walker	32	56	11	7	11.4	20%	0.0	1	1
Nnamdi Asomugha	24	46	15	9	8.2	33%	1.0	0	0
Stuart Schweigert	24	39	6	3	11.6	15%	0.0	0	0

Offensive Line

Year	Yards	AdjLineYd	Rank	Power	Rank	10+ Yds	Rank	Stuff	Rank	Sack	AdjSack%	Rank
2002	4.48	4.53	4	73%	10	17%	16	20%	3	36	5.9%	13
2003	4.27	4.36	12	71%	7	16%	13	19%	1	42	7.6%	27
2004	4.09	4.19	15	74%	3	18%	11	23%	13	30	5.7%	8

Year	LEnd	Rank	LTckl	Rank	MdGrd	Rank	RTckl	Rank	REnd	Rank
2002	4.71	6	4.82	5	4.55	5	4.65	7	4.04	15
2003	3.75	23	5.32	1	4.57	5	4.25	17	2.81	27
2004	4.44	13	4.34	19	4.10	21	5.57	1	3.26	24

The Raiders have been one of the league's best teams in short-yardage situations for a few years, and even if Jordan takes some of those carries away from Tyrone Wheatley or Zack Crockett, that shouldn't change; Jordan had only eight short-yardage carries last year, but he converted seven of them, indicating that he can do the job.

Gallery and fellow rookie Jake Grove, who played right guard last season, look like the future of the Raiders' right-side O-line for the next decade. Grove was moved to center, his college position, during the team's May minicamp. Ron Stone has been re-signed, but he may not start. The jury is still out on Langston Walker, a former first-round pick who was selected to replace Barry Sims at left tackle. Sims is still the starter, and Walker became a man without a position when Gallery moved past him on the depth chart. Walker was lined up as a guard at minicamp. Sims cut down on his penalties last year and is a fine run blocker, but he's slow-footed and gives up the corner too easily.

Defensive Front Seven

Year	Yards	AdjLineYd	Rank	Power	Rank	10+ Yds	Rank	Stuff	Rank	Sack	AdjSack%	Rank
2002	3.86	3.76	5	63%	10	15%	11	28%	6	42	7.5%	10
2003	4.73	4.47	26	70%	28	20%	23	22%	26	26	5.4%	25
2004	3.70	4.26	18	61%	14	9%	3	21%	29	26	5.0%	30

Year	LEnd	Rank	LTckl	Rank	MdGrd	Rank	RTckl	Rank	REnd	Rank
2002	3.23	5	3.80	9	3.98	8	3.26	3	4.13	17
2003	4.78	29	4.72	23	4.53	27	3.95	13	4.36	27
2004	3.85	8	5.05	28	4.19	17	4.66	28	3.45	8

The veteran rotation of Warren Sapp, Bobby Hamilton, John Parrella, and Ted Washington boasted little more than decades of combined NFL experience and millions of dollars of combined Raiders paychecks. Together, they managed only seven sacks and 18 tackles for a loss. In a 3-4 defense the lineman should occupy blocks so linebackers can make big plays, but Raiders linebackers recorded just 2.5 sacks and only three teams stuffed opposing runners at the line less often. The most impressive free agent signing on the front seven turned out to be the least heralded: linebacker Danny Clark, who led the team in tackles.

This past off-season the Raiders signed Derrick Burgess and Kenny Smith, two oft-injured free agents, to bolster the front three; Hamilton was re-signed but Ryan released Parrella in an effort to find the right combination of girth, athleticism, experience, and youth on the line. Burgess was hurt for nearly all of the 2002 and 2003 seasons and had just three sacks in the 2004 regular season, but his three sacks in the playoffs were enough to get the Raiders to fork over an $8 million signing bonus. He'll play the hybrid OLB/DE in Ryan's system. Look for Smith or 340-pound monster Terdell Sands to take over Ted Washington's role as the wide-load nose tackle.

Defensive Secondary

Year	DVOA vs. #1 WR	Rank	DVOA vs. #2 WR	Rank	DVOA vs. Other WR	Rank	DVOA vs. TE	Rank	DVOA vs. RB	Rank
2002	35.4%	32	-32.2%	6	-17.6%	9	-44.9%	1	9.0%	21
2003	4.8%	18	8.8%	22	-8.9%	18	31.7%	29	5.5%	19
2004	26.4%	24	2.8%	13	53.0%	32	19.2%	23	-3.9%	20

The Raiders had one of the most penalized secondaries in the NFL. Charles Woodson piled up nine flags, and nickel and dime defenders Denard Walker and Nnamdi Asomugha picked up eight apiece. Walker's four pass interference calls tied for the second-highest total in the league; Woodson's penalties included one interference call and a smorgasbord of illegal contact, face mask, and neutral zone violations. Asomugha also picked up three interference penalties. Not surprisingly, with the nickel defenders grasping and clutching for dear life, the Raiders were worst in the league in DVOA against third and fourth wideouts. Walker is finished, and Philip Buchanon is in Houston now, so rookies Fabian Washington and Stanford Routt will compete with free agent Renaldo Hill for the starting and nickel roles. Asomugha, a CB/safety, will draw the short straw and cover Tony Gonzalez and Antonio Gates frequently. With two rookies in key roles, a few illegal contact penalties may be better than the alternative; veteran receivers like Eddie Kennison, Keenan McCardell, and Rod Smith will be licking their chops if isolated against anyone but Woodson.

Special Teams

Year	DVOA	Rank	FG/XP	Rank	Net Punt	Rank	Punt Ret	Rank	Net Kick	Rank	Kick Ret	Rank
2002	-1.8%	21	2.1	11	-2.0	18	-2.6	21	-2.1	19	-5.6	25
2003	3.7%	5	9.7	6	8.9	6	12.8	2	-12.0	31	1.5	13
2004	-1.6%	21	7.5	5	-0.5	22	-0.1	7	-0.3	12	-15.4	31

Shane Lechler led the league in gross punting average, but critics say that he overkicked his coverage too often and was too willing to boot the ball into the end zone when he should have been trying to pin opponents deep. The "overkick" argument doesn't make sense—it's the job of the gunner units to get down the field, whether the ball travels 35 yards or 55 yards. The long punts yield longer returns, but if the coverage units are effective then the net average should be very good. According to our special teams measures, which consider the location of each punt but penalize touchbacks, Lechler's punts handed the Raiders 10.6 points worth of field position, and poor coverage of punt returns handed opponents 11.1 points worth of field position right back. When reviewing Lechler's 14 touchbacks, it's hard to find an egregious example of Lechler hurting the team by not pinning opponents inside the five. Some of his touchbacks came on punts from the opposing 40-yard line, where a pin is tough to execute. Others came from around the Raiders 45-yard line, where a booming punt yielded an acceptable 35-yard net.

The departure of Philip Buchanon means speedy but mediocre Doug Gabriel will return both kickoffs and punts. The blocking units could use an upgrade, but Gabriel doesn't have great open-field instincts and tends to run full speed into the heart of the coverage. Sebastian Janikowski is one of the league's better kickers.

Coaching Staff

Turner has a reputation for getting the most from his wide receivers. Moss's game doesn't need any fine-tuning; he just needs to be kept focused and motivated. Youngsters like Ronald Curry and Doug Gabriel have star potential; Turner will try to develop them despite the fact that there aren't many balls to go around with Moss and Jerry Porter battling for catches.

Turner was a defensive coordinator killer in Washington; both Mike Nolan and Ron Lynn were axed on his watch, and Ray Rhodes got his walking papers at the same time as Turner. Legend has it that when owner Dan Snyder took over the Redskins, he wanted to fire Lynn right away, but Turner ran interference for a whole season. If Turner tries to run interference between Al Davis and Rob Ryan, he'll get a pitchfork through the belly.

Pittsburgh Steelers

After going 6–10 in 2003—when Murphy's Law was ostensibly in full effect—the Pittsburgh Steelers reeled off 15 consecutive wins last season in route to another AFC championship matchup with the Patriots. And while they went on to lose that game, it shouldn't obscure the fact that their turnaround was nothing short of extraordinary—right up there with putting a man on the moon or John Travolta making his comeback in *Look Who's Talking.*

The 15–1 season is even more remarkable when you consider all the seemingly innocuous events that paved the way for Pittsburgh's resurgence.

- In March 2003, safety Dexter Jackson verbally agreed to a deal with the Steelers only to change his mind at the 11th hour, instead signing with the Cardinals for slightly more money. When Jackson left the Steelers hanging, Pittsburgh was forced to trade up in the 2003 draft to get safety Troy Polamalu with the 16th pick. And while there was much gnashing of teeth by Steelers fans during the 2003 season because of Polamalu's slow transition to the NFL, nary an unkind word was spoken last season. After two seasons, Polamalu is already one of the best safeties in the AFC, and he made his first Pro Bowl appearance this past February. Jackson, meanwhile, was released by Arizona after a season and a half and finished up the season back in Tampa. While no one knew it at the time, Dexter Jackson ended up doing the Steelers a big favor.
- In Week 17 of the 2003 season, the Steelers and the Ravens played in a game that was meaningless except for one thing: Jamal Lewis was trying to break the single-season rushing record. The Ravens, bound for the playoffs whatever the outcome of that game, would usually have rested their starters in preparation for a game against Tennessee the next week. But because of Lewis's shot at the record, Brian Billick threw everything into beating the Steelers. If Pittsburgh had managed to win the game, they wouldn't have ended up with the 11th-overall pick in the 2004 draft. Thanks, Brian Billick. Speaking of the draft...
- With hindsight being 20/20 and all, it seems almost impossible to believe that Ben Roethlisberger lasted until the 11th pick. If NFL teams knew then what they now know, the Chargers might have taken Robert

STEELERS PROSPECTUS

2004 Record: 15–1

DVOA Estimated Wins: 11.9 (4th)

Pythagorean Wins: 11.5 (4th)

DVOA: 35.4% total (2nd), 41.4% weighted (3rd)

Adjusted Offense: 25.9 points/game (16.6% DVOA, 7th)

Adjusted Defense: 17.5 points/game (−15.0% DVOA, 4th)

Adjusted Special Teams: +1.3 points/game (3.8% DVOA, 7th)

Variance: 17.2% (17th)

2004: Ben Roethlisberger's season turned into a pumpkin during the AFC championship game.

2005: The Steelers won't sneak up on teams this season, and their division rivals are improving.

2005 Projection

Leinart Land (0–4): 4%

Bad Team (5–6): 9%

Mediocre (7–8): 18%

Playoff Contender (9–10): 26%

Super Bowl Contender (11+): 43%

Projected Average Opponent: −3.0% DVOA (26th in NFL)

Gallery and Roethlisberger wouldn't have made it past the Giants with the 4th pick. As it turned out, the Chargers and Giants battled over Philip Rivers and Eli Manning, the pitiful Browns passed on their QB of the future to get Kellen Winslow (who'll miss another season after losing a game of chicken to a street curb), and miraculously Roethlisberger fell to the Steelers. This will probably be Butch Davis's legacy in Cleveland.

- During the 2003 off-season, Bill Cowher fired defensive coordinator Tim Lewis. Enter former Steelers defensive coordinator Dick LeBeau, who had been serving as a defensive consultant in Buffalo. LeBeau, credited with inventing the zone blitz, revitalized a defense that had been decidedly mediocre against the pass the four seasons prior to his arrival. Since 2000, Pittsburgh had ranked 11th, 16th, 13th, and 18th in pass defense DVOA. Last season, the Steelers finished 4th in overall defensive DVOA and 3rd in pass defense DVOA.

- In 2004, right guard Kendall Simmons went down in training camp and was lost for the season. This was one of those "I swallowed a bug" moments, right up there with watching Chris Webber call a timeout during the 1993 NCAA championship game or having to sit through a second showing of *Waterworld.* Injuries and setbacks decimated the offensive line in 2003, and it seemed to be starting all over again. Unlike a night stuck watching *Waterworld,* however, this story had a happy ending. Simmons's replacement, Keydrick Vincent, and tackle Oliver Ross were so capable on the right side of the line that you never heard their names unless it was laudatory. And when you consider how important the running game was to this Steelers team, Vincent and Ross were two of the biggest reasons for Pittsburgh's success.

- If OLB Clark Haggans hadn't broken his hand during training camp, a couple of things wouldn't have happened. First, backup Alonzo Jackson wouldn't have proclaimed, "I'm now the starter and Haggans has to earn his job back." (Of course, Haggans earned his job back simply due to Jackson's play, but that's another story.) Also, the Steelers never would have signed linebacker James Harrison. Harrison was passed over by all 32 teams in the draft and, after he was cut from the Ravens' practice squad, the Steelers signed him to fill out the roster as an afterthought. Harrison would go on to start four games in 2004, and he played a large part in a late-season win against the Ravens that cemented home-field advantage for the Steelers. Thanks again, Brian Billick.

- During Week 2, the Ravens again unwittingly had a hand in the Steelers' success when they knocked quarterback Tommy Maddox out of the game and out of a job. It was the turning point of the season, clearing the way for Roethlisberger. Thanks yet again, Brian Billick.

Roethlisberger, Vincent, and Harrison are all examples of players who began 2004 as backups and ended it as important pieces of Pittsburgh's stunning season. Like the team it played for the AFC title, New England, Pittsburgh was able to overcome a series of injuries with a seemingly bottomless roster of quality players. That depth, not the play of Big Ben, was the biggest difference between 2003 and 2004. At various points during the season, the Steelers were without four other starters: NT Casey Hampton and CB Chad Scott on defense and WR Plaxico Burress and RB Duce Staley on offense. But unlike the season before, players like Chris Hoke, Willie Williams, Ike Taylor, and Antwaan Randle El were able to successfully step into starting roles.

But the most important backup player, and the biggest surprise of the year, was a rejuvenated Jerome Bettis. Staley was brought in because the rushing attack of Bettis and Amos Zereoue had finished 31st in the league in yardage the season before. When Staley went down with a leg injury partway through last season, no one would have batted an eye if the Pittsburgh running game went the way of *Cop Rock.* Instead, the Bus—with a little help from Verron Haynes and Willie Parker—made everyone forget about the Tommy Maddox Passing Project, version 2003. Who would've guessed that a chubby, over-the-hill, asthmatic veteran would rack up 941 yards, score 13 touchdowns, and end up at the Pro Bowl?

Of course, most of the credit for the revitalized running game should go to the offensive line. The line, riddled with injuries in 2003, was never able to get into rhythm; in 2004, the front five played together every game of the season and Pittsburgh led the AFC in rushing. Going into 2005, the Steelers will have new players on the right side—one, Simmons, a proven veteran and former first-rounder, the other, Max Starks, a second-year player with very little experience. How well this new unit gels and avoids midseason injuries will go a long way in determining how successful the running game will be in 2005. It's not likely that Bettis can play this well yet again, but he won't have to with Staley around to help him wear down defenses while eating up the clock.

If the running game falters, there could be trouble, as Roethlisberger will be without one of his favorite targets from last season. Plaxico Burress signed with the New York Giants this off-season, and his replacement is Cedrick Wilson. And unless you're a member of the Wilson family, you probably haven't heard of him either. He spent the previous three seasons in San Francisco, and although he has the ability to stretch the field, he is much smaller and less physical than Burress. Currently the Steelers have three receivers—Hines Ward, Antwaan Randle El, and Wilson—who when stacked end-to-end still come up a few inches shorter than Burress. The Steelers did a good job of addressing these concerns during the draft. In the first round they got Heath Miller, the first tight end considered a legitimate downfield threat to come to Pittsburgh since Eric Green in the mid-1990s. Three rounds later, the Steelers nabbed 6' 4" WR Fred Gibson. He's similar in stature to Burress, but is considered a better athlete. He probably won't have much of an impact in 2005, but he has a chance to be better than Burress.

Roethlisberger will also not have the luxury of sneaking up on opponents. Defensive coordinators now have a season's worth of film on the second-year quarterback, and he can expect to see many of the same defensive schemes that gave him so much trouble during the playoffs. In preparation for this and the inevitable questions about a sophomore jinx, Roethlisberger has spent most of the off-season in Pittsburgh studying tape and getting a better grasp on the offense.

Even if Roethlisberger were to gain ten years worth of quarterbacking experience in a summer of film study, and not a single free agent had left the team in the off-season, the Steelers would be guaranteed to decline in 2005. You just don't win 15 games for two straight seasons. It would be like dating Mandy Moore, Lindsey Lohan, and Eva Longoria in succession. (Then again, actor Wilmer Valderrama actually completed that particular trifecta, which not only gives Pittsburgh fans a glimmer of hope but also serves as evidence that Valderrama probably has strange psychic powers.)

But Pittsburgh's success in 2004 has gone a long way in setting the course for its immediate future. The defense returns every starter from the AFC championship game and LeBeau will continue to mix schemes and coverages to confuse opponents. The offense will still be built around the running game, with Duce Staley and Jerome Bettis getting the bulk of the carries and Verron Haynes serving as the third-down back. This team is not going to go 15–1, but if Roethlisberger can avoid the sophomore jinx there is no reason they can't go 12–4 and march deep into the playoffs with the same motto as the Indianapolis Colts: New England has to lose sometime.

Ryan Wilson

Research: Cedrick Wilson's Tall Order

Consider this hypothetical situation: Team A sends its franchise player and former first-round draft pick packing and replaces him with a sixth-round afterthought. Since this is the Pittsburgh Steelers chapter, you know we aren't talking about Drew Bledsoe and Tom Brady. Instead the franchise player is wide receiver Plaxico Burress and the afterthought is the Steelers only off-season free agent acquisition, Cedrick Wilson.

When Burress was taken with the eighth-overall pick in 2000, he was expected to be the big-time deep threat the team had missed since losing Yancey Thigpen after the 1997 season. At 6′5″, 225 pounds, Burress created serious matchup problems for opposing defenses on paper. In reality, he struggled through a 23-catch, 0-TD rookie season and did little to assuage any concerns Pittsburgh had about the wideout position when they drafted him. Burress went on to have back-to-back 1,000-yard seasons, but then slumped in 2003 and was injured for part of 2004. After serving as the number two receiver in Pittsburgh, in 2005 he'll be the go-to guy for Eli Manning and the New York Giants.

Fast-forward a year and 161 picks to the San Francisco 49ers taking 5′11″ Cedrick Wilson out of Tennessee. The knock on Wilson at the time was that although he could stretch the field, he had an inexplicable knack for dropping passes. To glance at his receiving numbers during his three seasons in San Francisco would give no indication that he would be a viable replacement for a player like Burress, but upon closer inspection, maybe we shouldn't be so quick to pass judgment.

Last season, Wilson's DPAR (15.8) compared favorably to Burress's (20.5). Wilson actually was slightly more effective in the red zone (3.7 DPAR to 3.1) and on possessions starting inside the Steelers' own 20-yard line (1.6 to 1.3)—two areas of the field the Steelers have struggled in recent years. And it's not like Wilson was surrounded by Jerry Rice and Joe Montana; the 49ers ranked 29th in offensive DVOA, and Brandon Lloyd was second on the team in receiving yards with 563 (behind Wilson's team-leading 641), while the quarterbacking tandem of Tim Rattay and Ken Dorsey ranked near the bottom of the league in DPAR. Contrast that to a Pittsburgh team that was led by perennial Pro Bowler Hines Ward (1,004 yards), Burress (698), and slot receiver Antwaan Randle El (601). Having Offensive Rookie of the Year Ben Roethlisberger didn't hurt either—he was the tenth-best quarterback according to DPAR.

All of which raises the question: How important is height in a wide receiver? Wilson was more efficient in the red zone, though five inches shorter than Burress. Is anyone worried that he'll be teaming up with Ward and Randle El, two wideouts also known more for their ability to get open than for winning jump balls in the end zone?

In 2004, the average height of a team's number one receiver was an even 6′ while number two receivers came in 6′1″, which is just about where the Steelers currently are on the depth chart. More interesting still, there was no relationship between a receiver's height and his DPAR. So why are teams forever searching to find the next 6′5″ "game-changer"? Has the sight of Randy Moss making an acrobatic one-handed catch and outrunning the cornerback to the end zone made them fall too madly in love with height while undervaluing good hands and speed? Let's take a look.

Table 1 gives the average DPAR for all 2004 wide receivers based on height, then separates out the receivers who finished in the top 30 in average yards per catch—the downfield threats—from those who are primarily possession receivers. When you break down the number of players in the top 30 by height, the percentages of those 6′, 6′1″, 6′2″, and 6′3″-and-taller roughly mirrors their distribution among all receivers in the NFL.

As you might expect, receivers ranking in the top 30 in yards per reception also have significantly higher DPAR values than all receivers in the NFL. But statistically there

TABLE 1. DPAR FOR WR BY HEIGHT, 2004

Height	Top 30 in Yds/Catch		All NFL WRs	
	DPAR	% of Total	DPAR	% of Total
6′ and under	28.0	40.7	13.7	45.2
6′1″–6′2″	24.4	33.3	13.9	34.5
6′3″ and taller	28.1	25.9	11.1	20.2

TABLE 2. AVERAGE DPAR FOR WRs BY HEIGHT DIFFERENCE, 2004

A team's #1 WR compared to its #2 WR is...	Avg. DPAR
More than 4″ shorter	12.1
2″–3″ shorter	14.4
1″ shorter	19.6
The same height	19.2
1″ or more taller	8.7

is no difference in DPAR among these top 30 players simply based on height.

So what gives? If tall receivers are game changers, why aren't they better represented in the top 30? Well, first of all, there are a lot more receivers in the NFL who are closer to 6′ than 6′4″, and therefore it makes sense that there are more of them in the top 30. But there's another reason: Tall wideouts are more likely to be projects when coming into the league. They tend to have the physical tools that make coaches drool, but lack college game experience and need several years to blossom.

In 2004, Michael Clayton, Javon Walker, Terrell Owens, Ashley Lelie, and Drew Bennett had an average DPAR of 30.1—the highest among players 6′3″ or taller. But at the other end of the spectrum were guys like Bryant Johnson (−7.9 DPAR), Reggie Williams (−7.7 DPAR), Clarence Moore (−2.2 DPAR), Larry Fitzgerald (1.3 DPAR), and Rod Gardner (1.3 DPAR)—all players who are at least 6′3″, but are either early in their careers, long-term projects, or perennial underachievers. And while all receivers, no matter their height, can be put in these same categories, the difference is that it's much easier to replace a 6′ speedster who drops too many passes than it is to replace a 6′6″ former high jumper who struggles to run crisp routes. Consequently, these tall players with untapped potential have a tendency to stay with teams longer because of their tremendous upside.

Burress's size created matchup problems for smaller cornerbacks, but with him on the field the Steelers gave up speed for height. With Cedrick Wilson, they've traded in height for a player who can stretch the field. The question is whether the Burress-for-Wilson exchange is a net gain or loss in offensive production. Table 2 provides some definitive answers. There is no correlation between the difference in height between starting wideouts and their average DPAR. In fact, last season starting receivers of the same height had a higher average DPAR than when the number one receiver was more than two inches shorter than the number two receiver.

While it's easy to be infatuated by height, the numbers don't really justify the love. One lesson we can take from table 2 is that while height can be a game-changing advantage on specific plays, speed, toughness, and good hands are an advantage on every play.

In 2004, Randy Moss caught 29 passes when the score was within seven points. He used his speed, catching 10 passes for more than 20 yards and 6 for more than 40 yards, and he used his height, out-maneuvering and out-leaping defensive backs to catch eight touchdowns on plays that started from the four-yard line or closer. Numbers like these are why general managers are willing to take chances on tall, athletic players who might be a little raw, but who could eventually grow into legitimate outside threats. But because these diamonds in the rough are so rare, and take time to develop, front offices need more fearless receivers with sticky hands who are polished route runners, regardless of their height. This doesn't mean teams will quit looking for the next great physical specimen, it just means that until it's legal to start cloning Randy Moss, guys like Derek Mason, Torry Holt, and even Cedrick Wilson will always have jobs in the NFL.

Ryan Wilson

Steelers 2004 Stats by Week

Wk	vs.	W-L	PF	PA	YDF	YDA	TO	Total	Off	Def	ST
								DVOA			
1	OAK	W	24	21	234	353	+3	36.3%	-11.8%	-29.5%	18.6%
2	@BAL	L	13	30	310	259	-3	-50.7%	-10.9%	24.3%	-15.6%
3	@MIA	W	13	3	314	169	+3	54.4%	3.5%	-47.1%	3.8%
4	CIN	W	28	17	333	293	+1	28.4%	6.9%	-15.5%	5.9%
5	CLE	W	34	23	401	296	0	3.8%	25.1%	30.5%	9.2%
6	@DAL	W	24	20	297	348	+1	15.1%	30.5%	16.5%	1.1%
7	BYE										
8	NE	W	34	20	420	244	+4	114.4%	51.4%	-62.5%	0.5%
9	PHI	W	27	3	420	113	-1	83.5%	22.0%	-71.1%	-9.6%
10	@CLE	W	24	10	300	228	+3	42.1%	2.0%	-46.5%	-6.4%
11	@CIN	W	19	14	235	209	0	32.4%	11.7%	-7.3%	13.4%
12	WAS	W	16	7	207	156	+1	81.5%	19.3%	-39.3%	23.0%
13	@JAC	W	17	16	316	359	0	57.0%	68.0%	13.0%	2.0%
14	NYJ	W	17	6	262	296	+1	51.5%	-5.5%	-51.3%	5.7%
15	@NYG	W	33	30	469	278	-1	-31.7%	22.8%	35.6%	-18.9%
16	BAL	W	20	7	404	248	-1	51.9%	56.6%	6.0%	1.3%
17	@BUF	W	29	24	262	267	0	7.0%	-22.6%	-2.4%	27.2%
18	BYE										
19	NYJ	W	20	17	364	275	0	30.5%	5.0%	-29.9%	-4.4%
20	NE	L	27	41	388	322	-4	-14.0%	-12.0%	7.7%	5.8%

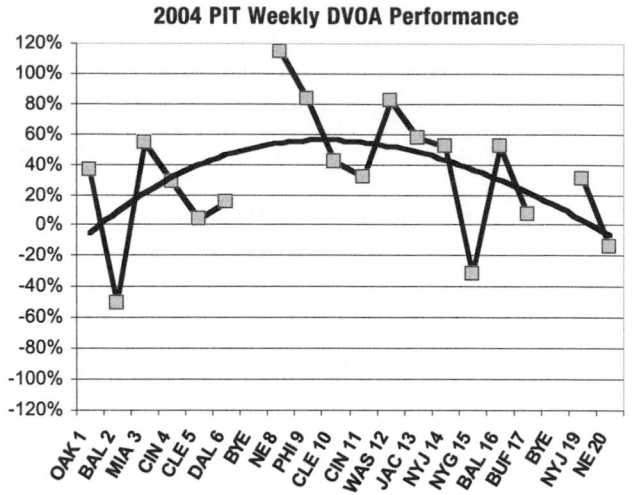

2004 PIT Weekly DVOA Performance

Trends and Splits

	Offense	Rank	Defense	Rank
Total DVOA	16.6%	7	-15.0%	4
Unadjusted VOA	12.1%	10	-21.1%	2
Weighted Trend	21.0%	5	-16.6%	3
Variance	6.6%	23	12.1%	9
Passing	28.6%	7	-19.6%	3
Rushing	9.4%	7	-9.2%	6
First Down	16.6%	5	-5.2%	11
Second Down	6.7%	15	-21.4%	2
Third Down	33.6%	6	-26.6%	4
Red Zone	18.9%	6	2.9%	20
Late and Close	15.8%	8	1.5%	20

Five-Year Performance

	2004	2003	2002	2001	2000
W-L	15-1	6-10	10-5-1	13-3	9-7
Pythagorean Wins	11.5	7.2	9.2	12.3	10.1
Estimated Wins	11.9	7.9	8.3	10.5	11.0
Total DVOA	35.4%	0.7%	5.6%	17.7%	24.6%
Rank	2	16	14	5	4
Offense	16.6%	-8.4%	6.4%	11.5%	11.2%
Rank	7	19	14	4	8
Defense	-15.0%	-6.0%	-2.5%	-8.9%	-12.1%
Rank	4	11	11	12	9
Special Teams	3.8%	3.2%	-3.4%	-2.7%	1.4%
Rank	7	8	25	23	15

Passing (min. 5 plays)

Player	DPAR	PAR	DVOA	Plys	NtYds	Avg	Cmpl	TD	Int
Ben Roethlisberger	75.3	62.8	40.3%	326	2413	7.4	66.4%	16	10
Tommy Maddox	-4.2	-6.0	-29.6%	67	282	4.2	50.0%	1	2

Rushing (min. 3 plays)

Player	DPAR	PAR	DVOA	Plys	Yds	Avg	TD	Fum	Suc
Jerome Bettis	27.4	26.7	11.8%	250	941	3.8	13	1	52%
Duce Staley	13.2	11.2	1.7%	192	834	4.3	1	3	48%
Verron Haynes	9.3	8.4	29.2%	55	272	4.9	0	0	47%
Willie Parker	6.1	5.3	36.1%	32	186	5.8	0	0	47%
Ben Roethlisberger	3.5	3.2	1.8%	28	173	6.2	1	0	—
Antwaan Randle El	0.1	-0.2	-29.9%	8	34	4.3	0	0	—
Tommy Maddox	-2.4	-2.4	-88.1%	5	16	3.2	0	1	—
Hines Ward	0.1	0.2	-27.6%	5	19	3.8	1	0	—
Dan Kreider	0.7	0.4	34.1%	4	18	4.5	0	0	50%

Receiving (min. 5 plays)

Player	DPAR	PAR	DVOA	Plys	Ctch	Yds	Y/C	TD	CPct
WR									
Hines Ward	32.9	31.3	30.4%	109	80	1010	12.6	4	75%
Antwaan Randle El	12.5	12.3	16.1%	62	43	590	13.7	3	68%
Plaxico Burress	20.5	20.0	36.8%	60	35	698	19.9	5	58%
Lee Mays	-1.7	-1.6	-26.3%	23	9	137	15.2	0	39%
TE									
Jerame Tuman	0.1	0.2	-12.6%	20	9	89	9.9	3	45%
Jay Riemersma	4.4	4.8	56.5%	9	7	82	11.7	2	78%
RB									
Verron Haynes	5.1	4.7	41.8%	23	18	142	7.9	2	78%
Dan Kreider	3.0	2.3	31.2%	14	10	75	7.5	1	71%
Duce Staley	-0.1	-0.3	-10.8%	12	6	55	9.2	0	50%
Jerome Bettis	1.2	0.9	21.0%	8	6	46	7.7	0	75%
Willie Parker	-1.4	-1.7	-70.0%	7	3	16	5.3	0	43%

Defensive Players (min. 20 plays)

Player	Age	Plys	Stop	Dfts	AvYds	StpRt	Sack	Int	FR	Player	Age	Plys	Stop	Dfts	AvYds	StpRt	Sack	Int	FR
Defensive Line										**Secondary**									
Aaron Smith	29	45	35	17	0.3	78%	8.0	0	2	Troy Polamalu	24	105	55	25	5.8	52%	1.0	5	0
Kimo von Oelhoffen	34	31	25	8	0.9	81%	1.0	0	2	Chris Hope	25	96	28	7	9.6	29%	0.0	1	0
Chris Hoke	29	23	18	3	1.8	78%	1.0	0	0	Deshea Townsend	30	70	28	16	6.3	40%	4.0	4	1
Linebackers										Willie Williams	35	59	18	8	7.6	31%	1.0	1	0
James Farrior	30	110	68	34	3.4	62%	3.0	4	3	Chad Scott	31	37	11	7	10.8	30%	0.0	1	0
Larry Foote	25	71	39	13	4.2	55%	3.0	1	1	Russell Stuvaints	25	23	7	4	11.5	30%	0.0	0	1
Joey Porter	28	66	55	24	0.8	83%	7.0	1	0										
Clark Haggans	28	37	28	16	1.6	76%	6.0	0	1										
James Harrison	27	26	16	10	1.7	62%	1.0	0	1										

Offensive Line

Year	Yards	AdjLineYd	Rank	Power	Rank	10+ Yds	Rank	Stuff	Rank	Sack	AdjSack%	Rank
2002	3.84	3.96	23	64%	20	14%	22	22%	7	35	6.0%	14
2003	3.30	3.82	26	62%	22	5%	32	28%	27	43	7.1%	23
2004	4.22	4.56	4	69%	10	11%	32	22%	9	36	8.9%	28

Year	LEnd	Rank	LTckl	Rank	MdGrd	Rank	RTckl	Rank	REnd	Rank
2002	3.63	25	4.36	12	4.16	19	3.93	22	2.96	28
2003	4.71	8	3.79	27	3.68	29	4.24	18	2.59	30
2004	4.41	14	4.81	5	4.76	2	3.64	29	3.97	14

They may not be the best pass blockers in the league, but the offensive linemen are the heart of the Pittsburgh power running game. The Steelers have finished last in the league in long runs for two straight years, so this isn't about Bettis running away from guys in the open field. The left side of the line is one of the best in football with Pro Bowler Alan Faneca at guard and Marvel Smith at tackle. Center Jeff Hartings is coming off a Pro Bowl season, although he's 33 and has knee issues. But a year after the line finally gelled, the right side is gone. Guard Keydrick Vincent and tackle Oliver Ross will be replaced by Kendall Simmons—who was supposed to start last season until he went down during training camp—and 2004 third-round pick Max Starks. The knock on Starks coming out of college was that he was soft, with poor footwork and questionable work habits. But after giving him a year of experience as a backup and in short-yardage situations last season, Cowher and offensive line coach Russ Grimm pronounced Starks ready to assume the right tackle position.

The question is not whether Simmons and Starks can succeed in the starting lineup but rather how to fill the holes they leave on the second level of the depth chart. The last time the Pittsburgh line was wracked by injuries, it resulted in a 6–10 record. Pittsburgh chose tackle Trai Essex out of Northwestern in the third round of this year's draft to provide some depth, but it will take him time to adjust to the pros. If this unit stays healthy, the Steelers could pick up where they left off in 2004. If any starter goes down, Staley and Bettis will struggle.

Defensive Front Seven

Year	Yards	AdjLineYd	Rank	Power	Rank	10+ Yds	Rank	Stuff	Rank	Sack	AdjSack%	Rank
2002	3.94	3.80	7	76%	27	21%	30	28%	8	51	8.0%	5
2003	3.93	3.82	7	51%	2	19%	22	30%	3	34	6.0%	19
2004	3.41	3.38	1	65%	21	16%	15	33%	1	42	7.8%	6

Year	LEnd	Rank	LTckl	Rank	MdGrd	Rank	RTckl	Rank	REnd	Rank
2002	4.51	25	4.00	12	3.93	7	3.66	8	2.71	5
2003	4.62	25	4.08	16	4.07	15	3.18	3	2.06	2
2004	3.92	11	3.47	1	3.40	1	3.71	6	2.48	1

A propensity for blitzing means that Pittsburgh responds to the run in a very different way compared to other 3-4 schemes around the league. Teams like New England and San Diego rarely stuff opposing runners at the line, but rarely allow long runs. The Steelers were the best team in the league when it came to stuffing opponents at the line, but runners who got to the second level could gain some yardage. But that's about the only weakness of this front seven, strong against both the run and the pass with good players returning at every position. Kendrell Bell, 2001 defensive rookie of the year, is now in Kansas City, but he played in only three games last season. Pittsburgh re-signed his replacement, Larry

(continued next page)

Defensive Front Seven *(continued)*

Foote, to a long-term deal. He will join Pro Bowler James Farrior in the middle and Joey Porter and Clark Haggans on the outside. Porter is always on the attack, and 83% of his plays resulted in failure for the offense, the highest Stop Rate for any starting linebacker in the league. Up front, nose tackle and 2003 Pro Bowler Casey Hampton missed most of the season with a knee injury but is now fully recovered and will once again clog up the middle for Farrior and Foote. Defensive end Aaron Smith may not be a well-known name, but he was rightfully selected to last year's Pro Bowl after a huge season that included eight sacks. For a defensive end in a 4-3 scheme, that's not a spectacular number, but in a 3-4 scheme where Smith is tying up blockers, it's remarkable—Smith was literally pushing blockers so far back that he got to the quarterback anyway.

Defensive Secondary

Year	DVOA vs. #1 WR	Rank	DVOA vs. #2 WR	Rank	DVOA vs. Other WR	Rank	DVOA vs. TE	Rank	DVOA vs. RB	Rank
2002	-11.4%	8	-21.9%	10	17.3%	26	-12.4%	10	-7.8%	8
2003	0.9%	16	22.8%	27	-18.1%	11	1.8%	17	-12.0%	9
2004	-10.0%	6	-12.5%	7	-26.9%	3	-7.0%	12	-4.0%	19

Pro Bowl strong safety Troy Polamalu will be the centerpiece of a young secondary that played surprisingly well under first-year coordinator Dick LeBeau. LeBeau is credited with inventing the zone blitz and this unit's success is a consequence of their ability to disguise their intentions. Free safety Chris Hope had a solid if not spectacular first season as a starter, and his physical skills coupled with his intelligence (he was an Academic All-American at Florida State) seldom left him out of position. The underrated Deshea Townsend holds one cornerback position, while the other currently belongs to the old man of the secondary, 34-year-old Willie Williams. The undersized (5'9") Williams had a surprisingly solid year after coming over from Seattle, where he had been limited to nickel situations, but he'll face a challenge for playing time from a slew of talented corners including third-year veteran Ike Taylor, last year's second-round pick Ricardo Colclough, and this year's second-round pick (and former teammate of Chris Hope) Bryant McFadden. With all this youth in the secondary, LeBeau can continue to use speed and athleticism to create matchup problems for opposing offenses.

Special Teams

Year	DVOA	Rank	FG/XP	Rank	Net Punt	Rank	Punt Ret	Rank	Net Kick	Rank	Kick Ret	Rank
2002	-3.4%	25	-6.1	26	6.0	10	-12.0	30	-9.1	28	2.6	12
2003	3.2%	8	-6.5	27	12.3	2	12.8	1	1.5	17	-2.5	20
2004	3.8%	7	6.4	8	19.5	1	-5.8	18	-1.2	14	2.3	13

Punter Chris Gardocki has yet to have a punt blocked in his 14-year career and the Steelers like the fact that he's less of a locker room distraction than his predecessor Josh Miller. Before joining the Steelers midway through the 2002 season, kicker Jeff Reed was laying bricks while waiting for his big break. Well, he got it and this off-season parlayed it into a big contract after hitting three game-winning kicks last season (including one to beat the Jets in the playoffs). Antwaan Randle El didn't return a punt for a touchdown last season, but was still one of the best return men in the league. He also teamed up with Colclough to return kickoffs, but if Randle El is promoted to the starting lineup at wide receiver he may hand that job off to Ike Taylor.

Coaching Staff

Bill Cowher is currently the longest tenured coach in the NFL. He's heading into his 13th season and has been criticized for not being able to win the big game, but it's hard to argue with his success: eight playoff appearances, four AFC championship games, and one Super Bowl. Former tight ends coach Ken Whisenhunt replaced Mike Mularkey as offensive coordinator last off-season and orchestrated an offense that led the AFC in rushing and successfully featured a rookie quarterback. His job should be a little easier this season given that Roethlisberger will have a year's worth of experience. Dick LeBeau returned to Pittsburgh to assume the defensive coordinator position and promptly turned a defense that had struggled against the pass into one of the best pass-defending teams in the NFL. Much of the success can be attributed to LeBeau's zone-blitz schemes that resulted in the Steelers registering 42 sacks. Russ Grimm is the offensive line coach, but has been mentioned in recent years as head coach material. Look for him to get more involved with the game planning in Pittsburgh as he prepares to take the next step.

San Diego Chargers

Hamlet, Act III, scene i, *as performed at Qualcomm Stadium:*
Drew Brees, or not Drew Brees, that is the question.
Whether 'tis wiser down the line to suffer
The picks and errors of our rookie's fortune,
Or take an arm that's seen a sea of troubles,
And by o'ercoming, end'd them?
What imports the nomination of this gentleman?

Philip Rivers, picked fourth overall in the 2004 draft and acquired by San Diego for Eli Manning, sat on the bench, $40 million contract and $14 million signing bonus in hand, for all but 18 meaningless plays of the Chargers' unlikely playoff run. Meanwhile Drew Brees, oft-replaced during his first three years by the ancient and now departed Doug Flutie, led the team to 12 victories, earning comeback player of the year honors and more than $8 million for 2005 as the franchise player.

The end of the Chargers' tale of two quarterbacks remains unwritten, and it may be either a comedy or a tragedy. They'll have to choose one or the other. More than $11 million of their 2005 salary cap is tied up in the quarterback position, and it is unlikely that the Chargers can keep both Brees and Rivers around for the long term. If they make the wrong decision about their quarterback of the future, their fans will be crying through another decade of futility. Pick right and they could be laughing all the way to a championship.

(Theoretically, either guy could be the guy, and they'll succeed no matter which they pick. But these are the Chargers. So each could also fail miserably.)

Though this be madness, yet there is method in't

If someone had told you, before last season began, that San Diego would go 12–4 and score nearly 30 points a game, you would have laughed at him. If that same person told you they would do this with LaDainian Tomlinson, the Chargers' one-man show, hampered by injuries most of the season, you may have questioned his sanity. But that's what happened. Tomlinson gained almost 600 fewer yards in 2004 than in 2003; compared with running backs throughout the league by DVOA, he was below average in 2004.

How did the passing game suddenly blossom? It certainly helped that defenses still focused on stopping Tomlinson, despite his off year. Drew Brees's breakout could

CHARGERS PROSPECTUS

2004 Record: 12–4
DVOA Estimated Wins: 10.7 (7th)
Pythagorean Wins: 11.2 (5th)
DVOA: 19.2% total (8th), 20.7% weighted (6th)
Adjusted Offense: 25.8 points/game (16.4% DVOA, 8th)
Adjusted Defense: 19.7 points/game (−6.6% DVOA, 11th)
Adjusted Special Teams: −1.3 points/game (−3.8% DVOA, 29th)
Variance: 10.2% (29th)
2004: Breakout team of the year, winning nine of its last ten games.
2005: Improving defense and stud running back mean this was no fluke. But that's what we all thought about the 2002 Bears.

2005 Projection
Leinart Land (0–4): 12%
Bad Team (5–6): 18%
Mediocre (7–8): 24%
Playoff Contender (9–10): 23%
Super Bowl Contender (11+): 22%
Projected Average Opponent: 6.4% DVOA (Hardest in NFL)

also be chalked up to more experience and familiarity with the system in his third season with head coach Marty Schottenheimer and offensive coordinator Cam Cameron.

But the biggest reason for Brees's spectacular improvement was a former Kent State basketball player and undrafted free agent tight end named Antonio Gates. Second only to Tony Gonzalez in DPAR and head and shoulders above the rest of the league's tight ends (not to mention the Chargers wide receivers), Gates was Brees's favorite receiver by far. He was thrown 114 passes, nearly as many as the Chargers' two top wideouts, Eric Parker (71) and Keenan McCardell (58), put together. He caught 29 passes that converted third downs into first downs, more than any other player in the NFL. He caught nearly half of Brees's TD passes and a third of his yards and became the indispensable man.

Neither a borrower nor a lender be

The Chargers will try to build on last season's offensive success with virtually identical personnel. All their receivers but the obsolescent Tim Dwight return, and while they lack a top-flight playmaker at wide receiver, they have significant depth. They expect to get a full year from both Reche Caldwell, who was lost in Week 6 to a knee injury, and Keenan McCardell, who didn't show up in San Diego until Week 7. Parker was a pleasant surprise as the number two receiver, first behind Caldwell and then McCardell. Behind these veterans, the Chargers will work on developing their second-round pick, Vincent Jackson, a raw physical talent from Northern Colorado whose basketball experience and TE-like size has San Diego anticipating a slimmed-down sequel to Gates.

The entire offensive line—a line that started two rookies and should benefit from being able to develop as a unit—will be back. So will the Chargers' biggest playmakers, Tomlinson and Gates. In short, the offense that Brees drove so well in 2004 will be the offense he gets to drive in 2005; a fully-functioning Tomlinson should even boost the horsepower.

There is nothing either good or bad, but thinking makes it so

The San Diego defense also returns remarkably intact, having lost only reserve linebacker Zeke Moreno to the Texans and backup nose tackle Jason Fisk to the Browns. That may not seem like such good news, if you look at official NFL rankings, which say the Chargers had the second-worst passing defense in the league. But this just demonstrates the absurdity of the official NFL rankings.

The Chargers allowed the second-most passing yards in the NFL because they faced more passes than any defense in the NFL. San Diego opponents, always playing from behind, threw 606 passes in 2004. That's 48 more passes than were thrown against any other team in the league. To put it in perspective, San Diego faced 48 more passes than second-place Seattle, and Seattle faced 48 more passes than *eighteenth*-place Oakland. All those yards and all those passes work out to 6.7 yards per pass, lower than the NFL average of 7.1 yards per pass. In addition, San Diego allowed only 3.7 yards per carry, the sixth-best mark in the league.

These numbers are even more remarkable when you consider that the Chargers play in the most offense-oriented division in the league. DVOA, which adjusts for all of these variables, ranked San Diego as the league's 11th-best defense. San Diego was even better—6th in the NFL—in weighted defensive DVOA, which considers a team's development over the course of the season.

The one area in which the Chargers defense clearly needed improvement was the pass rush. Only two teams registered fewer sacks than the Chargers, and—since they saw so many passes—only one had a worse Adjusted Sack Rate. Thanks to having the Giants' first-round pick as well as their own, the Chargers addressed the problem with defensive end Shawne Merriman, who will move to outside linebacker in San Diego's 3-4 defense, and nose tackle Luis Castillo. If the latter keeps off the juice and both can quickly assimilate into the professional ranks, this could become one of the premier defenses in the NFL.

Come, give us a taste of your quality

And so 2005 becomes for the San Diego Chargers a bit of a laboratory experiment. Was the 2004 Brees, who rated as the ninth-best passer in the NFL for 2004 with a DPAR of 75.6, real? Or is the real Brees the one who averaged just 3.65 DPAR during 2002 and 2003?

And, oh yeah, they'd like to know if this Rivers kid is the real deal, too.

The 2004 season may have been a fluke or it may have been a sign of genuine progress. The last time the Chargers won 12 games was a generation ago, in 1979, when Dan Fouts threw for 4,000 yards and Kellen Winslow Sr. was a rookie. Last year was San Diego's first winning season since 1995. This team is, customarily, *bad*. Ashlee Simpson bad.

A king of shreds and patches

But 2005 may prove that 2004 marked a genuine turning point. They aren't likely to play as well on third downs (an issue discussed later in this chapter) and rival coaches have had the entire off-season to study film and develop strategies against the now-dangerous Chargers. But while they may not be Super Bowl contenders, they can't be dismissed as hapless also-rans, either.

If 2005 does turn out to be a good year, Schottenheimer will get more credit than he deserves, but the glory belongs more to general manager A. J. Smith. Since taking over the position from the late John Butler right before the 2003 draft, Smith has orchestrated two highly successful drafts and turned around the franchise. Indeed, since the team of Butler and Smith arrived from Buffalo in 2001, the Chargers have posted a 29–35 record, easily the franchise's best four-season mark since the departure of Bobby Ross in 1996.

But curb your enthusiasm until the Chargers put together back-to-back winning seasons. If they can do that in 2005, this young team of homegrown stars would provide real reason for hope in San Diego. O day and night, but this is wondrous strange!

Tim Gerheim

Research: How We Predicted San Diego's Offensive Surge

Before the start of the 2004 season, FootballOutsiders.com introduced a complicated system for projecting team performance. The variables included everything from DVOA in specific situations and points scored and allowed over past seasons to the tenure of the offensive and defensive coordinators and the value of recent draft picks. And when we threw all the variables into the hopper to determine our final projections for 2004, the system spit out the following teams as the top three offenses in football: Kansas City, Philadelphia, and San Diego.

Excuse me?

Not only did this projection strain our credibility with the readers, but it made us question the projection system ourselves. Yes, the Chargers had finished 16th in points scored the year before, and 14th in offensive DVOA. But they had no receivers of note and a quarterback who in 2003 had thrown more interceptions than touchdowns. Their only quality offensive player was a running back who had gone from 3.6 yards per carry to 5.3 yards per carry in two seasons and couldn't possibly improve any further. When we ran the projections on our website, we manually dropped the Chargers projection, explaining that we thought something about the Chargers was confusing the equations.

As it turns out, nothing was confusing the equations. After a couple of mediocre games, San Diego exploded with a 38–17 win over Tennessee in Week 4. For the rest of the year, they were one of the top offenses in football. Seven times they scored over 30 points, and by season's end only Indianapolis and Kansas City had scored more points than San Diego's 446. The Chargers were the breakout team of the year, and nothing had predicted it.

Nothing except for our projection system, which even we didn't believe at the time.

Although no NFL expert saw it, there was a very clear sign that the Chargers were going to improve significantly from the year before. On both offense and defense, the 2003 Chargers were fine on first and second down but horrible on third down. And third-down performance, it turns out, is a particularly inconsistent portion of a team's total offense or defense.

When a team makes a small improvement on third downs, it creates a domino effect that dramatically improves the entire offense. Suddenly, a few drives that ended early get a chance to go longer, and "longer" could mean anything from a few extra yards to a TD.

In 2003, Drew Brees converted only 23 of 102 third-down passes for first downs or touchdowns. In 2004, he converted 54 of 128 third-down passes, meaning that drives were extended roughly twice as often. Part of this was improvement from Brees. Part of it was a full season from a more experienced Antonio Gates. And part of it was just plain blind luck and regression to the mean.

And while nobody noticed, the defense made a similar, though smaller, improvement, particularly against the run. In 2003, San Diego opponents converted 38% of passing plays on third down and 59% of rushing plays. In 2004, those numbers dropped to 32% conversion on passing plays and 46% on rushing plays.

San Diego's rebound from a year of poor third-down performance is not a one-time thing, but one example of a general NFL rule: Over time, a team will play as well on third and fourth down as it plays the rest of the time. Therefore, teams that play much better on third down tend to decline the next year, and teams that play much worse on third down tend to improve. To demonstrate, we'll use DVOA ratings, which take into account not just conversion rate on third down but also the value of big third-down plays and the importance of avoiding turnovers when in field goal range. These ratings include the occasional rushing or passing play on fourth down.

Table 1 gives the ten teams from 2000 through 2003 with the largest single-season differential between offensive DVOA overall and offensive DVOA on third down, along with points scored both that season and the following season. Not every team on this list had a better offense the following year, but four of these teams went from losing records to the playoffs and the one on top went to the Super Bowl. Just below the top ten are teams like the 2002 Bengals, the 2003 Falcons, and the 2003 Bills, each of which improved significantly the following year.

TABLE 1. TOP 10 OFFENSES WORSE ON THIRD DOWN, 2000–2003

Team	Year	DVOA	DVOA D3	Dif	PF	PF Y+1	Dif
CAR	2002	−23.9%	−66.0%	42.1%	258	325	67
HOU	2002	−38.0%	−69.8%	31.8%	213	255	42
SD	2003	−1.7%	−32.9%	31.3%	313	446	133
CHI	2001	−8.0%	−38.7%	30.7%	338	281	−57
TB	2003	−4.1%	−33.9%	29.8%	301	301	0
DEN	2003	2.8%	−26.2%	28.9%	381	381	0
BUF	2001	−13.3%	−40.9%	27.5%	265	379	114
DAL	2002	−23.9%	−51.0%	27.1%	217	289	72
STL	2002	−5.7%	−31.2%	25.5%	316	447	131
DET	2001	−14.8%	−40.0%	25.2%	270	306	36

TABLE 2. TOP 10 OFFENSES BETTER ON THIRD DOWN, 2000–2003

Team	Year	DVOA	DVOA D3	Dif	PF	PF Y+1	Dif
SF	2002	18.9%	59.8%	−40.9%	367	384	17
CAR	2000	−20.9%	19.4%	−40.3%	310	253	−57
PIT	2001	11.5%	49.1%	−37.6%	352	390	38
ARI	2002	−18.6%	18.6%	−37.1%	262	225	−37
SEA	2000	−9.8%	26.2%	−36.0%	320	301	−19
ATL	2001	−7.6%	25.2%	−32.7%	291	402	111
SEA	2003	17.3%	48.1%	−30.7%	404	371	−33
PHI	2000	−1.8%	27.6%	−29.3%	351	343	−8
STL	2001	25.6%	54.1%	−28.5%	503	316	−187
GB	2000	0.4%	28.3%	−27.9%	353	390	37

TABLE 4. TOP 10 DEFENSES BETTER ON THIRD DOWN, 2000–2003

Team	Year	DVOA	DVOA D3	Dif	PF	PF Y+1	Dif
CLE	2001	−22.1%	−68.4%	−46.3%	319	320	1
BAL	2003	−32.0%	−77.0%	−45.0%	281	268	−13
DEN	2001	−8.5%	−49.4%	−41.0%	339	344	5
BAL	2001	−18.1%	−49.8%	−31.6%	265	354	89
PHI	2002	−14.1%	−44.9%	−30.7%	241	287	46
MIA	2003	−18.4%	−47.2%	−28.9%	261	354	93
KC	2003	4.5%	−22.6%	−27.1%	332	435	103
TB	2003	−25.5%	−52.5%	−27.0%	264	304	40
NO	2000	−7.9%	−34.4%	−26.5%	305	409	104
PHI	2003	5.2%	−20.9%	−26.1%	287	260	−27

Table 2 shows the other side of the coin, the teams where offensive DVOA on third down was far better than offensive DVOA overall. This list isn't quite as impressive, but that's partly because of an Atlanta team that had a bit of a major quarterback change in 2002, and partly because the teams with the biggest offensive collapses are just below the top ten. That includes the 2003 Rams, the 2003 Titans, and the 2002 Raiders.

The ten teams from table 1 averaged 54 more points scored in the following season. The ten teams from table 2 averaged 14 fewer points scored in the following season. That second number doesn't seem like a big deal, but like we said, the teams with the biggest offensive collapses are just below the top ten. If you were to expand the table to include the top 20 teams where the offense was better on third down, those 20 teams averaged 40 fewer points scored in the following season.

The effect is similar when it comes to defense. The list of the top ten defenses that had the biggest decline on third down (table 3) includes two of the three years before

TABLE 3. TOP 10 DEFENSES WORSE ON THIRD DOWN, 2000–2003

Team	Year	DVOA	DVOA D3	Dif	PF	PF Y+1	Dif
ATL	2001	9.7%	55.1%	45.4%	377	314	−63
SF	2002	0.2%	43.0%	42.9%	351	337	−14
PIT	2002	−2.5%	34.1%	36.6%	345	327	−18
DET	2002	24.1%	56.5%	32.5%	451	379	−72
CLE	2000	11.8%	43.0%	31.2%	419	319	−100
KC	2000	4.1%	34.6%	30.5%	354	344	−10
NE	2002	−3.4%	25.9%	29.3%	346	238	−108
NYJ	2000	−21.6%	7.1%	28.7%	321	295	−26
MIN	2000	26.7%	55.2%	28.5%	371	390	19
NE	2000	5.7%	33.7%	27.9%	338	272	−66

the Patriots won their Super Bowls. Those ten teams gave up an average of 44 fewer points the following season. The list of the top ten defenses that had the biggest improvement on third down (table 4) includes the Dolphins and Chiefs before each team collapsed last year and two Baltimore teams that dropped out of the playoffs. Those ten teams gave up an average of 46 more points the following season.

Now that we've established the difference between overall performance and third-down performance as an indicator that helps predict a team's direction the following season, the next question is to figure out what this indicator says about our expectations for the 2005 season. Six teams stand out:

- Carolina had a defensive DVOA of −7.1%, but its third-down defensive DVOA was 33.4%, worse than every team in football except Minnesota and San Francisco. That makes it very likely the Panthers will allow fewer points this season.
- Indianapolis had a defensive DVOA of 2.3%, but its third-down defensive DVOA was the best in the league at −44.4%. Regression to the mean will lead to longer drives by opponents, which not only leads to more points against the Colts but also less time on the field for a certain record-setting quarterback.
- Minnesota had a great offensive DVOA of 28.0%, but the Vikings led the league with a ridiculous 80.6% DVOA on third downs. In 2003, by comparison, the Vikings had the same offensive DVOA on third downs that they had overall. The loss of Randy Moss makes it even more likely that there will be fewer extended Minnesota drives in 2005.
- Finally, three different teams had a significant drop in offensive efficiency on third down: Tennessee, Chicago, and Seattle. Seattle gives the best example of how fickle third down performance can be. Using the exact same personnel, the Seahawks had a 48.1%

DVOA on third downs in 2003, the best in the NFL, and a −34.0% DVOA on third downs in 2004, which ranked 27th. Pundits came up with numerous explanations for why Matt Hasselbeck was struggling last season, but a big part of it was just luck: abnormally good luck in 2003, abnormally bad luck in 2004. The most likely scenario for 2005 has Seattle playing just as well on third downs as it does the rest of the time, which means the Seahawks should rebound with an offensive performance closer to, though not as strong as, two years ago.

What about the Chargers? In 2003, they were the only team of the past five years to have both offensive and defensive DVOA at least 20% worse on third down. In 2004, that flipped around completely: Both offensive and defensive DVOA were 20% *better* on third down. It is a reason to believe that the Chargers, despite returning nearly all their young starters on both sides of the ball, are not likely to go 12–4 again this season.

Aaron Schatz

Chargers 2004 Stats by Week

Wk	vs.	W-L	PF	PA	YDF	YDA	TO	Total	Off	Def	ST
									DVOA		
1	@HOU	W	27	20	324	336	+4	23.0%	17.5%	-9.8%	-4.2%
2	NYJ	L	28	34	327	380	-4	-15.7%	-7.9%	14.7%	7.0%
3	@DEN	L	13	23	214	328	0	-19.5%	-13.0%	8.7%	2.2%
4	TEN	W	38	17	393	329	0	93.6%	88.3%	7.1%	12.4%
5	JAC	W	34	21	386	429	+3	40.9%	47.2%	15.9%	9.6%
6	@ATL	L	20	21	318	299	+1	-21.9%	-1.0%	25.8%	4.8%
7	@CAR	W	17	6	302	263	0	46.8%	26.3%	-21.2%	-0.8%
8	OAK	W	42	14	448	281	+2	58.1%	52.2%	-16.1%	-10.2%
9	NO	W	43	17	402	243	+2	32.0%	23.7%	-14.7%	-6.4%
10	BYE										
11	@OAK	W	23	17	402	273	0	-12.5%	11.0%	18.9%	-4.6%
12	@KC	W	34	31	498	310	+2	12.4%	39.8%	-4.6%	-32.0%
13	DEN	W	20	17	208	337	+2	34.7%	-37.5%	-65.0%	7.2%
14	TB	W	31	24	336	436	+1	-13.2%	1.4%	12.7%	-1.9%
15	@CLE	W	21	0	257	231	0	4.1%	9.6%	-13.6%	-19.2%
16	@IND	L	31	34	374	464	0	24.6%	18.2%	-28.2%	-21.7%
17	KC	W	24	17	363	443	+2	39.9%	10.1%	-33.6%	-3.8%
18	NYJ	L	17	20	408	396	-1	-9.3%	20.0%	22.8%	-6.5%

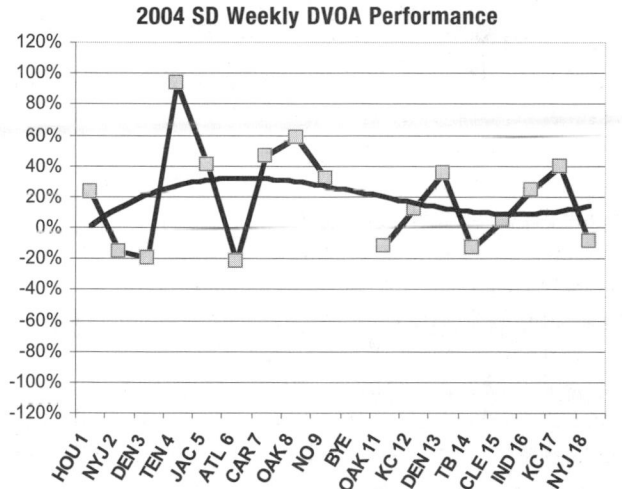

2004 SD Weekly DVOA Performance

Trends and Splits

	Offense	Rank	Defense	Rank
Total DVOA	16.4%	8	-6.6%	11
Unadjusted VOA	25.0%	4	-0.3%	17
Weighted Trend	13.9%	8	-14.4%	6
Variance	8.7%	17	5.7%	27
Passing	34.3%	5	-9.2%	12
Rushing	2.5%	11	-8.0%	8
First Down	2.0%	13	-4.3%	13
Second Down	20.4%	6	2.6%	16
Third Down	40.9%	4	-26.4%	5
Red Zone	23.8%	4	-21.5%	5
Late and Close	16.9%	7	-20.7%	5

Five-Year Performance

	2004	2003	2002	2001	2000
W-L	12-4	4-12	8-8	5-11	1-15
Pythagorean Wins	11.2	4.9	7.1	8.3	3.8
Estimated Wins	10.7	6.3	7.7	9.2	4.1
Total DVOA	19.2%	-14.6%	-2.7%	10.2%	-29.9%
Rank	8	25	21	9	28
Offense	16.4%	-1.7%	-0.6%	-3.8%	-39.0%
Rank	8	14	20	16	31
Defense	-6.6%	9.9%	2.1%	-13.9%	-12.9%
Rank	11	27	17	7	8
Special Teams	-3.8%	-3.1%	0.0%	0.2%	-3.9%
Rank	29	27	16	14	24

Passing (min. 5 plays)

Player	DPAR	PAR	DVOA	Plys	NtYds	Avg	Cmpl	TD	Int
Drew Brees	75.6	90.7	29.5%	420	3027	7.2	65.5%	27	7
Doug Flutie	10.2	12.8	60.6%	38	269	7.1	52.6%	1	0
Philip Rivers	-0.7	0.5	-36.8%	9	23	2.6	62.5%	1	0

Rushing (min. 3 plays)

Player	DPAR	PAR	DVOA	Plys	Yds	Avg	TD	Fum	Suc
LaDainian Tomlinson	14.0	16.3	-4.9%	340	1336	3.9	17	5	45%
Jesse Chatman	10.5	11.4	24.6%	65	392	6.0	3	1	52%
Drew Brees	4.6	4.7	4.0%	29	104	3.6	2	0	—
Michael Turner	1.8	3.0	10.4%	20	104	5.2	0	0	40%
Lorenzo Neal	0.3	0.5	-9.8%	16	53	3.3	0	1	81%
Andrew Pinnock	-4.3	-3.7	-110.1%	9	26	2.9	0	1	44%
Doug Flutie	4.2	4.3	126.2%	5	39	7.8	2	0	—
Reche Caldwell	2.4	2.6	78.9%	4	45	11.3	0	0	—
Tim Dwight	1.6	1.5	70.4%	4	54	13.5	0	0	—
Eric Parker	1.9	1.8	45.7%	4	53	13.3	0	0	—

Receiving (min. 5 plays)

Player	DPAR	PAR	DVOA	Plys	Ctch	Yds	Y/C	TD	CPct
WR									
Eric Parker	16.2	18.6	18.8%	71	47	690	14.7	4	66%
Keenan McCardell	1.2	3.4	-12.8%	58	31	393	12.7	1	53%
Kassim Osgood	5.5	5.9	10.3%	33	15	308	20.5	2	45%
Reche Caldwell	4.4	5.8	7.3%	29	18	310	17.2	3	62%
Bobby Shaw	-2.2	-1.9	-43.7%	13	5	59	11.8	0	38%
Malcom Floyd	-0.1	0.4	-18.7%	9	3	49	16.3	1	33%
Tim Dwight	0.6	0.7	0.2%	5	2	31	15.5	1	40%
TE									
Antonio Gates	35.3	39.5	36.1%	114	81	964	11.9	0	71%
Justin Peelle	-4.1	-4.1	-48.4%	20	10	84	8.4	0	50%
Ryan Krause	4.9	5.8	166.7%	6	5	81	16.2	0	83%
RB									
LaDainian Tomlinson	4.1	2.9	3.4%	66	53	450	8.5	13	80%
Lorenzo Neal	-0.9	-0.6	-21.0%	19	13	66	5.1	2	68%
Michael Turner	-4.5	-4.0	-195.2%	5	4	8	2.0	1	80%

Defensive Players (min. 20 plays)

Player	Age	Plys	Stop	Dfts	AvYds	StpRt	Sack	Int	FR
Defensive Line									
Igor Olshansky	23	41	28	5	2.5	68%	1.0	0	0
Jamal Williams	29	35	26	7	1.1	74%	4.0	0	0
Jason Fisk	33	31	22	5	2.6	71%	1.0	0	0
Jacques Cesaire	25	26	20	3	2.5	77%	0.5	0	0
DeQuincy Scott	27	21	15	10	3.3	71%	1.5	0	0
Linebackers									
Donnie Edwards	32	163	75	21	5.5	46%	1.0	5	0
Randall Godfrey	32	91	44	19	3.6	48%	2.0	0	1
Steve Foley	30	78	48	26	3.0	62%	10.0	2	2
Ben Leber	27	60	27	9	3.9	45%	2.0	0	1
Stephen Cooper	26	36	17	8	5.8	47%	0.0	0	1
Shaun Phillips	24	23	20	10	1.8	87%	4.0	1	2

Player	Age	Plys	Stop	Dfts	AvYds	StpRt	Sack	Int	FR
Secondary									
Terrence Kiel	25	109	40	16	8.7	37%	1.0	2	1
Jerry Wilson	32	79	16	11	11.9	20%	0.0	3	0
Quentin Jammer	26	78	17	8	10.7	22%	0.0	1	0
Sammy Davis	25	51	19	12	9.1	37%	0.0	1	0
Drayton Florence	25	41	16	11	7.6	39%	0.0	4	0
Jamar Fletcher	26	35	13	9	7.6	37%	0.0	1	1

Offensive Line

Year	Yards	AdjLineYd	Rank	Power	Rank	10+ Yds	Rank	Stuff	Rank	Sack	AdjSack%	Rank
2002	4.51	4.14	16	59%	28	22%	3	26%	23	23	4.7%	7
2003	5.04	4.21	16	70%	9	28%	1	24%	16	28	5.3%	8
2004	4.25	4.17	16	71%	7	20%	6	24%	16	19	4.8%	4

Year	LEnd	Rank	LTckl	Rank	MdGrd	Rank	RTckl	Rank	REnd	Rank
2002	3.65	24	3.57	29	4.12	21	4.70	5	4.89	4
2003	4.38	11	3.89	24	4.40	8	3.65	27	3.13	24
2004	2.87	28	5.09	2	4.10	20	4.73	7	3.45	23

The swift coalescence of the Chargers' offensive line was one of the biggest reasons for the team's surprising success in 2004. Yes, the rank in Adjusted Line Yards did not change, but that actually represents significant improvement on the line because injury-addled LaDainian Tomlinson was nowhere near his usual explosive self. Rookies Nick Hardwick and Shane Olivea outplayed their draft positions as third- and seventh-rounders, respectively. Roman Oben, from Tampa Bay, and Mike Goff, from Cincinnati, did the job in their first years in San Diego. Toniu Fonoti, a second-round pick in 2002 who played in 15 games that year, started every game after returning from the foot injury that cost him all of 2003. That 100 % turnover from 2003 to 2004 was justifiably worrying, but it looks like the Chargers found the right guys for the line, and they'll be sticking with them this year. They're hoping to find the same success with late-round offensive linemen from this year's draft—their last three picks were tackle Wesley Britt, guard Wes Sims, and center Scott Mruczkowski. It is worth noting that the Chargers successfully converted only 11 of 23 runs on the opposing first- or second-yard line in 2004, but were 25 of 28 in other short-yardage situations. League-wide the goal line rate of success is only slightly lower than the rate for other short-yardage situations, so regression to the mean should mean more touchdowns and fewer field goals in 2005.

Defensive Front Seven

Year	Yards	AdjLineYd	Rank	Power	Rank	10+ Yds	Rank	Stuff	Rank	Sack	AdjSack%	Rank
2002	4.11	3.91	9	68%	17	16%	12	29%	5	40	6.3%	15
2003	4.34	4.35	22	65%	15	15%	12	23%	20	31	5.9%	21
2004	3.74	4.17	16	62%	16	8%	2	21%	28	29	4.8%	31

Year	LEnd	Rank	LTckl	Rank	MdGrd	Rank	RTckl	Rank	REnd	Rank
2002	3.69	8	4.29	19	3.90	6	3.94	13	3.70	11
2003	4.43	19	4.45	18	4.46	26	4.42	21	3.76	16
2004	4.43	19	4.17	11	4.31	22	3.85	9	3.87	18

Nose tackle Jamal Williams and linebacker Donnie Edwards were two among the inevitable hordes with legitimate claims of being Pro Bowl snubs. They were the top performers on a defense that ranked eighth in DVOA against the run and tenth against passes to both running backs and tight ends. San Diego moved into a 3-4 formation in 2004, and you can see the effects in the combination of allowing very few long runs but also rarely stopping opposing runners at the line, very similar to the New England Patriots and Oakland Raiders. But the front seven may be the most worrisome area on the team—not necessarily in 2005, but soon. Four starters—Williams, Edwards, and linebackers Randall Godfrey and Steve Foley, who signed a contract extension in the off-season—are among the Chargers' oldest players. The team began to address this concern in the draft by taking outside linebacker Shawne Merriman and nose tackle Luis Castillo in the first round. Both figure to be major contributors in 2005, and Merriman in particular should help improve the weak pass rush. But otherwise, there is a notable dearth of experience behind San Diego's aging stalwarts.

Defensive Secondary

Year	DVOA vs. #1 WR	Rank	DVOA vs. #2 WR	Rank	DVOA vs. Other WR	Rank	DVOA vs. TE	Rank	DVOA vs. RB	Rank
2002	1.2%	17	33.5%	26	-18.6%	8	-13.7%	9	-12.8%	6
2003	27.2%	28	33.9%	32	-13.0%	15	24.6%	27	26.5%	30
2004	5.0%	10	-14.2%	5	-9.0%	13	-10.1%	10	-19.6%	10

Quentin Jammer. Sammy Davis. Terrence Kiel. Drayton Florence. Hanik Milligan. Teddy Gaines. That's the list of every defensive back the Chargers have drafted since 2002. Only 2002 seventh-rounder Gaines is no longer with the team. Jammer (CB), Davis (CB), and Kiel (SS) are all starters, Florence is the nickelback, and Milligan provides depth at safety. Bhawoh Jue was signed from Green Bay to compete with incumbent Jerry Wilson at free safety. This is a young, homegrown (and therefore relatively inexpensive) secondary that dramatically improved in all DVOA splits in 2004. Like everywhere else on the 2005 Chargers, everybody's back, so injury is the only real threat to another successful season.

Special Teams

Year	DVOA	Rank	FG/XP	Rank	Net Punt	Rank	Punt Ret	Rank	Net Kick	Rank	Kick Ret	Rank
2002	0.0%	17	-5.0	22	-5.4	21	4.9	11	5.8	8	-0.2	18
2003	-3.1%	27	-0.3	20	2.6	18	-5.1	21	-14.3	32	-0.1	17
2004	-3.8%	29	-3.2	25	4.5	16	-8.7	23	-20.2	32	6.2	9

Rookie kicker Nate Kaeding didn't exactly set the league on fire. He and his special teams battery mates ranked dead last on kickoffs and in the bottom ten for field goals, and you might remember how the Chargers' playoff game against the Jets *didn't* end: with a 40-yard Kaeding field goal in overtime. Nevertheless, he and punter Mike Scifres, whose punting was dead average, will be San Diego's kicking tandem in 2005. There will actually be a change in the return game, unlike everywhere else on this team: Tim Dwight, who performed solidly as the Chargers' primary kickoff returner, is now a Patriot. Rookie running back Darren Sproles figures to assume those duties, as well as taking punt returns from Eric Parker, a better complementary receiver than punt returner.

Coaching Staff

Martyball has always been built around running the ball and playing good defense. But last year Marty Schottenheimer added some new wrinkles to that old, regular season-tested formula, employing defensive coordinator Wade Phillips's 3-4 defense and using tight end Antonio Gates as the primary receiver. The major change this year comes along the offensive line, where the Chargers had that rare bird, a big-name free agent assistant coach. Hudson Houck will now try to repeat his trick of turning no-names and retreads into a solid blocking unit in Miami, where he'll get $850,000 a year. Taking over the Chargers' line is Carl Mauck, who was known at his last stop in Detroit for two things: a quarterback who didn't get sacked very often and a ferocious, somewhat frighteningly intense coaching style. If you are looking for a rising star on the coaching staff, try Greg Manusky, the linebackers coach who helped free agent additions Randall Godfrey and Steve Foley achieve their full potential in 2004.

Tennessee Titans

The Tennessee Titans' run of excellence came to an abrupt end with a 5–11 campaign in 2004. After being in the small group of teams considered Super Bowl contenders each year since 1999, the injury-ravaged Titans struggled mightily. They had the sharpest drop in DVOA of all teams, falling from 3rd in 2003 to 29th in 2004. Worse than the injuries, however, were the drastic economic measures management decided to take after the season. In early 2005, as an attempt to cure the team's long-term salary cap situation, Tennessee jettisoned six players still under contract, including such stars as WR Derrick Mason, CB Samari Rolle, and DE Kevin Carter.

During the off-season, our website featured a series of articles by economics Ph.D. Bruce Stram that examined a simplified economic model of the salary cap. In these articles, he discussed two financial strategies used by successful NFL teams: "Even Keel" and "Boom and Bust." The names are self-explanatory—Even Keel is the approach of the always cap-healthy Eagles, while Boom and Bust was most famously the modus operandi of the Baltimore Ravens, who imported talent, won a Super Bowl in 2000, and blew up their team two years later because of a salary cap crisis.

The Titans are this year's entry into the Boom and Bust category. After a near-miss in the Super Bowl in 1999 and their devastating loss in the 2000 playoffs to the aforementioned Ravens, the Titans tried to remain competitive by skirting the salary cap through the restructuring of important salaries. Although a few key contributors left, the Titans kept most of the team together and maintained hopes of getting back to the Super Bowl.

Now the Super Bowl seems light-years away. Not only was 2004 a complete disaster, but the Titans went into the off-season a whopping $27 million over the cap. Facing this brutal reality, they decided to follow the Ravens' successful strategy after the 2001 season—Baltimore swiftly released a number of contributors, fixed its cap situation, and was back in the playoffs within two years. The Ravens' model is a fantasy for any team facing salary cap problems. After one season out of contention, you are right back in the race the following year with a healthy cap and the ability to acquire talent for another run.

While every team would love to get out of salary cap jail as neatly as the Ravens did, is it practical to think that

TITANS PROSPECTUS

2004 Record: 5–11

DVOA Estimated Wins: 5.2 (30th)

Pythagorean Wins: 5.8 (26th)

DVOA: −22.5% total (29th), −29.8% weighted (30th)

Adjusted Offense: 18.7 points/game (−10.4% DVOA, 26th)

Adjusted Defense: 23.6 points/game (7.9% DVOA, 23rd)

Adjusted Special Teams: −1.5 points/game (−4.2% DVOA, 30th)

Variance: 21.4% (12th)

2004: Music City was hummin' those "Crumblin' Steve McNair Blues."

2005: With so many Titan toddlers, Music City may be humming Raffi's Greatest Hits.

2005 Projection

Leinart Land (0–4): 15%

Bad Team (5–6): 19%

Mediocre (7–8): 25%

Playoff Contender (9–10): 21%

Super Bowl Contender (11+): 19%

Projected Average Opponent: −1.7% DVOA (22nd in NFL)

the Titans are in a position to do so? To answer that, let us first look back at how they stumbled into this mess in the first place.

The 2003 Tennessee Titans were an excellent football team. They finished third in DVOA and came one dropped pass short of an easy field goal that would have forced overtime at New England in the playoffs. After the season ended, in a harbinger of things to come, the Titans had a few salary cap problems. Despite losing a few good players, including receiver Justin McCareins and defensive linemen Jevon Kearse and Robaire Smith, the team brought back most of its core for another run at the Super Bowl.

The best laid plans of mice, men, and NFL general managers often go awry. The problem with a star-laden team that's held together by salary cap manipulation is that the big salaries don't leave room for much depth, and so Tennessee's 2004 season disappeared under a torrent of injuries. Fourteen major contributors missed at least 4 games. Quarterback Steve McNair missed 8, both starting safeties missed at least 7, and the linebacking corps missed a combined 37 games. Altogether, Titans starters missed over 150 games last season.

Perhaps the most important injury was the one to third wide receiver Tyrone Calico, who effectively missed the whole season. In 2003, the Titans developed a dynamic passing offense that was held back only by the anemic play of the zombielike Eddie George. According to DVOA, the 2003 Titans had the league's best passing offense—yes, more efficient than the Colts'—but the third-*worst* rushing offense. With George being sent away in a "salary cap" move that actually improved the club, it was reasonable to believe that the Tennessee offense might get even better.

The Titans, in a true salary cap move, had traded number two receiver Justin McCareins to the New York Jets. Although McCareins had an excellent 2003, ranking eighth in DVOA, replacing him didn't seem like it would be a problem because number three receiver Drew Bennett ranked fourth in DVOA. But the Titans needed Calico to move into Bennett's old role to allow the team to use the three-receiver sets that played such a pivotal role in their spread offense. Calico went down early in the season's first game, reinjured himself when he tried to come back in Week 4, and the Titans never found an adequate replacement. In 2003, Mason, McCareins, and Bennett combined for 77.3 DPAR. In 2004, Mason and Bennett still produced 45.7 DPAR, but the next best Tennessee receiver was Eddie Berlin, worth only 2.7 DPAR, despite being thrown 41 passes.

The impact of losing McCareins and Calico was also felt in the lackluster performance of the Titans' quarterbacks. In 2003, Steve McNair was co-MVP of the league, with a passing DVOA of 34.1%. The Titans' passing offense was not all McNair, however; he missed two games due to injury, and Billy Volek and Neil O'Donnell stepped in with DVOAs of 37.1% and 73.5% in a limited sample size. But this year, hampered by injuries both to himself and his receivers, McNair posted a DVOA of −18.9%, and Volek was not much better at −10.2%.

The problems caused by the inability to find a third receiver loom large in the offense's overall context. The Titans' running game actually did improve as expected after posting a league-last DVOA of −13.5% in 2003. In 2004, it progressed modestly to −5.4% and 21st in the league, but the offense did not open up at all—because the passing game took several steps back.

While the offense slipped from 2003 to 2004 by a larger amount, Jeff Fisher had to be more upset at the decline of the defense. Once among the best in the NFL, the Titans posted a 7.9% defensive DVOA, good for just 23rd in the league. While Tennessee and Fisher have a strong defen-

sive reputation, it was actually the third time in four years that the Titans had a below-average defensive DVOA.

While the run defense was porous from the get-go, the pass defense was actually quite solid through the season's first ten games. Despite a 4–6 record, the Titans ranked fourth in the NFL with a −15.1% DVOA on pass defense (the run defense was 25th with a 6.0% DVOA).

The Week 11 game against Jacksonville—ironically a Titans victory—was the turning point. Tennessee entered that game without starting safeties Lance Schulters and Tank Williams, and then watched as three more defensive backs—Samari Rolle, Andre Woolfolk, and Scott McGarrahan—left the game due to injury. By the time the gun sounded, the Titans pass defense was left with Andre Dyson and some guys off the practice squad.

Over the season's final six weeks, Tennessee had a worse pass defense than every other team in the league except Oakland, Kansas City, and Minnesota (table 1). In Week 15 against Oakland, the Titans started only four defenders who had also started the season opener: linemen Kevin Carter and Carlos Hall, linebacker Keith Bulluck, and cornerback Andre Dyson.

In the NFL, it isn't enough to say that a team can be good if it can avoid injuries. A team has to be built to be good even *after* suffering injuries. Yes, the number of injuries was high, even by NFL standards, but last year's collapse showed that the Titans no longer had the depth to be playoff contenders. Usually a team coming off such an abnormal number of injuries could optimistically expect a rebound with injuries returning to a reasonable level. But, for every injured player coming back, the Titans lost a major contributor in the insane salary cap implosion that has trimmed this team's roster to Jack Sprat proportions. The team's best receiver and best defensive lineman are gone. So are both starting cornerbacks, the right tackle, and the fullback.

The quality and quantity of players shed mimics the Ravens' moves after their 2001 campaign, when they said goodbye to numerous players—including Shannon Sharpe, Rod Woodson, Elvis Grbac, Jamie Sharper, Sam Adams, and Qadry Ismail. But the Titans start their rebuilding from a very different position. Tennessee is coming off a

TABLE 1. 2004 TENNESSEE DEFENSE BY DVOA AND YARDS/PLAY

Period	Pass DVOA	Rank	Net Yds/ Pass	Run DVOA	Rank	Yds/ Rush
Weeks 1–11	-15.1%	4	5.9	6.0%	25	4.6
Weeks 12–17	32.4%	29	8.3	21.8%	30	5.2

5–11 campaign, whereas the 2001 Baltimore Ravens were a 10–6 playoff team.

The Titans have no proven second or third receiver and the problems caused by the loss of McCareins will be exacerbated by the departure of Derrick Mason. The running game is still substandard, and Brown has yet to prove he can remain healthy for an entire year. The underrated Keith Bulluck is still here to anchor the defense, but the line in front of him has no established pass rusher. Both veteran safeties return to a secondary that imploded down the stretch without them, and they will be playing inside of two brand-new corners.

The Titans did add a defensive playmaker with Adam "Pac-Man" Jones, the first defensive player taken in the draft. Maybe equal to his importance in replacing Rolle will be his impact on the return game. In 2004, the Titans were the second-worst team in the NFL in combined kick and punt returns, a weakness the electrifying Jones will likely improve.

While Jones is a potential game changer, the numerous holes meant that the Titans could not address their aging offensive line until the second round, and they were forced to draft three wide receivers in the third and fourth round, hoping that someone will emerge to play third receiver this season. Despite losing Carter and Carlos Hall, they did not add a defensive lineman; instead they are forced to rely on the large group of defensive lineman they drafted in 2004, none of whom impressed a season ago.

Finally, there is McNair, the face of the franchise since it moved to Nashville. In 2002 and 2003, the easiest story to write in football was the astounding tenacity of McNair. Of course, as he ages the potential for injury will increase, and the ability of his amazing body to absorb NFL abuse will decline. (McNair had the foresight to marry a registered nurse.) He will be playing hurt and missing games each season until he retires. He may be better this year than last year, but with his injury history it is unlikely he will ever again perform at the level he did two years ago.

Jeff Fisher has, throughout his career, consistently put a well-coached team on the field. Coaching in the NFL is the great equalizer, so maybe he can coach them up and get them competitive in the next several seasons. For now, however, the cupboard is bare. The Titans are facing consecutive losing seasons for the first time since the franchise was in Houston in 1994 and 1995. Though the cap situation will be improved going into the next off-season, Tennessee will be more than a key free agent away from recapturing past glory.

Ned Macey

Titans 2004 Stats by Week

Wk	vs.	W-L	PF	PA	YDF	YDA	TO	DVOA Total	Off	Def	ST
1	@MIA	W	17	7	243	262	+2	-3.2%	-23.3%	-26.4%	-6.3%
2	IND	L	17	31	389	373	-1	-8.8%	10.5%	17.2%	-2.1%
3	JAC	L	12	15	249	253	-1	-31.7%	-28.1%	2.8%	-0.8%
4	@SD	L	17	38	329	393	0	-88.2%	2.9%	80.4%	-10.8%
5	@GB	W	48	27	456	437	+6	85.1%	44.1%	-39.9%	1.1%
6	HOU	L	10	20	305	345	-2	-52.3%	-52.8%	3.3%	3.9%
7	@MIN	L	3	20	243	313	-4	-101.2%	-92.3%	12.3%	3.4%
8	CIN	W	27	20	358	274	+1	27.5%	19.1%	-5.6%	2.8%
9	BYE										
10	CHI	L	17	19	390	176	0	-9.5%	-22.7%	-47.6%	-34.4%
11	@JAC	W	18	15	295	274	0	-6.0%	-21.0%	-17.2%	-2.2%
12	@HOU	L	21	31	355	328	-2	-33.1%	12.4%	38.0%	-7.5%
13	@IND	L	24	51	340	567	+1	-48.9%	-37.6%	17.2%	5.9%
14	KC	L	38	49	542	383	-2	-7.8%	14.5%	-3.1%	-25.4%
15	@OAK	L	35	40	527	415	-1	-47.2%	-1.0%	50.6%	4.3%
16	DEN	L	16	37	153	496	0	-95.8%	-59.0%	48.4%	11.7%
17	DET	W	24	19	312	434	+2	-7.8%	20.7%	17.3%	-11.2%

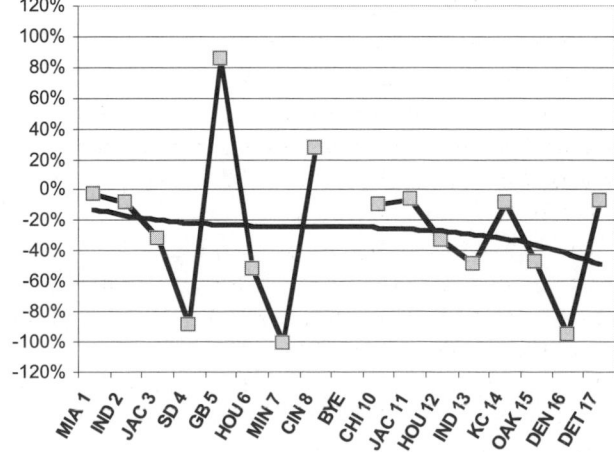

2004 TEN Weekly DVOA Performance

Trends and Splits

	Offense	Rank	Defense	Rank
Total DVOA	-10.4%	26	7.9%	23
Unadjusted VOA	-3.7%	20	12.7%	26
Weighted Trend	-13.1%	26	11.7%	24
Variance	12.6%	8	11.6%	11
Passing	-13.8%	25	4.4%	20
Rushing	-5.4%	21	12.2%	29
First Down	2.0%	14	3.9%	17
Second Down	4.6%	16	23.7%	27
Third Down	-57.0%	31	-12.6%	12
Red Zone	-29.7%	29	11.2%	25
Late and Close	-25.5%	26	13.5%	29

Five-Year Performance

	2004	2003	2002	2001	2000
W-L	5-11	12-4	11-5	7-9	13-3
Pythagorean Wins	5.8	10.7	9.2	6.6	12.9
Estimated Wins	5.2	10.6	9.1	7.5	12.6
Total DVOA	-22.5%	22.3%	8.5%	-10.4%	36.1%
Rank	29	3	13	22	1
Offense	-10.4%	15.6%	12.0%	1.9%	3.6%
Rank	26	5	7	9	12
Defense	7.9%	-6.6%	3.6%	11.8%	-27.2%
Rank	23	10	19	28	2
Special Teams	-4.2%	0.0%	0.1%	-0.5%	5.4%
Rank	30	18	15	17	5

Passing (min. 5 plays)

Player	DPAR	PAR	DVOA	Plys	NtYds	Avg	Cmpl	TD	Int
Billy Volek	5.0	24.8	-10.2%	383	2264	5.9	61.1%	18	10
Steve McNair	-6.0	1.9	-18.9%	229	1254	5.5	60.0%	8	9
Doug Johnson	1.1	0.6	6.9%	13	62	4.8	50.0%	0	0

Rushing (min. 3 plays)

Player	DPAR	PAR	DVOA	Plys	Yds	Avg	TD	Fum	Suc
Chris Brown	5.4	10.6	-8.0%	220	1072	4.9	6	6	43%
Antowain Smith	-0.9	1.5	-16.2%	137	509	3.7	4	2	40%
Steve McNair	3.9	4.0	18.6%	19	131	6.9	1	1	—
Robert Holcombe	-0.6	-0.2	-22.7%	17	62	3.6	0	0	35%
Billy Volek	1.9	1.9	11.1%	9	52	5.8	1	0	—
Troy Fleming	1.0	0.9	21.4%	7	40	5.7	0	0	43%

Receiving (min. 5 plays)

Player	DPAR	PAR	DVOA	Plys	Ctch	Yds	Y/C	TD	CPct
WR									
Derrick Mason	22.1	25.5	5.0%	158	96	1168	12.2	7	61%
Drew Bennett	23.6	26.9	8.4%	143	80	1244	15.6	11	56%
Eddie Berlin	2.7	4.0	-5.5%	41	20	278	13.9	1	49%
TE									
Ben Troupe	-5.4	-3.4	-29.9%	54	33	332	10.1	1	61%
Shad Meier	-8.4	-8.6	-47.2%	36	25	127	5.1	2	69%
Erron Kinney	5.7	6.7	13.7%	30	25	193	7.7	3	83%
RB									
Chris Brown	-2.5	-1.1	-26.1%	33	20	147	7.4	0	61%
Troy Fleming	0.1	1.8	-10.2%	28	19	164	8.6	2	68%
Antowain Smith	1.9	3.1	3.7%	26	22	169	7.7	0	85%
Robert Holcombe	-3.8	-3.6	-42.6%	21	11	60	5.5	0	52%

Defensive Players (min. 20 plays)

Player	Age	Plys	Stop	Dfts	AvYds	StpRt	Sack	Int	FR
Defensive Line									
Kevin Carter	32	50	42	20	0.7	84%	6.0	0	1
Carlos Hall	26	43	31	13	1.0	72%	2.5	0	1
Albert Haynesworth	24	39	29	15	1.1	74%	1.0	0	0
Randy Starks	22	34	32	13	-0.1	94%	4.5	0	2
Rien Long	24	26	22	10	0.3	85%	5.0	0	0
Antwan Odom	24	23	18	7	1.9	78%	2.0	0	0
Travis LaBoy	24	22	16	10	0.7	73%	3.5	0	1
Linebackers									
Keith Bulluck	28	165	93	32	4.5	56%	5.0	2	1
Brad Kassell	25	104	47	15	5.5	45%	0.0	0	1
Justin Ena	28	22	17	5	2.8	77%	0.0	0	0
Rocky Boiman	25	20	12	2	4.0	60%	0.0	0	0

Player	Age	Plys	Stop	Dfts	AvYds	StpRt	Sack	Int	FR
Secondary									
Lamont Thompson	27	72	10	8	13.6	14%	0.0	4	0
Andre Dyson	26	58	20	10	9.4	34%	0.0	6	0
Tank Williams	25	55	21	11	8.5	38%	1.0	1	1
Andre Woolfolk	25	47	18	7	6.6	38%	0.0	1	0
Michael Waddell	24	38	8	4	12.7	21%	0.0	1	2
Samari Rolle	29	36	12	6	9.4	33%	0.0	1	2
Donnie Nickey	25	33	9	3	8.2	27%	0.0	0	0
Scott McGarrahan	31	31	9	6	9.6	29%	0.5	1	0

Offensive Line

Year	Yards	AdjLineYd	Rank	Power	Rank	10+ Yds	Rank	Stuff	Rank	Sack	AdjSack%	Rank
2002	3.55	4.07	18	73%	9	9%	31	25%	18	21	4.0%	3
2003	3.38	3.64	30	46%	31	11%	29	32%	32	25	4.9%	7
2004	4.42	4.19	14	51%	28	18%	12	25%	18	44	8.0%	23

Year	LEnd	Rank	LTckl	Rank	MdGrd	Rank	RTckl	Rank	REnd	Rank
2002	4.60	9	4.03	20	4.25	16	3.51	29	3.96	17
2003	3.44	28	3.82	25	3.61	30	3.86	23	3.15	22
2004	3.19	26	4.18	21	4.32	14	4.60	10	3.67	19

For years, it was convenient to blame the minimal success of the Tennessee ground game on Eddie George's lack of speed and dexterity. With Chris Brown carrying the ball in 2005, however, the Titans still featured a substandard ground game. The big increase in double-digit runs shows the effect of a younger runner, but the Titans still struggled when they needed short yardage.

The Titans line is anchored by left tackle Brad Hopkins, now entering his 13th season. The once-elite Hopkins is clearly slowing down and missed 5 games due to injury. The Titans averaged 4.09 Adjusted Line Yards per carry in the 11 games started by Hopkins, but 4.42 Adjusted Line Yards per carry in the 5 games he missed—a stat even more remarkable than it seems because 3 of those 5 games featured veteran Antowain Smith as the starter instead of the oft-injured Brown. Those 5 games, however, were also responsible for the big jump in Tennessee's Adjusted Sack Rate, with 19 sacks compared to just 24 in the other 11 games. So while Hopkins can still do the job on pass blocking, the Titans might want to get a tight end over there to help him on running plays.

Besides Hopkins and center Justin Hartwig, the starting lineup is full of question marks. Right tackle Fred Miller frustrated the coaching staff with 14 penalties last year, second in the NFL; he was cut in the salary cap purge and is now a Chicago Bear. The Titans have three options for replacing Miller: last year's starting guard Jacob Bell, who needs to move with 2003 starter Zach Piller returning from injury; veteran backup Jason Mathews, who filled in for Hopkins during his injury; and second-round selection Michael Roos out of Eastern Washington, who will eventually succeed Hopkins on the left side.

Defensive Front Seven

Year	Yards	AdjLineYd	Rank	Power	Rank	10+ Yds	Rank	Stuff	Rank	Sack	AdjSack%	Rank
2002	3.70	3.58	2	46%	1	19%	19	32%	2	39	5.9%	20
2003	3.72	3.69	4	65%	17	16%	13	31%	2	37	6.5%	15
2004	4.80	4.12	12	48%	3	26%	32	26%	10	32	6.2%	24

Year	LEnd	Rank	LTckl	Rank	MdGrd	Rank	RTckl	Rank	REnd	Rank
2002	2.99	2	4.09	14	3.77	4	2.72	1	3.61	10
2003	4.97	32	3.86	12	3.17	1	3.81	11	4.26	23
2004	5.34	30	3.54	2	3.76	4	4.46	27	4.60	29

As Sam Cooke once said, a change is gonna come. Discussing the 2004 performance of the Tennessee front seven is a somewhat pointless exercise, because this is going to be a completely different group in 2005. Some veterans are gone for salary reasons, some are back from injuries, and lots of young players have had a year to develop and gain experience.

The defensive line had lost Robaire Smith and Jevon Kearse to free agency last off-season; this off-season, they lost Kevin Carter to the salary cap purge and Carlos Hall to a salary-driven trade. Veteran Albert Haynesworth returns after losing six weeks of 2004 to an elbow injury. The rest of the line will combine a number of second-year players from what defensive coordinator Jim Schwartz calls the "mutual fund" drafting theory: If you take enough young players in the draft, some of them will flop, some will become starters, and there's a good chance somebody will become a star. In 2004, the Titans took four linemen in rounds two through four: Travis LaBoy, Antwan Odom, Randy Starks, and Bo Schobel. Starks showed signs of being the star of the class as the only NFL defender to make at least 20 plays and post a Stop Rate above 90%.

(continued next page)

Defensive Front Seven *(continued)*

The linebackers were also decimated by injuries last year, with starters Peter Sirmon and Rocky Calmus playing just four games. That left Keith Bulluck to play with assorted parts, including Rocky Boiman and Brad Kassell. Kassell was competent at middle linebacker, Boiman not so much. Bulluck responded to the injuries by coming as close as possible to covering the entire field at once—according to our individual defensive stats he led the league in plays and stops while finishing tied for fourth in Defeats. Check out those Adjusted Line Yards numbers, and how good the Titans were against left-side runs behind the offensive line. Run around either end, and if you could get past Bulluck and Kassell, you had an open field because the Titan corners were cover guys, not tacklers. In 2005, Sirmon and Calmus should be healthy, with Kassell providing depth, so the linebackers should be the strength of the defense.

Defensive Secondary

Year	DVOA vs. #1 WR	Rank	DVOA vs. #2 WR	Rank	DVOA vs. Other WR	Rank	DVOA vs. TE	Rank	DVOA vs. RB	Rank
2002	3.0%	18	-61.6%	2	60.4%	32	-2.7%	13	19.0%	26
2003	-18.9%	7	20.8%	25	-39.5%	4	9.5%	22	-4.1%	12
2004	0.1%	17	7.2%	18	-2.8%	18	24.2%	26	-13.9%	12

The Titans opened the 2004 season with the same secondary that ranked ninth in DVOA pass defense for 2003. Then the injuries came, with starting safeties Lance Shulters and Tank Williams missing 13 and 9 games respectively. As tough, physical safeties, Shulters and Williams may have been missed in the running game more than the passing game, and the Titans were dead last in the league in preventing runs over ten yards. Starting cornerbacks Samari Rolle and Andre Dyson were relatively healthy, with Rolle missing four games and Dyson missing zero. The games Rolle missed, however, were embarrassing for the Titans' defense. He did not start a game after Week 12, and in their final five games, the Titans gave up 51, 49, 40, 37, and 19 points. Now the Titans will play all 16 games without Rolle, who signed with Baltimore, and Dyson, who signed with Seattle. Replacing them are Andre Woolfolk and Adam "Pac-Man" Jones. Woolfork was serviceable when forced into the lineup last season. Jones, the sixth-overall pick in this year's draft, is a little undersized, but he is extremely fast and can cover without using his hands. Rich Gardner, a 2004 third-rounder, will compete with 2005 fourth-rounder Vincent Fuller to be the team's nickelback. This may be the only secondary in the league to feature zwieback on the training table.

Special Teams

Year	DVOA	Rank	FG/XP	Rank	Net Punt	Rank	Punt Ret	Rank	Net Kick	Rank	Kick Ret	Rank
2002	0.1%	16	2.8	9	-10.5	26	-4.9	26	17.7	2	-4.8	23
2003	0.0%	18	9.7	7	6.4	9	-3.6	19	2.4	15	-14.6	31
2004	-4.2%	30	-2.6	24	7.8	12	-16.9	31	-3.7	21	-8.1	30

Hey, it wouldn't be a Titans season without an injury to kicker Joe Nedney, who in 2004 got his injury out of the way in the preseason instead of waiting for the first game like he did in 2003. That forced the Titans to get 45-year-old Gary Anderson out of mothballs, and while he remains accurate inside of 40 yards, he has very limited leg strength. Nedney is now in San Francisco and while Ola Kimrin is now technically the kicker according to the depth chart, nobody really knows who will be the kicker here. To be honest, it might be you. Please send a tape featuring kickoffs as well as field goal attempts from multiple distances to Baptist Sports Park, Nashville, TN 37228, Attn: Special Teams Coach Alan Lowry.

The kicking problems were nothing compared to the problems in the return game. Derrick Mason, once golden as a return man, had an odd off-year with an appallingly bad 3.9 yards per return. On kicks, Jason McAddley was not much better. There's no need for a résumé here, though, because Pac-Man Jones was an electric kick returner in college and could handle both kickoff and punt return duties for the Titans. The Titans have been throwing away points and field position for years thanks to their poor return game, so the addition of Jones is a big change. No change at punter, where Craig Hentrich is solid.

Coaching Staff

Jeff Fisher is entering his 11th full season as the Titans head coach, the second-longest tenure in the NFL. Following the cap purge, Fisher will be rebuilding a team for the first time since he originally took over midway through the 1994 season. To help in the rebuilding, he has brought in Norm Chow as his offensive coordinator. Chow is one of the most respected offensive minds in college football history, running the powerful national championship offense at USC the last two years. He has, however, no NFL experience, and he plans no major overhaul of the Titans' offensive system.

Those readers who have been reading FootballOutsiders.com know that Tennessee defensive coordinator Jim Schwartz is a big supporter of our site, and our editor in chief, Aaron Schatz, has worked with Schwartz on various projects over the past two off-seasons. From his early days as an assistant with the Belichick-era Cleveland Browns, Schwartz has always been on the cutting edge of combining statistical analysis with on-field football experience. But it is only fair to point out that in the four years he has been defensive coordinator, the Titans have only once had an above-average DVOA. We're sure Schwartz would rather be known as the architect of the defense that ranked 11th in DVOA after ten weeks of last season than as the man who had to call plays for the practice squad all-stars who were completely manhandled by opposing quarterbacks in the last seven weeks. With a rookie cornerback and a bunch of second-year defensive linemen, the plan in Tennessee is to reverse that trend in 2005, with players getting better as they gain experience. Statistical analysis helps Schwartz know what plays to run against opposing offenses, but only hands-on coaching by Schwartz and his positional coaches can teach these youngsters to run those plays with correct technique.

Arizona Cardinals

When Dennis Green arrived last winter, he had to do more than just find a franchise quarterback or get the Cardinals to .500. Green's job was to change the culture of complacency that has come to define the Arizona Cardinals, the institutionalized rot that has been weakening this organization since its last NFL title in 1948.

To understand the complacency culture in Arizona, a good place to start is the offensive line. In 1998, the team drafted Anthony Clement in the second round. In 1999, the Cardinals spent a first-round pick on L. J. Shelton. In 2001, the team used the second pick in the draft on Leonard Davis. All three players became starters, and with veteran guard/center Pete Kendall (a former first-round pick for the Seahawks), they became the nucleus of the Cardinals' offensive line. Clement missed most of the 2002 season, but for the most part the quartet stayed together for four full years, with players like Chris Dishman or Mike Gruttadauria rounding out the line.

Scouting reports always pointed out that the Cardinals linemen could be great—when they felt like it. In 2003, the *Sporting News*'s *Ultimate Pro Football Scouting Guide* listed Clement and Shelton 40th and 41st among tackles, saying that Clement's "mobility and conditioning are issues" and that Shelton "would benefit from losing weight." In its 2004 guide, *Pro Football Weekly* said that Davis could become a perennial Pro Bowler "if he applies himself, which has been a bit of a problem." The Cardinals linemen had grown fat, comfortable, and confident that their starting jobs were secure—in other words, complacent.

Green arrived to find a veteran offensive line filled with former high draft picks. But what had all of that stability and talent achieved? *Pro Football Prospectus* has several statistics for evaluating offensive lines, but the two key stats are Adjusted Line Yards and Adjusted Sack Rate (see table 1). By 2004, Clement, Shelton, Davis, and Kendall had spent years together, and the result was a line that was lousy at run blocking and mediocre at pass protection.

Green took one look at the situation and started cleaning house. Shelton was benched. Davis was moved to left tackle. Kendall, who may or may not have complained to the Players Association when Green's minicamp drills were too intense, was eventually cut. Kendall's complaints may have been valid: The Cardinals were penalized by the league for running off-season workouts that were more

intense than the collective bargaining agreement allowed, but Green's message was in either case painfully clear: No job was secure. Into the lineup came two inexperienced players: rookie center Alex Stepanovich, and second-year guard Reggie Wells, a small-school product raw enough to be a rookie.

The results: 3.71 Adjusted Line Yards, just 29th in the league, and a 6.0% Adjusted Sack Rate, which ranked 11th. Since those numbers aren't much improved over the previous years, it's not easy to call Green's maneuvers a success, but they were: Steponavich and Wells are young players with potential, and they don't come with high cap figures. Green replaced expensive old talent with cheap young talent and got the same results. In Arizona, that spells progress.

And the shakeup on the line continues. Free agent Oliver Ross has been signed to play right tackle, ending the Clement-Shelton era on the offensive line. Elton Brown, a

CARDINALS PROSPECTUS

2004 Record: 6–10

DVOA Estimated Wins: 5.3 (29th)

Pythagorean Wins: 6.8 (21st)

DVOA: −19.4% total (27th), −20.4% weighted (25th)

Adjusted Offense: 16.1 points/game (−20.5% DVOA, 30th)

Adjusted Defense: 21.1 points/game (−1.3% DVOA, 15th)

Adjusted Special Teams: −0.1 points/game (−0.2% DVOA, 18th)

Variance: 22.4% (9th)

2004: It seemed like the usual losing song, but if you listened closely you would have heard a different tune.

2005: The lines, not the new veteran quarterback, will determine if this team can finally win the division.

2005 Projection

Leinart Land (0–4): 30%

Bad Team (5–6): 24%

Mediocre (7–8): 22%

Playoff Contender (9–10): 15%

Super Bowl Contender (11+): 9%

Projected Average Opponent: 0.3% DVOA (15th in NFL)

TABLE 1. ARIZONA OFFENSIVE LINE, 2001–2003

Year	AdjLineYds	Rank	AdjSack%	Rank
2001	3.78	28	5.5%	9
2002	3.99	22	6.7%	20
2003	3.52	32	6.9%	19

TABLE 2. ARIZONA DEFENSIVE SACKS, 2000–2004

Year	Sacks	Rank
2000	25	30 (tie)
2001	19	31
2002	21	32
2003	21	30
2004	37	19

guard/tackle with starting potential, was drafted in the fourth round. Green saw that neither Clement nor Shelton had developed, so he took them off scholarship; now, no one can afford to rest on his reputation.

While the offensive line coasted for years, the defensive line was aggressively futile (table 2). Arizona finished last in the league in sacks in 2002 and 2003. Our Adjusted Sack Rate statistics, which modify sack totals based upon opponent and game situation, also ranked the Cardinals last both seasons. But they moved up to 19th in 2004. (As for run defense, the Cardinals ranked 31st, 20th, and 24th in Adjusted Line Yards from 2002 through 2004.)

Mediocrity ruled the defense from 2000 to 2003. The team didn't spend any free agent money on improving the defensive line; in fact, they let their best pass rusher, Simeon Rice, leave via free agency in 2001. The next year, a first-round pick was spent on defensive tackle Wendell Bryant, who promptly held out for the first two weeks of the season, got hurt in 2003, and has been a bust.

No, the Cardinals tried to improve their defensive line by drafting "high motor players" (Kyle Vanden Bosch), 6'7" oddities (Fred Wakefield), and undersized specialists (Calvin Pace). If there were a better tradition of player development in Arizona, then Bryant or one of these players could have emerged as solid starters. But there isn't, and the most noteworthy defensive lineman that the Cardinals drafted is the one they cut: Darwin Walker, who blossomed under better coaching in Philadelphia.

The 37-sack total for 2004 was the result of an aggressive approach by Green; the Cardinals signed DE Bertrand Berry from Denver while drafting DT Darnell Dockett and Karlos Dansby, a linebacker who can blitz. All three players made positive contributions. Historically, the Cardinals would have stood pat on the D-line at this point. That's the complacency culture for you; the unit goes from terrible to decent, and decent is good enough. But Green and coordinator Clancy Pendergast weren't satisfied with Pace and Peppi Zellner competing for one of the end positions. So they signed Chike Okeafor. Okeafor had nine sacks last season, three of them against the Cardinals. He isn't Bruce Smith, but the Berry-Dockett-Russell Davis-Okeafor line might actually be the best in the division. And third-round pick Daryl Blackstock, out of Virginia, who was ranked as a first-round pick by many draft experts, adds another pass rush dimension from the outside linebacker position.

There was some feeling in Arizona that Green's decision to bench Josh McCown in midseason kept the Cardinals from a fluke playoff berth. That's what once passed for ambition in this organization: Maybe we'll go 9–7 this year, sneak into the playoffs, and get beaten up by the Packers in the first round. It's true that Green's QB shuffle may have cost the Cardinals a chance to be the Rams or Vikings. A competent quarterback could easily have beaten the Lions, and a few breaks could have turned things around against the Jets (though McCown played poorly in relief in that game). The Cardinals offensive DVOA figures hovered between −20% and 20% with McCown starting. In the three games started by King and Navarre, they were −44.7%, −38.5%, and −62.5%.

To Green, the issue of whether the Cardinals *could* have backed into the playoffs was irrelevant. An 8-8 finish, a wild card spot, or the championship of an awful division—these are bogus accomplishments, consolation prizes. The Cardinals have an ingrained habit of building for 9–7; it's Green's job to shock the whole organization into thinking differently. That's why he went outside the box to create some competition at quarterback by signing Kurt Warner. In doing so, he confronted decades of quarterback complacency.

For a team that hasn't had a true franchise quarterback since Jim Hart, the Cardinals never seem to have a quarterback controversy. For five years, they went out of their way to make sure Jake Plummer never had any competition: His backup was always Kent Graham or Stoney Case or somebody. Before Plummer, the team was content to let a veteran like Dave Kreig or Boomer Esiason hold down the position. Most of the competitions for the quarterback job in Arizona in the last 15 years sound as absurd now as they did then: Stan Gelbaugh vs. Chris Chandler. Steve Beuerlein vs. Jay Schroeder vs. Case. Timm Rosenbach vs. a career in rodeo.

Nobody won the job from Plummer; the Cardinals just decided to move on. They brought in Jeff Blake, handed the ball to McCown when Blake went down with an injury late in 2003, and then shipped Blake off without making McCown work to keep his starting status. Lack of competition kept complacency alive. Plummer was good enough—he took us to the playoffs. McCown was good enough—he had a last-second win against the Vikings. Green wasn't buying it, so he gave King and Navarre a look. Now, with Warner, he has a former Super Bowl champion and two-time MVP, but, more important, a player with something to prove.

DPAR tells us that Warner ranked 22nd in the league last year, just a few slots above McCown. Scouts tell us that despite some solid starts last season, Warner gets anxious in the pocket and makes some bad decisions when rattled. But Green isn't looking for the Warner of 1999; he's looking for a training camp battle, a different attitude, a sense of urgency. Warner is good enough to ensure that Anquan Boldin and Larry Fitzgerald have a chance to develop. With better receivers and a better line than he had in New York, he could enjoy a mild renaissance. Even if he doesn't, he'll force McCown (or maybe Navarre) to elevate his game.

Denny Green can't afford to play it safe. Vince Tobin and Dave McGinnis played it safe. Here's what playing it safe in Arizona gets you: a 7–9 record and a chance to tell mediocre starters that they're the team's future.

For the first time since Don Coryell left the franchise, the Cardinals could have a truly scary offense. This is a team that has finished in the top 10 in offense only four times since Coryell left in 1978. But with Warner, rookie running back J. J. Arrington, the receivers, the rebuilt line, and some lousy defenses elsewhere in the division, the Cardinals will score points. Throw in a defense that was respectable last year, and the Cardinals have become a darling "sleeper" pick to win a division.

But Green isn't crossing his fingers, hoping to sneak away with a weak division. He's meeting the team's problems head on. He's not just patching weaknesses; he's also building on strengths. Management has followed suit by getting a new stadium deal, improving the team's image, and (lest we forget) overseeing the team's first major uniform design since the 1960s. That's now a much tougher-looking bird roosting on the helmet.

Mike Tanier

Research: The 1998 Cardinals Revisited

This season marks the 30th anniversary of the last Cardinals team to actually win their division. Since that 11–3 season in 1975, the Cardinals have appeared in the postseason only twice. In fact, since moving to Arizona in 1988, the Cardinals have only once had a winning record. With many people predicting that this will be the year that Arizona turns it around, it is worth looking back at the last time this franchise suddenly turned it around: the 1998 Arizona Cardinals, one of the greatest fluke teams in NFL history.

In their third year under head coach Vince Tobin, the 1998 Cardinals improved from 4–12 to 9–7 and snagged a wild card playoff birth. They finished only a game behind Dallas for the NFC East title and even went on the road to beat the Cowboys in the playoffs. The Cardinals looked like a team on the rise, one ready to take the proverbial next step and shake off about 40 years of organizational ineptitude. It was a young team led by a rising star at quarterback, Jake Plummer. The Cardinals played in a division ripe for the plundering: The Cowboys were fading fast, the Eagles were on skid row, and the Giants and Redskins were on a treadmill.

But while scouts and pundits predicted great things for those 1998 Cardinals, DVOA wasn't fooled. Calculated in retrospect, their DVOA of −15.0% was 21st in the NFL, and they were the only team in the league with a winning record and a negative DVOA value. Something was fishy in Arizona, and DVOA smelled out fluke.

That Cardinals team had glaring statistical deficiencies. They scored 325 points and allowed 378; even casual fans can spot trouble with a spread like that. (The Pythagorean projection for that point differential is just 6.6 wins.) In their first two games, the Cardinals were blown out 38–10 and 33–14. In Week 7, they lost 31–7 to the Giants. They went into their bye week 3–4, but went 6–3 in their final nine games. All six wins came by a field goal or less.

That late surge impressed observers at the time. The Cardinals "came of age" as the season wore on. Plummer "figured things out." They "found ways to win." That's how sportswriters rationalize the random bounces that can sometimes turn a 6–10 team into a postseason competitor. But DVOA tells another story: The Cardinals got extremely lucky in the second half of the 1998 season.

Rookie Charlie Batch threw three interceptions against the Cardinals in Week 9, but the Lions still had a 15–14 lead in the fourth quarter after Frank Reich replaced Batch and threw a touchdown pass on a flea-flicker to Johnnie Morton. Barry Sanders couldn't reach the end zone on a two-point conversion, and Plummer led a quick drive that ended with a career-long 53-yard field goal by Joe Nedney. That's a field goal that the average kicker misses over half the time.

In Week 10 against the Redskins, the Cardinals squandered a 26–17 fourth quarter lead, allowing the Redskins to score a touchdown, recover an onside kick, and kick a field goal in under a minute. Plummer was able to complete four passes in 29 seconds, and a 47-yard Nedney kick gave the Cardinals a 29–27 win.

The Cardinals trailed an awful Eagles team 17–10 with seven minutes left to play in Week 15; the only Cardinals touchdown came on a 70-yard interception return of a Koy Detmer pass by Tommy Bennett. Plummer engineered a 66-yard drive to force overtime, then moved the Cardinals 58 yards in overtime to set up a Chris Jacke field goal (Nedney was hurt). Plummer wouldn't have been in position for any late-game heroics if Eagles kicker Chris Boniol hadn't missed a 33-yard field goal earlier in the game.

In Week 16 against the Saints, Mike Ditka elected to try a fourth-and-one attempt from the Cardinals nine-yard line while trailing 13–10 early in the fourth quarter. NFL teams converted on two thirds of all runs in this situation. This happened to be one of the other third, as Aaron Craver was stuffed. The Cardinals still needed a late drive and a last-second field goal by Jacke to preserve a 19–17 win against another bad team.

In Week 17, Chargers QB Craig Whelihan threw four interceptions—all to Kwame Lassiter—and fumbled once. The Chargers racked up 377 yards of offense, but the Cardinals still needed a 52-yard field goal from Jacke (who missed two shorter kicks in the game) to clinch a playoff spot.

Saying that the Cardinals "got lucky" doesn't mean that they deserved to lose all of those games. But it took an amazing series of circumstances to win all five (plus a 45–42 win against Washington that nearly saw the Cardinals blow a 24-point lead). If the Lions make their two-point conversion, if Boniol hits a chipshot, if the Redskins force one incompletion, if Ditka doesn't go for it, if Craver gets a yard, if the kickers don't hit from 50-plus yards on two occasions…it's easy to see the Cardinals losing three of these games and having the Official 6–10 Season of the Arizona Cardinals.

The schedule didn't hurt the Cardinals either. A look at the quarterbacks mentioned above—Whelihan, Detmer, Reich, Batch—gives a good idea of who the Cardinals were playing. The Eagles finished 3–13, the Chargers and Lions 5–11, the Saints and Redskins 6–10. Arizona was facing weak teams in rebuilding mode and beating them with last-second miracles.

Still, people who should have known better were impressed. In their 1999 season preview, the *Sporting News* picked the Cardinals to play for the conference championship. "In the NFC East, this might finally be the year that the Bird is the word," began Lee Shappell's team preview, and he wasn't talking about the Eagles. Shappell later cautions that the Cardinals would face a tougher schedule in 1999, but elsewhere in the guide, *TSN* is decidedly pro-Cardinals, calling them "a team on the rise" and asking if they have caught the Cowboys, then the class of the division. In the 1999 *Stats Inc. Pro Football Scoreboard,* Tony Nistler called Plummer a player who "has

eaten pressure for lunch," later declaring that Plummer may be a few seasons away from the Super Bowl. The slightly more conservative *Sports Illustrated* still picked the Cardinals to go 9–7 again.

What do our numbers see that the experts did not? First, DVOA adjusts for the quality of the Cardinals' opponents. The Redskins ranked 28th in the league in points allowed in 1998, the Lions 26th, the Saints 21st, the Eagles dead last. The Redskins, Eagles, and Lions all ranked below average in defensive DVOA. The Chargers, on the other hand, ranked 18th in points allowed and first in yards allowed, but their quarterbacks couldn't stop tossing the ball back to the other team. They were third in defensive DVOA, last in offense.

Against these poor opponents, the Cardinals could score over 20 points only once, against Washington. They may have finished 15th in the league in scoring and 13th in yards gained, but when you take situation and opponent into account they end up with an offensive DVOA of −11.3%, 20th in the league that year.

The defense was even worse. A DVOA rating of 2.5% seems close to average, but that was because leaguewide offensive levels were down in 1998. Arizona's defensive DVOA rank of 23rd is in line with the team's ranks in points allowed (24th) and yards allowed (21st).

As for Plummer's late-game heroics, DVOA does take into account down, distance, and game situations, but it doesn't forget what happens in the other 58 minutes of the game. A 30-yard drive to set up a last-second field goal will boost your rating, but five futile three-and-outs and a fumble early in the game won't be wiped from the record. Plummer was sack- and interception-prone in 1998, running back Adrian Murrell had a low average of 3.8 yards per carry, and the Cardinals defense gave up long drive after long drive. There were plenty of plays on the negative side of the ledger before Plummer climbed on his horse at the two-minute warning. After a dramatic Cardinals victory, analysts forgot many of the negatives. Our numbers did not.

"You are what you are," Bill Parcells once said. That's often the response when our articles and statistics are quoted on message boards around the Internet. Maybe a playoff team actually has a negative DVOA, maybe the Pythagorean projection says they played more like a 7–9 team, but what do those guys at Football Outsiders know? If a team went 10–6, they are a 10–6 team, numbers be damned.

But in reality, "you are what you are" is simply not true. What is true instead is that "you were what you were." No advanced statistics can change wins and losses in the past. Instead, they tell us about what we might expect in the future. When a team's record doesn't match its statistical profile, DVOA can provide a more in-depth evaluation of the team's accomplishments. If DVOA and wins don't match, as they didn't for the 1998 Cardinals, then there's a good chance that the team had a fluke season. Barring major changes to the roster, that team's record should bounce back in the direction of its DVOA score the following year.

Sure enough, the Cardinals would fall to 6–10 in 1999 and 3–13 in 2000. The "team on the rise" from 1998 never developed. Plummer still retains his clutch reputation, but no one is comparing him to Joe Montana anymore, and he was exiled from Arizona three years ago. We're always in a hurry to attribute last-second wins to some intangible: to grit, to heart, to competitive drive or grace under pressure. Yes, those things matter, but chance plays just as big a role in the outcome of many close games—perhaps an even bigger role. The coin came up heads again and again for the 1998 Cardinals, but DVOA wasn't fooled. And when the next fluke team sneaks into the playoffs, we won't get fooled again.

Mike Tanier

Cardinals 2004 Stats by Week

Wk	vs.	W-L	PF	PA	YDF	YDA	TO	DVOA Total	Off	Def	ST
1	@STL	L	10	17	260	448	+3	-28.3%	-7.7%	31.6%	11.0%
2	NE	L	12	23	167	376	0	-47.3%	-50.3%	1.4%	4.3%
3	@ATL	L	3	6	240	283	0	26.2%	-37.8%	-69.4%	-5.5%
4	NO	W	34	10	373	279	+1	18.5%	19.4%	-10.6%	-11.5%
5	@SF	L	28	31	320	448	0	-68.9%	-8.1%	46.3%	-14.5%
6	BYE										
7	SEA	W	25	17	316	257	+2	67.3%	-20.6%	-66.6%	21.3%
8	@BUF	L	14	38	213	209	0	-16.3%	17.1%	-6.2%	-39.6%
9	@MIA	W	24	23	270	403	+1	-34.9%	-5.9%	30.1%	1.1%
10	NYG	W	17	14	178	308	0	-35.9%	-22.2%	26.6%	12.9%
11	@CAR	L	10	35	399	317	-3	-68.4%	-44.7%	19.4%	-4.2%
12	NYJ	L	3	13	245	325	-4	-15.8%	-38.5%	-19.3%	3.4%
13	@DET	L	12	26	254	398	-3	-78.1%	-62.5%	27.5%	11.8%
14	SF	L	28	31	374	352	-1	-62.4%	-6.7%	43.3%	-12.3%
15	STL	W	31	7	402	185	+1	84.2%	8.9%	-64.9%	10.4%
16	@SEA	L	21	24	317	301	-1	-14.2%	-40.1%	-25.7%	0.2%
17	TB	W	12	7	222	249	+3	30.7%	-28.3%	-51.5%	7.4%

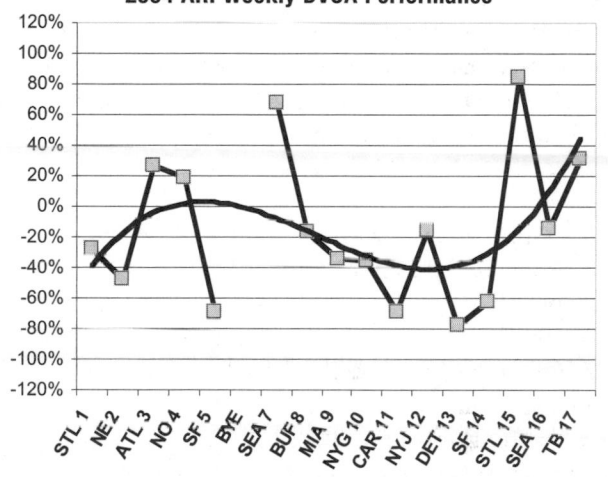

2004 ARI Weekly DVOA Performance

Trends and Splits

	Offense	Rank	Defense	Rank
Total DVOA	-20.5%	30	-1.3%	15
Unadjusted VOA	-16.7%	28	-6.6%	8
Weighted Trend	-23.2%	31	-1.3%	17
Variance	5.9%	26	16.4%	1
Passing	-22.4%	29	-0.8%	16
Rushing	-18.5%	31	-1.9%	15
First Down	-10.5%	27	-6.1%	9
Second Down	-19.2%	28	6.1%	19
Third Down	-42.8%	30	-2.5%	18
Red Zone	-34.2%	30	-10.7%	12
Late and Close	-37.1%	29	0.2%	19

Five-Year Performance

	2004	2003	2002	2001	2000
W-L	6-10	4-12	5-11	7-9	3-13
Pythagorean Wins	6.8	2.6	4	6.6	2.3
Estimated Wins	5.3	3.8	3.2	6.4	2.4
Total DVOA	-19.4%	-39.8%	-40.5%	-14.0%	-46.9%
Rank	27	32	31	24	31
Offense	-20.5%	-21.6%	-18.6%	1.2%	-21.4%
Rank	30	31	28	10	28
Defense	-1.3%	14.8%	17.3%	13.7%	24.0%
Rank	15	31	29	29	30
Special Teams	-0.2%	-3.4%	-4.6%	-1.5%	-1.5%
Rank	18	28	28	20	18

Passing (min. 5 plays)

Player	DPAR	PAR	DVOA	Plys	NtYds	Avg	Cmpl	TD	Int
Josh McCown	10.5	9.1	-7.6%	440	2251	5.1	57.1%	11	9
Shaun King	-10.0	-11.0	-38.6%	92	464	5.0	56.0%	1	4
John Navarre	-15.1	-15.1	-102.2%	41	160	3.9	45.0%	1	4

Rushing (min. 3 plays)

Player	DPAR	PAR	DVOA	Plys	Yds	Avg	TD	Fum	Suc
Emmitt Smith	-2.0	-3.5	-16.1%	267	937	3.5	9	4	39%
Troy Hambrick	2.1	2.6	-6.3%	63	283	4.5	1	0	40%
Obafemi Ayanbadejo	5.1	5.3	19.3%	30	122	4.1	3	0	63%
Larry Croom	-2.2	-3.1	-31.7%	29	76	2.6	0	0	28%
Josh Scobey	-0.6	0.1	-18.9%	27	89	3.3	0	0	41%
Josh McCown	0.3	1.0	-15.6%	26	124	4.8	2	1	—
Larry Fitzgerald	-1.1	-1.3	-55.8%	7	10	1.4	0	0	—
Shaun King	-0.2	-0.5	-24.6%	7	30	4.3	0	0	—

Receiving (min. 5 plays)

Player	DPAR	PAR	DVOA	Plys	Ctch	Yds	Y/C	TD	CPct
WR									
Larry Fitzgerald	1.3	2.4	-13.7%	116	58	784	13.5	8	51%
Anquan Boldin	-1.3	0.1	-17.3%	104	56	623	11.1	1	54%
Bryant Johnson	-7.9	-7.4	-27.1%	101	49	538	11.0	1	49%
Karl Williams	2.0	1.5	-4.9%	30	18	197	10.9	0	60%
Nathan Poole	0.8	0.7	-2.9%	11	5	70	14.0	0	45%
TE									
Freddie Jones	-2.8	-2.3	-19.2%	74	45	426	9.5	2	61%
Eric Edwards	0.7	1.6	-0.3%	8	5	51	10.2	0	63%
Lorenzo Diamond	-1.3	-0.9	-54.8%	5	3	19	6.3	0	60%
RB									
Obafemi Ayanbadejo	4.2	4.1	23.4%	25	19	171	9.0	1	76%
Josh Scobey	5.1	6.3	44.5%	21	18	191	10.6	0	86%
Emmitt Smith	0.9	0.2	-0.8%	20	15	105	7.0	0	75%
Larry Croom	0.3	0.0	5.2%	5	2	16	8.0	0	40%
Troy Hambrick	0.0	-0.1	-8.7%	5	4	16	4.0	1	80%

Defensive Players (min. 20 plays)

Player	Age	Plys	Stop	Dfts	AvYds	StpRt	Sack	Int	FR
Defensive Line									
Bertrand Berry	30	55	40	25	0.1	73%	14.5	0	2
Russell Davis	30	52	34	9	3.0	65%	1.0	0	0
Darnell Dockett	24	44	34	19	1.3	77%	3.5	1	1
Peppi Zellner	30	26	19	5	1.4	73%	2.0	0	1
Kyle Vanden Bosch	27	21	12	0	4.0	57%	0.0	0	0
Linebackers									
James Darling	31	92	47	22	4.7	51%	1.0	1	0
Ronald McKinnon	32	74	44	9	5.4	59%	0.0	0	0
Karlos Dansby	24	64	41	21	4.7	64%	5.0	1	3
Raynoch Thompson	28	36	16	7	7.1	44%	1.0	0	0
LeVar Woods	27	21	7	1	6.7	33%	0.0	0	1

Player	Age	Plys	Stop	Dfts	AvYds	StpRt	Sack	Int	FR
Secondary									
Adrian Wilson	26	114	68	30	6.2	60%	1.0	3	2
David Macklin	27	93	35	14	8.6	38%	0.5	4	1
Ifeanyi Ohalete	26	75	18	10	10.6	24%	0.0	0	2
Duane Starks	31	72	30	15	8.5	42%	1.0	3	2
Renaldo Hill	27	55	24	14	7.3	44%	1.0	1	0
Quentin Harris	28	26	6	7	12.1	23%	1.0	1	1

Offensive Line

Year	Yards	AdjLineYd	Rank	Power	Rank	10+ Yds	Rank	Stuff	Rank	Sack	AdjSack%	Rank
2002	4.14	3.99	22	62%	21	20%	7	22%	8	40	6.7%	20
2003	3.43	3.52	32	53%	29	11%	27	30%	31	42	6.9%	19
2004	3.62	3.71	29	47%	30	16%	25	29%	29	39	6.0%	11

Year	LEnd	Rank	LTckl	Rank	MdGrd	Rank	RTckl	Rank	REnd	Rank
2002	2.77	32	4.15	16	4.03	25	4.38	14	4.22	13
2003	4.87	5	3.67	30	3.69	28	2.64	31	3.08	25
2004	2.94	27	4.45	15	3.66	30	3.41	31	4.07	12

Anthony Clement was waived immediately after the draft, clarifying the situation on the front five. From left to right, the Cardinals will start Leonard Davis, Reggie Wells, Alex Stepanovich, Jeremy Bridges, and Oliver Ross. Elton Brown, a huge specimen who was voted the best offensive lineman in the ACC in 2004, may challenge Bridges. It's a very different line than the one Green inherited: younger, more motivated, and a little tougher.

Center Alex Stepanovich, the son of a Cleveland SWAT team lieutenant, is part of a new wave of NFL centers that also features Dan Koppen, Jeff Faine, Jake Grove, and Nick Hardwick. These players aren't superior athletes, but they combine a brawler's attitude with a quarterback's knowledge of defenses and pass rush schemes. Stepanovich could anchor this line for the next decade.

Defensive Front Seven

Year	Yards	AdjLineYd	Rank	Power	Rank	10+ Yds	Rank	Stuff	Rank	Sack	AdjSack%	Rank
2002	4.51	4.66	30	63%	9	14%	10	22%	25	21	4.5%	32
2003	4.08	4.07	19	73%	30	17%	16	29%	5	20	3.7%	32
2004	4.76	4.27	20	59%	12	25%	30	25%	13	37	6.6%	19

Year	LEnd	Rank	LTckl	Rank	MdGrd	Rank	RTckl	Rank	REnd	Rank
2002	4.55	27	4.12	15	4.78	31	4.86	31	4.60	26
2003	3.57	6	3.62	7	4.26	19	4.04	14	4.43	28
2004	4.65	24	4.36	17	4.25	19	3.79	7	5.38	31

Coordinator Clancy Pendergast likes to mix and match his fronts, and the arrival of DE/LB Chike Okeafor (free agent from Seattle) and rookie OLB Daryl Blackstock (rookie from Virginia) gives him multiple options. Okeafor and Bertrand Berry can both rush from an outside linebacker position or drop into short zone coverage. Blackstock is primarily a pass rusher, but he has some coverage experience, so opponents won't know his role when he enters the game. Second-year LB Karlos Dansby is also an effective blitzer. DE Peppi Zellner was re-signed, and he should be more effective as a situational player than he was as a starter. With a rookie as the Cardinals' top cornerback—and two rookies in the nickel package—the team will try to apply as much pressure as possible before the veteran receivers in Seattle and St. Louis have time to cook the fresh meat. (But not too much: Okeafor was called for roughing the passer four times last year, twice as often as any other NFL player.) The most questionable position is middle linebacker. Ronald McKinnon has been starting there since 1997, and the Cardinals have been trying to replace him for almost that long. Free agent Orlando Huff is younger, but his 45% Stop Rate was the lowest among Seattle's top five linebackers, so he might not be the ideal replacement.

Defensive Secondary

Year	DVOA vs. #1 WR	Rank	DVOA vs. #2 WR	Rank	DVOA vs. Other WR	Rank	DVOA vs. TE	Rank	DVOA vs. RB	Rank
2002	19.3%	27	12.5%	18	32.7%	29	18.1%	26	-3.6%	12
2003	33.0%	29	-11.4%	13	25.4%	31	-4.0%	14	19.9%	29
2004	-3.9%	13	-1.6%	9	-19.0%	7	15.7%	20	-2.8%	21

The starters appear to be Adrian Wilson, David Macklin, Robert Griffith, and rookie Antrell Rolle. This isn't the ideal secondary to line up against the Rams, but Rolle has outstanding potential, Macklin keeps plays in front of him, and Griffith, well, can at least regale his teammates with tales from the era of leather helmets and the Oorang Indians. He made tons of plays last year, but that's because tons of receivers were running around in the Cleveland backfield—he's far past his prime and may be beaten in camp by Quentin Harris. The underrated member of this foursome is Wilson, who according to our numbers has quite the nose for the ball on third downs. He led the league with 30 Defeats, plays that either forced a punt or lost yardage, and his 60% Stop Rate was the highest of any starting safety in the league. (We'll save you from paging to the Cleveland chapter; Griffith's was only 37%.) If someone gets injured here, depth is an issue, with Ifeanyi Ohalete, Robert Tate, and rookie Eric Green as the top backups.

Special Teams

Year	DVOA	Rank	FG/XP	Rank	Net Punt	Rank	Punt Ret	Rank	Net Kick	Rank	Kick Ret	Rank
2002	-4.6%	28	-5.1	23	-4.4	20	-6.5	27	-15.7	32	6.1	9
2003	-3.4%	28	-7.5	28	-10.8	30	-9.6	29	0.5	18	8.8	5
2004	-0.2%	18	7.2	7	-4.3	27	-8.9	24	11.4	5	-6.6	27

Karl Williams was ineffective as a punt returner, costing the Cardinals −13.0 points worth of field position. That was the second-worst mark in the league, behind Shaun McDonald of St. Louis. Josh Scobey was better on kickoffs, but the team needed to upgrade its return men and blocking units. The team didn't draft any potential return men, but rookie free agents Carlyle Holiday and Lamont Reid will get opportunities to challenge the incumbents.

The Cardinals are set everywhere else on the kick units. Neil Rackers is great on kickoffs and can boom long field goals, though he's occasionally inaccurate from short range. Scott Player is an adequate punter. The coverage units are sound. Nathan Hodel is a very good snapper, and Player is sure-handed on holds. These special teams won't beat you, but they won't beat themselves.

Coaching Staff

Denny Green's Vikings offenses were usually outstanding. Everyone remembers the Randall Cunningham-Randy Moss-Robert Smith-Cris Carter team, but the Vikings finished fourth in the NFL in points in Green's first season with Rich Gannon and Sean Salisbury at quarterback, Terry Allen and Roger Craig at running back, and Anthony Carter and Cris Carter at wideout. The one constant on Green's teams is the depth at wide receiver; there's always a Jake Reed, Hassan Jones, or Qadry Ismail lining up in the slot. The current Cardinals, of course, are deep but inexperienced at wideout.

Green was also usually flanked by a very good offensive coordinator; say what you will about Brian Billick, but his teams win, and he has made chicken-soup offenses out of some chicken-scratch personnel in Baltimore (granted, he drafted the chicken scratch). New coordinator Keith Rowan promises to balance the Cardinals attack; maybe Green is at his best when there's a run-first assistant on hand to keep the offense from becoming too predictable.

Atlanta Falcons

Led by a healthy Michael Vick, the Atlanta Falcons made a stunning turnaround from 5–11 in 2003 to 11–5, won the NFC South, and appeared in the NFC championship game. With another year of experience under his belt, Vick and the Falcons are poised to take the next step in 2005.

You might read a paragraph like the one above in some football guides, but not here. We have a little secret for the NFL's marketing machine: The Falcons improved in spite of Vick, not because of him.

No question: Michael Vick is the most spectacular player in the NFL, but his breathtaking athletic ability tends to obscure his considerable shortcomings. The numbers don't lie. According to DPAR, Vick was the 37th most effective passing quarterback in the NFL in 2004, 31st among primary starting quarterbacks. We think it's fair to expect more from a man who was taken in the first few picks of every fantasy draft in America last summer, not to mention the first overall pick of the reality draft in 2001.

A player with similar stats to a sport's immortals is sometimes said to "live in a very respectable neighborhood." Vick needs to call his real estate agent, because his neighbors in the projects of the 2004 DPAR rankings include Jonathan Quinn and Luke McCown. Meanwhile, if you paid enough attention to the hype surrounding Vick, you might believe that he actually lives up in Buckhead with the McNabbs and Bradys, right around the corner from Peyton's Place.

What about rushing? It's true that as a rushing QB, Vick has no peer. His DPAR of 29.3 dwarfs Daunte Culpepper's second-ranked 11.7. Put another way, if Vick were a running back, his DPAR neighbors would include Tiki Barber, Rudi Johnson, and Priest Holmes. Buckhead, indeed.

But the fact remains that Vick isn't a running back; he's a quarterback. And unless the Falcons plan on switching to the single-wing offense, Vick needs to do a much better job of throwing the ball in order for the Falcons to become true championship contenders. The Falcons nearly made the Super Bowl in the horrible NFC of 2004, but a team without a passing attack is not going to win the NFL title. Vick was a key cog in a three-headed rushing attack (with Warrick Dunn and T. J. Duckett) that ranked third in the NFL according to DVOA. But before we get carried away by visions of center Todd McClure sending his shotgun snaps to any of those three backs, let's get back to reality.

Despite the superior ground attack, the Falcons' overall offensive efficiency was just 24th in the league, because their passing game was a dismal 30th. That really isn't much better than the lost season of 2003, when those numbers were 26th and 31st.

We're not suggesting that Vick has no intangible positive impact on the Falcons. When he broke his leg in the 2003 preseason, the rest of the Falcons were handed a ready-made excuse to pack it in. With Vick back in the lineup and high hopes restored in 2004, the rest of the team elevated its play. Some of that can be attributed to Vick's mere presence. Football is the most emotional of sports, and a team that is emotionally flat will not fare well, no matter who is suiting up.

Vick polarizes NFL fans. There are those who simply don't want to hear that he's not one of the best quarterbacks in the league, while the more sabermetrically inclined among us (most likely including the readers of this book) love to harp on his shortcomings, among them the possibility that he'll never be able to master the Falcons' version of the West Coast offense. The truth probably lies somewhere in the middle. A few things need to be kept in perspective, primarily Vick's age and experience level. He's started only 36 NFL games, and when the 2005 season begins, he'll be just 25 years old. He also started just two years in college. Plenty of quarterbacks take time to master the pro game. Terry Bradshaw was widely considered a bust after being selected with the first-overall pick in 1970; he won his first of four Super Bowls in his fifth season. So there's still time for Vick to develop as a passer—with the emphasis on passer. More than anything, Vick needs to learn to use his legs to create big plays in the passing game, rather than taking off and running at the first hint of trouble. His breakaway runs may make the highlight films, but he'll do far more damage to a defense when he learns to use those pins to buy time to break down the defense and create open receivers downfield. In other words, become a midcareer John Elway.

Not only will that make Vick a more dangerous player, but it also might improve his life expectancy. Vick takes many licks on plays that would have been long whistled dead with other quarterbacks. How else do you explain that Vick, perhaps the best running quarterback in NFL history, was sacked nine more times than human statue Drew Bledsoe last year? He also went down 12 more times than Vinny Testaverde and 14 more than Trent Green, neither of whom could beat a three-legged horse in a foot race.

The Falcons will gladly take some of those sacks in exchange for Vick's big-play potential, but at some point the returns are not only diminishing, but career-shortening. Vick needs to learn some lessons in the art of self-preservation, and let's hope they're not too expensive. Sacrificing two yards to step out of bounds and avoid contact is a trade he should make every time, and it did appear that he was beginning to think along those lines at the end of last year. Perhaps that was in response to how beat up he was by December.

Enough Vick bashing. Not all of the passing-game struggles are his fault. To start, his receivers are awful. Atlanta threw fewer passes to its wide receivers than any team in the NFL (215 vs. NFL average of 302) and was one of only five teams whose receivers caught fewer than half the passes thrown to them. The combined DVOA of Atlanta's wideouts was −20.2%, better than only Chicago.

The most frustrating Atlanta receiver is Peerless Price, who looked like a star playing opposite Eric Moulds in Buffalo. Handed big money in Atlanta, he's been revealed as a lazy route runner who can't get open against top corners and loses interest if he doesn't see the ball early in the

game. Vick could find himself throwing to some different wideouts in 2005. While Price is expected to remain the number one receiver, the team has spent first-round draft choices on wide receivers the last two years. The Falcons want both those players, 2004 rookie Michael Jenkins and 2005 first-rounder Roddy White, to play significant roles in the offense this fall. Unfortunately, Jenkins was nearly invisible on offense as a rookie, and White's downside, according to the predraft chatter, is his difficulty running correct routes—not exactly a recipe for rookie success in a West Coast scheme.

So if the offense can't throw the ball, you might be thinking, how did the Falcons win 11 games in 2004? The answer is defense, rushing, special teams, and a healthy dose of luck. The defense in particular was a pleasant surprise. Boosted by the arrival of defensive-minded coach Jim Mora and the signing of tackle Rod Coleman, Atlanta improved in our defensive rankings from 26th to 16th. Coleman turned in one the best pass-rushing seasons by a defensive tackle in recent years, helping the Falcons to an Adjusted Sack Rate of 8.7%, second in the NFL. Getting a good push from the front four makes the rest of the defense better, and in 2004 it allowed Atlanta to break in a young secondary that improved greatly on the 2003 unit's performance.

After hitting it big in free agency with Coleman, the Falcons again moved to bolster the defense this off-season by signing linebacker Ed Hartwell from Baltimore. He will replace Chris Draft in the middle, and should make the Falcons' defense even stronger this year. The Falcons also used their second- through fifth-round picks on young defensive players, highlighted by second-round defensive tackle Jonathan Babineaux, a quick but raw talent from Iowa.

The other area where the Falcons excelled was special teams, ranking sixth in our ratings. The only area where they had negative value was field goal kicking, and that should improve with former 49er Todd Peterson replacing Jay Feely. The team also added a special teams ace in linebacker Ike Reese and re-signed Allen Rossum, the standout return man who broke open the playoff game against St. Louis.

The easy thing would be to predict that the 2005 Falcons will build on the success of 2004, Vick will continue to develop as a passer, the defense will get better in the second season under Mora, and the team will take up permanent residence among the NFL elite. But if we'd wanted to predict that, we would have been serious about that first paragraph.

The Falcons carry the stigma of never having had back-to-back winning seasons in franchise history, a more serious curse than that of, say, the Buccaneers, who have never returned a kickoff for a touchdown. The upcoming season probably represents Atlanta's best opportunity to end that streak, but some of our numbers suggest otherwise.

- Atlanta was the second-luckiest team in the NFL in 2004; only Pittsburgh further outperformed its Pythagorean win projection. The projection said that the Falcons were a .500 team masquerading as Super Bowl contenders last season. They were 11–5 despite outscoring opponents by just three points. To understand just how bizarre that figure is, consider that the 10–6 Packers outscored their opponents by 44 points and the 5–11 Buccaneers were outscored by just three points.

- Atlanta's defense was much better on third downs than it was on first and second downs. As we discuss in the San Diego chapter, it is more likely that the third-down defense will decline to match the defense's overall performance level than it is that the overall performance level will improve to match the –19.8% DVOA posted on third downs.

- According to our projections, Atlanta will play the hardest schedule in the NFC. The Falcons' first two games come against the two teams we project as the best in the conference, Philadelphia and Seattle. Divisional foes Carolina and Tampa are projected to improve substantially. The AFC East projects to be the best division in the league. They have to play in Detroit on Thanksgiving, when the Lions have a historical advantage, and they have to play in Chicago on a cold, windy December night.

The NFC South has produced surprise champions the last two seasons, and the Falcons could become the third straight division champ to fall apart the following year, after Tampa Bay in 2003 and Carolina last year. Looking at Atlanta's experience, team history, and 2004 performance in certain situations, our projections say that the 2005 Falcons are most likely a 7–9 team that the pundits will be touting as Super Bowl contenders. To avoid that distinction, it will take a major improvement from Vick. Or the single wing.

Russell Levine

Falcons 2004 Stats by Week

Wk	vs.	W-L	PF	PA	YDF	YDA	TO	DVOA			
								Total	Off	Def	ST
1	@SF	W	21	19	227	359	+1	-49.5%	-30.6%	21.2%	2.3%
2	STL	W	34	17	416	280	+2	65.3%	53.6%	-5.3%	6.4%
3	ARI	W	6	3	283	240	0	-43.2%	-68.0%	-17.8%	7.0%
4	@CAR	W	27	10	313	360	+3	60.5%	36.1%	-14.2%	10.3%
5	DET	L	10	17	279	227	-4	-34.0%	-42.5%	-5.9%	2.5%
6	SD	W	21	20	299	318	-1	38.6%	17.8%	-23.3%	-2.5%
7	@KC	L	10	56	222	540	-1	-106.0%	-85.4%	44.9%	24.3%
8	@DEN	L	41	28	467	567	+2	57.0%	56.4%	-0.6%	0.0%
9	BYE										
10	TB	W	24	14	325	193	0	22.6%	15.4%	-8.1%	-0.9%
11	@NYG	W	14	10	298	277	+2	13.9%	12.9%	-6.8%	-5.8%
12	NO	W	24	21	396	306	+2	10.5%	7.1%	-6.8%	-3.4%
13	@TB	L	0	27	255	247	-4	-74.4%	-59.8%	14.6%	0.0%
14	OAK	W	35	10	354	296	+3	39.5%	26.9%	2.5%	15.1%
15	CAR	W	34	31	334	375	0	43.0%	2.8%	-12.8%	27.4%
16	@NO	L	13	26	267	369	-1	-78.6%	-65.1%	-5.1%	-18.6%
17	@SEA	L	26	28	353	253	0	-9.3%	11.6%	19.9%	-1.0%
18	BYE										
19	STL	W	47	17	397	339	-1	60.9%	38.2%	22.1%	44.9%
20	PHI	L	10	27	202	326	-1	-45.6%	-33.0%	8.3%	-4.2%

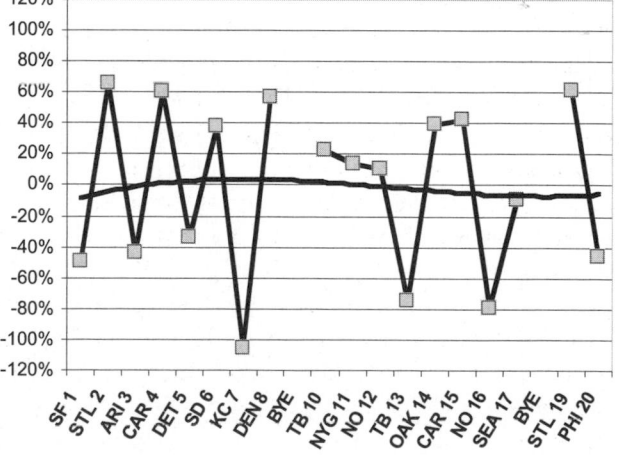

2004 ATL Weekly DVOA Performance

Trends and Splits

	Offense	Rank	Defense	Rank
Total DVOA	-6.2%	24	0.6%	16
Unadjusted VOA	-3.3%	19	-0.3%	16
Weighted Trend	-5.5%	22	1.2%	18
Variance	20.5%	1	3.0%	32
Passing	-34.9%	30	1.6%	19
Rushing	16.6%	3	-0.5%	17
First Down	3.9%	11	5.7%	19
Second Down	-12.4%	26	6.1%	20
Third Down	-17.1%	24	-19.8%	8
Red Zone	-3.7%	18	-7.9%	15
Late and Close	-13.9%	24	-15.7%	10

Five-Year Performance

	2004	2003	2002	2001	2000
W-L	11-5	5-11	9-6-1	7-9	4-12
Pythagorean Wins	8.1	4.9	10.3	5.6	3.8
Estimated Wins	8.1	4.9	9.3	7.0	4.4
Total DVOA	-2.9%	-21.9%	19.7%	-11.6%	-26.0%
Rank	19	30	5	23	27
Offense	-6.2%	-12.5%	13.5%	-7.6%	-28.4%
Rank	24	26	5	19	29
Defense	0.6%	9.5%	-1.8%	9.7%	1.9%
Rank	16	26	13	25	18
Special Teams	3.9%	0.1%	4.5%	5.7%	4.3%
Rank	6	17	6	2	9

Passing (min. 5 plays)

Player	DPAR	PAR	DVOA	Plys	NtYds	Avg	Cmpl	TD	Int
Michael Vick	-18.5	-14.3	-24.9%	366	2058	5.6	56.4%	14	11
Matt Schaub	-18.0	-14.4	-70.7%	74	315	4.3	47.1%	1	4

Rushing (min. 3 plays)

Player	DPAR	PAR	DVOA	Plys	Yds	Avg	TD	Fum	Suc
Warrick Dunn	11.9	12.6	-2.6%	265	1103	4.2	9	3	42%
Michael Vick	29.2	29.0	25.9%	106	919	8.7	3	2	—
T. J. Duckett	17.5	17.4	22.9%	104	509	4.9	8	2	61%
Justin Griffith	0.6	0.8	2.7%	9	39	4.3	0	0	44%
Stanley Pritchett	-0.7	-0.5	-41.2%	6	18	3.0	0	0	33%
Matt Schaub	-0.5	0.2	-32.9%	5	29	5.8	0	0	—
Peerless Price	2.1	2.2	91.0%	3	34	11.3	0	0	—
Dez White	-0.2	0.0	-42.1%	3	14	4.7	0	0	—
Jason Wright	0.5	0.3	46.6%	3	10	3.3	0	0	33

Receiving (min. 5 plays)

Player	DPAR	PAR	DVOA	Plys	Ctch	Yds	Y/C	TD	CPct
WR									
Peerless Price	-8.3	-7.8	-26.9%	106	45	575	12.8	3	42%
Dez White	-1.3	-1.4	-18.8%	56	30	370	12.3	2	54%
Brian Finneran	5.5	5.8	9.2%	33	23	258	11.2	2	70%
Michael Jenkins	-3.0	-2.8	-39.5%	20	7	119	17.0	0	35%
TE									
Alge Crumpler	23.6	24.6	37.8%	74	48	774	16.1	6	65%
Dwayne Blakely	-1.6	-1.4	-42.2%	8	4	35	8.8	0	50%
RB									
Warrick Dunn	3.3	3.4	7.6%	39	29	293	10.1	0	74%
Justin Griffith	5.1	4.9	21.8%	31	22	220	10.0	1	71%

Defensive Players (min. 20 plays)

Player	Age	Plys	Stop	Dfts	AvYds	StpRt	Sack	Int	FR
Defensive Line									
Patrick Kerney	29	73	53	27	1.1	73%	13.0	1	1
Rod Coleman	29	47	37	22	-0.2	79%	11.5	1	1
Ed Jasper	32	37	26	14	3.2	70%	2.0	0	2
Brady Smith	32	36	26	19	1.9	72%	6.0	1	2
Travis Hall	33	33	27	11	0.3	82%	3.0	0	1
Chad Lavalais	26	32	20	8	2.0	63%	0.0	0	2
Linebackers									
Keith Brooking	30	107	46	19	5.4	43%	2.5	3	1
M. Stewart	26	71	38	10	4.6	54%	1.5	0	0
Chris Draft	29	58	26	6	4.4	45%	0.0	1	0
Demorrio Williams	25	42	21	16	4.8	50%	2.5	0	0

Player	Age	Plys	Stop	Dfts	AvYds	StpRt	Sack	Int	FR
Secondary									
Bryan Scott	24	94	21	13	11.1	22%	2.5	1	1
Kevin Mathis	31	75	31	10	7.8	41%	0.0	2	0
Cory Hall	29	55	18	6	8.1	33%	0.0	0	1
Jason Webster	28	51	21	8	9.0	41%	0.0	1	0
DeAngelo Hall	22	41	13	7	8.2	32%	0.5	2	0
Allen Rossum	30	26	11	8	9.2	42%	1.0	2	1
Aaron Beasley	32	25	14	10	6.8	56%	1.0	4	0

Offensive Line

Year	Yards	AdjLineYd	Rank	Power	Rank	10+ Yds	Rank	Stuff	Rank	Sack	AdjSack%	Rank
2002	3.92	4.16	15	65%	18	16%	19	22%	11	40	7.5%	25
2003	4.48	4.16	18	78%	2	22%	6	24%	19	36	7.2%	24
2004	4.36	4.48	6	72%	5	16%	22	18%	1	49	11.3%	31

Year	LEnd	Rank	LTckl	Rank	MdGrd	Rank	RTckl	Rank	REnd	Rank
2002	4.07	15	4.31	13	4.43	8	4.04	19	3.39	23
2003	3.60	26	4.06	20	4.22	15	4.69	5	4.03	17
2004	4.48	12	4.79	6	4.54	9	4.50	11	3.50	22

"Hi, I'm Todd McClure. You may know me from such offensive lines as the Atlanta Falcons and Louisiana State." The names on the Atlanta line may not be well known, and Michael Vick's unique running ability makes the task of evaluating their performance more difficult. But our Adjusted Line Yards stat counts only the yardage of running backs, and it ranks Atlanta sixth in the NFL. One could argue that this metric shortchanges Atlanta because it doesn't count the running plays designed for Vick. It's also not fair to put Atlanta's poor ranking (31st) in Adjusted Sack Rate all on the shoulders of the linemen when it is Vick's superhuman ability to keep plays alive that ends up creating a lot of sacks—sacks that occur several seconds after most other quarterbacks have thrown the ball away. A look at some of our other offensive-line statistics backs up the solid performance of the unit: The Falcons have ranked in the top five in short-yardage situations for two seasons, and last year they led the league in preventing running backs from getting stuffed at the line.

Besides McClure, the Falcons got solid performance from Kevin Shaffer in his first full season as starting left tackle and veteran Todd Weiner at right tackle. Guard/center Matt Lehr was signed from the Rams and might end up being the only new face in the starting lineup if he beats out Michael Moore at left guard. There are some depth issues here, so an injury could cause problems. The biggest change comes in the coaching ranks. Legendary offensive-line coach Alex "Cut Block" Gibbs, who was lured out of retirement by Mora last year, is returning to semiretired status and will officially serve as a consultant. Gibbs, whose techniques offensive linemen swear by and defensive linemen swear at, will still take part in game planning. His replacement, former tight ends coach Jeff Jagodzinski, is not expected to depart from the style that Gibbs emphasized last year.

Defensive Front Seven

Year	Yards	AdjLineYd	Rank	Power	Rank	10+ Yds	Rank	Stuff	Rank	Sack	AdjSack%	Rank
2002	4.37	4.31	22	58%	7	19%	20	22%	24	48	8.6%	3
2003	4.82	4.53	30	67%	21	21%	25	22%	27	36	6.9%	9
2004	3.98	4.33	22	63%	18	14%	10	22%	23	48	8.7%	2

Year	LEnd	Rank	LTckl	Rank	MdGrd	Rank	RTckl	Rank	REnd	Rank
2002	3.20	4	4.77	28	4.26	19	4.56	22	4.47	22
2003	3.90	9	4.80	25	4.81	32	4.29	18	3.93	19
2004	5.93	32	3.56	3	4.18	16	3.81	8	5.02	30

While everyone else in the NFL is playing around with the 3-4 formation, Atlanta switched back to a 4-3 with the arrival of Mora and defensive coordinator Ed Donatell, and numerous players benefited. Rod Coleman was a force from one tackle spot, and Patrick Kerney enjoyed a career year rushing the quarterback off the edge. Donatell will be working with some new personnel on the line this season after Ed Jasper and Travis Hall were let go, but the team feels confident that Chad Lavalais is ready to step in after being used sparingly as a rookie in 2004. Jonathan Babineaux, taken out of Iowa in the second round, is a tackle in the light, quick mold that the Falcons prefer. He should see some time in the rotation this season, much as Lavalais did in 2004. Right end Brady Smith may be past his peak. He will be 32 when the season starts, and the Falcons ranked last in the league when an offense ran around left end.

The linebackers will also feature some new faces, with the departures of Matt Stewart and Chris Draft and the addition of Ed Hartwell from Baltimore and Ike Reese from the Eagles. Hartwell was the team's biggest move in free agency, and is expected to take Draft's spot in the middle, while Reese will contribute on special teams and compete for Stewart's spot on the strong side. The linemen are the strength of Atlanta's front seven, with their ability to pressure the passer without blitzing (second in Adjusted Sack Rate). The linebackers were below average in pass coverage, but the addition of the athletic Hartwell should help there.

Defensive Secondary

Year	DVOA vs. #1 WR	Rank	DVOA vs. #2 WR	Rank	DVOA vs. Other WR	Rank	DVOA vs. TE	Rank	DVOA vs. RB	Rank
2002	4.2%	21	-26.0%	7	3.4%	16	28.6%	29	12.6%	24
2003	15.7%	21	-5.4%	16	14.5%	26	11.7%	25	-0.5%	14
2004	10.8%	21	3.9%	15	-8.5%	14	25.1%	27	-0.6%	24

Atlanta's secondary made some strides last season but needs to continue improving for the Falcons to become an elite defense. The push that the front four gets ensures that the Atlanta DBs aren't stuck trying to cover receivers for seven seconds, which makes life easier in a division with outstanding wideouts like Steve Smith, Joe Horn, and Michael Clayton. The corners, 2004 rookie DeAngelo Hall and 49ers refugee Jason Webster, are solid. Hall could become a star, but the Falcons need more big plays out of the pair now. They combined for just three interceptions last year (although backups added eight more to the team's total). Safety Ronnie Heard, a free-agent signee from San Francisco this off-season, will compete for a starting spot opposite Bryan Scott after the Falcons released Corey Hall in a cost-cutting move.

Special Teams

Year	DVOA	Rank	FG/XP	Rank	Net Punt	Rank	Punt Ret	Rank	Net Kick	Rank	Kick Ret	Rank
2002	4.5%	6	-0.3	16	19.3	1	-3.3	24	7.8	5	1.4	14
2003	0.1%	17	-5.4	24	-2.3	22	12.4	3	15.8	2	-19.6	32
2004	3.9%	6	-3.9	28	9.6	11	5.3	5	10.1	6	0.7	15

If anything, the Falcons appear to have improved on their special teams, a unit that ranked sixth in the league last year according to DVOA. Allen Rossum is one of the best punt return men in the league (just ask the Rams), and in the 2005 draft the Falcons snagged Deandra Cobb, a standout kick returner from Michigan State. The addition of former Jet Toby Gowin should improve the punting game, and former San Francisco kicker Todd Peterson should be more accurate on field goals than Jay Feely.

Atlanta special teams coach Joe DeCamillis is one of the few who will use dual return men on punts when protecting field position is key. It's a mystery why more teams don't employ this approach, one that minimizes the possibility of the ball being kicked away from a returner and rolling for extra yardage. The Falcons also understand the importance of the guys on special teams who aren't carrying the ball. They signed linebacker Ike Reese, who was elected the NFC's Pro Bowl special teams specialist last year in Philadelphia. Reese excels on both returns and coverage units and had the highest special teams tackle total in 15 years for the Eagles last season. Rookie wideout Michael Jenkins may have been a disappointment on offense, but his speed and size made him one of the best outside gunners on punt coverage in the NFL.

Coaching Staff

In his first year as a head coach, Jim Mora turned out to be just what the doctor ordered after the dictatorial Dan Reeves regime. Mora, Donatell, and offensive coordinator Greg Knapp were able to put a team on the field each week that competed as if it expected to win. This season they face two challenges. First, they must convince the team that they had a lot of luck last year, and must play a lot better this season to get the same results. It's a cliché, but one that has merit: The Falcons will not sneak up on anyone this year. As the team at the center of the NFL's marketing campaign (eight national TV games, including preseason), they will get everyone's best effort.

The second challenge the Falcons' coaches face is dealing with Vick, a player who is a superstar in every respect except the one (passing) that defines his position. Like it or not, Vick is the face of the franchise, and he's the reason the Georgia Dome is sold out every week, so the staff almost has to treat him with kid gloves. But this could become a very delicate situation if he struggles throwing the ball the way he did in 2004 and the Falcons don't win as they did last year.

Carolina Panthers

It was difficult to predict the fortunes of the 2004 Carolina Panthers, a team coming off one of the strangest seasons in NFL history. The 2003 Panthers were propelled into the playoffs on the strength of a series of early-season fluke wins, going 11–5 despite outscoring opponents by only 21 points and ranking 20th for the year according to our DVOA ratings. When the postseason started, however, the Panthers suddenly put on a three-game clinic in dominating football and fell only three points short of an improbable Super Bowl title.

While many questioned if they were a one-year wonder, the Panthers were confident that the playoffs had displayed their true ability, and they expected further success in 2004. All the key players of the Super Bowl team returned, including linebacker Mark Fields from Hodgkin's disease. In the second half of Super Bowl XXXVIII, quarterback Jake Delhomme shook off a case of game-time jitters and torched New England's battered secondary. After negotiating a hefty new contract during the off-season, Jake was ready to join the ranks of the NFL's elite passers.

As a pre-insanity Mike Tyson once said, "Everyone has a plan—until they get hit."

Carolina's grand expectations lasted about as long as it took the team to sustain its first significant injury—a broken leg suffered by receiver Steve Smith in a season-opening loss to Green Bay. Then tackle Kris Jenkins, the heart of the Panther defense, was lost for the year after four games. Linebacker Dan Morgan missed four games in the middle of the year due to a concussion. The Panthers then had to put their top three tailbacks on injured reserve: Stephen Davis (knee), DeShaun Foster (collarbone), and even Rod "He Hate Me" Smart (knee). The injuries at tailback were so extensive that Nick Goings, who had arrived at training camp sixth on the depth chart, started much of the season.

With all the injuries to key players, nobody was surprised to see the Panthers stumble to a 1–7 start. But a funny thing happened on the way to becoming the 1999 Atlanta Falcons—nobody noticed that the Panthers didn't play that badly in most of their losses. As documented in the game-by-game table at the end of the chapter, the Panthers had a DVOA below −20% in only two of their first seven losses. At midseason, the Panthers seemed to accept their fate and became determined to rally with the players

PANTHERS PROSPECTUS

2004 Record: 7–9

DVOA Estimated Wins: 8.8 (13th)

Pythagorean Wins: 8.4 (12th)

DVOA: 4.2% total (12th), 10.5% weighted (11th)

Adjusted Offense: 21.5 points/game (0.1% DVOA, 15th)

Adjusted Defense: 19.6 points/game (−7.1% DVOA, 10th)

Adjusted Special Teams: −1.0 points/game (−3.0% DVOA, 25th)

Variance: 15.6% (23rd)

2004: Surgeon General's Warning: Playing for the Panthers may be harmful to your health.

2005: Whatever doesn't kill you makes you stronger. At least that's what John Fox hopes.

2005 Projection

Leinart Land (0–4): 5%

Bad Team (5–6): 10%

Mediocre (7–8): 18%

Playoff Contender (9–10): 25%

Super Bowl Contender (11+): 42%

Projected Average Opponent: −2.3% DVOA (24th in NFL)

they had left. What had looked like a lost season ended with a 6–2 run and a very real chance at a playoff berth in the weak NFC—a chance unfortunately squandered with a surprising loss to New Orleans in the final game of the year.

Last year's strong finish, combined with the expected full-strength return of their injured players, has created strong expectations for Carolina in 2005. There are reasons to believe that those expectations may be warranted, but also a few to believe they're not

Carolina is one of four teams that went 5–3 or better over its final eight games, and yet didn't make the playoffs. The others were Buffalo, Cincinnati, and New Orleans. There were 37 such teams in the NFL from 1990 through 2003, and only 14 of those teams made the playoffs the following season.

A more encouraging indicator for Carolina is that the team did not perform that badly in 2004, despite all its injuries. Minus a top receiver, its two best tailbacks, and its best defensive tackle, Carolina underperformed its Pythagorean projection by 1.4 wins. Due to all the luck of 2003, most indicators had the Panthers headed for a mediocre 2004 season. Considering the injuries, the fact that the team managed even a 7–9 campaign is impressive. Given a healthy roster, one could reasonably expect the Panthers to be much improved this year.

Foster and Smith should have no problems returning to full strength by the time training camp breaks. Jenkins also is expected to make a full recovery, although his injury, a torn labrum, could affect his ability to keep long-armed offensive linemen at bay.

Stephen Davis cannot be expected to be an every-down back at age 31, especially coming off microfracture knee surgery (he should be at full strength four to eight weeks into the season). However, as a part-time contributor he could be a valuable member of a running back committee consisting of Goings (a pleasant 2004 surprise), a healthy Foster, and potentially second-round rookie Eric Shelton.

Foster is not a favorite of our metrics because of his inconsistency. He hits some home runs but also often carries for little or no gain. In 2003, he had a running back success rate of only 36%, the worst among running backs with 100 carries. In limited action last year, his success rate was a still-low 42%. His penchant for occasionally breaking a big play has more value in a committee setup where he can be kept away from short-yardage downs, and his style differs enough from the plodding Davis and Goings to keep a defense off balance.

One player who will not be back is receiver Muhsin Muhammad, released after a career season because of a $10 million roster bonus that would have crippled Carolina's salary cap. Muhammad took advantage of Smith's absence and enjoyed career highs in receptions, yardage, and touchdowns—then parlayed his numbers into a huge free agent deal with receiver-starved Chicago. Yet Muhammad's release made fiscal sense—you cannot carry a number two receiver with a $12.5 million cap charge—and its impact was lessened by the emergence of Keary Colbert, a second-round pick in 2004. Colbert stepped in capably (16 yards per reception) as the number two receiver after Muhammad replaced Smith in the number one slot.

Muhammad's loss will be felt most acutely in the red zone. The Panthers excelled in red zone passing last season, thanks in large part to Muhammad's ability to use his 6′2″ frame to create space for himself in the tight confines of the end zone. You won't see that sort of above-the-rim end zone play from the 5′10″ Colbert or the 5′9″ Smith.

Carolina's calling card will continue to be its defense, which returns nearly everyone from a unit that ranked tenth in DVOA in 2004 despite the loss of Jenkins for

TABLE 1. CAROLINA DEFENSIVE DVOA, BY DOWN, 2004

Down	vs. Pass	Rank	vs. Run	Rank	Total	Rank
First	−31.6%	3	−3.0%	21	−16.0%	4
Second	−22.7%	2	−16.4%	4	−19.6%	4
Third/ Fourth	23.1%	28	55.8%	31	33.4%	30

much of the year. That defense did have one glaring weakness—third downs—and the Panthers used the money saved by cutting Muhammad to shore it up.

Carolina's defensive DVOA was fourth in the league on both first and second down, and then plunged to 30th on third down (table 1). As you'll learn from an essay in the San Diego chapter, a difference that large between total defense and third-down defense is almost always a fluke, and a sign that the defense will improve the following year. But there's nothing wrong with helping that improvement along with some wise personnel moves.

The Panthers started two young corners in 2004, Ricky Manning and Chris Gamble, and needed more depth in the secondary, so they signed cornerback Ken Lucas from Seattle and safety Marlon McCree from Houston as free agents. The physical Lucas is expected to start at one corner, leaving Gamble and Manning to fight for the other starting spot. Whoever loses that battle will still be an upgrade at nickel corner over Artrell Hawkins, who was part of the reason for the third-down struggles. Interestingly, Lucas and Gamble tied for the NFC lead in interceptions last season with six apiece.

Carolina's front seven gets plenty of attention due to playmakers like Julius Peppers, Jenkins, and linebacker Dan Morgan; yet for all the publicity, the unit struggled against the run, particularly in short-yardage situations. The Panthers ranked 28th defending the run in short-yardage situations, as measured by our power running metric, and only New Orleans had a worse DVOA against the run on third down. Jenkins's return should help bolster both of those figures in 2005. The Panthers, who struggled late in games, really missed his durability. Morgan is a tackling machine when healthy, but has been injury prone.

The Panthers also need to generate a better pass rush. For all the talent on the defensive line, they were just 27th in Adjusted Sack Rate. Again, the injury to Jenkins accounts for some of that, as well as the fact that Carolina likes to use Peppers, probably their top pass rusher, in pass coverage on zone blitz schemes.

Another area of need addressed was the offensive line. Lost in the attention paid to Smith's injury in the opener was the dreadful performance by a patchwork offensive line—a harbinger of season-long struggles for a unit that would finish the year ranked 26th in Adjusted Line Yards.

The signing of Mike Wahle from Green Bay should help. The Panthers' line was a unit in transition in 2004, and talented second-year tackle Jordan Gross really struggled after moving to the left side. Wahle, considered one of best guards in the NFL, will start at left guard and gives Carolina a second outstanding lineman to build around. Gross, meanwhile, will move back to his natural position, the right side.

Just as important for Carolina, both Wahle and Lucas are durable. Wahle has started 64 straight games, and Lucas missed just two starts the last four seasons—good news for an injury-ravaged squad.

Carolina's strong finish in 2004 doesn't automatically mean the Panthers will win the division in 2005, but they have a pretty good shot. Tampa Bay is rebuilding, New Orleans is a perennial head case of a team, and last year's champs, the Falcons, have yet to post back-to-back winning seasons in franchise history. Carolina's weaknesses have been shored up both through free agency and by the return of injured players. Assuming the injury plague stays away in 2005, expect the Panthers to be in the thick of the hunt for the division title.

Russell Levine

Research: Turning Things Around

Halfway through the 2004 season, the Carolina Panthers were living in a nightmare.

They had lost their season opener at home on Monday Night Football. Their best deep threat, Steve Smith, was lost for the year in that game. They were crushed by their biggest intradivision rival, the Falcons, as well by the team they had defeated to get to the Super Bowl, the Eagles. A knee injury ended the season of their best offensive player, Stephen Davis, after only 26 carries. In Week 4, they lost their best defensive player, Kris Jenkins. The Panthers had gone from Super Bowl participant to 1–7 losers in two months.

The nightmare ran its course and suddenly the team began playing like a dream. Carolina went 6–2 the rest of the way—losing both games by a field goal—and barely missed the playoffs in the weak NFC. Five of Carolina's six wins were by double-digit margins, although only one victory came against a playoff team, and that team was the 8–8 Rams.

What does a midseason revival of that magnitude portend? By going .750 in the second half of the season but still missing the playoffs, the Panthers joined an exclusive club (to which the 2004 Buffalo Bills were also admitted). Since the playoffs expanded to 12 teams in 1990, only 11 teams have gone 6–2 or better in the second half of the season but missed postseason play. Of the 11, only 5 made the playoffs the following year, and it's not a complete mystery why.

1990 Seattle started 3–5, finished 6–2; 7–9 in 1991 – Of the six games they won in the second half of the season, only one, a 30–10 victory over Detroit in the finale, looked particularly impressive. The other victories were by margins of one, three, three, six, and five points. Take note: When a team's boffo second-half finish is not followed by a playoff year, small margins of victory tend to be involved.

1991 Philadelphia started 3–5, finished 7–1; 11–5 in 1992 – These Eagles are the only team to miss the playoffs despite winning seven of their last eight. That 7–1 run down the stretch in Rich Kotite's first year as the replacement for Buddy Ryan was no mirage—they beat the Super Bowl champion Redskins and won two other games by three-touchdown margins. So it was no surprise that they made the playoffs the following year. The key to the turnaround halfway through 1991 was stability at quarterback. When Randall Cunningham went down with a torn ACL in the first game, the Eagles were still in good hands with Jim McMahon. But when McMahon went down a month later, the Eagles lost four straight behind cover-your-eyes-awful quarterbacks Brad Goebel and Pat Ryan. McMahon returned later in the season, and with Jerome Brown, Seth Joyner, Clyde Simmons, and Reggie White, the Eagles had one of the best front sevens in history. By 1992, Cunningham was healthy and the Eagles were a good team again.

1991 San Francisco started 4–4, finished 6–2; 14–2 in 1992 – Roger Craig retired, and Joe Montana was on the roster but missed the entire season because of an elbow injury. Steve Young began the year as the starting quarterback for the first time, but the 49ers were 4–5 after he injured the medial collateral ligament in his left knee against Atlanta. In the six games Young missed because of the injury, Steve Bono led the team to a 5–1 record, and Young then returned for a season-ending 52–14 romp over Chicago. Many who nonetheless concluded that the 49ers had finally gone into their inevitable decline conveniently overlooked the fact that the team's six losses were by two, three, six, five, three, and seven points. They won their last six games to finish 10–6 but missed a wild card spot on a tiebreaker. Although many fans thought Bono was a better quarterback than Young, in reality Young just had lousy luck. In 1992, the 49ers were again one of the best teams in the league, and Young proved himself to be Montana's equal.

1992 Green Bay started 3–5, finished 6–2; 9–7 in 1993 – This was Mike Holmgren's first year as head coach, and after a

2–5 start the Packers went 7–2. It may have appeared that Holmgren was already starting to build a winner, but what it really showed was that Brett Favre took the starting job from Don Majkowski. In 1993, the Packers added Reggie White as the NFL's first major free agent acquisition, Mark Clayton became a respectable number two receiver on a team that had only Sterling Sharpe the year before, and Holmgren wisely stuck with Favre because he showed great promise even as he struggled through a 24-interception season. Unlike the year before, 9–7 was enough to get Green Bay into the 1993 playoffs.

1994 New York Giants started 3–5, finished 6–2; 5–11 in 1995 – A die-hard Giants fan might call this the year that Michael Strahan began to emerge as one of the league's best defensive linemen, and the defense led the Giants to six straight wins to end the season. A closer look at that stretch reminds us that margin of victory and strength of schedule are better indicators of a team's quality than won-lost record. All six wins were by a touchdown or less, and three of the six were over the three worst teams in the league—Washington, Cincinnati, and Houston. New York's 5–11 record in 1995 confirmed the mirage of excellence.

1995 Seattle started 2–6, finished 6–2; 7–9 in 1996 – In Dennis Erickson's first year, the offense took off late in the season when he benched Rick Mirer for John Friesz, and Seattle won big 47–30 and 44–10 games down the stretch. But in 1996, Friesz and Mirer both struggled and Seattle continued the perpetual mediocrity of the pre-Holmgren era.

1996 Cincinnati started 2–6, finished 6–2; 7–9 in 1997 – David Shula coached the Bengals into the ground and was fired after seven games and a 1–6 record. Team's offensive coordinator Bruce Coslet became the coach for the rest of the season and did a phenomenal job, leading Cincinnati to a 7–2 record the rest of the way. He engineered the turnaround by routing the offense through receiver Carl Pickens, who finished the year with 100 catches for 1,180 yards. But as you can see, the party didn't last long into the following season.

1997 Cincinnati started 1–7, finished 6–2; 3–13 in 1998 – Coslet played the Shula role as well in the first half of 1997 before engineering a second-half turnaround by playing rookie Corey Dillon instead of Ki-Jana Carter, and benching youngster Jeff Blake for veteran Boomer Esiason late in the year. The numbers tell the whole story: Dillon averaged better than a yard per carry more than Carter; Blake had 6.7 yards per pass with 8 touchdowns and 7 interceptions, while Esiason averaged 7.9 yards per pass with 13 touchdowns and 2 interceptions. Unfortunately for the Bengals, Esiason was gone in 1998 and Coslet's team slumped to 3–13.

1997 Atlanta started 1–7, finished 6–2; 14–2 in 1998 – If, in August 1998, you had picked a surprise AFC contender based on which teams had played well at the end of 1997, you would have identified the Bengals. When they went 3–13, you would have looked like an idiot. If you had picked a surprise NFC contender based on the same method, you would have chosen the Atlanta Falcons. When they made it to Super Bowl XXXIII, you would have looked like a genius.

Like the Bengals in 1997, the Falcons started 1–7 in the first year with Dan Reeves in charge. But their resurgence in the second half was no false spring; it was, in fact, the beginning of a stretch of 21 victories in 24 games that got them to the Super Bowl in 1998. Chris Chandler led the 14–2 Falcons with the only 3,000-yard passing season of his career. Running back Jamal Anderson went from a mediocre plodder who gained 1,002 yards on 290 carries to one of the best backs in the league with 1,846 yards on 410 carries. The addition of wide receiver Tony Martin, previously of San Diego, had a huge impact as he gained 1,181 yards on 66 catches.

1999 New York Jets started 2–6, finished 6–2; 9–7 in 2000 – Bill Parcells's charges got off to a 1–6 start in his final year on the sidelines in New York. (It was also, he insisted, his final year on the sidelines anywhere. And some people were dumb enough to believe him.) Vinny Testaverde tore his Achilles tendon in Week 1, and when he was replaced by Rick Mirer (there's that name again!) the team fell apart. When Parcells finally decided he had had enough of Mirer and put Ray Lucas in, the team started to respond and finished in a respectable fashion. We don't wish to pick on Mirer, but when your teams are improving because they're benching you for John Friesz and Ray Lucas, it should tell you something.

2000 Green Bay started 3–5, finished 6–2; 12–4 in 2001 – Although it wasn't enough to get them into the playoffs, the Packers finished what began as a disappointing season in impressive fashion. Their last four games were against their four division rivals, and they systematically dismantled them all, beating Chicago 28–6, Detroit 26–13, eventual division champion Minnesota 33–28, and wild card team Tampa Bay 17–14. The Packers have made the playoffs every season since then.

Michael David Smith

Panthers 2004 Stats by Week

Wk	vs.	W-L	PF	PA	YDF	YDA	TO	Total	Off	Def	ST
								DVOA			
1	GB	L	14	24	300	279	-2	-15.2%	-6.8%	3.8%	-4.6%
2	@KC	W	28	17	358	281	0	19.4%	-27.1%	-44.6%	1.9%
3	BYE										
4	ATL	L	10	27	360	313	-3	-49.2%	-11.9%	29.1%	-8.2%
5	@DEN	L	17	20	227	434	+2	13.2%	12.5%	7.5%	8.3%
6	@PHI	L	8	30	344	283	-3	-16.1%	-19.7%	-16.2%	-12.6%
7	SD	L	6	17	263	302	0	-17.9%	-13.5%	-4.5%	-8.9%
8	@SEA	L	17	23	342	433	+1	9.3%	12.9%	14.8%	11.2%
9	OAK	L	24	27	304	297	+1	-44.8%	-12.8%	24.7%	-7.3%
10	@SF	W	37	27	358	357	+3	27.0%	25.1%	-13.3%	-11.4%
11	ARI	W	35	10	317	399	+3	60.8%	25.0%	-33.1%	2.7%
12	TB	W	21	14	300	398	+2	18.5%	34.3%	1.3%	-14.5%
13	@NO	W	32	21	401	280	+3	40.5%	23.8%	-19.6%	-2.9%
14	STL	W	20	7	308	289	+5	99.7%	-24.7%	-112.2%	12.2%
15	@ATL	L	31	34	375	334	0	-39.3%	-6.7%	2.3%	-30.2%
16	@TB	W	37	20	348	345	+3	29.2%	40.6%	20.2%	8.8%
17	NO	L	18	21	320	360	-3	-31.4%	-24.9%	14.4%	7.9%

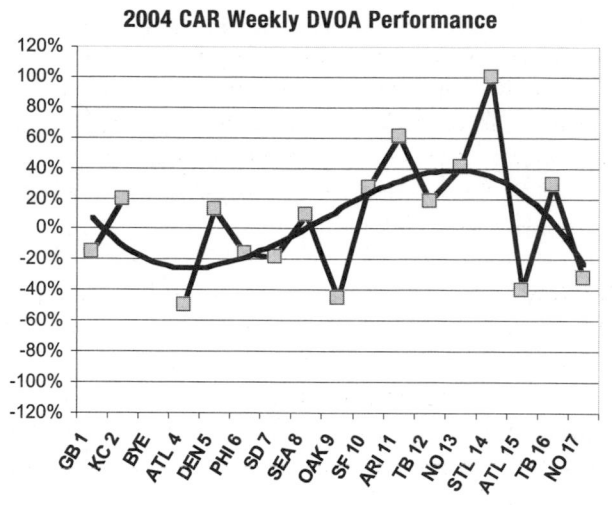

2004 CAR Weekly DVOA Performance

Trends and Splits

	Offense	Rank	Defense	Rank
Total DVOA	0.1%	15	-7.1%	10
Unadjusted VOA	5.9%	12	-5.5%	10
Weighted Trend	4.6%	13	-9.6%	9
Variance	5.2%	29	11.9%	23
Passing	7.4%	12	-13.8%	5
Rushing	-8.6%	25	0.1%	19
First Down	-9.1%	26	-16.0%	4
Second Down	15.1%	9	-19.6%	4
Third Down	-6.0%	16	33.4%	30
Red Zone	5.7%	13	-2.5%	17
Late and Close	1.9%	13	-4.8%	15

Five-Year Performance

	2004	2003	2002	2001	2000
W-L	7-9	11-5	7-9	1-15	7-9
Pythagorean Wins	8.4	8.6	6.5	3.9	8.0
Estimated Wins	8.8	7.0	6.0	4.5	6.8
Total DVOA	4.2%	-5.1%	-16.6%	-23.2%	-16.0%
Rank	12	20	25	28	23
Offense	0.1%	-9.6%	-23.9%	-32.8%	-20.9%
Rank	15	20	30	31	27
Defense	-7.1%	-3.8%	-7.0%	-3.9%	-1.3%
Rank	10	14	6	17	16
Special Teams	-3.0%	0.8%	0.3%	5.7%	3.7%
Rank	25	16	13	3	11

Passing (min. 5 plays)

Player	DPAR	PAR	DVOA	Plys	NtYds	Avg	Cmpl	TD	Int
Jake Delhomme	49.4	71.1	7.5%	569	3626	6.4	58.2%	29	15

Rushing (min. 3 plays)

Player	DPAR	PAR	DVOA	Plys	Yds	Avg	TD	Fum	Suc
Nick Goings	6.9	7.4	-6.8%	217	821	3.8	6	1	44%
Brad Hoover	0.6	0.0	-11.9%	68	246	3.6	0	0	38%
DeShaun Foster	3.1	4.6	-2.3%	59	255	4.3	2	0	42%
Stephen Davis	2.3	2.5	10.4%	24	92	3.8	0	0	46%
Jake Delhomme	2.4	2.3	6.6%	16	78	4.9	1	0	—
Joey Harris	0.2	0.1	-12.9%	15	53	3.5	0	0	33%
Brandon Bennett	0.4	0.7	-1.0%	6	17	2.8	1	0	33%

Receiving (min. 5 plays)

Player	DPAR	PAR	DVOA	Plys	Ctch	Yds	Y/C	TD	CPct
WR									
Muhsin Muhammad	41.5	43.2	23.8%	160	93	1407	15.1	16	58%
Keary Colbert	7.2	8.3	-3.4%	92	47	754	16.0	5	51%
Ricky Proehl	3.1	4.6	-8.8%	70	34	497	14.6	0	49%
Steve Smith	1.3	1.3	6.4%	9	6	60	10.0	0	67%
TE									
Kris Mangum	1.0	3.1	-10.7%	58	34	333	9.8	3	59%
Michael Gaines	-6.2	-6.2	-74.0%	14	4	34	8.5	0	29%
Mike Seidman	6.4	7.3	59.7%	13	13	123	9.5	2	100%
RB									
Nick Goings	8.8	9.3	19.4%	60	45	381	8.5	1	75%
Brad Hoover	0.5	1.7	-7.4%	31	21	161	7.7	2	68%
DeShaun Foster	0.3	0.5	-3.6%	9	9	66	7.3	0	100%

Defensive Players (min. 20 plays)

Player	Age	Plys	Stop	Dfts	AvYds	StpRt	Sack	Int	FR	Player	Age	Plys	Stop	Dfts	AvYds	StpRt	Sack	Int	FR
Defensive Line										**Secondary**									
Julius Peppers	25	74	53	23	3.7	72%	11.0	2	1	Mike Minter	31	92	32	13	9.7	35%	2.0	0	2
Mike Rucker	30	45	36	13	3.2	80%	3.5	0	1	Chris Gamble	22	81	31	15	7.4	38%	0.0	6	1
Brentson Buckner	34	44	34	10	1.6	77%	3.5	1	0	Ricky Manning	25	75	24	14	10.7	32%	0.0	4	0
Kindal Moorehead	27	42	33	14	1.0	79%	2.0	1	1	Colin Branch	25	62	19	7	10.2	31%	0.0	3	0
Al Wallace	31	24	18	10	2.1	75%	1.0	0	1	Artell Hawkins	29	33	17	11	7.4	52%	0.0	1	0
Linebackers																			
Will Witherspoon	25	116	62	23	4.9	53%	3.0	4	1										
Dan Morgan	27	109	50	21	5.3	46%	2.0	2	2										
Mark Fields	33	64	36	17	3.6	56%	4.0	1	1										
Brandon Short	28	42	19	6	5.2	45%	0.0	0	1										
Vinny Ciurciu	25	31	15	3	4.0	48%	0.0	0	0										

Offensive Line

Year	Yards	AdjLineYd	Rank	Power	Rank	10+ Yds	Rank	Stuff	Rank	Sack	AdjSack%	Rank
2002	3.61	3.75	29	59%	27	12%	27	29%	30	44	8.5%	29
2003	4.31	4.23	13	64%	19	16%	14	23%	14	26	5.4%	10
2004	3.80	3.92	26	61%	16	15%	26	25%	19	33	5.8%	9

Year	LEnd	Rank	LTckl	Rank	MdGrd	Rank	RTckl	Rank	REnd	Rank
2002	2.84	30	5.09	3	3.98	26	3.41	31	2.53	31
2003	4.14	14	3.80	26	4.34	11	3.45	29	4.78	3
2004	4.33	15	3.92	25	3.88	24	4.72	8	3.00	27

The Panthers did not expect their offensive line to be an area of concern when they released starting left tackle Todd Steussie following the Super Bowl season of 2003. Jordan Gross had looked so very promising as a rookie right tackle that Carolina planned to move him to the left side and signed free agent Adam Meadows to man the right tackle spot. However, Meadows abruptly retired and Gross, after moving to the left side, did not live up to expectations. Runs to the left tackle (behind Gross) ranked just 25th in the league, while runs behind the right tackle (primarily rookie Travelle Wharton) ranked 8th. Heading into minicamps, Carolina planned to move Gross back to the right side and replace him with Wharton on the left. The big upgrade on the line, however, comes from free agent guard Mike Wahle, perhaps the best offensive lineman available in free agency. Wahle was a huge part of Green Bay's rushing success, even though they were primarily a right-handed rushing team and he was the left guard. Wahle excels at pulling, and was frequently the lead blocker on runs to the right. His presence instantly upgrades the overall athleticism of Carolina's offensive line and should pave the way for a better rushing game, no matter who's toting the mail in the Panthers' backfield. He should also help to keep Jake Delhomme upright more often this season. Though Carolina ranked seventh in Adjusted Sack Rate, a lot of that was due to Delhomme's willingness to throw the ball away. Guard Evan Mathis, four-year starter and all-conference performer at Alabama, was drafted in the third round to provide depth at that spot.

Defensive Front Seven

Year	Yards	AdjLineYd	Rank	Power	Rank	10+ Yds	Rank	Stuff	Rank	Sack	AdjSack%	Rank
2002	3.24	3.58	3	79%	29	8%	1	30%	4	51	8.4%	4
2003	3.69	3.86	10	61%	6	11%	9	27%	11	38	7.1%	6
2004	4.13	4.01	9	74%	28	21%	25	23%	19	34	6.0%	27

Year	LEnd	Rank	LTckl	Rank	MdGrd	Rank	RTckl	Rank	REnd	Rank
2002	3.20	3	3.70	7	3.43	2	4.71	27	2.74	7
2003	3.12	3	3.79	10	3.99	10	3.76	8	4.33	26
2004	2.93	3	4.59	24	4.09	13	4.73	30	2.78	4

The defensive line is the heart of Carolina's team, and this is where the Panthers have invested a healthy portion of their salary cap. Ends Julius Peppers and Mike Rucker join tackles Kris Jenkins and Brentson Buckner to comprise one of the nastier foursomes in the league. (We do not mean nasty in an unhygienic, shoe-kissing fashion.) Jenkins is among the best in the league at his position, and Peppers is the reigning NFC Defensive Player of the Year. The linebackers, an active, mobile group, suffered a blow when it was announced that Mark Fields will miss the 2005 season after a relapse of his Hodgkin's disease. Added to the mix alongside Dan Morgan and Will Witherspoon is first-round draft pick Thomas Davis of Georgia. Primarily a safety in college, Davis is a sideline-to-sideline player who reminds some scouts of another college safety who made a successful transition to linebacker—Derrick Brooks. Jenkins's return from a shoulder injury should improve what was a suspect run defense, especially on short yardage, and improve the pass rush. Overall, the Carolina front seven did a good job protecting a secondary that featured three first-year starters in 2004, more than holding up its end of the bargain in underneath pass coverage—vital against short-passing division foes Atlanta and Tampa Bay. The Panthers ranked in the top ten in the league in pass defense against both tight ends and running backs.

Defensive Secondary

Year	DVOA vs. #1 WR	Year	DVOA vs. #2 WR	Rank	DVOA vs. Other WR	Rank	DVOA vs. TE	Rank	DVOA vs. RB	Rank
2002	-16.1%	6	35.1%	29	-18.9%	7	8.9%	19	2.9%	16
2003	1.4%	17	19.3%	24	22.1%	30	6.0%	18	-33.0%	3
2004	-3.5%	14	11.7%	21	-18.5%	9	-42.5%	3	-20.8%	9

Carolina's secondary was extremely green in 2004, with three first-year starters—cornerbacks Chris Gamble and Ricky Manning and safety Colin Branch—in the lineup alongside veteran Mike Minter. Though the Panthers felt they needed to upgrade by adding cornerback Ken Lucas from Seattle, all the experience gained by the young players should pay dividends this season. Whichever incumbent corner loses his starting job will be on the field plenty as a nickel corner (a guess says that will be Manning), providing a big upgrade at that spot. Minter is a decent safety, but needs to return to the playmaking form that saw him grab seven interceptions, returning three for scores in 2002–2003. Last year he was held without an interception for the first time since his rookie season, though he did force three fumbles, recovering a pair.

Special Teams

Year	DVOA	Rank	FG/XP	Rank	Net Punt	Rank	Punt Ret	Rank	Net Kick	Rank	Kick Ret	Rank
2002	0.3%	14	-11.4	32	11.3	7	0.0	17	7.5	6	-3.6	22
2003	0.8%	16	9.1	9	-7.8	27	-1.1	15	2.6	12	1.7	12
2004	-3.0%	25	-0.3	20	9.9	10	-13.8	28	-8.3	28	-4.1	23

Few punters in the NFL make more off-field noise than Todd Sauerbrun, whether it's for alleged steroid use, a drunk-driving arrest, or trash talking the entire Gramatica family. Carolina management may have finally had enough, and they traded him to Denver for Jason Baker this off-season. They also signed free agent Tom Rouen. Management might be happy, but the reality is that Rouen or Baker is a huge downgrade. Sauerbrun was one of the NFL's best special teams weapons, and was a lone bright spot as Carolina's special teams suffered from the injury bug that hit the team last year. In 2004, Sauerbrun's punts were worth 9.2 points of equivalent field position compared to an average punter. His off-year in 2003 was due to blocked punts, not short punts. Rouen's punts were worth just 1.1 points above average, and that was Rouen's best season in years. When he played in Denver, after adjusting for altitude, he was consistently one of the worst punters in the league. Baker is a little better than Rouen, but still a big step down from Sauerbrun.

John Kasay, a solid veteran kicker and an original Panther, missed two-plus games with a calf injury and struggled with depth on his kickoffs, but should be back to full strength this year. Carolina's return game should improve with Steve Smith back returning punts and Rod "He Hate Me" back to field kicks. A simple return to health of their return men should significantly boost the Panthers' ranking in special teams DVOA.

Coaching Staff

With the exception of a very few, NFL head coaches tend to be stronger in either motivational skills or game planning. Put another way, some are psychologists and others architects. In transforming the Panthers from a 1–15 squad to a Super Bowl team, by keeping them playing hard last year despite all the injuries and the dreadful start, John Fox has proven himself quite adept at the motivational aspects of coaching. Many teams tend to pack it in when things look hopeless (see Giants, New York) but Fox kept the Panthers playing hard. That suggests that his team would not accept being a loser and will play very hard in 2005.

Fox and his staff will have to recover from an emotional blow after linebackers coach Sam Mills passed away this spring. Fox, who is more involved with the defense, is well complemented by fourth-year offensive coordinator Dan Henning, who has proven to be a more effective coordinator than head coach during a lengthy NFL career. Defensive coordinator Mike Trgovac is entering his third year at that position. The only major change to the staff is special teams coach Danny Crossman, who takes over for the retired Scott O'Brien, generally considered one of the best special teams coaches in the NFL. Crossman, guaranteed to be the only special teams coach who was MVP of the first World Bowl, has some big shoes to fill. Overall, Carolina's staff continuity bodes well for a return to success in 2005. This team understands what it does well and plays to its strengths—a reflection of the staff that Fox has put together.

Chicago Bears

At the news conference introducing him as the fifteenth head coach of the Chicago Bears, Lovie Smith vowed that the Bears would beat Green Bay. And they did, in a big Week 2 upset at Lambeau Field. The 2004 season was going to determine whether quarterback Rex Grossman was going to lead the Bears for the rest of the decade, but in Week 3 Grossman tore his ACL, and for the rest of the year Chicago put on a clinic in bad quarterbacking that squandered the promise of a maturing young defense.

How well Grossman will develop under new offensive coordinator Ron Turner is one of the biggest question marks in 2005. Chicago's feeble air attack still needs major work before a win over Green Bay becomes a regular occurrence, not an occasional upset. Chicago's 2004 offensive DVOA of −39.4% was the worst in the league in the last five years—and this despite the fact that league-wide offensive levels were higher than they had been in two decades. Bears fans cheered when the team announced after the 2004 season that it had fired offensive coordinator Terry Shea, but Shea wasn't the offense's problem; the talent level was. A team that was already short on offensive talent traded away its best receiver, Marty Booker, during training camp because it thought acquiring defensive end Adewale Ogunleye was a more pressing need. The tight ends were a nonfactor, the running backs were mediocre, and the Bears started ten different offensive linemen because of injuries.

But absolutely nothing evinces Chicago's lack of offensive talent like the parade of backup quarterbacks who succeeded Grossman, a mixture of the washed-up, never-were, and weren't-about-to-be: Jonathan Quinn, Craig Krenzel, Chad Hutchinson, Jeff George. Cade McNown must've been tempted to call up and ask for his old job back. We think we even saw *The Replacements'* Shane "Footsteps" Falco taking a couple snaps for the Bears last year.

In the spring of 2005, the Bears tried to sign a veteran such as Kurt Warner, Brad Johnson, or Jeff Garcia, but they were the odd team out in the veteran quarterback sweepstakes. Fortunately, the quarterback position can't possibly be worse than it was last year. Even if Rex Grossman gets hurt again, the top backup will be Chad Hutchinson instead of Jonathan Quinn, and rookie Kyle Orton was added in the draft. If Shea can be blamed for anything in 2004, it's vouching for Quinn, who never threw a pass in the two

BEARS PROSPECTUS

2004 Record: 5–11

DVOA Estimated Wins: 4.3 (31st)

Pythagorean Wins: 4.8 (31st)

DVOA: −32.0% total (31st), −42.3% weighted (31st)

Adjusted Offense: 11.1 points/game (−39.4% DVOA, 32nd)

Adjusted Defense: 20.4 points/game (−4.1% DVOA, 12th)

Adjusted Special Teams: +1.1 points/game (3.3% DVOA, 9th)

Variance: 16.8% (18th)

2004: Bad backup at QB dooms the season.

2005: Talented young defense needs some help from the other side of the ball.

2005 Projection

Leinart Land (0–4): 28%

Bad Team (5–6): 25%

Mediocre (7–8): 23%

Playoff Contender (9–10): 14%

Super Bowl Contender (11+): 10%

Projected Average Opponent: −5.8% DVOA (easiest in NFL)

years he and Shea spent together in Kansas City. Quinn, Hutchinson, and Krenzel were three of the bottom five quarterbacks in our DPAR rankings, and the Bears as a team finished dead last in passing DVOA. Hutchinson signed with the team in the middle of last season and, while he wasn't very good, he wasn't Quinn or Krenzel, either. Of course, being a better quarterback than Jonathan Quinn is about as hard as being a better husband than Ike Turner. Some fans were disappointed when the Bears released Jeff George in February, but that, finally, was a correct move. George has had more second chances than Robert Downey Jr. It won't be long before everyone in the NFL will acknowledge that he's washed up.

The Bears' biggest off-season move wasn't about the quarterbacks, however; it was about finally providing the quarterbacks with good targets. The addition of wide receiver Muhsin Muhammad was a major proactive strike by a team with a reputation for standing back and waiting on free agency. Muhammad had an outstanding year in 2004 in Carolina. After Steve Smith got hurt, everyone in the stadium knew Muhammad was Jake Delhomme's only real target (rookie Keary Colbert was just medium, and Ricky Proehl was just about done), and yet Muhammad ran such great routes that he consistently got open and made big catches. The question about Muhammad is whether a player who had his best season at age 31 can be expected to have another great season at age 32. It seems unlikely. Muhammad was one of the best receivers in football last year, but before then many people questioned his dedication, and when he was younger he had a reputation for dropping balls and giving up on plays.

Of course, even a Muhammad regression-to-the-mean represents a clear upgrade for this team. In a weak crop of receivers, the Bears' best pass catcher last year was David Terrell, whom they cut two days after signing Muhammad. A high draft pick out of Michigan who got Chicago fans excited when he entered the league in 2001, Terrell had potential, but bad attitude and inconsistent play kept him mired in mere adequacy. The Bears' number two receiver, Bobby Wade, was brutal: bad hands, bad routes, and not much of an athlete. About the only good thing we can say about Wade is that when the Bears tried to keep the opposing defense off balance by using Wade on end-arounds, he usually was able to pick up some yardage. Tight ends Desmond Clark and Dustin Lyman both struggled as receivers, and neither is a great blocker. If anyone is going to break out for the Bears, it will probably be Bernard Berrian, who is still learning but as a rookie showed flashes of ability as a deep threat. This unit has a long way to go.

Optimists may want to focus more on the ground game. Cedric Benson, taken with the fourth overall pick to be Chicago's running back of the future, will compete for carries with Thomas Jones, who the Bears had previously said was their running back of the future. The Bears decided to add Benson because Jones, who turns 27 in August, has yet to show he can play a full season. His numbers don't look particularly impressive (−2.7% DVOA), but when you consider how often he faced eight-man fronts, and how bad the Bears' offensive line was, Jones actually played quite well when healthy. In the Bears' December game at Detroit, for instance, the Lions routinely stacked eight players in the box to stop them, practically begging the Bears to pass, but Jones still managed 109 yards on 22 carries. The Bears planned to use Jones often as a receiver out of the backfield, and he's talented enough to fill that role, but Chicago's atrocious quarterbacks couldn't get him the ball. Jones is a better and more consistent back, and a bigger threat to break off long runs, than Anthony Thomas, who had a terrible season and signed with Dallas. It's hard to figure out what became of Thomas, who was the NFL's Offensive Rookie of the Year when the Bears won their

division in 2001. Thomas, who took a lot of punishment with 924 career carries at Michigan, seems to have broken down after only a few NFL seasons. That has to worry Bears fans, because Benson had 1,112 career carries at Texas.

In an effort to upgrade the offensive line, the Bears signed Fred Miller to be their right tackle. Miller is competent but not spectacular, and at age 32 he's a little old to be getting a long-term deal. But Miller, who has started every game for the last six years, brings the Bears something they desperately need: stability. Last off-season, the Bears signed tackle John Tait away from Kansas City to man their right side, and he had a disappointing year. Tait has always been better as a pass blocker than a run blocker, so it makes sense that this year the Bears will move Tait to the left. In fact, it is a move that would have made just as much sense a year ago, when Chicago quarterbacks were spitting out Soldier Field sod on a regular basis after being blindsided by a defensive end blowing past Qasim Mitchell.

The Chicago offense may seem directionless, but the Chicago defense has no such problem. The Bears have a defense that is not only talented, but also young and still improving. The defensive line is one of the best in the league already, and the oldest member, right defensive end Alex Brown, just turned 26. Defensive tackle Tommie Harris, the Bears' first-round pick in 2004, looks like he's going to develop into an elite player, and he just turned 22. Left defensive end Michael Haynes, a first-round pick in 2003, has quietly developed into a solid run stopper. According to our line yards statistics, the Bears were the fifth-best team in the league at stopping runs to Haynes's side, but the 20th-best team in the league at stopping runs to Brown's side.

Lance Briggs and Hunter Hillenmeyer are both good linebackers who can form a very good unit with Brian Urlacher. At age 27, Urlacher is the old man of the linebacking group. Charles Tillman, who anchors the secondary, is entering only his third year in the league. He was one of the best young cornerbacks in the league as a rookie but missed eight games in 2004.

Some optimism about the Bears' D is tempered by looking more closely at the statistics. In 2004, the Bears were an incredible defense against the pass on third downs, with a −52% DVOA. But small differences in the ability to stop third down plays become huge differences in total yards and points because every third down play that converts becomes an opportunity for one more set of downs— or several. This makes pass defense on third down one of the most inconsistent elements of football. (For more on this issue, see the San Diego chapter.) It's very likely that the pendulum will swing the other way in 2005, back to 2003 numbers, when Chicago was worse than average at stopping the pass on third down.

However, all this talent and youth give us good reason to believe that the Bears will be stronger on first and second down. If the Bears can keep Urlacher and Tillman healthy, and the other players continue to develop, this could be one of the league's top defenses. With that and a little more offense, Lovie Smith will move these monsters of the mediocre a little closer to a new generation of Monsters of the Midway.

Michael David Smith

Research: The High Cost of Sacks

Nearly every NFL coach agrees that in any crucial situation, especially late in the game, the last thing a quarterback should do is take a sack. It sounds like the kind of conventional football wisdom that *Pro Football Prospectus* should be disproving—except it is absolutely true. As it turns out, a sack is disproportionately harmful to an offense in any situation.

To find out just how costly a sack is, we looked at every single offensive play from 2004, grouped by down and distance, and asked two questions: First, how often does a play with this down and distance lead to another first down (or a touchdown), and second, what is the average score on a drive that contains a play of this down and distance? Naturally, the average score on a drive with a first and ten at the offense's 20-yard line is different from the average score on a drive with a first and ten at midfield, but since we're considering first, second, and third downs all over the field, these issues even out.

In 2004, 66% of all first and ten plays eventually led, after one to four plays, to another first down or a touchdown. The average score on these drives was 2.30 points. On second and ten, only 53% of plays led to another first down, and the average score on these drives was 1.93 points. Life was much worse when the offense took a sack. Figure 1 shows the percentage of second down and third down plays that led to a first down, listed by the yardage needed for the first down. Naturally, there's a relatively smooth downward trend as an offense retreats farther and farther from the first down markers (and as you get to about second or thirdand 20, the small sample size wreaks havoc with the results). These second and third down distances are the results of first and second down plays, respectively, of various lengths. The first down percentage associated with a first or second down sack is interpolated into the appropriate line, giving the equivalent yardage lost. Likewise, the first down percentage of a first or second down holding penalty (the last-ditch sack prevention technique) is also included for comparison.

FIGURE 1. LIKELIHOOD OF FIRST DOWN BASED ON DOWN AND DISTANCE, 2004

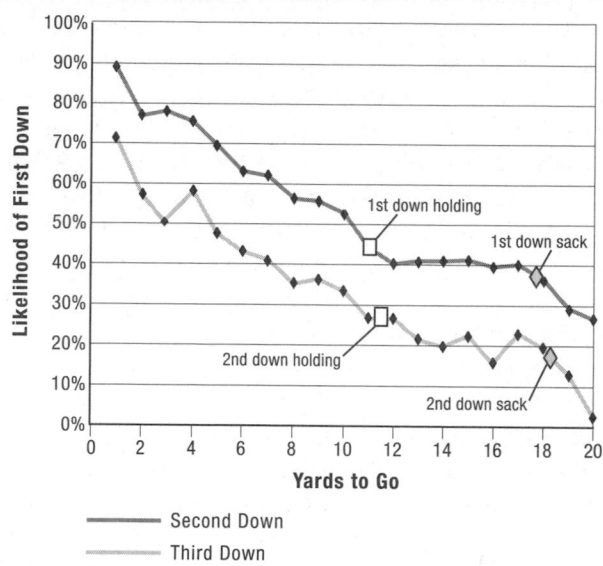

Taking a sack on first down reduces a team's likelihood of making a first down by as much as losing 7.8 yards does. On second down a sack is worth 8.4 yards. Sure, you say, but sacks cost a lot of yards, so this is no surprise. Well, that's only half true. Sacks do cost a lot of yards: the average first down sack lost 5.9 yards, and a second down sack lost 6.1 yards. But that means that there is something about a sack that makes it two yards (33%!) worse than you would expect based on just the lost yardage.

Figure 2 is identical to figure 1, but shows the average score on the drive instead of the first down percentage.

FIGURE 2. AVERAGE SCORE ON DRIVE BASED ON DOWN AND DISTANCE, 2004

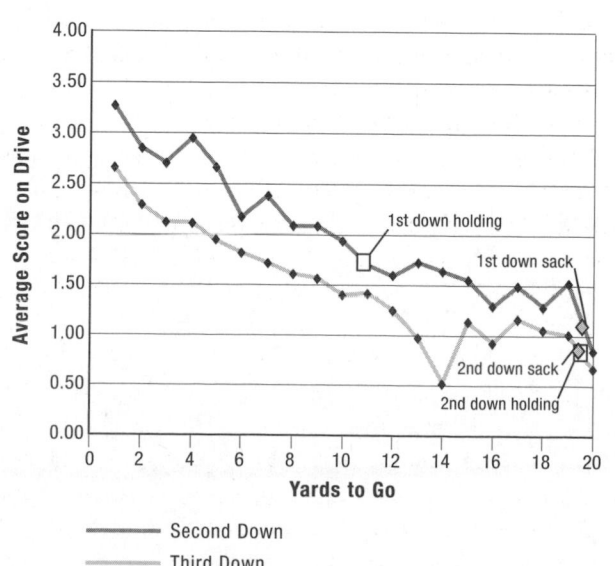

The results here are even more drastic: A sack on first down is equivalent to a loss of 9.6 yards, and on second down it is equivalent to a loss of 9.4 yards. The actual sack yardage is the same, of course, which means that in terms of the expected score on the drive, a sack is more than 50% worse than a comparable loss of yardage by another kind of play.

Why the seemingly irrational negative effect of taking a sack? Is it demoralization from the offensive players' having to watch a lumbering defensive lineman do a clumsy sack dance while their field general tries to pick himself off the turf? Does a sack "rattle" a quarterback, hampering his effectiveness on subsequent plays?

No, there's a simpler reason why a sack is the worst kind of bad play: fumbles. In general, on plays that are not sacks, a team turns the ball over once every 40 plays. But a fumble is lost once every 11 sacks. That may not sound like a lot. One lost fumble for every 11 sacks? For most teams, that means between two and four sack-generated fumbles a season. But not all fumbles are created equal. A quarterback who fumbles during a sack is behind the line of scrimmage, so that, although sack fumbles are actually lost at a lower rate than other fumbles, those lost fumbles do more damage. At best, the opponent has just acquired the ball farther upfield than the play started; at worst, a defender is streaking uncontested to the end zone while the offense continues running a play that has long since gone awry. This is why sacks are worse from the perspective of score on the drive than from the perspective of getting the next first down. All those fumbles returned for touchdowns make for drives where the offense has scored negative points.

Rex Grossman has been sacked 9 times in six starts over the past two seasons—a rate of about 24 sacks over a full season. By way of comparison, the estimable replacement trio of Chad Hutchinson, Craig Krenzel, and Jonathan Quinn was sacked 61 times in 13 games after Grossman's injury last year—a rate of 75 sacks over a full season. These 61 sacks alone won the Bears the award for "Most Likely to Help a Defensive End Earn an Incentive Bonus." (No other team in the NFL allowed more than 52 sacks over the entire season.) Not surprisingly, the Bears also led the league with 21 lost fumbles—only 3 of which occurred in the three games Grossman started. After Grossman went out at the end of Week 3, Chicago's offense scored about six points less per game, and the Bears' offensive DVOA went from averaging a poor −14.7% to a ghastly −46.4% per game. Of course the increased sack number is just one facet of the difference in the offense with and without Grossman, but it is a significant one.

Hutchinson actually had a better passer rating than Grossman, but his DPAR and DVOA were much lower. One reason for that is that our numbers penalize quarterbacks for sacks, and Hutchinson was sacked on 12.5% of his pass plays, compared to Grossman's 5.6%. The NFL average was 6.8%. Bears fans will welcome Grossman back to the field with open arms, but it may be his ability to avoid the sack more than his arm that they are grateful for.

Tim Gerheim

Bears 2004 Stats by Week

Wk	vs.	W-L	PF	PA	YDF	YDA	TO	DVOA Total	Off	Def	ST
1	DET	L	16	20	342	262	-3	-18.2%	-33.7%	-11.6%	3.9%
2	@GB	W	21	10	307	404	+1	5.5%	-2.9%	-16.2%	-7.8%
3	@MIN	L	22	27	385	443	+1	-13.6%	-7.7%	-3.8%	-9.8%
4	PHI	L	9	19	224	376	0	0.8%	4.7%	2.4%	-1.4%
5	BYE										
6	WAS	L	10	13	160	311	0	-23.5%	-24.5%	9.5%	10.5%
7	@TB	L	7	19	167	293	0	-37.7%	-23.4%	10.1%	-4.3%
8	SF	W	23	13	254	162	-1	-16.9%	-68.3%	-27.7%	23.7%
9	@NYG	W	28	21	231	258	+3	11.6%	-29.2%	-52.4%	-11.6%
10	@TEN	W	19	17	176	390	0	-53.9%	-94.8%	-18.5%	22.5%
11	IND	L	10	41	224	486	-4	-115.0%	-80.1%	38.7%	3.7%
12	@DAL	L	7	21	140	267	-2	-100.8%	-107.3%	-2.3%	4.2%
13	MIN	W	24	14	318	391	+3	31.8%	-8.0%	-30.3%	9.5%
14	@JAC	L	3	22	210	332	-1	-50.2%	-35.3%	10.2%	-4.8%
15	HOU	L	5	24	203	314	-4	-76.3%	-86.6%	5.0%	15.3%
16	@DET	L	13	19	229	314	0	-9.0%	-10.8%	-7.6%	-5.8%
17	GB	L	14	31	246	387	-1	-72.3%	-39.7%	37.6%	5.0%

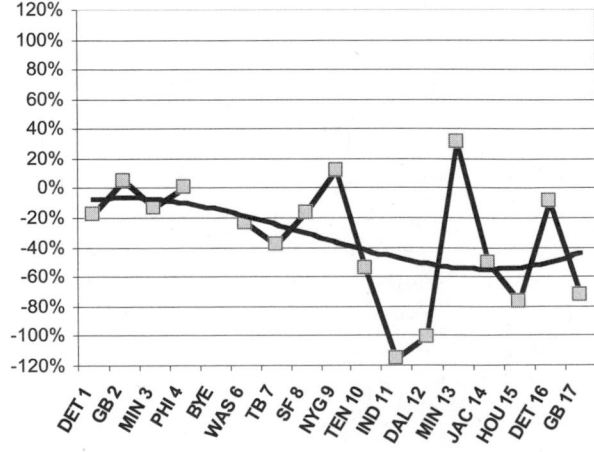

2004 CHI Weekly DVOA Performance

Trends and Splits

	Offense	Rank	Defense	Rank
Total DVOA	-39.4%	32	-4.1%	12
Unadjusted VOA	-37.7%	32	-3.7%	11
Weighted Trend	-50.1%	32	-2.7%	16
Variance	12.7%	7	5.5%	30
Passing	-61.6%	32	-3.4%	13
Rushing	-15.5%	28	-4.8%	12
First Down	-29.4%	31	5.2%	18
Second Down	-30.3%	32	-3.7%	11
Third Down	-75.7%	32	-26.0%	6
Red Zone	-77.3%	32	-37.1%	4
Late and Close	-59.5%	32	-18.4%	6

Five-Year Performance

	2004	2003	2002	2001	2000
W-L	5-11	7-9	4-12	13-3	5-11
Pythagorean Wins	4.8	6.1	5.3	12.3	3.8
Estimated Wins	4.3	6.4	6.1	8.7	5.9
Total DVOA	-32.0%	-15.7%	-16.6%	9.0%	-18.8%
Rank	31	26	26	10	25
Offense	-39.4%	-20.2%	-16.0%	-8.0%	-12.5%
Rank	32	28	27	20	23
Defense	-4.1%	-0.8%	3.0%	-12.3%	4.4%
Rank	12	17	18	10	20
Special Teams	3.3%	3.7%	2.3%	4.7%	-1.9%
Rank	9	6	11	4	21

Passing (min. 5 plays)

Player	DPAR	PAR	DVOA	Plys	NtYds	Avg	Cmpl	TD	Int
Chad Hutchinson	-25.0	-13.9	-46.0%	187	741	4.0	57.1%	4	3
Craig Krenzel	-41.7	-38.1	-82.6%	151	542	3.6	46.5%	3	6
Jonathan Quinn	-19.4	-23.3	-56.6%	113	318	2.8	52.0%	1	3
Rex Grossman	-2.2	4.2	-18.8%	88	583	6.6	56.0%	1	3

Rushing (min. 3 plays)

Player	DPAR	PAR	DVOA	Plys	Yds	Avg	TD	Fum	Suc
Thomas Jones	12.4	14.0	-2.6%	240	949	4.0	7	2	47%
Anthony Thomas	-9.0	-3.9	-31.5%	122	404	3.3	2	1	40%
Bobby Wade	2.5	2.7	10.1%	12	76	6.3	0	0	—
Curt Krenzel	-0.4	-0.9	-24.8%	11	45	4.1	0	0	—
Rex Grossman	-1.5	-1.3	-39.9%	9	50	5.6	1	1	—
Bernard Berrian	-0.7	-0.3	-44.1%	8	28	3.5	0	0	—
Adrian Peterson	-1.1	-0.8	-52.5%	6	19	3.2	0	0	17%
David Terrell	-1.7	-1.6	-130.4%	3	15	5.0	0	1	—
Chad Hutchinson	-2.5	-2.4	-147.1%	3	14	4.7	0	1	—
Jonathan Quinn	1.6	1.4	62.4%	3	35	11.7	0	0	—

Receiving (min. 5 plays)

Player	DPAR	PAR	DVOA	Plys	Ctch	Yds	Y/C	TD	CPct
WR									
David Terrell	6.8	7.1	-3.8%	90	42	699	16.6	1	47%
Bobby Wade	-14.4	-13.6	-40.6%	89	42	481	11.5	0	47%
Bernard Berrian	-8.1	-7.6	-43.5%	44	15	225	15.0	2	34%
Justin Gage	-2.8	-2.3	-30.9%	28	12	156	13.0	0	43%
TE									
Desmond Clark	-4.3	-1.6	-29.4%	49	24	282	11.8	1	49%
Dustin Lyman	-4.5	-4.5	41.7%	23	11	73	6.6	1	48%
RB									
Thomas Jones	2.3	4.8	-3.9%	72	56	427	7.6	0	78%
Bryan Johnson	-5.1	-5.1	-46.4%	25	14	55	3.9	2	56%
Anthony Thomas	2.0	1.8	10.0%	23	17	132	7.8	0	74%
Jason McKie	1.4	2.3	5.3%	17	13	70	5.4	2	76%

Defensive Players (min. 20 plays)

Player	Age	Plys	Stop	Dfts	AvYds	StpRt	Sack	Int	FR
Defensive Line									
Alex Brown	26	60	45	22	2.3	75%	6.0	0	1
Ian Scott	24	47	36	15	2.4	77%	2.0	0	1
Tommie Harris	22	45	37	14	1.2	82%	3.5	0	0
Adewale Ogunleye	28	40	26	15	2.4	65%	5.5	0	1
Michael Haynes	25	33	23	13	1.8	70%	2.0	1	0
Linebackers									
Lance Briggs	25	135	67	25	4.6	50%	0.5	1	0
Brian Urlacher	27	77	57	23	3.5	74%	5.0	1	0
Hunter Hillenmeyer	25	74	47	15	3.4	64%	2.0	0	1

Player	Age	Plys	Stop	Dfts	AvYds	StpRt	Sack	Int	FR
Secondary									
Mike Green	29	120	49	26	7.1	41%	1.5	2	4
R. W. McQuarters	29	78	20	9	11.8	26%	0.0	2	2
Todd Johnson	27	71	14	6	12.4	20%	0.0	0	1
Jerry Azumah	28	60	30	19	8.5	50%	1.5	4	0
Charles Tillman	24	45	14	7	9.2	31%	0.0	0	1
Nathan Vasher	24	33	13	12	6.8	39%	0.0	5	1
Bobby Gray	26	21	7	5	9.6	33%	0.0	1	0

Offensive Line

Year	Yards	AdjLineYd	Rank	Power	Rank	10+ Yds	Rank	Stuff	Rank	Sack	AdjSack%	Rank
2002	3.42	3.90	25	71%	11	9%	32	23%	15	43	6.8%	22
2003	3.98	4.01	22	68%	12	16%	16	28%	26	41	7.5%	26
2004	3.72	3.78	28	64%	15	14%	29	27%	24	66	12.1%	32

Year	LEnd	Rank	LTckl	Rank	MdGrd	Rank	RTckl	Rank	REnd	Rank
2002	2.77	31	4.31	14	4.12	22	4.13	17	2.62	30
2003	4.14	15	4.19	16	3.95	22	4.35	12	3.49	20
2004	4.24	18	4.43	17	3.85	26	4.25	13	1.79	32

With the exception of veteran center Olin Kreutz—the only lineman to start all 16 Chicago games in 2004—the Bears desperately need to upgrade their offensive line. Qasim Mitchell, the left tackle, was probably the worst of the lot, but the whole unit consistently failed to open holes for the running backs while opening up way too many holes for opposing pass rushers. With Fred Miller coming from Tennessee to play right tackle, John Tait will move over to left tackle and replace Mitchell. The Bears hope the change makes Tait look more like the player he was in Kansas City and less like a player who benefited from the guys around him in Kansas City. The guards are a mess: Veteran Ruben Brown looked shot in half a season, free agent signee Robert Garza (ex-Falcons) has bad knees, Rex Tucker and Marc Colombo can't stay healthy, and Steve Edwards and Terrence Metcalf are backups at best. Why the Bears didn't take an offensive lineman in the draft is a question we can't answer. Rex Grossman is advised to spend lots of time practicing snap counts in camp, because the Bears were fifth in the NFL with 31 false starts, while Miller was second among individual linemen with eight.

Defensive Front Seven

Year	Yards	AdjLineYd	Rank	Power	Rank	10+ Yds	Rank	Stuff	Rank	Sack	AdjSack%	Rank
2002	4.13	4.13	16	53%	4	16%	14	26%	12	36	6.5%	12
2003	4.36	4.06	18	69%	25	23%	27	24%	19	19	4.1%	31
2004	4.40	3.87	4	63%	17	22%	28	32%	3	34	6.2%	25

Year	LEnd	Rank	LTckl	Rank	MdGrd	Rank	RTckl	Rank	REnd	Rank
2002	4.14	20	3.89	10	4.10	12	3.92	10	4.52	24
2003	3.36	5	3.79	11	4.30	20	4.48	24	3.88	18
2004	4.03	12	4.26	12	3.80	5	3.63	4	3.63	14

Ask football fans to name the NFL's best front seven and you won't hear many people mention the Bears. In a year or two, you will. The Bears have two good defensive ends, Alex Brown and Adewale Ogunleye, and both of them are locked into long-term deals. The organization used its first two picks in the 2004 draft on promising defensive tackles Tommie Harris and Tank Johnson. Alfonso Boone provides good depth in the defensive line rotation; his size and upper-body strength make him a nice counterpoint to the team's other linemen, who are smaller and faster. Linebacker Lance Briggs is a hitter with speed, and Brian Urlacher, when he was healthy, had the best season since he burst onto the scene as a rookie—he's an athlete who forces turnovers. Second-year man Hunter Hillenmeyer surprised everyone with his impressive play when filling in for Urlacher. Lovie Smith is assembling a defense he can win with. The Bears led the league in stopping their opponents for negative yardage, and the front seven was a big part of that.

Defensive Secondary

Year	DVOA vs. #1 WR	Rank	DVOA vs. #2 WR	Rank	DVOA vs. Other WR	Rank	DVOA vs. TE	Rank	DVOA vs. RB	Rank
2002	0.6%	16	10.8%	17	5.3%	20	7.8%	18	20.6%	28
2003	-15.0%	8	-5.1%	17	-13.6%	13	8.0%	21	6.4%	22
2004	26.6%	25	-36.0%	1	-7.6%	15	-23.6%	6	-19.2%	11

Although the secondary still needs some work, it's going to develop nicely playing behind a good, young front seven. The Bears' secondary had only three illegal contact calls (St. Louis was the lowest in the league with two). That sounds like good news, but it might be an indication that they played too passively. Charles Tillman had a great rookie year in 2003 but struggled with injuries in his second season. The real unsung hero of the defense is Jerry Azumah, an athletic return man who is also underrated as a cornerback. That 26.6% DVOA against opposing number one receivers breaks out to an above-average −3.9% in the eight games Azumah started but a horrible 68.6% in the eight games Azumah did not. Azumah's abilities are even more impressive when you consider that he learned to play defensive back in the NFL; he was an excellent small-college running back at New Hampshire. If the Bears want to take a page from the Patriots' playbook and put some defensive players on offense, Azumah would be a natural.

Special Teams

Year	DVOA	Rank	FG/XP	Rank	Net Punt	Rank	Punt Ret	Rank	Net Kick	Rank	Kick Ret	Rank
2002	2.3%	11	9.6	2	15.6	3	0.3	16	-1.7	18	-10.9	30
2003	3.7%	6	-2.9	21	9.2	5	4.8	8	-8.7	30	18.1	1
2004	3.3%	9	-6.1	30	18.8	3	12.6	1	-5.4	25	-1.5	19

Speaking of Azumah, it was he, and not Dante Hall, who ranked as the most valuable kick returner of 2003 according to our methods. Azumah's injuries last year really hurt the Bears in the kick-return game, but they continued to be strong when it came to punting and returning punts. Several of their young players who haven't contributed on offense or defense are contributing on special teams. Backup running back Adrian Peterson is very good in coverage. He's such a sure tackler that it's surprising he's never played defense. One thing to note is that Chicago led the league with nine unnecessary roughness penalties, and five of those were on special teams.

Coaching Staff

Lovie Smith has assembled one of the youngest staffs in the league. Tight ends coach Rob Boras was born in 1970. Assistant offensive line coach Harold Goodwin was born in 1973. Assistant defensive backs coach Torrian Gray was born in 1974. Offensive quality control coach Mike Bajakian was born in 1974. Defensive quality control coach Lloyd Lee was born in 1976. Is this an NFL coaching staff or the cast of *The Real World?* New offensive coordinator Ron Turner insists he's going to install an offense that both pounds away in the running game and opens up the long passing game. But first the Bears will need more offensive talent. A big question is whether Wade Wilson, the longtime player who's now the Bears' quarterbacks coach, will be able to develop Rex Grossman.

Dallas Cowboys

For three quarters of the 2004 season, the Cowboys played like an above-average football team. The kind of team you would expect to win nine games and easily qualify for a wild card birth in the NFC. Heck, they would have been a favorite to knock off Seattle in the first round of the playoffs. Unfortunately, for the remaining quarter of the 2004 season, Dallas played as poorly as an NFL team can play. If the Cowboys had played as poorly over the entire 16-game schedule, they would have given the 1976 Tampa Bay Buccaneers a run for their money as the worst team to step foot on the gridiron since the merger of the AFL and NFL.

Now, if you're a Cowboys fan scouring the 2004 schedule trying to find 12 games where Dallas was above average, you can stop now. You're not going to find them. Even if you use our advanced metrics, there are only 7 games where Dallas had a positive DVOA.

But who says you have to divide a season by games? Table 1 looks at Dallas's 2004 season from a different angle.

After the third quarter, Dallas fell apart worse than the *Police Academy* series. The Cowboys outscored their opponents in the fourth quarter in only three games all season. In six games, Dallas was completely shut out in the final 15 minutes of game time.

How does a team go from perfectly respectable to amazingly atrocious at the 45-minute mark? On defense, Dallas's late-game collapses can be attributed almost completely to the deterioration of the defense's ability to contain opposing running backs. In the first three quarters, the Dallas run defense was the team's obvious strength, with a DVOA of −10.2%. If they could have kept that pace up for an entire game, the Cowboys would have finished with the sixth-best rushing defense in the league. Instead, Dallas had a fourth quarter DVOA of 24.6%. The middle of the Dallas run defense suffered the steepest decline in performance from the first three quarters to the last. On runs up

COWBOYS PROSPECTUS

2004 Record: 6–10

DVOA Estimated Wins: 6.6 (23rd)

Pythagorean Wins: 5.1 (29th)

DVOA: −14.9% total (24th), −18.3% weighted (24th)

Adjusted Offense: 20.6 points/game (−3.3% DVOA, 19th)

Adjusted Defense: 24.8 points/game (12.4% DVOA, 25th)

Adjusted Special Teams: +0.3 points/game (0.8% DVOA, 15th)

Variance: 9.9% (30th)

2004: Wanted: someone who can defend against the pass.

2005: Bill Simmons may want to get a head start on writing his "Bet Against Drew Bledsoe in the Playoffs" column.

2005 Projection

Leinart Land (0–4): 10%

Bad Team (5–6): 15%

Mediocre (7–8): 23%

Playoff Contender (9–10): 24%

Super Bowl Contender (11+): 28%

Projected Average Opponent: 2.1% DVOA (12th in NFL)

the middle or behind the guards, Dallas's DVOA dropped from −16.7% to 20.6% after the end of the third quarter.

On offense, a similarly drastic drop-off can be seen in the Dallas passing game. The Cowboys' passing attack in the first three quarters had an aggregate DVOA of 8.8%. In the fourth quarter the figure was −22.0%. Vinny Testaverde played like a Pro Bowler in the first quarter, but devolved into a NFL Europe benchwarmer by the fourth. This wasn't a new phenomenon for Vinny either; a similar decline, albeit in less than half as many attempts, can be seen in his 2003 performance (see table 2).

One might initially think that Testaverde's age was a big reason for his severe fourth quarter drop off in performance. At a cursory glance, the numbers from 2004 seem to support this theory. The ten quarterbacks who had the sharpest performance decline in the fourth quarter (see table 3) averaged 29.4 years of age in 2004. The ten quarterbacks whose performances improved the most in the fourth quarter were on average three years younger, at 26.3

TABLE 1. DALLAS COWBOYS BY QUARTER, 2004

Quarter	Pts For	OffDVOA	Pts Vs	DefDVOA	Pyth%
1–3	240	2.1%	225	−3.6%	.538
4	53	−18.6%	180	27.6%	.052

TABLE 2. VINNY TESTAVERDE BY QUARTER, 2003–2004

Qtr	DPAR	DVOA	Pass Plays
2004			
1	21.9	34.5%	107
2	13.0	7.0%	148
3	10.8	8.9%	120
4	−9.2	−27.2%	153
Total	36.5	3.2%	528
2003			
1	13.5	60.3%	43
2	10.1	33.8%	48
3	7.9	24.9%	49
4	5.5	7.7%	64
Total	37.0	29.4%	204

TABLE 3. TOP 10 QUARTERBACKS WHOSE DVOA DECLINED IN FOURTH QUARTER, 2004

Player	DVOA Q1-3	DVOA Q4	Difference	2004 Age
Steve McNair	0.6%	−66.2%	−66.8%	31
Billy Volek	11.4%	−51.2%	−62.6%	28
Tom Brady	52.4%	−9.3%	−61.8%	27
Trent Green	53.3%	−6.5%	−59.8%	34
Tim Rattay	14.4%	−37.3%	−51.7%	27
Vinny Testaverde	18.1%	−29.7%	−47.8%	41
Donovan McNabb	47.6%	4.1%	−43.5%	28
Chad Pennington	48.7%	7.5%	−41.2%	28
Carson Palmer	22.9%	−17.7%	−40.6%	25
Patrick Ramsey	2.6%	−36.4%	−39.1%	25

TABLE 4. TOP 10 QUARTERBACKS WHOSE DVOA INCREASED IN FOURTH QUARTER, 2004

Player	DVOA Q1-3	DVOA Q4	Difference	2004 Age
Kurt Warner	−19.6%	23.8%	43.4%	33
Ben Roethlisberger	33.2%	75.9%	42.6%	22
Jon Kitna	−13.4%	27.9%	41.4%	32
Craig Krenzel	−110.9%	−70.1%	40.8%	23
Eli Manning	−41.7%	−1.8%	39.9%	23
A. J. Feeley	−39.2%	−1.4%	37.8%	27
Michael Vick	−33.5%	−10.4%	23.1%	24
Aaron Brooks	−9.7%	12.4%	22.2%	28
Josh McCown	−17.3%	4.2%	21.5%	25
Joey Harrington	−11.6%	6.5%	18.1%	26

guard Marco Rivera in the off-season—Bledsoe will be given time to find open receivers downfield.

On defense, the Cowboys, like practically every other team in organized football—from Pop Warner leagues on up—have talked about switching to the 3-4 as their primary defense. Jason Ferguson was brought in from New York, where he helped the Jets have the sixth-best defense in the league against runs up the middle. He will anchor the middle of the Cowboy defensive front. In a 3-4, he's exactly the type of big, block-absorbing nose tackle the Cowboys were looking for. Even if Dallas stays with a 4-3, Ferguson will be a huge upgrade over Leonardo Carson, and along with La'Roi Glover, he gives Dallas one of the top tackle tandems in the league. Whether the addition of Ferguson will help the Cowboys in the fourth quarter remains to be seen, as the Jets also saw their run defense decline in the fourth quarter, though mainly on runs to the outside.

The one unit that Dallas needed to upgrade most, however, was the one unit that failed not only in the fourth quarter; the Dallas pass defense failed all game long (table 5). Dallas dropped from 10th the previous year to 27th in defensive DVOA against the pass. The secondary, in particular, was a major problem. While safety Roy Williams still played well, the other three starters played opposing receivers as if they carried infectious diseases. Greg Ellis

years old (table 4). The numbers are slightly skewed, however, merely by the presence of the 41-year-old Testaverde on the first list. If we take Testaverde out of table 3, the average drops to 28.1—lower, but still two years older than the ten quarterbacks who improved the most late in games.

Dallas took significant strides this off-season addressing the weaknesses at the root of their fourth quarter collapses. Drew Bledsoe is in as the new starting quarterback and, although he's no spring chicken at 33, Drew is eight years younger than Testaverde was last season. Bledsoe threw twice as many touchdowns and half as many interceptions as Testaverde did in the fourth quarter in 2004, despite having over 200 fewer passing attempts. If Bledsoe is going to be successful as a starting quarterback anywhere, it will be with the Cowboys. Behind an offensive line that has ranked in the top half of the league in Adjusted Sack Rate the past two seasons—and added perennial Pro Bowl

TABLE 5. DALLAS DEFENSIVE DVOA BY QUARTER, 2004

Qtr	Run Defense	Pass Defense
1	−13.9%	29.5%
2	−2.0%	11.4%
3	−14.1%	25.2%
4	25.5%	29.7%

and La'Roi Glover were able to create a bit of a pass rush, but the Cowboys got nothing out of what was left of free agent defensive end Marcellus Wiley (mercifully, now gone to Jacksonville).

Dallas did attempt to address its pass defense, both in the draft and through free agency. The Cowboys improved both their pass rush and the percentage of players on their team named Marcus by grabbing defensive end Marcus Spears from LSU and defensive end/linebacker Demarcus Ware from Troy State. Dallas also added linebacker Kevin Burnett from Tennessee in the second round, and he should help with intermediate pass coverage. After the draft, cornerback Aaron Glenn was cut by the Houston Texans and the Cowboys snapped him up. While neither he nor free agent signee Anthony Henry are "shut down" corners, they should provide Dallas with the quality depth they were lacking in the defensive backfield in 2004.

Our projection system is especially high on a Dallas bounce back this year. The Cowboy passing offense had a much higher DVOA on first (13.7%) and second (10.8%) down than on third down (−41.3%). Just a small improvement in third down performance could lead to a major offensive improvement overall, just as it did for the 2004 San Diego Chargers. (This indicator is discussed further in the San Diego chapter.) The system also expects the Cowboys' poor defense to rebound closer to their exceptional 2003 performance, and the additions to the defensive personnel should help the Cowboys do just that.

There is reason for optimism in Dallas, a good thing if the team hopes to win a Super Bowl in the Bill Parcells era. At 63, Parcells likely doesn't have too many years left on the sidelines. The Cowboys spent almost $30 million in free agent signing bonuses, most of which went to players on the wrong side of 30. That gives the Cowboys the horses they need to make a run for the roses in the NFC, but they have to make sure their thoroughbreds don't tire out once they hit the three-quarter-mile pole.

Al Bogdan

Research: In Defense of Drew Bledsoe

A career that offered limitless promise in New England and failed to rebound in Buffalo now begins its third act with Bledsoe's new three-year contract as the starting quarterback of the Dallas Cowboys.

In Dallas, Bledsoe is reunited with Bill Parcells, the head coach with whom he began his career and had his greatest success. Parcells and Bledsoe arrived in New England together in 1993 and in only two seasons took the Patriots from 2–14 to the playoffs. Two years later they took the Patriots to only their second Super Bowl. In those four

campaigns, Bledsoe twice passed for more than 4,000 yards and engineered numerous fourth quarter comebacks. He appeared to be on a clear path to a place as one of the greatest quarterbacks in NFL history.

Separated from Parcells, Bledsoe's career slowly deteriorated—along with the New England team around him. His penchant for fourth quarter comebacks was replaced by one for inexplicable on-field decisions. When an injury relegated Bledsoe to the sidelines, he had to watch his backup achieve what he never could—a Super Bowl title.

Traded to Buffalo, he had a strong 2002 but has been mediocre since. Thanks to his horrid performance in the season's final week, a Buffalo team that led our DVOA ratings for both defense and special teams couldn't make it into the playoffs. Fans who once saw Bledsoe as an elite quarterback—he made the Pro Bowl three times before the age of 26—now see him as a mistake-prone failure.

Bledsoe's reputation will always suffer because he is held to an unfair standard of comparison: Tom Brady. The list of quarterbacks in NFL history who lost their starting jobs to a multiple-Super Bowl-winning low-round draft pick consists of Bledsoe and . . . well, Bledsoe. When a team uses the number one overall pick on a quarterback, the general expectation is that the quarterback will lead the team to sustained greatness. Bledsoe's biography will always note that it was his backup who instead fulfilled this promise.

Is it fair of NFL fans to expect a quarterback taken number one overall to lead his team to multiple Super Bowl titles? Of the 15 other quarterbacks taken with the top pick in the NFL draft since 1960, only Elway, Troy Aikman, and Peyton Manning have more Pro Bowl appearances than Bledsoe's four (see table 6). Only four of the other 15 quarterbacks taken with the top pick led their teams to a Super Bowl (though the last few might still do so in the future).

The players we envision when we think of quarterbacks taken at the top of the draft are all-time greats: John Elway, Terry Bradshaw. But Tim Couch and Jeff George were also quarterbacks drafted number one overall. So was Terry Baker, the 1962 Heisman winner taken by the Los Angeles Rams with the number one pick in 1963. Baker played only three years in the NFL and never once started a game behind center.

Expand this view to look at first-round quarterbacks, not just first-*pick* quarterbacks, and the story stays the same. In the ten-year period from 1989 through1998, 16 different quarterbacks were taken in the first round of the draft (see table 7). Bledsoe, as the first pick in 1993, falls right in the middle of this period. Only five of these quarterbacks have taken their teams to the Super Bowl, and only Troy Aikman and Trent Dilfer own Super Bowl rings as starters. Only Aikman, Bledsoe, and Manning have

TABLE 6. QUARTERBACKS TAKEN FIRST OVERALL, 1960–2005

Name	Year	Team	Pro Bowls	Super Bowl W–L
Terry Baker	1963	RAM	0	0–0
Terry Bradshaw	1970	PIT	3	4–0
Jim Plunkett	1971	NE	0	2–0
Steve Bartkowski	1975	ATL	2	0–0
John Elway	1983	BAL	9	2–3
Vinny Testaverde	1987	TB	2	0–0
Troy Aikman	1989	DAL	6	3–0
Jeff George	1990	IND	0	0–0
Drew Bledsoe	1993	NE	4	0–1
Peyton Manning	1998	IND	5	0–0
Tim Couch	1999	CLE	0	0–0
Michael Vick	2001	ATL	2	0–0
David Carr	2002	HOU	0	0–0
Carson Palmer	2003	CIN	0	0–0
Eli Manning	2004	NYG	0	0–0
Alex Smith	2005	SF	0	0–0

TABLE 7. FIRST ROUND QUARTERBACKS, 1989–1998

Name	Year	Team	Pick	Pro Bowls	Years Starter*
Troy Aikman	1989	DAL	1	6	12
Jeff George	1990	IND	1	0	8
Andre Ware	1990	DET	7	0	0
Dan McGwire	1991	SEA	16	0	0
Todd Marinovich	1991	RAI	24	0	0
David Klingler	1992	CIN	6	0	1
Tommy Maddox	1992	DEN	25	0	2
Drew Bledsoe	1993	NE	1	4	11
Rick Mirer	1993	SEA	2	0	3
Heath Shuler	1994	WAS	3	0	1
Trent Dilfer	1994	TB	6	1	6
Steve McNair	1995	HOU	3	1	7
Kerry Collins	1995	CAR	5	1	9
Jim Druckenmiller	1997	SF	26	0	0
Peyton Manning	1998	IND	1	5	7
Ryan Leaf	1998	SD	2	0	0

* Years where player started at least ten games, including playoffs.

made multiple Pro Bowls. Seven of the 14 quarterbacks did not make it through even two seasons as a starting quarterback.

What if we expand the view another way, looking at all 39 first-overall picks since the combined AFL-NFL draft began in 1967? Only 11 of these number one overall picks own a Super Bowl ring, and only six own more than one: quarterbacks Aikman, Elway, Bradshaw, and Jim Plunkett, plus defensive linemen Russell Maryland and John Matuszak. Bledsoe's four Pro Bowl appearances put him in the upper one-third of first overall picks. Unless Keyshawn Johnson regains his old form, it is safe to say that the only number one draft choices from the 1990s who have had better careers then Bledsoe are Manning and Orlando Pace.

There is a historical precedent for Bledsoe to make a dramatic comeback in the third act of his career: Plunkett. Like Bledsoe, Plunkett was a number one overall pick by New England who lost a year to injury and found himself replaced by a young backup who quickly became a fan favorite, fifth-round selection Steve Grogan. Like Bledsoe, Plunkett was traded the following season; after disappointing a second team (with two seasons in San Francisco), he moved on to a third team. Plunkett resuscitated his career and led that third team, the Oakland Raiders, to Super Bowl titles in 1980 and 1983. That first title came when Plunkett was 33 years old—the same age Bledsoe will be in the 2005 season.

Unfortunately for Bledsoe, the team he joins in Dallas is far different from the one Plunkett joined in Oakland. Plunkett took over a Raiders team that had not suffered a losing season since 1964; Bledsoe is taking over a Dallas team that has lost ten or more games in four of the past five seasons.

The players Parcells will put around Bledsoe play to his strengths: a talented young running back to take the pressure off his arm, a strong offensive line to protect him in the pocket, and a strong tight end to serve as his main receiver. Slightly above average passing statistics won't save Bledsoe's reputation, however. If the rebuilt defense doesn't turn Dallas back into a winner, Bledsoe's third act will do nothing to turn his detractors back into fans. It might surprise those detractors that, when judged by the actual history of first-overall picks, Bledsoe's career has been a success.

Aaron Schatz

Cowboys 2004 Stats by Week

Wk	vs.	W-L	PF	PA	YDF	YDA	TO	DVOA Total	Off	Def	ST
1	@MIN	L	17	35	422	415	-2	-40.3%	7.4%	48.6%	0.9%
2	CLE	W	19	12	441	202	-1	47.5%	-1.3%	-54.7%	-5.9%
3	@WAS	W	21	18	287	384	0	20.7%	45.2%	24.0%	-0.5%
4	BYE										
5	NYG	L	10	26	278	336	-1	-27.5%	-18.0%	9.9%	0.5%
6	PIT	L	20	24	348	297	-1	13.3%	34.3%	27.8%	6.9%
7	@GB	L	20	41	362	480	0	-52.1%	9.5%	56.7%	-4.9%
8	DET	W	31	21	357	284	-2	-3.3%	-6.6%	16.5%	19.8%
9	@CIN	L	3	26	311	328	-5	-63.8%	-42.7%	24.5%	3.5%
10	PHI	L	21	49	317	485	-3	-47.5%	16.5%	63.2%	-0.8%
11	@BAL	L	10	30	222	287	-1	-39.0%	-27.8%	12.1%	0.8%
12	CHI	W	21	7	267	140	+2	27.7%	-9.3%	-53.8%	-16.9%
13	@SEA	W	49	39	405	507	0	2.6%	17.1%	33.7%	19.3%
14	NO	L	13	27	269	344	-2	-25.6%	-38.3%	-19.0%	-6.3%
15	@PHI	L	7	12	237	328	+1	-28.4%	-34.0%	-17.2%	-11.7%
16	WAS	W	13	10	306	233	+1	15.0%	1.3%	-11.6%	2.1%
17	@NYG	L	24	28	367	235	-1	-1.1%	8.0%	15.1%	6.0%

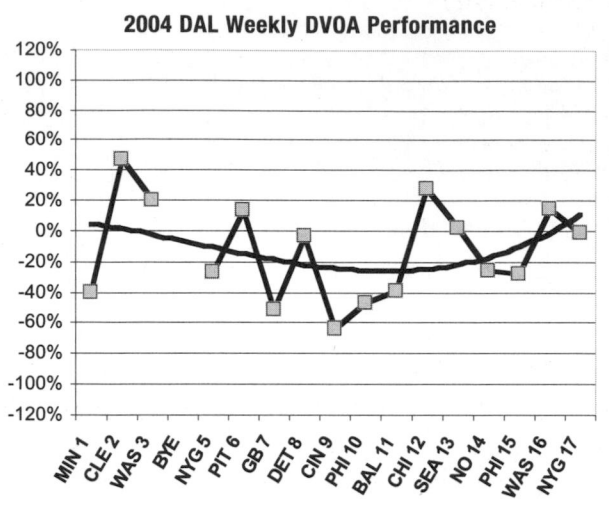

2004 DAL Weekly DVOA Performance

Trends and Splits

	Offense	Rank	Defense	Rank
Total DVOA	-3.3%	19	12.4%	25
Unadjusted VOA	-6.8%	23	10.8%	25
Weighted Trend	-8.2%	23	10.9%	23
Variance	6.4%	25	12.1%	8
Passing	-0.4%	17	23.4%	27
Rushing	-6.5%	22	0.0%	18
First Down	-8.2%	25	3.8%	16
Second Down	10.1%	12	25.0%	28
Third Down	-14.8%	22	8.5%	23
Red Zone	-18.9%	26	22.2%	27
Late and Close	-2.2%	14	4.2%	23

Five-Year Performance

	2004	2003	2002	2001	2000
W-L	6-10	10-6	5-11	5-11	5-11
Pythagorean Wins	5.1	9.0	4.3	5.1	6.1
Estimated Wins	6.6	7.8	5.2	5.8	5.6
Total DVOA	-14.9%	1.9%	-24.5%	-20.4%	-16.0%
Rank	24	15	28	26	24
Offense	-3.3%	-10.9%	-23.9%	-20.4%	-13.9%
Rank	19	22	31	29	24
Defense	12.4%	-14.4%	-1.9%	-1.3%	5.2%
Rank	25	5	12	22	21
Special Teams	0.8%	-1.7%	-2.4%	-1.4%	3.0%
Rank	15	25	23	19	13

Passing (min. 5 plays)

Player	DPAR	PAR	DVOA	Plys	NtYds	AvgCmpl	TD	Int
Vinny Testaverde	36.5	28.7	3.2%	528	3339	6.3	60.0%	17	20
Drew Henson	-2.5	-3.4	-42.4%	20	65	3.3	55.6%	1	1

Rushing (min. 3 plays)

Player	DPAR	PAR	DVOA	Plys	Yds	Avg	TD	Fum	Suc
Julius Jones	11.4	9.0	-0.8%	197	819	4.2	7	3	43%
Eddie George	-1.6	-1.5	-17.0%	131	433	3.3	4	2	44%
Richie Anderson	2.3	2.3	-3.6%	57	246	4.3	1	1	40%
ReShard Lee	4.4	4.7	23.4%	27	128	4.7	1	0	44%
Vinny Testaverde	0.5	0.1	-12.9%	11	48	4.4	1	0	—
Darian Barnes	-3.6	-3.4	-130.5%	5	10	2.0	0	1	40%

Receiving (min. 5 plays)

Player	DPAR	PAR	DVOA	Plys	Ctch	Yds	Y/C	TD	CPct
WR									
Keyshawn Johnson	23.6	20.1	13.5%	125	70	976	13.9	6	56%
Quincy Morgan	-3.8	-4.8	-26.4%	47	22	260	11.8	0	47%
Terry Glenn	11.6	11.3	32.6%	37	24	380	15.8	2	65%
Antonio Bryant	2.9	3.3	1.0%	27	16	267	16.7	0	59%
Terrance Copper	-0.3	-1.2	-16.2%	20	7	84	12.0	1	35%
Patrick Crayton	4.2	3.9	30.2%	14	12	132	11.0	1	79%
Dedric Ward	-4.3	-4.2	-103.5%	8	1	5	5.0	0	13%
TE									
Jason Witten	25.1	24.2	20.5%	122	87	982	11.3	6	71%
RB									
Richie Anderson	2.5	4.2	2.7%	41	26	227	8.7	0	63%
Julius Jones	-1.0	-1.3	-17.3%	26	17	109	6.4	0	65%
Darian Barnes	-0.3	0.0	-14.8%	14	10	59	5.9	1	71%
Eddie George	-1.5	-1.9	-31.8%	13	9	83	9.2	0	69%

Defensive Players (min. 20 plays)

Player	Age	Plys	Stop	Dfts	AvYds	StpRt	Sack	Int	FR
Defensive Line									
Greg Ellis	30	65	45	18	2.4	69%	9.0	0	0
La'Roi Glover	31	44	33	13	0.8	75%	7.0	0	0
Leonardo Carson	28	44	35	10	1.9	80%	0.5	0	1
Marcellus Wiley	31	37	24	6	2.5	65%	3.0	0	0
Linebackers									
Dat Nguyen	30	115	55	13	5.0	48%	1.0	3	1
Dexter Coakley	33	73	33	11	5.1	45%	0.0	0	1
Al Singleton	30	45	16	3	4.8	36%	0.0	0	0
Bradie James	24	31	19	4	3.9	61%	0.0	0	0
Scott Shanle	26	24	11	3	4.5	46%	0.0	0	0

Player	Age	Plys	Stop	Dfts	AvYds	StpRt	Sack	Int	FR
Secondary									
Roy Williams	25	97	32	14	8.0	33%	0.0	2	0
Terence Newman	27	88	30	16	8.3	34%	0.0	4	0
Lance Frazier	24	53	18	8	8.3	34%	0.0	2	2
Lynn Scott	28	42	12	6	9.4	29%	1.0	1	1
Tony Dixon	26	35	15	6	9.6	43%	3.0	0	0
Nate Jones	23	33	12	6	10.0	36%	1.0	0	0

Offensive Line

Year	Yards	AdjLineYd	Rank	Power	Rank	10+ Yds	Rank	Stuff	Rank	Sack	AdjSack%	Rank
2002	4.04	3.74	31	61%	23	15%	21	29%	29	55	10.1%	31
2003	3.83	3.83	25	63%	20	14%	20	27%	25	34	5.8%	14
2004	3.99	3.96	24	56%	25	16%	20	29%	28	37	6.2%	13

Year	LEnd	Rank	LTckl	Rank	MdGrd	Rank	RTckl	Rank	REnd	Rank
2002	4.10	13	3.98	21	3.19	32	5.17	1	3.27	26
2003	3.63	25	4.69	8	3.82	26	3.03	22	2.00	31
2004	5.44	2	4.73	9	3.59	31	3.71	27	2.94	29

Dallas needs this group to provide new quarterback Drew Bledsoe with as much time as humanly possible to throw the ball. That Adjusted Sack Rate is going to go up with the Human Monolith behind center—over his last five full seasons, Bledsoe has averaged 48 sacks per year. Marcos Rivera should be ready to start the season, but you never like hearing that your newly acquired Pro Bowl offensive lineman needs off-season surgery to repair a ruptured disk. Rivera is known as a quick healer, so he should be able to recover from what doesn't appear to be that serious of an operation. Rivera's right-side partner will most likely be Kurt Vollers, who moved into the starting lineup in Week 15 when Torrin Tucker was benched. On the left side, Flozell Adams was the Cowboys' top (pre-Rivera) blocker but led the league with nine false starts. Guard Larry Allen got a little bit of push back last year after an injured 2002 and a subpar 2003 (his Pro Bowl selection that year was essentially a lifetime achievement award). At center, 2003 second-rounder Al Johnson completes the group. The Cowboys are a good example of how different running styles can affect Adjusted Line Yards, despite our best efforts to attempt to isolate the value of blocking. The Cowboys actually dropped in Adjusted Line Yards on runs middle/guard after Julius Jones entered the starting lineup, from 3.89 yards/carry in the first nine games to just 3.32 yards/carry in the final seven. But Adjusted Line Yards on runs left tackle went up from 4.42 to 4.99, and runs left end went up from 5.03 to 6.03.

Defensive Front Seven

Year	Yards	AdjLineYd	Rank	Power	Rank	10+ Yds	Rank	Stuff	Rank	Sack	AdjSack%	Rank
2002	3.66	4.06	14	67%	13	11%	4	25%	14	25	4.7%	30
2003	3.55	3.81	6	67%	22	11%	8	26%	13	32	5.6%	24
2004	4.16	4.44	26	61%	13	17%	17	22%	25	33	6.0%	26

Year	LEnd	Rank	LTckl	Rank	MdGrd	Rank	RTckl	Rank	REnd	Rank
2002	4.02	17	4.68	27	4.12	13	3.65	7	3.90	15
2003	3.77	7	3.57	5	4.16	18	3.33	4	3.30	7
2004	4.89	28	4.61	25	4.29	21	4.26	19	4.52	26

As of press time, no one from the Cowboys has confirmed that they plan on switching to the 3-4 as their base defense, but all of their off-season moves indicate they're heading in that direction. Gone are Marcellus Wiley and Dexter Coakley and in are big defensive linemen like Jason Ferguson and Marcus Spears to absorb opposing linemen and tweener DE/LB Demarcus Ware to rush the passer on the outside. The switch may be what the Cowboys need to return their run defense to where it was in 2003. On third and fourth down with less than 3 yards to go, Dallas allowed 5.7 yards per

(continued next page)

Defensive Front Seven (continued)

rush, easily the worst in the league. Then again, since the biggest problem came from runs to the outside, perhaps what Dallas really needs is improved pursuit and tackling by the outside linebackers. Scott Shanle and Bradie James—two third-year players with a combined four starts—currently top the depth chart at those positions, and they happen to be the two Dallas linebackers who made plays closest to the line of scrimmage last season.

Defensive Secondary

Year	DVOA vs. #1 WR	Rank	DVOA vs. #2 WR	Rank	DVOA vs. Other WR	Rank	DVOA vs. TE	Rank	DVOA vs. RB	Rank
2002	13.2%	25	-34.9%	4	15.1%	25	9.7%	21	-28.2%	5
2003	-19.4%	6	-3.1%	18	-3.0%	22	-24.0%	3	-4.0%	13
2004	22.6%	22	44.1%	32	-21.9%	4	18.5%	22	-4.7%	17

Terrence Newman had a dreadful sophomore season, regularly getting picked on by opposing quarterbacks due to his penchant for leaving his receiver wide open by trying for an interception on every play. Newman's counterparts were even worse, as Dallas finished 22nd in the league defending against opposing number one receivers and dead last against number twos. The additions of Anthony Henry and Aaron Glenn won't turn the Cowboys' pass defense into the best in the league, but they do give the Cowboys a couple of legitimate defensive backs that they can run out onto the field every play.

Safety Roy Williams cemented his NFL legacy with the enactment of the so-called Roy Williams rule banning "horse collar" tackles like the one Williams has used to severely injured a number of opposing players, most notably Terrell Owens. It's unlikely the Roy Williams rule will reach the same level of notoriety as the Larry Bird rule in basketball (that allows a team to go over the cap to re-sign its own players), or the famous Tommy John elbow ligament replacement surgery. But for the moment, it is the most famous rule named after an NFL player, narrowly beating out the little-known Chris Hanson rule that forbids punters from swinging axes in NFL locker rooms.

Special Teams

Year	DVOA	Rank	FG/XP	Rank	Net Punt	Rank	Punt Ret	Rank	Net Kick	Rank	Kick Ret	Rank
2002	-2.4%	24	-8.5	29	-11.7	27	0.0	17	3.7	10	3.2	11
2003	-1.7%	26	1.6	18	4.8	14	-15.9	32	3.6	10	-3.3	21
2004	0.8%	15	0.6	18	3.8	17	-8.6	22	12.5	2	-3.8	21

Cowboys special teams were mediocre last year, which was a slight improvement on the year before when they were a shade below mediocre. The big improvement came on kickoffs and had nothing to do with Billy Cundiff, who registered as league-average in kick distance. But kick returns against the Cowboys cost the opposition −13.3 points worth of field position compared to average returns from the same catch locations. The Cowboys did not allow a kick return over 34 yards, and while a kick return generally ends at the 30-yard line, the average return against Dallas ended at the 26-yard line. Rashard Lee was a better kick returner than his teammates Terrance Copper and Jacques Reeves, so don't be surprised to see Dallas returns decline now that he's been cut.

Coaching Staff

Is "Tuna" the worst nickname in sports? The name was allegedly given to Bill Parcells after some players tried to play a practical joke on him, to which Parcells replied, "You must think I'm Charlie the Tuna." What does that mean? How do you get from such a ridiculous statement to a nickname that has stuck for over 25 years? Tuna is the most improbable nickname since radio producer Gary Dell'Abate mispronounced a cartoon character's name and became Baba Booey.

The Cowboys are going with a "running coordinator" and a "passing coordinator" this season, instead of an offensive coordinator. This was a common practice among coaching staffs in the 1960s but is very unusual today. Tony Sporano, not to be confused with Tony Soprano, is the running game coordinator, while Sean Payton will handle passing. Maurice Carthon (now in Cleveland) was listed as offensive coordinator last year, but Payton had significant control over the offense. Defensive coordinator Mike Zimmer, a holdover from the Barry Switzer era, cut his teeth coaching the team's secondary. In other words, his defenses were at their best when Deion Sanders and Darren Woodson were in their prime. The Cowboys website lists plenty of statistical accomplishments for Zimmer's secondaries in the late 1990s, but of course bad teams often have impressive pass defense stats—teams don't bother throwing much on them—so Zimmer's record may be more glitter than gold. Certainly, the decline of last year's defense suggests that he'll be on the hot seat this year.

Detroit Lions

Quick: Which NFL team has the fewest wins over the past four seasons?

Arizona Cardinals? Nope. They're the laughingstock of the NFL, but they've gone 22–42 over that span.

Cincinnati Bengals? Wrong again. They've gone 24–40.

Houston Texans? They didn't even play in 2001, so they have to have the fewest wins, right?

Well, it turns out that's half the answer. Over the past four seasons, the Houston Texans are 16–32. Those 16 wins tie them with the Detroit Lions, who have gone 16–48 since Matt Millen took over as general manager four years ago and ran a 9–7 team directly into the ground.

Last year there were finally signs of a light at the end of the tunnel. In Week 1, the Lions broke a three-year, 24-game road losing streak, and after six games they were 3–0 on the road and 4–2 overall. The team's top three draft picks, Roy Williams, Kevin Jones, and Teddy Lehman, made an immediate impact. In the weak NFC, the Lions looked like playoff contenders.

Then Williams, an early sensation, missed two games with ankle injuries, which hampered him even when he returned to action. Without his go-to receiver, quarterback Joey Harrington flailed around with no idea where to throw the football. By the time they were crushed by the Colts 41–9 on Thanksgiving, falling to 4–7, playoff talk was ancient history.

Now Williams has had an off-season to heal his injuries, and so have Detroit's top two picks from 2003, Charles Rogers and Boss Bailey. If these young players can stay healthy and reach their potential in 2005, Detroit may actually see the first winning record of the Matt Millen era.

Resist the temptation, however, to credit Millen for simply getting Detroit back to the same square one where he started four years ago. Millen claims that Detroit lacked talent when he arrived, but that talentless team had nine wins. Millen's 2004 team—he drafted, signed, or traded for 47 of the 53 players on last year's squad—had only six wins.

The 2004 draft haul of Williams, Jones, and Lehman is impressive, but not spectacular considering that the Lions had 3 of the first 37 selections. The Lions were only in a position to draft those players for two reasons: They were bad in 2003, and Cleveland's Butch Davis was willing to give up a king's ransom (the Browns' second-round pick) to move up one spot from seventh overall to sixth so he could draft Kellen Winslow.

LIONS PROSPECTUS

2004 Record: 6–10

DVOA Estimated Wins: 8.0 (18th)

Pythagorean Wins: 6.4 (24th)

DVOA: −2.9% total (18th), −7.0% weighted (21st)

Adjusted Offense: 20.6 points/game (−3.3% DVOA, 18th)

Adjusted Defense: 22.4 points/game (3.3% DVOA, 20th)

Adjusted Special Teams: +1.3 points/game (3.8% DVOA, 8th)

Variance: 19.8% (13th)

2004: Young team shows glimmer of promise.

2005: Detroit fans will revolt if Millen's players don't finally bring dividends.

2005 Projection

Leinart Land (0–4): 18%

Bad Team (5–6): 22%

Mediocre (7–8): 25%

Playoff Contender (9–10): 19%

Super Bowl Contender (11+): 15%

Projected Average Opponent: −5.1% DVOA (29th in NFL)

Millen's drafts have been notable for their lack of talent on the second day. Millen loves players from big schools, and every player he has taken on the first day of the draft has come from a BCS conference team with a winning tradition. But on the second day of the draft, the best general managers pick out underrated players who fit their system, or small-school gems who went unnoticed. Detroit's second-day hauls in the Millen era have been extraordinarily weak.

Millen's team-building method is the opposite of Bill Belichick's. The Lions sign big-money free agents (Az Hakim, Dré Bly, Damien Woody) and draft high-profile college players (Harrington, Rogers, Roy Williams, Mike Williams) that Millen thinks will be offensive stars. The Patriots, on the other hand, spread the money around to fill their roster with 53 players who can contribute, and constantly shift their draft position with trades, intelligently increasing the value of their picks. The difference in the results has been obvious.

In 2004, for the first time, the Lions drafted like the Patriots—they targeted Roy Williams and traded down, knowing he'd still be there, then they targeted Kevin Jones and traded up, worried he could be gone before their next pick. It worked well, and the draft was clearly Millen's best. But Woody, whom the Lions signed as a free agent from the Patriots, was a disappointment. A good rule of thumb: If the Patriots don't think a player is worth the money, he's not.

This year, there are signs that Millen is finally learning how to play the free agent market as well. In the off-season, Detroit added four important players without breaking the bank. Jeff Garcia, signed after one season with the Browns, took backup money even though he'll compete with Joey Harrington for the starting job, and possibly win it. Kenoy Kennedy is an upgrade at strong safety, Marcus Pollard is an upgrade at tight end (although perhaps, at age 33, on the downside of his career), and Rick DeMulling is an upgrade at left guard who comes at a reasonable price ($4.45 million for two years).

Trying to put a positive spin on last year's 6–10 record, both Millen and head coach Steve Mariucci have pointed out that in all but two of their ten losses the Lions kept the game close until the end. What they don't also point out is that in all but two of their six wins, the Lions' opponents kept it close until the end as well. This wasn't a 6–10 team that could have been better with a few breaks; this was a 6–10 team that illustrated the Bill Parcells maxim that you are what your record says you are.

Someone looking to put a positive spin on 2004 would be better served looking at a statistic that usually doesn't carry over from year to year: fumbles. The Lions were the second-best team in the league in holding on to the football; only 3.4% of their drives ended with a lost fumble. Mariucci constantly preaches the need to secure the football to his running backs. He has a standard speech he gives to his running backs about the "four points of pressure"—telling them that they must squeeze the ball with their hand, forearm, bicep, and rib cage. Losing fumbles tends to be a random occurrence, but the Lions weren't just second in the league in 2004; they were first in the league in 2003. And Mariucci's 49ers were fifth in 2002. Maybe Mariucci is onto something that defies what most statistical studies (including the one in the New Orleans chapter) have shown about fumbles.

Nearly every football pundit says that if the Lions are to become a playoff team in 2005 it will be because either Harrington turns into a high-quality NFL starter or Garcia replaces him and works the same magic he had with Mariucci in San Francisco. But the Lions' defense might deserve more attention in 2005. Defensive coordinator Dick Juaron had most of the elements he looks for in building a defense last year:

1. Two big tackles in Dan Wilkinson and Shaun Rogers, and a good run-stopping middle linebacker behind them in Earl Holmes;
2. A pass-rushing defensive end, James Hall;
3. Fast outside linebackers with James Davis and Teddy Lehman; and
4. A ball-hawking cornerback with Dré Bly.

The Lions return every starter except their safeties, a weak position improved by the signing of Kennedy. Boss Bailey is expected back at linebacker after missing 2004 with a knee injury, and new defensive lineman Shaun Cody should contribute immediately. It might turn out that the Lions don't need Harrington to turn into a spectacular quarterback who can lead the team to victory; they just need him to be a game manager who avoids turnovers as the defense leads the team.

That, however, is a best-case scenario. It's also entirely possible that the defense needed an overhaul rather than a tweak, and that the offense has structural problems that a quarterback controversy will exacerbate. If so, the Lions will have a losing record for the fifth straight year. And Lions fans will blame Millen for the fifth straight year.

Lions owner William Clay Ford has incredible patience. In a field where mass firings are an annual occurrence, Ford has kept unsuccessful coaches and personnel men around through years of futility. Russ Thomas was the Lions' general manager for 22 years despite a dreadful record. Coaches Monte Clark, Darryl Rogers, and Wayne Fontes all stayed long after the fans wanted them out. If Detroit puts up a fifth straight losing season, will he be able to resist the public call for Millen to be fired? Will he even want to?

Michael David Smith

Research: 'Tis Better to Have Rushed and Lost, Part II

The Lions had a surprising 4–2 record going into their Week 8 game against Dallas, but were down 21–14 at the start of the fourth quarter. A 25-yard punt return by Eddie Drummond gave the Lions prime field position to march down the field and tie the game, but after gaining 20 yards Detroit faced third and one at the Dallas 37-yard line.

This was the fourth time Detroit had faced third and one that day. On two occasions, they had run the ball for a new set of downs, once with Shawn Bryson and once with Kevin Jones. The other time, a pass to Tai Streets fell incomplete and they were forced to punt. With 12 minutes left in the game, Dallas wouldn't win the game with a defensive stop, but it would be very hard for Detroit to come back unless they could pick up this first down. Would they pass or run?

The answer was pass—not just once, but twice. On third and one, an attempted pass to Bryson was batted down at the line by safety Roy Williams. And on fourth and one, rather than lining his men up and trying to stuff that ball through—which had worked twice earlier in the game—Steve Mariucci called another pass play. Joey Harrington was sacked for a loss of ten yards, the ball went back to Dallas in good field position, and they came down the field to kick the field goal that made it a two-score game. A 50-yard touchdown pass to David Kircus couldn't overcome that field goal, and Detroit lost the game—and then the Lions lost the next four as well.

Did Detroit lose five straight games because they called two pass plays instead of trying a running play on that specific set of downs? No, of course not. But the passes were emblematic of how the Lions kick away offensive chances with bad play calls on short-yardage downs. Every single year, Detroit is one of the teams that most often calls a pass in short-yardage situations, and every single year, runs are far more likely to gain the necessary yardage than passes are.

The resistance of NFL coaches to just pound the ball down the middle on third-and-one is a particular bugaboo of Gregg Easterbrook, author of NFL.com's weekly column "Tuesday Morning Quarterback." He often writes about teams that throw incomplete passes at the goal line, or on third and one, in an recurring item he calls "'Tis Better to Have Rushed and Lost, Than Never to Have Rushed at All." Late in the 2003 season, he asked us to run the numbers to find out whether he was right in his insistence that runs were more likely than passes to achieve the necessary yardage on short-yardage downs.

The term *short-yardage down* is open to interpretation, so we ran through a series of different possible scenarios to determine how often runs and passes were successful in gaining a new set of downs. In almost every one of those scenarios, runs were not just more successful, but dramatically more successful. Now we've looked at the numbers for the last three years combined, and nothing has changed (table 1).

It isn't just third and one, either. Rushing plays are more likely to achieve a first down than passing plays on third and two, and even on third and three. Despite this, coaches call a pass play on third and three three times more often than a running play.

Among the plays we deem "power situations"—third or fourth down with one to two yards to go, or any play with goal to go from the one- or two-yard line—the only situations in which passing is as successful as rushing in terms of gaining a first down or touchdown are first and second down on the goal line, where the defense is particularly susceptible to play-action fakes.

The Lions have a particular weakness in this area, and they've had this problem since before Mariucci was their coach. In 2002 power situations, Detroit passed 36 times and ran only 34. The only other team that passed more often than it ran in similar situations was Buffalo. At least the Lions had an excuse that year, as both runs and passes converted for new first downs at the same terrible rate of 44%.

The next year, the Lions had a new coach, and the same play-calling problem. They were 12 for 31 when passing in power situations, and 21 for 28 when rushing in power situations. The only other team in 2003 that passed more often than it ran in similar situations was Cleveland.

In 2004, the Lions added a Pro Bowl offensive lineman from the world champion Patriots and a talented young running back. They had already shown the year before that they could gain a new first down much more often if they kept the ball on the ground, so you would

TABLE 1. PLAY CALLING AND SUCCESS ON SHORT-YARDAGE DOWNS

Situation	Pass	Rush	Pass Success	Rush Success	Passes as Pct of Total Plays
3rd and 1	528	1716	51.7%	70.6%	24%
3rd and 2	965	662	47.9%	60.4%	59%
3rd and 3	1149	390	52.0%	59.7%	75%
4th and 1	117	403	62.4%	73.7%	23%
4th and 2	104	50	36.5%	62.0%	68%
4th and 3	87	22	42.5%	63.6%	80%
3/4 and 1 or 2	1714	2831	49.4%	68.5%	38%
1/2 and 1 on the goal line	169	481	55.0%	55.3%	26%
1/2 and 1 or 2 on the goal line	298	769	50.3%	52.1%	28%
3/4 and 1 on the goal line	78	217	48.7%	64.5%	26%
3/4 and 1 or 2 on the goal line	182	295	46.2%	60.7%	38%
All Power Situations	**2012**	**3600**	**49.5%**	**65.0%**	**36%**

TABLE 2: AVERAGE YARDAGE AND NEXT SCORE RESULTING FROM SHORT-YARDAGE PLAYS, 2004

Situation	Play Type	Plays	1st Down Pct	Avg Yds	Avg Score on Drive	Avg Next Score Overall
3rd and 1	pass	182	58%	5.75	2.51	2.26
3rd and 1	rush	559	77%	2.87	2.72	2.38
3rd and 2	pass	293	53%	5.17	2.14	1.86
3rd and 2	rush	217	61%	3.97	2.43	2.47
4th and 1	pass	38	58%	7.82	2.07	1.60
4th and 1	rush	122	70%	3.33	2.89	1.68
4th and 2	pass	31	42%	4.48	1.51	0.45
4th and 2	rush	11	82%	10.18	3.72	4.08

expect them to try it a little more often. Instead, the Lions were 12 for 28 passing in power situations, and 15 for 25 rushing. No NFL team had a higher ratio of passes to runs when they needed just a yard or two.

When we have written about this issue in the past, the response is often the same: What about the fact that pass plays offer an opportunity for much longer gains? Isn't it worth it to trade a couple of first downs for a couple of 30-yard gains down the field?

We decided to test that theory by looking not just at how often a play results in a new set of downs, but how often a play results in a score. Table 2 shows every short-yardage play in 2004, along with the average yardage gain and how often each play resulted in a new first down. It also gives the average score on that drive whenever a rushing or passing play was called on this down and distance, as well as the average next score from the offense's perspective no matter how many drives away that next score was (as long as it took place in the same half). This latter measure takes into account the fact that field position is fluid, and gaining 30 yards and then punting puts a team in a better position to score next than gaining three yards and then punting.

In every situation except fourth and two, a passing play leads to more average yards than a rushing play. And yet, in every situation, a rushing play leads to a higher average score on that drive, and a higher overall chance of the offense scoring next. The difference is even greater on downs with two yards to go instead of just one yard to go. Despite this, coaches pass in three out of five third-and-two situations.

Why isn't there more value in taking a shot down the field on third and short? There are three reasons. First, a new set of downs does not preclude taking a shot down the field. In fact, if you can convert third down and gain four more opportunities, you can take your shot down the field on the first one and, if you miss, you don't have to punt; you still have two more chances to get the ten yards you need for another four more opportunities.

Second, the possibility of a turnover is higher on a pass play than on a rushing play. A turnover on third down generally gives the defense better field position than a punt return on fourth down. A turnover on third down in the red zone means the offense loses the opportunity for a field goal. Even if a running back fumbles the ball on a short-yardage carry, there is a good chance that one of his own linemen will jump on it and keep it away from the defense.

Third, most pass plays in short-yardage situations aren't teams taking a shot down the field. They are little sideline passes meant to get just a couple of yards, like the passes Joey Harrington was trying to throw to Tai Streets and Shawn Bryson during that game against Dallas. This is particularly true at the goal line, of course, where the pass play and the rushing play offer the exact same number of possible yards.

Unfortunately, because the NFL does not publish attempted yardage on passes, we cannot tell whether the possibility of a long touchdown makes a play-action fake on third and one from your own 30-yard line a worthwhile risk. But you can't defend the decision to throw a six-yard sideline out pattern instead of running the ball up the gut at midfield by saying, "Yes, but a pass could go for long yardage."

We're not suggesting that teams should run every single time they get into short-yardage situations. There is value in switching up your play calling to keep the defense honest. But the average NFL team ran in 64% of power situations last year. The happy medium between success and keeping the defense honest is likely higher than that. New England runs the ball in power situations more often than the average team every single year, including the years when Antowain Smith was their feature running back. Pittsburgh and Denver do the same. The one team that passed more often than it ran in power situations and still had success last season was Philadelphia, which at least had the excuse that it lost its up-the-gut back to an ACL tear in training camp and was left with the best pass-catching running back in football as the starter.

The good news for Detroit fans is that it doesn't have to be this way. Things can change. Before last season, when we complained about teams passing in short-yardage situations, it was nearly always a complaint about the Buffalo Bills. Last year, with ex-Pittsburgh coordinator Mike Mularkey as the new head coach, the Bills ran the ball 42 times in power situations, and threw only 14 passes. Steve Mariucci, this can be you.

Aaron Schatz

Lions 2004 Stats by Week

Wk	vs.	W-L	PF	PA	YDF	YDA	TO	DVOA Total	Off	Def	ST
1	@CHI	W	20	16	262	342	+3	-18.5%	-8.2%	-1.3%	-11.6%
2	HOU	W	28	16	266	386	+2	48.1%	16.4%	-13.8%	17.9%
3	PHI	L	13	30	256	402	0	-4.1%	1.5%	9.8%	4.2%
4	BYE										
5	@ATL	W	17	10	227	279	+4	20.6%	-3.3%	-28.6%	-4.7%
6	GB	L	10	38	125	434	-1	-111.3%	-94.4%	36.0%	19.0%
7	@NYG	W	28	13	325	325	+2	82.8%	59.7%	-22.9%	0.2%
8	@DAL	L	21	31	284	357	+2	-11.3%	6.2%	2.1%	-15.5%
9	WAS	L	10	17	322	229	-1	-34.0%	12.8%	20.2%	-26.7%
10	@JAC	L	17	23	100	415	-1	-11.3%	-30.4%	19.9%	44.9%
11	@MIN	L	19	22	213	319	0	12.5%	-28.2%	-11.5%	29.2%
12	IND	L	9	41	386	356	-5	-48.3%	2.0%	31.9%	-18.4%
13	ARI	W	26	12	398	254	+3	66.8%	30.1%	-38.3%	-1.6%
14	@GB	L	13	16	228	301	0	-14.8%	-28.1%	-10.3%	3.0%
15	MIN	L	27	28	463	461	-2	-21.8%	-12.5%	6.6%	-2.6%
16	CHI	W	19	13	314	229	0	-15.0%	-3.9%	24.6%	13.4%
17	@TEN	L	19	24	434	312	-2	-18.9%	3.7%	32.0%	9.3%

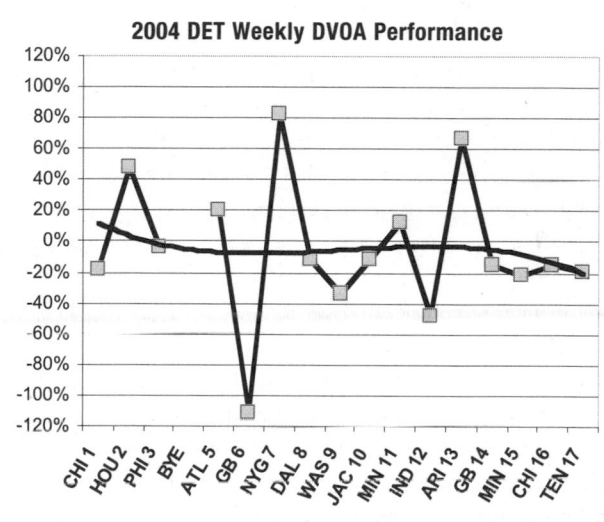

2004 DET Weekly DVOA Performance

Trends and Splits

	Offense	Rank	Defense	Rank
Total DVOA	-3.3%	18	3.3%	20
Unadjusted VOA	-0.3%	16	3.8%	20
Weighted Trend	-5.1%	21	6.8%	21
Variance	11.1%	10	5.3%	31
Passing	-7.7%	22	7.3%	23
Rushing	2.0%	13	-0.7%	16
First Down	-0.8%	20	6.1%	21
Second Down	-3.6%	21	-9.5%	6
Third Down	-7.9%	17	20.0%	26
Red Zone	-17.4%	25	-1.8%	18
Late and Close	-7.5%	19	-10.5%	13

Five-Year Performance

	2004	2003	2002	2001	2000
W-L	6-10	5-11	3-13	2-14	9-7
Pythagorean Wins	6.4	4.9	4.6	4.1	8.0
Estimated Wins	8.0	6.0	3.1	5.1	9.2
Total DVOA	-2.9%	-22.8%	-38.2%	-25.2%	6.6%
Rank	18	31	30	29	14
Offense	-3.3%	-23.5%	-20.3%	-14.8%	-17.1%
Rank	18	32	29	27	25
Defense	3.3%	1.8%	24.1%	11.1%	-18.2%
Rank	20	19	32	26	5
Special Teams	3.8%	2.5%	6.1%	0.8%	5.5%
Rank	8	9	3	10	4

Passing (min. 5 plays)

Player	DPAR	PAR	DVOA	Plys	NtYds	Avg	Cmpl	TD	Int
Joey Harrington	6.5	17.2	-10.2%	520	2843	5.5	56.0%	19	12
Mike McMahon	1.1	2.0	2.0%	16	65	4.1	73.3%	0	0

Rushing (min. 3 plays)

Player	DPAR	PAR	DVOA	Plys	Yds	Avg	TD	Fum	Suc
Kevin Jones	15.4	21.4	1.5%	241	1138	4.7	5	2	46%
Artose Pinner	1.1	1.2	-9.8%	57	174	3.1	2	0	58%
Shawn Bryson	8.3	8.6	26.7%	50	264	5.3	0	0	46%
Joey Harrington	0.3	1.4	-16.8%	34	185	5.4	0	0	—
Cory Schlesinger	-0.9	-0.8	-52.8%	4	7	1.8	0	0	25%

Receiving (min. 5 plays)

Player	DPAR	PAR	DVOA	Plys	Ctch	Yds	Y/C	TD	CPct
WR									
Roy Williams	4.5	2.5	-9.0%	118	54	817	15.1	8	46%
Az Hakim	14.1	13.1	22.6%	57	31	558	18.0	3	54%
Tai Streets	-7.1	-8.0	-33.6%	56	28	260	9.3	1	50%
Reggie Swinton	4.2	3.3	5.9%	31	18	213	11.8	1	58%
David Kircus	0.0	-0.4	-14.5%	10	3	68	22.7	1	30%
Scott Vines	-1.3	-0.7	-36.9%	9	3	51	17.0	0	33%
TE									
Stephen Alexander	-6.0	-4.4	-25.8%	76	41	377	9.2	1	54%
Casey FitzSimmons	1.6	2.1	3.4%	14	10	103	10.3	0	71%
RB									
Shawn Bryson	-2.1	0.2	-19.3%	56	44	297	6.8	0	79%
Kevin Jones	-2.0	-1.0	-19.4%	41	28	180	6.4	1	68%
Cory Schlesinger	2.6	3.4	15.2%	16	10	91	9.1	3	63%
Artose Pinner	0.7	1.2	2.5%	11	11	72	6.5	0	100%

Defensive Players (min. 20 plays)

Player	Age	Plys	Stop	Dfts	AvYds	StpRt	Sack	Int	FR
Defensive Line									
Shaun Rogers	26	75	57	21	1.8	76%	4.0	0	1
James Hall	28	53	39	20	0.7	74%	11.5	1	1
Cory Redding	25	42	34	10	0.2	81%	3.0	0	2
Marcus Bell	26	28	19	10	3.0	68%	2.0	0	0
Jared DeVries	29	25	19	7	2.0	76%	3.0	0	0
Dan Wilkinson	32	24	21	8	0.6	88%	1.5	0	0
Kalimba Edwards	26	24	17	10	1.5	71%	4.5	0	1
Linebackers									
Earl Holmes	32	113	56	12	3.9	50%	0.0	0	0
Teddy Lehman	24	99	48	23	5.4	48%	1.0	1	0
James Davis	26	83	41	14	4.2	49%	3.5	0	1
Alex Lewis	24	52	26	17	6.0	50%	2.0	1	0

Player	Age	Plys	Stop	Dfts	AvYds	StpRt	Sack	Int	FR
Secondary									
Brock Marion	35	97	32	13	9.1	33%	0.0	3	0
Bracy Walker	35	81	22	11	8.8	27%	1.0	1	2
Dré Bly	28	62	29	9	7.3	47%	0.0	4	0
Fernando Bryant	28	60	18	6	7.6	30%	0.0	0	0
Chris Cash	25	35	9	4	8.1	26%	0.0	1	0
Keith Smith	25	33	13	9	5.7	39%	0.0	1	0
André Goodman	27	25	5	3	8.0	20%	0.0	1	0

Offensive Line

Year	Yards	AdjLineYd	Rank	Power	Rank	10+ Yds	Rank	Stuff	Rank	Sack	AdjSack%	Rank
2002	4.07	3.74	30	44%	32	22%	4	32%	31	20	3.2%	1
2003	3.45	3.53	31	75%	4	14%	19	29%	28	14	2.6%	1
2004	4.50	4.06	21	60%	18	23%	1	30%	30	37	6.4%	16

Year	LEnd	Rank	LTckl	Rank	MdGrd	Rank	RTckl	Rank	REnd	Rank
2002	3.75	22	3.09	31	3.93	27	3.90	23	3.53	20
2003	3.30	31	4.53	12	3.82	27	3.09	30	0.92	32
2004	2.67	31	4.62	12	4.40	11	3.86	21	3.92	16

The Lions inked right guard Damien Woody to a huge free agent contract, and he took a long time before he provided results. He showed up to camp noticeably overweight, and it affected his play against faster defensive tackles; Atlanta's Rod Coleman had a very good game getting around Woody and to Joey Harrington. As the season went on, though, Woody played himself into shape, and the Lions' running game got better. On the left side of the line, Jim Backus returns at tackle; he'll play next to guard Rick DeMulling, who comes over from Indianapolis. Center Dominic Raiola had a somewhat disappointing season, but the Lions re-signed him nonetheless. The biggest question is who will replace Stockar McDougle at right tackle. The leading candidate seems to be Kyle Kosier, who played for Mariucci in San Francisco and joined the Lions in April as a free agent.

No matter how hard we try to analyze an offensive line and skill players separately, the success of one always affects the appearance of the other. Detroit running backs (primarily Kevin Jones) gained more of their yards on long runs than any other backs in the league, and the improvement of Detroit's running game from 2003 to 2004 in standard yards per carry was twice as large as the improvement in Adjusted Line Yards per carry. Jones often got stuffed at the line, but he took great advantage of the holes he did get, and that made the Detroit line look better in general. In pass protection, just the opposite took place, with a change in Harrington's style of play reflecting poorly on the offensive line. The Lions went from two years with the NFL's best Adjusted Sack Rate to middle of the pack, but this had little to do with a breakdown in pass protection. Rather, Harrington began to hold on to the ball longer instead of frequently throwing it out of bounds or into the arms of a defender at the first sign of pressure. Sacks went up, and interceptions went down.

Defensive Front Seven

Year	Yards	AdjLineYd	Rank	Power	Rank	10+ Yds	Rank	Stuff	Rank	Sack	AdjSack%	Rank
2002	4.05	4.36	24	70%	20	13%	6	19%	29	34	4.9%	29
2003	4.04	3.74	5	68%	24	18%	20	27%	12	28	5.1%	26
2004	3.78	4.04	10	79%	31	12%	5	26%	9	38	6.6%	20

Year	LEnd	Rank	LTckl	Rank	MdGrd	Rank	RTckl	Rank	REnd	Rank
2002	3.76	10	4.30	20	4.45	25	4.30	20	5.35	30
2003	3.91	11	3.38	2	3.82	6	3.83	12	3.38	10
2004	4.24	16	4.11	9	3.94	7	4.26	18	3.86	17

The interior linemen, Shaun Rogers and Dan Wilkinson, have been strong the last two years. Both men are huge, which is generally good but means they also sometimes run out of gas on long drives. Rogers was much better early in the season than he was later on. That lack of stamina explains why the Lions worked hard to re-sign backup defensive tackle Marcus Bell, who figures to get plenty of playing time. Linebacker Teddy Lehman did a great job making up for the loss of Boss Bailey to a knee injury. Lehman got lost in coverage a few times against the Texans, but he's so fast that he covered Andre Johnson better than the Lions' cornerbacks did. He also held Falcons tight end Alge Crumpler in check. If Bailey is back and healthy, and rookie Shaun Cody plays well, this could be a very solid group. But they need to improve on those all-important third-and-short situations.

Defensive Secondary

Year	DVOA vs. #1 WR	Rank	DVOA vs. #2 WR	Rank	DVOA vs. Other WR	Rank	DVOA vs. TE	Rank	DVOA vs. RB	Rank
2002	32.8%	30	31.1%	25	13.2%	23	20.7%	27	22.9%	30
2003	-14.8%	9	27.2%	30	-22.6%	9	49.8%	32	13.0%	27
2004	-1.4%	16	19.4%	26	-9.2%	12	20.8%	25	-13.5%	13

Dré Bly signed a five-year, $24.5 million contract at the beginning of the 2003 free agency period. Fernando Bryant signed a six-year, $24 million contract at the beginning of the 2004 free agency period. With a couple of pricey corners like that, the Lions should have had better play from their secondary last year. Bly makes a lot of big plays, but he also gives up a lot of them. The day after the draft, the Lions decided to get younger at safety by releasing 34-year-old Brock Marion and giving his job to 25-year-old Terrence Holt. That was an odd move because the Lions hadn't drafted a safety, but the Lions like Holt; free agent pickup Kenoy Kennedy and third-round pick Stanley Wilson, a cornerback out of Stanford, could play some safety if the Lions are thin. R. W. McQuarters was also signed to play nickelback.

Special Teams

Year	DVOA	Rank	FG/XP	Rank	Net Punt	Rank	Punt Ret	Rank	Net Kick	Rank	Kick Ret	Rank
2002	6.2%	3	-0.1	15	12.6	5	-2.2	20	8.5	4	15.5	2
2003	2.5%	9	10.5	4	-4.6	25	9.8	5	-4.7	24	2.8	10
2004	3.8%	8	-0.1	19	-5.0	29	0.0	6	11.5	4	14.4	3

Chuck Priefer has been the Lions' special teams coach since 1997, and designs some of the league's most effective blocking schemes. It's amazing that the Lions have been able to hold on to him for as long as they have. Special teams play in the NFL varies wildly from year to year, but the Lions are one of only three teams that have ranked in the top ten of our special teams ratings for five straight seasons (the others are Philadelphia and Miami). Eddie Drummond is a very talented return man who had an incredible season—two touchdowns on kick returns, two on punt returns—cut short when he broke his shoulder on Thanksgiving. Jason Hanson is a fine kicker, but punter Nick Harris has been near the bottom of our ratings for all four of his NFL seasons, including 2001–2002 in Cincinnati, and needs to be replaced.

Coaching Staff

Steve Mariucci hired Ted Tollner as the new offensive coordinator, replacing the retiring Sherman Lewis. Mariucci was an assistant under Tollner at USC in the 1980s, and Tollner was an assistant under Mariucci with the 49ers, so the two are comfortable working together. Tollner will take over play-calling duties, which last year shifted among Mariucci and several offensive assistants. Expect Tollner to use more no-huddle offense, especially if the young skill position players—Kevin Jones, Roy Williams, Mike Williams, and Charles Rogers—can develop into a nucleus that can stay on the field throughout the game. Defensive coordinator Dick Jauron also has a long working history with Mariucci; they were assistants together in Green Bay.

Green Bay Packers

Number 4 is back. Much of the Packers' roster changed during the off-season, but the return of Brett Favre eclipsed the bad news coming out of Green Bay.

Unfortunately, the bad news is still bad. This off-season, the Packers lost a lot and didn't add much. It's hard to imagine Green Bay being any better in 2005 than it was in 2004.

Last year's Packers seemed doomed after five games, starting off 1–4—including an unthinkable 0–3 at Lambeau Field. The game most frequently cited in discussing Green Bay's struggles is the 45–31 loss to Indianapolis. But getting torched by Peyton Manning is understandable. What's not understandable is that two weeks later the Packers lost 48–21 to Tennessee. In that game, the Titans scored on five of their first six possessions, including Chris Brown touchdowns of 37 and 29 yards on the first two series. The Titans ended the game with 456 yards, 23 first downs, and zero turnovers. Fans in Lambeau seemed to think the season ended that day.

Yet after that miserable start, the Packers rallied. They crushed the Lions, 38–10, and then proceeded to win five straight more, with three wins coming by two touchdowns or more. Heading into the playoffs, the Packers looked like they could challenge for the NFC title.

It wasn't to be. Favre had a terrible game as the Packers bowed out of the playoffs, losing at home to the Vikings in the wild card round. It's hard not to think that the real Packers were the ones that lost that playoff game. As impressive as their 9–2 record in the last 11 games sounds, they didn't win a single game all year against a team that finished better than .500. Favre is still a good quarterback, but the Packers wouldn't have drafted Aaron Rodgers in the first round if they thought Favre would be around much longer.

Favre may have thrown four interceptions in the game against Minnesota, but the signature moment of the contest was when a clearly hobbled Randy Moss managed to limp past cornerback Al Harris for a wide open touchdown. That completely blown coverage epitomized the collapse of the Green Bay defense. In 2003, the Packers ranked ninth in defensive DVOA, getting stronger as the year went along. By the end of that season, they had moved up to fourth in weighted defensive DVOA, our metric that emphasizes recent performance. In 2004, the Green Bay defense tumbled to 29th. Only San Francisco and Oak-

PACKERS PROSPECTUS

2004 Record: 10–6

DVOA Estimated Wins: 7.6 (20th)

Pythagorean Wins: 9.0 (10th)

DVOA: −5.0% total (21st), 3.0% weighted (16th)

Adjusted Offense: 25.0 points/game (13.3% DVOA, 9th)

Adjusted Defense: 26.8 points/game (20.0% DVOA, 29th)

Adjusted Special Teams: +0.6 points/game (1.7% DVOA, 13th)

Variance: 26.6% (6th)

2004: Packers overcome a horrible start, only to stumble in the playoffs.

2005: Loss of guards hurts, and for Favre to make one last Super Bowl run the defense has to improve.

2005 Projection

Leinart Land (0–4): 28%

Bad Team (5–6): 25%

Medioore (7–8): 23%

Playoff Contender (9–10): 14%

Super Bowl Contender (11+): 9%

Projected Average Opponent: −1.1% DVOA (19th in NFL)

land were worse against the pass. The Packers didn't do a lot to address their secondary in the off-season; free agent safety Earl Little was nothing special last year in Cleveland, and second-round pick Nick Collins of Bethune-Cookman is seen as a good athlete but also a project who won't contribute immediately.

Mike Sherman responded after the season by firing defensive coordinator Bob Slowik and defensive backs coach Kurt Schottenheimer. Sherman might have been better served by looking in the mirror. Sherman is the one who couldn't get along with the best cornerback on the team, Mike McKenzie, sending him to New Orleans as the result of a personality clash and a contract dispute. Sherman (in his former role as general manager) is the one who chose all those inexperienced cornerbacks who struggled against better passers. Sherman is the one who made Ed Donatell the scapegoat for the fourth-and-26 brain cramp that cost Green Bay a win in the 2003 playoffs. Donatell resurfaced in Atlanta after Sherman fired him and turned that team's defense around while Green Bay's defense disintegrated without him.

While firing Donatell to bring in Slowik was a mistake, firing Slowik and bringing in Jim Bates was not. Bates, as the defensive coordinator and then the interim head coach in Miami last year, did admirable work in a tough situation. He also brought two of his Miami assistants, Robert Nunn and Bob Sanders, with him to Green Bay as part of the Packers' defensive staff's off-season overhaul.

Bates will make significant changes to the Green Bay defense, starting with deemphasizing the blitz. Nearly all of the Dolphins' pass rush under Bates came from the defensive ends. As a result, Bates's defensive backs usually have to be able to hold their coverage for a long time, and he likes to keep his safeties deep.

Bates will look for a big contribution from pass-rushing defensive end Kabeer Gbaja-Biamila, who still has the quickness to rush outside but also often gets manhandled by stronger left tackles. When Gbaja-Biamila failed to rush the quarterback in 2004, it led to the secondary getting torched. On the other side of the line, third-year defensive end Aaron Kampman had his best season as a pro, and his continuing development will be important to Bates, who would love to have Gbaja-Biamila and Kampman develop into the type of defensive end duo that he had in Miami with Jason Taylor and Adewale Ogunleye.

Defensive tackle Grady Jackson was one of the most important parts of the Packers' defense in 2003, but he started to show his age in 2004. Jackson is 32 and, although he still has a good first step and the ability to clog the middle of the field, he can't move much beyond that first step anymore. Bates doesn't rely heavily on an inside pass rush from a defensive tackle, but it's a disappointment to the Packers that after averaging six sacks a season for the previous four years, Jackson had only one sack in 2004. It's highly unlikely he'll ever regain his 2003 form, and he'll be replaced in the lineup by promising youngster Cullen Jenkins more often in 2005.

Outside linebacker Na'il Diggs has the athleticism to chase running backs from sideline to sideline, and Bates will put him to good use. In the two games Diggs missed in 2004, the Packers gave up 156 yards on the ground to Kevin Jones and 165 yards to Fred Taylor.

The Packers were the worst team in the league at stopping passes to tight ends (54.1% DVOA) and to running backs (23.3% DVOA). That tells us that their safeties and linebackers were weak in coverage. Perhaps that's why they weren't sorry to see Darren Sharper go, but they did little in the off-season to address the problem. Bates will no doubt spend some sleepless nights in the film room searching for answers.

The subtractions on offense are a larger negative than those on defense because the Packers lost both their start-

ing guards to free agency. No NFL team relied more heavily on a pair of guards than the Packers did. The powerful Marco Rivera thwarted defenders at the point of attack, while pulling guard Mike Wahle led the way on sweeps and rollouts. They were the unsung heroes behind a running game that never suffered when it had to use second- or third-stringers, and a big reason why Favre has been one of the NFL's least-sacked quarterbacks.

The current plan for the Packers is to get center Mike Flanagan, who was lost for the season in the third game of 2004, back and healthy for 2005. That will allow the player who replaced Flanagan, Grey Ruegamer, to fill one of the guard spots. Either Kevin Barry or free agent pickup Adrian Klemm will fill the other spot. But no matter how the offensive line is assembled, it can't be as good without Wahle and Rivera.

Favre may have aged, but he hasn't lost his love for the deep ball. Favre threw deep more in 2004 than he had in 2003, and Javon Walker was his primary downfield target.

If there's any good news for the Packers' offense, it's that the 26-year-old Walker has emerged as one of the league's young stars. In his first full season as a starter, Walker delivered on the enormous promise he showed as a big-play receiver at Florida State. He and Donald Driver are a very good pair of wide receivers, although Driver is 30 and can't stretch the field the way Walker can. Walker missed the team's first minicamp and threatened a long holdout. David Martin contributed a lot to the Green Bay offense as an H-back. He's a good blocker and a good athlete. When he went out for the season with a knee injury, the Packers lost a solid lead blocker. If the Packers lose Bubba Franks in free agency, they'll count on Martin to take his place.

Favre is the Packers' most prominent player, but the most important to their chances of getting to the Super Bowl is Ahman Green. After having a phenomenal season in 2003, Green came back to earth in 2004. He didn't break as many long runs, wasn't as consistent, and couldn't shake the fumbling problems that have plagued him throughout his career. It's hard to imagine that he'll be better in 2005 because the offensive line in front of him will be worse.

If Green can somehow return to 2003 form, and Bates can get the defense turned around, and Favre still has enough gas left in the tank, this team has a shot. More likely, their last best chance for a while was 2003—their downward slide began in 2004, and it will continue in 2005.

Michael David Smith

Research: The Last Son of Gulfport

Faced with the impending destruction of their home planet of Krypton, Lara and Jor-El sent their baby son Kal-

El into space in a desperate attempt to save his life. By luck or by design, Kal-El's tiny spaceship landed on earth, where he was raised on a Kansas farm by Jonathan and Martha Kent. As the boy the Kents named Clark grew, so did his amazing powers. On his home planet, under its red sun, Kal-El would have been just another Kryptonian. But on Earth, Clark's alien cells absorbed the yellow sun's solar radiation, giving him super strength, super speed, and invulnerability. However, if the hero known to the world as Superman is denied exposure to the solar rays from a yellow sun for extended periods of time, his extraordinary powers begin to fade away.

Which brings us to Brett Favre. Although the Green Bay quarterback is allegedly not from a planet in a galaxy far, far away, like the Man of Steel, Favre's otherworldly abilities disappear once he's denied exposure to our sun's rays. When he plays outdoors, Favre is an unstoppable force, throwing spirals harder than a speeding bullet, leaping tall pass rushers in a single bound. Indoors, however, Favre becomes a mere mortal, like Jimmy Olsen or Joey Harrington.

Or at least that's the conventional wisdom. But this is *Pro Football Prospectus*. We're not satisfied with merely accepting the conventional wisdom. We scoff in its general direction. When we're not sitting around regretting all the time we spent reading comic books as teenagers, we're out there on the streets attempting to discover whether all these so-called truths we've come to believe as football fans have any basis in reality.

Using our play-by-play database, which stretches back to the 1998 season, we took a look at how Brett Favre has played on different fields over the past seven seasons and split the data in as many ways as we could think of: at home, on the road, in domes, outdoors, outdoors on the road, in a fortress of solitude built on an arctic glacier, and so on (table 1). Note that this data is from the regular season only, and not the playoffs.

Based on these figures, it doesn't look like Favre is hurt by playing indoors at all. His indoor numbers are pretty much the same as his outdoor numbers. In fact, he's played slightly better indoors than he has at home. His raw numbers have been much better indoors, averaging over 50 more passing yards per game underneath a roof. The most surprising statistic here may be that Favre has performed worse at home than he has on the road. Since 1998, Favre has been merely average at home, but excellent on the road.

So where did Brett get this reputation for playing so poorly indoors? Well, as it turns out, not all domes are created equal. Some are designed to allow a few of the sun's rays to seep through their roofs. But as you can see in table 2, one dome appears to be built with a roof coated in red kryptonite, causing our hero to act in unpredictable ways.

When Favre has played in a dome that isn't in Minnesota, he's actually performed better than he has at home or on the road overall over the past seven seasons. This includes seven games in Detroit and one each in St. Louis, New Orleans, Indianapolis, and Houston (with the roof closed due to rain). When he plays in Minnesota, however, Favre becomes a replacement-level quarterback, even considering his 358-yard, 22.0% DVOA performance in the Metrodome last season. That −6.8% DVOA overall in Minnesota is about what Josh McCown put up as Arizona's starter last season.

There isn't any good reason for Favre's poor performances only in Minnesota. The Vikings' pass defense has consistently been among the worst in the league over the past seven seasons: 12th in DVOA in 2003, 15th in 1998, and otherwise never above 25th. Table 2 also includes our

TABLE 1. BRETT FAVRE PERFORMANCE BASED ON LOCATION, 1998–2004

Location	Games	DPAR/G	DVOA	NetYds/G	NetYds/Pass
Home	56	2.5	0.6%	222.6	6.4
Road	56	3.3	12.0%	239.6	6.5
Outdoors	94	2.8	6.2%	222.8	6.4
Outdoors, Road Only	38	3.3	14.5%	223.1	6.4
Domes	18	3.1	6.8%	274.5	6.7

TABLE 2. BRETT FAVRE PERFORMANCE IN METRODOME VS. OTHER DOMES, 1998–2004

Location	Games	DPAR/G	PAR/G	DVOA	VOA	NetYds/G	NetYds/Pass
Metrodome	7	0.7	3.9	-6.8%	11.3%	250.9	6.3
Other Domes	11	4.7	5.6	15.5%	20.6%	289.5	6.9

stats without adjustment for opponent (PAR and VOA) to show that, when you consider how bad the Minnesota defense has been, Favre's track record in Minnesota is even worse than it looks. Familiarity doesn't seem to be the answer either, as Favre had an excellent DVOA of 18.4% when playing on the road against his other two division rivals, Detroit and Chicago.

Coincidentally, 1998, the beginning of the period used for this study, was the first year that Billy Joe "Red"

McCombs took over as owner of the team. McCombs's fiery mane brings to mind another red-headed billionaire who seemed to be the only person able to thwart an otherwise invincible being. Now comparing McCombs to a supervillian like Lex Luthor may seem a bit extreme, but in trying to figure out why Green Bay's Superman becomes a mere mortal in Minnesota, it may be the best explanation we have.

Al Bogdan

Packers 2004 Stats by Week

Wk	vs.	W-L	PF	PA	YDF	YDA	TO	DVOA Total	Off	Def	ST
1	@CAR	W	24	14	279	300	+2	13.3%	18.3%	10.5%	5.6%
2	CHI	L	10	21	404	307	-1	-39.3%	0.3%	37.0%	-2.6%
3	@IND	L	31	45	459	453	-2	1.5%	24.9%	29.1%	5.8%
4	NYG	L	7	14	301	403	-2	-55.8%	-24.4%	30.4%	-1.0%
5	TEN	L	27	48	437	456	-6	-98.1%	-33.0%	66.3%	1.2%
6	@DET	W	38	10	434	125	+1	105.2%	48.5%	-68.8%	-12.1%
7	DAL	W	41	20	480	362	0	33.2%	62.7%	40.9%	11.4%
8	@WAS	W	28	14	361	272	-2	-13.2%	-12.0%	3.8%	2.7%
9	BYE										
10	MIN	W	34	31	442	416	-1	12.5%	27.4%	26.0%	11.2%
11	@HOU	W	16	13	473	251	-2	27.2%	26.7%	-10.2%	-9.6%
12	STL	W	45	17	446	452	+3	55.0%	61.5%	11.3%	4.8%
13	@PHI	L	17	47	249	542	-1	-76.5%	-31.3%	44.8%	-0.4%
14	DET	W	16	13	301	228	0	22.6%	2.1%	-16.1%	4.4%
15	JAC	L	25	28	444	312	-3	-39.3%	-22.6%	23.9%	7.2%
16	@MIN	W	34	31	416	452	-1	-47.5%	13.3%	61.5%	0.8%
17	@CHI	W	31	14	387	246	+1	42.7%	52.8%	8.3%	-1.8%
18	MIN	L	17	31	306	384	-4	-87.2%	-68.2%	12.0%	-6.9%

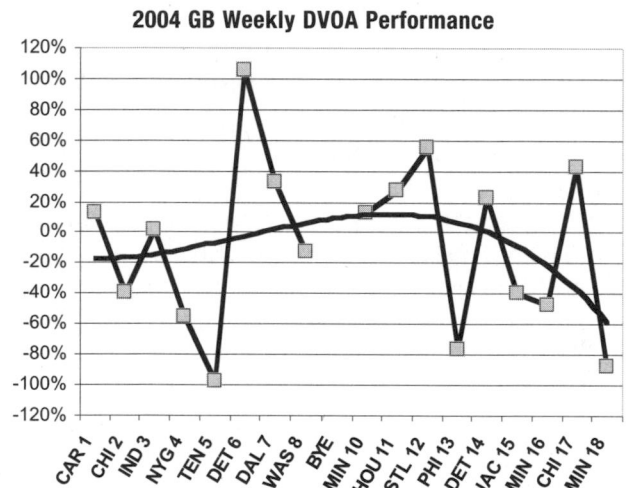

2004 GB Weekly DVOA Performance

Trends and Splits

	Offense	Rank	Defense	Rank
Total DVOA	13.3%	9	20.0%	29
Unadjusted VOA	18.4%	7	22.3%	30
Weighted Trend	16.8%	7	15.5%	27
Variance	10.6%	12	10.7%	12
Passing	26.0%	8	32.3%	30
Rushing	-2.9%	20	4.9%	23
First Down	1.4%	16	27.0%	32
Second Down	12.5%	11	13.2%	25
Third Down	42.0%	3	15.8%	25
Red Zone	14.6%	8	16.5%	26
Late and Close	8.1%	11	10.3%	28

Five-Year Performance

	2004	2003	2002	2001	2000
W-L	10-6	10-6	12-4	12-4	9-7
Pythagorean Wins	9.0	11.3	9.8	11.4	8.8
Estimated Wins	7.6	9.8	9.9	10.4	8.7
Total DVOA	-5.0%	18.9%	13.2%	13.8%	6.3%
Rank	21	5	10	8	16
Offense	13.3%	8.1%	2.8%	2.1%	0.4%
Rank	9	8	19	8	15
Defense	20.0%	-9.4%	-12.8%	-11.0%	-1.0%
Rank	29	9	4	11	17
Special Teams	1.7%	1.4%	-2.4%	0.7%	4.8%
Rank	13	12	24	11	8

Passing (min. 5 plays)

Player	DPAR	PAR	DVOA	Plys	NtYds	Avg	Cmpl	TD	Int
Brett Favre	83.5	96.4	22.0%	550	3996	7.3	64.1%	30	17
Craig Nall	17.0	16.7	98.2%	35	308	8.8	69.7%	4	0
Doug Pederson	-5.0	-5.1	-64.9%	23	120	5.2	47.8%	0	2

Rushing (min. 3 plays)

Player	DPAR	PAR	DVOA	Plys	Yds	Avg	TD	Fum	Suc
Ahman Green	12.3	14.2	-2.8%	259	1164	4.5	7	6	50%
Najeh Davenport	10.8	11.4	23.3%	71	359	5.1	2	0	51%
Tony Fisher	2.9	3.8	-3.5%	65	224	3.4	0	0	49%
Nick Luchey	-0.1	0.3	-17.9%	10	24	2.4	0	0	60%
Brett Favre	1.3	1.2	22.1%	6	46	7.7	0	0	—
Walter Williams	1.0	1.3	44.9%	6	42	7.0	0	0	33%
Antonio Chatman	-0.2	0.0	-36.1%	4	36	9.0	0	1	—
Donald Driver	-2.8	-2.9	-159.6%	3	4	1.3	0	1	—

Receiving (min. 5 plays)

Player	DPAR	PAR	DVOA	Plys	Ctch	Yds	Y/C	TD	CPct
WR									
Javon Walker	33.7	34.5	19.9%	144	89	1386	15.6	12	62%
Donald Driver	28.2	30.1	15.6%	138	84	1208	14.4	9	61%
Robert Ferguson	4.6	4.2	-0.5%	49	24	367	15.3	1	49%
Antonio Chatman	-0.9	0.3	-18.9%	45	22	246	11.2	1	49%
TE									
Bubba Franks	11.4	12.3	20.1%	50	34	361	10.6	7	68%
David Martin	0.7	1.7	-3.9%	12	5	88	17.6	0	42%
Ben Steele	-2.5	-2.3	-48.4%	11	4	42	10.5	0	36%
RB									
Ahman Green	-2.5	-0.8	-19.6%	51	40	275	6.9	1	78%
Tony Fisher	5.3	7.6	15.8%	44	38	277	7.3	2	86%
William Henderson	4.7	6.5	10.0%	40	34	239	7.0	3	85%

Defensive Players (min. 20 plays)

Player	Age	Plys	Stop	Dfts	AvYds	StpRt	Sack	Int	FR
Defensive Line									
Aaron Kampman	26	70	49	14	2.0	70%	4.5	0	1
Kabeer Gbaja-Biamila	28	46	35	19	0.4	76%	13.5	0	0
Cletidus Hunt	29	31	26	14	1.5	84%	2.0	0	0
Grady Jackson	32	25	21	6	1.6	84%	1.0	0	0
Corey Williams	25	22	12	3	2.9	55%	1.0	0	0
Linebackers									
Nick Barnett	24	126	66	25	5.0	52%	3.0	1	1
Na'il Diggs	27	80	40	14	4.6	50%	1.0	0	0
Hannibal Navies	28	49	20	6	5.4	41%	0.5	0	0
Paris Lenon	28	20	6	1	4.9	30%	0.0	0	0

Player	Age	Plys	Stop	Dfts	AvYds	StpRt	Sack	Int	FR
Secondary									
Al Harris	31	89	32	9	8.8	36%	0.0	1	0
Darren Sharper	30	79	24	9	9.6	30%	0.0	4	1
Mark Roman	28	70	24	9	9.5	34%	3.5	0	0
Ahmad Carroll	22	60	20	9	8.7	33%	2.0	1	1
Michael Hawthorne	28	42	16	9	8.4	38%	0.0	0	2
Bhawoh Jue	26	37	15	7	9.1	41%	0.0	1	0

Offensive Line

Year	Yards	AdjLineYd	Rank	Power	Rank	10+ Yds	Rank	Stuff	Rank	Sack	AdjSack%	Rank
2002	4.29	4.31	12	67%	17	17%	14	24%	16	27	4.6%	6
2003	5.30	4.55	2	78%	3	27%	3	20%	2	19	4.3%	5
2004	4.41	4.30	12	74%	2	20%	5	22%	8	14	1.8%	1

Year	LEnd	Rank	LTckl	Rank	MdGrd	Rank	RTckl	Rank	REnd	Rank
2002	4.07	14	4.58	6	4.21	18	4.56	9	4.30	11
2003	4.20	13	4.88	7	4.69	3	4.90	3	4.44	8
2004	3.54	24	4.47	13	4.34	13	5.03	4	4.18	11

The Packers had the deepest line in the league in 2004, but that will change. Guards Mike Wahle and Marco Rivera made a very good pair. Signing Chad Clifton to a big contract in 2003 pretty much assured that the Packers would have to cut costs elsewhere on their offensive line. If Clifton continues to develop, that will look like a smart move, but they might have overpaid for him a bit. The Packers' depth—six good offensive linemen—allowed them to line up in a run-oriented package that used tackle Kevin Barry as a tight end. That package could also draw the safeties close to the line of scrimmage and allow Favre to throw deep. With the loss of Wahle and Rivera, this formation will be less effective in 2005. The loss of center Mike Flanagan to an injury last year was difficult, although Grey Ruegamer filled in admirably. Still, Ahman Green didn't get a lot of easy yards running through huge holes last year, the way he had in 2003, and the absence of Flanagan was a big part of that. The Packers also have added Matt O'Dwyer and Adrian Klemm in free agency, and there's a chance that both could start, but neither player has been all that reliable. Combined, they have four starts in the last two years, and Klemm is the proper answer to the question, "Has Bill Belichick ever made a really bad draft pick?"

Defensive Front Seven

Year	Yards	AdjLineYd	Rank	Power	Rank	10+ Yds	Rank	Stuff	Rank	Sack	AdjSack%	Rank
2002	4.73	4.37	25	63%	8	21%	28	24%	17	44	7.8%	8
2003	4.09	3.89	12	71%	29	17%	15	24%	17	35	5.9%	20
2004	4.60	4.09	11	56%	9	26%	31	26%	8	40	7.3%	11

Year	LEnd	Rank	LTckl	Rank	MdGrd	Rank	RTckl	Rank	REnd	Rank
2002	4.46	24	5.16	31	4.13	14	4.38	21	4.32	21
2003	3.94	12	4.65	21	3.99	12	2.94	2	3.56	12
2004	4.17	13	3.57	4	4.50	27	3.62	3	3.61	13

As previously noted, the Packers got an inconsistent year from defensive end Kabeer Gbaja-Biamila, and would like to see him pair with Aaron Kampman to form a dynamic duo of defensive ends. Also noted was the speed and athleticism of outside linebacker Na'il Diggs, whose skill set balances nicely with tough middle linebacker Nick Barnett's. A defense needs more than two linebackers, however, and after Diggs and Barnett the Packers don't have any. Notice below that the Packers were the worst team in the league when it came to preventing successful pass plays to running backs, and that's a sign that the linebackers have problems in pass coverage as well as in pursuit and tackling on the edges of the field, where the backs are normally running after a screen or dump-off pass.

Defensive Secondary

Year	DVOA vs. #1 WR	Rank	DVOA vs. #2 WR	Rank	DVOA vs. Other WR	Rank	DVOA vs. TE	Rank	DVOA vs. RB	Rank
2002	-0.6%	15	-75.7%	1	4.8%	19	-13.9%	8	-29.1%	4
2003	-8.7%	13	4.8%	20	-33.8%	6	-36.9%	1	-14.0%	7
2004	25.4%	23	-15.3%	4	24.9%	29	54.1%	32	23.3%	32

This unit suffered through a tough year. Mike Sherman sent the best corner on the team, Mike McKenzie, to New Orleans because of a personality clash and a contract dispute. Veteran Al Harris is a physical corner, so the increased emphasis on illegal contact made the season tough on him. Darren Sharper was banged up for much of the year (and left for rival Minnesota in the off-season). The rest of the unit was inexperienced, and quarterbacks love picking on inexperienced cornerbacks. Rookie Ahmad Carroll, the team's first pick last year, struggled early but started making big plays as he acclimated to the pro game. The Packers occasionally used him as a blitzer off the edge, and that worked well. Third-round pick Joey Thomas out of Montana State didn't look ready for prime time. Carroll and Thomas both could turn out to be solid players, but the Packers' reliance on rookies caused them problems. Safeties Bhawoh Jue and Mark Roman both struggled, and the Packers hope new addition Arturo Freeman, who worked with Bates in Miami, can help the young guys adjust to Bates's coverage schemes. At 6'3", cornerback Michael Hawthorne should have been able to match up with the big receivers the Packers face, like the Lions' Roy Williams and the Vikings' Randy Moss, but Hawthorne was a disappointment and signed with St. Louis in the off-season. Rookie Nick Collins, as noted earlier, is not ready for full-time duty but will see as much action as he shows he can handle.

Special Teams

Year	DVOA	Rank	FG/XP	Rank	Net Punt	Rank	Punt Ret	Rank	Net Kick	Rank	Kick Ret	Rank
2002	-2.4%	23	3.0	8	4.7	13	-16.0	31	0.7	16	-5.7	27
2003	1.4%	12	9.4	8	-0.2	20	-8.4	28	-0.7	19	7.5	6
2004	1.7%	13	7.3	6	3.1	19	-4.0	14	-2.8	18	6.0	10

We would like to thank Green Bay for providing us with yet more evidence that supports our contention that teams should not take kickers and punters on the first day of the draft. The Packers used a third-round pick on punter B. J. Sander from Ohio State, and he couldn't even make the team. Bryan Barker, who beat him out last year during training camp, is a free agent, and Sander spent the summer in NFL Europe getting experience and eating schnitzel, so he may be back this year. Punt returns also have been a weakness for several years, including 2004, when Antonio Chatman cost the Packers −5.2 points' worth of field position. Their punt return number looks better than that because the guys up front did a good job of forcing opposing punters to rush and occasionally shank their punts. The one place Green Bay is consistently solid is field goal kicking, although the Packers should consider keeping a kickoff specialist on the roster. Even after adjusting for the Lambeau weather, kicker Ryan Longwell had below-average value on kickoffs four of the past five years.

Coaching Staff

Offensive coordinator Tom Rossley was one of the first people Mike Sherman brought on board when he became head coach in 2000. Rossley, who has coached in the CFL, USFL, and Arena League, has done a nice job of developing an offense that utilizes multiple formations and enough changes in personnel to keep opposing defenses off-guard. In that respect, he's similar to Cal coach Jeff Tedford, which means he should develop a good rapport with quarterback-in-waiting Aaron Rodgers. The defensive staff in Green Bay is undergoing a major overhaul with Jim Bates as the second new coordinator in two years. Defensive backs coach Kurt Schottenheimer was fired (he'll now coach the Rams' secondary) and defensive line coach Jethro Franklin left the Packers to become an assistant to Pete Carroll at USC.

Minnesota Vikings

The Vikings orchestrated perhaps the biggest move of the NFL's off-season when they traded Randy Moss to the Raiders for Napoleon Harris, the number seven pick overall, and the Raiders' seventh-round choice. On a team bogged down with questions—Can the owner find someone to buy his team? Can the coach find someone to buy his Super Bowl tickets? Will a number of off-season additions finally improve the defense?—the biggest question is whether the Vikings can win without Moss.

When the Vikings selected Moss with the 21st pick in the 1998 draft, the general consensus was that they had selected a player who had the talent to go number one overall but the attitude to go undrafted. Moss had his scholarship offer to Notre Dame rescinded and was kicked off the Florida State team by Bobby Bowden (not exactly a strict disciplinarian) before he settled for playing at Marshall, and he turned off several scouts with his attitude in predraft interviews.

Moss quickly became the best deep threat in football in his rookie year. He was universally praised as a draft steal, but it didn't take long before the criticisms started. Merril Hoge of ESPN pointed out that Moss frequently stood near the sidelines and rested on plays when the ball wasn't going to him. In November 2001, he made his infamous comment, "I play when I want to." Since then, there's been a steady decline in Moss's attitude and in the public and his teammates' acceptance of it. The last straw came in the Vikings' late-season game against the Redskins, when he walked off the field before the game ended, infuriating his teammates. The Vikings' front office decided that he had to go, and the natural choice for a trading partner was that refuge for troubled millionaires, Oakland. There's no question that the Vikings will miss Moss as a dangerous deep threat. But last year, injuries limited Moss's speed and he caught only 11 passes of 20 or more yards, by far the lowest of his career. (Nate Burleson actually topped Moss in that category, with 14 catches of 20 or more yards.) Where Moss really hurt opponents in 2005 was near the goal line: 13 of his 49 catches were touchdowns, by far the highest percentage of his career, and eight of those touchdowns came on passes thrown from the four-yard line or closer. It lends some credence to the quip attributed to Moss's former teammate, Cris Carter: "All he does is catch touchdowns."

VIKINGS PROSPECTUS

2004 Record: 8–8

DVOA Estimated Wins: 9.0 (11th)

Pythagorean Wins: 8.2 (13th)

DVOA: 1.5% total (13th), 4.8% weighted (13th)

Adjusted Offense: 28.9 points/game (28.0% DVOA, 3rd)

Adjusted Defense: 27.5 points/game (22.8% DVOA, 31st)

Adjusted Special Teams: −1.3 points/game (−3.7% DVOA, 28th)

Variance: 15.0% (24th)

2004: How far can this team go with such a talented but troubled offensive star?

2005: How far can this team go without such a talented but troubled offensive star?

2005 Projection

Leinart Land (0–4): 17%

Bad Team (5–6): 22%

Mediocre (7–8): 25%

Playoff Contender (9–10): 20%

Super Bowl Contender (11+): 17%

Projected Average Opponent: −5.5% DVOA (31st in NFL)

Before his injury, Moss was on track for another strong season and was clearly the Vikings' best receiver. After Moss got hurt in Week 7, Burleson picked up some, but not all, of the slack. The full-season stats make Burleson appear more valuable, but those stats are a bit misleading. Moss had 49 catches for 767 yards. Burleson had 68 for 1,006 yards. Burleson's DPAR of 35.0 and DVOA of 35.3% were better than Moss's 23.1 DPAR and 24.1% DVOA. Moss caught 57% of the passes thrown to him, significantly below the 67% that Burleson caught. But when we break the season into three parts, we see how much Burleson benefited from Moss drawing coverage away (see table 1).

Burleson didn't really play better when Moss pulled his hamstring, but he did have better numbers because Moss's absence made him Daunte Culpepper's primary target. His performance per pass didn't dramatically improve until Moss reentered the lineup in Week 12 and drew the attention of double teams and top cornerbacks away.

TABLE 1. RANDY MOSS AND NATE BURLESON BY WEEK, 2004

Week	DPAR	DVOA	Catch%
Burleson			
1–6	9.2	29.3%	61%
7–11	9.1	15.4%	67%
12–17	16.8	71.9%	71%
Moss*			
1–6	17.8	48.7%	67%
12–17	5.9	5.0%	50%

* One incomplete pass before injury in Week 7

TABLE 2. MINNESOTA RUSHING, WITH AND WITHOUT RANDY MOSS

	All Downs		First Down	
	Yd/Att	DVOA	Yd/Att	DVOA
With Moss	5.02	12.9%	4.78	0.5%
Without Moss	4.96	18.3%	5.74	25.7%

Burleson averaged 16.9 yards a catch for the first five games of 2004, 10.2 yards a catch during the five games Moss missed, and then 19.4 yards a catch in six regular-season games after Moss returned to the lineup. The same trend occurred in Minnesota's passing game as a whole, which averaged 8.4 yards per pass attempt over the first give games, 6.0 yards per pass attempt during the games Moss missed, and then 7.7 yards per pass attempt after he returned.

In 2002, Moss wasn't a great receiver, just a good one. The Raiders think they're getting the great Moss of 2003, but instead they might get the OK Moss of 2002, when he caught 106 balls but had career lows in yards per catch and touchdowns. Or they might get the injured Moss of 2004.

In any case, the team with one of the league's best offenses won't be as hobbled as most experts think by the disappearance of one player, even if that one player is the league's most talented wideout.

Now Burleson's number one; who's number two? The Vikings hope it's Troy Williamson, the speedster from South Carolina they drafted with the seventh pick. Williamson was the fastest receiver in the draft, but he played in the run-oriented offense of Lou Holtz and had only 1,754 yards in his three-year college career. Marcus Robinson's big season with the Bears in 1999 is a distant memory now, and at age 30 it's doubtful he'll approach those numbers again. Travis Taylor has had lousy numbers in Baltimore, but he's never had a quarterback like Culpepper throwing to him. Kelly Campbell is a small guy who has only 57 catches in his three-year career, but he's young and has shown great promise as a long-ball receiver. He averages better than 18 yards a catch, and he's the Vikings' primary kick returner to boot. Unfortunately, Moss wasn't the only receiver who had character issues. Campbell was arrested for possession of marijuana and a stolen handgun in February.

Many observers have said that the Vikings' ground game will suffer without Moss to keep opposing safeties

honest, but our numbers show that Minnesota's running numbers did not drop at all during the time Moss was out of the lineup (table 2). It's interesting that the Vikings averaged nearly a yard per carry more on first downs during the five games during which Moss was injured.

Even before the Moss trade, Mike Tice promised to run more in 2005, but it is unclear who will be doing it. Although Tice likes to use a running back-by-committee approach, his first choice has always been Onterrio Smith. In May, reports leaked that Smith—already a two-time loser in the league's drug policy—was caught in an airport with dried urine and a drug test cheating device called "The Whizzinator." A few days later, Smith was suspended for the season—but it's unclear why Tice favored him in the first place. Smith's DVOA was a pedestrian 2.1%, while the Vikings' next two backs, Mewelde Moore and Moe Williams, had much more impressive numbers. Moore's DVOA was 33.3%; Williams's was 42.7%. Both Moore and Williams were better in DPAR, even though Smith had 124 rushes, Moore had 65, and Williams had 30. The Vikings are among the best in the league at throwing passes to their running backs, and the speedy Michael Bennett, who can't seem to stay healthy, might be the best receiver of the bunch. Since Smith is also adept at catching passes out of the backfield, Bennett may have the best chance to take the top spot on the depth chart. The Vikings also have rookie Ciatrick Fason from the University of Florida, added in the fourth round of the draft.

Getting Harris in the Moss trade was the first sign that the Vikings had finally decided to upgrade their defense. At 6'2" and 255 pounds, Harris is big and athletic, having played both defensive end and linebacker (not to mention guard and forward on the basketball team) at Northwestern. Al Davis, who usually doesn't like drafting linebackers early, fell in love with Harris while scouting him, and in 2002 made him only the second linebacker in Raiders history to be taken in the first round.

But Harris never quite produced as expected. When the Raiders switched from a 4-3 to a 3-4 last season, defensive coordinator Rob Ryan said he had big plans to use Harris in a variety of defensive sets, and then Harris had the worst season out of his three in Oakland. He will fit better in the standard 4-3 favored by the Vikings' Ted Cottrell, and is under contract for two more years at reasonable salary cap numbers.

After Harris, the next step was to fix the secondary, so the Vikings hit the free-agent market. New cornerback Fred Smoot isn't a great tackler, but he's very good in coverage. Adding Darren Sharper as a free agent from the Packers also helps, and the secondary has two good holdovers in safety Corey Chavous, one of the smartest players in the league, and Antoine Winfield, who signed a big contract to become the Vikings' shutdown corner but had mixed results. Although Winfield goes 100 percent on every play (unlike a certain former teammate), he does sometimes give up catches, especially to bigger receivers. Still, he and Smoot will form one of the best cornerback tandems in the league.

With the linebacking corps and secondary bolstered, what about defensive line? That was the one place the Vikings already had a Pro Bowler, tackle Kevin Williams. Williams is extremely disruptive as a pass rusher, not only for the sacks he records himself but because his great first step draws extra blocking help from opposing running backs, opening up blitzing lanes for one of the Vikings' linebackers. Williams played particularly well in three games against the Packers' Pro Bowl guard, Marco Rivera.

Williams has been so successful that the Vikings went into the off-season looking to fill the other three spots on the defensive line with men named Williams. Moe Williams is still needed as a third-down back, so the Vikings instead signed free agent tackle Pat Williams away from the Bills. Williams is a big body (listed as 317 pounds, but he looks heavier) who stops running backs when they come directly at him but doesn't do much to stop outside runs or rush the passer. Since Pat Williams and Cottrell spent four years together in Buffalo, he should easily slot right into Cottrell's read-and-reach scheme for defensive linemen. But the downside of experience is age, and three years and $13 million is a lot to give someone who turns 33 in October.

Having added a slow, fat veteran, the Vikings next had to add a quick, lanky rookie. Unfortunately, the draft was devoid of defensive linemen named Williams, so the Vikings settled for Wisconsin's star pass-rushing defensive end Erasmus James, who was still available as the eighteenth pick in the draft.

Williams, Smoot, Sharper, Harris, James: That's a lot of new defensive blood to add in one off-season. Can the improvements make up for the loss of Moss? The Vikings were an average team last year, and another year of average probably won't be good enough for a return to the playoffs. That probably costs Mike Tice his job. Good thing he already has another source of income.

Michael David Smith

Research: What Happened to the Vikings in the Red Zone?

Between the 20-yard lines, the Vikings had one of the most dangerous offenses in the league. They finished sixth in the NFL in offensive points, second in net passing yards. The Vikings could beat you with Randy Moss or Nate Burleson, with Daunte Culpepper's arm or his legs, and with a four-headed backfield that averaged 4.7 yards per rush, second in the league.

But when the Vikings hit the red zone, it was like a mosquito hitting a windshield:

- Week 2 vs. Eagles: Five trips to the red zone result in one touchdown and two field goals. Penalties, incomplete passes, and a Culpepper fumble on the goal line contribute to a Vikings loss.

- Week 5 vs. Saints: The Vikings win a close game that was made closer by two red zone turnovers. Culpepper's pass to Marcus Robinson from the 18-yard line is intercepted in the end zone by Ashley Ambrose on the game's first drive. Later, a botched snap leads to a fumble and a long return by the Saints defense.

- Week 13 vs. Bears: Three red zone trips, one score: Culpepper is intercepted by Brian Urlacher at the three-yard line on one play and is sacked out of Morten Andersen's range (all the way back to the 20-yard line) on another. The Bears win 24–14.

- Week 14 vs. Seahawks: In a 27–23 loss, two drives end right smack on the 20-yard line (and so don't officially reach the "red zone," which starts inside the 20). One drive ends when a trick play goes awry: Randy Moss's pass to Nate Burleson is intercepted in the red zone.

- Week 17 vs. Redskins: The Vikings make one trip into the red zone. They execute six plays from inside the eight-yard line before settling for a short field goal. The Redskins would win by three.

These weren't the only games to feature red zone ineptitude. In Week 3 against the Bears, the Vikings botched a fake field goal from the 12-yard line and turned the ball over on a Kelly Campbell end-around from the 13-yard line. They settled for 25-yard and 21-yard field goals against the Packers and Colts, only to lose each game by three points. Another failed fake field goal from the 12-yard line prevented the Vikings from narrowing a 21–7 gap against the Eagles in the playoffs.

A casual glance at the stat sheet doesn't suggest that the Vikings were a bad red zone team in 2004. Culpepper threw 26 TD passes from inside the 20-yard line. The team as a whole scored 33 red zone touchdowns, fifth in the league behind the Chargers (44), Colts (42), Chiefs (40), and Patriots (37). They were 14th in points per red zone appearance with 4.66 points per red zone drive.

The conventional "red zone percentage" that shows up on NFL telecasts is a binary statistic with just two possibilities: touchdown and not touchdown. But that's just a small part of the story. Getting stopped at the 18-yard line is worse than getting stopped at the two-yard line (especially when your kicker has an AARP card). Turning the ball over is worse than just about anything else. The Vikings scored frequently, but they also cost themselves points by turning the ball over and frequently getting knocked out of field goal range.

DVOA gives a better appraisal of the Vikings' efforts. The Vikings offense finished third in the NFL with a DVOA of 28.0%, but in the red zone they had a −7.9% DVOA, 20th in the NFL. They weren't awful in the red zone, but they were far worse there than they were elsewhere on the field.

The Vikings reached the red zone 58 times last year; only the Steelers and Chiefs were there more frequently. But the Vikings were held without a score 12 times. Only nine teams were stopped a higher percentage of the time. With six red zone turnovers, the Vikings were tied for the third highest total in the league (the Bears had eight, the Saints seven). The Vikings turned the ball over on 10.3% of their journeys inside the 20, worse than 23 other teams.

And as the game summaries above show, the failures made a huge difference in the win-loss column. Early touchdowns would have completely changed the strategy of their Week 2 game against Philadelphia. The losses to the Colts and Packers in Weeks 13 and 14 could easily have been averted. Replace a short field goal with a touchdown against the Colts, Packers, or Redskins, and the Vikings would have won one or two of those games. They could have had home field throughout the playoffs with wins over the Eagles, Seahawks, and Packers.

So what was going on inside the red zone to make the Vikings so inept? Careful review of their play calling reveals some interesting trends:

1. The Vikings got cute inside the 20. Mike Tice isn't very cute, but he turns into Meg Ryan when he's calling plays near the goal line. Kelly Campbell end-arounds. Randy Moss option passes. Fake field goals. Daunte Culpepper draws. On fourth and one at the eight-yard line against the Lions in Week 11, Tice called a play-action pass to Campbell, fooling no one. Opponents routinely pounced on all of these gadget plays, many of which resulted in turnovers.

2. Moss was underused. Randy Moss was targeted for 21 passes inside the red zone. That's a high number, but Nate Burleson was actually the target of more

throws (22) than Moss. Granted, 11 of those passes were thrown to Burleson during the five games when Moss was either inactive or limping around. But Marcus Robinson (15) and Jermaine Wiggins (13) were also very frequent targets. Diversity is good, and Burleson was effective (six TD catches on ten goal-to-go passes), but sometimes you just have to go with the bread and butter. In the Week 13 loss to the Bears, Moss was targeted just once in the red zone; meanwhile, passes for Onterrio Smith and Moe Williams were intercepted. Moss caught a touchdown pass in Week 14 against the Seahawks, but it was one of only two red zone passes thrown to him, the same amount of passes Wiggins earned, while a Culpepper pass from the 20-yard line to Marcus Robinson was intercepted. When the Vikings failed to score on eight plays inside the eight-yard line against the Redskins in Week 17, Moss's lone contribution was an offsides penalty, as Burleson and Wiggins were the intended receivers for two Culpepper passes.

Perhaps Moss's diminished red zone role reflected the team's eroding trust in him. If that's the case, they should have just run the ball more often. That leads to the next point:

3. The "handoff" wasn't in the playbook. The Vikings ran the ball 64 times in the red zone, a very low total for their number of appearances inside the 20. But 17 of those runs were by Culpepper, leaving just 47 carries by non-quarterbacks in 58 drives that reached the red zone, by far the lowest percentage in the league (table 3). The NFL average is 1.32 rushes per red zone drive by non-QBs; the Vikings were far below that.

The Vikings use Moe Williams as their short-yardage runner; Williams had two short touchdown runs but also had several two-yard runs from the six-yard line among his nine goal-to-go carries. On first and ten from the 15-yard line, Williams or Onterrio Smith might get a carry, but

TABLE 3. RUSHES BY NON-QBs PER RED ZONE DRIVE

Team	Drives Reaching Red Zone	Non-QB Rushes	Rushes/ Drive
Vikings	64	47	.81
Eagles	47	42	.89
Dolphins	40	36	.95
Panthers	52	52	1.00
Lions	43	44	1.02

if they didn't gain eight yards on that attempt they would never see the ball again. On third and one or fourth and one, Tice would throw rather than giving Williams or Smith a chance to plow into the line. And the "Culpepper draw" was old news long before it failed in Week 2: Teams were ready for Culpepper to take off in goal-to-goal situations, and he only managed to score two one-yard TDs despite 17 red zone carries, seven of them in goal-to-go situations.

So the formula for fixing the red zone offense is simple: (1) Stop the shenanigans and rip the triple-reverses out of the playbook. (2) Moss is gone, but pick a go-to guy like Burleson and get him the ball when it counts. (3) Run the darn ball with Williams, Smith, or Ciatrick Fason, not Culpepper or Campbell. Other adjustments would help: A younger kicker might quell the urge to fake 38-yard field goal attempts; the return of Jim Kleinsasser gives Tice both a short-yardage blocker and an extra receiver.

Red zone offense should be simple: Win the line of scrimmage battle, pound the ball, set up play action or single coverage situations. Mike Tice and the Vikings must stop turning it into calculus.

Mike Tanier

Vikings 2004 Stats by Week

Wk	vs.	W-L	PF	PA	YDF	YDA	TO	DVOA Total	Off	Def	ST
1	DAL	W	35	17	415	422	+2	15.9%	61.9%	36.0%	-10.0%
2	@PHI	L	16	27	410	317	-1	-39.7%	18.1%	45.1%	-12.6%
3	CHI	W	27	22	443	385	-1	-14.4%	25.9%	41.5%	1.2%
4	BYE										
5	@HOU	W	34	28	510	410	0	-5.7%	46.1%	48.4%	-3.4%
6	@NO	W	38	31	605	385	-2	0.5%	33.4%	29.2%	-3.8%
7	TEN	W	20	3	243	313	+4	92.5%	30.9%	-62.5%	-1.0%
8	NYG	L	13	34	324	283	-3	-55.5%	-16.9%	16.8%	-21.8%
9	@IND	L	28	31	292	408	-1	17.3%	37.1%	44.2%	24.4%
10	@GB	L	31	34	416	442	+1	-9.0%	34.5%	35.2%	-8.2%
11	DET	W	22	19	319	213	0	-5.2%	12.5%	-8.0%	-25.7%
12	JAC	W	27	16	330	379	0	26.4%	18.3%	-3.1%	5.0%
13	@CHI	L	14	24	391	318	-3	-71.1%	-6.5%	51.2%	-13.5%
14	SEA	L	23	27	374	455	0	13.0%	21.2%	18.3%	10.1%
15	@DET	W	28	27	461	463	+2	30.1%	36.3%	9.2%	3.0%
16	GB	L	31	34	416	452	+1	57.0%	73.2%	18.3%	2.1%
17	@WAS	L	18	21	320	318	+2	6.9%	45.2%	32.8%	-5.4%
18	@GB	W	31	17	384	306	+4	82.3%	24.6%	-62.4%	-4.7%
19	@PHI	L	14	27	385	395	+3	-0.6%	6.2%	6.6%	-0.2%

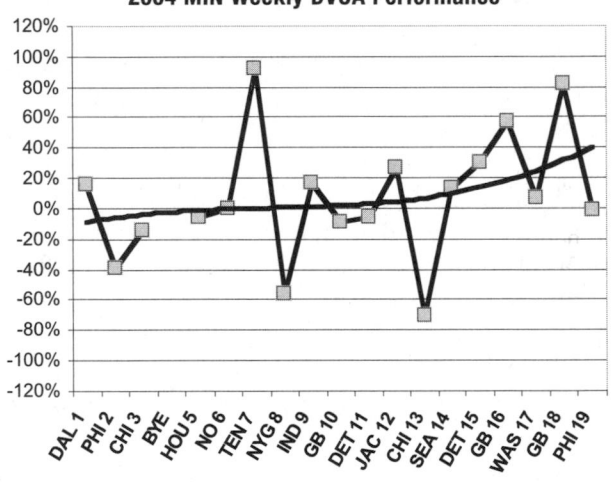

2004 MIN Weekly DVOA Performance

Trends and Splits

	Offense	Rank	Defense	Rank
Total DVOA	28.0%	3	22.8%	31
Unadjusted VOA	31.2%	2	23.6%	31
Weighted Trend	25.9%	3	18.7%	30
Variance	5.1%	30	8.3%	19
Passing	36.9%	3	30.7%	29
Rushing	14.6%	4	13.1%	31
First Down	10.6%	8	10.3%	24
Second Down	22.1%	4	29.1%	32
Third Down	80.6%	1	40.6%	32
Red Zone	-7.9%	20	-2.5%	16
Late and Close	33.7%	3	7.5%	25

Five-Year Performance

	2004	2003	2002	2001	2000
W-L	8-8	9-7	6-10	5-11	11-5
Pythagorean Wins	8.2	9.5	6.8	5.3	8.6
Estimated Wins	9.0	9.2	4.7	3.8	8.7
Total DVOA	1.5%	12.7%	-24.4%	-33.7%	-5.4%
Rank	13	10	27	31	21
Offense	28.0%	15.7%	4.8%	-7.1%	20.4%
Rank	3	4	16	17	3
Defense	22.8%	-2.7%	22.2%	23.5%	26.7%
Rank	31	15	31	31	31
Special Teams	-3.7%	-5.6%	-7.0%	-3.0%	0.8%
Rank	28	31	30	25	16

Passing (min. 5 plays)

Player	DPAR	PAR	DVOA	Plys	NtYds	Avg	Cmpl	TD	Int
Daunte Culpepper	136.4	144.4	38.9%	595	4446	7.5	69.2%	39	11

Rushing (min. 3 plays)

Player	DPAR	PAR	DVOA	Plys	Yds	Avg	TD	Fum	Suc
Onterrio Smith	8.4	8.5	2.4%	124	544	4.4	2	2	45%
Michael Bennett	0.7	0.0	-10.5%	70	276	3.9	1	1	41%
Daunte Culpepper	11.7	11.3	7.3%	70	418	6.0	2	2	—
Mewelde Moore	12.3	15.0	33.3%	65	379	5.8	0	0	57%
Moe Williams	8.8	8.9	42.8%	30	161	5.4	3	0	70%
Nate Burleson	4.1	4.0	87.9%	6	49	8.2	0	0	—
Kelly Campbell	-2.3	-2.2	-141.3%	3	15	5.0	0	1	—

Receiving (min. 5 plays)

Player	DPAR	PAR	DVOA	Plys	Ctch	Yds	Y/C	TD	CPct
WR									
Nate Burleson	35.0	34.7	35.3%	102	68	1006	14.8	9	67%
Randy Moss	23.1	21.5	24.1%	86	49	769	15.7	13	57%
Marcus Robinson	14.6	15.1	11.9%	79	47	657	14.0	8	59%
Kelly Campbell	9.0	8.9	26.6%	32	19	364	19.2	1	59%
TE									
Jermaine Wiggins	16.0	16.5	14.9%	92	71	706	9.9	4	77%
Sean Berton	2.1	2.2	15.1%	11	9	78	8.7	0	82%
Richard Owens	2.6	2.4	38.3%	8	—	69	—	0	100%
RB									
Onterrio Smith	13.5	15.8	43.2%	45	36	394	10.9	2	80%
Mewelde Moore	2.8	3.3	6.2%	33	27	238	8.8	0	82%
Moe Williams	6.9	8.1	44.9%	27	21	233	11.1	1	78%
Michael Bennett	7.3	9.0	54.3%	23	21	207	9.9	1	91%

Defensive Players (min. 20 plays)

Player	Age	Plys	Stop	Dfts	AvYds	StpRt	Sack	Int	FR
Defensive Line									
Kevin Williams	25	80	55	27	1.0	69%	12.0	1	3
Kenny Mixon	30	47	26	3	2.7	55%	2.5	0	0
Spencer Johnson	24	39	26	4	2.4	67%	1.0	0	0
Kenechi Udeze	22	37	27	9	0.8	73%	5.0	0	1
Lance Johnstone	32	31	20	14	0.7	65%	11.0	0	0
Darrion Scott	24	25	18	5	3.2	72%	0.0	0	2
Chris Hovan	27	22	14	5	2.7	64%	1.5	0	1
Steve Martin	31	21	14	2	1.8	67%	0.5	0	0
Linebackers									
E. J. Henderson	25	97	49	14	4.3	51%	1.0	0	0
Chris Claiborne	27	63	30	7	5.1	48%	1.0	1	1
Dontarrious Thomas	25	51	16	9	6.6	31%	0.5	0	1
Keith Newman	28	50	25	7	3.7	50%	3.0	0	0

Player	Age	Plys	Stop	Dfts	AvYds	StpRt	Sack	Int	FR
Secondary									
Antoine Winfield	28	89	34	19	7.1	38%	0.0	3	1
Brian Williams	26	85	28	13	8.3	33%	0.0	2	0
Brian Russell	27	85	20	12	12.2	24%	0.0	1	1
Corey Chavous	29	85	19	5	11.4	22%	0.0	1	0
Terrance Shaw	32	37	6	3	10.5	16%	0.0	1	0
Willie Offord	27	20	6	3	11.2	30%	0.0	0	0

Offensive Line

Year	Yards	AdjLineYd	Rank	Power	Rank	10+ Yds	Rank	Stuff	Rank	Sack	AdjSack%	Rank
2002	5.12	4.59	2	77%	4	25%	1	18%	2	52	8.4%	27
2003	4.65	4.60	1	86%	1	17%	11	20%	3	43	8.1%	30
2004	4.70	4.46	7	71%	6	18%	10	23%	12	45	7.4%	20

Year	LEnd	Rank	LTckl	Rank	MdGrd	Rank	RTckl	Rank	REnd	Rank
2002	4.59	10	4.43	10	4.33	12	4.61	8	5.64	1
2003	5.03	2	4.30	14	4.82	2	4.00	21	4.06	16
2004	3.79	22	5.06	3	4.56	7	4.76	6	3.81	17

The mark of a good offensive line is that any running back carrying the ball behind it can gain yardage. Denver gets all the press because that yardage tends to be gained by one feature running back at a time, but Minnesota's track record is just as strong when you look at the running game as a whole. The Vikings do give up sacks, but that's an effect mostly of Culpepper's efforts to make things happen when the play breaks down rather than throwing the ball away. Left tackle Bryant McKinnie, in his third year, is still too inconsistent, and he was burned a few times by Dwight Freeney on Monday Night Football, but for the most part he has become the solid tackle the Vikings thought he'd be when they drafted him. After just two games, the Vikings lost right tackle Mike Rosenthal, one of their best blockers, but rookies Adam Goldberg and Nat Dorsey filled in for him nicely. Three-time Pro Bowl center Matt Birk anchors the middle of the line along with guard Chris Liwienski, but the Vikings have probably said goodbye to starter David Dixon after 11 years. (Dixon still

(continued next page)

Offensive Line (*continued*)

wants to play, but only for the Vikings, so he may show up as the backup plan if this unit suffers injuries.) Liwienski will switch from left guard to right, with Goldberg likely taking the left guard spot. If Birk is completely recovered from a hernia, the Vikings should once again have a solid offensive line, and one that has depth thanks to the experience Goldberg and Dorsey gained in 2004 as well as the selection of Ole Miss tackle Marcus Johnson in the second round of the draft.

Defensive Front Seven

Year	Yards	AdjLineYd	Rank	Power	Rank	10+ Yds	Rank	Stuff	Rank	Sack	AdjSack%	Rank
2002	3.87	3.49	1	55%	5	23%	32	34%	1	27	5.4%	26
2003	4.54	3.86	9	69%	26	26%	31	32%	1	34	6.9%	8
2004	4.54	4.69	32	74%	29	16%	16	19%	32	39	7.1%	14

Year	LEnd	Rank	LTckl	Rank	MdGrd	Rank	RTckl	Rank	REnd	Rank
2002	3.87	12	5.10	30	3.22	1	3.57	4	2.73	6
2003	4.57	24	3.68	9	3.68	4	4.57	26	3.69	14
2004	4.66	25	5.28	31	4.87	32	4.45	25	3.51	10

Building up the front seven has been a major priority for the Vikings. In each of the last three years, they've picked a defensive lineman in the first round, and in three of the last four years they've taken a linebacker in the second round. The first-round pick of 2003, defensive lineman Kevin Williams, made the Pro Bowl in just his second season. But while 2004 first-round pick Kenechi Udeze has shown promise as a pass rusher, he's looked lousy against the run. The three linebackers, Dontarrious Thomas, Raonall Smith, and E. J. Henderson, have disappointed. The combined Stop Rate of Minnesota linebackers was just 46%, below every team in the league except New Orleans and Cincinnati. Shoring up the run defense is a major need, and the Vikings took more steps toward doing it this year by adding Napoleon Harris and Pat Williams.

Defensive Secondary

Year	DVOA vs. #1 WR	Rank	DVOA vs. #2 WR	Rank	DVOA vs. Other WR	Rank	DVOA vs. TE	Rank	DVOA vs. RB	Rank
2002	24.8%	29	19.6%	21	39.4%	31	25.7%	28	19.8%	27
2003	-10.7%	11	-38.2%	4	25.9%	32	7.4%	19	5.6%	20
2004	36.0%	30	18.9%	25	24.0%	28	48.4%	31	0.4%	25

Safety Corey Chavous might be the smartest player in the league; he always seems to know where the offense is going. Unfortunately, new defensive coordinator Ted Cottrell seems to like his safeties to hang back and wait to see what happens. Not surprisingly, Cottrell also uses the prevent defense too much. The best defensive player was cornerback Antoine Winfield, who made one big play after another, in particular a late interception that sealed the Vikings' victory over the Lions. Free agent pickup Fred Smoot will make an immediate difference—many people seem to consider him overrated, but Washington's pass defense improved despite the loss of Champ Bailey, so Smoot must be doing something right. Ex-Packer Darren Sharper completes the starting secondary, and third-round pick Dustin Fox and last year's starter Brian Williams will come in on nickel situations.

Special Teams

Year	DVOA	Rank	FG/XP	Rank	Net Punt	Rank	Punt Ret	Rank	Net Kick	Rank	Kick Ret	Rank
2002	-7.0%	30	-5.9	25	-6.6	23	3.5	12	-14.0	30	-15.9	32
2003	-5.6%	31	-5.9	26	-15.8	31	-5.4	22	1.6	16	-5.7	24
2004	-3.7%	28	-1.9	21	3.3	18	-0.9	9	-14.4	31	-6.7	28

Frankly, this is a complete mess, even though special teams coach Rusty Tillman has a good reputation in the NFL (he was a linebacker for eight years with the Redskins, has spent 20 years as an assistant, and was head coach of the XFL's New York/New Jersey Hitmen). The Vikings go through kickers the way Spinal Tap went through drummers. Morten Andersen simply doesn't have the leg strength to kick long field goals any more. Jose Cortez and Aaron Elling weren't so bad on kickoffs—based just on the kick distance, they were worth 1.2 and 0.7 points above average, respectively—but the kick coverage was atrocious, especially if the opposing returner happened to be wearing green and gold. The Vikings signed Paul Edinger after Chicago waived him, but he's coming off two poor years. Neither Kelly Campbell nor Mwelde Moore was that great overall on kick returns, Nate Burleson was better on punt returns, and Australian punter Darren Bennett remains Australian. Rushen Jones played well in punt coverage and was a rare bright spot on special teams.

Coaching Staff

Red McCombs wants to save money everywhere, and the coaching staff is a big part of that strategy. Mike Tice was the lowest-paid head coach in the league, and the NFL Coaches Association released a report saying that the Vikings' assistants made a combined $2,852,800—lowest in the league, only about 80% of the league-wide average of about $3.5 million, and much less than the Redskins, whose assistants got more than $5 million of Dan Snyder's money.

Losing offensive coordinator Scott Linehan was tough, but former offensive line coach Steve Loney was a good choice to replace him. Loney has done solid work with the Vikings' line the past three seasons. He's a disciple of Joe Bugel, the Redskins' offensive line guru, so it's likely that the Vikings will continue to run a Redskins-style offense with lots of counters and an emphasis on blocking tight ends and H-backs. Ted Cottrell is building a defense similar to the one he's had in his other stops in the NFL. The rest of the Vikings' defensive staff arrived before Cottrell, which raises questions about whether they're all on the same page. Although Cottrell got the added title of assistant head coach in the off-season, secondary coach Chuck Knox Jr. got the added (and unusual) title of coverage coordinator, which could raise questions of who has final say on what goes on in the Vikings' secondary.

New Orleans Saints

After 13 weeks of the 2004 season, the New Orleans Saints were 4–8 and rumors were spreading that head coach Jim Haslett would be canned at the end of the year. But with their season seemingly over, the Saints dramatically turned things around. A four-game win streak left the Saints on the threshold of the playoffs, only to have Seattle and St. Louis shut the door in their face by winning their final games. That four-game streak saved Haslett's job and raised expectations for the Saints in 2005. But in reality, it was the worst possible thing that could have happened to this terminally boring franchise.

In his first season after taking over for the disastrous Mike Ditka: The Sequel, Haslett turned a 3–13 team into a 10–6 division champion. With five Pro Bowlers and a promising young quarterback named Aaron Brooks, the Saints seemed ready to put together a string of winning seasons. Instead, the Saints have become a monument to mediocrity. Year after year, the team runs the same style of offense and defense with mostly the same personnel in an attempt to replicate that one flash of glory. The result: four straight seasons of seven to nine wins and no playoff appearances.

There is no player on the New Orleans offense or defense that could be considered among the ten best at his position in the NFL, with one exception: Joe Horn. And Horn, though unquestionably talented, is a 33-year-old receiver coming off an unrepeatable career year.

The only exception to the general rule of mediocrity in New Orleans has been special teams. The Saints were the only team to gain positive value from all five aspects of special teams in 2004; only Buffalo ranked higher in overall special teams play. But when a team's only above-average unit is special teams, you have a problem. It's like having a Big Mac that's got nothing in the bun but special sauce.

The Saints constantly believe that success is just over the next hill because they don't understand that individual player statistics do not equal team success. Many NFL observers make the same mistake. The final ESPN.com power ratings of 2004 said of New Orleans: "With players like Deuce McAllister, Joe Horn, and Aaron Brooks, the Saints should compete for the NFC South title next year." Yes, if you're talking about the title of NFC South fantasy football champion.

Brooks has now had four and a half years as the starting quarterback. Each year he throws for a lot of touch-

downs, and each year he ranks in the top ten in passing yardage. Each year, with the exception of 2003, he has also had a subpar completion percentage and at least 15 interceptions. He's not a bad quarterback, but, because of his superficially impressive numbers, the Saints think they have a star quarterback instead of what they really have: an average quarterback. The Saints chose Brooks over Marc Bulger and then again over Jake Delhomme, and both are better quarterbacks than the man they used to back up.

What about New Orleans' other erstwhile star, McAllister? Since he became the starter in 2002, McAllister's DVOA rank among running backs has gone from 20th to 27th to 36th. Every year, he ranks among the worst backs in the league according to our success rate metric because he's always getting stuffed at the line. His career average of 4.4 yards per carry isn't bad, but it is padded by a few spectacular long runs each season. No running back in the NFC runs for four to six yards less often. McAllister is the

SAINTS PROSPECTUS

2004 Record: 8–8

DVOA Estimated Wins: 6.9 (22nd)

Pythagorean Wins: 6.6 (23rd)

DVOA: −10.6% total (23rd), −5.9% weighted (20th)

Adjusted Offense: 20.4 points/game (−4.2% DVOA, 20th)

Adjusted Defense: 25.2 points/game (14.1% DVOA, 26th)

Adjusted Special Teams: +2.7 points/game (7.7% DVOA, 2nd)

Variance: 7.5% (32nd)

2004: December's Quixotic run at a playoff spot keeps this team from a much-needed cleansing.

2005: No truth to rumor that fleur-de-lis helmet logo will be replaced with hamster wheel.

2005 Projection

Leinart Land (0–4): 14%

Bad Team (5–6): 20%

Mediocre (7–8): 25%

Playoff Contender (9–10): 22%

Super Bowl Contender (11+): 19%

Projected Average Opponent: −0.8% DVOA (17th in NFL)

very definition of a boom-and-bust running back, which means lots of yards and touchdowns for your fantasy team and lots of New Orleans drives that stall out on third and eight. He did gain value from his durability in his first two seasons, but even that took a hit last year when an injury cost him two games and most of a third.

Offensively, the Saints are the anti-Patriots. New England is celebrated for being more than the sum of its parts, while New Orleans is definitely less than the sum of theirs. The Patriots win Super Bowls even though no player is particularly known for putting up big numbers. The Saints put up big numbers and go 8–8. But while the offensive stars of this team are severely overrated, they aren't the real problem.

No, the real reason why New Orleans hasn't been able to dig out of the 8–8 hole is the defense. Despite taking defensive linemen in the first round of the draft in 2002, 2003, and 2004, the Saints have finished in the bottom half of the league for three straight years in both our defensive line statistics, Adjusted Line Yards and Adjusted Sack Rate. For the last two seasons, New Orleans has been the worst team in the league at stopping opposing runners on what we call "power running situations" (third or fourth down and one to two yards to go) and the worst team in the league overall when it comes to stuffing opposing runners at the line.

Even worse for most of last season was the secondary. According to DVOA, the Saints haven't been above average in pass defense since 2000, but they were never the worst pass defense in the NFC until the first half of 2004. However, the New Orleans secondary improved in the last few weeks after Mike McKenzie and Fakhir Brown replaced Ashley Ambrose and Fred Thomas as the starting corners. The Saints had an above-average defensive DVOA in each of their final four wins, and their weighted defensive DVOA—which gives more influence to performance later in the season—ranked six places higher than their full-season defensive DVOA.

This turnaround by the secondary is the only real area of improvement for New Orleans in 2005. For the past four years, even when the pass defense wasn't very good overall, it was better than league average against passing in the red zone. The improvement should continue because of the one major roster change the Saints made in free agency, waiving safety Tebucky Jones and replacing him with former Buccaneer Dwight Smith, considered to have much better coverage skills. But other than Smith, the Saints made very few roster changes this off-season. In fact, they've made very few roster changes over the past couple of off-seasons, and that's the rub. The Saints keep thinking that they are a piece or two away. And they'd be right, if the pieces were Joe Montana and Lawrence Taylor. Since those guys are unavailable, the Saints keep running the

same veterans out there, hoping that 2000 will happen again. With a couple of exceptions, primarily defensive end Charles Grant, the few young players added to the mix have yet to develop.

In the NFL, where something unexpected happens every year, it is certainly possible for the Saints to make a sudden leap forward in 2005. If Aaron Brooks builds on 2003 instead of repeating 2004, if Joe Horn forgets how old he is, if the improvement in the secondary continues, if a couple of the young defensive linemen suddenly mature. If, if, if. It's like one of those courtroom scenes on *Law and Order,* where the defense attorney asks the expert witness, "Yes, but isn't it *possible* that Mr. Smith was actually killed by my client's separated-at-birth identical twin who just happens to own one of the other eight suits of this color and material sold in New York last year?"

As we went to press, our current mean DVOA projections put New Orleans 16th in offense and 18th in defense for 2005. The mean projection for New Orleans wins is 7.998. That means another season of the stagnation that keeps the Saints away from a Miami-like meltdown but also keeps them away from a Pittsburgh-like renaissance. This franchise desperately needs to blow up the roster and start over.

Aaron Schatz

Research: The Garbled Language of Fumbles

During the four-game win streak that ended their 2004 season, the Saints recovered eight fumbles from opposing offenses. Meanwhile, the Saints' offense fumbled the ball away only once. You know what they say: If you win the turnover battle, you usually win the game. Surely this favorable turnover ratio signals that the Saints will improve in 2005.

Actually, no. In reality, the fact that overall the 2004 Saints recovered twice as many opposition fumbles as they lost themselves is a very good indicator that the Saints will probably be worse in 2005.

Listen up: The New Orleans defense led the NFL in fumble recoveries in 2004, causing 24 fumbles and recovering 18 of them. Meanwhile, on offense, the Saints lost only nine fumbles, below the league average. It was a remarkable step forward for an offense that had led the league with 19 lost fumbles the year before. Quarterback Aaron Brooks lost 11 fumbles on his own in 2003, more than the entire offense put together in 2004. So why isn't this newfound ability to hold on to the ball a good thing?

The answer is that these numbers don't represent a newfound ability to hold onto the ball, or to strip the ball from opponents.

Once that ball comes out of an offensive player's hands and hits the ground, the question of which team will come up with the football is virtually random, dependent on, among other factors, how the ball bounces, who jumps on it first, who can grab it from another guy under the pile by gouging his private parts, how long it takes the refs to get over and clear the pile, who is pointing more strenuously as the refs are making their decision—none of which is an actual football skill.

Brooks himself provides an almost comical example of this. Over the past four seasons, Brooks has fumbled the ball 13, 11, 14, and 13 times. But the official count of his fumbles, according to the league—in other words, the fumbles recovered by the defense—are 2, 5, 11, and 2. The quarterback who lost only two fumbles in 2004 didn't suddenly learn to hold on to the ball. He's the same guy who lost 11 fumbles the year before, with much better luck.

Overall, half of all fumbles are recovered by the defense (53% in 2004, 50% in 2003). Whether, on a particular play, a fumble will be recovered by the offense correlates only with the kind of play on which the fumble occurs. Offenses recover three out of every four aborted snap fumbles, about half of all fumbles on sacks, and roughly 35% of all fumbles on running plays. The chances of the offense recovering a fumble on a reception change with the length of the reception; the longer the yardage, the more likely a fumble is going to be lost to the defense because the receiver is running out there all alone without a bunch of teammates around who can lunge for that loose ball.

Table 1 gives the five teams with the best and worst record when it came to recovering their own offensive fumbles in 2003. Table 2 is the same, but for 2004. What's the first thing you notice? How about the fact that three of the teams that lost the highest percentage of fumbles in 2003 show up again among the teams that lost the lowest percentage of fumbles in 2004? Miami, by the way, almost made that 2004 list as well—the 2004 Dolphins offense had a league-high 30 fumbles but lost only 13 of them after giving up two thirds of their fumbles the previous year.

This random year-to-year movement goes the other way as well. Yes, the Jets show up in both years among the

teams with the lowest percentage of lost fumbles. But Chicago and Tampa Bay, in the top five for 2003, were in the bottom five for 2004.

The year-to-year pattern is no different for defenses. In 2003, St. Louis led the league in defensive fumble recoveries (see table 3). Opposing offenses put the ball on the ground 24 times, and 19 times the Rams recovered and brought their high-flying offense back onto the field. There was absolutely no way this could continue, and in fact it did not; in 2004, the St. Louis defense recovered only 8 of the 15 fumbles it caused. This regression to the mean was a major reason why the St. Louis defense collapsed and the team dropped from 12–4 to 8–8.

Meanwhile, defensive coordinator Lovie Smith was promoted to head coach of the Bears, and the Chicago defense went from recovering just three out of ten opposition fumbles to recovering 13 out of 17 (see table 4). Lest you think that this is the effect of a new coach rather than random chance, note that the Cleveland Browns had four more fumble recoveries in 2004 even though they actually stripped the ball less often; the same is true for San Diego. The Oakland Raiders went from recovering 9 of 20 fumbles to recovering 9 of 13.

So rates of fumble recoveries are random, but is there any logic to a team's propensity to cause fumbles in the first place? While fumbles, like most football statistics, have a lot of year-to-year variation, there does seem to be an actual skill involved in avoiding them or causing them. Some teams are very good about protecting the ball year after year, and others are not so good.

To show you what we mean, let's use correlation coefficients. This is a common statistical measure between −1 and 1 that measures how closely two variables are related. The closer to 1, the stronger the relationship, like the correlation between scoring points and winning games. A negative correlation, closer to −1, means that when one number is high, the other is low, like the correlation between allowing points and winning games. A correlation of 0 means two numbers are unconnected.

The correlation between the number of fumbles per offensive play in 2003 and the number of fumbles per offen-

TABLE 1. BEST AND WORST AT RECOVERING FUMBLES, 2003 OFFENSES

Team	Fum	Lost	% Lost	Team	Fum	Lost	% Lost
Best				Worst			
DET	11	2	18%	PIT	15	9	60%
DEN	16	4	25%	NYG	26	16	62%
CHI	18	6	33%	MIA	21	14	67%
TB	19	7	37%	NO	27	19	70%
NYJ	16	6	38%	SD	15	11	73%

TABLE 2. BEST AND WORST AT RECOVERING FUMBLES, 2004 OFFENSES

Team	Fum	Lost	% Lost	Team	Fum	Lost	% Lost
Best				Worst			
NYJ	13	4	31%	CHI	28	18	64%
ARI	25	9	36%	NE	17	12	71%
NYG	25	9	36%	TB	24	17	71%
SD	21	8	38%	PHI	14	10	71%
NO	22	9	41%	CIN	13	10	77%

TABLE 3. BEST AND WORST AT RECOVERING FUMBLES, 2003 DEFENSES

Team	Fum	Lost	% Lost	Team	Fum	Lost	% Lost
Best				**Worst**			
STL	24	19	79%	BUF	19	8	42%
SF	13	9	69%	CLE	14	5	36%
KC	13	8	62%	SD	17	6	35%
NYJ	15	9	60%	CHI	10	3	30%
PHI	22	13	59%	MIN	21	6	29%

TABLE 4. BEST AND WORST AT RECOVERING FUMBLES, 2004 DEFENSES

Team	Fum	Lost	% Lost	Team	Fum	Lost	% Lost
Best				**Worst**			
CHI	17	13	76%	HOU	18	8	44%
CLE	12	9	75%	MIA	19	8	42%
NO	24	18	75%	KC	18	7	39%
OAK	13	9	69%	DEN	19	7	37%
BAL	18	12	67%	PHI	24	7	29%

sive play in 2004 was .39, so offenses that fumbled more than average two years ago did tend to fumble more than average last year. However, the correlation between the percentage of fumbles recovered in 2003 and the percentage of fumbles recovered in 2004 was −.29. Believe it or not, a team that recovered a high percentage of its own fumbles in 2003 generally was below average at recovering fumbles in 2004, and vice versa. On defense, the correlations were similar. The year-to-year correlation for fumbles caused per play was .26, slightly lower than it was for the offense. But the year-to-year correlation for the percentage of fumbles recovered was −.40, a stronger reverse effect.

Next year, that reverse effect is going to bite the Saints right where it matters. When Brooks drops the ball twice to lose an important game in November and commentators ask what happened to the discipline New Orleans showed in 2004, you'll understand that it was never there in the first place.

Aaron Schatz

Saints 2004 Stats by Week

Wk	vs.	W-L	PF	PA	YDF	YDA	TO	Total	Off	Def	ST
								DVOA			
1	SEA	L	7	21	281	415	-1	-25.9%	-16.3%	19.2%	9.6%
2	SF	W	30	27	302	370	+2	-37.1%	-29.1%	17.2%	9.2%
3	@STL	W	28	25	462	403	+1	2.4%	23.4%	36.6%	15.6%
4	@ARI	L	31	17	279	363	-1	-36.9%	-3.4%	53.9%	20.5%
5	TB	L	17	20	251	319	-1	-33.4%	-6.5%	28.2%	1.4%
6	MIN	L	31	38	385	605	+2	-3.1%	6.0%	17.2%	8.0%
7	@OAK	W	31	26	322	432	+2	-0.7%	-1.1%	27.7%	28.2%
8	BYE										
9	@SD	L	17	43	243	402	-2	-27.8%	-15.7%	16.8%	4.7%
10	KC	W	27	20	374	497	+3	-6.3%	-11.1%	-3.5%	1.3%
11	DEN	L	13	34	411	389	-4	-48.4%	4.6%	42.6%	-10.4%
12	@ATL	L	21	24	306	396	-2	-38.8%	-8.4%	29.0%	-1.4%
13	CAR	L	21	32	280	401	-3	-28.6%	-5.5%	32.2%	9.1%
14	@DAL	W	27	13	269	344	+2	-0.2%	-31.3%	-20.8%	10.3%
15	@TB	W	21	17	247	283	+2	29.1%	6.0%	-15.9%	7.3%
16	ATL	W	26	13	369	267	+1	54.2%	-6.1%	-39.5%	20.8%
17	@CAR	W	21	18	360	320	+3	16.4%	14.9%	-12.8%	-11.3%

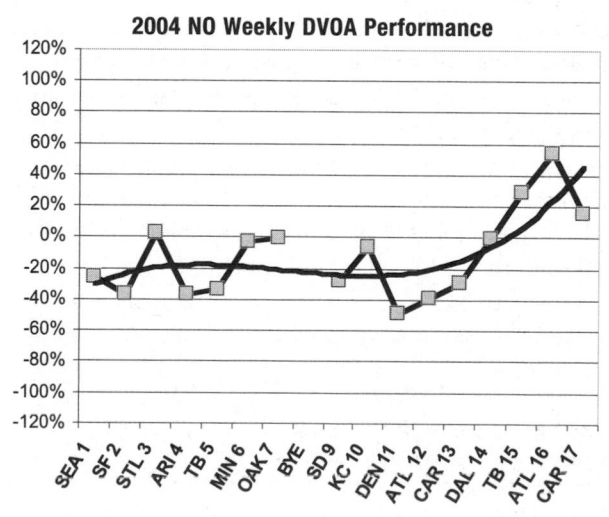

2004 NO Weekly DVOA Performance

Trends and Splits

	Offense	Rank	Defense	Rank
Total DVOA	-4.2%	20	14.1%	26
Unadjusted VOA	0.0%	15	10.7%	24
Weighted Trend	-4.5%	19	6.5%	20
Variance	2.1%	32	6.6%	24
Passing	-2.2%	18	18.1%	25
Rushing	-6.8%	23	9.8%	26
First Down	-4.0%	23	21.3%	30
Second Down	0.3%	18	13.0%	24
Third Down	-12.1%	19	-0.8%	21
Red Zone	-11.8%	22	-13.1%	10
Late and Close	-6.6%	16	8.0%	26

Five-Year Performance

	2004	2003	2002	2001	2000
W-L	8-8	8-8	9-7	7-9	10-6
Pythagorean Wins	6.6	8.4	9	6.1	9.4
Estimated Wins	6.9	8	10.1	7.1	8.2
Total DVOA	-10.6%	-2.4%	15.8%	-9.6%	-0.5%
Rank	23	17	7	21	19
Offense	-4.2%	5.2%	8.5%	-12.2%	-4.8%
Rank	20	11	10	24	18
Defense	14.1%	6.8%	5.4%	-2.1%	-7.9%
Rank	26	24	21	20	12
Special Teams	7.7%	-0.8%	12.7%	0.5%	-3.5%
Rank	2	22	1	13	23

Passing (min. 5 plays)

Player	DPAR	PAR	DVOA	Plys	NtYds	Avg	Cmpl	TD	Int
Aaron Brooks	23.2	33.1	-3.9%	590	3,552	6.0	57.0%	21	14

Rushing (min. 3 plays)

Player	DPAR	PAR	DVOA	Plys	Yds	Avg	TD	Fum	Suc
Deuce McAllister	9.0	5.0	-6.1%	269	1074	4.0	9	5	43%
Aaron Stecker	-1.2	-0.3	-19.7%	58	230	4.0	2	1	36%
Aaron Brooks	6.9	7.3	9.1%	40	210	5.3	4	0	—
Ki-Jana Carter	-2.2	-1.8	-60.0%	10	17	1.7	0	0	20%
Donté Stallworth	0.6	0.5	-8.1%	6	37	6.2	0	0	—
Mike Karney	0.3	0.0	3.1%	3	7	2.3	0	0	67%

Receiving (min. 5 plays)

Player	DPAR	PAR	DVOA	Plys	Ctch	Yds	Y/C	TD	CPct
WR									
Joe Horn	41.6	44.0	25.8%	153	94	1399	14.9	11	61%
Donté Stallworth	10.1	11.4	-1.0%	106	58	767	13.2	5	55%
Jerome Pathon	4.4	6.9	-5.7%	66	34	581	17.1	1	52%
Michael Lewis	4.5	4.6	40.2%	13	8	127	15.9	0	62%
TE									
Boo Williams	-10.6	-11.5	-35.6%	75	33	362	11.0	2	44%
Ernie Conwell	-1.3	-0.9	-23.6%	19	10	102	10.2	1	53%
RB									
Deuce McAllister	-3.3	-6.3	-24.1%	48	34	228	6.7	0	71%
Aaron Stecker	-1.6	-2.5	-17.8%	38	29	174	6.0	0	76%
Mike Karney	-0.4	-0.1	-19.2%	7	6	42	7.0	0	86%

Defensive Players (min. 20 plays)

Player	Age	Plys	Stop	Dfts	AvYds	StpRt	Sack	Int	FR
Defensive Line									
Charles Grant	27	87	66	31	0.7	76%	10.5	1	1
Brian Young	28	57	38	9	2.4	67%	2.5	0	1
Darren Howard	29	48	42	20	-0.4	88%	11.0	0	3
Will Smith	24	44	29	17	1.3	66%	7.5	0	1
Howard Green	26	28	18	2	2.4	64%	0.0	0	0
Linebackers									
Orlando Ruff	29	77	33	4	4.8	43%	0.0	1	0
Courtney Watson	25	58	31	10	4.7	53%	2.0	0	0
Derrick Rodgers	34	57	23	7	5.8	40%	0.0	0	0
James Allen	26	50	18	4	7.1	36%	0.0	0	2
Colby Bockwoldt	24	38	14	1	4.3	37%	1.0	0	1
Sedrick Hodge	27	27	17	6	5.3	63%	0.0	0	0

Player	Age	Plys	Stop	Dfts	AvYds	StpRt	Sack	Int	FR
Secondary									
Tebucky Jones	31	107	19	9	13.8	18%	0.0	1	1
Jay Bellamy	33	96	30	17	10.1	31%	0.0	0	3
Fakhir Brown	28	68	23	19	8.8	34%	0.0	2	3
Fred Thomas	32	50	13	8	12.1	26%	0.0	0	2
Mike McKenzie	29	47	20	10	8.8	43%	0.0	5	0
Ashley Ambrose	35	37	15	8	7.1	41%	0.0	3	1
Jason Craft	29	20	8	4	7.7	40%	0.0	0	0

Offensive Line

Year	Yards	AdjLineYd	Rank	Power	Rank	10+ Yds	Rank	Stuff	Rank	Sack	AdjSack%	Rank
2002	4.17	4.03	21	82%	2	22%	5	25%	20	38	6.1%	15
2003	4.67	4.22	15	71%	6	25%	4	22%	6	37	6.4%	16
2004	4.04	3.84	27	58%	21	21%	3	26%	22	42	7.1%	19

Year	LEnd	Rank	LTckl	Rank	MdGrd	Rank	RTckl	Rank	REnd	Rank
2002	4.04	17	3.97	22	3.81	28	4.37	15	4.58	8
2003	3.76	21	3.92	23	4.42	7	3.72	24	4.37	11
2004	3.49	25	3.45	29	3.85	25	5.01	5	2.99	28

This is the one area where the Saints are clearly better in 2005 than they were in 2004. They signed Jermane Mayberry as a free agent from the Eagles and then traded up in the draft to take Outland Trophy winner Jammal Brown out of the University of Oklahoma with the 13th pick. Brown should step right in at right tackle to replace unsigned free agent Victor Riley, who was near the top of the league with 12 penalties, including eight false starts. Of course, left tackle Wayne Gandy had 13 penalties and he's still here. The center is LeCharles Bentley, who looked like the league's next great lineman as a rookie but hasn't been as good since, and the left guard is undistinguished Kendyl Jacox.

Defensive Front Seven

Year	Yards	AdjLineYd	Rank	Power	Rank	10+ Yds	Rank	Stuff	Rank	Sack	AdjSack%	Rank
2002	4.24	4.13	17	67%	14	20%	22	23%	21	39	6.1%	18
2003	4.74	4.49	28	74%	31	21%	24	19%	30	31	6.1%	17
2004	4.64	4.49	28	81%	32	21%	24	20%	30	37	6.5%	21

Year	LEnd	Rank	LTckl	Rank	MdGrd	Rank	RTckl	Rank	REnd	Rank
2002	2.34	1	3.92	11	4.58	28	3.63	6	4.79	28
2003	4.53	23	4.98	26	4.42	25	4.39	20	4.26	24
2004	3.90	9	4.54	21	4.85	30	4.19	17	3.50	9

It's quite simple, really. On third and one, when you need to get a yard off the Saints' defense, you can get it. There's more to being a good front seven than stopping your opponents from picking up short yardage, but you're not a good front seven if you can't do it, and the Saints can't. Although Charles Grant is a solid and unappreciated defensive end who's good against the pass and strong against the run, we don't like the rest of the Saints' defensive line. Jonathan Sullivan in particular has been a disappointment; he was supposed to be Richard Seymour Part II when the Saints took him out of Georgia with the sixth pick in the draft, but that was two years and numerous hamburgers ago. The linebackers are also ineffectual, with the exception of Courtney Watson, who was athletic and good in pass coverage as a rookie last season. He's one of the few solid players to come out of talent-starved Notre Dame in recent years. Derrick Rodgers turns 34 this year and has never been more than a role player, but the Saints apparently plan to make him their starter on the weak side.

Defensive Secondary

Year	DVOA vs. #1 WR	Rank	DVOA vs. #2 WR	Rank	DVOA vs. Other WR	Rank	DVOA vs. TE	Rank	DVOA vs. RB	Rank
2002	-7.5%	10	33.6%	27	-6.2%	12	-33.4%	4	29.3%	32
2003	35.8%	31	-23.5%	8	-45.7%	3	-8.3%	12	11.0%	25
2004	35.7%	29	2.2%	12	-5.7%	17	17.7%	21	-4.3%	18

There's no question that the acquisition of Mike McKenzie greatly improved the Saints' defense (and greatly lessened the quality of the Packers' defense) in 2004. The late-season turnaround by the secondary was also helped by moving Fakhir Brown into the starting lineup. You can tell that opposing quarterbacks were picking on Fred Thomas—his Stop Rate is much worse than the other cornerbacks. Poor Tebucky Jones was usually stuck cleaning Thomas's mess—he led the Saints in tackles with 101, and his average defensive play came 13.8 yards past the line of scrimmage, the highest number in the league for a player with at least 20 plays. Jones was a salary cap cut and went to Miami, and free agent acquisition Dwight Smith comes over from Tampa Bay to replace him. Jay Bellamy is the expected starter at strong safety.

Special Teams

Year	DVOA	Rank	FG/XP	Rank	Net Punt	Rank	Punt Ret	Rank	Net Kick	Rank	Kick Ret	Rank
2002	12.7%	1	8.1	4	6.6	9	17.9	1	22.5	1	15.4	3
2003	-0.8%	22	-4.3	23	8.6	7	2.1	10	-5.7	26	-5.1	23
2004	7.7%	2	3.0	15	10.9	9	11.3	2	7.5	9	10.0	5

Ladies and gentlemen of the jury, I draw your attention to Exhibit A in special teams inconsistency. The Saints went from 3rd in the league to 23rd to 5th, with basically the same personnel and the same special teams coach, Al Everest. Kicker John Carney, punter Mitch Berger, and return man Michael Lewis are all back again in 2005, but given this track record it is pretty difficult to know what to expect.

Coaching Staff

One of Jim Haslett's first moves as the new head coach in 2000 was to hire Mike McCarthy as offensive coordinator. He figured that McCarthy, who was the quarterbacks coach for Joe Montana in Kansas City and Brett Favre in Green Bay, would be a good fit to run a similar style of offense in New Orleans. What he found out is that without the right personnel at quarterback, a lot of offensive coaches don't look so impressive. McCarthy moved on to become offensive coordinator in San Francisco, and he'll be replaced by Mike Sheppard, who had been quarterbacks coach the last three years. On defense, Rick Venturi, the only member of the staff who was in New Orleans before Haslett arrived, remains as coordinator. Venturi has twice been interim head coach when he was an assistant on a team whose head coach was fired in the middle of the year. If the Saints can't take the next step, he could do it a third time.

New York Giants

Tom Coughlin came into New York with a reputation for being a hard-nosed, disciplinarian coach. The media seemed evenly split on what to expect: Was he exactly the type of coach that the mistake-prone Giants needed—one who would create some structure and a sense of urgency in an organization that had become lackadaisical under Jim Fassel—or would Coughlin's unending list of rules rub a veteran team the wrong way? And would the team's resulting unhappiness with their inflexible coach lead to poor play and, worse, make it more difficult for the Giants to recruit players to work under Coughlin in years to come?

By the end of the season, however, any questions about Coughlin's personality were eclipsed by his controversial decision to replace quarterback Kurt Warner with rookie Eli Manning in Week 11, with the Giants still in the thick of the NFC playoff hunt at 5–4. Manning looked awful, leading New York to six straight losses before defeating Dallas in Week 17 to earn a tie for last place in the division. Manning had an absurd 5.3 yards per pass attempt, and our similarity scores system puts his rookie year alongside those of such nonentities as Steve Walsh, Craig Whelihan, Billy Joe Tolliver, Koy Detmer, and Eric Zeier. On the other hand, there were extenuating circumstances: Manning's starts came against some of the best pass defenses in the league: Philadelphia, Washington, Baltimore, Pittsburgh, and Cincinnati (remember, we said *pass* defenses). And while it may look like the decision to start Manning is what ultimately led to the Giants missing the playoffs, in reality he was an improvement over Warner in a number of key areas.

In the red zone, Eli Manning had a DVOA of −13.3%—bad, but nowhere near as bad as Kurt Warner's abysmal mark of −107.0%. Warner fumbled five times and threw two picks in the red zone, while Manning did each just once. Of course, it didn't help that everyone on the New York offense not named Jeremy Shockey evaporated once the team was in the red zone. Six Giants were thrown at least four red zone passes, and Shockey was the only one with a positive DVOA.

Manning was also much more mobile and quicker to release the ball than Warner. Warner was sacked an astonishing 39 times during his nine starts as a Giant, including 24 in his last four games. Some of the blame has to fall on the often porous offensive line, but Manning, despite playing behind a weaker line riddled with injuries, was sacked only 13 times on 208 passing downs. After considering opponent and situation, Warner had a 12.0% adjusted sack rate, more than twice as high as Manning's 5.5%. Toward the end of his run as a Giant starter, it seemed at times that Warner wouldn't release the ball unless a receiver was holding aloft a neon sign that said, "Look Over Here—I'm Open!" Even then, Warner would hold on for another second or two to make sure his offensive line got some more blocking practice.

Maybe the line was so tired from all that blocking that they couldn't remember the snap count, because the Giants finished sixth in the league in false starts, with starting offensive linemen David Diehl, Chris Snee, and Luke Petitgout all finishing in the top 25 in false start penalties. In fact, despite the arrival of the renowned disciplinarian Coughlin, the Giants were one of the ten most-penalized teams in the league. The Giants had six individual players

GIANTS PROSPECTUS

2004 Record: 6–10

DVOA Estimated Wins: 6.6 (24th)

Pythagorean Wins: 6.7 (22nd)

DVOA: −10.0% total (22nd), −24.2% weighted (28th)

Adjusted Offense: 20.1 points/game (−5.4% DVOA, 22nd)

Adjusted Defense: 23.2 points/game (6.3% DVOA, 22nd)

Adjusted Special Teams: +0.6 points/game (1.6% DVOA, 14th)

Variance: 29.8% (2nd)

2004: Hey, let's make the rookie run the gauntlet of the league's toughest defenses.

2005: With some big holes filled, it is time to learn if Eli can match the hype.

2005 Projection

D'Brickashaw D'erby (0–4): 18%

Bad Team (5–6): 22%

Mediocre (7–8): 26%

Playoff Contender (9–10): 20%

Super Bowl Contender (11+): 15%

Projected Average Opponent: 2.7% DVOA (11th in NFL)

penalized at least seven times in 2004 (Will Peterson, Frank Walker, Jason Whittle, Diehl, Snee, and Petitgout), the most of any team in the NFL. So much for tough love.

The other statistic that was supposed to improve with Coughlin's arrival was turnover margin. Coughlin's Jaguars teams were consistently able to hold on to the football, and his Giants followed suit. New York dropped from 38 turnovers to 24, the tenth-best mark in the league. This was partly luck; on offense, the Giants fumbled the ball only one fewer time than the year before, but the defense only recovered 9 of those 25 fumbles. (As an essay in the New Orleans chapter points out, the percentage of fumbles recovered by the defense is completely random.) But a reduction in interceptions thrown by Giants quarterbacks was real. So was the dramatic drop in fumbles after Manning (three fumbles) took over for Warner (12 fumbles), and a startling improvement from Tiki Barber, who averaged almost nine fumbles a year from 2000 to 2003 but only fumbled five times in 2004. Not coincidentally, Barber had his best year ever as a pro in 2004, setting career highs in total yards, touchdowns, rushing yards, rushing touchdowns, and yards per catch. The Giants will finally have some decent short-yardage/goal line options to pair with Tiki this year after relying on the abysmal Ron Dayne in recent years. With veteran Mike Cloud and 270-pound fourth-round pick Brandon Jacobs taking a pounding on third-and-ones, Barber should be able to keep up his new-found success even as he crosses into his thirties.

What about the idea that Coughlin's style would lead to a backlash from veteran Giants? Yes, a number of veterans were not happy with the way Coughlin ran things and were more than willing to voice their displeasure. Reportedly, six players filed complaints with the NFLPA over Coughlin's rules and workout schedule, including most infamously Michael Strahan, after he was fined $1,000 for showing up to a meeting two minutes *early*.

But such dissatisfaction with the team's coach hasn't stopped players from signing with Big Blue. The Giants were arguably the most successful team in free agency going into this season. The team's big three free agent signings—Antonio Pierce, Kareem McKenzie, and Plaxico Burress—should all have an immediate impact. Although the division rival Cowboys also brought in a number of potential big-impact players, the Giants' big three additions are all on the right side of 30, Burress being the oldest at 28.

Each player addresses an obvious Giants weakness. The 6'5" Burress is taller, stronger, and younger than the incumbent number one receiver, Amani Toomer. McKenzie should help Manning get a little of that protection that Chad Pennington has enjoyed so much. But the most significant of the three additions may be Pierce. One could make an argument that the Giants overpaid for a player coming off his first year as a starter. Pierce had more tackles last season than in his first three combined. However, the Giants were desperately in need of an upgrade at linebacker, especially in the middle, where Pierce is expected to play. New York has struggled mightily against speedy running backs who can catch the ball out of the backfield. The Giants were 27th in DVOA against passes to running backs, at 12.7%. Backs averaged 6.46 yards per intended pass against New York, fourth worst in the NFL. Philadelphia's Brian Westbrook in particular has torched the Giants. In 2004, Westbrook averaged 8.1 yards per intended pass. Against New York, that number jumped to 10.6 yards. Nearly half of Westbrook's receptions against New York ended up in first downs or touchdowns for the Eagles. With Pierce in the fold, the Giants may finally have someone who can bring Westbrook down before he crosses the computer-generated yellow line.

But it won't mean anything unless Manning can make dramatic improvements on his rookie performance. The Giants addressed all of their major weaknesses from 2004 through free agency and the draft save one—starting quarterback. Now we'll really see if Coughlin made the right decision last year by throwing Manning into the fire. If exposing Eli early to the best defenses in the NFL allowed him to confront his shortcomings in the off-season and enter 2005 as an improved, confident quarterback, the Giants have as good a chance as anyone else in the NFC to lose to Philadelphia in a championship game. Otherwise, 2005 will be another long year for Giants fans and Coughlin will be accused of stunting the growth of the player on whom the Giants have staked their future. At least this time they'll have a good first-round draft pick to show for it.

Al Bogdan

Giants 2004 Stats by Week

Wk	vs.	W-L	PF	PA	YDF	YDA	TO	DVOA Total	Off	Def	ST
1	@PHI	L	17	31	413	454	-1	-19.2%	19.0%	39.2%	1.0%
2	WAS	W	20	14	277	322	+6	63.2%	16.8%	-64.8%	-18.4%
3	CLE	W	27	10	390	285	+3	36.7%	43.7%	16.8%	9.8%
4	@GB	W	14	7	403	301	+2	24.0%	5.8%	-37.3%	-19.1%
5	@DAL	W	26	10	336	278	+1	0.5%	-8.7%	-8.1%	1.0%
6	BYE										
7	DET	L	13	28	325	325	-2	-101.5%	-35.4%	63.5%	-2.6%
8	@MIN	W	34	13	283	324	+3	55.6%	-5.1%	-46.8%	13.9%
9	CHI	L	21	28	258	231	-3	-53.6%	-64.4%	3.6%	14.4%
10	@ARI	L	14	17	308	178	0	11.5%	28.4%	2.5%	-14.4%
11	ATL	L	10	14	277	298	-2	-28.4%	-14.5%	17.5%	3.7%
12	PHI	L	6	27	272	390	-1	-77.9%	-60.1%	16.6%	-1.2%
13	@WAS	L	7	31	145	379	0	-76.4%	-21.2%	69.9%	14.7%
14	@BAL	L	14	37	196	353	-5	-95.6%	-74.3%	17.3%	-4.0%
15	PIT	L	30	33	278	469	+1	59.7%	49.4%	13.9%	24.2%
16	@CIN	L	22	23	326	233	+1	36.0%	9.9%	-22.4%	3.8%
17	DAL	W	28	24	235	367	+1	-17.1%	0.7%	16.9%	-0.9%

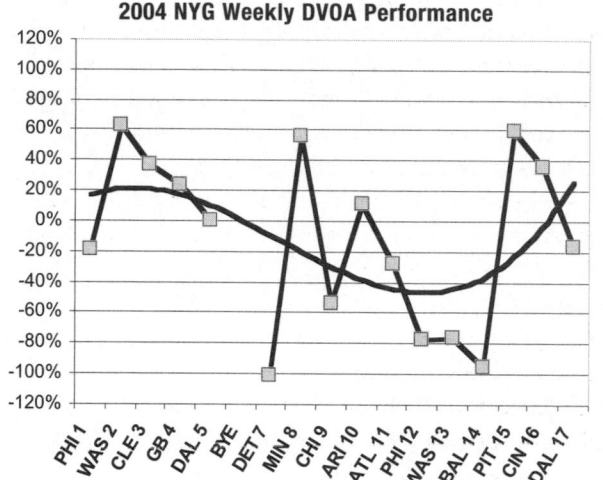

2004 NYG Weekly DVOA Performance

Trends and Splits

	Offense	Rank	Defense	Rank
Total DVOA	-5.4%	22	6.3%	22
Unadjusted VOA	-3.2%	18	2.7%	19
Weighted Trend	-14.7%	27	13.5%	26
Variance	13.6%	5	13.2%	4
Passing	-16.5%	26	7.1%	22
Rushing	6.5%	9	5.5%	24
First Down	-2.2%	21	11.2%	25
Second Down	7.4%	14	7.4%	22
Third Down	-36.1%	29	-3.7%	17
Red Zone	-20.6%	28	41.0%	32
Late and Close	-12.3%	23	-1.0%	18

Five-Year Performance

	2004	2003	2002	2001	2000
W-L	6-10	4-12	10-6	7-9	12-4
Pythagorean Wins	6.7	4.0	9.3	7.2	10.6
Estimated Wins	6.6	6.0	8.3	7.4	10.1
Total DVOA	-10.0%	-17.8%	2.1%	-6.2%	9.1%
Rank	22	28	15	20	13
Offense	-5.4%	-11.4%	9.8%	-3.8%	7.7%
Rank	22	25	9	15	10
Defense	6.3%	5.0%	3.8%	-6.0%	-7.2%
Rank	22	22	20	15	14
Special Teams	1.6%	-1.4%	-3.8%	-8.4%	-5.8%
Rank	14	23	27	30	28

Passing (min. 5 plays)

Player	DPAR	PAR	DVOA	Plys	NtYds	Avg	Cmpl	TD	Int
Kurt Warner	16.9	20.1	-0.5%	318	1861	5.9	62.8%	6	4
Eli Manning	-13.3	-22.1	-28.4%	208	961	4.6	48.2%	6	9

Rushing (min. 3 plays)

Player	DPAR	PAR	DVOA	Plys	Yds	Avg	TD	Fum	Suc
Tiki Barber	29.9	28.4	7.0%	322	1520	4.7	13	5	48%
Ron Dayne	2.6	2.4	-3.7%	52	179	3.4	1	0	46%
Mike Cloud	4.6	5.4	34.0%	21	90	4.3	3	0	57%
Kurt Warner	2.6	2.5	36.8%	7	34	4.9	1	0	—
Eli Manning	1.9	1.7	70.2%	4	36	9.0	0	0	—
Ike Hilliard	2.0	2.0	79.5%	3	34	11.3	0	0	—
Jim Finn	-0.8	-0.5	-76.5%	3	7	2.3	0	0	33%

Receiving (min. 5 plays)

Player	DPAR	PAR	DVOA	Plys	Ctch	Yds	Y/C	TD	CPct
WR									
Amani Toomer	4.9	0.6	-7.1%	107	51	747	14.6	0	48%
Ike Hilliard	-8.3	-11.1	-29.6%	81	49	441	9.0	0	60%
Tim Carter	7.2	6.4	43.9%	18	12	182	15.2	1	67%
David Tyree	4.5	4.1	23.6%	17	10	155	15.5	1	59%
Jamaar Taylor	-0.2	-0.3	-17.1%	17	6	146	24.3	0	35%
TE									
Jeremy Shockey	14.6	13.2	10.9%	97	61	666	10.9	6	63%
Marcellus Rivers	-2.3	-1.9	-40.5%	12	5	36	7.2	1	42%
Visanthe Shiancoe	0.8	1.1	3.3%	7	5	25	5.0	1	71%
RB									
Tiki Barber	11.8	11.8	21.1%	79	52	578	11.1	2	66%
Jim Finn	2.0	2.3	12.0%	18	15	112	7.5	0	83%

Defensive Players (min. 20 plays)

Player	Age	Plys	Stop	Dfts	AvYds	StpRt	Sack	Int	FR
Defensive Line									
Osi Umenyiora	24	66	49	32	1.7	74%	7.0	0	4
Fred Robbins	28	42	36	16	-0.2	86%	5.0	1	0
Michael Strahan	34	40	30	12	1.3	75%	4.0	0	3
Lance Legree	28	35	27	8	1.5	77%	2.0	0	0
William Joseph	26	25	20	11	0.9	80%	2.0	0	0
Kenderick Allen	27	20	15	2	2.0	75%	1.0	0	0
Linebackers									
Carlos Emmons	32	100	40	10	5.6	40%	1.0	0	0
Kevin Lewis	27	95	45	11	5.1	47%	1.0	0	1
Nick Greisen	26	78	44	13	4.2	56%	2.0	0	1
Barrett Green	28	44	18	5	4.9	41%	0.0	0	2
Reggie Torbor	24	22	10	8	3.2	45%	3.0	0	1

Player	Age	Plys	Stop	Dfts	AvYds	StpRt	Sack	Int	FR
Secondary									
Will Allen	27	99	36	17	7.5	36%	1.0	1	0
Will Peterson	26	90	31	13	7.9	34%	0.0	2	0
Brent Alexander	34	88	29	16	8.5	33%	2.0	3	2
Gibril Wilson	24	59	28	13	6.7	47%	3.0	3	0
Terry Cousin	30	44	9	5	11.0	20%	0.0	1	0
Curry Burns	24	21	6	4	8.3	29%	0.0	1	0

Offensive Line

Year	Yards	AdjLineYd	Rank	Power	Rank	10+ Yds	Rank	Stuff	Rank	Sack	AdjSack%	Rank
2002	4.22	4.05	19	50%	31	23%	2	27%	27	25	4.4%	5
2003	4.08	3.99	24	58%	27	14%	21	26%	22	42	6.1%	15
2004	4.51	4.35	10	57%	23	22%	2	24%	15	52	9.4%	29

Year	LEnd	Rank	LTckl	Rank	MdGrd	Rank	RTckl	Rank	REnd	Rank
2002	3.99	18	3.72	27	4.09	23	3.54	28	4.50	10
2003	4.40	10	3.64	31	3.59	32	5.19	2	4.07	15
2004	4.56	9	3.18	32	4.58	6	3.80	23	5.09	2

For the first time in years, New York appears to have some depth on its offensive line. The addition of right tackle Kareem McKenzie will allow David Diehl to move back into his natural guard position. That moves last year's starter at left guard, Jason Whittle, into a backup role, where he'll join veteran tackle Bob Whitfield. Right guard (and Coughlin's son-in-law) Chris Snee dismissed critics who viewed his acquisition as pure nepotism with a solid rookie season. Although Snee missed the last few games of the year with a glandular infection, his ability to bulk up so quickly back to his 320-pound playing weight is a good sign that he will be able to return to form. Luke Petitgout will start at left tackle for the sixth season. The Giants don't seem to be getting better at running behind him, although Tiki Barber sure does love to run *around* him.

Defensive Front Seven

Year	Yards	AdjLineYd	Rank	Power	Rank	10+ Yds	Rank	Stuff	Rank	Sack	AdjSack%	Rank
2002	3.96	3.75	4	66%	12	20%	23	28%	9	57	5.6%	23
2003	3.89	3.86	8	63%	10	16%	14	30%	4	46	7.6%	3
2004	4.34	4.48	27	54%	7	15%	13	23%	16	41	7.9%	5

Year	LEnd	Rank	LTckl	Rank	MdGrd	Rank	RTckl	Rank	REnd	Rank
2002	4.08	18	3.41	5	3.78	5	3.60	5	3.74	13
2003	4.35	17	3.89	14	3.76	5	2.88	1	4.51	29
2004	4.85	27	4.34	16	4.21	18	4.17	16	5.63	32

The Giants were good in short-yardage situations, but bad in long-yardage situations. On downs with more than ten yards to go, the Giants allowed more yards per play than any team in the league and had the third-worst DVOA of 47.3%. It will be tough for the Giant linebackers not to improve from their awful performance in 2004. Antonio Pierce is the biggest addition and should provide some stability in the middle of the field. Flanking him will be Carlos Emmons and Nick Greisen, who together make an interesting example of how players affect each other's numbers. Greisen had the highest Stop Rate among the Giants linebackers, playing behind Umenyiora, who had the lowest Stop Rate among Giants linemen. Emmons had the lowest Stop Rate among Giants linebackers, playing behind Fred Robbins, who had the highest Stop Rate among Giants linemen.

Former first-round pick William Joseph has been perceived as a disappointment at defensive tackle, but he anchored the strongest part of the Giants' run defense—split out the "MdGrd" section above, and the Giants are the best team in the league at stopping runs over the opposition's left guard, directly at the right defensive tackle position Joseph anchors. Where New York needs improvement is defending runs to the outside of the opposing team's right tackle. Michael Strahan missing half the season didn't help, but the Giants struggled even with him manning the left side of the defensive line. New York's DVOA defending runs to the outside went from 24.1% with Strahan in the lineup to 49.8% without him.

The Giants upgraded their pass rush in the draft, picking up Notre Dame pass rush specialist Justin Tuck in the third round. At best, Tuck will provide nice depth at defensive end, where there isn't much behind Strahan and Umenyiora. At worst, he'll be needed in the starting lineup if Strahan can't regain his effectiveness after coming back from a torn pectoral muscle. Some decrease in performance has to be expected, especially against longer-armed offensive tackles.

Defensive Secondary

Year	DVOA vs. #1 WR	Rank	DVOA vs. #2 WR	Rank	DVOA vs. Other WR	Rank	DVOA vs. TE	Rank	DVOA vs. RB	Rank
2002	-38.6%	3	27.7%	24	33.5%	30	7.3%	17	9.1%	22
2003	19.2%	22	23.3%	28	20.0%	29	28.5%	28	-9.3%	11
2004	-6.1%	9	41.8%	31	9.5%	21	2.3%	15	12.7%	27

Two business school professors, Cade Massey of Duke University and Richard H. Thaler of the University of Chicago, published a paper in March entitled "The Loser's Curse: Overconfidence vs. Market Efficiency in the National Football League Draft." The paper showed that higher draft picks are disproportionately expensive (and take up far more salary cap room) in relation to their slightly higher chance of succeeding than the players drafted later. Therefore, the best draft picks actually come later in the draft, but not too late. The inflection point—the actual most valuable pick in the draft, in terms of return on investment—turns out to be the 11th pick of the second round. And this year, that pick happened to belong to the New York Giants.

So come on down, former LSU cornerback Corey Webster! You're the next contestant on *The Price (When Considered in Comparison to Performance) Is Right!* Webster should be an immediate help to a team that struggled to take the ball away from opposing quarterbacks, averaging less than one interception per game. He'll also provide insurance should cornerback Will Allen leave after his contract runs out following the 2005 season. The other starting cornerback is Will Peterson, whose nine penalties were more than twice the total of any other New York defender. Safety Gibril Wilson was on his way to a great rookie season until suffering a stinger on a hit to Arizona quarterback Josh McCown in November. If the hard-hitting Wilson manages to play a full season, he'll stand a great chance at becoming only the second Giant safety to ever make the Pro Bowl.

Special Teams

Year	DVOA	Rank	FG/XP	Rank	Net Punt	Rank	Punt Ret	Rank	Net Kick	Rank	Kick Ret	Rank
2002	-3.8%	27	-6.3	27	-5.6	22	-3.3	23	-6.1	24	0.2	17
2003	-1.4%	23	-4.1	22	-3.1	23	9.7	6	2.6	13	-12.7	30
2004	1.6%	14	1.0	17	1.7	20	-1.7	10	-3.6	20	11.6	4

One of the goals of hiring Tom Coughlin was to improve the Giants' special teams and—will you look at that?—it seems to have worked. Actually, he just went out and got better kick returners. In 2003, Brian Mitchell was clearly so over the hill that he could no longer even see the hill in his rear view mirror. In 2004, Willie Ponder (11 games) and Derrick Ward (5 games) had a touchdown return each and only had two returns stopped short of the 20-yard line. Jay Feely is the new Giants kicker, which will cause frustration for fans who don't understand the value of kickoffs, since, after adjusting for the Georgia Dome, Feely has been worse than average on field goals for three straight seasons. However, each year he has also finished in the top six of our rankings for kickoffs. Jeff Feagles has been a good punter for two seasons (8.6 points above average last year on punt distance alone), but the punt coverage gives back some of his value.

Coaching Staff

Tom Coughlin's Jacksonville teams outplayed their expected Pythagorean record fairly consistently early on in his tenure. After their initial expansion season, the Jaguars won at least one more game than one would expect given their points scored and allowed for the next four seasons. That pattern abruptly ended, however, in 2000, and the Jaguars would go on to lose at least two games more than expected over Coughlin's last three seasons.

Year	Wins	PF	PA	Pyth	Dif	Year	Wins	PF	PA	Pyth	Dif
1996	9	325	335	7.7	+1.3	2000	7	367	327	9.1	−2.1
1997	11	394	318	10.0	+1.0	2001	6	294	286	8.3	−2.3
1998	11	392	338	9.4	+1.6	2002	6	328	315	8.4	−2.4
1999	14	396	217	12.9	+1.1						

Coughlin is the only coach since the 1970 merger to have two or more consecutive seasons of winning at least a game more than the Pythagorean projection followed by two or more consecutive seasons of winning at least a game less than the Pythagorean projection. This might not mean anything, or it could mean that Coughlin wore out his welcome in Jacksonville around 2000, and whatever he was doing before then stopped working. For Giants fans, this could mean that their favorite team has another few seasons before they get sick of their coach giving them PowerPoint presentations laying out team rules about what kind of socks players can wear and where they should wear them (no ankle socks on the field, no white socks on the road).

Philadelphia Eagles

With about five minutes left in Super Bowl XXXIX, when it became clear to all but the most optimistic Philadelphia fans (whoever they are) that the Eagles weren't going to come back against the Patriots, the Philly Phaithful began cursing into their beers and casting about for someone to blame.

The idea that there would be any blame at all after such a marvelous season might seem ridiculous to most non-Philadelphians. The Eagles were the best team in the NFC by a wide margin. Their only meaningful loss in the regular season came against a white-hot Steelers team that had just steamrolled the Patriots. For 52 minutes, right up until Donovan McNabb threw an interception to Tedy Bruschi with New England up by ten, the Eagles played the Patriots tough enough to prove conclusively that they were the second best team in the NFL, second only to a team of historic quality.

But second best isn't good enough. The Eagles had taken the next step after three years of NFC championship game losses, but didn't win it all. In the philosophy of the frustrated fan, teams don't lose simply because the opponent was better. There has to be a scapegoat.

McNabb shouldered some of the blame. He threw three interceptions. He couldn't rally the team late, and it's been rumored since that he was throwing up—from panic, his doubters claimed, or from fatigue, Terrell Owens later hinted. But McNabb threw three touchdowns, something no other passer could do against the Patriots in a single game. Neither Chad Pennington nor Peyton Manning could throw three touchdowns against New England in 2004, and they each had two cracks at it.

Andy Reid took his lumps too: for not having the two-minute offense ready for action, for managing the clock badly, for executing an onside kick when a deep kick might have been the better call. The Eagles haven't been a great two-minute offense team under Reid and McNabb. They've had one or two spectacular comebacks (think Packers, 2003 playoffs), but in 2004 the two-minute offense, usually executed before halftime, was a clumsy, listless affair that rarely scored.

The Eagles didn't need a great two-minute offense to go 13–3 and reach the Super Bowl. They spent most of their fourth quarters running out the clock; only against the Cowboys in Week 15 did they have to come from behind late. The Eagles didn't lose the Super Bowl because

EAGLES PROSPECTUS

2004 Record: 13–3

DVOA Estimated Wins: 12.3 (2nd)

Pythagorean Wins: 11.5 (3rd)

DVOA: 28.7% total (4th), 23.9% weighted (5th)

Adjusted Offense: 26.2 points/game (17.7% DVOA, 6th)

Adjusted Defense: 20.5 points/game (−3.5% DVOA, 13th)

Adjusted Special Teams: +2.6 points/game (7.4% DVOA, 3rd)

Variance: 28.2% (5th)

2004: So close. So very close.

2005: The class of the NFC again, but Philly fans believe anything short of a championship is a failure.

2005 Projection

Leinart Land (0–4): 0%

Bad Team (5–6): 1%

Mediocre (7–8): 4%

Playoff Contender (9–10): 14%

Super Bowl Contender (11+): 80%

Projected Average Opponent: −3.4% DVOA (27th in NFL)

of what they did when they were trailing by ten in the fourth quarter. They lost because they were trailing by ten in the fourth quarter in the first place.

As anger faded, blame failed to stick to McNabb and Reid. The defense, so marvelous in so many games, also got off easy. No, the vitriol of legions of disgruntled fans became focused on the two usual suspects: wide receivers Todd Pinkston and Freddie Mitchell, who suffered from a case of the yips (Pinkston) and the yaps (Mitchell).

Pinkston has long been a Philly whipping boy, a second-round pick who never lived up to expectations yet played just well enough to stay in the lineup. The spindly wideout was the goat of the 2003 NFC Championship loss to the Panthers when he couldn't beat the jam put on by rookie CB Ricky Manning, and even had one pass bounce right off his hands and into Manning's. Pinkston's stock dropped even further last season when he seemed afraid to go across the middle. Pinkston alligator-armed a pass against the Redskins in Week 14, then had an encore performance against the Cowboys in Week 15, pulling up in fear whenever Roy Williams was in the vicinity.

Meanwhile, Freddie Mitchell, a.k.a. The People's Champion, a.k.a. FredEx, spent most of the season as an invisible man. When Terrell Owens got hurt against the Cowboys, Mitchell was thrust into the starting role. He had a great game against the Vikings in the playoffs, but Mitchell tried to replace Owens by providing 40% of the production and 160% of the silliness and distractions.

Come the Super Bowl, neither receiver redeemed himself. Pinkston had two crucial catches in the Eagles' first scoring drive, but then left the game with cramps and never returned. Mitchell, who spent two weeks baiting the Patriots, had just one catch. With Owens battling an injury and TE Chad Lewis out, Pinkston and Mitchell needed to come through. They didn't.

The anti-Pinkston, anti-Mitchell sentiment had some fans grumbling that the Eagles should pursue Muhsin Muhammad or Plaxico Burress in the off-season. The two supporting wideouts may have been a weak link in a potent offense, but were they really that bad?

One way to look at the situation is to compare Owens's production to Pinkston's. Owens had 1,200 receiving yards in the 2004 regular season, Pinkston 676 yards. Owens missed two games, but Pinkston and Mitchell didn't play much in those games either. Is there something unusual about a 524-yard drop-off between a team's primary and secondary wide receivers (remembering that Brian Westbrook was actually second on the team in receiving yards)? Not really. Table 1 shows that there was nothing unusual about the gap between Owens and Pinkston in receiving yards.

Pinkston's DPAR of 12.4 ranked 43rd in the league; he ranked 34th in DVOA. Not too shabby: He ranks ahead of Eric Moulds and Amani Toomer, although he certainly benefits from a better quarterback. Mitchell didn't have enough catches to qualify for the league leaderboard, but a DPAR of 7.2 (10.0% DVOA) ranks him squarely among players like

Kelley Washington and Keary Colbert. Owens got a big share of the passes, and he also got the double coverage, but his subordinates came through when called upon.

In the final analysis, Pinkston and Mitchell did a pretty good job with the balls they got, and neither really deserves the Super Bowl scapegoat label. Pinkston will never be a superstar, but no matter what some fans and analysts believe, replacing him wasn't the Eagles' top priority in the off-season. Mitchell was a different story, but the reason behind his departure is his attitude, not his ability. Tired of his preening, the Eagles released Mitchell in May after drafting WR Reggie Brown from Georgia in the second round.

While Reid, McNabb, and Pinky and the Brainless were excoriated on Philly talk radio, the defense got a free pass. Few were willing to consider that the defense—which had minor problems early in the year, was embarrassed by the Steelers, then hardened in the second half into a championship-caliber unit—had let the team down at the worst time.

For the first eight games of the season, the Eagles had a defensive DVOA of 4.8%, slightly worse than league average. After the Steelers ran wild in Week 9, defensive coordinator Jimmy Johnson reinserted Jeremiah Trotter as the starting middle linebacker. Trotter, who had been relegated to special teams and spot duty after an unproductive two-year free agent stint in Washington, had an immediate positive impact. Over the next six games, the Eagles defense became one of the best in the NFL, sporting a defensive DVOA of −23.9%. The Eagles ranked 15th in run defense DVOA after 15 weeks, before the two meaningless December games in which few of the starters played.

Trotter didn't do it all himself, though. After he returned to the lineup, Corey Simon, injured and overweight at the start of the year, rounded into shape; Keith Adams was given a bigger role in the defense, replacing the less effective Mark Simoneau; Dhani Jones seemed to figure out the scheme and became more effective in pass coverage. But Trotter was the catalyst, and his gap-shooting style enabled the Eagles to shut down the run while intensifying the pass rush. By the time they reached the Super Bowl, all of the Eagles' question marks were on offense.

But the Patriots had the Eagles' defense figured out. Trotter was picked up by Corey Dillon or Patrick Pass on nearly every blitz. Deion Branch lined up in the slot, and neither Roderick Hood nor rookie Matt Ware could defend him. The Eagles were 27th in the league in DVOA against opponents' number one wideouts, in part because Johnson's cornerbacks aren't assigned to cover specific receivers. Against the Vikings in the playoffs, Hood sometimes covered Randy Moss while Pro Bowler Lito Sheppard matched up with Marcus Robinson. Bill Belichick and Charlie Weis exploited this tendency, and Branch was always open. Quick screens caught the Eagles off guard,

TABLE 1. NFL TEAMS WITH LARGEST GAP BETWEEN TOP TWO WRs, 2004

Team	#1 WR	#2 WR	Difference
Buccaneers	Clayton	Galloway	777
Seahawks	Jackson	Engram	708
Panthers	Muhammad	Colbert	651
Jaguars	Smith	Edwards	639
Saints	Horn	Stallworth	632
Cowboys	Keyshawn	Glenn	586
Eagles	Owens	Pinkston	524
Texans	Johnson	Gaffney	510

usually just when Trotter was abandoning the middle of the field to rush the quarterback. Cutback lanes suddenly opened up. The Patriots spent the second half in the Eagles red zone.

In other words, the defense let the Eagles down. That doesn't change the fact that it's an excellent defense, good enough to win the NFC despite some minor personnel losses. But it was three points short of Super last year, and it's up to Reid and Johnson to squeeze three points' worth of improvement out of young players like Sheppard, Ware, Sheldon Brown, Michael Lewis, and Jerome McDougle, and rookies like Mike Patterson.

Even if the defense doesn't improve at all, who will challenge Philadelphia in 2005? The second best team in the NFC last year was the Falcons. They lost to the Eagles 27–10 in the playoffs, and it wasn't even that close. The Eagles crushed the Packers, probably the third best team. The Rams, the fourth best team, beat the Eagles in a meaningless game, but it seemed that Philadelphia would have won, with or without Owens, if they had tried. The Eagles also beat the wild card Vikings twice, and while the Vikings certainly gained ground in the off-season, they also lost their most dangerous offensive weapon. The Eagles blew out the tough Panthers, too. Philadelphia also swept the Redskins and Cowboys, coached by legends Joe Gibbs and Bill Parcells. They've dominated the Giants for two years, and beaten Michael Vick and Brett Favre consistently. That covers the whole conference.

The Eagles' most dangerous opponent may be themselves. Owens turned back into a selfish pumpkin after his Super Bowl heroics, sniping at his teammates and grousing about the contract he signed just last year. Westbrook and Simon sniffed at the tender offers the team made to them. The Eagles are paying the price of success, but they've paid it before. When Jeremiah Trotter left in 2002, it was supposed to cut the heart out of the team. It didn't. When Troy Vincent, Bobby Taylor, and Duce Staley left in 2004, it was supposed to leave a leadership void. It didn't.

The Eagles had a DVOA of 28.7% in 2004. The Panthers were the second highest NFC team at 4.2%. The Redskins were second in the division at −2.4%. Our projection system predicts Philadelphia to be the best team in football with one of the easiest schedules. It gives the Eagles an 80% chance of 11 or more wins. Only one other team is over 50%. The projection system even gives them a 4.6% chance to have a perfect season. And nobody seems to be catching up.

The Eagles enter the 2005 season as heavy favorites in the NFC, just as they did last year. They should reach the Super Bowl. But can they win it?

They fought the Patriots to a 45-minute draw. All they need to do is find a way to survive another 15 minutes.

Mike Tanier

Research: The Secret of Their Success

The Eagles are often cited as the second best organization in football, as measured by their ability to sustain excellence, develop players, and manage the salary cap. Nothing illustrates the organization's overall quality quite like the play of the special teams in the last five years.

Last year, the Eagles had the third best special teams in the NFL, according to our analysis. The Eagles also ranked third in 2003, fourth in 2002, first in 2001, and sixth in 2000. Special teams are generally far more inconsistent than offense or defense, but Philadelphia has been an exception. Teams like the Panthers, Bills, and Saints have made one-year appearances among the league leaders in special teams, only to fall back to the pack the following year. Only the Eagles have been in the league's top five each year since 2001.

The Eagles' special teams are also consistent on a week-by-week basis, posting negative DVOA scores only twice during the regular season, the best mark in the league (table 2). The Eagles earned a −6.1% DVOA in Week 14 against the Redskins, when they allowed a 70-yard kickoff return to start the game and David Akers missed an important field goal. They earned a −18.0% DVOA in Week 17, when the season was in the bag and practice squad players were on the field. Every other week, special teams made a positive contribution. By comparison, the top-ranked Buffalo special teams only had a positive DVOA in eight games; their rating is based on a few huge touchdown returns instead of all-around dependability.

The special teams weren't always a strength. In 1995, for example, the Eagles allowed 25.8 yards per kick return, worst in the league, and 13.9 yards per punt return, second worst in the league. Philadelphia was the only team to allow two punt return touchdowns. The Eagles ranked near the bottom of the league in kick returns. Special teams

TABLE 2. MOST GAMES WITH POSITIVE SPECIAL TEAMS DVOA, 2004

Team	Games
Philadelphia Eagles	14
New Orleans Saints	13
Pittsburgh Steelers	12
Miami Dolphins	11
Arizona Cardinals	10
Cincinnati Bengals	10
Green Bay Packers	10
Jacksonville Jaguars	10
New England Patriots	10

remained a problem for years, as the team shifted coaches from Danny Smith to Joe Wessel before settling on John Harbaugh in 1998.

It took Harbaugh a couple years to solidify the special teams, which ranked 26th in DVOA in 1998 and 21st in 1999. But they've been uniformly excellent ever since. Under Harbaugh's guidance, every unit has excelled, which is why the Eagles are the only team that is always near the top of the rankings, usually surrounded by fly-by-night sensations. The Chiefs top them when their return man has a historic season, the Ravens when Ed Reed and company block lots of punts. But the Eagles kick well, punt well, cover well, and return well, year in and year out.

The key player has been Akers, the steadiest and most well-rounded kicker in football. Harbaugh signed him in 1999 as an undrafted free agent kickoff specialist, and his promotion to full-time kicker in 2000 coincides with the start of this current run of special teams excellence. But Akers and his entourage—snapper Mike Bartrum and holder Koy Detmer—have been the only constants. Return men like Brian Mitchell have come and gone. The team has changed punters. Coverage stars like Sean Morey and Dameane Douglas have moved on. Longtime standout and Pro Bowler Ike Reese is now in Atlanta, but Morey won accolades from analysts long before Reese, and the Eagles adjusted quickly to his loss. Reese's replacements are already

on the roster—Keith Adams (who the team prudently resigned), Jason Short, Quentin Mikell, and Dexter Wynn.

The Eagles special teams have won games. A Westbrook punt return touchdown against the Giants two years ago—a run sprung by a controversial Reese block—won the game and helped the Eagles overcome a very rough start to the season. Akers's two late kicks against the Browns turned a possible upset loss in 2004 into a win. And in the NFC Championship game against the Falcons, punter Dirk Johnson averaged 38.3 yards per punt in 26-mile-per-hour winds while the Eagles coverage unit stifled Allen Rossum, a player who had almost single-handedly beat the Rams the previous week. By forcing the Falcons to sustain long drives, the Eagles special teams did as much as the defense to keep them from scoring.

When analysts decide who will win the NFC this year, they'll talk about Donovan McNabb, Terrell Owens, Jeremiah Trotter, and Jevon Kearse. They'll ask whether the Vikings or Falcons have done enough to catch the Eagles. But many will forget that the Eagles have a secret weapon: special teams units that provide a few extra yards per game, a few precious points per season. Akers, the coverage units, and Harbaugh make up one of the key differences between a perennial title contender and just another playoff team.

Mike Tanier

Eagles 2004 Stats by Week

Wk	vs.	W-L	PF	PA	YDF	YDA	TO	DVOA Total	Off	Def	ST
1	NYG	W	31	17	454	413	+1	32.1%	49.6%	21.9%	4.4%
2	MIN	W	27	16	317	410	+1	81.7%	42.1%	-25.3%	14.2%
3	@DET	W	30	13	402	256	0	36.6%	25.3%	-7.2%	4.1%
4	@CHI	W	19	9	376	224	0	-12.3%	18.6%	34.9%	4.0%
5	BYE										
6	CAR	W	30	8	293	344	+3	63.1%	7.3%	-34.2%	21.6%
7	@CLE	W	34	31	488	394	+2	7.2%	38.7%	52.3%	20.8%
8	BAL	W	15	10	298	327	+1	44.8%	33.3%	0.6%	12.1%
9	@PIT	L	3	27	113	420	+1	-28.1%	-30.9%	8.5%	11.3%
10	@DAL	W	49	21	485	317	+1	55.3%	69.4%	17.5%	3.4%
11	WAS	W	28	6	334	213	-1	67.3%	43.9%	-16.5%	6.9%
12	@NYG	W	27	6	390	272	+1	101.4%	27.5%	-60.1%	13.9%
13	GB	W	47	17	542	249	+1	112.6%	36.6%	-60.4%	15.6%
14	@WAS	W	17	14	312	312	-1	-24.4%	-13.2%	5.1%	-6.1%
15	DAL	W	12	7	328	237	-1	31.4%	-8.1%	-34.9%	4.6%
16	@STL	L	7	20	155	419	0	-40.2%	-35.3%	10.8%	5.9%
17	CIN	L	10	38	342	308	-5	-83.9%	-46.3%	19.6%	-18.0%
18	BYE										
19	MIN	W	27	14	395	385	-3	53.5%	4.3%	-41.9%	7.2%
20	ATL	W	27	10	326	202	+1	73.6%	22.5%	-37.0%	14.1%
21	NE	L	21	24	369	331	-3	-17.8%	-2.0%	8.0%	-7.8%

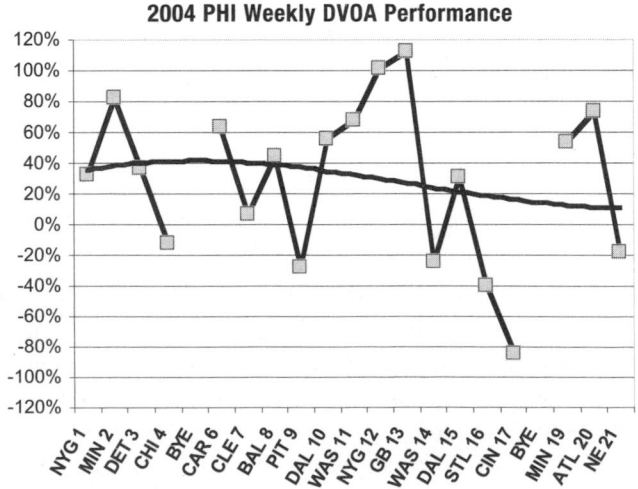

2004 PHI Weekly DVOA Performance

Trends and Splits

	Offense	Rank	Defense	Rank
Total DVOA	17.7%	6	-3.5%	13
Unadjusted VOA	15.0%	8	-2.0%	14
Weighted Trend	10.5%	10	-7.0%	11
Variance	11.4%	9	10.4%	13
Passing	21.8%	9	-7.2%	10
Rushing	11.4%	6	0.7%	20
First Down	11.8%	7	-8.1%	8
Second Down	33.5%	2	0.7%	13
Third Down	3.5%	13	-1.5%	19
Red Zone	31.1%	3	-8.2%	14
Late and Close	18.3%	5	-16.5%	8

Five-Year Performance

	2004	2003	2002	2001	2000
W-L	13-3	12-4	12-4	11-5	11-5
Pythagorean Wins	11.5	10.4	12.5	12.3	11.2
Estimated Wins	12.3	10.0	11.2	12.3	10.4
Total DVOA	28.7%	14.0%	28.0%	32.4%	12.5%
Rank	4	9	3	2	12
Offense	17.7%	15.1%	7.7%	-1.3%	-1.8%
Rank	6	6	11	12	16
Defense	-3.5%	5.2%	-14.1%	-24.6%	-9.1%
Rank	13	23	3	1	11
Special Teams	7.4%	4.1%	6.1%	9.1%	5.1%
Rank	3	3	4	1	6

Passing (min. 5 plays)

Player	DPAR	PAR	DVOA	Plys	NtYds	Avg	Cmpl	TD	Int
Donovan McNabb	107.1	102.9	35.8%	501	3677	7.3	64.0%	31	8
Koy Detmer	-9.2	-10.1	-62.8%	42	191	4.5	45.0%	0	2
Jeff Blake	-6.7	-6.9	-53.8%	38	109	2.9	48.6%	1	1

Rushing (min. 3 plays)

Player	DPAR	PAR	DVOA	Plys	Yds	Avg	TD	Fum	Suc
Brian Westbrook	15.7	15.0	8.1%	177	812	4.6	3	0	43%
Dorsey Levens	17.9	16.8	29.8%	94	410	4.4	4	0	55%
Donovan McNabb	8.7	7.6	40.2%	30	231	7.7	3	2	—
Reno Mahe	-0.4	-0.2	-17.8%	23	91	4.0	0	0	35%
Thomas Tapeh	0.4	0.2	-8.0%	12	42	3.5	0	0	33%
Eric McCoo	2.1	2.4	43.7%	9	54	6.0	0	0	67%
Greg Lewis	0.1	0.1	-25.0%	4	16	4.0	0	0	—
Terrell Owens	-1.3	-1.1	-109.0%	3	-5	-1.7	0	0	—

Receiving (min. 5 plays)

Player	DPAR	PAR	DVOA	Plys	Ctch	Yds	Y/C	TD	CPct
WR									
Terrell Owens	31.9	28.7	23.2%	127	77	1202	15.6	14	61%
Todd Pinkston	12.1	10.9	13.8%	63	36	676	18.8	1	57%
Freddie Mitchell	7.2	5.9	10.0%	44	22	377	17.1	2	50%
Greg Lewis	-1.1	-2.2	-18.8%	36	17	183	10.8	0	47%
Billy McMullen	-7.8	-8.5	-79.5%	17	3	24	8.0	0	18%
TE									
L. J. Smith	8.4	9.3	10.9%	54	34	377	11.1	5	63%
Chad Lewis	3.6	3.1	-1.3%	46	29	267	9.2	3	63%
Mike Bartrum	-1.8	-1.8	-48.5%	7	5	45	9.0	1	71%
RB									
Brian Westbrook	14.4	20.6	21.6%	87	73	703	9.6	6	84%
Josh Parry	-2.4	-1.5	-33.4%	18	9	75	8.3	0	50%
Reno Mahe	2.8	2.7	25.9%	16	14	123	8.8	0	88%
Dorsey Levens	1.8	1.9	14.3%	14	9	92	10.2	0	64%
Jon Ritchie	0.9	1.4	19.1%	6	4	36	9.0	0	67%
Eric McCoo	-0.5	-0.5	-27.4%	5	2	15	7.5	0	40%

Defensive Players (min. 20 plays)

Player	Age	Plys	Stop	Dfts	AvYds	StpRt	Sack	Int	FR
Defensive Line									
Jevon Kearse	29	36	31	13	1.2	86%	7.5	0	1
Darwin Walker	28	33	24	13	1.5	73%	4.5	0	0
Sam Rayburn	25	31	24	8	1.3	77%	6.0	0	0
Corey Simon	28	29	21	11	0.4	72%	5.5	0	0
Derrick Burgess	27	26	20	6	2.4	77%	2.5	0	0
Hollis Thomas	31	21	16	5	2.0	76%	0.0	0	1
Linebackers									
Dhani Jones	27	70	40	16	4.5	57%	0.5	1	1
Jeremiah Trotter	28	60	34	14	3.6	57%	1.0	0	0
Mark Simoneau	28	51	18	8	6.2	35%	1.5	0	1
Ike Reese	32	43	25	12	4.4	58%	1.0	2	0
Keith Adams	26	35	20	11	5.3	57%	0.0	0	0
Nate Wayne	30	31	16	4	4.6	52%	1.0	0	0

Player	Age	Plys	Stop	Dfts	AvYds	StpRt	Sack	Int	FR
Secondary									
Sheldon Brown	26	109	54	22	5.3	50%	3.0	2	0
Michael Lewis	25	105	43	19	7.9	41%	0.0	1	1
Brian Dawkins	32	84	35	15	6.5	42%	3.0	4	1
Lito Sheppard	24	74	29	13	8.8	39%	1.0	5	0
Roderick Hood	24	47	18	14	9.2	38%	0.0	1	3

Offensive Line

Year	Yards	AdjLineYd	Rank	Power	Rank	10+ Yds	Rank	Stuff	Rank	Sack	AdjSack%	Rank
2002	4.18	4.25	14	76%	6	14%	23	25%	17	37	6.8%	21
2003	4.72	4.41	4	73%	5	19%	8	23%	9	42	7.7%	29
2004	4.47	4.16	17	65%	13	19%	7	28%	27	36	5.9%	10

Year	LEnd	Rank	LTckl	Rank	MdGrd	Rank	RTckl	Rank	REnd	Rank
2002	5.06	5	3.77	26	4.46	7	3.95	21	3.96	16
2003	3.95	16	4.55	11	4.96	1	3.67	26	4.44	7
2004	4.29	17	4.45	14	4.55	8	3.73	26	3.52	21

The Eagles have had remarkable stability on the front five: Left tackle Tra Thomas, right tackle Jon Runyan, and center Hank Fraley have started together since 2001. Left guard Artis Hicks quietly emerged as a future Pro Bowl candidate in his first full-time season as the starter. The one change for 2005 will be Shawn Andrews, who looked good in half a game against the Giants before breaking a leg last season; he'll replace Jermane Mayberry at right guard. The Eagles' line is built for pass protection, and the team doesn't pull or trap very much. Many of Brian Westbrook's biggest gains have come on delays and stretch plays: slow-developing running plays that often lead defenders to commit to the pass rush. Blockers like Hicks and Runyan aren't that quick when blocking on the run, but they can crush flat-footed defenders when they try to switch gears.

Defensive Front Seven

Year	Yards	AdjLineYd	Rank	Power	Rank	10+ Yds	Rank	Stuff	Rank	Sack	AdjSack%	Rank
2002	4.17	3.96	11	69%	18	18%	17	26%	11	58	9.0%	1
2003	4.65	4.46	25	70%	27	18%	19	22%	24	39	6.4%	16
2004	4.31	4.14	13	51%	5	17%	19	24%	15	47	7.7%	8

Year	LEnd	Rank	LTckl	Rank	MdGrd	Rank	RTckl	Rank	REnd	Rank
2002	3.90	13	4.55	23	3.54	3	4.77	29	4.14	18
2003	4.39	18	4.06	15	4.55	28	4.47	22	4.55	30
2004	3.32	5	4.50	20	4.27	20	4.37	22	4.15	20

Defensive coordinator Jimmy Johnson used an eight-man rotation on the defensive line last year, and most of the key players are returning. Derrick Burgess signed with the Raiders; in 2004, he had just 2.5 sacks in the regular season but excelled in the playoffs. The Eagles have potential replacements in former first-round pick Jerome McDougle (who's been a disappointment), speed rusher Jamaal Green, and former starter N. D. Kalu. Defensive tackle is especially deep; first-round pick Mike Patterson out of USC joins a rotation featuring former Pro Bowler Corey Simon, up-and-comer Sam Rayburn, and consistent Darwin Walker. Hollis Thomas, a chubby spark plug and fan favorite, may be the odd man out. The team nearly traded Simon (their franchise player) to the Ravens; he skipped minicamp in a contract dispute and will be out of the picture in 2006 if Patterson plays well.

Jeremiah Trotter sets the tone for the defense, but he's not a conventional read-and-react linebacker. The Eagles' defense was most effective when Trotter attacked a lane at the snap, with Dhani Jones, Mark Simoneau, or Keith Adams sliding over to defend the cutback lanes or dropping into a zone. It's a strategy the Patriots exploited in the playoffs, so Johnson must make adjustments this year.

He also has to figure out what to do with Simoneau, who during the year went from middle linebacker to outside linebacker to the bench. He's adequate in coverage but was at the heart of Philadelphia's first-half troubles against the run. Only 35% of his plays stopped the offense short of success, while every other Philly linebacker had a Stop Rate above 50%, and his average play came 6.2 yards past the line of scrimmage, whereas the average for the rest of the Philly linebackers was 4.4 yards. In the playoffs, he was replaced by Keith Adams, who is undersized but slices through blockers and is fast enough to cover most running backs.

Defensive Secondary

Year	DVOA vs. #1 WR	Rank	DVOA vs. #2 WR	Rank	DVOA vs. Other WR	Rank	DVOA vs. TE	Rank	DVOA vs. RB	Rank
2002	-0.9%	14	-22.1%	9	7.8%	22	-5.0%	12	-11.8%	7
2003	-2.8%	14	-28.1%	6	19.1%	28	10.6%	24	1.7%	16
2004	27.6%	26	-5.8%	8	-20.1%	5	-36.5%	4	-33.1%	5

Cornerbacks Lito Sheppard and Sheldon Brown are similar in terms of size and coverage ability. Neither is personally responsible for Philadelphia's weakness against top wideouts, because neither was specifically assigned to the other team's main target. Each cornerback has a specific Achilles' heel: Brown gets clobbered in run support; Sheppard, despite five interceptions in 2004, has hands like feet. Sheppard's selection for the Pro Bowl was a little silly, but we have no beef with the selections of safeties Brian Dawkins and Michael Lewis, who were a big reason why the Eagles effectively shut down tight ends, running backs, and slot receivers. This unit also has very good depth with Roderick Hood, Dexter Wynn, and Matt Ware; Ware is expected to supplant Hood as the top nickelback this year. He was a Super Bowl goat because of his inability to cover Deion Branch, but his specialty is matching up against bigger receivers, and Branch would only qualify as big in the LFA (Lilliput Football Association).

Johnson loves to blitz the secondary. Eagles defensive backs had eight sacks, the fourth highest total in the NFL (behind the Bills, Redskins, and Ravens). The Eagles were the only team on which two defensive backs—Brown and Dawkins—had three or more sacks.

Special Teams

Year	DVOA	Rank	FG/XP	Rank	Net Punt	Rank	Punt Ret	Rank	Net Kick	Rank	Kick Ret	Rank
2002	6.1%	4	9.5	3	-1.2	17	9.6	6	6.7	7	9.4	6
2003	4.1%	3	7.5	11	-0.9	21	0.8	11	16.7	1	-1.1	18
2004	7.4%	3	13.7	2	19.3	2	-5.2	16	15.0	1	-1.6	20

In addition to what's written in the essay above, one thing worth noting is that the Eagles used different return men with very different results. The sample size is small, but J. R. Reed was worth +2.3 points on kick returns while Roderick Hood was worth −3.0 points, and Dexter Wynn was worth +0.7 points on punt returns while Reno Mahe was worth −4.9 points.

Coaching Staff

Andy Reid is as aggressive as any coach in the league. He'll throw deep on any down, design wicked gadget plays, and take bold risks. The Eagles' strategy in 2004 was to demolish opponents in the first half, raining McNabb-to-Owens bombs on them and counterpunching with Brian Westbrook. It usually worked, especially against the weaklings of the NFC. Reid's offensive style is similar to Mike Martz's, but his gift for management and his understated demeanor make him less of a target for criticism. And, of course, he's been more successful in the last three years. Key assistants like Jimmy Johnson, Brad Childress, John Harbaugh, and Marty Mornhinweg are back for another year, and the coaching stability allows Reid to juggle his coach-GM duties without dropping anything.

Though it is rarely discussed in the press, the Eagles are on the forefront of the NFL when it comes to using statistical analysis, both in game planning and in salary cap management. Reid hired two BYU professors, Shane Reese and Gil Fellingham, to design a Bayesian statistical model used in developing Philadelphia's postseason game plans. The Eagles are also among the teams that employ consultant Bud Goode, an early innovator in NFL analysis whose work paved the way for the book you are reading right now.

St. Louis Rams

A fluke playoff appearance can be the worst thing for an organization. When a team bottoms out like the Niners and Dolphins did last year, ownership has the good sense to press Ctrl-Alt-Delete and start over. But an 8–8 finish in a weak division can cause delusions. Management and the coaches may decide that tweaking the starting lineup could lead to 11 wins and real hope in the playoffs. With a team like the Rams, chock-full of former stars who've been to the Super Bowl, the urge to ignore the danger signs can be even greater.

With names like Faulk, Bruce, Holt, and Pace still on the roster, the Rams still have what sounds like the nucleus of a great team. A few 33–27 and 28–21 wins last year seduced casual observers into thinking that this Rams team wasn't that far removed from the 1999 or 2001 model. When they beat a good Jets team to advance to the playoffs, then defeated the Seahawks for a third straight time, it appeared that the Super Bowl window of opportunity was still open.

But against the Falcons, the window of opportunity closed. A 5'9", 180-pound return man slammed it shut.

Poor play on offense or defense is obvious on the field and evident all over the stat sheet—and teams with bad offenses or defenses usually make immediate, sweeping changes.

But special teams are different. A poor individual play on special teams, like a muffed punt or a long return allowed, can look like an isolated incident. Special teams statistics are often buried, and it takes seven or eight different numbers to get a picture of the strengths and weaknesses of the kick units. A team can have bad special teams for several years, but if the kicker makes all the easy field goals and the return men look the part, little will be done to solve the problem.

A look at annual DVOA for St. Louis special teams reveals that the team has had trouble for years (see table 1). In fact, the Rams' special teams DVOA of −14.4% in 2004 is the third worst total in the seven seasons for which we have broken down play-by-play and created DVOA ratings (see table 2). And the Rams' annual rankings would look worse if not for the abilities of kicker Jeff Wilkins, even though he had an off year in 2004. Our ratings estimate that Rams opponents gained more than 14 points of field position on kickoff returns when compared to the NFL average, but they gained only half a point of that field position based

on the actual length of the kickoff. The rest was just terrible tackling and pursuit by the St. Louis coverage team.

Special teams betrayed the 2004 Rams nearly every week. In Week 11 against the Bills, the coverage squads allowed punt returns of 86 and 53 yards, Erik Flowers muffed a squib kickoff, and Sean Landeta shanked a 29-yard punt. In Week 7, the Rams allowed a 20-yard punt return when rookie Tony Bua managed to block two gunners into each other, Keystone Kops–style.

These lapses foreshadowed what would happen against the Falcons in the playoffs. In that game, Allen Rossum returned a punt 68 yards for a touchdown and had two other key returns, for 39 and 45 yards. Rossum essentially accounted for ten points on his own and contributed to seven more: He wasn't the margin of victory in a 47–17 game, but his returns blew a close game wide open.

Mike Martz and special teams coach Mike Stock tried to fix things in midseason, bringing in punter Kevin

TABLE 1. ST. LOUIS SPECIAL TEAMS DVOA, 2000–2004

Year	DVOA	Rank
2000	−1.5%	17
2001	−6.8%	28
2002	−1.3%	18
2003	−1.7%	25
2004	−9.7%	32

TABLE 2. WORST SPECIAL TEAMS BY DVOA, 1998–2004

Year	Team	FG/XP	Net Kick	Kick Ret	Net Punt	Punt Ret	DVOA
2000	BUF	−6.8	−33.6	−9.6	−14.5	−15.2	−14.4%
2002	CIN	2.2	−13.8	7.0	−35.7	−23.7	−11.5%
2004	STL	1.2	−14.2	−15.6	−8.9	−16.3	−9.7%
2001	CIN	−13.5	−11.0	−8.5	−4.5	−13.3	−9.2%
2001	NYG	4.2	−17.2	−17.4	−6.1	−10.2	−8.4%
2002	WAS	−11.1	−3.0	−4.8	−23.0	−4.4	−8.3%
2001	BUF	−13.4	−4.5	−12.2	−5.4	−6.2	−7.5%
1999	SF	6.5	−4.5	−9.8	−25.3	−8.5	−7.5%
1998	OAK	−14.2	−13.7	−14.0	−1.6	2.6	−7.3%
1999	CLE	2.1	−0.1	−18.5	−10.5	−13.3	−7.3%

Stemke and return man Aveion Cason, and putting more starters onto the coverage units. Diagnosis: too little, too late. The Rams fired Stock in the off-season, and replaced him with Bob Ligashesky, a young coach who will try to erase the effects of five years of neglect. The team also signed free agent Mike Stone, a full-time kick gunner, and drafted punter Reggie Hodges in the sixth round to challenge Stemke.

Stone's a good player, and Ligashesky is a rising star in the assistant coaching ranks. But these moves are only small tweaks. The Rams didn't make an offer for Ike Reese, a special teams standout who could also have helped the defense. Hodges had four punts blocked for Ball State in 2004; there had to be safer options available in the sixth round. Some late draftees could become special teams gunners (Madison Hedgecock fits the mold), but the Rams passed on about a dozen potential standouts as return men. It's not clear if Ligashesky will have any roster authority; as it stands, Martz may pay lip service to improving the special teams, but he doesn't seem to know how to do it.

Would that the problems were confined to special teams, but the defense was awful week in and week out. The Super Bowl defenses of 1999 and 2001 forced lots of turnovers and kept opponents pinned to the mat after the offense knocked them silly. Those defenses were very good, though overshadowed by the offense.

The Rams have lost a lot of free agents since the glory years: Kevin Carter, London Fletcher, Dré Bly, Grant Wistrom, Dexter McCleon, and Mike Jones. Recent drafts brought few replacements: Adam Archuleta is the only true star the team has drafted on defense recently. The defense slipped steadily in 2002 and rebounded a little with a turnover-happy 2003. In 2004, without Lovie Smith to direct the show, it crumbled.

The Rams ranked 29th in the league in rushing yards allowed and 11th in the league in passing yards allowed. That makes it appear that the pass defense was adequate and the run defense was horrible. But yardage totals can be misleading, especially for a team that lost a lot of 31–14 and 45–17 games. You don't pass when you're up three touchdowns over a team with a quick-strike offense. DVOA cuts through the numerical pollution: The Rams ranked 28th in the league in run defense and 28th in the league in pass defense.

A look at the Rams' Week 2 loss to the Falcons illustrates both the overall futility of the defense and the distortions in the yards allowed totals. The Falcons rushed for 242 yards and 6.4 yards per carry in a 31–14 win. Michael Vick threw for just 179 yards. The run defense appears to be completely responsible for the loss. But Vick was 14 of 19 and averaged 9.4 yards per attempt, making the Rams game one of his best outings in 2004. The Falcons, like many opponents, had no trouble passing against the Rams; they just spent much of the second half running the ball and killing the clock.

Linebackers Tommy Polley and Robert Thomas received much of the blame for the team's defensive woes, and the Rams immediately targeted Dexter Coakley and Chris Claiborne as free agent replacements. Polley and Thomas are undersized linebackers who never developed great instincts in zone coverage. Coakley is a skilled coverage linebacker, and Claiborne's 250-pound frame will help him stand up to guards and fullbacks, but both have flaws. Coakley will turn 33 in October, and Clairborne has a history of weight issues.

Other units, though, were neglected. The Rams are still counting on Damione Lewis, Ryan Pickett, and Jimmy Kennedy to anchor an effective defensive line, but only Lewis has proven that he can be a quality starter. The Rams intercepted a league low six passes last season; Archuleta, Travis Fisher, and Jerametrius Butler form an average secondary. With a great pass rush harassing the opposing quarterback, they could be a playoff-caliber unit. With top pass rusher Bryce Fisher gone to Seattle, the Rams won't generate many sacks, and the defensive backs will be stretched thin.

Again, the Rams passed on players like Fred Smoot and Reggie Hayward, instead dropping a $3 million contact on Coakley, and slightly less on Claiborne. Cornerback Ronald Bartell of Howard was picked up in the draft, but he won't play a major role right away. It's as if the Rams took a quick glance at the stat sheet, decided that they just needed to tighten the run defense a little bit, and then tried to solve glaring problems on the line and in the secondary on the cheap with players like Bartell and DE Jay Williams. The Rams needed a rebuild and settled for a duct-tape job.

Martz spent the off-season girding the team for a finish somewhere between 7–9 and 9–7. For every step forward (finally getting Orlando Pace signed, picking up Coakley and Claiborne), there was an equal step backward (ticking off Kyle Turley, losing Fisher). The Rams are a borderline playoff team at best, weighed down by aging stars.

It didn't have to be this way. Martz and GM Charley Armey restructured Marshall Faulk and Torry Holt's contracts to free cap space. They could have restructured Isaac Bruce's deal as well, settled with Pace, placated Turley, and hit the free agent market with wallets wide open. A good haul there could have primed the Rams for one real last-gasp Super Bowl charge. Or the team could have cleared out the old vets, spent a year in salary cap purgatory, and rebuilt for 2006 around a Torry Holt–Marc Bulger–Steven Jackson nucleus.

But the Rams got false encouragement from their 2004 playoff run. They forgot the 31–7 blowout by the Cardinals, the 31–14 trouncing by the awful Dolphins. They forgot that they beat an Eagles team with nothing to play for in Week 16: Had the Eagles needed a win in that game, we would be writing about the Saints as the NFC's fluke playoff team. They forgot, because they ended up in the second round of the playoffs and figured that one or two more bodies could have gotten them to Jacksonville.

Quite simply, they forgot the lesson that Allen Rossum taught them in January. And it will soon come back to haunt them.

Mike Tanier

Research: In Defense of Mike Martz

A team loses to the Patriots on a last-second field goal in the Super Bowl. The following season this team is devastated by injuries to several Pro Bowl players, staggers out to a 1–5 start, and manages a 7–9 finish. The strong finish in the face of adversity gets the team coach lots of positive buzz and consideration as Coach of the Year.

That's the 2004 Carolina Panthers. It's also the 2002 St. Louis Rams, with one big exception. Unlike John Fox, Mike Martz was nobody's nominee for Coach of the Year.

He is considered one of the worst coaches in the league, criticized for poor game management and sometimes bizarre play calls. In the 2004 Football Outsiders Awards poll, readers chose him as the worst in pro football. One of his own players, Kyle Turley, rated him lower than that.

But is this fair?

The Pythagorean projection (explained in the Statistical Toolbox earlier in this book) is a simple method for projecting how many games a team might be expected to win based on points scored and allowed during the season. If a coach consistently leads teams that over- or underperform the Pythagorean projection, it may be a reflection of his ability (or inability) to win close games. Most coaches don't have definite trends in this area, but Martz does. The Rams are the only team to outperform their projected win total in each of the last five seasons. In fact, over his career Martz has the highest average number of wins over expected wins per season of any coach currently in the league (table 3).

It should be noted that not only is Martz the best by this measure, but his standard deviation is also the lowest, meaning he is also the most *consistent* at getting "extra" wins in each season.

(What about Bill Belichick, currently considered the NFL's best head coach by most observers? Belichick's Cleveland teams won fewer games than the Pythagorean projection all five years. If we discard his years with Cleveland and his first year with the Pats, and only look at 2001–2004, Belichick's average of 0.71 wins over projection is *still* second to Martz's average of 0.72.)

Perhaps what we are seeing here is not an effect of Martz's coaching, but an effect of the way the Rams play football. That might be true, except that the Rams won fewer games than projected during all three seasons with Dick Vermeil as head coach. And the Kansas City Chiefs, also coached by Vermeil and playing a similar style, have

TABLE 3. TOP FIVE CURRENT NFL COACHES, AVERAGE YEARLY DIFFERENCE BETWEEN ACTUAL WINS AND PYTHAGOREAN WINS (MIN. 2 SEASONS)

Rank	Coach	Avg. Win Difference
1	Mike Martz	0.66
2	Joe Gibbs	0.42
3	Dennis Green	0.41
4	Mike Sherman	0.33
5	Jim Haslett	0.32

won fewer games than projected in three of the past four seasons.

It's possible that the close wins indicated by outperforming the Pythagorean projection might come from frittering away big leads, not from overcoming adversity. Martz is often criticized for turning big wins into small wins, or even losses, due to game management. After losing to the Saints in Week 3, in a game that the Rams led by three in the fourth quarter, Bill Simmons of ESPN.com wrote that it was "the umpteenth time" the Rams had blown a late lead under Martz. In Week 5, the Rams completed a comeback against Seattle in a game that they had trailed by 17 points with less than six minutes to play. Instead of praising the Rams for their comeback (or knocking the Seahawks for allowing it to happen), Vic Carucci of NFL.com, simply used the opportunity to take another swing at Martz: "Aren't the Rams supposed to be the team that squanders big leads?"

Is it true Martz can't hold a lead in the fourth quarter? The answer is an emphatic "No."

Since the AFL-NFL merger in 1970, 114 different coaches have held a fourth quarter lead in at least 20 different games. During that period the average winning percentage for teams that have a lead at any point in the fourth quarter is .813. Table 4 lists the top ten coaches of the past 35 years, based on holding on to a fourth quarter lead and turning it into a win.

Simply put, Martz has the highest winning percentage of any coach over the last 35 years in games in which he has had a lead sometime during the fourth quarter. He does not fare as well in games in which he has a two-score

TABLE 4. TOP TEN NFL COACHES, WINNING PERCENTAGE WHEN HAVING ANY LEAD AT ANY TIME IN THE FOURTH QUARTER, 1970–2004 (MIN. 20 FOURTH QUARTER LEADS)

Rank	Coach	Win Pct.
1	Mike Martz	.914
2	Red Miller	.911
3	Barry Switzer	.898
4	Don McCafferty	.895
5	Joe Gibbs	.894
6	John Madden	.888
7	George Allen	.886
8	Mike Sherman	.885
9	Bobby Ross	.885
10	Brian Billick	.879

TABLE 5. TOP NFL COACHES, WINNING PERCENTAGE WHEN HAVING A TWO-SCORE LEAD AT ANY POINT IN A GAME, 1970–2004 (MIN. 15 GAMES WITH TWO-SCORE LEAD)

Rank	Coach	Win Pct.
1	Don McCafferty	.963
2	John Fox	.952
3	Jim Haslett	.939
4	Andy Reid	.935
5	Mike Sherman	.935
6	Red Miller	.933
7	Dennis Green	.929
8	Brian Billick	.925
9	John Madden	.921
10	George Allen	.918
27	Chuck Noll	.883
28	Mike Martz	.882
29	Don Shula	.881

lead. The league-average winning percentage in such games is .843. Table 5 lists the top ten coaches among the 114 coaches with at least 15 qualifying games since the merger. Added to the table are Martz and the two coaches that directly precede and follow him on the list.[1]

Obviously the Rams have squandered some big leads under Martz, but they're far better at protecting leads than most teams. Chuck Noll and Don Shula are generally considered good company when it comes to historical head coaches.

Another popular criticism of Martz goes something like this: "He's been handed the keys to the Cadillac and he's driven it right off a cliff!" That was the phrase Howie Long of FOX used in 2002. And again in 2003. And again last year. It means that Martz inherited a Super Bowl winning team and, through his poor coaching and mismanagement, irreparably damaged it.

Let's examine every other team that has won the Super Bowl, and then see what those teams did in the five seasons following each victory. In their five postchampionship seasons, the Rams have gone to the playoffs four times and made it to at least the divisional round three times. What about all of the previous Super Bowl winners? In their next five seasons, Super Bowl champions have averaged 2.88 postseason appearances and 2.45 trips that went as far as the divisional round. The Rams have done better than the average Super Bowl winner on both counts, and this includes the Super Bowl champions from before the salary cap era. Another myth debunked.

---

1. The full results for all 114 coaches are listed as tables 9 and 10 of the Statistical Appendix to this book.

Mike Martz is not the worst head coach in football. Given the weight of the evidence, Martz should be considered among the *best* head coaches in the NFL, maybe one of the top five. Martz is not an innocent bystander when the Rams win and the sole cause of any loss. As offensive coordinator, he helped turn a perennial also-ran into a perennial contender, and as head coach he has kept the team in the playoff hunt nearly every year. He is great at closing out games. If postseason records are included, he has the twelfth highest winning percentage of any head coach in history with at least five seasons. Before you decide that Martz is the head coach that he is reported to be, make sure you look at the head coach that he has actually been.

Jason McKinley

Research: The Slots Are Closed

It's late in your fantasy football draft—say, the 14th round. You have your starters, and now you are trying to acquire roster filler. You want value, players with upside, but the names on the draft board are no longer familiar to you. So you lapse into old habits. Torry Holt and Isaac Bruce left the board an hour ago, but you know the Rams like to throw the ball, so you thumb through your fantasy guide, find the name of their slot receiver, and figure you have a potential sleeper on your hands.

Don't do it. The days when the Rams' number three wideout could help your fantasy team are long gone.

In the halcyon days of the Rams offense, the slot receivers were major contributors: Ricky Proehl did the dirty work on third down, and Az Hakim provided quick strikes and explosive punt returns. Since Hakim and Proehl left, the productivity from the third and fourth wide receivers has slipped, though the newcomers see roughly the same number of passes thrown to them (table 6). Proehl and Hakim were thrown a total of 119 passes in 2000, while Kevin Curtis and Shaun McDonald were thrown a combined 118 passes last year.

There are several reasons why the Rams offense isn't as terrifying as it was four years ago: Marc Bulger isn't the young-ish Kurt Warner, Marshall Faulk is showing his age, and the offensive line has undergone transition. But the absence of Hakim and Proehl may be the biggest difference. Hakim was inconsistent, he fumbled, and he was miscast as a top receiver in Detroit, but there wasn't a nickel defender who could cover him, especially while the safety

TABLE 6. ST. LOUIS SLOT RECEIVERS, 1999–2004 (MIN. 25 RECEPTIONS)

Player	Year	Rec	Yards	TD	DPAR
Az Hakim	1999	36	677	8	23.3
Ricky Proehl	1999	33	349	0	8.5
Az Hakim	2000	53	734	4	17.6
Ricky Proehl	2000	31	441	4	24.5
Az Hakim	2001	39	374	4	2.0
Ricky Proehl	2001	40	563	5	24.7
Ricky Proehl	2002	43	466	4	11.4
Dane Looker	2003	47	495	3	2.2
Kevin Curtis	2004	32	421	2	5.6
Shaun McDonald	2004	37	494	3	6.3

was busy doubling Holt or Bruce. Proehl, meanwhile, was crafty at finding both the sticks and the end zone.

Martz has tried to replace Proehl and Hakim. The Rams drafted Shaun McDonald, Kevin Curtis, and Eric Crouch in search of a dangerous slot weapon. They also acquired free agent Terrance Wilkins, who had been an effective third wideout and return man in Indianapolis.

Wilkins was a bust, Crouch quit when he didn't get a chance at quarterback, and McDonald and Curtis were good, but not great, in 2004.

In addition to McDonald and Curtis, the names battling for the third receiver slot include Dane Looker, who actually started 2004 as the third wideout before an injury left him buried on the depth chart; Mike Furrey, who caught just one pass last season and is rumored to be moving to defensive back; and rookie Dante Ridgeway, who led the nation in receptions and caught 238 passes in three seasons at Ball State.

Curtis is the best prospect of the lot, which doesn't say much; these players smack of ordinariness, where Hakim and Proehl crackled with danger. Where's the 4.25 speed? The savvy of a decade of NFL experience? Why haven't the Rams pursued a 6′4″ possession weapon when so many have been available in the last two drafts?

Back in 2001, Proehl caught five touchdown passes in the red zone. Of his 40 receptions that year, 31 netted first downs. He averaged 14 yards per reception, squashing the myth that he was some slow guy who parked a yard past the line of scrimmage and waited for the defense to forget about him. None of the current Rams is capable of doing what Proehl did. If you find yourself thinking of drafting a third wideout whose name isn't "Brandon Stokley," think twice and take an extra running back instead.

Mike Tanier

Rams 2004 Stats by Week

Wk	vs.	W-L	PF	PA	YDF	YDA	TO	DVOA Total	Off	Def	ST
1	ARI	W	17	10	448	260	-3	3.1%	40.1%	31.7%	-5.2%
2	@ATL	L	17	34	280	416	-2	-68.3%	-1.8%	65.2%	-1.3%
3	NO	L	25	28	403	462	-1	-29.9%	18.2%	43.3%	-4.7%
4	@SF	W	24	14	360	332	+2	5.5%	36.8%	23.5%	-7.8%
5	@SEA	W	33	27	441	391	-3	-10.7%	3.6%	26.2%	11.9%
6	TB	W	28	21	324	332	+2	-9.3%	7.4%	-1.1%	-17.8%
7	@MIA	L	14	31	372	323	-1	-51.1%	35.8%	68.3%	-18.6%
8	BYE										
9	NE	L	22	40	336	377	-1	-15.0%	22.3%	22.9%	-14.4%
10	SEA	W	23	12	462	372	0	52.3%	55.2%	0.0%	-2.9%
11	@BUF	L	17	37	270	294	-3	-85.7%	-17.9%	21.7%	-46.2%
12	@GB	L	17	45	446	452	-3	-84.8%	-15.0%	64.0%	-5.9%
13	SF	W	16	6	350	160	-1	8.3%	-15.7%	-19.7%	4.3%
14	@CAR	L	7	20	289	308	-5	-104.0%	-104.3%	-11.3%	-11.1%
15	@ARI	L	7	31	185	402	-1	-95.2%	-49.3%	44.5%	-1.4%
16	PHI	W	20	7	419	155	0	38.1%	18.4%	-33.2%	-13.5%
17	NYJ	W	32	29	479	324	-3	16.4%	22.5%	-14.2%	-20.4%
18	@SEA	W	27	20	396	413	0	7.2%	28.9%	23.5%	1.8%
19	@ATL	L	17	47	339	397	+1	-02.5%	21.3%	46.4%	-37.4%

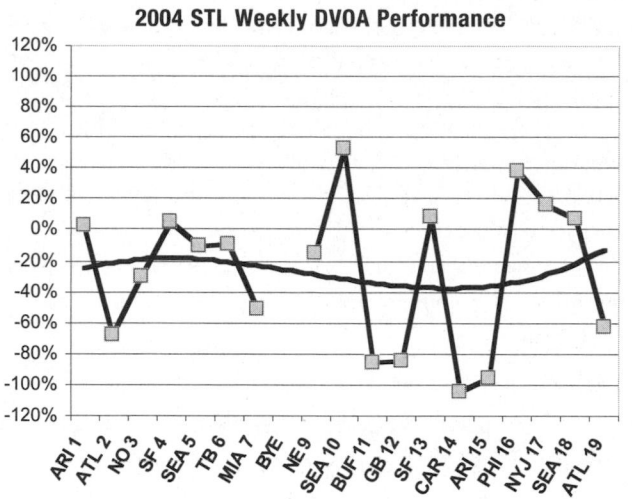

Trends and Splits

	Offense	Rank	Defense	Rank
Total DVOA	4.8%	12	21.0%	30
Unadjusted VOA	1.7%	14	17.0%	27
Weighted Trend	-3.7%	18	11.7%	25
Variance	15.3%	4	10.0%	16
Passing	6.6%	13	29.6%	28
Rushing	2.4%	12	12.0%	28
First Down	3.0%	12	13.2%	27
Second Down	0.7%	17	27.9%	31
Third Down	15.4%	10	26.2%	27
Red Zone	-0.4%	16	29.0%	29
Late and Close	6.2%	12	3.3%	21

Five-Year Performance

	2004	2003	2002	2001	2000
W-L	8-8	12-4	7-9	14-2	10-6
Pythagorean Wins	6.1	10.8	6.5	13.0	9.3
Estimated Wins	5.4	9.1	8.4	13.0	10.2
Total DVOA	-25.9%	9.1%	-2.0%	39.6%	18.0%
Rank	30	13	19	1	8
Offense	4.8%	-3.3%	-5.7%	25.6%	31.4%
Rank	12	16	25	1	1
Defense	21.0%	-14.0%	-5.1%	-20.8%	11.9%
Rank	30	6	9	3	26
Special Teams	-9.7%	-1.7%	-1.3%	-6.8%	-1.5%
Rank	32	26	18	28	17

Passing (min. 5 plays)

Player	DPAR	PAR	DVOA	Plys	NtYds	Avg	Cmpl	TD	Int
Marc Bulger	92.6	85.8	29.3%	523	3672	7.0	66.2%	21	14
Chris Chandler	-26.1	-24.5	-100.7%	69	406	5.9	56.5%	2	8
Jamie Martin	5.8	3.6	31.4%	33	178	5.4	53.3%	0	0

Rushing (min. 3 plays)

Player	DPAR	PAR	DVOA	Plys	Yds	Avg	TD	Fum	Suc
Marshall Faulk	9.8	8.2	-2.7%	195	774	4.0	3	1	47%
Steven Jackson	19.9	19.1	17.9%	134	673	5.0	4	1	57%
Arlen Harris	-0.5	-0.7	-20.3%	20	63	3.2	0	0	40%
Marc Bulger	2.7	3.1	7.7%	16	92	5.8	3	0	—
Shaun McDonald	-1.5	-1.8	-88.6%	4	0	0.0	0	0	—
Kevin Curtis	0.8	1.0	17.6%	3	24	8.0	0	0	—
Joey Goodspeed	1.0	1.1	32.9%	3	6	2.0	1	0	67%

Receiving (min. 5 plays)

Player	DPAR	PAR	DVOA	Plys	Ctch	Yds	Y/C	TD	CPct
WR									
Isaac Bruce	26.0	25.4	11.8%	148	89	1302	14.6	6	60%
Torry Holt	34.9	35.2	24.8%	137	94	1371	14.6	10	69%
Shaun McDonald	6.3	5.5	-0.6%	68	37	495	13.4	3	54%
Kevin Curtis	5.6	5.9	2.0%	50	32	421	13.2	2	64%
Dane Looker	-0.5	-1.1	-17.4%	26	13	183	14.1	0	50%
TE									
Brandon Manumaleuna	3.7	3.4	15.5%	21	15	174	11.6	1	71%
Cam Cleeland	0.5	0.0	-6.2%	12	7	57	8.1	0	58%
RB									
Marshall Faulk	-4.3	-5.2	-22.4%	65	50	310	6.2	1	77%
Steven Jackson	5.4	4.4	41.9%	24	19	189	9.9	0	79%
Joey Goodspeed	-2.2	-3.2	-34.3%	16	11	71	6.5	0	69%

Defensive Players (min. 20 plays)

Player	Age	Plys	Stop	Dfts	AvYds	StpRt	Sack	Int	FR
Defensive Line									
Leonard Little	31	53	43	23	1.1	81%	7.0	0	4
Ryan Pickett	26	47	36	11	1.4	77%	2.0	0	0
Bryce Fisher	28	45	39	14	0.4	87%	8.5	0	0
Damione Lewis	27	35	26	12	1.3	74%	5.0	0	0
Tony Hargrove	22	28	16	6	2.2	57%	1.0	0	0
Tyoka Jackson	34	26	19	12	1.3	73%	4.0	0	0
Linebackers									
Pino Tinoisamoa	24	96	57	22	4.1	59%	1.5	0	1
Tommy Polley	27	84	45	20	4.4	54%	2.0	0	0
Robert Thomas	25	53	31	8	3.6	58%	0.0	0	0
Trev Faulk	24	23	16	5	3.7	70%	0.0	0	0

Player	Age	Plys	Stop	Dfts	AvYds	StpRt	Sack	Int	FR
Secondary									
Jerametrius Butler	27	98	32	11	8.2	33%	0.0	5	1
Adam Archuleta	28	88	37	17	7.0	42%	2.0	0	1
Aeneas Williams	37	50	13	8	11.8	26%	0.0	0	0
Rich Coady	29	45	11	7	12.2	24%	0.0	0	1
Travis Fisher	27	41	13	6	8.7	32%	0.0	1	0
Antuan Edwards	28	33	10	3	10.6	30%	0.0	0	0
DeJuan Groce	25	31	10	2	9.6	32%	0.0	0	0

Offensive Line

Year	Yards	AdjLineYd	Rank	Power	Rank	10+ Yds	Rank	Stuff	Rank	Sack	AdjSack%	Rank
2002	4.16	3.89	27	60%	26	19%	9	28%	28	45	7.3%	23
2003	3.73	3.80	27	68%	13	15%	18	30%	29	44	6.9%	20
2004	4.31	4.26	13	66%	12	17%	16	21%	6	50	8.1%	25

Year	LEnd	Rank	LTckl	Rank	MdGrd	Rank	RTckl	Rank	REnd	Rank
2002	2.84	29	4.40	11	4.34	11	3.47	30	3.82	18
2003	3.41	29	4.18	17	3.94	23	5.34	1	2.60	29
2004	4.13	19	4.02	23	4.14	19	4.70	9	4.58	4

The Rams finally signed Orlando Pace to a long-term deal, but have uncertainty at three offensive line positions. Kyle Turley and Mike Martz are more likely to meet in a WWE ring than in a minicamp, so the team drafted Alex Barron, arguably the most athletic offensive lineman in the draft, to replace Turley. Richie Incognito will replace Turley as the team's resident wild man. Incognito was kicked off two college programs for a variety of assaults and locker-room brawls, but he's a great player when he channels his energy onto the football field. Incognito could play guard while waiting for center Andy McCollum to retire. Last year's interior line was filled with aging veterans (McCollum, Adam Timmerman) and already-aged retreads (Tom Nutten, Chris Dishman) so Incognito and third-year player Scott Tercero should provide a much-needed overhaul. The question is what happens to Grant Williams, who filled Turley's right tackle spot most of last season. Although he got a lot of help from tight end Brandon Manumaleuna, those strong numbers for the Rams' running right would seem to indicate that he's a bit underrated as a run blocker. As a pass blocker, he's horrible, with 12 sacks allowed.

Defensive Front Seven

Year	Yards	AdjLineYd	Rank	Power	Rank	10+ Yds	Rank	Stuff	Rank	Sack	AdjSack%	Rank
2002	4.18	4.25	20	56%	6	16%	13	26%	13	38	8.0%	6
2003	4.46	4.02	15	59%	4	23%	28	28%	9	42	7.2%	5
2004	4.59	4.26	19	76%	30	22%	27	24%	14	36	6.7%	16

Year	LEnd	Rank	LTckl	Rank	MdGrd	Rank	RTckl	Rank	REnd	Rank
2002	5.12	31	3.79	8	4.09	11	4.64	25	4.16	19
2003	4.52	21	3.86	13	3.89	8	4.83	30	2.55	3
2004	4.32	17	5.07	30	3.97	8	4.36	21	4.48	25

The Rams are making a concerted effort to get bigger on the front seven: 300-pound Damione Lewis is moving to end, 280-pound ex-Dolphin free agent Jay Williams was signed to be the other defensive end, and ex-Viking free agent Chris Claiborne is a big linebacker. (Plans to shift undersized linebacker Pisa Tinoisamoa to safety, however, seem to have been scuttled.) This is a philosophical shift: Former coordinator Lovie Smith emphasized quickness and preferred smaller linebackers. But the Rams ranked 30th in the league in Power Success last year, allowing opponents to convert 76% of their short-yardage plays, so the shift makes some sense. At the same time, it may be a reaction to the myth that the Rams run defense was significantly worse than the pass defense. That's what raw yardage totals say, but DVOA says that the Rams were just as bad against the pass because they ranked 13th in the NFC in passing plays faced and had just six interceptions. Dexter Coakley will improve the pass coverage, as Tommy Polley and Robert Thomas both had trouble defending their zones.

Defensive Secondary

Year	DVOA vs. #1 WR	Rank	DVOA vs. #2 WR	Rank	DVOA vs. Other WR	Rank	DVOA vs. TE	Rank	DVOA vs. RB	Rank
2002	3.4%	19	48.7%	32	-32.7%	5	-14.8%	7	8.7%	20
2003	-30.5%	2	-0.8%	19	-8.0%	19	-14.3%	8	-11.5%	10
2004	9.6%	20	15.6%	24	34.2%	31	20.7%	24	17.3%	30

The Rams secondary had just two pass interference penalties charged to them, and they weren't flagged once for illegal contact. Usually, that's a good thing, but for the Rams that suggests that: (1) opponents were so content to run the ball that the cornerbacks were rarely challenged, and (2) when challenged, undersized Travis Fisher and Jerametrius Butler didn't get pushy with their receivers. Rookie Ron Bartell stands at 6′1″ and has a rep as a good bump-and-run defender; he'll challenge Fisher for a starting job and may be the designated "cover the 6′4″ guy" defender. Bartell may not be effective immediately; as a rookie making the I-AA to NFL leap, he'll increase the penalty count without necessarily keeping his receiver in check. At safety, Aeneas Williams retired, Antuan Edwards was not re-signed, and Adam Archuleta spent the off-season rehabbing a herniated disc in his back. Rookies Oshiomogho Atogwe and Jerome Carter will battle for the right to play opposite Archuleta. While those of us who have to type these names frequently are rooting hard for Carter, Rams fans may want to root for Atogwe, who unlike Carter is a natural free safety.

Special Teams

Year	DVOA	Rank	FG/XP	Rank	Net Punt	Rank	Punt Ret	Rank	Net Kick	Rank	Kick Ret	Rank
2002	-1.3%	18	-1.5	17	-8.9	24	12.0	5	-5.9	23	-3.0	20
2003	-1.7%	25	15.2	2	-9.6	29	-2.3	16	-4.7	25	-7.8	28
2004	-9.7%	32	1.2	16	-8.9	31	-16.3	30	-14.2	30	-15.6	32

How can a team so obsessed with speedy players be so bad when it comes to returning kicks and punts? According to our numbers, Shaun McDonald cost the Rams an astonishing 17 points' worth of field position because he couldn't stop tripping over his own feet when returning punts. Look for the Rams to try rookie Dante Ridgeway in the role this year. Maybe he can return kicks, too, because the Rams had five players return at least four kicks last year and each one had negative value. Despite the poor coverage units, the Rams have several players who should be solid special teamers, including Brandon Chillar and Trev Faulk. The draft brought players like Jerome Carter and Ray Hodges; free agency brought Michael Stone and Michael Hawthorne. The best way to improve special teams is to make a serious commitment to doing so: Acquire and develop specialists, allocate extra practice time, make the kicking game a priority. The Rams have no other choice this year.

Coaching Staff

Defensive coordinator Larry Marmie was Mike Martz's boss at Arizona State in the late 1980s: Marmie was head coach, Martz offensive coordinator. Marmie coached the Sun Devils to an unimpressive 22–21 record and no bowl appearances from 1988 through 1991. New special teams coach Bob Ligashesky and tight ends coach Frank Falks were also on that Arizona State staff.

More recently, Marmie served as the defensive coordinator for the Cardinals of the Dave McGinnis era. From 2001 to 2003, the Cardinals finished 28th, 29th, and 31st in the league in DVOA, while last year's Rams finished 30th. Marmie's coaching philosophy is supposed to be similar to Lovie Smith's, but Smith gets results while Marmie's defenses flounder. If the Rams defense is awful again this year, Marmie will be fired, but he'll land on his feet: There's little accountability for assistant coaches, who can parachute from job to job as long as they have a network of friends and ex-assistants to call upon.

San Francisco 49ers

Another area of concern is the formula being implemented by [owner John] York's non-football people. The reliance on statistical analysis in putting together a football team is appalling to men who played the game; they would rather see such "Moneyball" tactics used as one limited tool, not an overall philosophy. "Football guys make football decisions, computers don't," one player said. "This product succeeds through emotion."

—ANN KILLON, SAN JOSE MERCURY NEWS, 1/10/05

[Ernie Adams] is officially the Pats' research director, with his main area of focus being statistical analysis. But he's really Bill Belichick's consigliore. Word is Belichick never makes an important football decision without him. Adams has a hand in game-planning and personnel, and during games he's in the coaches' booth wearing a headset.

—MICHAEL FELGER, BOSTON HERALD, 1/30/04

A team that finishes 2–14 is going to have a lot of needs. The 49ers went into the off-season needing new players at nearly every position on both sides of the ball. After a rash of injuries in 2004, they needed a better medical staff. After firing Terry Donahue and Dennis Erickson, they needed to find a new general manager and head coach.

But what the San Francisco 49ers needed most was a new public relations staff.

The 2003 49ers were a mediocre team filled with highly paid veterans. The last few drafts had been poor, and constant contract restructuring meant that the salary cap was choked with so-called dead money. The front office decided that the team had to start from scratch, and the only way to do it was to cut numerous veterans, get hit with salary cap penalties all at the same time, and finally wipe the slate clean. The team traded its franchise receiver and waived its starting quarterback, running back, and two starting offensive linemen. A number of defensive free agents left the team to sign elsewhere.

Going into 2004, everybody who followed football knew that the 49ers were going to be bad. But very few expected them to become the worst team in football. A wave of injuries cost them a veteran starting center, a Pro Bowl linebacker, and both starting cornerbacks for most of the season. Their promising young quarterback missed time due to problems in his feet, shoulders, and forearms. Their promising young running back apparently forgot how to run with the football. Keeping spending down to finally clear the salary cap meant there was no depth to make up for any of these injuries. The 49ers won only two games, both requiring overtime and both against the league's previous laughingstock, the Arizona Cardinals.

49ERS PROSPECTUS

2004 Record: 2–14

DVOA Estimated Wins: 2.3 (32nd)

Pythagorean Wins: 3.4 (32nd)

DVOA: −46.5% total (32nd), −50.3% weighted (32nd)

Adjusted Offense: 16.2 points/game (−19.9% DVOA, 29th)

Adjusted Defense: 28.5 points/game (26.7% DVOA, 32nd)

Adjusted Special Teams: 0.0 points/game (0.1% DVOA, 17th)

Variance: 16.0% (21st)

2004: Oh, we knew it would be bad, but not this bad.

2005: It's a long climb back up the team development curve.

2005 Projection

D'Brickashaw D'erby (0–4): 46%

Bad Team (5–6): 26%

Mediocre (7–8): 17%

Playoff Contender (9–10): 7%

Super Bowl Contender (11+): 4%

Projected Average Opponent: 1.4% DVOA (13th in NFL)

A 2–14 team needs a scapegoat, even two or three. For the ownership, the scapegoats were general manager Terry Donahue and head coach Dennis Erickson, both fired after the season. For the media and the fans, the scapegoats were the ownership and the secondary front office personnel who were left behind: Assistant General Manager Paarag Marathe and Assistant Director of Football Administration Terry Tumey.

One league personnel director with knowledge of the situation in San Francisco said, "They're trying to apply the 'Moneyball' principles to the NFL but they have a bunch of non-football guys in the front office. Their scouts have all lost their motivation because they feel their information isn't used. It's a terrible situation."
—RON BORGES, *BOSTON GLOBE*, 1/23/05

Andy Reid, a former BYU football player who coaches the Philadelphia Eagles, hopes a couple of number-crunchers can help his bone-crunching football team dominate the NFL. Reid has asked two BYU professors to prepare a report that statistically analyzes every play, every coach's decision and every player on the field.
—TAD WALCH, *DESERET MORNING NEWS*, 1/14/05

A couple of years ago it became clear to Donahue that the 49ers were going to face some tough economic times. He hired Marathe, a management consultant, to develop statistical programs that could predict market trends for player contracts and help the 49ers navigate salary cap ramifications. In 2004, promoted to assistant general manager, Marathe began to work on new methods of identifying and quantifying player talent.

While the 49ers were working on ways to lessen the strain on their salary cap, the book *Moneyball* focused the attention of the sports world on their baseball-playing neighbors across the bay. When talking to local reporters, Donahue compared his efforts to improve San Francisco's cap situation and talent base with Billy Beane's methods for producing a winning team despite financial constraints. A number of scouts and personnel people across the league, mindful of the cuts the Oakland A's had made in traditional scouting, were not very happy about this. When the 49ers collapsed, these scouts, and the journalists who used them as sources, quickly decided that Marathe was the reason—even though he had been involved in player personnel decisions for only a year, and never had final authority on any decisions. Tumey, a former defensive line coach with both UCLA and the Denver Broncos who had moved into financial administration, shared in the blame because he shared the same scarlet letters as Marathe: M.B.A.

Sportswriters wanted to know: Why were prospective coaches and general managers being interviewed by some guy who set the scouting budget and some other guy with a strange Indian name, and not by the organization's "football guys"? The answer, of course, was that the football guys—you know, the head coach and general manager—weren't available to interview prospective head coaches and general managers because *they hadn't been hired yet.*

All January long, the 49ers were mercilessly ripped by columnists, both local and national, for sacrificing their football team on the altar of raw mathematics. Meanwhile, the two most statistically oriented franchises in the NFL marched on to meet each other in Super Bowl XXXIX.

Football ability can't be quantified as easily as baseball talent can. Stats are largely meaningless in football. Donahue's attempt to copy Beane in the NFL was as pointless as a kitten trying to pull a dogsled. Different sports, different animals.
—GWEN KNAPP, *SAN FRANCISCO CHRONICLE*, 1/9/05

Now the sabermetric revolution may be gaining a toehold in football as well. And here too the center of the revolution can be found in Massachusetts, where Coach Bill Belichick has led the New England Patriots to victories in two of the last three Super Bowls.
—JON CHAIT AND PAUL CAMPOS, *NEW YORK TIMES MAGAZINE*, 12/12/04

This just in: What the San Francisco 49ers are doing is *not new*. It isn't just that baseball teams like Oakland and Boston (who, you may have heard, are the World Champions) are moving toward the use of statistical analysis in an attempt to maximize every spot on the roster and every dollar in the budget. Football teams have been using analysis to improve themselves since Gil Brandt first typed all the college prospects into a computer instead of drafting for the Dallas Cowboys out of a copy of *Street and Smith's*.

Bill Belichick owns an economics degree from that legendary football factory Wesleyan University. He reads papers on the relationship between probability theory and football by economics professors like David Romer and Harold Sackrowitz. His roster decisions are based on maximizing salary cap space, not "heart" and "chemistry." If you have heart and a $5 million cap number, well, it was nice knowing you. Just ask Troy Brown.

Andy Reid, meanwhile, employs a full-time research analyst to go with those BYU professors and the $20,000 a year he pays consultant Bud Goode, who also works for Dick Vermeil and helped advise the Rams on the roster changes that turned them into 1999 World Champions.

Each of the quotations criticizing the San Francisco front office could have easily been written about the Patriots in 2000 or the Eagles in 1999. In fact, they practically were—when New England hired Belichick in 2000, most local reporters saw him as a numbers geek with no social skills who had been a dismal failure in Cleveland. Some local reporters suggested that he was mentally unhinged. In Philadelphia, fans and writers slammed Reid for choosing Donovan McNabb over Ricky Williams in the 1999 draft.

For some reason, a number of writers both local and national have an axe to grind against the 49ers, so Ann Killon of the *San Jose Mercury News* can write, "I think number crunching tends to spit out the Ryan Leafs of the world, rather than the Tom Bradys," without mentioning that no head coach in the league uses number crunching more than the one who selected Tom Brady in the sixth round of the 2000 draft.

Somebody at the 49ers needs to stand up and explain to the world that the team is doing everything in its power to amass as much information as possible in order to improve the roster, develop a better game plan, and win football games. Information means subjective scouting reports from old guys smoking cigars, and it means numbers out of a computer. The conflict between scouting and statistics is a false dichotomy made up by reporters looking for an angle. The Patriots and Eagles don't choose between the two, and neither will the 49ers.

The "football guys" who were eventually hired to direct the 49ers are Head Coach Mike Nolan and Vice President of Player Personnel Scot McCloughan. Nolan is familiar with rebuilding after a salary cap purge, since he had to put the Baltimore defense back together in 2002. McCloughan spent the last five years as director of college scouting in Seattle, and was considered one of the rising stars in player personnel. Both men will combine years of football experience with the innovative research being done in the front office. Nolan told the *Sacramento Bee* before the draft that "there's a lot of common ground between who we think is a good player and what [Marathe's system] has put out."

Statistical analysis will be just one reason why this team succeeds or fails. Like Belichick and Reid, Nolan will need to use that analysis to draw up strong game plans, but he also needs to coach his players to execute them properly. Like Scott Pioli in New England and Tom Heckert in Philadelphia, McCloughan will have to find not just star players but low-round draft picks, undrafted rookies, and veteran free agents who can fill important roles and provide depth. Statistical analysis can help with some of that, but a lot of it is just good old-fashioned—yes, it's true—scouting.

The first big choice for this new administration was the first overall draft selection. With no team willing to trade up to get a specific player, and only offensive "skill players" as the consensus top prospects, and an injury-prone sixth-round pick as their current starter behind center, the new efficiency-focused 49ers were forced by circumstance to put the franchise in the hands of the riskiest, least economically efficient player possible: a highly paid rookie quarterback.

Welcome to the NFL, Alex Smith. Please, please, please don't torpedo our franchise.

We mean no disrespect to Smith or his abilities. But if the 49ers brass thinks the way we do (which is the problem, according to the local press) they would have much rather used that pick on an offensive tackle like D'Brickashaw Ferguson, or a defensive end like Julius Peppers. Unfortunately, this would have required a time machine.

The good news is that Smith's scouting report reads like a list of the skills possessed by the best quarterbacks in today's NFL. He's intelligent. He has pocket awareness and can recognize a blitz. He doesn't rush a throw to his primary target. He doesn't throw into traffic. If he can harness these skills, and learn to read the far more confusing defenses of the NFL, he sounds like a cross between Tom Brady and Steve McNair with a back transplant.

If Smith turns out for the best, he'll become the star around whom the 49ers can piece together a winning team. If he turns out to be a flop, he'll become a salary albatross that will handcuff the team whether the rest of the roster construction works out or not. It will take at least two years, maybe three, before we know whether he's the former or the latter.

In the meantime, the 49ers took 10 players in the 2004 draft and 11 players in the 2005 draft. The dead salary cap weight left over from a long run of success is finally cleared out of the budget. There is almost nobody in either the coaching staff or the administration who has held his position for more than a year. Very few players on the 2003 roster will be here when the young talent amassed over the last two drafts—and next year's draft, and the one after that—finally gels.

The bottom of the development curve is very painful. The year after isn't much better. What the 49ers are going through isn't new. The way they are trying to dig out of the hole isn't new either. There is no guarantee that the new administration in San Francisco will be able to build a championship team. But don't judge the quality of the rebuilding until they actually have time to rebuild.

Aaron Schatz

Research: How Long Do Terrible Teams Take to Reach Respectability?

San Francisco fans aren't used to this. It's just not natural for the 49ers, the team that dominated the 1980s and was still damn good throughout the 1990s, to have the first pick in the draft. All the questions about the 49ers—Is Mike Nolan ready to be a head coach? Is Alex Smith ready to be a starting quarterback?—boil down to this: How much longer until they're back in the playoffs? A look at some of the worst teams of recent seasons could give us an idea.

First, drafting a quarterback isn't necessarily a requirement for rebuilding. The Panthers set the gold standard for how to rebuild from a terrible season when they went from 1–15 to 7–9 to the Super Bowl. The Panthers didn't draft a quarterback in the first round; they just brought in three guys they thought could be acceptable—Chris Weinke, Rodney Peete, and Jake Delhomme—and found that one of them was more than just acceptable. That doesn't necessarily mean the 49ers were wrong to take Alex Smith, but there's no reason they couldn't have built with other positions and kept Tim Rattay for another go-round.

Second, if your coach has led your team to a 1–15 or 2–14 record, he needs to be replaced. Although not every team in our study fired its coach after its season of futility, firing the coach was a prerequisite for turning the team around. Might as well do it sooner rather than later. Replacing Dennis Erickson with Mike Nolan was a good move.

Below we examine every team that has finished 1–15 or 2–14 since 1992. Teams are ranked in order of how successfully they rebuilt, and we noted whether each team fired their coach and/or drafted a new quarterback, as the 49ers have.

2001 Panthers (1–15): Fired coach, didn't draft quarterback – At 1–15 in the last year of the Seifert era, the Panthers (who only a few years earlier exceeded everyone's expectations of how well an expansion team could play) looked like they had no direction. But the Panthers made a great decision by hiring John Fox, and Fox wisely signed Jake Delhomme as an inexpensive free agent and drafted Julius Peppers. Those moves, and several other smart signings, gave the Panthers immediate results: 7–9 in 2002 and 11–5 with a Super Bowl appearance in 2003.

1996 Jets (1–15): Fired coach, didn't draft quarterback – Hiring Bill Parcells wasn't an option available to the 49ers, but it would have been a good choice. Parcells took a team that looked much worse than this year's 49ers and made them winners: 9–7 in his first year and 12–4 in his second before going 8–8 in his final year. Perhaps the smartest move Parcells made was avoiding the temptation to draft a quarterback and instead keeping Neil O'Donnell around. One thing to remember: The Jets had the first overall pick but traded it to the Rams, who wanted Orlando Pace. They moved down and drafted James Farrior. But if Peyton Manning had left Tennessee as a junior, Parcells almost certainly would have kept the number one pick and used it on Manning. Parcells and Manning together in New York—now that would have been something.

1992 Patriots (2–14): Fired coach, drafted quarterback – Parcells took over in 1993 and made the Patriots 5–11 before getting them to 10–6 and the playoffs the next year. Although they then regressed to 6–10 in 1995 (Parcells teams always take a step backward after their first step forward), they went 11–5 in 1996 and made the Super Bowl before Parcells left for greener pastures. Here the Tuna's greatest decision was choosing Drew Bledsoe over Rick Mirer with the first choice in the 1993 draft, and Bledsoe moved right into the starting lineup. His reputation has faded in recent years, but as we pointed out in the Dallas chapter, Bledsoe is among the best number one overall selections of the past 20 years.

1994 Oilers (2–14): Fired coach, drafted quarterback – The best move the Oilers made was hiring assistant Jeff Fisher as interim coach in the middle of the '94 season

and giving him the job for good when the season ended. After 7–9 and 8–8 records, the Oilers moved to Tennessee in 1997, went 8–8 again, but then got to the Super Bowl with a 13–3 record in 1999. The key to the team's rebuilding was the decision to select Steve McNair in the first round of the 1995 draft. But unlike New England with Bledsoe, the Oilers left their top prospect on the bench to learn behind Chris Chandler until he was ready. Will the 49ers do the same with Smith and Rattay?

2000 Chargers (1–15): Didn't fire coach, didn't draft quarterback – Mike Riley was allowed to stay another year and brought the Chargers to 5–11 before he was fired. Still, that 1–15 record has to be viewed as a blessing in disguise for any Chargers fan. Unable to reach a contract deal with Michael Vick, the Chargers traded down with Atlanta. Instead of Vick, the Chargers chose LaDainian Tomlinson with the first-round pick that had belonged to the Falcons and Drew Brees with the first pick of round two (an additional pick from this trade became receiver Reche Caldwell in 2002). Riley was replaced by Marty Schottenheimer, who had a surprising 8–8 year in his first season, watched the team regress to 4–12, and then shocked everyone with a 12–4 record last year. San Francisco fans couldn't complain if the 49ers were to get results like these, although questions still remain about San Diego's quarterback situation, and it remains to be seen if that 12–4 season was a fluke or the beginning of a sustained period of winning.

2002 Bengals (2–14): Fired coach, drafted quarterback – A 2–14 record led to several changes in the Bengals' front office that haven't received enough attention. The biggest one is that Mike Brown, the team's owner, finally acknowledged—tacitly if not openly—that he's not the football man his father was. Brown still takes an active role in the front office, but when he fired Dick LeBeau and hired Marvin Lewis, he gave Lewis more control over personnel than previous Bengals coaches had received. The Bengals also raised their budget for scouting, which for years Brown had tried to do on the cheap. The results, so far, have been promising. Lewis spent the first pick in the draft on Carson Palmer, who looks like he's going to be a fine NFL quarterback. Even in 2003, with Palmer on the sidelines for every play of the season, the Bengals had a huge turnaround, from 2–14 to 8–8. The most credit for that belongs to Lewis, who made the league's laughingstock respectable.

1999 Browns (2–14): Didn't fire coach, didn't draft quarterback – As an expansion team, the Browns got the first pick in 1999 and the ability to take a quarterback of the future. They chose Tim Couch, who had reasonable growth over his first couple seasons before he inexplicably stagnated and watched his career fall apart. Head coach

Chris Palmer went 5–27 in two years before Butch Davis got the Browns up to 7–9 and 9–7 with a wild card win, but the team then languished due to poor drafting. Despite using numerous high draft picks on defensive linemen, running backs, and wide receivers, the Browns never saw a player at any of those positions actually mature into a star. After last year's implosion, the Browns are back to the drawing board.

1992 Seahawks (2–14): Didn't fire coach, drafted quarterback – After going 2–14, Seattle couldn't fire its head coach to hire a two-time Super Bowl champion head coach like Bill Parcells, because their head coach already was a two-time Super Bowl champion. The Seahawks had hired ex-Raiders coach Tom Flores the year before, only to watch the team crumble from 7–9 to 2–14 in his first season. New England didn't just end up with the better head coach; a draft tiebreaker also gave them the first pick and Drew Bledsoe, while the Seahawks were stuck with the second pick and Rick Mirer. The Mirer-led passing game was so bad that the Seahawks could go only 6–10 each of the next two seasons despite Pro Bowl seasons from running back Chris Warren and a reasonable defense led by youngsters like Cortez Kennedy and Sam Adams. Dennis Erickson then came in for four seasons of 7–9 or 8–8 before the Seahawks had a chance to hire Mike Holmgren, who led them back to the playoffs in 1999.

2001 Lions (2–14): Didn't fire coach, drafted quarterback – After taking over a 9–7 team that missed the playoffs on a last-second field goal on the last play of the last game of the season, Matt Millen's first year as general manager was an unmitigated disaster. His decision to hire Marty Mornhinweg proved disastrous, and the Lions plummeted to 2–14. Mornhinweg's ill-advised decision to bench Charlie Batch for Ty Detmer, who promptly threw seven interceptions in his first start, hurt the team. Millen got rid of solid players such as receiver Johnnie Morton and offensive lineman Jeff Hartings, without having a plan for replacing them. Other problems weren't the fault of Millen and Mornhinweg. Pro Bowl linebacker Stephen Boyd suffered a career-ending back injury. The career of Pro Bowl return man Desmond Howard ended when a teammate slapped him while celebrating a big play, injuring his neck. After a 3–13 season in 2002, Mornhinweg had a record identical to that of Palmer in Cleveland, although Palmer has the excuse that his was an expansion team. Steve Mariucci came on board, but the results haven't been much better, 5–11 and 6–10. Drafting Joey Harrington hasn't done much so far to help the team win.

Michael David Smith

Research: Does the Bye Week Matter?

This could finally be San Francisco's year...at least when it comes to the bye week. (What, you thought we were referring to Alex Smith pulling a Ben Roethlisberger and leading the 49ers deep into the playoffs?) If this claim doesn't immediately make sense, let us explain.

Historically the bye week is a time for teams to regroup from slow starts, recover from injuries, and get in some extra game planning for the next opponent. During the 2004 season, however, teams coming off a bye sported a 14–18 record. On the surface this may seem curious, but a closer look reveals that sometimes an extra week of preparation doesn't level the playing field against a superior opponent.

Of the 32 teams in the NFL, 15 had winning records entering the bye and 17 had records at or below .500. In aggregate, this works out to a combined record of 87–84 (a .509 winning percentage). How is it that there was such a precipitous drop-off in winning percentage for games immediately following the bye?

The question we're interested in is: Shouldn't teams perform better after the bye week? Specifically, given that teams have an extra week to prepare, shouldn't this increase the probability that they will win? To answer these questions, it's important to consider that this is really a question about trade-offs. Does an extra week of preparation equalize an opponent's strengths? In the extreme case, probably not. For example, if the 2004 49ers had had two weeks to prepare for the Eagles 16 times over a 16-game schedule, the Eagles would beat them about as often as the rules of probability would suggest, no matter how long the 49ers had to game-plan (which probably would have led to the 49ers being the first team since the 1976 Buccaneers to go winless in a full season). When teams are more evenly matched, however, there's sure to be some benefit to an extra week of preparation.

So, knowing all this, what should we expect from teams coming off a bye week? We separated data from the past four seasons into four different categories based on each team's winning percentage prior to the bye week and the winning percentage of the opponent following the bye week (see table 1).

On the surface, these numbers are interesting, but statistically they offer no insight into what role, if any, the bye week has on a team's performance. But all is not lost. Using a t-test, we can measure the statistical relationship between a team's winning percentage and the bye week. Looking at table 1, we find a statistically significant rela-

TABLE 1: W-L RECORDS BEFORE AND IMMEDIATELY FOLLOWING BYE WEEK

Situation	Pre-Bye WinPct	Post-Bye Game Results
Bye week team has <.500 record and opponent has >.500 record	.228	.321
Bye week team has <.500 record and opponent has <.500 record	.248	.480
Bye week team has >.500 record and opponent has >.500 record	.728	.478
Bye week team has >.500 record and opponent has <.500 record	.790	.810

tionship in the second and third cases, but the first and fourth cases are statistically identical.

In English this means that in the first case, the bye week has no impact on a team's winning percentage. And this is also true for the last case. When the bye week team has a losing record and the opposition has a winning record (or vice versa), the bye week doesn't make up for the on-field difference in talent. However, teams with win-

ning records coming off a bye week are significantly more likely to lose when their opponent also has a winning record. This is not to imply that a team with a winning record should petition to give up their bye week, but it does indicate that the bye week alone does not neutralize any on-field differences that may exist between two teams with winning records. Conversely, when two teams with losing records meet after one team has a bye (the third case), the bye week favors the team that gets an extra week of preparation.

So what does all of this have to do with San Francisco? First the bad news: By most accounts, the 49ers will struggle mightily in 2005, despite finally having a new coach and franchise quarterback in the making. But all is not lost, because based on these results the 49ers have a real shot in their Week 7 game against the Redskins. San Francisco has a bye during Week 6, and it's not a stretch to assume that both teams will be below .500 when they meet in Washington on October 23. So if you're a 49ers fan and you can only attend one game this season—and you wouldn't mind seeing them win—your best shot might be to fly 3,000 miles across the country and make your way to FedEx Field.

Ryan Wilson

49ers 2004 Stats by Week

Wk	vs.	W-L	PF	PA	YDF	YDA	TO	DVOA Total	Off	Def	ST
1	ATL	L	19	21	359	227	-1	-7.7%	-4.3%	2.3%	-1.1%
2	@NO	L	27	30	370	302	-2	-26.0%	-20.6%	-5.1%	-10.4%
3	@SEA	L	0	34	175	374	-4	-101.3%	-71.3%	25.1%	-4.9%
4	STL	L	14	24	332	360	-2	-70.3%	-16.4%	52.1%	-1.8%
5	ARI	W	31	28	448	320	0	13.4%	32.1%	34.0%	15.4%
6	@NYJ	L	14	22	374	371	-2	-29.6%	12.2%	36.0%	-5.8%
7	BYE										
8	@CHI	L	13	23	162	254	+1	-57.4%	-52.5%	-10.4%	-15.2%
9	SEA	L	27	42	317	453	-1	-39.2%	19.8%	67.2%	8.2%
10	CAR	L	27	37	357	358	-3	-60.4%	-34.3%	38.6%	12.6%
11	@TB	L	3	35	197	352	0	-48.6%	-26.5%	24.5%	2.4%
12	MIA	L	17	24	224	200	-1	-47.4%	-32.2%	4.9%	-10.3%
13	@STL	L	6	16	160	350	+1	-51.2%	-61.1%	0.4%	10.3%
14	@ARI	W	31	28	352	374	+1	3.7%	22.2%	34.4%	15.9%
15	WAS	L	16	26	254	337	-3	-69.0%	-57.7%	20.9%	9.6%
16	BUF	L	7	41	189	441	-3	-146.1%	-59.4%	65.4%	-21.3%
17	@NE	L	7	21	318	405	+1	-19.4%	-4.9%	12.4%	-2.1%

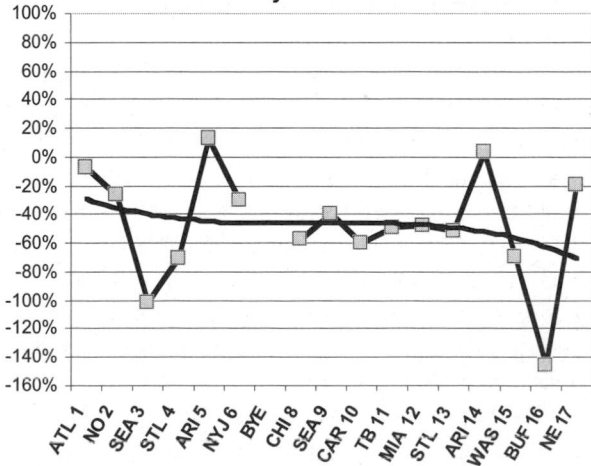

2004 SF Weekly DVOA Performance

Trends and Splits

	Offense	Rank	Defense	Rank
Total DVOA	-19.9%	29	26.7%	32
Unadjusted VOA	-28.2%	30	19.4%	28
Weighted Trend	-22.4%	30	29.2%	32
Variance	10.8%	11	5.7%	28
Passing	-17.1%	27	38.0%	32
Rushing	-23.4%	32	15.6%	32
First Down	-11.3%	28	19.9%	29
Second Down	-25.2%	31	27.8%	29
Third Down	-29.1%	26	40.2%	31
Red Zone	-15.5%	23	38.7%	31
Late and Close	-44.0%	30	16.9%	31

Five-Year Performance

	2004	2003	2002	2001	2000
W-L	2-14	7-9	10-6	12-4	6-10
Pythagorean Wins	3.4	9.2	8.4	11.3	7.2
Estimated Wins	2.3	8.4	9.2	9.5	6.7
Total DVOA	-46.5%	8.3%	13.2%	20.6%	-4.3%
Rank	32	14	9	4	20
Offense	-19.9%	10.6%	18.9%	16.1%	14.8%
Rank	29	7	3	2	4
Defense	26.7%	-1.5%	0.2%	-6.9%	15.2%
Rank	32	16	16	14	28
Special Teams	0.1%	-3.7%	-5.5%	-2.4%	-3.9%
Rank	17	29	29	21	26

Passing (min. 5 plays)

Player	DPAR	PAR	DVOA	Plys	NtYds	Avg	Cmpl	TD	Int
Tim Rattay	13.1	5.2	-4.6%	362	1947	5.4	60.9%	10	10
Ken Dorsey	-10.4	-16.3	-23.4%	240	1131	4.7	54.4%	6	9
Cody Pickett	-7.7	-9.3	-167.2%	12	41	3.4	40.0%	0	2

Rushing (min. 3 plays)

Player	DPAR	PAR	DVOA	Plys	Yds	Avg	TD	Fum	Suc
Kevan Barlow	-2.5	-7.0	-16.4%	244	822	3.4	7	2	37%
Maurice Hicks	-3.5	-6.4	-21.9%	96	362	3.8	2	3	35%
Terry Jackson	-6.6	-5.9	-72.2%	26	101	3.9	0	2	31%
Jamal Robertson	-2.3	-2.0	-42.8%	16	71	4.4	1	2	56%
Fred Beasley	-0.4	-0.6	-21.0%	9	15	1.7	0	0	44%
Tim Rattay	1.9	1.8	22.8%	9	56	6.2	0	0	—
Ken Dorsey	-0.4	-0.7	-35.2%	4	7	1.8	0	0	—

Receiving (min. 5 plays)

Player	DPAR	PAR	DVOA	Plys	Ctch	Yds	Y/C	TD	CPct
WR									
Brandon Lloyd	5.4	4.1	-5.6%	89	43	565	13.1	6	48%
Cedrick Wilson	15.8	13.8	14.3%	85	47	641	13.6	3	55%
Curtis Conway	-0.3	-2.0	-15.1%	75	38	403	10.6	3	51%
Rashaun Woods	0.1	-0.8	-13.0%	23	7	160	22.9	1	30%
Arnaz Battle	1.8	1.1	5.4%	15	8	146	18.3	0	53%
TE									
Eric Johnson	21.9	20.3	17.9%	117	82	825	10.1	2	70%
Aaron Walker	1.3	0.1	1.1%	15	10	115	11.5	0	67%
RB									
Kevan Barlow	3.7	3.0	5.9%	45	35	212	6.1	0	78%
Terry Jackson	-0.3	-1.2	-11.9%	29	21	136	6.5	0	72%
Maurice Hicks	4.0	3.4	20.6%	25	16	154	9.6	0	64%
Fred Beasley	-7.3	-8.1	-64.0%	25	10	44	4.4	0	40%
Jamal Robertson	2.3	2.0	86.3%	5	4	34	8.5	0	80%

Defensive Players (min. 20 plays)

Player	Age	Plys	Stop	Dfts	AvYds	StpRt	Sack	Int	FR
Defensive Line									
Bryant Young	33	51	40	18	1.3	78%	3.0	0	1
Anthony Adams	25	51	33	10	2.6	65%	0.0	1	0
John Engelberger	29	49	32	17	2.3	65%	6.0	0	1
Tony Brown	25	23	16	7	2.4	70%	1.0	0	0
Linebackers									
Derek Smith	30	113	51	17	5.0	45%	1.5	0	2
Jeff Ulbrich	28	91	52	20	4.4	57%	1.0	1	0
Jamie Winborn	26	72	41	16	3.9	57%	4.5	1	2
Julian Peterson	27	30	21	10	2.0	70%	2.5	0	0
Saleem Rasheed	24	21	12	4	5.2	57%	0.0	0	1

Player	Age	Plys	Stop	Dfts	AvYds	StpRt	Sack	Int	FR
Secondary									
Tony Parrish	30	89	23	16	9.2	26%	0.5	4	1
Ronnie Heard	29	76	19	7	11.0	25%	0.0	1	1
Shawntae Spencer	23	75	22	4	8.9	29%	0.0	0	0
Dwaine Carpenter	29	55	17	11	7.5	31%	2.0	1	1
Jimmy Williams	26	53	18	8	10.0	34%	1.0	0	1
Ahmed Plummer	29	29	12	3	7.0	41%	0.0	0	0
Joselio Hanson	24	26	10	7	10.3	38%	1.0	0	0

Offensive Line

Year	Yards	AdjLineYd	Rank	Power	Rank	10+ Yds	Rank	Stuff	Rank	Sack	AdjSack%	Rank
2002	4.47	4.37	8	82%	3	17%	13	23%	13	23	4.2%	4
2003	4.56	4.40	5	58%	26	19%	9	25%	21	29	5.4%	9
2004	3.50	3.59	31	56%	26	16%	24	28%	26	52	7.7%	21

Year	LEnd	Rank	LTckl	Rank	MdGrd	Rank	RTckl	Rank	REnd	Rank
2002	4.48	11	4.14	17	4.27	15	5.02	3	4.05	14
2003	4.91	4	5.14	3	4.25	14	4.48	9	4.39	9
2004	2.67	30	4.08	22	3.69	29	3.64	28	2.60	31

When rebuilding a team from the ground up, you start with two positions: quarterback and left tackle. Knowing it would snag the former in the draft, San Francisco's main goal in free agency was to find the latter. There was only one high-quality left tackle on the market, Jonas Jennings of Buffalo, and San Francisco snapped him up. You probably don't feel like paging all the way back to the Buffalo chapter, so we'll tell you here that while the Bills were 25th in Adjusted Line Yards last season, they ranked fourth on runs left end and 11th on runs left tackle. And while the conventional wisdom says that Jennings has problems with speed-rushing defensive ends, so would Anthony Munoz if he were forced to block for Drew "The Monolith" Bledsoe.

The other main part of the Protect Alex Smith Project is rookie David Baas, who should slip right into the starting lineup at right guard. Michigan has a reputation for producing solid, technically sound offensive linemen because the Wolverines run pro-style protection schemes. Baas is particularly strong when it comes to identifying defenses, and is expected to eventually move to the center position and make the line calls. For now, Jeremy Newberry will return to anchor the line and try to overcome the knee and back injuries that cost him nearly all of last season. He needed more surgery this summer, so he may not be ready for training camp. At least last year's injuries give the 49ers young players with experience for the last two spots on the line. Kwame Harris is currently penciled in at right tackle, with Justin Smiley or Eric Heitmann—assuming Baas starts right away—competing for the other guard slot and third-round pick Adam Snyder training for the future.

Defensive Front Seven

Year	Yards	AdjLineYd	Rank	Power	Rank	10+ Yds	Rank	Stuff	Rank	Sack	AdjSack%	Rank
2002	4.05	3.82	8	68%	16	20%	26	28%	7	31	5.7%	21
2003	4.10	4.05	17	87%	32	18%	17	24%	18	41	6.8%	10
2004	4.17	4.40	25	72%	27	13%	9	22%	22	29	5.4%	29

Year	LEnd	Rank	LTckl	Rank	MdGrd	Rank	RTckl	Rank	REnd	Rank
2002	3.69	9	4.17	17	4.04	9	4.28	19	2.24	1
2003	4.73	28	5.08	27	3.94	9	3.74	7	3.35	9
2004	5.16	29	4.32	15	4.14	14	5.04	32	4.18	21

3-4 Fever: Catch It! Mike Nolan brings the NFL's hottest fad with him from Baltimore along with a player who knows how to make it work, defensive end Marques Douglas. Given how much players on the Ravens defense like to talk about themselves, it seems ridiculous that any of them could be considered underrated, and yet Douglas qualifies. He came out of Howard University as an undrafted, slightly undersized free agent and, thanks to his outstanding technique, worked his way into the starting lineup of one of the NFL's best defenses. Our individual player stats credit him with more plays than any of last year's 49er linemen, even though he was playing in a system designed to funnel tackles to the linebackers. At a cost of just $1.45 million per year for three years, and a $1 million signing bonus, Douglas may have been the most economically sound signing of free agency.

Nolan will have to shift the rest of the 49er veterans into positions that fit the new formation. The current plan is to move defensive tackle Bryant Young to end, with either Anthony Adams or Isaac Sopoaga as nose tackle. Defensive end Andre Carter, who missed six games last year with back problems, will move into the "Elephant" linebacker position made famous by Charles Haley and Willie McGinest, but his problems in pass coverage may hand much of his playing time to Jamie Winborn. Winborn hasn't played a full season yet after four years in the league, but he will surprise many if he can stay healthy. There aren't many players with his speed and hustle. The other outside linebacker will be Julian Peterson, seeking to regain his Pro Bowl form of two years ago. Even before the Achilles' injury that cost him two thirds

(continued next page)

Defensive Front Seven (continued)

of 2004, Peterson wasn't the game-changing linebacker he had been the previous year. (The 49ers' website says he "excelled at shutting down athletic tight ends," but our numbers disagree.) The inside positions will be manned by Derek Smith and Jeff Ulbrich, with Winborn ready to move over in case of injury. Fifth-round nose tackle Ronald Fields from Mississippi State was the only draft choice for the front seven.

Defensive Secondary

Year	DVOA vs. #1 WR	Rank	DVOA vs. #2 WR	Rank	DVOA vs. Other WR	Rank	DVOA vs. TE	Rank	DVOA vs. RB	Rank
2002	-6.9%	11	-19.5%	11	0.0%	14	16.6%	25	-3.9%	11
2003	19.8%	23	-32.0%	5	-16.8%	12	0.0%	16	-0.1%	15
2004	64.1%	32	5.4%	16	23.6%	27	43.8%	30	-22.8%	8

San Francisco hasn't been on anyone's list of great secondaries for years now, but things really went down the tubes when both starting cornerbacks missed most of the season with injuries. Ahmed Plummer missed ten games with a bulging disc in his back but is expected to be a starter again this season. Mike Rumph broke his arm in an October game against St. Louis and was replaced by rookie Shawntae Spencer; the two will compete for the other starting corner position with the loser possibly moving to safety and knocking Dwaine Carpenter down the depth chart. Tony Parrish, by far the most valuable member of last year's secondary, is firmly ensconced at strong safety. The 49ers in 2003 played for the interception rather than the incomplete, picking off 23 passes but allowing plenty of yards. In 2004, they couldn't even get the interception, dropping to just nine.

Special Teams

Year	DVOA	Rank	FG/XP	Rank	Net Punt	Rank	Punt Ret	Rank	Net Kick	Rank	Kick Ret	Rank
2002	-5.5%	29	-8.2	28	-16.2	30	8.2	7	-8.7	27	-5.7	26
2003	-3.7%	29	-16.3	31	5.0	13	-5.5	23	-3.9	23	-0.1	16
2004	0.1%	17	4.4	11	7.2	13	-0.4	8	-6.8	27	-3.8	22

Oddly, while the offense and defense disintegrated in 2004, special teams went from the bottom of the league to the middle. Todd Peterson was effective as a field goal kicker but poor on kickoffs, which didn't stop the Falcons from signing him as a free agent. He's been replaced by Joe Nedney, who will probably be broken in three places by the time you read this. If he somehow can stay healthy and regain his 2002 form, he's an upgrade. Punter Andy Lee was fine in his first season and hopes to get better in his second. The 49ers gave the kick return job to Maurice Hicks after waiving Jamal Robertson halfway through the year, and he was a disappointment. Arnaz Battle wasn't very good as a punt returner either. Both may be replaced by sixth-round cornerback draftee Derrick "I'm not from Texas" Johnson or free agent signee Jason McAddley.

Coaching Staff

Mike Nolan is one of the few coaches who has recent experience as an assistant on both sides of the ball. Most of the people who became defensive coordinators had been defensive assistants before they got the job, but when the Ravens hired Mike Nolan from the Jets, they first made him their wide receivers coach before promoting him to defensive coordinator when Marvin Lewis left. Before that, Nolan was a Dan Reeves protégé, having worked for Reeves for six years in Denver and four with the Giants.

The coordinators, to be frank, don't have the best résumés. Defensive coordinator Billy Davis coached the underwhelming New York Giant linebackers last year, and before that coached the linebackers in Atlanta—you know, the ones who took a huge step forward after he left. On offense, coordinator Mike McCarthy comes over from New Orleans, where he ran an offense that we feel was generally overrated (this is discussed further in the New Orleans chapter). There are much more promising names among the position coaches. Legendary Chicago linebacker Mike Singletary, who coached the linebackers in Baltimore for the last two seasons, comes with Nolan to serve as linebackers coach and assistant head coach. Bishop Harris, freed from the Jets after his infamous shouting match with Herm Edwards on the sidelines of the San Diego playoff game, will try to salvage Kevan Barlow's ego and keep Frank Gore from getting injured again. He was great at getting the most out of two running backs in New York, and should really help things in San Francisco.

Seattle Seahawks

I s it possible for a team to win the division title *and* be considered a failure? If any team has ever earned this dubious distinction, it is the 2004 Seattle Seahawks.

The Seahawks looked like a serious Super Bowl contender after winning their first three games. But in Week 5, in St. Louis, they blew a double-digit fourth-quarter lead to the division rival Rams, and it was all downhill from there. They barely recovered in time to win the worst division in the NFL, and then meekly bowed out of the first round of the playoffs—thanks to a third straight loss to the Rams.

When Mike Holmgren took over in Seattle in 1999, conventional wisdom said he would return the football team from the Pacific Northwest to championship form. After all, this was the man who had won the Lombardi Trophy in Green Bay, and now he had access to owner Paul Allen's deep pockets in the quest to build a champion team. It seemed like just a matter of time before Holmgren took the Seahawks to the Super Bowl. Yet after six seasons, Seattle fans are still waiting for Holmgren to win a single playoff game.

The Seahawks won nine games last year, but they may have been the most unimpressive nine wins of all time. Although the Seahawks swept the NFC South, their wins against Tampa Bay and Carolina came by less than a touchdown apiece, and they barely beat Atlanta in the final week of the season when the Falcons were resting most of their top players. The Seahawks won three division games, sweeping the 49ers and barely beating the Cardinals at home. Their other two wins came by four points in Minnesota while the Vikings were going through their usual late-season tumble, and by seven points at home against the 4–12 Dolphins.

Front office turmoil followed the season, as Seattle fired team president Bob Whitsitt and general manager Bob Ferguson, and Green Bay hired away Seahawks vice president Ted Thompson. Combined with the previous removal of GM duties from Holmgren's job description, it looked like a front office in serious trouble. However, in February Seattle made Tim Ruskell its president of football operations, and he acted immediately to keep the core of the team intact.

Seattle's strength comes from its balanced offense. Although quarterback Matt Hasselbeck and running back Shaun Alexander get most of the attention, left tackle Walter Jones is the most important player on the team. The

SEAHAWKS PROSPECTUS

2004 Record: 9–7

DVOA Estimated Wins: 7.9 (19th)

Pythagorean Wins: 7.9 (16th)

DVOA: −3.3% total (20th), −13.2% weighted (23rd)

Adjusted Offense: 22.5 points/game (4.0% DVOA, 13th)

Adjusted Defense: 22.7 points/game (4.5% DVOA, 21st)

Adjusted Special Teams: −1.0 points/game (−2.8% DVOA, 24th)

Variance: 10.3% (28th)

2004: Mediocre team can't beat division rival.

2005: Holmgren needs to advance in playoffs or his tenure in Seattle is over.

2005 Projection

Leinart Land (0–4): 3%

Bad Team (5–6): 7%

Mediocre (7–8): 15%

Playoff Contender (9–10): 24%

Super Bowl Contender (11+): 52%

Projected Average Opponent: −5.3% DVOA (30th in NFL)

good news for Seattle is that these three players will all be with the team in 2005. That seemed nearly impossible a year ago, with all three players going into free agency this off-season. Ruskell, though, quickly signed Jones and Hasselbeck to long-term deals, and used the franchise player tag to keep Alexander in town for another year.

The biggest problem in the Hawks' balanced offense is the receiving corps, and the biggest problem for the receiving corps has been the inability to consistently catch the ball. Seattle was fourth in the league with 38 dropped passes—and that was actually an improvement over 2003, when the Seahawks were second with 41 dropped passes.

Koren Robinson is a great athlete with bad hands, a description that pretty much sums up every high-first-round receiver who ends up disappointing the team that drafts him. Robinson dropped ten passes despite playing in only nine games. Darrell Jackson is not as good an athlete as Robinson, but he does have better hands, which is like saying that the WFL was a more successful league than the XFL. Jackson dropped 11 passes. It was no surprise to see the Seattle season end on a dropped pass in the end zone; the surprise was that the receiver who let the ball go off his fingers was slot receiver Bobby Engram, who has actually been Seattle's most dependable pass catcher in recent years. New additions Jerome Pathon and Joe Jurevicius should help, but this receiving corps will continue to give Matt Hasselbeck fits.

Hasselbeck could greatly benefit from a reliable tight end, but former first-round pick Jerramy Stevens has been a bust, and Itula Mili doesn't have the athleticism or the hands to be a consistent receiving threat. The selection of Stevens is a good example of why Holmgren failed as a general manager: He chose a player because he was 6'7", 260 pounds, and a good athlete, and ignored his inconsistent play and consistent off-field trouble. In three seasons since being selected in the first round in 2002, Stevens has 63 catches for 673 yards.

The prize for Holmgren's worst draft move, however, is shared by the entire 1999 draft class. It was terrible. First-round pick Lamar King of Saginaw Valley State, considered a reach even at the time, has proven to be a bust. Seattle didn't have a second-round pick, and spent its two third-round choices on quarterback Brock Huard and receiver Karsten Bailey. Only backup defensive end Antonio Cochran, a fourth-round pick, remains with the team from that class.

Another questionable move came two years ago, when Holmgren brought in his old colleague Ray Rhodes to run the defense. Although the team performed well in his first year on the job, the Seattle defense took a big step backward in 2004. More specifically, the Seattle defense took a big step backward during that horrible fourth quarter against the Rams. Perhaps no defense in NFL history has had its flaws exposed so suddenly. Ken Hamlin was supposed to be a hitter, but Steven Jackson ran him over, and for the rest of the season backs were able to pick up additional yards against a secondary that couldn't tackle them. Terreal Bierria was supposed to be good in coverage, but he gave up the overtime touchdown and became a frequent target for the rest of the season until Rhodes took him out of the starting lineup in December.

Through the first three weeks of the season, the Seahawks had the NFL's top-ranked defense, not only by conventional measures but also by our DVOA ratings. In retrospect, that early success was due to the struggling offenses the Seahawks had played, not the inherent quality of the Seattle defense.

The Seahawks' defense was the second-worst in the league at stopping number one receivers (36.4% DVOA) but the best in the league at stopping third and fourth receivers (−44.4% DVOA). Why? Because when opposing teams went to three- or four-receiver formations, the Seahawks brought in rookie safety Michael Boulware, who showed in his first season that Seattle was very wise to draft him and move him from linebacker (where he played at Florida State) to safety. Rhodes frequently brought Boulware in on the nickel defense, and by the end of the season he was a part of the team's base defense. While Boulware is a very promising young player, those numbers against top receivers show that both starting cornerbacks, Ken Lucas and Marcus Trufant, struggled. Lucas signed with the Panthers in free agency, and Seahawks fans shouldn't be sad to see him go. He'll be replaced by Kelly Herndon, a restricted free agent from Denver who represents a slight (and slightly cheaper) improvement. Trufant is only 24 and still developing, and the Seahawks need a better year out of him. Seattle also needs Grant Wistrom, who signed in the 2004 off-season, to stay healthy. He got off to a good start but was limited to only nine games because of injuries.

With the exception of kicker Josh Brown, the Seahawks' special teams were lousy. But Seattle can take solace in knowing that offense is more consistent than defense or special teams, so a turnaround on defense and special teams while the offense stays strong is a realistic best-case scenario. And Brown, who missed only two field goal tries in 2004, is a 26-year-old who should have plenty of good years ahead of him.

One off-season trade seems more likely to hurt the Seahawks than to help them. Seattle picked up an extra fourth-round pick but lost Trent Dilfer, who was a trusted friend and mentor to Hasselbeck as well as someone the Seahawks could count on to play competently, if not spectacularly, in the event of a Hasselbeck injury. Was Florida State offensive tackle Ray Willis really worth losing a trusty veteran backup quarterback?

The best news for the Seahawks is that they still play in the NFC West, which still looks like the worst division in football. It appears that the Cardinals still need to do a little more work before they can take that next step, and the 49ers need to do a *lot* more work before they can take any step. That leaves St. Louis as the primary division rival. Can the Seahawks figure out how to beat the Rams this year?

If history is to be our guide, the answer is most likely yes. As the list below illustrates, one team has beaten a division rival three times in the same season seven times since the playoffs expanded in 1990. Four of these teams split with their rivals in the following year, and once the team that lost all three actually swept the next season's series.

2002 Steelers over Browns (In 2003, the teams split)
2000 Giants over Eagles (in 2001, the Eagles swept 2–0)
2000 Titans over Jaguars (in 2001, the teams split)

1997 Patriots over Dolphins (in 1998, the teams split)

1994 Steelers over Browns (in 1995, the Steelers swept 2–0)

1993 Raiders over Broncos (in 1994, the Raiders swept 2–0)

1991 Chiefs over Raiders (in 1992, the teams split)

So, the Rams may not own a psychological advantage over the Seahawks after all.

The problem Seattle has is that getting past the Rams isn't good enough. Nobody wants to see this team go 9–7

and lose in the first round of the playoffs again. With all the important offensive pieces coming back, and injured defensive players like Wistrom returning as well, this team has bigger expectations.

Holmgren is entering the seventh year of his eight-year contract. He's already had the general manager duties, which he demanded be part of the package that brought him to Seattle, stripped from him. If he doesn't have a good year, Seattle will strip his coaching duties as well.

Michael David Smith

Seahawks 2004 Stats by Week

Wk	vs.	W-L	PF	PA	YDF	YDA	TO	DVOA Total	Off	Def	ST
1	@NO	W	21	7	415	281	+1	23.9%	12.4%	-20.1%	-8.6%
2	@TB	W	10	6	182	271	+2	9.3%	-40.5%	-39.3%	10.5%
3	SF	W	34	0	374	175	+4	59.4%	10.9%	-51.5%	-3.1%
4	BYE										
5	STL	L	27	33	301	441	+3	4.0%	13.2%	-1.9%	-10.3%
6	@NE	L	20	30	443	363	0	10.3%	6.4%	-1.7%	2.2%
7	@ARI	L	17	25	257	316	-2	-53.6%	-52.8%	-1.8%	-2.6%
8	CAR	W	23	17	433	342	-1	6.6%	19.8%	2.5%	-10.8%
9	@SF	W	42	27	453	317	+1	-1.3%	51.6%	42.6%	-10.3%
10	@STL	L	12	23	372	462	0	-50.9%	-10.9%	53.3%	13.3%
11	MIA	W	24	17	293	288	0	-34.7%	-29.8%	-7.5%	-12.4%
12	BUF	L	9	38	230	434	+1	-24.5%	4.9%	23.0%	-6.3%
13	DAL	L	39	43	507	405	0	4.8%	29.1%	21.2%	-3.1%
14	@MIN	W	27	23	455	374	0	6.6%	5.1%	-7.7%	-6.2%
15	@NYJ	L	14	37	275	482	-3	-69.1%	4.1%	69.8%	-3.4%
16	ARI	W	24	21	301	317	+1	12.8%	-14.8%	-23.1%	4.5%
17	ATL	W	28	26	253	353	0	13.9%	27.1%	14.6%	1.4%
18	STL	L	20	27	413	396	0	-1.9%	11.1%	24.4%	11.5%

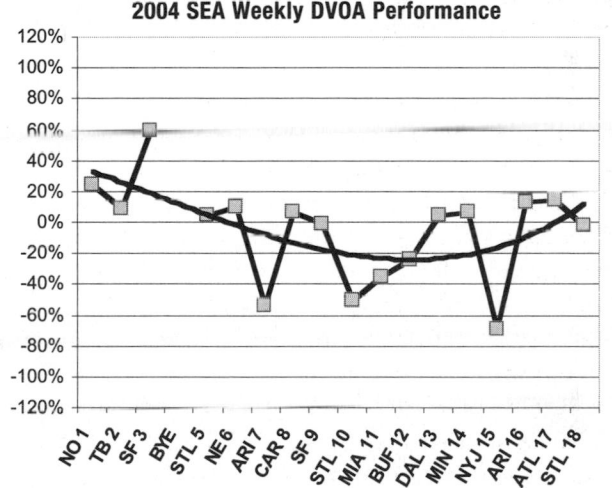

2004 SEA Weekly DVOA Performance

Trends and Splits

	Offense	Rank	Defense	Rank
Total DVOA	4.0%	13	4.5%	21
Unadjusted VOA	6.8%	11	-2.1%	13
Weighted Trend	5.7%	12	16.2%	29
Variance	7.2%	22	10.4%	14
Passing	6.2%	14	0.7%	17
Rushing	1.4%	14	9.1%	25
First Down	8.4%	9	5.7%	20
Second Down	20.0%	7	12.9%	23
Third Down	-34.0%	27	-11.7%	13
Red Zone	10.0%	11	8.8%	23
Late and Close	-7.4%	17	-12.7%	11

Five-Year Performance

	2004	2003	2002	2001	2000
W-L	9-7	10-6	7-9	9-7	6-10
Pythagorean Wins	7.9	10.0	7.6	7.3	5.8
Estimated Wins	7.9	10.7	6.9	8.0	5.6
Total DVOA	-3.3%	17.6%	-1.9%	-1.9%	-21.5%
Rank	20	7	18	18	26
Offense	4.0%	17.3%	7.3%	-3.1%	-9.8%
Rank	13	3	12	14	22
Defense	4.5%	-0.6%	9.1%	-4.0%	17.3%
Rank	21	18	25	16	29
Special Teams	-2.8%	-0.3%	0.0%	-2.8%	5.7%
Rank	24	19	17	24	3

Passing (min. 5 plays)

Player	DPAR	PAR	DVOA	Plys	NtYds	Avg	Cmpl	TD	Int
Matt Hasselbeck	52.5	57.7	10.3%	502	3215	6.4	58.9%	22	15
Trent Dilfer	-6.0	-9.5	-36.3%	62	312	5.0	43.1%	1	3

Rushing (min. 3 plays)

Player	DPAR	PAR	DVOA	Plys	Yds	Avg	TD	Fum	Suc
Shaun Alexander	36.7	37.9	10.6%	353	1696	4.8	16	5	46%
Mack Strong	-2.2	-2.3	-27.1%	36	131	3.6	0	2	58%
Maurice Morris	3.7	3.9	15.4%	30	126	4.2	0	0	60%
Matt Hasselbeck	0.8	1.0	-7.6%	15	105	7.0	1	1	—
Heath Evans	-2.5	-2.4	-76.5%	7	20	2.9	0	1	57%
Kerry Carter	1.0	1.1	41.9%	4	15	3.8	0	0	75%

Receiving (min. 5 plays)

Player	DPAR	PAR	DVOA	Plys	Ctch	Yds	Y/C	TD	CPct
WR									
Darrell Jackson	20.0	18.7	4.2%	155	87	1199	13.8	7	56%
Koren Robinson	6.3	4.9	-0.3%	67	31	495	16.0	2	46%
Bobby Engram	12.0	11.2	18.9%	53	36	499	13.9	2	68%
Jerry Rice	5.8	4.9	2.8%	48	25	362	14.5	3	52%
Jerheme Urban	3.2	3.5	42.3%	9	6	117	19.5	1	67%
TE									
Jerramy Stevens	8.5	9.7	14.3%	47	31	349	11.3	3	66%
Itula Mili	3.9	3.5	3.8%	36	23	240	10.4	1	64%
Ryan Hannam	3.3	3.2	28.9%	12	8	110	13.8	0	67%
RB									
Shaun Alexander	1.4	1.4	-3.2%	38	23	170	7.4	4	61%
Mack Strong	-2.1	-3.3	-22.3%	31	21	99	4.7	0	68%
Maurice Morris	-1.9	-2.9	-27.4%	20	9	53	5.9	0	45%

Defensive Players (min. 20 plays)

Player	Age	Plys	Stop	Dfts	AvYds	StpRt	Sack	Int	FR
Defensive Line									
Chike Okeafor	29	52	39	21	1.2	75%	8.5	0	0
Rashad Moore	26	50	35	6	1.9	70%	2.0	0	3
Cedric Woodard	28	48	31	6	3.0	65%	1.0	0	1
Rocky Bernard	26	44	36	12	1.5	82%	3.5	0	1
Grant Wistrom	29	43	28	14	1.8	65%	3.5	0	1
Antonio Cochran	29	40	29	15	0.5	73%	6.5	1	1
Linebackers									
Isaiah Kacyvenski	28	80	38	9	5.1	48%	1.0	0	0
Orlando Huff	27	56	25	8	4.6	45%	1.0	0	2
Anthony Simmons	29	46	24	10	4.5	52%	0.0	1	0
Niko Koutouvides	24	45	28	5	4.2	62%	1.0	0	0
Chad Brown	35	37	20	10	3.6	54%	1.0	0	1
Solomon Bates	23	27	10	4	5.3	37%	0.0	0	0
Tracy White	24	26	11	3	5.0	42%	1.0	0	0

Player	Age	Plys	Stop	Dfts	AvYds	StpRt	Sack	Int	FR
Secondary									
Marcus Trufant	25	116	36	16	8.0	31%	1.0	5	0
Ken Lucas	26	89	40	19	8.1	45%	0.0	6	2
Ken Hamlin	24	87	27	11	8.9	31%	2.0	4	0
Terreal Bierria	25	73	25	8	9.4	34%	0.0	1	0
Michael Boulware	24	56	23	14	7.5	41%	1.0	5	0
Kris Richard	26	25	6	4	10.4	24%	0.0	0	0

Offensive Line

Year	Yards	AdjLineYd	Rank	Power	Rank	10+ Yds	Rank	Stuff	Rank	Sack	AdjSack%	Rank
2002	4.02	4.04	20	67%	15	18%	11	26%	24	32	5.4%	10
2003	4.55	4.31	11	69%	10	21%	7	24%	18	43	7.7%	28
2004	4.62	4.35	9	61%	17	20%	4	21%	7	34	5.6%	7

Year	LEnd	Rank	LTckl	Rank	MdGrd	Rank	RTckl	Rank	REnd	Rank
2002	3.67	23	4.18	15	4.35	10	3.82	25	3.36	24
2003	4.81	6	4.92	5	4.36	9	4.46	10	2.74	28
2004	4.54	10	5.26	1	4.25	15	3.96	18	3.74	18

The left side of the line just might be the best in football. Tackle Walter Jones and guard Steve Hutchinson are two of the best run blockers in the game, and Jones is an excellent pass blocker as well. Center Robbie Tobeck has started every game for Seattle for the last four years, but he'll be challenged by first-round draft pick Chris Spencer. The problem with the line is the right side, where the Seahawks said goodbye and good riddance to last year's starting tackle, Chris Terry. It isn't every player who is prone to both injury and violation of the league's substance abuse policy, and then tops off the package by drawing twice as many penalties as any of his line-mates, despite playing only half a season. The left-overs on the right include guard Chris Gray, who is as unexciting a player as his name would suggest, and tackle Pork Chop Womack, who is as out of shape a player as his name would suggest.

Defensive Front Seven

Year	Yards	AdjLineYd	Rank	Power	Rank	10+ Yds	Rank	Stuff	Rank	Sack	AdjSack%	Rank
2002	4.98	4.70	31	67%	15	20%	25	18%	31	27	4.9%	28
2003	3.77	4.24	20	65%	16	9%	3	20%	28	43	6.6%	14
2004	4.50	4.29	21	69%	25	22%	26	22%	24	36	5.9%	28

Year	LEnd	Rank	LTckl	Rank	MdGrd	Rank	RTckl	Rank	REnd	Rank
2002	3.92	14	5.47	32	4.92	32	5.14	32	2.59	4
2003	3.91	10	4.73	24	4.15	17	4.25	17	4.13	20
2004	4.55	22	3.85	5	4.49	26	4.46	26	3.42	7

The biggest problem on the Seahawks' defense is the inability of the front four to generate a pass rush. Among teams that play the 4-3, only San Francisco had a worse Adjusted Sack Rate than Seattle did last year. Complicating the problem is the fact that Antonio Cochran, the best pass rusher on the defensive line, is a liability against the run. Grant Wistrom, who signed a lucrative free agent contract to leave St. Louis for Seattle, suffered through injuries and had only 3.5 sacks. The best player in the Seahawks' front seven is Anthony Simmons, who covers ten yards as fast as any linebacker in the league. Seattle signed two free agents who project as starters, strongside linebacker Jamie Sharper and end Bryce Fisher. But Chike Okeafor, the linebacker who led the Seahawks in sacks last year, signed with the Cardinals as a free agent.

Defensive Secondary

Year	DVOA vs. #1 WR	Rank	DVOA vs. #2 WR	Rank	DVOA vs. Other WR	Rank	DVOA vs. TE	Rank	DVOA vs. RB	Rank
2002	15.2%	26	22.3%	23	-41.0%	3	-40.8%	3	23.1%	31
2003	0.0%	15	27.1%	29	6.3%	24	-18.4%	6	6.0%	21
2004	36.4%	31	5.7%	17	-44.4%	1	-19.9%	7	-0.9%	23

Seattle's defensive backs were a little better in 2004 than they get credit for. Because the Seahawks did such a poor job of rushing opposing quarterbacks, Seattle's secondary had to hold its coverage longer than most teams. The most promising player to emerge last year was Michael Boulware, who is still learning the safety position but looks like he could be a Pro Bowler. Ken Lucas is gone, but two new free agent cornerbacks arrive to replace him: Andre Dyson and Kelly Herndon. Herndon had a particularly interesting season; playing across from Champ Bailey in Denver, opposing quarterbacks tended to pick on him, but he rose to the challenge with the highest Stop Rate of any starting defensive back in the NFL.

Special Teams

Year	DVOA	Rank	FG/XP	Rank	Net Punt	Rank	Punt Ret	Rank	Net Kick	Rank	Kick Ret	Rank
2002	0.5%	13	1.7	14	2.9	15	2.5	13	-4.6	21	0.3	16
2003	-0.3%	19	1.7	17	5.9	10	-2.9	17	-2.8	21	-3.5	22
2004	-2.8%	24	6.4	9	-0.7	24	-10.7	26	-3.6	19	-7.2	29

Another disappointing year for the Seahawks' special teams led to the dismissal of coach Mark Michaels. Bob Casullo replaces him. Although kicker Josh Brown had an excellent season, making 23 of 25 field goals, his kickoffs were below average. The Seahawks' return units were terrible, with Maurice Morris averaging only 21.1 yards on kickoffs and 5.0 yards on punts. Bobby Engram was better, with 11.8 yards on punt returns, but no matter who does the job in 2005, Casullo has his work cut out for him.

Coaching Staff

Mike Holmgren has turned over almost his entire coaching staff since joining the Seahawks in 1999. Only two assistants remain from his first staff: tight ends coach Jim Lind and running backs coach Stump Mitchell. Mitchell had a reputation as one of the smartest players in the league when he played for the Cardinals in the 1980s. He served three years as the head coach at Morgan State and could be an NFL head coach someday.

The biggest presence on Holmgren's staff, however, is Ray Rhodes. Because he's a defensive coach, many people forget to mention Rhodes when reciting the Bill Walsh family tree. But Rhodes—who played a season for Walsh in 1980 before becoming one of his assistants in 1981—actually spent more time with Walsh than Holmgren did. He's had mixed results since Holmgren hired him to take over Seattle's defense in 2003. According to our DVOA ratings, the Seahawks were 21st in the league on defense last year and 18th the year before. That's an improvement over where the Seahawks were before Rhodes arrived (25th in 2002), but not much of one.

Tampa Bay Buccaneers

Thank goodness Tampa Bay comes near the end of the alphabetical list of NFL teams, because if our explanation of the Buccaneers led off this book, you might not read much further.

Quite simply, the Buccaneers are Football Outsiders' "What the @#$%" team after two straight years of defying our advanced metrics. Things were going along swimmingly through the team's resurgence in the 1990s. Then something happened following the Super Bowl championship in 2002. On paper, Jon Gruden's retooled team was poised for plenty of success in 2003 and 2004, but the Buccaneeers' combined record of 12–20 the last two seasons has some Tampa Bay fans believing that the team must have sold its soul in exchange for that Super Bowl win.

Winning 12 of 32 games tells *what* happened to the 2003–2004 Buccaneers, but it doesn't say much about the *why*. Unfortunately, neither do our statistics. Tampa Bay managed a 5–11 mark in 2004 despite ranking 16th in total DVOA (7th on defense). Ten of the 16 teams ranked behind the Buccaneers in total DVOA still managed more victories.

Perhaps it was the 2004 schedule, you suggest? Try again. Tampa Bay's opponents had an average DVOA of −7.3%, the second lowest figure in the league.

Perhaps you would rather trust conventional numbers. If so, you'll have to explain how a team can gain 700 yards more than its opponents, give up only three more points than it scores, and still win only five games.

And before we label 2004 a fluke, let's consider that the Buccaneers were ranked eighth in total DVOA in 2003—a season in which they went 7–9 even though they outscored opponents 301 to 264.

Turnovers tell part of the story. Quarterback Brian Griese, who took over for an ineffective Brad Johnson and an injured Chris Simms, had a disturbing habit of having interceptions returned for touchdowns. Starting tailback Michael Pittman, who once again became the full-time ball carrier after free agent signee Charlie Garner tore the patella tendon in his knee, fumbled the ball six times, and Tampa Bay didn't recover a single one. (As noted in the New Orleans chapter, recovering fumbles is essentially random, but the only kind of luck in Tampa these days is bad luck.)

Special teams have been another boondoggle. According to DVOA, the Buccaneers ranked 30th and 31st in the NFL in overall special teams in 2003 and 2004, respec-

tively. That figure is thanks mostly to an absolutely dreadful kicking performance by Martin Gramatica, who last year was worth −14.7 points compared to an average field goal kicker. That's more than twice the negative value of last year's second worst kicker, Paul Edinger of Chicago, and it follows a 2003 campaign in which Gramatica's field goal inefficiency cost the Bucs approximately −9.9 points. When Todd Sauerbrun's favorite Argentinean was finally released after Week 12, it seemed like an almost merciful maneuver by the Buccaneers.

If you're thinking to yourself that a team whose won-loss record so defies its statistics must have some pretty bizarre losses, you'd be correct. In one memorable 2003 stretch, the Buccaneers managed to lose two games in a fashion never before seen in NFL annals. No team had ever missed a potential game-winning extra point with no time remaining before Tampa Bay did in an overtime loss to Carolina in Week 2. Three weeks later, the Buccaneers became the first team in NFL history to blow a 21-point lead with five minutes remaining.

While 2004's defeats were less gut-wrenching, the Buccaneers still suffered from an almost pathological inability to make the one play that could deliver a win, and at times appeared to actually be allergic to success. No matter what Gruden tried, he couldn't seem to find a Claritin tablet for what ailed his team. If Tampa Bay managed a big gain, it was negated by a flag. If they put together a potential game-tying drive, it ended in a turnover. If they needed a big kick, it was missed.

Tampa Bay's present problems are compounded by the fact that the front office still believed it could compete for championships the last two seasons—to be fair, a reasonable conclusion, given some of the statistics mentioned at the top. Thus, following a disappointing 2003 campaign, Gruden and GM Bruce Allen went on a shopping spree that netted the likes of tackles Todd Steussie and Derrick Deese to go with tailback Garner. None of these players worked out particularly well, and the signings only delayed the inevitable salary cap purge.

That purge began this summer. Quarterback Brad Johnson, wide receiver Joe Jurevicius, and linebacker Ian Gold were among those let go as Tampa Bay maneuvered to get under the cap and pare a huge salary excess from the 2006 budget. The cuts allowed the Buccaneers to get under the cap, but just barely, so Gruden—who makes no secret of his affection for veterans and free agents—was forced to largely sit on the sidelines in free agency. The team did little other than re-signing quarterback Brian Griese and receiver Joey Galloway and adding tight end Anthony Becht.

Receiving less attention, but perhaps having a bigger effect on the team's performance, were the exits via free agency of young, moderately priced starters such as right guard Cosey Coleman, defensive tackle Chartric Darby, and safety Dwight Smith.

OK, so the news isn't all bad in Buc-land. The cap cuts and lack of new signings should give the team much more flexibility next off-season. Additionally, the team had a full complement of draft choices for the first time in years and 12 picks overall, including extra selections in the third and fifth rounds.

The jewel of the draft class was first-round running back Carnell "Cadillac" Williams of Auburn, who can immediately expect 20-plus carries a game. That should allow Pittman to become more effective in the passing game. Pittman has struggled in the passing game as the feature back, but he's fast enough to hurt a defense if lined up wide and matched up on a linebacker. That's something the matchup mastermind Gruden will no doubt try to exploit with both Pittman and Williams deployed in a two-back set.

The 2005 draft comes on the heels of some encouraging results in 2004's selection meeting. Safety Will Allen, taken with a third-round pick in 2004, appears ready to step in at Smith's strong safety spot. Young holdover linemen Anthony Davis, Jeb Terry, and Sean Mahan could compete for starting spots, as could 2005 draftees Chris Colmer and Dan Buenning. Wide receiver Michael Clayton, taken with the fifteenth pick in 2004, would have been considered the steal of the draft in a normal year where no rookie quarterback was leading a 15–1 team.

Clayton easily outshined the four receivers taken ahead of him in last year's receiver-rich draft. He set franchise rookie records with 80 receptions for 1,198 yards and eight touchdowns. According to our advanced metrics, he was fourth in the league in DPAR (total value) and seventh in DVOA (value per pass). Even more impressive was his mastery of the less obvious aspects of wide receiver play. As Michael David Smith wrote in picking his 2004 All-Pro Team on our website, "watch him throw a block downfield some time and you'll see that his circus catches are only one part of his all-around game."

Actually, Clayton is so good at downfield blocking that perhaps he could give pointers to Tampa Bay's offensive line, which has been a troubled part of the team since the Tony Dungy years. Except for late in the 2002 season, when the unit gelled enough to help propel the Buccaneers to a Super Bowl title, the line has been a problem despite frequent turnover and the presence (since 2002) of renowned offensive line coach Bill Muir. Tampa Bay has struggled to run the ball consistently throughout Gruden's tenure, and sack totals were kept artificially low because of Brad Johnson's willingness to throw the ball away when rushed.

In 2005, the Buccaneers once again face an offensive line problem. Right tackle Kenyatta Walker, a former first-round pick, has become a serviceable starter, which is better than the bust he appeared to be after his rookie season, but he'll never be a star. Left tackle Derrick Deese was ageless as a 49er, but after signing with Tampa Bay a year ago he suddenly started playing like he was 49 himself.

And then there was the Steussie disaster. Signing Steussie was supposed to have a double-strength benefit, giving Tampa Bay a talented veteran tackle who was coming off a Super Bowl appearance (and also blocked for the highest-scoring team in NFL history, the 1998 Minnesota Vikings) while damaging a division rival. But Steussie, who began the year as the starting right tackle, suddenly and completely lost his effectiveness. He ended up allowing the sack that injured promising young quarterback Chris Simms during Simms's first start, and after that Steussie lost his starting spot to Walker. Now he finds himself in the middle of an emerging steroid scandal from his Panther days, making his future with the team even shakier.

On the other side of the ball, Tampa Bay withstood the loss of Warren Sapp and John Lynch to rank seventh in defensive DVOA. The Buccaneers continue to generate pressure with their undersized front four, ranking first in Adjusted Sack Rate even though they blitz infrequently. The team does have one defensive need: a run-stuffing tackle to play alongside injury-plagued tackle Anthony McFarland, who hasn't been able to stay healthy enough to fully deliver on his considerable promise.

But even without that upgrade, and despite some losses this off-season, Tampa Bay has enough talent left on the defense to keep the current team in contention. The Buccaneers may not have the dominating unit of three seasons ago, but this is still a fast, athletic group that tackles well. The secondary was excellent against number one receivers (third best in the league, according to DVOA), but struggled against number two and three receivers and tight ends.

Our metrics seem to view the Tampa sky through rose-colored glasses. As we go to press, our DVOA projections have the Buccaneers headed for a big bounce-back year and a mean projected win total of 10.2, good enough to win the NFC South. The projection system believes that the defense will once again be among the league's best, and looks favor-ably upon the team's offensive improvement with Griese under center in the second half of the year. Because of a schedule that projects to be among the league's easiest, our formulas give Tampa Bay a 50% chance of reaching at least 11 wins. Only Philadelphia and Seattle are listed with a higher-percentage chance of attaining "Super Bowl Contender" status.

But our DVOA projection system also viewed Tampa through rose-colored glasses last year, and the Buccaneers responded by grabbing the glasses, throwing them to the ground, and grinding them into rose-colored smithereens.

In a perfect world, the draft choices of 2004 and 2005, along with some core veterans—players like Griese, defensive end Simeon Rice, cornerbacks Ronde Barber and Brian Kelly, and weakside linebacker Derrick Brooks—would form the nucleus of a team that can contend for the NFC South title this season. But as Tampa Bay fans have come to learn the past two seasons, the world is rarely perfect. And as Tampa Bay has taught us, neither are statistical projection systems. More likely, the holes on this team will keep it fighting to reach .500 rather than returning to the postseason.

Russell Levine

Buccaneers 2004 Stats by Week

Wk	vs.	W-L	PF	PA	YDF	YDA	TO	DVOA			
								Total	Off	Def	ST
1	@WAS	L	10	16	169	291	-1	-39.3%	-42.2%	2.0%	5.0%
2	SEA	L	6	10	271	182	-2	9.8%	-40.0%	-56.6%	-6.8%
3	@OAK	L	20	30	389	399	+1	-60.9%	-17.4%	39.9%	-3.5%
4	DEN	L	13	16	269	249	-1	31.7%	11.5%	-17.7%	2.5%
5	@NO	W	20	17	319	251	+1	18.6%	4.8%	-15.9%	-2.0%
6	@STL	L	21	28	332	324	-2	-20.9%	-21.8%	-7.0%	-6.1%
7	CHI	W	19	7	293	167	0	6.9%	2.9%	-0.8%	3.3%
8	BYE										
9	KC	W	34	31	418	459	+3	37.9%	46.1%	-6.2%	-14.4%
10	@ATL	L	14	24	193	325	0	-12.8%	-15.2%	2.3%	4.7%
11	SF	W	35	3	352	197	0	14.7%	-2.4%	-16.8%	0.3%
12	@CAR	L	14	21	398	300	-2	-36.5%	3.8%	20.5%	-19.7%
13	ATL	W	27	0	247	255	+4	75.2%	8.5%	-62.4%	4.3%
14	@SD	L	24	31	436	336	-1	38.0%	11.8%	-32.0%	-5.8%
15	NO	L	17	21	283	247	-2	-44.9%	-30.8%	-2.9%	-17.0%
16	CAR	L	20	37	345	348	-3	-7.3%	37.5%	29.7%	-15.1%
17	@ARI	L	7	12	249	222	-3	-33.4%	-48.6%	-19.2%	-4.1%

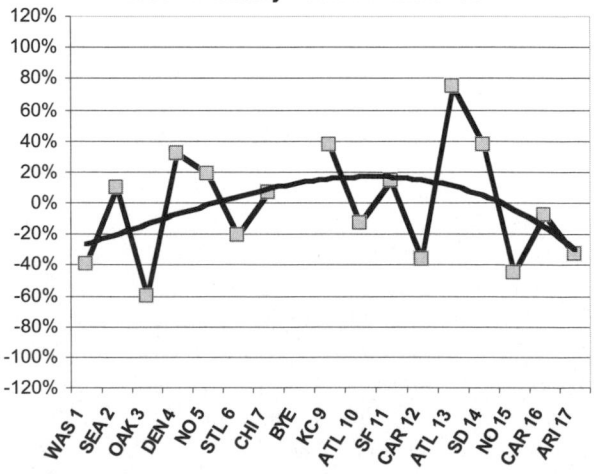

2004 TB Weekly DVOA Performance

Trends and Splits

	Offense	Rank	Defense	Rank
Total DVOA	-6.1%	23	-8.8%	7
Unadjusted VOA	-8.4%	25	-12.1%	6
Weighted Trend	0.4%	14	-9.9%	8
Variance	7.4%	21	7.4%	22
Passing	1.7%	15	-11.0%	6
Rushing	-16.4%	29	-6.8%	9
First Down	0.8%	17	-17.4%	3
Second Down	-12.0%	25	-1.3%	12
Third Down	-10.9%	18	-3.8%	16
Red Zone	1.1%	15	-21.0%	7
Late and Close	-26.6%	27	-26.3%	3

Five-Year Performance

	2004	2003	2002	2001	2000
W-L	5-11	7-9	12-4	9-7	10-6
Pythagorean Wins	7.9	9.2	12.7	9.4	11.3
Estimated Wins	8.0	10.1	12.6	10.1	10.1
Total DVOA	-2.0%	17.0%	40.9%	21.0%	21.5%
Rank	16	8	1	3	6
Offense	-6.1%	-4.1%	5.2%	-1.7%	0.8%
Rank	23	18	15	13	14
Defense	-8.8%	-25.5%	-32.4%	-19.5%	-16.7%
Rank	7	2	1	4	6
Special Teams	-4.7%	-4.4%	3.3%	3.2%	4.1%
Rank	31	30	8	7	10

Passing (min. 5 plays)

Player	DPAR	PAR	DVOA	Plys	NtYds	Avg	Cmpl	TD	Int
Brian Griese	50.4	60.6	19.3%	361	2460	6.8	69.3%	20	11
Brad Johnson	-2.4	-1.6	-18.2%	111	618	5.6	63.1%	3	3
Chris Simms	-7.6	-10.3	-33.1%	83	392	4.7	57.5%	1	3

Rushing (min. 3 plays)

Player	DPAR	PAR	DVOA	Plys	Yds	Avg	TD	Fum	Suc
Michael Pittman	1.9	2.2	12.5%	219	925	4.2	7	5	42%
Mike Alstott	1.7	2.1	-9.5%	67	232	3.5	2	1	55%
Charlie Garner	2.5	1.2	4.5%	30	111	3.7	0	0	40%
Brian Griese	-6.5	-6.4	-93.8%	14	26	1.9	0	1	—
Earnest Graham	3.1	3.3	45.4%	13	73	5.6	0	0	77%
Jamel White	-2.6	-3.0	-68.2%	13	20	1.5	0	0	15%
Michael Clayton	1.6	1.8	30.7%	5	30	6.0	0	0	—
Brad Johnson	1.1	1.0	26.4%	5	23	4.6	0	0	—
Chris Simms	-0.5	-0.6	-39.1%	4	20	5.0	0	0	—

Receiving (min. 5 plays)

Player	DPAR	PAR	DVOA	Plys	Ctch	Yds	Y/C	TD	CPct
WR									
Michael Clayton	39.8	38.6	33.9%	122	80	1196	15.0	7	66%
Joey Galloway	13.0	12.5	21.7%	53	33	416	12.6	5	62%
Joe Jurevicius	10.6	11.5	27.6%	37	27	333	12.3	2	73%
Tim Brown	-3.2	-3.6	-30.6%	31	24	200	8.3	1	77%
Charles Lee	4.1	4.4	12.8%	22	15	207	13.8	0	68%
Bill Schroeder	5.2	5.7	53.3%	11	7	156	22.3	1	64%
TE									
Ken Dilger	3.3	3.5	-3.6%	55	39	345	8.8	3	71%
Will Heller	-1.7	-1.4	-29.0%	16	12	98	8.2	1	75%
RB									
Michael Pittman	1.0	2.1	-7.0%	64	41	391	9.5	3	64%
Mike Alstott	-3.6	-2.6	-27.3%	41	29	202	7.0	0	71%
Charlie Garner	-2.1	-1.5	-45.4%	14	9	62	6.9	0	64%
Jameel Cook	0.0	1.0	-12.2%	12	7	44	6.3	1	58%
Jamel White	-2.3	-2.0	-70.9%	7	4	17	4.3	0	57%

Defensive Players (min. 20 plays)

Player	Age	Plys	Stop	Dfts	AvYds	StpRt	Sack	Int	FR
Defensive Line									
Greg Spires	31	63	52	28	0.7	83%	8.0	0	2
Chartric Darby	30	50	39	9	2.0	78%	0.0	0	1
Simeon Rice	31	43	33	20	-0.1	77%	12.0	0	0
Dewayne White	26	34	23	13	2.8	68%	6.0	0	1
Linebackers									
Derrick Brooks	32	139	69	27	4.6	50%	3.0	1	0
Shelton Quarles	34	107	57	16	4.2	53%	3.5	0	0
Ian Gold	27	74	40	19	4.7	54%	0.5	1	2
Jeff Gooch	31	22	12	2	3.6	55%	0.5	0	0

Player	Age	Plys	Stop	Dfts	AvYds	StpRt	Sack	Int	FR
Secondary									
Ronde Barber	30	109	52	24	5.4	48%	3.0	3	2
Dwight Smith	27	97	42	16	9.0	43%	0.0	3	0
Brian Kelly	29	82	39	14	5.9	48%	0.0	4	1
Jermaine Phillips	26	45	18	8	8.7	40%	1.0	1	0
Mario Edwards	30	27	8	7	8.6	30%	0.0	0	1

Offensive Line

Year	Yards	AdjLineYd	Rank	Power	Rank	10+ Yds	Rank	Stuff	Rank	Sack	AdjSack%	Rank
2002	3.81	3.91	24	61%	24	16%	18	25%	21	42	6.4%	17
2003	4.05	4.20	17	59%	25	13%	23	22%	7	23	3.8%	3
2004	4.03	4.00	23	56%	24	18%	14	24%	14	44	8.1%	24

Year	LEnd	Rank	LTckl	Rank	MdGrd	Rank	RTckl	Rank	REnd	Rank
2002	4.69	7	3.83	24	3.51	30	3.78	26	4.61	7
2003	3.92	17	5.27	2	4.33	12	3.52	28	3.70	19
2004	3.79	23	3.68	28	3.98	22	3.97	16	4.39	8

Tampa Bay's offensive line has seemingly been a work in progress going back to the Tony Dungy regime. The arrival of noted offensive line coach Bill Muir (who was hired as a precursor to the once expected, never realized arrival of Bill Parcells) was supposed to change that, but after three seasons under Muir the unit is still struggling. The Buccaneers are no better than mediocre by any of the statistics we use to measure offensive line performance. The problem appears to be the team's approach of signing new past-their-prime veterans each off-season to replace the previous year's signees who didn't work out. But with Tampa Bay tight up against the salary cap, that strategy appears to have been punted for 2005. Unheralded names like Jeb Terry, Sean Mahan, Anthony Davis, Chris Colmer, and Dan Buenning—none higher than a third-round pick—could all play significant roles on the line alongside holdovers Derrick Deese and Kenyatta Walker. (Veterans Todd Steussie and Matt Stinchcomb were both waived for cap purposes.) We'll find out this year if Muir really is a genius as he attempts to mold this group into a cohesive unit.

Defensive Front Seven

Year	Yards	AdjLineYd	Rank	Power	Rank	10+ Yds	Rank	Stuff	Rank	Sack	AdjSack%	Rank
2002	3.99	4.03	13	93%	32	17%	15	22%	23	46	7.9%	7
2003	3.72	3.89	11	66%	20	13%	10	27%	10	37	7.4%	4
2004	4.02	4.17	15	59%	11	17%	20	21%	26	45	9.5%	1

Year	LEnd	Rank	LTckl	Rank	MdGrd	Rank	RTckl	Rank	REnd	Rank
2002	3.62	6	3.05	3	4.29	21	3.75	9	4.18	20
2003	3.90	8	3.45	3	4.06	14	3.45	6	3.73	15
2004	4.21	15	3.99	7	4.06	11	4.72	29	4.36	23

The names may change, but it seems this group continues to perform among the league's best no matter who the Buccaneers plug in. The front seven will again feature some new faces in 2005, after the departures of tackle Chartric Darby and linebacker Ian Gold. Ryan Nece, a.k.a. Ronnie Lott's son, will compete to replace Gold on the strong side. The one-time starter is still raw after three seasons, but has the athletic and tackling ability that the Buccaneers love. Damien Gregory is likely to gain playing time from Darby's departure, with little drop-off in production, and the Buccaneers are also hoping to add depth at tackle by revitalizing the career of Chris Hovan. At end, Simeon Rice gets the headlines for his sack totals, but Greg Spires is a better all-around player, even though Rice is not as bad against the run as most people believe. The knock against the Buccaneers' undersized front four has always been that they are vulnerable to runs up the middle, but our Adjusted Line Yards metric doesn't agree, rating Tampa Bay stronger against runs between the tackles than on the ends. Derrick Brooks remains the leader of the linebacking corps. He may not be able to run down ball carriers from sideline to sideline anymore, but his football IQ is such that he's almost always in the right place, and he's still among the best linebackers in the league in pass coverage. Tampa Bay excels at covering opposing running backs on pass plays, a tribute to the overall athleticism of this unit, which is likely to start 30-somethings Brooks, Jeff Gooch, and Shelton Quarles in 2005, with Nece and second-round pick Barrett Ruud competing for time behind them.

Defensive Secondary

Year	DVOA vs. #1 WR	Rank	DVOA vs. #2 WR	Rank	DVOA vs. Other WR	Rank	DVOA vs. TE	Rank	DVOA vs. RB	Rank
2002	-47.0%	1	-57.9%	3	-15.7%	10	-41.1%	2	-44.6%	2
2003	-8.9%	12	-47.0%	2	-4.4%	21	-2.1%	15	-45.2%	2
2004	-25.6%	3	10.2%	20	18.4%	25	10.2%	18	-23.1%	7

Injuries have hurt the performance of this unit the last two seasons, and now Tampa Bay must cope with the departure via free agency of strong safety Dwight Smith. The Buccaneers hope to replace Smith with a familiar face—Super Bowl XXXVII MVP Dexter Jackson, back in Tampa Bay after a disastrous stint with the Cardinals. If Jackson can't do the job, fifth-round pick Donte Nicholson, a big hitter from Oklahoma, will be given a chance. Cornerbacks Ronde Barber and Brian Kelly form one of the best tandems in the league, though they don't receive much in the way of individual accolades because of Tampa Bay's reliance on zone coverage in its cover two scheme. Juran Bolden will be the nickelback in 2005, after Mario Edwards failed at the spot in 2004, and should help the Buccaneers' substandard performance against second and third receivers. The Buccaneers are counting on a return to full health of free safety Jermaine Phillips, who was limited by a broken forearm in 2004. It was the promise shown by Phillips that prompted the release of John Lynch last off-season, and he played well when he was in the lineup.

Special Teams

Year	DVOA	Rank	FG/XP	Rank	Net Punt	Rank	Punt Ret	Rank	Net Kick	Rank	Kick Ret	Rank
2002	3.8%	8	7.3	5	4.3	14	-2.1	19	11.0	3	0.7	15
2003	-4.4%	30	-9.9	29	0.6	19	-6.7	25	-1.1	20	-7.1	27
2004	-4.7%	31	-13.8	32	0.8	21	-19.6	32	-1.6	15	8.3	7

It might be the best-known quirky stat in NFL history, if only because every television announcer feels compelled to remind viewers at least once per game that the Buccaneers have never returned a kickoff for a touchdown in their history. The kick return unit, however, was the strongest area of Tampa Bay's abysmal special teams last season. The overall unit's poor ranking (31st and 30th in the NFL the last two seasons, according to DVOA) is primarily because of a shaky kicking game. Martin Gramatica finally wore out his welcome last November after costing the team several wins with missed kicks. Matt Bryant, signed in the off-season, should give Tampa Bay more reliable place-kicking.

The Buccaneers have never been afraid to use starters on their coverage units, and the team's other weak link, punt returns, should improve with a healthy Joey Galloway in 2005. Tampa Bay's league-worst punt return rating was actually more of a punt nonreturn rating. The Bucs were second in the league with 54 nonreturned punts: 22 fair catches, 18 downed by the punting team, 8 touchbacks, and 6 out of bounds. Part of the issue was that the Bucs were getting almost no rush on the punter, so opposing punters kicked the ball an average of 42.9 yards, tops in the NFL. Part of the problem was that with Galloway out of the lineup, Tampa often sent out 38-year-old Tim Brown to "return" punts, and he usually had his hand up in the air signaling fair catch before the ball was even kicked. When they weren't signaling fair catch, the Bucs were letting the ball bounce and roll until it invariably ended up close to the goal line. The NFL average for downed punts was the 19-yard line, but the 18 downed punts against Tampa Bay were downed, on average, at Tampa's *ten*-yard line.

Coaching Staff

Jon Gruden, who will be just 42 when the 2005 season kicks off, is still one of the youngest coaches in the NFL. The losing of the past two seasons has clearly worn on him, and there is a concern that a coach who has become accustomed to getting whatever he wants in free agency will be too impatient to wait out the rebuilding process if Tampa Bay struggles again this season. But Gruden, who is also de facto offensive coordinator even though Bill Muir holds that title, is still an excellent motivator and one of the NFL's best play callers, consistently finding ways to create matchups that exploit opposition weaknesses. Muir is considered one of the better offensive line coaches in the NFL, but he has had his hands full trying to create a cohesive unit in Tampa Bay, a process that will continue this season. Always looking for more offensive thinkers, Gruden added Paul Hackett to his staff as quarterbacks coach for 2005. For a team that has been successful, the Buccaneers have had surprisingly little turnover in their coaching staff. The team has denied some assistants the opportunity to interview elsewhere by giving them new titles, something that could cause friction down the road, especially if the losing continues. One man who doesn't appear to have any desire to leave is defensive coordinator Monte Kiffin, a holdover from the Dungy regime. Kiffin, whose unit always ranks among the NFL's best, has turned down head coaching opportunities and is one of the NFL's highest-paid assistants. If there's a coach on the hot seat, it's special teams coach Richard Bisaccia, based on the poor performance of the kicking game in recent seasons.

Washington Redskins

All right, class. Settle down. Today's lesson is about economic disparity. Having cities of different sizes and with populations of varying affluence has posed many challenges to professional sports leagues. Teams in cities with more people and more disposable income have a natural advantage—they generate more revenue and therefore have more to spend on the best players—over teams in smaller, poorer metropolitan areas. Many leagues have reacted to this economic disparity by adopting some sort of salary ceiling, or cap, which limits the amount of money a team can spend on players to give so-called small market teams a chance to compete against the large market teams. The NFL is one such league that has adopted a salary cap, which many observers believe has led to parity among teams and increased the league's appeal across America. Any questions?

OK, sorry if that was a bit too basic for the vast majority of *Pro Football Prospectus* readers. But if the front office of a professional football franchise like the Washington Redskins doesn't seem to understand the concept of a salary cap, there might be one or two of our readers who could use a quick explanation of how a salary cap works as well.

In 2004, the Washington Redskins had the highest payroll in NFL history, tipping the scales at around $120 million, including $70 million in signing bonuses. When you hand out that much in signing bonuses in the salary cap era, you have to get things right the first time, because those signing bonuses you pay this year count against your cap for years to come. If it turns out that you didn't spend that $70 million wisely, you've doomed your team to salary cap hell.

How bad have the Redskins' recent signings been? Let's take a look at the bonus money they've thrown away in the past few seasons. In 2004, 33-year-old quarterback Mark Brunell was given an $8.6 million signing bonus, even though he had been benched and replaced by a rookie in Jacksonville, and even though Patrick Ramsey had already shown in the second half of 2003 that he could be an adequate starter for a relatively small salary. That same off-season, Washington signed Clinton Portis to a $11.5 million signing bonus, even though he still had two years remaining on his rookie contract, and ex-Bronco running backs have a history of falling on their face once they have another offensive line blocking for them. Now there were many, including us, who thought Portis would be the one

running back to buck that trend, but taking a $11.5 million risk that this player will be different than all the others that have come before him is pretty foolhardy.

A large market team could try to avoid inevitable salary cap problems by taking advantage of the possibility of an uncapped year in 2007. Unless the NFL and NFLPA can come to terms on a new collective bargaining agreement, teams will have no restriction on how much money they can spend on players that season. Now, it's likely that the union and owners will come to an agreement by then. However, if the players take a hard-line stance in their desire to have an increased percentage of local revenues included in the overall salary pool that decides how much each team can spend on players, labor unrest may be more likely now than at any point since the 1987 strike.

Given this possibility, large market teams will want to have their normally backloaded contracts come due in 2007, when they're temporarily freed from the confines of the cap and can then use their large market status to their advantage. If a deal is struck before then, the teams will still have time to restructure these long-term deals, like they normally do anyway. Unfortunately, the Redskins didn't do this, as their biggest salary cap hits will come due this year and in 2006. In 2006, LaVar Arrington's salary cap value is scheduled to increase from $5.6 to over $12 million. Mark Brunell, Cornellius Griffin, Jon Jansen, Clinton Portis, Shawn Springs, and Marcus Washington will all see their 2006 salary cap value increase by at least $1 million from their 2005 value.

That doesn't begin to include the amount of dead money—salary cap space allocated to players no longer on the roster—that will undoubtedly be a part of the Redskins' cap in 2006. This season, Washington has $16 million dead money on its salary cap. This includes over $9 million owed to Laveraneus Coles, who was traded to the New York Jets for Santana Moss. (By the way, just before we went to press the Redskins signed Moss to a long-term deal roughly the same size as the one they had given Coles, which meant paying another $11 million in signing bonus.) The other $7 million in dead money will come almost entirely from contracts of players who didn't play a single down for the Redskins in 2004 and certainly won't play for Washington this season.

With no salary cap space to speak of, the Redskins were forced to restructure a number of contracts just to re-sign some of their own players who were due for a raise. Tackle Chris Samuels was re-signed to a big contract, which somewhat strangely has its lowest cap value in the potential uncapped 2007 season. At least the Redskins did enough restructuring to allow a slight dip in the free agency pool to bolster their woeful offensive line. Center Casey Rabach was one of the best free agent signings of the off-season, costing Washington only about $3 million a year for easily the best available center on the market.

But this team needed more than a new center and a slightly less disgruntled star receiver to fix what ailed them offensively. There was really nothing the Redskins did well. Mark Brunell started the season terribly, and while Patrick Ramsey was an improvement, that's merely damning with faint praise. Brunell was one of the ten worst quarterbacks according to both DPAR and DVOA. His replacement, Ramsey, was exactly that—a replacement-level quarterback, with a mere 1.0 DPAR. Unsatisfied with either of their two quarterbacks as long-term options behind center, the Redskins traded away three draft picks to move up to the end of the first round and grab Auburn quarterback Jason Campbell. (That included next year's first-round pick, which means that if Washington has the league's worst record they will have effectively traded Heisman Trophy winner Matt Leinart to the Denver Broncos for Campbell.)

The Brunell signing may have been the first clue that Joe Gibbs's triumphant return to the NFL wouldn't be quite

as triumphant as expected. Gibbs was the driving force behind the acquisition, convincing Brunell over dinner to agree to come to Washington. It was Gibbs's choice to add a second starting quarterback salary onto the already over-stuffed Washington budget, a tip-off that maybe he didn't quite understand the ramifications of a salary cap system that didn't exist during his first stint with the Redskins. At times, Gibbs seemed like an old poker player whose tricks and bluffs, which he'd once used to fleece tourists, no longer worked against the upstarts in the new era of tele-vised and online high-stakes Texas Hold 'Em. You had to wonder if Gibbs was going to end up slumped over a video slot machine, reminiscing about the flush days.

The biggest failure of Gibbs's return to Washington, however, was the running game. The Redskins dealt Pro Bowl cornerback Champ Bailey to Denver for Portis, signed him to the big new contract, and then saw him run for a dismal 3.8 yards per carry with only five touchdowns. Was the breakdown caused by an offensive line that could not open holes for Portis? Was Portis just being exposed as yet another product of the Denver running machine? Or was Gibbs at fault for using the same blocking scheme from his Super Bowl days, despite an offensive line that didn't fit the scheme?

The Gibbs–Joe Bugel blocking scheme, and the leg-endary counter-trey, calls for guards and tackles that are not only big but quick enough to pull across the line. The only member of the Redskins 2004 line that fit those job requirements was left guard Derrick Dockery. Right tackle Ray Brown, 320 pounds and 42 years of age, doesn't meet any conceivable definition of the word *quick*. Left tackle Chris Samuels is effective once he gets into position to level an opposing defender; it's just that he doesn't get into position as often as one might like.

In November, the Redskins showed that they were willing to change when they altered their schemes to include more of the zone blocking that Portis was used to in Denver. The result? A net nothing (table 1).

The total ineptitude of the Washington offense squan-dered an amazing turnaround season from the Washington defense. After finishing 28th in defensive DVOA in 2003, the Redskins catapulted all the way to third in 2004. They ranked number one with a −12.3% DVOA against the run,

TABLE 1. CLINTON PORTIS BEFORE AND AFTER NOVEMBER 1

	Sep/Oct	Nov/Dec
Yards/Game	94.7	81.5
Yards/Carry	3.92	3.77
DVOA	−21.8%	−9.5%

and seventh with a −10.9% DVOA against the pass. How does a team deal away its biggest-name defensive player, lose two of its starting linebackers for virtually the entire year with injuries, and still have such a remarkable change of fortune? The answer is: Improve up the middle.

Both starting defensive tackles, as well as the starting middle linebacker, were new in 2004. Cornelius Griffin, signed as a free agent from the New York Giants, improved his game to become the best run-stuffing defensive tackle in the league. He played next to veteran Joe Salave'a, signed away from San Diego, who was healthy for the first time in four seasons. And behind them was Antonio Pierce, a three-year backup who led Washington with 112 tackles and emerged as one of the league's best middle linebackers after injuries to Michael Barrow and LaVar Arrington.

The secondary, meanwhile, easily recovered from the loss of Bailey. Cornerback Fred Smoot was just as good as Bailey at covering the opposition's top wideout, free agent Shawn Springs had a strong season picking up the other side of the field, and rookie safety Sean Taylor came as advertised from the University of Miami (in both ability and attitude). Washington had the league's second highest DVOA on passes to the opposing team's best receiver, and the third best DVOA on passes to the opposing team's second best receiver.

The feeble offense that wasted this great defensive season won't get a second chance in 2005, because it is on defense where Washington suffered its biggest losses of the off-season. The lack of cap room prevented the Redskins from re-signing both Pierce and Smoot. Pierce's departure is doubly painful because he's moved over to the division rival New York Giants. After learning his craft down in the Chesapeake Valley Watershed Region, he'll get to spend his prime years stuffing Redskins running backs up in the New Jersey Swampland Region. The damage caused by Smoot's departure will be dampened slightly by Washington's top draft pick, Carlos Rogers. Washington reportedly had Rogers ranked as the top cornerback in the draft, even though he was the third one to come off the board. But the Redskins did not address their needs at linebacker until much later in the draft, thanks in part to the Jason Campbell trade.

It is possible that last year represented a short-term adjustment period, and Gibbs's on-field tactics will still work in today's NFL. Off the field, however, nothing has changed—this franchise makes one bad decision after another, changing long-term strategies at the drop of a hat. The old poker player might still bluff his way to a big pot, but that's hard to do when you keep tossing away all your good starting hands.

Al Bogdan

Research: The Assistant Coach Epidemic

Vince Lombardi won Super Bowl I with a six-man assistant coaching staff. Paul Brown coached one of the greatest teams in history with the help of five sturdy subordinates.

Brown and Lombardi wouldn't know what to do with today's 14- to 18-man coaching squadrons. The legendary coaches, not long removed from single-platoon football, might mistake the overstocked staff for the team itself.

There's no salary cap on coaches, so when teams had to limit spending on their rosters, they began to splurge in the coaching ranks. Since the 1990s, the ranks of assistant coaches have swelled, with predictable redundancy. And also redundancy.

No team is more redundant than the free-spending Redskins: Joe Gibbs is supported by an army of 20 assistants with similar-sounding titles. Joe Bugel is the assistant head coach: offense. Don Breaux is the offensive coordinator. Ernie Zampese is an offensive consultant.

It makes you wonder just how many coaches it takes to call a Clinton Portis counter 25 times every game. Too many assistant cooks can spoil the stew—just ask Patrick Ramsey, who answers to Gibbs, Breaux, Bugel, Zampese, and quarterbacks coach Bill Musgrave. Ramsey may still miss the open receiver, but he never forgets to staple a cover sheet on his TPS report.

The huge Redskins staff predates Gibbs, who no doubt likes having a NASCAR-sized battalion of assistants, right down to the pit crew and Spridle and Chim-Chim in the trunk. Back in 2003, 18 assistants made it look like Steve Spurrier was actually doing something. Spurrier was famous for not learning the names of his defensive players, a trait that the Washington media portrayed as charming during their six-month honeymoon with Spurrier in the summer of 2003. Anyone who ever worked for a boss who didn't bother to learn his name ("Smithers, who is that contemptible lay-about?") can imagine just how effective Spurrier was.

The myriad Redskins coaches demonstrate another strange trend on NFL coaching staffs: title proliferation. The Redskins have two assistant head coaches (Bugel and Gregg Williams) who aren't coordinators. In fairness to Gibbs and the Redskins, both coaches are seasoned veterans who could be expected to take over the team if Gibbs was suddenly called back to racing. Most teams keep an assistant who is the nominal "assistant head coach"; in reality, he's a prized underling who has been given a title so that he cannot negotiate with other teams for a promotion. The Ravens, for instance, list Chris Foertser as "Assistant Head Coach/Offensive Line," but if Brian Billick were ever called away by the United Nations to use his genius to solve the world's problems, Foertser would have to pry the headset out of Jim Fassel's cold, dead hand.

Title proliferation is rampant in NFL front offices, where there are usually a half dozen vice presidents with vague responsibilities (like "owner's son"), so a trickle-down effect to the coaching staff is inevitable. And small companies have a similar problem, as titles are often the only form of compensation. (The Football Outsiders Home Office has offered me a choice between the titles of "Vice President of Rambling Observations" or "Resident Stud." I'm still undecided.)

Before Gibbs, Denver's Mike Shanahan was the league's top staff builder. Dennis Dillon took note of the Broncos' burgeoning staff in a *Sporting News* column in 2001; at the time, the Broncos had 18 assistants (Alex Gibbs was a part-time consultant). Dillon joked at the time that his ideal 30-man staff would include a trick-play designer named Inspector Gadget. Shanahan had no such person, but he did have separate coaches for defensive tackles and ends, safeties and cornerbacks, all of which were considered extravagances at the time.

Shanahan still employs a "pass rush" coach to work with the defensive line and linebackers coach. The new pass rush coach in Denver is Andre Patterson, who coached for Butch Davis in Cleveland and brought the entire Browns defensive line with him to Denver. The Browns had 32 sacks last season, but maybe Patterson knows something we don't. Shanahan also kept Jimmy Spencer on the payroll as a player/assistant coach until last year. Official player-coaches are rarities in the NFL, though Terrell Owens occasionally nominates himself player–offensive coordinator.

Pass rush coaches and their ilk aren't unique to Denver. The Ravens employ Mike Pettine as an outside linebackers coach, while Jeff Fitzgerald is the traditional "linebackers coach." The Cowboys list separate coaches for defensive tackles and ends. And many teams feature various vague "defensive assistants" who may have similar responsibilities.

But some assistants have truly unique titles. The Dolphins currently list Jeff Dellanbach as "Fellowship Coach/Special Teams." Fellowship coach—sounds like Dellanbach is in charge of campfire sing-alongs. The Packers have two strength coaches, but also list Vince Workman as "Weight Room Assistant," by which we hope they don't mean that Workman, a former player, cleans mirrors and hands out towels. The Jets have promoted Dick Curl to "Senior Offen-sive Assistants/Special Projects." This special project, according to the team's website, is clock management. Jets fans agree: That's a promotion too long in coming.

Most teams employ at least one "quality control" coach; many teams have two or three. Despite the title, these guys don't inspect NFL-licensed apparel to make sure that the seams are straight. On most teams, they're film room assistants who log tendencies and chart the progress of plays while waiting for higher coaching jobs. "Generally, one thing that's consistent with all quality control coaches, they have to be very, very good on the computer," Terry Donahue said in 2003. Donahue is also very, very good on the computer. While ostensibly running the Niners in 2003, he found the time to create a 57th-level character in Everquest.

The defending champion Patriots, meanwhile, raised some eyebrows with their decision to replace offensive coordinator Charlie Weis with...nobody. Lombardi and Brown didn't need offensive coordinators, mind you, but both were offensive coaches, and Lombardi had Bart Starr to call his plays (Otto Graham could've called his own, but Brown wouldn't let him). Belichick's record as an offensive coach leaves something to be desired, but he'll have a hand in play calling, as will assistants Dante Scarnecchia and Josh McDaniels—and probably quarterback Tom Brady. There are rumors that the team will replace Weis's playbook with Tom Moore's scheme for the Colts, since the Patriots defenders know it by heart.

The Patriots list Berj Najarian as "Executive Administrator to the Head Coach." His job seems to include scheduling and logistics; it's easy to picture him as the Tom Hagen of the Patriots family. It's likely that most teams have someone with Najarian's duties on the payroll; the Patriots are unique in listing Najarian among the coaches. But if he's in charge of Belichick's wardrobe, he needs to be downsized.

We kid about the overspecialization of pro staffs, but let's think about baseball for a moment. What purpose does the "bench coach" serve? In baseball, where every at bat takes half an hour, why would a manager have to consult with anyone about his relatively limited strategic options? And if he had to consult with anyone, why would he choose Don Zimmer? Football coaches, myriad though they may be, all do something.

Well, all of them except maybe Ernie Zampese.

Mike Tanier

Redskins 2004 Stats by Week

Wk	vs.	W-L	PF	PA	YDF	YDA	TO	DVOA Total	Off	Def	ST
1	TB	W	16	10	291	169	+1	47.1%	-1.0%	-54.0%	-5.9%
2	@NYG	L	14	20	322	277	-6	-90.5%	-85.6%	7.9%	3.0%
3	DAL	L	18	21	384	287	0	-35.6%	-1.9%	34.6%	0.9%
4	@CLE	L	13	17	265	280	-1	-31.4%	-8.9%	17.8%	-4.8%
5	BAL	L	10	17	107	232	+1	-39.2%	-50.9%	-35.7%	-24.1%
6	@CHI	W	13	10	311	160	0	10.2%	-0.1%	-15.0%	-4.7%
7	BYE										
8	GB	L	14	28	272	361	+2	10.2%	-34.6%	-47.1%	-2.2%
9	@DET	W	17	10	229	322	+1	23.0%	3.1%	-2.2%	17.6%
10	CIN	L	10	17	268	316	0	-4.6%	-31.4%	-21.3%	5.5%
11	@PHI	L	6	28	213	334	+1	-38.9%	-20.1%	9.2%	-9.6%
12	@PIT	L	7	16	156	207	-1	-38.5%	-34.3%	-13.7%	-17.9%
13	NYG	W	31	7	379	145	0	80.0%	57.5%	-32.3%	-9.8%
14	PHI	L	14	17	312	312	+1	43.3%	-0.2%	-44.2%	-0.7%
15	@SF	W	26	16	337	254	+3	33.7%	-11.1%	-48.1%	-3.3%
16	@DAL	L	10	13	233	306	-1	-27.0%	-34.6%	-10.9%	-3.3%
17	MIN	W	21	18	318	320	-2	13.7%	0.5%	-5.4%	7.8%

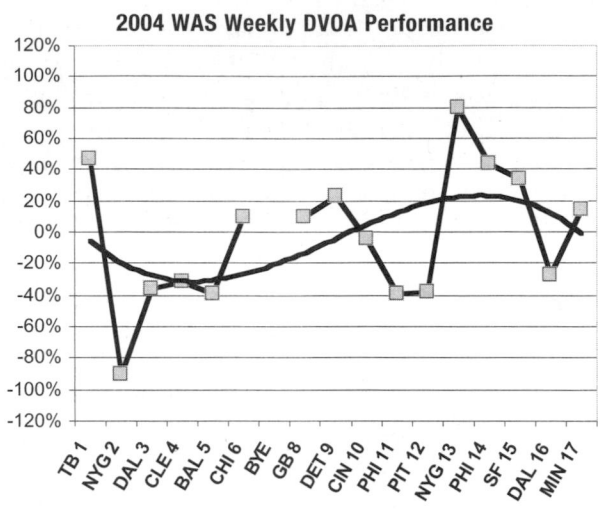

2004 WAS Weekly DVOA Performance

Trends and Splits

	Offense	Rank	Defense	Rank
Total DVOA	-15.3%	28	-16.0%	3
Unadjusted VOA	-14.3%	27	-17.3%	4
Weighted Trend	-8.6%	24	-18.9%	2
Variance	9.6%	14	6.8%	23
Passing	-17.5%	28	-10.9%	7
Rushing	-13.0%	27	-22.1%	1
First Down	-19.2%	30	-4.6%	12
Second Down	0.0%	19	-20.8%	3
Third Down	-34.9%	28	-31.2%	3
Red Zone	3.1%	14	0.9%	19
Late and Close	-36.3%	28	-1.1%	17

Five-Year Performance

	2004	2003	2002	2001	2000
W-L	6-10	5-11	7-9	8-8	8-8
Pythagorean Wins	7.1	5.6	6.4	6.4	8.4
Estimated Wins	7.0	5.6	8.0	8.5	9.6
Total DVOA	-2.4%	-13.5%	-5.4%	3.3%	13.7%
Rank	17	24	23	13	10
Offense	-15.3%	-4.1%	-3.2%	-9.7%	5.7%
Rank	28	17	23	22	11
Defense	-16.0%	11.0%	-6.2%	-13.0%	-14.2%
Rank	3	28	7	9	7
Special Teams	-3.2%	1.6%	-8.3%	0.1%	-6.2%
Rank	26	11	31	15	29

Passing (min. 5 plays)

Player	DPAR	PAR	DVOA	Plys	NtYds	Avg	Cmpl	TD	Int
Patrick Ramsey	1.0	-2.1	-12.4%	295	1520	5.2	62.1%	10	10
Mark Brunell	-10.2	-8.1	-22.8%	255	1086	4.3	49.8%	7	6

Rushing (min. 3 plays)

Player	DPAR	PAR	DVOA	Plys	Yds	Avg	TD	Fum	Suc
Clinton Portis	4.0	3.6	-11.3%	343	1319	3.8	5	5	45%
Ladell Betts	7.2	8.4	4.6%	90	371	4.1	1	0	51%
Mark Brunell	-1.6	-1.4	-39.1%	13	64	4.9	0	0	—
Patrick Ramsey	-0.1	-0.1	-25.2%	4	22	5.5	0	0	—
Laveranues Coles	0.2	0.4	-18.2%	3	-3	-1.0	0	0	—
Rod Gardner	0.3	0.3	-9.8%	3	7	2.3	0	0	—

Receiving (min. 5 plays)

Player	DPAR	PAR	DVOA	Plys	Ctch	Yds	Y/C	TD	CPct
WR									
Laveranues Coles	-1.7	-4.2	-16.2%	168	90	950	10.6	1	54%
Rod Gardner	1.3	-1.3	-12.7%	106	51	650	12.7	5	48%
Taylor Jacobs	0.0	-0.1	-15.2%	27	16	178	11.1	0	59%
James Thrash	6.5	6.2	32.7%	21	17	203	11.9	0	81%
Darnerien McCants	2.1	1.6	20.4%	9	5	71	14.2	0	56%
TE									
Chris Cooley	5.8	4.7	2.1%	63	37	314	8.5	6	59%
Robert Royal	2.1	2.5	10.4%	15	8	70	8.8	4	53%
Walter Rasby	1.1	0.6	7.9%	9	5	52	10.4	0	56%
Brian Kozlowski	0.5	0.0	0.9%	6	3	29	9.7	0	50%
RB									
Clinton Portis	-1.6	-0.8	-16.0%	57	40	235	5.9	2	70%
Ladell Betts	-0.5	-2.0	-12.5%	25	15	108	7.2	0	60%

Defensive Players (min. 20 plays)

Player	Age	Plys	Stop	Dfts	AvYds	StpRt	Sack	Int	FR
Defensive Line									
Corenlius Griffin	29	76	63	28	0.5	83%	6.0	0	1
Renaldo Wynn	31	38	31	8	1.4	82%	3.0	0	0
Demetric Evans	26	27	20	9	1.1	74%	2.5	0	0
Joe Salave'a	30	22	17	8	1.2	77%	2.0	0	0
Linebackers									
Antonio Pierce	27	115	60	23	5.1	52%	1.0	2	2
Marcus Washington	28	104	69	38	3.2	66%	4.5	0	1
Lemar Marshall	29	67	30	9	4.3	45%	1.5	0	0

Player	Age	Plys	Stop	Dfts	AvYds	StpRt	Sack	Int	FR
Secondary									
Sean Taylor	22	88	33	19	8.1	38%	1.0	4	0
Shawn Springs	30	80	36	18	6.9	45%	6.0	5	0
Fred Smoot	26	77	39	21	7.6	51%	0.0	3	1
Ryan Clark	26	76	23	9	9.7	30%	0.0	0	0
Matt Bowen	29	21	7	2	7.6	33%	2.0	0	0

Offensive Line

Year	Yards	AdjLineYd	Rank	Power	Rank	10+ Yds	Rank	Stuff	Rank	Sack	AdjSack%	Rank
2002	4.29	4.39	5	67%	16	14%	24	21%	5	38	6.5%	19
2003	3.98	4.30	12	63%	21	11%	28	23%	11	43	7.0%	22
2004	3.89	4.05	22	47%	31	14%	28	25%	17	38	6.4%	15

Year	LEnd	Rank	LTckl	Rank	MdGrd	Rank	RTckl	Rank	REnd	Rank
2002	4.35	12	3.81	25	4.33	13	5.12	2	4.80	5
2003	5.54	1	4.26	15	4.11	19	2.35	32	4.38	10
2004	3.84	21	4.02	24	3.92	23	4.38	12	4.37	10

On our website before last season, we argued that Clinton Portis would still be effective because the Washington offensive line was severely underrated. In 2002 and 2003, they were fine in Adjusted Line Yards, but the running backs could not do anything once they got through the initial hole. So we were even more shocked than most people when both Portis and the line imploded. Other than a new blocking scheme, the big difference last year was the loss of right tackle Jon Jansen for the season. While Jansen's torn Achilles' heel could have been career threatening as recently as five years ago, he should be able to make a full comeback, albeit maybe a step or two slower off the block. But can he still be effective executing the heavy pulling an offensive lineman must do in the Gibbs-Bugel scheme? Free agent center Casey Rabach is a big addition to a team that struggled at running up the middle. On the left, Washington features Chris Samuels at left tackle, finally pacified with a contract extension that includes $19 million in guaranteed bonuses, and third-year starter Derrick Dockery at left guard. Dockery is the quickest member of the line, but also the quickest to jump before the snap: He had 11 penalties (seven false starts, three holding, and, oddly, an ineligible downfield pass) while no other starter had more than six.

Defensive Front Seven

Year	Yards	AdjLineYd	Rank	Power	Rank	10+ Yds	Rank	Stuff	Rank	Sack	AdjSack%	Rank
2002	3.96	3.76	6	80%	31	20%	24	31%	3	39	6.7%	11
2003	4.41	4.50	29	63%	12	15%	11	20%	29	27	4.8%	27
2004	3.18	3.45	2	56%	8	12%	6	32%	2	39	6.7%	18

Year	LEnd	Rank	LTckl	Rank	MdGrd	Rank	RTckl	Rank	REnd	Rank
2002	4.00	16	3.05	2	4.27	20	4.23	18	2.34	2
2003	4.48	20	5.41	32	4.35	21	5.34	32	4.14	21
2004	2.85	2	4.56	22	3.42	2	4.39	23	2.59	3

Cornelius Griffin was the best run-stuffing defensive tackle in the league last year. Right tackles often are divided into two groups: Those who can free up their linebackers by taking on two offensive linemen, and those who can rush the passer. Griffin doesn't really fit into either group. He draws plenty of double teams, but he does much more than just free up the linebackers; he also makes plenty of tackles himself on running plays and had his best season as a pass rusher in 2004. The Giants made a big mistake in letting Griffin get away last year.

(continued next page)

Defensive Front Seven (continued)

Marcus Washington was a perfect fit for Gregg Williams's schemes because he's an aggressive player who flies to the ball with great speed. Drafted as a small defensive end out of Auburn by the Colts, he played well in Indianapolis when he was allowed to cut loose and go after the quarterback, but he struggled when he was asked to read and react. After signing with the Redskins in 2004, he was freed to improvise and responded with his best year.

The biggest question mark going into the season is the status of LaVar Arrington's injured knee. Arrington originally tore his lateral meniscus—the cartilage that goes between the femur and tibia and acts as a cushion—and required a second surgery on the same knee after suffering a bone bruise upon returning to action late in the year. If Arrington is getting bone-on-bone grinding—insert joke here—he'll need regular procedures and could lose some quickness.

Defensive Secondary

Year	DVOA vs. #1 WR	Rank	DVOA vs. #2 WR	Rank	DVOA vs. Other WR	Rank	DVOA vs. TE	Rank	DVOA vs. RB	Rank
2002	-18.5%	5	-25.5%	8	-13.5%	11	15.0%	23	-6.3%	10
2003	-23.5%	4	11.3%	23	11.3%	25	38.3%	31	18.2%	28
2004	-28.7%	2	-18.1%	3	4.9%	19	3.7%	16	-11.0%	16

Because Gregg Williams likes his safeties to attack, it's important that he has cornerbacks who won't let receivers behind them. Fred Smoot excelled at that last year and was also solid when it came to tackling running backs on the outside. Unfortunately for Washington, Smoot is now a Viking and Shawn Springs now will be expected to handle opposing teams' top receivers. Springs is a good cover corner, but he turned 30 this year and is not quite at the level he was a few years ago. Of course, opposing quarterbacks will probably avoid Springs so they can spend more time testing the education of rookie Carlos Rogers. Safeties Sean Taylor and Ryan Clark round out the unit, with Pierson Prioleau signing from Buffalo to provide depth.

Special Teams

Year	DVOA	Rank	FG/XP	Rank	Net Punt	Rank	Punt Ret	Rank	Net Kick	Rank	Kick Ret	Rank
2002	-8.3%	31	-11.1	31	-23.0	31	-4.4	25	-3.0	20	-4.8	24
2003	1.6%	11	3.1	15	6.6	8	-13.9	31	7.0	5	6.0	7
2004	-3.2%	26	-6.6	31	-4.6	28	-6.7	20	-3.8	22	3.9	12

Thanks to John Hall's love of making special teams tackles—and the injuries that result—the Redskins went through three kickers last year. While both Hall and Ola Kimrin were below average on both field goals and kickoffs, Jeff Chandler was worth 1.2 points on field goals and 1.8 points on kickoffs. Could Chandler finally be living up to the promise that led San Francisco to waste a fourth-round pick on him in 2002? Or is this small sample size? We're going with the latter. Hall will be healthy again in 2005 but he may battle Chandler for the position in training camp. James Thrash returns kicks well and punts not so well. The low net punting rating comes not because Tom Tupa couldn't punt for distance—he was third in the league with an gross punting average of 44.1 yards per punt—but because he couldn't put it where it wouldn't be returned: 63% of Washington punts were returned in some way; the only other team over 56% was Cincinnati.

Coaching Staff

Before last season, a great case could be made that Joe Gibbs was the greatest coach of all time, or at least should be part of the conversation. He won three Super Bowls with three different quarterbacks. Washington only had one losing season and made the playoffs eight times during Gibbs's original 12-year run, losing in the first round only once. So, of course, he had to fall on his face in his first year back in coaching, making those of us who argued he should be mentioned in the same breath as Vince Lombardi and Paul Brown look like idiots. Combine that with his orchestration of the terrible Mark Brunell signing and the failures of the Washington running game, and his legacy is now up in the air.

Although his personality is much different, in terms of defensive scheme, defensive coordinator Gregg Williams is the most similar coach to Buddy Ryan that the NFL has in 2005. Williams and Ryan emphasize the same things on defense: Attack the quarterback, try to make big plays, don't worry about giving up yardage at times as long as your defense can force turnovers. Williams was an assistant when Ryan was the defensive coordinator with the Houston Oilers, so he's well versed in Ryan's defensive philosophy.

Quarterbacks

2004 was a banner year for quarterbacks. Peyton Manning set the all-time NFL record for passer rating. Daunte Culpepper, as we note earlier in the book, also had one of the ten best quarterback seasons in modern NFL history. Tom Brady and Donovan McNabb had by far the best numbers of their careers before meeting in the Super Bowl. Ben Roethlisberger came close to having the best rookie year by any quarterback in history.

2004 was also a banner year for bad quarterbacks. While Peyton was cruising to 49 touchdowns, his brother Eli managed to throw just 6, with nine interceptions. He wasn't the worst rookie to see regular playing time (Craig Krenzel), nor was he the most overhyped player to post a severely negative DPAR (hello, Michael Vick). But he was part of the league's soft white underbelly of overmatched signal callers. From Jonathan Quinn to Luke McCown to Jay Fiedler to Matt Schaub, 2004 produced a bumper crop of awful passers, the yang to Peyton and Daunte's yin.

Using standard deviation, we can easily see how unusual the quarterback data was in 2004. Standard deviation is a statistical tool for measuring how far away from the mean individual items in a data set are; in other words, it measures how "spread out" the data is. Standard deviation isn't affected much by one aberrant bit of data, like Peyton Manning's touchdown total or his brother's low completion percentage. Each data item is accounted for, and the larger the standard deviation is, the greater the spread between the great, the average, and the Krenzelian.

Table 1 shows the standard deviation of passing DPAR in each of the last six seasons (for all quarterbacks with over 100 attempts). Over the past few years, fans knew what to expect at the top of the league leaderboards (30 TDs, 7.5 yards

per attempt) and at the bottom (52% completions, TD/INT ratios under 1.0). Suddenly, 2004 hit, and stakes were higher: Five QBs passed for over 4,000 yards, three attempted over 100 passes but completed less than 50% of them.

There doesn't appear to be any root cause for the increase in both great and terrible quarterback performances. Conventional arguments—the new defensive holding rules, diluted talent at the NFL level due to expansion—don't bear out under scrutiny. (Expansion was three years ago, not last year.) Quarterback performance is not a zero sum game where one passer benefits from the failures of another; Marc Bulger isn't throwing touchdowns because John Navarre can't cover his receivers, he's throwing touchdowns because John Navarre's teammates can't cover his receivers. (Frankly, Bulger's teammates can't cover Navarre's receivers either, but that didn't help because Navarre couldn't get them the ball.) Many offenses fell completely apart last year for very different reasons, while a handful of defenses (particularly in the NFC) proved to be completely inept. As teams like the Niners, Browns, and Bears rebuild, and as age and the salary cap erode the lineups of better teams, it's likely that the standard deviation of quarterback performance will return to normal.

What does that mean for the average fan? Don't bank on another 49 touchdowns from Peyton, for one thing. And rest assured that the bottom feeders will staunch the offensive bleeding.

In the following section we give the last three years' worth of numbers for every quarterback who played a role in 2004—major or minor—and/or will likely play a role in 2005 (see table 2). We also give projections for quarterbacks expected to receive starts in 2005.

The first line contains biographical data—the player's name, height, weight, college, birthdate, and age. Height and weight are the best data we could find; weight, of course, can fluctuate during the off-season. Age is very simple, the number of years between the player's birth year and 2005, and the full birthdate is given for anyone who wants to either do research involving more complexity or buy their favorite player a cake.

Next we give the last three years of player stats. Passing stats are on the left side, and rushing stats are on the right.

The first few columns are standard numbers: games, pass attempts, pass completions, completion percentage, passing yards, passing touchdowns, and interceptions.

TABLE 1. STANDARD DEVIATION OF PASSING DPAR, 1999–2004

Year	Stan. Dev.
2004	48.4
2003	34.8
2002	38.0
2001	32.4
2000	37.6
1999	33.6

TABLE 2. QUARTERBACK STATISTICS SAMPLE

Tom Brady Height: 6-4 Weight: 225 College: Michigan Born: 3-Aug-1977 Age: 28

Year	Team	G	Att	Comp	Pct	Yds	TD	INT	FUM	Sck%	NtY/P	Rank	DVOA	Rank	DPAR	Rank	PAR	Runs	Yds	TD	DPAR	DVOA
2002	NE	16	594	373	62.8%	3764	29	14	9	5.0%	5.7	30	6.8%	18	53.9	13	66.1	42	110	1	3.4	-0.5%
2003	NE	16	526	317	60.3%	3620	23	12	13	5.4%	6.0	18	5.2%	14	43.2	10	52.0	42	63	1	-0.4	-21.9%
2004	NE	16	474	288	60.8%	3692	28	14	7	5.0%	7.1	9	41.6%	2	113.4	3	95.6	43	28	0	1.1	-8.1%
2005	*NE*	*16*	*511*	*324*	*63.3%*	*3731*	*27*	*14*	—	—	*6.7*	—	—	—	—	—	—	*24*	*10*	*1*		

These numbers are official NFL totals and therefore include plays we leave out of our own metrics, such as spikes, and leave out plays we include in our metrics, like sacks and aborted snaps. Note that "games" is all games the player appeared in, not games started, which is why a quarterback who also holds on field goals will be listed with 16 games played.

The next column is fumbles (FUM), which adds together all fumbles by the player, whether turned over to the defense or recovered by the offense (to see why, read the New Orleans chapter). Even though it is with the passing numbers on the left, this number includes all fumbles on sacks, aborted snaps, or rushing attempts. We wanted it to be next to interceptions to give a general idea of how many turnovers each player is responsible for.

Next comes Adjusted Sack Rate (Sck%). This is the same statistic you'll find in the team chapters, only here it is separated by quarterback. It represents sacks per pass play (pass attempts plus sacks) adjusted based on down, distance, and strength of schedule. For reference, the NFL average was 6.8% in 2004, 6.1% in 2003, and 6.5% in 2002.

The next two columns are Net Yards per Pass, a standard stat but a particularly good one, and the player's rank in Net Yards per Pass for that season. Consider the inclusion of this number our tribute to the godfather of football stats, Bud Goode. It consists of passing yards minus yards lost on sacks, divided by pass plays.

The five columns remaining in passing stats give our advanced metrics: DVOA (Defense-Adjusted Value Over Average), DPAR (Defense-Adjusted Points Above Replacement), and PAR (Points Above Replacement), along with the player's rank in both DVOA and DPAR. These metrics compare each quarterback's passing performance to a league-average baseline based on the game situations that quarterback faced. DVOA and DPAR are also adjusted based on the opposing defense. The methods used to compute these numbers are described in detail in the front of the book. The important distinctions between them are:

- Higher DVOA means more value per pass play. Higher DPAR means more total value over the 16-game season.
- A player whose DPAR is higher than his PAR faced a harder-than-average schedule. A player whose PAR is higher than his DPAR faced an easier-than-average schedule.

To qualify for ranking in Net Yards per Pass, passing DVOA, and passing DPAR, a quarterback must have 100 pass plays in the given season. 42 quarterbacks are ranked for 2004, 47 each for 2003 and 2002.

The final five columns represent rushing stats, starting with runs, rushing yards, and rushing touchdowns. Once again, these are official NFL totals and include kneeldowns, meaning you get to enjoy numbers like Tom Brady running 43 times for 28 yards. (Yes, this is a run stat, if by "run" you mean "falls to the ground.") Rushing touchdowns by quarterbacks, by the way, fell 33% last season compared to the last few years.

The final two columns give DPAR and DVOA for quarterback rushing, which are calculated separately from passing. Rankings as well as numbers that are not adjusted for defense (PAR and VOA) can be found on our website, FootballOutsiders.com.

Finally, we have the last row of numbers, our 2005 projections. Right now we are only projecting conventional statistics, although in future years we hope to project advanced metrics like DVOA and DPAR. Projections are based on a complicated regression analysis that takes into account numerous variables including projected role, performance over the past two years, performance on third down vs. all downs, historical comparables, height, age, and strength of schedule. Inspired by our partners at *Baseball Prospectus,* who named their projection system PECOTA after the Kansas City utility infielder of the 1980s, we have named our projection system KUBIAK. The letters don't stand for anything except that we're fans of Gary Kubiak.

It is difficult to accurately project statistics for a 162-game baseball season, but it is exponentially more difficult to accurately project statistics for a 16-game football season. Consider the listed projections not as a prediction of exact numbers, but the mean of a range of possible performances. What's important is less the exact number of yards we project, more which players are projected to improve or decline. We are projecting the 2005 offensive environment to be similar to the heightened offensive environment of 2002 and 2004, but with a lower standard deviation.

The other problem we face is that of backup quarterbacks. With other positions, backups will see some playing time even if starters are healthy the entire season. But while a number of backup quarterbacks will see significant time this season, we have very little ability to predict who they will be. At the same time, KUBIAK projects a majority of starting quarterbacks to play "15.2 games" or some such thing. Therefore, we have projected most starting quarterbacks to play 16 games, even though we know that many will not, and we have made only cursory projections for backup quarterbacks unless we feel they are particularly likely to see action because:

a. They play behind starters with a higher chance of injury due to style or age.
b. They play behind starters with a good chance of losing their jobs due to subpar play.

c. They are rookies playing behind average quarterbacks on teams that are unlikely to be in playoff contention come December.
d. They are old veterans returning home for one final season.

There are no projections for more than two quarterbacks on any team, even though we know that a few third- and even fourth-string quarterbacks will inevitably take the field at one point or another. These players, unless they have thrown more than a handful of passes in the last couple seasons, are briefly discussed at the end of the chapter in a section called "Going Deep." FA signifies a player who was still a free agent at press time.

TABLE 3. TOP 20 QB BY PASSING DPAR (TOTAL VALUE), 2004

Rank	Player	Team	DPAR	Rank	Player	Team	DPAR
1	Peyton Manning	IND	170.1	11	Jake Plummer	DEN	56.4
2	Daunte Culpepper	MIN	136.4	12	Matt Hasselbeck	SEA	52.5
3	Tom Brady	NE	113.4	13	Brian Griese	TB	50.4
4	Donovan McNabb	PHI	107.1	14	Jake Delhomme	CAR	49.4
5	Trent Green	KC	102.9	15	Carson Palmer	CIN	39.0
6	Marc Bulger	STL	92.6	16	Vinny Testaverde	DAL	36.5
7	Brett Favre	GB	83.5	17	Byron Leftwich	JAC	30.2
8	Chad Pennington	NYJ	77.2	18	David Carr	HOU	27.5
9	Drew Brees	SD	75.6	19	Aaron Brooks	NO	23.2
10	Ben Roethlisberger	PIT	75.3	20	Kyle Boller	BAL	23.1

TABLE 4. TOP 20 QB BY PASSING DVOA (VALUE PER PASS), 2004

Rank	Player	Team	DVOA	Rank	Player	Team	DVOA
1	Peyton Manning	IND	62.8%	11	Brian Griese	TB	19.3%
2	Tom Brady	NE	41.6%	12	Jake Plummer	DEN	11.5%
3	Ben Roethlisberger	PIT	40.3%	13	Matt Hasselbeck	SEA	10.3%
4	Daunte Culpepper	MIN	38.9%	14	Jake Delhomme	CAR	7.5%
5	Donovan McNabb	PHI	35.8%	15	Carson Palmer	CIN	7.2%
6	Chad Pennington	NYJ	31.6%	16	Jon Kitna	CIN	5.9%
7	Drew Brees	SD	29.5%	17	Vinny Testaverde	DAL	3.2%
8	Marc Bulger	STL	29.3%	18	Byron Leftwich	JAC	2.3%
9	Trent Green	KC	27.7%	19	Kurt Warner	NYG	-0.5%
10	Brett Favre	GB	22.0%	20	David Carr	HOU	-0.6%

Tony Banks

Height: 6-4   **Weight: 230**   **College: Michigan State**   **Born: 5-Apr-1973**   **Age: 32**

Year	Team	G	Att	Comp	Pct	Yds	TD	INT	FUM	Sck%	NtY/P	Rank	DVOA	Rank	DPAR	Rank	PAR	Runs	Yds	TD	DPAR	DVOA
2002	HOU	0	0	0	0.0%	0	0	0	—	—	—	—	—	—	—	—	—	0	0	0	—	—
2003	HOU	7	102	61	59.8%	693	5	3	1	10.3%	5.6	27	21.1%	8	16.1	21	11.8	6	27	0	0.7	4.5%
2004	HOU	5	2	1	50.0%	16	0	0	—	0.0%	8.0	—	696.8%	—	1.3	—	1.3	0	0	0	—	—
2005	*HOU*	*—*	*—*	*—*	*—*	*—*	*—*	*—*	*—*	*—*	*—*	*—*	*—*	*—*	*—*	*—*	*—*	*—*	*—*	*—*		

Have you ever looked at the numbers Tony Banks put up with the 1998 Rams and contrasted them with the numbers Kurt Warner put up with the 1999 Rams? Banks in 1998: 408 attempts, 241 completions (59.1%), 2,535 yards, 6.21 yards per throw, 7 touchdowns, 14 interceptions, sacked 41 times. Warner in 1999: 499 attempts, 325 completions (65.1%), 4,353 yards, 8.72 yards per throw, 41 touchdowns, 13 interceptions, sacked 29 times. The amazing thing is that Warner was on the Rams' roster in 1998 but Dick Vermeil & Co. chose to start Banks ahead of him. In fairness, we should say that Banks played fairly well two years ago when David Carr was hurt.

Jeff Blake

Height: 6-1   **Weight: 223**   **College: East Carolina**   **Born: 4-Dec-1970**   **Age: 35**

Year	Team	G	Att	Comp	Pct	Yds	TD	INT	FUM	Sck%	NtY/P	Rank	DVOA	Rank	DPAR	Rank	PAR	Runs	Yds	TD	DPAR	DVOA
2002	BAL	10	295	165	55.9%	2084	13	11	7	8.6%	5.7	29	-7.5%	30	7.8	31	5.4	39	106	1	1.8	-2.4%
2003	ARI	13	368	208	56.5%	2252	13	15	7	4.7%	5.6	28	-15.8%	34	-4.2	35	-10.8	31	179	2	2.5	-2.5%
2004	PHI	3	37	18	48.6%	126	1	1	1	6.0%	2.9	—	-53.8%	—	-6.7	—	-6.9	3	6	0	0.4	56.7%

Because he spent most of his starting career as a Bengal in the 1990s, the average fan would probably drastically underestimate Jeff Blake's career numbers. Do you realize he has 21,656 yards, 133 touchdowns, and 99 interceptions? Blake might not make an NFL roster at the start of training camp, but some team that suffers an injury will want him around as an insurance policy. Blake and Koy Detmer both have horrid DVOA ratings because we don't have a "Game Full of Backups-Adjusted" VOA.

Drew Bledsoe

Height: 6-5   **Weight: 238**   **College: Washington State**   **Born: 14-Feb-1972**   **Age: 33**

Year	Team	G	Att	Comp	Pct	Yds	TD	INT	FUM	Sck%	NtY/P	Rank	DVOA	Rank	DPAR	Rank	PAR	Runs	Yds	TD	DPAR	DVOA
2002	BUF	16	610	375	61.5%	4359	24	15	10	8.5%	6.0	19	5.7%	21	54.3	12	67.7	27	67	2	2.8	8.1%
2003	BUF	16	471	274	58.2%	2860	11	12	14	9.1%	4.7	40	-12.9%	30	0.5	30	-1.6	24	29	2	0.1	-15.5%
2004	BUF	16	450	256	56.9%	2932	20	16	9	7.8%	5.5	26	-2.0%	22	22.5	21	13.7	22	37	0	-1.4	-41.5%
2005	*DAL*	*14*	*411*	*248*	*60.3%*	*2896*	*17*	*12*	*—*	*—*	*5.9*	*—*	*—*	*—*	*—*	*—*	*—*	*18*	*16*	*0*		

In the Dallas Chapter, you'll find an article arguing that Bledsoe, despite never having won the Super Bowl, is actually one of the more successful first overall selections in the history of the NFL draft. But that article is about the Bledsoe of 1992–2004, not the Bledsoe of 2005. The Bledsoe of 2005 is an aging, average quarterback who makes poor decisions on the field and takes too many sacks. A list of the most similar quarterbacks over a two-year period consists almost entirely of players who never again played a full season: Boomer Esiason and Jeff Hostetler 1993–1994, Troy Aikman 1996–1997, Joe Ferguson 1982–1983, Tommy Maddox 2002–2003 (the exception is Joe Theismann 1979–1980). The move to Dallas gives him a better offensive line and his favorite kind of target, a good young tight end, but will he have the self-discipline to be the kind of game-manager quarterback that a team built on defense and Julius Jones needs?

Kyle Boller

Height: 6-3   **Weight: 220**   **College: California**   **Born: 17-Jun-1981**   **Age: 24**

Year	Team	G	Att	Comp	Pct	Yds	TD	INT	FUM	Sck%	NtY/P	Rank	DVOA	Rank	DPAR	Rank	PAR	Runs	Yds	TD	DPAR	DVOA
2003	BAL	11	224	116	51.8%	1260	7	9	9	6.7%	4.8	38	-40.8%	45	-26.7	46	-22.0	30	52	0	-5.0	-58.6%
2004	BAL	16	464	258	55.6%	2559	13	11	11	6.9%	4.7	34	-2.0%	21	23.1	20	3.1	53	189	1	1.5	-12.0%
2005	*BAL*	*16*	*472*	*275*	*58.3%*	*3004*	*18*	*14*	*—*	*—*	*5.8*	*—*	*—*	*—*	*—*	*—*	*—*	*53*	*188*	*2*		

It's hard to figure out what to think of this guy. DVOA says he was not a horrible quarterback, just an average one, who looked worse than he really was because of the difficult schedule faced by the AFC North. His DVOA was −29.0% in Baltimore's first five games, but 6.5% after the bye week, which makes you think perhaps he can continue improving in 2005. On the other hand, if you watch him on tape, his footwork is just awful. Sometimes he'll take too many steps in his drop, which leads to things like Jonathan Ogden pushing a defensive end into Boller instead of behind Boller. He'll throw off his back foot, which is why the ball sails on him so often. The Ravens finally solved this issue by finding a 6'6" receiver, Clarence Moore. But the big free agent acquisition for 2005, Derrick Mason, is a whopping 5'10". So is the high-profile first round pick, Mark Clayton. We sure hope you guys like watching passes go over your heads.

Brooks Bollinger

Height: 6-0 Weight: 205 College: Wisconsin Born: 15-Nov-1979 Age: 26

Year	Team	G	Att	Comp	Pct	Yds	TD	INT	FUM	Sck%	NtY/P	Rank	DVOA	Rank	DPAR	Rank	PAR	Runs	Yds	TD	DPAR	DVOA
2004	NYJ	1	9	5	55.6%	60	0	0	0	9.2%	5.2	—	4.2%	—	0.7	—	0.3	1	2	0	-0.6	-117.9%
2005	NYJ	—	—	—	—	—	—	—	—	—	—	—	—	—	—	—	—	—	—	—	—	—

Brooks Bollinger was more of a running threat than a passing threat at Wisconsin and it's a bit surprising that he's in the league as a quarterback. If your team ends up with him under center, it's time to turn off the TV.

Tom Brady

Height: 6-4 Weight: 220 College: Michigan Born: 3-Aug-1977 Age: 28

Year	Team	G	Att	Comp	Pct	Yds	TD	INT	FUM	Sck%	NtY/P	Rank	DVOA	Rank	DPAR	Rank	PAR	Runs	Yds	TD	DPAR	DVOA
2002	NE	16	601	373	62.1%	3764	28	14	9	5.0%	5.7	30	6.8%	18	53.9	13	66.1	42	110	1	3.4	-0.5%
2003	NE	16	528	317	60.0%	3620	23	12	13	5.5%	6.0	18	5.2%	14	43.2	10	52.0	42	63	1	-0.4	-21.9%
2004	NE	16	474	288	60.8%	3692	28	14	7	5.0%	7.1	9	41.6%	2	113.4	3	95.6	43	28	0	1.1	-8.1%
2005	NE	16	511	324	63.3%	3731	27	14	—	—	6.7	—	—	—	—	—	—	24	10	1		

We're all sick to death of the arguments about whether or not Tom Brady is better than Peyton Manning. The real question is how on earth every single team in the NFL missed on this guy through five rounds of the 2000 draft. Was it because he was sandwiched at Michigan between the son of a legend and the biggest name recruit in the country? Word is that scouts laughed at Brady's not-quite-chiseled body at the scouting combine, and he doesn't have the world's strongest arm. But you are talking about a quarterback with near-perfect awareness and mechanics and an excellent feel for where the rush is coming from. That's why he made it through the first 13 games of the season without having a pass tipped at the line of scrimmage. Watch the way he gets the ball up high at the point of release, as opposed to the shot-put motion of David Carr. His only weakness before this year was occasional inaccuracy when throwing the deep ball, so he made that his project during the 2004 off-season and is now one of the league's best at throwing it long. On top of everything else, his numbers finally caught up with and then surpassed his reputation last year, so that people who still think of Brady as a game-manager quarterback are now really selling him short.

Drew Brees

Height: 6-0 Weight: 221 College: Purdue Born: 15-Jan-1979 Age: 26

Year	Team	G	Att	Comp	Pct	Yds	TD	INT	FUM	Sck%	NtY/P	Rank	DVOA	Rank	DPAR	Rank	PAR	Runs	Yds	TD	DPAR	DVOA
2002	SD	16	526	320	60.8%	3284	17	16	1	4.7%	5.7	31	-3.6%	28	22.0	23	38.9	38	130	1	0.6	-13.6%
2003	SD	11	356	205	57.6%	2108	11	15	5	5.7%	5.1	33	-22.8%	37	-14.7	41	-22.1	21	84	0	4.0	33.1%
2004	SD	15	400	262	65.5%	3159	27	7	7	5.0%	7.2	8	29.5%	7	75.6	9	90.7	53	85	2	4.6	4.0%
2005	SD	16	417	264	63.2%	3226	27	13	—	—	7.1	—	—	—	—	—	—	33	113	2		

Over and over last season, we were told that nobody could have expected Drew Brees to suddenly become one of the best quarterbacks in the NFL. This is a whole lot of nonsense. Throughout recent NFL history there have been a number of quarterbacks who, like Brees, followed a league-average performance in their first full starting season with a step backward instead of a step forward. Nearly every one of those quarterbacks bounced back in the third year: Steve DeBerg, Mark Rypien, Jake Plummer, Stan Humphries. (No, those aren't superstars, but two of them went to the Super Bowl.) There was also the fact, discussed in the San Diego chapter, that a small improvement in third down performance would lead to a much greater improvement in San Diego's overall offense. Thanks to a much harder defensive schedule that exchanges the two southern divisions for the two eastern divisions, his conventional numbers are going to drop a little, but there's no reason to believe he can't play at this skill level for the next few years.

Aaron Brooks

Height: 6-4 Weight: 210 College: Virginia Born: 24-Mar-1974 Age: 31

Year	Team	G	Att	Comp	Pct	Yds	TD	INT	FUM	Sck%	NtY/P	Rank	DVOA	Rank	DPAR	Rank	PAR	Runs	Yds	TD	DPAR	DVOA
2002	NO	16	529	284	53.7%	3574	27	15	11	6.1%	5.9	26	12.7%	13	60.4	10	35.5	61	256	2	5.7	0.9%
2003	NO	16	518	306	59.1%	3546	24	8	14	6.4%	5.9	21	11.3%	10	57.0	6	64.0	52	183	2	4.0	-1.9%
2004	NO	16	542	309	57.0%	3810	21	16	13	7.1%	6.0	19	-3.9%	24	23.2	19	33.1	58	173	4	6.9	9.1%
2005	NO	16	520	311	59.7%	3627	23	13	—	—	6.2	—	—	—	—	—	—	51	124	2		

An average quarterback masquerading as a star. In the summer of 2004, we ran an article on FootballOutsiders.com about what we called "failed completes," passes that despite being caught did not achieve the number of yards needed to be considered a "successful play" according to the DVOA system. Aaron Brooks led the league in this category in 2004 with

(continued next page)

Aaron Brooks (continued)

82 failed completes, which gives you a pretty good idea of why his raw yardage totals are always better than his actual value when it comes to winning. That total includes an absurd 11 different passes of ten or more yards on third down that still didn't convert for first down. Brooks was also responsible for the funniest play of the season in Week 9 when in midscramble he inexplicably pitched the ball backward to an area where the only possible receivers were tackle Wayne Gandy and the back judge.

Mark Brunell
Height: 6-1 Weight: 217 College: Washington   **Born: 17-Sep-1970 Age: 35**

Year	Team	G	Att	Comp	Pct	Yds	TD	INT	FUM	Sck%	NtY/P	Rank	DVOA	Rank	DPAR	Rank	PAR	Runs	Yds	TD	DPAR	DVOA
2002	JAC	15	416	245	58.9%	2788	17	7	5	7.9%	5.8	27	8.8%	16	41.1	19	45.5	43	207	0	3.5	0.8%
2003	JAC	3	82	54	65.9%	484	2	0	0	9.3%	4.7	—	9.5%	—	8.8	—	7.4	8	19	1	-0.1	-19.7%
2004	WAS	9	237	118	49.8%	1194	7	6	6	5.7%	4.3	38	-22.8%	34	-10.2	33	-8.1	19	62	0	-1.6	-39.1%
2005	WAS	—	—	—	—	—	—	—	—	—	—	—	—	—	—	—	—	—	—	—	—	—

It looks terrible in retrospect, but let's be honest—nobody expected him to fall of the cliff like this. After the 2003 season, in our online awards balloting, we asked our readers which one of eight possible trade bait/free agent quarterbacks they would most want leading their team. Brunell got 36% of the vote, ahead of Kurt Warner and Marc Bulger (Drew Brees, by the way, got less than 2%). Jason Campbell's arrival in Washington now makes him completely superfluous, while his contract renders him untradable. Happy happy joy joy.

Marc Bulger
Height: 6-3 Weight: 215 College: West Virginia   **Born: 5-Apr-1977 Age: 28**

Year	Team	G	Att	Comp	Pct	Yds	TD	INT	FUM	Sck%	NtY/P	Rank	DVOA	Rank	DPAR	Rank	PAR	Runs	Yds	TD	DPAR	DVOA
2002	STL	7	214	138	64.5%	1826	14	6	2	6.6%	7.7	1	34.2%	2	42.4	18	54.0	12	-13	1	0.9	85.0%
2003	STL	15	532	336	63.2%	3845	22	22	8	6.8%	6.3	13	0.7%	19	32.7	15	45.6	29	75	4	4.1	30.6%
2004	STL	14	485	321	66.2%	3964	21	14	5	8.0%	7.0	10	29.3%	8	92.6	6	85.8	19	89	3	2.7	7.7%
2005	STL	16	544	346	63.6%	3976	24	18	—	—	6.5	—	—	—	—	—	—	34	136	2		

Among the ironies of 2004 is that the St. Louis Rams went from 12–4 to 8–8 despite improvement from the passing game. Bulger was the only quarterback besides Peyton Manning to have no negative DPAR games (minimum four starts). He cut down significantly on both incompletes and interceptions except in one very important situation: at the goal line. Bulger threw 20 passes in goal-to-go situations and only 6 of them went for touchdowns. Three of them were intercepted, costing the Rams a chance not just at a touchdown but a field goal as well.

Jason Campbell
Height: 6-4 Weight: 223 College: Auburn   **Born: 31-Dec-1981 Age: 23**

Year	Team	G	Att	Comp	Pct	Yds	TD	INT	FUM	Sck%	NtY/P	Rank	DVOA	Rank	DPAR	Rank	PAR	Runs	Yds	TD	DPAR	DVOA
2005	WAS	7	206	113	54.8%	1182	6	7	—	—	5.0	—	—	—	—	—	—	20	80	1		

Jason Campbell, welcome to the NFL's most dysfunctional family—the Washington Redskins, a team where the owner is a legend only in his own mind and the head coach's legend is fading in the mind of many of the team's fans. Welcome, too, to a situation where you'll be one of three quarterbacks earning a starter's paycheck in 2005, and another huge chunk of the salary cap is devoted to players no longer with the team. Oh, and the team traded a bunch of picks to move up and select you, so there won't be much help coming next year when they elevate you to starter. On the plus side, Campbell is used to turmoil, having starred at Auburn, where he played for four offensive coordinators and nearly saw his coach fired by the school's top booster after his junior year, only to return and pilot the team to a 13–0 season.

David Carr
Height: 6-3 Weight: 223 College: Fresno State   **Born: 21-Jul-1979 Age: 26**

Year	Team	G	Att	Comp	Pct	Yds	TD	INT	FUM	Sck%	NtY/P	Rank	DVOA	Rank	DPAR	Rank	PAR	Runs	Yds	TD	DPAR	DVOA
2002	HOU	16	444	233	52.5%	2592	9	15	21	14.1%	4.1	47	-45.2%	47	-66.8	47	-61.5	58	279	3	2.8	-5.4%
2003	HOU	12	295	167	56.6%	2013	9	13	2	4.8%	6.2	14	-11.4%	27	2.3	27	1.5	27	151	2	7.7	39.9%
2004	HOU	16	466	285	61.2%	3531	16	14	10	10.6%	6.3	16	-0.6%	20	27.5	18	46.3	73	299	0	5.9	-0.4%
2005	HOU	16	469	292	62.1%	3493	23	16	—	—	6.5	—	—	—	—	—	—	56	230	2		

He would like very much not to get sacked. One more season spent getting helped off the turf by an apologetic offensive tackle and Carr may be too shell shocked to live up to his full potential. He has thus far resisted the temptation to respond to his critics by disparaging his teammates, justified as he might be to do so, but in 2004 he finally began to show outward frustration in games that were being lost by his teammates despite his best efforts. Maybe that's part of why Carr was the most-penalized quarterback in 2004 with five delays of game, four intentional groundings, and an unsportsmanlike conduct. While our projection likes him to have a repeat season with more touchdowns, here's the scare for Houston: Carr had a 64% completion rate and averaged 270 yards per game over the first eight games of the season, but a 59% completion rate with just 172 yards per game over the final eight games.

Quincy Carter

Height: 6-2 **Weight:** 231 **College:** Georgia **Born:** 13-Oct-1977 **Age:** 28

Year	Team	G	Att	Comp	Pct	Yds	TD	INT	FUM	Sck%	NtY/P	Rank	DVOA	Rank	DPAR	Rank	PAR	Runs	Yds	TD	DPAR	DVOA
2002	DAL	7	221	125	56.6%	1465	7	8	5	8.0%	5.6	34	-16.3%	37	-3.1	37	-4.3	25	94	0	-1.0	-25.1%
2003	DAL	16	506	292	57.7%	3302	17	21	8	5.9%	5.8	23	-15.1%	33	-4.1	34	1.6	68	257	2	3.3	-7.9%
2004	NYJ	6	58	35	60.3%	498	3	1	2	16.3%	6.1	—	15.9%	—	8.8	—	4.9	12	20	0	-2.5	-72.5%

Here's a good example of how the quarterback is partially responsible for the number of times he gets sacked. Chad Pennington started 13 games for the Jets and was sacked 18 times. Carter started the other 3 games and was sacked 12 times, including 6 by the lowly Browns. Unsigned at press time, and given the way the Cubs are hitting this year, perhaps he should consider a reverse-Henson.

Chris Chandler

Height: 6-4 **Weight:** 224 **College:** Washington **Born:** 13-Oct-1965 **Age:** 40

Year	Team	G	Att	Comp	Pct	Yds	TD	INT	FUM	Sck%	NtY/P	Rank	DVOA	Rank	DPAR	Rank	PAR	Runs	Yds	TD	DPAR	DVOA
2002	CHI	9	162	104	64.2%	1023	4	4	3	12.6%	4.7	44	-33.2%	45	-16.1	43	-8.0	10	32	0	1.0	26.3%
2003	CHI	8	192	107	55.7%	1050	3	7	3	6.2%	4.7	42	-29.7%	41	-13.8	40	-9.4	14	35	0	1.4	4.9%
2004	STL	6	62	35	56.5%	463	2	8	—	10.1%	5.9	—	-100.7%	—	-26.1	—	-24.5	1	2	0	—	—

Chris Chandler played so badly for the Rams last year that Mike Martz said he was essentially holding the team hostage, with everyone else playing well but Chandler keeping the team from having a chance. Needless to say, he won't be back in St. Louis. If his career is over, he'll probably spend his Sundays sharing some beers with Kyle Turley and rooting for Martz to waste a timeout challenging the spot of a ball on an unimportant play early in the third quarter.

Kerry Collins

Height: 6-5 **Weight:** 250 **College:** Penn State **Born:** 30-Dec-1972 **Age:** 32

Year	Team	G	Att	Comp	Pct	Yds	TD	INT	FUM	Sck%	NtY/P	Rank	DVOA	Rank	DPAR	Rank	PAR	Runs	Yds	TD	DPAR	DVOA
2002	NYG	16	545	335	61.5%	4076	19	14	7	4.4%	6.8	5	22.7%	5	85.7	3	90.9	43	-3	0	-2.6	-75.1%
2003	NYG	13	500	284	56.8%	3110	13	16	11	4.8%	5.6	26	-0.5%	20	28.4	18	17.9	17	49	0	-1.9	-55.2%
2004	OAK	14	513	289	56.3%	3495	21	20	7	5.8%	6.2	17	-11.1%	29	4.8	29	19.4	16	36	0	1.1	11.8%
2005	*OAK*	*16*	*553*	*328*	*59.3%*	*4138*	*28*	*19*	—	—	*6.9*	—	—	—	—	—	—	*16*	*45*	*0*		

Wow, did this guy win the off-season teammate lottery. He should be buying everyone in the Oakland front office gift baskets for handing him a running game and a game-breaking wide receiver who dramatically transforms defensive strategy. Part of the KUBIAK projection system involves trying to square the receiver projections with the quarterback projections, and the difference between the projection for Collins and the projection for his receivers was by far the greatest. They'll probably meet somewhere in the middle, and it should halt the drop in his DVOA/DPAR.

Todd Collins

Height: 6-4 **Weight:** 219 **College:** Michigan **Born:** 5-Nov-1971 **Age:** 34

Year	Team	G	Att	Comp	Pct	Yds	TD	INT	FUM	Sck%	NtY/P	Rank	DVOA	Rank	DPAR	Rank	PAR	Runs	Yds	TD	DPAR	DVOA
2002	KC	2	6	5	83.3%	73	1	0	0	0.0%	12.2	—	120.8%	—	4.2	—	4.5	1	7	0	-0.1	-34.7%
2003	KC	6	12	9	75.0%	74	0	0	—	0.0%	6.7	—	17.5%	—	1.5	—	1.8	8	-7	0	—	—
2004	KC	2	5	1	20.0%	42	0	0	0	0.0%	8.4	—	25.8%	—	0.8	—	0.6	1	4	0	-0.2	-85.7%
2005	*KC*	—	—	—	—	—	—	—	—	—	—	—	—	—	—	—	—	—	—	—	—	—

As the Bills' starter for 13 games in 1997, Todd Collins probably saw himself as a 26-year-old who was moving up in the league. When the Bills' idiotic signing of Rob Johnson to a big-money contract ensured that Collins's days as the starter in Buffalo were done, he thought he would have a chance of competing with Rich Gannon and Elvis Grbac for the job in Kansas City. Since he moved to Kansas City, Collins has never started and has thrown 27 passes. The best-laid plans of mice and men, and so forth.

Daunte Culpepper

Height: 6-4 **Weight: 264** **College: Central Florida** **Born: 28-Jan-1977 Age: 28**

Year	Team	G	Att	Comp	Pct	Yds	TD	INT	FUM	Sck%	NtY/P	Rank	DVOA	Rank	DPAR	Rank	PAR	Runs	Yds	TD	DPAR	DVOA
2002	MIN	16	551	334	60.6%	3859	18	23	23	8.2%	6.0	22	-5.1%	29	20.9	24	12.3	105	603	10	15.0	5.3%
2003	MIN	14	454	295	65.0%	3479	25	11	15	8.3%	6.7	5	16.0%	9	62.0	5	73.2	72	422	4	13.6	22.0%
2004	MIN	16	548	379	69.2%	4717	39	11	9	7.5%	7.5	2	38.9%	4	136.4	2	144.4	89	406	2	11.7	7.3%
2005	MIN	16	509	328	64.4%	4062	27	13	—	—	7.0	—	—	—	—	—	—	95	428	3		

Peyton Manning wasn't the only quarterback in 2004 to enjoy one of the greatest seasons in NFL history. By the method we use to measure quarterbacks in a long essay elsewhere in the book, Culpepper's 2004 performance comes out just below Manning's as one of the top five seasons by any passer since the AFL-NFL merger. That being said, Culpepper is likely headed for a significant falloff. Start with his third down performance: On the whole, NFL quarterbacks converted 35% of these plays for new first downs, but Culpepper converted 76 of 134, nearly half. That's not going to continue. There's also the absence of his best receiver, now clad in silver and black. In the 5 games where Moss was injured at mid-season, Culpepper averaged 215 net passing yards, 1.8 touchdowns, and 5.2 DPAR per game. In the other 11 games, Culpepper averaged 306 passing yards, 2.7 touchdowns, and 10.0 DPAR per game. Culpepper is also going to see a lot more blitzing this year—opposing defensive coordinators would have preferred root canal without anesthetic to leaving Randy Moss in man coverage, but they don't feel quite the same way about Nate Burleson or Travis Taylor.

Rohan Davey

Height: 6-2 **Weight: 245** **College: LSU** **Born: 14-Apr-1978 Age: 27**

Year	Team	G	Att	Comp	Pct	Yds	TD	INT	FUM	Sck%	NtY/P	Rank	DVOA	Rank	DPAR	Rank	PAR	Runs	Yds	TD	DPAR	DVOA
2002	NE	2	2	1	50.0%	3	0	0	—	0.0%	1.5	—	-74.4%	—	-0.6	—	-0.7	2	-4	0	—	—
2003	NE	1	6	3	50.0%	31	0	0	—	0.0%	4.4	—	-1.4%	—	0.4	—	0.3	0	0	0	—	—
2004	NE	4	10	4	40.0%	54	0	0	0	0.0%	5.4	—	49.0%	—	2.3	—	2.3	4	-1	0	-1.1	-109.8%
2005	NE	—	—	—	—	—	—	—	—	—	—	—	—	—	—	—	—	—	—	—	—	—

A big QB with a cannon of an arm. He threw for 3,347 yards in his senior year at LSU. Davey led last year's NFL Europe Berlin Thunder to the World Bowl title and was named the offensive MVP with 19 TDs and a passer rating of 105.9. The rewards of such success? He got the chance to throw a career-high ten NFL passes. Then the Patriots signed Doug Flutie and drafted Matt Cassel. This should be considered a signal for Davey to call his real estate broker. He'll be dangled to every team that has a backup quarterback go down during training camp, looking for the best possible draft choice. Of course, his old coach is now with division rival Miami, and the Dolphins could sure use a backup quarterback. Maybe even a starter.

Jake Delhomme

Height: 6-2 **Weight: 205** **College: Louisiana-Lafayette** **Born: 10-Jan-1975 Age: 30**

Year	Team	G	Att	Comp	Pct	Yds	TD	INT	FUM	Sck%	NtY/P	Rank	DVOA	Rank	DPAR	Rank	PAR	Runs	Yds	TD	DPAR	DVOA
2002	NO	3	10	8	80.0%	113	0	0	0	8.0%	9.7	—	87.2%	—	4.1	—	3.4	3	4	0	0.4	29.6%
2003	CAR	16	449	266	59.2%	3219	19	16	15	4.9%	6.3	12	-3.5%	22	19.4	19	25.5	42	43	1	-2.7	-38.6%
2004	CAR	16	533	310	58.2%	3886	29	15	12	5.9%	6.4	14	7.5%	14	49.4	14	71.1	25	71	1	2.4	6.6%
2005	CAR	16	505	299	59.1%	3486	23	15	—	—	6.3	—	—	—	—	—	—	30	81	1		

We always enjoyed the *Twilight Zone* episode where the Super Bowl quarterback wakes up and discovers everyone else on the team has been replaced with fourth-stringers. After his breakout performance in the 2003 playoffs, Delhomme was set for a huge year in 2004. Then it seemed like everyone around him got injured, including his best wide receiver, all his running backs, and himself (he spent much of the season throwing with a broken thumb on his throwing hand). Then his agent stubbed his toe and the kid who mows his lawn got chicken pox. We expect his DVOA to get even better in 2005—the projected drop in his conventional numbers is partly projected improvement by Carolina's defense, keeping Delhomme from chucking the ball downfield to make up a two-touchdown deficit.

Koy Detmer

Height: 6-1 **Weight: 195** **College: Colorado** **Born: 5-Jul-1973   Age: 32**

Year	Team	G	Att	Comp	Pct	Yds	TD	INT	FUM	Sck%	NtY/P	Rank	DVOA	Rank	DPAR	Rank	PAR	Runs	Yds	TD	DPAR	DVOA
2002	PHI	9	28	19	67.9%	224	2	0	1	4.7%	7.4	—	66.0%	—	9.5	—	9.2	2	4	1	-1.3	-96.3%
2003	PHI	16	5	3	60.0%	32	0	0	—	0.0%	6.2	—	13.9%	—	1.0	—	0.4	0	0	0	—	—
2004	PHI	16	40	18	45.0%	207	0	2	1	6.1%	4.5	—	-62.8%	—	-9.2	—	-10.1	10	-7	0	-0.4	-123.0%
2005	PHI	—	—	—	—	—	—	—	—	—	—	—	—	—	—	—	—	—	—	—	—	—

If you like quarterback-playing brothers, you're living in a Golden Age. In NFL history only six pairs of brothers have played quarterback, and five of the six are active now—the Detmers, Hasselbecks, Huards, Mannings, and McCowns. Where have you gone, Craig Bradshaw?

Trent Dilfer
Height: 6-4 Weight: 225 College: Fresno State Born: 13-Mar-1972 Age: 33

Year	Team	G	Att	Comp	Pct	Yds	TD	INT	FUM	Sck%	NtY/P	Rank	DVOA	Rank	DPAR	Rank	PAR	Runs	Yds	TD	DPAR	DVOA
2002	SEA	6	168	94	56.0%	1182	4	6	2	5.0%	6.5	11	-19.2%	39	-4.4	40	3.1	10	27	0	1.1	7.5%
2003	SEA	5	8	4	50.0%	31	1	1	—	11.0%	2.4	—	-190.5%	—	-6.6	—	-5.7	2	-1	0	—	—
2004	SEA	5	58	25	43.1%	333	1	3	1	5.6%	5.0	—	-36.3%	—	-6.0	—	-9.5	10	14	0	-1.2	-141.9%
2005	*CLE*	*11*	*325*	*171*	*52.6%*	*2084*	*9*	*13*	*—*	*—*	*6.3*	*—*	*—*	*—*	*—*	*—*	*—*	*24*	*85*	*1*		

Trent Dilfer is the worst quarterback ever to start on a team that won the Super Bowl, but maybe the Ravens should have hung onto him all this time. They could have paid Dilfer the league minimum and spent all that money they gave to Elvis Grbac on keeping the rest of the team together. If they had done that, the Ravens would have won another Super Bowl, and all those silly people who think you judge a quarterback by his won-loss record would make silly comments about how great Dilfer is.

Ken Dorsey
Height: 6-4 Weight: 205 College: Miami Born: 22-Apr-1981 Age: 24

Year	Team	G	Att	Comp	Pct	Yds	TD	INT	FUM	Sck%	NtY/P	Rank	DVOA	Rank	DPAR	Rank	PAR	Runs	Yds	TD	DPAR	DVOA
2003	SF	0	0	0	0.0%	0	0	0	—	—	—	—	—	—	—	—	—	0	0	0	—	—
2004	SF	9	226	123	54.4%	1231	6	9	5	4.4%	4.7	35	-23.4%	35	-10.4	34	-10.3	5	7	0	0.1	35.2%
2005	*SF*	*—*	*—*	*—*	*—*	*—*	*—*	*—*	*—*	*—*	*—*	*—*	*—*	*—*	*—*	*—*	*—*	*—*	*—*	*—*		

It was hard to judge Dorsey's skill in college because the talent around him was so great that he hardly ever faced a challenge. Alex Smith's arrival means Dorsey is now a third-stringer, but he can live out the next few years as a clipboard holder knowing that, contrary to expectations, he showed last year that he could hold his own in the NFL. Dorsey had the same number of touchdowns and interceptions as Eli Manning, with more yards and a better completion percentage. Every excuse used for Manning's poor performance—difficult schedule, no offensive line, poor receivers—applied to Dorsey as well.

Brett Favre
Height: 6-2 Weight: 225 College: Southern Mississippi Born: 10-Oct-1969 Age: 36

Year	Team	G	Att	Comp	Pct	Yds	TD	INT	FUM	Sck%	NtY/P	Rank	DVOA	Rank	DPAR	Rank	PAR	Runs	Yds	TD	DPAR	DVOA
2002	GB	16	551	341	61.9%	3658	27	16	9	4.7%	6.0	20	5.6%	22	47.7	16	57.2	25	73	0	-4.4	-63.7%
2003	GB	16	472	308	65.3%	3361	32	21	5	4.4%	6.6	6	7.4%	12	43.2	9	47.7	18	15	0	-1.1	-39.6%
2004	GB	16	540	346	64.1%	4088	30	17	4	1.8%	7.3	7	22.0%	10	83.5	7	96.4	16	36	0	1.3	22.1%
2005	*GB*	*16*	*524*	*314*	*59.8%*	*3728*	*24*	*19*	*—*	*—*	*6.8*	*—*	*—*	*—*	*—*	*—*	*—*	*16*	*44*	*0*		

Brett Favre has become more of a symbol than a human being, representing the platonic ideal of "quarterback" in the minds of most television analysts and print writers. By midyear, the constant overglorification of Favre had reached a level of annoyance so high that it spawned an equally irritating countermovement of fans who couldn't stop complaining on Internet message boards about the constant overglorification of Brett Favre. Lost in all of this nonsense is the performance of Brett Favre, the actual human being, who is still a pretty good quarterback though not at the level of a decade ago. He'll probably be good again in 2005 but you have to figure the entire Green Bay offense will be negatively affected by the loss of both Pro Bowl-level guards, and if Favre is getting hurried more often by the pass rush he's likely to throw more of those completely wacko interceptions that make Green Bay fans bang their cheeseheads against the wall.

A. J. Feeley
Height: 6-3 Weight: 225 College: Oregon Born: 16-May-1977 Age: 28

Year	Team	G	Att	Comp	Pct	Yds	TD	INT	FUM	Sck%	NtY/P	Rank	DVOA	Rank	DPAR	Rank	PAR	Runs	Yds	TD	DPAR	DVOA
2002	PHI	6	154	86	55.8%	1011	6	5	3	4.8%	5.9	24	3.0%	24	10.7	29	8.4	12	6	0	-2.5	-134.0%
2003	PHI	0	0	0	0.0%	0	0	0	—	—	—	—	—	—	—	—	—	0	0	0	—	—
2004	MIA	11	356	191	53.7%	1893	11	15	10	6.1%	4.6	36	-20.5%	33	-11.6	35	-33.0	14	13	1	-0.6	-33.3%
2005	*MIA*	*8*	*251*	*136*	*54.2%*	*1693*	*10*	*9*	*—*	*—*	*5.8*	*—*	*—*	*—*	*—*	*—*	*—*	*10*	*24*	*0*		

(continued next page)

A. J. Feeley (continued)

Is there another NFL player whose performance is harder to judge because of the quality of his teammates? When he was good in Philadelphia, was he good or was he in a good situation? When he was bad in Miami, was he bad or was he in a bad situation? Given the record of the other two quarterbacks who took a snap in Miami last year, plus the reemergence of Brian Griese in Tampa, we're betting the latter. Of course, the bad situation will be just as bad this year, and so will Feeley. His −42.1% DVOA on first down was the worst of any quarterback in the league with at least 300 plays. Double projection if Dolphins knock off this "Gus Frerotte is starting" nonsense.

Jay Fiedler
Height: 6-2   Weight: 225   College: Dartmouth   Born: 29-Dec-1971 Age: 33

Year	Team	G	Att	Comp	Pct	Yds	TD	INT	FUM	Sck%	NtY/P	Rank	DVOA	Rank	DPAR	Rank	PAR	Runs	Yds	TD	DPAR	DVOA
2002	MIA	11	292	179	61.3%	2024	14	9	2	5.2%	6.3	14	6.5%	19	25.6	21	39.2	27	108	3	5.9	25.3%
2003	MIA	13	314	179	57.0%	2138	11	13	7	6.0%	6.0	19	−5.3%	23	11.0	24	10.5	33	95	3	3.7	3.4%
2004	MIA	8	190	101	53.2%	1186	7	8	8	11.6%	4.7	33	−39.0%	38	−22.9	40	−27.2	12	59	0	−1.5	−40.7%
2005	NYJ	2	10	6	60.0%	68	0	0	—	—	6.8	—	—	—	—	—	—	3	5	0		

It's been an interesting career for Jay Fiedler. You probably don't remember that he spent four years on the Eagles without ever getting into a game, or that he spent a year each in Minnesota and Jacksonville. The Dolphins stuck with him for too long, figuring that they had a good enough defense that they could get by without a high-quality quarterback. In New York he'll play the role he was born to play: backup.

Doug Flutie
Height: 5- 10 Weight: 180   College: Boston College   Born: 23-Oct-1962 Age: 43

Year	Team	G	Att	Comp	Pct	Yds	TD	INT	FUM	Sck%	NtY/P	Rank	DVOA	Rank	DPAR	Rank	PAR	Runs	Yds	TD	DPAR	DVOA
2002	SD	2	11	3	27.3%	64	0	0	0	0.0%	6.4	—	18.0%	—	1.2	—	1.0	1	6	0	−0.2	−39.9%
2003	SD	7	167	91	54.5%	1097	9	4	6	4.5%	6.1	17	6.5%	13	14.3	22	16.2	33	168	2	3.0	1.0%
2004	SD	2	38	20	52.6%	276	1	0	0	3.5%	7.1	—	60.6%	—	10.2	—	12.8	5	39	2	4.2	126.2%
2005	NE	2	26	15	57.7%	185	1	1	—	—	6.6	—	—	—	—	—	—	5	26	1		

The Natick-Framingham metropolitan area is known for three things: the Twinkie factory where Peter Griffin took his family after the Y2K nuclear holocaust, the worldwide headquarters of Football Outsiders, Inc., and Doug Flutie. Last year our favorite son came in to replace Drew Brees in Week 2 and the result was classic Flutie, with first down throws on fourth and 10 and fourth and 15 plus a six-yard rushing TD to prolong a comeback that fell just short. If the Patriots can clinch their playoff spot before the final week of the season, Our Doug will get one final start to say goodbye to the home fans, on New Year's Day against Miami. We hope they'll wear their orange Hurricane-like unis.

Gus Frerotte
Height: 6-3   Weight: 225   College: Tulsa   Born: 3-Jul-1971   Age: 34

Year	Team	G	Att	Comp	Pct	Yds	TD	INT	FUM	Sck%	NtY/P	Rank	DVOA	Rank	DPAR	Rank	PAR	Runs	Yds	TD	DPAR	DVOA
2002	CIN	5	85	44	51.8%	437	1	5	2	10.7%	3.9	—	−63.2%	—	−19.8	—	−17.3	4	22	0	1.5	84.0%
2003	MIN	16	65	38	58.5%	690	7	2	2	6.8%	9.4	—	20.7%	—	10.5	—	13.9	12	−2	0	−3.6	−203.1%
2004	MIN	16	1	0	0.0%	0	0	0	—	0.0%	0.0	—	−75.3%	—	−0.2	—	−0.3	0	0	0	—	—
2005	MIA	8	250	139	55.6%	1605	10	10	—	—	6.2	—	—	—	—	—	—	12	22	0		

There is no point in a rebuilding team taking its starting quarterback position away from a 28-year-old who still has something to prove, especially when the alternative is a 34-year-old veteran who saw action last year only as a field goal holder and has not had 100 pass attempts in a season since 2000. And yet, every report out of Miami says that's exactly what the Dolphins plan on doing, because new offensive coordinator Scott Linehan is comfortable with Frerotte from their days together in Minnesota. At the last minute, we cut Feeley's projection in half and gave Frerotte half a season, so just double the numbers for whoever gets the job, and then keep your fantasy team far, far away.

Charlie Frye
Height: 6-4   Weight: 228   College: Akron   Born: 28-Aug-1981 Age: 24

Year	Team	G	Att	Comp	Pct	Yds	TD	INT	FUM	Sck%	NtY/P	Rank	DVOA	Rank	DPAR	Rank	PAR	Runs	Yds	TD	DPAR	DVOA
2005	CLE	5	134	70	52.1%	875	7	5	—	—	5.9	—	—	—	—	—	—	14	67	1		

Frye fits the mold of the modern quarterback prospect from the MAC. He's well-built, poised, and reads the field very well. He's known as a gutsy leader and film room junkie. He runs well but isn't a scrambler, and has a fine arm but comes with questions about the level of competition he faced and the style of offense he executed. Chad Pennington, Byron

Leftwich, and Ben Roethlisberger all had similar line items on their résumés. Frye won't be asked to start right away, but Cleveland will start chanting for local boy Frye soon after Trent Dilfer throws his second incompletion.

Rich Gannon Height: 6-3 Weight: 210 College: Delaware Born: 20-Dec-1965 Age: 39

Year	Team	G	Att	Comp	Pct	Yds	TD	INT	FUM	Sck%	NtY/P	Rank	DVOA	Rank	DPAR	Rank	PAR	Runs	Yds	TD	DPAR	DVOA
2002	OAK	16	616	417	67.7%	4676	26	10	9	5.9%	6.9	4	25.5%	3	112.4	2	128.8	50	156	3	3.4	0.4%
2003	OAK	7	225	125	55.6%	1274	6	4	2	7.5%	4.9	37	-7.5%	26	5.8	26	6.6	6	18	0	-0.3	-27.7%
2004	OAK	3	68	41	60.3%	524	3	2	3	5.2%	7.0	—	39.8%	—	15.7	—	5.7	5	26	0	0.9	70.6%

Gannon retired in May after missing 22 games the past two years because of injury. His mid-30s resurgence with Oakland is what every career backup playing today's dreams are made of. Gannon threw for nearly as many yards in his first three years in Oakland (11,098) as he had over his ten pre-Oakland seasons (11,158).

Jeff Garcia Height: 6-1 Weight: 195 College: San Jose State Born: 24-Feb-1970 Age: 35

Year	Team	G	Att	Comp	Pct	Yds	TD	INT	FUM	Sck%	NtY/P	Rank	DVOA	Rank	DPAR	Rank	PAR	Runs	Yds	TD	DPAR	DVOA
2002	SF	16	528	328	62.1%	3344	21	10	1	3.8%	6.0	21	17.0%	10	70.1	7	74.1	72	358	3	14.3	24.9%
2003	SF	13	392	225	57.4%	2704	18	13	8	5.5%	6.3	11	5.0%	15	32.3	16	31.2	54	325	7	12.8	25.2%
2004	CLE	11	252	144	57.1%	1731	10	9	8	8.1%	5.9	22	-2.8%	23	11.2	24	-4.3	35	169	2	7.5	22.1%
2005	*DET*	*9*	*238*	*136*	*57.0%*	*1716*	*8*	*7*	*—*	*—*	*6.2*	*—*	*—*	*—*	*—*	*—*	*—*	*34*	*162*	*2*		

Wow, let's all pretend that didn't happen. Garcia's Cleveland experience looks a bit like Brian Griese's Miami experience three entries down from here. Like Carson Palmer, he got whacked by a killer schedule. When Detroit signed him, Garcia said all the right things about how he was just there to back up Harrington, but let's be realistic. Harrington may have a stronger arm, but Garcia is more mobile, makes better decisions, and is more comfortable in the type of offense Steve Mariucci wants to run. It is pretty easy to concoct a scenario where Garcia takes over the reins in Detroit sometime in October and turns the Lions into this year's out of nowhere, Chargers-like Super Bowl contender.

David Garrard Height: 6-1 Weight: 238 College: East Carolina Born: 14-Feb-1978 Age: 27

Year	Team	G	Att	Comp	Pct	Yds	TD	INT	FUM	Sck%	NtY/P	Rank	DVOA	Rank	DPAR	Rank	PAR	Runs	Yds	TD	DPAR	DVOA
2002	JAC	4	46	23	50.0%	231	1	2	1	12.9%	3.7	—	-26.5%	—	-2.8	—	-2.2	25	139	2	4.5	15.1%
2003	JAC	2	12	9	75.0%	86	1	0	—	0.0%	7.2	—	79.2%	—	5.3	—	4.8	0	0	0	—	—
2004	JAC	4	72	38	52.8%	374	2	1	0	7.0%	4.3	—	-9.5%	—	1.2	—	1.0	12	76	1	2.8	20.1%
2005	*JAC*	*3*	*15*	*9*	*60.0%*	*87*	*0*	*0*	*—*	*—*	*5.8*	*—*	*—*	*—*	*—*	*—*	*—*	*3*	*7*	*0*		

Garrard is a talented guy from a mid-Atlantic state school, has an arm like a cannon, legs like Crazy Horse, but his brief time behind center suggests that he is too inaccurate to start right now. Perhaps he needed better marketing. We would have suggested a name change—let's see, "Michael Vick" is taken, so how about "Ron Mexico"?—but we were too late. Garrard signed a long-term deal to stay locked behind Byron Leftwich on the Jacksonville depth chart, much to the surprise of many who expected him to bask in the glow of free agency.

Trent Green Height: 6-3 Weight: 217 College: Indiana Born: 9-Jul-1970 Age: 35

Year	Team	G	Att	Comp	Pct	Yds	TD	INT	FUM	Sck%	NtY/P	Rank	DVOA	Rank	DPAR	Rank	PAR	Runs	Yds	TD	DPAR	DVOA
2002	KC	16	470	287	61.1%	3690	26	13	1	5.6%	7.1	2	21.9%	6	74.8	6	85.6	31	225	1	11.1	52.9%
2003	KC	16	523	330	63.1%	4039	24	12	5	4.2%	7.2	2	28.6%	5	97.1	2	102.9	26	83	2	4.3	28.1%
2004	KC	16	556	369	66.4%	4591	27	17	10	6.7%	7.4	3	27.7%	9	102.9	5	114.3	25	85	0	4.4	37.3%
2005	*KC*	*16*	*486*	*304*	*62.4%*	*3541*	*25*	*14*	*—*	*—*	*6.5*	*—*	*—*	*—*	*—*	*—*	*—*	*25*	*73*	*1*		

The closest historical parallel to Trent Green is so clear after a little research that it's astonishing nobody ever brings it up: Warren Moon. Like Moon, Trent Green doesn't get enough credit for his big numbers because of the offense that surrounds him. Like Moon, Green didn't get a chance to start in the NFL until much later than usual, though Moon spent his formative years in Canada while Green spent his in the trainer's room. And like Moon, Green is an underappreciated scrambler. His senior year at Indiana he ran for 13 touchdowns. He doesn't run often in the NFL, but when he sees something open up he's quick and very smart about getting the yardage he needs. Moon continued to have strong seasons into his early 40s, and Green doesn't seem to be slowing down either. Unfortunately for Green, the same cannot be said for the rest of his offense.

Brian Griese Height: 6-3 Weight: 215 College: Michigan Born: 18-Mar-1975 Age: 30

Year	Team	G	Att	Comp	Pct	Yds	TD	INT	FUM	Sck%	NtY/P	Rank	DVOA	Rank	DPAR	Rank	PAR	Runs	Yds	TD	DPAR	DVOA
2002	DEN	13	422	281	66.6%	3112	15	15	2	7.4%	6.3	13	10.2%	15	48.0	15	53.1	37	107	1	2.2	-6.7%
2003	MIA	5	130	74	56.9%	813	5	6	4	8.0%	5.1	34	-31.0%	42	-10.6	38	-12.8	5	15	0	0.4	24.6%
2004	TB	11	336	233	69.3%	2632	20	12	5	6.9%	6.8	11	19.3%	11	50.4	13	60.6	30	17	0	-6.5	-93.8%
2005	TB	16	507	322	63.5%	3736	21	18	—	—	6.9	—	—	—	—	—	—	33	43	0		

This was the first year of Griese's career where nobody wanted him to be somebody else. In Michigan, they wanted him to be his father. In Denver, they always wanted him to be John Elway. In Miami, they wanted him to be his father again, only they forgot to give him his father's offensive line. Tampa just wanted him to be a good quarterback, and he finally was able to relax and pay well. In the past, he would always go into a shell when things went wrong, but when he made mistakes in Tampa he finally showed the ability to bounce back. The entire off-season there were rumors that the Bucs would replace him, but here he is, still the starter. He'll have another above-average year as long as they let him be a component and not insist he be the star of the show.

Rex Grossman Height: 6-1 Weight: 222 College: Florida Born: 23-Aug-1980 Age: 25

Year	Team	G	Att	Comp	Pct	Yds	TD	INT	FUM	Sck%	NtY/P	Rank	DVOA	Rank	DPAR	Rank	PAR	Runs	Yds	TD	DPAR	DVOA
2003	CHI	3	72	38	52.8%	437	2	1	—	5.3%	5.0	—	-11.6%	—	0.6	—	0.9	3	-1	0	—	—
2004	CHI	3	84	47	56.0%	607	1	3	3	6.3%	6.6	—	-18.8%	—	-2.2	—	4.2	11	48	1	-1.5	-39.9%
2005	CHI	16	524	297	56.7%	3681	21	19	—	—	6.9	—	—	—	—	—	—	45	172	1		

Rex Grossman's ACL tear won't affect him terribly because he never relied very much on his ability to move. But the Bears' offense was a disaster last year, and Grossman still hasn't shown that he can be the solution. By the way, the Bears have started 19 different quarterbacks, the most in the NFL, since Brett Favre began his consecutive games streak.

Joey Harrington Height: 6-4 Weight: 220 College: Oregon Born: 21-Oct-1978 Age: 27

Year	Team	G	Att	Comp	Pct	Yds	TD	INT	FUM	Sck%	NtY/P	Rank	DVOA	Rank	DPAR	Rank	PAR	Runs	Yds	TD	DPAR	DVOA
2002	DET	14	430	215	50.0%	2294	12	16	2	2.1%	5.1	39	-23.5%	43	-19.4	44	-22.4	7	4	0	-3.9	-136.3%
2003	DET	16	554	309	55.8%	2880	17	22	5	2.5%	5.0	36	-23.5%	38	-24.6	44	-25.6	28	98	0	3.0	7.9%
2004	DET	16	489	274	56.0%	3047	19	12	6	6.3%	5.5	28	-10.2%	28	6.5	27	17.2	48	175	0	0.3	-16.8%
2005	DET	9	333	199	59.7%	2025	14	10	—	—	5.3	—	—	—	—	—	—	36	128	1		

In his first two seasons, Harrington threw the ball away at the slightest hint that his receivers might be covered, which meant fewer sacks but also more interceptions. Last year, he held onto the ball longer, which meant fewer interceptions but three times as many sacks. He also may be the least-effective scrambler of all time, king of the one-yard run on second and 10 and the five-yard run on third and 13. He's now entering his fourth season and he'll face off against David Carr in the "Put Up or Shut Up" Olympics. Carr has the early lead, but Harrington has been given three highly drafted young receivers, a veteran tight end, our projected NFL rushing champion, and a ridiculously easy schedule. He's also been given actual job competition for the first time. We have a soft spot for a quarterback who says his favorite video game is Ms. Pac-Man, but that projection shows that we think Jeff Garcia will be running the Lions by December.

Matt Hasselbeck Height: 6-4 Weight: 233 College: Boston College Born: 25-Sep-1975 Age: 30

Year	Team	G	Att	Comp	Pct	Yds	TD	INT	FUM	Sck%	NtY/P	Rank	DVOA	Rank	DPAR	Rank	PAR	Runs	Yds	TD	DPAR	DVOA
2002	SEA	14	419	267	63.7%	3075	15	10	4	5.6%	6.6	9	21.8%	7	65.8	8	68.7	40	202	1	8.1	20.2%
2003	SEA	16	513	313	61.0%	3844	26	15	4	7.7%	6.5	8	23.5%	7	87.1	3	80.2	36	125	2	1.3	-8.5%
2004	SEA	14	474	279	58.9%	3382	22	15	4	5.6%	6.4	13	10.3%	13	52.5	12	57.7	27	90	1	0.8	-7.6%
2005	SEA	16	528	329	62.2%	4104	27	16	—	—	7.0	—	—	—	—	—	—	38	137	2		

Last year, Hasselbeck killed anyone who took him in fantasy football. For the first few weeks, even though Hasselbeck had a few subpar games, it looked like Seattle was a strong team so people held onto him rather than dumping him to get someone off the waiver wire like, say, Drew Brees. Ironically, as we discuss in the San Diego chapter, Hasselbeck himself is a very good candidate to become this year's version of Brees. Last year Hasselbeck had a 15.7% DVOA on first downs, 18.2% DVOA on second downs, but −12.9% DVOA on third downs. Every additional third down he converts this season opens up the possibility of not just another ten yards but another extended drive and touchdown. A healthy Bobby "The Third Down Machine" Engram will do a lot to make the rebound a reality. Fantastic fantasy sleeper and a big reason why Seattle is a better Super Bowl contender than most people realize.

Drew Henson
Height: 6-4 Weight: 223 College: Michigan   **Born: 13-Feb-1980 Age: 25**

Year	Team	G	Att	Comp	Pct	Yds	TD	INT	FUM	Sck%	NtY/P	Rank	DVOA	Rank	DPAR	Rank	PAR	Runs	Yds	TD	DPAR	DVOA
2004	DAL	7	18	10	55.6%	78	1	1	1	6.4%	3.3	—	-42.4%	—	-2.5	—	-3.4	1	7	0	0.6	143.3%
2005	DAL	3	92	53	57.4%	519	3	4	—	—	9.8	—	—	—	—	—	—	6	15	0		

Probably has a better chance of becoming the starting 3B for the Yankees than he does ever becoming the starting QB of the Cowboys. Even when Dallas was out of realistic playoff contention in November, Parcells gave Henson a single start on Thanksgiving, and then promptly benched the QB after a poor first half against Chicago. If you're not willing to give your young QB playing time at the end of November when your team is 3–7 and your starter is a 41-year-old Vinny Testaverde, you're never going to give your young QB a shot. With Drew Bledsoe behind center for ostensibly the next two seasons, Henson will likely have to go elsewhere if he ever wants to get a shot at starting regularly.

Kelly Holcomb
Height: 6-2 Weight: 212 College: Middle Tennessee State   **Born: 9-Jul-1973 Age: 32**

Year	Team	G	Att	Comp	Pct	Yds	TD	INT	FUM	Sck%	NtY/P	Rank	DVOA	Rank	DPAR	Rank	PAR	Runs	Yds	TD	DPAR	DVOA
2002	CLE	6	106	64	60.4%	790	8	4	1	5.3%	6.8	6	12.5%	14	12.3	27	17.5	8	9	0	0.9	20.3%
2003	CLE	10	302	193	63.9%	1797	10	12	5	6.2%	5.0	35	-12.2%	29	1.4	29	-2.7	8	7	0	-0.6	-49.9%
2004	CLE	4	87	59	67.8%	737	7	5	—	5.1%	7.7	—	21.4%	—	13.7	—	11.4	0	2	0	—	—
2005	BUF	4	120	74	61.7%	898	8	6	—	—	6.6	—	—	—	—	—	—	3	1	0		

Reasonable contract demands, and he would have been handed the starting quarterback job in Cleveland. Instead he heads to Buffalo to presumably back up a first-round draft pick. If Losman gets hurt, Holcomb should flash enough brilliance to create a full-fledged quarterback controversy. Cleveland fans know what that looks like. This is the only projection in this chapter that we don't expect to see fulfilled, but we did want to present a "what if" in case Losman is hurt or just horrible.

Chad Hutchinson
Height: 6-5 Weight: 237 College: Stanford   **Born: 21-Feb-1977 Age: 28**

Year	Team	G	Att	Comp	Pct	Yds	TD	INT	FUM	Sck%	NtY/P	Rank	DVOA	Rank	DPAR	Rank	PAR	Runs	Yds	TD	DPAR	DVOA
2002	DAL	9	250	127	50.8%	1555	7	8	12	12.0%	4.7	45	-42.7%	46	-32.2	46	-29.9	18	74	0	1.0	-4.2%
2003	DAL	2	2	1	50.0%	8	0	0	—	0.0%	4.0	—	-110.7%	—	-0.4	—	-0.1	2	-3	0	—	—
2004	CHI	6	161	92	57.1%	903	4	3	8	12.5%	4.0	40	-46.0%	39	-25.0	41	-13.9	6	14	0	-2.5	-147.1%
2005	CHI	—	—	—	—	—	—	—	—	—	—	—	—	—	—	—	—	—	—	—		

In 2001, Hutchinson made his pro debut—as a pitcher for the St. Louis Cardinals. Hutchinson was so bad that Bobby Bonilla actually had a lower ERA that year (18.00 to Chad's 27.54). That must have been humiliating and prepared him well for his lack of NFL success. He will probably be an acceptable backup to Rex Grossman, but if Craig Krenzel beats him for the job, maybe Hutch should try his hand as a scab NHL player. Note: His official photo on ESPN.com is useful for scaring small children.

Brad Johnson
Height: 6-5 Weight: 226 College: Florida State   **Born: 13-Sep-1968 Age: 37**

Year	Team	G	Att	Comp	Pct	Yds	TD	INT	FUM	Sck%	NtY/P	Rank	DVOA	Rank	DPAR	Rank	PAR	Runs	Yds	TD	DPAR	DVOA
2002	TB	13	451	281	62.3%	3049	22	6	7	4.1%	6.2	17	24.7%	4	77.4	5	74.7	13	30	0	0.9	-3.9%
2003	TB	16	570	354	62.1%	3811	26	21	6	3.4%	6.3	10	4.0%	16	43.0	11	50.3	25	33	0	-3.5	-55.0%
2004	TB	4	103	65	63.1%	674	3	3	2	8.6%	5.6	25	-18.2%	31	-2.4	31	-1.6	5	23	0	1.1	26.4%
2005	MIN	3	6	3	50.0%	39	0	0	—	—	6.5	—	—	—	—	—	—	4	-3	0		

For years Johnson has been steady if unexciting but last season he suddenly looked completely lost. Assuming he can get back up after plummeting off the cliff, he should make a good fit for the role of Minnesota's "unspectacular veteran backup who could fall out of bed and be ready to play in 10 minutes."

Doug Johnson Height: 6-2 Weight: 225 College: Florida Born: 27-Oct-1977 Age: 28

Year	Team	G	Att	Comp	Pct	Yds	TD	INT	FUM	Sck%	NtY/P	Rank	DVOA	Rank	DPAR	Rank	PAR	Runs	Yds	TD	DPAR	DVOA
2002	ATL	6	57	37	64.9%	448	2	3	3	3.8%	7.3	—	38.2%	—	13.1	—	4.6	8	16	1	1.2	27.4%
2003	ATL	10	243	136	56.0%	1655	8	12	2	7.6%	5.8	22	-22.8%	36	-10.6	37	-16.1	14	21	1	1.4	20.8%
2004	TEN	3	12	6	50.0%	68	0	0	—	9.7%	4.8	—	6.9%	—	1.1	—	0.6	2	-2	0	—	—

Three years ago when Michael Vick was knocked out of a game against Tampa, Johnson came off the bench. He threw three picks—who didn't against the Bucs that year?—but the next week was 19-for-25 for 257 yards in a 17–10 win over the Giants. The next year, when Vick broke his leg in preseason, a number of analysts—including the head writer of a brand-new website called Football Outsiders—held up that game as proof Johnson could keep the Falcons afloat until Vick was ready to return. Instead, he was awful. And thus was born the Doug Johnson Effect, the rule that says never to expect a season's worth of good performance based on one big game by a part-time player the year before. Johnson will never start an NFL game again, but not every third-stringer is immortalized with his own rule. A free agent at press time and coming soon to a scout team practice near you.

Shaun King Height: 6-0 Weight: 225 College: Tulane Born: 29-May-1977 Age: 28

Year	Team	G	Att	Comp	Pct	Yds	TD	INT	FUM	Sck%	NtY/P	Rank	DVOA	Rank	DPAR	Rank	PAR	Runs	Yds	TD	DPAR	DVOA
2002	TB	3	27	10	37.0%	80	0	1	0	1.7%	2.7	—	-62.4%	—	-5.8	—	-6.6	4	25	0	0.6	5.5%
2003	TB	3	22	15	68.2%	130	1	1	0	11.8%	4.2	—	-30.9%	—	-2.1	—	-3.1	4	20	0	1.0	10.4%
2004	ARI	3	84	47	56.0%	502	1	4	4	7.1%	5.0	—	-38.6%	—	-10.0	—	-11.0	9	30	0	-0.2	-24.6%

In 1999, this highly touted Tulane graduate took the offensive reigns of Tampa Bay, which had the league's leading defense, but he was never able to generate enough offense to get them over the hump. Buffalo fans, this is your nightmare. King's 343-yard performance against Carolina in Week 11 wins the "garbage time stat-padding performance of the year" award.

Jon Kitna Height: 6-2 Weight: 220 College: Central Washington Born: 21-Sep-1972 Age: 33

Year	Team	G	Att	Comp	Pct	Yds	TD	INT	FUM	Sck%	NtY/P	Rank	DVOA	Rank	DPAR	Rank	PAR	Runs	Yds	TD	DPAR	DVOA
2002	CIN	13	473	294	62.2%	3178	16	16	9	4.1%	6.2	18	7.8%	17	43.8	17	36.3	25	52	4	-1.4	-24.5%
2003	CIN	16	521	325	62.4%	3605	26	15	9	6.7%	6.0	20	8.9%	11	52.3	7	54.8	38	117	0	2.6	5.1%
2004	CIN	4	104	61	58.7%	623	5	4	2	4.3%	5.2	30	5.9%	16	8.7	26	0.8	10	42	0	1.1	10.0%
2005	CIN	2	12	7	58.3%	69	1	0	—	—	5.8	—	—	—	—	—	—	2	4	0		

The best backup quarterback in football. One point of view: He gracefully handled his demotion to reserve behind the untested Carson Palmer. Another point of view: You have to wonder about the competitiveness of a guy who didn't seem to mind at all when he lost his starting job to Carson Palmer. Arizona would have been much better off trying to pry him away from the Bengals instead of giving Kurt Warner a shot at his 47th comeback.

Craig Krenzel Height: 6-3 Weight: 227 College: Ohio State Born: 1-Jul-1981 Age: 24

Year	Team	G	Att	Comp	Pct	Yds	TD	INT	FUM	Sck%	NtY/P	Rank	DVOA	Rank	DPAR	Rank	PAR	Runs	Yds	TD	DPAR	DVOA
2004	CHI	6	127	59	46.5%	718	3	6	—	14.6%	3.6	41	-82.6%	42	-41.7	42	-38.1	18	41	0	—	—

Ladies and gentlemen, we give you the least valuable quarterback of 2004. Krenzel converted only 9 of 56 third and fourth down pass plays. He was also the best possible example of why quarterbacks should not be judged based solely on their ability to "win games." He won his first three starts despite completing just 42% of his passes for a miserable 143 yards per game. The third win, Week 10 in Tennessee, Krenzel was 10-for-28 for 116 yards and two picks, but the Bears won 19–17 thanks to an interception return for a touchdown, a punt return for a touchdown, and a safety in overtime. As you may have read 1,000 times during the season, Krenzel was a molecular biology major at Ohio State and the winner of the academic equivalent of the Heisman Trophy. We hope he invests his NFL money well and has a good career ahead of him afterward, because it would be shocking to see him actually start again in this league. Waived in June.

Byron Leftwich　　　Height: 6-5　Weight: 245　　College: Marshall　　　　　　Born: 14-Jan-1980　Age: 25

Year	Team	G	Att	Comp	Pct	Yds	TD	INT	FUM	Sck%	NtY/P	Rank	DVOA	Rank	DPAR	Rank	PAR	Runs	Yds	TD	DPAR	DVOA
2003	JAC	15	418	239	57.2%	2819	14	16	10	3.9%	6.2	15	-6.7%	25	12.1	23	8.6	25	108	2	2.6	2.4%
2004	JAC	14	441	267	60.5%	2941	15	10	—	5.7%	6.1	18	2.3%	18	30.2	17	43.6	39	148	2	—	—
2005	JAC	16	501	310	61.8%	3627	22	16	—	—	6.7	—	—	—	—	—	—	48	189	2		

There is an unwritten rule prevalent in sports journalism, one that prescribes that African American players can be compared only to other African Americans and whites only to other whites. Thus you'll hear Leftwich compared to Daunte Culpepper. Yes, they're both huge. And black. Culpepper can run. Leftwich can't. Not a lick. What Leftwich can do is stand in the pocket and deliver the ball. He took some baby steps last season, but those early-season fourth quarter comebacks made his game look more mature than it actually is. Leftwich is still learning to run a pro-style offense after playing in a shotgun-and-chuck-it set at Marshall. New coordinator Carl Smith will simplify the passing game, removing many of the West Coast-style timing routes, but what he really needs to do is get Leftwich to look for someone other than Jimmy Smith. Smith had 137 passes thrown his way, while no other Jags receiver had more than 80. Smith is a great receiver, but you generally don't want your young quarterback's security blanket to be 36 years old.

J. P. Losman　　　Height: 6-2　Weight: 217　　College: Tulane　　　　　　Born: 12-Mar-1981　Age: 24

Year	Team	G	Att	Comp	Pct	Yds	TD	INT	FUM	Sck%	NtY/P	Rank	DVOA	Rank	DPAR	Rank	PAR	Runs	Yds	TD	DPAR	DVOA
2004	BUF	4	5	3	60.0%	32	0	1	1	17.7%	5.0	—	-167.4%	—	-4.9	—	-5.2	2	15	0	0.7	36.9%
2005	BUF	16	478	287	60.1%	3086	20	14	—	—	5.8	—	—	—	—	—	—	36	103	2		

Losman showed off a good arm and excellent athleticism in college, and he's been put in an excellent situation with a strong defense and a potential stud running back. Of course, Losman was also known for taking too many sacks and trying to squeeze the ball into tight coverage, not the best combination for a first-year starter playing behind a mediocre offensive line. If he plays as well as that projection, the Bills are headed for the playoffs. If he struggles early and the Bills lose a number of 16–13 games, we're going to be seeing Kelly Holcomb. Either way, a first-year starter on a defense-first team is someone you want to keep far away from your fantasy team.

Tommy Maddox　　　Height: 6-4　Weight: 220　　College: UCLA　　　　　　Born: 2-Sep-1971　Age: 34

Year	Team	G	Att	Comp	Pct	Yds	TD	INT	FUM	Sck%	NtY/P	Rank	DVOA	Rank	DPAR	Rank	PAR	Runs	Yds	TD	DPAR	DVOA
2002	PIT	13	377	234	62.1%	2836	20	16	5	6.3%	6.7	7	17.8%	9	52.7	14	38.7	18	49	0	-3.7	-91.2%
2003	PIT	16	519	298	57.4%	3414	18	17	4	7.0%	5.7	25	2.6%	18	36.8	13	31.7	13	12	0	-2.5	-89.7%
2004	PIT	4	60	30	50.0%	329	1	2	3	8.9%	4.2	—	-29.6%	—	-4.2	—	-6.0	9	15	0	-2.4	-88.1%
2005	PIT	2	11	6	54.5%	65	0	0	—	—	5.9	—	—	—	—	—	—	2	4	0		

Pittsburgh fans were apoplectic when Ben Roethlisberger went down in Week 16, afraid that they would be stuck with Maddox at quarterback in the playoffs. We think they doth protest too much. Yes, Big Ben was an improvement over Mr. XFL, but how many backup quarterbacks in the NFL would you rather have running your team if the starter went down to an injury? Garrard, Volek, Kitna, and Flutie, that's about it. Anyone else is either an untested youngster or fairly inept.

Eli Manning　　　Height: 6-4　Weight: 218　　College: Mississippi　　　　　　Born: 3-Jan-1981　Age: 24

Year	Team	G	Att	Comp	Pct	Yds	TD	INT	FUM	Sck%	NtY/P	Rank	DVOA	Rank	DPAR	Rank	PAR	Runs	Yds	TD	DPAR	DVOA
2004	NYG	9	197	95	48.2%	1043	6	9	3	5.5%	4.6	37	-28.4%	37	-13.3	36	-22.1	6	35	0	1.9	70.2%
2005	NYG	16	478	271	56.7%	3264	21	18	—	—	6.1	—	—	—	—	—	—	33	146	1		

Just a horrible rookie year. Look at the list of the most similar first-year QBs: Steve Walsh, Todd Marinovich (played one game in previous year), Billy Joe Tolliver, Ken Dorsey, Eric Zeier, Jim Everett, Quincy Carter, Craig Whelihan, and Koy Detmer. Those seasons weren't just similar, they were better: Every single one of those quarterbacks averaged more yards per attempt than Manning, and every single one except Tolliver had a higher completion percentage. Donovan McNabb had a miserable 4.4 yards per attempt as a rookie, but at least he threw more touchdowns than interceptions and added 313 rushing yards. Vinny Testaverde completed only 43% of his passes, but he averaged 6.6 yards per attempt. None of those quarterbacks (except Dorsey) played in a season with an offensive environment as conducive to scoring as 2004. Yes, Manning had to face a number of hard defenses. Yes, he looked good against Pittsburgh. But there is no historical precedent for a QB who has a rookie season this bad to turn into a superstar, let alone Eli's brother. His ceiling right now looks like Vinny Part II.

Peyton Manning
Height: 6-5 **Weight:** 230 **College:** Tennessee **Born:** 24-Mar-1976 **Age:** 29

Year	Team	G	Att	Comp	Pct	Yds	TD	INT	FUM	Sck%	NtY/P	Rank	DVOA	Rank	DPAR	Rank	PAR	Runs	Yds	TD	DPAR	DVOA
2002	IND	16	591	392	66.3%	4199	27	19	5	3.8%	6.6	8	16.5%	11	79.5	4	77.1	38	148	2	6.6	24.3%
2003	IND	16	566	379	67.0%	4267	29	10	6	3.5%	7.1	3	36.0%	2	126.8	1	125.4	27	29	0	-5.3	-82.3%
2004	IND	16	497	336	67.6%	4557	49	10	5	3.2%	8.7	1	62.8%	1	170.1	1	189.2	25	38	0	0.8	-3.1%
2005	IND	16	535	363	67.9%	4494	36	13	—	—	8.0	—	—	—	—	—	—	27	41	1		

Since we've already addressed the standing of this season among the best of all time elsewhere in this book, we'd like to use this space to address last year's playoff loss to New England. The common media storyline was "Patriots own Peyton," ignoring the fact that Manning had a very good game—worth 10.5 DPAR, in fact, once you take into account the quality of the Patriots defense. It is not Peyton Manning's fault that Edgerrin James averaged 2.8 yards per carry and that the Colts had 16 first downs passing and *zero* rushing. It is not Peyton Manning's fault that his receivers coughed up the ball twice. And as much as people like to talk about how Manning adjusts plays on the field, he does not draw up the game plan. Offensive coordinator Tom Moore is the one who decided to base everything on screen passes and short throws instead of going long against the patchwork Patriots secondary. If Manning holds any responsibility for the loss, it is because he became more and more visibly frustrated on the sidelines as his running back kept going nowhere and his receivers kept dropping the ball. He needs to learn to act like a leader even if he doesn't feel like things are going well. The Colts don't need a quarterbacks coach, they need an acting coach.

Some may take issue with our projected touchdown total for 2005, but Dan Marino threw "only" 30 touchdowns the year after his record-setting 48 (and led the league anyway). Brett Favre is the only quarterback in NFL history with consecutive years of 33 or more passing touchdowns (four of them, from 1994–1997) and Manning will be the second despite the projected drop.

Jamie Martin
Height: 6-2 **Weight:** 205 **College:** Weber State **Born:** 8-Feb-1970 **Age:** 35

Year	Team	G	Att	Comp	Pct	Yds	TD	INT	FUM	Sck%	NtY/P	Rank	DVOA	Rank	DPAR	Rank	PAR	Runs	Yds	TD	DPAR	DVOA
2002	STL	5	195	124	63.6%	1216	7	10	2	6.6%	5.6	32	-21.2%	41	-7.0	41	-0.8	5	6	0	-1.0	-97.9%
2003	NYJ	0	0	0	0.0%	0	0	0	—	—	—	—	—	—	—	—	—	0	0	0	—	—
2004	STL	1	30	16	53.3%	188	0	0	—	6.3%	5.4	—	31.4%	—	5.8	—	3.6	0	0	0	—	—
2005	STL	—	—	—	—	—	—	—	—	—	—	—	—	—	—	—	—	—	—	—	—	—

Mike Martz is said to like Jamie Martin, but the guy's been around forever and has never given any indication that he's capable of doing more than holding a clipboard. The Rams drafted Jeff Smoker last year and Ryan Fitzpatrick this year, so it's possible they'll say goodbye to Martin and keep the two young guys behind Marc Bulger.

Shane Matthews
Height: 6-3 **Weight:** 199 **College:** Florida **Born:** 1-Jun-1970 **Age:** 35

Year	Team	G	Att	Comp	Pct	Yds	TD	INT	FUM	Sck%	NtY/P	Rank	DVOA	Rank	DPAR	Rank	PAR	Runs	Yds	TD	DPAR	DVOA
2002	WAS	8	237	124	52.3%	1251	11	6	1	4.1%	5.0	41	-10.1%	32	3.0	33	7.7	12	31	0	0.7	-0.3%
2003	CIN	0	0	0	0.0%	0	0	0	—	—	—	—	—	—	—	—	—	0	0	0	—	—
2004	BUF	4	3	2	66.7%	44	1	0	—	0.0%	14.7	—	222.7%	—	2.7	—	3.1	2	-3	0	—	—
2005	BUF	—	—	—	—	—	—	—	—	—	—	—	—	—	—	—	—	—	—	—	—	—

How has Shane Matthews managed to hold a job in the NFL for 12 years? He's thrown a pass in only six of those seasons, and never appeared in more than eight games in a year. He was given a couple of opportunities as a starter, but lost those jobs to such luminaries as Jim Miller and Danny Wuerffel. Kudos to Matthews for sticking around so long, but the half-life of a backup quarterback should be much shorter than this.

Josh McCown
Height: 6-4 **Weight:** 212 **College:** Sam Houston State **Born:** 4-Jul-1979 **Age:** 26

Year	Team	G	Att	Comp	Pct	Yds	TD	INT	FUM	Sck%	NtY/P	Rank	DVOA	Rank	DPAR	Rank	PAR	Runs	Yds	TD	DPAR	DVOA
2002	ARI	2	18	7	38.9%	66	0	2	1	22.4%	0.7	—	-191.2%	—	-15.5	—	-13.3	1	20	0	1.2	172.3%
2003	ARI	8	166	95	57.2%	1018	5	6	10	11.3%	4.3	44	-34.9%	43	-17.4	42	-17.3	28	158	1	5.2	12.4%
2004	ARI	14	408	233	57.1%	2511	11	10	12	5.9%	5.1	32	-7.6%	26	10.5	25	9.1	36	112	2	0.3	-15.6%
2005	ARI	5	138	75	54.1%	789	5	4	—	—	4.5	—	—	—	—	—	—	20	62	1		

Winner of the McCown Brother of the Year Award from the National Institute for Damning with Faint Praise. He's nobody's idea of a star quarterback, but when he was in the lineup he played much better than the year before, and most of that time he was without Anquan Boldin. Warner hasn't played a full season since 2001 so McCown will see starts in 2005.

Luke McCown Height: 6-3 Weight: 208 College: Louisiana Tech Born: 12-Jul-1981 Age: 24

Year	Team	G	Att	Comp	Pct	Yds	TD	INT	FUM	Sck%	NtY/P	Rank	DVOA	Rank	DPAR	Rank	PAR	Runs	Yds	TD	DPAR	DVOA
2004	CLE	5	98	48	49.0%	608	4	7	2	11.4%	4.2	39	-58.0%	41	-20.0	39	-26.9	6	25	0	1.1	47.6%
2005	TB	—	—	—	—	—	—	—	—	—	—	—	—	—	—	—	—	—	—	—	—	—

What the Comellas are to second-rate NFL fullbacks, the fighting McCowns are to second-rate NFL quarterbacks. Still, investing a sixth-round pick in a young quarterback with starting experience—as the Bucs did in acquiring McCown from Cleveland on draft day—can't be considered a bad move.

Mike McMahon Height: 6-2 Weight: 213 College: Rutgers Born: 8-Feb-1979 Age: 26

Year	Team	G	Att	Comp	Pct	Yds	TD	INT	FUM	Sck%	NtY/P	Rank	DVOA	Rank	DPAR	Rank	PAR	Runs	Yds	TD	DPAR	DVOA
2002	DET	8	147	62	42.2%	874	7	9	4	6.4%	5.0	40	-29.4%	44	-10.4	42	-18.3	14	96	3	3.6	22.2%
2003	DET	4	31	9	29.0%	87	0	2	1	5.7%	2.4	—	-93.9%	—	-10.3	—	-10.9	5	32	0	-1.2	-62.9%
2004	DET	1	15	11	73.3%	77	0	1	0	10.4%	4.1	—	2.0%	—	1.1	—	2.0	2	18	0	0.1	-7.2%
2005	PHI	—	—	—	—	—	—	—	—	—	—	—	—	—	—	—	—	—	—	—	—	—

Look, we're sure he's a nice fellow, but you can't take any team seriously as a playoff threat when they're thinking about voluntarily starting Mike McMahon. McMahon is a very athletic quarterback, but you also need this thing called "accuracy" to succeed in the NFL.

Donovan McNabb Height: 6-2 Weight: 226 College: Syracuse Born: 25-Jan-1976 Age: 29

Year	Team	G	Att	Comp	Pct	Yds	TD	INT	FUM	Sck%	NtY/P	Rank	DVOA	Rank	DPAR	Rank	PAR	Runs	Yds	TD	DPAR	DVOA
2002	PHI	10	361	211	58.4%	2289	17	6	6	7.9%	5.5	37	5.6%	23	32.1	20	32.3	62	464	6	23.8	48.6%
2003	PHI	16	478	275	57.5%	3215	16	11	8	7.8%	5.7	24	3.3%	17	36.8	14	32.1	71	354	3	10.6	11.7%
2004	PHI	15	469	300	64.0%	3875	31	8	8	5.7%	7.3	6	35.8%	5	107.1	4	102.9	41	220	3	8.7	40.2%
2005	PHI	16	508	319	62.8%	3974	28	12	—	—	7.1	—	—	—	—	—	—	52	245	3		

As McNabb improved as a passer last year, not many people noticed that he began to rely a lot less on his running ability. He became much more of a pocket quarterback, and when he did scramble, he scrambled to find a receiver rather than just trying to run. But McNabb's big leap forward was really just a combination of two things: fewer sacks and Terrell Owens. The total DVOA for Eagle receivers (i.e., the passing game without sacks and interceptions) was 2.2% in 2003, and the total DVOA for Eagle receivers not counting T.O. was 2.0% in 2004. McNabb's projection, like pretty much every Eagles projection, assumes that T.O. is full of bluster and will be back in September; if he really doesn't play, McNabb is in serious trouble. At least his beard will still be super badass.

Steve McNair Height: 6-2 Weight: 235 College: Alcorn State Born: 14-Feb-1973 Age: 32

Year	Team	G	Att	Comp	Pct	Yds	TD	INT	FUM	Sck%	NtY/P	Rank	DVOA	Rank	DPAR	Rank	PAR	Runs	Yds	TD	DPAR	DVOA
2002	TEN	16	492	301	61.2%	3387	22	15	7	4.1%	6.3	15	16.3%	12	64.1	9	62.7	82	440	3	20.5	42.3%
2003	TEN	14	400	250	62.5%	3215	24	7	12	4.9%	7.4	1	34.1%	3	85.1	4	95.3	37	138	4	2.7	1.2%
2004	TEN	8	215	129	60.0%	1343	8	9	5	6.3%	5.5	27	-18.9%	32	-6.0	32	1.9	23	128	1	3.9	18.6%
2005	TEN	12	350	207	59.2%	2560	16	11	—	—	6.8	—	—	—	—	—	—	32	174	2		

McNair's body finally gave out on him last year, and so did the team around him. He's coming back in 2005 but you have to wonder what the point is. The Titans have been ripped apart by the salary cap for two years now and are currently at the bottom of the rebuilding curve. Yes, there is a small chance that the youth on this team could solidify faster than Magic Shell, but it is more likely that McNair will go through another one or two years of very painful football and then be forced into retirement just as the new Titans core is ready to take the leap back into the playoffs.

Adrian McPherson   Height: 6-3   Weight: 218   College: Florida State   Born: 8-May-1983   Age: 22

Year	Team	G	Att	Comp	Pct	Yds	TD	INT	FUM	Sck%	NtY/P	Rank	DVOA	Rank	DPAR	Rank	PAR	Runs	Yds	TD	DPAR	DVOA
2005	NO	2	28	14	50.0%	184	1	1	—	—	6.1	—	—	—	—	—	—	5	23	1		

Our Arena Football to NFL projection formula states that McPherson will throw for 2,718 yards, 19 touchd … What? We don't have an Arena Football to NFL projection formula? While Aaron works on that, we'll outline the obvious: (1) McPherson was one of the best high school athletes in Florida history; (2) He got himself into some horrible trouble in 2002 by passing bad checks; (3) The Indiana Firebirds are a long way from the New Orleans Saints, but McPherson did a fine job of dusting himself off in the minor leagues. Forget projections: If Brooks gets injured, McPherson becomes an instant fantasy sleeper because he runs.

Craig Nall   Height: 6-3   Weight: 230   College: Northwestern (La.) State   Born: 21-Apr-1979   Age: 26

Year	Team	G	Att	Comp	Pct	Yds	TD	INT	FUM	Sck%	NtY/P	Rank	DVOA	Rank	DPAR	Rank	PAR	Runs	Yds	TD	DPAR	DVOA
2003	GB	1	0	0	0.0%	0	0	0	—	—	—	—	—	—	—	—	—	2	-2	0	—	—
2004	GB	6	33	23	69.7%	314	4	0	1	4.3%	8.8	—	98.2%	—	17.0	—	16.7	3	7	0	-0.2	-54.1%
2005	GB	—	—	—	—	—	—	—	—	—	—	—	—	—	—	—	—	—	—	—	—	—

Make that "ex-heir apparent to Brett Favre." His fabulous DVOA rating from last season is the result of an entire quarter of garbage time against Tennessee fourth-stringers on *Monday Night Football*. Back when the Tennessee fourth-stringers were still fourth-stringers, not first-stringers like they were in December.

John Navarre   Height: 6-6   Weight: 246   College: Michigan   Born: 9-Sep-1980   Age: 25

Year	Team	G	Att	Comp	Pct	Yds	TD	INT	FUM	Sck%	NtY/P	Rank	DVOA	Rank	DPAR	Rank	PAR	Runs	Yds	TD	DPAR	DVOA
2004	ARI	2	40	18	45.0%	168	1	4	—	2.5%	3.9	—	-102.2%	—	-15.1	—	-15.1	0	0	0	—	—
2005	ARI	2	17	8	47.1%	83	0	1	—	—	4.3	—	—	—	—	—	—	2	-1	0		

Navarre, Jim Sorgi, Jeff Smoker, Craig Krenzel—apparently whenever a team couldn't think of someone to take on the second day of the 2004 draft, they threw a dart at a list of Big Ten quarterbacks. Because he is a Denny Green QB, there is a significant possibility that Navarre will end up behind center for at least a few snaps in 2005. In fact, find a friend, and offer him the non-Navarre side of this prop bet: completions by Navarre versus wins by the Redskins. Imagine how cool you will look if you win.

Kyle Orton   Height: 6-3   Weight: 226   College: Purdue   Born: 14-Nov-1982   Age: 23

Year	Team	G	Att	Comp	Pct	Yds	TD	INT	FUM	Sck%	NtY/P	Rank	DVOA	Rank	DPAR	Rank	PAR	Runs	Yds	TD	DPAR	DVOA
2005	CHI	2	10	5	50.0%	54	0	1	—	—	4.5	—	—	—	—	—	—	3	3	0		

Orton's senior season fell apart faster than the Yankees in the 2004 ALCS. But he didn't forget the skills that made him the first-half Heisman leader, and he should be an upgrade over Craig Krenzel and Jonathan Quinn behind Rex Grossman.

Carson Palmer   Height: 6-5   Weight: 230   College: USC   Born: 27-Dec-1979   Age: 25

Year	Team	G	Att	Comp	Pct	Yds	TD	INT	FUM	Sck%	NtY/P	Rank	DVOA	Rank	DPAR	Rank	PAR	Runs	Yds	TD	DPAR	DVOA
2003	CIN	0	0	0	0.0%	0	0	0	—	—	—	—	—	—	—	—	—	0	0	0	—	—
2004	CIN	14	432	263	60.9%	2897	18	18	2	5.0%	6.0	20	7.2%	15	39.0	15	15.7	18	47	1	3.5	51.2%
2005	CIN	16	519	314	60.4%	3720	22	18	—	—	6.6	—	—	—	—	—	—	30	85	1		

You are going to hear a lot about Palmer's big second-season leap forward from people who don't understand how schedule strength works. His rookie numbers were dampened by a schedule littered with good defenses like those of Pittsburgh, Baltimore, Washington, and Miami. He still has to play the Steelers and Ravens twice each, but he gets to exchange the AFC East and NFC East for the AFC South and NFC North, including Green Bay, Indianapolis, and the Tennessee Teen Titans. People also forget that Palmer was injured early in Week 15 and would have passed for 3,500 yards had he stayed healthy.

Doug Pederson   Height: 6-3   Weight: 220   College: Louisiana-Monroe   Born: 31-Jan-1968 Age: 37

Year	Team	G	Att	Comp	Pct	Yds	TD	INT	FUM	Sck%	NtY/P	Rank	DVOA	Rank	DPAR	Rank	PAR	Runs	Yds	TD	DPAR	DVOA
2002	GB	11	28	19	67.9%	134	1	0	—	3.0%	4.3	—	28.0%	—	4.9	—	4.6	1	-1	0	—	—
2003	GB	16	2	2	100.0%	16	0	0	—	—	—	—	—	—	—	—	—	8	-7	0	—	—
2004	GB	4	23	11	47.8%	120	0	2	0	0.0%	5.2	—	-64.9%	—	-5.0	—	-5.1	2	15	0	0.8	68.3%

Pederson spent years backing up Brett Favre, had two terrible seasons as a part-time starter in Philadelphia and Cleveland, and then came back to back up Favre some more. It's nice to find something you are good at. Retired this off-season.

Chad Pennington   Height: 6-3   Weight: 225   College: Marshall   Born: 26-Jun-1976 Age: 29

Year	Team	G	Att	Comp	Pct	Yds	TD	INT	FUM	Sck%	NtY/P	Rank	DVOA	Rank	DPAR	Rank	PAR	Runs	Yds	TD	DPAR	DVOA
2002	NYJ	15	400	276	69.0%	3128	22	6	1	5.6%	7.1	3	50.2%	1	112.7	1	122.0	30	49	2	0.8	-8.1%
2003	NYJ	10	297	189	63.6%	2139	13	12	8	7.2%	6.1	16	-0.8%	21	17.2	20	11.2	21	42	2	1.0	-4.2%
2004	NYJ	13	370	242	65.4%	2673	16	9	5	4.4%	6.6	12	31.6%	6	77.2	8	60.5	34	126	1	5.3	15.5%
2005	*NYJ*	16	447	285	63.7%	3526	23	14	—	—	7.4	—	—	—	—	—	—	41	172	2		

Pennington is best when he's able to throw intermediate-range balls that give his receivers room to run after the catch. As the rest of his team was going through spring minicamps, Pennington could only stand by and watch. Although the Jets say he'll be ready to go for the preseason, Pennington's shoulder injury is serious. With Curtis Martin a year older and LaMont Jordan gone, the Jets will need Pennington more than ever.

Cody Pickett   Height: 6-3   Weight: 227   College: Washington   Born: 30-Jun-1980 Age: 25

Year	Team	G	Att	Comp	Pct	Yds	TD	INT	FUM	Sck%	NtY/P	Rank	DVOA	Rank	DPAR	Rank	PAR	Runs	Yds	TD	DPAR	DVOA
2004	SF	3	10	4	40.0%	55	0	2	1	15.5%	3.4	—	-167.2%	—	-7.7	—	-9.3	1	5	0	0.0	-26.2%
2005	*SF*	—	—	—	—	—	—	—	—	—	—	—	—	—	—	—	—	—	—	—		

Cody Pickett entered the Week 16 game against Buffalo with 9:38 remaining. His first pass was nearly intercepted. His next pass was overthrown. His third was completed. His fourth was intercepted. Then he got sacked twice and threw another interception. In the fourth quarter he finally led a touchdown drive that made the score Buffalo 41, San Francisco 7. So ends the career of Cody Pickett.

Jake Plummer   Height: 6-2   Weight: 197   College: Arizona State   Born: 19-Dec-1974 Age: 30

Year	Team	G	Att	Comp	Pct	Yds	TD	INT	FUM	Sck%	NtY/P	Rank	DVOA	Rank	DPAR	Rank	PAR	Runs	Yds	TD	DPAR	DVOA
2002	ARI	16	530	286	54.0%	2979	18	20	11	6.1%	4.8	43	-21.3%	42	-19.7	45	-14.1	47	283	2	10.2	23.3%
2003	DEN	11	302	189	62.6%	2183	15	7	2	5.3%	6.7	4	24.4%	6	49.6	8	62.3	37	205	3	7.7	27.6%
2004	DEN	16	521	303	58.2%	4089	27	20	4	3.8%	7.4	4	11.5%	12	56.4	11	72.5	62	202	1	-2.6	-27.4%
2005	*DEN*	16	495	295	59.6%	3541	26	17	—	—	6.7	—	—	—	—	—	—	44	133	2		

Plummer took a step back in his second year under Mike Shanahan, with a lower DVOA, a lower completion percentage, and nearly three times the interceptions. On the other hand, he set the Denver record for passing yards in a season, which pretty much says it all about raw passing yardage as the main yardstick for quarterback performance. His play is still punctuated by too many bone-headed plays (such as a left-handed toss for an interception last season) and the jury is out as to whether he's really an upgrade over the man he replaced, Brian Griese.

Jonathan Quinn   Height: 6-6   Weight: 240   College: Middle Tennessee State   Born: 27-Feb-1975 Age: 30

Year	Team	G	Att	Comp	Pct	Yds	TD	INT	FUM	Sck%	NtY/P	Rank	DVOA	Rank	DPAR	Rank	PAR	Runs	Yds	TD	DPAR	DVOA
2002	KC	1	0	0	0.0%	0	0	0	—	—	—	—	—	—	—	—	—	1	-1	0	—	—
2003	KC	0	0	0	0.0%	0	0	0	—	—	—	—	—	—	—	—	—	0	0	0	—	—
2004	CHI	5	98	51	52.0%	413	1	3	—	13.0%	2.8	42	-56.6%	40	-19.4	38	-23.3	3	35	0	—	—

The Bears actually had a good scheme set up to protect the journeyman Quinn, leaving him a short receiver if the blitz got to him, but most of the time Quinn just threw the ball away. It's hard to believe he'll get a job with another team this year.

Patrick Ramsey   Height: 6-2   Weight: 218   College: Tulane   Born: 14-Feb-1979 Age: 26

Year	Team	G	Att	Comp	Pct	Yds	TD	INT	FUM	Sck%	NtY/P	Rank	DVOA	Rank	DPAR	Rank	PAR	Runs	Yds	TD	DPAR	DVOA
2002	WAS	10	228	117	51.3%	1539	9	8	8	7.0%	5.7	28	1.2%	26	14.2	26	7.0	13	-1	1	0.2	-10.8%
2003	WAS	11	338	180	53.3%	2169	14	9	7	7.4%	5.3	31	-6.4%	24	10.3	25	6.5	15	62	1	1.9	13.2%
2004	WAS	9	272	169	62.1%	1665	10	11	6	7.1%	5.2	31	-12.4%	30	1.0	30	-2.1	10	19	0	-0.1	-25.2%
2005	*WAS*	*10*	*254*	*150*	*59.2%*	*1687*	*12*	*9*	—	—	*5.7*	—	—	—	—	—	—	*7*	*29*	*0*		

Right now the Redskins say Patrick Ramsey is their starter, but they'll obviously give every opportunity to Jason Campbell, and Joe Gibbs seems to be the only man left in America who hasn't completely given up on Mark Brunell. Will Ramsey start the season as the starter? Probably. Will he end the season as the starter? It's anyone's guess. That projection sort of gives away our opinion, doesn't it?

Tim Rattay   Height: 6-0   Weight: 215   College: Louisiana Tech   Born: 15-Feb-1977 Age: 28

Year	Team	G	Att	Comp	Pct	Yds	TD	INT	FUM	Sck%	NtY/P	Rank	DVOA	Rank	DPAR	Rank	PAR	Runs	Yds	TD	DPAR	DVOA
2002	SF	4	43	26	60.5%	232	2	0	2	8.8%	4.4	—	4.4%	—	3.6	—	2.7	5	0	0	-0.1	-32.4%
2003	SF	11	118	73	61.9%	856	7	2	0	5.1%	6.4	9	45.2%	1	29.6	17	24.1	8	0	0	-0.2	-62.7%
2004	SF	9	325	198	60.9%	2169	10	10	11	9.6%	5.4	29	-4.6%	25	13.1	23	5.2	12	55	0	1.9	22.8%
2005	*SF*	*3*	*50*	*30*	*60.0%*	*353*	*3*	*2*	—	—	*6.2*	—	—	—	—	—	—	*7*	*43*	*0*		

Or, as we like to call him, "Mr. Glass." Last year Rattay tore a groin muscle in spring minicamp, lost three weeks during training camp to an "inflamed forearm," separated his shoulder getting sacked in Week 1, missed another game with the same forearm issue, and then tore a tendon on the bottom of his right foot in December. Rattay actually had a 24.7% DVOA in his first four starts, before the forearm flared up again, but a −32.7% DVOA in the five starts after. We have no doubt that if he could stay healthy, he'd be an above-average NFL quarterback. But the 49ers were stuck with the top pick in a draft, no defensive players worth using it on, and nobody who wanted to trade for it. Now they'll roll the economic dice paying big money to Alex Smith rather than roll the medical dice trying to keep Rattay upright. No matter what Mike Nolan says in July, we'll be stunned if Rattay is starting when the season begins.

Philip Rivers   Height: 6-4   Weight: 226   College: North Carolina State   Born: 8-Dec-1981   Age: 23

Year	Team	G	Att	Comp	Pct	Yds	TD	INT	FUM	Sck%	NtY/P	Rank	DVOA	Rank	DPAR	Rank	PAR	Runs	Yds	TD	DPAR	DVOA
2004	SD	2	8	5	62.5%	33	1	0	—	0.0%	2.6	—	-36.8%	—	-0.7	—	0.5	5	-5	0	—	—
2005	*SD*	*3*	*39*	*24*	*61.5%*	*265*	*2*	*1*	—	—	*6.2*	—	—	—	—	—	—	*6*	*12*	*0*		

Listen here, young man, this town ain't big enough for the both of us. The Chargers are in a very awkward situation because they were much higher on Rivers than were most other teams. At North Carolina State he showed an awkward delivery and not a great arm. Excess cap room allowed the Chargers to keep both for this year, but unless Drew Brees comes out of the gate having a lousy year, the Chargers will have to try to trade Rivers. There's no way they'll get anything close to the fourth pick in the draft for him. Trading down and picking up extra choices was a wise move by the Chargers, but adding Rivers wasn't.

Ben Roethlisberger   Height: 6-4   Weight: 242   College: Miami (Ohio)   Born: 2-Mar-1981   Age: 24

Year	Team	G	Att	Comp	Pct	Yds	TD	INT	FUM	Sck%	NtY/P	Rank	DVOA	Rank	DPAR	Rank	PAR	Runs	Yds	TD	DPAR	DVOA
2004	PIT	14	295	196	66.4%	2621	17	11	2	9.0%	7.4	5	40.3%	3	75.3	10	62.8	56	144	1	3.5	1.8%
2005	*PIT*	*16*	*456*	*291*	*63.8%*	*3507*	*22*	*16*	—	—	*6.6*	—	—	—	—	—	—	*55*	*182*	*2*		

Since 1978, the first-year starting quarterbacks with the most statistical similarity to Big Ben are Tom Brady in 2001, Joe Montana in 1980, Jim McMahon in 1982, and Brett Favre in 1992. There's no doubt that he's something special, and the future looks very good. That being said, his role in Pittsburgh's 15–1 season was a bit overrated—he had only one game with more than 25 pass attempts—and the team has to be worried about the Walter Hudson-sized case of the yips that he picked up during the playoffs. Teams discovered that you could, in fact, pressure him with a blitz, and he went from being sacked 9 times in his first seven games to 21 times in his last seven. Brady in 2002, Favre in 1993, and Brad Johnson in 1997 (also on Big Ben's comparables list) each saw both yards per attempt and completion percentage drop in year two and then took a big leap forward in year three. The Steelers won't win 15 games again and the running backs might show their age, so Big Ben will have to throw more, and it is very reasonable to believe that he may face a similar sophomore slump and then raise his game in 2006.

Aaron Rodgers Height: 6-2 Weight: 210 College: California Born: 2-Dec-1983 Age: 22

Year	Team	G	Att	Comp	Pct	Yds	TD	INT	FUM	Sck%	NtY/P	Rank	DVOA	Rank	DPAR	Rank	PAR	Runs	Yds	TD	DPAR	DVOA
2005	GB	3	41	24	57.8%	249	2	2	—	—	5.5	—	—	—	—	—	—	5	23	0		

Every sportswriter in America has now had the chance to advise Rodgers how much better off he is for having plummeted in the first round from potential first-overall selection to the Packers at number 24, and most of them have taken advantage of the opportunity. We recognize that there's a certain $12 million or so missing from Rodgers's bank account that might suggest otherwise, but it's hard to argue against the merits of his current situation. Unlike most high-first-round QBs who get thrown to the wolves on bad teams, Rodgers could probably read the paper on the sidelines in Green Bay this fall à la Steamin' Willie Beamon without missing much. Really, can you name a Packers' backup QB of the Brett Favre era? So our advice to the big-armed, but Jeff Tedford-tainted Rodgers—sit back, watch Brett work, and plan your long-term investment strategy. In three years you can reintroduce yourself to the American sporting public.

Sage Rosenfels Height: 6-4 Weight: 218 College: Iowa State Born: 6-Mar-1978 Age: 27

Year	Team	G	Att	Comp	Pct	Yds	TD	INT	FUM	Sck%	NtY/P	Rank	DVOA	Rank	DPAR	Rank	PAR	Runs	Yds	TD	DPAR	DVOA
2002	MIA	4	3	0	0.0%	0	0	0	—	22.3%	-1.8	—	-108.3%	—	-1.5	—	-1.9	1	-2	0	—	—
2003	MIA	2	6	4	66.7%	50	1	0	—	0.0%	8.3	—	98.1%	—	2.7	—	2.4	1	-1	0	—	—
2004	MIA	3	39	16	41.0%	264	1	3	—	7.1%	5.7	—	-67.8%	—	-9.8	—	-13.3	0	0	0	—	—
2005	MIA	—	—	—	—	—	—	—	—	—	—	—	—	—	—	—	—	—	—	—	—	—

"The Ultimate Sage Rosenfels Experience" was the name of an auction item that was available last off-season to the hard-core fan who wanted to see what it was like to hang around with a real, live NFL quarterback. Fans could bid big bucks for the opportunity to hang with Sage. That he succeeded at raising money with the venture (all the money went to a charity for people with disabilities in his native Iowa) indicates that he's a better self-promoter than he is a quarterback. The Dolphins had so much faith in his backup abilities that they signed Gus Frerotte.

Matt Schaub Height: 6-5 Weight: 237 College: Virginia Born: 25-Jun-1981 Age: 24

Year	Team	G	Att	Comp	Pct	Yds	TD	INT	FUM	Sck%	NtY/P	Rank	DVOA	Rank	DPAR	Rank	PAR	Runs	Yds	TD	DPAR	DVOA
2004	ATL	6	70	33	47.1%	330	1	4	1	5.6%	4.3	—	-70.7%	—	-18.0	—	-14.4	8	26	0	-0.5	-32.9%
2005	ATL	3	74	40	53.5%	511	2	3	—	—	6.1	—	—	—	—	—	—	6	18	0		

After lighting it up last August, Schaub went from preseason promise to in-season implosion faster than you can say Michael Bishop. Still, he'll be the first guy to get the call when Michael Vick's inevitable first injury of the season occurs.

Chris Simms Height: 6-4 Weight: 220 College: Texas Born: 29-Aug-1980 Age: 25

Year	Team	G	Att	Comp	Pct	Yds	TD	INT	FUM	Sck%	NtY/P	Rank	DVOA	Rank	DPAR	Rank	PAR	Runs	Yds	TD	DPAR	DVOA
2003	TB	0	0	0	0.0%	0	0	0	—	—	—	—	—	—	—	—	—	0	0	0	—	—
2004	TB	5	73	42	57.5%	467	1	3	2	12.5%	4.7	—	-33.1%	—	-7.6	—	-10.3	7	14	0	-0.5	-39.1%
2005	TB	—	—	—	—	—	—	—	—	—	—	—	—	—	—	—	—	—	—	—	—	—

Simms's early NFL career seems to be suffering the fate of his star-crossed career at the University of Texas: plenty of promise, an occasional eye-opening play, and little production when it actually matters. Injury short-circuited his starting opportunity in 2004, and now he finds himself stuck behind Brian Griese on the depth chart. Still, if he's going to develop into a quality NFL quarterback, it'll probably be in Tampa Bay under Jon Gruden, who has squeezed career years out of nearly every QB he's worked with.

Alex Smith Height: 6-3 Weight: 212 College: Utah Born: 7-May-1984 Age: 21

Year	Team	G	Att	Comp	Pct	Yds	TD	INT	FUM	Sck%	NtY/P	Rank	DVOA	Rank	DPAR	Rank	PAR	Runs	Yds	TD	DPAR	DVOA
2005	SF	16	502	278	55.3%	3186	17	17	—	—	5.4	—	—	—	—	—	—	45	180	2		

Did San Francisco make the correct choice in selecting Smith the first-overall pick in the draft? Check back in three years for the answer. Certainly, Smith is an intriguing prospect after serving as the trigger man in Utah's explosive spread-option offense for two seasons. The offense Smith ran in college barely resembles an NFL attack, but then again, neither

(continued next page)

Alex Smith (continued)

did San Francisco's offense last year. Still, there is always concern any time a QB comes out of a shotgun-oriented attack into the NFL, but Smith is one of the brightest prospects to enter the league in years. He earned a college economics degree in under three years and carried a 3.74 GPA, indications that he should be able to shorten the learning curve.

Jim Sorgi

Jim Sorgi Height: 6-3 Weight: 194 College: Wisconsin Born: 3-Dec-1980 Age: 25

Year	Team	G	Att	Comp	Pct	Yds	TD	INT	FUM	Sck%	NtY/P	Rank	DVOA	Rank	DPAR	Rank	PAR	Runs	Yds	TD	DPAR	DVOA
2004	IND	4	29	17	58.6%	175	2	0	1	6.5%	5.2	—	4.8%	—	2.6	—	1.3	8	-5	0	-0.3	-73.6%
2005	IND	—	—	—	—	—	—	—	—	—	—	—	—	—	—	—	—	—	—	—	—	—

Let's see... he's a sixth-round quarterback, from a Big Ten school, going into his second season, playing behind the highest-paid quarterback in football. We feel very confident that if the Colts can just get Peyton Manning injured, three out of four Super Bowls will follow.

Kordell Stewart

Kordell Stewart Height: 6-1 Weight: 217 College: Colorado Born: 16-Oct-1972 Age: 33

Year	Team	G	Att	Comp	Pct	Yds	TD	INT	FUM	Sck%	NtY/P	Rank	DVOA	Rank	DPAR	Rank	PAR	Runs	Yds	TD	DPAR	DVOA
2002	PIT	8	166	109	65.7%	1155	6	6	4	4.9%	6.4	12	6.3%	20	14.6	25	19.2	43	191	2	-1.4	-28.0%
2003	CHI	9	251	126	50.2%	1418	7	12	6	9.2%	4.6	43	-39.2%	44	-28.9	47	-27.4	59	290	3	5.9	-4.5%
2004	BAL	2	0	0	0.0%	0	0	0	—	—	—	—	—	—	—	—	—	1	-1	0	—	—
2005	BAL	—	—	—	—	—	—	—	—	—	—	—	—	—	—	—	—	—	—	—	—	—

Stewart threw no passes last year but punted five times after Dave Zastudil got injured early in the Week 10 game against the Jets. Twice he pinned the Jets behind their own ten-yard line. You heard lots of jokes last year about how "If X was quarterback in Arizona, the Cardinals would have won the NFC West," but here's one you didn't hear—if Kordell Stewart was the punter in St. Louis all season, the Rams would have won the NFC West. Instead, he's still a lousy backup quarterback in Baltimore.

Vinny Testaverde

Vinny Testaverde Height: 6-5 Weight: 235 College: Miami Born: 13-Nov-1963 Age: 42

Year	Team	G	Att	Comp	Pct	Yds	TD	INT	FUM	Sck%	NtY/P	Rank	DVOA	Rank	DPAR	Rank	PAR	Runs	Yds	TD	DPAR	DVOA
2002	NYJ	5	83	54	65.1%	499	3	3	2	9.5%	4.8	—	-16.1%	—	-1.2	—	-3.3	2	23	0	1.2	148.8%
2003	NYJ	7	198	123	62.1%	1385	7	2	1	3.0%	6.5	7	29.4%	4	37.0	12	33.5	6	13	0	1.0	62.8%
2004	DAL	16	495	297	60.0%	3532	17	20	7	6.2%	6.3	15	3.2%	17	36.5	16	28.7	21	38	1	0.5	-12.9%

Testaverde is the NFL equivalent of what our buddies at *Baseball Prospectus* call an "innings eater." Once considered a colossal bust, he has done well to fashion an 18-year NFL career, during which he was mostly at least an average QB. He is the only player in the NFL to hold the passing yards record both for a team and against that team (Baltimore, to be precise). Unsigned at press time, he'll end up as somebody's backup this season, and you could certainly do worse than to have him on your bench.

Michael Vick

Michael Vick Height: 6-0 Weight: 210 College: Virginia Tech Born: 28-Jun-1980 Age: 25

Year	Team	G	Att	Comp	Pct	Yds	TD	INT	FUM	Sck%	NtY/P	Rank	DVOA	Rank	DPAR	Rank	PAR	Runs	Yds	TD	DPAR	DVOA
2002	ATL	15	421	231	54.9%	2936	16	8	9	8.0%	5.9	23	18.5%	8	58.5	11	49.9	112	796	8	23.6	21.4%
2003	ATL	5	100	50	50.0%	585	4	3	3	9.4%	4.7	41	-19.9%	35	-3.2	33	-4.7	40	255	1	12.1	45.1%
2004	ATL	15	321	181	56.4%	2313	14	12	15	12.6%	5.6	24	-24.9%	36	-18.5	37	-14.3	120	902	3	29.2	25.9%
2005	ATL	14	369	213	57.8%	2585	16	14	—	—	5.7	—	—	—	—	—	—	103	761	4		

Nobody thinks less of what Michael Vick did last year than we do. Yes, it says he ranked 36th among quarterbacks in DVOA, and for all those scoring at home, there can only be 32 starting quarterbacks. If you factor in his impressive rushing DPAR, he becomes slightly more valuable than a replacement player. Of course, look back to his first full season in 2002, when at the age of 22, he had a DVOA higher than that of any Tom Brady or Donovan McNabb season until last year. The question is, who stole the Michael Vick of 2002, and where did they hide him? Most people blame the West Coast offense, which takes several years to learn and could be poorly suited for Vick's talents. Of course, Vick posted equally bad numbers in 2003 after returning from his injury, before Atlanta was playing the West Coast. And no offensive system causes you to sail one pass ten yards over Alge Crumpler's head and then bounce the next one six yards in front of Peerless Price. If the Vick of 2002 comes back, our low expectations for the 2005 Falcons will look awfully silly. But if the Vick of 2002 doesn't come back soon, Vick's supporters will look awfully silly.

Billy Volek Height: 6-2 Weight: 214 College: Fresno State Born: 28-Apr-1976 Age: 29

Year	Team	G	Att	Comp	Pct	Yds	TD	INT	FUM	Sck%	NtY/P	Rank	DVOA	Rank	DPAR	Rank	PAR	Runs	Yds	TD	DPAR	DVOA
2002	TEN	0	0	0	0.0%	0	0	0	—	—	—	—	—	—	—	—	—	0	0	0	—	—
2003	TEN	7	69	44	63.8%	545	4	1	1	7.8%	6.8	—	37.1%	—	16.9	—	17.4	11	4	1	0.4	-3.9%
2004	TEN	10	357	218	61.1%	2486	18	10	6	9.0%	5.9	21	-10.2%	27	5.0	28	24.8	11	50	1	1.9	11.1%
2005	*TEN*	*8*	*142*	*81*	*57.0%*	*961*	*8*	*5*	—	—	*5.8*	—	—	—	—	—	—	*5*	*46*	*1*		

This year's least-consistent quarterback. How many fantasy playoff games were lost when Volek went from 492 yards and four TDs to 111 yards and zero TDs in one week? Still, Volek showed enough in his stint as the starter last year that he'll probably be the Titans' next full-time starter once Steve McNair is eventually driven into retirement by his injuries.

Kurt Warner Height: 6-2 Weight: 220 College: Northern Iowa Born: 22-Jun-1971 Age: 34

Year	Team	G	Att	Comp	Pct	Yds	TD	INT	FUM	Sck%	NtY/P	Rank	DVOA	Rank	DPAR	Rank	PAR	Runs	Yds	TD	DPAR	DVOA
2002	STL	7	220	144	65.5%	1431	3	11	8	7.9%	5.4	38	-16.8%	38	-3.8	39	-20.7	8	33	0	0.6	-4.8%
2003	STL	3	65	38	58.5%	365	1	1	—	8.1%	4.4	—	-56.1%	—	-12.9	—	-10.2	1	0	0	—	—
2004	NYG	10	277	174	62.8%	2054	6	4	12	12.0%	5.9	23	-0.5%	19	16.9	22	20.1	13	30	1	2.6	36.8%
2005	*ARI*	*13*	*380*	*221*	*58.2%*	*2737*	*14*	*11*	—	—	*6.4*	—	—	—	—	—	—	*16*	*55*	*0*		

Kurt Warner is the football version of Charley from the book *Flowers for Algernon.* For those of you who never had to read this novel in high school, Charley is a mentally disabled janitor who submits to a scientific experiment that turns him into a genius intellect. Unfortunately, the effect is only temporary, and as Charley gradually loses his intelligence he is stuck with the knowledge that he used to be able to do things that he can't do today, and tomorrow it is going to be worse, and there's nothing he can do about it. Warner's change was physical, not mental—a meteoric rise from grocery bagger to NFL MVP. But since a thumb injury in 2002, Warner has gotten worse and worse, unable to do the marvelous things he once could do, constantly trying to prove that he is still an NFL starter and not once again the football equivalent of a mentally disabled janitor. A couple big games early had people thinking he had the magic again, but eventually he showed he couldn't hit receivers in stride anymore. He held onto the ball when he should have thrown it (39 sacks), and he dropped it when he should have held onto it (12 fumbles). He was horrific in the red zone, with a −107% DVOA. In Arizona he'll have better receivers, but a worse running game, and while they don't expect the Warner of 1999, his skills keep slipping away like Charley's intellect.

Going Deep

Derek Anderson, BAL: Quarterback math: Huge QB (6′6″, 239 lbs.) + great arm + couldn't beat Drew Bledsoe in a foot race = late-sixth-round pick.

Charlie Batch, PIT: Quarterback math: David Woodley + Bubby Brister − Mark Malone = Charlie Batch.

Todd Bouman, NO: Looked great in three starts in 2001 (5.8% DVOA) but has thrown 20 passes since. Bouman is the only player from St. Cloud State ever to score an NFL touchdown.

Travis Brown, IND: Will battle with Jim Sorgi for the number two job in Indianapolis. If Manning actually gets hurt, they start scheduling tractor pulls inside the dome on Sundays.

Matt Cassel, NE: Cassel never started a game at USC and threw fewer career passes than Matt Leinart does in a day's work. Yet he merited a seventh-round pick. How'd that taste, Jason White?

Timmy Chang, ARI: The NCAA's all-time passing leader, Chang has a weak arm and earned college fame by throwing six-yard passes in a run 'n' shoot offense. Unpredictable Denny Green could still give him a look.

Tim Couch, FA: A quarterback haiku: "Another big bust/Consigned to the great scrap heap/Just like Akili."

Ryan Fitzpatrick, STL: We have a soft spot for Ivy Leaguers in the NFL, and this seventh-round pick out of Harvard gives Mike Martz someone to play chess with. Fitzpatrick had 448 rushing yards last year, 384 more than the next-highest Ivy League QB.

Chad Friehauf, DEN: An undrafted free agent from the Colorado School of Mines who won the Harlon Hill Trophy as the best player in Division II. We just like saying "Colorado School of Mines."

Andy Hall, PHI: A practice-squad QB from Delaware whom Andy Reid hopes to parlay into a future high draft pick, A. J. Feeley style.

Jason Garrett, MIA: Quarterback math: Earl Morrall – Steve DeBerg = Jason Garrett.

David Greene, SEA: Greene is similar to Eric Zeier, the Georgia quarterback of the mid-1990s who was drafted by the Browns and hung around several benches for half a decade. Both players were heady leaders with good "game management" skills and so-so arms. "Game management" often means "He was good at handing off to Thomas Brown or Garrison Hearst and letting the defense win games for him."

Tim Hasselbeck, NYG: A quarterback haiku: "Play near your wife's job/But we have some sage advice/Steer clear of Star Jones."

Shaun Hill, MIN: Has three years of clipboard experience. Local prep star and University of North Dakota star John "Cougar" Bowenkamp will beat him for the number three job in August.

Brock Huard, SEA: The better-looking Huard brother by far. Brock has sort of a Dolph Lundgren thing going; Damon looks like the love child of Morten Andersen and Tyne Daly.

Damon Huard, KC: The Huard brothers have thrown 21 passes since the 2001 season. But those paychecks are nice.

Danny Kanell, DEN: Denver's quarterback depth chart also features Bradlee Van Pelt and Matt Mauck. If Jake Plummer goes down with an injury, it is not going to be pretty.

Kurt Kittner, CHI: In the Star Trek Mirror Universe, Kittner is the starting quarterback for the Falcons, as Michael Vick was eaten by the Jem Hadar. He has a really cool goatee, too.

Stefan LeFors, CAR: At 6′4″, LeFors probably would have been a first-round pick. At 6′1″, he fell in the draft but is still a nice backup to groom behind Jake Delhomme. (How tall is he, exactly? Oh yeah, 6′2″.)

Jared Lorenzen, NYG: At over 325 pounds, he may not be a suitable backup quarterback for the Giants. But he would be a fine mascot.

Jim Miller, FA: Pointless fact: Miller has carried the ball 55 times for 4 yards in his career, or .072 yards per attempt and 0.33 yards per year, roughly the same rate at which Madagascar is moving away from Africa.

Rick Mirer, FA: Will be looking for employer number eight this off-season. Cats have nine lives, but former first-round picks don't have quite as many.

J. T. O'Sullivan, GB: Had the rug pulled from under his career faster than you can say "Aaron Rodgers."

Daniel Orlovsky, DET: Not to be confused with Russian history scholar Daniel Orlovsky of Southern Methodist University. This fifth-round pick led the Connecticut Huskies into the big time of Division I-A football and now gets a front row seat for the coming Harrington-Garcia quarterback controversy.

Jesse Palmer, NYG: Think reality TV is good for your football career? Ask Brian Billick how that appearance on *Match Game* turned out.

Dave Ragone, HOU: Ragone has been unable to unseat Tony Banks as David Carr's primary backup, but he was the leading passer this summer in NFL Europe.

Bryan Randall, ATL: Randall is a Virginia Tech product that was likely brought in to be a training camp arm. Will he cause tension because he kept Michael Vick's younger brother largely on the bench in their one season together with the Hokies?

Chris Redman, FA: Redman had a 0.6% DVOA in 2002, his only year of significant playing time, with 7 touchdowns and only 3 interceptions. The Ravens drafted Kyle Boller to replace him, and he was terrible in limited time in 2003, then missed all of 2004 with back surgery. He had signed with the Patriots but lost his roster spot to Doug Flutie. Will somebody please give this guy a chance?

Tony Romo, DAL: Teacher's pet to Cowboys coach Sean Payton. If he were Jerry Jones's pet project, he'd have started nine games by now.

Rod Rutherford, CAR: After not getting into a game as a rookie, Rutherford could be the odd man out on Carolina's depth chart now that the Panthers have drafted Stefan LeFors.

Brian St. Pierre, PIT: Pierre is apparently the patron saint of the kneeldown. St. Pierre will be out of work unless the Steelers trade either Tommy Maddox or Charlie Batch to a team in need of a veteran backup.

Akili Smith, TB: Smith turns 30 in August, so he can't really sell himself as a prospect anymore. A fine candidate to rise Tommy Maddox-like if Vince McMahon ever starts another football league.

Jeff Smoker, STL: A 2004 sixth-round pick out of Michigan State who spent the year behind Marc Bulger and Jamie Martin. Headline writers are dying for this guy to get a shot.

Marques Tuiasosopo, OAK: A quarterback haiku: "Woe! One-game wonder/Stricken with a last name that/Al Davis can't spell."

Seneca Wallace, SEA: Exciting college player on the way out in Seattle. Wallace could shine in the CFL or Arena Football.

Andrew Walter, OAK: A separated throwing shoulder during Arizona State's regular-season finale likely kept Walter from being drafted higher. He's huge, but still has decent mobility and a strong-enough arm. He's also landed in what could be quarterback heaven with the Randy Moss Raiders where he gets to back up Kerry Collins and polish his deep throws.

Anthony Wright, BAL: Wright got hot for seven games in 2003 (–27.9% DVOA was higher than Kyle Boller's that year), but Brian Billick has forgotten about him for now. A survivor type who could pull a Vince Evans and still be on a bench in 2019.

Running Backs

You've heard about "the graying of America" as the Baby Boomer generation gets older. In 2004, we learned about "the graying of the backfield."

Of the 32 players who led their teams in rushing in 2004, seven of them were 30 or older by season's end: Curtis Martin, Jerome Bettis, Emmitt Smith, Marshall Faulk, Priest Holmes, Corey Dillon, and Warrick Dunn (who turned 30 in the playoffs).

Yes, for running backs, college undergrads, and supermodels, 30 is old. And having seven old men among the league's rushing leaders is rare. Back in 1994, only two running backs over 30 led their teams in rushing: Marcus Allen and Herschel Walker (in fact, Faulk, Emmitt, and Bettis were among the 1994 rushing leaders as well). Back in 1984, only three 30-somethings led their teams in rushing: John Riggins, Tony Dorsett, and Walter Payton.

There are many causes for the upswing in graybeards. Emmitt, Bettis, and Martin are all-time greats with almost preternatural durability; every generation has one or two players who can still play regularly well into their 30s. Bettis and Martin also had the advantage of particularly strong offensive lines. Dillon, who turned 30 in October, could prove to be one of those players now that he has escaped Cincinnati. Faulk and Dunn held off younger running backs last year and are starting to fade. Holmes is a unique case because of an early career as a part-time player, but he too can hear the music swelling after missing the second half of last season.

In other words, the rise of the ancient running back isn't a trend, but a bubble that will burst faster than you can say "Eddie George." The new generation of featured runner has arrived: Willis McGahee, Steven Jackson, Julius Jones, Kevin Jones, Ronnie Brown, and others. Not only are these youngsters pushing players like Faulk to the sidelines, they are also ready to push some younger veteran runners like Ahman Green down a few rungs on the league leaderboard.

That's why some of the projections on the pages to come may shock you, like Kevin Jones as the NFL rushing champion. Most fantasy guides project future stats using a glorified cut 'n' paste method: They take last year's stats, add a few hundred yards to the young players getting their first starting jobs, take a few hundred off old-timers like Bettis, and produce statistics that look almost identical to last year's. In reality, there is a great deal of turnover among the top 20 running backs. The KUBIAK projection system reflects this ever-changing landscape.

In the following section we give the last three years' worth of numbers as well as a 2005 projection for every running back who played a role in 2004—major or minor—and/or will likely play a role in 2005 (table 1).

The first line contains biographical data—the player's name, height, weight, college, birthdate, and age. Height and weight are the best data we could find; weight, of course, can fluctuate during the off-season. Age is very simple, the number of years between the player's birth year and 2005, and the full birthdate is given for anyone who wants to either do research involving more complexity or perform an astrological reading on Reuben Droughns.

Next we give the last three years of player stats. The first number is games played. This is the official NFL total and may include games where a player was on special teams but did not carry the ball or catch a pass. The next four columns are familiar: runs, rushing yards, yards per rush (Yd/R, to mark it differently from yards per catch), and rushing touchdowns.

The entry for fumbles (FUM) includes all fumbles by the running back, no matter whether they are recovered by the offense or defense. Holding onto the ball is an identifiable skill; fumbling it so that your own offense can recover

TABLE 1. RUNNING BACK STATISTICS SAMPLE

Corey Dillon   Height: 6-1   Weight: 225   College: Washington   Born: 24-Oct-1975   Age: 30

Year	Team	G	Runs	Yds	Yd/R	TD	FUM	DVOA	Rank	DPAR	Rank	PAR	Suc%	Rec	Pass	Yds	CPct	Yd/C	TD	DVOA	Rank	DPAR	Rank
2002	CIN	16	314	1301	4.1	7	5	1.0%	23	20.5	16	16.8	50%	43	61	298	70%	6.9	1	-3.8%	32	1.8	30
2003	CIN	13	138	540	3.9	2	0	-5.2%	32	5.6	35	5.7	43%	11	18	71	61%	6.5	1	-24.6%	-	-0.9	—
2004	NE	15	345	1646	4.8	12	5	19.8%	8	50.4	2	49.5	54%	15	21	103	71%	6.9	1	0.8%	-	1.0	—
2005	NE	14	290	1226	4.2	10	—	—	—	—	—	—	—	12	—	78	—	6.5	1				

it is not. (For more on this issue, see the New Orleans chapter.) This entry also combines fumbles on both carries and receptions.

The next five columns give our advanced metrics for rushing: DVOA (Defense-adjusted Value Over Average), DPAR (Defense-adjusted Points Above Replacement), and PAR (Points Above Replacement), along with the player's rank in both DVOA and DPAR. These metrics compare every carry by the running back to a league-average baseline based on the game situations in which that running back carried the ball. DVOA and DPAR are also adjusted based on the opposing defense. The methods used to compute these numbers are described in detail in the front of the book. The important distinctions between them are:

- Higher DVOA means more value per carry. Higher DPAR means more total value over the 16-game season.
- A player whose DPAR is higher than his PAR faced a harder-than-average schedule. A player whose PAR is higher than his DPAR faced an easier-than-average schedule.

To qualify for ranking in rushing DVOA and DPAR, a running back must have 75 carries in the given season. 52 running backs are ranked for 2004, 53 for 2003, and 51 for 2002.

The final rushing statistic is Success Rate (Suc%). This number represents running back consistency, measured by successful running plays divided by total running plays. (The definition for success is explained in the "Statistical Toolbox" at the start of the book.) A player with high DVOA and a low Success Rate mixes long runs with downs getting stuffed at the line of scrimmage. A player with low DVOA and a high Success Rate generally gets the yards needed, but doesn't often get more. The league-average Success Rate in 2004 was 46.4%. Success Rate is not adjusted based on defenses faced.

After Success Rate, the remaining numbers give data for each running back as a pass receiver. Receptions (Rec) counts passes caught, while Passes (Pass) counts passes thrown to the player, complete or incomplete. The next four columns list receiving yards, catch percentage (CPct), yards per catch (Yd/C), and receiving touchdowns.

Catch percentage, or receptions divided by total passes, is an attempt to rectify a major problem in conventional statistics, which lay the blame for incomplete passes entirely on quarterbacks. Historical study shows that receivers definitely have an impact on whether a ball is complete or incomplete. We're still working on an estimate of how much responsibility for an incomplete belongs to the quarterback as opposed to the receiver, but it is clearly closer to 50–50 than it is to the 100–0 currently reflected in NFL stats. The average NFL running back caught 73% of passes in 2004.

Finally we have receiving DVOA and DPAR, which are entirely separate from rushing DVOA and DPAR. To qualify for ranking in receiving DVOA and DPAR, a running back must have 25 passes thrown to him in the given season. 59 running backs are ranked for 2004, 52 for 2003, and 59 for 2002. Numbers without opponent adjustment (PAR/VOA) can be found on our website, FootballOutsiders.com.

Finally, we have the last row of numbers, 2005 projections. Right now we are only projecting conventional statistics, although in future years we hope to project advanced metrics like DVOA and DPAR. The KUBIAK projection system is based on a complicated regression analysis that takes into account numerous variables including projected role, performance over the past two years, projected team offense and defense, historical comparables, height, weight, age, and strength of schedule.

It is difficult to accurately project statistics for a 162-game baseball season, but it is exponentially more difficult to accurately project statistics for a 16-game football season. Consider the listed projections not as a prediction of exact numbers, but the mean of a range of possible performances. What's important is less the exact number of yards we project, more which players are projected to improve or decline. Actual performance will vary from our projection less for veteran starters and more for rookies and fourth-stringers. Touchdown numbers will vary more than yardage numbers.

A few low-round rookies, guys listed at seventh on the depth chart, and players who are listed as running backs but really only play special teams are briefly discussed at the end of the chapter in a section called "Going Deep." *FA* signifies a player who was still a free agent at press time.

TABLE 2. TOP 20 RB BY RUSHING DPAR (TOTAL VALUE), 2004

Rank	Player	Team	DPAR	Rank	Player	Team	DPAR
1	Curtis Martin	NYJ	54.4	11	Steven Jackson	STL	19.9
2	Corey Dillon	NE	50.3	12	Willis McGahee	BUF	19.6
3	Shaun Alexander	SEA	36.7	13	LaMont Jordan	NYJ	19.2
4	Edgerrin James	IND	34.8	14	Dorsey Levens	PHI	17.9
5	Rudi Johnson	CIN	30.6	15	T. J. Duckett	ATL	17.5
6	Tiki Barber	NYG	29.9	16	Reuben Droughns	DEN	17.0
7	Jerome Bettis	PIT	27.4	17	Jamal Lewis	BAL	16.2
8	Priest Holmes	KC	26.9	18	Brian Westbrook	PHI	15.7
9	Larry Johnson	KC	24.0	19	Tatum Bell	DEN	15.5
10	Derrick Blaylock	KC	22.1	20	Kevin Jones	DET	15.4

TABLE 3. TOP 20 RB BY RUSHING DVOA (VALUE PER RUSH), 2004

Rank	Player	Team	DVOA	Rank	Player	Team	DVOA
1	LaMont Jordan	NYJ	36.0%	11	Tyrone Wheatley	OAK	14.0%
2	Tatum Bell	DEN	33.9%	12	Jerome Bettis	PIT	11.8%
3	Dorsey Levens	PHI	29.8%	13	Shaun Alexander	SEA	10.6%
4	Larry Johnson	KC	28.0%	14	Edgerrin James	IND	9.9%
5	Derrick Blaylock	KC	25.9%	15	Brian Westbrook	PHI	8.1%
6	T. J. Duckett	ATL	22.9%	16	Chester Taylor	BAL	7.8%
7	Corey Dillon	NE	19.7%	17	Tiki Barber	NYG	7.0%
8	Curtis Martin	NYJ	19.7%	18	Sammy Morris	MIA	6.2%
9	Steven Jackson	STL	17.9%	19	Rudi Johnson	CIN	5.1%
10	Priest Holmes	KC	16.3%	20	Ladell Betts	WAS	4.6%

TABLE 4. TOP 10 RB BY RECEIVING DPAR (TOTAL VALUE), 2004

Rank	Player	Team	DPAR
1	Edgerrin James	IND	14.7
2	Brian Westbrook	PHI	14.4
3	Onterrio Smith	MIN	13.5
4	Larry Johnson	KC	13.0
5	Domanick Davis	HOU	12.3
6	Tiki Barber	NYG	11.8
7	Nick Goings	CAR	8.8
8	Kevin Faulk	NE	8.2
9	Jerald Sowell	NYJ	7.1
10	Moe Williams	MIN	6.9

TABLE 5. TOP 10 RB BY RECEIVING DVOA (VALUE PER PASS), 2004

Rank	Player	Team	DVOA
1	Larry Johnson	KC	76.9%
2	Kevin Faulk	NE	46.8%
3	Moe Williams	MIN	44.9%
4	Onterrio Smith	MIN	43.2%
5	Edgerrin James	IND	40.2%
6	Obafemi Ayanbadejo	ARI	23.4%
7	Justin Griffith	ATL	21.8%
8	Brian Westbrook	PHI	21.6%
9	Tiki Barber	NYG	21.1%
10	Maurice Hicks	SF	20.6%

Rabih Abdullah

Height: 6-0 **Weight:** 220 **College:** Lehigh **Born:** 27-Apr-1975 **Age:** 30

Year	Team	G	Runs	Yds	Yd/R	TD	FUM	DVOA	Rank	DPAR	Rank	PAR	Suc%	Rec	Pass	Yds	CPct	Yd/C	TD	DVOA	Rank	DPAR	Rank
2002	CHI	0	0	0	0.0	0	—	—	—	—	—	—	—	0	—	0	—	0.0	0	—	—	—	—
2003	CHI	15	18	37	2.1	0	0	-56.5%	—	-3.4	—	-3.1	28%	8	9	55	89%	6.9	0	10.1%	—	0.6	—
2004	NE	9	13	13	1.0	1	0	-19.6%	—	-0.3	—	-0.9	23%	1	2	9	50%	9.0	0	-64.3%	—	-0.4	—
2005	NE	13	19	79	4.2	0	—	—	—	—	—	—	—	3	—	20	—	7.6	0				

The Patriots like his size and drive on special teams, but he's strictly garbage time when it comes to actually carrying the ball. Shaun Alexander is very angry that he finished one yard short of the alphabetical rushing title.

Shaun Alexander

Height: 5-11 **Weight:** 220 **College:** Alabama **Born:** 30-Aug-1977 **Age:** 28

Year	Team	G	Runs	Yds	Yd/R	TD	FUM	DVOA	Rank	DPAR	Rank	PAR	Suc%	Rec	Pass	Yds	CPct	Yd/C	TD	DVOA	Rank	DPAR	Rank
2002	SEA	16	295	1175	4.0	16	3	-2.7%	28	14.6	23	14.2	42%	59	78	460	76%	7.8	2	-1.3%	30	3.2	25
2003	SEA	16	326	1435	4.4	14	4	8.0%	12	31.8	5	33.4	48%	42	59	295	71%	7.0	2	1.6%	23	2.9	16
2004	SEA	16	353	1696	4.8	16	5	10.6%	13	36.7	3	37.9	46%	23	38	170	61%	7.4	4	-3.2%	31	1.4	32
2005	SEA	16	351	1547	4.4	13	—	—	—	—	—	—	—	34	—	257	—	7.6	2				

One thing we haven't heard anyone mention in the controversy over Shaun Alexander selfishly wanting the league rushing title is what Barry Sanders did in the last game of his rookie year. The Chiefs' game was already over, and Kansas City's Christian Okoye had finished the season as the league leader with 1,480 yards. The Lions' game was still going on, and Sanders had 1,470 yards. The Lions had a comfortable lead in the fourth quarter, and Sanders had already gained 158 yards that day, so they could easily have just handed off to Sanders as many times as they needed to until he got those 11 yards. Instead, Sanders went to Wayne Fontes and asked him to give the ball to fullback Tony Paige, saying Paige had worked hard all year and deserved to get some carries. Shaun Alexander could learn a lot from Barry Sanders.

Mike Alstott

Height: 6-1 **Weight:** 248 **College:** Purdue **Born:** 21-Dec-1973 **Age:** 31

Year	Team	G	Runs	Yds	Yd/R	TD	FUM	DVOA	Rank	DPAR	Rank	PAR	Suc%	Rec	Pass	Yds	CPct	Yd/C	TD	DVOA	Rank	DPAR	Rank
2002	TB	16	146	548	3.8	5	4	-7.4%	34	5.5	34	2.9	44%	35	48	242	73%	6.9	2	-5.8%	37	1.0	37
2003	TB	4	27	77	2.9	2	0	-9.0%	—	0.9	—	1.5	48%	10	12	83	83%	8.3	0	44.8%	—	2.7	—
2004	TB	14	67	230	3.4	2	2	-9.5%	—	1.7	—	2.1	55%	29	41	202	71%	7.0	0	-27.3%	54	-3.6	53
2005	TB	13	61	213	3.5	2	—	—	—	—	—	—	—	18	—	136	—	7.3	0				

He's 31, he's slowed down, and he's not much of a lead blocker. It's hard to imagine him making much of an impact in the league in 2005 and beyond. With Carnell Williams in the mix, he's not likely to see many goal line carries, his one-time specialty. But off the field, he's the most popular player in Buccaneers team history. A year after Tampa Bay released community icon John Lynch, the team agreed to a reworked deal that should allow Alstott to retire a Buccaneer. Whether that happens in training camp or following the 2005 season or beyond remains to be seen.

Mike Anderson

Height: 6-0 **Weight:** 230 **College:** Utah **Born:** 21-Sep-1973 **Age:** 32

Year	Team	G	Runs	Yds	Yd/R	TD	FUM	DVOA	Rank	DPAR	Rank	PAR	Suc%	Rec	Pass	Yds	CPct	Yd/C	TD	DVOA	Rank	DPAR	Rank
2002	DEN	15	84	386	4.6	2	2	-2.0%	26	5.2	35	7.3	54%	17	25	165	72%	9.7	2	9.9%	18	3.0	26
2003	DEN	12	70	257	3.7	3	2	-29.6%	—	-4.7	—	-2.1	46%	12	15	53	80%	4.4	2	-25.5%	—	-1.1	—
2004	DEN	0	0	0	0.0	0	—	0.0%	0	0.0	0	0.0	0%	0	—	0	—	0.0	0	—	—	—	—
2005	DEN	13	17	73	4.2	1	—	—	—	—	—	—	—	6	—	39	—	6.0	1				

When Clinton Portis emerged, Anderson moved to fullback, and when Portis was traded, Anderson was excited to return to halfback. That lasted long enough for Anderson to tear his groin in a preseason game and go on injured reserve for the season. He's supposed to be part of the competition for the starting halfback job, but we expect he'll generally be making his appearances at fullback again.

Richie Anderson

Height: 6-2 **Weight:** 230 **College:** Penn State **Born:** 13-Sep-1971 **Age:** 34

Year	Team	G	Runs	Yds	Yd/R	TD	FUM	DVOA	Rank	DPAR	Rank	PAR	Suc%	Rec	Pass	Yds	CPct	Yd/C	TD	DVOA	Rank	DPAR	Rank
2002	NYJ	16	5	27	5.4	0	0	27.0%	—	0.8	—	0.8	40%	45	56	257	80%	5.7	1	-5.3%	35	1.4	34
2003	DAL	15	70	306	4.4	1	2	-0.6%	—	3.7	—	4.3	44%	69	87	493	79%	7.1	4	9.3%	18	6.6	9
2004	DAL	12	57	246	4.3	1	1	-3.6%	—	2.3	—	2.3	40%	26	41	207	63%	8.0	0	2.7%	29	2.5	28

We've likely seen the last of Anderson in the NFL, although as of press time he had not yet announced his retirement. The Cowboys cut Anderson after off-season surgery to fix a pinched nerve in his neck. Known mainly for his receiving ability, Anderson managed only 1,274 rushing yards over his 12-year NFL career. Lorenzo Neal and Fred McAfee are the only other running backs to have had fewer rushing yards than Anderson over a 12-year career.

J. J. Arrington
Height: 5-9   Weight: 214   College: California   Born: 23-Jan-1983 Age: 22

Year	Team	G	Runs	Yds	Yd/R	TD	FUM	DVOA	Rank	DPAR	Rank	PAR	Suc%	Rec	Pass	Yds	CPct	Yd/C	TD	DVOA	Rank	DPAR	Rank
2005	ARI	16	282	1116	4.0	7	—	—	—	—	—	—	—	27	—	183	—	6.9	0				

Arrington ran for 2,000 yards in a major college conference last season, had at least 100 yards in every game, and averaged over seven yards per carry. So why did he last until the second round of the NFL draft? Must be the 40 time, right? Uh, no. Arrington was one of the fastest backs at the NFL combine. Must be the size, right? Uh, no. Yes, he's 5'9". But so are Emmitt Smith and Barry Sanders and they turned out all right. So what was it? Here's a hint. Starts with a "b" and rhymes with "knocking." As a public service message, we'd like to tell Kurt Warner to think twice about calling any play that requires Arrington to pick up a blitzing linebacker. Still, this was a good pick by Arizona. Arrington can run, and they can teach him the rest.

B. J. Askew
Height: 6-3   Weight: 233   College: Michigan   Born: 19-Aug-1980 Age: 25

Year	Team	G	Runs	Yds	Yd/R	TD	FUM	DVOA	Rank	DPAR	Rank	PAR	Suc%	Rec	Pass	Yds	CPct	Yd/C	TD	DVOA	Rank	DPAR	Rank
2003	NYJ	16	2	9	4.5	0	—	130.8%	—	1.2	—	1.1	100%	0	—	0	—	0.0	0	—	—	—	—
2004	NYJ	10	6	23	3.8	0	0	-23.2%	—	-0.3	—	-0.2	33%	2	2	12	100%	6.0	0	8.4%	—	0.2	—
2005	NYJ	14	12	53	4.3	0	—	—	—	—	—	—	—	5	—	37	—	7.5	0				

It's a truism that players who are good at a lot of little things don't get as much credit as players who are really good at one big thing, and that certainly applies to Askew. He'll never be a team's leading rusher or receiver, but you can line him up as a fullback and he'll block for you, line him up on the kickoff team and he'll tackle for you, or line him up on the punt team and he'll protect for you. Every team needs a few guys like that.

Obafemi Ayanbadejo
Height: 6-2   Weight: 235   College: San Diego State   Born: 5-Mar-1975   Age: 30

Year	Team	G	Runs	Yds	Yd/R	TD	FUM	DVOA	Rank	DPAR	Rank	PAR	Suc%	Rec	Pass	Yds	CPct	Yd/C	TD	DVOA	Rank	DPAR	Rank
2003	MIA	16	1	-2	-2.0	0	1	-115.3%	—	-0.6	—	-0.6	0%	12	13	53	92%	4.4	0	-80.9%	—	-3.7	—
2004	ARI	16	30	122	4.1	3	1	19.3%	—	5.1	—	5.3	63%	19	25	171	76%	9.0	1	23.4%	6	4.2	18
2005	ARI	14	24	103	4.4	1	—	—	—	—	—	—	—	8	—	71	—	8.4	0				

A fullback/special teamer who bounced around with the Dolphins and Ravens, Ayanbadejo appeared to be having one of those careers that consists of 12 NFL seasons and about 20 carries per. Then he landed in Arizona, where he found work as a short-yardage back and receiver out of the backfield, and he wasn't bad at either job. He's a long shot to repeat those roles in 2005, and Denny Green will not be happy if he has to give Ayanbadejo 50 touches.

Marion Barber
Height: 5-11 Weight: 221   College: Minnesota   Born: 10-Jun-1983 Age: 22

Year	Team	G	Runs	Yds	Yd/R	TD	FUM	DVOA	Rank	DPAR	Rank	PAR	Suc%	Rec	Pass	Yds	CPct	Yd/C	TD	DVOA	Rank	DPAR	Rank
2005	DAL	15	49	192	3.9	1	—	—	—	—	—	—	—	4	—	59	—	13.3	0				

Barber won't be the explosive back in the NFL he was in college; he lacks the straight-line speed. He could be a nice insurance policy behind Julius Jones if he can get past the typical problems that Big Ten backs have in the NFL. He'll need to learn to find the right hole and let his blocks develop rather than just running straight ahead when he gets the ball.

Tiki Barber
Height: 5-10 Weight: 200   College: Virginia   Born: 7-Apr-1975   Age: 30

Year	Team	G	Runs	Yds	Yd/R	TD	FUM	DVOA	Rank	DPAR	Rank	PAR	Suc%	Rec	Pass	Yds	CPct	Yd/C	TD	DVOA	Rank	DPAR	Rank
2002	NYG	16	303	1386	4.6	11	8	1.5%	22	21.6	12	17.6	43%	69	95	598	73%	8.7	0	-6.3%	38	1.5	32
2003	NYG	16	278	1216	4.4	2	9	-6.0%	35	10.5	27	11.4	47%	69	98	461	70%	6.7	1	-16.7%	39	-2.7	46
2004	NYG	16	322	1518	4.7	13	5	7.0%	17	29.9	6	28.4	48%	52	79	578	66%	11.1	2	21.1%	9	11.8	6
2005	NYG	16	332	1474	4.4	11	—	—	—	—	—	—	—	56	—	473	—	8.4	2				

(continued next page)

Tiki Barber (continued)

Tiki had one of the five best age 29 seasons of all time. Only Priest Holmes and Jim Brown scored more touchdowns at the age of 29 and only Holmes and Barry Sanders gained more yards. Barber is one of six running backs who have gained over 1,500 combined yards and set their career high in combined yards in their age 29 season or later. All but one of the peak seasons has occurred within the last three years. Curtis Martin and Corey Dillon also achieved the feat last season. The other three running backs had mixed success after their peak season. Holmes had another amazing season, which was then followed by his injury-marred 2004 campaign. Barry Sanders was productive at the age of 30 before unexpectedly retiring. Charlie Garner gained less than 1,000 total yards following his 2002 season and barely played at all for Tampa last season. It will be interesting to see how much of a decline, if any, Barber, Martin, and Dillon will see after reaching their peak at an advanced age.

Kevan Barlow

Height: 6-1 Weight: 238 College: Pittsburgh Born: 7-Jan-1979 Age: 26

Year	Team	G	Runs	Yds	Yd/R	TD	FUM	DVOA	Rank	DPAR	Rank	PAR	Suc%	Rec	Pass	Yds	CPct	Yd/C	TD	DVOA	Rank	DPAR	Rank
2002	SF	14	145	675	4.7	4	2	9.8%	10	15.2	22	19.3	53%	14	21	136	67%	9.7	1	-0.2%	—	1.3	—
2003	SF	16	201	1024	5.1	6	5	6.8%	15	18.1	15	18.6	50%	35	44	307	80%	8.8	1	6.5%	20	3.0	14
2004	SF	15	244	822	3.4	7	2	-16.4%	47	-2.5	49	-7.0	37%	35	45	212	78%	6.1	0	5.9%	25	3.7	22
2005	*SF*	*16*	*227*	*889*	*3.9*	*4*	—	—	—	—	—	—	—	*42*	—	*312*	—	*7.3*	*1*				

We're not sure who wants a do-over more, Barlow for last season or the 49ers for the five-year contract and $8 million signing bonus they gave him before it began. His problems in 2004 were the combination of every imaginable factor. Teams keyed on him with eight in the box because they had no fear of the SF receivers. His offensive line was awful. And his struggles got into his head. He would get to the hole and then pause to figure out where he was going, afraid to get hit. As the 49ers improve the team around him, he's going to need to psychologically get back into the place where he trusts his teammates. There's a good chance he'll be sharing the job again, this time with third-round pick Frank Gore.

Darian Barnes

Height: 6-2 Weight: 250 College: Hampton Born: 28-Feb-1980 Age: 25

Year	Team	G	Runs	Yds	Yd/R	TD	FUM	DVOA	Rank	DPAR	Rank	PAR	Suc%	Rec	Pass	Yds	CPct	Yd/C	TD	DVOA	Rank	DPAR	Rank
2002	TB	6	0	0	0.0	0	—	—	—	—	—	—	—	0	—	0	—	0.0	0	—	—	—	—
2003	TB	14	0	0	0.0	0	—	—	—	—	—	—	—	1	1	6	100%	6.0	0	77.7%	—	0.5	—
2004	DAL	16	5	10	2.0	0	1	-130.5%	—	-3.6	—	-3.4	40%	10	14	59	71%	5.9	1	-14.8%	—	-0.3	—
2005	*DAL*	*14*	*9*	*40*	*4.3*	*0*	—	—	—	—	—	—	—	*20*	—	*152*	—	*7.4*	*1*				

The heir apparent to Richie Anderson as a pass-catching fullback in the Cowboy offense. Anderson's departure probably means another 30–40 passes for Barnes. He just has to get past the line of scrimmage with them. He had three catches for zero yards and a fourth for just one.

Fred Beasley

Height: 6-0 Weight: 246 College: Auburn Born: 18-Sep-1974 Age: 31

Year	Team	G	Runs	Yds	Yd/R	TD	FUM	DVOA	Rank	DPAR	Rank	PAR	Suc%	Rec	Pass	Yds	CPct	Yd/C	TD	DVOA	Rank	DPAR	Rank
2002	SF	15	27	75	2.8	0	1	-11.0%	—	1.1	—	1.4	63%	22	32	152	69%	6.9	1	-11.9%	45	-0.3	45
2003	SF	16	17	24	1.4	0	0	-58.7%	—	-3.9	—	-4.2	29%	19	28	184	68%	9.7	1	7.5%	19	2.1	20
2004	SF	13	9	15	1.7	0	0	-21.0%	—	-0.4	—	-0.6	44%	10	25	44	40%	4.4	0	-64.0%	57	-7.3	57
2005	*SF*	*13*	*12*	*51*	*4.3*	*0*	—	—	—	—	—	—	—	*7*	—	*49*	—	*6.7*	*0*				

After making the Pro Bowl in 2003, Beasley battled injuries and was blocking in tandem with one of the worst lines in football. He hardly gets carries at this point, and to add insult to injury, Beasley ranked last in DVOA among all backs who were the target of at least 25 passes.

Tatum Bell

Height: 5-11 Weight: 212 College: Oklahoma State Born: 2-Mar-1981 Age: 24

Year	Team	G	Runs	Yds	Yd/R	TD	FUM	DVOA	Rank	DPAR	Rank	PAR	Suc%	Rec	Pass	Yds	CPct	Yd/C	TD	DVOA	Rank	DPAR	Rank
2004	DEN	14	75	396	5.3	3	1	33.9%	2	15.5	19	17.5	57%	5	7	80	71%	16.0	0	-82.7%	—	-2.5	—
2005	*DEN*	*14*	*228*	*994*	*4.4*	*8*	—	—	—	—	—	—	—	*26*	—	*207*	—	*8.0*	*1*				

Tatum Bell was the best and most consistent running back in Denver last year, but since he was making just a couple plays a week nobody noticed until he finally ran for 123 yards against Miami in Week 14. On the other hand, last year on ESPN's *NFL Matchup* they showed him getting completely destroyed by the Chiefs linebackers and safeties when he tried to pass block. It was just brutal. Plummer got sacked six times, a third of his total for 2004 in one game. If the Broncos don't spend all summer working on Bell's blocking, they're going to have to take him out of the game whenever they have to pass the ball.

Brandon Bennett

Height: 5-11 **Weight:** 220 **College:** South Carolina **Born:** 3-Feb-1973 **Age:** 32

Year	Team	G	Runs	Yds	Yd/R	TD	FUM	DVOA	Rank	DPAR	Rank	PAR	Suc%	Rec	Pass	Yds	CPct	Yd/C	TD	DVOA	Rank	DPAR	Rank
2002	CIN	12	33	155	4.7	0	1	9.0%	—	3.3	—	3.5	42%	18	25	109	72%	6.1	0	-21.4%	50	-1.4	47
2003	CIN	16	56	173	3.1	0	1	-35.0%	—	-4.7	—	-4.8	32%	25	32	176	78%	7.0	1	4.0%	21	1.5	25
2004	CAR	8	6	17	2.8	1	—	-1.0%	—	0.4	—	0.7	33%	0	—	0	—	0.0	0	—	—	—	—
2005	CAR	12	18	74	4.2	0	—	—	—	—	—	—	—	2	—	8	—	4.0	0				

Was signed in the middle of the year after the Panthers put DeShaun Foster on IR, but he didn't do much of note. Sources seem confused on whether he re-signed with Carolina or not, but at this point the Panthers' depth chart at running back includes any man between the ages of 22 and 40 who lives within five hours of the Charlotte metropolitan area.

Michael Bennett

Height: 5-9 **Weight:** 211 **College:** Wisconsin **Born:** 13-Aug-1978 **Age:** 27

Year	Team	G	Runs	Yds	Yd/R	TD	FUM	DVOA	Rank	DPAR	Rank	PAR	Suc%	Rec	Pass	Yds	CPct	Yd/C	TD	DVOA	Rank	DPAR	Rank
2002	MIN	16	255	1296	5.1	5	4	8.5%	11	22.9	10	23.9	50%	37	41	351	90%	9.5	1	32.6%	8	9.5	7
2003	MIN	8	90	447	5.0	1	1	7.1%	13	9.3	30	8.4	45%	12	14	132	86%	11.0	0	57.3%	—	3.5	—
2004	MIN	11	70	276	3.9	1	1	-10.5%	—	0.7	—	0.0	41%	21	23	207	91%	9.9	1	54.3%	—	7.3	—
2005	MIN	14	210	904	4.3	7	—	—	—	—	—	—	—	32	—	262	—	8.1	2				

In terms of straight-ahead speed, Michael Bennett is the fastest running back in the NFL. In 2000, he won the Big Ten championships in the 60-meter dash, the 100-meter dash, and the 200-meter dash (both indoors and outdoors). Track-star speed is of limited value for a running back, which is why the Vikings are always drafting players like Mewelde Moore (better hands, more shake-'n'-bake), Onterrio Smith (more power, better instincts), and Ciatrick Fason (better blocker and interior runner). Bennett's main role is to run draws and sweeps out of four-WR sets, where his speed can be deadly if he gets to the second level. He's an expensive, oft-injured specialist. He's also seems to be the likely starter thanks to Onterrio Smith's suspension.

Cedric Benson

Height: 5-10 **Weight:** 222 **College:** Texas **Born:** 28-Dec-1982 **Age:** 22

Year	Team	G	Runs	Yds	Yd/R	TD	FUM	DVOA	Rank	DPAR	Rank	PAR	Suc%	Rec	Pass	Yds	CPct	Yd/C	TD	DVOA	Rank	DPAR	Rank
2005	CHI	16	297	1166	3.9	7	—	—	—	—	—	—	—	28	—	219	—	7.8	0				

Benson is everything a team could want in a power back, but you have to wonder if there is a little too much wear on the tires after over 1,100 carries—nearly all of them between the tackles—in college at Texas. Worried about predraft comparisons to über-flake Ricky Williams, Benson cut his dreads before the NFL combine. Now that you're in Chicago, Cedric, feel free to grow those babies back. The last Bears running back drafted this high, Penn State's Curtis Enis (number five overall in 1998), once delivered a fire-and-brimstone religious harangue to guests at his own wedding, at which he had married a three-months pregnant former stripper. Chances are it's going to take more than a hairstyle to make Bears fans think Benson's weird. And as long as he punishes the defense for 25 carries a game, nothing else will matter.

Jerome Bettis

Height: 5-11 **Weight:** 252 **College:** Notre Dame **Born:** 16-Feb-1972 **Age:** 33

Year	Team	G	Runs	Yds	Yd/R	TD	FUM	DVOA	Rank	DPAR	Rank	PAR	Suc%	Rec	Pass	Yds	CPct	Yd/C	TD	DVOA	Rank	DPAR	Rank
2002	PIT	12	187	666	3.6	9	1	7.0%	14	16.7	20	15.5	49%	7	9	57	78%	8.1	0	51.1%	—	2.7	—
2003	PIT	16	246	811	3.3	7	5	-14.1%	44	-1.8	46	4.3	48%	13	22	86	59%	6.6	0	-45.0%	—	-3.0	—
2004	PIT	15	250	941	3.8	13	1	11.8%	12	27.4	7	26.7	52%	6	8	46	75%	7.7	0	21.0%	—	1.2	—
2005	PIT	14	154	520	3.4	8	—	—	—	—	—	—	—	6	—	47	—	8.0	0				

Bettis is almost certain to return for a George Blanda-like 40th season in the league. Burned out by 375 carries in 1997, he had three years of decline, made a huge comeback in 2001, had two more years where he seemed at the end of the road, and then had an even more surprising comeback last year. Bettis had 8.8 DPAR on goal-to-go situations inside the

(continued next page)

Jerome Bettis *(continued)*

five-yard line, the best in the NFL. Not all big backs are great short-yardage runners (Ron Dayne), and not all great short-yardage runners are big backs (Priest Holmes). Bettis combines raw size and power with experience and patience, allowing him to consistently get the toughest yards in football. But last season came completely out of nowhere because of the way he also consistently gained the other yards, in the non-short-yardage situations. He's made some noise about retiring, but we're expecting one more season in tandem with Duce Staley. When he does finally decide to call it quits, he'll make a smooth transition to the broadcast booth.

Ladell Betts Height: 5-11 Weight: 220 College: Iowa Born: 27-Aug-1979 Age: 26

Year	Team	G	Runs	Yds	Yd/R	TD	FUM	DVOA	Rank	DPAR	Rank	PAR	Suc%	Rec	Pass	Yds	CPct	Yd/C	TD	DVOA	Rank	DPAR	Rank
2002	WAS	11	65	307	4.7	1	1	-8.6%	—	1.8	—	0.5	40%	12	17	154	71%	12.8	0	59.0%	—	5.0	—
2003	WAS	9	77	255	3.3	2	0	-4.9%	31	3.2	38	3.5	48%	15	23	167	65%	11.1	0	28.1%	—	3.2	—
2004	WAS	16	90	371	4.1	1	0	4.6%	20	7.2	35	8.4	51%	15	25	108	60%	7.2	0	-12.5%	40	-0.5	39
2005	*WAS*	*12*	*35*	*149*	*4.3*	*0*	—	—	—	—	—	—	—	*10*	—	*81*	—	*7.9*	*0*				

Betts was the Redskins' best RB in 2004, putting up a higher DVOA and DPAR than Clinton Portis despite having 250 fewer carries. When given a chance to start in Week 17, Betts gained 118 yards and scored one touchdown in 26 carries. Even if Portis is productive to start the season, it would behoove the Redskins to keep Betts involved in their offense.

Derrick Blaylock Height: 5-9 Weight: 200 College: Stephen F. Austin Born: 23-Aug-1979 Age: 26

Year	Team	G	Runs	Yds	Yd/R	TD	FUM	DVOA	Rank	DPAR	Rank	PAR	Suc%	Rec	Pass	Yds	CPct	Yd/C	TD	DVOA	Rank	DPAR	Rank
2002	KC	9	16	72	4.5	0	0	-1.0%	—	0.7	—	0.8	38%	5	10	47	50%	9.4	0	-36.5%	—	-1.5	—
2003	KC	16	22	112	5.1	2	1	26.0%	—	3.8	—	4.6	55%	15	22	181	68%	12.1	1	-5.0%	—	0.4	—
2004	KC	12	118	539	4.6	8	0	25.9%	5	22.1	10	22.0	57%	25	36	244	69%	9.8	1	17.6%	15	4.6	17
2005	*NYJ*	*16*	*132*	*581*	*4.4*	*6*	—	—	—	—	—	—	—	*26*	—	*217*	—	*8.2*	*1*				

Chiefs' running backs finished 8th, 9th, and 10th in the NFL in DPAR last year, which says a little about their quality and a lot about the Chiefs' offensive line and Al Saunders's system. Blaylock is an outstanding special teamer but a Brand X running back who has no real weaknesses but no overwhelming strengths. He can be effective with the Jets, who also have a strong offensive line, but he won't elevate the offense.

Chris Brown Height: 6-3 Weight: 219 College: Colorado Born: 17-Apr-1981 Age: 24

Year	Team	G	Runs	Yds	Yd/R	TD	FUM	DVOA	Rank	DPAR	Rank	PAR	Suc%	Rec	Pass	Yds	CPct	Yd/C	TD	DVOA	Rank	DPAR	Rank
2003	TEN	11	56	221	3.9	0	1	-20.4%	—	-1.1	—	-2.4	39%	8	9	61	89%	7.6	0	28.1%	—	1.5	—
2004	TEN	11	220	1067	4.9	6	6	-8.0%	38	5.4	37	10.6	43%	20	33	147	61%	7.4	0	-26.1%	52	-2.5	50
2005	*TEN*	*12*	*237*	*999*	*4.2*	*8*	—	—	—	—	—	—	—	*31*	—	*239*	—	*7.7*	*1*				

Handed the starting running back job with the departure of Eddie George, Brown showed flashes of greatness, but his season was undone by injury and fumbles. He averaged almost five yards a carry, but his six fumbles tied for the league lead, despite only 220 carries. Brown can't stay healthy, with ankle issues and then a fairly serious case of turf toe that caused him to miss the final three games of the season. An off-season of rest had him at 100% until he broke his hand at minicamp. He's supposed to be back for the start of 2005, but his upright running style is a huge risk for injury and he will likely have minor ailments whenever he plays.

Ronnie Brown Height: 6-0 Weight: 233 College: Auburn Born: 12-Dec-1981 Age: 23

Year	Team	G	Runs	Yds	Yd/R	TD	FUM	DVOA	Rank	DPAR	Rank	PAR	Suc%	Rec	Pass	Yds	CPct	Yd/C	TD	DVOA	Rank	DPAR	Rank
2005	*MIA*	*16*	*365*	*1381*	*3.8*	*10*	—	—	—	—	—	—	—	*30*	—	*224*	—	*7.5*	*0*				

It was Brown's all-around skills that helped him emerge from the running back pack at the top of this year's draft class. He can run inside or out, is a tremendous receiver out of the backfield, and has less mileage on him than either college teammate Cadillac Williams or Cedric Benson of Texas. New Dolphins coach Nick Saban knows Brown's skills well from coaching against him in the SEC and is likely to build his fledgling offense around the back's diverse skill set. We ran a second projection in case Ricky Williams is serious about coming back and Brown has to split time in 12 of 16 games: 892 yards rushing, 170 yards receiving, and 7 TDs.

Shawn Bryson

Height: 6-1 **Weight:** 233 **College:** Tennessee **Born:** 26-Aug-1976 **Age:** 29

Year	Team	G	Runs	Yds	Yd/R	TD	FUM	DVOA	Rank	DPAR	Rank	PAR	Suc%	Rec	Pass	Yds	CPct	Yd/C	TD	DVOA	Rank	DPAR	Rank
2002	BUF	5	13	35	2.7	0	1	-91.7%	—	-4.3	—	-4.6	38%	1	3	9	33%	9.0	0	-38.7%	—	-0.5	—
2003	DET	16	158	606	3.8	3	2	-10.0%	38	3.4	37	2.6	41%	54	72	340	75%	6.3	0	-33.3%	49	-6.0	51
2004	DET	16	50	264	5.3	0	1	26.7%	—	8.3	—	8.6	46%	44	56	322	79%	7.3	0	-19.3%	45	-2.1	46
2005	*DET*	*14*	*87*	*391*	*4.5*	*2*	—	—	—	—	—	—	—	*35*	—	*281*	—	*8.0*	*1*				

He has decent hands, decent speed, and a good understanding of the passing game, so Bryson can help a team out as a third down back. But as Kevin Jones emerged in the second half of the season, Bryson's importance to the offense declined.

Correll Buckhalter

Height: 6-0 **Weight:** 222 **College:** Nebraska **Born:** 6-Oct-1978 **Age:** 27

Year	Team	G	Runs	Yds	Yd/R	TD	FUM	DVOA	Rank	DPAR	Rank	PAR	Suc%	Rec	Pass	Yds	CPct	Yd/C	TD	DVOA	Rank	DPAR	Rank
2002	PHI	0	0	0	0.0	0	—							0	—	0	—	0.0	0	—	—	—	—
2003	PHI	15	126	542	4.3	8	3	-0.2%	25	7.1	34	6.7	46%	10	14	133	71%	13.3	1	44.5%	—	3.6	—
2004	PHI	0	0	0	0.0	0	—	0.0%	0	0.0	0	0.0	0%	0	—	0	—	0.0	0	—	—	—	—
2005	*PHI*	*13*	*63*	*231*	*3.6*	*2*	—	—	—	—	—	—	—	*10*	—	*72*	—	*7.4*	*0*				

You can't spell Buckhalter without "ACL." Buckhalter is coming off his second season in three missed with an ACL tear, but he knows the Eagles' system and is well-liked by the coaching staff. He's a one-cut runner who takes what the defense gives him, has some speed and power, and isn't useless as a receiver. A respectable DPAR as the third member of a three-headed backfield in 2003 shows what he can do. He's a fine complement to Brian Westbrook and a low-priced second banana.

Joe Burns

Height: 5-9 **Weight:** 215 **College:** Georgia Tech **Born:** 15-Apr-1973 **Age:** 32

Year	Team	G	Runs	Yds	Yd/R	TD	FUM	DVOA	Rank	DPAR	Rank	PAR	Suc%	Rec	Pass	Yds	CPct	Yd/C	TD	DVOA	Rank	DPAR	Rank
2002	BUF	9	5	7	1.4	0	—	-60.0%	—	-1.0	—	-1.1	20%	0	—	0	—	0.0	0	—	—	—	—
2003	BUF	16	39	113	2.9	0	1	-53.6%	—	-4.9	—	-5.6	38%	7	9	62	78%	8.9	0	39.2%	—	1.7	—
2004	BUF	16	20	73	3.7	0	0	-25.6%	—	-1.0	—	-1.1	25%	1	3	7	33%	7.0	0	-27.2%	—	-0.2	—
2005	*BUF*	*13*	*31*	*130*	*4.2*	*0*	—	—	—	—	—	—	—	*7*	—	*53*	—	*7.5*	*0*				

Burns has contributed very little in the few chances he's had, although it's possible that he'll get more use if the Bills succeed in trading Travis Henry.

Kerry Carter

Height: 6-1 **Weight:** 238 **College:** Stanford **Born:** 19-Dec-1980 **Age:** 24

Year	Team	G	Runs	Yds	Yd/R	TD	FUM	DVOA	Rank	DPAR	Rank	PAR	Suc%	Rec	Pass	Yds	CPct	Yd/C	TD	DVOA	Rank	DPAR	Rank
2003	SEA	16	3	-2	-0.7	0	—	-149.7%	—	-1.1	—	-1.2	0%	0	—	0	—	0.0	0	—	—	—	—
2004	SEA	16	4	15	3.8	0	0	41.9%	—	1.0	—	1.1	75%	0	1	0	0%	0.0	0	-121.8%	—	-0.6	—
2005	*SEA*	*14*	*9*	*40*	*4.3*	*0*	—	—	—	—	—	—	—	*6*	—	*37*	—	*6.6*	*0*				

Carter was born in Spain, went to high school in Canada, and played only one football game in his senior season because a teachers' strike led to the cancellation of most of the schedule. Stanford recruited him after watching him play in a summer league, and he had a fine but injury-riddled college career, highlighted by a four-TD game against USC in 2000. He made the Seahawks as an undrafted rookie and has seen little playing time, but he could pull a "Nick Goings" and do all right if the Seahawks suffer multiple injuries.

Rock Cartwright

Height: 5-7 **Weight:** 223 **College:** Kansas State **Born:** 3-Dec-1979 **Age:** 26

Year	Team	G	Runs	Yds	Yd/R	TD	FUM	DVOA	Rank	DPAR	Rank	PAR	Suc%	Rec	Pass	Yds	CPct	Yd/C	TD	DVOA	Rank	DPAR	Rank
2002	WAS	14	3	22	7.3	0	0	82.5%	—	1.4	—	1.4	67%	11	13	121	85%	11.0	1	58.3%	—	4.6	—
2003	WAS	15	107	411	3.8	4	1	9.6%	11	14.6	20	10.3	53%	18	27	176	67%	9.8	0	12.3%	14	2.0	22
2004	WAS	13	2	0	0.0	0	0	-93.7%	—	-0.5	—	-0.4	0%	0	1	0	0%	0.0	0	-97.2%	—	-0.8	—
2005	*WAS*	*12*	*17*	*71*	*4.1*	*0*	—	—	—	—	—	—	—	*6*	—	*39*	—	*6.9*	*0*				

In the spring of 2004 we wrote an article at FootballOutsiders.com explaining why Rock Cartwright was a far better running back than DeShaun Foster. Cartwright was a first down machine playing against some of the best run defenses in

(continued next page)

Rock Cartwright *(continued)*

the NFL. So what happened in 2004? Beats us. Joe Gibbs decided to stick mainly to 205-pound starter Clinton Portis in short yardage situations, instead of the converted fullback Cartwright. The results? Not so good. Among running backs with at least 30 rushes in short-yardage (three yards or less needed for a first down) situations, Portis had the fifth-worst DVOA in the NFL at −16.1%. Maybe it's time to get Rock the, uh, rock again in short-yardage situations.

Jesse Chatman Height: 5-8 Weight: 215 College: Eastern Washington Born: 22-Sep-1979 Age: 26

Year	Team	G	Runs	Yds	Yd/R	TD	FUM	DVOA	Rank	DPAR	Rank	PAR	Suc%	Rec	Pass	Yds	CPct	Yd/C	TD	DVOA	Rank	DPAR	Rank
2002	SD	10	6	19	3.2	0	0	-50.9%	—	-0.9	—	-1.0	17%	3	3	44	100%	14.7	0	98.8%	—	2.0	—
2003	SD	16	8	17	2.1	0	0	-62.3%	—	-1.8	—	-1.6	25%	5	5	54	100%	10.8	0	96.3%	—	2.1	—
2004	SD	15	65	392	6.0	3	1	24.6%	—	10.5	—	11.4	52%	2	2	17	100%	8.5	0	65.0%	—	0.8	—
2005	*SD*	*14*	*25*	*108*	*4.2*	*1*	*—*	*—*	*—*	*—*	*—*	*—*	*—*	*5*	*—*	*42*	*—*	*7.7*	*0*				

Chatman is a good special teams player who had a great fluke season as LaDainian Tomlinson's backup. 278 of his 392 yards were gained with the Chargers leading by at least 10 points in the second half. The Chargers used Chatman less and less as the year went along, and he had only 18 carries after Week 10, 14 of which came on a single snowy Sunday in Cleveland. Despite the big 2004 numbers, Chatman may have lost his backup role to second-year back Michael Turner.

Maurice Clarett Height: 6-0 Weight: 234 College: Ohio State Born: 29-Oct-1983 Age: 22

Year	Team	G	Runs	Yds	Yd/R	TD	FUM	DVOA	Rank	DPAR	Rank	PAR	Suc%	Rec	Pass	Yds	CPct	Yd/C	TD	DVOA	Rank	DPAR	Rank
2005	*DEN*	*14*	*59*	*257*	*4.3*	*1*	*—*	*—*	*—*	*—*	*—*	*—*	*—*	*10*	*—*	*86*	*—*	*8.5*	*1*				

In all the hubbub over his Ohio State eligibility, Ohio State ineligibility, draft eligibility, draft ineligibility, draft re-eligibility, aborted combine workout, somewhat better private workout, and finally his selection by the Broncos with the final pick of the third round, everyone lost focus on Maurice Clarett, the football player. As a true freshman in 2002, Clarett was nearly impossible to tackle. And though he ran a 4.8 40 at the combine, he was fast enough to catch Sean Taylor from behind and strip the ball on an interception, a play that was key in Ohio State's upset win for the 2002 national championship. He also proved his worth as a blocker and pass catcher. In Denver, which has become the land where running back dreams come true, he just might end up being worth that 101st pick after all.

Mike Cloud Height: 5-10 Weight: 205 College: Boston College Born: 1-Jul-1975 Age: 30

Year	Team	G	Runs	Yds	Yd/R	TD	FUM	DVOA	Rank	DPAR	Rank	PAR	Suc%	Rec	Pass	Yds	CPct	Yd/C	TD	DVOA	Rank	DPAR	Rank
2002	KC	13	49	115	2.3	2	0	-26.1%	—	-3.0	—	-1.1	45%	6	9	48	67%	8.0	0	-3.5%	—	0.3	—
2003	NE	5	27	118	4.4	5	0	60.6%	—	6.7	—	6.0	57%	1	2	8	50%	8.0	0	-63.0%	—	-0.2	—
2004	NYG	10	21	90	4.3	3	0	34.0%	—	4.6	—	5.4	57%	1	1	3	100%	3.0	0	-46.1%	—	-0.2	—
2005	*NYG*	*11*	*22*	*94*	*4.2*	*2*	*—*	*—*	*—*	*—*	*—*	*—*	*—*	*3*	*—*	*23*	*—*	*8.2*	*0*				

In the two games Cloud served as the primary backup/short-yardage running back for the Giants, he was nothing but successful. Against Cleveland, Cloud gained a first down on half of his carries, including a five-yard TD run. Against Minnesota, Cloud had five first downs on nine carries, including two touchdowns. The departure of Ron Dayne leaves Cloud and rookie Brandon Jacobs battling for carries in short-yardage situations. If Cloud can hold off the rookie, he might be worth a late-round flier in deeper fantasy leagues. He has a chance of being a Moe Williams-like fantasy performer this year.

Cedric Cobbs Height: 6-0 Weight: 221 College: Arkansas Born: 9-Jan-1981 Age: 24

Year	Team	G	Runs	Yds	Yd/R	TD	FUM	DVOA	Rank	DPAR	Rank	PAR	Suc%	Rec	Pass	Yds	CPct	Yd/C	TD	DVOA	Rank	DPAR	Rank
2004	NE	3	22	50	2.3	0	—	—	—	—	—	—	—	0	—	0	—	0.0	0	—	—	—	—
2005	*NE*	*11*	*25*	*106*	*4.3*	*0*	*—*	*—*	*—*	*—*	*—*	*—*	*—*	*7*	*—*	*51*	*—*	*6.9*	*0*				

Cobbs seemed like a particularly astute pick a year ago. He comes from the SEC, which has a record of producing running backs who have substantial careers as late-round picks. (Rudi Johnson, Stephen Davis, and Domanick Davis were all fourth-round selections out of the SEC, like Cobbs.) He would apprentice under a veteran with a similar style, Corey Dillon. But he spent most of the year on the physically-unable-to-perform list with a "mysterious injury" (likely called "rookie disease") and then showed up for some garbage-time carries against Cleveland and San Francisco that went nowhere. Consider it a red shirt year; word out of Foxboro says he's been among the most diligent attendees of off-season workouts.

Greg Comella

Height: 6-1 **Weight:** 248 **College:** Stanford **Born:** 29-Jul-1975 **Age:** 30

Year	Team	G	Runs	Yds	Yd/R	TD	FUM	DVOA	Rank	DPAR	Rank	PAR	Suc%	Rec	Pass	Yds	CPct	Yd/C	TD	DVOA	Rank	DPAR	Rank
2002	TEN	12	1	0	0.0	0	1	-100.3%	—	-0.6	—	-0.8	0%	10	15	70	67%	7.0	0	-16.3%	—	-0.7	—
2003	HOU	5	0	0	0.0	0	—	—	—	—	—	—	—	0	1	0	0%	0.0	0	-110.4%	—	-0.6	—
2004	TB	7	0	0	0.0	0	—	—	—	—	—	—	—	1	1	12	100%	12.0	0	110.1%	—	0.7	—
2005	*TB*	*10*	*4*	*15*	*4.3*	*0*	—	—	—	—	—	—	—	*2*	—	*10*	—	*5.0*	*0*				

Comella is the eldest of three would-be NFL fullback brothers, which has to be some sort of first in the annals of parenting.

Jameel Cook

Height: 5-10 **Weight:** 237 **College:** Illinois **Born:** 8-Feb-1979 **Age:** 26

Year	Team	G	Runs	Yds	Yd/R	TD	FUM	DVOA	Rank	DPAR	Rank	PAR	Suc%	Rec	Pass	Yds	CPct	Yd/C	TD	DVOA	Rank	DPAR	Rank
2002	TB	13	0	0	0.0	0	—	—	—	—	—	—	—	4	6	43	67%	10.8	0	20.8%	—	1.1	—
2003	TB	14	1	-1	-1.0	0	0	-103.3%	—	-0.3	—	-0.4	0%	20	30	120	67%	6.0	1	-17.9%	41	-1.1	38
2004	TB	12	0	0	0.0	0	—	—	—	—	—	—	—	7	12	44	58%	6.3	1	-12.2%	—	0.0	—
2005	*TB*	*13*	*5*	*21*	*4.3*	*0*	—	—	—	—	—	—	—	*7*	—	*54*	—	*7.3*	*1*				

Cook's skills as a lead blocker and pass catcher out of the backfield were good enough to earn him a new contract with Tampa Bay this off-season. His playing time could increase as Mike Alstott is phased out of the offense, but he's never going to show up real high on the stat sheet.

Zack Crockett

Height: 6-2 **Weight:** 240 **College:** Florida State **Born:** 2-Dec-1972 **Age:** 33

Year	Team	G	Runs	Yds	Yd/R	TD	FUM	DVOA	Rank	DPAR	Rank	PAR	Suc%	Rec	Pass	Yds	CPct	Yd/C	TD	DVOA	Rank	DPAR	Rank
2002	OAK	15	40	118	3.0	8	—	20.2%	—	8.1	—	12.0	78%	0	—	0	—	0.0	0	—	—	—	—
2003	OAK	16	48	145	3.0	7	1	-9.6%	—	1.1	—	1.8	46%	7	12	53	58%	7.6	0	-13.3%	—	-0.1	—
2004	OAK	16	48	232	4.8	2	0	17.6%	—	7.4	—	8.7	61%	16	20	87	80%	5.4	0	-0.6%	—	1.0	—
2005	*OAK*	*16*	*45*	*166*	*3.7*	*3*	—	—	—	—	—	—	—	*7*	—	*47*	—	*6.7*	*0*				

Now entering his seventh season with the Raiders as a part-time fullback and goal line special... wait a minute. How does a goal line specialist end up with only two touchdowns? For some reason the Raiders pulled Crockett out of the goal line role in 2004, and he had just four carries until Week 14. Then, with the Raiders in "throw it against the wall to see if it sticks" mode, Crockett suddenly became a normal back, and he was really good, including 134 yards in the final game of the season. Then the Raiders signed LaMont Jordan and now they say Crockett will be back in his old role. We suspect that Jordan will keep a few of those goal line carries to himself.

Larry Croom

Height: 5-10 **Weight:** 205 **College:** UNLV **Born:** 29-Oct-1981 **Age:** 24

Year	Team	G	Runs	Yds	Yd/R	TD	FUM	DVOA	Rank	DPAR	Rank	PAR	Suc%	Rec	Pass	Yds	CPct	Yd/C	TD	DVOA	Rank	DPAR	Rank
2004	ARI	6	29	76	2.6	0	0	-31.7%	—	-2.2	—	-3.1	28%	2	5	16	40%	8.0	0	5.2%	—	0.3	—
2005	*ARI*	*12*	*27*	*114*	*4.3*	*0*	—	—	—	—	—	—	—	*12*	—	*81*	—	*6.7*	*0*				

Against the Jets in Week 12, the Cardinals started seventh-round pick John Navarre at quarterback and undrafted rookie Larry Croom at halfback. Croom carried the ball 18 times in the game and averaged 2.7 yards per rush; Navarre threw four picks and averaged 4.2 yards per attempt. Herm Edwards neglected to mention any of this in his Christmas card to Denny Green.

Najeh Davenport

Height: 6-1 **Weight:** 245 **College:** Miami **Born:** 8-Feb-1979 **Age:** 26

Year	Team	G	Runs	Yds	Yd/R	TD	FUM	DVOA	Rank	DPAR	Rank	PAR	Suc%	Rec	Pass	Yds	CPct	Yd/C	TD	DVOA	Rank	DPAR	Rank
2002	GB	8	39	184	4.7	1	1	1.2%	—	2.8	—	2.0	41%	5	9	33	56%	6.6	0	-56.5%	—	-2.1	—
2003	GB	15	77	420	5.5	2	4	-10.5%	40	0.9	43	1.1	52%	6	10	38	60%	6.3	0	-16.1%	—	-0.3	—
2004	GB	11	71	359	5.1	2	0	23.3%	—	10.8	—	11.4	51%	4	4	33	100%	8.3	0	76.7%	—	1.6	—
2005	*GB*	*13*	*62*	*244*	*3.9*	*2*	—	—	—	—	—	—	—	*11*	—	*86*	—	*7.9*	*0*				

Davenport is a freak of nature. Men who weigh 250 pounds are not supposed to be that fast or elusive. Davenport has struggled with fumbles, but if he can learn to hang onto the ball, he's going to do big things in the NFL. He's one of the most consistent backs in the league at grinding out yardage without being stopped at the line of scrimmage, and he's only 26.

Domanick Davis Height: 5-9 Weight: 216 College: LSU Born: 1-Oct-1980 Age: 25

Year	Team	G	Runs	Yds	Yd/R	TD	FUM	DVOA	Rank	DPAR	Rank	PAR	Suc%	Rec	Pass	Yds	CPct	Yd/C	TD	DVOA	Rank	DPAR	Rank
2003	HOU	14	238	1031	4.3	8	4	-1.9%	28	11.6	26	11.9	41%	47	67	351	70%	7.5	0	-5.1%	29	1.1	28
2004	HOU	15	302	1188	3.9	13	4	-2.9%	32	14.5	21	19.8	43%	68	85	588	81%	8.6	1	19.1%	12	12.3	5
2005	*HOU*	*16*	*322*	*1429*	*4.4*	*11*	—	—	—	—	—	—	—	*61*	—	*492*	—	*8.0*	*2*				

"He is a good number two back but not the guy you want starting for you. He is tough, slippery, more quick than fast, and a very hard worker who has had some big games against some bad teams." This wasn't said about Domanick Davis, but it may as well have been. It was said about Priest Holmes, who's also a little guy—about 3 pounds lighter than Davis—and, oh yeah, a pretty good runner too. The point is, Davis can be a very good back in the NFL; he has enough talent, and he has plenty of tenacity and drive. What he needs is a better line in front of him and a year free of injuries. He struggled for two months with a sprained ankle and then a bruised thigh, and in Weeks 1–8 was worth −8.7 DPAR with a 2.9-yard average and only three TDs. In Weeks 9–17, Davis was worth 23.2 DPAR with a 4.5-yard average and ten TDs.

Stephen Davis Height: 6-0 Weight: 235 College: Auburn Born: 8-Feb-1979 Age: 26

Year	Team	G	Runs	Yds	Yd/R	TD	FUM	DVOA	Rank	DPAR	Rank	PAR	Suc%	Rec	Pass	Yds	CPct	Yd/C	TD	DVOA	Rank	DPAR	Rank
2002	WAS	12	207	820	4.0	7	4	0.7%	24	14.1	24	12.9	50%	23	33	142	70%	6.2	1	0.4%	29	1.6	31
2003	CAR	14	318	1444	4.5	8	3	3.7%	20	24.8	9	26.9	46%	14	17	159	82%	11.4	0	62.4%	—	5.1	—
2004	CAR	2	24	92	3.8	0	0	10.4%	—	2.3	—	2.5	46%	2	2	32	100%	16.0	0	156.3%	—	1.9	—
2005	*CAR*	*11*	*63*	*184*	*2.9*	*1*	—	—	—	—	—	—	—	*8*	—	*62*	—	*7.4*	*0*				

Davis is still not fully healed after microfracture surgery on his right knee back in November. Some reports out of Charlotte say that Davis could return to practice by July, other rumors say he might retire. A number of athletes have returned after microfracture surgery, but it permanently sidelined Terrell Davis. This is a last ditch effort to get something from a guy who might not have much left. You know when you squeeze the juice out of an orange, then give it that one last hard squeeze, thinking there might be some left? That's what the doctors are trying, and Davis is the orange.

Ron Dayne Height: 5-10 Weight: 253 College: Wisconsin Born: 14-Mar-1978 Age: 27

Year	Team	G	Runs	Yds	Yd/R	TD	FUM	DVOA	Rank	DPAR	Rank	PAR	Suc%	Rec	Pass	Yds	CPct	Yd/C	TD	DVOA	Rank	DPAR	Rank
2002	NYG	16	125	428	3.4	3	1	-9.2%	40	3.6	40	2.1	42%	11	12	49	92%	4.5	0	-36.2%	—	-1.5	—
2003	NYG	0	0	0	0.0	0	—	—	—	—	—	—	—	0	—	0	—	0.0	0	—	—	—	—
2004	NYG	14	52	179	3.4	1	0	-3.7%	—	2.6	—	2.4	46%	1	4	7	25%	7.0	0	-97.1%	—	-1.6	—
2005	*DEN*	*12*	*19*	*80*	*4.3*	*0*	—	—	—	—	—	—	—	*1*	—	*10*	—	*8.6*	*0*				

What Keanu Reeves is to actors, Ron Dayne is to running backs. If you give Reeves a solid script that calls for him to express only one emotion, you get *The Matrix*. Ask Keanu to change things up and show some range and you get stinkers like *Sweet November* and *The Replacements*. Likewise, if you give Ron Dayne some good blocking and ask him to run in one direction he has a very good chance at gaining a few yards. If you don't give Dayne a giant hole to run through directly in front of him, you'll soon be punting away. Thankfully for Giants fans, Dayne will not be brought back to gain half a yard on third-and-ones in 2005. Now in Denver, we may finally get to see exactly how good the Denver blocking scheme really is. If the Broncos can get 1,000 yards out of Dayne, Mike Shanahan should be next in line for sainthood.

Corey Dillon Height: 5-11 Weight: 225 College: Washington Born: 24-Oct-1974 Age: 31

Year	Team	G	Runs	Yds	Yd/R	TD	FUM	DVOA	Rank	DPAR	Rank	PAR	Suc%	Rec	Pass	Yds	CPct	Yd/C	TD	DVOA	Rank	DPAR	Rank
2002	CIN	16	314	1311	4.2	7	5	1.0%	23	20.5	16	16.8	50%	43	61	298	70%	6.9	0	-3.8%	32	1.8	30
2003	CIN	13	138	541	3.9	2	0	-5.2%	32	5.6	35	5.7	43%	11	18	71	61%	6.5	0	-19.7%	—	-0.7	—
2004	NE	15	345	1635	4.7	12	5	19.7%	7	50.3	2	49.5	54%	15	21	103	71%	6.9	1	0.8%	—	1.0	—
2005	*NE*	*14*	*290*	*1226*	*4.2*	*10*	—	—	—	—	—	—	—	*12*	—	*78*	—	*6.5*	*1*				

Malcontent? Cancer in the locker room? Turns out that Corey Dillon just didn't like losing. A model citizen both on and off the field in 2004, he earned a contract extension that will likely make him a Patriot for at least the next two years. But it is going to be hard for him to repeat the success he had last year. Not only is he on the wrong side of 30, but he set a career high with 345 carries and then tossed another 65 on top of that during the playoffs. The Patriots need to use him less and keep him fresh in 2005.

Reuben Droughns

Height: 5-11 **Weight:** 207 **College:** Oregon **Born:** 21-Aug-1978 **Age:** 27

Year	Team	G	Runs	Yds	Yd/R	TD	FUM	DVOA	Rank	DPAR	Rank	PAR	Suc%	Rec	Pass	Yds	CPct	Yd/C	TD	DVOA	Rank	DPAR	Rank
2002	DEN	14	4	11	2.8	1	0	35.2%	—	0.7	—	1.0	50%	5	7	53	71%	10.6	1	51.7%	—	2.1	—
2003	DEN	15	6	14	2.3	0	0	-32.5%	—	-0.5	—	-0.2	17%	9	12	87	75%	9.7	2	99.3%	—	5.5	—
2004	DEN	16	275	1240	4.5	6	5	-0.3%	26	17.0	16	21.2	51%	32	44	241	73%	7.5	2	10.6%	20	4.9	14
2005	*CLE*	*15*	*191*	*711*	*3.7*	*5*	—	— —		— —		— —		*36*	—	*278*	—	*7.8*	*1*				

Escape from the Planet of the Cut Blocks. Reuben Droughns was a nice story last year, and he can be a powerful force between the tackles, but there's very little reason to believe that he can avoid the drop-off that seems to hit every runner after leaving Denver.

T. J. Duckett

Height: 6-0 **Weight:** 254 **College:** Michigan State **Born:** 17-Feb-1981 **Age:** 24

Year	Team	G	Runs	Yds	Yd/R	TD	FUM	DVOA	Rank	DPAR	Rank	PAR	Suc%	Rec	Pass	Yds	CPct	Yd/C	TD	DVOA	Rank	DPAR	Rank
2002	ATL	12	130	507	3.9	4	0	11.3%	8	13.7	25	13.7	51%	9	11	61	82%	6.8	0	20.6%	—	1.7	—
2003	ATL	16	197	779	4.0	11	3	2.9%	22	14.3	21	12.6	47%	11	13	94	85%	8.5	0	34.8%	—	2.3	—
2004	ATL	13	104	509	4.9	8	2	22.9%	6	17.5	15	17.4	61%	3	3	15	100%	5.0	0	24.4%	—	0.4	—
2005	*ATL*	*16*	*187*	*812*	*4.3*	*6*	—	— —		— —		— —		*17*	—	*128*	—	*7.7*	*0*				

An interesting first-round draft selection in 2002 given the team's previous six-year contract with Warrick Dunn, Duckett has emerged as a successful inside rusher. Out of his 104 carries in 2004, only one was for negative yards. In 2004, he was the team's third rushing option behind Dunn and QB Vick, but we expect that may change in 2005, and if he has a 2005 like or better than his 2004, Dunn may be seeking new employment in 2006.

Warrick Dunn

Height: 5-9 **Weight:** 180 **College:** Florida State **Born:** 5-Jan-1975 **Age:** 30

Year	Team	G	Runs	Yds	Yd/R	TD	FUM	DVOA	Rank	DPAR	Rank	PAR	Suc%	Rec	Pass	Yds	CPct	Yd/C	TD	DVOA	Rank	DPAR	Rank
2002	ATL	15	230	927	4.0	7	4	-7.5%	35	6.6	33	5.0	44%	50	65	377	77%	7.5	2	13.4%	15	6.8	14
2003	ATL	11	125	672	5.4	3	2	10.4%	10	12.9	22	13.0	42%	37	52	336	71%	9.1	2	-1.3%	28	1.6	24
2004	ATL	16	265	1106	4.2	9	3	-2.6%	29	11.9	29	12.6	42%	29	39	294	74%	10.1	0	7.6%	23	3.3	24
2005	*ATL*	*16*	*171*	*704*	*4.1*	*5*	—	— —		— —		— —		*27*	—	*216*	—	*8.0*	*1*				

You'd never know it looking at him, but the 180-pound Warrick Dunn is tough when he picks up the blitz. Dunn is surprisingly strong, and he embarrassed Jeremetrius Butler with a stiff-arm on his long touchdown run against the Rams. In goal-to-go situations, Dunn still gets more carries than T. J. Duckett: He had 15 carries to Duckett's 9 last season. That situation will change this year. Dunn's quick feet and instincts made him a good short-yardage runner, but he's slowing down, and Duckett proved last season that he can move the pile. Age and Duckett's emergence account for Dunn's slip in the projections for 2005. He'll still get a lot of opportunities because he catches the ball well, can pass block, and is a bigger threat than Duckett to break a long gain.

Adimchinobe Echemandu

Height: 5-10 **Weight:** 226 **College:** California **Born:** 21-Nov-1980 **Age:** 25

Year	Team	G	Runs	Yds	Yd/R	TD	FUM	DVOA	Rank	DPAR	Rank	PAR	Suc%	Rec	Pass	Yds	CPct	Yd/C	TD	DVOA	Rank	DPAR	Rank
2004	CLE	4	8	25	3.1	0	1	-83.8%	—	-2.9	—	-3.3	38%	3	4	25	75%	8.3	0	15.1%	—	0.5	—
2005	*CLE*	*12*	*14*	*60*	*4.3*	*0*	—	— —		— —		— —		*11*	—	*75*	—	*6.7*	*0*				

Echemandu played under the name Joey Echu for most of his college career, then returned to his birth name before the NFL draft in 2004, just in time to make our spell-checking responsibilities that much more onerous.

Marc Edwards

Height: 6-0 **Weight:** 249 **College:** Notre Dame **Born:** 17-Nov-1974 **Age:** 31

Year	Team	G	Runs	Yds	Yd/R	TD	FUM	DVOA	Rank	DPAR	Rank	PAR	Suc%	Rec	Pass	Yds	CPct	Yd/C	TD	DVOA	Rank	DPAR	Rank
2002	NE	16	31	96	3.1	0	1	-1.5%	—	1.9	—	2.5	58%	23	32	196	72%	8.5	0	-2.0%	31	1.5	33
2003	JAC	16	7	13	1.9	1	0	22.0%	—	1.4	—	1.1	57%	31	43	226	72%	7.3	0	-7.1%	30	0.5	32
2004	JAC	13	0	0	0.0	0	—	— —		— —		— —		7	8	41	88%	5.9	0	-20.8%	—	-0.5	—

Three years ago, the Patriots used him to run in surprise situations. Two years ago, the Jaguars handed him the ball only seven times, but they used him a lot in the passing offense. Last year, he was mostly just used to block. This spring, he was waived, and may retire. Thank you for watching Hallmark Hall of Fame's production of *Requiem for a Fullback*.

Heath Evans Height: 6-0 Weight: 245 College: Auburn Born: 30-Dec-1978 Age: 26

Year	Team	G	Runs	Yds	Yd/R	TD	FUM	DVOA	Rank	DPAR	Rank	PAR	Suc%	Rec	Pass	Yds	CPct	Yd/C	TD	DVOA	Rank	DPAR	Rank
2002	SEA	12	17	53	3.1	0	1	-42.0%	—	-1.6	—	-2.1	59%	8	12	41	67%	5.1	0	-22.9%	—	-0.9	—
2003	SEA	14	7	24	3.4	0	0	-10.0%	—	0.1	—	0.2	43%	2	2	34	100%	17.0	0	146.6%	—	1.7	—
2004	SEA	15	7	20	2.9	0	1	-76.5%	—	-2.5	—	-2.4	57%	2	4	12	50%	6.0	0	-88.1%	—	-2.1	—
2005	MIA	14	12	50	4.3	0	—	—	—	—	—	—	—	5	—	41	—	7.9	0				

Evans was an acceptable lead blocker and all-purpose special teamer in Seattle. He'll do the same job in Miami.

Justin Fargas Height: 6-1 Weight: 220 College: USC Born: 25-Jan-1980 Age: 25

Year	Team	G	Runs	Yds	Yd/R	TD	FUM	DVOA	Rank	DPAR	Rank	PAR	Suc%	Rec	Pass	Yds	CPct	Yd/C	TD	DVOA	Rank	DPAR	Rank
2003	OAK	10	40	203	5.1	0	1	-6.6%	—	1.0	—	2.0	40%	2	3	2	67%	1.0	0	-121.6%	—	-1.0	—
2004	OAK	12	35	126	3.6	1	1	6.0%	—	3.1	—	3.7	54%	11	14	68	79%	6.2	0	-26.2%	—	-1.2	—
2005	OAK	13	34	147	4.3	1	—	—	—	—	—	—	—	9	—	64	—	7.4	0				

Huggy Bear's son was always injured in college and has had a hard time staying healthy as a pro. He's had more than seven carries in a game only once in two pro seasons, so it's hard to gauge his actual ability level. He can catch the ball and has some open-field elusiveness, making him similar to Amos Zereoue. There's only room for one of these guys behind LaMont Jordan.

Ciatrick Fason Height: 6-0 Weight: 211 College: Florida Born: 29-Oct-1982 Age: 23

Year	Team	G	Runs	Yds	Yd/R	TD	FUM	DVOA	Rank	DPAR	Rank	PAR	Suc%	Rec	Pass	Yds	CPct	Yd/C	TD	DVOA	Rank	DPAR	Rank
2005	MIN	14	67	306	4.6	2	—	—	—	—	—	—	—	13	—	136	—	10.5	0				

Fason probably should have stayed for his senior year at Florida. He was the first Gator to lead the SEC in rushing since 1993, which says more about the state of Florida's passing game last year than it does about Fason. In Minnesota, he takes over the important position of fifth-string running back. One Minnesota running back caught with dried urine and the Whizzinator means he'll occasionally see the field. If they catch the other three Minnesota running backs with dried urine and the Whizzinator, Fason becomes a major fantasy sleeper.

Kevin Faulk Height: 5-8 Weight: 202 College: LSU Born: 5-Jun-1976 Age: 29

Year	Team	G	Runs	Yds	Yd/R	TD	FUM	DVOA	Rank	DPAR	Rank	PAR	Suc%	Rec	Pass	Yds	CPct	Yd/C	TD	DVOA	Rank	DPAR	Rank
2002	NE	15	52	271	5.2	2	1	25.0%	—	8.3	—	10.1	54%	37	53	379	70%	10.2	3	4.9%	23	4.2	21
2003	NE	15	178	638	3.6	0	4	-17.9%	47	-1.9	47	-2.2	45%	48	66	440	73%	9.2	0	18.7%	12	7.8	8
2004	NE	11	54	255	4.7	2	1	39.8%	—	11.4	—	11.2	50%	26	30	248	87%	9.5	1	46.8%	2	8.2	8
2005	NE	14	91	392	4.3	3	—	—	—	—	—	—	—	26	—	214	—	8.3	1				

Kevin Faulk is the very definition of a change-of-pace running back. His 2004 performance shows what he can do when used in a way that matches his skills, and his 2003 performance shows what he does when used in a way that does not match his skills. He simply cannot carry the ball on a regular basis. Antowain Smith's decline forced him into a regular role in 2003, and his rushing DVOA by quarter went like this: −1.2% in Q1, −9.5% in Q2, −15.0% in Q3, and −48.5% in Q4. That trend didn't exist in 2004 because he was used only in spots. By trading for Corey Dillon, the Patriots actually upgraded two running back positions, not one. It's hard to believe he had only one fumble last year; Pats fans had to feel a little nervous when Faulk, not Dillon, was running out the clock in the Super Bowl.

Marshall Faulk Height: 5-10 Weight: 211 College: San Diego State Born: 26-Feb-1973 Age: 32

Year	Team	G	Runs	Yds	Yd/R	TD	FUM	DVOA	Rank	DPAR	Rank	PAR	Suc%	Rec	Pass	Yds	CPct	Yd/C	TD	DVOA	Rank	DPAR	Rank
2002	STL	14	212	953	4.5	8	4	7.1%	13	18.6	18	21.1	50%	80	102	537	78%	6.7	2	-13.6%	46	-1.7	48
2003	STL	11	209	818	3.9	10	0	5.8%	17	17.7	16	19.5	45%	45	61	290	74%	6.4	1	-18.0%	42	-1.9	43
2004	STL	14	195	774	4.0	3	2	-2.7%	30	9.8	32	8.2	47%	50	65	310	77%	6.2	1	-22.4%	49	-4.3	54
2005	STL	11	105	412	3.9	3	—	—	—	—	—	—	—	24	—	167	—	6.9	0				

DPAR and DVOA have seen Faulk as a below-average receiver over the last three years. Faulk's raw receiving numbers remain high, but there's a lot of roughage in the data: He catches a lot of four-yard swing passes on third and 5 and eight-yard screens on second and 20. It's hard to make a major contribution when averaging 6.2 yards per reception and under 5 yards per pass attempt; do it for 65 passes in a year, and you are doing a little more harm than good. Faulk still has some elusiveness and makes good decisions with the ball, but the replacement level is rapidly rising to meet him. His experience and a reworked, cap-friendly contract should keep him in St. Louis until he's ready to go. Still, he won't provide much that a good fourth-round pick couldn't provide this year, except of course for memories.

Jim Finn Height: 6-0 Weight: 245 College: Pennsylvania Born: 2-Dec-1976 Age: 29

Year	Team	G	Runs	Yds	Yd/R	TD	FUM	DVOA	Rank	DPAR	Rank	PAR	Suc%	Rec	Pass	Yds	CPct	Yd/C	TD	DVOA	Rank	DPAR	Rank
2002	IND	11	5	8	1.6	0	2	-64.3%	—	-1.0	—	-1.3	40%	6	9	31	67%	5.2	0	-117.5%	—	-5.3	—
2003	NYG	15	0	0	0.0	0	—	—	—	—	—	—	—	14	20	115	70%	8.2	0	14.3%	—	1.9	—
2004	NYG	16	3	7	2.3	0	0	-76.5%	—	-0.8	—	-0.5	33%	15	18	112	83%	7.5	0	12.0%	—	2.0	—
2005	NYG	16	10	44	4.3	1	—	—	—	—	—	—	—	11	—	92	—	8.0	0				

Very good hands. Finn caught 83.3% of all passes intended for him, the highest percentage among Giants with more than ten intended passes.

Tony Fisher Height: 6-1 Weight: 222 College: Notre Dame Born: 12-Oct-1979 Age: 26

Year	Team	G	Runs	Yds	Yd/R	TD	FUM	DVOA	Rank	DPAR	Rank	PAR	Suc%	Rec	Pass	Yds	CPct	Yd/C	TD	DVOA	Rank	DPAR	Rank
2002	GB	14	70	283	4.0	2	2	0.0%	—	3.8	—	2.1	47%	18	22	70	82%	3.9	0	-75.6%	—	-7.2	—
2003	GB	15	40	200	5.0	1	0	17.3%	—	4.2	—	5.3	40%	21	25	206	84%	9.8	2	61.9%	1	6.0	10
2004	GB	16	65	224	3.4	0	1	-3.5%	—	2.9	—	3.8	49%	38	44	277	86%	7.3	2	15.8%	16	5.3	12
2005	GB	16	39	171	4.4	1	—	—	—	—	—	—	—	24	—	189	—	7.8	1				

Fisher hasn't gotten many opportunities with Ahman Green and Najeh Davenport ahead of him on the depth chart. He was mostly a third down back in 2004 and continued to show ability as a receiver out of the backfield, but he doesn't run until the game is basically over. Seventy-three of his 105 runs over the last two seasons have come in the second half, and 49 of those were in the fourth quarter.

Troy Fleming Height: 6-0 Weight: 230 College: Tennessee Born: 1-Oct-1980 Age: 25

Year	Team	G	Runs	Yds	Yd/R	TD	FUM	DVOA	Rank	DPAR	Rank	PAR	Suc%	Rec	Pass	Yds	CPct	Yd/C	TD	DVOA	Rank	DPAR	Rank
2004	TEN	16	7	40	5.7	0	0	21.4%	—	1.0	—	0.9	43%	19	28	164	68%	8.6	2	-10.2%	36	0.1	36
2005	TEN	14	16	70	4.4	0	—	—	—	—	—	—	—	19	—	140	—	7.4	1				

With the departure of Robert Holcombe, Fleming becomes the starting fullback for the Titans. He showed some promise as a rookie, but needs to establish himself as a better blocker this season and do a better job of catching balls thrown his way.

Brock Forsey Height: 5-11 Weight: 203 College: Boise State Born: 11-Feb-1980 Age: 25

Year	Team	G	Runs	Yds	Yd/R	TD	FUM	DVOA	Rank	DPAR	Rank	PAR	Suc%	Rec	Pass	Yds	CPct	Yd/C	TD	DVOA	Rank	DPAR	Rank
2003	CHI	9	50	191	3.8	2	0	18.2%	—	7.1	—	6.3	54%	3	5	37	60%	12.3	0	58.2%	—	1.4	—
2004	MIA	7	19	53	2.8	0	—	-55.9%	—	-3.8	—	-4.8	37%	0	—	0	—	0.0	0	—	—	—	—
2005	WAS	12	21	80	3.8	0	—	—	—	—	—	—	—	3	—	22	—	7.3	0				

Forsey was a very good runner at Boise State and developed into something of a cult hero in Chicago when for one game in 2003 he became the Bears' starting running back and gained 134 yards on 27 carries in a 28–3 win against Arizona. Rick Telander of the *Chicago Sun-Times* wrote a column that day noting that in a game in which both starting quarterbacks were black and no one noticed, it was almost unheard of in the 21st-century NFL to see a white running back gaining 100 yards. Alas, since Forsey's game against Arizona, he has totaled 49 yards in a season and a half. Signed with Washington in the off-season.

DeShaun Foster   Height: 6-0   Weight: 222   College: UCLA   Born: 10-Jan-1980   Age: 25

Year	Team	G	Runs	Yds	Yd/R	TD	FUM	DVOA	Rank	DPAR	Rank	PAR	Suc%	Rec	Pass	Yds	CPct	Yd/C	TD	DVOA	Rank	DPAR	Rank
2002	CAR	0	0	0	0.0	0	—	—	—	—	—	—	—	0	—	0	—	0.0	0	—	—	—	—
2003	CAR	14	113	429	3.8	0	4	-27.9%	51	-6.1	51	-5.4	36%	26	35	207	74%	8.0	2	-18.1%	43	-1.1	36
2004	CAR	4	59	255	4.3	2	—	-2.3%	—	3.1	—	4.6	42%	9	—	76	—	8.4	0	—	—	—	—
2005	CAR	15	160	677	4.2	5	—	—	—	—	—	—	—	25	—	196	—	7.9	0				

DeShaun Foster is a bit of a whipping boy for Football Outsiders, because he mixes a few highlights with a ton of runs that go absolutely nowhere. Note the horrible Success Rate. He made a couple of good plays on national television in the playoffs, and suddenly people thought he was a star. He's not. He's not a good runner (one game against a terrible Kansas City front doesn't prove anything), and he doesn't do the little things a running back needs to do. (He missed a block on the blitz pickup when Jake Delhomme threw his costly interception that Atlanta's Kevin Mathis returned for a touchdown.) With improvement and experience, Foster could become the player people think he is now. But you have to understand that Foster is not *now* the player people think he is now.

Chris Fuamatu-Ma'afala   Height: 5-11   Weight: 254   College: Utah   Born: 4-Mar-1977   Age: 28

Year	Team	G	Runs	Yds	Yd/R	TD	FUM	DVOA	Rank	DPAR	Rank	PAR	Suc%	Rec	Pass	Yds	CPct	Yd/C	TD	DVOA	Rank	DPAR	Rank
2002	PIT	8	23	115	5.0	0	—	25.6%	—	3.9	—	3.8	57%	2	—	12	—	6.0	0	—	—	—	—
2003	JAC	13	35	144	4.1	1	—	9.9%	—	4.7	—	3.7	57%	1	—	2	—	2.0	0	—	—	—	—
2004	JAC	7	20	69	3.5	1	0	16.2%	—	3.2	—	2.9	65%	4	6	19	67%	4.8	0	-29.7%	—	-0.6	—
2005	JAC	12	20	84	4.2	0	—	—	—	—	—	—	—	4	—	26	—	7.3	0				

Fu repositioned himself as a fullback for the Jaguars last season and proved to be an effective short-yardage runner and good-enough pass blocker. Jaguars fans will be trying to sing his name to the tune of Gwen Stefani's "Hollaback Girl" on third and one this season, assuming that they can spell it.

Charlie Garner   Height: 5-10   Weight: 195   College: Tennessee   Born: 13-Feb-1972   Age: 33

Year	Team	G	Runs	Yds	Yd/R	TD	FUM	DVOA	Rank	DPAR	Rank	PAR	Suc%	Rec	Pass	Yds	CPct	Yd/C	TD	DVOA	Rank	DPAR	Rank
2002	OAK	16	180	959	5.3	7	0	29.2%	4	31.8	4	38.9	54%	91	110	941	83%	10.3	4	47.2%	3	32.2	1
2003	OAK	14	120	553	4.6	3	1	11.4%	7	12.5	24	12.9	44%	48	69	386	70%	8.0	1	-7.6%	32	0.7	31
2004	TB	3	30	111	3.7	0	0	4.5%	—	2.5	—	1.2	40%	9	14	62	64%	6.9	0	-45.4%	—	-2.1	—
2005	TB	11	25	103	4.1	0	—	—	—	—	—	—	—	5	—	23	—	4.8	0				

When Garner crumpled to the turf in Oakland in Week 3, it was a fitting metaphor for Tampa Bay's season. Garner is exactly the type of veteran player coach Jon Gruden imported to the Tampa roster in bunches in an effort to get back to the Super Bowl. Unfortunately, Garner looked a step slow before he went down with a torn patella tendon on a non-contact injury and was lost for the year. Tampa's other veteran acquisitions didn't fare much better, and this year the team is attempting to retool with youth, which probably won't leave a roster spot for Garner. That patella tear is likely to rob him of some of his quickness, which is both Garner's biggest asset and something that was already in a dwindling supply.

Eddie George   Height: 6-3   Weight: 240   College: Ohio State   Born: 24-Sep-1973   Age: 32

Year	Team	G	Runs	Yds	Yd/R	TD	FUM	DVOA	Rank	DPAR	Rank	PAR	Suc%	Rec	Pass	Yds	CPct	Yd/C	TD	DVOA	Rank	DPAR	Rank
2002	TEN	16	343	1165	3.4	12	1	0.2%	25	20.5	15	21.1	46%	36	46	255	78%	7.1	2	33.9%	7	10.1	6
2003	TEN	16	312	1031	3.3	5	1	-9.0%	37	7.8	32	5.2	39%	22	31	163	71%	7.4	0	-10.4%	33	-0.2	33
2004	DAL	14	132	432	3.3	4	3	-17.0%	48	-1.6	46	-1.5	44%	9	13	83	69%	9.2	0	-31.8%	—	-1.5	—
2005	FA	10	45	183	4.1	2	—	—	—	—	—	—	—	3	—	22	—	8.7	0				

George was still looking for a job as of press time, having not yet realized that his days as a productive running back were over a few seasons ago. 403 carries in 2000 completely burned him out. George averaged 3.9 yards per carry from 1996 through 2000 but only 3.2 yards per carry since. As a result, he is one of only three backs in NFL history to carry the ball more than 2,500 times and average less than 4.0 yards per carry over their career. His rushing average of 3.64 yards per carry is well below Jerome Bettis (3.94) and John Riggins (3.89). If he does re-sign with the Titans as rumored, it won't be the prodigal son returning, but rather a warrior headed to his final resting place.

Nick Goings

Height: 6-0 Weight: 225 College: Pittsburgh   Born: 26-Jan-1978 Age: 27

Year	Team	G	Runs	Yds	Yd/R	TD	FUM	DVOA	Rank	DPAR	Rank	PAR	Suc%	Rec	Pass	Yds	CPct	Yd/C	TD	DVOA	Rank	DPAR	Rank
2002	CAR	14	50	188	3.8	0	2	-42.6%	—	-5.2	—	-5.7	37%	18	29	91	62%	5.1	0	-30.0%	56	-2.5	51
2003	CAR	15	10	69	6.9	0	0	97.5%	—	4.7	—	4.4	80%	12	14	97	86%	8.1	1	36.8%	—	3.0	—
2004	CAR	16	217	821	3.8	6	1	-6.8%	37	6.9	36	7.4	44%	45	60	394	75%	8.8	1	19.4%	11	8.8	7
2005	*CAR*	*16*	*141*	*596*	*4.2*	*4*	—	— —		— —		— —		*36*	—	*287*	—	*8.0*	*1*				

If Reuben Droughns hadn't gotten all the attention, he might have been the breakout RB of the year. Began training camp as the number two fullback, became starting tailback because of injuries and immediately produced, sparking Carolina's late playoff run. Bruising style with a little bit of speed.

Joey Goodspeed

Height: 6-1 Weight: 247 College: Notre Dame   Born: 22-Feb-1978 Age: 27

Year	Team	G	Runs	Yds	Yd/R	TD	FUM	DVOA	Rank	DPAR	Rank	PAR	Suc%	Rec	Pass	Yds	CPct	Yd/C	TD	DVOA	Rank	DPAR	Rank
2002	SD	12	0	0	0.0	0	—	— —		— —		— —		0	—	0	—	0.0	0	—	— —		—
2003	STL	8	0	0	0.0	0	—	— —		— —		— —		0	1	0	0%	0.0	0	-88.4%	—	-0.4	—
2004	STL	16	3	6	2.0	1	1	32.9%	—	1.0	—	1.1	67%	11	16	71	69%	6.5	0	-34.3%	—	-2.2	—
2005	*STL*	*16*	*11*	*49*	*4.3*	*1*	—	— —		— —		— —		*11*	—	*79*	—	*7.2*	*0*				

The Rams need fullbacks the way men need nipples. Goodspeed helps out on special teams and plays on about 20% of the team's snaps.

Lamar Gordon

Height: 6-1 Weight: 218 College: North Dakota State   Born: 7-Jan-1980 Age: 25

Year	Team	G	Runs	Yds	Yd/R	TD	FUM	DVOA	Rank	DPAR	Rank	PAR	Suc%	Rec	Pass	Yds	CPct	Yd/C	TD	DVOA	Rank	DPAR	Rank
2002	STL	13	65	228	3.5	1	2	-35.8%	—	-6.0	—	-6.5	38%	30	38	278	79%	9.3	2	55.0%	2	12.5	4
2003	STL	10	71	298	4.2	1	1	-0.2%	—	5.4	—	6.0	49%	8	13	59	62%	7.4	0	-33.5%	—	-1.1	—
2004	MIA	3	35	64	1.8	0	1	-81.6%	—	-9.1	—	-7.8	29%	13	19	74	68%	5.7	0	-37.2%	—	-2.4	—
2005	*MIA*	*12*	*62*	*227*	*3.6*	*1*	—	— —		— —		— —		*15*	—	*115*	—	*7.5*	*0*				

The man some tabbed as the heir to Ricky Williams had 35 carries for 64 yards. When Nick Saban arrived in Miami, his first words must have been, "We traded a third-round pick for this?" Cancel that projection if America's favorite running back-turned-holistic medicine man actually returns to the Dolphins as rumored.

Frank Gore

Height: 5-9 Weight: 217 College: Miami   Born: 14-May-1983 Age: 22

Year	Team	G	Runs	Yds	Yd/R	TD	FUM	DVOA	Rank	DPAR	Rank	PAR	Suc%	Rec	Pass	Yds	CPct	Yd/C	TD	DVOA	Rank	DPAR	Rank
2005	*SF*	*14*	*204*	*845*	*4.1*	*6*	—	— —		— —		— —		*19*	—	*152*	—	*8.1*	*1*				

Back in 2001, Gore rushed for 562 yards as the change-up back behind Clinton Portis. In 2002, he was listed at the Hurricanes' starting halfback, with a kid named "McGahee" second on the depth chart. Then came a torn right ACL. Then, after a year of rehab, came a torn left ACL. Gore played well enough in 2004 to merit a third-round pick, especially if you subscribe to the theory that it takes two years to fully recover from ACL injuries. He's sure to get his chances once Kevan Barlow goes into one of those stretches where he averages 2.3 yards per carry over four games. Remember, Priest Holmes had injury problems in college too.

Earnest Graham

Height: 5-9 Weight: 215 College: Florida   Born: 15-Jan-1980 Age: 25

Year	Team	G	Runs	Yds	Yd/R	TD	FUM	DVOA	Rank	DPAR	Rank	PAR	Suc%	Rec	Pass	Yds	CPct	Yd/C	TD	DVOA	Rank	DPAR	Rank
2004	TB	9	13	73	5.6	0	0	45.4%	—	3.1	—	3.3	77%	0	1	0	0%	0.0	0	-77.4%	—	-0.4	—
2005	*TB*	*12*	*24*	*104*	*4.3*	*0*	—	— —		— —		— —		*12*	—	*85*	—	*6.8*	*0*				

Graham is a 5'9", 215-pound bowling ball of a back out of the University of Florida, but the Emmitt Smith comparisons should stop right there.

Ahman Green

Height: 6-0 **Weight: 217** **College: Nebraska** **Born: 16-Feb-1977 Age: 28**

Year	Team	G	Runs	Yds	Yd/R	TD	FUM	DVOA	Rank	DPAR	Rank	PAR	Suc%	Rec	Pass	Yds	CPct	Yd/C	TD	DVOA	Rank	DPAR	Rank
2002	GB	14	286	1240	4.3	7	4	4.9%	18	23.3	9	18.1	45%	57	74	393	77%	6.9	2	1.1%	27	4.2	20
2003	GB	16	355	1883	5.3	15	7	10.9%	8	38.5	3	43.0	49%	50	59	367	83%	7.3	5	28.3%	8	9.1	6
2004	GB	15	259	1163	4.5	7	7	-2.8%	31	12.3	27	14.2	50%	40	51	275	78%	6.9	1	-19.6%	47	-2.5	48
2005	GB	14	252	1069	4.2	6	—	—	—	—	—	—	—	45	—	343	—	7.6	1				

Green was nowhere near as good in 2004 as he was in 2003. He looked a step slower. He couldn't break the long runs. The Packers couldn't rely on him to grind out carries. He looked hesitant when catching passes out of the backfield. His fumbling problems, seemingly solved in the second half of 2003, returned. Some of his regression was related to an early-season injury to center Mike Flanagan: Green's DVOA was 9.3% before Flanagan's injury and −7.7% afterwards. Flanagan may be back, but Mike Wahle and Marco Rivera are gone. At 28, Green should still have a couple of productive years, but last season's performance must worry Packers fans.

William Green

Height: 6-1 **Weight: 221** **College: Boston College** **Born: 17-Dec-1979 Age: 25**

Year	Team	G	Runs	Yds	Yd/R	TD	FUM	DVOA	Rank	DPAR	Rank	PAR	Suc%	Rec	Pass	Yds	CPct	Yd/C	TD	DVOA	Rank	DPAR	Rank
2002	CLE	16	243	887	3.7	6	4	-15.8%	43	-2.1	45	-2.9	42%	16	27	113	59%	7.1	0	-40.4%	58	-4.6	56
2003	CLE	7	142	559	3.9	1	5	-22.0%	49	-3.7	50	-3.7	45%	10	14	50	71%	5.0	0	-28.3%	—	-1.1	—
2004	CLE	15	163	585	3.6	2	3	-17.4%	49	-1.8	47	-3.8	36%	14	22	84	64%	6.0	0	-19.7%	—	-1.0	—
2005	CLE	12	89	346	3.9	2	—	—	—	—	—	—	—	10	—	67	—	7.0	0				

If *COPS* ever decides to do an NFL episode, William Green should get a lot of face time. Since coming back to Cleveland in 1999, the Browns are probably best known for making really bad first-round picks, and Green could serve as the poster boy. Green doesn't figure in the Browns' plans for 2005 and he could be looking for a new team by training camp.

Quentin Griffin

Height: 5-7 **Weight: 195** **College: Oklahoma** **Born: 12-Jan-1981 Age: 24**

Year	Team	G	Runs	Yds	Yd/R	TD	FUM	DVOA	Rank	DPAR	Rank	PAR	Suc%	Rec	Pass	Yds	CPct	Yd/C	TD	DVOA	Rank	DPAR	Rank
2003	DEN	10	94	345	3.7	0	3	-32.4%	53	-6.5	53	-5.0	48%	8	11	61	73%	7.6	0	19.7%	—	1.3	—
2004	DEN	6	85	311	3.7	2	3	-33.0%	52	-6.9	51	-6.0	33%	10	14	68	71%	6.8	1	-32.8%	—	-1.9	—
2005	DEN	15	91	360	3.9	3	—	—	—	—	—	—	—	17	—	130	—	7.5	0				

From 2000 through 2004, 15 different running backs carried the ball at least 20 times for the Denver Broncos. Out of those 15, the lowest DVOA belongs to Quentin Griffin in 2004. The second-lowest DVOA belongs to Quentin Griffin in 2003. The other Denver backs, running behind the same line, combined in 2004 for 8.5% DVOA, 37.7 DPAR, and a Success Rate of 53%. Griffin tore his ACL, then had a second surgery in April to fix a cartilage tear. Why is Denver still futzing around with this guy?

Justin Griffith

Height: 5-11 **Weight: 232** **College: Mississippi State** **Born: 13-Apr-1981 Age: 24**

Year	Team	G	Runs	Yds	Yd/R	TD	FUM	DVOA	Rank	DPAR	Rank	PAR	Suc%	Rec	Pass	Yds	CPct	Yd/C	TD	DVOA	Rank	DPAR	Rank
2003	ATL	16	38	168	4.4	0	0	35.5%	—	8.8	—	7.9	63%	21	34	122	62%	5.8	2	-21.1%	46	-1.6	41
2004	ATL	12	9	39	4.3	0	0	2.7%	—	0.6	—	0.8	44%	22	31	220	71%	10.0	1	21.8%	7	5.1	13
2005	ATL	15	20	85	4.3	1	—	—	—	—	—	—	—	23	—	187	—	8.3	1				

A very effective Swiss Army knife of a fullback who can lead and pass block well, catches the ball, and won't kill you if he takes four or five handoffs a game. Griffith is the type of player who was indispensable 20 years ago but has a hard time holding onto work today.

Troy Hambrick

Height: 6-1 **Weight: 233** **College: Savannah State** **Born: 6-Nov-1976 Age: 29**

Year	Team	G	Runs	Yds	Yd/R	TD	FUM	DVOA	Rank	DPAR	Rank	PAR	Suc%	Rec	Pass	Yds	CPct	Yd/C	TD	DVOA	Rank	DPAR	Rank
2002	DAL	16	79	317	4.0	1	2	-17.0%	44	-0.9	43	-0.2	42%	21	24	99	88%	4.7	0	-62.8%	—	-5.5	—
2003	DAL	16	275	972	3.5	5	4	-14.3%	45	0.6	44	3.0	44%	17	24	99	71%	5.8	0	-24.3%	—	-1.3	—
2004	ARI	10	63	283	4.5	1	0	-6.3%	—	2.1	—	2.6	40%	4	5	16	80%	4.0	1	-8.7%	—	0.0	—
2005	ARI	14	108	446	4.1	2	—	—	—	—	—	—	—	11	—	87	—	7.8	0				

Hambrick followed Emmitt Smith from Dallas to Arizona, washing out in his one chance to be the Cowboys' featured back in 2003. He's big, fast, and completely unreliable: Hambrick can't find a hole, doesn't make good down-and-distance decisions, gets hurt a lot, and is about one-fourth the player he thinks he is. Take away Hambrick's 62-yard run against the Dolphins, and his per carry average last season drops from 4.5 to 3.8. He'll try to stick as the power back who complements J. J. Arrington, but Hambrick would be better off hanging around Emmitt's house and doing odd jobs.

Arlen Harris
Height: 5-10 Weight: 212   College: Hofstra   Born: 22-Apr-1980 Age: 25

Year	Team	G	Runs	Yds	Yd/R	TD	FUM	DVOA	Rank	DPAR	Rank	PAR	Suc%	Rec	Pass	Yds	CPct	Yd/C	TD	DVOA	Rank	DPAR	Rank
2003	STL	16	85	255	3.0	4	1	-10.1%	39	1.3	41	-0.6	46%	15	19	102	79%	6.8	0	-12.2%	—	-0.2	—
2004	STL	14	20	63	3.2	0	1	-20.3%	—	-0.5	—	-0.7	40%	4	4	44	100%	11.0	0	-43.4%	—	-0.7	—
2005	*STL*	*13*	*37*	*155*	*4.2*	*0*	—	—	—	—	—	—	—	*10*	—	*80*	—	*7.6*	*0*				

A Brand X runner. Harris is short but works well between the tackles. He takes what the defense gives him and can catch and block a little, but isn't a breakaway threat. He's below average as a kick returner but takes care of the ball, and he hasn't been terrible in spot starts. The Rams re-signed him for 2005, mainly to be a useful spare part.

Joey Harris
Height: 5-10 Weight: 205   College: Purdue   Born: 18-Dec-1980 Age: 24

Year	Team	G	Runs	Yds	Yd/R	TD	FUM	DVOA	Rank	DPAR	Rank	PAR	Suc%	Rec	Pass	Yds	CPct	Yd/C	TD	DVOA	Rank	DPAR	Rank
2004	CAR	4	15	53	3.5	0	0	-12.9%	—	0.2	—	0.1	33%	0	3	0	0%	0.0	0	-104.2%	—	-1.8	—
2005	*CAR*	*11*	*22*	*95*	*4.3*	*0*	—	—	—	—	—	—	—	*12*	—	*81*	—	*6.8*	*0*				

Rushed for 1,100 yards for Purdue in 2002, but was ignored by the NFL because he was a straight-line runner who excelled in a spread offense. Got a chance last year because the Panthers were looking though the phone book for warm bodies. Harris's 95-yard projection reflects the total futility of guessing how the carries will be spread out in Carolina this year.

Verron Haynes
Height: 5-10 Weight: 223   College: Georgia   Born: 17-Feb-1979 Age: 26

Year	Team	G	Runs	Yds	Yd/R	TD	FUM	DVOA	Rank	DPAR	Rank	PAR	Suc%	Rec	Pass	Yds	CPct	Yd/C	TD	DVOA	Rank	DPAR	Rank
2002	PIT	12	10	51	5.1	0	0	-15.9%	—	0.1	—	0.5	30%	3	7	10	43%	3.3	0	-97.3%	—	-2.8	—
2003	PIT	12	20	63	3.2	0	2	-65.7%	—	-3.3	—	-3.4	35%	7	10	57	70%	8.1	0	-63.0%	—	-2.0	—
2004	PIT	13	55	272	4.9	0	0	29.2%	—	9.3	—	8.4	47%	18	23	142	78%	7.9	2	41.8%	—	5.1	—
2005	*PIT*	*14*	*73*	*314*	*4.3*	*2*	—	—	—	—	—	—	—	*19*	—	*154*	—	*7.9*	*1*				

Haynes might be the best third down back no one's heard of. He's a nice change of pace from Staley and Bettis and if he can avoid injuries he may eventually take over starting duties in the next year or so.

Garrison Hearst
Height: 5-11 Weight: 215   College: Georgia   Born: 4-Jan-1971   Age: 34

Year	Team	G	Runs	Yds	Yd/R	TD	FUM	DVOA	Rank	DPAR	Rank	PAR	Suc%	Rec	Pass	Yds	CPct	Yd/C	TD	DVOA	Rank	DPAR	Rank
2002	SF	16	215	972	4.5	8	4	11.2%	9	22.3	11	25.7	52%	48	69	317	70%	6.6	1	-22.7%	52	-4.2	54
2003	SF	12	178	768	4.3	3	2	7.1%	14	16.4	18	12.6	44%	25	38	211	66%	8.4	1	11.4%	16	2.8	17
2004	DEN	6	20	81	4.1	1	0	16.9%	—	2.9	—	3.8	45%	2	3	20	67%	10.0	0	-14.5%	—	0.0	—

This guy was a warrior. Hearst is a model for "injury-prone" players because every time he got hurt, he kept fighting and fighting to get back onto the field. You have to really give him credit for losing two years of his career and then still coming back to rush for 1,200 yards in 2001. He had 34.0 DPAR that year, third in the NFL behind Priest Holmes and Marshall Faulk. His run is probably over at this point, but as of press time Hearst was still trying to find a job as a role player instead of retiring.

William Henderson
Height: 6-1 Weight: 249   College: North Carolina   Born: 19-Feb-1971 Age: 34

Year	Team	G	Runs	Yds	Yd/R	TD	FUM	DVOA	Rank	DPAR	Rank	PAR	Suc%	Rec	Pass	Yds	CPct	Yd/C	TD	DVOA	Rank	DPAR	Rank
2002	GB	14	7	27	3.9	1	0	13.6%	—	0.9	—	0.8	43%	26	32	168	81%	6.5	3	28.1%	10	6.6	15
2003	GB	16	0	0	0.0	0	—	—	—	—	—	—	—	24	34	214	71%	8.9	3	27.2%	9	5.5	12
2004	GB	16	0	0	0.0	0	—	—	—	—	—	—	—	34	40	239	85%	7.0	3	10.0%	21	4.7	16
2005	*GB*	*16*	*6*	*28*	*4.4*	*1*	—	—	—	—	—	—	—	*17*	—	*127*	—	*7.3*	*1*				

(continued next page)

William Henderson (continued)

Henderson got to the Pro Bowl in his tenth season, but the Packers seemed to be phasing him out. Although Henderson is still fine as a lead blocker and receiver out of the backfield, Green Bay's coaching staff seemed to like the younger Nick Luchey just as much, using him in many situations that in years past had been Henderson's bread and butter. At age 34, Henderson won't be around much longer.

Leonard Henry							Height: 6-1	Weight: 210		College: East Carolina								Born: 5-Jan-1978		Age: 27	
Year	Team	G	Runs	Yds	Yd/R	TD	FUM	DVOA	Rank	DPAR	Rank	PAR	Suc%	Rec	Pass	Yds	CPct	Yd/C	TD	DVOA	Rank	DPAR	Rank
2004	MIA	6	46	141	3.1	0	1	-34.2%	—	-3.7	—	-5.9	29%	3	6	12	50%	4.0	0	-60.4%	—	-1.2	—

Henry was about as terrible as a running back can be in 2004, but thanks to Lamar Gordon, he wasn't the Dolphins' worst running back. He was signed by the Jets on April 6 and then released by the Jets on May 5, which pretty much gives you an indication of where his career is going.

Travis Henry							Height: 5-9	Weight: 215		College: Tennessee								Born: 29-Oct-1978		Age: 27	
Year	Team	G	Runs	Yds	Yd/R	TD	FUM	DVOA	Rank	DPAR	Rank	PAR	Suc%	Rec	Pass	Yds	CPct	Yd/C	TD	DVOA	Rank	DPAR	Rank
2002	BUF	16	325	1438	4.4	13	11	-9.1%	39	7.6	32	16.4	50%	43	59	309	73%	7.2	1	-8.1%	40	0.8	38
2003	BUF	15	331	1356	4.1	10	7	-7.3%	36	9.5	29	10.2	45%	28	40	158	70%	5.6	1	-24.1%	48	-2.1	44
2004	BUF	10	94	326	3.5	0	0	-10.6%	39	1.4	41	0.2	43%	10	14	45	71%	4.5	0	-13.8%	—	-0.2	—
2005	BUF	15	113	434	3.8	2	—	—	—	—	—	—	—	16	—	120	—	7.3	0				

The Bills' brass said they couldn't figure out why no team would offer them a high draft pick for Henry. Here's a clue, fellas: He's no good. For three years all we heard was that if Henry could start to hang onto the ball he'd be a very good runner. Then in 2004 he held onto the ball and still stunk. No one wants to pay high NFL currency for your backup, Buffalo.

Maurice Hicks							Height: 5-10	Weight: 200		College: North Carolina A&T								Born: 22-Jul-1978		Age: 27	
Year	Team	G	Runs	Yds	Yd/R	TD	FUM	DVOA	Rank	DPAR	Rank	PAR	Suc%	Rec	Pass	Yds	CPct	Yd/C	TD	DVOA	Rank	DPAR	Rank
2004	SF	9	96	362	3.8	2	3	-21.9%	50	-3.5	50	-6.4	35%	16	25	154	64%	9.6	0	20.6%	10	4.0	20
2005	SF	12	52	189	3.7	0	—	—	—	—	—	—	—	17	—	137	—	7.8	0				

Hicks spent two years on the Chicago practice squad before finally seeing the field in San Francisco. Despite his size, he's a north-south runner rather than a shifty outside guy. With Kevan Barlow scuffling, San Francisco considered making Hicks and Barlow equal parts of a running back committee this season. Frank Gore's arrival probably ends that idea.

Robert Holcombe							Height: 5-11	Weight: 208		College: Illinois								Born: 11-Dec-1975		Age: 29	
Year	Team	G	Runs	Yds	Yd/R	TD	FUM	DVOA	Rank	DPAR	Rank	PAR	Suc%	Rec	Pass	Yds	CPct	Yd/C	TD	DVOA	Rank	DPAR	Rank
2002	TEN	8	47	242	5.1	0	1	26.3%	—	7.8	—	7.9	51%	10	11	91	91%	9.1	0	46.0%	—	2.4	—
2003	TEN	15	63	201	3.2	1	2	-30.0%	—	-2.7	—	-5.2	29%	19	25	121	76%	6.4	1	15.6%	13	2.1	21
2004	TEN	16	17	62	3.6	0	0	-22.7%	—	-0.6	—	-0.2	35%	11	21	60	52%	5.5	0	-42.6%	—	-3.8	—
2005	KC	12	28	120	4.2	0	—	—	—	—	—	—	—	7	—	48	—	7.0	0				

Holcombe was asked to bulk up and switch to fullback by the Titans last season, a move he made with some success. He now heads to Kansas City to be reunited with his former coach in St. Louis, Dick Vermeil. He is behind Tony Richardson at fullback and Priest Holmes and Larry Johnson at tailback.

Tony Hollings							Height: 5-10	Weight: 216		College: Georgia Tech								Born: 1-Dec-1981		Age: 24	
Year	Team	G	Runs	Yds	Yd/R	TD	FUM	DVOA	Rank	DPAR	Rank	PAR	Suc%	Rec	Pass	Yds	CPct	Yd/C	TD	DVOA	Rank	DPAR	Rank
2003	HOU	14	38	102	2.7	0	2	-46.7%	—	-4.6	—	-6.0	29%	2	6	25	33%	12.5	0	-91.8%	—	-1.8	—
2004	HOU	7	11	47	4.3	0	0	21.3%	—	1.7	—	1.5	64%	5	7	46	71%	9.2	0	-1.8%	—	0.2	—
2005	HOU	14	28	120	4.2	0	—	—	—	—	—	—	—	8	—	61	—	7.3	0				

Tony Hollings is currently in the middle of the transition from "promising young backup" to "yeah, whatever happened to that guy?" If they had had any inkling prior to the 2003 season that Domanick Davis would be a starting-quality running back in the NFL, the Texans never would have taken Hollings with a second-round pick in the supplemental draft. He wasn't even able to beat out Jonathan Wells as Davis's top backup. If he can't keep ahead of rookie Vernand Morency on the depth chart, Hollings probably won't be on the roster in 2006.

Priest Holmes

Height: 5-9 Weight: 213 College: Texas Born: 7-Oct-1973 Age: 32

Year	Team	G	Runs	Yds	Yd/R	TD	FUM	DVOA	Rank	DPAR	Rank	PAR	Suc%	Rec	Pass	Yds	CPct	Yd/C	TD	DVOA	Rank	DPAR	Rank
2002	KC	14	313	1615	5.2	21	1	33.4%	2	64.5	1	69.6	55%	70	81	672	86%	9.6	3	45.1%	4	22.2	2
2003	KC	16	320	1420	4.4	27	1	26.6%	4	56.6	1	58.8	58%	74	90	690	82%	9.3	0	32.2%	6	16.0	1
2004	KC	8	196	892	4.6	14	4	16.3%	10	26.9	8	26.0	53%	19	25	187	76%	9.8	1	18.5%	13	3.6	23
2005	KC	14	287	1218	4.2	14	—	—	—	—	—	—	—	30	—	235	—	7.8	1				

Holmes's role in the passing game decreased significantly in 2004, falling from 81 passes thrown to him in 2002 and 90 in 2003 to 25 last year. That's a sign of decline in a running back, one that presages a significant drop in rushing yardage. Emmitt Smith caught over 50 passes per year in his prime; that number dropped into the 20s and then the teens as he became less and less Emmitt-like. Thurman Thomas went from 50 catches in 1994 to 26 in 1995; his yardage totals slipped in 1997. Marshall Faulk's receiving stats took a sharp dip between 1999 and 2001, about a year ahead of his rushing totals. The drop-off, combined with Holmes's injury history, suggests that the end of the road isn't far away.

Brad Hoover

Height: 6-0 Weight: 242 College: Western Carolina Born: 11-Nov-1976 Age: 29

Year	Team	G	Runs	Yds	Yd/R	TD	FUM	DVOA	Rank	DPAR	Rank	PAR	Suc%	Rec	Pass	Yds	CPct	Yd/C	TD	DVOA	Rank	DPAR	Rank
2002	CAR	16	31	129	4.2	0	1	-7.9%	—	1.5	—	1.6	52%	17	30	187	57%	11.0	2	-7.2%	39	0.4	40
2003	CAR	16	6	21	3.5	0	0	16.9%	—	0.9	—	0.8	83%	12	20	72	60%	6.0	1	-27.0%	—	-1.3	—
2004	CAR	14	68	246	3.6	0	0	-11.9%	—	0.6	—	0.0	38%	21	31	161	68%	7.7	2	-7.4%	34	0.5	34
2005	CAR	15	23	101	4.4	0	—	—	—	—	—	—	—	14	—	113	—	8.1	0				

One Monday night in 2000, when injuries forced the Panthers to put undrafted free agent fullback Brad Hoover in the game as their primary ballcarrier, he shocked the opposing Packers and the rest of the football world by gaining 117 yards on 24 carries. Chants of "HOO-VER! HOO-VER!" echoed throughout the stadium. Since then he's gone right back into the undrafted free agent fullback mode, although he did have a couple of nice weeks last year, gaining 63 and 99 yards in consecutive games when both Stephen Davis and DeShaun Foster were hurt. DVOA is still not impressed, and this year he'll return to fullback duties and make some meaningless short-yardage catches.

Cedric Houston

Height: 5-11 Weight: 225 College: Tennessee Born: 28-Jun-1982 Age: 23

Year	Team	G	Runs	Yds	Yd/R	TD	FUM	DVOA	Rank	DPAR	Rank	PAR	Suc%	Rec	Pass	Yds	CPct	Yd/C	TD	DVOA	Rank	DPAR	Rank
2005	NYJ	16	34	130	3.8	1	—	—	—	—	—	—	—	12	—	111	—	8.9	1				

Houston is a good complement to Curtis Martin because he picks up the blitz well and can fill a role on third downs. If Houston performs well in camp, he could force Derrick Blaylock to share the carries that used to go to LaMont Jordan. More likely, if Martin gets hit with nagging injuries because of age and overuse last year, Houston will be backing up Blaylock in a few games.

James Jackson

Height: 5-10 Weight: 215 College: Miami Born: 4-Aug-1976 Age: 29

Year	Team	G	Runs	Yds	Yd/R	TD	FUM	DVOA	Rank	DPAR	Rank	PAR	Suc%	Rec	Pass	Yds	CPct	Yd/C	TD	DVOA	Rank	DPAR	Rank
2002	CLE	11	12	54	4.5	0	0	-3.3%	—	0.6	—	0.5	33%	3	5	9	60%	3.0	0	-82.3%	—	-2.0	—
2003	CLE	12	102	382	3.7	3	3	-5.6%	33	3.7	36	2.9	53%	14	18	114	78%	8.1	0	26.2%	—	2.6	—
2004	CLE	4	12	81	6.8	0	—	—	—	—	—	—	—	6	8	22	75%	3.7	0	-67.4%	—	-1.5	—
2005	CLE	12	39	162	4.2	0	—	—	—	—	—	—	—	7	—	54	—	7.4	0				

The last five running backs drafted out of Miami before this season are Edgerrin James, James Jackson, Clinton Portis, Najeh Davenport, and Willis McGahee. Is there something in the water at the Browns training facility that just sucks the talent out of players?

Steven Jackson   Height: 6-2   Weight: 233   College: Oregon State   Born: 22-Jul-1983   Age: 22

Year	Team	G	Runs	Yds	Yd/R	TD	FUM	DVOA	Rank	DPAR	Rank	PAR	Suc%	Rec	Pass	Yds	CPct	Yd/C	TD	DVOA	Rank	DPAR	Rank
2004	STL	14	134	673	5.0	4	—	17.9%	9	19.9	11	19.1	57%	19	24	189	79%	9.9	0	41.9%	—	5.4	—
2005	STL	16	271	1215	4.5	9	—	—	—	—	—	—	—	32	—	259	—	8.1	0				

Scouts and statniks agree: Jackson can play. He has a high Success Rate, surprising receiving ability, and a scary size-speed combination. Big backs can be deadly in a pass-oriented offense, plowing through 195-pound nickelbacks on their way to big gains. Jackson can do that, but he can also turn the corner, square his shoulders, and outrun linebackers up the sidelines. He still strings too many plays to the outside and will make mistakes in blitz pickup, but Jackson is the real deal. Sharing a few carries with the aging Marshall Faulk will hurt his fantasy value but keep him from wearing out.

Terry Jackson   Height: 6-0   Weight: 232   College: Florida   Born: 10-Jan-1976   Age: 29

Year	Team	G	Runs	Yds	Yd/R	TD	FUM	DVOA	Rank	DPAR	Rank	PAR	Suc%	Rec	Pass	Yds	CPct	Yd/C	TD	DVOA	Rank	DPAR	Rank
2002	SF	5	0	0	0.0	0	—	—	—	—	—	—	—	0	—	0	—	0.0	0	—	—	—	—
2003	SF	16	0	0	0.0	0	—	—	—	—	—	—	—	0	—	0	—	0.0	0	—	—	—	—
2004	SF	16	26	101	3.9	0	2	-72.2%	—	-6.6	—	-5.9	31%	21	29	139	72%	6.6	0	-11.9%	38	-0.3	37
2005	SF	14	25	112	4.4	0	—	—	—	—	—	—	—	11	—	83	—	7.7	0				

Here's another third down back/special teams standout. San Francisco threw to Jackson 9 times on first or second down but 20 times on third or fourth down. The 49ers like him and signed him to a two-year contract in the off-season, but if he wants to expand his role he has to get in line behind Barlow, Gore, and Hicks.

Brandon Jacobs   Height: 6-4   Weight: 256   College: Southern Illinois   Born: 6-Jul-1982   Age: 23

Year	Team	G	Runs	Yds	Yd/R	TD	FUM	DVOA	Rank	DPAR	Rank	PAR	Suc%	Rec	Pass	Yds	CPct	Yd/C	TD	DVOA	Rank	DPAR	Rank
2005	NYG	10	33	121	3.7	2	—	—	—	—	—	—	—	10	—	59	—	6.1	1				

Ron Dayne Jr., or Tyrone Wheatley III. It looked like the running of the bulls when Jacobs plowed through the secondaries of the Gateway Conference, but all of those 1-AA linebackers and safeties kept catching up to him and bringing him down (eventually). Pro defenders won't let this 4×4 get off road.

Edgerrin James   Height: 6-0   Weight: 214   College: Miami   Born: 1-Aug-1978   Age: 27

Year	Team	G	Runs	Yds	Yd/R	TD	FUM	DVOA	Rank	DPAR	Rank	PAR	Suc%	Rec	Pass	Yds	CPct	Yd/C	TD	DVOA	Rank	DPAR	Rank
2002	IND	14	277	989	3.6	2	4	-5.0%	31	11.6	28	9.1	46%	61	80	353	76%	5.8	1	-23.8%	53	-5.6	58
2003	IND	13	309	1257	4.1	11	5	2.0%	23	24.9	8	18.4	50%	51	71	292	72%	5.7	0	-19.6%	44	-2.7	45
2004	IND	16	334	1548	4.6	9	5	9.9%	14	34.8	4	41.0	57%	51	60	483	85%	9.5	0	40.2%	5	14.7	1
2005	IND	15	318	1412	4.4	11	—	—	—	—	—	—	—	50	—	413	—	8.2	1				

2004 marked the return of the real Edgerrin James, the dominant back that burst on the scene in 1999 and lead the league in rushing his first two seasons. After missing most of 2001 due to his knee injury and struggling mightily in 2002, James showed flashes of his old self in 2003. This past season, however, he was all the way back, ranking third among all backs in DPAR (rushing and receiving). James lacks big-play ability, but his Success Rate, our measurement of whether a given run was successful given the context, was first in the NFL. Playing under the franchise tag and with the Colts apparently unwilling to offer a long-term contract, this could be James's last season as a Colt.

Bryan Johnson   Height: 6-1   Weight: 245   College: Boise State   Born: 18-Jan-1978   Age: 27

Year	Team	G	Runs	Yds	Yd/R	TD	FUM	DVOA	Rank	DPAR	Rank	PAR	Suc%	Rec	Pass	Yds	CPct	Yd/C	TD	DVOA	Rank	DPAR	Rank
2002	WAS	16	1	0	0.0	0	0	-112.1%	—	-0.4	—	-0.3	0%	15	19	114	79%	7.6	0	9.4%	—	1.9	—
2003	WAS	16	2	5	2.5	0	0	-117.6%	—	-0.6	—	-0.5	0%	9	12	71	75%	7.9	0	14.6%	—	1.2	—
2004	CHI	12	0	0	0.0	0	—	—	—	—	—	—	—	14	25	55	56%	3.9	2	-46.4%	55	-5.1	55
2005	CHI	14	6	26	4.3	0	—	—	—	—	—	—	—	10	—	72	—	7.2	1				

Johnson occasionally catches passes out of the backfield, but that's not his strength. He's mostly a blocking back and a special teamer.

Jeremi Johnson
Height: 5-11 **Weight:** 265 **College:** Western Kentucky **Born:** 4-Sep-1980 **Age:** 25

Year	Team	G	Runs	Yds	Yd/R	TD	FUM	DVOA	Rank	DPAR	Rank	PAR	Suc%	Rec	Pass	Yds	CPct	Yd/C	TD	DVOA	Rank	DPAR	Rank
2003	CIN	16	15	41	2.7	1	0	-14.9%	—	0.1	—	0.4	47%	15	20	82	75%	5.5	1	-6.9%	—	0.2	—
2004	CIN	16	3	5	1.7	0	1	-241.0%	—	-3.9	—	-3.8	0%	16	18	53	89%	3.3	1	-31.9%	—	-2.5	—
2005	CIN	15	10	44	4.3	0	—	—	—	—	—	—	—	14	—	94	—	6.8	1				

The less heralded member of Cincinnati's Johnson and Johnson backfield, Jeremi is a solid blocker and a valuable part of the Bengals' improving offense.

Kyle Johnson
Height: 6-1 **Weight:** 242 **College:** Syracuse **Born:** 15-Dec-1978 **Age:** 26

Year	Team	G	Runs	Yds	Yd/R	TD	FUM	DVOA	Rank	DPAR	Rank	PAR	Suc%	Rec	Pass	Yds	CPct	Yd/C	TD	DVOA	Rank	DPAR	Rank
2004	DEN	14	0	0	0.0	0	—	—	—	—	—	—	—	9	13	126	69%	14.0	2	62.1%	—	5.6	—
2005	DEN	13	6	27	4.3	0	—	—	—	—	—	—	—	6	—	52	—	9.3	1				

Stepped in as the fullback last year when Mike Anderson got hurt and Ruben Droughns became the next Davis/Gary/Anderson/Portis. With Anderson back, Clarett drafted, and Ron Dayne acquired, Johnson will struggle to make the team.

Larry Johnson
Height: 6-1 **Weight:** 228 **College:** Penn State **Born:** 19-Nov-1979 **Age:** 26

Year	Team	G	Runs	Yds	Yd/R	TD	FUM	DVOA	Rank	DPAR	Rank	PAR	Suc%	Rec	Pass	Yds	CPct	Yd/C	TD	DVOA	Rank	DPAR	Rank
2003	KC	6	20	85	4.3	1	0	26.2%	—	2.9	—	2.9	55%	1	3	2	33%	2.0	0	-109.5%	—	-1.2	—
2004	KC	10	120	581	4.8	9	0	28.0%	4	24.0	9	21.8	53%	22	28	278	79%	12.6	2	76.9%	1	13.0	4
2005	KC	14	102	464	4.6	5	—	—	—	—	—	—	—	16	—	150	—	9.4	0				

Johnson appeared destined to join the scrap heap of cursed Penn State running backs as late as October of last season. He even put yellow police tape around his locker area when he saw his name linked to every trade rumor in the country (the joke was lost on the local media). He proved to be a difference maker once he got some carries. Johnson's receiving ability is an asset that Penn State alums like Curtis Enis and Ki-Jana Carter lacked, and whatever disagreements he had with management have been smoothed over for now. If Priest Holmes suffers another major injury, Johnson will step into the lineup for good.

Rudi Johnson
Height: 5-10 **Weight:** 220 **College:** Auburn **Born:** 1-Oct-1979 **Age:** 26

Year	Team	G	Runs	Yds	Yd/R	TD	FUM	DVOA	Rank	DPAR	Rank	PAR	Suc%	Rec	Pass	Yds	CPct	Yd/C	TD	DVOA	Rank	DPAR	Rank
2002	CIN	6	17	67	3.9	0	0	7.0%	—	1.5	—	1.6	47%	6	10	34	60%	5.7	0	-14.3%	—	-0.3	—
2003	CIN	14	214	967	4.5	9	0	10.5%	9	22.5	10	24.6	51%	21	23	146	91%	7.0	0	9.0%	—	1.8	—
2004	CIN	16	361	1454	4.0	12	4	5.1%	19	30.6	5	21.8	46%	15	28	84	54%	5.6	0	-48.6%	—	-5.3	—
2005	CIN	16	348	1485	4.3	12	—	—	—	—	—	—	—	23	—	154	—	6.8	1				

This off-season the Bengals signed Johnson to a long-term deal because it looks like last year's first-rounder, Chris Perry, is in the running for the "Ki-Jana Carter Award." Johnson actually had a better DPAR last season (30.6) than Corey Dillon ever had while in Cincinnati. Of course, Dillon had a better DPAR than Johnson last year, which once again shows how the trade helped both teams. That drop in Success Rate came from an odd source, as Johnson's average dropped by over a yard per carry on second downs.

Greg Jones
Height: 6-1 **Weight:** 250 **College:** Florida State **Born:** 4-Apr-1981 **Age:** 24

Year	Team	G	Runs	Yds	Yd/R	TD	FUM	DVOA	Rank	DPAR	Rank	PAR	Suc%	Rec	Pass	Yds	CPct	Yd/C	TD	DVOA	Rank	DPAR	Rank
2004	JAC	16	62	162	2.6	3	1	-24.2%	—	-3.2	—	-2.2	48%	3	10	13	30%	4.3	0	-72.1%	—	-3.4	—
2005	JAC	14	67	235	3.5	2	—	—	—	—	—	—	—	12	—	83	—	7.1	0				

Drafted to be a physical short-yardage back and eventual successor to Fred Taylor, Jones is supposed to be shifted full-time to fullback this season. He was featured mostly as the short-yardage back throughout his rookie year, but struggled in that role. Given a chance to start in Week 17, he gained 30 yards on 16 carries. We still projected him as a backup tailback because Taylor's injury status will likely force the Jaguars to give him more carries than they would prefer.

Julius Jones Height: 5-9 Weight: 217 College: Notre Dame Born: 14-Aug-1981 Age: 24

Year	Team	G	Runs	Yds	Yd/R	TD	FUM	DVOA	Rank	DPAR	Rank	PAR	Suc%	Rec	Pass	Yds	CPct	Yd/C	TD	DVOA	Rank	DPAR	Rank
2004	DAL	8	197	819	4.2	7	3	-0.8%	27	11.4	30	9.0	43%	17	26	109	65%	6.4	0	-17.3%	43	-1.0	42
2005	DAL	16	366	1584	4.3	11	—	—	—	—	—	—	—	39	—	293	—	7.4	1				

He's for real. Amazing eye for the holes, no matter how small. Shirked two Seattle tackles on the way to a TD that put Dallas ahead with 39 seconds left in Week 13. When you replace Eddie George in the backfield, you don't need to do much to be a huge improvement. The biggest difference between the two was on runs up the middle. Running behind center, George averaged 2.7 yards per carry, with a DVOA of −43.0%. Jones was nearly a yard per carry better, with a 3.6 average and a DVOA of 3.4%. Last year, Parcells held him back in the first half so he could improve at blitz pickup, but he'll be a workhorse in 2005.

Kevin Jones Height: 5-11 Weight: 221 College: Virginia Tech Born: 21-Aug-1982 Age: 23

Year	Team	G	Runs	Yds	Yd/R	TD	FUM	DVOA	Rank	DPAR	Rank	PAR	Suc%	Rec	Pass	Yds	CPct	Yd/C	TD	DVOA	Rank	DPAR	Rank
2004	DET	15	241	1133	4.7	5	2	1.5%	24	15.4	20	21.4	46%	28	41	180	68%	6.4	1	-19.4%	46	-2.0	45
2005	DET	16	356	1605	4.5	11	—	—	—	—	—	—	—	38	—	291	—	7.6	1				

Considered elusive and quick coming out of Virginia Tech, Jones lived up to his billing as the best of the rookie Joneses despite a nagging injury in Week 3 that limited him until midseason. Of his 1,133 yards, 911 came in the last eight games of the season, and he had a 7.4% DVOA in those games after −11.8% DVOA in the first eight. Combine those facts with Detroit's easy projected schedule, and KUBIAK says Jones is the most likely candidate for 2005 NFL rushing champion.

Thomas Jones Height: 5-10 Weight: 220 College: Virginia Born: 19-Aug-1978 Age: 27

Year	Team	G	Runs	Yds	Yd/R	TD	FUM	DVOA	Rank	DPAR	Rank	PAR	Suc%	Rec	Pass	Yds	CPct	Yd/C	TD	DVOA	Rank	DPAR	Rank
2002	ARI	9	138	511	3.7	2	3	-22.9%	47	-5.4	47	-7.8	40%	20	30	113	67%	5.7	0	-24.0%	54	-2.0	50
2003	TB	16	137	627	4.6	3	4	-11.4%	41	1.3	42	4.0	45%	24	31	180	77%	7.5	0	0.9%	26	1.3	27
2004	CHI	14	240	948	4.0	7	2	-2.6%	28	12.4	26	14.0	47%	56	72	427	78%	7.6	0	-3.9%	32	2.3	29
2005	CHI	14	89	388	4.3	2	—	—	—	—	—	—	—	30	—	238	—	8.0	0				

Jones managed a career high with 240 carries, bettering his previous best by more than 100. That number is sure to drop after the Bears drafted Cedric Benson of Texas with the fourth pick. Benson is likely to get 25 carries a game, reducing Jones to backup duty. Jones's 2004 numbers don't look particularly impressive, but when you consider how often he faced eight-man fronts and how bad the Bears' offensive line was, Jones actually played quite well when healthy. Still, he tends to be a boom-or-bust player. He had four games with more than 100 yards, but he also had some terrible performances, like his 13-carry, 26-yard day against Jacksonville and his 15-carry, 40-yard game against Houston.

LaMont Jordan Height: 5-10 Weight: 230 College: Maryland Born: 11-Nov-1978 Age: 27

Year	Team	G	Runs	Yds	Yd/R	TD	FUM	DVOA	Rank	DPAR	Rank	PAR	Suc%	Rec	Pass	Yds	CPct	Yd/C	TD	DVOA	Rank	DPAR	Rank
2002	NYJ	14	84	316	3.8	3	4	-43.6%	50	-10.3	50	-9.0	39%	17	23	160	74%	9.4	0	28.9%	—	4.3	—
2003	NYJ	16	46	190	4.1	4	0	4.2%	—	3.8	—	4.5	48%	11	13	101	85%	9.2	0	43.2%	—	2.6	—
2004	NYJ	16	93	479	5.2	2	0	36.0%	1	19.2	13	20.6	55%	15	16	112	94%	7.5	0	42.7%	—	4.4	—
2005	OAK	16	221	971	4.4	7	—	—	—	—	—	—	—	32	—	250	—	7.9	1				

According to DVOA, Jordan was actually more effective than Curtis Martin in his limited opportunities. The biggest question is whether he can stay effective if the Raiders give him 300 carries—and, hopefully, zero chances to throw the halfback option. The last time LaMont Jordan was a feature back, during his senior year at Maryland, he spent the season battling nagging injuries. He also needs to cut down on the time he spends dancing around the line of scrimmage, because the Oakland offensive line isn't the New York offensive line, and sometimes he's just going to have to put his head down and fight for three tough yards instead of trying to break a long run on every play.

Mike Karney Height: 5-11 Weight: 254 College: Arizona State Born: 6-Jul-1981 Age: 24

Year	Team	G	Runs	Yds	Yd/R	TD	FUM	DVOA	Rank	DPAR	Rank	PAR	Suc%	Rec	Pass	Yds	CPct	Yd/C	TD	DVOA	Rank	DPAR	Rank
2004	NO	16	3	7	2.3	0	0	3.1%	—	0.3	—	0.0	67%	6	7	42	86%	7.0	0	-19.2%	—	-0.4	—
2005	NO	13	9	40	4.3	0	—	—	—	—	—	—	—	13	—	82	—	6.5	1				

Karney was expected to give the Saints a good blocker in the backfield. But he struggled at picking up blitzes.

Rob Konrad

Height: 6-3 **Weight:** 255 **College:** Syracuse **Born:** 12-Nov-1976 **Age:** 29

Year	Team	G	Runs	Yds	Yd/R	TD	FUM	DVOA	Rank	DPAR	Rank	PAR	Suc%	Rec	Pass	Yds	CPct	Yd/C	TD	DVOA	Rank	DPAR	Rank
2002	MIA	16	3	2	0.7	0	2	-278.0%	—	-3.7	—	-3.7	0%	34	45	233	76%	6.9	3	10.3%	17	5.0	18
2003	MIA	14	4	17	4.3	0	0	30.9%	—	0.8	—	0.6	50%	16	19	166	84%	10.4	0	69.5%	—	6.8	—
2004	MIA	10	2	18	9.0	0	0	52.4%	—	0.9	—	0.7	100%	8	18	69	44%	8.6	1	-10.4%	—	-0.2	—

Purely a blocking fullback and never a runner, Konrad signed with the Raiders in the off-season and then changed his mind and decided to retire.

Dan Kreider

Height: 5-11 **Weight:** 246 **College:** New Hampshire **Born:** 11-Mar-1977 **Age:** 28

Year	Team	G	Runs	Yds	Yd/R	TD	FUM	DVOA	Rank	DPAR	Rank	PAR	Suc%	Rec	Pass	Yds	CPct	Yd/C	TD	DVOA	Rank	DPAR	Rank
2002	PIT	13	6	16	2.7	0	1	14.2%	—	0.9	—	0.8	67%	18	25	122	72%	6.8	1	9.1%	19	2.3	27
2003	PIT	16	7	29	4.1	1	0	26.5%	—	1.1	—	1.7	71%	9	24	107	38%	11.9	0	-28.4%	—	-1.9	—
2004	PIT	16	4	18	4.5	0	0	34.1%	—	0.7	—	0.4	50%	10	14	75	71%	7.5	1	31.2%	—	3.0	—
2005	PIT	14	11	46	4.3	0	—	—	—	—	—	—	—	7	—	57	—	8.0	1				

How often does your fullback weigh less than your tailback? And Dan Kreider isn't exactly a small guy.

ReShard Lee

Height: 5-10 **Weight:** 232 **College:** Middle Tennessee State **Born:** 12-Oct-1980 **Age:** 25

Year	Team	G	Runs	Yds	Yd/R	TD	FUM	DVOA	Rank	DPAR	Rank	PAR	Suc%	Rec	Pass	Yds	CPct	Yd/C	TD	DVOA	Rank	DPAR	Rank
2004	DAL	14	27	128	4.7	1	0	23.4%	—	4.4	—	4.7	44%	1	3	4	33%	4.0	0	-113.3%	—	-1.5	—
2005	BUF	13	22	95	4.3	0	—	—	—	—	—	—	—	6	—	45	—	7.5	0				

Although ReShard received some carries backing up Eddie George early in the season, his complete inability to block on passing plays relegated him to the bench for the second half of the year. Cut by Dallas after the draft, he signed with the Bills, who already have four running backs and a great return guy, so what's the point?

Dorsey Levens

Height: 6-1 **Weight:** 230 **College:** Georgia Tech **Born:** 21-May-1970 **Age:** 35

Year	Team	G	Runs	Yds	Yd/R	TD	FUM	DVOA	Rank	DPAR	Rank	PAR	Suc%	Rec	Pass	Yds	CPct	Yd/C	TD	DVOA	Rank	DPAR	Rank
2002	PHI	16	75	411	5.5	1	1	15.0%	7	7.9	30	9.1	41%	19	28	124	68%	6.5	1	0.8%	28	1.2	35
2003	NYG	11	68	197	2.9	3	0	-19.1%	—	-1.5	—	-0.4	41%	5	7	39	71%	7.8	0	23.7%	—	0.9	—
2004	PHI	15	94	410	4.4	4	0	29.8%	3	17.9	14	16.8	55%	9	14	92	64%	10.2	0	14.3%	—	1.8	—
2005	PHI	12	90	323	3.6	4	—	—	—	—	—	—	—	3	—	17	—	4.9	0				

He's expected to retire; that projection is just in case he does come back. Levens had an impressive career as a system running back who did all the little things well. He never had great natural talent, but he spent several years as a featured back for a playoff team because he was a good receiver and blocker, followed his linemen, and made good decisions.

Jamal Lewis

Height: 5-11 **Weight:** 240 **College:** Tennessee **Born:** 29-Aug-1979 **Age:** 26

Year	Team	G	Runs	Yds	Yd/R	TD	FUM	DVOA	Rank	DPAR	Rank	PAR	Suc%	Rec	Pass	Yds	CPct	Yd/C	TD	DVOA	Rank	DPAR	Rank
2002	BAL	16	308	1327	4.3	6	8	-3.0%	29	15.7	21	12.9	50%	47	60	442	78%	9.4	1	16.5%	14	7.0	12
2003	BAL	16	387	2066	5.3	14	9	3.4%	21	30.3	6	32.4	45%	26	38	205	68%	7.9	0	10.3%	17	2.9	15
2004	BAL	12	235	1006	4.3	7	2	2.4%	21	16.2	17	14.5	46%	10	12	116	83%	11.6	0	47.1%	—	3.5	—
2005	BAL	16	259	1038	4.0	6	—	—	—	—	—	—	—	24	—	192	—	7.9	1				

Lewis broke several records in the Ron LeFlore league while serving time, but it will be very interesting to see how he bounces back from incarceration and an ankle injury that caused him to miss part of the 2004 season. Lewis's role over the last few years as the Ravens' only offensive weapon has to be taking a toll on his body. For Lewis's sake, Brian Billick's ability to cultivate QB talent needs to arrive soon.

Nick Luchey   Height: 6-2   Weight: 273   College: Miami   Born: 30-Mar-1977 Age: 28

Year	Team	G	Runs	Yds	Yd/R	TD	FUM	DVOA	Rank	DPAR	Rank	PAR	Suc%	Rec	Pass	Yds	CPct	Yd/C	TD	DVOA	Rank	DPAR	Rank
2002	CIN	14	12	59	4.9	2	—	—	—	—	—	—	—	7	—	46	—	6.6	0	—	—	—	—
2003	GB	11	1	3	3.0	0	0	-37.5%	—	-0.1	—	0.0	100%	1	2	12	50%	12.0	0	-2.6%	—	0.1	—
2004	GB	16	10	24	2.4	0	0	-17.9%	—	-0.1	—	0.3	60%	2	4	20	50%	10.0	0	-23.9%	—	-0.3	—
2005	*GB*	*12*	*10*	*43*	*4.2*	*0*	—	—	—	—	—	—	—	*4*	—	*33*	—	*8.6*	*0*				

Nick Luchey is an odd man, and we mean that in the best of ways. He changed his last name from Williams to Luchey just before the start of the 2002 season, saying he wanted to honor his father and grandfather. He collects giant centipedes and tarantulas. He plays chess. He studies Egyptian and Roman history. He's also an enormous fullback (at 273 pounds, maybe the biggest in the league), and at age 28 he's getting more playing time and seems likely to surpass William Henderson as the Packers' top fullback.

Reno Mahe   Height: 5-10 Weight: 195   College: BYU   Born: 3-Jun-1980 Age: 25

Year	Team	G	Runs	Yds	Yd/R	TD	FUM	DVOA	Rank	DPAR	Rank	PAR	Suc%	Rec	Pass	Yds	CPct	Yd/C	TD	DVOA	Rank	DPAR	Rank
2003	PHI	2	0	0	0.0	0	—	—	—	—	—	—	—	1	2	5	50%	5.0	0	22.0%	—	0.2	—
2004	PHI	11	23	91	4.0	0	0	-17.8%	—	-0.4	—	-0.2	35%	14	16	123	88%	8.8	0	25.9%	—	2.8	—
2005	*PHI*	*13*	*24*	*106*	*4.4*	*0*	—	—	—	—	—	—	—	*12*	—	*89*	—	*7.6*	*0*				

The typical Eagles roster player: a good citizen and effective special-teams player, can catch the ball out of the backfield, and would be used as a third down back if Brian Westbrook wasn't around. Most of Mahe's carries last season were in the meaningless Rams and Bengals games. He won't play a major role in the offense.

Curtis Martin   Height: 5-11 Weight: 205   College: Pittsburgh   Born: 1-May-1973 Age: 32

Year	Team	G	Runs	Yds	Yd/R	TD	FUM	DVOA	Rank	DPAR	Rank	PAR	Suc%	Rec	Pass	Yds	CPct	Yd/C	TD	DVOA	Rank	DPAR	Rank
2002	NYJ	16	261	1094	4.2	7	0	7.2%	12	21.2	14	25.6	44%	49	56	362	88%	7.4	0	16.8%	13	7.6	10
2003	NYJ	16	323	1308	4.0	2	2	6.3%	16	27.8	7	19.1	45%	42	53	262	79%	6.2	0	-15.5%	35	-1.3	39
2004	NYJ	16	371	1697	4.6	12	2	19.7%	8	54.4	1	51.1	53%	41	50	245	84%	6.0	2	10.7%	19	4.7	15
2005	*NYJ*	*13*	*251*	*1067*	*4.2*	*9*	—	—	—	—	—	—	—	*26*	—	*174*	—	*6.8*	*1*				

Curtis Martin is the same age as Marshall Faulk, who peaked four years ago. He's older than Eddie George, who is totally washed up. He's older than Stephen Davis and Priest Holmes, whose injuries raise questions about whether they're breaking down. He is currently fourth on the all-time rushing list and will pass Barry Sanders sometime in 2006. He has an outside shot at passing Emmitt Smith for the all-time record. He has played ten seasons and every single year has gained at least 1,450 combined rushing and receiving yards.

Martin has fumbled only 27 times in his career. Considering that he has 3,298 carries and 460 receptions, that's a rate of one fumble for every 139 touches, which is the best in NFL history. Take a look at some of the league's other top backs, both today and all-time:

Player	Touches per Fumble	Player	Touches per Fumble	Player	Touches per Fumble
Curtis Martin	139	Jerome Bettis	87	Ahman Green	57
Priest Holmes	129	Eddie George	85	Earl Campbell	54
Marshall Faulk	103	Barry Sanders	83	Jim Brown	51
Corey Dillon	97	Emmitt Smith	81	Walter Payton	50
Fred Taylor	93	Edgerrin James	69	Eric Dickerson	42
Terrell Davis	91	Marcus Allen	59	Tiki Barber	41

Curtis Martin is a sure Hall of Famer. Unfortunately, he's also poised for a breakdown. Running backs generally begin to decline after age 28, and Martin carried the ball 371 times last year at the age of 31. Martin is one of only two running backs to ever carry the ball over 325 times after the age of 30. The other was John Riggins. He is one of only two RBs to ever run for over 1,500 yards after the age of 30. The other was Walter Payton. Martin didn't just break these barriers—he demolished them. No matter how well he takes care of his body in the off-season, past history says that Martin will see a steep decline next season. The Jets insured themselves against this possibility by signing free agent Derrick Blaylock, and if you want to draft Curtis Martin in your fantasy league, you better plan to do the same.

Jamar Martin
Height: 5-11 **Weight:** 256 **College:** Ohio State **Born:** 12-Apr-1980 **Age:** 25

Year	Team	G	Runs	Yds	Yd/R	TD	FUM	DVOA	Rank	DPAR	Rank	PAR	Suc%	Rec	Pass	Yds	CPct	Yd/C	TD	DVOA	Rank	DPAR	Rank
2003	DAL	14	4	7	1.8	0	0	-28.6%	—	-0.3	—	-0.1	50%	2	4	9	50%	4.5	0	-54.4%	—	-0.9	—
2004	MIA	10	0	0	0.0	0	—	—	—	—	—	—	—	4	8	15	50%	3.8	0	-90.1%	—	-3.9	—
2005	*MIA*	*14*	*6*	*25*	*4.3*	*0*	—	—	—	—	—	—	—	*4*	—	*27*	—	*6.5*	*0*				

Backup fullback for the Dolphins who will remain as such with the signing of Heath Evans.

Fred McAfee
Height: 5-10 **Weight:** 193 **College:** Mississippi College **Born:** 20-Jun-1968 **Age:** 37

Year	Team	G	Runs	Yds	Yd/R	TD	FUM	DVOA	Rank	DPAR	Rank	PAR	Suc%	Rec	Pass	Yds	CPct	Yd/C	TD	DVOA	Rank	DPAR	Rank
2002	NO	10	1	11	11.0	0	—	55.5%	—	0.6	—	0.5	100%	0	—	0	—	0.0	0	—	—	—	—
2003	NO	14	1	13	13.0	0	—	90.2%	—	0.8	—	0.7	100%	0	—	0	—	0.0	0	—	—	—	—
2004	NO	11	2	54	27.0	0	—	13.5%	—	0.5	—	0.7	50%	0	—	0	—	0.0	0	—	—	—	—
2005	*NO*	*11*	*3*	*12*	*4.1*	*0*	—	—	—	—	—	—	—	*0*	—	*0*	—	*0.0*	*0*				

Has there ever been a player who played 14 years in the NFL at a skill position and had a lower profile than McAfee? Does anyone even remember the three years he spent in New Orleans in the early 1990s before he moved on to five years in Pittsburgh, one in Tampa, and then back to New Orleans again in 2000? As a third-round draft pick out of Mississippi College, the Saints thought McAfee would be an every down running back, but after getting 109 carries as a rookie he never again had even half that many. Still, he developed into a solid blocker, a special teams player, and a good presence in the locker room. Whether he's still on a roster this year at age 37 or not, Fred McAfee, we salute you.

Deuce McAllister
Height: 6-1 **Weight:** 221 **College:** Mississippi **Born:** 27-Dec-1978 **Age:** 26

Year	Team	G	Runs	Yds	Yd/R	TD	FUM	DVOA	Rank	DPAR	Rank	PAR	Suc%	Rec	Pass	Yds	CPct	Yd/C	TD	DVOA	Rank	DPAR	Rank
2002	NO	15	325	1388	4.3	13	4	3.4%	20	23.5	8	15.5	42%	47	74	352	64%	7.5	3	2.7%	26	4.5	19
2003	NO	16	351	1641	4.7	8	6	-1.8%	27	19.2	14	15.8	41%	69	86	516	80%	7.5	0	20.2%	11	10.0	5
2004	NO	14	269	1074	4.0	9	5	-6.1%	36	9.0	33	5.0	43%	34	48	228	71%	6.7	0	-24.1%	50	-3.3	51
2005	*NO*	*15*	*319*	*1355*	*4.2*	*9*	—	—	—	—	—	—	—	*47*	—	*358*	—	*7.6*	*1*				

Maybe the most inconsistent running back in the league and, like inconsistent backs tend to be, he is overrated because the highlights on ESPN show only his spectacular runs, not the plays when he tiptoes around behind the line before getting stopped for a gain of a yard.

Eric McCoo
Height: 5-10 **Weight:** 209 **College:** Penn State **Born:** 6-Sep-1980 **Age:** 25

Year	Team	G	Runs	Yds	Yd/R	TD	FUM	DVOA	Rank	DPAR	Rank	PAR	Suc%	Rec	Pass	Yds	CPct	Yd/C	TD	DVOA	Rank	DPAR	Rank
2004	PHI	1	9	54	6.0	0	0	43.7%	—	2.1	—	2.4	67%	2	5	15	40%	7.5	0	-27.4%	—	-0.5	—
2005	*PHI*	*11*	*23*	*100*	*4.3*	*0*	—	—	—	—	—	—	—	*13*	—	*92*	—	*6.9*	*0*				

NFL Europe's 2004 rushing champion, McCoo finally got a carry in Week 17 when the Eagles rested their regulars. He has an uphill fight to make the roster again, but the NFL needs more players named "McCoo." If he cannot stick in Philly, he is good enough to be a backup for someone.

Fred McCrary
Height: 6-0 **Weight:** 247 **College:** Mississippi State **Born:** 19-Sep-1972 **Age:** 33

Year	Team	G	Runs	Yds	Yd/R	TD	FUM	DVOA	Rank	DPAR	Rank	PAR	Suc%	Rec	Pass	Yds	CPct	Yd/C	TD	DVOA	Rank	DPAR	Rank
2002	SD	15	2	1	0.5	0	1	-106.4%	—	-0.9	—	-1.0	0%	22	31	96	71%	4.4	3	-44.1%	59	-5.7	59
2003	NE	6	3	3	1.0	0	0	-40.3%	—	-0.5	—	-0.5	33%	2	5	12	40%	6.0	0	-38.1%	—	-0.6	—
2004	ATL	3	0	0	0.0	0	—	—	—	—	—	—	—	2	4	23	50%	11.5	0	12.5%	—	0.5	—
2005	*ATL*	*9*	*4*	*15*	*4.2*	*0*	—	—	—	—	—	—	—	*2*	—	*9*	—	*4.5*	*0*				

Various injuries and his impending 33rd birthday probably spell the end of McCrary's career, but he deserves to be remembered for the solid years he turned in as the blocking back in front of LaDainian Tomlinson.

Willis McGahee   Height: 6-0   Weight: 223   College: Miami   Born: 20-Oct-1981   Age: 24

Year	Team	G	Runs	Yds	Yd/R	TD	FUM	DVOA	Rank	DPAR	Rank	PAR	Suc%	Rec	Pass	Yds	CPct	Yd/C	TD	DVOA	Rank	DPAR	Rank
2003	BUF	0	0	0	0.0	0	—	—	—	—	—	—	—	0	—	0	—	0.0	0	—	—	—	—
2004	BUF	16	284	1128	4.0	13	4	1.2%	25	19.6	12	18.3	46%	22	36	169	61%	7.7	0	-12.2%	39	-0.5	40
2005	BUF	16	348	1505	4.3	12	—	—	—	—	—	—	—	29	—	218	—	7.5	1				

We see good things for McGahee this year. He should be a step faster because his infamous Fiesta Bowl knee injury is a year further in the past. He was clearly better than Travis Henry last year and will be the number one back from Day One in 2005. If the Bills' passing game is good enough that he doesn't see many eight-man fronts and their line makes up for the loss of Jonas Jennings, McGahee could lead the league in rushing. OK, maybe not.

Jason McKie   Height: 5-11   Weight: 231   College: Temple   Born: 22-May-1980   Age: 25

Year	Team	G	Runs	Yds	Yd/R	TD	FUM	DVOA	Rank	DPAR	Rank	PAR	Suc%	Rec	Pass	Yds	CPct	Yd/C	TD	DVOA	Rank	DPAR	Rank
2002	DAL	1	0	0	0.0	0	—	—	—	—	—	—	—	1	1	7	100%	7.0	0	53.7%	—	0.2	—
2003	CHI	6	0	0	0.0	0	—	—	—	—	—	—	—	0	—	0	—	0.0	0	—	—	—	—
2004	CHI	16	1	1	1.0	0	0	-104.9%	—	-0.3	—	-0.3	0%	13	17	70	76%	5.4	2	5.3%	—	1.4	—
2005	CHI	13	7	28	4.3	0	—	—	—	—	—	—	—	11	—	76	—	7.1	1				

McKie is an occasional threat to catch passes out of the backfield. He hasn't done it often, but he's shown some promise when he does.

Travis Minor   Height: 5-10   Weight: 205   College: Florida State   Born: 30-Jun-1979   Age: 26

Year	Team	G	Runs	Yds	Yd/R	TD	FUM	DVOA	Rank	DPAR	Rank	PAR	Suc%	Rec	Pass	Yds	CPct	Yd/C	TD	DVOA	Rank	DPAR	Rank
2002	MIA	16	44	180	4.1	2	—	27.0%	—	6.6	—	6.6	45%	0	—	0	—	0.0	0	—	—	—	—
2003	MIA	16	41	193	4.7	1	0	31.4%	—	8.1	—	7.3	49%	4	5	13	80%	3.3	0	-52.4%	—	-0.8	—
2004	MIA	11	109	388	3.6	3	0	-5.1%	35	4.2	38	3.3	37%	13	27	75	48%	5.8	0	-26.5%	53	-2.5	49
2005	MIA	14	28	121	4.3	1	—	—	—	—	—	—	—	6	—	39	—	6.9	0				

A few optimists said Minor would step into the incense-scented void created by Ricky Williams's departure and play just as well as Williams. Although we've never been fans of Ricky's (and that has nothing to do with his off-field activities), Minor proved that he lacked the durability that made Williams at least somewhat valuable. He had 109 carries, almost twice what he had ever had in a season in the past, and it's doubtful he'll ever break the 100 mark again.

Ryan Moats   Height: 5-8   Weight: 210   College: Louisiana Tech   Born: 17-Dec-1982   Age: 22

Year	Team	G	Runs	Yds	Yd/R	TD	FUM	DVOA	Rank	DPAR	Rank	PAR	Suc%	Rec	Pass	Yds	CPct	Yd/C	TD	DVOA	Rank	DPAR	Rank
2005	PHI	12	36	188	5.2	1	—	—	—	—	—	—	—	10	—	99	—	9.7	1				

The Eagles flirted with the idea of trading for Travis Henry, then gave up on the idea when Henry Jr. was available in the third round. Moats is a tough little runner like Henry: He has a low center of gravity (yes, that means he's short) and drives his legs after contact, dragging defenders for an extra yard or two. He'll complement Brian Westbrook in 2005; in 2006, he'll be on hand to keep Westbrook's contract demands under control.

Mewelde Moore   Height: 5-10   Weight: 205   College: Tulane   Born: 24-Jul-1982   Age: 23

Year	Team	G	Runs	Yds	Yd/R	TD	FUM	DVOA	Rank	DPAR	Rank	PAR	Suc%	Rec	Pass	Yds	CPct	Yd/C	TD	DVOA	Rank	DPAR	Rank
2004	MIN	10	65	379	5.8	0	1	33.3%	—	12.3	—	15.0	57%	27	33	238	82%	8.8	0	6.2%	24	2.8	26
2005	MIN	16	129	590	4.6	4	—	—	—	—	—	—	—	35	—	279	—	8.0	1				

Moore was one of the best players in the league in October, but that was the only point in the season that he got significant playing time as he struggled with injuries and finding a spot on the Vikings' crowded running back depth chart. Although he slipped to the fourth round because he ran a slow 40, Moore proved during his rookie year that he can be a very valuable asset to the Vikings' offense. The Onterrio Smith silliness opens up more playing time for him.

Vernand Morency   Height: 5-9   Weight: 212   College: Oklahoma State   Born: 4-Feb-1980   Age: 25

Year	Team	G	Runs	Yds	Yd/R	TD	FUM	DVOA	Rank	DPAR	Rank	PAR	Suc%	Rec	Pass	Yds	CPct	Yd/C	TD	DVOA	Rank	DPAR	Rank
2005	HOU	12	54	194	3.6	0	—	—	—	—	—	—	—	10	—	90	—	8.8	1				

Morency, who spent time in the Colorado Rockies organization, is eight months older than Domanick Davis. He's a full year older than Tony Hollings, with whom he will likely battle for a roster spot. Morency's age makes him a suspicious prospect: His 1,400 yards in the Big 12 don't stack up well against the younger Davis's 1,200 yards in the NFL. Davis and Morency are similar: short, one-cut runners who can make the most of a slight crack in the defense. Morency will make the team but is no lock to supplant Davis.

Maurice Morris   Height: 5-11   Weight: 202   College: Oregon   Born: 1-Dec-1979   Age: 26

Year	Team	G	Runs	Yds	Yd/R	TD	FUM	DVOA	Rank	DPAR	Rank	PAR	Suc%	Rec	Pass	Yds	CPct	Yd/C	TD	DVOA	Rank	DPAR	Rank
2002	SEA	11	32	153	4.8	0	1	15.5%	—	3.6	—	5.0	56%	3	3	25	100%	8.3	0	-148.1%	—	-1.9	—
2003	SEA	16	38	239	6.3	0	1	36.2%	—	6.9	—	6.8	45%	4	6	32	67%	8.0	1	36.6%	—	1.3	—
2004	SEA	15	30	126	4.2	0	0	15.4%	—	3.7	—	3.9	60%	9	20	53	45%	5.9	0	-27.4%	—	-1.9	—
2005	SEA	16	34	144	4.3	1	—	—	—	—	—	—	—	9	—	67	—	7.7	0				

The failure of the Seahawks to move Shaun Alexander has the biggest impact on Morris. He has been very useful in limited touches as Alexander's backup, and it would have been interesting to see what he did in a full season as a starter. He could be a perfect example of the fungible nature of running backs, as while he might not match Alexander's stats, he would probably get 1,200 yards as an every down player. If he never gets a chance to start in the NFL, at least everyone who watched Oregon beat Colorado in the 2002 Fiesta Bowl will remember a spectacular run in which he somehow kept his balance as he was nearly on his back. Morris and the nearest official were the only people in the stadium who realized he wasn't down.

Sammy Morris   Height: 6-0   Weight: 220   College: Texas Tech   Born: 23-Mar-1977   Age: 28

Year	Team	G	Runs	Yds	Yd/R	TD	FUM	DVOA	Rank	DPAR	Rank	PAR	Suc%	Rec	Pass	Yds	CPct	Yd/C	TD	DVOA	Rank	DPAR	Rank
2002	BUF	15	2	5	2.5	0	0	-81.8%	—	-0.7	—	-0.6	0%	3	4	48	75%	16.0	0	101.5%	—	2.5	—
2003	BUF	9	19	70	3.7	1	0	13.9%	—	2.3	—	1.7	47%	14	17	100	82%	7.1	0	-14.7%	—	-0.2	—
2004	MIA	13	132	523	4.0	6	1	6.2%	18	12.4	25	11.3	45%	22	28	124	79%	5.6	0	-11.0%	37	-0.3	38
2005	MIA	13	26	113	4.4	2	—	—	—	—	—	—	—	10	—	77	—	7.3	0				

Morris never did anything special in Buffalo and didn't look great in his first year in Miami. But when you take a closer look at his numbers with the Dolphins, he actually played pretty well. Behind a horrid offensive line, our DVOA stats indicate that he was an above-average runner. That's hard to do. If he ever got to start a game for a team with professional blockers, Morris might surprise some people.

James Mungro   Height: 5-9   Weight: 214   College: Syracuse   Born: 13-Feb-1978   Age: 27

Year	Team	G	Runs	Yds	Yd/R	TD	FUM	DVOA	Rank	DPAR	Rank	PAR	Suc%	Rec	Pass	Yds	CPct	Yd/C	TD	DVOA	Rank	DPAR	Rank
2002	IND	9	97	336	3.5	8	3	-5.3%	32	4.0	38	-1.2	41%	13	16	81	81%	6.2	0	-26.4%	—	-1.5	—
2003	IND	9	24	60	2.5	2	0	-9.4%	—	0.6	—	0.2	38%	1	5	-4	20%	-4.0	0	-109.2%	—	-2.0	—
2004	IND	15	5	19	3.8	0	0	12.7%	—	0.4	—	0.3	60%	7	8	36	88%	5.1	3	50.3%	—	3.4	—
2005	IND	13	27	117	4.3	0	—	—	—	—	—	—	—	7	—	49	—	6.8	1				

Mungro's career has two notable accomplishments: a 2002 game where he rushed for 114 yards and two touchdowns against the Eagles and the fact that he caught Peyton Manning's record-tying 48th touchdown last season. Other than that, he serves mostly as an emergency running back and the fullback in those rare sets where the Colts use one. When a guy like Mungro is catching three touchdown passes, you know you have a prolific offense.

Damien Nash   Height: 5-10   Weight: 218   College: Missouri   Born: 14-Apr-1982   Age: 23

Year	Team	G	Runs	Yds	Yd/R	TD	FUM	DVOA	Rank	DPAR	Rank	PAR	Suc%	Rec	Pass	Yds	CPct	Yd/C	TD	DVOA	Rank	DPAR	Rank
2005	TEN	12	41	160	3.9	0	—	—	—	—	—	—	—	9	—	84	—	8.9	1				

Nash had limited college experience: He blew out his knee at the juco level, spent a year as a backup at Missouri, then started eight games in 2004 and entered the draft because of financial needs. He catches the ball well and could help out as a third down specialist, but he's a real project.

Lorenzo Neal   Height: 5-11   Weight: 245   College: Fresno State   Born: 27-Dec-1970   Age: 34

Year	Team	G	Runs	Yds	Yd/R	TD	FUM	DVOA	Rank	DPAR	Rank	PAR	Suc%	Rec	Pass	Yds	CPct	Yd/C	TD	DVOA	Rank	DPAR	Rank
2002	CIN	16	9	31	3.4	0	0	13.5%	—	1.0	—	0.8	44%	21	29	133	76%	6.3	1	3.1%	25	2.1	28
2003	SD	16	18	40	2.2	1	0	-8.0%	—	0.6	—	0.9	61%	16	25	62	64%	3.9	0	-60.5%	51	-5.1	49
2004	SD	16	16	53	3.3	0	1	-9.8%	—	0.3	—	0.5	81%	13	19	66	68%	5.1	0	-21.0%	—	-0.9	—
2005	*SD*	*15*	*20*	*67*	*3.4*	*0*	—	—	—	—	—	—	—	*10*	—	*49*	—	*4.9*	*0*				

The closest thing to a superstar at the pure blocking fullback position since Sam Gash retired. We have nothing but respect for a man who earns his living enabling his comrades to achieve riches and glory—he has been the starting fullback for five consecutive 1,000-yard backs. We're betting dollars to donuts he stretches that to six. It does not quite reach Brett Favre levels, but Neal has played in every game since 1994, a streak of 176 consecutive games.

Moran Norris   Height: 6-1   Weight: 250   College: Kansas   Born: 16-Jun-1978   Age: 27

Year	Team	G	Runs	Yds	Yd/R	TD	FUM	DVOA	Rank	DPAR	Rank	PAR	Suc%	Rec	Pass	Yds	CPct	Yd/C	TD	DVOA	Rank	DPAR	Rank
2002	HOU	13	0	0	0.0	0	—	—	—	—	—	—	—	0	—	0	—	0.0	0	—	—	—	—
2003	HOU	16	0	0	0.0	0	—	—	—	—	—	—	—	7	10	40	70%	5.7	0	-34.5%	—	-1.1	—
2004	HOU	12	1	0	0.0	0	0	-94.7%	—	-0.4	—	-0.4	0%	4	5	13	80%	3.3	0	-43.9%	—	-1.0	—
2005	*HOU*	*14*	*6*	*24*	*4.3*	*0*	—	—	—	—	—	—	—	*4*	—	*28*	—	*6.6*	*0*				

What can we say about Moran Norris that hasn't already been said? Well, anything, since nobody talks about fullbacks, particularly ones that only carry the ball once in two seasons. Moran Norris's career goal is to be Lorenzo Neal.

Willie Parker   Height: 5-10   Weight: 208   College: North Carolina   Born: 11-Nov-1980   Age: 25

Year	Team	G	Runs	Yds	Yd/R	TD	FUM	DVOA	Rank	DPAR	Rank	PAR	Suc%	Rec	Pass	Yds	CPct	Yd/C	TD	DVOA	Rank	DPAR	Rank
2004	PIT	8	32	186	5.8	0	0	36.1%	—	6.1	—	5.3	47%	3	7	16	43%	5.3	0	-70.0%	—	-1.4	—
2005	*PIT*	*12*	*25*	*107*	*4.3*	*0*	—	—	—	—	—	—	—	*13*	—	*91*	—	*6.9*	*0*				

Parker made the team as an undrafted free agent and showed glimpses of promise during the Week 17 Bills game. He rushed for 102 yards on 19 carries against one of the league's best defenses. He's small for a starter but he's the fastest player on the team and could eventually become a third down back.

Josh Parry   Height: 6-2   Weight: 250   College: San Jose State   Born: 5-Apr-1978   Age: 27

Year	Team	G	Runs	Yds	Yd/R	TD	FUM	DVOA	Rank	DPAR	Rank	PAR	Suc%	Rec	Pass	Yds	CPct	Yd/C	TD	DVOA	Rank	DPAR	Rank
2004	PHI	13	0	0	0.0	0	—	—	—	—	—	—	—	9	18	75	50%	8.3	0	-33.4%	—	-2.4	—
2005	*PHI*	*13*	*7*	*30*	*4.3*	*0*	—	—	—	—	—	—	—	*14*	—	*95*	—	*6.8*	*0*				

Parry went from practice squad player to Super Bowl starter when Jon Ritchie got hurt. The Eagles don't use a fullback that often, roughly 30% of their offensive snaps, so it doesn't really matter who plays the position as long as he can block a little.

Patrick Pass   Height: 5-10   Weight: 217   College: Georgia   Born: 31-Dec-1977   Age: 27

Year	Team	G	Runs	Yds	Yd/R	TD	FUM	DVOA	Rank	DPAR	Rank	PAR	Suc%	Rec	Pass	Yds	CPct	Yd/C	TD	DVOA	Rank	DPAR	Rank
2002	NE	12	4	27	6.8	0	—	119.8%	—	1.5	—	1.7	50%	0	—	0	—	0.0	0	—	—	—	—
2003	NE	13	6	27	4.5	0	0	31.3%	—	1.3	—	1.3	83%	4	8	21	50%	5.3	0	-60.3%	—	-1.4	—
2004	NE	14	39	141	3.6	0	1	-6.7%	—	1.2	—	0.6	46%	28	32	215	88%	7.7	0	11.2%	18	2.9	25
2005	*NE*	*14*	*26*	*116*	*4.4*	*1*	—	—	—	—	—	—	—	*19*	—	*153*	—	*8.1*	*0*				

Pass is the only fullback on the Pats roster, and he's not even a true fullback. He's a change-of-pace back for the change-of-pace back. In the red zone, he had nine carries for just 16 yards and no first downs. If 2004 isn't his career high in carries and catches, we'll be shocked.

Alvin Pearman

Height: 5-9 Weight: 208 College: Virginia Born: 10-Aug-1982 Age: 23

Year	Team	G	Runs	Yds	Yd/R	TD	FUM	DVOA	Rank	DPAR	Rank	PAR	Suc%	Rec	Pass	Yds	CPct	Yd/C	TD	DVOA	Rank	DPAR	Rank
2005	JAC	13	15	89	5.9	0	—	—	—	—	—	—	—	11	—	76	—	7.1	1				

A little back with good hands but no speed, Pearman will try to stick as a third down back. He will get a chance to replace Jermaine Lewis and David Allen as a punt returner.

Chris Perry

Height: 6-0 Weight: 224 College: Michigan Born: 27-Dec-1981 Age: 23

Year	Team	G	Runs	Yds	Yd/R	TD	FUM	DVOA	Rank	DPAR	Rank	PAR	Suc%	Rec	Pass	Yds	CPct	Yd/C	TD	DVOA	Rank	DPAR	Rank
2004	CIN	2	2	1	0.5	0	0	-123.4%	—	-0.6	—	-0.5	0%	3	3	33	100%	11.0	0	159.7%	—	2.4	—
2005	CIN	12	47	204	4.4	1	—	—	—	—	—	—	—	7	—	52	—	7.6	0				

Whoops! Taking Perry in the 2004 draft was a bit unconventional for the Bengals, who already had a young running back, and things could not have gone worse. The Bengals drafted Perry ahead of the more highly regarded Kevin Jones, who now has star written all over him. Perry fought injuries all season and contributed nothing. Perry's injury and Rudi Johnson's excellent season combined to make the Bengals offer Rudi a long-term deal, eliminating any chance Perry would have of starting without an injury to Johnson. At least Perry can catch passes, something Johnson is unable to do, so maybe he'll develop into a decent third down back.

Adrian Peterson

Height: 5-10 Weight: 210 College: Georgia Southern Born: 1-Jul-1979 Age: 26

Year	Team	G	Runs	Yds	Yd/R	TD	FUM	DVOA	Rank	DPAR	Rank	PAR	Suc%	Rec	Pass	Yds	CPct	Yd/C	TD	DVOA	Rank	DPAR	Rank
2002	CHI	8	19	101	5.3	1	0	38.0%	—	3.8	—	4.7	63%	3	4	18	75%	6.0	0	-10.1%	—	0.0	—
2003	CHI	6	22	70	3.2	0	0	-6.8%	—	0.6	—	-0.1	50%	1	1	5	100%	5.0	0	-42.0%	—	-0.1	—
2004	CHI	14	6	19	3.2	0	0	-52.5%	—	-1.1	—	-0.8	17%	2	2	30	100%	15.0	0	119.8%	—	1.3	—
2005	CHI	12	24	104	4.3	0	—	—	—	—	—	—	—	5	—	40	—	8.0	0				

One of the best players in the history of NCAA Division I-AA football, Peterson is a solid backup who can contribute on special teams.

Artose Pinner

Height: 5-10 Weight: 229 College: Kentucky Born: 5-Jan-1978 Age: 27

Year	Team	G	Runs	Yds	Yd/R	TD	FUM	DVOA	Rank	DPAR	Rank	PAR	Suc%	Rec	Pass	Yds	CPct	Yd/C	TD	DVOA	Rank	DPAR	Rank
2003	DET	3	39	99	2.5	0	0	-41.4%	—	-4.7	—	-4.6	36%	5	7	40	71%	8.0	0	18.3%	—	0.7	—
2004	DET	9	57	174	3.1	2	0	-9.8%	—	1.1	—	1.2	58%	11	11	72	100%	6.5	0	2.5%	—	0.7	—
2005	DET	13	32	137	4.3	1	—	—	—	—	—	—	—	9	—	70	—	7.4	0				

Pinner led the SEC in rushing during his senior year at Kentucky, but his draft stock plummeted when he broke his ankle in the Senior Bowl. The Lions still think he has potential, but he won't get to show it much as long as Kevin Jones is around.

Michael Pittman

Height: 6-0 Weight: 218 College: Fresno State Born: 14-Aug-1975 Age: 30

Year	Team	G	Runs	Yds	Yd/R	TD	FUM	DVOA	Rank	DPAR	Rank	PAR	Suc%	Rec	Pass	Yds	CPct	Yd/C	TD	DVOA	Rank	DPAR	Rank
2002	TB	16	204	718	3.5	1	3	-8.8%	37	4.8	36	-0.4	44%	59	86	477	69%	8.1	0	-5.4%	36	1.8	29
2003	TB	16	187	751	4.0	0	4	-3.1%	30	9.7	28	9.2	49%	75	120	597	63%	8.0	2	-21.4%	47	-5.3	50
2004	TB	13	219	926	4.2	7	6	-12.5%	42	1.9	40	2.2	42%	41	64	391	64%	9.5	3	-7.0%	33	1.0	33
2005	TB	14	113	471	4.2	3	—	—	—	—	—	—	—	33	—	274	—	8.2	1				

Pittman may not be the best NFL running back, or even a very good one, but it's not for lack of running hard. There are few backs in the league that hit the pile with the blunt force of Pittman. The problem for Tampa Bay's human battering ram is that he's always hitting the pile, rarely showing the patience to let holes develop or making anyone miss. It says here that Tampa Bay's much maligned offensive line will actually look more competent with Carnell Williams, a back who won't just run into the first defender in front of him, getting the bulk of the carries. Pittman could still find an effective role as a late-game finisher, punishing an already worn-down defense, or as a receiver out of the backfield in two-back sets.

Clinton Portis

Height: 5-11 Weight: 205   College: Miami   Born: 1-Sep-1981   Age: 24

Year	Team	G	Runs	Yds	Yd/R	TD	FUM	DVOA	Rank	DPAR	Rank	PAR	Suc%	Rec	Pass	Yds	CPct	Yd/C	TD	DVOA	Rank	DPAR	Rank
2002	DEN	16	273	1508	5.5	15	5	24.5%	5	45.3	2	54.0	60%	33	48	364	69%	11.0	2	17.5%	12	7.1	11
2003	DEN	13	290	1591	5.5	14	3	15.2%	6	36.1	4	45.5	53%	38	51	314	75%	8.3	0	-17.2%	40	-1.4	40
2004	WAS	15	343	1315	3.8	5	5	-11.3%	40	4.0	39	3.6	45%	40	57	235	70%	5.9	2	-16.0%	42	-1.6	43
2005	WAS	16	356	1466	4.1	7	—	—	—	—	—	—	—	55	—	400	—	7.3	2				

Clinton Portis was arguably the most disappointing player in all of football in 2004. After ranking fifth and sixth in DVOA in his first two seasons in Denver, Portis dropped all the way to number 40 in his first season as a Redskin. Of course some of the drop-off was to be expected after moving from the infamous Broncos offensive line to an injury-riddled Redskins line that was anchored for most of the season by 42-year-old Ray Brown. As a rookie, Brown played in St. Louis—for the Cardinals. But a decline in offensive line quality can't be the only explanation for Portis's catastrophic decline from 5.5 yards per carry to 3.8. We went looking for players since 1978 who:

1. Carried the ball at least 200 times for three straight years,
2. In the third year, had a drop of at least one yard per carry compared to each of the two years before, and
3. Were in the first five years of their careers.

Those are pretty loose requirements compared to what happened to Portis, and yet Portis is the only running back who qualifies. There are two other running backs who had a similar drop in their sixth year, Joe Morris and Thurman Thomas, but then those guys were not as young as Portis, and they only dropped a yard per carry, not a yard and a half per carry, and Morris only counts because we pro-rated his 1987 stats to 16 games.

Stanley Pritchett

Height: 6-2 Weight: 250   College: South Carolina   Born: 22-Dec-1973 Age: 31

Year	Team	G	Runs	Yds	Yd/R	TD	FUM	DVOA	Rank	DPAR	Rank	PAR	Suc%	Rec	Pass	Yds	CPct	Yd/C	TD	DVOA	Rank	DPAR	Rank
2002	CHI	13	1	2	2.0	0	0	20.1%	—	0.2	—	0.3	100%	19	27	165	70%	8.7	1	29.2%	9	5.5	17
2003	CHI	16	21	93	4.4	2	0	23.9%	—	3.9	—	4.3	57%	18	27	83	67%	4.6	0	-45.9%	50	-4.3	48
2004	ATL	14	6	18	3.0	0	0	-41.2%	—	-0.7	—	-0.5	33%	2	4	5	50%	2.5	1	-33.4%	—	-0.6	—

His long, solid career is coming to an end. Pritchett for years has been the type of player the average fan doesn't notice but the knowledgeable fan appreciates: He throws blocks, he contributes on special teams, and he catches outlet passes when no one else is open.

J. R. Redmond

Height: 5-11 Weight: 215   College: Arizona State   Born: 28-Sep-1977 Age: 28

Year	Team	G	Runs	Yds	Yd/R	TD	FUM	DVOA	Rank	DPAR	Rank	PAR	Suc%	Rec	Pass	Yds	CPct	Yd/C	TD	DVOA	Rank	DPAR	Rank
2002	NE	8	4	2	0.5	0	0	-80.7%	—	-0.9	—	-0.9	50%	2	3	5	67%	2.5	0	-85.9%	—	-1.0	—
2003	OAK	1	9	30	3.3	0	0	-20.9%	—	-0.2	—	0.2	44%	1	2	6	50%	6.0	0	-95.0%	—	-0.4	—
2004	OAK	16	21	119	5.7	0	2	-15.1%	—	-0.1	—	-0.5	43%	32	50	233	64%	7.3	0	-24.8%	51	-3.5	52
2005	OAK	15	30	133	4.4	1	—	—	—	—	—	—	—	18	—	142	—	8.1	0				

A replacement-level running back. Unsure if the Raiders are bringing him back or not.

Dominic Rhodes

Height: 5-9 Weight: 203   College: Midwestern State   Born: 17-Jan-1979 Age: 26

Year	Team	G	Runs	Yds	Yd/R	TD	FUM	DVOA	Rank	DPAR	Rank	PAR	Suc%	Rec	Pass	Yds	CPct	Yd/C	TD	DVOA	Rank	DPAR	Rank
2002	IND	0	0	0	0.0	0	—	—	—	—	—	—	—	0	—	0	—	0.0	0	—	—	—	—
2003	IND	11	37	157	4.2	0	0	0.9%	—	2.1	—	2.6	41%	6	7	62	86%	10.3	1	146.0%	—	3.2	—
2004	IND	16	53	254	4.8	1	1	8.1%	—	4.6	—	4.3	45%	2	4	24	50%	12.0	0	41.4%	—	0.8	—
2005	IND	13	88	353	4.0	4	—	—	—	—	—	—	—	15	—	119	—	7.8	0				

Rhodes has done little since he burst on the scene in 2001 to run for 1,000 yards after the injury to Edgerrin James. Rhodes suffered his own injury the following year and started to get back into form only last season. With Edge's status for the future up in the air, Rhodes got a two-year, $4.75 million extension in February. His work filling in for James will go a long way to determining whether the Colts trust him to take over as the starter in 2006.

Alan Ricard

Height: 5-11 **Weight:** 237 **College:** Louisiana-Monroe **Born:** 17-Jan-1977 **Age:** 28

Year	Team	G	Runs	Yds	Yd/R	TD	FUM	DVOA	Rank	DPAR	Rank	PAR	Suc%	Rec	Pass	Yds	CPct	Yd/C	TD	DVOA	Rank	DPAR	Rank
2002	BAL	15	14	58	4.1	2	0	56.5%	—	3.9	—	3.4	64%	10	14	60	71%	6.0	0	-8.8%	—	0.1	—
2003	BAL	16	19	79	4.2	0	0	-17.5%	—	-0.1	—	0.7	42%	9	15	62	60%	6.9	0	-22.7%	—	-0.8	—
2004	BAL	16	10	36	3.6	0	0	7.5%	—	1.2	—	1.1	70%	11	14	39	79%	3.5	0	-47.5%	—	-2.9	—
2005	*BAL*	*14*	*23*	*98*	*4.3*	*0*	—	—	—	—	—	—	—	*10*	—	*69*	—	*6.9*	*0*				

It is almost cliché to say a fullback is underappreciated, but Ricard does an excellent job for the Ravens. Fullbacks are supposed to be tough guys, but when Ricard leads into a hole and sees both safeties and a linebacker, do you think he ever wonders what it would be like to see only seven men in the box? He must get so jealous when he sees highlights where a fullback gets into the second level to take out a corner. Not with Kyle Boller or Anthony Wright at QB.

Tony Richardson

Height: 6-1 **Weight:** 232 **College:** Auburn **Born:** 17-Dec-1971 **Age:** 33

Year	Team	G	Runs	Yds	Yd/R	TD	FUM	DVOA	Rank	DPAR	Rank	PAR	Suc%	Rec	Pass	Yds	CPct	Yd/C	TD	DVOA	Rank	DPAR	Rank
2002	KC	14	22	81	3.7	2	1	-1.3%	—	0.7	—	1.0	45%	18	23	125	78%	6.9	1	9.9%	—	2.4	—
2003	KC	16	24	59	2.5	0	0	-18.8%	—	-0.5	—	-0.9	42%	12	16	76	75%	6.3	0	11.1%	—	1.3	—
2004	KC	16	12	56	4.7	0	0	33.8%	—	2.4	—	2.2	58%	19	23	118	74%	6.2	0	-23.4%	—	-1.5	—
2005	*KC*	*13*	*22*	*94*	*4.3*	*0*	—	—	—	—	—	—	—	*7*	—	*39*	—	*5.9*	*0*				

Richardson blocked for Marcus Allen early in his career and has played on three Chiefs teams that finished 13–3. He made the Pro Bowl in 2003, more or less by default. His role as an occasional change-up for Priest Holmes will be taken by Larry Johnson. He's had about as good a career as a fullback can have in modern football.

Jon Ritchie

Height: 6-2 **Weight:** 250 **College:** Stanford **Born:** 4-Sep-1974 **Age:** 31

Year	Team	G	Runs	Yds	Yd/R	TD	FUM	DVOA	Rank	DPAR	Rank	PAR	Suc%	Rec	Pass	Yds	CPct	Yd/C	TD	DVOA	Rank	DPAR	Rank
2002	OAK	16	0	0	0.0	0	—	—	—	—	—	—	—	10	21	66	48%	6.6	1	-62.0%	—	-5.3	—
2003	PHI	16	1	1	1.0	0	0	-110.4%	—	-0.3	—	-0.3	0%	17	26	86	65%	5.1	3	1.2%	24	1.3	26
2004	PHI	3	0	0	0.0	0	—	—	—	—	—	—	—	4	6	36	67%	9.0	0	19.1%	—	0.9	—
2005	*PHI*	*14*	*4*	*17*	*4.3*	*0*	—	—	—	—	—	—	—	*2*	—	*11*	—	*6.2*	*0*				

A tough guy and fan favorite, Ritchie is a good lead blocker and outlet receiver, but he's getting older and has limited usefulness in the Eagles system. There wasn't much drop-off when Josh Parry replaced him last year. In fact, since both Parry and Ritchie have scruffy long hair and beards, we're not exactly sure they're different people.

Jamal Robertson

Height: 5-10 **Weight:** 210 **College:** Ohio Northern **Born:** 10-Jan-1977 **Age:** 28

Year	Team	G	Runs	Yds	Yd/R	TD	FUM	DVOA	Rank	DPAR	Rank	PAR	Suc%	Rec	Pass	Yds	CPct	Yd/C	TD	DVOA	Rank	DPAR	Rank
2002	SF	6	0	0	0.0	0	—	—	—	—	—	—	—	0	—	0	—	0.0	0	—	—	—	—
2003	SF	9	32	136	4.3	0	0	-10.4%	—	0.8	—	0.9	34%	0	2	0	0%	0.0	0	-134.1%	—	-1.5	—
2004	SF	7	16	71	4.4	1	2	-42.8%	—	-2.3	—	-2.0	56%	4	5	34	80%	8.5	0	86.3%	0	2.3	0
2004	CAR	5	0	0	0.0	0	—	—	—	—	—	—	—	0	0	0	0%	0.0	0	—	—	—	—
2005	*CAR*	*12*	*28*	*118*	*4.3*	*0*	—	—	—	—	—	—	—	*7*	—	*56*	—	*7.7*	*0*				

Robertson started the year as Kevan Barlow's backup, was released because he couldn't hold onto the ball, and showed up in Carolina in November just like pretty much every other out-of-work running back. Carolina tendered him a one-year contract this past March as insurance against Davis not being able to return, and he's somewhere between 2nd and 37th on the depth chart.

B. J. Sams

Height: 5-10 **Weight:** 173 **College:** McNeese State **Born:** 29-Oct-1980 **Age:** 25

Year	Team	G	Runs	Yds	Yd/R	TD	FUM	DVOA	Rank	DPAR	Rank	PAR	Suc%	Rec	Pass	Yds	CPct	Yd/C	TD	DVOA	Rank	DPAR	Rank
2004	BAL	16	4	19	4.8	1	0	75.1%	—	1.8	—	1.6	75%	1	4	2	25%	2.0	0	-127.2%	—	-2.4	—
2005	*BAL*	*16*	*13*	*56*	*4.3*	*0*	—	—	—	—	—	—	—	*4*	—	*27*	—	*6.8*	*0*				

Rookies can be inconsistent. Primarily a special teams return man, Sams was being hailed as the next Dante Hall and named special teams player of the month in October after two touchdown returns. By December, fans were clamoring for his benching after his fifth special teams fumble.

Cecil Sapp

Height: 5-11 **Weight:** 229   **College:** Colorado State   **Born:** 12-Dec-1978 **Age:** 26

Year	Team	G	Runs	Yds	Yd/R	TD	FUM	DVOA	Rank	DPAR	Rank	PAR	Suc%	Rec	Pass	Yds	CPct	Yd/C	TD	DVOA	Rank	DPAR	Rank
2003	DEN	1	12	31	2.6	0	—	-51.6%	—	-1.7	—	-1.9	25%	0	—	0	—	0.0	0	—	—	—	—
2004	DEN	5	4	32	8.0	0	0	117.8%	—	2.3	—	2.3	100%	0	2	0	0%	0.0	0	-79.5%	—	-0.8	—
2005	DEN	11	13	54	4.3	0	—	—	—	—	—	—	—	6	—	38	—	6.6	0				

If you're looking for a player who could be the next Reuben Droughns, remember this: Denver drafted Cecil Sapp as yet another of their many running backs, but he now seems to be entrenched as a fullback, where he shows promise. Then again, we all thought Ruben Droughns was entrenched as a fullback until a whole lot of running backs got injured.

Cory Schlesinger

Height: 6-0 **Weight:** 247   **College:** Nebraska   **Born:** 23-Jun-1972 **Age:** 33

Year	Team	G	Runs	Yds	Yd/R	TD	FUM	DVOA	Rank	DPAR	Rank	PAR	Suc%	Rec	Pass	Yds	CPct	Yd/C	TD	DVOA	Rank	DPAR	Rank
2002	DET	16	49	139	2.8	2	2	-45.2%	—	-6.8	—	-9.1	37%	35	54	263	65%	7.5	0	-22.2%	51	-3.6	53
2003	DET	16	9	16	1.8	0	0	-19.1%	—	-0.3	—	-0.2	56%	34	49	247	69%	7.3	2	-0.9%	27	1.8	23
2004	DET	13	4	7	1.8	0	0	-52.8%	—	-0.9	—	-0.8	25%	10	16	91	63%	9.1	3	15.2%	—	2.6	—
2005	DET	13	9	40	4.3	0	—	—	—	—	—	—	—	6	—	36	—	6.0	1				

Schlesinger was the best blocking fullback in the league during the Marty Mornhinweg era, but the Lions were so bad that no one noticed. Now he's slowing down (he was never very fast to begin with) and he's still a good blocker, but he doesn't hit linebackers with quite the impact that he once did.

Josh Scobey

Height: 6-0 **Weight:** 222   **College:** Kansas State   **Born:** 11-Dec-1979 **Age:** 25

Year	Team	G	Runs	Yds	Yd/R	TD	FUM	DVOA	Rank	DPAR	Rank	PAR	Suc%	Rec	Pass	Yds	CPct	Yd/C	TD	DVOA	Rank	DPAR	Rank
2003	ARI	15	0	0	0.0	0	—	—	—	—	—	—	—	1	1	9	100%	9.0	0	61.5%	—	0.3	—
2004	ARI	12	27	89	3.3	0	0	-18.9%	—	-0.6	—	0.1	41%	18	21	191	86%	10.6	0	44.5%	—	5.1	—
2005	ARI	15	28	121	4.4	0	—	—	—	—	—	—	—	10	—	90	—	8.7	0				

The Cardinals collect this kind of player: 220-pound all-purpose backs who aren't very durable. Scobey doubles as a mediocre kickoff returner when he's not pressed into service as a third down back. There's only room for one of this type of player on the roster, unless they all plan to spend four games on the injured list, in which case you can have four of them.

Daimon Shelton

Height: 6-0 **Weight:** 262   **College:** Sacramento State   **Born:** 15-Sep-1972 **Age:** 33

Year	Team	G	Runs	Yds	Yd/R	TD	FUM	DVOA	Rank	DPAR	Rank	PAR	Suc%	Rec	Pass	Yds	CPct	Yd/C	TD	DVOA	Rank	DPAR	Rank
2002	CHI	10	0	0	0.0	0	—	—	—	—	—	—	—	7	9	34	78%	4.9	0	2.0%	—	0.7	—
2003	CHI	0	0	0	0.0	0	—	—	—	—	—	—	—	0	—	0	—	0.0	0	—	—	—	—
2004	BUF	16	0	0	0.0	0	—	—	—	—	—	—	—	17	24	114	71%	6.7	0	-3.3%	—	0.7	—
2005	BUF	13	4	20	4.4	0	—	—	—	—	—	—	—	7	—	50	—	7.0	0				

Shelton is a solid lead blocker who never runs the ball but is occasionally used as an outlet receiver.

Eric Shelton

Height: 6-1 **Weight:** 246   **College:** Louisville   **Born:** 23-Jun-1983 **Age:** 22

Year	Team	G	Runs	Yds	Yd/R	TD	FUM	DVOA	Rank	DPAR	Rank	PAR	Suc%	Rec	Pass	Yds	CPct	Yd/C	TD	DVOA	Rank	DPAR	Rank
2005	CAR	13	134	525	3.9	4	—	—	—	—	—	—	—	16	—	118	—	7.4	1				

Dan Henning likes big backs, and he cannot lie. When he was head coach of the Falcons, he gave William Andrews and Gerald Riggs about 330 carries per year, most of them right up the gut. In San Diego, when Marion Butts wasn't enough of a battering ram, he would give the ball to converted tight end Rod Bernstine. Last year, when Brad Hoover had to move from fullback to halfback, Henning didn't seem too upset. So big, wide, heavy-hitting Shelton should be a Henning favorite.

Marcel Shipp

Height: 5-11 **Weight:** 230 **College:** Massachusetts **Born:** 8-Aug-1978 **Age:** 27

Year	Team	G	Runs	Yds	Yd/R	TD	FUM	DVOA	Rank	DPAR	Rank	PAR	Suc%	Rec	Pass	Yds	CPct	Yd/C	TD	DVOA	Rank	DPAR	Rank
2002	ARI	15	188	844	4.5	6	4	-6.4%	33	7.6	31	8.4	41%	39	50	420	78%	10.8	3	39.6%	6	10.7	5
2003	ARI	16	227	828	3.6	0	3	-12.2%	43	2.8	39	0.1	43%	30	37	184	81%	6.1	0	-16.3%	36	-0.9	35
2004	ARI	0	0	0	0.0	0	—	0.0%	0	0.0	0	0.0	0%	0	—	0	—	0.0	0	—	—	—	—
2005	ARI	14	97	399	4.1	3	—	—	—	—	—	—	—	12	—	91	—	7.3	1				

A nothing-special runner coming off a bad injury, Shipp is a big back with little-back skills. He cuts back well, catches the ball OK, but isn't durable and fumbles too often. Shipp missed all of 2004 but is a better option as the number two running back in Arizona than Troy Hambrick, Larry Croom, or Josh Scobey.

Ian Smart

Height: 5-8 **Weight:** 192 **College:** C.W. Post **Born:** 28-Feb-1980 **Age:** 25

Year	Team	G	Runs	Yds	Yd/R	TD	FUM	DVOA	Rank	DPAR	Rank	PAR	Suc%	Rec	Pass	Yds	CPct	Yd/C	TD	DVOA	Rank	DPAR	Rank
2004	TB	4	2	26	13.0	0	0	134.1%	—	1.2	—	1.2	50%	2	2	10	100%	5.0	0	30.6%	—	0.5	—
2005	TB	11	8	35	4.3	0	—	—	—	—	—	—	—	11	—	69	—	6.3	1				

Smart's first NFL carry went for 25 yards. His career average after two carries is 13.0. He should have quit while he was ahead.

Rod Smart

Height: 5-11 **Weight:** 201 **College:** Western Kentucky **Born:** 9-Jan-1977 **Age:** 28

Year	Team	G	Runs	Yds	Yd/R	TD	FUM	DVOA	Rank	DPAR	Rank	PAR	Suc%	Rec	Pass	Yds	CPct	Yd/C	TD	DVOA	Rank	DPAR	Rank
2002	CAR	15	1	2	2.0	0	—	41.3%	—	0.4	—	0.4	100%	0	—	0	—	0.0	0	—	—	—	—
2003	CAR	16	20	49	2.5	0	0	-26.7%	—	-1.1	—	-1.3	35%	3	3	11	100%	3.7	0	-34.5%	—	-0.3	—
2004	CAR	3	3	4	1.3	0	0	-81.2%	—	-0.5	—	-0.4	0%	1	1	5	100%	5.0	0	-85.3%	—	-0.3	—
2005	CAR	14	22	93	4.3	0	—	—	—	—	—	—	—	4	—	25	—	6.8	0				

Considering his lack of success as an RB and coming off a season-ending injury, it's a bit of a surprise that Carolina signed the back formerly known as "He Hate Me" to a four-year contract extension this past off-season. Smart is used as a kick-off return specialist.

Antowain Smith

Height: 6-2 **Weight:** 232 **College:** Houston **Born:** 14-Mar-1972 **Age:** 33

Year	Team	G	Runs	Yds	Yd/R	TD	FUM	DVOA	Rank	DPAR	Rank	PAR	Suc%	Rec	Pass	Yds	CPct	Yd/C	TD	DVOA	Rank	DPAR	Rank
2002	NE	16	252	982	3.9	6	2	-2.2%	27	13.0	27	16.5	50%	31	42	243	74%	7.8	2	5.2%	21	3.4	23
2003	NE	13	182	642	3.5	3	1	-5.8%	34	7.4	33	5.2	45%	14	16	92	88%	6.6	0	-18.8%	—	-0.4	—
2004	TEN	13	137	509	3.7	4	2	-16.2%	46	-0.9	45	1.5	40%	22	26	169	85%	7.7	0	3.7%	26	1.9	31
2005	NO	11	47	199	4.2	2	—	—	—	—	—	—	—	8	—	59	—	7.3	0				

Smith came to Tennessee after being let go by the Patriots, and he got extensive work behind injury-prone starter Chris Brown. His production has declined for three straight years, and at age 33, he offers no real value to a team. He moves to New Orleans this year to back up Deuce McAllister.

Emmitt Smith

Height: 5-10 **Weight:** 221 **College:** Florida **Born:** 15-May-1969 **Age:** 36

Year	Team	G	Runs	Yds	Yd/R	TD	FUM	DVOA	Rank	DPAR	Rank	PAR	Suc%	Rec	Pass	Yds	CPct	Yd/C	TD	DVOA	Rank	DPAR	Rank
2002	DAL	16	254	975	3.8	5	3	-9.0%	38	4.6	37	4.9	44%	16	24	89	67%	5.6	0	-44.9%	—	-4.2	—
2003	ARI	10	90	256	2.8	2	2	-31.7%	52	-6.4	52	-8.6	39%	14	19	107	74%	7.6	0	-0.9%	—	0.7	—
2004	ARI	15	267	937	3.5	9	4	-16.1%	45	-2.0	48	-3.5	39%	15	20	105	75%	7.0	0	-0.8%	—	0.9	—

Smith had career lows in yards, average gain, and touchdowns during an injury-plagued 2003 season and was only marginally better through a relatively healthy 2004. It's questionable whether Smith could have found a team to sign him even if he wanted to come back for a 16th season in 2005. When he becomes eligible in five years, Smith will be a unanimous selection for the Pro Football Hall of Fame. People will talk about Super Bowl XXVIII, when he gained 132 yards and scored two touchdowns on 30 carries. On one drive, he carried on seven of the Cowboys' eight plays, gaining 61 of the team's 64 yards, culminating in a 15-yard touchdown run. Decades from now, when fans not yet born turn on NFL Films, that's how they'll see Emmitt Smith. These two years in the desert will disappear from our memories like a mirage.

Jonathan Smith
Height: 5-10 Weight: 194   College: Washington State   Born: 28-Nov-1981 Age: 24

Year	Team	G	Runs	Yds	Yd/R	TD	FUM	DVOA	Rank	DPAR	Rank	PAR	Suc%	Rec	Pass	Yds	CPct	Yd/C	TD	DVOA	Rank	DPAR	Rank
2004	BUF	9	2	11	5.5	0	—	—	—	—	—	—	—	3	6	21	50%	7.0	0	-48.8%	—	-1.4	—
2005	BUF	12	7	31	4.3	0	—	—	—	—	—	—	—	11	—	70	—	6.3	1				

Primarily a special teams player, Smith shows great promise as a punt returner.

Musa Smith
Height: 6-0 Weight: 232   College: Georgia   Born: 31-May-1982 Age: 23

Year	Team	G	Runs	Yds	Yd/R	TD	FUM	DVOA	Rank	DPAR	Rank	PAR	Suc%	Rec	Pass	Yds	CPct	Yd/C	TD	DVOA	Rank	DPAR	Rank
2003	BAL	11	9	31	3.4	2	—	-75.0%	—	-1.7	—	-1.1	44%	0		0		0.0	0	—	—	—	—
2004	BAL	9	12	48	4.0	0	0	0.6%	—	0.9	—	0.5	33%	2	4	31	50%	15.5	0	74.7%	—	1.3	—
2005	BAL	13	18	77	4.3	0	—	—	—	—	—	—	—	6	—	49	—	8.4	0				

Smith got drafted in more fantasy drafts last year than he ever will for the rest of his career. He lost out to Chester Taylor in the battle to start when Jamal Lewis was otherwise engaged. Taylor was even better than Lewis over the course of last season, making Smith's battle for carries decidedly uphill. The Ravens' decision to keep Taylor is almost as much an indictment of Smith as it is a compliment to Taylor.

Onterrio Smith
Height: 5-10 Weight: 214   College: Oregon   Born: 8-Dec-1980 Age: 24

Year	Team	G	Runs	Yds	Yd/R	TD	FUM	DVOA	Rank	DPAR	Rank	PAR	Suc%	Rec	Pass	Yds	CPct	Yd/C	TD	DVOA	Rank	DPAR	Rank
2003	MIN	15	107	579	5.4	5	1	34.7%	1	21.3	11	21.7	57%	15	20	129	75%	8.6	0	14.9%	—	2.2	—
2004	MIN	11	124	544	4.4	2	2	2.4%	22	8.4	34	8.5	45%	36	45	394	80%	10.9	2	43.2%	4	13.5	3

So, finally we discover why the Vikings had to carry five running backs. Apparently, the Whizzinator of OS just loves that ganja. Suspended for the year.

Terrelle Smith
Height: 6-0 Weight: 246   College: Arizona State   Born: 12-Mar-1978 Age: 27

Year	Team	G	Runs	Yds	Yd/R	TD	FUM	DVOA	Rank	DPAR	Rank	PAR	Suc%	Rec	Pass	Yds	CPct	Yd/C	TD	DVOA	Rank	DPAR	Rank
2002	NO	14	5	11	2.2	0	1	-32.3%	—	-0.4	—	-0.3	40%	9	13	30	69%	3.3	0	-70.7%	—	-4.6	—
2003	NO	15	0	0	0.0	0	—	—	—	—	—	—	—	6	10	28	60%	4.7	0	-33.4%	—	-1.0	—
2004	CLE	16	4	9	2.3	0	0	31.8%	—	1.2	—	1.0	100%	7	12	39	58%	5.6	0	-33.7%	—	-1.7	—
2005	CLE	13	9	38	4.3	0	—	—	—	—	—	—	—	5	—	35	—	7.4	0				

The NFL has only 32 teams and a limited number of starting positions, but is there anything less glamorous than being the starting fullback for the Cleveland Browns? It is sort of like being nominated for an Oscar for Best Animated Short. Sure, it's an Oscar nomination, but once you have said, "I was nominated for an Oscar," you sort of dread the follow-up question of "What for?" Smith likely quickly exits conversations after telling people he is a starter in the NFL.

Jerald Sowell
Height: 6-0 Weight: 237   College: Tulane   Born: 21-Jan-1974 Age: 31

Year	Team	G	Runs	Yds	Yd/R	TD	FUM	DVOA	Rank	DPAR	Rank	PAR	Suc%	Rec	Pass	Yds	CPct	Yd/C	TD	DVOA	Rank	DPAR	Rank
2002	NYJ	14	1	0	0.0	0	0	-116.2%	—	-0.7	—	-0.7	0%	9	13	85	69%	9.4	1	43.6%	—	3.8	—
2003	NYJ	16	1	2	2.0	0	0	-40.6%	—	-0.1	—	-0.2	0%	47	60	436	78%	9.3	1	32.3%	5	11.5	3
2004	NYJ	16	2	28	14.0	0	1	301.9%	—	1.3	—	1.3	50%	45	59	342	76%	7.6	1	13.0%	17	7.1	9
2005	NYJ	16	9	42	4.5	1	—	—	—	—	—	—	—	29	—	230	—	7.9	1				

Reports said the infamous sideline confrontation between Herman Edwards and running backs coach Bishop Harris during the San Diego playoff game stemmed from Edwards wanting both Curtis Martin and LaMont Jordan on the field at the same time. If that's true, Harris was in the right. When Martin and Jordan were both on the field, Jerald Sowell had to come out, and Sowell is one of the league's best fullbacks. Jordan and Martin are both good runners, but neither is in the same league as Sowell as a blocker (neither is Derrick Blaylock, Jordan's replacement for 2005). A good example came on a second-and-12 play in the playoff game against the Steelers. Jordan motioned right and didn't block anyone, and then the ball went to Martin, who got stuffed going to the right. If it had been Sowell instead of Jordan on the field, Martin would have had room to run.

Darren Sproles Height: 5-6 Weight: 181 College: Kansas State Born: 20-Jun-1983 Age: 22

Year	Team	G	Runs	Yds	Yd/R	TD	FUM	DVOA	Rank	DPAR	Rank	PAR	Suc%	Rec	Pass	Yds	CPct	Yd/C	TD	DVOA	Rank	DPAR	Rank
2005	SD	16	11	49	4.5	0	—	—	—	—	—	—	—	12	—	151	—	12.3	2				

Every writer grading drafts seemed to like the pick of Sproles in the fourth round by the Chargers. Apparently, like all of us, they saw Sproles dominate Oklahoma in the Big 12 championship game two years ago. Very fast, but very small. The plan is for him to return kicks, but it will be hard for someone this little to compete.

Duce Staley Height: 5-11 Weight: 220 College: South Carolina Born: 27-Feb-1975 Age: 30

Year	Team	G	Runs	Yds	Yd/R	TD	FUM	DVOA	Rank	DPAR	Rank	PAR	Suc%	Rec	Pass	Yds	CPct	Yd/C	TD	DVOA	Rank	DPAR	Rank
2002	PHI	16	269	1030	3.8	5	2	-3.0%	30	13.5	26	13.3	47%	51	69	541	74%	10.6	3	39.9%	5	18.2	3
2003	PHI	16	97	457	4.7	5	2	29.9%	3	16.6	17	15.7	57%	36	47	382	77%	10.6	2	30.4%	7	8.0	7
2004	PIT	10	192	830	4.3	1	3	1.7%	23	13.2	24	11.2	48%	6	12	55	50%	9.2	0	-10.8%	—	-0.1	—
2005	PIT	14	191	795	4.2	5	—	—	—	—	—	—	—	18	—	132	—	7.3	1				

Staley missed six games in 2004 because of a hamstring injury and still managed twice as many carries as he had with the Eagles the year before. Staley has battled injuries during his eight-year career but the Steelers are betting that his time in Philadelphia's West Coast offense helped prolong his career. He'll be the starter in 2005, but expect to see a lot of the Bus too.

Aaron Stecker Height: 5-10 Weight: 205 College: Western Illinois Born: 13 Nov 1975 Age: 30

Year	Team	G	Runs	Yds	Yd/R	TD	FUM	DVOA	Rank	DPAR	Rank	PAR	Suc%	Rec	Pass	Yds	CPct	Yd/C	TD	DVOA	Rank	DPAR	Rank
2002	TB	16	28	174	6.2	0	1	15.0%	—	3.2	—	2.5	46%	13	16	69	81%	5.3	0	-20.1%	—	-0.9	—
2003	TB	16	37	125	3.4	0	0	-7.3%	—	1.2	—	1.1	44%	9	12	48	75%	5.3	1	-11.3%	—	0.0	—
2004	NO	16	58	244	4.2	2	1	-19.7%	—	-1.2	—	-0.3	36%	29	38	174	76%	6.0	0	-17.8%	44	-1.6	44
2005	NO	15	35	152	4.3	2	—	—	—	—	—	—	—	17	—	131	—	7.7	0				

Stecker is a little small and doesn't find holes very well as a running back, although he's a consistent contributor on special teams. He got a big opportunity for playing time when Deuce McAllister was hurt, and his 108-yard performance against St. Louis in Week 3 set off a fantasy stampede. Those who won their waiver claims were treated to a grand total of 9 rushing yards the following week, after which McAllister came back and Stecker got only 17 carries and 74 yards the rest of the year.

Mack Strong Height: 6-0 Weight: 245 College: Georgia Born: 11-Sep-1971 Age: 34

Year	Team	G	Runs	Yds	Yd/R	TD	FUM	DVOA	Rank	DPAR	Rank	PAR	Suc%	Rec	Pass	Yds	CPct	Yd/C	TD	DVOA	Rank	DPAR	Rank
2002	SEA	16	23	94	4.1	0	0	38.0%	—	6.1	—	6.9	78%	22	32	120	69%	5.5	2	-5.2%	34	0.8	39
2003	SEA	16	37	174	4.7	1	1	23.1%	—	6.8	—	7.1	68%	29	33	216	88%	7.4	0	27.1%	10	4.4	13
2004	SEA	16	36	131	3.6	0	2	-27.1%	—	-2.2	—	-2.3	58%	21	31	99	68%	4.7	0	-22.3%	48	-2.1	47
2005	SEA	14	23	98	4.3	0	—	—	—	—	—	—	—	9	—	47	—	5.1	0				

Meet the ultimate short-yardage specialist. Over the last three seasons, Seattle has handed the ball to Strong on third and one 13 times and every single one of them has ended in a first down (although he did fail once last year on fourth and one). Alexander, in the same situation, is 16-for-28. On the other hand, Strong had just a single run over eight yards last year.

Lee Suggs Height: 6-0 Weight: 205 College: Virginia Tech Born: 11-Aug-1980 Age: 25

Year	Team	G	Runs	Yds	Yd/R	TD	FUM	DVOA	Rank	DPAR	Rank	PAR	Suc%	Rec	Pass	Yds	CPct	Yd/C	TD	DVOA	Rank	DPAR	Rank
2003	CLE	7	56	289	5.2	2	1	6.7%	—	5.4	—	5.3	48%	2	4	0	50%	0.0	0	-90.8%	—	-1.4	—
2004	CLE	10	199	744	3.7	2	6	-14.9%	44	-0.5	44	-6.5	45%	20	35	178	57%	8.9	1	-13.5%	41	-0.7	41
2005	CLE	12	68	259	3.8	1	—	—	—	—	—	—	—	11	—	84	—	7.6	0				

Lee Suggs looked like he would be the starter heading into training camp only to have the Browns trade for Reuben Droughns before the draft. Still, in two seasons Suggs has been a very capable backup. In 2004 he started four games and finished the season with 744 rushing yards. He's battled injuries during his short career, but when he's healthy he's been a solid contributor.

Thomas Tapeh Height: 6-1 Weight: 245 College: Minnesota Born: 28-Mar-1980 Age: 25

Year	Team	G	Runs	Yds	Yd/R	TD	FUM	DVOA	Rank	DPAR	Rank	PAR	Suc%	Rec	Pass	Yds	CPct	Yd/C	TD	DVOA	Rank	DPAR	Rank
2004	PHI	7	12	42	3.5	0	0	-8.0%	—	0.4	—	0.2	33%	2	2	15	100%	7.5	0	58.0%	—	0.6	—
2005	PHI	12	12	51	4.3	0	—	—	—	—	—	—	—	13	—	92	—	6.9	0				

Tapeh dislocated his hip with 28 seconds left in Philadelphia's meaningless loss to St. Louis last year. He is apparently ahead of schedule in his rehabilitation, so he may be healthy enough to make the team, play on some kickoff coverage, and finally get a few carries when the Eagles have clinched a playoff spot and are playing a meaningless game at the end of 2005.

Chester Taylor Height: 5-11 Weight: 213 College: Toledo Born: 22-Sep-1979 Age: 26

Year	Team	G	Runs	Yds	Yd/R	TD	FUM	DVOA	Rank	DPAR	Rank	PAR	Suc%	Rec	Pass	Yds	CPct	Yd/C	TD	DVOA	Rank	DPAR	Rank
2002	BAL	14	33	122	3.7	0	0	1.7%	—	2.0	—	1.1	42%	14	22	129	64%	9.2	2	48.3%	—	5.4	—
2003	BAL	16	63	276	4.4	2	1	-14.7%	—	0.3	—	3.0	41%	20	27	132	74%	6.6	0	0.9%	25	0.9	30
2004	BAL	16	160	714	4.5	2	1	7.8%	16	14.0	22	12.5	41%	30	36	184	78%	6.1	0	-9.6%	—	0.2	—
2005	BAL	16	87	377	4.3	1	—	—	—	—	—	—	—	27	—	205	—	7.5	0				

2005 could be his breakout year because of the uncertainty surrounding Jamal Lewis's comeback. The former fifth-round pick successfully filled in for Lewis last season and the Ravens consider him so important that they matched the Browns' offer this off-season to keep him from going to Cleveland. If Lewis can't go, don't be surprised if Taylor has a good season.

Fred Taylor Height: 6-1 Weight: 234 College: Florida Born: 27-Jan-1976 Age: 29

Year	Team	G	Runs	Yds	Yd/R	TD	FUM	DVOA	Rank	DPAR	Rank	PAR	Suc%	Rec	Pass	Yds	CPct	Yd/C	TD	DVOA	Rank	DPAR	Rank
2002	JAC	16	287	1314	4.6	8	3	6.0%	17	23.7	7	22.1	44%	49	57	408	86%	8.3	0	18.2%	11	7.8	9
2003	JAC	16	345	1572	4.6	6	6	-1.4%	26	21.0	12	23.2	46%	48	73	370	66%	7.7	1	-10.9%	34	-0.3	34
2004	JAC	14	260	1224	4.7	2	3	-3.5%	33	10.1	31	13.7	45%	36	58	345	62%	9.6	1	3.2%	28	3.8	21
2005	JAC	13	211	915	4.3	4	—	—	—	—	—	—	—	35	—	283	—	8.1	1				

And so Fred Taylor begins the gradual decline that gets almost every back in his late 20s. Taylor posted a conventionally excellent 4.7 yards per carry, but according to DVOA, he was a below-average back. After battling the injury-prone label for a long time, Taylor ran off 46 consecutive starts until he missed the last two games of 2004 with a knee strain that required surgery. Rehab took longer than expected, a troubling sign given Taylor's past. By late May, the Jags were making scary noises about Taylor missing the season.

Anthony Thomas Height: 6-2 Weight: 228 College: Michigan Born: 7-Nov-1977 Age: 28

Year	Team	G	Runs	Yds	Yd/R	TD	FUM	DVOA	Rank	DPAR	Rank	PAR	Suc%	Rec	Pass	Yds	CPct	Yd/C	TD	DVOA	Rank	DPAR	Rank
2002	CHI	12	214	721	3.4	6	5	-22.4%	46	-7.2	49	-9.4	44%	24	41	163	59%	6.8	0	-25.6%	55	-3.3	52
2003	CHI	13	244	1024	4.2	6	1	-2.8%	29	12.1	25	15.8	45%	9	14	36	64%	4.0	0	-61.3%	—	-2.5	—
2004	CHI	12	122	404	3.3	2	1	-31.5%	51	-9.0	52	-3.9	40%	17	23	132	74%	7.8	0	10.0%	—	2.0	—
2005	DAL	14	102	435	4.3	3	—	—	—	—	—	—	—	14	—	112	—	7.8	0				

We'll never really know what became of that great rookie running back from the 13–3 Chicago Bears of 2001. The Thomas of 2002 and beyond is a completely different guy. That guy is now part of the crowded backfield in Dallas, but Parcells likes to pound the big guys in there in short-yardage situations, so that's probably where Thomas will get most of his carries. If you have Julius Jones on your fantasy team this year, prepare to swear at the television whenever Thomas vultures a touchdown.

LaBrandon Toefield Height: 5-11 Weight: 232 College: LSU Born: 24-Sep-1980 Age: 25

Year	Team	G	Runs	Yds	Yd/R	TD	FUM	DVOA	Rank	DPAR	Rank	PAR	Suc%	Rec	Pass	Yds	CPct	Yd/C	TD	DVOA	Rank	DPAR	Rank
2003	JAC	16	53	212	4.0	2	0	3.7%	—	3.7	—	3.4	48%	14	16	105	88%	7.5	1	55.1%	—	4.0	—
2004	JAC	14	51	169	3.3	0	1	-11.5%	—	0.4	—	1.6	49%	28	34	151	82%	5.4	1	1.3%	30	2.0	30
2005	JAC	16	81	334	4.1	2	—	—	—	—	—	—	—	31	—	216	—	7.2	1				

After a promising rookie campaign in 2003, the man that Mexicans call "the Brandon" struggled and was gradually phased out of the offense in 2004. Questions about Fred Taylor's knees may resuscitate his career.

LaDainian Tomlinson
Height: 5-10 **Weight:** 221 **College:** TCU **Born:** 23-Jun-1979 **Age:** 26

Year	Team	G	Runs	Yds	Yd/R	TD	FUM	DVOA	Rank	DPAR	Rank	PAR	Suc%	Rec	Pass	Yds	CPct	Yd/C	TD	DVOA	Rank	DPAR	Rank
2002	SD	16	372	1683	4.5	14	3	1.9%	21	24.5	6	35.3	46%	79	101	489	78%	6.2	1	-19.4%	49	-4.5	55
2003	SD	16	313	1645	5.3	13	1	18.8%	5	42.2	2	42.9	44%	100	137	725	73%	7.3	4	-7.5%	31	1.1	29
2004	SD	15	339	1335	3.9	17	6	-4.9%	34	14.0	23	16.3	45%	53	66	441	80%	8.3	1	3.4%	27	4.1	19
2005	*SD*	*16*	*358*	*1532*	*4.3*	*13*	—	—	—	—	—	—	—	*61*	—	*477*	—	*7.9*	*2*				

Don't be deceived by the 17 touchdowns. San Diego somehow went 12–4 despite a subpar year from Tomlinson, who ran straight into two major historical trends. First, 30 different backs in NFL history have risen at least .5 yards per carry from one season to the next, with a minimum of 250 carries both years, and those backs on average drop by .75 yards per carry in year three. Second, running backs who go over 370 carries generally suffer a major injury or drop in yards per carry within two years. Newsflash: Overuse leads to injuries and, as Dennis Miller once noted, "There is no such thing as a minor groin injury." Tomlinson's likely rebound is one reason to believe the Chargers will not regress to 6–10.

Michael Turner
Height: 5-10 **Weight:** 237 **College:** Northern Illinois **Born:** 13-Feb-1982 **Age:** 23

Year	Team	G	Runs	Yds	Yd/R	TD	FUM	DVOA	Rank	DPAR	Rank	PAR	Suc%	Rec	Pass	Yds	CPct	Yd/C	TD	DVOA	Rank	DPAR	Rank
2004	SD	13	20	104	5.2	0	1	10.4%	—	1.8	—	3.0	40%	4	5	8	80%	2.0	0	-195.2%	—	-4.5	—
2005	*SD*	*13*	*27*	*116*	*4.3*	*0*	—	—	—	—	—	—	—	*12*	—	*81*	—	*7.0*	*0*				

Promising stats from the fifth-round rookie who battled Jesse Chatman for the number two role. His potential is not yet fully known since 15 of his 20 carries came from one game in Week 17.

Kenny Watson
Height: 5-11 **Weight:** 214 **College:** Penn State **Born:** 13-Mar-1978 **Age:** 27

Year	Team	G	Runs	Yds	Yd/R	TD	FUM	DVOA	Rank	DPAR	Rank	PAR	Suc%	Rec	Pass	Yds	CPct	Yd/C	TD	DVOA	Rank	DPAR	Rank
2002	WAS	16	116	534	4.6	1	0	21.4%	6	17.5	19	18.9	53%	32	43	253	74%	7.9	1	-8.2%	41	0.3	41
2003	CIN	8	0	0	0.0	0	—	—	—	—	—	—	—	0	—	0	—	0.0	0	—	—	—	—
2004	CIN	16	26	161	6.2	0	2	-2.0%	—	1.2	—	0.3	48%	25	35	171	71%	6.8	1	9.1%	22	2.7	27
2005	*CIN*	*14*	*29*	*126*	*4.4*	*1*	—	—	—	—	—	—	—	*16*	—	*123*	—	*7.8*	*0*				

Back in August 2003, one of the first articles ever posted on FootballOutsiders.com discussed three running backs who, according to DVOA, were particularly underrated. Moe Williams went on to have two more strong years, Stacey (Big) Mack ate himself out of the league, and nobody would give Kenny Watson a chance. All those Penn State runners who never develop, and this guy can't get a job. Cincinnati finally picked him up as a special teamer, he did well with a few carries last year, and if Chris Perry still isn't ready to backup Rudi Johnson in 2005, Watson can easily fill the role.

Jonathan Wells
Height: 6-1 **Weight:** 243 **College:** Ohio State **Born:** 21-Jul-1979 **Age:** 26

Year	Team	G	Runs	Yds	Yd/R	TD	FUM	DVOA	Rank	DPAR	Rank	PAR	Suc%	Rec	Pass	Yds	CPct	Yd/C	TD	DVOA	Rank	DPAR	Rank
2002	HOU	16	197	529	2.7	3	3	-44.0%	51	-23.7	51	-26.0	27%	9	12	48	75%	5.3	0	-24.9%	—	-0.9	—
2003	HOU	13	5	14	2.8	0	0	-66.0%	—	-1.5	—	-1.2	40%	2	4	17	50%	8.5	0	-23.8%	—	-0.2	—
2004	HOU	16	82	299	3.6	3	1	-11.6%	41	0.9	42	3.6	48%	11	16	79	69%	7.2	2	9.2%	—	1.6	—
2005	*HOU*	*13*	*26*	*112*	*4.3*	*1*	—	—	—	—	—	—	—	*7*	—	*51*	—	*7.6*	*0*				

From the Eddie George School of Running Backs (also known as The Ohio State University), Wells is big and slow and has no wiggle. Despite his size, he's actually a terrible short-yardage back, so he's mostly used as a change-of-pace back. He's the kind of player you expect to find on an expansion team, but he's destined to be a special teamer for most of his career.

Brian Westbrook
Height: 5-8 **Weight:** 200 **College:** Villanova **Born:** 2-Sep-1979 **Age:** 26

Year	Team	G	Runs	Yds	Yd/R	TD	FUM	DVOA	Rank	DPAR	Rank	PAR	Suc%	Rec	Pass	Yds	CPct	Yd/C	TD	DVOA	Rank	DPAR	Rank
2002	PHI	15	46	193	4.2	0	2	-5.1%	—	2.3	—	1.4	48%	9	13	86	69%	9.6	0	-9.8%	—	0.0	—
2003	PHI	15	117	613	5.2	7	0	33.5%	2	20.7	13	19.6	45%	37	49	332	78%	9.0	4	41.7%	3	10.0	4
2004	PHI	13	177	812	4.6	3	1	8.1%	15	15.7	18	15.0	43%	73	87	703	84%	9.6	6	21.6%	8	14.4	2
2005	*PHI*	*16*	*243*	*1127*	*4.6*	*5*	—	—	—	—	—	—	—	*61*	—	*512*	—	*8.4*	*5*				

(continued next page)

Brian Westbrook (*continued*)

Westbrook's high finishes in receiving DPAR weren't lost on the Eagles. He lines up in the slot or split wide frequently; he's more likely to catch a pass on a slant or crossing route than Todd Pinkston is, and he was targeted 11 times in the end zone, more than Pinkston, Freddie Mitchell, and Greg Lewis combined. Westbrook tries to bounce too many carries to the outside, earning some 15-yard gains but leaving him with a low Success Rate. The Eagles will take the trade-off because of the number of big plays Westbrook produces, but they'll always need a conventional running back in the rotation who works inside.

Tyrone Wheatley
Height: 6-0 Weight: 235 College: Michigan Born: 19-Jan-1972 Age: 33

Year	Team	G	Runs	Yds	Yd/R	TD	FUM	DVOA	Rank	DPAR	Rank	PAR	Suc%	Rec	Pass	Yds	CPct	Yd/C	TD	DVOA	Rank	DPAR	Rank
2002	OAK	14	105	411	3.9	2	1	-8.2%	36	2.7	41	7.5	53%	12	20	71	60%	5.9	0	-42.9%	—	-3.0	—
2003	OAK	15	159	678	4.3	4	2	5.2%	19	12.8	23	15.4	50%	12	18	120	67%	10.0	0	16.9%	—	1.8	—
2004	OAK	8	85	327	3.8	4	0	14.0%	11	12.1	28	8.0	51%	15	15	78	100%	5.2	0	13.0%	—	1.6	—
2005	FA	10	46	193	4.2	2	—	—	—	—	—	—	—	6	—	36	—	5.8	0				

The Raiders released Wheatley in March; he's probably finished. He had a fine second career for a player who appeared to be headed for the All Time Draft Busts column after he washed out of New York.

Jamel White
Height: 5-9 Weight: 222 College: South Dakota Born: 11-Feb-1978 Age: 27

Year	Team	G	Runs	Yds	Yd/R	TD	FUM	DVOA	Rank	DPAR	Rank	PAR	Suc%	Rec	Pass	Yds	CPct	Yd/C	TD	DVOA	Rank	DPAR	Rank
2002	CLE	14	106	470	4.4	3	0	4.8%	19	8.1	29	10.0	47%	63	86	452	73%	7.2	0	-9.4%	42	0.2	42
2003	CLE	16	70	266	3.8	1	1	-10.3%	—	1.3	—	0.8	44%	46	69	303	67%	6.6	1	-20.8%	45	-2.9	47
2004	TB	7	13	20	1.5	0	0	-68.2%	—	-2.6	—	-3.0	15%	4	7	17	57%	4.3	0	-70.9%	—	-2.3	—
2004	BAL	6	14	62	4.4	0	0	-23.9%	—	-0.5	—	0.0	36%	2	2	4	100%	2.0	0	-79.4%	—	-0.8	—
2005	DET	13	31	131	4.2	0	—	—	—	—	—	—	—	10	—	78	—	7.7	0				

White is the kind of do-a-little-bit-of-everything back that most teams need somewhere on the depth chart, as he can run, catch, and return kicks if the top three guys are out. In 2004, however, "can" did not mean "can do well," so "is" might end up meaning "was." White will fight with Artose Pinner to be third string in Detroit.

Carnell "Cadillac" Williams
Height: 5-11 Weight: 217 College: Auburn Born: 21-Apr-1982 Age: 23

Year	Team	G	Runs	Yds	Yd/R	TD	FUM	DVOA	Rank	DPAR	Rank	PAR	Suc%	Rec	Pass	Yds	CPct	Yd/C	TD	DVOA	Rank	DPAR	Rank
2005	TB	16	285	1121	3.9	8	—	—	—	—	—	—	—	27	—	224	—	8.2	0				

Bucs coach Jon Gruden may drive an expensive foreign car, but he's thrilled to hitch his star to a Cadillac. Williams caught Gruden's eye when the Buccaneers staff coached the South squad in the Senior Bowl. After three years of watching Michael Pittman do a poor imitation of an every down NFL back, Gruden is thrilled to have a stud in Williams to tote the ball 25 times a game. Gruden is known as a master of matchups and finesse, but at his core, he loves to "pound the rock," something that Williams will be given every chance to do this season.

Moe Williams
Height: 6-1 Weight: 205 College: Kentucky Born: 26-Jul-1974 Age: 31

Year	Team	G	Runs	Yds	Yd/R	TD	FUM	DVOA	Rank	DPAR	Rank	PAR	Suc%	Rec	Pass	Yds	CPct	Yd/C	TD	DVOA	Rank	DPAR	Rank
2002	MIN	16	84	414	4.9	11	1	51.0%	1	26.9	5	24.4	59%	28	42	257	67%	9.2	0	-4.0%	33	1.2	36
2003	MIN	16	174	745	4.3	5	2	5.4%	18	15.0	19	15.5	48%	65	85	644	76%	9.9	3	32.8%	4	15.0	2
2004	MIN	14	30	161	5.4	3	0	42.8%	—	8.8	—	8.9	70%	21	27	233	78%	11.1	1	44.9%	3	6.9	10
2005	MIN	16	69	259	3.7	2	—	—	—	—	—	—	—	24	—	194	—	8.1	1				

The most unappreciated "skill player" in the NFL, period. He's been in the league nine years and has gotten to carry the ball more than 85 times only once. But with those limited opportunities, Williams always produces impressive results. When the Vikings decided to make him their goal line back in 2002, he responded with 11 touchdowns. When they made him more of an all-purpose back in 2003, he responded with nearly 1,400 total yards from scrimmage. He's older than the other backs in the Vikings' stable, but he can still contribute. Just give him a chance.

Ricky Williams

Height: 5-10   Weight: 226   College: Texas   Born: 21-May-1977 Age: 28

Year	Team	G	Runs	Yds	Yd/R	TD	FUM	DVOA	Rank	DPAR	Rank	PAR	Suc%	Rec	Pass	Yds	CPct	Yd/C	TD	DVOA	Rank	DPAR	Rank
2002	MIA	16	383	1853	4.8	16	7	6.8%	15	32.4	3	42.3	51%	47	59	363	80%	7.7	1	8.9%	20	5.8	16
2003	MIA	16	392	1372	3.5	9	7	-11.6%	42	2.4	40	-2.0	39%	50	62	351	81%	7.0	1	-16.7%	38	-1.7	42
2004		420	0	0	0.0	0	—	0.0%	0	0.0	0	0.0	0%	0	—	0	—	0.0	0	—	—	—	—
2005	MIA	12	151	632	4.2	4	—	—	—	—	—	—	—	15	—	118	—	7.9	1				

There is nothing wrong with Ricky Williams's decision that a life of smoking dope and studying holistic medicine is better than one of regularly getting hammered by 300-pound linemen. The problem is that the correct time to make that decision is in February, not in July. The damage to the Dolphins was the psychological blow of his retirement, not the retirement itself. Ricky Williams owns two of the top 13 rushing attempt seasons of all time, and nearly every running back in history with at least 370 carries in a season has lost his speed or blown out his knee within two years. Williams was toast as an effective NFL running back, and the only difference between him and Sammy Morris or Leonard Henry was that opposing coaches respected Williams, which freed up the Miami passing game. If Williams had played last year, those coaches would have eventually wised up. Lawsuits about bonus money aside, we don't think he's coming back. But in case he does, that projection approximates what we think he would do splitting time evenly with Ronnie Brown after he serves a four-game drug suspension.

Shaud Williams

Height: 5-7   Weight: 193   College: Alabama   Born: 2-Oct-1980   Age: 25

Year	Team	G	Runs	Yds	Yd/R	TD	FUM	DVOA	Rank	DPAR	Rank	PAR	Suc%	Rec	Pass	Yds	CPct	Yd/C	TD	DVOA	Rank	DPAR	Rank
2004	BUF	4	42	167	4.0	2	0	5.1%	—	3.2	—	4.4	48%	3	3	19	100%	6.3	0	34.5%	—	0.5	—
2005	BUF	12	43	173	4.0	1	—	—	—	—	—	—	—	12	—	81	—	6.8	0				

SEC Sleeper Alert! If Buffalo can finally get someone to take Travis Henry off its hands, Williams becomes Willis McGahee's backup and he will blow that projection away. He went undrafted because he is so small, but this guy led the SEC in rushing in 2003. The Bills brought him in last year as a free agent and he was inactive for most of the season. When he finally got some playing time in the last four weeks he did very well against the very bad Browns and 49ers. Williams was, believe it or not, second among AFC rookies in rushing yards.

Amos Zereoue

Height: 5-8   Weight: 212   College: West Virginia   Born: 8-Oct-1976   Age: 29

Year	Team	G	Runs	Yds	Yd/R	TD	FUM	DVOA	Rank	DPAR	Rank	PAR	Suc%	Rec	Pass	Yds	CPct	Yd/C	TD	DVOA	Rank	DPAR	Rank
2002	PIT	16	193	762	3.9	4	2	-10.5%	41	3.9	39	3.6	40%	42	53	341	79%	8.1	0	3.1%	24	3.3	24
2003	PIT	16	132	433	3.3	2	0	-19.1%	48	-2.0	48	0.1	39%	40	51	310	78%	7.8	0	3.8%	22	2.7	18
2004	OAK	15	112	425	3.8	3	1	-14.3%	43	0.2	43	1.2	42%	39	47	284	83%	7.3	0	18.2%	14	6.8	11
2005	FA	14	58	252	4.3	2	—	—	—	—	—	—	—	23	—	177	—	7.8	0				

The best players in history with a last name that begins with Z: (1) Garry Zimmerman, perennial Pro Bowl tackle for the Broncos; (2) Jim Zorn, longtime Seahawks quarterback; (3) Roger Zatkoff, three-time Pro Bowl linebacker for the Packers in the 1950s; (4) Mike Zordich, who played safety for the Jets, Eagles, and Cardinals and made two All Madden teams; (5) Chris Zorich, Bears defensive lineman of the mid-1990s and noted philanthropist; (6) Zereoue, who leapt past John Zook by leading the Raiders in rushing last season. He's always been a low Success Rate runner who gets by on his big-play ability and receiving, but he'll have a hard time moving up the "All Z" list even if someone signs him for 2005. At least he has safely lapped the Scott Zolaks of the world.

Going Deep

David Allen, JAC: Allen is an adequate kick and punt returner riding fourth or fifth on the depth chart at running back.

Damien Anderson, ARI: The Cardinals re-signed Anderson in the off-season. He's one of about a dozen guys (Marcel Shipp, Larry Croom) vying to back up J. J. Arrington.

Jarrod Baxter, HOU: Baxter is trapped behind Moran Norris at fullback on a team that uses one-back sets most of the time. In other words, he's a special teams gunner.

Dante Brown, BUF: Was waived by the Bills in mid-May. Brown looks good whenever he gets preseason carries (he had three preseason TDs in 2004), but he's not much of a blocker, receiver, or special teams player, so he has a hard time staying on the active roster.

Kory Chapman, NE: Jacksonville State product who had a strong summer in Europe for the Cologne Centurions, with nearly six yards per carry. In college, returned kicks and showed talent as a receiver out of the backfield. Could be Kevin Faulk Lite for some team with an aging backup and a need for special teams help, like the Rams.

Deandra Cobb, ATL: Cobb is an excellent kick returner, something that could help him win a roster spot backing up Atlanta running backs T. J. Duckett, Warrick Dunn, and Michael Vick.

Anthony Davis, IND: The Colts continued to show an affinity for Big Ten players by selecting Davis, a diminutive, but very productive back at Wisconsin. He could be an effective third down player for the Colts.

Omar Easy, KC: Easy was drafted three years ago to ease into Tony Richardson's fullback/halfback role, but he was a disappointment as a receiver and pass blocker. He's fighting for a roster spot.

Lionel Gates, BUF: Gates was part of a productive committee backfield after transferring from Florida State to Louisville, where he played alongside second-rounder Eric Shelton and top prospect Michael Bush. He should stick as a number three running back.

Noah Herron, PIT: Herron has solid all-around skills and could win a roster spot in Pittsburgh as fullback or H-back. He's an excellent receiver and blocker.

Chris Hetherington, OAK: A veteran fullback and special teams player who was re-signed by the Raiders in March. He touches the ball about once every three weeks.

Jason Isom, NO: Isom spent two years on the 49ers practice squad, seeing limited action in a handful of games. He was signed by the Saints to back up FB Mike Karney.

Vick King, NYJ: A former Dolphin, King will battle for the number four running back spot on the Jets, a team that may not have a number four running back spot.

George Layne, ATL: Carried the ball once in 2003 and gained 15 yards, then once more in 2004 and gained 12 yards. Maybe he's earned two carries this year.

Larry Ned, FA: Ned spent two years on the Vikings as a kick gunner, was signed by the Cardinals, then was quickly released for stealing a laptop from an Arizona airport. In fact, it was Aaron Schatz's laptop, so Ned now knows the DVOA of every player in the league.

Jarrett Payton, TEN: The Titans had two players among the NFL Europe rushing leaders this spring: Payton (Walter's son) and Joe Smith. Both have sleeper potential if Chris Brown's broken hand doesn't heal by training camp.

Andrew Pinnock, SD: After playing all 16 games as a rookie, Pinnock was inactive the first nine weeks of last season. His solution? Anabolic steroids, apparently. At least football's testing policy has been in play a long time, so a backup fullback testing positive did not make the lead on *SportsCenter* like he would have if he were a lousy Tampa Bay Devil Rays outfielder with no power.

Lousaka Polite, DAL: A scrappy, hard-working fullback battling for a roster spot. Polite's college teammates at Pitt reported that Polite ate the same meal three times every day: Polish sausage, milk, and a large Kool-Aid. For some reason, he was never nicknamed "Kielbasa Polite."

Rick Razzano, TB: On the day he was drafted, Razzano was on trial for assault of a fellow Ole Miss student. "An abuse and manipulation of the [legal] system," said his attorney of the trial, which ended in a hung jury. Thus Razzano is free to pursue a roster spot as the Buccaneers' starting fullback.

Joe Smith, TEN: Smith had a productive season in NFL Europe. His chances of seeing some real playing time increased when Chris Brown broke his hand in minicamp.

Stephen Trejo, DET: A special teams blocker and third-string fullback. Four seasons, 59 games played, one carry.

Manuel White, WAS: A tailback/fullback at UCLA, White looks like a blocking back or an H-back in the NFL.

Walter Williams, GB: Williams played in exactly one game last season, against the Texans on November 21, and cracked the highlight reel with a 28-yard run. If Ahman Green, Najeh Davenport, and Tony Fisher get hurt, look out.

Jason Wright, ATL: Wright was an effective college runner, racking up 1,257 yards and 12 TDs for Northwestern in 2003. He should stick as the Falcons' number three running back but will see little action.

Wide Receivers

The NFL adjusted its rules on illegal contact and defensive holding against receivers before the 2004 season. Just in time, too: All of those 6′3″, 220-pound rookie wide receivers entering the league really needed protection from all of the 5′11″, 195-pound defenders who wanted to harass them.

Some experts predicted that the new rules (to be precise, the new emphasis on existing rules) would create a surge in penalties, or passing totals, or both. The penalty surge never happened. Penalties against defensive backs (the players usually flagged for holding and downfield contact) rose from 510 in 2003 to 541 in 2004, but pass interference penalties against defensive backs dropped from 205 in 2003 to 151 in 2002. Referees doled out a few more five-yard prizes, but they paid out far fewer jackpots when a receiver and defender bumped into each other 30 yards downfield.

As for the offensive increase, it occurred, but it was subtle: Teams averaged 3,207 net passing yards and 20.8 passing TDs in 2003, 3,367 net passing yards and 22.8 passing TDs in 2004. Pass attempts actually decreased from 515.6 per team in 2004 to 511.2 per team in 2003, as the Steelers, Jets, and Falcons proved that a team could make the playoffs with a run-dominated offense.

The mild increase in passing offense was partly a result of rules changes, but an exceptional rookie class also deserves some of the credit. Michael Clayton, Lee Evans, Roy Williams, Larry Fitzgerald, and Keary Colbert made an immediate splash as part of the best rookie crop since 1988 (Tim Brown, Michael Irvin, Sterling Sharpe, Anthony Miller). Most of the players drafted in 2004 (excluding Evans but including Reggie Williams and Michael Jenkins) are tall, thickly built individuals far removed from the lanky sprinters of yesteryear or the Smurfs of the 1980s. These guys can run, but they are also so big and strong that bump 'n' run coverage is now called

"the Crouton" (get tossed 'n' toasted). The 2005 draft brings Braylon Edwards and Mike Williams, two more small forward-sized football players ready to cause mismatches in coverage.

While young receivers arrive with imposing physical tools, there is still plenty of work available for veteran receivers who have mastered the double move and know how to pick apart a zone defense. In fact, 2004 saw abnormal results on both ends of the age spectrum, with seven receivers above the age of 30 (the usual peak for receivers) ranking among the top 20 in DPAR, compared to just three in 2003. Veterans like Muhsin Muhammad, Joe Horn, Jimmy Smith, Isaac Bruce, Rod Smith, and Terrell Owens all reversed their age-related decline last season. The liberated contact rules may be part of the reason why 2004 was such a big year for veterans, but even if the rules are called in a similar fashion in 2005, we cannot expect 33- and 34-year-old receivers to hold on to unexpected late-career improvement in their numbers.

In the following section, we give the last three years' worth of numbers as well as a 2005 projection for every wide receiver who played a role in 2004—major or minor—and/or will likely play a role in 2005 (table 1).

The first line contains biographical data—each player's name, height, weight, college, birthdate, and age. Height and weight are the best data we could find; weight, of course, can fluctuate during the off-season. Age is very simple, the number of years between the player's birth year and 2005, and the full birthdate is given for anyone who wants to either do research involving more complexity or print a fake ID which identifies the holder as "Craphonso Thorpe."

Next we give the last three years of player stats. Note that rushing stats are not included here for wide receivers; any receiver with at least three carries last year will have stats in the team chapters.

TABLE 1. WIDE RECEIVER STATISTICS SAMPLE

David Patten Height: 5-10 Weight: 190 College: Western Carolina Born: 19-Aug-1974 Age: 31

Year	Team	G	Rec	Pass	Yds	CPct	Yd/C	TD	DVOA	Rank	DPAR	Rank	PAR
2002	NE	16	61	120	824	51%	13.5	6	-3.6%	58	9.1	49	8.7
2003	NE	6	9	21	140	43%	15.6	0	-26.0%	—	-1.4	—	-0.9
2004	NE	16	44	95	800	46%	18.2	7	15.5%	30	18.6	32	17.2
2005	WAS	12	40	—	592	44%	14.8	4					

The first number is games played. This is the official NFL total and may include games in which a player was on special teams but did not play wide receiver.

Receptions (Rec) counts passes caught, while Passes (Pass) counts passes thrown to this player, complete or incomplete. The next four columns list receiving yards, catch percentage (CPct), yards per catch (Yd/C), and receiving touchdowns.

Catch percentage, or receptions divided by total passes, is an attempt to rectify a major problem in conventional statistics, which lay the blame for incomplete passes entirely on quarterbacks. Historical study shows that receivers definitely have an impact on whether a ball is complete or incomplete. We're still working on an estimate of how much responsibility for an incomplete belongs to the quarterback as opposed to the receiver, but it is clearly closer to 50–50 than it is to the 100–0 currently reflected in NFL stats. Wide receivers who are used in longer pass patterns will generally catch a lower percentage of passes. The average NFL wide receiver caught 56% of passes in 2004. (Incomplete pass does not mean dropped pass; dropped passes are not specified in publicly available play-by-play, and we cannot yet correct for dropped passes in our metrics.)

The next five columns give our advanced metrics for receiving: DVOA (Defense-Adjusted Value Over Average), DPAR (Defense-Adjusted Points Above Replacement), and PAR (Points Above Replacement), along with the player's rank in both DVOA and DPAR. These metrics compare every pass intended for a receiver to a league-average baseline based on the game situations in which passes were thrown to that receiver. DVOA and DPAR are also adjusted based on the opposing defense. The methods used to compute these numbers are described in detail in the front of the book. The important distinctions between them are:

- Higher DVOA means more value per pass attempt. Higher DPAR means more total value over the 16-game season.
- A player whose DPAR is higher than his PAR faced a harder-than-average schedule. A player whose PAR is higher than his DPAR faced an easier-than-average schedule.

To qualify for ranking in receiving DVOA and receiving DPAR, a wide receiver must have 50 passes thrown to him in that season. 84 receivers are ranked for 2004 and 2003, 86 for 2002. Receivers with multiple teams are only ranked once, based on full-year stats.

Finally, we have the last row of numbers, 2005 projections. Right now we are projecting only conventional statistics, although in future years we hope to project advanced metrics like DVOA and DPAR. The KUBIAK projection system is based on a complicated regression analysis that takes into account numerous variables including projected role, performance over the past two years, KUBIAK projection for that team's quarterbacks, historical comparables, height, age, and strength of schedule.

It is difficult to accurately project statistics for a 162-game baseball season, but it is exponentially more difficult to accurately project statistics for a 16-game football season. Consider the listed projections not as a prediction of exact numbers, but the mean of a range of possible performances. What's important is less the exact number of yards we project, and more which players are projected to improve or decline. Actual performance will vary from our projection less for veteran starters and more for rookies and fourth-string receivers. Touchdown numbers will vary more than yardage numbers.

A few low-round rookies, guys listed at seventh on the depth chart, and players who are listed as wide receivers but really only play special teams are briefly discussed at the end of this chapter in a section we call "Going Deep." *FA* signifies a player who was still a free agent at press time.

A couple of caveats: We cannot yet fully separate the performance of a receiver from the performance of his quarterback. Be aware that one will affect the other. In addition, these statistics measure only passes thrown to a receiver, not performance on plays when he is not thrown the ball, such as blocking and drawing double teams.

TABLE 2. TOP 20 WR BY DPAR (TOTAL VALUE), 2004

Rank	Player	Team	DPAR		Rank	Player	Team	DPAR
1	Reggie Wayne	IND	44.0		11	T. J. Houshmandzadeh	CIN	31.0
2	Joe Horn	NO	41.6		12	Marvin Harrison	IND	28.6
3	Muhsin Muhammad	CAR	41.5		13	Donald Driver	GB	28.2
4	Michael Clayton	TB	39.8		14	Lee Evans	BUF	26.7
5	Brandon Stokley	IND	38.4		15	Isaac Bruce	STL	26.0
6	Nate Burleson	MIN	35.0		16	Ashley Lelie	DEN	25.4
7	Torry Holt	STL	34.9		17	Eddie Kennison	KC	24.7
8	Javon Walker	GB	33.7		18	Santana Moss	NYJ	24.6
9	Hines Ward	PIT	32.9		19	Chad Johnson	CIN	24.0
10	Terrell Owens	PHI	31.9		20	Keyshawn Johnson	DAL	23.6

TABLE 3. TOP 20 WR BY DVOA (VALUE PER PASS), 2004

Rank	Player	Team	DVOA		Rank	Player	Team	DVOA
1	Brandon Stokley	IND	41.7%		11	T. J. Houshmandzadeh	CIN	28.8%
2	Reggie Wayne	IND	40.8%		12	Joe Horn	NO	25.8%
3	Lee Evans	BUF	39.4%		13	Torry Holt	STL	24.8%
4	Plaxico Burress	PIT	36.8%		14	Johnnie Morton	KC	24.4%
5	Deion Branch	NE	36.2%		15	Randy Moss	MIN	24.1%
6	Nate Burleson	MIN	35.3%		16	Muhsin Muhammad	CAR	23.8%
7	Michael Clayton	TB	33.9%		17	Terrell Owens	PHI	23.2%
8	Santana Moss	NYJ	32.6%		18	Ashley Lelie	DEN	22.7%
9	Hines Ward	PIT	30.4%		19	Az Hakim	DET	22.6%
10	Ronald Curry	OAK	29.7%		20	Joey Galloway	TB	21.7%

Sam Aiken Height: 6-2 Weight: 204 College: North Carolina Born: 14-Dec-1980 Age: 24

Year	Team	G	Rec	Pass	Yds	Ctch%	Yd/C	TD	DVOA	Rank	DPAR	Rank	PAR
2003	BUF	5	3	8	35	38%	11.7	0	-50.3%	—	-1.4	—	-1.3
2004	BUF	15	11	18	148	61%	13.5	0	-1.1%	—	1.6	—	0.8
2005	BUF	13	10	—	135	—	13.4	1					

Aiken isn't very fast but has good hands and makes a nice possession receiver. The Bills may give him a few more opportunities this year to figure out if he can step into Josh Reed's slot next year when Reed is a free agent, but it is more likely that slot will go to Roscoe Parrish.

Derick Armstrong Height: 6-2 Weight: 196 College: Arkansas-Monticello Born: 2-Apr-1979 Age: 26

Year	Team	G	Rec	Pass	Yds	Ctch%	Yd/C	TD	DVOA	Rank	DPAR	Rank	PAR
2003	HOU	8	7	13	75	54%	10.7	1	0.5%	—	1.1	—	0.9
2004	HOU	14	29	39	415	74%	14.3	1	42.9%	—	14.5	—	16.6
2005	HOU	15	39	—	584	—	14.9	3					

DVOA loves Derick Armstrong, and why not? He had the second best catch percentage of any receiver with more than ten receptions in 2004, and seemed to have a knack for picking up big first downs. He ought to be no lower than third on the depth chart in 2005, and could even push Jabar Gaffney for his starting spot. He might be the best thing to come out of the Canadian Football League since Doug Flutie.

Arnaz Battle   Height: 6-1   Weight: 217   College: Notre Dame   Born: 22-Feb-1980 Age: 25

Year	Team	G	Rec	Pass	Yds	Ctch%	Yd/C	TD	DVOA	Rank	DPAR	Rank	PAR
2003	SF	8	0	1	0	0%	0.0	0	-114.1%	—	-0.5	—	-0.5
2004	SF	14	8	15	143	53%	17.9	0	5.4%	—	1.8	—	1.1
2005	*SF*	*16*	*36*	*—*	*513*	*—*	*14.3*	*2*					

You know he is going to be great. How so? He is a former Notre Dame quarterback playing in San Francisco, and the last guy who did that had a town named after him. In all seriousness, Battle may be the next QB-cum-WR to have a big year... it just won't be in 2005. Do not be surprised if he leads all Niner receivers in receiving yards, as the competition for that honor is weak and Battle can be quite the deep threat—three of his eight catches were for 20 or more yards.

Drew Bennett   Height: 6-5   Weight: 206   College: UCLA   Born: 26-Aug-1978 Age: 27

Year	Team	G	Rec	Pass	Yds	Ctch%	Yd/C	TD	DVOA	Rank	DPAR	Rank	PAR
2002	TEN	15	33	64	478	52%	14.5	2	4.8%	38	7.9	54	6.5
2003	TEN	12	32	54	504	59%	15.8	4	29.6%	4	12.8	29	12.5
2004	TEN	16	80	143	1247	56%	15.6	11	8.4%	38	23.6	21	26.9
2005	*TEN*	*16*	*71*	*—*	*1028*	*—*	*14.5*	*8*					

Bennett surprised many people with his outstanding 2004 season, but his DVOA numbers were excellent the year before. Increased opportunities with the departure of Justin McCareins allowed him to post such impressive numbers. What was particularly odd was his connection with Billy Volek. When McNair was quarterback, he posted a DVOA of −18.2% compared with 29.6% with Volek. The number with McNair would have placed him among the ten worst receivers in football, while with Volek he would have been sixth best. Bennett was successful with McNair in 2003, so with McNair's favorite target, Derrick Mason, no longer on the team, he should look for Bennett often.

Eddie Berlin   Height: 5-11   Weight: 195   College: Northern Iowa   Born: 14-Jan-1978 Age: 27

Year	Team	G	Rec	Pass	Yds	Ctch%	Yd/C	TD	DVOA	Rank	DPAR	Rank	PAR
2002	TEN	13	1	1	14	100%	14.0	0	140.4%	—	0.9	—	0.9
2003	TEN	14	1	2	50	50%	50.0	1	115.4%	—	1.5	—	1.5
2004	TEN	16	20	41	278	49%	13.9	1	-5.5%	—	2.7	—	4.0
2005	*CHI*	*12*	*12*	*—*	*159*	*—*	*13.1*	*1*					

Given a chance to be the number three receiver following the injury to Tyrone Calico, Berlin offered basically nothing to the Titans' offense. He caught fewer than half the passes intended for him, a function of both his role as a deep threat and his lack of skill in that role. Around Baptist Sports Park, they still remember his two kick return fumbles against Indianapolis that cost the Titans the AFC South in 2003. He now moves to Chicago, where he will struggle for playing time, even in their suspect receiving corps.

Bernard Berrian   Height: 6-1   Weight: 183   College: Fresno State   Born: 27-Dec-1980 Age: 24

Year	Team	G	Rec	Pass	Yds	Ctch%	Yd/C	TD	DVOA	Rank	DPAR	Rank	PAR
2004	CHI	16	15	44	225	34%	15.0	2	-43.5%	—	-8.1	—	-7.6
2005	*CHI*	*14*	*17*	*—*	*232*	*—*	*13.9*	*1*					

Bernard Berrian, the Bears' third-round pick in 2004, is a good athlete who has the potential to be a big-play threat, but the Bears' quarterbacks rarely got him the ball, and when they did he often had trouble holding on. Let's try again in 2005, shall we?

Anquan Boldin   Height: 6-1   Weight: 218   College: Florida State   Born: 3-Oct-1980   Age: 25

Year	Team	G	Rec	Pass	Yds	Ctch%	Yd/C	TD	DVOA	Rank	DPAR	Rank	PAR
2003	ARI	16	101	165	1377	61%	13.6	8	3.2%	37	15.9	15	15.9
2004	ARI	10	56	104	623	54%	11.1	1	-17.3%	72	-1.3	72	0.1
2005	*ARI*	*16*	*76*	*—*	*1011*	*—*	*13.3*	*7*					

By "below replacement level" we mean "below replacement level after Dennis Green decided to play Wheel of Quarterbacks." Boldin actually posted a DPAR of 2.7 with Josh McCown at QB. Navarre targeted Boldin 13 times in the loss to the Lions: Two of the passes were intercepted, one was batted at the line, Boldin dropped one, and three of their five connections yielded eight yards or less. Boldin looked like his old self in late games against the Niners and Seahawks, so he'll be back at full speed in 2005.

Marty Booker

Height: 6-0 Weight: 212 College: Louisiana-Monroe Born: 31-Jul-1976 Age: 29

Year	Team	G	Rec	Pass	Yds	Ctch%	Yd/C	TD	DVOA	Rank	DPAR	Rank	PAR
2002	CHI	16	97	167	1183	58%	12.2	6	-8.0%	65	8.0	52	8.1
2003	CHI	13	52	105	715	50%	13.8	4	-15.9%	71	-0.3	71	0.3
2004	MIA	15	50	105	638	48%	12.8	1	-19.6%	74	-3.2	76	-3.9
2005	MIA	14	33	—	435	—	13.4	2					

Quick: Can you name the wide receiver most similar to Marty Booker over a three-year span? That's right, it's everyone's favorite whipping boy, Peerless Price. The Dolphins, like the Falcons with Price, thought they were getting a 1,000-yard receiver, but Booker dropped too many balls and wasn't the threat in the red zone the Dolphins hoped he would be. Booker's DVOA in 2002 was 0% with Jim Miller behind center, −19.0% otherwise. Maybe all along Booker really wasn't that good, and Jim Miller was.

David Boston

Height: 6-2 Weight: 240 College: Ohio State Born: 19-Aug-1978 Age: 27

Year	Team	G	Rec	Pass	Yds	Ctch%	Yd/C	TD	DVOA	Rank	DPAR	Rank	PAR
2002	ARI	8	32	75	512	43%	16.0	1	-5.9%	63	4.3	67	2.6
2003	SD	14	70	115	880	61%	12.6	7	9.5%	28	14.4	20	13.7
2004	MIA	0	0	0	0	0%	0.0	0	0.0%	—	0.0	—	0.0
2005	MIA	13	29	—	412	—	14.3	2					

Was it really only a few years ago that Boston looked like one of the most promising young receivers in football? Now he's about as popular as Ward Churchill on Fox News. From testing positive for steroids to feuding with coaches to losing seasons to injury, you have to wonder how many more chances Boston has. Miami tossed him one more, re-signing him at a lower salary after waiving him earlier in the off-season.

Larry Brackins

Height: 6-4 Weight: 205 College: Pearl River CC Born: 5-Nov-1982 Age: 23

Year	Team	G	Rec	Pass	Yds	Ctch%	Yd/C	TD	DVOA	Rank	DPAR	Rank	PAR
2005	TB	11	4	—	81	—	19.5	0					

Brackins, a talented but extremely raw receiver, opted to turn pro after two seasons of junior college football rather than pursue scholarship offers from Florida State and USC. He has a good shot to make weekly appearances in receiver-starved Tampa Bay, which has Michael Clayton, Joey Galloway, and little else.

Corey Bradford

Height: 6-1 Weight: 197 College: Jackson State Born: 8-Dec-1975 Age: 30

Year	Team	G	Rec	Pass	Yds	Ctch%	Yd/C	TD	DVOA	Rank	DPAR	Rank	PAR
2002	HOU	16	45	106	697	42%	15.5	6	-20.3%	80	-3.4	82	-3.2
2003	HOU	16	24	62	460	39%	19.2	4	-19.8%	74	-1.6	74	-1.3
2004	HOU	15	27	54	399	50%	14.8	3	-7.4%	60	3.1	64	4.3
2005	HOU	13	15	—	214	—	13.9	1					

In their first year, Bradford was the Texans' best receiver. In 2003, he was the starter opposite Andre Johnson for most of the season. By 2004, Jabar Gaffney had moved ahead of him into the starting lineup, and Bradford came in for three receiver sets. In 2005, he ought to be the fourth receiver, called in to run straight, very, very fast, and hopefully catch the ball. The Texans like to keep five receivers on their roster; at this rate, in 2006 he'll be a special teamer, and after that he'll be on another team.

Mark Bradley   Height: 6-2   Weight: 198   College: Oklahoma   Born: 29-Jan-1982   Age: 23

Year	Team	G	Rec	Pass	Yds	Ctch%	Yd/C	TD	DVOA	Rank	DPAR	Rank	PAR
2005	CHI	13	17	—	224	—	13.4	2					

Bradley's fine senior season was marred by an Orange Bowl brain cramp of Leon Lett–like proportions. As the ball was rolling dead near the end zone after a USC punt, Bradley decided to scoop it up and make something happen. Unfortunately, he was surrounded by defenders: USC's Collin Ashton tipped the ball, the Trojans scored one play later to break a 7–7 tie, and the rout was on. The Bears hope that Bradley's poor decision was an isolated incident; they need the son of Sooners QB Danny Bradley to break a logjam at wide receiver, where Justin Gage, Bobby Wade, and Bernard Berrian keep playing hot potato with the starting job. *Pro Football Weekly*'s 2005 Draft Preview compares Bradley to Chad Johnson. If he's that good, he'll make Midway fans very happy.

Deion Branch   Height: 5-9   Weight: 193   College: Louisville   Born: 18-Jul-1979   Age: 26

Year	Team	G	Rec	Pass	Yds	Ctch%	Yd/C	TD	DVOA	Rank	DPAR	Rank	PAR
2002	NE	13	43	68	489	63%	11.4	2	3.0%	42	7.9	53	7.7
2003	NE	15	57	104	803	55%	14.1	3	2.6%	40	9.7	37	9.7
2004	NE	9	35	51	454	69%	13.0	4	36.2%	5	16.7	35	17.2
2005	NE	16	65	—	832	—	12.7	5					

Branch's Super Bowl MVP award was no fluke. Although a good receiver in his first two years, he really broke out in 2004 despite being healthy for only nine games. Conventional stats hide the importance of his high catch percentage, and of course in the Super Bowl he caught every single pass that Tom Brady threw to his hands instead of his rear end. Over a two-year span, the most similar receiver to Branch is should-be Hall of Famer Henry Ellard in 1985–1986, so this projection might be a little low.

Reggie Brown   Height: 6-1   Weight: 195   College: Georgia   Born: 13-Jan-1981   Age: 24

Year	Team	G	Rec	Pass	Yds	Ctch%	Yd/C	TD	DVOA	Rank	DPAR	Rank	PAR
2005	PHI	16	19	—	296	—	15.5	2					

Brown has some Darrell Jackson attributes: He's a great route runner, he reads zones well, and at times he'll drop a pass thrown right between the numbers. He's also a fine blocker, a must in Andy Reid's system. Brown is Terrell Owens insurance, he's the fire under Todd Pinkston's heels, and he's the reason callers to Philadelphia talk shows now refer to Freddie Mitchell in the past tense.

Tim Brown   Height: 6-0   Weight: 195   College: Notre Dame   Born: 22-Jul-1966   Age: 39

Year	Team	G	Rec	Pass	Yds	Ctch%	Yd/C	TD	DVOA	Rank	DPAR	Rank	PAR
2002	OAK	16	81	127	930	64%	11.5	2	3.3%	41	16.2	27	17.1
2003	OAK	16	52	93	567	55%	10.9	2	-12.8%	66	1.2	65	1.7
2004	TB	15	24	31	200	77%	8.3	1	-30.6%	—	-3.2	—	-3.6

Brown is expected to retire rather than return for an 18th NFL season after a disappointing one-year reunion with Jon Gruden in Tampa Bay. Brown mostly served as the Buccaneers' designated fair-catch man on punt returns, which often drew boos from the home crowd. It was a rather undignified end for a likely Hall of Famer.

Troy Brown   Height: 5-10   Weight: 196   College: Marshall   Born: 2-Jul-1971   Age: 34

Year	Team	G	Rec	Pass	Yds	Ctch%	Yd/C	TD	DVOA	Rank	DPAR	Rank	PAR
2002	NE	14	97	141	890	69%	9.2	3	-10.1%	72	4.6	65	4.1
2003	NE	12	40	60	472	67%	11.8	4	0.3%	46	4.9	49	5.4
2004	NE	12	17	29	184	59%	10.8	1	5.2%	—	3.6	—	3.0
2005	NE	12	14	—	177	—	13.1	1					

Brown's contribution to the 2004 Super Bowl champions, as the first significant two-way player since Deion Sanders in 1996, is addressed in the Patriots chapter. But Troy Brown, football legend, is different from Troy Brown, declining 34-year-old backup with injury issues. Only the Saints and Patriots were really interested in him, so he went back to the

Patriots for a reduced salary and becomes part of a logjam at slot receiver that includes David Terrell, Bethel Johnson, Tim Dwight, and P. K. Sam.

Isaac Bruce

Height: 6-0 Weight: 188 College: Memphis Born: 10-Nov-1972 Age: 33

Year	Team	G	Rec	Pass	Yds	Ctch%	Yd/C	TD	DVOA	Rank	DPAR	Rank	PAR
2002	STL	16	79	130	1075	61%	13.6	7	11.4%	21	22.2	17	21.4
2003	STL	15	69	119	981	58%	14.2	5	12.6%	22	17.6	12	19.9
2004	STL	16	89	148	1292	60%	14.5	6	11.8%	37	26.0	15	25.4
2005	STL	15	63	—	864	—	13.7	5					

Back in the mid-1990s, when Bruce rose to stardom, the number one cornerbacks of the NFC West were Eric Allen, Marquez Pope, Eric Davis, and D. J. Johnson. Now, he typically lines up against number two cornerbacks like Shantae Spencer and David Macklin. Bruce has kept himself in exceptional shape, is a very smart receiver, and will be able to put up 1,000-yard seasons for another year or two. But if he ever became the number one option again or the defenses on the Rams schedule drastically improved, Bruce would suddenly start posting the stat lines of a 33-year-old receiver.

Antonio Bryant

Height: 6-1 Weight: 192 College: Pittsburgh Born: 9-Mar-1981 Age: 24

Year	Team	G	Rec	Pass	Yds	Ctch%	Yd/C	TD	DVOA	Rank	DPAR	Rank	PAR
2002	DAL	16	44	93	733	47%	16.7	6	-3.2%	55	7.1	57	6.0
2003	DAL	16	39	83	550	47%	14.1	2	-10.8%	62	1.8	62	1.3
2004	DAL	5	16	27	266	58%	16.6	0	1.0%	—	2.0		2.2
2004	CLE	10	42	72	546	59%	13.0	4	7.1%	42	9.9	41	8.8
2005	CLE	16	36	—	507	—	14.2	2					

The highlight of Bryant's 2004 season was throwing a jersey in the face of his then-coach Bill Parcells during training camp. That chip on his shoulder didn't go away with his trade to Cleveland. The two closest historical comparables to Bryant's last two seasons are Todd Pinkston 2001–2002 and Travis Taylor 2001–2002, which sounds about right: overextended as a number one but likely to have value as a number two. In the Cleveland mess, for all we know, he could be number four or five.

Nate Burleson

Height: 6-0 Weight: 192 College: Nevada Born: 19-Aug-1981 Age: 24

Year	Team	G	Rec	Pass	Yds	Ctch%	Yd/C	TD	DVOA	Rank	DPAR	Rank	PAR
2003	MIN	16	29	57	455	51%	15.7	2	-8.0%	55	2.2	61	2.8
2004	MIN	16	68	102	1006	67%	14.8	9	35.3%	6	35.0	6	34.7
2005	MIN	16	77	—	978	—	12.7	5					

In his second pro season, Burleson emerged as a solid receiver, especially when injuries to Randy Moss meant Daunte Culpepper needed a new go-to guy. Although he doesn't have Moss's size or speed, he's a good route runner and knows where to find holes in opposing secondaries. Just be aware (as we note in the Minnesota chapter) that Burleson's best games came after Moss returned, and he won't benefit this year from playing against defenses with their attention focused elsewhere.

Plaxico Burress

Height: 6-5 Weight: 226 College: Michigan State Born: 12-Aug-1977 Age: 28

Year	Team	G	Rec	Pass	Yds	Ctch%	Yd/C	TD	DVOA	Rank	DPAR	Rank	PAR
2002	PIT	16	78	144	1325	54%	17.0	7	15.1%	17	29.1	8	30.3
2003	PIT	16	60	124	860	48%	14.3	4	-9.1%	58	4.0	51	4.3
2004	PIT	11	35	60	698	58%	19.9	5	36.8%	4	20.5	28	20.0
2005	NYG	16	62	—	937	—	15.1	6					

Burress missed parts of six games with a hamstring injury, but when he played he was Ben Roethlisberger's security blanket. He's now in New York, and Eli Manning will find out how much easier it is to throw to receivers when they can actually get open (or aren't named Shockey). Incidentally, early odds in Las Vegas have Burress leading the Giants in fines from coach Tom Coughlin for "being only three minutes early to team meetings."

Reche Caldwell
Height: 5-11 Weight: 194   College: Florida   Born: 28-Mar-1979 Age: 26

Year	Team	G	Rec	Pass	Yds	Ctch%	Yd/C	TD	DVOA	Rank	DPAR	Rank	PAR
2002	SD	14	22	43	208	51%	9.5	3	-26.5%	—	-3.2	—	-2.8
2003	SD	9	8	34	80	24%	10.0	0	-64.3%	—	-8.6	—	-9.2
2004	SD	6	18	29	310	62%	17.2	3	7.3%	—	4.4	—	5.8
2005	SD	16	37	—	558	—	15.2	4					

Injuries have plagued most of Caldwell's 2003 and 2004 campaigns. Beginning the year as a starter, Caldwell showed some promise. However, his injury on October 19 did more than kill his season; it dropped him down on this year's depth chart. The tear in his right ligament caused San Diego to go out and trade for Keenan McCardell.

Tyrone Calico
Height: 6-4 Weight: 223   College: Middle Tennessee State   Born: 9-Nov-1980 Age: 25

Year	Team	G	Rec	Pass	Yds	Ctch%	Yd/C	TD	DVOA	Rank	DPAR	Rank	PAR
2003	TEN	14	18	43	297	42%	16.5	4	-2.1%	—	2.9	—	3.0
2004	TEN	1	2	4	13	50%	6.5	0	-47.4%	—	-0.9	—	-0.9
2005	TEN	15	36	—	523	—	14.7	3					

Calico injured his left knee on a horse collar tackle by Roy Williams in a preseason game, then hurt himself again when he tried to come back, and basically missed the whole year. Originally the injury was thought to be a torn meniscus, but Dr. Jim Andrews discovered that an old high school injury to Calico's ACL was the root cause and fixed that. Calico should be 100 percent by the season opener and is a reminder that injuries are cumulative. Of course, so is experience, and Calico has very little of it for a third-year veteran expected to step in as a starter.

Kelly Campbell
Height: 5-10 Weight: 173   College: Georgia Tech   Born: 23-Jul-1980 Age: 25

Year	Team	G	Rec	Pass	Yds	Ctch%	Yd/C	TD	DVOA	Rank	DPAR	Rank	PAR
2002	MIN	6	13	32	176	41%	13.5	3	-23.4%	—	-1.8	—	-2.0
2003	MIN	15	25	44	522	57%	20.9	4	8.1%	—	5.6	—	6.2
2004	MIN	16	19	30	364	57%	19.2	1	9.3%	21	4.1	22	3.0
2005	MIN	14	15	—	205	—	13.5	1					

Campbell has shown he can go long with the best of them, but the question now is whether he can catch passes over the middle and become a more consistent presence in the Vikings' offense. Troy Williamson will provide the same speed in a bigger package.

Jonathan Carter
Height: 6-0 Weight: 180   College: Troy State   Born: 20-Mar-1979 Age: 26

Year	Team	G	Rec	Pass	Yds	Ctch%	Yd/C	TD	DVOA	Rank	DPAR	Rank	PAR
2002	NYJ	1	0	—	0	—	—	0	—	—	—	—	—
2003	NYJ	9	4	6	93	67%	23.3	1	60.8%	—	2.5	—	2.6
2004	NYJ	13	10	16	173	63%	17.3	1	42.0%	—	6.1	—	5.8
2005	NYJ	13	12	—	160	—	13.6	1					

Carter played only a minor role as a receiver and was an adequate but not great kickoff return man.

Tim Carter
Height: 6-0 Weight: 200   College: Auburn   Born: 21-Sep-1979 Age: 26

Year	Team	G	Rec	Pass	Yds	Ctch%	Yd/C	TD	DVOA	Rank	DPAR	Rank	PAR
2002	NYG	4	2	3	37	67%	18.5	0	84.7%	—	1.8	—	1.6
2003	NYG	12	26	52	309	50%	11.9	0	-15.3%	70	-0.2	70	-1.1
2004	NYG	5	12	18	182	67%	15.2	1	43.9%	—	7.2	—	6.4
2005	NYG	12	15	—	221	—	14.7	1					

Suffered a fractured hip in October against Dallas. He's missed time because of injury in every one of his three seasons. Could be an acceptable number three receiver if he ever stayed healthy, but his constant injuries have likely pushed him below David Tyree on the Giants depth chart.

Chris Chambers

Height: 5-11 Weight: 210   College: Wisconsin   Born: 12-Aug-1978 Age: 27

Year	Team	G	Rec	Pass	Yds	Ctch%	Yd/C	TD	DVOA	Rank	DPAR	Rank	PAR
2002	MIA	15	52	100	734	52%	14.1	3	-4.7%	59	7.1	58	7.4
2003	MIA	16	64	130	963	49%	15.0	11	7.8%	29	15.4	16	13.4
2004	MIA	15	69	138	898	50%	13.0	7	-9.2%	63	5.0	57	2.8
2005	MIA	16	61	—	783	—	12.9	7					

One of the few promising signs for the Dolphins' offense is that Chambers continues to be a big-play threat who also has good hands and runs good routes. Although Miami quarterbacks have struggled to get him the ball, expect big things from him if that ever changes.

Antonio Chatman

Height: 5-9 Weight: 177   College: Cincinnati   Born: 12-Feb-1979 Age: 26

Year	Team	G	Rec	Pass	Yds	Ctch%	Yd/C	TD	DVOA	Rank	DPAR	Rank	PAR
2003	GB	0	0	1	0	0%	0.0	0	-88.1%	—	-0.4	—	-0.5
2004	GB	16	22	45	246	49%	11.2	1	-18.9%	—	-0.9	—	0.3
2005	GB	13	14	—	174	—	12.9	1					

The Packers liked what they saw out of Chatman when they signed him as an undrafted free agent, but he has been a disappointment both as a receiver and as a kick returner. Chatman is fast, but someone with his lack of size needs to have blinding speed, and Chatman falls a bit short.

Wayne Chrebet

Height: 5-10 Weight: 188   College: Hofstra   Born: 14-Aug-1973 Age: 32

Year	Team	G	Rec	Pass	Yds	Ctch%	Yd/C	TD	DVOA	Rank	DPAR	Rank	PAR
2002	NYJ	15	51	80	691	64%	13.5	9	28.0%	7	22.1	18	20.9
2003	NYJ	7	27	44	289	61%	10.7	1	-12.4%	—	0.6	—	0.0
2004	NYJ	16	31	54	397	57%	12.8	1	2.6%	46	6.2	52	6.6
2005	NYJ	14	27	—	358	—	13.1	2					

Chrebet gave the Jets a solid season as a possession receiver, but he's definitely on his last legs and his career might be over. Seven of the top nine guys on his historical comparables list never played again.

Mark Clayton

Height: 5-10 Weight: 193   College: Oklahoma   Born: 2-Jul-1982 Age: 23

Year	Team	G	Rec	Pass	Yds	Ctch%	Yd/C	TD	DVOA	Rank	DPAR	Rank	PAR
2005	BAL	16	41	—	556	—	13.6	3					

Clayton is the opposite of a "workout wonder" like Matt Jones, the QB-cum-receiver taken one pick ahead of him in the first round of the 2005 draft. All Clayton did the last two seasons at Oklahoma was produce nearly 150 receptions for more than 2,300 yards and 23 touchdowns the last two seasons at Oklahoma. Receiver is a notoriously tough position for rookies to make an impact, because most of the high draftees dominated the college game simply with overwhelming physical skills. But Clayton is more of a technician, having had to learn to read defenses and run crisp routes in order to dominate at Oklahoma. If Kyle Boller can show a similar master in his third season running Baltimore's offense, Clayton could produce the type of season Michael Clayton—no relation—did as a rookie wideout in Tampa Bay last year.

Michael Clayton

Height: 6-3 Weight: 197   College: LSU   Born: 13-Oct-1982 Age: 23

Year	Team	G	Rec	Pass	Yds	Ctch%	Yd/C	TD	DVOA	Rank	DPAR	Rank	PAR
2004	TB	16	80	122	1193	66%	14.9	7	33.9%	7	39.8	4	38.6
2005	TB	16	83	—	1155	—	13.9	6					

Clayton was the fifth wide receiver taken in the 2004 draft, and had the best rookie year by a substantial margin. We have our advanced metrics computed for play-by-play back to 1998, and in the last seven years the only other rookie to rank in the top ten in DPAR was Randy Moss. Clayton is the poster child for why teams that run a complex offense (such as Jon Gruden's version of the West Coast) should draft intelligent, polished college wideouts rather than "workout wonders." He's an adept route runner with good hands and more speed and quickness than his 40 time at the combine would suggest. But what's most impressive about him is the all-around maturity of his game beyond just catching the football. He throws some harsh crackback blocks and could probably teach Tampa Bay's linemen a thing or two.

Keary Colbert Height: 5-10 Weight: 193 College: USC Born: 21-May-1982 Age: 23

Year	Team	G	Rec	Pass	Yds	Ctch%	Yd/C	TD	DVOA	Rank	DPAR	Rank	PAR
2004	CAR	15	47	92	754	51%	16.0	5	-3.4%	52	7.2	48	8.3
2005	CAR	16	52	—	738	—	14.3	4					

A decent, if somewhat inconsistent, year from the second-round rookie out of USC. Given his success in the USC program (he owns the USC career reception record with 207), he entered the league with a reputation as being a sure-handed, big-play guy. Colbert produced two 100-plus-yard games last year, and has likely positioned himself as the number two receiver going into 2005.

Laveranues Coles Height: 5-11 Weight: 193 College: Florida State Born: 29-Dec-1977 Age: 27

Year	Team	G	Rec	Pass	Yds	Ctch%	Yd/C	TD	DVOA	Rank	DPAR	Rank	PAR
2002	NYJ	15	89	134	1264	66%	14.2	5	30.6%	5	40.7	3	42.4
2003	WAS	16	82	158	1204	52%	14.7	6	3.9%	36	15.3	17	13.2
2004	WAS	16	90	168	950	54%	10.6	1	-16.2%	71	-1.7	73	-4.2
2005	NYJ	16	74	—	947	—	12.8	6					

There are some internal disagreements within the *Pro Football Prospectus* staff about the question of whether Laveranues Coles is really a better receiver than Santana Moss, who had much better numbers but also a much better quarterback. But we all agree that spending $9 million in salary cap space to trade Coles for a player who is at best his equal is ridiculous.

Curtis Conway Height: 6-1 Weight: 196 College: USC Born: 13-Jan-1971 Age: 34

Year	Team	G	Rec	Pass	Yds	Ctch%	Yd/C	TD	DVOA	Rank	DPAR	Rank	PAR
2002	SD	13	57	94	852	61%	14.9	5	6.9%	34	13.9	32	16.4
2003	NYJ	16	46	102	640	45%	13.9	2	-13.7%	69	0.6	68	-0.9
2004	SF	15	38	75	403	51%	10.6	3	-15.1%	70	-0.3	70	-2.0
2005	FA	14	16	—	173	—	10.5	0					

At age 34, Curtis Conway's career seems to be winding down. He had two solid seasons in Chicago in 1995 and 1996, then entered into a decline, suffering injuries and moving on to San Diego, where he surprised everyone with a career high in receiving yards in 2001. But last year he was with his third team in three seasons and looked just about finished.

Terrance Copper Height: 6-0 Weight: 204 College: East Carolina Born: 12-Mar-1982 Age: 23

Year	Team	G	Rec	Pass	Yds	Ctch%	Yd/C	TD	DVOA	Rank	DPAR	Rank	PAR
2004	DAL	10	7	20	84	35%	12.0	1	-16.2%	—	-0.3	—	-1.2
2005	DAL	14	14	—	194	—	14.1	1					

Terrance Cooper was a possession receiver and punt returner at East Carolina who didn't show much when he got the opportunity to be a receiver and returner with the Cowboys last year. His chances of earning a roster spot improved when the Cowboys went heavy on the defense in April and didn't draft any receivers.

Jerricho Cotchery Height: 6-0 Weight: 199 College: North Carolina State Born: 16-Jun-1982 Age: 23

Year	Team	G	Rec	Pass	Yds	Ctch%	Yd/C	TD	DVOA	Rank	DPAR	Rank	PAR
2004	NYJ	12	6	11	60	55%	10.0	0	-16.1%	—	-0.1	—	-0.3
2005	NYJ	14	13	—	170	—	13.4	1					

As a rookie out of North Carolina State, Cotchery didn't impress anyone with his offense, but he has the makings of a dynamic kick returner and a solid all-around contributor on special teams.

Patrick Crayton Height: 6-1 Weight: 205 College: NW Oklahoma State Born: 7-Apr-1979 Age: 26

Year	Team	G	Rec	Pass	Yds	Ctch%	Yd/C	TD	DVOA	Rank	DPAR	Rank	PAR
2004	DAL	7	12	14	162	79%	13.5	1	30.2%	—	4.2	—	3.9
2005	DAL	13	12	—	166	—	13.9	1					

After coming off the practice squad to replace the injured Terry Glenn, Crayton finally saw some playing time at wide receiver the last two weeks of the season and took advantage of the opportunity. In those two games, he caught all seven passes thrown his way, with six converting for a first down or touchdown. Don't forget his name if Glenn, Keyshawn Johnson, or Quincy Morgan go down with an injury this season.

Airese Currie		Height: 5-10	Weight: 186		College: Clemson						Born: 16-Nov-1982	Age: 23	
Year	Team	G	Rec	Pass	Yds	Ctch%	Yd/C	TD	DVOA	Rank	DPAR	Rank	PAR
2005	CHI	12	17	—	209	—	12.6	1					

A sprint champion who is gunning for the Bernard Berrian role as return man and fly pattern specialist.

Ronald Curry		Height: 6-2	Weight: 220		College: North Carolina						Born: 28-May-1979	Age: 26	
Year	Team	G	Rec	Pass	Yds	Ctch%	Yd/C	TD	DVOA	Rank	DPAR	Rank	PAR
2002	OAK	1	0	—	0	—	—	0	—	—	—	—	—
2003	OAK	16	5	10	31	50%	6.2	0	-46.6%	—	-1.7	—	-2.0
2004	OAK	12	50	70	679	71%	13.6	6	29.7%	10	20.8	26	22.6
2005	OAK	14	41	—	588	—	14.4	3					

DPAR loves Curry, who had the misfortune of suffering an Achilles' tendon injury just as the Raiders offense was starting to improve late in the season. Curry is a converted quarterback and former basketball star with Hines Ward–like talent, but the frequent Achilles' injuries—he had a similar injury in 2000—are a concern. A ruptured Achilles' tendon is generally an old athlete's injury, and it's rare to see a young player like Curry plagued by it. Curry would have been a great candidate for a breakout season had the Raiders not traded for Randy Moss and re-signed Jerry Porter. Now, he's just another talented slot receiver with injury issues.

Kevin Curtis		Height: 5-11	Weight: 186		College: Utah State						Born: 17-Jul-1978	Age: 27	
Year	Team	G	Rec	Pass	Yds	Ctch%	Yd/C	TD	DVOA	Rank	DPAR	Rank	PAR
2003	STL	5	4	5	13	80%	3.3	0	-62.1%	—	-1.3	—	-1.2
2004	STL	14	32	50	421	64%	13.2	2	2.0%	47	5.6	54	5.9
2005	STL	14	31	—	433	—	14.1	3					

Curtis was drafted in 2003 after Ricky Proehl left and the team gave up on Terrence Wilkins, Troy Williams, and Yo Murphy. Prior to the 2003 draft, Rams receivers coach John Ramsdell had Curtis ranked second among wideouts, ahead of Charles Rogers and everyone else but Andre Johnson. Ramsdell must've known Rogers would break his collarbone every year, but apparently he didn't know Curtis was fragile too. After a broken leg cost him his rookie year, Curtis found himself the number five receiver at the start of the 2004 season, but he was outperforming Shaun McDonald by the playoffs: He had four catches for 107 yards in the postseason win against the Seahawks and seven catches for 128 yards in the loss to the Falcons. Curtis is advertised as a faster version of Proehl: He has great hands, works the middle, knows coverages, and runs crisp routes. He lacks McDonald's shiftiness, but he's more versatile because he's big enough to beat a jam and fast enough to stretch the seam. Curtis has the best chance of any Rams receiver not named Holt or Bruce to post a 50-catch, 600-yard, six-TD stat line, and he's also most likely to start if Holt or Bruce gets hurt.

DeVard Darling		Height: 6-1	Weight: 213		College: Washington State						Born: 16-Apr-1982	Age: 23	
Year	Team	G	Rec	Pass	Yds	Ctch%	Yd/C	TD	DVOA	Rank	DPAR	Rank	PAR
2004	BAL	3	2	2	5	100%	2.5	0	-215.0%	—	-2.7	—	-2.8
2005	BAL	11	7	—	101	—	13.9	0					

DeVard Darling is probably best known because his teammate and identical twin brother, DeVaughn, collapsed and died during a strenuous workout at Florida State. The Seminoles were concerned that DeVard might share some kind of heart problem with DeVaughn and told him he could no longer play there, but he transferred to Washington State, passed his physical, and became a solid possession receiver. Baltimore had high hopes for him until an early-season quad strain changed his gait and led to a heel injury, which led to him basically doing nothing all season. Hopes are high again, but chronic leg injuries are not good for a wide receiver.

André Davis

Height: 6-1 Weight: 195 College: Virginia Tech Born: 12-Jun-1979 Age: 26

Year	Team	G	Rec	Pass	Yds	Ctch%	Yd/C	TD	DVOA	Rank	DPAR	Rank	PAR
2002	CLE	16	37	72	420	51%	11.4	6	-5.8%	62	4.4	66	5.4
2003	CLE	16	40	62	576	65%	14.4	5	34.4%	2	16.0	14	16.2
2004	CLE	7	16	33	416	48%	26.0	2	34.1%	—	10.2	—	8.6
2005	CLE	16	31	—	493	—	16.0	3					

The best thing to happen to Davis this off-season was the Browns' drafting Braylon Edwards. Davis isn't a true number one receiver, and, with the addition of Edwards, Davis will now be the number two guy.

Donald Driver

Height: 6-0 Weight: 188 College: Alcorn State Born: 2-Feb-1975 Age: 30

Year	Team	G	Rec	Pass	Yds	Ctch%	Yd/C	TD	DVOA	Rank	DPAR	Rank	PAR
2002	GB	16	70	113	1064	62%	15.2	9	20.7%	13	27.0	11	27.7
2003	GB	15	52	86	621	60%	11.9	2	4.4%	33	9.0	39	9.0
2004	GB	16	84	138	1208	61%	14.4	9	15.6%	29	28.2	13	30.1
2005	GB	14	49	—	652	—	13.3	3					

Driver had his best year as a pro in 2004. At age 30, it's hard to imagine he'll be able to top that in 2005, but he's still a good possession receiver who understands his role in the Packers' offense.

Tim Dwight

Height: 5-9 Weight: 180 College: Iowa State Born: 13-Jul-1975 Age: 30

Year	Team	G	Rec	Pass	Yds	Ctch%	Yd/C	TD	DVOA	Rank	DPAR	Rank	PAR
2002	SD	16	50	93	623	54%	12.5	2	-8.0%	66	4.6	64	6.2
2003	SD	9	14	31	193	45%	13.8	0	-6.1%	—	1.3	—	0.2
2004	SD	12	2	5	31	40%	15.5	1	0.2%	—	0.6	—	0.7
2005	NE	13	6	—	89	—	13.8	0					

Better known as a special teamer, Dwight's responsibilities will primarily be as a punt returner—an area the Pats had some trouble with last year. His overall role will greatly depend on the development of Bethel Johnson and P. K. Sam.

Braylon Edwards

Height: 6-1 Weight: 211 College: Michigan Born: 21-Feb-1983 Age: 22

Year	Team	G	Rec	Pass	Yds	Ctch%	Yd/C	TD	DVOA	Rank	DPAR	Rank	PAR
2005	CLE	16	53	—	717	—	13.6	5					

Braylon Edwards should be the poster child for the stay-in-school crowd. Returning to Michigan for his senior year probably boosted Edwards's rookie signing bonus on the order of $12 million or so—no wonder he was driving a $140,000 Bentley before draft day. Rookie receivers rarely make a big impact—for every Michael Clayton there are two Reggie Williams, it seems—but Edwards will be given every chance to do so in Cleveland. The knock on him in college was dropped balls, but Edwards really cut down in that category his senior year and almost never lost a battle for the ball once it was in the air. If Kellen Winslow returns to health, there should be plenty of room for both to operate in opposing secondaries.

Troy Edwards

Height: 5-10 Weight: 191 College: Louisiana Tech Born: 7-Apr-1977 Age: 28

Year	Team	G	Rec	Pass	Yds	Ctch%	Yd/C	TD	DVOA	Rank	DPAR	Rank	PAR
2002	STL	12	18	24	157	75%	8.7	2	-13.0%	—	0.3	—	0.0
2003	JAC	13	35	62	487	56%	13.9	3	2.3%	42	5.8	46	6.2
2004	JAC	16	50	80	533	63%	10.7	1	-20.9%	76	-2.6	75	-0.8
2005	JAC	12	16	—	191	—	12.2	1					

Edwards re-signed with the Jaguars after they failed to land any outside free agent receiver help. His contributions as a third receiver look acceptable only when compared to the output of number two receiver Reggie Williams. He is undersized and has limited ability. He was also good for a few laughs when, against Houston, he channeled the ghost of Aaron Brooks and tossed a backward lateral to nobody. The drafting of Matt Jones could relegate him to number four receiver.

Bobby Engram Height: 5-10 Weight: 188 College: Penn State Born: 7-Jan-1973 Age: 32

Year	Team	G	Rec	Pass	Yds	Ctch%	Yd/C	TD	DVOA	Rank	DPAR	Rank	PAR
2002	SEA	15	50	72	619	69%	12.4	0	21.0%	12	17.0	25	18.0
2003	SEA	16	52	74	640	70%	12.3	6	39.1%	1	20.6	7	20.2
2004	SEA	13	36	53	499	68%	13.9	2	18.9%	25	12.0	44	11.2
2005	SEA	14	36	—	493	—	13.7	3					

Among receivers who have never reached the 1,000-yard mark in a season, Engram is probably the best in the league. If that sounds like damning with faint praise, it's not intended to; he'll never play a starring role, but the role he plays is important and he plays it well. At age 32, Engram doesn't appear to have lost a step, but he was never very fast to begin with. He does have good hands and a good sense for getting to the first down marker. Although a fairly reliable possession receiver for Seattle, Engram will ironically be remembered for dropping the potential game-tying catch in the wild card game against St. Louis last year.

Lee Evans Height: 5-10 Weight: 197 College: Wisconsin Born: 11-Mar-1981 Age: 24

Year	Team	G	Rec	Pass	Yds	Ctch%	Yd/C	TD	DVOA	Rank	DPAR	Rank	PAR
2004	BUF	16	48	75	843	64%	17.6	9	39.4%	3	26.7	14	26.9
2005	BUF	16	58	—	796	—	13.8	4					

Last year it seemed like all of Evans's catches were highlight-reel long bombs, but Evans was Buffalo's most valuable receiver no matter what down it was or how close the Bills were to the end zone. If the Bills needed a tough first down, they could go to Evans, who converted 10 of the 11 passes thrown to him on third and six or less. In the red zone, he caught 6 of 11 balls with five touchdowns while Moulds caught only 8 of 24 with three touchdowns. If you cut the field into five 20-yard zones, he had a higher DVOA than Moulds did in each one. And yes, if you needed to throw it long, Evans averaged 27 yards per catch on first down, five yards more than any other receiver with at least ten first down catches. Since Evans struggles at fighting through bump coverage, the Bills played to his strengths by putting him in motion and sending him straight downfield at the snap. The most similar rookie seasons were put up by Chris Chambers and James Lofton, and that basically gives you two directions for his career: Either he enjoys countless 1,000-yard seasons, or he spends years stuck on a team that can't find a quarterback.

Robert Ferguson Height: 6-1 Weight: 209 College: Texas A&M Born: 17-Dec-1979 Age: 25

Year	Team	G	Rec	Pass	Yds	Ctch%	Yd/C	TD	DVOA	Rank	DPAR	Rank	PAR
2002	GB	15	22	52	293	42%	13.3	3	-22.1%	82	-2.2	80	-1.1
2003	GB	15	38	59	520	64%	13.7	4	24.7%	10	12.3	32	12.3
2004	GB	13	24	49	367	49%	15.3	1	-0.5%	—	4.6	—	4.2
2005	GB	14	25	—	369	—	14.7	2					

Although Ferguson has speed and can catch deep balls, he got hit by numerous injuries in 2004 and watched Javon Walker steal his spot as the next star Packer receiver. What most people didn't know was that Ferguson had awful vision problems and refused to wear contacts. He had LASIK surgery in the off-season and believes it will help him track the ball deep. A study by Matthew Namee (HardballTimes.com) showed no improvement pattern among baseball players after LASIK, but perhaps pass receiving is different. If Walker's threatened holdout causes him to start the season out of shape and rusty, Ferguson will be an important part of Green Bay's early passing game and an interesting fantasy sleeper.

Brian Finneran Height: 6-5 Weight: 210 College: Villanova Born: 31-Jan-1976 Age: 29

Year	Team	G	Rec	Pass	Yds	Ctch%	Yd/C	TD	DVOA	Rank	DPAR	Rank	PAR
2002	ATL	16	56	102	838	55%	15.0	6	7.6%	31	15.5	29	15.3
2003	ATL	12	26	54	368	48%	14.2	2	2.4%	41	4.8	50	4.7
2004	ATL	12	23	33	258	70%	11.2	2	9.2%	—	5.5	—	5.8
2005	ATL	12	8	—	91	—	11.4	0					

A very good athlete, a good leaper, and a good special teams player, the biggest problem for Finneran is that the Falcons don't use him enough. For two straight years, he's been the Falcons' best receiver according to DPAR and DVOA. He's a big target, and Michael Vick needs to find him more often.

Larry Fitzgerald

Height: 6-2 Weight: 223 College: Pittsburgh Born: 31-Aug-1983 Age: 22

Year	Team	G	Rec	Pass	Yds	Ctch%	Yd/C	TD	DVOA	Rank	DPAR	Rank	PAR
2004	ARI	16	58	116	780	51%	13.4	8	-13.7%	68	1.3	66	2.4
2005	ARI	16	59	—	866	—	14.6	5					

Like Anquan Boldin, Fitzgerald saw his numbers dip as Denny Green experimented with Shaun King and John Navarre at quarterback. Fitzgerald's DPAR was an impressive 9.5 when Josh McCown was under center, but it dipped to −4.8 and −3.4 with King and Navarre. Fitzgerald is still raw as a route runner, but he showed potential both as a possession receiver (36 first down receptions) and a big play threat (five TD catches of 20 or more yards). He looks a lot like Houston's Andre Johnson, a big receiver who can out-jump or out-muscle defenders or use his body as a shield. Unlike Johnson, Fitzgerald has the luxury of being a number two wideout. The potential of the Boldin-Fitzgerald combo has not yet really been tapped.

Malcom Floyd

Height: 6-6 Weight: 215 College: Wyoming Born: 8-Sep-1981 Age: 24

Year	Team	G	Rec	Pass	Yds	Ctch%	Yd/C	TD	DVOA	Rank	DPAR	Rank	PAR
2004	SD	4	3	9	49	33%	16.3	1	-18.7%	—	-0.1	—	0.4
2005	SD	12	7	—	81	—	11.9	0					

A select few of you may have heard of a wide receiver named Malcolm Floyd. He had 26 catches and two touchdowns during a four-year career with the Oilers and the Rams. He has a younger brother named Malcom, who was an undrafted rookie with the 2004 Chargers. Apparently their parents just love the name. We'd be surprised if Malcom's career looked much different from Malcolm's.

Mike Furrey

Height: 6-0 Weight: 185 College: Northern Iowa Born: 12-May-1977 Age: 28

Year	Team	G	Rec	Pass	Yds	Ctch%	Yd/C	TD	DVOA	Rank	DPAR	Rank	PAR
2003	STL	13	20	33	189	61%	9.5	0	-19.3%	—	-0.7	—	-0.3
2004	STL	8	1	3	8	33%	8.0	0	-51.0%	—	-0.6	—	-0.5
2005	STL	13	9	—	122	—	13.7	1					

Furrey hails from Kurt Warner's alma mater (Northern Iowa) and makes his living as a special teamer. He caught 20 passes in 2003, many of them when Isaac Bruce was hurt late in the year, then hauled in four more in the overtime loss to the Panthers in the playoffs. Last year, he was trapped behind three better players and caught just one pass. The Rams are talking about moving him to defensive back, a sure sign that he'll spend the rest of his career on the coverage units.

Doug Gabriel

Height: 6-2 Weight: 215 College: Central Florida Born: 27-Aug-1980 Age: 25

Year	Team	G	Rec	Pass	Yds	Ctch%	Yd/C	TD	DVOA	Rank	DPAR	Rank	PAR
2003	OAK	12	1	1	17	100%	17.0	0	142.7%	—	0.8	—	0.8
2004	OAK	16	33	79	551	42%	16.7	2	-12.6%	65	1.5	65	2.8
2005	OAK	16	20	—	353	—	17.7	2					

Gabriel was a buzz player in training camp last year: The coaches loved him, he has sprinter's speed, and he seemed destined to average 19 yards per catch and score eight or nine touchdowns. In fact, Gabriel followed in the long tradition of Raiders "deep threats" like James Jett, providing a scant handful of highlights but dozens of long incompletions. If Ronald Curry is healthy, Gabriel will be the fourth wideout in Oakland. Every team has a guy with 4.4 speed that they bring off the bench to run fly routes; Gabriel is no better than Kelly Campbell, Greg Lewis, or a half dozen other backups around the league.

Jabar Gaffney

Height: 6-1 Weight: 193 College: Florida Born: 1-Dec-1980 Age: 25

Year	Team	G	Rec	Pass	Yds	Ctch%	Yd/C	TD	DVOA	Rank	DPAR	Rank	PAR
2002	HOU	16	41	81	483	51%	11.8	1	-15.7%	75	-0.1	75	0.7
2003	HOU	16	34	57	402	60%	11.8	2	5.5%	31	6.0	45	6.0
2004	HOU	16	41	68	632	60%	15.4	2	20.9%	21	16.7	34	18.7
2005	HOU	16	53	—	783	—	14.6	5					

Exhibit 847 in the "don't expect too much out of Florida receivers" argument, Gaffney is a number three slot receiver type playing the number two receiver position. He's fairly reliable when he doesn't showboat, trying to stretch the ball forward across the goal line only to fumble it into the end zone for a touchback against Jacksonville. His DVOA is partly a result of opposing defenses paying more attention to Andre Johnson, but at least Gaffney was able to take advantage of the opportunity. That's more than you can say for Donté Stallworth or Reggie Williams.

Justin Gage Height: 6-4 Weight: 208 College: Missouri Born: 25-Jan-1981 Age: 24

Year	Team	G	Rec	Pass	Yds	Ctch%	Yd/C	TD	DVOA	Rank	DPAR	Rank	PAR
2003	CHI	10	17	35	338	49%	19.9	2	6.2%	—	3.8	—	4.6
2004	CHI	16	12	28	156	43%	13.0	0	-30.9%	—	-2.8	—	-2.3
2005	CHI	14	21	—	312	—	14.5	1					

A former basketball player, Gage has the height and athleticism to be a real threat, particularly in the red zone. But so far he hasn't delivered, in large part because Bears quarterbacks haven't given him the opportunity. It's time for him to show what he can do.

Joey Galloway Height: 5-11 Weight: 197 College: Ohio State Born: 20-Nov-1971 Age: 34

Year	Team	G	Rec	Pass	Yds	Ctch%	Yd/C	TD	DVOA	Rank	DPAR	Rank	PAR
2002	DAL	16	61	120	908	51%	14.9	6	-7.1%	64	6.1	61	4.7
2003	DAL	15	34	83	672	41%	19.8	2	-8.6%	56	3.2	58	5.0
2004	TB	10	33	53	416	62%	12.6	5	21.7%	20	13.0	40	12.5
2005	TB	14	36	—	448	—	12.4	3					

Tampa Bay did well to get Galloway for the disgruntled Keyshawn Johnson before the 2004 season. They knew what they were getting—a receiver who still possessed great speed at age 32, but with a knack for injuries and dropped balls. Galloway is nothing if not true to form. On the first pass thrown his way in the season opener, he dropped a sure touchdown and crumpled to the turf with a groin injury that would cost him six games. When he got healthy, Galloway showed enough to merit his re-signing for 2005. He can still stretch a defense, although it's tough to tell in Tampa Bay's forever-throwing-short passing game.

Rod Gardner Height: 6-2 Weight: 213 College: Clemson Born: 26-Oct-1977 Age: 28

Year	Team	G	Rec	Pass	Yds	Ctch%	Yd/C	TD	DVOA	Rank	DPAR	Rank	PAR
2002	WAS	16	71	141	1006	50%	14.2	8	1.6%	44	15.1	30	13.2
2003	WAS	16	59	115	600	51%	10.2	5	-23.7%	80	-5.4	81	-6.1
2004	WAS	16	51	106	650	48%	12.7	5	-12.7%	66	1.3	67	-1.3
2005	WAS	16	31	—	426	—	13.8	2					

The Redskins had two unhappy wide receivers seeking a trade. Instead of unloading Rod Gardner and the $2.5 million left on his contract, Washington decided to add $9 million in dead money to their cap and traded Laveranues Coles away instead. Now, Washington has an unhappy Gardner, who will likely see his role in the offense reduced after the team brought in Santana Moss to replace Coles and David Patten to serve as the team's number two receiver. As of press time, the Skins were still looking to move the unhappy Gardner, but odds are he's wearing maroon and gold in Week 1.

Talman Gardner Height: 6-1 Weight: 205 College: Florida State Born: 10-Mar-1980 Age: 25

Year	Team	G	Rec	Pass	Yds	Ctch%	Yd/C	TD	DVOA	Rank	DPAR	Rank	PAR
2003	NO	10	3	15	29	20%	9.7	0	-72.2%	—	-4.1	—	-4.2
2004	NO	11	1	1	23	100%	23.0	0	235.2%	—	1.5	—	1.4
2005	NO	16	13	—	182	—	14.0	1					

Despite playing very little offense, this 2003 seventh-round pick has provided good value to the Saints in kick coverage. He's got good speed but was known at Florida State for running bad routes. KUBIAK inexplicably loves him and gives him 660 yards if you change his expected role to "third receiver." Not likely, but he does have sleeper potential if New Orleans has injuries.

Fred Gibson   Height: 6-4   Weight: 202   College: Georgia   Born: 26-Oct-1981   Age: 24

Year	Team	G	Rec	Pass	Yds	Ctch%	Yd/C	TD	DVOA	Rank	DPAR	Rank	PAR
2005	PIT	15	10	—	166	—	17.2	1					

A two-sport star at Georgia who started for the Bulldogs for four years, Gibson was ranked above teammate Reggie Brown by some scouts but lasted into the fourth round because he's thin-framed and has a rep for getting the yips over the middle. He'll be a number four wideout in 2005.

Bryan Gilmore   Height: 6-0   Weight: 200   College: Midwestern State   Born: 21-Jul-1978   Age: 27

Year	Team	G	Rec	Pass	Yds	Ctch%	Yd/C	TD	DVOA	Rank	DPAR	Rank	PAR
2002	ARI	3	1	4	14	25%	14.0	0	-42.8%	—	-0.7	—	-0.9
2003	ARI	14	17	45	213	38%	12.5	2	-26.0%	—	-2.7	—	-2.9
2004	MIA	16	15	34	206	44%	13.7	1	-13.6%	—	0.2	—	-0.3
2005	MIA	13	12	—	163	—	13.4	1					

Gilmore made the Dolphins' roster after four years in Arizona more for his special teams contributions, which are OK but not great, than for his receiving skills, which are somewhat less than OK.

David Givens   Height: 6-0   Weight: 212   College: Notre Dame   Born: 16-Aug-1980   Age: 25

Year	Team	G	Rec	Pass	Yds	Ctch%	Yd/C	TD	DVOA	Rank	DPAR	Rank	PAR
2002	NE	11	9	15	92	60%	10.2	1	-19.1%	—	-0.5	—	-1.0
2003	NE	13	34	54	510	63%	15.0	6	32.6%	3	13.4	26	14.1
2004	NE	15	56	106	874	53%	15.6	3	16.6%	27	21.4	24	19.8
2005	NE	16	58	—	813	—	14.1	5					

Typical of a New England Patriot, Givens is small, tough, and underrated. He turned in solid performances against some top pass defenses, particularly in both games against the Bills. Starting from the beginning of the season, he had 30 straight receptions that were all first downs or touchdowns, a streak that didn't end until he caught a 13-yard pass on second and 24 in the final minutes of the Week 8 loss to Pittsburgh. His role in the game plan declined after Deion Branch returned from his injury, but David Patten's departure for Washington makes him the clear number two.

Terry Glenn   Height: 5-11   Weight: 195   College: Ohio State   Born: 23-Jul-1974   Age: 31

Year	Team	G	Rec	Pass	Yds	Ctch%	Yd/C	TD	DVOA	Rank	DPAR	Rank	PAR
2002	GB	15	56	106	817	53%	14.6	2	2.1%	43	12.0	37	10.9
2003	DAL	16	52	96	754	54%	14.5	5	1.5%	44	8.3	40	8.4
2004	DAL	6	24	37	400	65%	16.7	2	32.6%	—	11.6	—	11.3
2005	DAL	13	24	—	333	—	13.9	2					

Not many people noticed it because of the Cowboys' disappointing season, but Terry Glenn, the guy Bill Parcells once called "she," actually played very well before an injury ended his season early. Glenn was a fairly productive receiver in 2002 and 2003, but our projections don't see him reaching those levels again this year. An aging number three receiver coming off a serious foot injury isn't a recipe for success.

Az-Zahir Hakim   Height: 5-10   Weight: 189   College: San Diego State   Born: 3-Jun-1977   Age: 28

Year	Team	G	Rec	Pass	Yds	Ctch%	Yd/C	TD	DVOA	Rank	DPAR	Rank	PAR
2002	DET	10	37	82	541	45%	14.6	3	-8.2%	68	3.4	70	2.1
2003	DET	14	49	107	449	45%	9.2	4	-36.8%	85	-12.4	85	-13.5
2004	DET	12	31	57	533	54%	17.2	3	22.6%	19	14.1	39	13.1
2005	NO	12	25	—	351	—	13.9	2					

Hakim finally put together a fairly good season after two bad years in Detroit, but he still hasn't done anywhere near enough to justify the huge contract Matt Millen gave him. Signed with New Orleans right before press time.

Dante Hall

Height: 5-8   **Weight: 187**   **College: Texas A&M**   **Born: 1-Sep-1978**   **Age: 27**

Year	Team	G	Rec	Pass	Yds	Ctch%	Yd/C	TD	DVOA	Rank	DPAR	Rank	PAR
2002	KC	16	20	35	322	57%	16.1	3	6.7%	—	4.9	—	4.8
2003	KC	16	40	60	423	67%	10.6	1	-13.3%	68	0.4	69	-0.4
2004	KC	16	25	36	230	64%	9.2	0	-11.2%	—	1.1	—	2.1
2005	KC	13	8	—	85	—	10.2	1					

A phenomenal return man; an ordinary slot receiver. Coaches always bend over backward to find offensive roles for players like Hall, to "get them the ball in space." The best way to get Hall the ball in space is to let him field kickoffs and punts, block like the dickens for him, and then give him a Gatorade on the sidelines.

Cortez Hankton

Height: 6-0   **Weight: 200**   **College: Texas Southern**   **Born: 20-Jan-1981**   **Age: 24**

Year	Team	G	Rec	Pass	Yds	Ctch%	Yd/C	TD	DVOA	Rank	DPAR	Rank	PAR
2003	JAC	16	17	41	166	41%	9.8	0	-52.7%	—	-7.5	—	-6.9
2004	JAC	12	9	9	81	100%	9.0	2	42.0%	—	3.3	—	3.7
2005	JAC	14	16	—	223	—	14.4	1					

Cortez Hankton entered the league as an undrafted free agent from Texas Southern, and while he hasn't made a huge impact, he has earned a reputation as a hard worker and someone the Jaguars think can contribute. The presence of first-round pick Matt Jones might cut down a bit on Hankton's playing time.

Karl Hankton

Height: 6-2   **Weight: 202**   **College: Trinity**   **Born: 24-Jul-1970**   **Age: 35**

Year	Team	G	Rec	Pass	Yds	Ctch%	Yd/C	TD	DVOA	Rank	DPAR	Rank	PAR
2002	CAR	15	9	17	146	53%	16.2	0	20.2%	—	3.9	—	3.7
2003	CAR	14	2	4	27	50%	13.5	0	8.9%	—	0.5	—	0.4
2004	CAR	15	2	2	25	100%	12.5	0	77.1%	—	1.2	—	1.2
2005	CAR	13	2	—	33	—	13.3	0					

Karl Hankton of the Panthers is a little-known special teams player, but he had one of the heads-up plays of the year in the season finale. When the Saints' Mel Mitchell shoved him in the face, Hankton didn't just decline to retaliate; he put up both hands so the officials could clearly see that he wasn't retaliating. Mitchell got a 15-yard penalty in a situation that often results in offsetting penalties.

Marvin Harrison

Height: 6-0   **Weight: 175**   **College: Syracuse**   **Born: 25-Aug-1972**   **Age: 33**

Year	Team	G	Rec	Pass	Yds	Ctch%	Yd/C	TD	DVOA	Rank	DPAR	Rank	PAR
2002	IND	16	143	205	1722	70%	12.0	11	21.2%	11	49.6	1	49.5
2003	IND	15	94	142	1272	66%	13.5	10	10.1%	27	19.7	9	20.5
2004	IND	16	86	139	1113	62%	12.9	15	14.6%	32	28.6	12	31.4
2005	IND	16	78	—	1001	—	12.9	11					

Lost amid all the hubbub surrounding the Colts' record-setting offense was the beginning of Marvin Harrison's decline. Harrison remained Manning's top red zone target, leading the team with 15 touchdowns, but his overall numbers were down for the second straight year. Much of this is attributable to the rise of Reggie Wayne, but more troubling could be Harrison's 32nd ranking in DVOA. Harrison is still a highly productive receiver but the days when he was the best receiver in football appear to be over.

Devery Henderson

Height: 5-11   **Weight: 200**   **College: LSU**   **Born: 26-Mar-1982**   **Age: 23**

Year	Team	G	Rec	Pass	Yds	Ctch%	Yd/C	TD	DVOA	Rank	DPAR	Rank	PAR
2004	NO	1	0	—	0	—	—	0	—	—	—	—	—
2005	NO	16	36	—	481	—	13.4	4					

Last year's second-round pick held out of camp for the first eight days, fell behind the rest of his teammates, and spent the whole year doing nothing. Henderson couldn't beat out Jerome Pathon as the third receiver, and he couldn't beat out Talman Gardner for a spot on special teams. Since New Orleans hasn't been able to sign a veteran slot receiver as of this writing, the door is open for him to get on the field, and he's apparently impressed coaches with a ton of strength training in the off-season.

Chris Henry Height: 6-4 Weight: 197 College: West Virginia Born: 17-May-1983 Age: 22

Year	Team	G	Rec	Pass	Yds	Ctch%	Yd/C	TD	DVOA	Rank	DPAR	Rank	PAR
2005	CIN	12	10	—	140	—	14.3	1					

In his final college game, West Virginia's 30–18 loss to Florida State in the Gator Bowl, Henry got angry when QB Rasheed Marshall didn't see him get open on a first quarter play. According to the *Pittsburgh Post Gazette,* Henry "waved his arms, took off his helmet, waved his arms angrily again and then walked petulantly off the field," earning him a head session with coach Rich Rodriguez. Henry was infamous at West Virginia for taking shots at Marshall (saying once that his numbers would be better if a "real quarterback" were throwing him the ball) and giving Rutgers fans (both of them) the finger at the end of a game. He'll have to unseat Kelley Washington or T. J. Houshmandzadeh to be anything more than a roster filler in Cincinnati. Stay tuned for how this paragon of maturity adjusts to life in the NFL.

Ike Hilliard Height: 5-11 Weight: 210 College: Florida Born: 5-Apr-1976 Age: 29

Year	Team	G	Rec	Pass	Yds	Ctch%	Yd/C	TD	DVOA	Rank	DPAR	Rank	PAR
2002	NYG	7	27	47	386	57%	14.3	2	18.2%	—	10.4	—	11.3
2003	NYG	13	60	102	608	59%	10.1	6	-2.6%	50	6.5	43	6.2
2004	NYG	16	49	81	437	60%	8.9	0	-29.6%	81	-8.3	82	-11.1
2005	TB	12	22	—	270	—	12.4	2					

Never developed into the reliable number two WR Giants fans had hoped he would. Had very good years in 1999 and 2000, but since then has only managed to play a full 16 games only once. A perennial favorite in our online anti-fantasy "Loser League" game, since he is always good for two or three catches, a handful of yards, and zero touchdowns.

Torry Holt Height: 6-0 Weight: 190 College: North Carolina State Born: 5-Jun-1976 Age: 29

Year	Team	G	Rec	Pass	Yds	Ctch%	Yd/C	TD	DVOA	Rank	DPAR	Rank	PAR
2002	STL	16	91	160	1302	57%	14.3	4	12.9%	20	28.8	9	26.0
2003	STL	16	117	183	1696	64%	14.5	12	27.9%	6	40.9	1	43.8
2004	STL	16	94	137	1372	69%	14.6	10	24.8%	13	34.9	7	35.2
2005	STL	16	96	—	1302	—	13.6	9					

Holt has been in the top ten among receivers in DPAR every year since 2000 and hasn't posted a mark under 28.8 in that span. He led the league in DPAR in 2003. His Catch % usually isn't particularly high (though it was great in 2004), but Holt is almost always working downfield and doesn't have many six-yard hitches on his stat sheet. He typically outperforms Randy Moss in DPAR and has out-paced Terrell Owens and Rodney Harrison the past two seasons. He doesn't get as much attention as the other top receivers, but he can dominate games.

Chris Horn Height: 5-11 Weight: 195 College: Rocky Mountain Born: 13-Jul-1977 Age: 28

Year	Team	G	Rec	Pass	Yds	Ctch%	Yd/C	TD	DVOA	Rank	DPAR	Rank	PAR
2004	KC	14	15	17	178	59%	11.9	1	9.1%	—	2.8	—	3.0
2005	KC	13	12	—	161	—	13.5	1					

An undrafted free agent who spent two years on the practice squad, Chris Horn is the living embodiment of the concept of "replacement level." If Horn is starting, this is a pretty good sign that our prediction about the collapse of the Kansas City offense is going to be accurate.

Joe Horn Height: 6-1 Weight: 206 College: Itawamba Junior College Born: 16-Jan-1972 Age: 33

Year	Team	G	Rec	Pass	Yds	Ctch%	Yd/C	TD	DVOA	Rank	DPAR	Rank	PAR
2002	NO	16	89	150	1314	59%	14.8	7	20.5%	14	34.8	5	32.6
2003	NO	15	78	130	973	60%	12.5	10	3.1%	38	12.8	28	14.7
2004	NO	16	94	153	1399	61%	14.9	11	25.8%	12	41.6	2	44.0
2005	NO	16	81	—	1063	—	13.2	8					

Teams that draft projects often find that they develop nicely…and then pay off for another team. A good example is the Chiefs, who took Joe Horn out of junior college in the fifth round of the 1996 draft, got just 53 catches from him over four years as he developed, and then watched him sign with the Saints and become a star. It isn't much of a draft steal if the team that takes you doesn't benefit from the selection. Horn was one of the many receivers who watched the effects of aging seemingly reverse in 2004, but when you prepare for your fantasy draft, don't delude yourself into thinking that a 33-year-old who just set career highs in catches, yards, and touchdowns is going to do it again.

T. J. Houshmandzadeh
Height: 6-1   Weight: 197   College: Oregon State   Born: 26-Sep-1977 Age: 28

Year	Team	G	Rec	Pass	Yds	Ctch%	Yd/C	TD	DVOA	Rank	DPAR	Rank	PAR
2002	CIN	16	41	70	492	59%	12.0	1	1.3%	45	7.5	56	7.5
2003	CIN	2	0	—	0	—	—	0	—	—	—	—	—
2004	CIN	16	73	109	978	67%	13.4	4	28.8%	11	31.0	11	27.5
2005	CIN	16	63	—	834	—	13.2	4					

For a seventh-round afterthought, T. J. Whosyourdaddy has done pretty well for himself. He was able to avoid injuries in 2004 and turned in such a good performance he got a new contract out of it. Overall, he had a DPAR of 31.0, and actually bettered his teammate Chad Johnson in red zone DPAR. Houshmandzadeh is the number two receiver on this team no matter what Peter Warrick might tell you.

Keenan Howry
Height: 5-10 Weight: 172   College: Oregon   Born: 17-Jun-1981 Age: 24

Year	Team	G	Rec	Pass	Yds	Ctch%	Yd/C	TD	DVOA	Rank	DPAR	Rank	PAR
2003	MIN	16	2	6	15	33%	7.5	0	-56.7%	—	-1.4	—	-1.2
2004	MIN	3	1	1	3	100%	3.0	0	-96.4%	—	-0.4	—	-0.5
2005	MIN	14	11	—	157	—	13.0	1					

Howry is small and fast, and the Vikings would like him to be a kick returner like the Lions have had in Eddie Drummond. But so far he hasn't shown that potential, and there's concern that he's too injury-prone.

Randy Hymes
Height: 6-3   Weight: 211   College: Grambling   Born: 7-Aug-1979 Age: 26

Year	Team	G	Rec	Pass	Yds	Ctch%	Yd/C	TD	DVOA	Rank	DPAR	Rank	PAR
2002	BAL	6	6	13	123	46%	20.5	0	6.4%	—	1.7	—	1.4
2003	BAL	0	0	—	0	—	—	0	—	—	—	—	—
2004	BAL	14	26	44	323	55%	12.4	2	-6.0%	—	2.5	—	1.8
2005	BAL	14	19	—	241	—	12.5	1					

Hymes is a converted quarterback who also served as the team's backup long snapper. If anything screams "We need more depth at the wideout position!" it's when your third receiver is also the long snapper. Hymes is 6'3", and the Ravens hope he can grow into a downfield threat who can complement Mark Clayton. Actually, with Boller as quarterback, they are just hoping he can grow another inch or two.

Darrell Jackson
Height: 6-0   Weight: 201   College: Florida State   Born: 6-Dec-1978 Age: 27

Year	Team	G	Rec	Pass	Yds	Ctch%	Yd/C	TD	DVOA	Rank	DPAR	Rank	PAR
2002	SEA	13	62	112	877	55%	14.1	4	-8.2%	67	5.5	62	7.2
2003	SEA	16	68	130	1137	52%	16.7	9	16.5%	15	21.5	5	20.2
2004	SEA	16	87	155	1199	56%	13.8	7	4.2%	45	20.0	29	18.7
2005	SEA	16	79	—	1141	—	14.5	7					

Jackson had career highs in catches and yards last year, not because he was really playing better but because the Seahawks relied on him more than ever. With Koren Robinson out six games, Jackson became the clear number one receiver in Seattle, and he should reprise that role in 2005.

Frisman Jackson
Height: 6-3   Weight: 215   College: Western Illinois   Born: 12-Jun-1979 Age: 26

Year	Team	G	Rec	Pass	Yds	Ctch%	Yd/C	TD	DVOA	Rank	DPAR	Rank	PAR
2002	CLE	6	1	1	6	100%	6.0	0	40.3%	—	0.4	—	0.5
2003	CLE	5	2	5	29	40%	14.5	0	-20.0%	—	-0.1	—	-0.2
2004	CLE	10	13	19	168	68%	12.9	0	37.7%	—	6.4	—	5.6
2005	CLE	12	10	—	122	—	12.6	1					

(continued next page)

Frisman Jackson (continued)

The Browns say that Jackson will grow into a nice red zone target because of his size. To test this theory, they threw to him past the opposing 30-yard line a grand total of once last year. But he's cheap and plays on coverage teams, so he fits nicely into the last spot on the depth chart. Braylon Edwards is stuck in the first spot, and the spots between the two of them may change roughly every five minutes.

Nate Jackson Height: 6-3 Weight: 223 College: Menlo College Born: 4-Jun-1979 Age: 26

Year	Team	G	Rec	Pass	Yds	Ctch%	Yd/C	TD	DVOA	Rank	DPAR	Rank	PAR
2003	DEN	1	0	2	0	0%	0.0	0	-94.9%	—	-0.8	—	-0.9
2004	DEN	12	8	11	73	73%	9.1	0	1.5%	—	1.1	—	1.0
2005	*DEN*	*13*	*9*	—	*113*	—	*12.8*	*1*					

A Division III All-American, Nate Jackson became an important part of the Broncos' special teams and an occasional fourth receiver last year, but a broken ankle late in the season will hamper his chances to make the team again.

Vincent Jackson Height: 6-5 Weight: 241 College: Northern Colorado Born: 14-Jan-1983 Age: 22

Year	Team	G	Rec	Pass	Yds	Ctch%	Yd/C	TD	DVOA	Rank	DPAR	Rank	PAR
2005	*SD*	*13*	*12*	—	*174*	—	*14.3*	*1*					

Two Antonio Gateses are better than one. Jackson, a two-time All-American at the Division I-AA level, had Gates-like dimensions and skills. The plan, once Jackson ramps up to the speed of the pro game: Put both players in the formation, sprinkle in some LaDainian, then see who the defense tries to cover with a linebacker or a slow strong safety. Who said Marty Schottenheimer lacks creativity?

Taylor Jacobs Height: 6-0 Weight: 198 College: Florida Born: 30-May-1981 Age: 24

Year	Team	G	Rec	Pass	Yds	Ctch%	Yd/C	TD	DVOA	Rank	DPAR	Rank	PAR
2003	WAS	8	3	6	37	50%	12.3	1	14.4%	—	0.9	—	0.5
2004	WAS	15	16	27	178	59%	11.1	0	-15.2%	—	0.0	—	-0.1
2005	*WAS*	*15*	*27*	—	*375*	—	*13.9*	*2*					

Jacobs is the likely beneficiary of a potential deal sending Rod Gardner out of Washington, as he probably could beat out James Thrash for playing time behind Santana Moss and David Patten. In the department of statistical oddities, he had 155 receiving yards on plays that started between the 40s, and 23 receiving yards on plays that started everywhere else. This projection drops significantly if Gardner isn't traded.

Michael Jenkins Height: 6-4 Weight: 217 College: Ohio State Born: 18-Jun-1982 Age: 23

Year	Team	G	Rec	Pass	Yds	Ctch%	Yd/C	TD	DVOA	Rank	DPAR	Rank	PAR
2004	ATL	16	7	20	119	35%	17.0	0	-39.5%	—	-3.0	—	-2.8
2005	*ATL*	*16*	*27*	—	*409*	—	*15.1*	*2*					

Obviously a disappointment on offense, but his numbers don't tell the whole story. Jenkins was one of the best special teams players in the league: excellent in punt coverage, flying down the field, and a fierce blocker. You don't take special teams players in the first round, so the Falcons obviously want more out of him, but he's already a contributor.

Andre Johnson Height: 6-2 Weight: 221 College: Miami Born: 11-Jul-1981 Age: 24

Year	Team	G	Rec	Pass	Yds	Ctch%	Yd/C	TD	DVOA	Rank	DPAR	Rank	PAR
2003	HOU	16	66	119	976	55%	14.8	4	4.9%	32	12.6	30	12.3
2004	HOU	16	79	137	1142	58%	14.5	6	4.5%	44	18.4	33	22.8
2005	*HOU*	*16*	*76*	—	*1107*	—	*14.6*	*7*					

Johnson has a lot of potential, but he's not an elite receiver yet. Those highlight-reel catches tended to come against weak opposition, with his best games coming against the Vikings, Jets, Packers, Raiders, Chiefs, and Lions. Meanwhile, he suffered against tough secondaries—Champ Bailey shut him down—and he disappeared at the end of the season, with only

11 catches for 124 yards in the last four games of the season combined. Most similar historical receivers after two seasons are Chris Collinsworth (pro-rated for the strike) and Andre Rison, so Johnson should consider broadcasting school and fire insurance.

Bethel Johnson   Height: 5-11   Weight: 200   College: Texas A&M   Born: 11-Feb-1979   Age: 26

Year	Team	G	Rec	Pass	Yds	Ctch%	Yd/C	TD	DVOA	Rank	DPAR	Rank	PAR
2003	NE	15	16	34	209	47%	13.1	2	-21.7%	—	-1.1	—	-0.8
2004	NE	13	10	21	174	48%	17.4	1	-6.5%	—	1.3	—	2.3
2005	NE	13	11	—	157	—	13.8	1					

An extremely fast receiver and kickoff return man who shows flashes of brilliance. Recall his 48-yard fingertip catch to lock up the game against Seattle. However, he inexplicably seems to consistently be in Bill Belichick's doghouse. Johnson has a low catch percentage, but that is a reflection of the deep routes that he runs. With David Patten gone, this is Johnson's year to step up and battle David Terrell for the number three spot.

Bryant Johnson   Height: 6-2   Weight: 214   College: Penn State   Born: 7-Mar-1981   Age: 24

Year	Team	G	Rec	Pass	Yds	Ctch%	Yd/C	TD	DVOA	Rank	DPAR	Rank	PAR
2003	ARI	15	35	77	438	45%	12.5	1	-29.9%	83	-5.9	82	-6.0
2004	ARI	16	49	101	537	49%	11.0	1	-27.1%	79	-7.9	81	-7.4
2005	ARI	16	32	—	458	—	14.3	3					

If this offense gets humming the way Denny Green hopes it will, Johnson will have the Jake Reed role, running deep routes while Boldin and Fitzgerald attract all of the defensive attention. Johnson was overmatched as a starter when Boldin was hurt last season, but he had some fine games as a slot receiver against the Niners and Rams late in the year. He wasn't worth a first-round pick in 2003, but the team redeemed itself by taking Boldin in the next round.

Chad Johnson   Height: 6-1   Weight: 192   College: Oregon State   Born: 9-Jan-1978   Age: 27

Year	Team	G	Rec	Pass	Yds	Ctch%	Yd/C	TD	DVOA	Rank	DPAR	Rank	PAR
2002	CIN	14	69	137	1166	50%	16.9	5	9.8%	25	22.7	16	22.0
2003	CIN	16	90	154	1355	58%	15.1	10	18.7%	13	28.1	4	28.5
2004	CIN	16	95	169	1274	56%	13.4	9	6.7%	40	24.0	19	20.8
2005	CIN	16	83	—	1171	—	14.1	8					

When he's not taking plays off, Johnson might be the best wide receiver in the AFC North. According to similarity scores, the list of comparable receivers is led by Torry Holt, Laveranues Coles, Keyshawn Johnson, Al Toon, Antonio Freeman, and Randy Moss. And given that Carson Palmer has a year's worth of game experience under his belt, things should only get better for Johnson. If things go really well, rumor has it that he will upgrade to titanium teeth for pregame warm-ups and postgame press conferences.

Kevin Johnson   Height: 5-11   Weight: 195   College: Syracuse   Born: 15-Jul-1976   Age: 29

Year	Team	G	Rec	Pass	Yds	Ctch%	Yd/C	TD	DVOA	Rank	DPAR	Rank	PAR
2002	CLE	16	67	120	703	56%	10.5	4	-17.0%	76	-1.2	76	0.3
2003	CLE	9	41	65	381	63%	9.3	2	-10.9%	—	1.5	—	1.8
2003	JAC	6	17	30	253	57%	14.9	1	8.9%	51	3.8	47	4.1
2004	BAL	16	35	58	373	57%	10.7	1	-14.0%	69	0.2	69	-0.8
2005	DET	13	17	—	213	—	12.3	1					

Three seasons into his career, the most similar receivers to Kevin Johnson included Ernest Givins, Anthony Miller, Keyshawn Johnson, Chris Chambers, and Hines Ward. Then Johnson completely imploded, bouncing to a different team every year with fewer receptions and fewer yards. Team number four is Detroit, home of the first-round wide receiver draft pick and our projected NFL rushing leader. Even if Charles Rogers doesn't play, there are too many hands looking for the ball.

Keyshawn Johnson

Height: 6-4 **Weight:** 212 **College:** USC **Born:** 22-Jul-1972 **Age:** 33

Year	Team	G	Rec	Pass	Yds	Ctch%	Yd/C	TD	DVOA	Rank	DPAR	Rank	PAR
2002	TB	16	76	141	1088	54%	14.3	5	6.0%	36	19.9	20	20.8
2003	TB	10	45	74	600	61%	13.3	3	19.9%	12	13.7	23	13.8
2004	DAL	16	70	125	981	56%	14.0	6	13.5%	35	23.6	20	20.1
2005	DAL	16	64	—	849	—	13.3	5					

The pairing of Keyshawn with his old buddies Bill Parcells and Vinny Testaverde had mixed results. There's no question that Keyshawn has talent, and his numbers would look better if the Cowboys hadn't played so many top secondaries. But 33 is old for a wide receiver, and it's hard to imagine Keyshawn being a Pro Bowler again.

Brandon Jones

Height: 6-1 **Weight:** 208 **College:** Oklahoma **Born:** 6-Oct-1982 **Age:** 23

Year	Team	G	Rec	Pass	Yds	Ctch%	Yd/C	TD	DVOA	Rank	DPAR	Rank	PAR
2005	TEN	14	17	—	235	—	13.5	2					

A career number three wideout for a pass-oriented Oklahoma offense, Jones passes the tape measure and stopwatch tests but also drops a lot of passes. He caught just two passes for seven yards against USC in the Orange Bowl, but Titans offensive coordinator Norm Chow (who coached the Trojans offense in January) must have seen something he liked, because Jones will compete for a major role in the Titans offense.

Matt Jones

Height: 6-6 **Weight:** 242 **College:** Arkansas **Born:** 22-Apr-1983 **Age:** 22

Year	Team	G	Rec	Pass	Yds	Ctch%	Yd/C	TD	DVOA	Rank	DPAR	Rank	PAR
2005	JAC	14	26	—	394	—	14.9	3					

Jones is one of the more intriguing draftees in recent NFL history. The draft has seen plenty of "workout wonders"—guys whose performances in predraft workouts sent their draft stock soaring—but rarely if ever has a player who will have to learn an entirely new position at the NFL level been selected so high. We found it interesting that it was the Lions who took all the abuse for their third straight first-round receiver, but didn't Jacksonville draft a wideout early in round one last year? If Reggie Williams, a fairly polished college receiver, barely made an impact despite starting his entire rookie season, how is Jones going to justify his lofty draft status while trying to learn the fundamentals of his position? Being 6′6″ with freakish size and speed won't hurt.

Joe Jurevicius

Height: 6-5 **Weight:** 230 **College:** Penn State **Born:** 23-Dec-1974 **Age:** 30

Year	Team	G	Rec	Pass	Yds	Ctch%	Yd/C	TD	DVOA	Rank	DPAR	Rank	PAR
2002	TB	14	37	52	423	71%	11.4	4	26.0%	8	13.5	34	13.1
2003	TB	4	12	24	118	50%	9.8	2	-6.1%	—	1.0	—	0.8
2004	TB	10	27	37	333	73%	12.3	2	27.6%	—	10.6	—	11.5
2005	SEA	14	23	—	303	—	13.4	2					

Jurevicius has been through a lot the last two-plus years. There was the starring role during Tampa Bay's Super Bowl run, which occurred in the midst of a personal tragedy—the death of his infant son. That was followed by serious knee and back injuries that cost him much of the 2003–2004 seasons. But if he can stay healthy he's exactly the type of team-first, competent pro the Seahawks desperately needed to add to their receiver corps. He possesses great hands and body control, things that have been sorely lacking in Seattle.

Eddie Kennison

Height: 6-1 **Weight:** 201 **College:** LSU **Born:** 20-Jan-1973 **Age:** 32

Year	Team	G	Rec	Pass	Yds	Ctch%	Yd/C	TD	DVOA	Rank	DPAR	Rank	PAR
2002	KC	16	53	92	906	58%	17.1	2	28.2%	6	26.2	12	26.6
2003	KC	16	56	99	854	57%	15.3	5	14.3%	18	15.1	18	14.8
2004	KC	14	62	106	1086	58%	17.5	8	19.2%	24	24.7	17	27.1
2005	KC	15	61	—	917	—	15.1	6					

Kennison was targeted 17 times in the red zone, second on the team to Gonzo, but he wasn't particularly effective: He scored three red zone touchdowns but recorded a DPAR of 0.5, just a hair above replacement level. Kennison is an aging burner who does his best work when the threat of a fly pattern is there. He will remain effective as long as opponents have to stack the box against the run and Gonzo is there to occupy a safety.

Andre King			Height: 5-11	Weight: 195	College: Miami						Born: 26-Nov-1973		Age: 32
Year	Team	G	Rec	Pass	Yds	Ctch%	Yd/C	TD	DVOA	Rank	DPAR	Rank	PAR
2002	CLE	10	5	6	41	83%	8.2	0	-12.2%	—	0.1	—	0.1
2003	CLE	15	9	14	88	64%	9.8	0	-5.3%	—	0.8	—	1.1
2004	CLE	9	5	8	49	63%	9.8	0	-24.6%	—	-0.4	—	-0.3
2005	CLE	13	7	—	94	—	13.1	0					

King was selected in the second round of the 1993 Major League Baseball amateur draft by the Atlanta Braves and played with four different minor league teams in five seasons before deciding to take up college football. He was never a starter at Miami, playing behind Santana Moss and Reggie Wayne, among others. But during his senior year the coaching staff gave him the team's Leadership Award for his hard work in practice and his stellar special teams play. With his college coach, Butch Davis, gone, he might not be around in Cleveland much longer, but even if his athletic career is over it's been an admirable one.

David Kircus			Height: 6-1	Weight: 185	College: Grand Valley State						Born: 19-Feb-1980		Age: 25
Year	Team	G	Rec	Pass	Yds	Ctch%	Yd/C	TD	DVOA	Rank	DPAR	Rank	PAR
2003	DET	5	3	12	53	25%	17.7	0	-48.2%	—	-1.9	—	-1.6
2004	DET	7	3	10	68	30%	22.7	1	-14.5%	—	0.0	—	-0.4
2005	DET	14	14	—	193	—	14.2	1					

The coaches frequently rave about Kircus's hands. Maybe he shows them off in practice. He sure doesn't show them off in games.

Charles Lee			Height: 6-2	Weight: 210	College: UCF						Born: 19-Nov-1977		Age: 28
Year	Team	G	Rec	Pass	Yds	Ctch%	Yd/C	TD	DVOA	Rank	DPAR	Rank	PAR
2002	TB	1	0	—	0	—	—	0	—	—	—	—	—
2003	TB	8	33	46	432	72%	13.1	2	15.5%	—	7.9	—	9.3
2004	TB	7	15	22	207	68%	13.8	0	12.8%	—	4.1	—	4.4
2005	ARI	11	9	—	115	—	12.9	1					

When a player has as many chances to stick in a regular role with an NFL team as Lee has had and doesn't do it, well, you can pretty much assume it's not going to happen. Lee has played for Green Bay and Tampa Bay during his five-year career, and is waiting for the NFL to add an expansion team in Montego Bay. Until then, he'll be buried on the depth chart in Arizona, where he signed a one-year deal this summer.

Ashley Lelie			Height: 6-3	Weight: 200	College: Hawaii						Born: 16-Feb-1980		Age: 25
Year	Team	G	Rec	Pass	Yds	Ctch%	Yd/C	TD	DVOA	Rank	DPAR	Rank	PAR
2002	DEN	15	32	53	505	66%	15.8	2	31.6%	4	16.0	28	17.3
2003	DEN	16	37	81	628	46%	17.0	2	1.4%	45	6.8	42	5.2
2004	DEN	16	54	101	1084	53%	20.1	7	22.7%	18	25.4	16	26.5
2005	DEN	16	58	—	938	—	16.3	6					

A year ago, all we were hearing from the Denver press was how Mike Shanahan had fallen in love with Darius Watts, and Ashley Lelie's days as an underachieving starter were nearing an end. Well, that second part was certainly true. Lelie finally put the mental aspects of football together with his physical talent, and the new emphasis on illegal contact helped the slight-of-build Lelie break free of stronger cornerbacks. He made big catches nearly every week, with 11 games of 60 yards or more. None of the players who was similar to Lelie over a three-year period gave back his third-year gains, so we expect Lelie to have another big season. But you don't truly qualify as a star Denver receiver until you have your own mustard.

Greg Lewis Height: 6-0 Weight: 180 College: Illinois Born: 12-Feb-1980 Age: 25

Year	Team	G	Rec	Pass	Yds	Ctch%	Yd/C	TD	DVOA	Rank	DPAR	Rank	PAR
2003	PHI	11	6	9	95	67%	15.8	0	33.6%	—	2.4	—	2.9
2004	PHI	16	17	46	183	63%	10.8	0	-1.3%	25	3.6	25	3.1
2005	*PHI*	*16*	*38*	*—*	*550*	*—*	*14.5*	*3*					

A playoff hero who played well against the Vikings and Falcons and scored a touchdown in the Super Bowl, Lewis is the fastest receiver on the Eagles roster, Andy Reid's favorite option for end-arounds, and a hardworking special teamer. He has a new contract and will battle Todd Pinkston and Reggie Brown for playing time and catches. This is the type of player good teams draft, cultivate, and find roles for, while bad teams scramble for the same caliber of player in free agency.

Michael Lewis Height: 5-8 Weight: 165 College: None Born: 14-Nov-1971 Age: 34

Year	Team	G	Rec	Pass	Yds	Ctch%	Yd/C	TD	DVOA	Rank	DPAR	Rank	PAR
2002	NO	16	8	19	200	42%	25.0	0	-26.0%	—	-1.3	—	-1.7
2003	NO	13	12	24	226	50%	18.8	1	15.3%	—	3.8	—	4.3
2004	NO	14	8	13	127	62%	15.9	0	40.2%	—	4.5	—	4.6
2005	*NO*	*13*	*2*	*—*	*10*	*—*	*4.5*	*0*					

The former beer man who never played college ball is still one of the league's best return men. He also plays well at receiver in the rare times that the Saints use him in that role. Although he turns 34 this season, he's only played four seasons of football since he was a teenager, so he has much less wear and tear on his body than most players his age.

Brandon Lloyd Height: 6-0 Weight: 184 College: Illinois Born: 5-Jul-1981 Age: 24

Year	Team	G	Rec	Pass	Yds	Ctch%	Yd/C	TD	DVOA	Rank	DPAR	Rank	PAR
2003	SF	16	14	30	212	47%	15.1	2	-14.2%	—	0.1	—	0.0
2004	SF	13	43	89	565	48%	13.1	6	-5.6%	57	5.4	55	4.1
2005	*SF*	*16*	*56*	*—*	*739*	*—*	*13.1*	*4*					

Brandon Lloyd is the kind of player who makes a few spectacular, incredible catches, the kind who makes you think he's destined for greatness. Then you watch him the rest of the game and remember that a few great plays don't mean as much when you disappear for long stretches at other times. Come to think of it, that makes Lloyd the DeShaun Foster of wide receivers.

Dane Looker Height: 6-0 Weight: 194 College: Washington Born: 5-Apr-1976 Age: 29

Year	Team	G	Rec	Pass	Yds	Ctch%	Yd/C	TD	DVOA	Rank	DPAR	Rank	PAR
2002	STL	3	0	—	0	—	—	0	—	—	—	—	—
2003	STL	16	47	75	495	63%	10.5	3	-11.2%	63	1.7	63	3.2
2004	STL	14	13	26	183	50%	14.1	0	-17.4%	—	-0.5	—	-1.1
2005	*STL*	*13*	*10*	*—*	*131*	*—*	*13.0*	*1*					

Looker, not Shaun McDonald or Kevin Curtis, started the 2004 season as the number three wideout for the Rams. He got hurt after some productive early-season games, then had a hard time getting back on the field once Curtis and McDonald started getting opportunities. McDonald does all the things that Looker does, he does them a little better, and his name doesn't conjure the image of a peeping Tom from Copenhagen. Looker signed a one-year contract in April and will be given a chance to compete for playing time.

Triandos Luke Height: 5-10 Weight: 189 College: Alabama Born: 24-Dec-1981 Age: 23

Year	Team	G	Rec	Pass	Yds	Ctch%	Yd/C	TD	DVOA	Rank	DPAR	Rank	PAR
2004	DEN	10	6	8	52	75%	8.7	0	-29.5%	—	-0.7	—	-0.2
2005	*DEN*	*14*	*12*	*—*	*164*	*—*	*13.5*	*1*					

Mike Shanahan raves about the athletic ability of Triandos Luke. His college production was nothing special, but after a good Senior Bowl and a good combine Shanahan took a chance on him in the sixth round. As a rookie he played almost exclusively on special teams but did enough that the Broncos think he has a solid career ahead of him.

Rasheed Marshall

| | Height: 6-0 | Weight: 185 | | College: West Virginia | | | | | | Born: 11-Jul-1981 | Age: 24 |

Year	Team	G	Rec	Pass	Yds	Ctch%	Yd/C	TD	DVOA	Rank	DPAR	Rank	PAR
2005	SF	14	17	—	234	—	13.6	1					

As an option QB in the Big East, Marshall rushed for more yards (2,039) than either Michael Vick or Donovan McNabb. Marshall looks more like Bert Emmanuel than Hines Ward, but Emmanuel had a pretty fine career.

Derrick Mason

| | Height: 5-10 | Weight: 190 | | College: Michigan State | | | | | | Born: 17-Jan-1974 | Age: 31 |

Year	Team	G	Rec	Pass	Yds	Ctch%	Yd/C	TD	DVOA	Rank	DPAR	Rank	PAR
2002	TEN	14	79	125	1012	63%	12.8	5	16.2%	16	25.6	14	25.8
2003	TEN	16	95	134	1303	72%	13.7	8	26.1%	9	30.4	3	33.3
2004	TEN	16	96	158	1168	61%	12.2	7	5.0%	43	22.1	23	25.5
2005	BAL	16	77	—	812	—	10.5	5					

O salary cap, is no man spared your merciless wrath? Between 2000 and 2004, Mason was quietly the third most productive receiver in football, according to DPAR. Only Torry Holt and Marvin Harrison offered more production for their teams. It didn't take long for Mason to find a place in Baltimore, where he may be the best wide receiver the team has had since moving from Cleveland. Nonetheless, given that no receiver on this team has caught even 40 passes in either of the last two seasons, his numbers are bound to suffer.

Jerome Mathis

| | Height: 5-11 | Weight: 181 | | College: Hampton | | | | | | Born: 26-Jun-1983 | Age: 22 |

Year	Team	G	Rec	Pass	Yds	Ctch%	Yd/C	TD	DVOA	Rank	DPAR	Rank	PAR
2005	HOU	13	11	—	157	—	14.6	1					

He'll mostly play on special teams as a rookie in 2005. Mathis was a dangerous kick returner at the I-AA level. However, the Texans might bring him in on offense once in a while and tell him to run as fast as he can toward the goal line and look back from time to time for a football. We're not sure, but we think he and Corey Bradford have the same Indian name: Runs like the Wind, Hands like a Seahawk.

Lee Mays

| | Height: 6-2 | Weight: 200 | | College: UTEP | | | | | | Born: 18-Sep-1978 | Age: 27 |

Year	Team	G	Rec	Pass	Yds	Ctch%	Yd/C	TD	DVOA	Rank	DPAR	Rank	PAR
2002	PIT	16	0	2	0	0%	0.0	0	-97.4%	—	-1.1	—	-1.1
2003	PIT	16	2	3	17	67%	8.5	0	-3.2%	—	0.2	—	0.3
2004	PIT	16	9	23	137	39%	15.2	0	-26.3%	—	-1.7	—	-1.6
2005	PIT	14	10	—	133	—	13.3	1					

This is the make-or-break season for Mays. A former seventh-round pick, he has a chance to see more playing time with Burress now in New York, but he'll need to use his frame to his advantage and do a better job of holding on to the ball.

Jason McAddley

| | Height: 6-2 | Weight: 200 | | College: Alabama | | | | | | Born: 28-Jul-1979 | Age: 26 |

Year	Team	G	Rec	Pass	Yds	Ctch%	Yd/C	TD	DVOA	Rank	DPAR	Rank	PAR
2002	ARI	9	25	69	362	36%	14.5	1	-30.6%	84	-7.0	85	-6.1
2003	ARI	2	4	12	53	33%	13.3	0	-37.6%	—	-1.5	—	-1.5
2004	TEN	11	2	4	28	50%	19.0	0	-29.1%	—	-0.4	—	-0.2
2005	SF	14	18	—	276	—	15.3	1					

McAddley was one of the top high-school decathletes in Tennessee, but unfortunately being good at the hammer throw doesn't necessarily translate into NFL success. 49ers wide receivers coach Jerry Sullivan was in Arizona when they drafted McAddley, so there's a level of comfort that might give McAddley the third receiver job. He wins the title of WR Most Likely to Screw Up Alex Smith's Completion Percentage.

Darnerien McCants

Height: 6-3 **Weight: 214** **College: Delaware State** **Born: 1-Aug-1977** **Age: 28**

Year	Team	G	Rec	Pass	Yds	Ctch%	Yd/C	TD	DVOA	Rank	DPAR	Rank	PAR
2002	WAS	9	21	41	256	51%	12.2	2	-9.9%	—	1.2	—	0.0
2003	WAS	15	27	55	360	49%	13.3	6	11.0%	24	7.4	41	6.6
2004	WAS	5	5	9	71	56%	14.2	0	20.4%	—	2.1	—	1.6
2005	WAS	12	7	—	85	—	12.8	0					

Thanks to the departure of Laveraneus Coles, Darnerien has a stranglehold on the best name in Washington's receiver corps.

Keenan McCardell

Height: 6-1 **Weight: 191** **College: UNLV** **Born: 6-Jan-1970** **Age: 35**

Year	Team	G	Rec	Pass	Yds	Ctch%	Yd/C	TD	DVOA	Rank	DPAR	Rank	PAR
2002	TB	14	61	100	670	61%	11.0	6	-5.6%	61	6.5	59	7.0
2003	TB	16	84	138	1174	61%	14.0	8	12.9%	21	20.3	8	20.9
2004	SD	7	31	58	393	53%	12.7	1	-12.8%	67	1.2	68	3.4
2005	SD	14	45	—	642	—	14.1	5					

Every so often when you are reading analysis by our baseball compadres you will come across the phrase "Ken Phelps all-star." It's a reference to an article by Bill James in which he named a team full of minor leaguers who would produce in the major leagues if just given a chance (the titular Seattle DH being a good example). If we had such a team in the NFL, it might be called the Keenan McCardell all-stars. McCardell didn't get a chance to play regularly until his fourth season, 1995 in Cleveland, and he didn't blossom until he went to Jacksonville in the expansion draft the next year. Possibly because of this, he's had one of the strangest aging curves in NFL history, which included his best season in 2003 at the age of 33. Then he went and held out half the year, got dealt to San Diego, and got thrown a lot of incomplete passes in an offense that didn't throw many incomplete passes. Given how unusual his career path has been, it's pretty difficult to project how good he'll be this year.

Justin McCareins

Height: 6-2 **Weight: 215** **College: Northern Illinois** **Born: 11-Dec-1978** **Age: 26**

Year	Team	G	Rec	Pass	Yds	Ctch%	Yd/C	TD	DVOA	Rank	DPAR	Rank	PAR
2002	TEN	16	19	48	301	40%	15.8	2	-26.2%	—	-3.6	—	-4.4
2003	TEN	16	47	82	813	57%	17.3	7	26.4%	8	18.7	11	20.7
2004	NYJ	16	56	90	770	62%	13.8	4	19.8%	23	20.8	27	20.0
2005	NYJ	15	54	—	770	—	14.3	5					

At first, McCareins didn't play quite as well as the Jets were expecting when they traded for him after his breakout season with the Titans in 2003. McCareins had 3.7 DPAR in Weeks 1 through 7 but righted the ship in Week 8 and from then on had 17.1 DPAR. All four touchdowns came in the second half of the year as well. He should improve his numbers now that he's been reunited with former Titans offensive coordinator Mike Heimerdinger. Watch for the fact that McCareins is consistently better on first down—over the last three seasons, he has caught 75% of passes thrown to him on first down compared to just 50% on second down and 45% on third down. (For 2004, those numbers were 77%, 53%, and 57%.)

Leron McCoy

Height: 6-1 **Weight: 211** **College: Indiana (Pa.)** **Born: 24-Jan-1982** **Age: 23**

Year	Team	G	Rec	Pass	Yds	Ctch%	Yd/C	TD	DVOA	Rank	DPAR	Rank	PAR
2005	ARI	12	7	—	78	—	11.1	1					

McCoy was a touchdown machine in the Pennsylvania State Athletic Conference, scoring 30 times in his college career while battling opponents like Kutztown and Bloomsburg. Don't laugh: Andre Reed played for Kutztown. McCoy has a good chance to take over Karl Williams's role as the Cardinals' fourth wideout.

Shaun McDonald

Height: 5-10 **Weight: 183** **College: Arizona State** **Born: 13-Jun-1981** **Age: 24**

Year	Team	G	Rec	Pass	Yds	Ctch%	Yd/C	TD	DVOA	Rank	DPAR	Rank	PAR
2003	STL	8	10	21	62	48%	6.2	0	-67.5%	—	-5.7	—	-5.2
2004	STL	16	37	68	494	54%	13.4	3	-0.6%	49	6.3	50	5.5
2005	STL	13	21	—	284	—	13.6	1					

McDonald drew comparisons to Deion Branch coming out of Arizona State, but he wasn't ready to make a major contribution in 2003. He got a chance to play in 2004 and registered very good games against the Seahawks, Dolphins, Bills, and Packers. There's still a McDonald-shaped scorch mark on Terreal Bierra's chest from that first Rams-Seahawks game. Like most small receivers, he gets by on his lateral quickness and route running. He'd have trouble if he had to beat top cornerbacks off the line, so he's in an ideal situation as long as Bruce and Holt keep the heat off. The Rams tried to make a red zone threat out of McDonald, throwing him the ball eight times inside the 20, often on short crossing routes 10 to 15 yards from the end zone. McDonald scored twice inside the red zone, but five of the passes thrown his way fell incomplete.

Billy McMullen

Height: 6-4 Weight: 210 College: Virginia Born: 8-Mar-1980 Age: 25

Year	Team	G	Rec	Pass	Yds	Ctch%	Yd/C	TD	DVOA	Rank	DPAR	Rank	PAR
2003	PHI	5	1	3	2	33%	2.0	0	-85.8%	—	-1.2	—	-1.3
2004	PHI	9	3	17	24	18%	8.0	0	-79.5%	—	-7.8	—	-8.5
2005	PHI	13	4	—	39	—	10.0	0					

McMullen supposedly has great hands, but he hasn't figured out the offense and hasn't been good enough on special teams to be activated for most games. Now, he's caught in a numbers crisis and may not make the Eagles. It takes three years for some players to learn the West Coast offense, but some of them don't have that kind of time.

Freddie Mitchell

Height: 5-11 Weight: 184 College: UCLA Born: 28-Nov-1978 Age: 27

Year	Team	G	Rec	Pass	Yds	Ctch%	Yd/C	TD	DVOA	Rank	DPAR	Rank	PAR
2002	PHI	13	12	24	105	50%	8.8	0	-44.8%	—	-4.7	—	-5.2
2003	PHI	16	35	59	498	59%	14.2	2	16.8%	14	9.6	38	8.7
2004	PHI	16	22	44	377	50%	17.1	2	10.0%	—	7.2	—	5.9
2005	FA	14	16	—	226	—	13.8	1					

Mitchell Forrest Gump-ed his way into many of the major events of Eagles history. When McNabb threw the late interception against the Rams in Futility Bowl I (the Eagles' 2001 NFC Championship loss), Mitchell was the intended receiver. Mitchell caught the fourth-and-26 pass against the Packers in the 2003 playoffs and was on the receiving end of McNabb's video-game scramble-and-throw on Monday Night Football against the Cowboys. When L. J. Smith fumbled at the end zone against the Vikings in last year's playoffs, the ball plopped into Mitchell's hands. Then two weeks of posturing and inane chatter before the Super Bowl changed Mitchell's image from cocky clutch player to arrogant buffoon. For all his big talk, Mitchell is just a possession receiver who doesn't read coverage very well. That makes him a limited-use player, and a bust as a first-round pick. He'll look very silly wearing that wrestling belt when playing for the Colorado Crush.

Clarence Moore

Height: 6-6 Weight: 211 College: Northern Arizona Born: 24-Sep-1982 Age: 23

Year	Team	G	Rec	Pass	Yds	Ctch%	Yd/C	TD	DVOA	Rank	DPAR	Rank	PAR
2004	BAL	15	24	56	293	41%	12.2	4	-20.0%	75	-2.2	74	-4.1
2005	BAL	14	20	—	242	—	12.0	1					

The Ravens hope Moore eventually develops into another deep threat for Kyle Boller. He's 6'6" and will need to put on some weight as he learns the position. Moore caught only 11 of the 32 passes he was thrown on first or second down, but 12 of the 24 passes on third down. He's also 6'6". Did we mention that he's 6'6"?

Quincy Morgan

Height: 6-1 Weight: 210 College: Kansas State Born: 23-Sep-1977 Age: 28

Year	Team	G	Rec	Pass	Yds	Ctch%	Yd/C	TD	DVOA	Rank	DPAR	Rank	PAR
2002	CLE	15	56	97	964	58%	17.2	7	0.5%	46	10.6	42	13.0
2003	CLE	16	38	80	516	49%	13.6	3	-22.3%	77	-2.9	77	-3.2
2004	CLE	6	9	21	144	43%	16.0	3	-11.1%	—	0.5	—	0.0
2004	DAL	9	22	47	260	47%	11.8	0	-26.4%	77	-3.8	77	-4.8
2005	DAL	16	40	—	588	—	14.7	4					

That 2002 season is looking more and more like an aberration. Since averaging over 17 yards per catch in 2002, Morgan has been nearly four yards per catch worse the past two seasons. Maybe Drew Bledsoe will be exactly what Morgan needs to return to 2002 form. The more likely scenario, though, is that he's riding the pine by Week 9.

Johnnie Morton

Johnnie Morton			**Height: 6-0**	**Weight: 190**		**College: USC**					**Born: 7-Oct-1971**		**Age: 34**
Year	Team	G	Rec	Pass	Yds	Ctch%	Yd/C	TD	DVOA	Rank	DPAR	Rank	PAR
2002	KC	14	29	64	397	45%	13.7	1	-8.4%	69	2.8	71	2.3
2003	KC	16	50	92	740	54%	14.8	4	13.7%	20	13.5	24	12.8
2004	KC	13	55	74	795	68%	14.5	3	24.4%	14	19.3	31	21.0
2005	*FA*	*12*	*19*	*—*	*240*	*—*	*12.8*	*1*					

Morton has lost a step and doesn't work the middle of the field well, but with defenses turning their attention elsewhere he had the best of his three Kansas City seasons in 2004. The Chiefs thanked him with a big fat June release so they could save cap space. Some combination of Chris Horn, Dante Hall, Marc Boerigter, and Craphonso Thorpe should easily replace his production, and Morton joins the parade of veteran receivers trying to grab a spot on a roster somewhere. On the helpful scale, he's somewhere below Az Hakim and above Tai Streets.

Randy Moss

Randy Moss			**Height: 6-4**	**Weight: 200**		**College: Marshall**					**Born: 13-Feb-1977**		**Age: 28**
Year	Team	G	Rec	Pass	Yds	Ctch%	Yd/C	TD	DVOA	Rank	DPAR	Rank	PAR
2002	MIN	16	106	184	1347	58%	12.7	7	0.3%	47	18.7	22	15.0
2003	MIN	16	111	172	1632	65%	14.7	17	27.4%	7	39.1	2	38.8
2004	MIN	13	49	86	767	57%	15.7	13	24.1%	15	23.1	22	21.5
2005	*OAK*	*16*	*81*	*—*	*1090*	*—*	*13.5*	*10*					

Randy Moss is better on turf than he is on grass. A lot better. A receiver like Moss, who relies on his speed to blow past opposing defensive backs, thrives in a dome. Moss has been so explosive on turf that it's gone largely unnoticed that he turns into a tall possession receiver on grass. That has been OK because in each of the past four seasons, the Vikings have played 11 games on turf and five on grass. In 2005, the Raiders play all 16 games on grass. An analysis of the numbers shows just how pronounced the difference between Moss on grass and Moss on turf is:

Year	Grass				Turf			
	Rec	Yds	Y/C	TD	Rec	Yds	Y/C	TD
2001	20	293	14.7	2	62	940	15.2	8
2002	25	302	12.1	2	81	1045	12.9	5
2003	38	444	11.7	4	73	1188	16.3	13
2004	22	256	11.6	4	27	511	18.9	9

Santana Moss

Santana Moss			**Height: 5-10**	**Weight: 185**		**College: Miami**					**Born: 1-Jun-1979**		**Age: 26**
Year	Team	G	Rec	Pass	Yds	Ctch%	Yd/C	TD	DVOA	Rank	DPAR	Rank	PAR
2002	NYJ	15	31	53	441	58%	14.2	4	11.1%	22	9.1	48	9.4
2003	NYJ	16	74	117	1105	63%	14.9	10	16.0%	16	19.1	10	18.7
2004	NYJ	15	45	78	838	58%	18.6	5	32.6%	8	24.6	18	22.9
2005	*WAS*	*16*	*68*	*—*	*921*	*—*	*13.6*	*5*					

Moss turned in a very good year in 2004, becoming the kind of big-play threat the Jets always wanted him to be. Unfortunately, he's now moving to a team, Washington, that is uniquely ill-suited to his strengths. The Redskins' offense isn't designed to stretch the field with speedsters like Moss, and even if it were, none of the Redskins' quarterbacks has shown an ability to find open receivers downfield. Expect Moss to fall well short of his 2004 performance, in both catch percentage and yards per catch.

Eric Moulds

Eric Moulds			**Height: 6-2**	**Weight: 210**		**College: Mississippi State**					**Born: 17-Jul-1973**		**Age: 32**
Year	Team	G	Rec	Pass	Yds	Ctch%	Yd/C	TD	DVOA	Rank	DPAR	Rank	PAR
2002	BUF	16	100	180	1287	56%	12.9	10	-9.4%	71	7.6	55	11.1
2003	BUF	13	64	120	780	53%	12.2	1	-8.6%	57	3.8	54	1.2
2004	BUF	16	88	152	1043	58%	11.9	5	-4.0%	54	11.1	45	10.5
2005	*BUF*	*16*	*65*	*—*	*853*	*—*	*13.1*	*5*					

Moulds and Hines Ward offer an important lesson on why Passes is as important a statistic for receivers as Receptions. Moulds caught 88 balls for 1,043 yards, while Ward caught 80 balls for 1,004 yards. But Moulds was involved in 64 plays on which a pass to him went absolutely nowhere (a.k.a. an incomplete or interception). Ward was only involved in 29 such plays. That's 35 plays on which Pittsburgh could do something else with the ball, worth roughly 210 more yards based on the average of six yards that the Steelers gained on plays that didn't go to Ward.

Muhsin Muhammad Height: 6-2 Weight: 217 College: Michigan State Born: 5-May-1973 Age: 32

Year	Team	G	Rec	Pass	Yds	Ctch%	Yd/C	TD	DVOA	Rank	DPAR	Rank	PAR
2002	CAR	14	63	108	823	58%	13.1	3	-1.4%	53	10.4	44	11.7
2003	CAR	15	54	100	837	54%	15.5	3	-5.3%	52	5.1	48	4.8
2004	CAR	16	93	160	1405	58%	15.1	16	23.8%	16	41.5	3	43.2
2005	CHI	16	71	—	929	—	13.1	7					

Certainly picked a nice time to have a career year, didn't he? Right before a bonus in his contract that made him impossible to keep, Muhammad turned into one of the best receivers in football—he was third in the league in DPAR even though a Week 1 injury to Steve Smith meant that everyone in the stadium every week knew that he was the guy Jake Delhomme would look to first. Anyone who picks him up for fantasy purposes would be advised to think carefully about how likely it is that a 32-year-old who switches to a team with an unproven quarterback will come close to replicating the best numbers he's ever had.

Terrence Murphy Height: 0-0 Weight: 202 College: Texas A&M Born: 15-Dec-1982 Age: 22

Year	Team	G	Rec	Pass	Yds	Ctch%	Yd/C	TD	DVOA	Rank	DPAR	Rank	PAR
2005	GB	14	21	—	272	—	13.3	2					

Murphy is a poor man's Mark Clayton, a disciplined route runner and student of the game who uses guile to get open. He's also a very good blocker who played for a team that ran the option frequently, so he'll help Ahman Green turn the corner on some sweeps. He'll push Robert Ferguson for playing time, and Murphy's work habits and blocking ability may give him the edge.

Dennis Northcutt Height: 5-11 Weight: 175 College: Arizona Born: 22-Dec-1977 Age: 27

Year	Team	G	Rec	Pass	Yds	Ctch%	Yd/C	TD	DVOA	Rank	DPAR	Rank	PAR
2002	CLE	13	39	50	614	78%	15.7	5	70.7%	1	28.5	10	29.0
2003	CLE	15	62	92	729	67%	11.8	2	15.0%	17	14.4	19	13.9
2004	CLE	16	55	94	806	59%	14.7	2	-5.4%	56	5.7	53	4.6
2005	CLE	14	27	—	394	—	14.4	2					

Northcutt has never developed into the big-play WR many thought he would be coming out of Arizona, but he's still a dangerous punt returner who is also a solid slot receiver. Of course, Cleveland has roughly 37 different guys to whom that sentence applies, and they are all battling for playing time.

Kassim Osgood Height: 6-5 Weight: 209 College: San Diego State Born: 20-May-1980 Age: 25

Year	Team	G	Rec	Pass	Yds	Ctch%	Yd/C	TD	DVOA	Rank	DPAR	Rank	PAR
2003	SD	16	13	33	278	39%	21.4	2	-1.2%	—	2.5	—	2.4
2004	SD	16	15	33	308	45%	20.5	2	10.3%	—	5.5	—	5.9
2005	SD	13	10	—	120	—	12.2	1					

An excellent blocker and wedge buster, Osgood was one of the most prolific receivers in the nation in college but has settled into a role as a special teams ace and "mismatch" receiver who toasts 5′9″ nickelbacks. Osgood is capable of bigger things, but the Chargers have a crowd at wide receiver.

Terrell Owens

| Height: 6-3 | Weight: 226 | College: Tennessee-Chattanooga | Born: 7-Dec-1973 | Age: 32 |

Year	Team	G	Rec	Pass	Yds	Ctch%	Yd/C	TD	DVOA	Rank	DPAR	Rank	PAR
2002	SF	14	100	159	1300	63%	13.0	13	13.0%	19	29.5	7	30.4
2003	SF	15	80	145	1102	55%	13.8	9	2.9%	39	14.0	22	13.4
2004	PHI	14	77	127	1200	61%	15.6	14	23.2%	17	31.9	10	28.7
2005	PHI	16	79	—	1127	—	14.3	11					

The top DPAR scores by Eagles wideouts, 2000–2004: (1) Terrell Owens, 2004: 31.9; (2) Todd Pinkston, 2004: 12.1; (3) Freddie Mitchell, 2004: 12.0; (4) Antonio Freeman, 2002: 11.7; (5) Todd Pinkston, 2002: 9.8. That probably qualifies as a "major impact." Owens not only posted the highest score but made the next two scores possible by drawing coverage. As this book went to print, Owens had stopped speaking to the media about his contract situation and was trying to distance himself from a suggestion that one of his teammates was out of shape in the Super Bowl (the remark was supposedly leveled at McNabb, but could also have been a shot at Pinkston, who left the game with cramps). Owens may hold out of camp; with him, the Eagles remain odds-on favorites in the NFC, but without him, they're another 11–5 team.

Eric Parker

| Height: 6-0 | Weight: 180 | College: Tennessee | Born: 14-Apr-1979 | Age: 26 |

Year	Team	G	Rec	Pass	Yds	Ctch%	Yd/C	TD	DVOA	Rank	DPAR	Rank	PAR
2002	SD	8	17	30	268	57%	15.8	1	22.2%	—	7.3	—	8.1
2003	SD	8	18	31	244	58%	13.6	3	20.8%	—	5.9	—	5.0
2004	SD	15	47	71	690	66%	14.7	4	18.8%	26	16.2	36	18.6
2005	SD	16	45	—	670	—	14.7	4					

Parker came around late last year with solid games against the Buccaneers in Week 15 (six catches, 118 yards, one TD), the Colts in Week 17 (seven catches, 103 yards, one TD), and the Jets in the playoffs (nine catches, 93 yards). He's not flashy, but he has good hands and is a good blocker. He's also a capable punt returner. Parker is a good example of how often NFL scouts miss good prospects: He entered the league as an undrafted free agent despite having a good career at Tennessee.

Samie Parker

| Height: 5-10 | Weight: 178 | College: Oregon | Born: 25-Mar-1981 | Age: 24 |

Year	Team	G	Rec	Pass	Yds	Ctch%	Yd/C	TD	DVOA	Rank	DPAR	Rank	PAR
2004	KC	4	9	13	137	69%	15.2	1	36.8%	—	4.5	—	5.0
2005	KC	16	41	—	574	—	13.9	4					

A 175-pound speedster and former college track star, Parker made the highlight reel with one 48-yard catch against the Broncos in Week 15 after being inactive for 13 of the previous 14 games. With Johnnie Morton gone he may be a starter, and Al Saunders will try to "get him the ball in space," which means a lot of four-yard crossing routes on third and 17.

Roscoe Parrish

| Height: 5-10 | Weight: 168 | College: Miami | Born: 16-Jul-1982 | Age: 23 |

Year	Team	G	Rec	Pass	Yds	Ctch%	Yd/C	TD	DVOA	Rank	DPAR	Rank	PAR
2005	BUF	14	18	—	373	—	20.3	2					

The Bills have one of the best kickoff returners in the league in Terrence McGee, but last season they pressed starting CB Nate Clements into punt return duties. Parrish, who returned three punts for touchdowns at Miami (including a school-record 92-yarder in 2003), will take over for Clements. He will also push Josh Reed for playing time. Parrish weighs 170 pounds after a Waffle House breakfast, so he won't cut it as a starting wideout, but he's a jackrabbit with the ball in his hands.

Jerome Pathon

| Height: 6-0 | Weight: 182 | College: Washington | Born: 16-Dec-1975 | Age: 29 |

Year	Team	G	Rec	Pass	Yds	Ctch%	Yd/C	TD	DVOA	Rank	DPAR	Rank	PAR
2002	NO	14	43	80	523	54%	12.2	4	-4.7%	60	5.0	63	4.0
2003	NO	16	44	79	578	56%	13.1	4	-5.7%	53	3.8	53	3.5
2004	NO	15	34	66	581	52%	17.1	1	-5.7%	58	4.4	61	6.9
2005	SEA	16	39	—	627	—	16.1	4					

The Colts took Peyton Manning with the first pick in the 1998 draft and then took Pathon with the first pick of the second round. They thought they had a QB-WR combination for the ages, and were half right. Pathon is now on his third team, and although last year he showed more of a penchant for catching long balls than he had in the past, he's no better than a third receiver. That's also what he does best: Pathon over the past three seasons has a −16.0% DVOA on first down, −7.9% DVOA on second down, and 8.2% DVOA on third down. As we go to press, Pathon is the most likely winner of the Koren Robinson Gets Drunk sweepstakes, but while Pathon is perceived as a starter and Bobby Engram is seen as the third option, we think the Seahawks would be a lot better the other way around.

David Patten

Height: 5-10 Weight: 190 College: Western Carolina Born: 18-Aug-1974 Age: 31

Year	Team	G	Rec	Pass	Yds	Ctch%	Yd/C	TD	DVOA	Rank	DPAR	Rank	PAR
2002	NE	16	61	120	824	51%	13.5	5	-3.6%	58	9.1	49	8.7
2003	NE	6	9	21	140	43%	15.6	0	-26.0%	—	-1.1	—	-0.8
2004	NE	16	44	95	800	46%	18.2	7	15.5%	30	18.6	32	17.2
2005	WAS	16	46	—	599	—	13.1	3					

Patten picked a good year to be a free agent—his best of the last three (which includes 2003, when he was injured for most of the year). He's moving to a team with an inferior quarterback who likes to throw shorter routes, so he's unlikely to reproduce last year's results.

Todd Pinkston

Height: 6-2 Weight: 174 College: SMU Born: 23-Apr-1977 Age: 28

Year	Team	G	Rec	Pass	Yds	Ctch%	Yd/C	TD	DVOA	Rank	DPAR	Rank	PAR
2002	PHI	15	60	113	798	53%	13.3	7	-1.8%	54	9.8	47	6.9
2003	PHI	16	36	85	575	42%	16.0	2	-21.4%	76	-3.0	79	-4.2
2004	PHI	16	36	63	676	57%	18.8	1	13.8%	34	12.1	43	10.9
2005	PHI	14	37	—	619	—	16.7	2					

Pinkston's a "little things" player who was miscast as a top wideout but makes a good second option (when he doesn't have the yips). McNabb did not throw a single pass to Pinkston in the red zone last season, which isn't exactly a vote of confidence. But despite his preying-mantis physique, he's a terrific downfield blocker and he draws a lot of contact penalties. He's useless when jammed but can glide by defenders in zone coverage. Best of all, he has a number two receiver's mentality and doesn't expect ten throws every game. He finds himself in a crunch because the Eagles now have a better deep option in Greg Lewis and a potentially better blocking wideout in Fred Gibson. Look for Pinkston to still have a role, though it may be a reduced role.

Nathan Poole

Height: 6-2 Weight: 210 College: Marshall Born: 1-Feb-1977 Age: 28

Year	Team	G	Rec	Pass	Yds	Ctch%	Yd/C	TD	DVOA	Rank	DPAR	Rank	PAR
2002	ARI	5	13	22	108	59%	8.3	1	-23.6%	—	-1.2	—	-0.9
2003	ARI	15	13	19	177	68%	13.6	1	42.6%	—	5.8	—	5.9
2004	ARI	9	5	11	70	45%	14.0	0	-2.9%	—	0.8	—	0.7
2005	NO	13	9	—	118	—	13.3	0					

Green Bay fans will always have a special place in their hearts for Poole, thanks to his last-second touchdown catch that gave the Cardinals a win over the Vikings, taking Minnesota out of the playoffs and putting the Packers in in 2003. Although Poole will almost certainly never be a Pro Bowler, he can spend the rest of his life knowing he'll never have to pay for his own meal if he visits Wisconsin.

Jerry Porter

Height: 6-2 Weight: 220 College: West Virginia Born: 14-Jul-1978 Age: 27

Year	Team	G	Rec	Pass	Yds	Ctch%	Yd/C	TD	DVOA	Rank	DPAR	Rank	PAR
2002	OAK	16	51	70	688	73%	13.5	9	47.6%	2	29.9	6	30.5
2003	OAK	10	28	57	361	49%	12.9	1	-7.2%	54	2.3	60	2.2
2004	OAK	16	64	136	998	47%	15.6	9	-9.5%	64	5.3	56	6.9
2005	OAK	15	48	—	747	—	15.5	5					

(continued next page)

Jerry Porter *(continued)*

Now one of the best—and highest paid—number two receivers in pro football. Only Tony Gonzalez and Muhsin Muhammad (26 each) had more passes thrown to them in the red zone than Porter (25) did last year (Marvin Harrison also had 25). No other Raiders player was targeted more than seven times. Presumably, Randy Moss will take away most of that red zone action, especially since Porter wasn't very effective: His catch percentage was 40%, his red zone DPAR −0.9.

Peerless Price			Height: 5-11	Weight: 190		College: Tennessee					Born: 27-Oct-1976		Age: 29
Year	Team	G	Rec	Pass	Yds	Ctch%	Yd/C	TD	DVOA	Rank	DPAR	Rank	PAR
2002	BUF	16	94	148	1252	64%	13.3	9	9.3%	26	24.5	15	25.3
2003	ATL	16	64	141	838	45%	13.1	3	-23.3%	79	-6.1	83	-5.9
2004	ATL	16	45	106	575	42%	12.8	3	-26.9%	78	-8.3	83	-7.8
2005	*ATL*	*16*	*51*	*—*	*672*	*—*	*13.2*	*4*					

Everyone talks about how the Lions have used first-round picks on receivers the last three years, but hardly anyone points out that the Falcons have too. They've taken Michael Jenkins and Roddy White in the last two years, and the year before that they traded their first-round pick to acquire Price from the Bills. What a waste. If Price has taught the Falcons anything, it's that you don't give a guy number one money if he's not a number one receiver.

Ricky Proehl			Height: 6-0	Weight: 190		College: Wake Forest					Born: 7-Mar-1968		Age: 37
Year	Team	G	Rec	Pass	Yds	Ctch%	Yd/C	TD	DVOA	Rank	DPAR	Rank	PAR
2002	STL	16	43	70	466	61%	10.8	4	10.8%	23	11.4	40	10.6
2003	CAR	16	27	52	389	52%	14.4	4	-0.9%	47	3.7	56	4.1
2004	CAR	16	34	70	497	49%	14.6	0	-8.8%	61	3.1	63	4.6
2005	*CAR*	*15*	*21*	*—*	*288*	*—*	*13.8*	*2*					

Ever since Proehl left St. Louis, they have been seeking to find a replacement who can as effectively work the middle. Although he's made some highlight plays, Carolina may soon be looking to find the Ricky Proehl that St. Louis misses.

Antwaan Randle El			Height: 5-10	Weight: 186		College: Indiana					Born: 17-Aug-1979		Age: 26
Year	Team	G	Rec	Pass	Yds	Ctch%	Yd/C	TD	DVOA	Rank	DPAR	Rank	PAR
2002	PIT	16	47	65	489	72%	10.4	2	-0.7%	—	6.2	—	6.5
2003	PIT	16	37	56	364	66%	9.8	1	-1.7%	49	3.9	52	3.6
2004	PIT	16	43	62	601	68%	14.0	3	16.1%	28	12.5	42	12.3
2005	*PIT*	*16*	*52*	*—*	*708*	*—*	*13.7*	*4*					

While he's a different kind of receiver than Plaxico Burress, Randle El thrived as a starter last year. In the 11 games Burress started, Randle El averaged two catches for 22 yards with a −11.3% DVOA. In the five games he started in Burress's absence, he averaged four catches for 70 yards with a 51.7% DVOA. Randle El is a versatile athlete: Not only is he one of the NFL's top punt returners, but he gained 3,895 rushing yards and 7,469 passing yards as a quarterback at Indiana, and he played college basketball for Bobby Knight.

Josh Reed			Height: 5-10	Weight: 208		College: LSU					Born: 1-May-1980		Age: 25
Year	Team	G	Rec	Pass	Yds	Ctch%	Yd/C	TD	DVOA	Rank	DPAR	Rank	PAR
2002	BUF	16	37	59	514	63%	13.9	2	7.3%	33	8.7	50	10.2
2003	BUF	16	58	102	588	57%	10.1	2	-12.4%	64	1.2	64	0.6
2004	BUF	12	16	36	153	44%	9.6	0	-36.8%	—	-5.1	—	-5.7
2005	*BUF*	*16*	*25*	*—*	*314*	*—*	*12.5*	*2*					

Reed lost a large part of the season, and his starting slot, to knee injuries. He had a good rookie year as a slot receiver, because his strength is the ability to break free of nickelbacks and linebackers on short routes. We also like the fact that, like most receivers coached by Nick Saban in college, he's a strong blocker. But he's a bit slow, a bit short, and gets jammed easily, so he was horribly miscast as a starter. Even though he was still gimpy, he had a higher DVOA and catch percentage when he came back from his injury and moved back into his old role. With health, perhaps he can repeat his 2002 numbers. It's the last year of his rookie contract, so he has incentive, but any team that signs him to be a starter in 2006 is making a mistake.

Jerry Rice Height: 6-2 Weight: 200 College: Mississippi Valley State Born: 13-Oct-1962 Age: 43

Year	Team	G	Rec	Pass	Yds	Ctch%	Yd/C	TD	DVOA	Rank	DPAR	Rank	PAR
2002	OAK	16	92	150	1211	61%	13.2	7	10.1%	24	25.7	13	26.9
2003	OAK	16	63	124	869	51%	13.8	2	-9.1%	59	3.8	55	3.2
2004	OAK	4	5	15	67	33%	13.4	0	-23.1%	—	-0.8	—	-1.3
2004	SEA	13	25	48	362	52%	14.5	3	2.8%	51	5.8	58	4.9
2005	DEN	15	14	—	200	—	14.6	1					

It is not unusual for extended greatness to end in sudden collapse. In the history of failures that shouldn't ruin our memories of what came before, Jerry Rice's 2004 season ranks alongside Willie Mays with the Mets, Joe Namath with the Rams, Johnny Unitas in San Diego, the seventh season of *Homicide: Life on the Street, Rocky V,* the last Clash album, and the final episode of *Seinfeld.* Instead of retiring, Rice signed in Denver, where he'll block the development of Darius Watts. Mike Shanahan just doesn't use extra receivers, and the Broncos haven't had four wideouts with 100 yards or more since 1996.

Koren Robinson Height: 6-1 Weight: 205 College: North Carolina State Born: 19-Mar-1980 Age: 25

Year	Team	G	Rec	Pass	Yds	Ctch%	Yd/C	TD	DVOA	Rank	DPAR	Rank	PAR
2002	SEA	16	78	141	1240	55%	15.9	5	3.3%	40	17.4	23	19.9
2003	SEA	15	65	119	896	55%	13.8	4	1.6%	43	10.5	35	10.6
2004	SEA	10	31	67	495	46%	16.0	2	-0.3%	48	6.3	51	4.9
2005	FA	12	26	—	381	—	14.7	2					

Koren Robinson is a great athlete with bad hands. That's a little better than being a bad athlete with great hands, but it is clear he will never live up to the promise he showed coming out of college. When Mike Holmgren selected him with the ninth pick in the 2001 draft, Koren Robinson looked like the perfect fit to become a deep threat in an offense that had possession receivers Darrell Jackson and Bobby Engram. Although his second year looked very promising, it hasn't worked out. Robinson drops far too many passes, doesn't run good routes, and last season was suspended four games for a substance abuse violation and another two for breaking team rules. After he was arrested for drunken driving during the off-season, the Seahawks decided enough was enough and cut their losses. Robinson should hook up with a coach who believes he can turn people around and badly needs receiving depth, but he may face more disciplinary action first.

Marcus Robinson Height: 6-3 Weight: 215 College: South Carolina Born: 27-Feb-1975 Age: 30

Year	Team	G	Rec	Pass	Yds	Ctch%	Yd/C	TD	DVOA	Rank	DPAR	Rank	PAR
2002	CHI	15	21	53	244	40%	11.6	3	-40.1%	86	-8.8	86	-9.3
2003	BAL	15	31	62	451	50%	14.5	6	4.1%	34	6.3	44	7.4
2004	MIN	16	47	79	657	59%	14.0	8	11.9%	36	14.6	38	15.1
2005	MIN	13	28	—	406	—	14.3	2					

When Robinson burst onto the scene in 1999, gaining 1,400 yards with the Bears, who would have predicted that he would never again total even 800 yards in a season? Because he showed so much promise in Chicago, Robinson has to be labeled a disappointment. But he's still a solid third receiver who makes a difference in the Vikings' passing game.

Courtney Roby Height: 6-0 Weight: 189 College: Indiana Born: 10-Jan-1983 Age: 22

Year	Team	G	Rec	Pass	Yds	Ctch%	Yd/C	TD	DVOA	Rank	DPAR	Rank	PAR
2005	TEN	16	23	—	297	—	12.9	2					

Look for Roby, a rookie third-rounder out of Indiana, to spend some time as Tennessee's third receiver. He has good speed, but doesn't always show it on the field and looks more like a possession guy. But the important question is: What are the odds that the NFL will allow him to wear a watch on the field in tribute to his late cousin Reggie Roby?

Charles Rogers

Height: 6-2   **Weight:** 202   **College: Michigan State**   **Born: 23-May-1981   Age: 24**

Year	Team	G	Rec	Pass	Yds	Ctch%	Yd/C	TD	DVOA	Rank	DPAR	Rank	PAR
2003	DET	5	22	52	243	42%	11.0	3	-23.7%	81	-2.5	76	-3.1
2004	DET	1	0	1	0	0%	0.0	0	-93.7%	—	-0.5	—	-0.6
2005	DET	14	33	—	505	—	15.2	3					

After two years, the second overall pick in the 2003 draft has given the Lions nothing. Two years, two broken collarbones. Actually, one collarbone (the right one), two separate breaks. The Lions are praying that the aggressive surgery that plated two portions of Rogers's clavicle will help once the hitting starts. Team orthopedist David Collon speculated after the second break that Rogers may be falling wrong. "Whenever you fall on your shoulder or hit your shoulder, you've got potential to break it," Collon told the *Detroit News* in 2004. "He seems to fall on that shoulder every single time he goes out for a pass. It's unbelievable how much he falls [on it]." Rogers won't have many opportunities to fall down and go boom if Roy Williams and Mike Williams are now the starters, as appears to be the case.

P. K. Sam

Height: 6-1   **Weight:** 196   **College: Florida State**   **Born: 26-Dec-1983   Age: 21**

Year	Team	G	Rec	Pass	Yds	Ctch%	Yd/C	TD	DVOA	Rank	DPAR	Rank	PAR
2004	NE	2	0	—	0	—	—	0	—	—	—	—	—
2005	NE	13	14	—	200	—	14.3	1					

There was a lot of talk before the draft that the Patriots needed to take a wide receiver for depth. But the Patriots already had their rookie wide receiver: Sam. Last year, draft gurus all agreed that Sam would have been a second- or third-round pick had he stayed another year at Florida State, but he fell to the fifth round because he came out way too early and way too raw. He played only two games last year before going on injured reserve, so 2005 is in effect his rookie season. He could surprise or disappear; the Seminoles have developed some big talents (Javon Walker, Laveranues Coles, Anquan Boldin) and some big busts (Snoop Minnis, Ron Dugans) with very little in between.

Bill Schroeder

Height: 6-3   **Weight:** 200   **College: Memphis**   **Born: 9-Jan-1971   Age: 34**

Year	Team	G	Rec	Pass	Yds	Ctch%	Yd/C	TD	DVOA	Rank	DPAR	Rank	PAR
2002	DET	11	36	77	595	47%	16.5	5	5.8%	37	10.4	45	11.1
2003	DET	16	36	80	397	45%	11.0	2	-22.5%	78	-3.0	78	-3.2
2004	TB	7	7	11	156	64%	22.3	1	53.3%	—	5.2	—	5.7

Says much about the state of Tampa Bay's receiving corps early in the season that Schroeder started a game, although he did have one of the more fun small sample size DVOA ratings of the year. Was released once Michael Clayton emerged and Joey Galloway returned from injury. Probably done.

Bobby Shaw

Height: 6-1   **Weight:** 185   **College: California**   **Born: 23-Apr-1975   Age: 30**

Year	Team	G	Rec	Pass	Yds	Ctch%	Yd/C	TD	DVOA	Rank	DPAR	Rank	PAR
2002	JAC	16	44	73	525	60%	11.9	1	8.7%	28	11.1	41	10.1
2003	BUF	16	56	86	732	65%	13.1	4	14.2%	19	12.8	27	13.2
2004	BUF	10	5	13	59	38%	11.8	0	-43.7%	—	-2.2	—	-1.9

It is an understatement to say that Bobby Shaw, signed when Reche Caldwell went down in October, was not the impact player San Diego had hoped for. He wasn't even thrown a pass in a Charger uniform. Unsigned free agent at press time.

Edell Shepherd

Height: 6-1   **Weight:** 175   **College: San Jose State**   **Born: 18-May-1980   Age: 25**

Year	Team	G	Rec	Pass	Yds	Ctch%	Yd/C	TD	DVOA	Rank	DPAR	Rank	PAR
2003	TB	2	4	6	38	67%	9.5	0	-2.8%	—	0.3	—	0.1
2004	TB	0	0	—	0	—	—	0	—	—	—	—	—
2005	TB	15	10	—	146	—	14.2	1					

Shepherd was incredibly prolific at San Jose State, catching 83 passes and scoring 14 TDs as a senior while topping the 250-yard mark twice. He has spent three full seasons bouncing around practice squads and has a good chance to be Tampa Bay's fourth wideout.

Jimmy Smith

Height: 6-1 Weight: 213 College: Jackson State Born: 9-Feb-1969 Age: 36

Year	Team	G	Rec	Pass	Yds	Ctch%	Yd/C	TD	DVOA	Rank	DPAR	Rank	PAR
2002	JAC	16	80	136	1027	59%	12.8	7	8.7%	27	21.2	19	20.3
2003	JAC	12	54	112	805	48%	14.9	4	-10.6%	61	2.8	59	2.8
2004	JAC	16	74	137	1172	54%	15.8	6	6.6%	41	19.7	30	20.8
2005	JAC	16	58	—	818	—	14.2	5					

Jimmy Smith continues to hold off Father Time, bouncing back from a disappointing 2003 campaign (where he was suspended four games for a failed drug test) to post solid numbers in 2004. He was the only weapon in the Jaguars passing offense, which has never really clicked since Keenan McCardell left in 2002. Smith is 36 years old, so a decline must be around the corner, but he was very solid last season with the second highest average yards per reception of his career.

Rod Smith

Height: 6-0 Weight: 200 College: Missouri Southern State Born: 15-May-1970 Age: 35

Year	Team	G	Rec	Pass	Yds	Ctch%	Yd/C	TD	DVOA	Rank	DPAR	Rank	PAR
2002	DEN	16	88	147	1012	61%	11.5	5	-0.7%	50	13.8	33	13.7
2003	DEN	15	74	114	846	65%	11.4	3	7.1%	30	13.4	25	13.1
2004	DEN	16	79	136	1144	58%	14.5	7	7.5%	39	20.9	25	23.8
2005	DEN	16	70	—	961	—	13.7	6					

Smith is another veteran receiver who saw the effects of aging reverse in 2004, bouncing back from a slightly down 2003 with his highest yards per catch in five years. Smith has 1,000 yards receiving seven times in the last eight years, and he has a good chance to make it eight of nine. His one weakness last year came on third down, where he caught just 38% of passes. That's either a statistical quirk or a sign that Smith got more defensive attention on third downs with Shannon Sharpe retired.

Steve Smith

Height: 5-9 Weight: 179 College: Utah Born: 12-May-1979 Age: 26

Year	Team	G	Rec	Pass	Yds	Ctch%	Yd/C	TD	DVOA	Rank	DPAR	Rank	PAR
2002	CAR	15	54	97	872	56%	16.1	3	0.2%	48	9.9	46	10.6
2003	CAR	16	88	141	1110	62%	12.6	7	-1.4%	48	10.3	36	11.6
2004	CAR	1	6	9	60	67%	10.0	0	6.4%	—	1.3	—	1.3
2005	CAR	16	60	—	762	—	12.6	5					

Carted off the field in Week 1 with a broken leg, Steve Smith was placed on IR in late October after all optimism was washed out. With Muhsin Muhammad now in Chicago, Smith has no competition for his old role as Jake Delhomme's favorite wideout. Fractures heal pretty cleanly and don't tend to be a problem again unless you're Charles Rogers, but alas the surgery didn't make Smith any taller. What Smith really needs is another receiver (maybe Colbert) to step up and keep him from seeing blanket coverage.

Donté Stallworth

Height: 6-0 Weight: 197 College: Tennessee Born: 10-Nov-1980 Age: 25

Year	Team	G	Rec	Pass	Yds	Ctch%	Yd/C	TD	DVOA	Rank	DPAR	Rank	PAR
2002	NO	13	42	—	594	—	—	8	—	—	—	—	—
2003	NO	11	25	55	485	45%	19.4	3	-12.5%	65	0.9	66	1.7
2004	NO	16	58	106	767	55%	13.2	5	-1.0%	50	10.1	46	11.4
2005	NO	16	52	—	719	—	13.7	4					

Stallworth never should have been the 13th pick in the draft. He had only 41 receptions in his junior year at Tennessee, but he decided to turn pro and amazed scouts with a blazing 40 time in the 4.25 range. That sent him flying up draft boards despite only so-so production. The Saints have found that speed is nice, but it ain't everything. Like a lot of players with great speed, Stallworth relies too heavily on outrunning people and doesn't run precise routes. He also doesn't have very good hands. He'll always be a deep threat, but he'll never be much more than that. Vikings fans might think long and hard about Stallworth before getting too excited about Troy Williamson.

Brandon Stokley Height: 5-11 Weight: 197 College: Louisiana-Lafayette Born: 23-Jun-1976 Age: 29

Year	Team	G	Rec	Pass	Yds	Ctch%	Yd/C	TD	DVOA	Rank	DPAR	Rank	PAR
2002	BAL	8	24	52	357	46%	14.9	2	-3.5%	57	3.8	69	2.8
2003	IND	6	22	32	211	69%	9.6	3	7.1%	—	3.8	—	4.7
2004	IND	16	68	102	1077	67%	15.8	10	41.7%	1	38.4	5	40.8
2005	*IND*	*16*	*54*	*—*	*740*	*—*	*13.8*	*5*					

An injury cost Stokley much of 2003, but a few big games at the end of the year gave a glimpse of what he could offer in the Colts offense. What he could offer, it turned out, was more value per play than any receiver in football. Stokley is the undisputed top slot receiver in football, a perfect fit in the Colts' offense with his ability to work across the middle. Stokley was Manning's favorite third down target, and he's too good for nickel corners or safeties, the sort of coverage he often gets playing with Marvin Harrison and Reggie Wayne. Along with his quarterback from college, Jake Delhomme, he provides evidence that Louisiana-Lafayette might be the nation's best small school when it comes to developing NFL talent. He is also the answer to the trivia question of who caught Manning's 49th TD.

John Stone Height: 5-11 Weight: 180 College: Wake Forest Born: 7-Jul-1979 Age: 26

Year	Team	G	Rec	Pass	Yds	Ctch%	Yd/C	TD	DVOA	Rank	DPAR	Rank	PAR
2003	OAK	1	0	—	0	—	—	0	—	—	—	—	—
2004	OAK	4	3	5	80	60%	26.7	0	50.5%	—	2.1	—	2.3
2005	*OAK*	*12*	*10*	*—*	*136*	*—*	*13.6*	*1*					

Well, someone has to be ahead of Johnnie Morant on the depth chart. If the Raiders are hit with so many injuries that Stone actually gets serious game time, this is a sign to immediately drop Kerry Collins from your fantasy roster.

Tai Streets Height: 6-3 Weight: 207 College: Michigan Born: 20-Apr-1977 Age: 28

Year	Team	G	Rec	Pass	Yds	Ctch%	Yd/C	TD	DVOA	Rank	DPAR	Rank	PAR
2002	SF	15	72	109	756	66%	10.5	5	-1.4%	52	10.5	43	11.7
2003	SF	16	47	85	595	55%	12.7	7	10.5%	26	11.0	34	9.7
2004	DET	13	28	56	260	50%	9.3	1	-33.6%	82	-7.1	78	-8.0
2005	*FA*	*12*	*11*	*—*	*139*	*—*	*12.6*	*1*					

Streets was one of the biggest free agent disappointments the Lions have had in recent years, and that's saying a lot. Steve Mariucci, who coached Streets in San Francisco, thought he'd be a perfect fit. Instead he dropped balls and generally looked lost. There's a glut of veteran receivers on the market as we go to press, so Streets will have a hard time even finding a team that wants him this year.

Reggie Swinton Height: 6-0 Weight: 186 College: Murray State Born: 24-Jul-1975 Age: 30

Year	Team	G	Rec	Pass	Yds	Ctch%	Yd/C	TD	DVOA	Rank	DPAR	Rank	PAR
2002	DAL	14	7	10	63	70%	9.0	0	7.1%	—	1.3	—	0.9
2003	DET	11	9	14	100	64%	11.1	0	7.1%	—	1.7	—	2.2
2004	DET	13	18	31	213	58%	11.8	1	5.9%	—	4.2	—	3.3
2005	*DET*	*13*	*12*	*—*	*162*	*—*	*13.3*	*1*					

Swinton has talent as a receiver and a special teams player. He'll never be a great player, but he's the kind of athlete who does a lot of things well, and teams need those guys in order to build a deep roster. Statistical completists should note that Swinton had one game and one incomplete pass in Dallas before going to Detroit in 2003.

Jamaar Taylor Height: 6-0 Weight: 197 College: Texas A&M Born: 25-Feb-1981 Age: 24

Year	Team	G	Rec	Pass	Yds	Ctch%	Yd/C	TD	DVOA	Rank	DPAR	Rank	PAR
2004	NYG	8	6	17	146	35%	24.3	0	-17.1%	—	-0.2	—	-0.3
2005	*NYG*	*13*	*12*	*—*	*169*	*—*	*13.6*	*1*					

Taylor missed most of last season with various injuries. He may have missed his chance at regular playing time after David Tyree had three productive games as the team's third wideout at the end of the season.

Travis Taylor

Height: 6-1   Weight: 200   College: Florida   Born: 30-Mar-1978   Age: 27

Year	Team	G	Rec	Pass	Yds	Ctch%	Yd/C	TD	DVOA	Rank	DPAR	Rank	PAR
2002	BAL	16	61	118	869	52%	14.2	6	0.0%	49	12.3	35	12.9
2003	BAL	16	39	90	632	43%	16.2	3	-20.3%	75	-2.2	75	-0.9
2004	BAL	10	34	80	421	43%	12.4	0	-29.1%	80	-7.8	80	-9.2
2005	MIN	14	18	—	278	—	15.3	2					

The highlight of Taylor's career was being selected with the tenth overall pick of the 2000 draft. After that, everything went downhill pretty fast. In Baltimore, Taylor usually had one game per season where he would tease you into thinking that he could be a star, like his 138-yard, two-TD day against the Bengals in 2003 or his 127-yard, one-TD game against the Falcons in 2002. Last year, he didn't even bother to have that one good game. The Vikings don't quite count as a second chance, because he's way down on the depth chart.

David Terrell

Height: 6-3   Weight: 215   College: Michigan   Born: 13-Mar-1979   Age: 26

Year	Team	G	Rec	Pass	Yds	Ctch%	Yd/C	TD	DVOA	Rank	DPAR	Rank	PAR
2002	CHI	5	9	10	127	90%	14.1	3	104.2%	—	7.8	—	7.9
2003	CHI	16	43	85	361	52%	8.4	1	-34.6%	84	-8.8	84	-9.3
2004	CHI	16	42	90	699	47%	16.6	1	-3.8%	53	6.8	49	7.1
2005	NE	14	32	—	522	—	16.4	3					

"On a day when they could have had impact players David Terrell or Koren Robinson or the second best tackle in the draft in Kenyatta Walker, they took Georgia defensive tackle Richard Seymour, who had one sack last season in the pass-happy SEC and is too tall to play tackle at 6–6 and too slow to play defensive end." That report on the 2001 draft by *Boston Globe* sportswriter Ron Borges is legendary among Patriot fans, who find Terrell's arrival in New England bitterly ironic. The undisciplined Terrell led NFL wideouts with 11 penalties, including four offensive pass interference calls, a couple false starts, and three illegal blocks. That doesn't sound like a player who will fit in New England, but Tom Brady vouched for his old Wolverine teammate.

Derrius Thompson

Height: 6-2   Weight: 220   College: Baylor   Born: 5-Jul-1977   Age: 28

Year	Team	G	Rec	Pass	Yds	Ctch%	Yd/C	TD	DVOA	Rank	DPAR	Rank	PAR
2002	WAS	16	53	93	773	57%	14.6	4	4.2%	39	11.8	38	10.9
2003	MIA	16	26	59	359	44%	13.8	0	-17.3%	73	-0.8	72	-1.4
2004	MIA	16	23	47	359	49%	15.6	4	14.3%	—	8.5	—	8.2
2005	MIA	14	23	—	329	—	14.1	1					

Thompson looked pretty good in limited action in 2004, but in general he's nothing more than a fourth receiver who can provide an occasional deep threat.

Craphonso Thorpe

Height: 6-0   Weight: 188   College: Florida State   Born: 27-Jun-1983   Age: 22

Year	Team	G	Rec	Pass	Yds	Ctch%	Yd/C	TD	DVOA	Rank	DPAR	Rank	PAR
2005	KC	16	38	—	520	—	13.5	3					

Exhibit A as to how far one's anger at his parents over the name he was given can carry a young man. Thorpe will get a chance to contribute in Kansas City, which has to have the worst group of receivers any explosive offense has ever had.

James Thrash

Height: 6-0   Weight: 200   College: Missouri Southern State   Born: 28-Apr-1975   Age: 30

Year	Team	G	Rec	Pass	Yds	Ctch%	Yd/C	TD	DVOA	Rank	DPAR	Rank	PAR
2002	PHI	16	52	107	635	49%	12.2	6	-18.3%	77	-2.5	81	-3.9
2003	PHI	16	49	92	558	53%	11.4	1	-16.6%	72	-0.9	73	-2.0
2004	WAS	16	17	21	203	81%	11.9	0	32.7%	—	6.5	—	6.2
2005	WAS	12	8	—	106	—	12.6	1					

What a wasted name. It should belong to a game-breaking receiver who can win a game at any moment in a single play. Instead, it belongs to a possession receiver, on the last legs of his career. The Redskins didn't throw to him often, but he played well when they did. This is what happens when you use a limited player in the correct role (see also: Kevin Faulk). Thrash is also one of the best special teams coverage men in the league.

Andrae Thurman   Height: 5-11 Weight: 192   College: College of Southern Oregon   Born: 25-Oct-1980 Age: 25

Year	Team	G	Rec	Pass	Yds	Ctch%	Yd/C	TD	DVOA	Rank	DPAR	Rank	PAR
2004	GB	2	2	2	12	100%	6.0	0	-31.3%	—	-0.2	—	0.0
2005	GB	14	12	—	169	—	13.7	1					

Ranked fifth in the NAIA in 2003 with 55 receptions in 2003 for the Raiders of Southern Oregon. Was activated from the Packers' practice squad when Robert Ferguson and Charles Lee were hurt last year. He'll only meet this projection if the Packers have injuries.

Amani Toomer   Height: 6-3 Weight: 208   College: Michigan   Born: 8-Sep-1974 Age: 31

Year	Team	G	Rec	Pass	Yds	Ctch%	Yd/C	TD	DVOA	Rank	DPAR	Rank	PAR
2002	NYG	16	82	134	1343	61%	16.4	8	32.5%	3	41.6	2	41.6
2003	NYG	16	63	152	1057	41%	16.8	5	-10.3%	60	3.3	57	0.3
2004	NYG	15	51	107	747	48%	14.6	0	-7.1%	59	4.9	59	0.6
2005	NYG	15	43	—	636	—	14.8	4					

Amani Toomer gained 747 yards without catching a single touchdown pass. How rare of a feat is that? Toomer is only the sixth WR of all time to gain over 700 receiving yards but not catch a single touchdown. Al Toon's 963 yards in 1991 is the most receiving yards by a wide receiver in a season without catching a single touchdown. Toomer's failure to find the end zone is somewhat surprising, as he was one of Kurt Warner's favorite red zone targets with ten intended passes. Those ten passes resulted in a DVOA of −239.1%. Not very good. It looks like Eli noticed Toomer's poor red zone performance, as Manning didn't throw a single red zone pass to Toomer.

David Tyree   Height: 6-0 Weight: 205   College: Syracuse   Born: 3-Jan-1980 Age: 25

Year	Team	G	Rec	Pass	Yds	Ctch%	Yd/C	TD	DVOA	Rank	DPAR	Rank	PAR
2003	NYG	16	16	31	211	52%	13.2	0	-15.0%	—	-0.1	—	-0.9
2004	NYG	16	10	17	155	59%	15.5	1	23.6%	—	4.5	—	4.1
2005	NYG	16	30	—	444	—	14.7	3					

The Giants' best special teams player also worked well with Eli Manning last year, putting up a 30.1% DVOA after the rookie replaced Warner as the starter. If the Giants are smart, they'll make Tyree their number three receiver, over Jamaar Taylor or Tim Carter.

Jerheme Urban   Height: 6-3 Weight: 212   College: Trinity International   Born: 26-Nov-1980 Age: 25

Year	Team	G	Rec	Pass	Yds	Ctch%	Yd/C	TD	DVOA	Rank	DPAR	Rank	PAR
2004	SEA	7	6	9	117	67%	19.5	1	42.3%	—	3.2	—	3.5
2005	SEA	14	11	—	144	—	13.3	1					

Honestly, where do people get these spellings? And who would win in a fight between Urban and TE Jerame Tuman of Pittsburgh? Urban's one of those guys you have to root for, an undrafted free agent out of Division III who put in his time on the practice squad and finally made the roster in 2004. The signings of Pathon and Jurevicius drop him to fifth on the depth chart (yikes), but the Seahawks seem to like him so he might be someone worth watching in the future.

Scott Vines   Height: 6-2 Weight: 203   College: Wyoming   Born: 17-Apr-1979 Age: 26

Year	Team	G	Rec	Pass	Yds	Ctch%	Yd/C	TD	DVOA	Rank	DPAR	Rank	PAR
2004	DET	6	3	9	51	33%	17.0	0	-36.9%	—	-1.3	—	-0.7
2005	DET	14	11	—	153	—	13.6	1					

Not to be confused with Stevie Strokes or Tommy White Stripes. Vines is locked in an epic battle with David Kircus for the fifth wideout spot in Detroit.

Bobby Wade

Height: 5-10 **Weight:** 193 **College:** Arizona **Born:** 25-Feb-1981 **Age:** 24

Year	Team	G	Rec	Pass	Yds	Ctch%	Yd/C	TD	DVOA	Rank	DPAR	Rank	PAR
2003	CHI	12	12	18	137	67%	11.4	0	1.2%	—	1.6	—	1.8
2004	CHI	16	42	89	481	47%	11.5	0	-40.6%	84	-14.4	84	-13.6
2005	CHI	16	39	—	520	—	13.4	3					

At only 5′10″ and not particularly fast, it's doubtful that Wade can make much of an impact. About the nicest thing that can be said of Wade is that he was the Bears' most consistent receiver. Unfortunately, he was consistently bad.

Javon Walker

Height: 6-3 **Weight:** 220 **College:** Florida State **Born:** 14-Oct-1978 **Age:** 27

Year	Team	G	Rec	Pass	Yds	Ctch%	Yd/C	TD	DVOA	Rank	DPAR	Rank	PAR
2002	GB	15	23	50	319	46%	13.9	1	-21.5%	81	-2.0	78	-1.1
2003	GB	16	41	74	716	55%	17.5	9	21.2%	11	14.2	21	14.7
2004	GB	16	89	144	1382	62%	15.5	12	19.9%	22	33.7	8	34.5
2005	GB	16	75	—	1078	—	14.4	8					

It sounds counterintuitive, but the emergence of Javon Walker had a lot to do with the Packers' use of the run-oriented package that used tackle Kevin Barry as a tight end. It brought opposing safeties closer to the line and opened up the long ball. Brett Favre improved from 42 throws of more than 20 yards in 2003 to 50 in 2004 and from seven throws of more than 40 yards in 2003 to 12 in 2004. Walker had 19 catches of more than 20 and seven of more than 40.

Kevin Walter

Height: 6-3 **Weight:** 221 **College:** Eastern Michigan **Born:** 4-Aug-1981 **Age:** 24

Year	Team	G	Rec	Pass	Yds	Ctch%	Yd/C	TD	DVOA	Rank	DPAR	Rank	PAR
2003	CIN	11	3	4	18	75%	6.0	0	-21.5%	—	-0.1	—	-0.1
2004	CIN	16	8	9	67	89%	8.4	0	4.6%	—	1.1	—	0.7
2005	CIN	14	6	—	72	—	12.0	0					

Walter was already buried on the depth chart, and that was before Cincinnati invested a pair of draft picks in more receivers this April.

Troy Walters

Height: 5-7 **Weight:** 172 **College:** Stanford **Born:** 15-Dec-1976 **Age:** 28

Year	Team	G	Rec	Pass	Yds	Ctch%	Yd/C	TD	DVOA	Rank	DPAR	Rank	PAR
2002	IND	16	18	25	207	72%	11.5	0	4.3%	—	3.3	—	3.3
2003	IND	15	36	52	456	69%	12.7	3	29.1%	5	12.3	31	11.8
2004	IND	5	1	1	5	100%	5.0	0	-22.6%	—	0.0	—	0.0
2005	IND	14	13	—	153	—	11.7	1					

Welcome to "What Could Have Been." Walters was the third wide receiver going into the season, which, on most teams, means 30 or so catches, 200 to 400 yards, and maybe a few touchdowns. You know, like his 2003 season. But on Planet Peyton, it was good for 68–1,077–10. That would have resembled Walters's line (maybe) had he not missed almost the entire season due to a broken arm suffered during a preseason game against the Jets. Instead, Brandon Stokely took that line to the bank, and Walters is hoping that Tony Dungy uses some four receiver sets. We are pessimistic.

Hines Ward

Height: 6-0 **Weight:** 205 **College:** Georgia **Born:** 8-Mar-1976 **Age:** 29

Year	Team	G	Rec	Pass	Yds	Ctch%	Yd/C	TD	DVOA	Rank	DPAR	Rank	PAR
2002	PIT	16	112	161	1329	70%	11.9	12	19.4%	15	36.1	4	36.9
2003	PIT	16	95	156	1163	61%	12.2	10	10.6%	25	21.4	6	21.8
2004	PIT	16	80	109	1004	75%	12.6	4	30.4%	9	32.9	9	31.3
2005	PIT	16	88	—	1125	—	12.8	7					

Probably the most complete WR in football, Ward will have to have another Ward-like season since big-play threat Plaxico Burress is now a New York Giant. If the running game picks up where it left off in 2004, expect Ward to have his regular, run-of-the-mill, ho-hum Pro Bowl–type season.

Peter Warrick
Height: 5-11 Weight: 192   College: Florida State   Born: 19-Jun-1977 Age: 28

Year	Team	G	Rec	Pass	Yds	Ctch%	Yd/C	TD	DVOA	Rank	DPAR	Rank	PAR
2002	CIN	15	53	82	606	66%	11.4	6	6.7%	35	12.1	36	12.8
2003	CIN	15	80	124	833	65%	10.4	7	3.9%	35	12.2	33	12.1
2004	CIN	5	11	17	127	65%	11.5	0	12.0%	—	3.0	—	3.6
2005	*CIN*	*13*	*10*	*—*	*136*	*—*	*13.2*	*1*					

Wally Pipp, meet Peter Warrick. Peter Warrick, Wally Pipp. Warrick was one of the best all-purpose players to come out of college since Gordie Lockbaum, but that never translated to the NFL. He was injured for most of 2004 and given the emergence of T. J. Houshmandzadeh, and an improving Kelley Washington, Warrick could have trouble getting on the field.

Kelley Washington
Height: 6-3 Weight: 218   College: Tennessee   Born: 21-Aug-1979 Age: 26

Year	Team	G	Rec	Pass	Yds	Ctch%	Yd/C	TD	DVOA	Rank	DPAR	Rank	PAR
2003	CIN	16	22	47	299	47%	13.6	4	-7.2%	—	2.0	—	2.2
2004	CIN	16	31	50	378	64%	12.2	3	14.8%	31	9.5	47	9.5
2005	*CIN*	*14*	*31*	*—*	*443*	*—*	*14.3*	*3*					

Washington has improved in each of his two seasons in the league, and in 2004 he sported a 9.5 DPAR, which ranked better than 26 other WRs who were either number one or number two starters for their respective teams. If he continues to improve, he could replace Warrick as the number three receiver on the Bengals depth chart.

Darius Watts
Height: 6-1 Weight: 188   College: Marshall   Born: 19-Dec-1981 Age: 23

Year	Team	G	Rec	Pass	Yds	Ctch%	Yd/C	TD	DVOA	Rank	DPAR	Rank	PAR
2004	DEN	16	31	53	385	58%	12.4	1	-5.3%	55	3.4	62	4.3
2005	*DEN*	*16*	*34*	*—*	*510*	*—*	*15.1*	*3*					

No, it turned out he wasn't the fantasy football sleeper of the year, but he still had a pretty reasonable rookie campaign. A list of the most similar rookie receivers since 1978 features a mixture of the good (Quinn Early, Carl Pickens, Tony Martin) and the bad (David Terrell, Peerless Price, every second-round Cleveland draft pick since the dawn of time). As long as the Broncos don't bring in Tim Couch to play quarterback, Watts should develop and be ready to join Lelie in the starting lineup when Rod Smith finally retires. They must resist the urge to give Jerry Rice his playing time.

Reggie Wayne
Height: 6-0 Weight: 203   College: Miami   Born: 17-Nov-1978 Age: 27

Year	Team	G	Rec	Pass	Yds	Ctch%	Yd/C	TD	DVOA	Rank	DPAR	Rank	PAR
2002	IND	15	49	72	716	68%	14.6	4	14.3%	18	14.1	31	13.5
2003	IND	16	68	107	838	64%	12.3	7	12.4%	23	16.0	13	17.4
2004	IND	16	77	115	1210	67%	15.7	12	40.8%	2	44.0	1	46.5
2005	*IND*	*16*	*80*	*—*	*1104*	*—*	*13.8*	*9*					

What happens when a slow-developing first-round pick suddenly becomes the most productive receiver in football? Nobody notices, apparently. Wayne has increased all his major stats (both advanced and traditional) every season he has been in the league. Last year he was the top receiver in DPAR and number two in DVOA. His battle with Denver cornerback Roc Alexander during the playoffs was the most one-sided battle the world has seen since Reagan invaded Grenada. Of course, Wayne got to abuse Alexander only because Champ Bailey was blanketing Marvin Harrison, so it is fair to wonder what sort of numbers Wayne would put up if he were the one who got the attention of the opposing defenses. This year we're probably going to find out.

Dez White
Height: 6-1 Weight: 215   College: Georgia Tech   Born: 23-Aug-1979 Age: 26

Year	Team	G	Rec	Pass	Yds	Ctch%	Yd/C	TD	DVOA	Rank	DPAR	Rank	PAR
2002	CHI	16	51	94	656	54%	12.9	4	-11.6%	73	2.1	73	1.6
2003	CHI	15	49	106	583	46%	11.9	3	-24.3%	82	-5.0	80	-4.2
2004	ATL	16	30	56	370	54%	12.3	2	-18.8%	73	-1.3	71	-1.4
2005	*ATL*	*14*	*22*	*—*	*323*	*—*	*14.4*	*2*					

A possession receiver who doesn't run particularly good routes, White was a big disappointment as a free agent signing for the Falcons, who for some reason thought he could be a solid addition to their passing game even though he hadn't done much in Chicago. With all the young blood the Falcons have added, White doesn't seem likely to keep his starting job.

Roddy White Height: 6-1 Weight: 201 College: Alabama-Birmingham Born: 2-Nov-1981 Age: 24

Year	Team	G	Rec	Pass	Yds	Ctch%	Yd/C	TD	DVOA	Rank	DPAR	Rank	PAR
2005	ATL	16	27	—	373	—	13.9	3					

Atlanta is another team, along with the Jaguars and Lions, that has double-dipped on first-round wide receivers the past two drafts. A year after taking Michael Jenkins in the latter stages of round one, the Falcons tapped White at a similar point in the draft. Jenkins managed just seven catches as a rookie but appears poised for a much larger role in 2005. Our guess is that White, who led the nation in receiving yardage his senior season at Alabama-Birmingham, might be given a bit more opportunity to showcase his skills than Jenkins was last year.

Alvis Whitted Height: 6-0 Weight: 185 College: North Carolina State Born: 4-Sep-1974 Age: 31

Year	Team	G	Rec	Pass	Yds	Ctch%	Yd/C	TD	DVOA	Rank	DPAR	Rank	PAR
2002	OAK	9	0	—	0	—	—	0	—	—	—	—	—
2003	OAK	16	7	24	106	29%	15.1	1	-51.2%	—	-4.5	—	-4.6
2004	OAK	12	9	25	227	36%	25.2	2	-0.7%	—	2.4	—	2.6
2005	OAK	13	12	—	164	—	14.3	1					

Whitted had receptions of 52, 38, 38, and 37 yards last season, but Doug Gabriel will fill his role as "guy who comes off the bench and goes deep."

Ernest Wilford Height: 6-3 Weight: 220 College: Virginia Tech Born: 14-Jan-1979 Age: 26

Year	Team	G	Rec	Pass	Yds	Ctch%	Yd/C	TD	DVOA	Rank	DPAR	Rank	PAR
2004	JAC	15	19	35	271	54%	14.3	2	-5.4%	—	2.5	—	4.1
2005	JAC	13	13	—	181	—	13.6	1					

Wilford's first NFL catch was a game-winning touchdown in Week 1. His second catch was also a touchdown, and through those two weeks he had the Jaguars' only two touchdowns. Based on these two touchdowns, our buddy Gregg "TMQ" Easterbrook couldn't stop writing about the guy, but Wilford caught only 17 more balls over the rest of the season, and none of them was for a touchdown. Wilford is a big, physical receiver, so the addition of Matt Jones could limit his role in the offense.

Karl Williams Height: 5-10 Weight: 177 College: Texas A&M Born: 10-Apr-1971 Age: 34

Year	Team	G	Rec	Pass	Yds	Ctch%	Yd/C	TD	DVOA	Rank	DPAR	Rank	PAR
2002	TB	16	7	11	77	64%	11.0	1	22.0%	—	2.5	—	3.0
2003	TB	14	7	17	114	41%	16.3	0	-15.2%	—	0.0	—	0.0
2004	ARI	15	18	30	197	60%	10.9	0	-4.9%	—	2.0	—	1.5
2005	FA	12	6	—	75	—	11.9	0					

An aging return man, Williams caught six passes for 90 yards against the Falcons in Week 3, then returned to the bench, whence he came. He was released by the Cardinals in the off-season.

Mike Williams Height: 6-5 Weight: 229 College: USC Born: 4-Jan-1984 Age: 21

Year	Team	G	Rec	Pass	Yds	Ctch%	Yd/C	TD	DVOA	Rank	DPAR	Rank	PAR
2005	DET	16	44	—	606	—	13.7	3					

When the Lions took Mike Williams, we were starting to believe they may only draft receivers in the first round from here on out. At some point you have to wonder where they're going to play all these guys. On the upside, however, they should dominate those NFL off-season made-for-television events in which they drop balls out of hot air balloons and

(continued next page)

Mike Williams *(continued)*

see which players can catch them. So kudos to Matt Millen for his foresight on that. Still, Detroit's selection of Williams was smarter than Minnesota's drafting Troy Williamson three picks earlier. Williams was a monster in his two seasons at USC. The stopwatches may say he's not that fast, but nobody in college could cover him. With Roy Williams and maybe even brittle-boned Charles Rogers across the field, there should be plenty of room for this Williams to operate.

Reggie Williams   Height: 6-3   Weight: 223   College: Washington   Born: 17-May-1983   Age: 22

Year	Team	G	Rec	Pass	Yds	Ctch%	Yd/C	TD	DVOA	Rank	DPAR	Rank	PAR
2004	JAC	16	27	54	268	50%	9.9	1	-36.3%	83	-7.7	79	-7.0
2005	*JAC*	*16*	*42*	—	*622*	—	*14.8*	*4*					

So this is what a first-round bust looks like. Williams had just 27 catches and one touchdown despite starting 15 games, and only two starting receivers in the league were below him in DVOA. Averaging less than ten yards a reception is also a special talent. Yes, Williams was drafted in front of Lee Evans, Michael Clayton, and Keary Colbert. Williams would seemingly have to improve this season, if only because he cannot be worse. New coordinator Carl Smith was brought in to help make the passing game vertical, a move specifically designed to benefit Williams because he struggled in the timing-based routes of last year's West Coast scheme. With a more favorable offense, Williams will have no excuses.

Roy Williams   Height: 6-2   Weight: 212   College: Texas   Born: 20-Dec-1981   Age: 23

Year	Team	G	Rec	Pass	Yds	Ctch%	Yd/C	TD	DVOA	Rank	DPAR	Rank	PAR
2004	DET	14	54	118	817	46%	15.1	8	-9.0%	62	4.5	60	2.5
2005	*DET*	*16*	*63*	—	*929*	—	*14.7*	*6*					

Roy Williams had a season that showed great promise but didn't deliver great results. In his first three games as a pro, Williams had 17 catches for 277 yards and four touchdowns. Lions fans were ecstatic, even though they had lost Charles Rogers for the second straight season. But in his fourth game, Williams injured his ankle, and although he tried to keep playing, he wasn't the same for the rest of the season. He missed two games completely and was a shell of his former self in a few others. Toward the end of the year he began to recover, but the Lions need him to be healthy from start to finish in 2005. We can't help but wonder if the Lions would have been better off resting him completely instead of trotting him out in games when he limped noticeably.

Roydell Williams   Height: 6-0   Weight: 192   College: Tulane   Born: 14-Mar-1981   Age: 24

Year	Team	G	Rec	Pass	Yds	Ctch%	Yd/C	TD	DVOA	Rank	DPAR	Rank	PAR
2005	*TEN*	*16*	*26*	—	*347*	—	*13.3*	*2*					

A tough-guy wideout who played the 2003 season with screws in his foot and still caught 66 passes, Williams would be a top possession target if he were 6'3" and 220 pounds. At 190 pounds, he's fifth wideout material.

Troy Williamson   Height: 6-1   Weight: 203   College: South Carolina   Born: 30-Apr-1983   Age: 22

Year	Team	G	Rec	Pass	Yds	Ctch%	Yd/C	TD	DVOA	Rank	DPAR	Rank	PAR
2005	*MIN*	*16*	*35*	—	*559*	—	*16.0*	*4*					

We hope Troy Williamson enjoys pressure, because he's been handed a double dose of it by the Vikings. Fair or not, he'll be judged by his ability to replace Randy Moss in Minnesota's downfield attack. And if that weren't enough, he'll also be expected to outperform Mike Williams, a more-heralded receiver ahead of whom he was drafted. Still, the Minnesota offense is a receiver's dream, and Williamson will be given plenty of opportunities to show off the speed that made him such a high pick in the first place.

Cedrick Wilson

Height: 5-10 Weight: 183   College: Tennessee   Born: 17-Dec-1978 Age: 26

Year	Team	G	Rec	Pass	Yds	Ctch%	Yd/C	TD	DVOA	Rank	DPAR	Rank	PAR
2002	SF	14	15	22	166	68%	11.1	1	25.6%	—	5.8	—	6.6
2003	SF	16	35	63	396	56%	11.3	2	-12.9%	67	0.7	67	0.6
2004	SF	15	47	85	641	55%	13.6	3	14.3%	33	15.8	37	13.8
2005	PIT	16	45	—	563	—	12.5	3					

Wilson should fit right in with the Steelers, who seem to have a love of sub-6′ receivers these days. Who knows, maybe they're planning to replace the 6′5″ Plaxico Burress by having Wilson climb onto Antwaan Randle El's shoulders. Wilson should see the field enough to approach last year's numbers, but he's likely to be not better than the third option (or even fourth, given that Pittsburgh might actually throw to the tight end, since they drafted one in the first round).

Rashaun Woods

Height: 6-2 Weight: 202   College: Oklahoma State   Born: 17-Oct-1980 Age: 25

Year	Team	G	Rec	Pass	Yds	Ctch%	Yd/C	TD	DVOA	Rank	DPAR	Rank	PAR
2004	SF	13	7	23	160	30%	22.9	1	-13.0%	—	0.1	—	-0.8
2005	SF	12	11	—	148	—	13.6	0					

Mike Nolan's current starting receivers are Brandon Lloyd (43 catches in 2004) and Arnaz Battle (8 catches). Behind them, the Niners have one receiver with just two catches last year, another who didn't even have one catch, two rookies, and this guy. A first-round pick in his second season can't work his way into the top four spots on that depth chart, let alone the starting lineup? Woods is setting an all-time record for getting buried on the roster.

Going Deep

Alex Bannister, SEA: NFC Pro Bowl special teams specialist in 2003, injured part of last year, listed at receiver on the roster but rarely plays there (two catches for ten yards in 2004). Also an aspiring music mogul; Lord knows we don't have enough of those in professional football.

Ronald Bellamy, MIA: This Michigan alum was one of 15 people to catch a pass for Miami in 2004.

Craig Bragg, GB: A hamstring injury at the combine likely pushed Bragg down a couple of rounds in the draft. He could end up returning kicks for the Packers.

Zamir Cobb, PIT: Undrafted free agent from Temple who ran a 4.4-second 40-yard dash, but spent last year on IR after breaking his leg in August.

Eddie Drummond, DET: Is a wide receiver a wide receiver if he hasn't caught a pass in two seasons? Drummond's purely a return specialist, and a damn fine one at that. He ranks first in our punt return stats for 2004, 8.8 points above average, and third in kick returns, 14.4 points above average.

P. J. Fleck, SF: Last year he hung around on the 49ers practice squad as an undrafted rookie out of Northern Illinois University. This year he's part of the San Francisco quest to bury Reshaun Woods as far down the depth chart as possible.

Antonio Freeman, FA: No, he does not consider himself retired, and yes, every NFL team apparently disagrees. Still trying to get invited to camp somewhere.

D. J. Hackett, SEA: A 2004 fifth-rounder out of the University of Colorado who didn't play last year, he's part of the receiver depth that allowed the Seahawks to cut their ties with Koren Robinson. Tall, strong, and fast, but he allegedly has trouble tracking the ball in the air.

Derrick Hamilton, SF: Last year's third-round pick was penciled in as the number three receiver until he tore his ACL in May. He'll try again in 2006.

Cedric James, NE: A fourth-round pick of the Vikings in 2001 who's never made it in the league, but he had a strong summer in NFL Europe.

Chase Lyman, NO: Lyman is big (6′3″, 217 pounds) and fast (4.46 40), but had an injury-plagued college career while catching passes from Aaron Rodgers at Cal. If healthy, he has plenty of sleeper potential—in 2006. Lyman tore his ACL at minicamp.

Ruvell Martin, SD: This summer's leading receiver in NFL Europe, with an astonishing 18.4 yards per catch and 12 touchdowns, twice the total of any other wideout.

Marcus Maxwell, SF: Big, fast, but very raw receiver who was at least drafted by a team that needs lots of help at the position.

Aaron Moorehead, IND: He's on the Colts roster, so he may be only an injury or two away from a ten-touchdown season.

Sean Morey, PIT: Our favorite player because he went to Brown, alma mater of half the Football Outsiders staff. A kick coverage dynamo with a grand total of one career reception.

Chad Owens, JAC: A tiny (5′7″) rookie out of Hawaii who will probably serve as the Jaguars' return man. Think of him as a destitute man's Antwaan Randle El. With Kyle Turley unlikely to play this year, Owens assumes the title of "most-tattooed NFL player."

Tab Perry, CIN: You can do worse than to pick up a 6′2½″, 229-pound receiver with a 4.46 40 time at the 190th spot in the NFL draft.

Willie Ponder, NYG: Ponder quietly was the NFL's leader in kickoff return average in the NFL. If he hadn't been inactive or injured for five games in 2004, more people would realize how good of a return man he is.

Brad Pyatt, IND: Primary a return man, Pyatt has missed most of the past two years because of injury.

Dante Ridgeway, STL: Did St. Louis really draft a possession receiver who is better known for his hands than his speed? Did the earth's magnetic poles reverse or something? The Rams actually took two Ball State Cardinals in the sixth round, Ridgeway and punter Reggie Hodges.

Cliff Russell, CIN: Helped the Bengals to become one of the worst teams in the league in kick returns as their primary return man for most of the 2004 season.

J. R. Russell, TB: Russell was another productive college player selected by the Buccaneers in the late rounds of the draft. He was a major contributor at Louisville last season, but lacked the speed to be a high or even mid-round draft pick.

Paris Warren, TB: In their quest to add some much-needed receiver depth, the Buccaneers looked for productive college players late in the draft. That's what they found in Warren, who was Alex Smith's favorite target at Utah last season.

Harry Williams, NYJ: Seventh-round pick of the Jets out of Tuskegee Institute, he's super-fast with the Body Mass Index of a pencil.

Randal Williams, FA: Cut by Dallas. A special teams specialist who has his own footnote in NFL history by scoring the quickest TD in NFL history after returning a failed onside kick by Philadelphia on the opening play of a 2003 game, three seconds into the contest.

Tight Ends

Last season was a banner year for tight ends. The big guys averaged 58.6 receptions, 613.3 yards, and 5.8 touchdowns per team in 2004, continuing a steady upward trend in tight end usage (table 1).

Most of the increase in tight end production can be attributed to a handful of players: Antonio Gates, Jason Witten, Eric Johnson, and a few others. Nine teams got 80 or more receptions from their tight ends last season: the Chiefs, Chargers, Niners, Cowboys, Vikings, Dolphins, Titans, and Ravens. In 2003, no team received 80 catches from their tight ends; in 2002, only three teams benefited from such production (Giants, Broncos, Ravens).

Tight ends should continue to enjoy an expanded role in NFL offenses over the next few years. While 29-year-old Tony Gonzalez tops our list of tight ends, most of the players directly under him are 27 or younger: Antonio Gates (25), Randy McMichael (26), Jason Witten (23), Eric Johnson (26), Jeremy Shockey (25), Alge Crumpler (27). Todd Heap, hurt for much of last season, is 25. Most of these players are just entering their primes, while youngsters like Chris Cooley, Ben Troupe, Heath Miller, and Kellen Winslow (assuming he ever takes the field) all have the potential to produce 70-catch, 800-yard, nine-TD seasons if given the opportunity.

Many of these young tight ends will have that opportunity. As linebackers have gotten smaller, offensive coordinators have discovered that they just can't cover 6′5″ tight ends. Today's breed of tight end is fast enough to line up as a third wide receiver; players like Gates and Shockey are often covered by cornerbacks. A curmudgeon might suggest that some of these new tight ends are just beefed-up wide receivers who cannot block, but several (Shockey, Heap, Bubba Franks, Daniel Graham) are formidable run blockers, and most are called upon to help stop defensive ends like Julius Peppers (who is too fast for most left tackles) from pulverizing the quarterback in pass protection. Tight ends are multipurpose weapons, and colleges are merrily churning out chiseled, 260-pound speedsters to meet an increasing NFL demand.[1]

In the following section, we give the last three years' worth of numbers as well as a 2005 projection for every tight end who played a role in 2004—major or minor—and/or will likely play a role in 2005 (table 2).

The first line contains biographical data—each player's name, height, weight, college, birthdate, and age. Height and weight are the best data we could find; weight, of course, can fluctuate during the off-season. Age is very simple, the number of years between the player's birth year and 2005, and the full birthdate is given for anyone who wants to either do research involving more complexity or pick up girls by pretending to be Jeremy Shockey.

Next we give the last three years of player stats. The first number is games played. This is the official NFL total and may include games in which a player was on special teams but did not play tight end.

TABLE 1. TIGHT END STATS PER TEAM

Year	Rec	Yds	Yd/R	TD
2004	58.6	613.3	10.5	5.8
2003	53.2	561.4	10.6	3.8
2002	53.5	553.6	10.4	4.2
2001	47.2	486.9	10.3	4.8

TABLE 2. TIGHT END STATISTICS SAMPLE

Tony Gonzalez Height: 6-4 Weight: 248 College: California Born: 27-Feb-1976 Age: 29

Year	Team	G	Rec	Pass	Yds	CPct	Yd/C	TD	DVOA	Rank	DPAR	Rank	PAR
2002	KC	16	63	99	773	64%	12.3	7	19.5%	10	20.0	2	20.2
2003	KC	16	71	106	915	67%	12.9	10	28.2%	5	22.3	1	23.2
2004	KC	16	102	141	1258	70%	12.3	7	35.9%	3	43.1	1	43.6
2005	KC	16	83	—	938	—	11.3	7					

---

1. For more information on the rise of the tight end in recent years, check out the article "Tight Ends Break Loose," by Michael Horn, which can be found on our website here: http://www.footballoutsiders.com/ramblings.php?p=2458.

Receptions (Rec) counts passes caught, while Passes (Pass) counts passes thrown to this player, complete or incomplete. The next four columns list receiving yards, catch percentage (CPct), yards per catch (Yd/C), and receiving touchdowns.

Catch percentage, or receptions divided by total passes, is an attempt to rectify a major problem in conventional statistics, which lay the blame for incomplete passes entirely on quarterbacks. Historical study shows that receivers definitely have an impact on whether a ball is complete or incomplete. We're still working on an estimate of how much responsibility for an incomplete belongs to the quarterback as opposed to the receiver, but it is clearly closer to 50–50 than it is to the 100–0 currently reflected in NFL stats. The average NFL tight end caught 63% of passes in 2004.

The next five columns give our advanced metrics for receiving: DVOA (Defense-Adjusted Value Over Average), DPAR (Defense-Adjusted Points Above Replacement), and PAR (Points Above Replacement), along with the player's rank in both DVOA and DPAR. These metrics compare every pass intended for a receiver to a league-average baseline based on the game situations in which passes were thrown to that receiver. DVOA and DPAR are also adjusted based on the opposing defense. The methods used to compute these numbers are described in detail in the front of this book. The important distinctions between them are:

- Higher DVOA means more value per pass attempt. Higher DPAR means more total value over the 16-game season.
- A player whose DPAR is higher than his PAR faced a harder-than-average schedule. A player whose PAR is higher than his DPAR faced an easier-than-average schedule.

To qualify for ranking in receiving DVOA and receiving DPAR, a tight end must have 25 passes thrown to him in that season. 37 tight ends are ranked for 2004, 42 for 2003 as well as 2002.

Finally, we have the last row of numbers, 2005 projections. Right now we are only projecting conventional statistics, although in future years we hope to project advanced metrics like DVOA and DPAR. The KUBIAK projection system is based on a complicated regression analysis that takes into account numerous variables, including projected role, performance over the past two years, KUBIAK projection for that team's quarterbacks, historical comparables, height, age, and strength of schedule.

It is difficult to accurately project statistics for a 162-game baseball season, but it is exponentially more difficult to accurately project statistics for a 16-game football season. Consider the listed projections not as a prediction of exact numbers, but the mean of a range of possible performances. What's important is less the exact number of yards we project, and more which players are projected to improve or decline. Actual performance will vary from our projection less for veteran starters and more for players used primarily in the red zone. Touchdown numbers will vary more than yardage numbers.

There are no numbers yet to measure tight end blocking, but we do mention in the comments when a tight end is a particularly good or bad blocker.

A few low-round rookies and players who are listed as tight ends but really only play special teams are briefly discussed at the end of this chapter in a section we call "Going Deep." *FA* signifies a player who was still a free agent at press time.

TABLE 3. TOP 10 TE BY DPAR (TOTAL VALUE), 2004

Rank	Player	Team	DPAR
1	Tony Gonzalez	KC	43.1
2	Antonio Gates	SD	35.3
3	Jason Witten	DAL	25.1
4	Alge Crumpler	ATL	23.6
5	Eric Johnson	SF	21.9
6	Jeb Putzier	DEN	16.8
7	Jermaine Wiggins	MIN	16.0
8	Jeremy Shockey	NYG	14.6
9	Daniel Graham	NE	13.6
10	Bubba Franks	GB	11.4

TABLE 4. TOP 10 TE BY DVOA (VALUE PER PLAY), 2004

Rank	Player	Team	DVOA
1	Alge Crumpler	ATL	37.8%
2	Antonio Gates	SD	36.1%
3	Tony Gonzalez	KC	35.9%
4	Jeb Putzier	DEN	35.9%
5	Daniel Graham	NE	32.5%
6	Marcus Pollard	IND	27.1%
7	Jason Witten	DAL	20.5%
8	Bubba Franks	GB	20.1%
9	Todd Heap	BAL	19.9%
10	Eric Johnson	SF	17.9%

Stephen Alexander Height: 6-4 Weight: 250 College: Oklahoma Born: 7-Nov-1975 Age: 30

Year	Team	G	Rec	Pass	Yds	CPct	Yd/C	TD	DVOA	Rank	DPAR	Rank	PAR
2002	SD	12	45	76	510	59%	11.3	1	-9.5%	30	1.5	28	0.9
2003	SD	3	0	6	0	0%	0.0	0	-104.9%	—	-2.7	—	-2.7
2004	DET	16	41	76	377	54%	9.2	1	-25.8%	34	-6.0	36	-4.4
2005	DEN	10	11	—	110	—	10.0	1					

Alexander was a disappointment for the Lions, who thought he would be a good blocker and receiver but found out that he was neither. He'll battle Jeb Putzier for playing time in Denver. Mike Shanahan and his staff are high on Putzier, so Alexander's role may be limited.

Courtney Anderson Height: 6-6 Weight: 269 College: San Jose State Born: 19-Nov-1980 Age: 25

Year	Team	G	Rec	Pass	Yds	CPct	Yd/C	TD	DVOA	Rank	DPAR	Rank	PAR
2004	OAK	9	13	21	175	62%	13.5	1	11.6%	—	3.5	—	3.1
2005	OAK	15	30	—	303	—	10.1	4					

A good blocking tight end with decent hands, Anderson went from seventh-round pick to Norv Turner favorite before a knee injury ended his season after nine games. He's the reason why Teyo Johnson was on the inactive list for the first eight games of last season. With Doug Jolley gone, he gets to battle Johnson for the starting job, and he'll probably win it. Stephen Alexander, Freddie Jones, Randy McMichael—remember, Norv Turner loves his tight ends, and all those guys going deep leave space underneath.

Chris Baker Height: 6-3 Weight: 258 College: Michigan State Born: 18-Nov-1979 Age: 26

Year	Team	G	Rec	Pass	Yds	CPct	Yd/C	TD	DVOA	Rank	DPAR	Rank	PAR
2002	NYJ	10	2	3	14	67%	7.0	0	-49.7%	—	-0.8	—	-0.6
2003	NYJ	16	14	18	137	78%	9.8	0	3.1%	—	1.5	—	1.7
2004	NYJ	15	18	29	182	62%	10.1	4	14.1%	14	5.3	20	3.5
2005	NYJ	16	18	—	198	—	11.0	2					

Baker is more a blocker than a receiver, although in 2004 he played very well when he got his limited opportunities, especially in the red zone. He probably won't be the target of many more passes in 2005, but he's a solid player who will split time with Doug Jolley. Heimerdinger always has liked two-TE sets.

Mike Bartrum Height: 6-4 Weight: 245 College: Marshall Born: 23-Jun-1970 Age: 35

Year	Team	G	Rec	Pass	Yds	CPct	Yd/C	TD	DVOA	Rank	DPAR	Rank	PAR
2002	PHI	13	1	2	8	50%	8.0	0	-1.9%	—	0.1	—	-0.1
2003	PHI	16	0	1	0	0%	0.0	0	-91.9%	—	-0.4	—	-0.5
2004	PHI	16	5	7	45	71%	9.0	1	-48.5%	—	-1.8	—	-1.8
2005	PHI	13	6	—	43	—	7.0	1					

In Week 3 against Detroit, long snapper Bartrum actually caught a touchdown pass from Donovan McNabb. He celebrated by long snapping the ball back to McNabb, and for this was given a 15-yard taunting penalty. David Akers sent the ensuing kickoff 80 yards, all the way back to the Detroit five-yard line. We tell you this to remind you that (1) throwing to the long snapper is fun; (2) NFL officials have absolutely no sense of humor; and (3) David Akers, in case we haven't drilled this into your head yet, is the best kicker in football.

Anthony Becht Height: 6-5 Weight: 272 College: West Virginia Born: 8-Aug-1977 Age: 28

Year	Team	G	Rec	Pass	Yds	CPct	Yd/C	TD	DVOA	Rank	DPAR	Rank	PAR
2002	NYJ	16	28	44	243	64%	8.7	5	2.0%	24	4.7	22	6.8
2003	NYJ	16	40	58	356	69%	8.9	4	0.0%	24	3.9	21	2.8
2004	NYJ	16	13	28	100	46%	7.7	1	-25.4%	33	-2.4	32	-3.7
2005	TB	13	22	—	187	—	8.4	2					

Becht signed with the Bucs in the off-season, and he won't be missed. He's just not a good enough receiver to justify the number of passes Chad Pennington threw his way.

Sean Berton Height: 6-4 Weight: 272 College: North Carolina State Born: 31-Oct-1979 Age: 26

Year	Team	G	Rec	Pass	Yds	CPct	Yd/C	TD	DVOA	Rank	DPAR	Rank	PAR
2003	MIN	16	0	—	0	—	—	0	—	—	—	—	—
2004	MIN	14	9	11	78	82%	8.7	0	15.1%	—	2.1	—	2.2
2005	MIN	8	11	—	79	—	7.3	1					

Mostly a blocker and special teams player, Berton won't play much offense if Jimmy Kleinsasser is healthy in 2005.

Dwayne Blakely Height: 6-4 Weight: 257 College: Missouri Born: 10-Aug-1979 Age: 26

Year	Team	G	Rec	Pass	Yds	CPct	Yd/C	TD	DVOA	Rank	DPAR	Rank	PAR
2004	ATL	15	4	8	35	50%	8.8	0	-42.2%	—	-1.6	—	-1.4
2005	ATL	15	5	—	37	—	8.0	0					

Blakely will battle Derek Rackley for the right to back up Alge Crumpler. Rackley is a veteran special teams player, so Blakely will have a lot to prove.

Kyle Brady Height: 6-6 Weight: 278 College: Penn State Born: 14-Jan-1972 Age: 33

Year	Team	G	Rec	Pass	Yds	CPct	Yd/C	TD	DVOA	Rank	DPAR	Rank	PAR
2002	JAC	16	43	67	461	64%	10.7	4	9.4%	16	9.5	13	10.0
2003	JAC	16	29	45	281	64%	9.7	1	-17.5%	34	-1.1	36	-1.8
2004	JAC	11	14	23	103	61%	7.4	1	-36.9%	—	-3.4	—	-2.1
2005	JAC	13	13	—	119	—	9.5	1					

Few people remember that Bill Belichick absolutely loved Kyle Brady when Brady was coming out of Penn State. He thought a man of Brady's size and agility was going to be a unique weapon, and he made no secret of the fact that he planned to take him with the tenth overall pick. When the Jets stunned everyone by taking Brady (whom they had never invited for a predraft interview or workout) with the ninth pick, Belichick was despondent and he traded down to the 30th pick, grabbed Ohio State linebacker Craig Powell, and was soon out of a job. It turns out that Belichick, like nearly all observers, was wrong about Brady: He's been an OK tight end, but nowhere near the dominant force that so many thought he'd be. He's getting old, had some injuries last year, and won't be around much longer.

Mark Bruener Height: 6-4 Weight: 260 College: Washington Born: 16-Sep-1972 Age: 33

Year	Team	G	Rec	Pass	Yds	CPct	Yd/C	TD	DVOA	Rank	DPAR	Rank	PAR
2002	PIT	11	13	18	66	72%	5.1	1	-17.3%	—	-0.6	—	-0.7
2003	PIT	14	2	5	12	40%	6.0	1	-50.7%	—	-1.1	—	-1.2
2004	HOU	16	4	10	52	40%	13.0	0	-38.2%	—	-1.8	—	-1.5
2005	HOU	14	4	—	53	—	12.9	0					

He caught four passes last year. He'll probably catch about four passes next year, too. He's a blocking tight end, and a pretty good one, but only his mom has him on her fantasy team.

Steve Bush Height: 6-3 Weight: 280 College: Arizona State Born: 4-Jul-1974 Age: 31

Year	Team	G	Rec	Pass	Yds	CPct	Yd/C	TD	DVOA	Rank	DPAR	Rank	PAR
2002	ARI	14	19	27	121	70%	6.4	1	-23.6%	38	-1.8	37	-1.2
2003	ARI	16	11	17	71	65%	6.5	1	-20.5%	—	-0.7	—	-1.1
2004	SF	5	2	3	10	67%	5.0	1	43.5%	—	1.1	—	0.7
2005	SF	10	5	—	28	—	5.6	0					

Bush was the target of 27 passes in one season? Oh, those wacky Cardinals. Bush averages eight catches per season for his career. He won't match that average in 2005.

Dan Campbell   Height: 6-5   Weight: 263   College: Texas A&M   Born: 13-Apr-1976   Age: 29

Year	Team	G	Rec	Pass	Yds	CPct	Yd/C	TD	DVOA	Rank	DPAR	Rank	PAR
2002	NYG	15	22	—	175	—	—	1	—	—	—	—	—
2003	DAL	16	20	30	195	67%	9.8	1	-18.0%	35	-0.6	33	0.9
2004	DAL	3	2	2	16	100%	8.0	0	94.1%	—	0.9	—	0.7
2005	*DAL*	*16*	*8*	*—*	*50*	*—*	*6.3*	*0*					

Campbell was limited to only two games last season after suffering a severe sprain to his foot in Week 3. He should be back lining up on the other side of the offensive line from Jason Witten, confusing defenses who for some strange reason think the Cowboys are going to run a play for Dan Campbell.

Mark Campbell   Height: 6-6   Weight: 255   College: Michigan   Born: 6-Dec-1975   Age: 30

Year	Team	G	Rec	Pass	Yds	CPct	Yd/C	TD	DVOA	Rank	DPAR	Rank	PAR
2002	CLE	16	25	46	179	54%	7.2	3	-35.4%	43	-6.5	42	-5.5
2003	BUF	16	34	50	339	68%	10.0	1	2.5%	21	3.8	22	4.1
2004	BUF	12	17	30	203	57%	11.9	5	9.3%	—	4.1	—	3.0
2005	*BUF*	*13*	*19*	*—*	*173*	*—*	*9.2*	*2*					

Campbell is a fairly good blocker, and Mike Mularkey loves calling his name in the red zone, where, at 6'6" and 255 pounds, he can bang away at smaller defensive backs for position in the corner.

Dwayne Carswell   Height: 6-3   Weight: 260   College: Liberty   Born: 10-Jan-1972   Age: 33

Year	Team	G	Rec	Pass	Yds	CPct	Yd/C	TD	DVOA	Rank	DPAR	Rank	PAR
2002	DEN	14	18	29	149	72%	8.3	1	3.5%	22	3.1	27	3.4
2003	DEN	16	6	17	53	35%	8.8	1	-48.1%	—	-3.0		-2.6
2004	DEN	15	22	36	198	61%	9.0	1	-19.3%	31	-1.3	30	0.0
2005	*DEN*	*12*	*12*	*—*	*114*	*—*	*9.7*	*1*					

The Broncos keep trying to make Carswell a tackle, inevitably switching him back to tight end when they decide that he's better than whatever backup they signed. When it comes to blocking, he is. When it comes to pass catching, he's not. He's always near the bottom of our ratings, while the starting Denver tight end is near the top. Now they're talking about making him a guard. Make up your minds, guys.

Dallas Clark   Height: 6-3   Weight: 257   College: Iowa   Born: 12-Jun-1979   Age: 26

Year	Team	G	Rec	Pass	Yds	CPct	Yd/C	TD	DVOA	Rank	DPAR	Rank	PAR
2003	IND	11	29	42	340	69%	11.7	1	13.2%	15	5.6	15	5.2
2004	IND	15	25	39	423	64%	16.9	5	17.2%	11	7.6	16	7.4
2005	*IND*	*16*	*38*	*—*	*585*	*—*	*15.4*	*4*					

Clark was a surprising first-round choice for the defense-needy Colts in 2003, but with the departure of Marcus Pollard this year he will have a vital role with the Colts. Of course, Clark wears a fullback number (44) and nearly always splits out wide, so calling him a tight end seems fairly absurd. Oddly enough, since 1978 the tight end most similar to Clark over a two-year period is another 2003 draft pick, Philadelphia's L. J. Smith. With comparables like Alge Crumpler, it is no wonder our projection system likes Clark to have a big 2005, but nothing is ensured—one of his other top comparables, O. J. Santiago, saw his career crumble after 428 yards and five touchdowns in 1998.

Desmond Clark   Height: 6-3   Weight: 255   College: Wake Forest   Born: 20-Apr-1977   Age: 28

Year	Team	G	Rec	Pass	Yds	CPct	Yd/C	TD	DVOA	Rank	DPAR	Rank	PAR
2002	MIA	10	2	3	42	67%	21.0	0	85.4%	—	1.8	—	1.9
2003	CHI	15	44	71	433	62%	9.8	2	-13.7%	31	-0.2	31	0.6
2004	CHI	15	24	49	282	49%	11.8	1	-29.4%	35	-4.3	34	-1.6
2005	*CHI*	*16*	*28*	*—*	*293*	*—*	*10.4*	*1*					

In a year in which tight end production flourished, here's a preseason sleeper who went down in flames. He had some really bad drops and did not help any of the Bears' quarterbacks at all. Offensive coordinator Terry Shea would love to have a pass-catching tight end like he had in Kansas City with Tony Gonzalez, but Clark will never be anything close to that.

Cam Cleeland

Height: 6-4   Weight: 272   College: Washington   Born: 15-Aug-1975   Age: 30

Year	Team	G	Rec	Pass	Yds	CPct	Yd/C	TD	DVOA	Rank	DPAR	Rank	PAR
2002	NE	12	16	21	112	76%	7.0	1	-0.4%	—	1.6	—	0.8
2003	STL	16	10	16	145	63%	14.5	0	7.1%	—	1.7	—	1.5
2004	STL	16	7	12	57	58%	8.1	0	-6.2%	—	0.5	—	0.0
2005	FA	14	6	—	55	—	8.6	0					

An unrestricted free agent at press time. Cleeland never developed as a receiving threat but can help a team as a blocker.

Ernie Conwell

Height: 6-2   Weight: 265   College: Washington   Born: 17-Aug-1972   Age: 33

Year	Team	G	Rec	Pass	Yds	CPct	Yd/C	TD	DVOA	Rank	DPAR	Rank	PAR
2002	STL	15	34	48	419	71%	12.3	2	20.8%	8	9.8	11	9.6
2003	NO	10	26	44	290	59%	11.2	2	-8.8%	28	0.8	29	0.6
2004	NO	16	10	19	102	53%	10.2	1	-23.6%	—	-1.3	—	-0.9
2005	NO	16	16	—	161	—	10.1	1					

With only ten catches last year, Conwell has pretty much stopped being a part of the passing game, but he's still an important part of the Saints' special teams and can earn a roster spot that way.

Chris Cooley

Height: 6-3   Weight: 265   College: Utah State   Born: 11-Jul-1982   Age: 23

Year	Team	G	Rec	Pass	Yds	CPct	Yd/C	TD	DVOA	Rank	DPAR	Rank	PAR
2004	WAS	16	37	63	314	59%	8.5	6	2.1%	24	5.8	18	4.7
2005	WAS	16	40	—	400	—	10.0	4					

Cooley had the Clint Didier season last year. When Joe Gibbs coached the Redskins in the 1980s, Didier would often have a 35-catch, five-TD season as part of a two-TE attack. Cooley is an H-back who often goes in motion before the snap, putting him in ideal position to lead block or isolate a linebacker in pass coverage. He was one of the few components of the Redskins offense that actually worked last season.

Alge Crumpler

Height: 6-2   Weight: 262   College: North Carolina   Born: 23-Dec-1977   Age: 27

Year	Team	G	Rec	Pass	Yds	CPct	Yd/C	TD	DVOA	Rank	DPAR	Rank	PAR
2002	ATL	16	36	58	455	62%	12.6	5	33.4%	3	16.3	3	15.1
2003	ATL	16	44	80	552	55%	12.5	3	-4.7%	26	3.2	24	3.0
2004	ATL	14	48	74	774	65%	16.1	6	37.8%	1	23.6	4	24.6
2005	ATL	16	52	—	645	—	12.5	7					

Just about the only bright spot in the Falcons' passing game, Crumpler is an outstanding pass catcher and also a good blocker. He's not as tall or as athletic as the league's other elite tight ends, but he has very good hands and is a smart player who finds holes in coverage. Just about the only way to slow him down is to put both a linebacker and a strong safety on him. Unfortunately for the Falcons, toward the end of the year teams started to figure out that they could do that without anyone else in the Falcons' passing game beating them.

Ken Dilger

Height: 6-5   Weight: 250   College: Illinois   Born: 2-Feb-1971   Age: 34

Year	Team	G	Rec	Pass	Yds	CPct	Yd/C	TD	DVOA	Rank	DPAR	Rank	PAR
2002	TB	14	34	48	329	71%	9.7	2	-3.2%	28	3.1	26	3.7
2003	TB	15	22	41	244	54%	11.1	1	-30.8%	40	-4.0	40	-4.4
2004	TB	16	39	55	345	71%	8.8	3	-3.6%	26	3.3	26	3.5

Once one of the best downfield tight ends in the league, age and injuries have taken a toll on the ten-year veteran. Dilger was still an effective receiver on occasion as part of a tight end–by–committee approach in Tampa Bay last season, but looks to be at the end of the line. He turned down a chance to interview with the Jets this off-season and may retire.

Darnell Dinkins Height: 6-3 Weight: 255 College: Pittsburgh Born: 20-Jan-1977 Age: 28

Year	Team	G	Rec	Pass	Yds	CPct	Yd/C	TD	DVOA	Rank	DPAR	Rank	PAR
2002	NYG	2	0	—	0	—	—	0	—	—	—	—	—
2003	NYG	7	2	5	16	40%	8.0	0	-68.3%	—	-1.6	—	-1.3
2004	BAL	10	9	15	94	60%	10.4	1	9.5%	—	2.1	—	1.8
2005	*BAL*	*15*	*10*	—	*91*	—	*9.4*	*0*					

Dinkins started four games last season and played well against the Cowboys, but the Ravens prefer Dan Wilcox as their third tight end/H-back. Dinkins may not make the roster.

Rickey Dudley Height: 6-6 Weight: 255 College: Ohio State Born: 15-Jul-1972 Age: 33

Year	Team	G	Rec	Pass	Yds	CPct	Yd/C	TD	DVOA	Rank	DPAR	Rank	PAR
2002	TB	13	16	26	192	62%	12.0	3	11.9%	13	4.2	24	4.7
2003	TB	7	7	11	42	64%	6.0	1	-11.7%	—	0.0	—	0.0
2004	TB	3	3	4	48	75%	16.0	0	80.1%	—	2.0	—	1.7

Dudley was Antonio Gates before Gates was, lettering in basketball as well as football at Ohio State. At 6'6", 255 pounds, and with freakish athletic ability, he should have developed into the prototype tight end in the NFL in the 1990s. One small problem: hands of stone. A free agent.

Jason Dunn Height: 6-6 Weight: 270 College: Eastern Kentucky Born: 15-Nov-1973 Age: 32

Year	Team	G	Rec	Pass	Yds	CPct	Yd/C	TD	DVOA	Rank	DPAR	Rank	PAR
2002	KC	9	2	3	16	67%	8.0	0	-28.4%	—	-0.4	—	-0.4
2003	KC	16	5	8	35	63%	7.0	3	45.2%	—	2.7	—	2.4
2004	KC	16	17	21	120	67%	7.1	3	-3.1%	—	1.3	—	1.5
2005	*KC*	*16*	*16*	—	*128*	—	*8.3*	*1*					

Early in his career, Dunn was Gonzo-lite: a college hoops player who had a couple of big games for the Eagles and was miscast as a potential offensive star. Dunn didn't have the hands to be a primary target, but he turned into a very good blocking tight end with sneaky speed. Dunn has had a fine little career, but like many of the Chiefs' featured players, he's starting to hear the music swell.

Eric Edwards Height: 6-4 Weight: 249 College: LSU Born: 4-Aug-1980 Age: 25

Year	Team	G	Rec	Pass	Yds	CPct	Yd/C	TD	DVOA	Rank	DPAR	Rank	PAR
2004	ARI	16	5	8	51	63%	10.2	0	-0.3%	—	0.7	—	1.6
2005	*ARI*	*15*	*21*	—	*223*	—	*10.6*	*2*					

Edwards made the Cardinals as an undrafted rookie last year. He's considered a block-first tight end but showed some promise as a receiver with a three-catch game against the Niners. Arizona waived Lorenzo Diamond and let Freddie Jones leave for Carolina, which leaves Edwards as the starter. Good sleeper if you play in a fantasy league that uses, say, 30 tight ends.

Tim Euhus Height: 6-4 Weight: 247 College: Oregon State Born: 2-Oct-1980 Age: 25

Year	Team	G	Rec	Pass	Yds	CPct	Yd/C	TD	DVOA	Rank	DPAR	Rank	PAR
2004	BUF	12	11	15	98	73%	8.9	2	28.1%	—	3.8	—	2.9
2005	*BUF*	*13*	*18*	—	*166*	—	*9.0*	*2*					

As a rookie, Euhus was used primarily in the red zone, where Mike Mularkey loves going to his tight ends. Any tight end on the Bills is a threat to score more touchdowns than most people would think. If they ever settle on one, he'll be a fantasy sleeper.

Kevin Everett   Height: 6-4   Weight: 241   College: Miami   Born: 5-Feb-1982   Age: 23

Year	Team	G	Rec	Pass	Yds	CPct	Yd/C	TD	DVOA	Rank	DPAR	Rank	PAR
2005	BUF	3	7	—	80	—	11.4	1					

Everett is a great athlete in the tradition of Miami tight ends from Bubba Franks to Jeremy Shockey to Kellen Winslow Jr. But he lacks the superior blocking ability of Franks and the great hands of Shockey and Winslow. He does not, however, lack the fragility of Shockey and Winslow—Everett tore a knee ligament on the first day of minicamp and is out most or all of the season.

Christian Fauria   Height: 6-4   Weight: 250   College: Colorado   Born: 22-Sep-1971   Age: 34

Year	Team	G	Rec	Pass	Yds	CPct	Yd/C	TD	DVOA	Rank	DPAR	Rank	PAR
2002	NE	15	27	40	253	68%	9.4	7	31.5%	5	11.5	9	11.6
2003	NE	16	28	45	285	62%	10.2	2	11.4%	16	5.4	16	5.3
2004	NE	16	16	20	195	80%	12.2	2	42.3%	—	8.0	—	8.1
2005	NE	15	15	—	157	—	10.3	1					

Fauria is on local television so much that his team should be listed as WHDH instead of NE. As a free agent in 2002, he was exactly the right fit for the Patriots, and he got two Super Bowl rings out of three very good seasons. Ben Watson's return makes him the third-stringer, so while he'll show up for a few plays this is probably the last hurrah before he has to start boning up on his Red Sox and Celtics for Sports Xtra.

Casey FitzSimmons   Height: 6-3   Weight: 250   College: Carroll   Born: 10-Oct-1980   Age: 25

Year	Team	G	Rec	Pass	Yds	CPct	Yd/C	TD	DVOA	Rank	DPAR	Rank	PAR
2003	DET	16	23	40	160	58%	7.0	2	-27.0%	38	-3.1	38	-3.5
2004	DET	16	10	14	103	71%	10.3	0	3.4%	—	1.6	—	2.1
2005	DET	13	15	—	143	—	9.8	1					

Marcus Pollard's age means nagging injuries, which probably means more time for FitzSimmons, and we hope he does something with it. He's got a great back story. He grew up playing eight-man football, and the Lions went out on a limb by signing him to their active roster two years ago as an undrafted free agent out of NAIA Carroll College. FitzSimmons also gives editors fits with his odd name. The Lions issued an unintentionally hilarious press release a year ago explaining that the capitalization of the *S* was a big issue in his family. That still doesn't explain LaVar Arrington and LaMont Jordan.

Bubba Franks   Height: 6-6   Weight: 263   College: Miami   Born: 6-Jan-1978   Age: 27

Year	Team	G	Rec	Pass	Yds	CPct	Yd/C	TD	DVOA	Rank	DPAR	Rank	PAR
2002	GB	16	54	70	442	77%	8.2	7	11.5%	15	12.3	7	14.5
2003	GB	16	30	44	241	68%	8.0	4	1.5%	23	3.2	25	3.9
2004	GB	16	34	50	361	68%	10.6	7	20.1%	8	11.4	10	12.3
2005	GB	16	29	—	327	—	11.3	4					

The question about Franks is, why hasn't he improved? He looked so good early in his career that he seemed destined to become one of the best tight ends in the league, but he's essentially the same player now as he was coming out of Miami. The Hurricanes provide the league with NFL-ready tight ends, but those tight ends don't seem to make the jump from good player to superstar.

Michael Gaines   Height: 6-2   Weight: 275   College: Central Florida   Born: 30-Mar-1980   Age: 25

Year	Team	G	Rec	Pass	Yds	CPct	Yd/C	TD	DVOA	Rank	DPAR	Rank	PAR
2004	CAR	14	4	14	34	29%	8.5	0	-74.0%	—	-6.2	—	-6.2
2005	CAR	15	4	—	32	—	7.4	0					

A glorified right tackle who started several games when the Panthers operated out of a two-TE set, Gaines will make the roster once the Panthers stop wasting time with Freddie Jones. Any receptions by Gaines will purely be accidental.

Antonio Gates Height: 6-4 Weight: 260 College: None Born: 18-Jun-1980 Age: 25

Year	Team	G	Rec	Pass	Yds	CPct	Yd/C	TD	DVOA	Rank	DPAR	Rank	PAR
2003	SD	15	24	42	389	57%	16.2	2	18.2%	11	6.7	14	6.7
2004	SD	15	81	114	964	71%	11.9	13	36.1%	2	35.3	2	39.5
2005	*SD*	*16*	*70*	*—*	*858*	*—*	*12.3*	*9*					

Have you noticed a lot more gentlemen wearing NFL team polos sitting behind the bench of your favorite Division I college basketball team, furiously scribbling notes about power forwards? You can thank Antonio Gates for that. When a guy can go from a college basketball player who hasn't played football since high school to arguably the NFL's best receiving tight end in under two years, it kind of changes the way you scout the position. The only bad news for Gates fans is that with more receiving options on the field—Keenan McCardell and Reche Caldwell will both be around all season, Eric Parker has a year as a starter under his belt, and Vincent Jackson was drafted up in the second round—Gates probably won't catch 13 touchdowns again.

Tony Gonzalez Height: 6-4 Weight: 248 College: California Born: 27-Feb-1976 Age: 29

Year	Team	G	Rec	Pass	Yds	CPct	Yd/C	TD	DVOA	Rank	DPAR	Rank	PAR
2002	KC	16	63	99	773	64%	12.3	7	19.5%	10	20.0	2	20.2
2003	KC	16	71	106	915	67%	12.9	10	28.2%	5	22.3	1	23.2
2004	KC	16	102	141	1258	70%	12.3	7	35.9%	3	43.1	1	43.6
2005	*KC*	*16*	*83*	*—*	*938*	*—*	*11.3*	*7*					

With Gonzalez and Antonio Gates in the same division, opponents are stocking up on big cornerbacks like Lonny Walls and fast safeties like Nmandi Asomugha. You can't beat the Chiefs and Chargers unless you can match up with their tight ends. No strategy has totally neutralized Gonzo, but he's starting to get jammed at the line by Father Time, which is the subject of a longer essay back in the Kansas City chapter.

Daniel Graham Height: 6-3 Weight: 257 College: Colorado Born: 16-Nov-1978 Age: 27

Year	Team	G	Rec	Pass	Yds	CPct	Yd/C	TD	DVOA	Rank	DPAR	Rank	PAR
2002	NE	11	15	23	150	65%	10.0	1	-7.8%	—	0.8	—	1.3
2003	NE	14	38	62	409	61%	10.8	4	1.7%	22	4.4	17	3.6
2004	NE	14	30	48	364	63%	12.1	7	32.5%	5	13.6	9	12.2
2005	*NE*	*16*	*33*	*—*	*352*	*—*	*10.5*	*4*					

When Graham and Jeremy Shockey left college after the 2001 season, it was Graham who won the John Mackey Trophy as the nation's best tight end. If you look like a refugee from a *Road Warrior* movie and benefit from New York hype, you spend three years as a "budding superstar." Contribute quietly (but significantly) to two Super Bowl teams, and you're just another player. Graham is the king of the "wam" block, pulling to take on linebackers so Corey Dillon can run up the middle. When injuries hit the offensive line at midseason, he was held back to block more often, and his passes per game dropped by half.

Ryan Hannam Height: 6-2 Weight: 248 College: Northern Iowa Born: 24-Feb-1980 Age: 25

Year	Team	G	Rec	Pass	Yds	CPct	Yd/C	TD	DVOA	Rank	DPAR	Rank	PAR
2002	SEA	11	1	1	16	100%	16.0	1	265.0%	—	1.8	—	1.9
2003	SEA	5	0	—	0	—	—	0	—	—	—	—	—
2004	SEA	16	8	12	110	67%	13.8	0	28.9%	—	3.3	—	3.2
2005	*SEA*	*14*	*13*	*—*	*132*	*—*	*10.3*	*1*					

Mostly a special teams player, Hannam played well on the rare occasions the offense called on him.

Patrick Hape Height: 6-4 Weight: 262 College: Alabama Born: 6-Jun-1974 Age: 31

Year	Team	G	Rec	Pass	Yds	CPct	Yd/C	TD	DVOA	Rank	DPAR	Rank	PAR
2002	DEN	13	5	14	19	43%	3.8	2	-39.6%	—	-2.7	—	-2.5
2003	DEN	16	3	4	30	75%	10.0	0	32.8%	—	0.9	—	1.0
2004	DEN	16	8	17	35	47%	4.4	4	-25.1%	—	-1.3	—	-0.7
2005	*DEN*	*16*	*11*	*—*	*45*	*—*	*4.1*	*2*					

(continued next page)

Patrick Hape *(continued)*

Hape is listed as a tight end but actually plays more at blocking fullback. He's part of the endless string of seemingly interchangeable parts in the Broncos' backfield. If you are watching a Broncos game and the announcer sounds surprised when the Broncos throw to Hape at the goal line, it is a signal that the announcer has not done any preparation.

Ben Hartsock			Height: 6-3	Weight: 264	College: Ohio State					Born: 5-Jul-1980		Age: 25
Year	Team	G	Rec	Pass	Yds	CPct	Yd/C	TD	DVOA	Rank	DPAR	Rank	PAR
2004	IND	16	4	8	33	50%	8.3	0	-33.4%	—	-1.3	—	-2.4
2005	*IND*	*16*	*20*	*—*	*210*	*—*	*10.6*	*2*				

With the departure of Marcus Pollard, Hartsock will see a serious increase in playing time. A third-round pick in 2004, Hartsock is a very good blocker who is still developing his receiving skills. He needs to develop in order for the Colts to successfully run their two-tight-end offense.

Todd Heap			Height: 6-5	Weight: 252	College: Arizona State					Born: 16-Mar-1980		Age: 25
Year	Team	G	Rec	Pass	Yds	CPct	Yd/C	TD	DVOA	Rank	DPAR	Rank	PAR
2002	BAL	16	68	122	836	56%	12.3	6	-0.5%	26	9.8	12	10.6
2003	BAL	16	57	112	693	51%	12.2	3	-10.8%	29	1.0	28	0.4
2004	BAL	6	27	44	303	61%	11.2	3	19.9%	9	8.6	13	7.5
2005	*BAL*	*15*	*47*	*—*	*582*	*—*	*12.3*	*5*				

Heap only played in six games last season because of an ankle injury, and then couldn't show up for minicamp because he had shoulder surgery. He should only get better now that QB Kyle Boller is a year older and wide receivers like Derrick Mason and Mark Clayton are making plays down the field. But this is the final year on his contract, so if he keeps struggling with injuries, you wonder if the Ravens might just be better off going with someone like Daniel Wilcox.

Steve Heiden			Height: 6-5	Weight: 265	College: South Dakota State					Born: 21-Sep-1976		Age: 29
Year	Team	G	Rec	Pass	Yds	CPct	Yd/C	TD	DVOA	Rank	DPAR	Rank	PAR
2002	CLE	14	17	19	105	89%	6.2	1	-4.0%	—	1.4	—	2.5
2003	CLE	9	18	31	134	58%	7.4	0	-40.8%	41	-4.5	41	-4.7
2004	CLE	13	28	42	287	67%	10.3	5	12.6%	16	6.7	17	5.5
2005	*CLE*	*14*	*19*	*—*	*164*	*—*	*8.6*	*3*				

Not bad for a guy who was supposed to back up Kellen Winslow. Of course, Heiden and Aaron Shea teamed up at TE to put up numbers that Winslow probably would've reached by Week 10, but given all that the Browns went through last season this was actually one of the bright spots. Guess what: Now it gets to be one of the few bright spots again. If there's a knock on Heiden, it's that despite his soft hands he's not a great blocking tight end.

Will Heller			Height: 6-6	Weight: 250	College: Georgia Tech					Born: 28-Feb-1981		Age: 24
Year	Team	G	Rec	Pass	Yds	CPct	Yd/C	TD	DVOA	Rank	DPAR	Rank	PAR
2003	TB	7	2	4	15	50%	7.5	1	18.0%	—	0.7	—	0.4
2004	TB	10	12	16	98	75%	8.2	1	-29.0%	—	-1.7	—	-1.4
2005	*TB*	*14*	*10*	*—*	*98*	*—*	*9.8*	*1*				

Heller looked like he might get an opportunity in Tampa Bay with Ken Dilger and Rickey Dudley hitting unrestricted free agency, but the team promptly signed Anthony Becht and drafted Alex Smith. Heller looks like a roster-depth guy.

Eric Johnson			Height: 6-3	Weight: 256	College: Yale					Born: 15-Sep-1979		Age: 26
Year	Team	G	Rec	Pass	Yds	CPct	Yd/C	TD	DVOA	Rank	DPAR	Rank	PAR
2002	SF	12	36	65	321	55%	8.9	0	-11.1%	31	0.2	32	-3.5
2003	SF	0	0	—	0	—	—	0	—	—	—	—	—
2004	SF	16	82	117	825	70%	10.1	2	17.9%	10	21.9	5	20.3
2005	*SF*	*15*	*58*	*—*	*652*	*—*	*11.3*	*5*				

Not a bad return from a year lost to injury. Tim Rattay had to throw to someone, and he picked Johnson as his favorite receiver. In nine games started by Rattay, Johnson averaged 8.8 passes, 6.2 catches, and 65 yards per game with a DVOA of 24.1%. In seven games started by Ken Dorsey, Johnson averaged 5.3 passes, 3.6 catches, and 33 yards per game with a DVOA of 1.4%. Our advice to Johnson is to buy Alex Smith dinner a couple times and get on his good side. Johnson was a wide receiver in college and he's a poor blocker, so DVOA and DPAR will overvalue him.

Teyo Johnson

Height: 6-5 **Weight: 260** **College: Stanford** **Born: 29-Nov-1981** **Age: 24**

Year	Team	G	Rec	Pass	Yds	CPct	Yd/C	TD	DVOA	Rank	DPAR	Rank	PAR
2003	OAK	16	14	24	128	58%	9.1	1	-7.4%	—	0.6	—	0.3
2004	OAK	9	9	13	131	69%	14.6	2	51.7%	—	5.7	—	6.1
2005	*OAK*	*16*	*17*	*—*	*155*	*—*	*8.9*	*2*					

An intriguing wideout/tight end tweener who may not have a role on this Raiders team. Norv Turner likes tight ends who can catch, but he also needs a dependable pass blocker at the position. Johnson blocks like a big wide receiver. He would be deadly as a second tight end in the Dallas Clark mold, but how many balls are there to go around in Oakland? An offensive coordinator like Al Saunders would find a role for Johnson; in Oakland, he'll catch 15 passes and take up roster space.

Doug Jolley

Height: 6-4 **Weight: 250** **College: BYU** **Born: 2-Jan-1979** **Age: 26**

Year	Team	G	Rec	Pass	Yds	CPct	Yd/C	TD	DVOA	Rank	DPAR	Rank	PAR
2002	OAK	14	31	37	396	86%	12.8	2	49.8%	1	15.8	4	16.9
2003	OAK	15	31	53	250	58%	8.1	1	-28.0%	39	-4.0	39	-3.0
2004	OAK	16	27	48	313	56%	11.6	2	-4.8%	28	2.4	27	2.7
2005	*NYJ*	*16*	*35*	*—*	*386*	*—*	*11.2*	*3*					

Jets GM Terry Bradway is one of the few people in America who thinks that Jolley was worth trading a first-round pick for. Jolley switched from quarterback to tight end early in his college career, then left school with a reputation as a clever player who could dissect coverage and get open in critical situations. He was ridiculously good as a rookie but never developed. In fact, he somewhat un-developed. His low catch percentages show that he's not effective as a safety valve receiver, and he caught just two of seven balls thrown to him in the red zone last season. Jolley will get more opportunities in New York, but Jets fans will still be wondering in December why the team didn't just take that first-round pick and select Heath Miller.

Brian Jones

Height: 6-3 **Weight: 235** **College: Arkansas–Pine Bluff** **Born: 23-Aug-1981** **Age: 24**

Year	Team	G	Rec	Pass	Yds	CPct	Yd/C	TD	DVOA	Rank	DPAR	Rank	PAR
2004	JAC	16	6	19	87	32%	14.5	1	-35.5%	—	-2.7	—	-2.3
2005	*JAC*	*15*	*8*	*—*	*89*	*—*	*11.9*	*0*					

The weakest of the Rolling Stones guitar players in terms of pure talent, but still a vital part of the group in their formative years. Jones's vibe playing added vitality to songs like "Under My Thumb," and the band's sound changed immeasurably when Jones gave way to Mick Taylor and later Ronnie Wood.

Freddie Jones

Height: 6-4 **Weight: 260** **College: North Carolina** **Born: 16-Sep-1974** **Age: 31**

Year	Team	G	Rec	Pass	Yds	CPct	Yd/C	TD	DVOA	Rank	DPAR	Rank	PAR
2002	ARI	16	44	81	358	54%	8.1	1	-29.7%	40	-8.5	43	-8.4
2003	ARI	16	55	88	517	64%	9.4	3	-14.8%	32	-0.6	34	0.6
2004	ARI	16	45	74	426	61%	9.5	2	-19.2%	30	-2.8	33	-2.3
2005	*CAR*	*14*	*30*	*—*	*305*	*—*	*10.1*	*3*					

Jones is a Grand High Black Belt in the art of the one-catch, six-yard statline, the tight end equivalent of haiku. He had four one-catch games and three two-catch games in 2004, averaging less than ten yards per reception in each game and only netting two first downs. In past seasons, he produced such gems as the two-catch, four-yard game (Week 7 vs. Dallas, 2002), the three-catch, nine-yard game (Week 12 vs. Oakland, 2002), and the transcendently beautiful three-catch,

(continued next page)

Freddie Jones *(continued)*

seven-yard game (Week 11 vs. Cleveland, 2003). No, sensei, none of those catches was a one-yard touchdown: They were all just really, really short throws. Jones hauls in the occasional 40-yard reception to make his numbers look better, but he has milked a long career out of lots and lots of mediocre games. Signed in Carolina, where the Panthers claim he'll be more of a blocker. Ye gods.

Terry Jones Height: 6-3 Weight: 265 College: Alabama Born: 3-Dec-1979 Age: 26

Year	Team	G	Rec	Pass	Yds	CPct	Yd/C	TD	DVOA	Rank	DPAR	Rank	PAR
2002	BAL	11	11	21	106	52%	9.6	1	-23.2%	—	-1.4	—	-1.2
2003	BAL	16	19	25	159	76%	8.4	3	21.7%	10	4.2	20	4.8
2004	BAL	15	20	24	152	71%	7.6	1	-15.4%	—	-0.5	—	-1.5
2005	*BAL*	*16*	*14*	*—*	*130*	*—*	*9.1*	*0*					

Jones complements Todd Heap well and filled in adequately as a blocker when Heap was hurt last season. H-back Dan Wilcox was actually the target of more throws than Jones, so there will be a battle for the number two tight end spot in Baltimore. Try not to hyperventilate with enthusiasm.

Reggie Kelly Height: 6-4 Weight: 255 College: Mississippi State Born: 22-Feb-1977 Age: 28

Year	Team	G	Rec	Pass	Yds	CPct	Yd/C	TD	DVOA	Rank	DPAR	Rank	PAR
2002	ATL	14	14	20	162	70%	11.6	0	4.8%	—	2.4	—	2.5
2003	CIN	12	13	21	81	62%	6.2	1	-28.7%	—	-1.7	—	-1.4
2004	CIN	16	15	21	85	71%	5.7	0	-34.1%	—	-3.1	—	-3.6
2005	*CIN*	*13*	*14*	*—*	*111*	*—*	*7.8*	*2*					

The good news is that Kelly is one of the best blocking tight ends in the league. The bad news is he catches more like an offensive tackle than a wideout. The Bengals would like for him to improve on those numbers and become a viable option in the middle of the field for Carson Palmer, but maybe they should try running him on some longer patterns. In 2002, running plays usually meant for Alge Crumpler, he had roughly as many yards as his two Bengal seasons combined.

Erron Kinney Height: 6-5 Weight: 275 College: Florida Born: 28-Jul-1977 Age: 28

Year	Team	G	Rec	Pass	Yds	CPct	Yd/C	TD	DVOA	Rank	DPAR	Rank	PAR
2002	TEN	13	13	19	173	68%	13.3	0	19.3%	—	4.1	—	4.1
2003	TEN	16	41	58	381	71%	9.3	3	18.1%	12	8.9	8	8.8
2004	TEN	10	25	30	193	83%	7.7	3	13.7%	15	5.7	19	6.7
2005	*TEN*	*14*	*15*	*—*	*149*	*—*	*9.9*	*2*					

With the retirement of Frank Wycheck, Kinney became the Titans' primary tight end but battled injuries all season. While most football players blow their money on sports cars or tricked-out Cadillac Escalades, Kinney drives a cross between an SUV and a fire truck that he uses in his off-season job as a volunteer fireman. Seriously.

Jim Kleinsasser Height: 6-3 Weight: 272 College: North Dakota Born: 31-Jan-1977 Age: 28

Year	Team	G	Rec	Pass	Yds	CPct	Yd/C	TD	DVOA	Rank	DPAR	Rank	PAR
2002	MIN	14	37	50	393	74%	10.6	1	25.0%	7	11.7	8	10.9
2003	MIN	16	46	59	401	78%	8.7	4	28.9%	3	11.8	6	12.8
2004	MIN	1	2	3	24	67%	12.0	0	28.4%	—	0.8	—	1.0
2005	*MIN*	*14*	*29*	*—*	*311*	*—*	*10.7*	*3*					

The damage from losing Kleinsasser was less about his blocking and more about the fact that, without him, Mike Tice shied away from running the ball despite a stable of good running backs and a strong offensive line. He'll still be one of the best blockers in the league, and he's versatile enough to play both tight end and fullback, but Jermaine Wiggins will take away a lot of the passes he used to see.

Brian Kozlowski Height: 6-3 Weight: 250 College: Connecticut Born: 4-Oct-1970 Age: 35

Year	Team	G	Rec	Pass	Yds	CPct	Yd/C	TD	DVOA	Rank	DPAR	Rank	PAR
2002	ATL	13	6	9	59	67%	9.8	0	17.2%	—	1.6	—	1.3
2003	ATL	16	10	27	87	37%	8.7	0	-51.1%	42	-5.4	42	-5.1
2004	WAS	11	3	6	29	50%	9.7	0	0.9%	—	0.5	—	0.0
2005	WAS	14	5	—	31	—	6.8	0					

Brian is the all-time leader in career receiving yards by a Kozlowski, with his 946 topping former Chicago Bear Glen's 471. He also blocks. He was the only UConn product on an NFL roster until LB Alfred Fincher and QB Dan Orlovsky were drafted in 2005. Did we mention he blocks?

Donald Lee Height: 6-3 Weight: 255 College: Mississippi State Born: 31-Aug-1980 Age: 25

Year	Team	G	Rec	Pass	Yds	CPct	Yd/C	TD	DVOA	Rank	DPAR	Rank	PAR
2003	MIA	16	7	11	110	64%	15.7	1	20.6%	—	2.2	—	2.1
2004	MIA	16	13	20	110	65%	8.5	1	-28.1%	—	-2.2	—	-3.7
2005	MIA	15	18	—	193	—	10.5	2					

Someone needs to explain to us what kind of tight end never gets thrown the ball on third down. One out of every four passes to a tight end is thrown on third down. To Lee, zippo, the only tight end thrown at least 15 passes but none on third down. Lee is a strong blocker and good special teams player, but the Dolphins need to stop throwing him the ball—he just doesn't work as a receiver.

Chad Lewis Height: 6-6 Weight: 252 College: BYU Born: 5-Oct-1971 Age: 34

Year	Team	G	Rec	Pass	Yds	CPct	Yd/C	TD	DVOA	Rank	DPAR	Rank	PAR
2002	PHI	16	42	67	398	63%	9.5	3	-11.4%	32	0.5	31	-0.2
2003	PHI	16	23	40	293	58%	12.7	1	22.7%	8	7.0	13	5.8
2004	PHI	15	29	46	267	63%	9.2	3	-1.3%	—	3.6	—	3.1

Lewis has caught more touchdown passes from Donovan McNabb than any other player. He's now likely to retire as a result of his foot injury.

Dustin Lyman Height: 6-4 Weight: 245 College: Wake Forest Born: 5-Aug-1976 Age: 29

Year	Team	G	Rec	Pass	Yds	CPct	Yd/C	TD	DVOA	Rank	DPAR	Rank	PAR
2002	CHI	8	14	20	121	70%	8.6	2	12.8%	—	3.2	—	3.0
2003	CHI	9	11	13	80	85%	7.3	0	-8.5%	—	0.4	—	1.3
2004	CHI	16	11	23	73	48%	6.6	1	-41.7%	—	-4.5	—	-4.5
2005	CHI	16	19	—	159	—	8.4	2					

Lyman doesn't have very good hands and isn't a very good athlete. Nothing more than a backup.

Kris Mangum Height: 6-4 Weight: 249 College: Mississippi Born: 15-Aug-1973 Age: 32

Year	Team	G	Rec	Pass	Yds	CPct	Yd/C	TD	DVOA	Rank	DPAR	Rank	PAR
2002	CAR	14	16	29	159	55%	9.9	0	-12.1%	34	0.1	34	0.1
2003	CAR	16	17	29	199	59%	11.7	0	-5.8%	27	1.1	27	1.9
2004	CAR	15	34	58	323	59%	9.5	3	-10.7%	29	1.0	29	3.1
2005	CAR	16	23	—	225	—	9.6	2					

Had his best season last year, filling in admirably on a team with injuries everywhere. He's a good blocker and a good special teams player.

Brandon Manumaleuna   Height: 6-2   Weight: 288   College: Arizona   Born: 4-Jan-1980   Age: 25

Year	Team	G	Rec	Pass	Yds	CPct	Yd/C	TD	DVOA	Rank	DPAR	Rank	PAR
2002	STL	15	8	14	106	57%	13.3	1	16.9%	—	2.6	—	3.3
2003	STL	16	29	45	238	64%	8.2	2	-20.3%	36	-1.8	37	-2.4
2004	STL	16	15	21	174	71%	11.6	1	15.5%	—	3.7	—	3.4
2005	*STL*	*15*	*24*	*—*	*282*	*—*	*11.8*	*1*					

A huge, block-first tight end who isn't that great a blocker (though he does his best work against Julius Peppers), Manumaleuna should be a great end zone target but isn't: He was thrown to just twice in goal-to-go situations last year, scoring once. The Rams could really use a better receiving threat at tight end; free agent acquisition Roland Williams probably isn't the answer.

David Martin   Height: 6-4   Weight: 260   College: Tennessee   Born: 13-Mar-1979   Age: 26

Year	Team	G	Rec	Pass	Yds	CPct	Yd/C	TD	DVOA	Rank	DPAR	Rank	PAR
2002	GB	7	8	11	33	73%	4.1	1	-34.1%	—	-1.5	—	-0.9
2003	GB	16	13	17	79	76%	6.1	2	-1.6%	—	1.0	—	1.1
2004	GB	9	5	12	88	42%	17.6	0	-3.9%	—	0.7	—	1.7
2005	*GB*	*16*	*11*	*—*	*114*	*—*	*10.1*	*1*					

Martin contributed a lot to the Green Bay offense as an H-back. He's a good blocker and a good athlete. Joe Gibbs would love to have him.

Randy McMichael   Height: 6-3   Weight: 250   College: Georgia   Born: 28-Jun-1979   Age: 26

Year	Team	G	Rec	Pass	Yds	CPct	Yd/C	TD	DVOA	Rank	DPAR	Rank	PAR
2002	MIA	16	39	68	485	57%	12.4	4	4.2%	20	7.2	15	8.2
2003	MIA	16	49	83	598	59%	12.2	2	7.1%	18	8.1	10	7.3
2004	MIA	16	73	118	791	62%	10.8	4	3.9%	22	11.1	11	4.5
2005	*MIA*	*16*	*67*	*—*	*716*	*—*	*10.6*	*5*					

Never let it be said that the Dolphins' offense is without talent. McMichael is actually one of the league's best pass-catching tight ends. He managed career highs in yards, receptions, DPAR, and catch percentage even though the offense around him was scuffling. Mild warning: His list of most comparable tight ends over a three-year span includes a few guys who just fell off the bridge, including Stephen Alexander in 2001 (from 510 yards and 2 TD to 105 yards and 0 TD) and Mike Barber in 1981 (from 712 yards and 5 TD to 203 yards and 1 TD).

Shad Meier   Height: 6-4   Weight: 255   College: Kansas State   Born: 6-Jul-1978   Age: 27

Year	Team	G	Rec	Pass	Yds	CPct	Yd/C	TD	DVOA	Rank	DPAR	Rank	PAR
2002	TEN	11	1	4	17	25%	17.0	1	9.2%	—	0.5	—	0.3
2003	TEN	15	13	19	159	68%	12.2	0	-11.5%	—	0.2	—	0.3
2004	TEN	14	25	36	127	69%	5.1	2	-47.2%	38	-8.4	38	-8.6
2005	*NO*	*15*	*19*	*—*	*121*	*—*	*6.5*	*1*					

What's worse than averaging 5.1 yards per catch? Averaging 4.1 yards per catch. That's what Meier averaged if you take away his 29-yard reception against the Chiefs. Meier is expected to battle Boo Williams for the starting job in New Orleans, but he'll have to gain more than 15 feet per reception to crack the lineup.

Itula Mili   Height: 6-4   Weight: 260   College: BYU   Born: 20-Apr-1973   Age: 32

Year	Team	G	Rec	Pass	Yds	CPct	Yd/C	TD	DVOA	Rank	DPAR	Rank	PAR
2002	SEA	14	43	64	508	67%	11.8	2	1.7%	25	6.2	19	6.5
2003	SEA	16	46	62	492	74%	10.7	4	28.4%	4	13.7	3	13.4
2004	SEA	15	23	36	240	64%	10.4	1	3.8%	23	3.9	24	3.5
2005	*SEA*	*16*	*32*	*—*	*291*	*—*	*9.1*	*2*					

Mike Holmgren likes passing to the tight end, and Matt Hasselbeck does too. Because of that, Mili will always get some balls thrown his way, even though he's really more of a blocking tight end.

Billy Miller Height: 6-3 Weight: 230 College: USC Born: 24-Apr-1977 Age: 28

Year	Team	G	Rec	Pass	Yds	CPct	Yd/C	TD	DVOA	Rank	DPAR	Rank	PAR
2002	HOU	14	51	80	613	64%	12.0	3	35.2%	2	22.0	1	20.3
2003	HOU	16	40	64	355	63%	8.9	3	-0.2%	25	3.7	23	3.0
2004	HOU	16	17	34	178	50%	10.5	1	-20.9%	32	-1.7	31	-1.8
2005	HOU	16	21	—	219	—	10.6	2					

The best receiving tight end on an expansion team since Pete Mitchell was a Jaguar in 1995, Miller must rue the day that the Texans drafted Andre Johnson, their first honest-to-goodness wide receiver. Miller just hopes L.A. gets an expansion team for him to lead in receptions its first year. Until that happens, he'll be in Houston, trying to reverse his steady decline in receptions, yardage, and DVOA. Since Bennie Joppru is out for the year yet again, Miller is still the starter.

Heath Miller Height: 6-5 Weight: 256 College: Virginia Born: 22-Dec-1982 Age: 22

Year	Team	G	Rec	Pass	Yds	CPct	Yd/C	TD	DVOA	Rank	DPAR	Rank	PAR
2005	PIT	14	27	—	292	—	10.8	3					

No Steelers tight end has caught over 30 passes in a season since Eric Green caught 46 in 1994. Mark Bruener was the starting tight end for much of the past decade; he was a great run blocker who averaged about 15 receptions per year, and Bill Cowher liked him that way. Miller, with 144 catches and 19 TDs to his credit in three college seasons, will bring back the threat of the occasional 15-yard pass over the middle to the tight end. Miller isn't just a king-sized wide receiver; he's a dependable blocker, and he should unseat Jerame Tuman as the starter early in training camp.

Dave Moore Height: 6-2 Weight: 250 College: Pittsburgh Born: 11-Nov-1969 Age: 36

Year	Team	G	Rec	Pass	Yds	CPct	Yd/C	TD	DVOA	Rank	DPAR	Rank	PAR
2002	BUF	11	16	24	141	67%	8.8	2	6.5%	—	3.3	—	3.3
2003	BUF	15	7	18	82	39%	11.7	2	-37.4%	—	-2.3	—	-3.6
2004	TB	15	3	4	17	75%	5.7	0	-8.6%	—	0.2	—	0.4
2005	TB	14	4	—	11	—	2.7	0					

You too can have a 14-year NFL career, just like Dave Moore. You don't have to be huge, fast, or even particularly athletic. What's the secret? Just learn to throw a 15-yard spiral through your legs. Once a better-than-average tight end, Moore has kept his NFL career alive as a long snapper, a role he is likely to again fill this season in Tampa.

Ryan Neufeld Height: 6-4 Weight: 250 College: UCLA Born: 22-Nov-1975 Age: 30

Year	Team	G	Rec	Pass	Yds	CPct	Yd/C	TD	DVOA	Rank	DPAR	Rank	PAR
2003	BUF	16	3	5	41	60%	13.7	0	-1.8%	—	0.4	—	0.6
2004	BUF	16	6	14	61	43%	10.2	0	-25.8%	—	-1.3	—	-1.9
2005	BUF	16	5	—	63	—	12.6	0					

Primarily a special teams player, Neufeld occasionally plays some tight end.

Richard Owens Height: 6-4 Weight: 273 College: Louisville Born: 4-Nov-1980 Age: 25

Year	Team	G	Rec	Pass	Yds	CPct	Yd/C	TD	DVOA	Rank	DPAR	Rank	PAR
2004	MIN	6	8	8	69	100%	8.6	0	38.3%	—	2.6	—	2.4
2005	MIN	14	9	—	70	—	7.9	0					

The 273-pounder looks more like a tackle than a tight end, but he actually showed some promise as a receiver in limited action as a rookie.

Justin Peelle   Height: 6-4   Weight: 255   College: Oregon   Born: 15-Mar-1979 Age: 26

Year	Team	G	Rec	Pass	Yds	CPct	Yd/C	TD	DVOA	Rank	DPAR	Rank	PAR
2002	SD	13	3	7	15	43%	5.0	0	-75.9%	—	-2.7	—	-2.7
2003	SD	15	16	25	133	64%	8.3	1	-21.9%	37	-1.1	35	-0.6
2004	SD	16	10	20	84	50%	8.4	2	-48.4%	—	-4.1	—	-4.1
2005	SD	14	11	—	102	—	9.4	1					

Before Antonio Gates came around, there were some in the Chargers organization who thought Peelle would develop into a quality receiving threat. Those were lean, lean years for the Chargers organization.

Marcus Pollard   Height: 6-3   Weight: 247   College: Bradley   Born: 8-Feb-1972   Age: 33

Year	Team	G	Rec	Pass	Yds	CPct	Yd/C	TD	DVOA	Rank	DPAR	Rank	PAR
2002	IND	15	43	69	478	62%	11.1	6	3.2%	23	6.8	16	5.8
2003	IND	14	40	57	541	70%	13.5	3	23.7%	7	10.8	7	11.0
2004	IND	13	29	41	309	71%	10.7	6	27.1%	6	10.6	12	11.8
2005	DET	15	25	—	231	—	9.3	2					

With Dallas Clark set to take over the top tight end spot, the only Indianapolis Colt left from the 1995 AFC Championship team will finally move on. Pollard's production has dropped over the past several seasons, with fewer catches and fewer yards per catch. He still ranked high in our ratings last year, but remember that he was usually the fifth option whenever he was on the field, and therefore wasn't exactly being smothered by opposing defenses. Pollard signed with the Detroit Lions, and since Joey Harrington loves nothing more than checking down, many balls could be heading Pollard's way. But the drafting of Mike Williams means that Pollard will have competition for the role of big, strong red zone target.

Jeb Putzier   Height: 6-4   Weight: 256   College: Boise State   Born: 20-Jan-1979 Age: 26

Year	Team	G	Rec	Pass	Yds	CPct	Yd/C	TD	DVOA	Rank	DPAR	Rank	PAR
2002	DEN	3	0	1	0	0%	0.0	0	-79.3%	—	-0.5	—	-0.6
2003	DEN	4	4	5	34	80%	8.5	0	39.7%	—	1.4	—	1.0
2004	DEN	16	36	54	572	67%	15.9	2	35.9%	4	16.8	6	19.6
2005	DEN	16	40	—	466	—	11.7	3					

Denver is so busy pumping out 1,000-yard rushers that nobody notices their constant stream of impressive tight ends. One thing to remember for you fantasy leaguers is that, unlike most tight ends, Putzier sees the ball less in the red zone, not more. Putzier was thrown only 2 of his 54 passes in the red zone, and he wasn't thrown a single pass in a goal-to-go situation. That explains why a tight end with over 300 yards had just two touchdowns. It also helps explain why Putzier was second to only Alge Crumpler in yards per catch among tight ends—you can run farther when there's farther to go.

Walter Rasby   Height: 6-3   Weight: 252   College: Wake Forest   Born: 7-Sept-1972 Age: 33

Year	Team	G	Rec	Pass	Yds	CPct	Yd/C	TD	DVOA	Rank	DPAR	Rank	PAR
2002	WAS	12	9	13	85	69%	9.4	0	-3.2%	—	0.7	—	0.3
2003	NO	16	6	7	55	86%	9.2	0	38.2%	—	2.0	—	1.9
2004	WAS	6	5	9	52	56%	10.4	0	7.9%	—	1.1	—	0.6
2005	PIT	14	5	—	54	—	10.3	1					

Signed by Pittsburgh to serve as their fourth-string tight end.

Jay Riemersma   Height: 6-5   Weight: 255   College: Michigan   Born: 17-May-1973 Age: 32

Year	Team	G	Rec	Pass	Yds	CPct	Yd/C	TD	DVOA	Rank	DPAR	Rank	PAR
2002	BUF	16	32	48	350	67%	10.9	0	19.7%	9	9.9	10	9.8
2003	PIT	11	10	23	138	43%	13.8	1	-15.1%	—	-0.2	—	0.3
2004	PIT	11	7	9	82	78%	11.7	2	56.5%	—	4.4	—	4.8
2005	FA	12	11	—	91	—	8.4	1					

Now that, my friends, is a decline phase. It becomes even clearer if you look at the 2001 numbers: 53 catches, 590 yards, three TD, sixth in the league with 13.5 DPAR. The Steelers threw to him only once after Week 9, so don't get too excited over a high DVOA on seven catches. Unsigned as of press time and probably done.

Marcellus Rivers			Height: 6-4		Weight: 250	College: Oklahoma State					Born: 26-Oct-1978		Age: 27
Year	Team	G	Rec	Pass	Yds	CPct	Yd/C	TD	DVOA	Rank	DPAR	Rank	PAR
2002	NYG	14	2	2	25	100%	12.5	1	189.6%	—	2.3	—	2.5
2003	NYG	12	17	22	155	77%	9.1	0	16.5%	—	3.5	—	3.4
2004	NYG	16	5	12	36	42%	7.2	1	-40.5%	—	-2.3	—	-1.9
2005	*HOU*	*15*	*5*	*—*	*31*	*—*	*5.7*	*1*					

Rivers signed in Houston as a backup TE/special teams player when Bennie Joppru was lost for the 48th straight year due to injury. Nothing to see here.

Robert Royal			Height: 6-4		Weight: 257	College: LSU					Born: 15-May-1979		Age: 26
Year	Team	G	Rec	Pass	Yds	CPct	Yd/C	TD	DVOA	Rank	DPAR	Rank	PAR
2003	WAS	7	5	11	48	45%	9.6	0	-65.0%	—	-3.2	—	-2.9
2004	WAS	14	8	15	70	53%	8.8	4	10.4%	—	2.1	—	2.5
2005	*WAS*	*14*	*13*	*—*	*118*	*—*	*9.0*	*1*					

Royal was a touchdown machine at the end of the season, scoring four times on only five receptions over the last five weeks.

Matt Schobel			Height: 6-5		Weight: 257	College: TCU					Born: 4-Nov-1978		Age: 27
Year	Team	G	Rec	Pass	Yds	CPct	Yd/C	TD	DVOA	Rank	DPAR	Rank	PAR
2002	CIN	15	27	36	212	75%	7.9	2	7.9%	18	4.5	23	4.3
2003	CIN	15	24	30	332	80%	13.8	2	49.1%	1	8.7	9	8.4
2004	CIN	16	21	33	201	64%	9.6	4	11.2%	17	3.9	23	0.8
2005	*CIN*	*16*	*33*	*—*	*349*	*—*	*10.6*	*3*					

57% of passes to Matt Schobel were on third down. No other TE with at least 15 passes was used on first and second down less than half the time. Now, check out Schobel's DVOA on the three downs. On first down, −6.7% DVOA. On second down, −24.4% DVOA. On third down, +37.6% DVOA. For receivers, unlike quarterbacks, these trends are consistent. In 2003, he also received half his passes on third downs, and was very good. If Schobel's in the game on third down, guess who's getting the ball?

Mike Seidman			Height: 6-4		Weight: 261	College: UCLA					Born: 11-Feb-1981		Age: 24
Year	Team	G	Rec	Pass	Yds	CPct	Yd/C	TD	DVOA	Rank	DPAR	Rank	PAR
2003	CAR	12	5	9	35	56%	7.0	0	-31.4%	—	-1.0	—	-1.5
2004	CAR	16	13	13	123	100%	9.5	2	59.7%	—	6.4	—	7.3
2005	*CAR*	*16*	*18*	*—*	*182*	*—*	*10.2*	*3*					

Isn't much of a blocker and doesn't have a lot of speed but has soft hands and runs good routes.

Aaron Shea			Height: 6-3		Weight: 255	College: Michigan					Born: 5-Dec-1976		Age: 29
Year	Team	G	Rec	Pass	Yds	CPct	Yd/C	TD	DVOA	Rank	DPAR	Rank	PAR
2002	CLE	7	7	8	49	88%	7.0	0	-15.6%	—	-0.1	—	0.2
2003	CLE	4	2	5	9	40%	4.5	0	-69.6%	—	-1.4	—	-1.7
2004	CLE	15	26	48	252	54%	9.7	4	-4.4%	27	2.1	28	0.3
2005	*CLE*	*11*	*16*	*—*	*174*	*—*	*10.5*	*1*					

Shea got a lot of playing time last season due to Kellen Winslow's missing most of the year with a broken leg. He's an all-purpose player who doesn't excel at any one part of the game but somehow finds a way to make plays. He's battled injuries in the past and will need to do the same if the Browns are going to have an effective run-blocking tight end.

Visanthe Shiancoe   Height: 6-4   Weight: 250   College: Morgan State   Born: 18-Jun-1980 Age: 25

Year	Team	G	Rec	Pass	Yds	CPct	Yd/C	TD	DVOA	Rank	DPAR	Rank	PAR
2003	NYG	16	10	23	56	43%	5.6	2	-30.8%	—	-2.3	—	-3.1
2004	NYG	16	5	7	25	71%	5.0	1	3.3%	—	0.8	—	1.1
2005	*NYG*	*14*	*5*	*—*	*20*	*—*	*3.6*	*0*					

According to the U.S. Census Bureau, Visanthe has not been one of the 1,000 most popular baby names at any point in the past 100 years.

Jeremy Shockey   Height: 6-5   Weight: 253   College: Miami   Born: 18-Aug-1980 Age: 25

Year	Team	G	Rec	Pass	Yds	CPct	Yd/C	TD	DVOA	Rank	DPAR	Rank	PAR
2002	NYG	15	74	127	894	58%	12.1	2	4.2%	21	13.0	6	10.0
2003	NYG	9	48	70	535	69%	11.1	2	21.7%	9	12.2	5	10.5
2004	NYG	15	61	97	666	63%	10.9	6	10.9%	19	14.6	8	13.2
2005	*NYG*	*14*	*43*	*—*	*477*	*—*	*11.1*	*5*					

The biggest non-story of the Giants' off-season was Jeremy Shockey's absence from the team's involuntary-voluntary workouts. Eli Manning went to the media to voice his desire to get extra time to work with Shockey. Manning was right to want to get some extra reps with Shockey, as the tight end was much more productive with Kurt Warner throwing to him. Shockey with Warner: 41 catches, 484 yards, four TD, 68% catch percentage, 15.4 DPAR, 26.6% DVOA. Shockey with Manning: 20 catches, 182 yards, two TD, 54% catch percentage, −0.8 DPAR, −15.8% DVOA.

Alex Smith   Height: 6-4   Weight: 258   College: Stanford   Born: 22-May-1982 Age: 23

Year	Team	G	Rec	Pass	Yds	CPct	Yd/C	TD	DVOA	Rank	DPAR	Rank	PAR
2005	*TB*	*14*	*17*	*—*	*158*	*—*	*9.1*	*2*					

Jon Gruden is hoping to turn the "other" Alex Smith in the 2005 draft class into the Buccaneers' version of Antonio Gates. He's a huge target who showed the ability to get down the field in his senior year at Stanford, and should make a nice bookend in two tight end sets (along with Anthony Becht) that Gruden is sure to employ. He won't become an every-down player until he learns to block better, though.

L. J. Smith   Height: 6-3   Weight: 258   College: Rutgers   Born: 13-May-1980 Age: 25

Year	Team	G	Rec	Pass	Yds	CPct	Yd/C	TD	DVOA	Rank	DPAR	Rank	PAR
2003	PHI	15	27	46	320	59%	11.9	1	-12.8%	30	0.0	30	-0.6
2004	PHI	16	34	54	377	63%	11.1	5	10.9%	18	8.4	15	9.3
2005	*PHI*	*16*	*44*	*—*	*464*	*—*	*10.5*	*4*					

Smith is a fumbler and a pass dropper, but he works the middle of the field very well and has sneaky speed. Opponents rarely have the luxury of covering Smith with a nickelback or safety (TO and Westbrook occupy most of their attention), and Smith can eat up linebackers. Smith and Chad Lewis had 16 passes thrown to them in the red zone last year (eight each); with Lewis's future in doubt, Smith will get more opportunities.

Ben Steele   Height: 6-4   Weight: 233   College: Mesa   Born: 27-May-1978 Age: 27

Year	Team	G	Rec	Pass	Yds	CPct	Yd/C	TD	DVOA	Rank	DPAR	Rank	PAR
2004	GB	15	4	11	42	36%	10.5	0	-48.4%	—	-2.5	—	-2.3
2005	*GB*	*14*	*4*	*—*	*42*	*—*	*11.8*	*0*					

An H-back type and coverage ace. Steele's 2004 highlight was a fumble recovery in the 34–31 victory over the Vikings: Robert Ferguson fumbled a kick return; Steele beat Minnesota's Kevin Ross to the ball at the bottom of the pile. Steele may push David Martin for the number two tight end job.

Jerramy Stevens   Height: 6-7   Weight: 260   College: Washington   Born: 13-Nov-1979   Age: 26

Year	Team	G	Rec	Pass	Yds	CPct	Yd/C	TD	DVOA	Rank	DPAR	Rank	PAR
2002	SEA	11	26	42	252	62%	9.7	3	-14.7%	35	-0.5	35	-0.3
2003	SEA	16	6	19	72	32%	12.0	0	-45.8%	—	-3.1	—	-3.7
2004	SEA	16	31	47	349	66%	11.3	3	14.3%	13	8.5	14	9.7
2005	*SEA*	*16*	*29*	*—*	*273*	*—*	*9.6*	*2*					

An example of why Mike Holmgren no longer calls the shots in the Seahawks' draft room. Stevens has size and athleticism but was known in college as an underachiever and has done nothing in the NFL to shake that image.

Tony Stewart   Height: 6-5   Weight: 260   College: Penn State   Born: 9-Aug-1979   Age: 26

Year	Team	G	Rec	Pass	Yds	CPct	Yd/C	TD	DVOA	Rank	DPAR	Rank	PAR
2002	CIN	3	1	1	6	100%	6.0	0	-5.0%	—	0.1	—	0.1
2003	CIN	16	21	33	212	64%	10.1	0	2.7%	20	2.8	26	3.0
2004	CIN	16	10	25	48	40%	4.8	1	-50.3%	39	-6.4	37	-8.1
2005	*CIN*	*14*	*9*	*—*	*73*	*—*	*8.6*	*0*					

Stewart is in the last year of a two-year deal and last season he ranked near the bottom of the NFL in DPAR for tight ends. He may struggle for playing time behind Matt Schobel and Reggie Kelly.

Ben Troupe   Height: 6-4   Weight: 262   College: Florida   Born: 1-Sep-1982   Age: 23

Year	Team	G	Rec	Pass	Yds	CPct	Yd/C	TD	DVOA	Rank	DPAR	Rank	PAR
2004	TEN	14	33	54	329	61%	10.0	1	-29.9%	36	-5.4	35	-3.4
2005	*TEN*	*14*	*36*	*—*	*367*	*—*	*10.3*	*3*					

Expected to take over the role traditionally played by Frank Wycheck, Troupe struggled with injuries in training camp, and that slowed his development. He is a great athlete, however, and he closed the season with 13 catches for 174 yards in his final three games. With a full off-season and training camp, and with the limited wide receiver options the Titans have, Troupe could really emerge as a threat this season.

Jerame Tuman   Height: 6-4   Weight: 253   College: Michigan   Born: 24-Mar-1976   Age: 29

Year	Team	G	Rec	Pass	Yds	CPct	Yd/C	TD	DVOA	Rank	DPAR	Rank	PAR
2002	PIT	10	4	14	63	29%	15.8	1	-17.3%	—	-0.6	—	-1.4
2003	PIT	16	12	19	113	63%	9.4	0	-14.2%	—	-0.2	—	-0.2
2004	PIT	16	9	20	89	45%	9.9	3	-12.6%	—	0.1	—	0.2
2005	*PIT*	*14*	*14*	*—*	*119*	*—*	*8.2*	*1*					

Tuman, the tight end with the funny spelling and the hometown that's an oxymoron (Liberal, Kansas), has proven in six years that he's basically a replacement-level NFL player. Not that he's had much of an opportunity to prove otherwise: The Steelers threw a combined 29 passes to Tuman and Jay Riemersma last year. Tuman won't get many looks after the Steelers invested a first-round pick in Heath Miller this April.

Aaron Walker   Height: 6-6   Weight: 252   College: Florida   Born: 14-Mar-1980   Age: 25

Year	Team	G	Rec	Pass	Yds	CPct	Yd/C	TD	DVOA	Rank	DPAR	Rank	PAR
2003	SF	16	8	13	116	62%	14.5	1	42.9%	—	3.8	—	4.0
2004	SF	16	10	15	115	67%	11.5	0	1.1%	—	1.3	—	0.1
2005	*SF*	*16*	*18*	*—*	*202*	*—*	*11.0*	*2*					

Walker looks like strictly a backup after the emergence of Eric Johnson last season, but KUBIAK likes him.

Ben Watson

Height: 6-3 **Weight: 253** **College: Georgia** **Born: 18-Dec-1980 Age: 24**

Year	Team	G	Rec	Pass	Yds	CPct	Yd/C	TD	DVOA	Rank	DPAR	Rank	PAR
2004	NE	1	2	4	16	50%	8.0	0	-49.4%	—	-0.7	—	-0.4
2005	*NE*	*15*	*35*	*—*	*392*	*—*	*11.3*	*4*					

Watson had an excellent 2004 preseason, then got hurt in the opener against the Colts and missed the rest of the season with a knee injury of some kind. The Patriots would rather eat shards of glass than publicly reveal the details of player injuries. Watson is a Dallas Clark type with fine speed and agility who can line up in the slot or motion out of the back-field. Expect to see a lot of two-tight end sets, and Watson ain't gonna be the one blocking.

Jed Weaver

Height: 6-4 **Weight: 258** **College: Oregon** **Born: 11-Aug-1976 Age: 29**

Year	Team	G	Rec	Pass	Yds	CPct	Yd/C	TD	DVOA	Rank	DPAR	Rank	PAR
2002	MIA	13	6	9	75	67%	12.5	3	58.0%	—	4.8	—	4.8
2003	SF	16	35	53	437	66%	12.5	1	17.1%	13	7.8	11	7.5
2004	NE	10	8	12	93	67%	11.6	0	16.8%	—	2.5	—	3.1

Peripatetic tight end for hire who can catch a little bit. Yeah, we pulled *peripatetic* out of the thesaurus. Currently on the New England roster along with Fauria, Graham, and Watson, but likely to be somewhere else by the first week of the season. Like his house.

Jermaine Wiggins

Height: 6-2 **Weight: 255** **College: Georgia** **Born: 18-Jan-1975 Age: 30**

Year	Team	G	Rec	Pass	Yds	CPct	Yd/C	TD	DVOA	Rank	DPAR	Rank	PAR
2002	IND	3	2	5	17	40%	8.5	0	-108.4%	—	-3.1	—	-3.3
2002	CAR	4	8	10	45	80%	5.6	1	2.7%	—	0.8	—	-0.1
2003	CAR	16	8	20	80	40%	10.0	1	-40.2%	—	-2.7	—	-2.4
2004	MIN	14	71	92	705	77%	9.9	4	14.9%	12	16.0	7	16.5
2005	*MIN*	*16*	*46*	*—*	*508*	*—*	*11.0*	*5*					

From East Boston, which Chris Berman will not stop reminding us, Wiggins emerged in 2004 as a very good possession receiver after several years as more of a special teams/role player. He looks like he needs to lose some weight, and at 30 he's getting a little old, but the Vikings will get a lot of value out of Wiggins and the returning Jim Kleinsasser. And if you are looking for a candidate for the next undrafted free agent tight end to suddenly catch 71 passes for 705 yards, let us introduce you to...

Daniel Wilcox

Height: 6-1 **Weight: 245** **College: Appalachian State** **Born: 23-Mar-1977 Age: 28**

Year	Team	G	Rec	Pass	Yds	CPct	Yd/C	TD	DVOA	Rank	DPAR	Rank	PAR
2003	TB	2	0	—	0	—	—	0	—	—	—	—	—
2004	BAL	16	25	35	219	71%	8.8	1	10.7%	20	4.6	21	1.9
2005	*BAL*	*16*	*22*	*—*	*224*	*—*	*10.4*	*3*					

Todd Heap's ankle injury gave Wilcox a chance, and at the end of the season he started four games as an "H-back"-style tight end. In those four games, he hauled in 19 receptions for 147 yards, scored a touchdown, and looked strong taking out linebackers in front of Jamal Lewis. Wilcox even ranked third on the Ravens in DPAR in the red zone (2.0), behind only Heap and Clarence Moore. Terry Jones is more of a traditional tight end, but Heap and Wilcox together in two-TE sets would be very dangerous, and Wilcox comes at a nice low price. Small-sample-size caveats, of course.

Boo Williams

Height: 6-4 **Weight: 270** **College: Arkansas** **Born: 22-Jun-1979 Age: 26**

Year	Team	G	Rec	Pass	Yds	CPct	Yd/C	TD	DVOA	Rank	DPAR	Rank	PAR
2002	NO	16	13	31	143	42%	11.0	2	-30.2%	41	-3.3	40	-2.0
2003	NO	16	41	62	436	66%	10.6	5	29.9%	2	12.7	4	12.1
2004	NO	16	33	75	362	44%	11.0	2	-35.6%	37	-10.6	39	-11.5
2005	*NO*	*16*	*30*	*—*	*333*	*—*	*10.9*	*3*					

According to our statistics, Williams had a great year in 2003 but provided more negative value to his team than any other tight end in football in 2004. The question isn't what happened in 2004, but what happened in 2003, because he was just as bad in 2002. If Williams can't catch the ball at least half the time it is thrown to him, there's not much reason to have him around.

Kellen Winslow   Height: 6-4   Weight: 243   College: Miami   Born: 21-Jul-1983   Age: 22

Year	Team	G	Rec	Pass	Yds	CPct	Yd/C	TD	DVOA	Rank	DPAR	Rank	PAR
2004	CLE	2	5	11	50	45%	10.0	0	-28.4%	—	-1.0	—	-0.6

Some life advice: If you are biking down the freeway next to Peter Fonda and Dennis Hopper while Bob Dylan's "It's Alright Mama, I'm Only Bleeding" plays in the background, for the love of God please don't cheese off the dude in the pickup truck. And if you have a nonguaranteed, multimillion-dollar contract to play football, maybe you should lay off the bike altogether. Like everyone else, we're assuming he won't play at all in 2005.

Jason Witten   Height: 6-5   Weight: 257   College: Tennessee   Born: 6-May-1982   Age: 23

Year	Team	G	Rec	Pass	Yds	CPct	Yd/C	TD	DVOA	Rank	DPAR	Rank	PAR
2003	DAL	15	35	54	347	65%	9.9	1	3.2%	19	4.2	19	4.0
2004	DAL	16	87	122	980	71%	11.3	6	20.5%	7	25.1	3	24.2
2005	*DAL*	*16*	*71*	*—*	*848*	*—*	*12.0*	*9*					

He'll be one of the top three tight ends in football, and possibly the best. But in fantasy football, he could likely be had two or three rounds after Antonio Gates and Tony Gonzalez are off the board. Let someone else spend a third-round pick on Gates or Gonzo and swoop in during the sixth to get Witten. They'll end up with a good tight end and Kevan Barlow in their starting lineup. You'll have a good tight end and NFL rushing leader Kevin Jones. Don't say we didn't warn you.

George Wrighster   Height: 6-3   Weight: 260   College: Oregon   Born: 1-Apr-1981   Age: 24

Year	Team	G	Rec	Pass	Yds	CPct	Yd/C	TD	DVOA	Rank	DPAR	Rank	PAR
2003	JAC	15	13	20	150	65%	11.5	2	21.6%	—	3.6	—	4.0
2004	JAC	4	10	14	69	71%	6.9	1	-38.9%	—	-1.9	—	-2.0
2005	*JAC*	*14*	*16*	*—*	*153*	*—*	*9.8*	*3*					

Wrighster is a promising player as a pass-catching tight end, but missed the last 12 games of 2004 with a back injury and eventually had surgery to remove a bulging disc. That type of injury is often career-threatening, but Wrighster looked to be on track in April minicamps; if he's recovered, the Jags might release Kyle Brady. If he's not, you'll be seeing more of...

Todd Yoder   Height: 6-4   Weight: 250   College: Vanderbilt   Born: 18-Mar-1978   Age: 27

Year	Team	G	Rec	Pass	Yds	CPct	Yd/C	TD	DVOA	Rank	DPAR	Rank	PAR
2002	TB	14	2	5	26	40%	13.0	0	-3.3%	—	0.2	—	-0.5
2003	TB	16	7	11	68	64%	9.7	2	34.2%	—	2.7	—	2.5
2004	JAC	16	14	22	157	64%	11.2	0	-27.1%	—	-1.9	—	-1.2
2005	*JAC*	*14*	*19*	*—*	*179*	*—*	*9.3*	*1*					

One of a half dozen undistinguished journeymen hoping for a starting job in Jacksonville. May the best blocker win.

Going Deep

Adam Bergen, ARI: Bergen was a two-time Division I-AA All-American at Lehigh and is extremely muscular. Most people expected him to be drafted, and as a free agent, he certainly picked the right organization. Arizona's projected starting tight end, Eric Edwards, has five career catches. The backup, Lorenzo Diamond, was waived in May. No matter how often they go with a three-receiver set, you have to figure the Cardinals will at least have tight ends on the roster.

Bobby Blizzard, ARI: Next in line after Bergen, this North Carolina alum has a great name and spent the summer in NFL Europe.

Jerome Collins, STL: Collins played wide receiver, linebacker, and tight end—the position he was drafted to play—at Notre Dame, though he never started a game at TE. Yep, sounds like a Mike Martz pick.

Matt Cushing, PIT: A six-year vet, special teamer, H-back, and second tight end. Cushing is a valuable player even though he only catches one pass per year.

John Gilmore, CHI: Gilmore occasionally gets playing time on offense, but he's primarily in the league because he can block and tackle on special teams.

Lamont Hall, NO: Yet another cog in the Saints' special teams.

Keith Heinrich, CLE: Out for the year after an ACL tear, an injury which is apparently contagious in Cleveland.

Zachary Hilton, NO: An undrafted free agent now in his third year, Hilton is a 6′6″ ex–basketball player, which means he has coaches dreaming wild fantasies of Antonio Gates–like production. Given how badly Boo Williams played last year, they may decide to indulge them.

Tony Jackson, SEA: Jackson is a plus-size tight end who could play on the goal line or grow into a tackle à la Denver's Matt Lepsis.

Bennie Joppru, HOU: Concerned that Kellen Winslow would match him by losing his first two seasons to injury, Joppru tore his ACL in minicamp. That means he has now lost his first *three* seasons to injury.

Nate Lawrie, TB: Lawrie is a second-year tight end out of Yale who will compete for a roster spot. In 2003, the Bucs drafted both Lawrie and Dartmouth FB Casey Cramer, which must set some sort of record for Ivy League blockers in one draft.

Chad Mustard, CLE: Invited to training camp with Cleveland. Attempting to come back from a torn planter fascia in his left foot. Cleveland has a thousand tight ends, 999 of whom do not ride motorcycles.

Jeff Robinson, DAL: You too can become a millionaire by bending over and accurately throwing an oblong spheroid seven yards through your legs.

Bo Sciafe, TEN: Appropriately chosen in the sixth round of the draft after finishing his sixth year of eligibility at the University of Texas. Yes, sixth—Sciafe missed both 2000 and 2002 due to knee injuries. We hope he used the extra time and free tuition to get a doctorate or something. Good hands as a receiver, but he's a better run blocker than pass blocker.

Andy Stokes, NE: Mr. Irrelevant!

Rod Trafford, BUF: When Trafford was 13 he was in a car crash that seriously injured his father and brother. Although Trafford was left relatively unscathed, doctors examining him discovered a hole in his heart, ultimately repairing an atrial septal defect that could have proved fatal if not treated at such an early age. This medical intervention led the way for Trafford to eventually catch three passes for 25 yards as a fourth-string tight end.

Kickers

Sometime in the past year or so, the major NFL statistical services discovered that kickers do more than kick field goals and convert extra points. Kickoff data magically appeared on NFL.com sometime during the 2004 season, charting each kicker's total attempts, yards per kickoff, yards per return, and touchbacks.

Finally, a gaping statistical void had been filled. Think kickoff data isn't important? Compare Neil Rackers's 23 touchbacks and 67.5 yards per kickoff with Steve Christie's two touchbacks and 57.7 yards per kickoff. Rackers kicked off 70 times, Christie 71, so a net difference of 9.8 yards per kickoff amounts to just under 700 yards (690.9) over the course of 16 games. Is there any team in the NFL willing to give away 700 yards?

Field goal statistics also make little sense. Kickers are often ranked by points scored, which is silly (the guys on the best offenses win) or by raw percentages, which are primitive. Rian Lindell scored 117 points and converted 86% of his attempts last year but attempted 25 kicks of 39 yards or shorter, including 14 of 20 to 29 yards. The captain of your local high school girl's soccer team would convert a high percentage of 25-yard field goals. Matt Stover also scored 117 points and had an even better percentage (91%), but he was 11 for 13 from 40 yards and beyond.

The raw data for field goals by distance has been available for years, but our numbers collect the data into an easy-to-interpret format. We also adjust for weather and altitude, because it is easier to kick in a dome or Denver than in Buffalo in December.

In the following section, we give the last three years' worth of numbers for every kicker who played a role in 2004—major or minor—and/or will likely play a role in 2005, along with a 2005 projection of placekicking numbers (table 1).

The first line contains biographical data—each player's name, college, birthdate, and age. There is no height or weight data for kickers. If you are looking for height and weight data for kickers, you may require psychological counseling. Age is very simple, the number of years between the player's birth year and 2005, and the full birthdate is given for anyone who wants to either do research involving more complexity or register to vote in Swedish elections under the name "Ola Kimrin."

Next we give the last three years of player stats, starting with placekicking data. The first column is the official NFL total of games played, followed by extra points (XP) and field goals separated by distance: 18–29 yards, 30–39 yards, 40–49 yards, and 50+ yards. Then comes the total number of field goals made and attempted in each season and standard field goal percentage.

The following columns represent our estimate of the value of this kicker's field goals compared to how an average kicker would fare from the same down and distance (FGPts+). This number is adjusted for weather and altitude, and followed by rank among each year's kickers. To qualify for ranking in FGPts+, a kicker must attempt 20 field goals that season. 33 kickers are ranked for 2004, 34 for 2003, and 35 for 2002.

The next few columns give kickoff data. The first five columns represent kickoffs (KO), average gross length of kickoff (Avg), touchbacks (TB), kicks out of bounds (OoB), and average length of kickoff return (RetAv). These numbers are official NFL totals with the exception of kicks out of bounds, which we compute ourselves.

Then come our advanced metrics for kickoff value. Yards of field position are translated into points using a method that gives each yard line a point value based on the average next score an NFL offense is worth from that

TABLE 1. KICKER STATISTICS SAMPLE

Mike Vanderjagt College: West Virginia Born: 24-Mar-1970 Age: 35

Year	Team	G	XP	18-29	30-39	40-49	50+	Total	FG%	FGPts+	Rank	KO	Avg	TB	OoB	RetAv	KickPts+	Rank	NetPts+	Rank	WEA
2002	IND	16	34	8-9	6-7	6-12	3-3	23-31	74%	-3.9	27	77	59.0	1	0	20.5	-5.7	31	-0.4	18	-4.4
2003	IND	16	46	17-17	7-7	12-12	1-1	37-37	100%	18.1	1	99	60.2	4	0	21.5	-5.3	30	-7.3	29	-5.2
2004	IND	15	59	6-6	9-11	5-7	0-1	20-25	80%	-1.6	25	32	58.1	0	1	20.4	-4.9	32	-6.5	27	-3.5
2005	IND	16	49	—	—	—	—	25-29	84%	6.0											

point on the field. (This method is discussed further in the Statistical Toolbox at the beginning of this book; look for the special teams section.) Kickoff values are also adjusted for weather and altitude. We give both value of gross kickoffs compared to average (KickPts+) and value of net kickoffs compared to average (NetPts+) to help show how performance on kickoffs is split between a kicker and his coverage team.

Each number is also followed by rank among each year's kickers. To qualify for ranking in kickoff stats, a kicker must attempt 32 kickoffs that season. 34 kickers are ranked for 2004, 32 for 2003 as well as 2002. Onside kicks are not included in these metrics.

The final number is the weather adjustment for each kicker (WEA), combining the difference between weather-adjusted and nonadjusted value on FGPts+ and KickPts+. A higher number reflects a kicker who faced more difficult conditions, while a lower number reflects a kicker who faced easier conditions. In 2004, the highest WEA belongs to Jeff Reed of Pittsburgh (5.6) and the lowest WEA by a full-time kicker belongs to Jeff Wilkins of St. Louis (−4.6; punter/kickoff specialist Micah Knorr of Denver has a WEA of −4.8).

The last line gives a projection of placekicking numbers for 2005. All kickers are listed with a 16-game projection, even if two kickers are currently competing for a role on the same team.

Punters who were also used as kickoff specialists are included if they are expected to be used as kickoff specialists again in 2005, but punting statistics are found in a statistical appendix at the end of the book. A handful of free agent kickers and possible kickoff specialists are briefly discussed at the end of this chapter in a section we call "Going Deep." *FA* signifies a player who was still a free agent at press time, and the free agents most likely to be called upon in case of injury have generic six-game projections.

TABLE 2. TOP 10 KICKERS BY FG VALUE, KICKOFF VALUE, AND TOTAL VALUE, 2004

Rnk	Player	Tm	FGPts+	Rnk	Player	Tm	KckPts+	Rnk	Player	Tm	TotPts+
1	Adam Vinatieri	NE	15.2	1	Neil Rackers	ARI	11.9	1	David Akers	PHI	25.0
2	David Akers	PHI	13.7	2	David Akers	PHI	11.3	2	Neil Rackers	ARI	19.1
3	Matt Stover	BAL	12.9	3	Sebastian Janikowski	OAK	5.3	3	Adam Vinatieri	NE	18.6
4	Shayne Graham	CIN	12.1	4	Olindo Mare	MIA	5.3	4	Matt Stover	BAL	14.9
5	Josh Brown	SEA	8.3	5	Jay Feely	ATL	4.9	5	Sebastian Janikowski	OAK	12.9
6	Sebastian Janikowski	OAK	7.5	6	Jason Hanson	DET	4.6	6	Shayne Graham	CIN	12.0
7	Ryan Longwell	GB	7.3	7	Kris Brown	HOU	4.0	7	Josh Brown	SEA	8.2
8	Neil Rackers	ARI	7.2	8	Toby Gowin	NYJ	3.7	8	Jeff Reed	PIT	7.6
9	Jeff Reed	PIT	6.4	9	Adam Vinatieri	NE	3.5	9	Jason Elam	DEN	6.7
10	Jason Elam	DEN	6.3	10	Josh Scobee	JAC	3.2	10	Olindo Mare	MIA	6.5

David Akers

College: Louisville   **Born: 9-Dec-1974   Age: 31**

Year	Team	G	XP	18-29	30-39	40-49	50+	Total	FG%	FGPts+	Rank	KO	Avg	TB	OoB	RetAv	KickPts+	Rank	NetPts+	Rank	WEA
2002	PHI	16	43	9-9	14-16	6-7	1-2	30-34	88%	9.5	3	89	62.1	10	1	21.5	5.5	4	6.7	8	4.0
2003	PHI	16	42	9-9	7-7	6-10	2-3	24-29	83%	7.5	12	83	63.3	8	1	21.5	7.2	3	16.7	1	4.5
2004	PHI	16	41	4-4	6-7	15-18	2-3	27-32	84%	13.7	2	86	64.9	12	0	23.2	11.3	2	15.0	1	3.0
2005	PHI	16	42	—	—	—	—	26-32	83%	7.7											

We apologize to those of you who have heard this from us before, but we want to make this clear for the new folks: David Akers is the best kicker in football. Not Adam Vinatieri, not Sebastian Janikowski, and certainly not Mike Vanderjagt. Some kickers can kick field goals but not kickoffs, others have length on kickoffs but no accuracy on field goals. Most kickers alternate good and bad years with no consistency. Only Akers ranks among the league's top kickers in both field goal and kickoff value year after year. The only reason he's never nailed a last-second field goal to win the Super Bowl is that he's never had the chance.

Morten Andersen

College: Michigan State   Born: 19-Aug-1960 Age: 45

Year	Team	G	XP	18-29	30-39	40-49	50+	Total	FG%	FGPts+	Rank	KO	Avg	TB	OoB	RetAv	KickPts+	Rank	NetPts+	Rank	WEA
2002	KC	14	51	6-6	10-10	5-9	1-1	22-26	85%	5.3	7	64	59.2	6	0	21.4	-2.1	26	-6.2	28	1.2
2003	KC	16	58	3-3	8-8	5-8	0-1	16-20	80%	5.1	14	0	0.0	0	0	0.0	3.5	9	-3.6	24	2.8
2004	MIN	16	45	9-9	5-7	4-6	0-0	18-22	82%	-1.9	26	8	54.1	0	0	23.9	-0.4	—	-2.4	—	-2.7
2005	FA	6	13	—	—	—	—	6-8	75%	-0.5											

Morten Andersen is the NFL's all-time record holder for most games played, with 354. (That's one more than the Titans' Gary Anderson, who missed one game in 2004 and is now one game behind Morten.) Although he's the league's career leader in 50-yard field goals, having made 40 of his 83 career attempts, Andersen's leg strength is nothing like what it used to be. He hasn't kicked off regularly in two years, and he hasn't made a field goal of more than 50 yards in the last two years. Minnesota isn't bringing him back, but he could show up in midseason if somebody has an injury.

Gary Anderson

College: Syracuse   Born: 16-Jul-1959 Age: 46

Year	Team	G	XP	18-29	30-39	40-49	50+	Total	FG%	FGPts+	Rank	KO	Avg	TB	OoB	RetAv	KickPts+	Rank	NetPts+	Rank	WEA
2002	MIN	14	36	9-9	5-5	3-8	1-1	18-23	78%	-3.3	25	8	55.0	0	0	19.6	-1.4	—	-2.2	—	-1.5
2003	TEN	15	42	5-5	12-12	10-14	0-0	27-31	87%	9.3	8	0	0.0	0	0	0.0	0.7	14	1.6	18	-0.7
2004	TEN	15	37	4-5	4-4	9-12	0-1	17-22	77%	0.8	21	0	0.0	0	0	0.0	0.0	—	0.0	—	-0.2

"Just when I thought I was out, they pull me back in." Gary Anderson is the first number on the Tennessee Titans' speed dial every time Joe Nedney hurts himself. Like the other old Anderson(en), he has accuracy but no longer distance, and he should be home with the family for good.

Doug Brien

College: California   Born: 24-Nov-1970 Age: 35

Year	Team	G	XP	18-29	30-39	40-49	50+	Total	FG%	FGPts+	Rank	KO	Avg	TB	OoB	RetAv	KickPts+	Rank	NetPts+	Rank	WEA
2002	MIN	6	5	3-3	1-1	1-2	0-0	5-6	83%	-2.6	—	31	60.7	2	0	22.0	-0.5	—	-3.1	—	-1.6
2003	NYJ	16	24	5-5	15-15	7-8	0-4	27-32	84%	8.9	10	72	59.9	1	0	21.1	-4.1	27	-7.1	28	3.0
2004	NYJ	16	33	9-10	4-6	10-11	1-2	24-29	83%	3.7	12	3	66.3	0	0	19.3	0.2	—	1.0	—	0.4
2005	CHI	16	30	—	—	—	—	22-28	79%	3.5											

There is a good chance that Brien will have a better field goal percentage in Chicago than his famous replacement in New York, Mike Nugent. The real problem with Brien isn't his field goal accuracy but his difficulty with kickoffs, which is why the Jets had their punter kicking off last year. Brien can't be much worse than Edinger, though.

Josh Brown

College: Nebraska   Born: 29-Apr-1979 Age: 26

Year	Team	G	XP	18-29	30-39	40-49	50+	Total	FG%	FGPts+	Rank	KO	Avg	TB	OoB	RetAv	KickPts+	Rank	NetPts+	Rank	WEA
2003	SEA	16	48	5-5	10-11	6-11	1-3	22-30	73%	1.7	17	84	60.2	3	2	20.6	-2.9	24	-2.9	22	2.5
2004	SEA	16	40	8-8	8-9	6-7	1-1	23-25	92%	8.3	5	82	61.4	5	1	21.8	-0.1	21	-3.3	23	0.3
2005	SEA	16	42	—	—	—	—	25-30	84%	8.6											

Brown has improved on kickoffs. He had 21 kickoffs of 60 yards or less last season (not counting onside kicks or squib kicks to end a half) and did not reach the end zone with a normal kickoff until Week 8. After that, he had five touchbacks and several other kicks into the end zone . . . Both of Brown's missed field goals were wide left . . . Once kicked a 61-yarder in the Oklahoma State 8-on-8 high school championships. Also rushed for 471 yards and six TDs in a high school game.

Kris Brown

College: Nebraska   Born: 23-Dec-1976 Age: 28

Year	Team	G	XP	18-29	30-39	40-49	50+	Total	FG%	FGPts+	Rank	KO	Avg	TB	OoB	RetAv	KickPts+	Rank	NetPts+	Rank	WEA
2002	HOU	16	20	3-4	1-1	11-14	2-5	17-24	71%	2.1	14	56	60.8	2	1	22.4	2.4	11	1.8	15	2.1
2003	HOU	16	27	4-4	8-8	5-6	1-4	18-22	82%	5.3	13	61	63.8	8	0	21.9	5.1	6	6.1	6	1.6
2004	HOU	16	34	7-7	3-5	6-9	1-3	17-24	71%	-4.2	31	69	63.8	9	1	23.2	4.0	7	-1.9	19	-3.9
2005	HOU	16	38	—	—	—	—	24-29	81%	1.3											

This might seem obvious, but it's hard to be an NFL kicker when you have an injured pelvis. Through the first seven games, Brown was 13 for 14 on field goals, but after that he was just 4 for 10, missing a field goal in every game in which he attempted one. Brown had off-season surgery to correct the injury, and the Texans are confident enough in Brown and his recovery to sign him to a five-year extension.

Matt Bryant College: Baylor Born: 29-May-1975 Age: 30

Year	Team	G	XP	18-29	30-39	40-49	50+	Total	FG%	FGPts+	Rank	KO	Avg	TB	OoB	RetAv	KickPts+	Rank	NetPts+	Rank	WEA
2002	MIA	16	30	9-9	14-19	3-4	0-0	26-32	81%	-3.8	26	75	60.4	2	1	22.5	-1.9	25	-6.1	27	3.3
2003	NYG	11	17	3-4	4-5	4-5	0-0	11-14	79%	-0.3	22	39	60.4	2	2	20.4	-1.8	22	2.1	17	0.8
2004	IND	1	5	0-0	0-0	0-1	0-0	0-1	0%	-2.0	—	6	59.5	0	0	20.0	-0.8	—	-0.7	—	-0.3
2004	MIA	3	7	1-1	0-0	2-2	0-0	3-3	100%	2.5	—	12	63.7	0	0	18.9	0.0	—	2.5	—	-0.2
2005	*TB*	*16*	*35*	—	—	—	—	*23-29*	*79%*	*0.5*											

Signed in the off-season to shore up Tampa Bay's shaky kicking situation, Bryant faces a likely training camp challenge from NFL Europe vet Todd France.

John Carney College: Notre Dame Born: 20-Apr-1964 Age: 41

Year	Team	G	XP	18-29	30-39	40-49	50+	Total	FG%	FGPts+	Rank	KO	Avg	TB	OoB	RetAv	KickPts+	Rank	NetPts+	Rank	WEA
2002	NO	16	37	9-9	11-13	11-12	0-1	31-35	89%	8.1	5	26	64.2	2	1	22.6	-0.3	—	2.9	—	-4.1
2003	NO	16	36	6-6	10-12	5-9	1-3	22-30	73%	-4.3	26	20	55.5	1	0	22.6	0.2	—	-7.3	—	-3.1
2004	NO	16	38	3-3	12-15	5-6	2-3	22-27	82%	3.0	16	42	62.4	0	0	21.6	0.8	17	10.4	7	-4.3
2005	*NO*	*16*	*37*	—	—	—	—	*19-24*	*81%*	*-0.5*											

In 2003, when John Carney missed an extra point with no time left after a spectacular touchdown against Jacksonville, the Saints could have overreacted like a certain team in New Jersey did this year and wasted a high draft pick on a new kicker. But the Saints kept Carney around, and he rewarded them with a solid year. He was accurate from long range and kicked off as well as he ever has.

Jeff Chandler College: Florida Born: 18-Jun-1979 Age: 26

Year	Team	G	XP	18-29	30-39	40-49	50+	Total	FG%	FGPts+	Rank	KO	Avg	TB	OoB	RetAv	KickPts+	Rank	NetPts+	Rank	WEA
2002	SF	6	14	3-3	1-1	4-7	0-1	8-12	67%	-1.8	20	29	59.3	1	1	21.8	-2.5	—	-9.1	—	0.4
2003	SF	2	7	5-5	1-1	0-1	0-0	6-7	86%	-1.9	—	16	60.1	1	1	20.8	-0.5	—	-0.1	—	-1.2
2004	WAS	5	14	4-4	0-2	1-1	0-1	5-8	63%	-3.4	29	14	62.2	0	0	20.0	0.6	—	1.8	—	1.0
2005	*WAS*	*16*	*28*	—	—	—	—	*21-27*	*77%*	*-2.2*											

Exhibit A in the Case against Drafting a Kicker. Since wasting a fourth-round pick on the University of Florida star three years ago, San Francisco has had five different guys attempt field goals for them, none of whom is on their roster as we head to press.

Steve Christie College: William and Mary Born: 13-Nov-1967 Age: 38

Year	Team	G	XP	18-29	30-39	40-49	50+	Total	FG%	FGPts+	Rank	KO	Avg	TB	OoB	RetAv	KickPts+	Rank	NetPts+	Rank	WEA
2002	SD	16	35	8-8	5-6	4-9	1-3	18-26	69%	-5.0	29	21	54.6	0	0	17.1	-1.1	—	0.7	—	2.7
2003	SD	16	36	7-7	3-3	3-7	2-3	15-20	75%	-0.3	21	43	56.2	0	0	19.9	-5.7	31	-8.1	30	0.4
2004	NYG	16	33	9-9	6-8	4-7	3-4	22-28	79%	1.0	19	71	57.7	2	1	19.4	-4.0	31	-3.6	24	2.3

For $3,000 this past April (flights not included), a website offered a five-day tour of Scotland hosted by Steve Christie. Your trip would have included rounds of golf at the legendary Old Course at St. Andrew's and Carnoustie, plus luxury suite seats for a Glasgow Celtic FC home game. Now, playing golf at St. Andrew's and Carnoustie sounds amazing, but are there really that many Steve Christie fans out there that would sign up for this package? And why Scotland? If any of our readers went on the trip, please let us know how it was.

Jose Cortez College: Oregon State Born: 27-May-1975 Age: 30

Year	Team	G	XP	18-29	30-39	40-49	50+	Total	FG%	FGPts+	Rank	KO	Avg	TB	OoB	RetAv	KickPts+	Rank	NetPts+	Rank	WEA
2002	SF	10	25	8-10	7-8	3-6	0-0	18-24	75%	-6.4	34	53	62.8	5	0	23.3	0.1	15	0.4	10	-2.0
2002	WAS	4	9	3-3	1-1	1-4	0-0	5-8	63%	-2.1	—	18	60.6	2	0	21.6	1.3	—	3.5	—	3.3
2003	MIN	2	0	0-0	0-0	0-0	0-0	0-0	0%	-2.2	25	8	66.1	1	0	22.4	0.2	17	2.9	11	0.3
2004	MIN	8	0	0-0	0-0	0-0	0-0	0-0	0%	0.0	—	38	63.9	4	1	27.0	1.2	14	-12.3	32	-0.3

A former XFL player, Cortez has only moderate leg strength and little accuracy. He's only a marginal player, someone teams pick up when they're desperate for a kicker, and if does show up somewhere it will likely be as a kickoff specialist.

Billy Cundiff

College: Drake   Born: 30-Mar-1980   Age: 25

Year	Team	G	XP	18-29	30-39	40-49	50+	Total	FG%	FGPts+	Rank	KO	Avg	TB	OoB	RetAv	KickPts+	Rank	NetPts+	Rank	WEA
2002	DAL	16	25	3-3	5-7	4-8	0-1	12-19	63%	-8.5	32	30	58.1	1	0	21.6	-0.3	—	1.3	—	-0.5
2003	DAL	15	30	11-11	5-6	4-7	3-5	23-29	79%	1.6	18	3	63.7	0	0	27.0	0.0	—	-0.8	—	0.5
2004	DAL	16	31	7-7	4-4	9-13	0-2	20-26	77%	3.3	15	67	61.7	3	1	17.5	-0.4	22	12.5	3	2.4
2005	*DAL*	*16*	*35*	—	—	—	—	*24-29*	*82%*	*5.1*											

You can do a lot better than Billy Cundiff for your fantasy team. Heck, the Cowboys could do better than Cundiff for their real team, but they have more important things to deal with than replacing a perfectly acceptable yet lackluster kicker.

Phil Dawson

College: Texas   Born: 23-Jan-1975   Age: 30

Year	Team	G	XP	18-29	30-39	40-49	50+	Total	FG%	FGPts+	Rank	KO	Avg	TB	OoB	RetAv	KickPts+	Rank	NetPts+	Rank	WEA
2002	CLE	16	34	9-10	6-8	5-7	2-3	22-28	79%	-2.4	23	77	59.7	7	1	20.4	0.3	18	2.0	14	1.8
2003	CLE	13	20	9-9	4-5	3-5	2-2	18-21	86%	3.0	16	54	60.3	1	1	20.4	-1.0	20	2.4	15	1.9
2004	CLE	16	28	11-11	6-8	6-9	1-1	24-29	83%	3.3	14	69	60.5	5	1	22.6	2.5	12	-0.9	15	1.2
2005	*CLE*	*16*	*28*	—	—	—	—	*22-28*	*79%*	*1.0*											

Dawson has been with the Browns since they returned to Cleveland, and he's easily their most consistent player. He converted 83% of his field goal attempts last season and didn't miss a kick inside of 30 yards.

Paul Edinger

College: Michigan State   Born: 17-Jan-1978   Age: 27

Year	Team	G	XP	18-29	30-39	40-49	50+	Total	FG%	FGPts+	Rank	KO	Avg	TB	OoB	RetAv	KickPts+	Rank	NetPts+	Rank	WEA
2002	CHI	16	29	4-4	5-6	8-10	5-8	22-28	79%	9.6	2	67	60.3	2	2	22.5	-0.2	20	-1.6	20	0.8
2003	CHI	16	27	5-5	9-13	9-14	3-4	26-36	72%	-0.8	23	69	57.7	1	1	21.4	-4.2	28	-8.7	31	2.7
2004	CHI	16	22	6-7	2-5	4-7	3-5	15-24	63%	-6.1	32	56	58.4	0	1	21.7	-3.0	28	-5.4	26	2.2
2005	*MIN*	*16*	*44*	—	—	—	—	*20-25*	*81%*	*3.4*											

Edinger once seemed like one of the league's most promising young kickers, but he's had problems kicking field goals for two years and his kickoffs are too short. Chicago signed Doug Brien to replace him, and he headed to Minnesota, where he becomes a viable fantasy option thanks to at least 20 more extra points.

Jason Elam

College: Hawaii   Born: 8-Mar-1970   Age: 35

Year	Team	G	XP	18-29	30-39	40-49	50+	Total	FG%	FGPts+	Rank	KO	Avg	TB	OoB	RctAv	KickPts+	Rank	NetPts+	Rank	WEA
2002	DEN	16	42	10-10	7-9	5-11	4-6	26-36	72%	-5.9	30	44	63.1	1	2	22.8	-2.7	27	-0.8	19	-5.2
2003	DEN	16	39	10-11	6-6	9-11	2-3	27-31	87%	7.8	11	0	0.0	0	0	0.0	-0.2	—	-0.4	—	-1.8
2004	DEN	16	42	10-10	7-8	9-12	3-4	29-34	85%	6.3	10	1	18.0	0	0	36.0	0.4	—	0.4	—	-2.4
2005	*DEN*	*16*	*41*	—	—	—	—	*25-30*	*83%*	*4.8*											

How many people have had better lives than Jason Elam? First, he spends his college years in Hawaii studying communications and setting team and conference records for scoring. Then he gets picked up by Denver, hands down the greatest place a kicker could ever spend his career. At some point during all of this, he marries a Bronco cheerleader. Not a bad way to live.

Aaron Elling

College: Wyoming   Born: 31-May-1978   Age: 27

Year	Team	G	XP	18-29	30-39	40-49	50+	Total	FG%	FGPts+	Rank	KO	Avg	TB	OoB	RetAv	KickPts+	Rank	NetPts+	Rank	WEA
2003	MIN	16	48	7-7	6-8	4-7	1-3	18-25	72%	-4.9	27	74	59.8	1	3	21.3	-5.0	29	0.3	19	-4.5
2004	TEN	1	2	1-1	0-1	0-0	0-0	1-2	50%	-2.5	—	4	62.0	0	0	24.8	-0.3	—	-0.9	—	-0.3
2004	MIN	7	0	0-0	0-0	0-0	0-0	0-0	0%	0.0	—	35	63.8	0	0	23.6	0.7	18	-0.3	16	-1.4
2005	*MIN*	*16*	*44*	—	—	—	—	*20-25*	*80%*	*1.2*											

Aaron Elling was cut by Minnesota in the preseason because he couldn't kick field goals, signed with Tennessee after Joe Nedney got injured, was waived after one game, then signed back in Minnesota to be a kickoff specialist. Then he broke his ankle halfway into the season. This year Elling is back in Minnesota, where he will compete for a job with Paul Edinger. A role as a kickoff specialist is more likely than beating out Edinger entirely.

Jay Feely

College: Michigan · Born: 23-May-1976 Age: 29

Year	Team	G	XP	18-29	30-39	40-49	50+	Total	FG%	FGPts+	Rank	KO	Avg	TB	OoB	RetAv	KickPts+	Rank	NetPts+	Rank	WEA
2002	ATL	16	42	8-10	12-14	11-13	1-3	32-40	80%	-0.3	17	92	64.2	16	2	22.0	5.4	5	7.8	6	-4.4
2003	ATL	16	32	6-6	9-11	4-7	0-3	19-27	70%	-5.4	28	69	63.5	7	2	19.8	5.1	5	15.7	2	-4.3
2004	ATL	16	40	8-8	7-9	3-6	0-0	18-23	78%	-3.9	30	73	63.8	13	2	20.0	4.9	5	10.5	6	-4.2
2005	NYG	16	35	—	—	—	—	21-26	82%	4.2											

For four full years, fantasy football fans feared Feely's failed figgies. For some reason, he and the Georgia Dome did not mix, and now he leaves a rather good offense in Atlanta for a rather bad one at Giants Stadium. He has a strong leg and has been a serviceably good kicker outside of Atlanta (46 for 57, or about 80%), so expect any drop-off in extra points attempted to be offset by gains in field goals made.

Shayne Graham

College: Virginia Tech · Born: 9-Dec-1977 Age: 27

Year	Team	G	XP	18-29	30-39	40-49	50+	Total	FG%	FGPts+	Rank	KO	Avg	TB	OoB	RetAv	KickPts+	Rank	NetPts+	Rank	WEA
2002	CAR	11	21	3-5	2-3	6-8	2-2	13-18	72%	-1.4	18	5	66.0	0	0	21.0	0.0	—	0.2	—	0.1
2003	CIN	16	40	5-5	10-10	7-8	0-2	22-25	88%	10.2	5	77	62.2	4	2	20.7	0.9	13	3.5	10	3.5
2004	CIN	16	41	7-7	10-12	7-8	3-4	27-31	87%	12.1	4	82	60.5	2	0	19.6	0.0	20	13.0	2	5.1
2005	CIN	16	37	—	—	—	—	23-29	81%	3.7											

Prior to a solid 2004 season, Graham was best known for his stirring performance as Opie Taylor in the stage production of *The Andy Griffith Show*. Seriously, Graham ranked fifth in the NFL in field goal percentage last season and his ability to consistently kick gives Marvin Lewis one less thing to worry about.

Martin Gramatica

College: Kansas State · Born: 27-Nov-1975 Age: 30

Year	Team	G	XP	18-29	30-39	40-49	50+	Total	FG%	FGPts+	Rank	KO	Avg	TB	OoB	RetAv	KickPts+	Rank	NetPts+	Rank	WEA
2002	TB	16	32	7-8	14-15	6-10	5-6	32-39	82%	7.3	6	81	64.5	6	2	21.8	4.1	8	11.0	3	-0.5
2003	TB	16	33	9-9	3-6	3-8	1-3	16-26	62%	-9.9	32	67	61.4	5	1	23.6	0.7	15	-1.2	21	-0.9
2004	TB	11	21	6-7	3-6	1-5	1-1	11-19	58%	-14.7	33	46	62.5	6	1	21.6	-2.0	—	7.7	—	-2.7
2004	IND	4	0	0-0	0-0	0-0	0-0	0-0	0%	0.0	—	21	60.4	1	1	22.1	0.7	25	-2.8	10	-1.2
2005	FA	6	13	—	—	—	—	7-9	78%	-0.2											

Gramatica went from "Automatica" to "Auto-shankica" in five years and provides a good example for the Jets as to why it's dangerous to invest a high-round pick in a kicker. Namely—that they're all flakes who will eventually hit a major slump and get released. Because of the third-round pick invested in him and the big contract he carried, the Buccaneers gave Gramatica every chance imaginable to kick himself out of his slump, but he couldn't do it. And when you go 4 for 11 from 30 to 49 yards, as Gramatica did last year, you can't kick in the NFL. A brief stint as a kickoff specialist in Indianapolis didn't work out, so Gramatica finds himself out of work as we go to press.

John Hall

College: Wisconsin · Born: 17-Mar-1974 Age: 31

Year	Team	G	XP	18-29	30-39	40-49	50+	Total	FG%	FGPts+	Rank	KO	Avg	TB	OoB	RetAv	KickPts+	Rank	NetPts+	Rank	WEA
2002	NYJ	16	35	9-9	9-11	6-10	0-1	24-31	77%	-2.2	22	79	62.4	5	0	21.3	1.4	16	2.6	12	3.5
2003	WAS	16	26	8-8	7-9	6-9	4-7	25-33	76%	3.1	15	72	61.5	11	0	20.6	3.7	8	7.0	5	2.6
2004	WAS	8	13	4-4	3-3	1-3	0-1	8-11	73%	-2.8	28	30	60.8	1	0	23.0	-0.5	—	-4.8	—	0.4
2005	WAS	16	29	—	—	—	—	22-28	81%	3.9											

Hall missed half the 2004 season because of an injury to his kicking groin. He'll be competing with Jeff Chandler for the starting job in 2005.

Jason Hanson

College: Washington State · Born: 17-Jun-1970 Age: 35

Year	Team	G	XP	18-29	30-39	40-49	50+	Total	FG%	FGPts+	Rank	KO	Avg	TB	OoB	RetAv	KickPts+	Rank	NetPts+	Rank	WEA
2002	DET	16	31	8-8	8-9	7-8	0-3	23-28	82%	2.6	11	74	64.5	5	0	22.9	5.3	6	8.5	4	-4.4
2003	DET	16	26	7-7	6-6	5-6	4-4	22-23	96%	10.5	3	66	64.2	10	2	24.8	3.9	7	-4.7	25	-5.2
2004	DET	16	28	9-9	10-11	5-8	0-0	24-28	86%	0.9	20	71	64.3	14	2	19.3	4.6	6	12.3	4	-4.3
2005	DET	16	38	—	—	—	—	24-30	80%	0.3											

Hanson is a solid kicker whose reputation is probably a little better than it should be because he kicks in a dome. The Lions love him as much because he's been a good guy off the field as for what he's done on the field. He'll probably retire a Lion.

Sebastian Janikowski

College: Florida State — Born: 3-Mar-1978 — Age: 27

Year	Team	G	XP	18-29	30-39	40-49	50+	Total	FG%	FGPts+	Rank	KO	Avg	TB	OoB	RetAv	KickPts+	Rank	NetPts+	Rank	WEA
2002	OAK	16	50	10-11	7-8	7-12	2-2	26-33	79%	2.1	13	97	66.6	22	1	24.7	9.2	1	-2.1	21	-1.9
2003	OAK	16	28	6-6	6-6	9-10	1-3	22-25	88%	9.7	6	66	62.9	7	2	25.9	0.5	16	-12.0	32	-1.6
2004	OAK	16	31	8-8	7-8	8-10	2-2	25-28	89%	7.5	6	76	64.1	12	0	23.5	5.3	3	-0.3	14	-2.5
2005	OAK	16	38	—	—	—	—	25-30	82%	6.0											

He's fat, has a bad attitude, tends to forget that God gave him a brain, and worst of all, you know that whenever his name appears in the newspaper it is for a bad reason. But he can sure kick a football, which is why the Raiders like him. You know the only thing that kept them from going after Todd Sauerbrun was that they already had a good punter.

Nate Kaeding

College: Iowa — Born: 26-Mar-1982 — Age: 23

Year	Team	G	XP	18-29	30-39	40-49	50+	Total	FG%	FGPts+	Rank	KO	Avg	TB	OoB	RetAv	KickPts+	Rank	NetPts+	Rank	WEA
2004	SD	16	54	10-12	2-2	5-6	3-5	20-25	80%	-0.3	23	89	61.1	2	5	22.3	-7.3	33	-20.6	34	-2.9
2005	SD	16	43	—	—	—	—	19-25	77%	-2.3											

You may remember Nate Kaeding as the guy who honked the field goal in overtime of the Chargers' playoff game with the Jets. That's the kind of kick that a third-round draft pick misses, but a second-round draft pick nails down the middle. Nothing ever appears to rattle him, so there shouldn't be any lingering effects from one bad play.

John Kasay

College: Georgia — Born: 27-Oct-1969 — Age: 36

Year	Team	G	XP	18-29	30-39	40-49	50+	Total	FG%	FGPts+	Rank	KO	Avg	TB	OoB	RetAv	KickPts+	Rank	NetPts+	Rank	WEA
2002	CAR	2	5	2-2	0-0	0-2	0-1	2-5	40%	-5.6	—	0	0.0	0	0	0.0	0.0	0	0.0	0	-0.3
2003	CAR	16	29	13-13	6-8	11-13	2-4	32-38	84%	9.1	9	74	62.4	4	1	20.7	-0.8	19	2.9	12	-0.1
2004	CAR	14	27	11-11	4-4	1-2	3-5	19-22	86%	3.7	13	56	59.9	2	1	21.9	-3.6	30	-8.2	30	-2.5
2005	CAR	16	37	—	—	—	—	25-30	83%	7.3											

Among the players who made their living with their feet for Carolina last season, Kasay is the one who (1) is an original Panther; (2) has never been caught up in a steroid scandal; and (3) doesn't carry on a feud with a family of diminutive, soccer-loving, Argentinian kickers. Kasay remains an accurate field goal kicker (he didn't miss under 40 yards last season), but his kickoff length has dropped noticeably. The Panthers may need to look into using a kickoff specialist.

Ola Kimrin

College: Texas-El Paso — Born: 24-Feb-1972 — Age: 33

Year	Team	G	XP	18-29	30-39	40-49	50+	Total	FG%	FGPts+	Rank	KO	Avg	TB	OoB	RetAv	KickPts+	Rank	NetPts+	Rank	WEA
2004	WAS	5	6	3-3	2-3	1-3	0-1	6-10	60%	-4.9	—	17	53.3	0	2	20.0	-1.5	—	-0.3	—	0.5
2005	TEN	16	34	—	—	—	—	18-25	75%	-5.1											

Arguably the greatest Swedish place kicker in NFL history, Kimrin was signed by Tennessee in the off-season. Kimrin originally made a name for himself by kicking a 65-yard field goal in a preseason game in 2002, which would have set an NFL record had it come in a real game. Of course, Kimrin couldn't hit a long one in his brief time with the Redskins.

Rian Lindell

College: Washington State — Born: 20-Jan-1977 — Age: 28

Year	Team	G	XP	18-29	30-39	40-49	50+	Total	FG%	FGPts+	Rank	KO	Avg	TB	OoB	RetAv	KickPts+	Rank	NetPts+	Rank	WEA
2002	SEA	16	38	10-10	8-10	4-5	1-4	23-29	79%	1.7	16	79	58.0	0	2	21.8	-1.7	24	-4.6	25	2.3
2003	BUF	16	24	11-12	3-3	3-7	0-2	17-24	71%	-5.7	29	60	60.5	3	1	19.6	-1.1	21	2.4	14	2.3
2004	BUF	16	45	13-14	10-11	1-3	0-0	24-28	86%	0.4	22	83	58.3	3	3	18.3	-1.1	24	9.9	8	4.8
2005	BUF	16	39	—	—	—	—	22-28	79%	1.4											

Take a quick look at Lindell's numbers (24 of 28 field goals made) and you might think he's a good field goal kicker. But he's just not accurate enough from long range to be reliable. Last year the Bills never even tried to use him on a field goal of more than 50 yards, and his longest successful kick came from 43 yards.

Ryan Longwell

College: California   Born: 16-Aug-1974   Age: 31

Year	Team	G	XP	18-29	30-39	40-49	50+	Total	FG%	FGPts+	Rank	KO	Avg	TB	OoB	RetAv	KickPts+	Rank	NetPts+	Rank	WEA
2002	GB	16	44	9-10	12-13	7-10	0-1	28-34	82%	3.0	9	85	61.0	2	0	21.7	0.2	19	0.7	16	2.2
2003	GB	16	51	5-5	11-11	6-9	1-1	23-26	89%	9.4	7	92	58.6	4	3	20.8	-3.9	26	-0.7	20	2.2
2004	GB	16	48	8-8	8-9	6-8	2-3	24-28	86%	7.3	7	83	58.6	2	0	20.2	-1.8	26	-2.1	20	1.2
2005	*GB*	*16*	*35*	—	—	—	—	*21-26*	*79%*	*1.2*											

Longwell is very reliable on field goals, especially from close range, and he's good at navigating his kicks in windy conditions. But Packers fans probably lost some faith in his clutch ability when he missed what should have been a chip shot in the playoffs. His kickoffs are too short, and that has caused the Packers some problems.

Olindo Mare

College: Syracuse   Born: 6-Jun-1973   Age: 32

Year	Team	G	XP	18-29	30-39	40-49	50+	Total	FG%	FGPts+	Rank	KO	Avg	TB	OoB	RetAv	KickPts+	Rank	NetPts+	Rank	WEA
2002	MIA	16	42	13-14	2-3	7-11	2-3	24-31	77%	-2.1	21	84	63.9	12	2	22.3	4.1	7	3.6	11	-1.6
2003	MIA	16	33	9-9	3-6	6-8	4-6	22-29	76%	0.7	19	72	65.8	24	0	21.9	11.0	1	15.4	3	0.9
2004	MIA	11	18	1-2	6-7	3-4	2-3	12-16	75%	1.2	17	44	64.6	11	0	23.5	5.3	4	3.6	11	0.3
2005	*MIA*	*16*	*36*	—	—	—	—	*21-27*	*80%*	*1.7*											

Olindo Mare was injured for half of last season, but when he was healthy he was the same kicker he usually is: average on field goals, superb on kickoffs. No kicker outside of Denver is more likely to kick a touchback.

Joe Nedney

College: San Jose State   Born: 22-Mar-1973   Age: 32

Year	Team	G	XP	18-29	30-39	40-49	50+	Total	FG%	FGPts+	Rank	KO	Avg	TB	OoB	RetAv	KickPts+	Rank	NetPts+	Rank	WEA
2002	TEN	16	36	9-9	10-12	5-8	1-2	25-31	81%	2.8	10	84	64.0	9	0	20.0	5.8	3	17.6	2	0.3
2003	TEN	1	0	0-0	0-0	0-0	1-1	1-1	100%	0.3	—	3	68.0	1	0	31.0	0.5	—	-0.3	—	-0.2
2004	TEN	0	0	0-0	0-0	0-0	0-0	0-0	0%	0.0	0	0	0.0	0	0	0.0	0.0	0	0.0	0	0.0
2005	*SF*	*16*	*28*	—	—	—	—	*18-25*	*73%*	*-6.7*											

Ladies and gentlemen, the world's first injury-prone kicker. He was great after replacing Richie Cunningham on the 2000 Panthers, had a disappointing 2001 season in Tennessee, but bounced back in 2002 to finish in the top ten of our kicker rankings. But a torn ACL in 2003 and a torn hamstring in 2004 have held Nedney to only one regular-season field goal attempt in two seasons. Signed by San Francisco, he should be an upgrade over Todd Peterson, assuming Nedney can make it to opening day in one piece.

Mike Nugent

College: Ohio State   Born: 2-Mar-1982   Age: 23

Year	Team	G	XP	18-29	30-39	40-49	50+	Total	FG%	FGPts+	Rank	KO	Avg	TB	OoB	RetAv	KickPts+	Rank	NetPts+	Rank	WEA
2005	*NYJ*	*16*	*39*	—	—	—	—	*22-28*	*78%*	*-0.4*											

The problem with taking a kicker, even one as talented as Nugent, in the second round is that nearly all kickers will eventually hit a slump. And what happens to a kicker when he slumps? He gets cut. It's not like other positions, where a team might bench a slumping player and replace him with a backup to motivate him. There is no backup for the slumping kicker, so he gets released. Sure, Nugent could be worth a win this season, but chances are he'll be kicking for someone else in five years.

Todd Peterson

College: Georgia   Born: 4-Feb-1970   Age: 35

Year	Team	G	XP	18-29	30-39	40-49	50+	Total	FG%	FGPts+	Rank	KO	Avg	TB	OoB	RetAv	KickPts+	Rank	NetPts+	Rank	WEA
2002	PIT	10	25	3-4	6-10	3-7	0-0	12-21	57%	-14.5	35	49	55.5	1	2	21.4	-3.7	28	-7.0	29	0.9
2003	SF	8	22	5-7	3-3	4-4	0-1	12-15	80%	0.0	20	44	57.9	1	0	21.5	-2.4	23	-2.9	23	3.0
2004	SF	16	23	4-4	7-8	5-6	2-4	18-22	82%	4.4	11	61	56.4	1	1	20.0	-7.4	34	-6.8	28	-0.8
2005	*ATL*	*16*	*30*	—	—	—	—	*19-25*	*76%*	*-6.3*											

If someone kicks a field goal in San Francisco, will anyone hear it? Peterson quietly had an effective season as a field goal kicker with the 49ers, despite the few opportunities the 49ers gave him to ply his trade. Forty-four-year-old Morten Anderson was the only other player to appear in all 16 games as a field goal kicker in 2004 and have fewer field goal attempts than Peterson. In Atlanta he'll wait for the rare drive that doesn't end in either a Michael Vick highlight-worthy touchdown run or an interception.

Neil Rackers

College: Illinois   Born: 16-Aug-1976 Age: 29

Year	Team	G	XP	18-29	30-39	40-49	50+	Total	FG%	FGPts+	Rank	KO	Avg	TB	OoB	RetAv	KickPts+	Rank	NetPts+	Rank	WEA
2002	CIN	16	30	7-7	3-3	3-5	2-3	15-18	83%	2.2	12	64	55.0	3	0	21.1	-3.8	30	-13.1	30	3.3
2003	ARI	7	8	5-5	1-4	3-3	0-0	9-12	75%	-1.5	24	27	59.5	5	1	24.2	3.3	—	1.7	—	2.3
2004	ARI	16	28	6-6	5-7	6-7	5-9	22-29	76%	7.2	8	70	67.5	23	1	22.1	11.9	1	11.4	5	-0.1
2005	*ARI*	*16*	*33*	*—*	*—*	*—*	*—*	*20-26*	*77%*	*-1.7*											

The staff of Football Outsiders has been making fun of Neil Rackers since before Football Outsiders existed, when the original staff was just a bunch of frat buddies in a fantasy league. As the inaccurate kicker of a Bengals team with no offense, he was the king of the Loser League, our reverse-fantasy game where the object is to draft the worst players. But over the past two seasons the strangest thing has happened: Neil Rackers has become one of the top kickers in football. He's still inaccurate, but he's built up so much strength in his leg that he booms kickoffs and tosses on a few long field goals for good measure. Our prediction: On October 2 in Mexico City, Rackers will set a new NFL record by kicking a 65-yard field goal against San Francisco.

Jeff Reed

College: North Carolina   Born: 9-Apr-1979 Age: 26

Year	Team	G	XP	18-29	30-39	40-49	50+	Total	FG%	FGPts+	Rank	KO	Avg	TB	OoB	RetAv	KickPts+	Rank	NetPts+	Rank	WEA
2002	PIT	6	10	5-5	5-5	6-7	1-2	17-19	90%	8.4	4	35	58.3	1	0	21.4	-1.5	23	-2.2	22	4.7
2003	PIT	16	31	9-12	6-7	7-12	1-1	23-32	72%	-6.5	30	70	63.0	5	1	20.7	3.0	10	2.3	16	4.0
2004	PIT	16	40	9-10	12-13	5-8	2-2	28-33	85%	6.4	9	84	62.1	7	3	21.6	1.2	15	-1.2	17	5.6
2005	*PIT*	*16*	*39*	*—*	*—*	*—*	*—*	*23-28*	*82%*	*5.3*											

When you consider that Reed was laying bricks in 2002 before the Steelers signed him off the street, it's pretty impressive to think that he signed a five-year, $7.5 million contract this off-season. He won three games on last-minute field goals in 2004 and is 22 for 28 on kicks at Heinz Field, which in four seasons has been a notoriously difficult place to kick.

Wade Richey

College: LSU   Born: 19-May-1976 Age: 29

Year	Team	G	XP	18-29	30-39	40-49	50+	Total	FG%	FGPts+	Rank	KO	Avg	TB	OoB	RetAv	KickPts+	Rank	NetPts+	Rank	WEA
2002	SD	12	0	0-0	0-0	0-0	0-0	0-0	0%	0.0	—	50	65.5	16	3	20.6	3.7	9	6.2	9	-1.8
2003	BAL	15	0	0-0	0-0	0-0	1-2	1-2	50%	0.6	—	81	63.9	14	1	21.3	8.9	2	8.5	4	2.9
2004	BAL	12	0	0-0	0-0	0-0	0-0	0-0	0%	0.0	—	53	63.1	7	0	24.1	2.9	11	-7.7	29	1.0
2005	*BAL*	*16*	*0*	*—*	*—*	*—*	*—*	*0-0*	*—*	*0.0*											

Most teams that split their kicking duties have a field goal kicker and a punter/kickoff specialist. The Ravens are the only team that uses three players, with Matt Stover kicking the field goals, Richey the kickoffs, and Dave Zastudil the punts. But they've gotten good value out of that use of an extra roster spot each week. In 2003, Wamatt Stoverichey would have been the second-ranked kicker in the league, behind Jeff Wilkins and just ahead of David Akers. Last year, Richey had some leg problems that forced Stover to kick off for part of the year, but he'll be back to full health in 2005.

Josh Scobee

College: Louisiana Tech   Born: 23-Jun-1982 Age: 23

Year	Team	G	XP	18-29	30-39	40-49	50+	Total	FG%	FGPts+	Rank	KO	Avg	TB	OoB	RetAv	KickPts+	Rank	NetPts+	Rank	WEA
2004	JAC	16	21	10-10	8-11	5-7	1-3	24-31	77%	-2.5	27	62	65.2	11	1	19.9	3.2	10	8.0	9	-2.7
2005	*JAC*	*16*	*29*	*—*	*—*	*—*	*—*	*20-27*	*76%*	*-4.0*											

The Jets took Mike Nugent to appease their angry fans, but last year's Jaguars actually had a gaping hole that needed to be filled. According to our numbers, Seth Marler was worth −16.8 points on field goals and another −3.9 points on kickoffs in 2003. And yet, did the Jaguars grab a kicker high in the draft? No, they waited until the fifth round, when many draft choices often become special teamers anyway. Our good friend Marc Helmick submitted the best waiver claim of the fantasy football season when he picked up Scobee and then added Josh Scobey of Arizona to his bench "just to own both Josh Scobee/ys." Unless you are shooting for humor, don't follow his lead; Scobee's strong but scattershot leg makes him great on kickoffs but mediocre on field goals, and Jacksonville's offense isn't really going to get him many opportunities anyway.

Matt Stover

College: Louisiana Tech

Born: 27-Jan-1968 Age: 37

Year	Team	G	XP	18-29	30-39	40-49	50+	Total	FG%	FGPts+	Rank	KO	Avg	TB	OoB	RetAv	KickPts+	Rank	NetPts+	Rank	WEA
2002	BAL	15	33	9-9	4-5	7-10	1-1	21-25	84%	5.2	8	40	57.5	1	0	20.5	0.3	17	0.2	17	4.0
2003	BAL	16	35	16-16	6-6	11-14	0-2	33-38	87%	10.3	4	7	60.0	1	0	21.7	0.0	—	-1.2	—	1.5
2004	BAL	16	30	11-11	7-8	9-10	2-3	29-32	91%	12.9	3	23	62.7	2	0	21.8	2.0	—	4.9	—	3.6
2005	BAL	16	30	—	—	—	—	25-30	81%	5.1											

Coming into 2005, Stover was Baltimore's best offensive weapon who didn't spend time in the can this spring. In fact, Stover accounted for 37% of all the Raven's points last season. People talk about how the addition of Derrick Mason and Mark Clayton should take some of the workload off Jamal Lewis, but no one should be happier about the off-season acquisitions than Matt Stover.

Jay Taylor

College: West Virginia

Born: 23-Oct-1976 Age: 29

Year	Team	G	XP	18-29	30-39	40-49	50+	Total	FG%	FGPts+	Rank	KO	Avg	TB	OoB	RetAv	KickPts+	Rank	NetPts+	Rank	WEA
2004	TB	5	11	0-0	2-3	1-1	1-1	4-5	80%	1.0	—	21	57.0	0	0	24.8	-1.6	—	-9.3	—	0.6
2005	FA	6	13	—	—	—	—	8-9	89%	0.2											

The release this off-season of Taylor, who was brought in to replace Martin Gramatica once the Buccaneers had finally had enough of his inconsistency, is sad for one reason: It reduces by one the number of former XFL players who are currently earning an NFL paycheck.

Lawrence Tynes

College: Troy State

Born: 3-May-1978 Age: 27

Year	Team	G	XP	18-29	30-39	40-49	50+	Total	FG%	FGPts+	Rank	KO	Avg	TB	OoB	RetAv	KickPts+	Rank	NetPts+	Rank	WEA
2004	KC	16	58	5-5	7-8	3-6	2-4	17-23	74%	-1.2	24	94	60.5	7	0	22.4	0.2	19	-4.2	25	1.9
2005	KC	16	41	—	—	—	—	19-25	76%	-3.9											

One of two kickers (Mike Vanderjagt is the other) who had 60 extra point attempts in 2004. Fantasy football players should remember that, when drafting kickers, the differential in extra point opportunities is vast. Josh Scobee had just 21 opportunities, Paul Edinger 22, and Todd Peterson 23 in a full season's work. Peterson's a better kicker than Tynes, but a difference of over 30 "free" points in a season is tough to make up. When drafting kickers, it often makes sense to just draft whoever kicks for the best available offense. (Of course, there's a reasonable possibility that Kansas City falls from those ranks in 2005.)

Mike Vanderjagt

College: West Virginia

Born: 24-Mar-1970 Age: 35

Year	Team	G	XP	18-29	30-39	40-49	50+	Total	FG%	FGPts+	Rank	KO	Avg	TB	OoB	RetAv	KickPts+	Rank	NetPts+	Rank	WEA
2002	IND	16	34	8-9	6-7	6-12	3-3	23-31	74%	-3.9	27	77	59.0	1	0	20.5	-5.7	31	-0.4	18	-4.4
2003	IND	16	46	17-17	7-7	12-12	1-1	37-37	100%	18.1	1	99	60.2	4	0	21.5	-5.3	30	-7.3	29	-5.2
2004	IND	15	59	6-6	9-11	5-7	0-1	20-25	80%	-1.6	25	32	58.1	0	1	20.4	-4.9	32	-6.5	27	-3.5
2005	IND	16	49	—	—	—	—	25-29	84%	6.0											

Going into the 2004 season, many people considered Vanderjagt the best kicker in the league thanks to his perfect field goal record the year before. This belief ignored a few important facts: that the inconsistent nature of field goal kicking rendered his 2004 record unrepeatable, that Vanderjagt benefits from kicking in a dome, and that despite kicking in a dome his kickoffs are terrible. On top of this, he's a prima donna who throws a hissy fit whenever the Colts try to bring in a kickoff specialist, and his constant ridicule of the Patriots is like a permanent IV drip of growth hormone plugged directly into the continent-sized chip on Rodney Harrison's shoulder. Idiot kicker? No kidding.

Adam Vinatieri

College: South Dakota State

Born: 28-Dec-1972 Age: 32

Year	Team	G	XP	18-29	30-39	40-49	50+	Total	FG%	FGPts+	Rank	KO	Avg	TB	OoB	RetAv	KickPts+	Rank	NetPts+	Rank	WEA
2002	NE	16	36	6-6	12-12	8-10	1-2	27-30	90%	13.9	1	83	60.4	6	3	20.5	-0.8	21	2.5	13	3.2
2003	NE	16	37	16-17	4-8	5-8	0-1	25-34	74%	-9.2	31	79	62.9	2	0	21.4	2.7	11	4.1	9	1.8
2004	NE	16	48	13-13	7-7	11-12	0-1	31-33	94%	15.2	1	94	63.0	6	1	23.3	3.5	9	-1.6	18	4.0
2005	NE	16	43	—	—	—	—	24-28	83%	7.3											

Even after the heroics of the 2004 Red Sox, there's no risk of Vinatieri getting bumped from the free-dinner-for-life club in the Hub, not after the pair of Super Bowl game-winning kicks and the greatest kick ever made (against Oakland in the snow in the 2001 playoffs). He may not be the best kicker in the NFL (see Akers, David), but he's pretty darn close. He's accurate, never misses a chippy, and has improved his kickoff distance. The back issues he faced in 2003 seem like a distant memory. No wonder the Patriots made him their franchise player, and will probably sign him to a long-term deal at some point this year.

Jeff Wilkins
College: Youngstown State　　　　　　**Born: 19-Apr-1972　Age: 33**

Year	Team	G	XP	18-29	30-39	40-49	50+	Total	FG%	FGPts+	Rank	KO	Avg	TB	OoB	RetAv	KickPts+	Rank	NetPts+	Rank	WEA
2002	STL	16	37	5-5	8-10	6-9	0-1	19-25	76%	-1.5	19	71	61.8	9	2	23.8	3.1	10	-6.0	26	-3.4
2003	STL	16	46	16-16	11-13	8-9	4-4	39-42	93%	15.2	2	96	65.1	12	1	24.0	5.6	4	-4.9	26	-5.4
2004	STL	16	32	7-7	5-6	3-6	4-5	19-24	79%	1.2	18	70	63.6	3	1	25.5	-0.5	23	-14.2	33	-4.6
2005	*STL*	*16*	*38*	—	—	—	—	*26-31*	*85%*	*7.6*											

Why kickers are strange birds: Over the past three seasons, Wilkins is 100% on kicks of 29 yards or less, 83% on kicks of 30–39 yards, 71% on kicks of 40–49 yards, and 80% on kicks of 50+ yards. He clearly has a strong, accurate leg based on the performance from 50+, so why the struggles at 40–49 yards? He had an off year, both in field goal accuracy and kickoff length, but the horrendous returns are the fault of the ten guys on kickoff coverage, not Wilkins.

Going Deep

Paul Ernster, DEN: Punter/kickoff specialist, drafted by Denver in the seventh round. Highly unlikely to see any time kicking field goals (he was a lackluster 9 of 18 in college last year) unless Jason Elam's leg falls off, and the trade for Todd Sauerbrun means he's unlikely to see any time punting, either.

Todd France, TB: As of press time, France stood a good chance of breaking the NFL Europe record for points in a season. Don't laugh: David Akers kicked for Berlin in 1999 and Adam Vinatieri for Amsterdam in 1996. He gets Matt Bryant's projection if he wins the Tampa Bay kicking job.

Bill Gramatica, FA: He could show up if a kicker goes down with an injury, and he's never been that bad, just average.

Remy Hamilton, TEN: One of the best kickers in Arena League history, Hamilton will be competing for the starting job in Tennessee. More teams should look at successful Arena League kickers instead of wasting second-round picks on guys from Ohio State. The uprights are half as narrow in the Arena League as they are in the NFL. If someone is successful kicking the ball between uprights that are only nine feet wide, you'd think they'd be able to kick through NFL uprights that are twice that.

Dave Rayner, IND: Looks like Mike Vanderjagt has a new teammate to glower at on the sidelines. The Colts presume that Vandy will be gone as a free agent in another year, and will have Rayner kick off this season before taking over in 2006.

Joe Rheem, BUF: Undrafted free agent from Kansas State who signed with the Bills. Buffalo could use a kicker upgrade, but Rheem and incumbent Rian Lindell share the same strength (accuracy on shorter field goals) and the same weakness (short kickoffs and the inability to consistently hit field goals over 40 yards).

Clay Rush, FA: Another Arena League kicker garnering interest after hitting the Arena Bowl–winning field goal for the Colorado Crush.

The Five Injuries You Meet in Football Hell

Will Carroll

If you're mad at your kid, you can either raise him to be a nose tackle or send him out to play in the freeway. It's about the same.

—BOB GOLIC

t's not often that the wit and wisdom of a former *Saved by the Bell* cast member (It's true, you could look it up) shows up in a treatise on injury. In this case, Golic is absolutely correct. The modern game of football is not just "a collision sport," as the oft-quoted Vince Lombardi stated, but one that approaches and too often exceeds the physical capacities of mortal men.

"Ten years ago, I couldn't believe the hits these guys took," said an NFL physician who cannot be named due to the strict restrictions placed on medical personnel. "Now, it's worse. It's a question of when, not if, now. When the injury will happen. When they'll recover. Once a game we have the one moment where the stadium gasps, and too often now, that's an injury."

Injuries in the NFL are no longer just something that the medical staff can handle out of the tape trunk. X rays and MRI machines are on site. Teams travel not only with a team of certified athletic trainers, but with the team doctors and often an orthopedist on the sideline. Injuries have gone from simple abrasions to complex situations that require antibiotics to avoid "turf burn." There's a whole garment industry based on dealing with the fake grass.

While the NFL strictly limits the information available about injuries due to the gambling implications of injury "scoops," there is nonetheless a great deal of confusion surrounding injuries in football. When team doctors and trainers cannot comment and injuries are grouped into broad categories and vague descriptions, Vinny Boombatz down the block certainly isn't the only person interested in the diagnosis.

The first thing to note is that the categories used by the NFL to describe and delineate injuries are extremely accurate. The categories—out, unlikely, questionable, probable—separate the chance of a player touching the field into simple quartiles. An internal study done by an NFL team showed that the accuracy of the descriptors was very close to the appropriate tolerances. The strict control and occasional penalty for those teams foolhardy enough to try and game the system keep the system usable. For the players who did manage to play, there appears to be a noticeable "grade out" when analyzed on film.

Of course, not all injuries are the same. Last year, I wrote an article called "The Five Injuries You Meet in Fantasy Hell" for Rotowire's *Baseball Magazine* that—ahem—won a Fantasy Sportswriters Association Award for best fantasy baseball magazine article. (My publicist insisted I put that in.) Football magnifies the effects of the five worst injuries. There are certain injuries that, in the car-crash modern game of football, can and do end a player's effective career, derail a playoff season, and even force a team into a massive rebuilding program.

Don't think so? Just ask Dick Vermeil.

1. The Terrible Triad

The first injury that causes significant problems is one you'll almost never hear called by its proper name. Sure, even the densest "analyst" on TV can rattle off ACL recovery times, but the worry today is not the easily repaired and predictably rehabbed simple ACL, it is "O'Donoghue's Triad." This is not the opening act for the Dropkick Murphys. Instead, it is the combined tearing of three essential structures inside the knee, the ACL and MCL along with the medial meniscus. While it is an uncommon injury in normal society, the "terrible triad" is becoming all too common in the NFL, especially among running backs.

The injury normally occurs on a lateral hit (from the player's outside), buckling the knee and causing a cascade of tearing. Because of the complexity of this injury, it is difficult to assess the repaired structure of the knee and return proprioception properly. (*Proprioception* is a medical term for the ability of the body to sense itself in space.) An athlete that loses quickness, cutting ability, and the sense of his body in space—all at the same time—is an athlete we soon see in the "retired" column. Be sure to note whether or not your running back or cornerback who just had his ACL repaired was not in fact the latest to suffer the curse of O'Donoghue. If not for this type of injury, suffered by Trent Green while in St Louis, we may not have had Kurt Warner or his wife to enjoy. More indicative of both the injury and the rehab for a triad injury is Willis McGahee. I'm sure most football fans remember the cringe-inducing injury in the Fiesta Bowl as well as the agent-influenced rehab procedures. McGahee has come back, but not without a full year of nonstop physical therapy.

2. Shoulder Dislocations

Other injuries reflect the sheer violence of the postmillennial game. As players get bigger, stronger, and faster, the colliding forces have worse, different, and more traumatic consequences than ever. What once caused a bruise or even a fracture is now causing tears and dislocations. For many players, a dislocation is the worst injury possible. While being exceptionally painful is bad enough—the apocryphal story of the player dislocating a finger and running to the wrong sideline probably has some basis in truth—dislocations to three-dimensional joints like the ankle and shoulder can be career-threatening or at the very least career-altering. Depending on position, a shoulder dislocation can leave chronic weakness and instability behind even after it's healed. This is most important for players who use their arms as leverage or anchors, such as linemen. It's also a serious problem for cornerbacks, due to their use of "jam" moves in coverage. Their often graceful yet awkward in-air moves and hellacious landings leave them with shoulder dislocations in far too many situations. An example of this type of injury would be the brutal fall and dislocation suffered by Bengals receiver Kelley Washington.

3. Ankle Dislocations

Ankle dislocations are rarer, but are almost always career-enders. For any player reliant on quickness—and this defines nearly all players in the modern game—an ankle dislocation is going to take away an explosive first step. While some players can get by at 90% of their peak capacity, many cannot, and the salary cap, nonguaranteed structure of NFL contracts often makes these one-step slow players waiver wire casualties. It's interesting to note that in the NFL, almost 90% of ankle dislocations take place on artificial turf, and the percentage actually went up on Field-Turf fields. With 22 of 32 teams now playing on this surface, this is an injury that could become more prevalent. We must also note the dangers of cut blocks here. Defensive tackle Tony Williams of the Jaguars had both a fracture and dislocation of his ankle after a Denver cut block last year when he played with Cincinnati.

4. Turf Toe

Turf toe: It just doesn't sound serious. It is. The hyperextension injury to the capsuloligamentous structure of the first metatarsophalangeal joint—you can see why we call it "turf toe"—usually takes place when a player is in a three- or four-point stance, his toes extended to start quickly. While on grass, that explosive start will result in a divot. On turf, a grippier and ungiving surface, the toe is forced into extension. Add in tighter shoes with engineered cleats and you have a situation just begging to tax the toes. One factor that is only now being researched is whether the current bulk of players is contributing to the injury. It appears that larger players—and let's face it, most of the guys in the trenches redefine *large*—plant their feet at different angles than smaller people. This new "pes valgus" stress gives team physicians a new direction to go in attempting to prevent the injury. The worst statistics seen in regards to turf toe are the increase in both frequency and severity, the increased number of receivers and runners suffering the injury, and the extended period of time that players seem to be affected by the injury, even after returning to play. It could be that it takes a full off-season to return a player to full function after this injury. Peter Boulware, Steve McNair, and Chris Brown have all had recent turf toe injuries, especially painful for players like Boulware who rely on burst speed.

5. Lumbar-Sacral Hyperextension

There is no more serious injury than a spinal injury, in football or any other sport. While sadly some athletes are still struck down by this devastating injury at all levels, it was one football injury—to Marc Buoniconti—that has led to new techniques that have not only made football a safer game in regards to spinal injuries, but may lead to advances and perhaps cures. The back, however, is still a significant injury risk. The complex structure of the spine and its surrounding supports is often taxed and overtaxed by the demands and stresses of the game. Lumbar-sacral hyperextension is the next buzzword and a rapidly expanding and debilitating condition that has been caused by the changes in the game over the last decade. This is an exceptionally underreported injury, likely due to the broad categories that the NFL uses in public. Almost any lower back injury to linemen likely involves some hyperextension.

A player attempting to either block or run through blocks is often moving forward, and when the proverbial unstoppable force meets the immovable object, something has to give. In a game full of barrel chests, massive biceps, and thighs the size of tree trunks, the back is perhaps the only thing left on the body that gives. It's the weakest link in the chain. If the player—and it can be either player—is forced backward rapidly, before the back muscles and abdominals can sufficiently stabilize the spine, both trauma and tearing will often occur with the hyperextension. In order to protect itself, the body will initiate an inflammation and spasm response. This sounds painful, and it is—it's simply the worst possible injury for a lineman. The game is also starting to see hyperextension injuries in linebackers. It's impossible to tell if this is a result of changes in the way linebackers play ("rushbackers" and blitzes) or if linemen who are bigger and faster are getting to the second level, creating more opportunity for the dangerous collisions that case these injuries.

Injuries often decide games or even seasons. In the modern salary cap NFL, with rules that make midseason trading basically impossible, shortened drafts, more pre-season games, more turf facilities, further specialization, and a one-level injured reserve (as opposed to the various lengths of the baseball disabled list), it is little wonder that teams are beginning to spend more and more of their research dollars attempting to decrease both the frequency and the severity of injuries. Unless there is a rapid advance in protective technologies or a reduction in the forces that the players are subjected to, the best that the league can hope for is some kind of painful stasis.

It's hard to expect less when we send these guys out to play in traffic.

OPE: How Do I Explain It?

A Frame-by-Frame Way to Improve Your Fantasy Drafting

Dan Lewis

1 Take only running backs in the first two rounds, Peyton Manning and maybe Randy Moss being the only exceptions.

2. Stock up on running backs and wide receivers.

3. Wait until the middle to late rounds to grab your quarterback.

4. Tight ends should be drafted late. Make exceptions only if Tony Gonzalez or Antonio Gates falls further than expected. Don't reach to get Jeremy Shockey, Jason Witten, or Alge Crumpler; you'll be fine with a Bubba Franks or Daniel Graham.

5. Kickers should be drafted even later, if at all. Face it, last year you could have grabbed Lawrence Tynes (109 points) off waivers, while David Akers (122 points) would have cost you a middle- to late-round pick.

6. Defenses? Don't bother. Check the waiver wire every week, and take the team that is facing the weakest offensive line.

7. Stay active on the waiver wire. Be the first to uncover this year's Rudi Johnson, Domanick Davis, Reuben Droughns, or Nick Goings.

Call them the Seven Habits of Highly Effective Fantasy Footballers. The strategy is simple and straightforward; fail to follow it, and you'll almost certainly fail to compete for your league title.

Unfortunately for you, almost everyone follows those rules, and not everyone can win the league title.

If you follow the Seven Habits and finish 6–7 to miss the playoffs, it is probably for one of a few reasons. Perhaps your top two picks—running backs—were Clinton Portis and Fred Taylor, who rushed for a grand total of seven touchdowns. Maybe you had Deuce McAllister, who put up good numbers but missed three weeks to injury. Or maybe you settled on Jeff Garcia or Brad Johnson as your quarterback, while your opponent landed Ben Roethlisberger or Jake Plummer. And you probably gambled by taking guys like Thomas Jones and Justin Gage in the middle or late rounds, while the eventual champion hit pay dirt with Willis McGahee and Nate Burleson.

In other words, you can sum up your team's disappointment with one of two garden-variety complaints: "My top guys didn't pan out" (also known as "I got unlucky!") or "Your flyers were incredible" (also known as "You were soooooooooo lucky!").

Even though you didn't make mistakes according to the Seven Habits, you could have mitigated the impact of what befell your team. One of the keys to a successful fantasy football season is to identify undervalued guys and grab them (typically, but not always, in the later rounds). Another key is to identify overvalued guys and avoid them. Easier said than done? Sure. Talent evaluation itself is key, but it is not enough.

So how do you separate your team from the rest? It's as easy as O-P-E.

OPE stands for opportunity, perception, and environment. These are three things that you don't see when looking at stats, be it yards, touchdowns, or even DVOA. But in the world of fantasy football, they are equally important. Let's take a closer look.

Opportunity

Opportunity is rather straightforward: You can't score a lot of fantasy points if you're not in the game often. It is also the hardest thing to determine at draft time. The problem is not whether an opportunity exists; often, that is rather obvious. The better question is, who will fill the slot?

Take the Denver backfield. Last year, the job could have gone to one of five players: Quentin Griffin, Ahmaad Galloway, Tatum Bell, Mike Anderson, or Garrison Hearst. Come August, it was still anybody's guess who would emerge as the starter. Not even Mike Shanahan appeared to have a foothold on it. And if you tried to guess, you were wrong; as we all know, Reuben Droughns won the Olandis Gary Award. What does this teach us? Easy: Opportunity is a requirement for success—but it is hardly a guarantee.

When you see a backfield with no clear starter, it is not a worthwhile gamble to grab any one of the players who could win the job. In fact, had you avoided the messy running games in Denver, Miami, Arizona, Tampa Bay, and Minnesota last year, you would have been no worse for your indifference.

That said, opportunity is still a requirement for fantasy success. Take Green Bay's Najeh Davenport. I call him the Genie of the Lamp because his buzz is so good that he has to be talented, but there is that whole Ahman Green problem. It's as if Najeh has phenomenal cosmic powers, but an itty-bitty living space. And there are plenty of players like him. He and his brethren will only see significant playing time if the men they back up get hurt.

So, Davenport lacks opportunity, which suggests that he is not worth taking. In some cases, this may be wrong, but it is usually sound reasoning. The exception is what some fantasy theorists call a "handcuff": If you have Green in a league with a reasonably sized bench, take Davenport as a late-round insurance policy.

Another cardinal rule is that when one player has opportunity, it is an asset. When numerous players have the same opportunity, tread lightly.

Take this year's Carolina running back situation. Going into camp, there is certainly opportunity for a number one running back to emerge, but who is going to get the shot? Steven Davis? Maybe if he's healthy. DeShaun Foster, perhaps? Even Nick Goings and Eric Shelton will get some touches. While the smart money is on Foster, notice how quickly his chance will evaporate if he fails to succeed. That is not to say you should erase Foster from your list of sleepers. But it does mean that further investigation of him needs to be positive.

The exception to this rule is wide receiver. Most teams have two guys who get a lot of touches; some go as deep as three. When a team has an open opportunity for a receiver to step up, further investigation is warranted.

Even when a team has an unquestioned number one receiver, the opportunity is there for someone to gain yards and catch touchdowns. You should keep your eye on guys whose opportunity seems to be neutral (if not positive) and will be fighting for an open job. Last year saw Brandon Stokley, Nate Burleson, Marcus Robinson, Drew Bennett, and Ashley Lelie become serviceable if not strong wide receiver candidates. Some were more visible than others, but all were given a chance they had not seen in years prior.

Even a receiver like Kelley Washington could become a sleeper possibility with a minor change in opportunity. While Washington has been good in limited time (with a strong DVOA) and is a former first-day draft pick in his "likely breakout" third year, he's stuck behind three veterans: Chad Johnson, T. J. Houshmandzadeh, and Peter War-

rick. But all it takes is a training camp injury to one of the first two players, and the door is open for Washington to pass Warrick and gain a starting slot in a passing offense on the rise.

Of course, opportunity alone is not enough to ensure fantasy success. Not even close.

Perception

Perception is how a player's team views the player. If a player is perceived to be lackluster or a backup-variety player, that is most likely where he'll be.

An example: If you read Football Outsiders last year, you may have looked at the 2003 wide receiver DVOA rankings and noticed that Bobby Engram was number one. Deciding he was a stud in the making, you grabbed him and thought you had the king of sleepers on your hands.

You were wrong. And the fact is, you knew better.

You knew Engram was not going to be a superstar because Mike Holmgren liked him in the Ricky Proehl role—a good guy to have as a third receiver. He's reliable, he can even turn in a big play now and then, but if you go to him as the number one guy, all the Champ Baileys and Chris McAllisters of the world are going to have a field day. That is how he's used, because that's how he's perceived, *even if it's not true.*

Even after Koren Robinson was suspended and Matt Hasselbeck nearly repeated his 2003 numbers, Engram didn't come close to vaulting into the middle, let alone the upper echelon of fantasy receivers. He is viewed, perhaps wrongfully, as a third option, and because of this he will never be an impact fantasy player. In fact, while Robinson sat out six games, Engram totaled a mere two touchdowns and 24 catches, and never broke 80 yards. That's the type of player he is expected to be, and the Seahawks likely arranged their game plan accordingly. It's all about perception.

Engram is an obvious example. But what about the less obvious and outright tempting players? Here is a rather incomplete list of guys who are looked upon negatively, but will almost certainly go in your league's draft:

- Brian Griese. His touchdowns thrown, especially considering he did not play a full season, make him an interesting risk. Same with his DVOA (11th) and DPAR (13th). But look at the facts: He did not win the job outright; he came out of training camp third on the depth chart; the Bucs almost opted to let him go this off-season; Jon Gruden considered trading up to draft Alex Smith. All these facts signal that Tampa Bay does not look at Griese as Mr. Right, but merely Mr. Right Now.

- Lee Suggs. He will probably be the starting running back in Cleveland, but the acquisition of Reuben

Droughns suggests that he is more Capulet than Juliet as far as Romeo is concerned. Someone in your league will take him in a middle or late round, hoping he becomes a big-time running back; you should downgrade those odds significantly.

- T. J. Duckett. In 2003, he rushed for 11 scores and almost 800 yards, all while splitting carries with Warrick Dunn (and, yes, Michael Vick). Last year, with a better offensive line, and with a better DVOA rank (sixth, up from 22nd the year before), he scored only eight times and barely surpassed 500 yards. These experiences came under two different coaching staffs; in the eyes of Jim Mora, the term *committee-back* is etched permanently on Duckett's lapel.

Taking these guys comes with a great deal of peril. The fact that they are likely to split time or, at the very least, lose snaps or carries because something better comes along means that you do not want them as a starter. If you are banking on them to be a backup if your starter goes down, there really is not a lot of upside here—but there is a ton of downside. You are better off opting for others.

Look for the guys who are perceived as extremely positive. These players are probably *better* risks than you would expect. The most obvious are recent high draft picks who have been silent due to lack of opportunity. Last year, the list of such players would have included Roethlisberger, McGahee, and Carson Palmer. In 2005, you can add any rookie who survives the opportunity test and the environment test (explained below) to that list, as well as guys who have "good buzz"—a coach who believes that last year's positive results were the real deal. Compare Houshmandzadeh or Deion Branch to Droughns or Thomas Jones; while all four had solid years, the former two head into 2005 with a buzz around them and a starting slot, while the latter's performances earned them the right to compete for a starting role in camp.

There is a pitfall to avoid when grading how a player is perceived. Don't assume that no buzz means bad news. That is anything but the case. While many players already are pigeonholed into the third down or goal-line back category or labeled "the future of the franchise," a great many are just kind of out there. T. J. Houshmandzadeh and Nate Burleson would have fallen into this realm before last season. Writing them off because they had not done anything was as silly as promoting them simply because they had not yet received a strike against them.

While that, too, seems obvious, you'd be surprised how often perfectly good prospects are overlooked because of even a salmon of doubt. It's not limited to fantasy owners, either. Let's say that you are the GM of a real NFL team. Two years ago, you had a strong duo of wide receivers—together, they had almost 2,000 yards receiving. When one got hurt early last year, the other made up

for it and then some. But this off-season, the second receiver departed via free agency and the first is just preparing to return from injury. The saving grace is that you drafted a rookie in the first round of last year's draft, and he put up serviceable but by no means stellar numbers when given the chance to play. Now, with a pick in the low teens this year, the conventional wisdom says that one of the positions you are looking to improve is, indeed, wide receiver.

You have probably surmised that I'm talking about the Carolina Panthers and, specifically, Keary Colbert. Given the above scenario, your reaction is probably "Man, the Panthers just don't trust him to be the number two." His situation greatly resembles the one Josh Reed was in last year, when the Bills were desperately in need of someone to complement Eric Moulds. When Buffalo gave Reed the big vote of no confidence by selecting Lee Evans in the draft, you rightfully soured on Reed.

But the resemblances are only skin deep. Ask yourself these two questions:

1. Are the Panthers (or the Bills) drafting a wide receiver because they have decided that their other one is best suited as a slot receiver or third option?
2. Are the Panthers (or the Bills) drafting a wide receiver because they are collecting them, hoping to see who pans out as a first or second option?

Carolina is doing the latter, especially if Steve Smith is still hurt. Buffalo, having seen what Josh Reed could do (drop passes and misrun routes) did the former. That is how Colbert and Reed are perceived—and the difference is very important. Reed will never be a fantasy success; Colbert is a bona fide sleeper candidate.

Environment

Unlike opportunity and perception, environment can affect all players, even superstars. By definition, a superstar is perceived to be a good player, and in almost all cases guys of that caliber are going to have the opportunity to shine.

When a player perceived as a superstar doesn't produce to expectations, many think that the problem is one of talent, but that's probably not the case. More likely than not, it is the player's environment that has gone sour.

Consider the 1999 Cleveland Browns, who began their rebirth by selecting Tim Couch with the first overall pick. Daunte Culpepper was taken ten picks later by the Minnesota Vikings. Both were perceived to be quality players, and within two seasons both had the opportunity they needed to become stars.

Now for some environmental factors:

- Couch's Browns were an expansion team, the definition of awful. Culpepper's team was coming off a 15–1 season.

- Couch had a baptism by fire: The only other Browns quarterback who took a snap in his rookie year was Ty Detmer. Culpepper? One game, no snaps, three rushes for six yards, and the tutelage of Randall Cunningham and Jeff George.
- In 1999, the Browns' top two wide receivers were fellow rookies Kevin Johnson and Darrin Chiaverini. The 2000 Vikings, in Culpepper's first season as the starter, featured Cris Carter and Randy Moss, both of whom had made the previous Pro Bowl.
- The 1999 Browns as a team rushed for 1,150 yards. A year later, Viking RB Robert Smith alone rushed for over 1,500.
- Couch entered the league, took 80% of his team's snaps, and was sacked over 50 times. Culpepper's first year as a starter resulted in almost all his team's snaps and only 30 sacks, perhaps a benefit of having two Pro Bowl offensive linemen.

Six years later, Couch is basically out of the NFL. Culpepper is the second best fantasy quarterback in the league, and that is only because of some guy named Manning. What gives?

It's not talent. There is simply no way that talent and talent alone makes up for such a stark difference. Culpepper entered a fantastic environment, and Couch not so much. Differences like this matter in the fantasy world, too, even for superstars. Take Clinton Portis, 2003 Denver Broncos, vs. Clinton Portis, 2004 Washington Redskins, in table 1.

That drop-off is incredible. Did Portis just forget to eat his Wheaties in Washington? Or should the blame be placed on a bad team that lost tackle Jon Jansen for the season?

If it is the former, well, fantasy football is a crapshoot and all one needs to win is luck. If it is the latter, perhaps we need to rethink the role environment plays in our fantasy selections.

But environment is almost entirely overlooked. According to his ESPN.com player card, Clinton Portis's average draft position was 5.0. Corey Dillon—having gone from battling Rudi Johnson for carries in Cincinnati to the unquestioned top back for the defending champs in New England—had an average draft slot of 18.2. But a blind man could see that Portis's situation went from incredibly good to incredibly bad, while Dillon's went from eh . . . to *yeehaw!* Are people that obtuse?

Yep.

Except when a player has actual competition at his position (see Travis Henry, who averaged out at slot 27.2), fantasy owners tend to neglect environment. Portis is younger than Dillon and put up better numbers; he therefore should go much higher. Forget the fact that Dillon's situation was much better.

There are two obvious big-ticket players who should fall off this year due to a negative change in their environments: Mushin Muhammed and Ahman Green. Muhammed goes from a team with a decent offensive outlook and a seasoned quarterback (Carolina) to Chicago, where, if he's *lucky,* he will end up with Rex Grossman as his quarterback. Green? No, he wasn't traded to Arizona. But he did lose two offensive linemen, and Brett Favre is declining. Note that one does not need to change teams in order for his environment to alter.

Some vets will improve as their environment does. Last year, Donovan McNabb benefited greatly from the arrival of Terrell Owens, and there is little reason to think that Kerry Collins will not have a similar improvement with Randy Moss on his team in Oakland. Whoever wins the starting running back job in Carolina will benefit from the addition of ex-Packers guard Mike Wahle. These are all guesses, of course, but do your homework about players' environments and you will be better off.

Environment may be even more important when looking for draft sleepers. Last year, in my long-running fantasy keeper league, I drafted both Justin Gage and Nate Burleson. Gage, as you know, stunk it up like Maurice Clarett at the combine. Burleson became the greatest thing since sliced bread.

Along with Burleson, I was also considering Marcus Robinson. Both were going into the season with a clean slate (perception: neutral). There was a big need for a number two guy to complement Randy Moss—as there had been since Cris Carter's departure (opportunity: positive). While the veteran Robinson appeared to be the more likely guy to get the chances, there was a sudden buzz around Burleson, and, this being a keeper league, I figured to go with the young'n. My reasoning was flawless.

But a few picks earlier, I had blown it. Gage was getting all sorts of hype, so I figured that was a good sign. And since David Terrell may be the wide receiver equivalent of Ryan Leaf, there was an opportunity, too. Where I erred was in not realizing how bad the environment was in

TABLE 1. CLINTON PORTIS: 2003 BRONCOS VS. 2004 REDSKINS

Year	Runs	Yards	Yd/Rush	TD	DPAR	Rank	DVOA	Rank
2003	290	1591	5.5	14	36.1	4	15.2	6
2004	343	1319	3.8	5	4.2	39	-11.2	40

Chicago—a second-year quarterback, no established passing game, a rather murky running game, and general malaise all over.

Had I factored environment into my analysis, I would have realized that the Minnesota passing game was so much better than the Bears' that two Viking receivers—even the number two and number three—were arguably better than a guy who had a legit shot at being the Chicago number one. A minor mistake? Perhaps, but an entirely avoidable one.

OPE's Foe

He was taken in the first round of the 2004 NFL draft by a team that was prepared to start him right away as the number two wide receiver. The team that drafted him had a young, recent high draft pick at quarterback. All three elements were in place—high perception, good opportunity, and, potentially, a good environment. He even had a good last name: Williams.

Reggie did not do so well.

But Roy did.

Rookie wide receivers pose a real problem. Very rarely do teams draft a wide receiver early when they are already stocked at the position, so we already know what the team thinks of the player (future starter). Sometimes you get lucky and the team announces that their player—Atlanta's Michael Jenkins and San Francisco's Rashaun Woods, for example—is going to be eased into the lineup (opportunity: low). But for every Roy Williams, there's a Reggie. For every Andre Johnson, there's a Bryant. Perhaps Michael Clayton's season speaks ill for Mark? But how do we explain Larry Fitzgerald and Lee Evans?

The fact is that there are no easy answers. The best I can offer is this: So long as all the OPE factors are favorable, go with higher ranked players based on the NFL draft, unless, of course, you have some sort of reason to distrust the selecting team's talent evaluation. That means that Charles Rogers and Andre Johnson made for good picks in 2003, while Bryant Johnson did not. It also meant that Fitzgerald and Roy Williams were good ideas last year. But then it puts Reggie Williams over both Evans and Clayton, not to mention second-rounder Anquan Boldin. We're stuck until there's more research on how to identify low-risk rookie receivers.

Applying OPE

Ron Dayne: Stop. Do not be fooled by the opportunity presented by Droughns's departure, nor by the running back–friendly environment in Denver. Even if you assume that Dayne comes in with a clean slate (perception: neutral), he has still had five years to prove that he's a bust.

Remember, OPE is not a substitute for your everyday talent evaluation.

Chester Taylor: Last year, Taylor had the chance to be the starting running back for the team that happens to have Jonathan Ogden at tackle (opportunity and environment: both positive). But even though he averaged 4.5 yards per carry and had an 8.1% DVOA—16th overall and five spots above Jamal Lewis—he is considered a backup or committee-back by both teams (the Ravens and Browns) that showed interest in him (perception: negative).

Najeh Davenport: As seen above, Davenport has the buzz and (had) the environment, but not the opportunity. Assuming Ahman Green does not tear his ACL, it is unlikely that his opportunity will come in 2005. Before, I suggested that with some exceptions this was a good reason for the right team to draft him late. That team, of course, is the only team for whom Davenport's lack of opportunity is a *good* thing—namely, the guy who owns Green. Normally, "handcuffing" is a fool's errand; you trick yourself into thinking that the backup is going to be a suitable replacement for your Pro Bowl–caliber starter. Take a deep breath, exhale, and you will realize that Aaron Stecker is no Deuce McAllister; Jesse Chatman cannot replace LaDanian Tomlinson; If Corey Dillon gets injured, Kevin Faulk of 2004 becomes the incorrectly used Kevin Faulk of 2002 again. But when you have a guy who can truly replace the injured star, grab him as an insurance policy.

DeShaun Foster: Our metrics aside—he put up a −2.3% DVOA in a meager 59 carries—Foster's team appears to see him as the running back of the very near future. At the very least, they see him as a guy who should have a shot at claiming that mantle. The opportunity is there, with Stephen Davis aging and Nick Goings hardly a solution. And the team, generally speaking, is strong on both sides of the ball. Note that on a pure talent level, factoring in injury history, Foster may not be the best of this bunch. And even the Panthers know it—why else would they have drafted a running back (Eric Shelton) in the second round of this year's draft? Still, the situation is good for Foster; or, at least, good enough to warrant you selecting him as a flyer in hopes that he turns into the next Rudi Johnson or Domanick Davis. DVOA doesn't like that he mixes so many one-yard runs with a couple of highlight runs. But if those highlight runs go into the end zone, you have a great fantasy player, even if Carolina doesn't have a great running back. It's the football equivalent of one of those baseball players who steals tons of bases and never walks.

Note that everything about Foster reeks of cautious optimism: The window of opportunity is small, he is perceived positively but with an air of disappointment, and the Panthers are a good but hardly great offensive squad. But that is what we are after—if the signals were more positive (as with, for example, Tatum Bell), well, the guy would be an obvious choice, and OPE would be a redundant tool in identifying him.

Summing It Up

In drafting your team, follow the Seven Habits. Not doing so is a recipe for disaster. That will get you the core you need: two starting running backs, a deep wide receiver pool, a solid quarterback, and the flexibility to make the right picks in later rounds.

In the opening rounds, OPE comes in to help you avoid the star players who are likely to decline due to a poor environment. In later rounds, OPE is your best tool to grab the Burlesons over the Gages, the Delhommes over the Garcias, and the Fosters over the Taylors, Davenports, and Smiths. It won't help you figure out which rookie wide receiver will be this year's Michael Clayton, but nobody's perfect.

Except Peyton Manning.

Fantasy Risers and Fallers

Al Bogdan and Aaron Schatz

Everyone has lists of fantasy sleepers and busts. But what exactly are sleepers and busts? Is a former backup who's been handed a starting job somewhere really a "sleeper"? Can a 32-year-old former stud running back relegated to a backup role really be considered a "bust"? We don't think so. Anyone can tell you that LaMont Jordan will do better than last year now that he's a starter in Oakland. No one expects Marshall Faulk to be a top-notch fantasy back now that he's relegated to backup/third down duty in St. Louis. But you'll find both those names prominently displayed in different lists of "sleepers" or "busts" in various fantasy publications this year.

We're all about objectivity here at *Pro Football Prospectus,* so our lists of fantasy players to watch aren't based on any subjective criteria like being a "sleeper" or "bust." Below you'll find the players who, based on our projections, will deviate the most from last year's performances. We expect these players to either rise or fall at least eight places in their respective positional rankings. In larger leagues, this could be the difference between being a valid number one option at the position to a borderline number two or three. In smaller leagues, these are players that could go from being a must-start to completely unplayable.

Top 10 Fantasy Fallers

Curtis Martin   RB   Jets

2004: 371 carries	1697 rushing yards	41 receptions	245 receiving yards	14 TD	Rank: 4
2005: 251 carries	1067 rushing yards	26 receptions	174 receiving yards	10 TD	Rank: 17

Martin cemented his place in the Hall of Fame last year, but he is just too old to keep this up. He'll be 32 this season. Only nine players in NFL history have topped 1,000 yards at the age of 32 or older. Only four of those cracked 1,100 yards, with John Riggins's 1,347 rushing yards in 1983 setting the record for old running backs. Martin was the only running back last year to surpass the 370-carry barrier, which is generally followed by injury (Jamal Anderson, Edgerrin James, Terrell Davis), loss of effectiveness (Eddie George, Ricky Williams), or incoherent sideline reporting (Eric Dickerson). Martin's receptions have also steadily declined each of the past five seasons, another sign that a running back is about to fall off the career cliff. New York made a great move by signing Derrick Blaylock as Martin's backup. It's more likely that Blaylock will end up splitting time with Martin by midseason.

Corey Dillon   RB   Patriots

2004: 345 carries	1635 rushing yards	15 receptions	103 receiving yards	13 TD	Rank: 7
2005: 290 carries	1226 rushing yards	12 receptions	78 receiving yards	11 TD	Rank: 16

Dillon reached career highs in carries, rushing yards, and rushing touchdowns in 2004, all at the age of 30. Running backs who reach their peak at the age of 30 or older are few and far between. Even rarer are those who are able to sustain that newfound level of performance. Only 12 other running backs in NFL history have had career highs in carries, yards, and touchdowns after turning 30. Only three did so while amassing over 1,000 rushing yards. John Riggins, the dean of older running backs, was able to have two more 1,000-yard seasons after peaking after 30. Rocky Bleier and Lamar Smith never topped 1,000 yards again.

Reuben Droughns   RB   Browns

2004: 275 carries	1240 rushing yards	32 receptions	241 receiving yards	8 TD	Rank: 13
2005: 191 carries	711 rushing yards	36 receptions	278 receiving yards	6 TD	Rank: 30

Did you take Clinton Portis in your fantasy league last year? Did you take Olandis Gary the year before? Well, Reuben Droughns is this summer's hottest sequel, *Denver Running Backs: Episode III.* After the converted fullback excelled behind the legendary Bronco offensive line, Cleveland picked him up in exchange for defensive linemen Ebenezer

Ekuban and Michael Myers, and he'll battle Lee Suggs for the role of primary halfback. But Droughns is no better as a halfback than Suggs or even that other guy on Cleveland's roster, William Green. Even if Droughns wins the job as Cleveland's number one running back, it shouldn't be long before he's exposed as yet another ex-Bronco runner who loses his connection to the Force after leaving the side of Darth Shanahan and settles back into his natural role as a blocking back or third down option.

Brett Favre   QB   Packers

2004: 4088 passing yards	30 TD	17 INT	Rank: 6
2005: 3728 passing yards	24 TD	19 INT	Rank: 19

Brett's entering his 15th NFL season, a feat that has been accomplished by 50 other quarterbacks in the history of the NFL. None of those 50 ever threw for 4,000 yards in a season in their 15th year or later. Only eight ever topped 3,000 yards, and only four ever threw 20 or more touchdowns in a season. His streak of games started is commendable, but sooner or later the constant pounding he's suffered in all of those games will take its toll on his performance. He'll also be without Marco Rivera and Mike Wahle, two of the best guards in football, blocking for him. With less time to throw the ball, Favre, we're guessing, will spend too much time as "Bad Brett," throwing the ball up into triple coverage.

Jake Delhomme   QB   Panthers

2004: 3886 passing yards	29 TD	15 INT	Rank: 7
2005: 3486 passing yards	23 TD	15 INT	Rank: 20

When Steve Smith went down for the year, everyone expected Delhomme's numbers to nosedive. Instead, they went up. There were two reasons. First, Muhsin Muhammad's incredible year: Take away passes intended for the now-departed Muhammad, and Delhomme's DVOA drops from 8.2% to −25.8%. But Delhomme's yards per attempt went up only slightly despite all those long bombs to Muhammad. The biggest reason why Delhomme threw for over 600 more yards compared to 2003 is that he had more pass attempts than in 2003, and the biggest reason for that was a defense that allowed 339 points instead of 304. Instead of playing from ahead and running out the clock, Carolina was playing from behind and throwing the ball. If Carolina's defense improves as we expect it will, Delhomme won't constantly be throwing late in games trying to make up a deficit.

Joey Harrington   QB   Lions

2004: 3047 passing yards	19 TD	12 INT	Rank: 16
2005: 2025 passing yards	14 TD	10 INT	Rank: 29

The over/under for Jeff Garcia's first start with Detroit is Week 6. After starting the season 1–4, Steve Mariucci will have no choice but to bench Harrington and allow Garcia to take revenge against the Cleveland Browns. We don't necessarily think Garcia will be a huge upgrade over Harrington, but with his former quarterback sitting on the sidelines Mariucci won't have much patience for another year of poor performances from Detroit's incumbent starter.

Donald Driver   WR   Packers

2004: 84 receptions	1208 yards	9 TD	Rank: 10
2005: 49 receptions	652 yards	3 TD	Rank: 51

Since we think Favre's going to decline, his receivers are likely to feel the sting as well, and that probably means Donald Driver and not Javon Walker. J-Walk is three years younger than Driver and has seen his numbers steadily increase over his first three seasons. Walker was also much more productive than Driver in the red zone, with a DVOA of 109.6% to Driver's 0.6%. With fewer red zone opportunities, Favre will likely concentrate on throwing to the receiver who's going to successfully make the six.

Jimmy Smith   WR   Jaguars

2004: 74 receptions	1172 rec yards	6 TD	Rank: 21
2005: 58 receptions	818 rec yards	5 TD	Rank: 29

Isaac Bruce   WR   Rams

2004: 89 receptions	1292 rec yards	6 TD	Rank: 12
2005: 63 receptions	864 rec yards	5 TD	Rank: 25

Both Jimmy Smith and Isaac Bruce are entering their eleventh seasons as starters for their teams. Both had a bit of a resurgence in 2004, gaining more yardage than in any recent season. It's highly unlikely, though, that receivers with as many years behind them as Smith and Bruce have will be able to keep up that level of performance. Instead, they're more likely to revert back to the slightly lower levels they had established in the two to three years leading up to 2004. They are both still going to be effective receivers, but as fantasy options they'll go from every-week starters to "play depending on opponent."

Brandon Stokley   WR   Colts

2004: 68 receptions	1077 yards	10 TD	Rank: 11
2005: 54 receptions	740 yards	5 TD	Rank: 38

Peyton Manning isn't going to throw for 49 touchdowns again. With Marcus Pollard gone and Marvin Harrison half a step slower than he once was, Stokley won't be able to catch defenses by surprise this season. Stokley may still be the best third receiver in football, but he won't reach 1,000 yards or double-digit touchdowns in 2005.

Bonus Faller

Tony Gonzalez   TE   Chiefs

2004: 102 receptions	1258 yards	7 TD	Rank: 2
2005: 83 receptions	938 yards	7 TD	Rank: 3

Tony Gonzalez has been either the number one or number two tight end in fantasy football for the past six years. Tony Gonzalez has a good chance of being the number one or number two tight end in fantasy football in 2005 as well. So what is he doing under "fantasy fallers"? The other tight ends in the NFL have finally caught up with him. Your typical fantasy draft since 2000 would see Gonzalez go in the third round, one or two other owners would reach for players like Shannon Sharpe or Jeremy Shockey in the fifth or sixth, and everyone else would grab whatever was left in the seventh or eighth round after filling out the rest of their starting lineups. And from 1999 to 2003, that was where Gonzalez deserved to go. Over that five-year span, Gonzo scored 27.7% more fantasy points than the tight end who finished behind him.

But we expect all that to change. Antonio Gates emerged last year as the new top tight end in football. With a bit less fanfare, Jason Witten developed into the Cowboys' top receiving option. Gonzo himself is now 29, entering his ninth year in the league, the point at which other top tight ends through history began the decline phase of their careers. Factor in decent production from tight ends like Shockey, Alge Crumpler, Randy McMichael, Dallas Clark, Jermaine Wiggins, and Todd Heap (if he's ever healthy), and the difference in quality between Gonzalez and the tight end you'll draft if you don't get Gonzalez is smaller than at any point since Gonzalez's emergence as a fantasy machine.

This doesn't mean that Gonzalez won't go in the third round of fantasy drafts this year, just that he shouldn't. You'll be much better off picking up the best available running back or wide receiver in round three and waiting until the sixth or seventh round to pick up a tight end who will give you solid production for a fraction of the cost.

Top 10 Fantasy Risers

Kevin Jones   RB   Lions

2004: 241 carries	1133 rushing yards	28 receptions	180 receiving yards	6 TD	Rank: 21
2005: 356 carries	1605 rushing yards	38 receptions	291 receiving yards	12 TD	Rank: 5

Julius Jones   RB   Cowboys

2004: 197 carries	819 rushing yards	17 receptions	109 receiving yards	7 TD	Rank: 28
2005: 366 carries	1584 rushing yards	39 receptions	293 receiving yards	12 TD	Rank: 6

Ladies and gentlemen, meet the top two rushers in the NFL in 2005, Kevin and Julius Jones. LT2 and Shaun Alexander may find the end zone more, while Tiki Barber and Domanick Davis will gain more receiving yards out of the backfield. Besides those four, we don't think you'll find better fantasy running backs than either of these two. (Though Edgerrin James will be pretty close.) The issue is age: young, like the Joneses, is better than old, like Priest Holmes and Curtis Martin. Kevin adds ex-Colt Rick DeMulling to his offensive line; Julius adds ex-Packer Marco Rivera. And both had strong finishes to 2004: Kevin averaged 113 yards per game over the last eight weeks, while Julius averaged 114 yards per game after entering the Cowboys' starting lineup in Week 11. Kevin gets a bonus reason for optimism: We project Detroit to have one of the four easiest schedules in the league, including a number of defenses that are much weaker against the run than the pass (Carolina, Cincinnati, and New Orleans among them).

Anquan Boldin   WR   Cardinals

2004: 56 receptions	623 receiving yards	1 TD	Rank: 59
2005: 76 receptions	1011 receiving yards	7 TD	Rank: 14

Don't forget about Anquan Boldin. Two years ago he was a rookie sensation. Last year, he missed six games because of knee surgery and struggled early upon returning to the Cardinal lineup. But Boldin excelled toward the end of the season, putting up a DVOA of 82.9% over the last four games. Kurt Warner wasn't much of a starting quarterback last season, but he was better than anything the Cardinals put on the field. Even if Warner broke his hand during training camp, a full year of Josh McCown would be better than screwing around with John Navarre and Shaun King. Fully healthy, Boldin will reemerge as a fantasy fixture this year.

Laveraneus Coles   WR   Jets

2004: 90 receptions	950 receiving yards	1 TD	Rank: 40
2005: 74 receptions	947 receiving yards	6 TD	Rank: 17

The list of the ten most similar receivers to Coles over a three-year span includes players who would go on to 12 Pro Bowl appearances and 22 1,000-yard seasons over the rest of their careers. Coles had his lowest yards per catch numbers with Washington last season, but the blame for that falls more on the poor quarterback play of Mark Brunell and Patrick Ramsey than on Coles. Both Rod Gardner and James Thrash also saw their yards per catch drop by at least half a yard last season from their career average. Reunited with Chad Pennington, Coles should jump right back into the mix as a legitimate fantasy option. It's not easy to gain 900 yards and score only one touchdown.

Randy Moss   WR   Raiders

2004: 49 receptions	767 receiving yards	13 TD	Rank: 18
2005: 81 receptions	1090 receiving yards	10 TD	Rank: 3

OK, this one's a gimme. No one expects Moss to struggle like he did last year after missing three games and having limited effectiveness in others because of a hamstring injury. But, if you look at the projection, we're not expecting a full season of Moss in Oakland to be the same as a full season of Moss in Minnesota. Moss will miss the friendly confines of the Metrodome and the friendly deep tosses of Daunte Culpepper. He will suffer from a schedule that includes the great defenses of the AFC East and the improving defenses of the NFC East. Moss should be back among the top fantasy receivers in football this year, but don't expect him to be worth a first-round pick as in years past.

Andre Johnson   WR   Texans

2004: 79 receptions	1142 receiving yards	7 TD	Rank: 23
2005: 79 receptions	1107 receiving yards	7 TD	Rank: 11

No, that's not a typo. We expect Johnson to be pretty much the same player he was last year, but to jump 12 spots in the wide receiver rankings. Our projections aren't specific predictions of exact numbers; they're "mean projections" that represent the middle of a range of possibilities. Like any projection system based on statistical regression, there is going to be regression to the mean. The two phrases are, after all, related. Andre Johnson's mean projection is exactly what he did last year. He could be better, could be worse. However, for most of last year's top receivers who are not named Randy Moss or Torry Holt, the projection is a drop from last year, because last year represented a performance more toward the upper boundary of what we would expect from them in 16 random games. Thus, guys like Muhammad and Horn and Smith drop, very few guys move up, and guys who stay the same move up in rank. Like Andre Johnson.

Hines Ward   WR   Steelers

2004: 80 receptions	1004 receiving yards	4 TD	Rank: 30
2005: 88 receptions	1125 receiving yards	7 TD	Rank: 9

Plaxico Burress   WR   Giants

2004: 35 receptions	698 receiving yards	5 TD	Rank: 42
2005: 62 receptions	937 receiving yards	6 TD	Rank: 19

We're projecting Ben Roethlisberger to throw almost 1,000 more yards than he did last season. Those extra passing yards have to go somewhere. With Plaxico Burress out of town, Hines Ward is the natural beneficiary. Ward put up his highest yards per catch numbers of his career in 2004, but his fantasy numbers were hurt by the Steelers' increased attention on the running game. Ward was Roethlisberger's favorite red zone target last year. With Burress gone, Ward should see even more looks inside the 20. If he can convert a few more of those targets into touchdowns, Ward will be back as a number one fantasy wide receiver.

Burress will become the clear number one receiver in New York, after playing Robin to Ward's Batman in Pittsburgh. Plaxico is exactly the type of receiver a young quarterback like Eli Manning needs. At 6′5″, 225 pounds, Burress will provide a big target for Manning to throw to. He also gives Manning a legitimate big play option. Burress's 16.0 career yards per catch is the highest on the Giants' current roster.

Matt Hasselbeck　　QB　Seahawks

　2004: 3382 passing yards　　22 TD　　　15 INT　　　Rank: 14
　2005: 4104 passing yards　　27 TD　　　16 INT　　　Rank: 4

There were two reasons why Hasselbeck's numbers went down in 2004 while league-wide quarterback numbers went up. First, he missed two games to injury. Second, his third down performance fell through the floor, and as we point out in the San Diego chapter, a small rebound in that area has huge consequences. If Hasselbeck can stay on the field for a full 16 games, there's no reason he won't put up similar numbers to those he compiled in 2003. Two more games on the field move Matt from a fantasy backup to a fantasy starter. Average performance on third downs moves him from a fantasy starter to a first-tier starter. He's another example of why it doesn't make sense to grab for a quarterback in the first two rounds of a fantasy draft. Wait until the fourth or fifth round and grab Hasselbeck instead of using a late first-round pick on Daunte Culpepper.

Kerry Collins　　QB　Raiders

　2004: 2495 passing yards　　21 TD　　　20 INT　　　Rank: 15
　2005: 4138 passing yards　　28 TD　　　19 INT　　　Rank: 5

Randy Moss + LaMont Jordan + Jerry Porter > Jerry Porter + Amos Zereoue + Ronald Curry.

In the past, 1,000-yard receivers who switched teams generally didn't have much of an impact on the statistics of their new quarterbacks. That's because in the past, nearly all of those receivers were glorified number two options like Peerless Price and Qadry Ismail, not superstars like Terrell Owens and Randy Moss. It should surprise nobody if Moss has the same effect on Kerry Collins that Owens had on Donovan McNabb, especially since the Raiders are also getting a major upgrade in the running department—and aren't getting a major upgrade in the "keep other teams off the board" department. Hey, Randy, we're down by 14 with 10 minutes left. Go long.

Drive-Based Win Probability

Jim Armstrong

In Week 1 of the 2004 season, the Minnesota Vikings were leading the Dallas Cowboys 28–17 when Antoine Winfield recovered a Richie Anderson fumble, giving the Minnesota offense possession of the ball at their own 19 yard line with an 11-point lead and 9:35 left to play in the game. The turnover ended any realistic hopes the Cowboys might have had of winning the game. The Vikings then proceeded to drive down the field 81 yards to score another touchdown to put the final nail in the coffin at 35–17, the eventual final score. Although the game was pretty much already decided before that final touchdown, Minnesota still racked up an additional seven points and 81 yards of offense.

Meanwhile, earlier that day in Buffalo, the Jacksonville Jaguars received the ball after a punt with 2:07 remaining, trailing the Bills 10–6. The Jaguars started their drive at their own 20 yard line and drove 80 yards down the field, converting two fourth-down plays along the way, and culminating in a seven-yard touchdown pass from Byron Leftwich to Ernest Wilford as time expired. The scoring play was upheld after review, giving the Jaguars a 13–10 victory.

Viewed out of context, these two drives look pretty similar. They both put seven points up on the board and gained about the same number of yards. And in the final season statistics, the numbers from these two drives add up all the same. Yet one drive was clearly the difference between winning and losing, while the other was an afterthought to an already decided outcome. What we would like is a way to determine how much each of these drives contributes to its team's ultimate goal of winning the game.

Baseball researchers, or sabermetricians, as they are called, have been studying Win Probabilities for dozens of years. Many different names have been given to these metrics, including Win Averages, Game Percentages, Win Expectancies, Game State Wins, and Win Values, but the process is pretty much all the same. At any given point in a game, an average team has a certain likelihood of winning the game based on the current game state. The probability is determined by analyzing hundreds or thousands of games looking for similar game states, and then calculating how often each team ended up winning those games. Taking it a step further, each time a game moves from one state to the next, the change in win probability can be computed.

That change can then be credited to the teams and even divided among individual players. Finally, adding them all together over the course of a game or a season results in a reasonable approximation of how much each team's units or players contributed to the success of the team.

In baseball, there are 24 possible base-out situations of runners on base and number of outs. Ignoring extra-inning games, there are 18 time periods, or half-innings, in a baseball game. And realistically, there are about 15 possible score differentials, ranging from behind seven runs to ahead seven runs. That leaves 6,480 possible combinations of score, inning, base runners, and innings. A Major League Baseball season has 2,430 games. Each game has a minimum of 54 game states and usually many more. Play-by-play accounts of baseball games are publicly available for the last 30 seasons. It's pretty easy to see that baseball analysts have quite a bit of data to work with to derive very accurate Win Probabilities.

It's a much more complex problem in football. First of all, there are 99 yard lines on a football field. In a nonovertime game there are 60 minutes, or 3,600 ticks of the clock. And a reasonably close game would give you about 31 score differentials, ranging from behind by 15 points to ahead by 15 points. There are four possible downs and perhaps 20 different yards commonly needed for a first down. That leaves 14,731,200 possible situations, or nearly 1 billion if you're a stickler for time accuracy. Thank goodness the NFL hasn't gone to tenths of a second in the final minute like basketball! There are only 256 games in an NFL season, each with about 130 plays. And obtaining historical play-by-play data of NFL games has been a rather difficult task. Obviously using such a fine-grained approach is not very feasible, so it's not really surprising that Win Probability metrics aren't as common as they are in baseball.

In *The Hidden Game of Football,* authors Bob Carroll, Pete Palmer, and John Thorn did compute Win Probabilities using a simplified approach. They ignored the down and distance factors and used two seasons' worth of drive charts to estimate Win Probabilities only at the beginning and end of each drive. They also grouped the time units into larger intervals. After computing the baseline values, they worked through three games in detail in order to determine the net effect of each team's units on the eventual outcome.

We took a similar approach of using drive charts to estimate Win Probabilities. Using drive charts from all 1,752 regular-season games from 1998 to 2004, we looked only at game states at the beginning and end of drives. The yard lines were broken into 20 five-yard units, the time units were simplified to 12 five-minute intervals, and 31 score differentials were considered as described above. That left us with a much more manageable 7,440 possible situations. For each of these situations, its Win Probability baseline was computed by tabulating the number of times the team with possession of the ball in that situation went on to win the game and dividing by the total number of occurrences of that situation. For those situations where the number of occurrences was below a certain threshold, neighboring yard line units were combined and in some uncommon instances neighboring time units were also combined. Then these baselines were used to compute the values of various drive-based events of every game.

To show how this works, let's look at the examples above. In situations similar to the one Minnesota found itself in, leading by 11 points with 9:35 remaining and the ball at their own 19 yard line, the Win Probability baseline based on all those years of previous NFL games was 0.96. That is, an average team against an average opponent in similar situations ended up winning the game 96% of the time. After they scored the touchdown to take an 18-point lead, their Win Probability baseline increased to 0.993. That means for all that work in driving 81 yards for the touchdown, Minnesota's offense only increased its team's chances of winning the game by about 3%. Likewise, the performance of the Cowboy defense on that drive decreased its team's chances of winning by 3%.

In the other example described earlier, when Jacksonville gained possession of the ball on their own 20 with 2:07 remaining and trailing by 4 points, their Win Probability baseline was 0.234, meaning that results from previous comparable situations indicated that their chances of winning the game was about 23%. Of course, their 81-yard drive not only ended in a touchdown but it also ended with no time remaining in the game, meaning that Buffalo had no subsequent chance to win. At the end of a (nontie) game, the Win Probability baseline for the winning team is always 1.0, so Jacksonville's drive increased their chances of winning by a whopping 76.6%! And Buffalo's defense on that drive netted a −0.766 Win Probability value. So those seven points and 81 yards were about 25 times more important to Jaguars in that game's context than the seven points and 80 yards were to the Vikings in their game.

Of course, those are two of the more extreme examples. But we can work through every drive of every game of the season in similar fashion and assign a Win Probability value to each team's offense and defense for each drive. And by noting the last line of scrimmage and spe-

cific result of each drive, such as punts and field goal attempts, and the situation prior to the next drive, we can also compute Win Probability values for special teams units. Although the baselines are computed on a drive-by-drive basis, the values assigned to each team's units are cumulative for the game, representing how much each contributed to its team's win or loss.

Before we get too far with this, we need to emphasize that the Win Probability baselines are just averages. Besides down and distance, there are several other factors that are not considered in these baselines—for example, the relative strengths of the teams, the game location (that is, weather effects and home field advantage), and player injuries. Perhaps even more important, Win Probabilities are not necessarily predictive. They can be used to analyze and evaluate what has already happened, but they may not be as meaningful in determining what will happen in the future. (This is the answer to the frequently asked question of why Win Probabilities are not part of the computation of the DVOA ratings seen throughout this book.) In particular, Win Probabilities can fluctuate greatly in critical situations, as we described with the Jacksonville-Buffalo game, but further research is required to determine whether performance in clutch situations is a distinct skill or simply the residue of opportunity. Finally, there are some limitations with the methodology used here. Clearly, some situations are more common than others and not uniformly distributed within our chosen groupings. Thus, the varying sample sizes of game state occurrences imply that the observed Win Probabilities for some situations are probably more accurate than those for other situations. Later we will discuss alternative approaches to calculating Win Probabilities.

However, despite these limitations, we believe that a set of average Win Probabilities is still a very useful tool. Once we've computed the Win Probability values for each team's units (offense, defense, and special teams), we can also figure the average contribution per game toward a team's success over the course of the season. This suggests an alternate metric for evaluating and ranking teams and their individual units.

Table 1 shows the results as tallied up for the 2004 regular season, and here's a bit of an explanation. In every game, each change in Win Probability for one team is the exact negative for the other team. Thus the sum of Win Probability values assigned in a game is always zero. At the beginning of a game, each team has a 50% chance of winning, so after the game is over the winning team's Win Probability value is about 50% and the losing team's value is about −50%. The team averages shown are computed on a per-game basis. For example, Pittsburgh's offensive value of 0.675 means that their offensive unit improved their chances of winning by about 67.5% each game. Because a

TABLE 1. TOTAL WIN PROBABILITY VALUES BY TEAM AND UNIT, 2004

Team	Total	Rank	Offense	Rank	Defense	Rank	Special Teams	Rank
PIT	0.480	1	0.675	5	−0.261	1	0.066	4
NE	0.424	2	0.614	7	−0.303	4	0.113	2
PHI	0.335	3	0.559	14	−0.262	2	0.038	10
GB	0.291	4	0.612	8	−0.529	15	0.208	1
SD	0.264	5	0.727	3	−0.428	8	−0.035	24
IND	0.214	6	0.794	2	−0.578	23	−0.002	17
ATL	0.185	7	0.580	12	−0.406	7	0.011	13
NYJ	0.148	8	0.582	11	−0.430	9	−0.004	19
DEN	0.140	9	0.624	6	−0.528	14	0.044	8
JAC	0.113	10	0.586	10	−0.533	18	0.061	5
NO	0.082	11	0.533	16	−0.538	19	0.087	3
BAL	0.072	12	0.525	17	−0.284	3	−0.169	31
BUF	0.069	13	0.363	27	−0.342	5	0.049	6
CIN	0.013	14	0.482	22	−0.502	12	0.033	12
SEA	−0.021	15	0.595	9	−0.552	21	−0.063	29
CAR	−0.034	16	0.515	18	−0.505	13	−0.044	26
STL	−0.038	17	0.558	15	−0.533	17	−0.063	28
DET	−0.066	18	0.495	20	−0.559	22	−0.003	18
MIN	−0.084	19	0.714	4	−0.659	29	−0.140	30
WAS	−0.109	20	0.285	31	−0.398	6	0.005	14
HOU	−0.114	21	0.468	23	−0.543	20	−0.039	25
DAL	−0.119	22	0.512	19	−0.632	26	0.000	16
KC	−0.120	23	0.807	1	−0.921	32	−0.006	20
NYG	−0.127	24	0.427	24	−0.596	24	0.042	9
OAK	−0.185	25	0.567	13	−0.786	31	0.035	11
TB	−0.192	26	0.291	30	−0.530	16	0.047	7
CHI	−0.214	27	0.222	32	−0.439	10	0.002	15
TEN	−0.221	28	0.492	21	−0.658	28	−0.054	27
ARI	−0.236	29	0.410	25	−0.473	11	−0.173	32
MIA	−0.239	30	0.369	26	−0.600	25	−0.008	21
CLE	−0.342	31	0.321	29	−0.642	27	−0.021	23
SF	−0.371	32	0.343	28	−0.698	30	−0.016	22

team's defense usually leaves their team worse off than when they came onto the field, defensive Win Probability values are almost always negative. Pittsburgh's defense decreased their changes of winning by just 26.1% per game, tops in the league. And their special teams increased their chances of winning by 6.6% per game.

As you would probably expect, ranking of the totals for each team mirrors pretty close the won-loss record of the team. This makes sense because Win Probabilities are based on moving your team toward victory. Where things start to get interesting is in the rankings of the individual units. According to these numbers, no team's offensive unit did more to help itself win than Kansas City's. And no team's defensive unit did more to help itself lose than, yep,

those Chiefs again. The units fed off each other, and not in a cooperative manner. Their offense had lots of opportunities to keep the Chiefs in every game, and their defense had lots of opportunities to screw things right back up again. Put it together and you get a 7–9 team. Still, one could argue that no player did more to help his team win than Trent Green did for the Chiefs, who played without the injured Priest Holmes for half the season.

Green Bay's special teams units weren't much better than average by most rankings. But in terms of helping the team win games, it matters greatly *when* the big plays were made. The Packers won four games on last-second Ryan Longwell field goals. And two of those game-winning field goals were set up by key special teams plays. In their first game against their division-rival Vikings, Robert Ferguson's 37-yard kickoff return gave them excellent field position. And later in the season at Detroit, they benefited from a 19-yard Nick Harris punt leading up to another field goal in the final seconds. Of course, that may have been just good luck, just as opposing kickers converted field goals against the Packers at only a 68% rate, boosting their field goal defense ranking. That's one reason why these rankings are not predictive. On the other hand, if there really is ice water running through Longwell's veins, it shows up nicely here.

Besides revealing how some teams and units have more critical opportunities based on the game situations, the cumulative nature of Win Probability values is affected by the interaction of a team's units. For example, a team with a strong defense will force a lot of punts, suggesting that its punt return unit will have more than its fair share of opportunities to influence the outcome of its games.

Other Applications of Win Probabilities

Football coaches make most of their pregame and in-game decisions based on intuition and experience. They generally have an instinctual feel for which choices help their team win the game and which hinder their team's chances. We could also use Win Probability baselines as a set of guidelines to evaluate strategy questions in the context of the game situation. However, our drive-based baselines may not be granular enough to be appropriate for specific down and distance situations.

Win Probabilities can also be used to determine the average values of various in-game events. For example, knowing the average effect of a turnover on the outcome of a game, as well as understanding how often they occur, can help shape a coach's philosophies and threshold for taking risks. We computed the Win Probability values of some common events and present them in table 2 along with their frequencies. These represent the average change in Win Probability according to actual distribution of occurrences among the game situations, not the theoretical effects as if the events were equally likely to occur in any game situation. For example, the average touchdown occurs from the opponent's 16-yard line, but would be more valuable in terms of Win Probability if scored from midfield.

One interesting conclusion is that an average touchdown is worth about six times more than an average turnover costs. This suggests that teams should not be afraid to risk turnovers in their quest to score touchdowns. It also indicates that the NFL's passer rating, which penal-

TABLE 2. WIN PROBABILITY VALUES OF FOOTBALL EVENTS

Event	Value	Frequency
Turnover	−0.031	0.027 per play
Interception	−0.032	0.028 per pass attempt
Fumble Lost	−0.028	0.011 per play
Touchdown	0.183	0.036 per play
Field Goal	0.083	0.794 per attempt
Field Goal Missed	−0.016	0.197 per attempt
Field Goal Blocked	−0.047	0.009 per attempt
Punt	−0.011	0.414 per drive
Punt Blocked	−0.069	0.003 per punt
Safety	−0.030	0.0007 per play
Turnover on Downs	−0.012	0.484 per 4th-down attempt
First Down	0.001	0.258 per play

izes interceptions more than it rewards touchdowns, puts too much emphasis on avoiding interceptions. Also of note from the table is that interceptions are actually more costly than lost fumbles. Previous analysis has suggested that interceptions are less costly because they tend to occur farther downfield. However, our research shows that interceptions are more damaging because they are nearly 50% more likely to be returned for touchdowns.

We can also use Win Probability values to break down turnovers based on where they occur on the football field. In *Hidden Game,* the authors present a chart estimating that turnovers are worth about the same whether they occur at midfield or near either end zone. A 2003 article on FootballOutsiders.com, "How Many Points Is a Turnover Worth?", updated this research by using a nonlinear equation to estimate the value of having the ball at each point on the field (showing, of course, that turnovers are more costly at either end of the field, and less costly the closer they occur to midfield).[1]

Win Probability values suggest that this statement is half correct: Turnovers are indeed most costly near your own goal, but they are least costly in your opponent's end (see table 3). The reason appears to be that turnovers near your own goal are more likely to be returned for touchdowns, which results in seven points for your opponent with no chance for a defensive stand.

Future Research

In order to estimate more fine-grained Win Probabilities that consider down and distance to go, play-by-play data needs to be analyzed. As discussed earlier, it may not be

---

1. This article can be found at: www.footballoutsiders.com/ramblings.php?p=48.

TABLE 3: TURNOVER WIN PROBABILITY VALUES BY FIELD LOCATION

Own 1–19	−0.038
Own 20–39	−0.034
Own 40–Opp. 40	−0.030
Opp. 39–20	−0.024
Opp. 19–1	−0.015

computationally feasible to use an empirical approach, as we did for drive-based Win Probabilities. However, advanced statistical modeling techniques such as dynamic programming may help with deriving approximations and minimize inaccuracies.

Reasonably accurate guidelines would be a particularly useful tool for evaluating strategies involving fourth down plays, point-after-touchdown decisions, penalty acceptance, and instant replay challenges. Even ordinary play calling might benefit from determining the distribution of outcomes for a set of possible actions (for example, run middle, run wide, short pass, or long pass) based on the given situation. A play-by-play methodology also has potential for evaluating individual players, particularly quarterbacks, by dividing the Win Probability values among key players.

Because Win Probabilities can measure how crucial game situations are, they could also be the foundation for assessing proficiency in clutch situations as well as exploring whether certain teams, players, or coaching strategies are more suited for come-from-behind victories or more susceptible to squandering large leads.

Debunking the Myth of Drive Momentum

Tim Gerheim and Jim Armstrong

Wearing out the defense: It's an important goal of offensive football, if the punditry is to be believed. You run the ball to wear out the defense and set up the pass. You want to put together a long drive to wear out the defense and make it easier to move the ball, both now and for the rest of the game. Everyone knows that defensive players tire faster than offensive ones, right?

Not so fast. Offenses don't get better as drives progress. They don't get better as games progress. They don't get better after the half. They don't get better if you laugh. They don't get better if they're Rams. They don't get better, Sam I Am.

Conventional wisdom says that offenses gain "momentum" with each successful play, but defenses are just as likely to stop an offense (that is, force a punt, turnover, or field goal attempt) that has made five first downs as one that has made none.

We came to this conclusion after looking at every regular-season drive from 1998 to 2004, with the exception of those that consisted of nothing but taking a knee (drives at the end of a half with three or fewer plays and negative yardage). By noting how many first downs were gained in each drive, we were able to determine how often a drive stalls after each first down. Table 1 shows the results: No matter how long the drive has been, there's about a 34%

chance that it will stall before the next first down—put a different way, there's a 66% chance that an offense will get its next first down.

The difference between 33.5% and 34.5% is just not meaningful, particularly given the lack of any kind of trend. The numbers for six and seven first downs are more varied because of small sample size. So much for a drive's momentum. So much for wearing out the defense, either physically or psychologically. A drive is a laborious war of wills and attrition as much for the offense as it is for the defense. Your job doesn't get any easier until you've put the ball in the end zone and retired to the bench, with its simple comforts of Gatorade and oxygen.

Debunking the myth of drive momentum offers important lessons for defenses just as much as offenses. Keeping in mind the facts of the situation allows the defensive players to keep their confidence up, knowing, even as the offense scores first down after first down, that on average they will get a stop on one of every three sets of downs.

These results also underscore the importance of both big plays and good field position. A play that gains substantially more than ten yards reduces the number of first downs needed to reach the end zone. Likewise, having good starting field position means not only fewer yards but also fewer first downs required to reach the Promised Land. And that means fewer opportunities for the defense to make the best-laid schemes o' Weis and Hen(ning) gang aft agley.

The insight that an average offense facing an average defense has a 66% chance of getting another first down suggests a new metric to add to our toolbox to judge the efficiency of offensive and defensive teams: Drive Success Rate (or more precisely, series of downs success rate), or DSR. It measures the likelihood that a team's offense will get another first down (or a touchdown, which the official NFL statisticians also count as a first down) in a given set of downs. And the equivalent defensive number measures how often a defense will allow another first down. Tables 2 and 3 show each team's 2004 offensive and defensive DSR, along with its traditional NFL rank by total yardage and its DVOA rank.

TABLE 1. FIRST DOWNS AND STALLED DRIVES

First Downs	Percent Stalled	Stalled/Total
0	0.340	13,791/40,570
1	0.335	8,687/25,895
2	0.339	5,438/16,059
3	0.345	3,124/9,055
4	0.339	1,437/4,244
5	0.344	488/1,417
6	0.276	84/304
7	0.361	13/36

TABLE 2. 2004 DRIVE SUCCESS RATE, OFFENSE

Team	DSR	DSR Rank	Yds Rank	DVOA Rank	Team	DSR	DSR Rank	Yds Rank	DVOA Rank	Team	DSR	DSR Rank	Yds Rank	DVOA Rank
IND	0.783	1	2	1	SEA	0.682	12	8	13	CIN	0.644	23	18	11
KC	0.770	2	1	2	PHI	0.679	13	9	6	TB	0.637	24	22	23
MIN	0.755	3	4	3	HOU	0.679	14	19	14	DET	0.632	25	24	18
SD	0.737	4	10	8	TEN	0.665	15	11	26	ARI	0.626	26	27	30
NE	0.733	5	7	4	DAL	0.662	16	14	19	SF	0.618	27	26	29
GB	0.725	6	3	9	ATL	0.662	17	20	24	BAL	0.618	28	31	16
DEN	0.703	7	5	10	NO	0.658	18	15	20	WAS	0.613	29	30	28
STL	0.699	8	6	12	OAK	0.656	19	17	17	MIA	0.601	30	29	31
NYJ	0.697	9	12	5	JAC	0.653	20	21	25	CLE	0.592	31	28	27
PIT	0.691	10	16	7	NYG	0.652	21	23	22	CHI	0.553	32	32	32
CAR	0.688	11	13	15	BUF	0.645	22	25	21					

TABLE 3. 2004 DRIVE SUCCESS RATE, DEFENSE

Team	DSR	DSR Rank	Yds Rank	DVOA Rank	Team	DSR	DSR Rank	Yds Rank	DVOA Rank	Team	DSR	DSR Rank	Yds Rank	DVOA Rank
DEN	0.598	1	4	5	PHI	0.663	12	10	13	ATL	0.688	23	14	16
WAS	0.603	2	3	3	NE	0.666	13	9	6	DAL	0.692	24	16	25
BAL	0.613	3	6	2	JAC	0.668	14	11	8	NO	0.696	25	32	26
BUF	0.614	4	2	1	CLE	0.67	15	15	24	SF	0.697	26	24	32
PIT	0.623	5	1	4	SEA	0.978	16	26	21	TEN	0.699	27	27	23
TB	0.625	6	5	7	CAR	0.684	17	20	10	GB	0.703	28	25	29
ARI	0.625	7	12	15	NYG	0.684	18	13	22	IND	0.709	29	29	18
MIA	0.629	8	8	9	SD	0.685	19	18	11	KC	0.723	30	31	28
CHI	0.634	9	21	12	DET	0.687	20	22	20	OAK	0.744	31	30	27
NYJ	0.656	10	7	19	HOU	0.688	21	23	14	MIN	0.748	32	28	31
CIN	0.659	11	19	17	STL	0.688	22	17	30					

DSR runs generally congruent with traditional NFL and DVOA rankings, but there are some interesting disagreements. DSR much prefers San Diego's offense and Arizona's defense, and it distinctly downgrades Philadelphia's offense and New England's defense. The discrepancy probably traces back primarily to third down percentage.

San Diego on offense and Arizona on defense, although they ranked as mediocre in terms of yards, had elite third down percentages, 46.6% and 31.6%, respectively. Philadelphia's offense converted third downs at a rate of just 36.9%, which, unlike their top ten yardage and DVOA numbers, is fairly average. Likewise, New England's top ten defense had just the 21st-ranked third down percentage, allowing opponents to convert 38.8% of the time.

It only makes sense that DSR should be heavily influenced by third down efficiency. The average first down (as we've seen) ultimately leads to another first down 66% of the time, but the average third down is converted only about 41% of the time. So improving upon third down efficiency will have the greatest impact on a team's first down conversion rate.

(Of course, DVOA is also adjusted for situation and strength of opponent, and considers the effect of turnovers. The former is part of the disagreement about the San Diego offense and Arizona defense, the latter part of the disagreement about the Philadelphia offense and New England defense.)

If momentum doesn't show up during a drive, does it show up *after* a drive, particularly a long touchdown drive in which a defense was dominated all the way down the field? We wondered whether long drives resulted in any physical effect of fatigue on the defense or any psychological effects of demoralizing the defense.

To help answer this question, we defined long drives as those gaining 80 or more yards and resulting in a touchdown. For each of these drives, we looked at the drives in the same game immediately preceding and immediately following the long drive and involving the same offensive and defensive units. If there is some negative effect on the defense after long drives, we would expect the defense to perform worse their next time out on the field than they did prior to the long drive. Since the set of *before* drives and the set of *after* drives contain the same team matchups, no adjustment for offensive or defensive quality is necessary.

"But wait!" you're saying. "Everyone knows that offenses get better during games, since defenses tire. That's why you need to establish the run—to open up the pass." Of course, you didn't really say that. You're a sophisticated *Pro Football Prospectus* reader, you understand cause and effect, and you know there's no such thing as "establishing the run."[1] But let's just pretend you did say it.

To see whether offenses indeed gain an advantage later in games, we looked at every regular-season drive from 1998 to 2004, throwing out kneel-down drives and drives that began with under five minutes left in a half—since at that point the shortage of time drastically changes teams' playing styles and strategies and reduces their chances of scoring points. We grouped the drives by the quarter in which the drive began, and calculated the average points, yards, and number of plays per drive, as well as DSR (table 4).

Once again, there is no significant trend. Points and yards per drive fall off in the second half after peaking in the second quarter, which actually implies that defenses gain a slight upper hand later in the game. Plays per drive tell a bit of a different story: It falls in each quarter until the fourth, when it rises noticeably. Teams get fewer points in more plays in the fourth quarter—everyone running out the clock or playing a prevent defense, please raise your hand. The long and the short of it is that neither the offense nor the defense gains a significant advantage over the other as the game progresses.

Back to those long drives. We identified 738 sets of long drives fitting our definition after again discarding

TABLE 5: EFFECTS BEFORE AND AFTER LONG DRIVES

Drive	Points	Yards	Plays	DSR
Before	1.925	27.31	5.348	0.662
After	1.905	28.94	5.686	0.683

those in which the *after* drive started with less than five minutes remaining in the half or started in a different half than the long drive or the *before* drive. The long drives in our data set gained, on average, 85 yards in about eight plays, using up nearly five minutes off the game clock. We then looked at how successful the *before* drives were compared to the *after* drives using several metrics (table 5).

At first it appears that the *after* drives do slightly favor the offense, at least in terms of moving the ball even though points scored are nearly equal—indeed slightly lower. But take a look at the same numbers, broken down by the score of the game during the long drive (see table 6), and you will get a much clearer picture. When the long drive occurs in a close game, the difference between *before* and *after* drives is reminiscent of the difference between the third and fourth quarter: slightly fewer points and slightly more plays per drive. In other words, the effect attributable to the long drive is negligible.

The results are much different in blowouts. The *before* drives, for teams either leading or trailing by eight or more points, are very different from average, and even more different from each other. It's basically the difference between good teams and bad teams. Leading teams' *before* drives are spectacularly efficient: more than 150% of the scoring on slightly more yards and plays than the drives in close games. Trailing teams' *before* drives, by contrast, are terrible across the board.

By the time a leading team gets to the *after* drive, it is almost always ahead by two touchdowns. Is it any wonder that teams leading by such a margin aren't such effective scoring machines anymore? The clock, at that point, is their enemy more than the opponent, and they have adjusted their strategy accordingly.

The case of a trailing team managing to put together a long drive may be a cautionary tale against the use of the prevent defense. From immediately before to immediately after a long drive, these teams go from scoring at a rate less than half the average to above-average productivity. Maybe it really is a form of momentum—the crowd is fired up (or fearful, depending which is the home team) about an impending comeback, and its spirit infects both the trail-

TABLE 4. SCORING AND PERFORMANCE PER DRIVE BY QUARTER

Quarter	Points	Yards	Plays	DSR
1	1.742	27.777	5.676	0.665
2	1.806	28.309	5.657	0.654
3	1.763	27.803	5.641	0.67
4	1.682	27.727	5.740	0.657
OT	1.611	30.473	5.556	0.629

---

1. Running the ball more often early in the game has very little correlation with winning percentage; this was the subject of the first article ever written for Football Outsiders, which can be read here: http://www.footballoutsiders.com/ramblings.php?p=3.

TABLE 6. EFFECTS BEFORE AND AFTER LONG DRIVES, BY SCORE DIFFERENTIAL

Drive	Score Differential	Points	Yards	Plays	DSR
Before	+/− 7 points	1.919	27.560	5.436	0.666
After	+/− 7 points	1.879	29.285	5.673	0.679
Before	leading by 8+ points	3.164	33.947	5.781	0.763
After	leading by 8+ points	1.693	23.702	5.447	0.645
Before	trailing by 8+ points	0.853	20.481	4.628	0.562
After	trailing by 8+ points	2.194	32.248	5.946	0.728

ing offense and the leading defense. Maybe the defense, comfortably ahead late in the game, relaxed into an "it only prevents victories" defense and, when that got defeated (the long drive), couldn't get its base back under it.

It's unclear exactly why teams improve on offense upon closing the gap in the score with a long drive. When one team is leading by a large margin, there are several other factors that affect strategy. What is clear is that those comeback games featuring long drives are by far the least common; close games and long drives by winning teams are much more the norm, and those show very little support for either fatigue or demoralization effects of long drives. So the next time you see your friendly neighborhood strength and conditioning coach, give him your thanks; he's tired of having matters of team strategy blamed on his tired players.

The Most Important Real Estate in Football:

The Maroon Zone Revisited

Aaron Schatz

One of football's commonly stated maxims is that the most important area of the football field is the red zone, defined as the area between your opponent's 20-yard line and the goal line. The red zone is so important that it has its own name. In fact, some head coaches feel the need to call it something else to emphasize to their team that while the red zone is important to most teams, to their team it is *really, really important.* The Giants call it the "green zone" because playing well there is how you make your money. The Chargers call it the "gold zone" because their salaries are apparently paid in krugerrands.

Gregg Easterbrook, who writes the column "Tuesday Morning Quarterback" for NFL.com, believes that another area of the field is just as important as the red zone. He calls it the maroon zone, and he introduced the term in a column back in October 2003:

> The Maroon Zone is the area from the opponent's 40-yard line to 30-yard line—where logic usually dictates going on fourth down, since it's too far for an easy field goal, but too close to punt. Once in the Maroon Zone, make a first down and you've converted a mere possession into a scoring opportunity; fail to get the first and it's either an embarrassing turnover on downs, a long-shot figgie try that gives the opponent great field position if it fails or, worst, launching a ridiculous, mincing fraidy-cat punt. In the Maroon Zone, the team that wants to win simply must get a first down.

I thought this was such an interesting idea that I decided to test it in a column on FootballOutsiders.com immediately afterward, which I called "Maroon Zone vs. Scarlet Zone." (You can find it here: http://www.football-outsiders.com/ramblings.php?p=72.) I calculated the VOA ratings (explained in the Statistical Toolbox that opens this book) for every team during the first half of the 2003 season, separating the plays into 10- and 20-yard chunks based on line of scrimmage, and compared those numbers to each team's record at the time. For example, the red zone went from the opponent's 1 to 20, the "front" zone from the 21 to 40, and so forth. The ten-yard chunks went 1 to 10, 11 to 20, and so on. Based on those nine weeks, I found that:

1. The two most important 20-yard portions of the field were the red zone and what I called the "back" zone, from the offense's 20-yard line to their 40-yard line.

2. The correlation coefficient between performance in TMQ's maroon zone and wins was just .11, lower than any 20-yard chunk except the one between the offense's own goal line and their own 20 yard line. (Correlation coefficient is a statistical tool that measures how two variables are related by using a number between 1 and −1. The closer to −1 or 1, the stronger the relationship, but the closer to 0, the weaker the relationship.)

3. A much better indicator of a team's winning percentage, better even than the red zone, was how the team performed in the area from the opponent's 30-yard line through the opponent's 11-yard line. I dubbed this area the "scarlet zone."

But the strangest result was the following: When I broke the field down into 10-yard chunks and examined offensive and defensive performance separately, there was zero correlation between a team's offensive VOA in goal-to-go situations and their winning percentage.

Let's look at that last, strangest result in more detail. As we wrote at the time:

> Could it really be that the quality of a team's offense in a goal-to-go situation has virtually no impact on whether that team wins the game, or even scores more points? Could quality defense be that much more important than quality offense in these situations? I don't know if this is small sample size based on having only eight (in the case of four teams, nine) games to study, or if this is a definite fact about the NFL. More study will illuminate, once we have two or three years of data to put together.

Well, here we are two years later, and we've managed to accumulate seven years' worth of data, for all games between 1998 and 2004. We also have more advanced VOA formulas that are more accurate than the ones we used in our early days. We can now revisit those early conclusions to find out how they hold up over the long term.

I'll use the last three seasons for this study, because we're trying to analyze what works for teams in the enhanced offensive environment of the current NFL. Over the past two decades, the last three seasons rank first, fifth, and second in average points scored.

I'm using VOA ratings rather than simply yards or first downs, because VOA rewards progress toward both. However, I'm using VOA, and not the adjusted-for-opponent DVOA, because if we're going to compare performance to actual wins and points, we need to use actual performance. (After all, at the end of the season nobody says, "Well, Baltimore had a hard schedule, so let's give them an extra half a win.") The other change I've made is to remove the adjustments in VOA that give teams extra credit based on their performance in the red zone and the "back zone," since those parts of the formula were based on the original research that I'm trying to re-create.

Let's start by looking at the correlation between offensive VOA and points scored as well as winning percentage (table 1). I've split the field into the five zones we use when we figure the VOA ratings, which are roughly (although not always) 20 yards apiece. The table also has VOA in the red zone split into goal-to-go plays and other red zone plays, and includes both TMQ's maroon zone and the scarlet zone from our first version of this study.

With the exception of when a team is backed into its own end, the correlation between VOA and scoring points seems to be roughly the same throughout most of the field. The correlation with winning seems to drop a bit in the front zone, past the opponent's 40-yard line but not yet in the red zone. Since half of that is TMQ's maroon zone, the correlation between maroon zone performance and scoring ends up being smaller than the correlation for any of the 20-yard portions of the field. Meanwhile, the scarlet zone that I defined in the first version of this study is still important but on offense, at least, no more important than any other 20-yard chunk of the field.

The most interesting number here, however, is the correlation between how well an offense plays in goal-to-go situations and how many points it scores or games it wins. While this correlation is not .02, like it was in the first version of the study, offensive performance in goal-to-go situations still seems to be less important than offensive performance in the rest of the red zone. In fact, when you break the field down into ten chunks of ten yards apiece, offensive in goal-to-go situations has a lower correlation with winning than offense over any other ten-yard chunk on the field except for the one between the offense's own ten-yard line and their own goal line.

A number of the top 2004 offenses were very strong in the zone I call Red2 but actually had a negative VOA in goal-to-go situations: St. Louis, Philadelphia, New England, Indianapolis, and Green Bay. What do these teams have in common? They were all strong passing offenses, which might mean that they weren't getting a lot of experience in goal-to-go situations because they had already passed for touchdowns of 10 to 20 yards. They may have been below average once they got close to the goal line, but that really wasn't a big deal because the bar representing "average" is set so high. In 2004, 73% of drives that reached first and goal ended in a touchdown. And, excepting turnovers, the other 27% ended in either three points or a defense in great field position.

Next, let's check out defensive performance on various parts of the field (table 2). Remember that since VOA represents efficiency at scoring points, defensive VOA is better when it is negative. That also means that the correlation with wins will be negative, because a higher defensive VOA means a team that wins fewer games. And I'm looking at zones here from the offense's perspective, so the red zone, for example, is the defense's own goal line to their 20-yard line.

The first thing you may notice is that, with the exception of the front zone, where the offense is 21 to 39 yards from the goal line, defensive VOA has a much lower correlation

TABLE 1. CORRELATION BETWEEN WINS/PTS AND OFFENSIVE VOA BY LOCATION, 2002–2004

Zone	Location	Crl w/ Pts For	Crl w/ Wins
Red	offense on opponent 1–20	.62	.53
Front	offense on opponent 21–39	.57	.37
Mid	between the 40s	.66	.48
Back	offense on own 20–39	.66	.51
Deep	offense on own 1–19	.45	.33
Red 1	any goal-to-go, opp. 1–10	.39	.33
Red 2	all other red zone plays	.52	.43
Maroon	offense on opponent 30–40	.46	.35
Scarlet	offense on opponent 11–30	.65	.44

TABLE 2. CORRELATION BETWEEN WINS/PTS AND DEFENSIVE VOA BY LOCATION, 2002–2004

Zone	Location	Crl w/ Pts Vs.	Crl w/ Wins
Red	offense on opponent 1–20	.59	−.36
Front	offense on opponent 21–39	.56	−.40
Mid	between the 40s	.54	−.28
Back	offense on own 20–39	.61	−.38
Deep	offense on own 1–19	.21	−.17
Red 1	any goal-to-go, opp. 1–10	.35	−.19
Red 2	all other red zone plays	.48	−.32
Maroon	offense on opponent 30–40	.41	−.30
Scarlet	offense on opponent 11–30	.57	−.37

with winning percentage than offensive VOA. There's no getting around it: In the current NFL, it is better to have offense than defense. (Of course, it's best to have both.) On nearly every stat—yards, yards per play, DVOA—offensive numbers correlate better with wins than defensive numbers do. And as noted in the Buffalo chapter, team offense is more consistent from year to year than team defense. People often confuse this with "defense wins championships" because what we think is defense is often offense. Pittsburgh kept other teams from scoring, in part, by holding on to the ball for so long. Miami's defense gave up 354 points because their offense couldn't stop handing the ball back to the other team in good field position. Even the 2002 Buccaneers and the 2000 Ravens (once Dilfer took over at quarterback) had, according to our metrics, league-average offenses to support their stellar defenses.

As far as the correlation of defensive VOA by location to points allowed, it is very similar to the correlation of offensive VOA by location to points scored. Two zones, red and back, still stand out by a tiny margin. Performance in goal-to-go situations still isn't as important as performance in the rest of the red zone. And the maroon zone still doesn't seem to be particularly important.

The final step is to add both offensive and defensive performance together (actually, offensive VOA and the reverse of defensive VOA, so that better defense makes for a bigger number) and compare it to the difference between the points a team scores and the points it allows (table 3). There's no special teams involved here, just offense and defense.

Combine both offense and defense and you get the somewhat surprising result that the red zone is not the most important 20-yard chunk on the field. The most important area on the field is the area where the offense is between its own 20-yard line and its own 39-yard line, what I call the back zone. In 2004, eight of the top ten teams in back zone VOA (offense and defense) had winning records, and the other two teams were 7–9 Houston and 7–9 Kansas City (see table 4). Only one of the bottom ten teams in back zone VOA had a winning record, 2004 NFC West champion Seattle. And let's be honest, the phrase "2004 NFC West champion" is very similar to the phrase "losing record."

The odd exception for 2004 was Super Bowl champion New England, which was just average in back zone performance but one of the top teams in the league in every other location on the field. In fact, in 2004, red zone VOA actually correlated slightly better with wins (.70) than back zone VOA (.67). But the correlation coefficient between red zone performance and wins was just .57 in 2003 and .53 in 2002. Over the larger data set, the importance of the back zone wins out.

What is so important about plays when the offense is between its own 20- and 39-yard lines? Get your offense past this area, and you have a sustained drive that will generally either score points or lead to a punt that gives the other offense the ball without good field position. Three-and-out in this area, however, means a punt that lets the other offense usually start close to midfield. The back zone is also the place to get the big plays—if your offensive arsenal includes a receiver who can beat a corner deep, you can't really use that weapon when you are on the opponent's 30-yard line. And a turnover in this area basically hands at least three points to the other team.

Other than the importance of the back zone, both on offense and defense, here's what we can take away from this study:

- The red zone is still a very important part of the field, particularly on offense.
- While the correlation between goal-to-go offense and wins isn't zero like I thought two years ago, and a team that can't run it in from the goal line is still going to have some problems (hello, Indianapolis), performance between your opponent's 11 and 20 is much more important than performance in goal-to-go situations.
- While Gregg Easterbrook is still our buddy, and we anxiously look forward to TMQ every week, the maroon zone really isn't that important. Sorry, Gregg.
- The scarlet zone, introduced by Football Outsiders two years ago, is really no big deal either.

TABLE 3. CORRELATION BETWEEN WINS/PTS AND TOTAL VOA BY LOCATION, 2002–2004

Zone	Location	Crl w/ Pts Dif	Crl w/ Wins
Red	offense on opponent 1–20	.66	.61
Front	offense on opponent 21–39	.57	.51
Mid	between the 40s	.64	.58
Back	offense on own 20–39	.76	.67
Deep	offense on own 1–19	.37	.34
Red 1	any goal-to-go, opp. 1–10	.40	.43
Red 2	all other red zone plays	.56	.55
Maroon	offense on opponent 30–40	.47	.46
Scarlet	offense on opponent 11–30	.63	.56

FIGURE 1. CORRELATION BETWEEN WINS AND TOTAL VOA BY FIELD LOCATION, 2002–2004

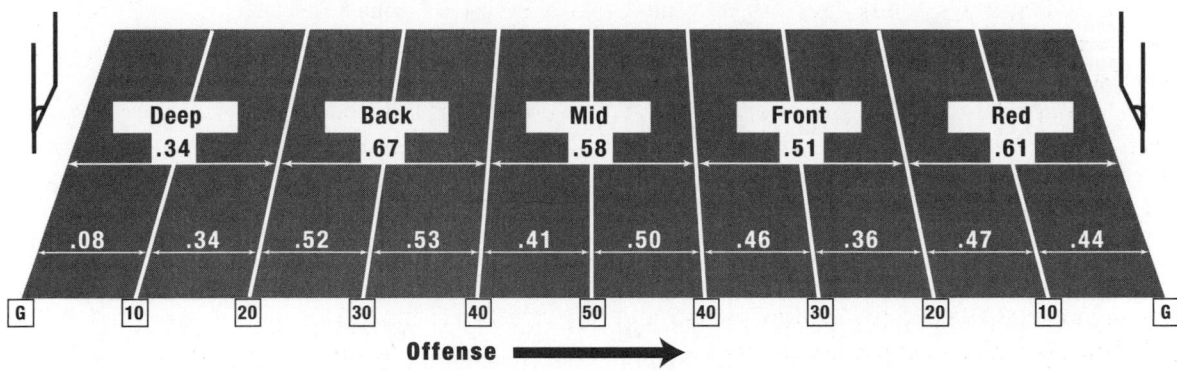

TABLE 4. TOTAL VOA BY ZONE, 2004

Team	Red	Front	Mid	Back	Deep	Team	Red	Front	Mid	Back	Deep
ARI	−11.8%	−24.2%	−3.4%	−17.3%	−2.3%	MIA	−30.2%	−12.1%	−39.1%	−45.3%	45.6%
ATL	5.9%	−6.5%	−2.7%	3.8%	−43.3%	MIN	−9.5%	7.8%	17.1%	−1.8%	49.2%
BAL	69.9%	−55.7%	−3.0%	34.2%	−6.8%	NE	55.8%	41.1%	49.8%	−1.7%	36.4%
BUF	9.1%	36.9%	−22.2%	34.1%	77.7%	NO	0.3%	−7.8%	23.6%	−29.5%	−72.5%
CAR	10.8%	1.2%	22.0%	5.1%	33.4%	NYG	−53.6%	29.1%	8.3%	−19.9%	28.9%
CHI	−43.1%	−65.7%	−37.2%	−19.8%	−15.6%	NYJ	27.6%	10.2%	30.3%	37.9%	−45.9%
CIN	3.3%	−11.8%	2.5%	3.8%	−31.6%	OAK	−45.4%	−2.6%	−20.9%	−32.2%	−39.4%
CLE	−45.4%	−31.2%	−30.0%	−31.9%	18.2%	PHI	27.5%	28.6%	−7.6%	18.8%	39.4%
DAL	−47.0%	−18.4%	−12.8%	−11.9%	9.7%	PIT	13.9%	43.9%	9.8%	55.2%	−5.7%
DEN	−10.8%	3.6%	29.3%	29.8%	26.8%	SD	43.5%	−13.6%	17.3%	29.5%	64.9%
DET	−16.1%	−16.9%	17.5%	−11.5%	1.9%	SEA	−0.2%	68.2%	4.3%	−20.1%	60.3%
GB	7.0%	11.0%	−23.6%	6.1%	−29.1%	SF	−54.0%	−56.1%	−43.4%	−26.7%	−96.5%
HOU	9.4%	−22.7%	−43.4%	35.0%	14.9%	STL	−30.5%	−27.1%	−10.5%	−28.6%	55.9%
IND	44.3%	56.4%	36.4%	35.3%	−8.8%	TB	34.8%	−13.5%	−0.5%	7.7%	−20.0%
JAC	24.8%	20.6%	18.0%	−19.9%	−86.1%	TEN	−47.3%	−0.9%	0.9%	−27.1%	1.9%
KC	−6.2%	0.3%	1.2%	13.2%	30.8%	WAS	10.4%	−4.8%	21.9%	4.2%	−64.5%

NOTE: Offensive VOA minus Defensive VOA, not adjusted for strength of opponents.

Football—It's Not Just for Sundays Anymore

Russell Levine and Vinny Gauri

The book you are reading is called *Pro Football Prospectus,* and from the day Football Outsiders went online, our analysis has always focused on professional football. But as you may know, they also play football on Saturdays. And while college football—with over 100 Division 1-A teams, different styles played in each conference, and uniform play-by-play logs close to nonexistent—doesn't provide a good venue for the statistical analysis that is our bread and butter, a number of us enjoy the college game just as much as the NFL. In fact, a couple of us even hold the heretical belief that the college game is more fun.

Of course, it can be tough to convince people to embrace a sport that seemingly awards its championship the way your local deli awards free lunches—by picking business cards out of a goldfish bowl. But there are many reasons to follow college football, not the least of which is that you'll gain a new appreciation for Mel Kiper Jr. on draft weekend. When Mr. Hair-Helmet is setting a new world record for most words featuring the suffix *-ability* in a single sentence (all while rambling about a seventh-round receiver) you might just find yourself nodding along in agreement.

And if you can get past the absurdity of the BCS, you might just learn to love the college game for its unique regular season. Top teams routinely have their championship aspirations made or broken in early-season games. It may not be fair, but it sure makes for exciting September Saturdays.

If tradition is your thing, then the college game is also for you. Dotting the "i," Howard's Rock, Ralphie, the Volunteer Navy, "Fight On," Touchdown Jesus, "War Eagle," "Hail to the Victors," between the hedges, the Tomahawk Chop, Saturday nights on the Bayou. Each immediately calls to mind decades-old football culture at places where the college game rules: Columbus and Clemson, Knoxville and the L.A. Coliseum, South Bend and the Alabama plains. Spend a few Saturdays with the college game and you too will be waxing poetic like Keith Jackson.

But for the pure NFL junkie, the best reason to follow college football is to learn the names that you'll spend next April fretting over. What follows is a week-by-week guide to the big games and big names in the upcoming college season—for the uninitiated and the die-hards alike.

Note: All players listed are seniors eligible for the 2006 NFL Draft unless denoted by * (juniors who are also eligible for the 2006 NFL Draft) or ** (sophomores who are eligible for the 2007 NFL Draft).

September 3

Notre Dame at Pitt: The first Pats-Phins matchup of the year with Charlie Weiss and Dave Wannstedt both making their debuts in the college game. Will Weiss's mastery of the passing game elevate marginal prospects like Irish QB Brady Quinn* and WRs Maurice Stovall and Rhema McKnight? Don't tell Beano Cook, but Wanny has better "material" in Pitt QB Tyler Palko,* WR Greg Lee,* and ILB H. B. Blades* (Bennie's son).

September 5

Miami (FL) at Florida State: There's nothing like a big rivalry game for a season opener, one of the ways college football has it over the NFL. (When the Bears beat the Packers early last year, it didn't exactly end Green Bay's playoff hopes.) As is usually the case when these two teams get together, there will be plenty of NFL talent on the field, including some burners in 'Noles CB Antonio Cromartie* (four interceptions in 2004) and 'Canes CB/KR Devin Hester,* who returned four kicks for scores last year. Other prospects to keep an eye on include 'Noles RB Leon Washington and OLB Ernie Sims,* and Canes OT Eric Winston, DT Orien Harris, and DE Baraka Atkins.

September 10

Texas at Ohio State: The Buckeyes will spend their entire nonconference slate in Columbus this year, as has been their recent custom, but at least they scheduled Texas for the intersectional matchup of the year. Can 'Horns QB Vince Young* repeat his Michael Vick imitation from the Rose Bowl against standout Buckeyes OLB A. J. Hawk? Doubtful, especially if he's forced to throw more than ten yards downfield. Young has the running skills of Vick, but it's questionable whether he throws accurately enough to play QB in the NFL. Buckeyes WR Santonio Holmes will be off the draft board early, as will 'Horns DT Rodrique Wright—who still disappears too much for our liking—and OT Jonathan Scott. Two of the better defensive backs in the land, 'Horns S Michael Huff and Buckeyes S Nate Salley, could also be first-day selections.

Notre Dame at Michigan: The Irish continue their brutal early-season schedule in Ann Arbor. Even after the departure of Braylon Edwards, the Wolverines have plenty of talent on the offensive side of the ball, including WRs Jason Avant and Steve Breaston* along with G Matt Lentz and TE Tim Massaquoi. On defense, DT Gabe Watson—who really needs to improve his stamina—and DE LaMarr Woodley* must make amends for a late-season collapse in 2004 by the Wolverine defense. With Michigan's linebackers and safeties often out of position, Irish TE Anthony Fasano* may be able to free himself for a score or two.

September 17

Tennessee at Florida: Urban Meyer brings his wide-open offensive attack to Gainesville, where he has some great pupils in QB Chris Leak* (think Drew Brees, but more mobile), WR Andre Caldwell,* and C Mike Degory. The Vols' returning stars include S Jason Allen, RB Gerald Riggs Jr., and QB Eric Ainge.** Tennessee's inexperienced offensive line must surpass expectations for the Vols to win the SEC crown.

Oklahoma at UCLA: Bob Stoops doesn't have to worry about his team getting dismantled in the national title game for the third straight year—the Sooners lost too much talent to even get there. Sooners RB Adrian Peterson** gets the headlines in this matchup, but he's not the only standout. Sooners OG Davin Joseph and Bruins TE Mercedes Lewis should be early selections on day one of the draft. Sooners DT Dusty Dvoracek can be a force when he's focused—he's back for a fifth year after getting dismissed from the team early last season. Bruins OLB Spencer Havner and Sooners WR Travis Wilson are others to watch.

Oregon State at Louisville: Louisville's offense may not be as explosive as in 2004. But as long as the coach with the perennial wandering eye, Bobby Petrino, hasn't sold his home, they're going to put up some good numbers. It certainly helps when four fifths of the nation's most underrated offensive line returns, including OT Travis Leffew and C Jason Spitz. Cardinals QB Brian Brohm** and RB Michael Bush* step into the spotlight as full-time starters in 2005. Beavers TE Joe Newton* could improve his measurables, but has shown good hands thus far in his career. Teammate WR Mike Hass snuck behind defenses with frequency last year, but expect his production to drop with QB Derek Anderson now in the NFL.

September 24

Iowa at Ohio State: Iowa coach Kirk Ferentz will make the jump to the NFL sooner or later, but in the meantime he's coaching some great prospects in OLB Chad Greenway—perhaps the best defensive prospect in the draft—ILB Abdul Hodge, OG Mike Jones,* and WR Clinton Solomon. The Buckeyes may be utilizing the speed and playmaking of WR/KR Ted Ginn Jr.** on defense at this point of the season. Hawkeye QB Drew Tate* reminds some of a taller (6'0"), poor man's Doug Flutie. Buckeye QBs Troy Smith* and Justin Zwick* can make plays with their feet, but their passing accuracy can be streaky.

October 1

USC at Arizona State: Even after back-to-back national titles, the cupboard is hardly bare at USC, where Heisman-winning QB Matt Leinart is still in the backfield with Marshall Faulk clone Reggie Bush.* Other potential first-day draft prospects include TE Dominique Byrd (who has some academic issues to address), S Darnell Bing,* and DE Frostee Rucker. Arizona State should put up points with QB Sam Keller* throwing to WR Derek Hagan (83 receptions in 2004).

Virginia at Maryland: This matchup might not be the ACC game of the year, but it's the All-Name Hall of Fame game when it features Virginia OT D'Brickashaw Ferguson and Maryland LB D'Qwell Jackson. Ferguson could have been a top pick in the 2005 draft and will go in the upper reaches of round one next April if things go as expected during his senior season. Jackson, who piled up 124 tackles as a junior, projects to be a top outside linebacker in the 2006 draft. Some see him as a better player than former teammate Shawne Merriman (the number 12 pick in 2005). Jackson isn't the only linebacker worth watching in this game. Cavs ILB Ahmad Brooks* is rated by some as the nation's best defensive player.

October 8

Georgia at Tennessee: Pick any SEC game and you're likely watching a bunch of first-day NFL draft candidates. Georgia-Tennessee is no different. The best of the bunch at Georgia is probably OG Max-Jean Gilles, who will pave the way for RB Danny Ware.** Also keep an eye on Georgia TE Leonard Pope,* who has the potential to be the top tight end selected in 2006 or 2007.

October 15

Florida at LSU: The Gators head into Death Valley to face an LSU team that still has vestiges of the talent that earned a share of the 2003 national title, including S LaRon Landry.* Les Miles has come over from Stillwater to replace Nick Saban, and he's hoping RBs Joseph Addai and Justin Vincent find plenty of holes running behind OT Andrew Whitworth and OG Nate Livings.

Wisconsin at Minnesota: This is usually where things fall apart for Minnesota and coach Glen Mason. The Gophers typically pile up gaudy wins against nonconference patsies, then crumble once they face the Big Ten big boys. Minnesota will look to pound the ball behind RB Laurence Maroney, who managed better than 1,300 yards while splitting time with Marion Barber III last year. Maroney is the better NFL prospect of the two, and he should have even bigger numbers running behind a pair of NFL-caliber linemen in OG Mark Setterstrom and C Greg Eslinger, both of whom can move and cut-block with the best of them (Alex Gibbs, are you reading this?). Wisconsin was hit hard by graduation, but keep an eye on Badgers C Donovan Raiola, who could come off the board not long after Eslinger.

October 22

Miami (Ohio) at Eastern Michigan: Sure, there are better games on this date—Auburn-LSU, Tennessee-Alabama, Texas Tech-Texas—but if you are an NFL fan trying to catch the players you'll need to know in 2006, the "other" Miami is a team worth checking out at least once. RedHawks QB Josh Betts looks to follow Ben Roethlisberger to the pros, and while he'll draw an NFL paycheck, he's probably limited to life as a backup. A better pro prospect is his frequent target, WR Martin Nance.

October 29

Clemson at Georgia Tech: Tigers QB Charlie Whitehurst had a disastrous junior season (17 INTs, 7 TDs) but is still considered the top senior signal caller in the 2006 draft after Leinart. Jackets DE Eric Henderson had a similarly disappointing junior campaign, but hopes to find Whitehurst a few times in the backfield in this one. Also worth watching is Georgia Tech RB P. J. Daniels, a smallish powerhouse back who was also banged up in 2004.

Oklahoma at Nebraska: Once upon a time this was the most important game on the college schedule. But the arrival of the Big XII conference's two-division format (and Nebraska's recent decline) has lessened its impact on the national-title scene. Nebraska's second-year coach Bill Callahan needs to get things turned around or his stay in Lincoln won't last any longer than his stint with the Raiders. He'll be counting on NFL prospects DT LeKevin Smith and TE Matt Herian to play a big role in the Huskers' turnaround.

November 5

Miami (FL) at Virginia Tech: QB Marcus Vick* gets the starting nod for the Hokies, who hope he can put both

defenders and his legal problems behind him. Vick is actually much less polished than his brother was at this stage, but Frank Beamer cares little about polish in his simplistic offense. Vick might be looking at a position switch if he wants to play in the NFL. CB Jimmy Williams (5.5 TFLs and 5 INTs in 2004) and DE Darryl Tapp (16.5 TFLs and 8.5 sacks) are the returning stars on the Hokie defense.

November 12

North Carolina State at Boston College: The two best defensive end prospects in the land should be on display at the Heights, along with Chuck Amato's funky shades. Eagles DE Mathias Kiwanuka is a proven performer (over 20 sacks the last two years) while Wolfpack DE Mario Williams* (6'7", 285 pounds) landed on draftniks' radar last season with six sacks and 15 TFLs. Let's see if Kiwanuka can maintain his productivity against the quality linemen he'll now face in the ACC. Others to watch include Eagles OT Jeremy Trueblood (6'9", 330 pounds) and CB/KR William Blackmon, along with Wolfpack DE Manny Lawson and TE T. J. Williams.

Memphis at Tennessee: This, admittedly, is not the first game that comes to mind when you think of classic late-season, nonconference matchups. But this game is worth keeping an eye on just to see Memphis RB DeAngelo Williams, who was injured in the Tigers' bowl game last year and wisely returned for his senior year (rather than enter a draft already deep in running backs). He is a great combination of power and speed, and could be the first running back off the board in 2006.

Oregon at Washington State: Do not adjust your set: These teams really do look like they bought their uniforms from the Eastbay Catalog. Ducks QB Kellen Clemens put up good numbers again in 2004, but his lack of mobility (and a porous offensive line) forced him to take a staggering number of sacks (40). Ducks DT Haloti Ngata, TE Tim Day and WR Demetrius Williams will be playing on Sundays in 2006 and beyond, as will Cougars OLB Will Derting and WR Jason Hill.*

November 19

Alabama at Auburn: Late November means one thing in college football: rivalry games. November 19 alone offers Cal-Stanford, Oregon-Oregon State, Clemson-South Carolina, Michigan-Ohio State, Virginia-Virginia Tech, and Washington-Washington State, all worth watching for the sheer intensity that only a big college grudge match can produce. Auburn-Alabama (a.k.a. "The Iron Bowl") doesn't take a backseat to any of those on the pure hate scale, and it also features plenty of NFL talent. The 2005 draft hit Auburn hard, but there are some Tigers who are not yet Washington Redskins, including mammoth OT Marcus McNeill

(6'9", 340 pounds) and standout WR Ben Obomanu. For Alabama, watch ILB Freddie Roach and QB Brodie Croyle, whose injury in 2004 destroyed the Tide's season.

November 22

Toledo at Bowling Green: MAC quarterbacks are getting plenty of attention from NFL scouts these days after the recent successes of Chad Pennington, Byron Leftwich, and Roethlisberger. This game presents one of the best QB matchups not just in the MAC, but in all of college football. Bowling Green's Omar Jacobs* put up incredible numbers in his first season as the starter in 2004: better than 4,000 yards and 41 TDs with just four interceptions. Another year like that will have him thinking long and hard about entering the 2006 draft. He will be opposed by Toledo's Bruce Gradkowski, who completed 70% of his passes last year with 27 TDs. Neither of these guys will find the success that their predecessors have had in the NFL, but the track record of MAC quarterbacks makes them good risks as second-day choices. Jacobs is very raw, while Gradkowski lacks a prototypical NFL arm.

Finally, here are some lesser known prospects that could be fast risers on draft boards next April: QB Paul Pinegar (Fresno State), RB Dontrell Moore (New Mexico), OT Daryn Colledge (Boise State), OG Aaron Lips (Louisiana Tech), C Kyle Young* (Fresno State), Leon Moore (UNLV), OLBs Thomas Howard (UTEP) and Dennis Burke (Middle Tennessee State), DB Shannon James (UMass), and S Kedrick Alexander (Tulsa).

For more analysis on these games and many others, read our weekly college football preview column "Seventh Day Adventure," appearing Thursdays on FootballOutsiders.com.

Statistical Appendix

Fantasy Projections

Table 1 has the top 180 players according to the KUBIAK projection system, ranked by projected fantasy value in 2005. Fantasy value does not include adjustments for week-to-week consistency and there are no projections for team defenses/special teams. We've used the following generic scoring system:

- 1 point for each 10 yards rushing, 10 yards receiving, or 20 yards passing
- 6 points for each rushing or receiving TD, 4 points for each passing TD
- −2 points for each interception
- 1 point for each extra point, 3 points for each field goal.

The final four columns give projected draft order based on marginal value of each player, the idea that you draft based on how many more points a player will score compared to the worst starting player at that position, not how many points a player scores overall. Ranks are given for four different generic league setups:

- 12-3WR: 12 teams starting QB, 2 RB, 3 WR, 1 TE, 1 K
- 12-FX: 12 teams starting QB, 2 RB, 2 WR, 1 TE, 1 K, 1 FLEX (any RB/WR/TE)
- 10-3WR: 10 teams starting QB, 2 RB, 3 WR, 1 TE, 1 K
- 10-FX: 10 teams starting QB, 2 RB, 2 WR, 1 TE, 1 K, 1 FLEX (any RB/WR/TE).

TABLE 1. 2005 FANTASY PROJECTIONS

Name	Team	Pos	PaYD	PaTD	Int	RuYD	RuTD	RecYD	RecTD	XP	FG	Fant	12-3WR	12-FX	10-3WR	10-FX
LaDainian Tomlinson	SD	RB	0	0	0	1532	13	477	2	0	0	291	1	1	1	1
Tiki Barber	NYG	RB	0	0	0	1474	11	473	2	0	0	273	2	2	2	2
Shaun Alexander	SEA	RB	0	0	0	1547	13	257	2	0	0	270	3	3	3	3
Domanick Davis	HOU	RB	0	0	0	1429	11	492	2	0	0	270	4	4	4	4
Kevin Jones	DET	RB	0	0	0	1605	11	291	1	0	0	262	5	5	6	5
Julius Jones	DAL	RB	0	0	0	1584	11	293	1	0	0	260	6	6	7	6
Peyton Manning	IND	QB	4494	36	13	41	1	0	0	0	0	353	7	15	5	15
Edgerrin James	IND	RB	0	0	0	1412	11	413	1	0	0	255	8	7	9	7
Willis McGahee	BUF	RB	0	0	0	1505	12	218	1	0	0	250	9	8	11	8
Torry Holt	STL	WR	0	0	0	0	0	1302	9	0	0	184	10	25	10	23
Daunte Culpepper	MIN	QB	4062	27	13	428	3	0	0	0	0	346	11	18	8	16
Antonio Gates	SD	TE	0	0	0	0	0	858	9	0	0	140	12	19	13	18
Jason Witten	DAL	TE	0	0	0	0	0	848	9	0	0	139	13	20	15	20
Terrell Owens	PHI	WR	0	0	0	0	0	1127	11	0	0	179	14	29	12	24
Rudi Johnson	CIN	RB	0	0	0	1485	12	154	1	0	0	242	15	9	14	9
Tony Gonzalez	KC	TE	0	0	0	0	0	938	7	0	0	136	16	21	19	22
Clinton Portis	WAS	RB	0	0	0	1466	7	400	2	0	0	241	17	10	16	10
Priest Holmes	KC	RB	0	0	0	1218	14	235	1	0	0	235	18	11	21	11
Randy Moss	OAK	WR	0	0	0	0	0	1090	10	0	0	169	19	34	18	30
Donovan McNabb	PHI	QB	3974	28	12	245	3	0	0	0	0	329	20	27	17	21
Deuce McAllister	NO	RB	0	0	0	1355	9	358	1	0	0	231	21	12	24	12
Marvin Harrison	IND	WR	0	0	0	0	0	1001	11	0	0	166	22	36	20	32

Name	Team	Pos	PaYD	PaTD	Int	RuYD	RuTD	RecYD	RecTD	XP	FG	Fant	12-3WR	12-FX	10-3WR	10-FX
Chad Johnson	CIN	WR	0	0	0	0	0	1171	8	0	0	165	23	37	22	35
Reggie Wayne	IND	WR	0	0	0	0	0	1104	9	0	0	164	24	38	23	37
Brian Westbrook	PHI	RB	0	0	0	1127	5	512	5	0	0	224	25	13	29	13
Darrell Jackson	SEA	WR	0	0	0	0	0	1141	7	0	0	156	26	42	25	41
Javon Walker	GB	WR	0	0	0	0	0	1078	8	0	0	156	27	43	26	42
Ronnie Brown	MIA	RB	0	0	0	1381	10	224	0	0	0	221	28	14	33	14
Hines Ward	PIT	WR	0	0	0	0	0	1125	7	0	0	155	29	44	27	43
Joe Horn	NO	WR	0	0	0	0	0	1063	8	0	0	154	30	45	28	44
Andre Johnson	HOU	WR	0	0	0	0	0	1107	7	0	0	153	31	46	30	45
Michael Clayton	TB	WR	0	0	0	0	0	1155	6	0	0	152	32	49	31	47
Drew Bennett	TEN	WR	0	0	0	0	0	1028	8	0	0	151	33	50	32	48
Alge Crumpler	ATL	TE	0	0	0	0	0	645	7	0	0	107	34	39	36	40
Matt Hasselbeck	SEA	QB	4104	27	16	137	2	0	0	0	0	307	35	40	34	34
Anquan Boldin	ARI	WR	0	0	0	0	0	1011	7	0	0	143	36	54	35	54
Randy McMichael	MIA	TE	0	0	0	0	0	716	5	0	0	102	37	41	38	46
Steven Jackson	STL	RB	0	0	0	1215	9	259	0	0	0	201	38	16	40	17
Eric Johnson	SF	TE	0	0	0	0	0	652	5	0	0	95	39	51	45	49
Muhsin Muhammad	CHI	WR	0	0	0	0	0	929	7	0	0	135	40	61	37	63
Rod Smith	DEN	WR	0	0	0	0	0	061	6	0	0	132	41	64	39	67
Corey Dillon	NE	RB	0	0	0	1226	10	78	1	0	0	196	42	17	48	19
Laveranues Coles	NYJ	WR	0	0	0	0	0	947	6	0	0	131	43	67	41	72
Ashley Lelie	DEN	WR	0	0	0	0	0	938	6	0	0	130	44	71	42	73
Plaxico Burress	NYG	WR	0	0	0	0	0	937	6	0	0	130	45	72	43	74
Todd Heap	BAL	TE	0	0	0	0	0	582	5	0	0	88	46	53	53	56
Roy Williams	DET	WR	0	0	0	0	0	929	6	0	0	129	47	75	44	78
Nate Burleson	MIN	WR	0	0	0	0	0	978	5	0	0	128	48	78	46	97
Eddie Kennison	KC	WR	0	0	0	0	0	917	6	0	0	128	49	79	47	98
Dallas Clark	IND	TE	0	0	0	0	0	585	4	0	0	83	50	55	62	65
Kerry Collins	OAK	QB	4138	28	19	45	0	0	0	0	0	285	51	56	49	50
Mike Vanderjagt	IND	K	0	0	0	0	0	0	0	49	25	124	52	57	51	55
Marc Bulger	STL	QB	3976	24	18	136	2	0	0	0	0	284	53	59	50	53
Santana Moss	WAS	WR	0	0	0	0	0	921	5	0	0	122	54	88	52	107
Jermaine Wiggins	MIN	TE	0	0	0	0	0	508	5	0	0	81	55	60	68	69
Chris Chambers	MIA	WR	0	0	0	0	0	783	7	0	0	120	56	92	55	112
Curtis Martin	NYJ	RB	0	0	0	1067	9	174	1	0	0	184	57	22	66	25
David Akers	PHI	K	0	0	0	0	0	0	0	42	26	120	58	62	54	57
Jeremy Shockey	NYG	TE	0	0	0	0	0	477	5	0	0	78	59	63	79	79
Ahman Green	GB	RB	0	0	0	1069	6	343	1	0	0	183	60	23	70	26
Cadillac Williams	TB	RB	0	0	0	1121	8	224	0	0	0	183	61	24	73	27
Isaac Bruce	STL	WR	0	0	0	0	0	864	5	0	0	116	62	102	60	119
Josh Brown	SEA	K	0	0	0	0	0	0	0	42	25	117	63	70	56	58
Cedric Benson	CHI	RB	0	0	0	1166	7	219	0	0	0	181	64	26	81	28
Eric Moulds	BUF	WR	0	0	0	0	0	853	5	0	0	115	65	108	63	122
Jason Elam	DEN	K	0	0	0	0	0	0	0	41	25	116	66	73	58	61
Jeff Wilkins	STL	K	0	0	0	0	0	0	0	38	26	116	67	74	59	62
Keyshawn Johnson	DAL	WR	0	0	0	0	0	849	5	0	0	115	68	111	64	123
Jake Plummer	DEN	QB	3541	26	15	133	2	0	0	0	0	276	69	76	57	60
Adam Vinatieri	NE	K	0	0	0	0	0	0	0	43	24	115	70	77	61	64

(continued next page)

TABLE 1. 2005 FANTASY PROJECTIONS *(continued)*

Name	Team	Pos	PaYD	PaTD	Int	RuYD	RuTD	RecYD	RecTD	XP	FG	Fant	12-3WR	12-FX	10-3WR	10-FX
Deion Branch	NE	WR	0	0	0	0	0	832	5	0	0	113	71	112	69	127
Chris Brown	TEN	RB	0	0	0	999	8	239	1	0	0	178	72	28	88	29
Sebastian Janikowski	OAK	K	0	0	0	0	0	0	0	38	25	113	73	80	67	68
Jimmy Smith	JAC	WR	0	0	0	0	0	818	5	0	0	112	74	115	74	128
Tom Brady	NE	QB	3731	27	14	10	1	0	0	0	0	274	75	81	65	66
L. J. Smith	PHI	TE	0	0	0	0	0	464	4	0	0	70	76	82	104	99
David Givens	NE	WR	0	0	0	0	0	813	5	0	0	111	77	117	75	130
Derrick Mason	BAL	WR	0	0	0	0	0	812	5	0	0	111	78	118	76	132
John Kasay	CAR	K	0	0	0	0	0	0	0	37	25	112	79	83	71	70
Aaron Brooks	NO	QB	3627	23	13	124	2	0	0	0	0	272	80	85	72	71
Larry Fitzgerald	ARI	WR	0	0	0	0	0	793	5	0	0	109	81	123	83	134
Tatum Bell	DEN	RB	0	0	0	994	8	207	1	0	0	174	82	30	101	31
Jason Hanson	DET	K	0	0	0	0	0	0	0	38	24	110	83	86	77	75
Kris Brown	HOU	K	0	0	0	0	0	0	0	38	24	110	84	87	78	76
Jabar Gaffney	HOU	WR	0	0	0	0	0	783	5	0	0	108	85	127	86	135
David Carr	HOU	QB	3493	23	16	230	2	0	0	0	0	270	86	89	80	80
Chad Pennington	NYJ	QB	3526	23	14	172	2	0	0	0	0	270	87	90	82	81
T. J. Houshmandzadeh	CIN	WR	0	0	0	0	0	834	4	0	0	107	88	129	90	137
Jeff Reed	PIT	K	0	0	0	0	0	0	0	39	23	108	89	91	85	83
Justin McCareins	NYJ	WR	0	0	0	0	0	770	5	0	0	107	90	131	92	138
J. J. Arrington	ARI	RB	0	0	0	1116	7	183	0	0	0	172	91	31	107	33
Byron Leftwich	JAC	QB	3627	22	16	189	2	0	0	0	0	268	92	94	84	82
Steve Smith	CAR	WR	0	0	0	0	0	762	5	0	0	106	93	133	94	139
Bill Cundiff	DAL	K	0	0	0	0	0	0	0	35	24	107	94	95	87	84
Michael Bennett	MIN	RB	0	0	0	904	7	262	2	0	0	171	95	32	110	36
Jeb Putzier	DEN	TE	0	0	0	0	0	466	3	0	0	65	96	96	118	109
LaMont Jordan	OAK	RB	0	0	0	971	7	250	1	0	0	170	97	33	111	38
Shayne Graham	CIN	K	0	0	0	0	0	0	0	37	23	106	98	98	91	86
Chris Cooley	WAS	TE	0	0	0	0	0	400	4	0	0	64	99	99	119	110
Jerry Porter	OAK	WR	0	0	0	0	0	747	5	0	0	105	100	135	100	142
Drew Brees	SD	QB	3226	27	13	113	2	0	0	0	0	267	101	101	89	85
Ben Watson	NE	TE	0	0	0	0	0	392	4	0	0	63	102	103	121	113
Matt Stover	BAL	K	0	0	0	0	0	0	0	30	25	105	103	104	95	89
Rian Lindell	BUF	K	0	0	0	0	0	0	0	39	22	105	104	105	96	90
Mike Nugent	NYJ	K	0	0	0	0	0	0	0	39	22	105	105	106	97	91
Brandon Stokley	IND	WR	0	0	0	0	0	740	5	0	0	104	106	138	102	146
Lee Evans	BUF	WR	0	0	0	0	0	796	4	0	0	104	107	139	103	147
Michael Vick	ATL	QB	2585	16	14	761	4	0	0	0	0	265	108	107	93	87
Paul Edinger	MIN	K	0	0	0	0	0	0	0	44	20	104	109	109	98	93
Matt Bryant	TB	K	0	0	0	0	0	0	0	35	23	104	110	110	99	94
Braylon Edwards	CLE	WR	0	0	0	0	0	717	5	0	0	102	111	143	108	148
Trent Green	KC	QB	3541	25	14	73	1	0	0	0	0	262	112	113	105	100
Daniel Graham	NE	TE	0	0	0	0	0	352	4	0	0	59	113	114	128	120
Jamal Lewis	BAL	RB	0	0	0	1038	6	192	1	0	0	165	114	35	123	39
Ben Roethlisberger	PIT	QB	3507	22	16	182	2	0	0	0	0	262	115	116	106	101

Name	Team	Pos	PaYD	PaTD	Int	RuYD	RuTD	RecYD	RecTD	XP	FG	Fant	12-3WR	12-FX	10-3WR	10-FX
Nate Kaeding	SD	K	0	0	0	0	0	0	0	43	19	100	116	119	109	102
Olindo Mare	MIA	K	0	0	0	0	0	0	0	36	21	99	117	120	112	103
Brandon Lloyd	SF	WR	0	0	0	0	0	739	4	0	0	98	118	149	116	150
Keary Colbert	CAR	WR	0	0	0	0	0	738	4	0	0	98	119	150	117	151
Bubba Franks	GB	TE	0	0	0	0	0	327	4	0	0	57	120	121	133	125
Doug Jolley	NYJ	TE	0	0	0	0	0	386	3	0	0	57	121	122	134	126
Jay Feely	NYG	K	0	0	0	0	0	0	0	35	21	98	122	126	113	106
Lawrence Tynes	KC	K	0	0	0	0	0	0	0	41	19	98	123	125	114	105
Ryan Longwell	GB	K	0	0	0	0	0	0	0	35	21	98	124	124	115	104
Donte' Stallworth	NO	WR	0	0	0	0	0	719	4	0	0	96	125	151	122	153
Ben Troupe	TEN	TE	0	0	0	0	0	367	3	0	0	55	126	128	135	129
Courtney Anderson	OAK	TE	0	0	0	0	0	303	4	0	0	54	127	130	137	131
Doug Brien	CHI	K	0	0	0	0	0	0	0	30	22	96	128	132	120	111
Antwaan Randle El	PIT	WR	0	0	0	0	0	708	4	0	0	95	129	152	124	154
Keenan McCardell	SD	WR	0	0	0	0	0	642	5	0	0	94	130	154	126	156
Matt Schobel	CIN	TE	0	0	0	0	0	349	3	0	0	53	131	134	140	133
Boo Williams	NO	TE	0	0	0	0	0	333	3	0	0	51	132	137	141	136
Rex Grossman	CHI	QB	3681	21	19	172	1	0	0	0	0	253	133	140	125	115
Peerless Price	ATL	WR	0	0	0	0	0	672	4	0	0	91	134	156	130	159
Eric Parker	SD	WR	0	0	0	0	0	670	4	0	0	91	135	157	131	160
Carson Palmer	CIN	QB	3720	22	18	85	1	0	0	0	0	253	136	141	127	116
Jim Kleinsasser	MIN	TE	0	0	0	0	0	311	3	0	0	49	137	142	144	140
Freddie Jones	CAR	TE	0	0	0	0	0	305	3	0	0	49	138	144	145	141
Jake Delhomme	CAR	QB	3486	23	15	81	1	0	0	0	0	250	139	145	129	121
Heath Miller	PIT	TE	0	0	0	0	0	292	3	0	0	47	140	146	147	144
Amani Toomer	NYG	WR	0	0	0	0	0	636	4	0	0	88	141	159	136	162
Brett Favre	GB	QB	3728	24	19	44	0	0	0	0	0	249	142	147	132	124
Jerome Pathon	SEA	WR	0	0	0	0	0	627	4	0	0	87	143	160	138	163
Reggie Williams	JAC	WR	0	0	0	0	0	622	4	0	0	86	144	161	139	164
Kevan Barlow	SF	RB	0	0	0	889	4	312	1	0	0	150	145	47	149	51
Fred Taylor	JAC	RB	0	0	0	915	4	283	1	0	0	150	146	48	151	52
Donald Driver	GB	WR	0	0	0	0	0	652	3	0	0	83	147	164	142	167
Ronnie Brown*	MIA	RB	0	0	0	892	7	170	0	0	0	148	147	51	153	56
Quincy Morgan	DAL	WR	0	0	0	0	0	588	4	0	0	83	148	165	143	168
Samie Parker	KC	WR	0	0	0	0	0	574	4	0	0	81	149	167	146	169
Troy Williamson	MIN	WR	0	0	0	0	0	559	4	0	0	80	150	168	150	170
Reche Caldwell	SD	WR	0	0	0	0	0	558	4	0	0	80	151	169	152	171
Mike Williams	DET	WR	0	0	0	0	0	606	3	0	0	79	152	171	153	172
David Patten	WAS	WR	0	0	0	0	0	599	3	0	0	78	153	172	154	173
Brian Griese	TB	QB	3736	21	18	43	0	0	0	0	0	239	154	158	148	145
Ronald Curry	OAK	WR	0	0	0	0	0	588	3	0	0	77	155	173	155	174
Frank Gore	SF	RB	0	0	0	845	6	152	1	0	0	142	156	52	161	59

(continued next page)

---

* Because Ricky Williams's comeback was unsure at press time, there are two projections for Ronnie Brown. The second Brown projection represents Brown and Williams splitting time in Miami.

TABLE 1. 2005 FANTASY PROJECTIONS *(continued)*

Name	Team	Pos	PaYD	PaTD	Int	RuYD	RuTD	RecYD	RecTD	XP	FG	Fant	12-3WR	12-FX	10-3WR	10-FX
Derick Armstrong	HOU	WR	0	0	0	0	0	584	3	0	0	76	157	174	156	175
Cedrick Wilson	PIT	WR	0	0	0	0	0	563	3	0	0	74	158	178	157	178
Todd Pinkston	PHI	WR	0	0	0	0	0	619	2	0	0	74	159	179	158	179
Mark Clayton	BAL	WR	0	0	0	0	0	556	3	0	0	74	160	180	159	180
Reuben Droughns	CLE	RB	0	0	0	711	5	278	1	0	0	135	161	58	164	77
Eli Manning	NYG	QB	3264	21	18	146	1	0	0	0	0	232	162	166	160	152
J. P. Losman	BUF	QB	3086	20	14	103	2	0	0	0	0	229	163	170	162	157
T. J. Duckett	ATL	RB	0	0	0	812	6	128	0	0	0	130	164	65	165	88
Ricky Williams*	MIA	RB	0	0	0	790	5	147	1	0	0	130	165	66	166	92
Duce Staley	PIT	RB	0	0	0	795	5	132	1	0	0	129	166	68	167	95
Kyle Boller	BAL	QB	3004	18	14	188	2	0	0	0	0	225	167	176	163	161
Warrick Dunn	ATL	RB	0	0	0	704	5	216	1	0	0	128	168	69	168	96
Derrick Blaylock	NYJ	RB	0	0	0	581	6	217	1	0	0	122	169	84	169	108
Nick Goings	CAR	RB	0	0	0	596	4	287	1	0	0	118	170	93	170	114
DeShaun Foster	CAR	RB	0	0	0	677	5	196	0	0	0	117	171	97	171	117
Mewelde Moore	MIN	RB	0	0	0	590	4	279	1	0	0	117	172	100	172	118
Jerome Bettis	PIT	RB	0	0	0	520	8	47	0	0	0	105	173	136	173	143
Michael Pittman	TB	RB	0	0	0	471	3	274	1	0	0	99	174	148	174	149
Eric Shelton	CAR	RB	0	0	0	525	4	118	1	0	0	94	175	153	175	155
Larry Johnson	KC	RB	0	0	0	464	5	150	0	0	0	91	176	155	176	158
Shawn Bryson	DET	RB	0	0	0	391	2	281	1	0	0	85	177	162	177	165
Kevin Faulk	NE	RB	0	0	0	392	3	214	1	0	0	85	178	163	178	166
Marshall Faulk	STL	RB	0	0	0	412	3	167	0	0	0	76	179	175	179	176
Thomas Jones	CHI	RB	0	0	0	388	2	238	0	0	0	75	180	177	180	177

* This projection is only applicable if Williams does return this season.

Special Teams

Punters

Table 2 represents individual punting performance in 2004 according to the methods described in the Statistical Toolbox at the beginning of the book. Kickoff value is also given for punters used as kickoff specialists. (Kickoff value for most kickers is found in the player comments section.) Nick Murphy punted for both Baltimore and Kansas City. Jason Baker punted for both Kansas City and Denver, and kicked off for both Indianapolis and Denver. Punters are listed if they had a minimum of ten punts.

PtPts+: Points worth of field position gained on punts before returns, compared to league average, adjusted based on weather and altitude.

PtNet+: Points worth of field position gained on net punts and punt returns, compared to league average, adjusted based on weather and altitude.

PtYd: Official NFL average gross yardage per punt.

NtYd: Official NFL average net yardage per punt.

In50: Number of opportunities this punter had from the fifty-yard line or inside opponent territory.

Pin: Number of times this punter pinned the opposing team inside their own ten-yard line on punts from the fifty-yard line or closer.

Pin%: Pin percentage (Pin divided by In50).

Down: Punts downed by the punting team.

FC: Punts resulting in fair catch.

TB: Touchbacks.

OoB: Punts out of bounds.

Kicks: Kickoffs.

KOPts+: Points worth of field position gained on kickoffs before returns, compared to league average, adjusted based on weather and altitude.

KONet+: Points worth of field position gained on net kickoffs and kick returns, compared to league average, adjusted based on weather and altitude.

TABLE 2. 2004 PUNTING PERFORMANCE

Punter	Team	G	Punts	PtPts+	PtNet+	PtYd	NtYd	In50	Pin	Pin%	Down	FC	TB	OoB	Kicks	KOPts+	KONet+
Hunter Smith	IND	16	54	14.3	5.6	45.2	36.8	12	4	33%	8	13	3	1	8	−1.1	−2.5
Chris Gardocki	PIT	16	67	13.7	19.5	43.0	37.4	16	9	56%	15	8	6	4	—	—	—
Tom Tupa	WAS	16	103	11.1	−4.7	44.1	35.2	18	5	28%	10	11	8	9	—	—	—
Shane Lechler	OAK	16	73	10.6	−0.5	46.7	37.2	17	4	24%	10	10	14	4	—	—	—
Todd Sauerbrun	CAR	16	76	9.6	10.9	44.1	37.5	20	5	25%	17	12	8	1	17	−1.2	0.0
Brian Moorman	BUF	16	77	9.2	12.3	43.2	36.8	16	8	50%	13	6	9	12	—	—	—
Brad Maynard	CHI	16	108	8.7	19.0	42.9	38.7	12	5	42%	14	21	5	13	—	—	—
Mitch Berger	NO	16	85	8.7	10.7	43.6	39.0	13	6	46%	10	25	4	3	37	1.2	−2.9
Mat McBriar	DAL	16	75	7.6	3.1	42.4	35.1	17	5	29%	6	16	7	7	—	—	—
Chris Hanson	JAC	16	84	6.9	−3.2	42.8	35.5	22	10	45%	19	13	9	5	—	—	—
Josh Miller	NE	16	56	6.0	−0.5	42.0	33.7	11	6	55%	7	7	5	6	—	—	—
Dirk Johnson	PHI	16	72	5.6	19.3	42.1	37.4	12	6	50%	14	12	6	5	—	—	—
Nick Murphy	2TM	5	18	3.6	4.2	43.9	37.4	4	1	25%	3	3	3	2	—	—	—
Sean Landeta	STL	10	40	2.5	−12.0	43.3	32.5	6	2	33%	3	9	3	1	—	—	—
Jeff Feagles	NYG	16	74	2.4	0.9	41.5	34.6	17	8	47%	11	14	4	6	—	—	—
Jason Baker	3TM	10	15	2.2	−2.3	38.8	31.6	11	6	55%	5	5	1	3	57	−2.5	−9.1
Dave Zastudil	BAL	13	73	1.2	7.2	40.4	34.6	28	6	21%	14	19	12	4	—	—	—
Tom Rouen	SEA	4	26	1.1	1.0	42.0	37.8	5	1	20%	5	10	1	0	—	—	—
Andy Lee	SF	16	96	0.6	7.2	41.6	35.3	17	6	35%	14	17	8	6	—	—	—
Scott Player	ARI	16	98	0.2	−4.3	43.2	36.4	18	6	33%	17	16	7	2	—	—	—
Matt Turk	MIA	16	98	−0.1	13.3	41.7	37.2	21	5	24%	16	19	10	9	—	—	—
Mike Scifres	SD	16	69	−0.5	4.5	43.1	38.4	18	8	44%	11	23	8	4	—	—	—
Kyle Larson	CIN	16	83	−0.7	6.1	42.2	35.5	14	3	21%	10	10	7	5	—	—	—
Josh Bidwell	TB	16	82	−0.8	1.0	42.3	36.8	16	4	25%	17	24	7	3	—	—	—
Kevin Stemke	STL	6	28	−1.5	3.2	39.8	36.1	10	1	10%	3	8	3	3	—	—	—
Craig Hentrich	TEN	16	73	−1.6	6.7	42.7	38.0	12	1	8%	6	25	8	5	69	−3.1	−2.8
Bryan Barker	GB	16	66	−1.8	3.1	40.1	33.4	14	3	21%	10	10	7	5	—	—	—

(continued next page)

TABLE 2. 2004 PUNTING PERFORMANCE *(continued)*

Punter	Team	G	Punts	PtPts+	PtNet+	PtYd	NtYd	In50	Pin	Pin%	Down	FC	TB	OoB	Kicks	KOPts+	KONet+
Derrick Frost	CLE	16	85	−1.9	17.0	40.0	35.4	16	3	19%	9	10	4	14	—	—	—
Toby Gowin	NYJ	16	80	−3.2	16.9	38.2	33.5	24	12	50%	15	14	8	9	76	3.7	0.8
Ken Walter	SEA	6	24	−3.4	0.4	38.3	33.0	4	0	0%	4	7	1	1	—	—	—
Darren Bennett	MIN	15	57	−3.8	3.3	39.3	35.3	14	3	21%	9	15	3	4	—	—	—
Chad Stanley	HOU	16	73	−6.2	−3.9	41.2	35.7	11	2	18%	8	24	7	4	—	—	—
Steve Cheek	KC	12	42	−6.3	−8.4	39.1	31.6	11	3	27%	3	10	6	5	—	—	—
Nick Harris	DET	16	92	−8.1	−5.0	40.9	34.2	22	8	36%	12	24	7	3	—	—	—
Chris Mohr	ATL	16	76	−8.3	9.6	40.6	36.9	13	3	23%	10	21	7	5	—	—	—
Donnie Jones	SEA	6	26	−9.5	−2.2	38.0	32.2	6	2	33%	8	4	2	2	—	—	—
Micah Knorr	DEN	12	54	−10.5	−8.7	41.5	34.2	12	4	33%	10	8	6	4	58	1.0	2.5

Kick Returns

Table 3 represents individual kick return value in 2004 according to the methods described in the Statistical Toolbox at the beginning of the book. RetPts+ is the value in points of field position gained by this kick returner compared to NFL average. This is based on location of each kick and catch, so the baseline for a kickoff that starts on the 30-yard line and is caught on the 10-yard line is different from the baseline for a kickoff that starts on the 25-yard line and is caught on the 20-yard line. Players are listed if they had a minimum of three kick returns. Wes Welker returned kicks for two teams, San Diego and Miami.

TABLE 3. 2004 INDIVIDUAL KICK RETURN VALUE

Player	Tm	RetPts+	Ret	Player	Tm	RetPts+	Ret	Player	Tm	RetPts+	Ret
D. Hall	KC	21.8	67	A. Peterson	CHI	1.1	3	A. Thurman	GB	−0.2	3
T. McGee	BUF	20.1	52	J. Robertson	SF	0.9	25	H. Evans	SEA	−0.2	3
E. Drummond	DET	14.4	41	R. Droughns	DEN	0.8	14	T. Stewart	CIN	−0.2	3
B. Johnson	NE	9.2	40	J. Williams	SF	0.7	3	E. Edwards	ARI	−0.2	3
W. Ponder	NYG	8.7	36	R. Colclough	PIT	0.7	26	B. Pyatt	IND	−0.2	10
J. Cotchery	NYJ	7.3	13	L. Fletcher	BUF	0.6	4	I. Smart	TB	−0.2	8
D. Rhodes	IND	7.2	48	F. McAfee	NO	0.5	8	J. Azumah	CHI	−0.2	42
T. Dwight	SD	6.9	50	C. Morton	WAS	0.4	16	M. Cloud	NYG	−0.4	8
T. Cox	TB	6.6	33	J. White	TB	0.4	4	R. Smart	CAR	−0.4	8
A. Stecker	NO	5.8	18	T. Edwards	JAC	0.4	15	D. Allen	JAC	−0.4	11
W. Welker	2TM	5.7	60	G. Jones	JAC	0.3	5	L. Brightful	MIA	−0.4	6
R. Ferguson	GB	5.1	22	M. Cushing	PIT	0.3	3	L. Jordan	NYJ	−0.4	14
R. Alston	CLE	4.7	46	B. Johnson	ARI	0.3	6	R. Mahe	PHI	−0.5	3
D. Ward	NYG	4.4	16	M. Sellers	WAS	0.2	4	R. Curry	OAK	−0.5	4
M. Lewis	NO	4.0	51	A. King	CLE	0.2	5	O. Ayanbadejo	ARI	−0.6	3
J. Robertson	CAR	2.8	6	K. Kasper	NE	0.2	3	M. Waddell	TEN	−0.6	16
A. Chatman	GB	2.7	24	R. Swinton	DET	0.2	18	T. J. Houshmandzadeh	CIN	−0.7	10
A. Randle El	PIT	2.7	21	J. Chatman	SD	0.1	4	L. Hall	NO	−0.7	3
J. Reed	PHI	2.3	33	E. Graham	TB	0.1	3	B. Bennett	CAR	−0.7	8
R. Lee	DAL	2.1	41	N. Davenport	GB	0.1	14	J. R. Redmond	OAK	−0.8	8
C. Russell	CIN	1.7	39	J. Thrash	WAS	0.0	9	A. Battle	SF	−0.8	13
L. Betts	WAS	1.5	23	C. Horn	KC	0.0	4	C. Wilson	SF	−0.8	10
B. Gilmore	MIA	1.5	5	L. Toefield	JAC	0.0	3	J. Mungro	IND	−0.9	7
F. Murphy	TB	1.4	8	R. Proehl	CAR	0.0	3	A. Cason	STL	−1.0	14
T. Luke	DEN	1.4	15	B. Berrian	CHI	−0.1	17	B. J. Sams	BAL	−1.1	59

Player	Tm	RetPts+	Ret	Player	Tm	RetPts+	Ret	Player	Tm	RetPts+	Ret
K. Campbell	MIN	−1.1	35	D. Jones	CHI	−1.9	6	F. Jackson	CLE	−3.4	4
R. Holcombe	TEN	−1.2	3	T. Copper	DAL	−1.9	16	T. Fleming	TEN	−3.4	18
S. Jackson	STL	−1.2	4	K. Carter	SEA	−2.0	21	L. Croom	ARI	−3.5	16
P. Pass	NE	−1.2	7	J. Broussard	CAR	−2.1	24	J. Carter	NYJ	−3.9	17
K. Faulk	NE	−1.3	4	K. Watson	CIN	−2.2	13	M. Hicks	SF	−3.9	31
Q. Griffin	DEN	−1.5	4	R. Alexander	DEN	−2.4	19	M. Moore	MIN	−4.2	20
M. Furrey	STL	−1.5	8	J. McKie	CHI	−2.4	3	M. Morris	SEA	−4.7	47
D. Anderson	STL	−1.7	4	J. McAddley	TEN	−2.8	38	J. Lewis	JAC	−5.1	21
O. Smith	MIN	−1.7	9	D. Brown	CLE	−2.8	14	D. Gabriel	OAK	−5.5	53
I. Taylor	PIT	−1.7	11	J. J. Moses	HOU	−3.0	59	A. Harris	STL	−6.0	47
A. Rossum	ATL	−1.8	58	R. Hood	PHI	−3.0	15	C. Francis	OAK	−9.5	14
J. Scobey	ARI	−1.8	32	J. Reeves	DAL	−3.3	13				

Punt Returns

Table 4 represents individual punt return value in 2004 according to the methods described in the Statistical Toolbox at the beginning of the book. RetPts+ is the value in points of field position gained by this punt returner compared to NFL average. This is based on location of each punt and catch, so the baseline for a punt from midfield that is caught on the 10-yard line is different from the baseline for a punt from the 20-yard line that is caught at midfield. Players are listed if they had a minimum of three punt returns.

There are more negative players than positive because 2004 was a particularly poor year for punt returns compared to previous seasons.

TABLE 4. 2004 INDIVIDUAL PUNT RETURN VALUE

Player	Tm	RetPts+	Ret	Player	Tm	RetPts+	Ret	Player	Tm	RetPts+	Ret
E. Drummond	DET	8.8	24	J. McCareins	NYJ	−1.4	14	C. Morton	WAS	−3.5	13
J. Smith	BUF	7.8	10	J. Galloway	TB	−1.4	20	A. Brown	WAS	−3.9	10
A. Rossum	ATL	4.0	37	B. J. Sams	BAL	−1.5	55	D. Allen	JAC	−4.0	15
K. Ratliff	CIN	2.0	17	R. Smith	DEN	−1.6	22	N. Clements	BUF	−4.3	34
M. Lewis	NO	1.6	34	D. Starks	ARI	−1.6	7	L. Frazier	DAL	−4.4	24
B. Engram	SEA	1.1	10	T. Brown	NE	−1.7	12	M. Morris	SEA	−4.5	15
R. W. McQuarters	CHI	0.8	42	B. Johnson	NE	−1.7	4	R. Mahe	PHI	−4.9	18
D. Wynn	PHI	0.7	18	D. O'Neal	CIN	−1.8	7	K. Faulk	NE	−5.0	20
W. Welker	MIA	0.5	42	E. Baker	CAR	−2.0	8	A. Chatman	GB	−5.2	32
D. Hall	KC	0.3	23	J. Lewis	JAC	−2.1	23	A. Randle El	PIT	−5.5	42
P. Crayton	DAL	−0.2	4	T. J. Houshmandzadeh	CIN	−2.2	11	P. Buchanon	OAK	−5.8	21
T. Edwards	JAC	−0.2	3	T. Walters	IND	−2.3	7	M. Jones	NYG	−7.0	34
N. Burleson	MIN	−0.5	25	D. Ward	DAL	−2.3	14	E. Parker	SD	−7.1	26
C. Gamble	CAR	−0.6	9	E. Berlin	TEN	−2.4	6	R. Swinton	DET	−7.3	16
M. Moore	MIN	−0.6	4	B. Pyatt	IND	−2.5	8	J. Broussard	CAR	−7.4	10
K. Richard	SEA	−0.8	4	J. David	IND	−2.6	8	J. J. Moses	HOU	−8.0	36
D. Sanders	BAL	−0.9	5	B. Schroeder	TB	−2.8	6	T. Luke	DEN	−9.0	19
I. Hilliard	NYG	−1.0	4	J. Thrash	WAS	−2.9	19	D. Mason	TEN	−9.6	24
A. Glenn	HOU	−1.0	4	L. Brightful	MIA	−2.9	9	K. Williams	ARI	−13.0	42
T. Brown	TB	−1.1	6	S. Moss	NYJ	−3.0	27	S. McDonald	STL	−17.0	30
D. Northcutt	CLE	−1.1	36	D. Stallworth	NO	−3.1	6				
A. Battle	SF	−1.2	32	M. Waddell	TEN	−3.4	10				

Offensive Pace, 2002–2004

Table 5 gives offensive pace for the past three seasons based on game clock seconds per offensive play. Two numbers are given for each season. The first number (Situation Neutral Pace) represents seconds per offensive play based on the definition from the pace essay in the New York Jets chapter: No drives starting in the fourth quarter or the last five minutes of the first half, and only drives with the score within six points. The second number (General Pace) represents game pace on all offensive plays.

TABLE 5. OFFENSIVE PACE, 2002–2004

Team	2004				2003				2002			
	Situation Neutral Pace	Rank	General Pace	Rank	Situation Neutral Pace	Rank	General Pace	Rank	Situation Neutral Pace	Rank	General Pace	Rank
NYG	32.41	1	27.55	15	29.10	26	25.22	32	28.44	24	27.07	17
JAC	32.05	2	28.44	4	30.47	9	26.50	26	31.28	4	28.14	7
HOU	31.51	3	27.81	8	32.42	2	28.25	8	30.83	5	27.42	13
ARI	31.46	4	27.70	12	32.68	1	28.01	10	28.66	22	26.06	25
NYJ	31.45	5	29.83	2	32.20	3	28.65	3	31.69	1	28.45	5
TEN	31.45	6	27.34	20	31.83	4	30.31	1	31.68	2	29.13	2
WAS	31.06	7	27.39	19	28.36	31	26.42	28	26.75	32	26.44	21
TB	31.03	8	28.00	7	30.35	14	28.41	4	31.68	3	29.16	1
STL	30.88	9	28.19	5	28.67	29	26.77	24	30.13	10	26.70	20
ATL	30.77	10	27.75	10	29.90	23	26.84	23	29.92	13	28.63	3
PIT	30.66	11	30.31	1	29.48	24	26.90	22	29.64	19	27.36	15
DAL	30.63	12	27.58	14	30.39	12	28.26	7	29.12	20	27.63	11
BAL	30.56	13	27.45	18	30.03	18	27.43	15	27.98	25	26.22	22
CHI	30.51	14	27.47	16	30.06	16	26.75	25	29.64	18	25.93	28
CAR	30.51	15	27.77	9	31.65	5	28.20	9	30.50	7	27.96	9
SD	30.28	16	29.13	3	28.67	30	26.44	27	29.74	16	28.27	6
CLE	29.98	17	27.26	21	31.49	6	27.82	11	29.86	14	27.93	10
MIN	29.71	18	27.46	17	30.27	15	28.41	5	30.03	11	26.10	24
DEN	29.64	19	27.74	11	31.28	7	29.31	2	30.33	8	26.03	26
DET	29.56	20	27.69	13	29.98	20	27.10	20	27.52	30	24.64	32
KC	29.55	21	26.28	27	30.47	8	27.27	17	29.95	12	26.71	19
SF	29.50	22	26.06	29	30.42	11	26.91	21	29.79	15	28.05	8
GB	29.32	23	26.17	28	29.99	19	27.51	14	28.73	21	27.50	12
IND	29.20	24	26.98	25	30.38	13	27.60	13	30.51	6	27.20	16
NO	29.11	25	26.62	26	30.05	17	27.13	19	27.19	31	25.52	30
BUF	29.09	26	28.16	6	29.98	21	27.75	12	29.69	17	27.38	14
NE	29.08	27	27.15	22	29.28	25	27.14	18	28.64	23	26.01	27
CIN	28.87	28	27.02	24	30.47	10	27.34	16	27.62	29	25.58	29
PHI	28.69	29	27.03	23	28.74	28	26.34	29	27.67	28	26.13	23
OAK	27.63	30	26.05	30	28.93	27	25.85	30	27.96	26	26.88	18
MIA	27.55	31	25.15	32	29.90	22	28.31	6	30.25	9	28.59	4
SEA	27.52	32	25.36	31	26.10	32	25.76	31	27.84	27	25.19	31
Avg	30.03	—	27.40	—	30.11	—	27.39	—	29.40	—	27.05	—

Drive Stats

The stats in tables 6–8 are computed from NFL drive charts and are not adjusted for strength of schedule or situation. FUM/Dr represents Fumbles Lost per drive. LOS/Dr represents average starting field position (line of scrimmage) per drive. Kneeldowns at the end of a half are discarded. NET values are simply offense minus defense.

TABLE 6. 2004 OFFENSIVE DRIVE STATS

Team	Drives	Yds/Dr	Rnk	Pts/Dr	Rnk	TD/Dr	Rnk	Punt/Dr	Rnk	TO/Dr	Rnk	INT/Dr	Rnk	FUM/Dr	Rnk	LOS/Dr	Rnk
IND	166	39.8	1	2.93	1	0.37	1	0.33	2	0.102	3	0.060	4	0.042	3	30.4	18
MIN	161	39.0	2	2.38	4	0.29	4	0.35	4	0.124	10	0.075	9	0.050	12	26.5	31
KC	177	37.8	3	2.58	2	0.33	2	0.31	1	0.147	18	0.096	21	0.051	15	30.7	15
GB	179	35.4	4	2.16	6	0.25	6	0.37	6	0.156	22	0.106	25	0.050	14	28.5	30
DEN	188	34.3	5	1.95	8	0.21	9	0.37	5	0.149	19	0.106	26	0.043	4	28.7	29
NE	169	34.0	6	2.37	5	0.26	5	0.33	3	0.154	20	0.083	13	0.071	26	31.4	11
SD	170	33.5	7	2.54	3	0.31	3	0.41	10	0.094	2	0.047	1	0.047	9	32.7	4
STL	172	32.9	8	1.72	16	0.20	14	0.40	8	0.209	32	0.128	32	0.081	29	26.2	32
NYJ	170	31.5	9	1.82	12	0.20	13	0.47	24	0.088	1	0.065	6	0.024	1	30.1	22
PHI	184	30.5	10	2.04	7	0.23	7	0.40	9	0.114	6	0.060	3	0.054	19	30.4	17
SEA	189	29.9	11	1.85	11	0.21	10	0.41	12	0.143	16	0.095	20	0.048	10	29.4	26
PIT	174	29.9	12	1.93	9	0.21	11	0.39	7	0.121	8	0.075	10	0.046	7	32.7	3
CAR	179	28.7	13	1.86	10	0.22	8	0.44	20	0.128	11	0.084	14	0.045	5	31.7	9
HOU	174	28.5	14	1.58	21	0.18	20	0.42	16	0.138	15	0.080	12	0.057	22	30.3	19
JAC	174	28.1	15	1.46	24	0.15	24	0.48	27	0.121	7	0.063	5	0.057	23	28.8	27
OAK	178	28.1	16	1.76	13	0.19	18	0.41	13	0.180	26	0.124	29	0.056	20	30.2	21
DAL	184	28.0	17	1.58	20	0.18	21	0.41	14	0.196	30	0.125	30	0.071	25	31.5	10
ATL	180	27.8	18	1.66	19	0.19	16	0.42	18	0.161	23	0.089	17	0.072	27	31.1	13
TEN	194	27.8	19	1.70	17	0.20	12	0.41	11	0.155	21	0.098	23	0.057	21	29.8	24
NO	187	26.7	20	1.70	18	0.19	17	0.46	23	0.134	12	0.086	15	0.048	11	30.2	20
DET	179	26.5	21	1.42	25	0.15	26	0.51	29	0.106	4	0.073	8	0.034	2	29.7	25
NYG	180	26.4	22	1.53	22	0.17	23	0.42	15	0.122	9	0.072	7	0.050	13	31.9	8
CIN	195	25.8	23	1.74	15	0.19	19	0.43	19	0.164	24	0.113	28	0.051	16	32.0	7
TB	187	25.8	24	1.48	23	0.18	22	0.44	22	0.187	28	0.096	22	0.091	31	30.0	23
BUF	185	24.6	25	1.75	14	0.20	15	0.42	17	0.146	17	0.092	19	0.054	18	36.3	1
BAL	185	23.7	26	1.38	26	0.13	30	0.52	30	0.114	5	0.059	2	0.054	17	34.2	2
ARI	196	23.5	27	1.37	27	0.15	25	0.50	28	0.138	14	0.092	18	0.046	6	30.6	16
SF	199	22.6	28	1.19	30	0.13	29	0.48	26	0.201	31	0.106	24	0.095	32	28.8	28
WAS	194	22.2	29	1.16	31	0.12	31	0.53	31	0.134	13	0.088	16	0.046	8	31.3	12
CLE	195	22.0	30	1.34	28	0.14	28	0.44	21	0.185	27	0.108	27	0.077	28	32.6	5
MIA	206	21.4	31	1.26	29	0.14	27	0.48	25	0.189	29	0.126	31	0.063	24	31.0	14
CHI	205	17.7	32	0.87	32	0.09	32	0.54	32	0.166	25	0.078	11	0.088	30	32.1	6

TABLE 7. 2004 DEFENSIVE DRIVE STATS

Team	Drives	Yds/Dr	Rnk	Pts/Dr	Rnk	TD/Dr	Rnk	Punt/Dr	Rnk	TO/Dr	Rnk	INT/Dr	Rnk	FUM/Dr	Rnk	LOS/Dr	Rnk
BUF	188	22.5	1	1.40	5	0.14	4	0.42	19	0.197	3	0.128	2	0.069	7	30.8	19
DEN	191	23.0	2	1.54	13	0.17	13	0.50	4	0.099	30	0.063	28	0.037	31	32.4	29
WAS	189	23.4	3	1.16	1	0.13	2	0.54	1	0.132	22	0.095	14	0.037	30	29.9	12
PIT	172	23.7	4	1.30	3	0.13	3	0.46	10	0.174	7	0.110	7	0.064	10	28.3	1
TB	184	24.1	5	1.43	9	0.16	9	0.47	8	0.136	19	0.087	17	0.049	21	31.9	26
BAL	195	24.4	6	1.23	2	0.12	1	0.48	7	0.169	11	0.108	9	0.062	14	28.8	3
MIA	198	24.8	7	1.43	11	0.16	11	0.52	2	0.116	25	0.076	21	0.040	26	30.9	20
ARI	199	24.9	8	1.43	10	0.15	6	0.48	6	0.151	17	0.075	23	0.075	5	29.6	8
CHI	206	25.6	9	1.47	12	0.16	7	0.45	13	0.141	18	0.083	18	0.058	16	31.7	25
CLE	190	27.3	10	1.82	19	0.21	16	0.45	12	0.126	23	0.079	19	0.047	23	32.5	30
NYJ	177	27.4	11	1.42	8	0.16	12	0.50	3	0.169	10	0.107	10	0.062	13	29.5	7
CIN	191	27.4	12	1.69	15	0.18	14	0.41	20	0.168	12	0.105	12	0.063	12	31.4	22
NYG	184	27.8	13	1.89	21	0.22	25	0.42	17	0.152	15	0.076	20	0.076	4	32.4	28
PHI	181	28.0	14	1.40	6	0.16	10	0.49	5	0.133	21	0.094	16	0.039	29	29.7	9
NE	172	28.0	15	1.36	4	0.16	8	0.40	22	0.203	2	0.116	6	0.087	2	30.6	17
ATL	179	28.4	16	1.79	18	0.22	23	0.44	14	0.173	8	0.106	11	0.067	9	29.5	6
SF	189	28.9	17	2.21	29	0.26	29	0.42	18	0.101	29	0.048	30	0.053	18	34.6	32
SEA	189	29.4	18	1.95	22	0.22	22	0.39	24	0.185	5	0.122	5	0.063	11	32.4	27
DET	185	29.6	19	1.75	16	0.21	21	0.45	11	0.124	24	0.076	22	0.049	22	28.9	4
STL	178	29.6	20	1.98	25	0.21	19	0.40	23	0.079	32	0.034	32	0.045	25	32.5	31
DAL	177	29.9	21	2.14	27	0.25	26	0.44	15	0.113	27	0.073	25	0.040	28	30.1	13
SD	181	29.9	22	1.65	14	0.19	15	0.35	30	0.177	6	0.127	3	0.050	20	29.1	5
JAC	169	30.0	23	1.41	7	0.15	5	0.44	16	0.166	13	0.095	15	0.071	6	28.8	2
HOU	174	30.1	24	1.83	20	0.21	18	0.39	25	0.172	9	0.126	4	0.046	24	30.3	14
CAR	179	30.1	25	1.78	17	0.21	17	0.35	31	0.207	1	0.145	1	0.061	15	29.8	11
TEN	184	31.3	26	2.16	28	0.26	27	0.40	21	0.152	16	0.098	13	0.054	17	31.3	21
GB	175	31.4	27	2.09	26	0.26	28	0.46	9	0.080	31	0.046	31	0.034	32	31.6	24
NO	190	32.6	28	1.96	24	0.21	20	0.37	27	0.163	14	0.068	26	0.095	1	29.7	10
OAK	177	33.6	29	2.31	30	0.29	32	0.38	26	0.102	28	0.051	29	0.051	19	30.5	16
IND	174	33.7	30	1.96	23	0.22	24	0.30	32	0.190	4	0.109	8	0.080	3	30.4	15
KC	175	34.1	31	2.36	31	0.29	31	0.37	28	0.114	26	0.074	24	0.040	27	30.8	18
MIN	163	34.7	32	2.37	32	0.28	30	0.36	29	0.135	20	0.067	27	0.067	8	31.5	23

TABLE 8. 2004 NET DRIVE STATS

Team	Yds/Dr	Rnk	Pts/Dr	Rnk	TD/Dr	Rnk	Punt/Dr	Rnk	TO/Dr	Rnk	INT/Dr	Rnk	FUM/Dr	Rnk	LOS/Dr	Rnk
DEN	11.3	1	0.41	6	0.04	8	−0.13	1	0.049	24	0.044	26	0.006	20	−3.7	29
PIT	6.2	2	0.63	5	0.08	4	−0.07	4	−0.054	6	−0.036	8	−0.018	6	4.4	3
IND	6.1	3	0.97	2	0.15	1	0.03	22	−0.087	1	−0.049	3	−0.038	3	0.0	20
NE	6.0	4	1.01	1	0.10	3	−0.07	5	−0.050	8	−0.033	10	−0.016	9	0.8	11
MIN	4.3	5	0.00	16	0.02	11	−0.01	14	−0.011	18	0.007	19	−0.018	7	−5.0	30
NYJ	4.2	6	0.41	7	0.04	9	−0.03	9	−0.081	3	−0.043	6	−0.039	2	0.5	14
GB	4.0	7	0.07	12	−0.01	19	−0.09	2	0.076	28	0.060	30	0.016	25	−3.1	28
KC	3.7	8	0.22	9	0.04	7	−0.06	6	0.033	23	0.022	24	0.011	22	0.0	21
SD	3.5	9	0.89	3	0.12	2	0.05	27	−0.083	2	−0.080	1	−0.003	16	3.6	4
STL	3.4	10	−0.26	23	−0.01	20	0.00	15	0.131	32	0.094	32	0.036	30	−6.4	32
PHI	2.5	11	0.63	4	0.07	5	−0.09	3	−0.018	14	−0.034	9	0.016	24	0.7	12
BUF	2.1	12	0.35	8	0.06	6	0.01	18	−0.051	7	−0.036	7	−0.015	12	5.5	1
TB	1.7	13	0.05	15	0.02	10	−0.03	8	0.051	25	0.009	21	0.042	31	−1.9	26
SEA	0.5	14	−0.10	19	−0.01	18	0.02	20	−0.042	10	−0.026	12	−0.016	10	−3.0	27
ATL	−0.5	15	−0.13	20	−0.02	24	−0.02	11	−0.012	17	−0.017	13	0.005	18	1.6	6
BAL	−0.7	16	0.15	10	0.01	12	0.04	25	−0.056	5	−0.048	4	−0.007	15	5.4	2
WAS	−1.2	17	0.00	17	0.00	17	−0.01	13	0.002	20	0.000	14	0.009	21	1.4	7
NYG	−1.3	18	−0.35	26	−0.06	26	0.00	16	−0.030	12	−0.004	16	−0.026	5	−0.5	24
CAR	−1.4	19	0.08	11	0.01	14	0.08	30	−0.078	4	−0.061	2	−0.017	8	2.0	5
ARI	−1.4	20	−0.06	18	0.00	16	0.02	21	−0.013	16	0.016	22	−0.029	4	1.1	9
CIN	−1.6	21	0.06	13	0.01	13	0.01	19	−0.003	19	0.008	20	−0.012	14	0.6	13
HOU	−1.6	22	−0.25	22	−0.02	23	0.03	23	−0.034	11	−0.046	5	0.011	23	0.1	19
DAL	−1.9	23	−0.55	30	−0.08	30	−0.03	10	0.083	30	0.052	28	0.031	29	1.4	8
JAC	−1.9	24	0.05	14	0.00	15	0.05	26	−0.045	9	−0.031	11	−0.014	13	0.0	22
DET	−3.1	25	−0.33	25	−0.07	28	0.06	28	−0.018	15	−0.003	17	−0.015	11	0.9	10
MIA	−3.3	26	−0.17	21	−0.02	22	−0.04	7	0.073	27	0.050	27	0.023	26	0.1	17
TEN	−3.5	27	−0.46	27	−0.05	25	0.01	17	0.002	21	0.000	18	0.002	17	−1.5	25
CLE	−5.3	28	−0.48	28	−0.07	29	−0.01	12	0.058	26	0.029	25	0.030	28	0.1	18
OAK	−5.5	29	−0.55	29	−0.10	31	0.03	24	0.078	29	0.073	31	0.005	19	−0.4	23
NO	−5.9	30	−0.26	24	−0.02	21	0.09	31	−0.029	13	0.017	23	−0.047	1	0.5	15
SF	−6.3	31	−1.03	32	−0.13	32	0.06	29	0.100	31	0.058	29	0.043	32	−5.8	31
CHI	−7.9	32	−0.60	31	−0.06	27	0.09	32	0.025	22	−0.004	15	0.030	27	0.5	16

Coaching History

Tables 9 and 10 give the historical totals referenced in the essay in the St. Louis chapter, "In Defense of Mike Martz."

TABLE 9. WINNING PERCENTAGE FOR COACHES WITH A FOURTH-QUARTER LEAD, 1970–2004 (MINIMUM 20 QUALIFYING GAMES)

Rnk	Coach	Win%	Rnk	Coach	Win%	Rnk	Coach	Win%
1	Mike Martz	.914	39	Herman Edwards	.837	77	Hank Stram	.774
2	Red Miller	.911	40	Jimmy Johnson	.837	78	Mike McCormack	.769
3	Barry Switzer	.898	41	Joe Walton	.831	78	John Mackovic	.769
4	Don McCafferty	.895	42	Marty Schottenheimer	.830	80	Jim Mora	.767
5	Joe Gibbs	.894	43	Jim Hanifan	.830	81	Charley Winner	.762
6	John Madden	.888	44	Pete Carroll	.829	82	Leeman Bennett	.761
7	George Allen	.886	45	Gene Stallings	.828	83	Joe Schmidt	.758
8	Mike Sherman	.885	46	Dom Capers	.825	84	Bart Starr	.757
9	Bobby Ross	.885	47	Dick Vermeil	.821	85	Chuck Fairbanks	.754
10	Brian Billick	.879	48	Bill Walsh	.821	85	Wade Phillips	.754
11	Jim Haslett	.875	49	Forrest Gregg	.821	87	Ron Erhardt	.750
12	Tony Dungy	.874	50	Bill Belichick	.819	87	Dave McGinnis	.750
13	Bill Cowher	.871	51	Lindy Infante	.814	87	Daryl Rogers	.750
14	Nick Skorich	.865	52	Ray Rhodes	.813	90	Jack Patera	.745
15	Chuck Knox	.864	53	Dave Wannstedt	.812	91	Norm Van Brocklin	.744
16	Steve Mariucci	.864	54	Raymond Berry	.810	92	Rich Kotite	.741
17	Don Shula	.864	54	John Ralston	.810	93	Chan Gailey	.739
18	Andy Reid	.863	56	Mike Holmgren	.809	94	Sam Rutigliano	.738
19	Tom Landry	.862	57	Weeb Ewbank	.808	94	John McKay	.738
20	Chuck Noll	.862	58	John Gruden	.807	96	John Fox	.737
21	Mike Ditka	.861	58	Wayne Fontes	.807	97	Dennis Erickson	.736
22	George Seifert	.858	60	Neill Armstrong	.806	98	Bruce Coslet	.730
23	John Robinson	.857	61	Jerry Glanville	.805	99	Gunther Cunningham	.727
23	Ron Meyer	.857	62	Lou Saban	.804	100	Norv Turner	.720
23	Bill Johnson	.857	63	Tom Coughlin	.802	101	Ray Perkins	.717
26	Bud Grant	.856	64	Dick Jauron	.800	102	Monte Clark	.714
27	Dennis Green	.856	64	Dan Devine	.800	102	Mike White	.714
28	Marv Levy	.852	64	Mike Tice	.800	104	Butch Davis	.697
29	Bum Phillips	.851	64	Alex Webster	.800	105	Gregg Williams	.680
30	Don Coryell	.851	68	Jack Pardee	.798	106	Tommy Protho	.679
31	Mike Shanahan	.850	69	Ray Malavasi	.796	107	June Jones	.656
32	Dan Reeves	.845	70	Sam Wyche	.792	108	Dan Henning	.650
33	Art Shell	.844	70	Walt Michaels	.792	109	Joe Bugel	.649
34	Jeff Fisher	.841	72	Ted Marchibroda	.789	110	Marion Campbell	.642
35	Vince Tobin	.839	73	Paul Brown	.787	111	John McVay	.636
36	Jim Fassel	.838	74	Buddy Ryan	.778	112	David Shula	.581
37	Bill Parcells	.838	75	Dick Nolan	.775	113	Dave Campo	.577
38	Tom Flores	.837	76	Jerry Burns	.775	114	Mike Riley	.538

TABLE 10. WINNING PERCENTAGE FOR COACHES WITH A TWO-SCORE LEAD, 1970–2004 (MINIMUM 15 QUALIFYING GAMES)

Rank	Coach	Win%	Rank	Coach	Win%	Rank	Coach	Win%
1	Don McCafferty	.963	39	Bill Parcells	.872	77	Chuck Fairbanks	.809
2	John Fox	.952	40	Walt Michaels	.872	78	Joe Walton	.807
3	Jim Haslett	.939	40	Marty Schottenheimer	.872	79	Buddy Ryan	.804
4	Andy Reid	.935	42	Jeff Fisher	.871	79	Art Shell	.804
5	Mike Sherman	.935	43	Jerry Glanville	.865	81	Dick Vermeil	.802
6	Red Miller	.933	44	Chuck Knox	.865	82	Dick Nolan	.797
7	Dennis Green	.929	45	Jerry Burns	.864	83	Lou Saban	.795
8	Brian Billick	.925	46	Bum Phillips	.864	84	Jim Mora	.793
9	John Madden	.921	46	Nick Skorich	.864	85	Tommy Protho	.789
10	George Allen	.918	48	Don Coryell	.863	85	Mike White	.789
11	Bill Cowher	.915	49	Sam Wyche	.861	87	John Ralston	.784
12	Ron Erhardt	.913	50	Bill Belichick	.860	88	Jim Hanifan	.780
12	George Seifert	.913	51	Vince Tobin	.857	89	Ted Marchibroda	.773
14	Tom Landry	.908	52	Steve Mariucci	.852	90	Ray Malavasi	.773
15	Joe Gibbs	.907	53	Joe Schmidt	.852	91	Dennis Erickson	.763
16	Neill Armstrong	.900	54	Wade Phillips	.851	92	Monte Clark	.763
16	John Robinson	.900	54	Hank Stram	.851	93	Dom Capers	.756
18	Bill Walsh	.899	56	Dan Reeves	.850	94	Rich Brooks	.750
19	Tony Dungy	.897	57	Chan Gailey	.850	94	John Mackovic	.750
19	Mike Holmgren	.897	57	Gene Stallings	.850	96	Jack Patera	.744
21	Bobby Ross	.897	59	Jack Pardee	.848	97	Weeb Ewbank	.739
22	Tom Flores	.894	60	Tom Coughlin	.847	98	John McVay	.733
23	Raymond Berry	.889	61	Mike McCormack	.846	99	Rich Kotite	.730
23	Bill Callahan	.889	62	John Gruden	.844	100	John McKay	.727
23	Jimmy Johnson	.889	62	Ray Rhodes	.844	101	Ray Perkins	.725
26	Marv Levy	.886	64	Dan Devine	.840	102	Dick Jauron	.710
27	Chuck Noll	.883	64	Mike Tice	.840	103	Leeman Bennett	.708
28	Mike Martz	.882	66	Bart Starr	.839	104	Ray Handley	.706
29	Don Shula	.881	67	Sam Rutigliano	.838	105	Dan Henning	.700
30	Ron Meyer	.878	68	Wayne Fontes	.833	106	Marion Campbell	.697
30	Barry Switzer	.878	69	Mike Shanahan	.832	107	Bruce Coslet	.696
32	Paul Brown	.875	70	Lindy Infante	.828	108	Al Saunders	.688
32	Pete Carroll	.875	71	Alex Webster	.826	109	Butch Davis	.684
32	Mike Ditka	.875	72	Dave Wannstedt	.824	110	June Jones	.650
32	Herman Edwards	.875	73	Bill Johnson	.824	110	Daryl Rogers	.650
32	Jim Fassel	.875	74	Norv Turner	.818	112	Joe Bugel	.567
32	Charley Winner	.875	75	Norm Van Brocklin	.815	113	Mike Riley	.556
38	Bud Grant	.873	76	Forrest Gregg	.813	114	David Shula	.524

Author Biographies

Lead Writer and Statistician

Aaron Schatz is a regular contributor to ESPN.com Page 2 and covers the NFL for the *New York Sun.* He has also written for the *New York Times,* the *Boston Globe,* the New Republic Online, and Slate, and has done custom research for NFL.com and a number of NFL teams. Before creating Football Outsiders, he spent three years tracking search trends online for the Internet column "The Lycos 50." He has a B.A. in economics from Brown University and lives in Framingham, Massachusetts, with his wife, Kathryn, and daughter, Mirinae.

Football Outsiders Staff

Al Bogdan is one of the original Brown alumni who started Football Outsiders, and still co-writes the weekly column "Scramble for the Ball. " He lives in Queens and is a third-year student at St. John's University School of Law, and a member of the St. John's Law Review and the Entertainment and Sports Law Society.

Will Carroll is our Bo Jackson, best known as an award-winning columnist for *Baseball Prospectus.* The Indianapolis resident is the author of two books, *Saving the Pitcher* and *The Juice: The Real Story of Baseball's Drug Problems.* He will begin a weekly column covering NFL injuries for Football Outsiders this fall.

Like much of the website staff, **Tim Gerheim** attended Brown University, but he also holds a master's degree in sport management from the University of Texas, where he begins law school this fall.

Web producer **Russell Levine** covers college football for the *New York Sun* and writes two columns for Football Outsiders: "Confessions of a Football Junkie" and "Seventh Day Adventure" (with Chicago lawyer and fellow Michigan grad **Vinny Gauri,** who also co-wrote the college preview in this book). He lives in West Orange, New Jersey, with his wife, Susan, and their children, Trevor and Lindsay, who can already do a mean duet on "Hail to the Victors."

Ned Macey is a graduate of Haverford College, a school proud to be undefeated in football since 1972, and begins law school this fall at the University of Michigan. Over the past year, living in Australia and Germany, he discovered that "football" is globally confused with a sport where the foot is actually central to the action.

During the season, **Michael David Smith** writes the weekly Football Outsiders column "Every Play Counts," analyzing "non–skill position" football skills such as line play and pass coverage. He has also written for the *Orange County Register, New York Sun,* and the New Republic Online, and contributed a chapter on steroids in football to Will Carroll's *The Juice.* He lives in Chicago with his wife, Sarah, and, contrary to popular belief, is neither the Michael Smith who writes for ESPN.com nor the Michael Smith who coordinates the Jacksonville defense.

When not teaching high school math, **Mike Tanier** writes for both Football Outsiders and Sports Forecaster, a syndicated sports service that provides content for over 20 newspaper websites in the United States and Canada. Mike is a graduate of La Salle University and lives in Mount Ephraim, New Jersey (elevation: 72 feet above sea level) with his wife, Karen, and son, C. J.

Economist **Ryan Wilson** was raised in North Carolina but went to school in Pittsburgh, where he became a maniacal Steelers fan. He manages the Football Outsiders weblog, "Extra Points," and lives near Washington, D.C. with his wife, Audrey.

Special Contributors

Dr. Benjamin Alamar is the founding editor of the *Journal of Quantitative Analysis in Sports* and has consulted for various NFL and NBA franchises. He holds a doctorate in economics from U.C. Santa Barbara.

Jim Armstrong is a Boston software developer by day and a Packers fan by birthright.

Dan Lewis is an aspiring lawyer and Manhattan-based sportswriter whose work has appeared in the *Washington Times,* FOXSports.com, National Review Online, and *Reason.*

St. Louis resident **Jason McKinley** is a former molecular microbiologist now studying actuarial science.